Medical Law and Ethics

Medical Law and Ethics

2nd Edition

By

Shaun D. Pattinson
LL.B., M.A., Ph.D., F.R.S.A.
Reader in Law at Durham University

SWEET & MAXWELL

THOMSON REUTERS

First edition   2006

*Published in 2009 by Thomson Reuters (Legal) Limited (Registered in England &
Wales, Company No 1679046. Registered Office and address for service: 100 Avenue
Road, London NW3 3PF) trading as
Sweet & Maxwell Limited*

*For further information about our products and services, visit
www.sweetandmaxwell.co.uk
Typeset by LBJ Typesetting Ltd of Kingsclere
Printed and bound in Great Britain by
Ashford Colour Press Ltd, Gosport, Hampshire*

No natural forests were destroyed to make this product;
only farmed timber was used and re-planted.

A CIP catalogue record for this book is available from the British Library

ISBN–13 978-1-84703-819-7

CONTENTS

At some point all of those who live in developed countries such as the UK will be assisted by doctors, nurses, and other health professionals. Medical law, operating in the background of medical practice, thereby has an impact on all of us. It does more than address high profile aberrations, such as the murders committed by Dr Harold Shipman or the systemic failures highlighted by a number of recent inquiries. We shall see that the law plays a role that runs much wider and deeper than addressing patient grievances and fishing out the bad apples that "contaminate every professional barrel".[1] In turn, the law governing medical practice and related technologies is subject to many ethical and contextual pressures. This book seeks to question, analyse, and explain medical law in terms of moral theory and the pressures created by the rapidly changing context of healthcare. The context in which the law operates includes the impact of market forces and patient consumerism, political interests, medical and professional interests, changing perceptions of medicine, developing technologies, limited resources, and the impact of increasingly direct (international and domestic) recognition of human rights. These are themes that are relevant to many of the topics covered in this book.

The law addressing medical practice and its implications draws from more traditional categories of law—such as tort, contract, criminal, family, and public law—while still having a strong claim to being a subject in its own right. Whether or not medical law is better categorised as a subcategory of another subject or itself separated into subcategories depends on the purpose of the categorisation. My purpose is simply to explain and examine the law of England and Wales as it addresses medical practice, including features of its background and context. It is increasingly common to refer to this field as "healthcare" or "health" law, instead of "medical" law.[2] According to Brazier and Glover,

> Medical law which focuses on a relationship between doctors and patients remains in essence a creature of private law. . . . Health care law is located more firmly in public law. Doctors are shifted to the margins of debate. The needs, and even rights, of individual patients must be viewed within a wider context of protecting health and promoting public goods.[3]

Why, then, does the title of this book refer to "medical" and not "healthcare"? Well, medical law remains the title of most of the relevant university courses and some selectivity was required, even for a book of this size. The result is a book which focuses more on the clinical context than on the promotion of health,[4] but which remains alert to the changing nature of medical practice and

---

[1] Brazier 2005, 13.
[2] See e.g. Montgomery 2002 and McHale and Fox 2006.
[3] Brazier and Glover 2000, 372.
[4] This book does not, e.g., address public health law, such as the law on immunisation, screening, and health promotion programmes.

the growing impact of consumer and public law. I have also focused more on doctors and nurses than other health professionals. Similarly, the title uses "medical ethics" instead of "bioethics", because bioethics has a wider ambit and steps beyond the ethics of medical treatment and research aimed at developing types of medical treatment. Medical ethics also steps well beyond the professional ethics of medical practitioners; it is a branch of applied ethics, of moral philosophy.

As already indicated, this book focuses on the law of England and Wales. For convenience this is often referred to as English law. On many issues English and Scottish law coincide, but these two legal systems occasionally adopt very different approaches. Following devolution there are even occasionally differences in the medical law and practice of England and Wales, where this is the case this book will focus on the English position. Other jurisdictions will be mentioned only to provide a comparative context or to indicate the possibility of travel to another jurisdiction for treatment or research opportunities that are not available in the England and Wales.

Stylistic issues

For ease of expression, this book uses "he" to mean "he or she" (unless otherwise apparent or appropriate), "claimant" to refer to the person bringing a private law action, and "EU" to refer to the European Union and the European Community. False implications should not be drawn from this usage. Health professionals and patients can clearly be of either sex and, in practice, doctors are disproportionately male and patients are disproportionately female. Similarly, not all my uses of claimant comply with historical practice, as pre-Woolf reform cases used the term "plaintiff", and not all my uses of EU adhere to the increasingly ignored distinction between the EC and the EU.

Structural issues

Structurally this book has a number of unusual features, designed to facilitate its use by students taking medical law and ethics courses, and by academics and researchers with selective interests.

First, since the topics covered vary from one course or research project to another, this book is written with the general aim of facilitating selective reading. The first and final chapters are designed to be read with any combination of intermediate chapters. Occasional references to others chapters have, however, been required by the book's interconnected topics and themes. Each chapter begins with a list of the headings used in the text. Chapter 2 provides an explanation of a number of institutional and contextual issues that readers might also find useful. There are, however, some chapters that should be read together. The two chapters on consent (Chs 4 and 5) should be read as if they were one chapter, as should the two chapters on transplantation (Chs 13 and 14) and the two on end of life decisions (Chs 15 and 16). They have been divided simply to make their reading more manageable.

Second, a list of selected further reading is provided at the end of each chapter. These lists are by no means comprehensive or directed towards views with which I agree.

Third, the references in the chapters are given in footnotes using the Harvard style (author(s) followed by the date and page number). This is to ensure that the footnotes do not dominate the text while avoiding the distracting effect of putting the references in the text itself. Complete reference information is given in the bibliography. For similar reasons the footnoted case references use the neutral citation where available,[5] leaving other citations to the *List of Cases* at the front of the book.

Fourth, while philosophical reasoning is utilised throughout, many underlying philosophical issues are left unaddressed until the final chapter. This is designed to maximise the likelihood that the relevance of these issues will be understood before the reader is launched into the deeper philosophical debate.

Although this book addresses amazingly protean area of law and practice, I have sought to ensure that the law and web links were accurate as of 1 April 2009.

Changes from the first edition

Readers familiar with the first edition of this book will notice that just about every chapter has been updated and reworked. In the relatively short period since the last edition the Mental Capacity Act 2005 and the Human Tissue Act 2004 have been fully implemented and Parliament has enacted the Compensation Act 2006, NHS Act 2006, NHS Redress Act 2006, Mental Health Act 2007, Health and Social Care Act 2008, and the Human Fertilisation and Embryology Act 2008. In addition, there have been major changes to the regulation of the medical profession and the patient complaint procedures. Medical law is rapidly becoming a creature of statute. That is not to say that the judiciary have been sitting on their hands during the last three years, this second edition addresses a great many new decisions and common law developments.

I regard this edition as a substantial improvement over the last. Of the many changes to the book's content, a handful are structurally significant. *First*, Ch.3 on clinical negligence contains a complete reworking of the theoretical and ethical discussion (3.8) and a new section addressing the procedural issues of malpractice litigation (3.5). *Second*, Ch.5 on capacity now addresses a topic almost completed ignored in the last edition—the detention and treatment of *mentally ill patients* (5.5). *Third*, the first edition's largest chapter, which addressed transplantation, has been split into two for more manageable reading (Chs 13 and 14).

---

[5] See the following Practice Directions: [2001] 1 W.L.R. 194 and [2002] 1 W.L.R. 346.

ACKNOWLEDGMENTS

The first edition of this book was assisted by the financial support of the Arts and Humanities Research Council (AHRC) and I received many helpful comments from the publisher's reviewers, two research assistants, and the academic colleagues whom I listed in the preface of the previous edition. Here I wish to reiterate those thanks and extend them to include those who have offered advice on this new edition, including the publisher's three reviewers, Allan Beever, Alex Williams, and those studying on the "Law and Medicine" module at Durham who were kind enough to offer comments on the draft chapters.

I dedicate this book to those closest to my heart, not least of which is my dearest Zoe.

SDP

TABLE OF CASES

TABLE OF LEGISLATION

Chapter 1

....

MEDICAL ETHICS

1.1 Introduction

Should a doctor kill a suffering patient who begs for an early release from life? Should a doctor withdraw food and water from an insensate patient who could survive for years without ever regaining consciousness? Should a doctor perform an abortion on a woman who does not want to carry a disabled child? Such questions pulse with significance for the doctor, the patient, and the law.

The controversy and complexity of the issues faced by modern medicine is often deeper than is immediately apparent. Consider the weight to be given to the free and informed decision of a pregnant woman who steadfastly refuses the Caesarean section advised by her doctor. If your initial reaction is to support the woman's decision *in all circumstances* as long as she is competent, ask yourself whether you would still hold this view if the baby was ready to take its first breath and without a Caesarean section would be dead in the womb within the next 15 minutes, followed within hours by the death of the woman herself. What if the pregnant woman is refusing the Caesarean section solely to punish the baby's father? If your initial reaction is to support the doctor's view *in all circumstances* irrespective of the competence of the pregnant woman, ask yourself whether you would still hold this view if the pregnant woman's decision was supported by her husband, there was only a low chance that the surgery would save the baby and a high chance that it would accelerate the woman's imminent death from secondary lung cancer.[1] If your initial reaction was that it all depends on the precise circumstances, ask yourself who should make the decision as to what follows from a particular set of circumstances. What if there is insufficient time to get the issue before a court or other decision-making body?

Fortunately, many issues of medical practice are not nearly as ethically complicated or as detrimental to the imperturbable rhythms of commonplace routine. Few pregnant women refuse medical assistance when advised that their unborn child's life depends upon it. Medical law must, however, address the most controversial as well as the most straightforward aspects of medical practice. It is an inescapable feature of the lives of all health professionals (not just doctors) and the patients they treat.

1.2 Medical law and medical ethics

Medical practice and the law regulating medical practice play out in an overtly moral arena. From the Hippocratic Oath to modern times, this has (at least ostensibly) been recognised by the medical profession itself. This is not surprising when we consider that medicine deals with the deepest ethical and spiritual questions about life itself. By dealing with the beginning, end, and process of human life, medicine and medical law are rendered ineluctably ethical in nature. Still it is reasonable to ask just how law is connected to morality or ethics.[2] Is the connection between medical law and medical ethics simply carried by the common medical subject-matter or does it run deeper? The deepest and most theoretical response is also the most controversial. This claims that the very concept (or idea) of law is connected with the concept of morality. According to this conceptual claim, if we are to understand the nature of law and the legal enterprise, then we must understand that it necessarily connects with morally required procedures, morally required substance, or both. This *natural law* (or legal idealist) position is now out of favour in British legal theory. More popular are *legal positivism*, which holds that regulatory orders can be objectively recognised as legally valid without reference to morality, and *conventionalism*, which holds that the debate between the natural lawyer and legal positivist is merely one of empty word play. This book evades much of this debate because the

---

[1] These were the facts of the American case *Re AC*. At first instance the court authorised the involuntary Caesarean section. The District of Columbia Court of Appeals refused to stay this decision on appeal (533 A.2d 611 (DC, 1987)). However, the Court of Appeals later vacated its earlier judgment following the death of both the mother and fetus (573 A.2d 1235 (1990)).

[2] I shall use the terms "morality" and "ethics" interchangeably. Unless the context requires otherwise, they will be used to refer to standards of conduct that are at least *other-regarding* (prescribed for the benefit of others) (see Ch.17 (17.2)). The context will be otherwise when discussing "virtue ethics", as these positions focus on character rather than action (see below).

unequivocal (albeit contingent) connection between morality and medical law doctrine should be sufficient for even the most ardent legal positivist to see the relevance of moral theory.[3] Morality is sometimes explicitly incorporated into positive legal doctrine. It is unavoidably incorporated where the law addresses the ethically controversial issues raised by medical care.

Judges cannot escape the ethical nature of medical law by retreating into the fortress of legal doctrine. Consider the life and death decision in *Re A*, where the courts had been asked to rule on the lawfulness of separating conjoined twins.[4] The court had to decide whether to require doctors to stand by and watch the twins, who were unable to survive for long conjoined, die or allow the doctors to separate them in the knowledge that this would vastly increase the stronger twin's chances of survival but would kill the weaker twin. Despite judicial protestations that the "court is a court of law, not of morals",[5] the court was inescapably in moral territory and the moral arguments advanced on such issues need to be scrutinised for their adequacy.

1.3 Understanding medical ethics

A proper understanding of medical ethics, as a branch of applied ethics, requires an understanding of moral theory. However, the merest mention of "theory" can suck the enthusiasm out of even the most committed of law students. This threat looms ominously over moral theory because most students already have deep-rooted moral beliefs and hard thinking about those beliefs can be distinctly uncomfortable. Unfortunately, there is no escaping such hard thinking on any medical law and ethics course. You should not be discouraged by the initial unfamiliarity of new words and concepts, and it is hoped that you are encouraged to avoid the temptation to retreat towards the comfort of the familiar or hide from questioning the hitherto unquestioned. Thinking about one's belief system and ethical assumptions can be immensely rewarding. At the very least, moral theory should enable you to put those beliefs into their wider context. An unexamined reason is no reason at all.

In some respects philosophical study differs markedly from the study of legal doctrine. Legal doctrine carries reassuringly authoritative sources and source interpreters. In contrast, our society is no longer characterised by value homogeneity and shared religious beliefs. There are deep controversies about what we ought to do and how (and indeed if) we can determine what we ought to do. We can, nonetheless, still seek to understand these ethical disagreements. Since medical law is inseparable from medical ethics, we cannot properly understand medical law without understanding the ethical tensions in play.

---

[3] For convenience, throughout this book I use the term "law" and related terms to refer to "positive law". A legal idealist would not, of course, recognise positive law as valid law unless it is moral (either substantively or procedurally).

[4] [2001] Fam. 147.

[5] [2001] Fam. 147 at 155 (Ward L.J.).

1.3.1 Moral relativism, moral objectivism, and moral pluralism

There are two diametrically opposed views on the validity of moral beliefs. On the one hand are the *moral objectivists*, who hold that moral beliefs are capable of being objectively valid in the sense of being capable of being true or false, or capable of being rational or irrational.[6] On the other hand are the *moral relativists*, who hold that moral beliefs are not capable of being objectively valid. According to moral relativists all moral theories are *on a par* with regard to their truth or rationality. Denials that moral values can be objectively true or rational are made by those who deny all moral knowledge and those who wish to claim that moral values are *relative* to a particular culture or individual.

Widely accepted beliefs often contain an incompatible mix of moral objectivism and moral relativism. This can be seen when moral debates are ended by a statement that, in the end, it is just a matter of opinion and we ought to respect moral differences. The view that moral beliefs are just a matter of opinion is in fact incompatible with the view that we morally ought to tolerate the beliefs and actions of those with whom we disagree, unless toleration itself is held to be a matter of opinion. The view that moral beliefs are all just a matter of opinion is a moral relativist view. Yet, if the claim that there is an obligation to respect the differing moral views of others is to be more than a matter of opinion, then it amounts to the claim that there is at least one objectively valid moral obligation, which is a variant of moral objectivism. Moral relativism is the denial of moral objectivism. To be consistent, one cannot simultaneously accept liberalism as an objectively valid moral position and accept moral relativism.

Moral beliefs do, in fact, differ from person to person, culture to culture, and generation to generation. Some issues seem to attract almost as many ethical views as view holders. Consider, for example, views on when and if abortion is permissible. *Moral pluralism*, the existence of many different moral viewpoints, is an incontestable empirical fact. Despite this, there are few adherents to theoretically pure moral relativism. A consistent moral relativist would have to accept that the moral beliefs of Hitler and Gandhi are *on a par*. If moral beliefs can be neither false nor irrational, then there can be nothing objectively true or rational about the belief that it is wrong for doctors to torture patients for their own enjoyment or to engage in any other conduct generally regarded as repulsive. Moral pluralism does not imply moral relativism, because the existence of divergent views does not imply the equal validity of those views. Divergent moral views do not imply moral relativism any more than different views on whether the earth is flat or spherical, or different views on the answer to a mathematical question imply the equal truth or rationality of all those views. Moral relativism seems so plausible because the alternative seems so arrogant. Moral objectivism must hold that many moral beliefs are wrong. It does not imply that *every* moral question must have a single, *uncontroversial* answer.

---

[6] Cognitivism and rationalism, respectively. There are three variants of moral objectivism, which hold that moral beliefs are capable of being *true* (moral intuitionism or arational cognitivism), *rational* (moral rationalism or rational noncognitivism), or *both* (moral naturalism or rational cognitivism).

The reality of pluralism itself should not be overemphasised. Even in largely secular societies some level of moral consensus is actually quite common. If it were not, no stable polity could exist. It should therefore be no surprise that English legal doctrine actually encompasses many moral values shared by the majority of the population. Indeed, a more widespread developed-world consensus can be seen in international instruments such as the Helsinki declaration[7] and the innumerable human rights instruments that pepper the international arena. These instruments proclaim the universal nature of moral values such as respect for patient autonomy and the democratic process. This still, however, leaves ethical disagreement on many of the issues raised by medical law and the consensus that exists operates only at the level of regulatory or policy outcome. There is no universally accepted ethical theory; no consensus on the underlying ethical principles or their application. How, then, is a lawyer to understand these moral issues?

The first step is surely to understand the debates. Even *if* moral relativism is to be rejected in favour of objectivism, there are many different variations of moral objectivism. If, as will soon become clear, the law cannot be neutral between different moral theories which should the lawyer adopt? This chapter will focus on a more humble question: what are the principal moral theories vying for consideration? The more difficult questions will be left until Ch.17.

1.3.2 Criteria of moral permissibility

There are innumerable criteria capable of distinguishing the morally permissible from the morally impermissible. Some of these are religious—English case law is littered with examples of the tension between legal doctrine and the views of Catholics, Jehovah's Witnesses, and adherents of other faiths. Some of these are secular—modern bioethics[8] is often presented as a two-cornered contest between what are known as "deontological" and "teleological" theories.[9] There is an almost infinite range of possibilities. Let us start by examining the five major groups of moral theories: utilitarianism, duty-based theories, rights-based theories, virtue ethics, and compromise positions. The precise requirements and implications of each vary with the specific theory in play, but these general positions do explain much of the debate within controversial areas of medical practice.

---

[7] The Helsinki declaration is a set of principles for medical research on human subjects issued by the World Medical Association (WMA). See *http://www.wma.net* and the discussion in Ch.11.

[8] Bioethics has a wider subject-matter than medical ethics, as it encompasses all applied ethics concerned with healthcare and biological science. For present purposes this distinction is ignored.

[9] *Teleological* theories hold that moral permissibility depends on the effect of actions on some non-moral good or property, such as pain or pleasure. *Deontological* theories hold that the morally permissible is to be determined independently of any non-moral good or property. It has become commonplace to refer to teleological theories as *consequentialist*. I have avoided this practice because it implies that deontological theories are not concerned with consequences. Yet, many deontological positions are concerned with the consequences to moral goods or properties (see e.g. Gewirth 1978 and Rawls 1973, esp. 30). Thus, one must either define the deontological as compatible with some form of consequential evaluation or adopt a third category (of consequentialist deontological theories).

1.3.2.1 Utilitarianism

Utilitarianism is a collection of moral theories holding that we are morally required to seek the best possible balance of utility over disutility.[10] Classical or hedonistic utilitarianism is the most famous version and requires us to seek to maximise pleasure over pain. More recently, preference utilitarianism has come to the fore. In its most popular form, preference utilitarianism requires us to maximise the subjective preferences of persons.[11] All forms of utilitarianism invoke a calculus in which the relevant interests of all individuals count equally. This commitment to equality has led to the common association of utilitarianism with the phrase "the greatest benefit to the greatest number". This association is somewhat misleading, not least because the differences between utilitarians do not stop with the difference between classical and preference utilitarianism.

Faced with the objection that utilitarianism rides roughshod over widely accepted moral norms and requires endless utility evaluation, another version appeared requiring us to adopt rules that *generally* achieve the best utility balance. This version, known as rule-utilitarianism, seeks to answer concerns that act-utilitarianism creates uncertainty, is impractical, and can result in what are generally considered abhorrent conclusions. Standard act-utilitarianism can have a difficult time considering the consequences of every act. Imagine a doctor faced with a number of patients in need of life-saving donations of organs and tissue in circumstances where there is a suitable but unwilling potential "donor" from whom such tissue can be removed relatively safely.[12] For an act-utilitarian set on maximising utility, the permissibility of removing some tissue (say, a single kidney, a liver segment, some bone marrow, and some blood), to save the lives of four patients will depend on the overall utility balance of so doing. The utility of saving four patients' lives is likely to be very high, especially where those patients contribute to the lives of others. High enough that in some circumstances the disutility of using an unwilling "donor" could be outweighed! Imagine, for example, that the donor patient has no loved ones, needs major surgery for an unconnected purpose, and is unlikely to complain about any mistreatment, in circumstances where many of the participating medics could be kept in the dark to protect them from any feelings of guilt. Utilitarians have presented many responses to such difficult and controversial consequence balancing. Rule-utilitarianism is one such response.[13] According to supporters of rule-utilitarianism, adopting rules that track the best utility balance, rather than evaluating all individual acts, avoids the need for such

---

[10] See Gandjour and Lauterbach 2003 for a brief summary of many popular versions of utilitarianism.

[11] Preferences can be understood either as choices (see e.g. Hare 1981 and Harris 1985) or as interests/desires (see e.g. Singer 1993). Used in the latter sense, preference utilitarianism is little different to classical utilitarianism (cf. Singer 1993, 14).

[12] See further Harris 1975 and Thomson 1985 and 1976. Thomson considers situations where numbers also cause intuitive difficulties for rights and duty-based theories.

[13] Other common responses include rejecting unpopular conclusions as purely hypothetical and implausible, and invoking other moral principles to supplement the Principle of Utility.

calculations and the possibility of concluding that removing these organs is permissible. Others disagree.[14]

Utilitarians are actually quite a disparate bunch. Although utilitarianism can be said to hold that the permissibility of any particular action (for act-utilitarians) or rule (for rule-utilitarians) is dependent on its consequences for the utility balance, the utility balance itself is a source of some disagreement. There are many ways of balancing many different types of utility. Utility could be maximised (Positive Utilitarianism) or disutility minimised (Negative Utilitarianism), and some claim that there are higher or lower types of utility (Ideal Utilitarianism).

What do utilitarians agree on? Utilitarians are unified by acceptance of at least four tenets. *First*, utility is not itself a moral property. Utility is defined as something non-moral (such as pain or preferences), rather than something that is itself inherently moral (such as rights or duties). *Second*, the Principle of Utility—"we ought to achieve the best balance of utility over disutility"—is the supreme principle of morality. *Third*, individual interests can be meaningfully added together (for aggregation or averaging) and compared. Utilitarianism holds that it makes sense for A, B, and C's interests to be added in some way and weighed against the interests of D. In classical (pain/pleasure) utilitarianism, it is possible to aggregate the suffering of the four patients in need of life-saving tissue to outweigh the suffering of the unwilling donor patient. *Fourth*, what matters are the predicted consequences to the utility balance and nothing is intrinsically good irrespective of its consequences.

For the sake of convenience, unless otherwise specified, explanations of the implications of utilitarianism will focus on *utility-maximising preference utilitarianism*.

1.3.2.2 Rights-based theories and duty-based theories

Both rights-based and duty-based theories, as I define them, focus on the interests of individuals rather than the collective.[15] Unlike utilitarianism, they do not allow the aggregation or averaging of individual interests. They are distributive rather than aggregative. What matters is the weight of the relevant right or duty, not the number of persons involved. It follows that, unlike many versions of utilitarianism, if everything else is equal, the combined moral claims of a large number in need of wart removal cannot outweigh the claim of someone dying of a heart attack.

The difference between rights-based and duty-based theories rests on the waivability of the benefit of any moral obligation. Rights-based theories hold that all moral obligations reduce to moral rights, understood as justifiable

---

[14] David Lyons (1965) famously argued that rule-utilitarianism collapses into act-utilitarianism, because adequate rules are not absolute. Any adequate rule prohibiting a particular activity will be a rule prohibiting that activity in particular circumstances, where those circumstances depend on the consequences of particular acts. The rule against lying, for example, is not "Do not lie" but "Do not lie in circumstances x, y, or z". In response, J. J. C. Smart (1973) has presented a version of utilitarianism that requires us to *sometimes* obey rules (though, paradoxically, he sees this as a version of act-utilitarianism).

[15] In philosophical parlance, both are strictly deontological.

claims imposing correlative duties, the benefits of which are waivable by the rights-holder.[16] Rights are justifiable claims against unwanted interference (negative rights) or justifiable claims for wanted assistance (positive rights), or both. In contrast, duty-based theories do not automatically entitle the recipient of the duty to waive its benefit, in the sense of releasing the duty-bearer from an otherwise binding obligation. Duty-based theories are thus more compatible with paternalism. For some this distinction is one within rights-theories—a distinction between the will (or choice) conception of rights and the benefit (or interest) conception. This is simply a matter of terminology. Care must be taken with labels. The same concept can be described by different labels (compare the American "potato chip" with the English "crisp"), and the same label can describe different concepts (compare the American "jelly" with English "jelly"). The linguistic flexibility of "rights" is particularly prone to such confusion. Rights-speak is frequently hijacked by supporters of moral and political positions that do not hold that all moral obligations reduce to justifiable claims imposing duties on others, the benefits of which can be waived by the rights-holder. If we are to avoid misunderstandings, then we need to be consistent with our use of such terms. Not all usage of rights-speak is compatible with rights-based moral theories as defined here.

Both duty-based and rights-based theories are sometimes described as "Kantian", because of their association with the work of Immanuel Kant. Kant's theory is, however, often viewed as a duty-based theory because he is usually taken to reject the view that the benefits of all duties can be waived by the duty holder.[17] Kant famously presented four formulae of his supreme moral principle, the Categorical Imperative.[18] Two of these have received considerable attention in the literature on medical ethics. These are the *Formula of the Universal Law* (which requires us to take as guiding principles only those that can be willed as universal moral rules) and the *Formula of the End in Itself* (which requires us to treat others never as simply means to our ends but also as ends in themselves). The first conveys a message that is *superficially* similar to the Golden rule accepted by just about all religions—"treat your neighbour as you wish your neighbour to treat you" or, as it is sometimes expressed, "do unto others as you would have them do unto you". Unlike the Golden rule, however, what this version of the Categorical Imperative is concerned with what can *rationally* be willed.[19] The second demands that we never instrumentalise other persons in the sense of using them merely for our own benefit. For Kant "persons" were those who are able to voluntarily choose their purposes (agents

---

[16] Some theorists equate waiving the benefit of a right (i.e. the duty that is correlative to the right) with waiving the right itself. There is, however, a conceptual difference. The difference turns on whether it is possible to waive one's claim to being a rights-holder (which waiving one's rights would imply). Thus, I use the narrower expression to allow for those theories holding that individuals cannot possess the properties of a rights-holder without possessing rights. See e.g. the theory of Gewirth (1978).

[17] See, however, Beyleveld and Brownsword 2001, 109–110.

[18] The Formula of the Universal Law (see Kant 1785, as translated in Paton 1948, 83–84), the Formula of the End in itself (Paton 1948, 90–91), the Formula of Autonomy (Paton 1948, 93), and the Formula of the Kingdom of Ends (Paton 1948, 95–96).

[19] See further see Ch.17 (17.3.1.1).

or, in Kant's words, "rational beings with a will"). However, many subsequent theorists have chosen to ignore this aspect of his theory so as to derive more intuitively appealing conclusions.

Kant's work is at times dense and impenetrable (and often read in translation). The number of interpretations of his work is such that a cynic might be tempted by the view that much of its continuing popularity stems from the ability of contemporary theorists to read whatever they are looking for into it. The formula of the End in Itself is now widely accepted within contemporary bioethics and is particularly at home with rights and duty-based theories (due to their rejection of the idea that individual moral interests can be aggregated).

All rights- and duty-based theories must deal with conflicts between rights or duties. There can be, at most, only one absolute right or duty, otherwise conflict between them creates an insurmountable impasse. Imagine, for example, that a patient confides that he has an overwhelming desire to kill his girlfriend to his physician.[20] If the physician has a duty to keep the patient's confidence and a duty to protect innocent people from being harmed by a dangerous patient (i.e. there is a conflict between the rights of the patient and the rights of the patient's girlfriend), both duties (rights) cannot be of equal weight. This means that all such theories require a hierarchy of rights or duties, which in turn requires an objective criterion ranking those rights or duties.

1.3.2.3 Virtue ethics

Virtue ethics rejects all action-based moralities—including utilitarian, rights-based, and duty-based theories—in favour of character-based values.[21] Such positions reject the idea that judgments of duty, obligations to perform the right action, or moral rules and principles are the most basic moral concepts. Instead, ethics is understood to be primarily concerned with character and virtuous traits. Virtuous traits are held to be intrinsically good and, typically, linked to human flourishing (assessed according to some "objective" criterion).[22] In this way virtue ethics contrasts with action-based moralities, for which a virtuous character is simply one predisposing towards *actions consistent with one's moral obligations*. For virtue theory, virtuous character traits are not dispositions that are merely instrumental to compliance with moral rules or principles; they are dispositions about feeling, reacting, and acting that are in some sense intrinsically valuable or linked to human flourishing.

Virtue ethics dates back at least as far as the Ancient Greeks and is particularly associated with the work of Aristotle. Different versions offer different criteria of value. What virtues a doctor must have to be virtuous varies from theory to theory. According to Hursthouse, three tenets unify such theories: an action is only morally right if a virtuous person would choose that action, a

---

[20] This was the situation faced by the psychotherapist in the Californian case of *Tarasoff v Regents of the University of California* (1976) 131 Cal. Rptr. 14.

[21] See e.g. the articles on virtue ethics in Statman 1997a.

[22] Some theorists reject the necessity of a link between the virtues and human flourishing: see Statman 1997b, 7–8.

virtuous person is one who has or exercises virtues, and the virtues track human flourishing.[23] For Hursthouse's theory at least, since different virtuous persons exercising the same virtues can choose to act differently in identical circumstances, some ethical dilemmas have no single, universal moral answers.[24] To have any practical application, virtue theories need to tell us how to recognise virtuous persons and virtuous traits.[25] Even then, virtue ethics does not aim to provide universal rules or principles like the principle of utility (the aim is *not* to maximise virtuous conduct) or those associated with rights- and duty-based theories.

1.3.2.4 Compromise positions

The fifth moral camp, compromise positions, is a collection of eclectic moral positions typically drawing elements from the other four. These positions are rarely foundationalist and usually adhere more closely to the ethical reasoning of the layperson. It is essentially a miscellaneous category, capturing almost innumerable moral positions, *not all of which are coherent*. Some consider rule-utilitarianism to be a compromise position because of its reliance on general rules even where the strict application of the principle of utility requires a different conclusion.

The classic compromise position in medical ethics is represented by the "principlism" of Beauchamp and Childress. These two authors advocate four principles of biomedical ethics:

> (1) *respect for autonomy* (a norm of respecting the decision-making capacities of autonomous persons), (2) *nonmaleficence* (a norm of avoiding the causation of harm), (3) *beneficence* (a group of norms for providing benefits and balancing benefits against risks and costs), and (4) *justice* (a group of norms for distributing benefits, risks, and costs fairly).[26]

Their position explicitly seeks a compromise between overarching deep moral theory and practical ethics by adopting elements of utilitarianism, rights and duty-based theories, and virtue ethics. Beauchamp and Childress make no claims to foundationalist grounding for these principles. Nonetheless, "very few critics argue that any one of the four principles is incompatible with his or her preferred theory or approach to biomedical ethics".[27]

Beauchamp and Childress' principles are intended to act as rules of thumb, providing a checklist of ethical issues to consider when evaluating a medical issue. The problem is that just about all contentious medical issues can be understood as conflicts between one or more of these principles. Consider, for example, the question of whether it is permissible to allow living persons to

---

[23] See Hursthouse 1991, 225–226. Hursthouse herself defines human flourishing in terms of "*eudaimonia*", which she loosely specifies as "(human) rational happiness" (Hursthouse 1991, 226). Others contest the generality of these criteria. According to Statman, the unifying tenet is simply that "*the basic judgments in ethics are about character*" (1997b, 7, original emphasis).

[24] See Hursthouse 1991, 225 (n.1).

[25] For a basic application of a virtue ethics approach to medical practice, see Gardiner 2003.

[26] Beauchamp and Childress 2001, 12.

[27] Gillon 1995, 324.

voluntarily sell their organs. Beauchamp and Childress do not directly address commercial dealings in human organs, except to say that it is "appropriate to consider potential donors' motives, at least to the extent of investigating whether financial gain is the motivating factor".[28] This issue raises a conflict between, at least, two principles. On the one hand, the principle of autonomy tells us to respect the autonomous decision of the person who wishes to sell, say, a kidney or a liver segment. On the other hand, the principle of nonmaleficence tells the doctor not to inflict harm on a patient by removing an organ where there is no medical indication for its removal. The resolution of this conflict must either revert to deep theory or rely on the idiosyncratic, contingent intuitions of the decision-maker.

Another compromise position undergoing something of a revival is casuistry. Casuistry rejects overarching theories resting on abstract principles in favour of a case-based approach to bioethics. Although it has its origins in the theological reasoning of the Middle Ages, it has many contemporary supporters among secular bioethicists. The process involved should be easy to grasp for law students because it is similar to common law reasoning. It works by taking a paradigm case and arguing analogically from it. Any principles thereby derived are "subject to further revision and articulation in the light of new cases".[29] The difference is that, by rejecting the authority of any underlying abstract moral theory, casuistry lacks the authoritative structure of the common law. It also lacks the authoritative decision-makers, judges, who are so essential to the workability of the common law system. Thus, casuistry requires an authoritative mechanism for identifying a paradigm case and for identifying relevant similarities between the paradigm case and the one in question. As a response to this, some commentators have sought to find a middle way between casuistry and principle-based ethics.[30] The result is simply a different type of compromise position.

1.3.3 Religious and issue-perspective approaches

It might be objected that the five-fold classification of major theories in medical ethics presented above fails to give sufficient consideration to approaches derived from religious views (religious bioethics) or from issue specific perspectives (issue-perspective bioethics). The above classificatory framework is, however, consistent with more approaches to medical ethics than is at first apparent. The "compromise" group, in particular, encompasses theories drawing elements from the other four groups *and* purely miscellaneous theories.

Despite the obvious differences between religions, religious approaches to medical ethics have a number of common features. *First*, religious positions tend to place great value on human life as God's most special creation (see sanctity of life, 1.4.3.1, below) and adhere to some form of the Golden rule ("treat

---

[28] Beauchamp and Childress 2001, 50.
[29] Arras 1991, 35.
[30] See e.g. Richardson 2000.

your neighbour as you wish your neighbour to treat you"). *Second*, religious positions appeal to authoritative sources, usually an authoritative text (such as the Bible or Koran), figure (such as the Pope), or oral tradition. The above classificatory framework is consistent with religious perspectives. Most of these are variants of duty-based theories, rejecting consequentialist evaluation of non-moral properties, attempts to aggregate the interests of individuals, and the waivability of all moral benefits. Buddhism is different (indeed, some argue that it lacks the theism necessary to be characterised as a religion) and is best understood as a virtue-based position.

Issue-perspective bioethics is a diverse group of theories all of which examine ethical issues from the perspective of a particular issue. This does not mean that such theories ignore other issues, but that they are unified in their view that one particular issue is of central importance to moral theory.[31] These issues are usually those that are thought to be underplayed by traditional moral theories. Divergences exist on both the specific issues unifying a particular variant and the approach taken towards such issues. Feminist ethics, which is the dominant issue-perspective position, has many variants. All these variants fit into the framework presented above. Feminist "care ethics",[32] for example, is best understood as a form of virtue ethics. Not surprisingly, few feminists are act-utilitarians, as few would be prepared to accept the continued subordination of women where it maximises utility. Feminist ethics has played an important part in evaluating contemporary medical practices because, as many feminists have pointed out, patients tend to be disproportionately female and doctors disproportionately male. Also, many medical issues directly impact on women, particularly those concerned with abortion and reproductive medicine.

A distinction cutting across the moral positions defined above is that between positive and negative duties. Negative duties are duties not to interfere, whereas positive duties are duties to provide assistance. So, a duty not to kill a patient by lethal injection would be a negative duty and a duty to resuscitate a patient would be a positive duty. Within the rights-based, duty-based, and compromise camps it is possible to accept negative duties while rejecting positive duties. In practice, however, few bioethicists hold that the state has *no* positive obligations to provide any medical treatment to those unable to obtain access unaided. Heated debate between supporters of minimal positive duties on the state and supporters of more extensive duties is much more prevalent. Healthcare provision in the US leans more towards the minimalist end than that in the UK.

Until now we have not looked at communitarianism. Unlike most other moral theories, communitarianism rejects the focus on the individual in favour of the community or collective good. Membership of the community is presented as part of an individual's identity. It is a community-based ethical view with more in common with utilitarianism than rights-based or duty-based theories, but it also rejects the utilitarian requirement that every individual is to count as one and no more than one. Insofar as it purports to lay down criteria of moral permissibility, those criteria derive from social and communal

---

[31] Cf. Herring 2008, 27 (n.134).
[32] See e.g. Kittay 1998 and Steinbock *et al.* 2003, esp. 30.

values, putting it in the compromise camp. In practice, like virtue ethics, communitarianism also has strong relativistic tendencies—which is an issue to which we will return in Ch.17. This disparate group encompasses positions with a "distinctly conservative political" agenda (which emphasise history, tradition, and social practices) and positions adopting "a highly progressive, even Marxist, critique of existing social relationships".[33]

1.4 Common arguments in medical ethics

Medical ethics has often focused on the tension between rights-based and utility-based reasoning. This tension can also be found in judicial reasoning, particularly in matters concerned with resource allocation. Compare the approach adopted at first instance by Laws J. in the *Ex p. B* case with the approach adopted in the Court of Appeal by Sir Thomas Bingham M.R.[34] The two courts reached opposed conclusions on whether to quash a health authority's refusal to fund further experimental treatment for a ten-year-old girl suffering from acute myeloid leukaemia. Laws J. required the health authority to reconsider its decision on the basis that the girl's right to life had been compromised by their failure to reveal the details of their resource allocation policy. Sir Thomas Bingham rejected the justiciability of this issue, noting the complex policy nature of allocating a limited budget "to the maximum advantage of the maximum number of patients".[35] On one level, this is a conflict between a utilitarian and a rights-based position.[36] On another level, it is a conflict over the proper role of the court and whether the court is suited to what Lon Fuller famously called "polycentric" disputes, i.e. complex disputes whose resolution is likely to have repercussions on wider policy concerns or persons who are not party to the proceedings.[37] Both debates are morally loaded.

In addition to utility and rights-based reasoning, a number of ethical arguments make regular appearances in medical ethics. Three make particularly frequent appearances: concerns about "human dignity", the danger of stepping onto a "slippery slope", and the "sanctity of life". These concerns can, but do not always, convey moral reasons and arguments. Where they do convey moral reasons, these moral reasons will be underpinned by one of the five moral groups outlined above.

1.4.1 Human dignity

Historically, much of bioethics was a two-cornered contest between utilitarian and human rights perspectives, with the latter prioritising individual autonomy

---

[33] Steinbock *et al.* 2003, 26–29. See also Howard-Hassmann 1995, 2–5.
[34] *R. v Cambridge HA Ex p. B* [1995] 1 F.L.R. 1055, High Court and [1995] 2 All E.R. 129, CA.
[35] [1995] 2 All E.R. 129 at 137.
[36] See Mullender 1996.
[37] See Fuller 1978.

and pleading individual entitlements against collective welfare. More recently, bioethical debates have been peppered with claims that certain practices violate human dignity irrespective of their beneficial consequences or the existence of free and informed consent. Practices to be examined in later chapters, such as reproductive cloning, germ-line gene therapy, sex selection (particularly for social reasons), the commercialisation and commodification of the human body (particularly organ selling and commercial surrogacy), and research on embryos have been rejected as violating human dignity in this way. This new "Dignitarian alliance" draws on Kantian, Catholic, and communitarian credos.[38] It is, in essence, an alliance of different (duty-based and compromise) moral theories, all of which reject certain practices irrespective of their consequences or consensual nature. And it is a position with an evident influence on English law; on both the judiciary (see *R. v Brown*)[39] and Parliament (see s.32 of the Human Tissue Act 2004). Beyleveld and Brownsword insightfully refer to this concep-tion of human dignity as "dignity as constraint".[40] This constraint can be the "collective good that represents each society's vision of the kind of society it wants to be" (the communitarian reading) or the wrong of compromising one's own dignity as much as that of others (the Kantian reading).[41]

To confuse matters, the concept of human dignity is also invoked outside of the new Dignitarian alliance of duty-based and compromise theories. Utilitarians are reluctant to present their concerns about disutility in the terminology of human dignity, but they have, at times, quite happily hijacked the terminology of rights and might well start to use dignity in this way. Paradoxically, the human rights perspective often grounds its entire position in respect for human dignity. The premise that human rights are grounded in human dignity is reflected in post-Second World War human rights instru-ments. The Preamble and art.1 of the Universal Declaration of Human Rights, for example, takes as a fundamental premise the claim that we each have inalienable and intrinsic human dignity. Within the human rights tradition, however, dignity is used to emphasise individual choice and autonomy, rather than constraint. Beyleveld and Brownsword refer to this conception of dignity as "dignity as empowerment".[42] The only constraint here stems from the rights of others, rather than one's duties to oneself.

The famous exchange between Hart and Devlin on the enforcement of "private morality" can be understood as a clash of the empowerment and constraint perspectives.[43] It follows from the existence of two competing conceptions of human dignity—"dignity as a constraint" and "dignity as empowerment"—that human dignity can be cited by opposing sides on issues of medical controversy. Consider the request of a patient to be put to death by a doctor, often referred to as "voluntary euthanasia". Those relying on dignity as

---

[38] See Brownsword 2003b, esp. 26.
[39] [1994] 1 A.C. 212.
[40] See Beyleveld and Brownsword 2001, esp. ch.2.
[41] Beyleveld and Brownsword 2001, 11.
[42] See Beyleveld and Brownsword 2001, esp. ch.1.
[43] See Devlin 1959 and 1965, and Hart 1963. See the discussion in Beyleveld and Brownsword 2001, 34–35.

a constraint typically condemn such a practice as violating human dignity, even where the patient makes a free and informed decision. Those relying on dignity as empowerment will point to this free and informed decision-making as a reason why prohibiting the doctor from acting on the patient's request may prevent the patient from "dying with dignity".

It is also possible to use "dignity" to refer to something else, as this terminology can carry many loads down many paths.[44] The language of dignity is at its most insightful as an articulation of a modern conflict within bioethics. It usefully explains why otherwise opposed moral positions find themselves in what appears to be a two-cornered contest between, on the one hand, an "empowerment" alliance attracting the support of rights-based theories and, on the other, a "constraint" or "dignitarian" alliance of duty-based and (conservative) compromise positions.

1.4.2 Slippery slopes

It is also common for commentators on issues of medical law and ethics to appeal to the dangers of the "slippery slope".[45] One argument against voluntary euthanasia, for example, asserts that allowing this practice would cause us to slide towards involuntary euthanasia (killing a patient against the patient's will) as respect for life ebbs away. Such metaphorical appeals object to a particular practice or approach on the basis that it represents the first step on a slippery slope heading towards something undesirable. The fear is that allowing (or, occasionally, not allowing) the relevant activity will *lead to* a practice or outcome that is unequivocally unacceptable. Understood in this way, the argument usually has the following underlying form:

Permitting *A* will *lead to* B. Therefore, we ought to prohibit *A*.[46]

Here *A* might appear to be morally permissible in itself but *B* is considered a morally impermissible outcome. *A* might be said to "lead to" *B* on logical or empirical grounds, or both. In the above euthanasia example, the claimed link is empirical.

The underlying argumentative strategy employed by the slippery slope metaphor is that of a "feared endpoint". This strategy can also be invoked by metaphorical fears of "opening the floodgates". The floodgate metaphor does, however, carry subtly different associations to the slippery slope metaphor. For a start, the consequence of opening genuine floodgates is a flood, whereas the consequence of stepping onto a genuinely slippery slope is a slide to the bottom of that slope. Thus, the metaphor of "opening the floodgates" seems to carry

---

[44] See e.g. Beyleveld and Pattinson 2004b, where dignity is used to refer to the possession of moral status or standing on the basis of the characteristics or properties possessed.

[45] See Pattinson 2000 and 2002a, 144–153.

[46] This argument could also be expressed in positive form: Prohibiting *A* will *lead to* B. Therefore, we ought to permit *A*.

associations of greater urgency and unstoppability than the metaphor of "sliding down the slope". As a result the floodgate metaphor seems particularly appropriate for describing the threat that a particular decision or policy will lead to a sudden increase in legal actions, or will lead to uncontrollable or unpredictable liability.[47] The slippery slope metaphor, in contrast, seems more appropriate for describing situations where A is likely to lead to B in a more gradual way, such as where what is predicted is an incremental failure to make or uphold relevant distinctions. Nonetheless, where such metaphors are used to convey an argument—rather than used as rhetorical conversation stopping devices—they can describe any sub-instance of the general feared endpoint argument.

Some instances of the feared endpoint argument render the slippery slope metaphor superfluous. Where the underlying argument is that A will *logically* lead to B *because* the justification for prohibiting A also justifies prohibiting B purely logically, the metaphor is completely dispensable. It is merely an argument for consistency.[48] The metaphor has more relevance where the reason for allowing A is vague or expressed in vague language so that future applications will, in practice, incrementally take us towards allowing B. Here the link between A and B is an empirical prediction about what will be treated as purely logical developments, even though there is no straightforward logical link between A and B.[49]

The danger of metaphors is that they can cloak poor underlying arguments. Metaphors are only useful where they elucidate rather than obscure. Appeals to the dangers of a slippery slope based on an empirical prediction often fail to appreciate that the moral benefits of allowing A might outweigh the risk of B occurring. Those who, for example, argue that a particular medical advance is unacceptable because it might facilitate abuse must be careful to specify why the predicted abuse outweighs all the likely benefits of the activity. Humanity has an inherent ability to use (just about) anything for an immoral purpose. The discovery of fire created a means of deliberately burning others. The creation of the World Wide Web provided a means of disseminating bomb-making instructions to evil terrorists. The arrival of germ-line gene therapy will provide another means for evil dictators to conduct large-scale eugenic programmes. Yet, fire has the potential to prevent people from freezing, the World Wide Web has the potential to disseminate medical and educational information, and germ-line gene therapy has the potential to prevent some otherwise fatal conditions. If we ignore the potential benefits, then we become obliged to prohibit every new development. Such broad-brush claims would require regression to a state of being that is incompatible with human freedom of action, simply

---

[47] Personified by Cardozo C.J.'s fear that wide liability for negligence would result in "liability in an indeterminate amount for an indeterminate time to an indeterminate class": *Ultramares Corporation v Touche* (1931) 174 N.E. 441 at 444. This phrase carries the rhetorical flourish of an uncontroversially unacceptable outcome (no complex society could function with the legal and economic uncertainty created by indeterminate liability unless legal claims were unlikely to be brought or enforced).

[48] More precisely, such an argument is a substitutive instance of the logical principle of universalisability. For an explanation of this principle, see Gewirth 1978, 105.

[49] Cf. the Sorites paradox: "if one grain of sand is not a heap and one more does not make it a heap, there can never be a heap". This *paradox* relies on the grey area produced by reliance on vague or undefined terms, such as a "heap". It is fallacious insofar as it seeks to imply the absence of a distinction solely from the absence of a determinate cut-off point: see Pattinson 2002a, 143.

because human freedom enables the occurrence of immoral outcomes.[50] Thus, the fact that a medical development (or medical research towards it) could lead to abuses is not, without more, a sufficient argument. Dressing the claim in the clothing of the slippery slope metaphor does not change this.

Fears of stepping onto a slippery slope are not always empty or rhetorical. The metaphor can cloak sound arguments. But, if the metaphor is to enlighten rather than obscure, the underpinning argument needs to be carefully unpacked and all its premises exposed.

1.4.3 Sanctity of human life and the moral status of humans

1.4.3.1 The sanctity of human life

Most ethical positions hold human life to have intrinsic value. There are, however, many different views on the precise nature of this value. Keown has sought to distinguish three of these views:

(a) *vitalism*: the view that human life has absolute moral value, so that it is wrong either to shorten it or fail to lengthen it;

(b) *sanctity of life*: the view that it is always wrong to intentionally kill a human being, but there is no moral obligation to preserve life at all costs; and

(c) *quality of life*: the view that what matters is the worthwhileness of the patient's life and it is permissible to end the life of a person when it is not worth living.[51]

Keown's framework needs to be treated carefully because a large number of otherwise unrelated positions are put together in (c). Both utilitarian and rights-based positions are consistent with (c), but a rights-based theorist will usually restrict quality of life decision-making to the patient himself. Sometimes virtue ethics will also be consistent with (c). In fact, since for virtue ethics it is all a matter of one's motive and intentions vis-à-vis the virtues and human flourishing, virtue ethics is inconsistent with the absolute values in "vitalism" and "sanctity of life" as defined by Keown.

Vitalism as defined by Keown is a rather extreme position.[52] Few, if any, theorists adhere to this position. Keown claims that vitalism "is as ethically untenable as its attempt to maintain life indefinitely is physically impossible".[53] If it is to be action-guiding, it cannot require the impossible.[54] Even requiring all possible attempts to be made to save every human life would, to say the least, be very exhausting for health professionals.

---

[50] See Beyleveld 1997.
[51] See Keown 1997, 482–486.
[52] Keown (1997, esp. 503) accuses the House of Lords in *Airedale NHS Trust v Bland* [1993] A.C. 789 of confusing "sanctity of life" with "vitalism", so that it could be easily dismissed.
[53] Keown 1997, 482.
[54] Otherwise it violates the philosophical principle "ought" implies "can".

Only the duty-based and compromise camps are consistent with "sanctity of life" as defined by Keown (which is not to say that all such theories adhere to this position). This is a dignitarian position. Keown's own position is a duty-based position closely connected to Catholicism. As such it denies a free reign to patient self-determination (as do many other religious positions that hold human life to be a special gift from God). The duty not to intentionally kill is usually interpreted by supporters of this position by reference to the "principle of double effect" (sometimes called the "doctrine of double effect"). This principle holds that an act with two predicted consequences, one good and one bad, can be morally permissible where the intention is to achieve the good and the bad is as undesired as it is unavoidable.[55] Accordingly, this principle holds that it is sometimes permissible for a doctor to undertake a course of treatment that is intended to achieve a good outcome, even though it is known that a bad consequence will also follow. So a doctor is permitted to perform a hysterectomy on a pregnant woman with life-threatening womb cancer, despite it being impermissible to intentionally kill the fetus. Similarly, a doctor is sometimes permitted to administer morphine to relieve the suffering of a terminally ill patient even though it will accelerate the patient's death. In practice, it is often difficult to non-arbitrarily distinguish intended effects from unintended side-effects (double-effects). Many theorists doubt the moral significance of this distinction.[56] Some simply dismiss this principle as an ad hoc means of avoiding "the counterintuitive implications of an absolutist ethic that insists that some acts (like directly causing the death of an innocent person) are absolutely wrong, regardless of reason or context".[57] This is discussed further in Ch.15 (15.2.1).

The sanctity of life position, as defined by Keown, distinguishes between quality of life decisions and quality of treatment decisions. Only the latter are compatible with sanctity of life. According to Keown, "the sanctity principle holds that there can be no moral obligation to administer or undergo a treatment which is not worthwhile".[58] This position does not require treatment when it offers no reasonable hope of benefit or when the benefit is outweighed by its burdens. By way of example, Keown suggests that treatment to remove an intestinal blockage on an otherwise healthy Down's syndrome child would be required, but painful treatment on a terminally ill child that will only delay the dying process is not required. Since the worthwhileness of treatment involves an evaluation of whether the treatment's benefits are proportionate to its burdens, there is some scope for different judgments within this position.

Keown's position is not the only sanctity of life position. Other moral positions appeal to less stringent versions, some of which will be consistent with all the five bioethical positions outlined above. Thus, care needs to be taken when reading appeals to the sanctity of life because, like appeals to human dignity, the phrase means different things to different people.

---

[55] This doctrine has many formulations. See the more detailed discussion in Ch.16 (16.2.1).
[56] See e.g. Harris 1985, 43–45, and Singer 1993, 209–211.
[57] Steinbock *et al.* 2003, 22.
[58] Keown 1997, 485.

1.4.3.2 The moral status of human beings

The sanctity of life view adopted by orthodox Catholicism grants full moral status to all those who are biologically human. All human beings are owed *the same level* of moral duties by virtue of being members of the human species. This is not the only position that can be taken. Different moral positions imply or rest on different criteria of moral status and take different positions on whether *all* members of the human species have the same status.[59] The moral status of the patient is ethically controversial where the patient is an early human (an embryo or fetus) or permanently unconsciousness (such as an anencephalic baby or a human in a permanent vegetative state). In theory, such "patients" could be granted *full, no, or limited* moral status, depending on the positions taken with regard to the moral duties that we owe directly to them. For the purpose of exposition it will be assumed that all theories grant cognitively normal adult humans full moral status. This is certainly true of all the major theories of medical ethics.

With regard to the embryo, the *full status* position would grant the embryo the same moral protection as the mother, the *no status* position would grant the embryo no more status than the mother's hair or nails, and the *limited status* position would grant the embryo a fixed or gradual status between those two extremes. These positions and their connection to the five criteria for moral permissibility outlined above will be developed in subsequent chapters. It should be noted that a being with less than full status can attain additional protection by virtue of the interests of others with greater status. See, in particular, Ch.7 on abortion (7.2.1).[60]

With regard to the permanently unconscious human, the *full status* position would grant such humans the same level of status as you or I, the *no status* position would view such humans as having no intrinsic worth, and the *limited status* position would again grant such humans a fixed or gradual status between those two extremes. The implications of these positions will be outlined in Chs 13 and 15.

1.5 Pressures on medical law and the Human Rights Act 1998

The law rarely appeals *directly* to any one moral position. In an age of moral pluralism, any attempt to do so would be likely to provoke vociferous attacks. This does not, of course, mean that adherents of particular moral positions do not seek to press their views in the legal and political arena. Recent years have seen increased lobbying by pressure groups. For a time this was largely restricted to attempts to influence debates in the media and in parliamentary debates. A notorious incident of such lobbying occurred during the parliamentary debate

---

[59] See further Ch.7 (7.2.1.2).
[60] See also Chs 8 (8.2.1), 10 (10.3.1), and 15 (15.4.1).

leading up to the enactment of the Human Fertilisation and Embryology Act 1990. After lobbying hard to persuade the Government to amend the Abortion Act at the same time as passing legislation on assisted reproduction, one pro-life group went as far as sending replica fetuses to individual MPs. (Ironically, the result of fresh parliamentary consideration was a liberalisation of British abortion law—the very opposite of what the groups lobbying for a reopening of the abortion debate had wanted.)

Denied the support of the major political parties, many pressure groups are now increasingly looking towards the judicial process. In some cases, the courts have accepted submissions from groups and individuals who were not parties to the action. In the conjoined twin case *Re A*, for example, the Court of Appeal took the exceptional step of allowing submissions from the Archbishop of Westminster and the Pro-Life Alliance. In the *Burke* case, the Court of Appeal allowed submissions from no less than seven interveners.[61] It still remains comparatively rare for the courts to allow third party interventions in medical law cases.[62] Another trend has been for such groups and individuals to bring cases themselves. I know of no case where a group or individual with a "genuine and legitimate interest"[63] has been denied standing by the courts to challenge the legality of the decision of a public body on a topic of medical controversy. The famous *Gillick* case was, for example, a challenge to a Department of Health circular that had not, at the time, directly affected the applicant.[64]

Individuals and groups holding the full status view (i.e. those who hold that the embryo has the same moral status as you or I) have been particularly eager to invoke the judicial process. The Pro-Life Alliance and Comment on Reproductive Ethics (CORE), led by the Quintavalles,[65] have been particularly active in this regard. Their activities have largely failed to achieve their desired judicial outcome. In one week in 2003 the appeal courts decided two separate cases against the Quintavalles, and they had already lost a case in the House of Lords only a month earlier![66] Other full status groups have fared little better.[67] But all succeeded in attracting publicity for their cause.

The appeal courts have been understandably reluctant to drive judicial reasoning in the direction desired by pro-life groups. In medical law as a whole the courts are rarely unwilling to step back and consider the whole picture. At times this makes it difficult to avoid the view that the judges are reasoning backwards from a desired conclusion. In the conjoined twins case, *Re A*, for example, the appeal court judges agreed on little other than the outcome.

---

[61] *R. (Burke) v GMC* [2005] EWCA Civ 1003, para.20.

[62] Other examples, where the House of Lords has allowed third party interventions, include *Re F* [1990] 2 A.C. 1 and *R. v Bournewood Community and Mental Health NHS Trust Ex p. L* [1999] 1 A.C. 458.

[63] Sir Thomas Bingham M.R. in *Re S* [1996] Fam. 1 at 18.

[64] *Gillick v West Norfolk and Wisbech AHA* [1986] A.C. 112.

[65] Josephine Quintavalle and her son Bruno Quintavalle.

[66] *R. (Pro-Life Alliance) v BBC* [2003] UKHL 23 (reasons handed down on 16 May 2003), *R. (Josephine Quintavalle) v HFEA* [2003] EWCA Civ 667 (reasons handed down on 15 May 2003, later upheld by the House of Lords: : [2005] UKHL 28), and *R. (Bruno Quintavalle) v Secretary of State for Health* [2003] UKHL 13, HL, March 2003.

[67] See e.g. *R. (Smeaton) v Secretary of State for* Health [2002] EWHC 610.

It should, therefore, come as no surprise to discover that our judges have not used the Human Rights Act 1998 to radically reshape the substance of medical law. This Act could yet have such an effect. It is, after all, one of the most radical pieces of legislation ever enacted in this country. The Human Rights Act (HRA) 1998 requires the courts to give domestic effect to the rights of the *European Convention on Human Rights and Fundamental Freedoms* (hereafter the Convention) in two ways. *First*, "so far as possible", all legislation must be interpreted "in a way which is compatible with the Convention rights" (s.3(1)). If it cannot be so interpreted, the court may make a declaration of incompatibility (s.4(2)). The Government should then amend the relevant legislation to remove this incompatibility by making a "remedial order" (s.10).[68] *Second*, s.6(1) makes it unlawful for a "public authority" to act incompatibly with a Convention right. The victim of such an act may bring proceedings against the public authority or rely on the Convention rights concerned in any legal proceedings (s.7(1)). If the court finds a violation, it "may grant such relief or remedy, or make such order, within its powers as it considers just and appropriate" (s.8(1)).

The first, s.3(1), obviously applies to legislation addressing issues of medical law, such as the Human Fertilisation and Embryology Act 1990, the Human Tissue Act 2004, and the Mental Capacity Act 2005. The second, s.6(1), renders the decisions of public bodies directly challengeable under the Act and it is beyond debate that relevant bodies include the institutions of the National Health Service (NHS) and statutory bodies such as the Human Fertilisation and Embryology Authority and the General Medical Council.[69] What is more controversial is whether (and to what extent) the Act enables individuals to plead the HRA against other individuals (i.e. those who are not public authorities). There is no provision explicitly granting individuals actions against other individuals in the Act. Most of the controversy rests on the effect of s.6(3), which provides that a "public authority" includes "a court or tribunal". Reading s.6(1) with s.6(3), the Act states that "[i]t is unlawful for a . . . [court] to act in a way which is incompatible with a Convention right". Commentators are divided on whether this means that the courts must enable individuals to invoke the Convention rights against other individuals. At one extreme are commentators who argue that claimants need only plead that their Convention rights have been violated and, if the court agrees, it is required to enforce these rights.[70] At the other extreme are those who hold that the Act "does nothing to create private law rights".[71] Most commentators take a position somewhere between these extremes,[72] as have recent decisions of the appeal courts.[73]

---

[68] If the Government does not remove this incompatibility the patient could bring an action against the Government before the European Court of Human Rights in Strasbourg.

[69] See e.g. *R. (Burke) v GMC* [2004] EWHC 1879, paras 31 and 117.

[70] See Wade 2000, and Beyleveld and Pattinson 2002.

[71] Buxton 2000, 65.

[72] See e.g. Hunt 1998 and Brazier 2003, 21–22. According to Hunt, the Act requires any existing law governing private relations be applied and developed to achieve compatibility with the Convention, but it does not create any new causes of action against individuals.

[73] See e.g. *Douglas v Hello* [2001] Q.B. 967, esp. 1001–1002 (Sedley L.J.), and *Campbell v MGN* [2004] UKHL 22, esp. para.132 (Baroness Hale). See also the discussion of the latter case in J. Morgan 2004.

Many of the Convention rights that are given effect by the HRA impact on areas that are central to medical practice. Most notable are the right to life (art.2), the prohibition on torture, and inhuman or degrading treatment (art.3), the right to liberty (art.5), the right to a fair trial (by an independent and impartial tribunal for determinations of one's civil rights and obligations: art.6), the right to respect for private and family life (art.8), the right to freedom of thought, conscience and religion (art.9), the right to freedom of expression (art.10), the right to marry and found a family (art.12), and the prohibition of discrimination with regard to the enjoyment of these rights (art.14). This is a limited range of rights and many are qualified. Some impose positive duties on the state,[74] but none provide for a positive right to healthcare equivalent to the right to health recognised by other international instruments to which the UK is a signatory.[75]

The courts are unlikely to respond positively to ill-considered and opportunist attempts to use the HRA as a means of attacking inconvenient laws. It is not "a catchall means to put right all previous rules of law which are against a client's case".[76] For several years the courts have, after all, sought to take account of the Convention when interpreting Acts of Parliament and developing the common law. It is, therefore, no surprise that a number of early decisions applying the HRA merely confirmed the compatibility of the existing law with the Convention rights. It has, for example, been held that the legislative prohibition on assisting persons to commit suicide, and the common law on withdrawing nutrition and hydration from severely incapacitated patients are compatible with the Convention rights.[77]

The HRA is still likely to have a profound effect on some aspects of medical law.[78] The Convention right least protected by the existing law is the art.8 right to respect for private and family life—the so-called right to privacy. Before the Act, some invasions of privacy gave rise to no cause of action at common law.[79] Despite the Convention's qualifications to this right,[80] it has a wider ambit than the pre-Act common law. Following the enactment of the HRA 1998, developments in this area have already started to take place (see Ch.6).

---

[74] See e.g. *Osman v UK* (2000) 29 E.H.R.R. 245, para.115 at 305 (art.2), *A v UK* (1999) 27 E.H.R.R. 611, para.22 at 629–630 (art.3), *X and Y v The Netherlands* (1986) 8 E.H.R.R. 235, para.23 at 239–240 (art.8), *Otto-Preminger Institute v Austria* (1995) 19 E.H.R.R. 34, para. 47–48 at 56 (art.9 via art.10(2)), and *X and Y v UK* (1982) 28 D.R. 77, para.11 at 82 (art.10).

[75] e.g. the Universal Declaration of Human Rights 1948 (art.25) and the European Social Charter 1961, as revised in 1996 (arts 11 and 13).

[76] Hodgson 2001, 28.

[77] *R. (Pretty) v DPP* [2001] UKHL 61 and *NHS Trust A v M* [2001] Fam. 348, respectively. The decision on the former has been upheld by the European Court of Human Rights (*Pretty v UK* (2002) 35 E.H.R.R. 1) and the decision in the latter has subsequently been followed (*NHS Trust v I* [2003] EWHC 2243).

[78] Such as mental health law: see *HL v UK* (2005) 40 E.H.R.R. 32 and the discussion in Ch.5 (5.5.3).

[79] See *Kaye v Robertson* [1991] F.S.R. 62 and *Wainwright v Home Office* [2003] UKHL 53.

[80] Art.8(2) allows interference with this right if it is "in accordance with the law and is necessary in a democratic society" in the interests specified. Thus, interference with a patient's privacy can be justified on grounds of public safety, the protection of health or morals, or the protection of the rights and freedoms of others.

On the face of it the Convention appears to fit comfortably with rights-based theories. One should, nonetheless, remember that other moral theories can also use the language of rights. There are reasons to wonder whether this is the case with the Convention's use of rights-language. The Convention jurisprudence denies the rights-holder the authority to waive the benefit of some of the Convention rights, suggesting adherence to a duty-based position. In *Pretty v UK*, for example, the Strasbourg court held that the art.2 right to life did not "create a right to self-determination in the sense of conferring on an individual the entitlement to choose death rather than life".[81] Also, some of the Convention rights have qualifications that smack of utilitarian values. Article 8(2), for example, separates the protection of the rights and freedoms of others from other limitations on the ambit of art.8(1). Thus, like most international instruments, the Convention appears to represent a compromise position.[82]

Another possible source of future changes is the *European Convention on Human Rights and Biomedicine* (the "Biomedicine Convention"). Although the UK has neither signed nor ratified this Convention, there is jurisprudence suggesting that the provisions of the general human rights Convention are likely to be interpreted in the light of the Biomedicine Convention.[83] Interpreting a binding Convention in the light of a non-binding Convention can surely only be acceptable where the relevant provision from the non-binding Convention is uncontroversial and plausibly implicit in the binding provision. Thus, one would expect such an approach to be used to do little more than re-affirm an interpretation that would be given anyway. In practice, only time will tell what affect the HRA 1998 will have on more controversial issues.

1.6 Additional themes and pressures

For the reasons explained in this chapter, no study of the medical law of England and Wales would be complete without devoting attention to medical ethics. This chapter has not, however, been concerned about the types of reasons offered for accepting a particular moral position over other moral positions. It has, instead, mapped the moral territory in such a way as to enable the debates underpinning the law to be clarified in subsequent chapters. The dispute over justificatory strategies can be left until Ch.17, by which time the reader should have a more concrete understanding of both medical law and medical ethics.

Medical law has other themes that have not yet been brought to the reader's attention. No study of medical law can ignore the developing *consumerism* of patients, its corollary, *medical tourism*, and the impact of *market forces* on the NHS. Consumerism and medical tourism can take the form of patients

---

[81] (2002) 35 E.H.R.R. 1, para.39 at 29.
[82] See, however, Beyleveld and Brownsword 2001, 80–82, who argue that the Convention is most coherently explained as relying on a rights-based moral theory.
[83] See *Glass v UK* (2004) 39 E.H.R.R. 15, para.58.

shopping around both within and outside of the UK. While patients shopping around within the UK will be a key theme for some chapters, patients seeking medical services in other jurisdictions will be a theme of many more. Well publicised examples of patients evading regulatory restrictions by travelling to other jurisdictions include Diane Blood's visit to Belgium for posthumous insemination, Reg Crew's visit to Switzerland for physician assisted suicide, the Whitaker family's visit to the US for tissue-typing, and the Irish women who travel to mainland Britain for abortion (see Chs 7, 8, and 14).

Medical law also faces a continual challenge from the *changing nature of medicine and technology*. Not only do technological advances threaten to undermine outdated regulatory structures, the field of medical practice is expanding as conditions are re-defined as medical (a process which can be called "*medicalisation*"). Consider, for example, the way that medically assisted procreation turns the anxiety of involuntary childlessness into a medical condition treatable by infertility treatment, and how scientific advances (such as the creation of Dolly the sheep) raise new expectations and render existing law out-of-date (see Chs 8 and 10, respectively). Or consider how artificial nutrition and hydration, originally administered to treat short-term digestive problems, is now keeping patients alive who might never regain consciousness (see Chs 14 and 15). Medicalisation, however, threatens to disguise ethical decision-making as purely medical decision-making. It moves doctors away from weighing medical evidence and making diagnostic and prognostic judgments to making decisions about what *ought* to be done. Health professionals are participating in ethical decision-making. A clear example of this is presented by the current law on abortion, which treats doctors as the gatekeepers of access (see Ch.7).

The reality of *limited resources* is also constantly hammering at the door of medical practice (see Ch.2). No society can afford to grant universal access to expensive medical treatments. Limited finance is just the most apparent resource difficulty. There are also limitations in medical expertise and, sometimes, raw materials. Hundreds of patients are, for example, dying on waiting lists because of a shortage of human organs for transplantation (see Ch.13). The *global inequality* of resources, especially economic resources, is such that the preoccupations of this country are not those of some developing countries (see especially Ch.12).[84]

What should medical law do to deal with these realities? The law needs to be internally consistent, attract the broad support of the populace, and tailored to its specific goals, but there is more to defensible regulation than consistency, acceptance, and instrumental rationality. Regulatory attempts also need to display sufficient expertise, be sufficiently proactive, and be ethically defensible.

The regulation of medical practice cannot be left to the courts alone and, in practice, it is not. In reality, medical practice is regulated both formally and informally by a combination of professional and institutional rules, guidance, and practices (see, in particular, Ch.2). Medical law is more than legislation and case law. It is more than the application of legal doctrine to medical practice.

---

[84] See Chs 2 (2.6), 11 (11.2), 12 (12.4.2.2), and 13 (13.5 and 13.7).

1.7 Further reading

Beauchamp, Tom L. and Childress, James F. (2001) *Principles of Biomedical Ethics.* (5th ed.) (Oxford: Oxford University Press).

Beyleveld, Deryck and Brownsword, Roger (2001) *Human Dignity in Bioethics and Biolaw.* (Oxford: Oxford University Press), chs 1 and 2.

Harris, John (1985) *The Value of Life: An Introduction to Medical Ethics.* (London: Routledge).

Gandjour, Afschin and Lauterbach, Karl W. (2003) "Utilitarian Theories Reconsidered: Common Misconceptions, More Recent Developments, and Health Policy Implications." 11(3) *Health Care Analysis* 229–244.

Gardiner, P. (2003) "A Virtue Ethics Approach to Moral Dilemmas in Medicine." 29 *Journal of Medical Ethics* 297–302.

Singer, Peter (1993) *Practical Ethics.* (2nd ed.) (Cambridge: Cambridge University Press).

Steinbock, Bonnie, Arras, John D., and London, Alex John (2003) "Introduction: Moral Reasoning in the Medical Context." In Bonnie Steinbock et al. (eds) *Ethical Issues in Modern Medicine.* (New York: McGraw-Hill), 1–41.

Chapter 2

REGULATION, COMPLAINTS, AND THE PROVISION OF MEDICAL CARE

2.1 Introduction

The skills of the medical profession bring powers over health and illness, over life and death. Such skills are capable of evoking not only respect and esteem, but also fear and distrust. Consider the repercussions of the discovery that an unusually large percentage of children had died or suffered brain damage after heart surgery at Bristol Royal Infirmary. A public investigation reported findings of inadequate care and treatment,[1] and revealed evidence of questionable practices taking place elsewhere, which led to an inquiry into the removal and retention of tissue and organs at Alder Hey Hospital in Liverpool.[2] That inquiry discovered that a large amount of human material, removed during post-mortems, had been retained and stored without the knowledge or consent of relatives. Many organs had been stored without further use. Bristol and Alder Hey were not isolated incidents.[3] Media attention has also been provoked by the actions of a number of rogue individuals. Harold Shipman, a GP, was convicted of murdering fifteen of his patients and is thought to have killed hundreds more.[4] Some years earlier, Beverly Allitt, a nurse, was convicted of murdering four patients, all of whom were young children.[5] Another widely-reported case was that of the gynaecologist Rodney Ledward who was struck off by the General Medical Council for botching many operations.[6] These and many other recent "scandals" have drawn attention to a few bad health professionals and some failures of NHS systems.[7] As we shall see, the consequence has been the introduction of a number of wide-ranging reforms, including radical moves away from the traditional of professional self-regulation within medicine.

This chapter is concerned with attempts to balance the interests of patients, the public, and the medical profession. Essential to the regulatory structure is the way in which patient grievances are addressed. As we shall see, in addition to *ex post facto* grievance mechanisms—complaint procedures, litigation, and other professional accountability procedures—patients are increasingly gaining consumer-like powers to seek services from elsewhere. In theory at least, patients can now shop around for medical care within and outside the National Health Service (NHS), and within and outside the UK. This chapter seeks to examine the interplay between various mechanisms of professional accountability, as they operate in the context of the resource limitations and consumer expectations.

2.2 The structure and responsibilities of the NHS

The vast majority of healthcare in the UK is provided by the NHS—amounting to around 380 million treatments every year![8] Nothing more than a brief overview of the NHS will be attempted here, as it is a moving target, constantly being reformed for largely political reasons. Its position, close to the hearts *and*

---

[1] See the Bristol Report: Kennedy et al. 2001.
[2] See the Alder Hey Report: Redfern et al. 2001.
[3] See e.g. the Isaacs Report: HM Inspector of Anatomy 2003.
[4] The subsequent inquiry reported that Shipman had killed at least 215 patients and there was "real cause to suspect" that he might have killed 260 patients: see Shipman 2002, para.14.2.
[5] See Clothier et al. 1994.
[6] See the Ritchie Inquiry: DH 2000a.
[7] See e.g. Healthcare Commission 2006.
[8] See Healthcare Commission 2007, 4.

votes of the UK electorate, makes it a constant political football.[9] As a previous chair of the British Medical Association put it, the NHS is "the Punch and Judy show of British politics".[10]

The NHS Act 2006 consolidates numerous enactments addressing the NHS. Section 1(1) of this Act requires the Secretary of State to promote "a comprehensive health service designed to secure improvement (a) in the physical and mental health of the people of *England*, and (b) in the prevention, diagnosis and treatment of illness".[11] In the absence of contrary legislation, such healthcare services must be provided free of charge (s.1(3)).[12] While the Secretary of State and Department of Health have responsibility for the overall direction of the NHS, much of the day-to-day responsibility is delegated to other bodies within the NHS. The structure of these bodies has seen major reform. The latest reforms began in October 2002 and follow the Government's ten-year programme of investment and reform, outlined in the *NHS Plan*.[13] Initially, 28 Strategic Health Authorities replaced the 95 Health Authorities as the local headquarters of the NHS in England.[14] In July 2006, the number of Strategic Health Authorities was reduced to ten.[15] These bodies are responsible for managing the NHS locally by, for example, developing plans for improving local health services and ensuring high-quality performance.[16]

All NHS bodies have legal duties and responsibilities to patients. At the end of January 2009, the rights and privileges of patients within the NHS were brought together in the new NHS Constitution.[17] While this document does not seek to create or replace patient rights, it does serve as a useful summary of patients' rights and legitimate expectations and illustrates the consumer orientation that the NHS is increasingly been shaped to deliver.

2.2.1 Primary Care Trusts and NHS Trusts

Primary Care Trusts (PCTs) are the local bodies responsible for securing and planning both *primary care* (through family doctors, dentists, opticians, and pharmacists) and *secondary care* (through hospitals and ambulance services) for patients.[18] They can commission healthcare from public, private, or voluntary providers. There are now just over 150 PCTs. Since they control about 80 per cent

---

[9] See e.g. BBC 2005c.
[10] Dr Ian Bogle, quoted in Eaton 2002.
[11] The equivalent provision for Wales is s.1(1) of the National Health Service (Wales) Act 2006.
[12] Charges can, for example, be made for the supply of drugs, and optical and dental services: ss.172–181.
[13] DH 2000b.
[14] NHS Reform and Health Care Professions Act 2002 s.1, and NHS Act 1977 (as amended) ss.8 and 12.
[15] Strategic Health Authorities (Establishment and Abolition) (England) Order 2006/1408.
[16] See further *http://www.osha.nhs.uk*.
[17] See DH 2009a and 2009b.
[18] See NHS Act 2006 ss.18–24.

of the NHS budget (around £58 billion),[19] the majority of litigation over the provision of particular treatments will be directed at PCTs.

While PCTs can commission care from independent hospitals, most hospital care continues to be provided by *NHS Trusts*, increasingly referred to as NHS Hospital Trusts or Acute Trusts. These run NHS hospitals and employ most of the NHS workforce. These are supplemented by *NHS Foundation Trusts* (or foundation hospitals), which have even more financial, managerial, and operational freedom.[20] Given their role, the majority of patient complaints and compensation claims are unavoidably directed at NHS Trusts and NHS Foundational Trusts.

All NHS bodies have duties to monitor and improve the quality of healthcare.[21] The performance of the Strategic Health Authorities, PCTs, NHS Trusts, and Foundation Trusts is overseen by the Special Health Authorities (see below). Although the accountability of healthcare bodies is not the focus of this chapter, it is worth noting that there is also a statutory duty on these NHS bodies to consult and involve patients and the public in the planning and management of healthcare provision, which is imposed by s.242 of the NHS Act 2006. In addition, after the abolition of the existing consultative bodies (Patient's Forums) in March 2008, Local Involvement Networks (LINks) were established to discover what people want, monitor local services, and hold services to account.[22]

2.2.2 Special Health Authorities

The Special Health Authorities provide a health service to the whole of England, not just a specific region.[23] These bodies are part of the NHS and accountable, through the Secretary of State for Health, to Parliament. As public bodies their actions are amenable to judicial review. I will briefly outline the functions of the National Institute for Health and Clinical Excellence (NICE).[24] Other Special Health Authorities include the NHS Litigation Authority, the National Patient Safety Agency, and NHS Blood and Transplant.

NICE was created to respond to criticisms that the NHS was operating a "postcode lottery", whereby the quality and range of services available depended on geographical location.[25] NICE provides guidance on best practice, and, significantly, evaluates the cost-effectiveness of drugs and treatments,

---

[19] See King's Fund 2006.
[20] See Pt I of the Health and Social Care (Community Health and Standards) Act 2003, as discussed in Brown 2004.
[21] Health and Social Care (Community Health and Standards) Act 2003 s.45.
[22] See NHS Act 2006, Pt 14 (esp. ss.221–227).
[23] See NHS Act 2006 ss.13–17.
[24] Its short title was kept as NICE after its long title changed from the "National Institute for Clinical Excellence" on 1 April 2005.
[25] NICE (Establishment and Constitution) Order 1999/220 (amended by 1999/2219 and 2002/1760), and NICE Regulations 1999/260 (amended by 1999/2218, 2002/1759, and 2005/498). NICE's jurisdiction does not extend to Scotland.

especially new drugs and treatments. PCTs and NHS Trusts are required, unless otherwise directed by the Health Minister, to make treatments recommended by NICE (following a health technology appraisal) available to patients within three months.[26] In the words of the NHS Constitution: "You have the right to drugs and treatments that have been recommended by NICE for use in the NHS, if your doctor says they are clinically appropriate for you".[27] This role, with its effects on the allocation of healthcare resources, has received intense academic and political scrutiny.[28] NICE has not ended the postcode lottery. The resources needed to fund and follow its guidelines have to come from somewhere, and different PCTs will redistribute resources in different ways. Indeed, a recent House of Comments Health Committee report noted that a positive NICE technology appraisal carries the risk that "treatments which NICE has not examined, or other areas of healthcare, will be 'crowded out' as PCTs are forced to prioritise NICE-evaluated approaches".[29] Assessing the cost-effectiveness of health treatments and procedures cannot be an ethically neutral or purely technical process where funding decisions are tied to the resulting recommendations. Despite the apparently neutral connotations of evidence-based medicine, NICE's functions have an inescapable ethical dimension. And, as we shall see (2.4.2, below), resource allocation is underpinned by profound ethical controversy.

2.2.3 Other specialist bodies

There are a number of other regulatory and advisory bodies that are not formally part of any government department *or the NHS*. Some are known as Commissions, such as the *Human Genetics Commission* (the advisory functions of which are addressed in Ch.12).

The *Care Quality Commission*, which was established under s.1 of the Health and Social Care Act 2008, is worthy of specific mention. In April 2009, this Commission took over the functions of the Healthcare Commission,[30] the Commission for Social Care Inspection and the Mental Health Act Commission. The result is a body whose many functions include monitoring the detention of mental health patients, assessing the performance of health services, coordinating investigations into whether public funds are being used effectively within healthcare, and overseeing of the NHS complaints procedure. (We will return to the complaints procedure below, 2.3.2.) Importantly, this Commission

---

[26] Directions to Primary Care Trusts and NHS Trusts in England concerning Arrangements for the Funding of Technology Appraisal Guidance from the National Institute for Clinical Excellence (NICE) (July 1, 2003).

[27] DH 2009a, section 2a. See also DH 2009b, 32–35.

[28] See e.g. Syrett 2002 and 2003; Newdick 2004, 62–65; and House of Commons Health Committee 2008.

[29] House of Commons Health Committee 2008, para.219.

[30] This was formally known as the Commission for Healthcare Audit and Inspection and set up under s.41 of the Health and Social Care (Community Health and Standards) Act 2003.

has the task of reviewing the implementation of the National Service Frameworks (NSFs), which set national standards and seek to raise quality and ensure appropriate levels of care in local NHS services. This is a mammoth oversight body. To perform all these functions, the Commission has an extensive array of powers.[31] These *include* the power to enter premises that are used to provide NHS healthcare, without consent if necessary, and the power to inspect, copy, and remove from the premises *any* relevant document and require the person holding such information to produce it.

Some of the specialist bodies under discussion are not commissions. The *Medicines and Healthcare products Regulatory Agency* (MHRA) is responsible for licensing and regulating medicines and medical devices, including clinical research into such products. Various functions of this body are addressed in the chapters on medical research, genetics, and transplantation (see Chs 11–14). The *Human Fertilisation and Embryology Authority* (HFEA) has roles as licensor, regulator, and advisor in the area of assisted reproduction. Its functions are addressed in some depth in Ch.8 (esp. 8.3.1). A similar body, the *Human Tissues Authority* (HTA), regulates matters concerning the removal, storage, use, and disposal of human tissue failing outside of the regulatory remit of the HFEA. The functions of this body are addressed in the chapters on transplantation (see Chs 13 and 14).

2.3 Regulation, discipline and complaints

A number of procedures exist to ensure that medical practitioners are held accountable for their actions. If a doctor's conduct gives rise to concern it can lead to:

(a) a patient complaint to the health service provider;

(b) litigation by a patient;

(c) disciplinary action by the employing body;

(d) (after exhaustion of (a)) investigation by the Health Service Commissioner (the Ombudsman);

(e) investigation by the General Medical Council (GMC); or

(f) in extreme cases, investigation by the police or, where death results, an inquiry by the Coroner.

These are the main procedures. In exceptional circumstances there could also be a public inquiry. A famous example was the public inquiry into children's heart surgery at Bristol Royal Infirmary.[32]

---

[31] Health and Social Care Act 2008 ss.62–65 (previously: Health and Social Care (Community Health and Standards) Act 2003 ss.66–69).

[32] See Kennedy et al. 2001. This public inquiry was conducted under s.84 of the NHS Act 1977. This provision has subsequently been repealed and replaced by those of the Inquiries Act 2005.

This chapter covers professional regulation and complaints ((a), (d), and (e) above). Patient litigation is principally covered in other chapters, with the exception of patient initiated actions challenging the allocation of resources or seeking to take advantage of European law on free movement (see below). The sheer breadth of these procedures makes some selectivity unavoidable. Consequently, this book does not provide detailed coverage of disciplinary actions by the employing body,[33] criminal procedures, or coroner procedures ((c) and (f) above).

2.3.1 Regulation of the medical profession

Patient and public confidence in the medical profession is, at least in part, based on trust in its regulation and control. That trust has been damaged by high-profile scandals such as those summarised at the beginning of this chapter. As the Chief Medical Officer has pointed out,

> However atypical their behaviour, names like Beverley Allitt and Harold Shipman are now fixed in the public memory. The mounting pressure of scrutiny from the Bristol Royal Infirmary Inquiry, Alder Hey, Neale, Ayling, and the Kerr and Haslam inquiries, and other cases, has led to growing doubt in the public's mind about the adequacy of our arrangements for professional regulation.[34]

As a result, the regulation of the medical profession is currently undergoing major reform.

2.3.1.1 Regulatory overview

The regulation of the medical profession has been entrusted to the General Medical Council (GMC) since its creation by the Medical Act 1858.[35] This role continues under the Medical Act 1983, as amended. Most other health professionals have their own professional bodies. Nurses have the Nursing and Midwifery Council, dentists have the General Dental Council, opticians have the General Optical Council, osteopaths have the General Osteopathic Council, chiropractors have the General Chiropractic Council, and pharmacists have the Royal Pharmaceutical Society of Great Britain (to be replaced by the General Pharmaceutical Council).[36] These professional bodies maintain registers of qualified practitioners, oversee professional education, and are responsible for removing those who are unfit to practise from the register.

---

[33] For discussion of the rules governing NHS procedures and the disciplinary framework applying to GPs, see O'Rourke and Holl-Allen 2004, esp. 112–119.

[34] Donaldson 2007, 17.

[35] It was originally called the "General Council of Medical Education and Registration".

[36] See the Nursing and Midwifery Order 2001 (2002/253), the Dentists Act 1984, the Opticians Act 1989, the Osteopaths Act 1993, the Chiropractors Act 1994, and *http://www.rpsgb.org.uk*, respectively.

Since 2003, the regulatory functions of these bodies have been supervised by the Council for Healthcare Regulatory Excellence (CHRE).[37] One of the many oversight powers of this body is the power to refer the disciplinary/performance decisions of the professional bodies that it considers to be "unduly lenient" to the High Court.[38] It can in effect appeal on behalf of patients, even where the doctor has been acquitted by the GMC.[39] In the *Ruscillo* case, the Court of Appeal accepted that this power creates an element of "double jeopardy", but thought that such concerns were to take second place when this is necessary to protect the public.[40] The test of undue leniency is, however, much higher than one asking whether the decision was merely wrong.[41]

Our focus is the regulation of the medical profession. This is a role that the GMC is responsible for performing in the public interest.[42] Unfortunately, in recent years it has been attacked for failing both the patients and doctors. In 2000, the British Medical Association (BMA)—a non-affiliated trade union representing and protecting the interests of doctors—passed a motion of no confidence in the GMC. The GMC's response was to seek consultation on a fundamental review of its structure and processes.[43] After statutory consultation,[44] the Government gave legal effect to the GMC's proposed reforms by Orders of Council.[45] No new primary legislation was required (by virtue of s.60 of the Health Act 1999).

These reforms failed to satisfy critics. Dame Janet Smith in particular, made a number of poignant criticisms in the fifth report of the Shipman Inquiry.[46] This led to further reviews by the Chair Medical Officer (CMO), the Department of Health, and the GMC.[47] In February 2007, the Government issued a White Paper entitled *Trust, Assurance and Safety: The Regulation of Health Professionals*.[48] It signals the end of the GMC's role as adjudicator in fitness to practise cases. The Health and Social Care Act 2008 will, when implemented, establish an independent adjudicator by setting up the Office of the Health Professions Adjudicator (OHPA).[49]

---

[37] See NHS Reform and Health Care Professions Act 2002 ss.25–29, and *http://www.chre.org.uk*. This body was originally called the "Council for the Regulation of Healthcare Professionals". Its new name is given statutory force by s.113 of the Health and Social Care Act 2008.

[38] NHS Reform and Health Care Professions Act 2002 s.29. Referrals are to the Court of Session in Scotland and the High Court of Northern Ireland in Ireland.

Such referrals initially excluded decisions concerning impairment to the fitness to practise of a medical practitioner by reason of his physical or mental health, but this exclusion is removed by s.118(5) of the Health and Social Care Act 2008.

[39] *Council for the Regulation of Healthcare Professionals v GMC and Ruscillo* [2004] EWCA Civ 1356.

[40] [2004] EWCA Civ 1356, para.42.

[41] *Council for the Regulation of Healthcare Professionals v GMC and Leeper* [2004] EWHC 1850.

[42] According to the new s.1A of the Medical Act 1983, "The main objective of the General Council in exercising their functions is to protect, promote and maintain the health and safety of the public".

[43] See GMC 2001a and 2001b.

[44] See DH 2002a.

[45] These included the Medical Act 1983 (Amendment) Order 2002/3135, GMC (Constitution) Order 2002/3136, and the GMC (Fitness to Practise) Rules Order of Council 2004/2608.

[46] See Shipman Inquiry 2004.

[47] See CMO 2006, DH 2006a, and GMC 2006c, respectively.

[48] See HM Government 2007.

[49] See ss.98–110.

The Health and Social Care Act 2008 makes two other changes that are worthy of note here. *First*, it grants the GMC powers to appeal the outcome of fitness to practise cases heard by OHPA to the High Court.[50] *Second*, it creates "responsible officers", who will perform functions concerned with the regulation of doctors, including monitoring their conduct and performance.[51] These will be senior doctors within local healthcare organisations.[52]

2.3.1.2 Constitution and functions of the GMC

Who regulates doctors is almost as important to the retention of public confidence as the stringency of that regulation. Reforms have seen the GMC move away from the tradition of regulation of doctors by doctors. A large professional-dominated Council has been replaced by a smaller, more independent Council. The 2002 reforms saw a Council of 35 replace the previous 104 members.[53] Those 35 members comprised 19 elected by registered doctors, 14 members of the public appointed by the Appointments Commission,[54] and two academics appointed by education bodies (the universities and royal medical colleges). The lay membership thereby increased from 25 to 40 per cent. This did not, however, satisfy critics.[55] The 2007 White Paper therefore proposed that *all* members be appointed by the Appointments Commission and there be a minimum parity of membership between professional and lay members.[56] The Council now comprises only 24 members, made up of 12 lay and 12 professional members, all appointed by the Appointments Commission.[57]

The principal responsibilities of the GMC concern the maintenance of the official register of medical practitioners, oversight of medical education,[58] the provision of advice to the medical professional on professional conduct, professional performance, and medical ethics, and (subject to the reforms mentioned earlier) the operation of professional disciplinary procedures.[59] The maintenance of the register is one of the most high-profile of these responsibilities. There are currently 240,000 doctors on the register.[60] It exists to protect the public from those who lack appropriate medical qualifications. Perhaps surprisingly, no specific offence is committed by an unqualified person practising most types of medicine in the UK. A criminal offence is only committed when such a person

---

[50] Schedule 7, para.11 inserting s.40A into the Medicine Act 1983.
[51] Section 119, inserting ss.45A–45F into the Medicine Act 1983.
[52] See further DH 2008d.
[53] General Medical Council (Constitution) Order 2002/3136.
[54] S.57 of the Health Act 2006.
[55] See the recommendations of the CMO (CMO 2006, recommendation 43) and the GMC's response (GMC 2006c, esp. para.32).
[56] See HM Government 2007, ch. 1 (esp. para.1.12) and the opposition of the BMA (BMA 2007b).
[57] The GMC (Constitution) Order 2008/2554. The appointment powers granted to the Privy Council are delegated to the Appointments Commission.
[58] The GMC has responsibility for overseeing undergraduate education and continuing professional development. Postgraduate education is overseen by the Postgraduate Medical Education and Training Board (PMETB).
[59] Medical Act 1983, ss.2 and 30–34 (registration), ss.5–7 (education), and s.35 (advice).
[60] See DH 2008c, para.3.1.

(a) "wilfully and falsely" pretends to be a registered medical practitioner or possess a medical qualification,[61]

(b) seeks to perform a function statutorily limited to registered practitioners (such as prescribing medication and signing death certificates), or

(c) (with the implementation of the license to practise procedures) falsely holds himself out as being licensed to practise.[62]

The rationale for this is that patients should be able to seek advice on medical matters from whomever they wish, as long as they have not been deceived as to the qualifications, registration, or licence to practise of such persons. This is consistent with the development of patient freedom and consumerism, which will be explored later in this chapter.

The 2002 Amendment Order significantly reformed the GMC's committees.[63] In fact, the Education Committee was the only one to survive these reforms, though the responsibilities of that committee were subsequently transferred to the GMC itself.[64] I mention this only to explain references to committees that no longer exist (particularly the Professional Conduct Committee) in the case law and other materials that you might read. In the place of the old committees, the amended Medical Act provides for an Investigation Committee, Interim Order Panels, Fitness to Practise Panels, Registration Decisions Panels, and Registration Appeal Panels. These committees can include non-Council members.[65] In fact, only persons who are not members of the Council are allowed to sit on the Interim Orders, Registration Appeals, or Fitness to Practise Panels.[66] These are the adjudicatory committees. This restriction exists to ensure a separation of the investigatory/prosecution and adjudicatory functions of the GMC and thereby avoid challenge under the HRA 1998. Article 6 of the European Convention on Human Rights and Fundamental Freedoms (hereafter the Convention) requires the determination of an individual's civil rights and obligations to be undertaken in a fair and public hearing by an independent and impartial tribunal. The old procedures had failed to separate these functions, which had undermined their independence and impartiality.[67] Unfortunately, the 2002 procedures are not paragons of independence and impartiality.[68] As mentioned earlier, an independent adjudicator is in the

---

[61] Medical Act 1983 s.49.

[62] This includes engaging in conduct calculated to falsely suggest that one has such a licence: Medical Act 1983 s.49A.

[63] Medical Act 1983 (Amendment) Order 2002/3135, art.5.

[64] Medical Act 1983 s.10A, as amended by the Medical Profession (Miscellaneous Amendments) Order 2008/3131.

[65] Medical Act 1983 Sch.1 para.25(1A), inserted by the 2002 Order.

[66] Sch.1 para.23(a).

[67] See Panting 2001, 121. In *Ghosh v GMC* [2001] UKPC 29, the Privy Council refused to consider whether the old Professional Conduct Committee satisfied the requirements of independence and impartiality, because they were "satisfied that their own jurisdiction is sufficient to remedy any deficiency there may be in these respects" (para.32).

[68] See e.g. Shipman Inquiry 2004, para.25.37.

process of being established to address these concerns. The GMC's adjudica-tory panels—i.e. the Interim Order, Fitness to Practise, and Registration Appeals Panels—will therefore cease to exist and their powers will pass to the OHPA.

2.3.1.3 The "licence to practise" and revalidation procedures

Another significant change to the responsibilities of the GMC will be the introduction of a "licence to practise".[69] From late 2009, all doctors who want to practise will have to be registered *and* licensed. Such a licence is to be granted on first registration and will thereafter be subject to *revalidation*, whereby practitioners will be evaluated to ensure that they are up-to-date and fit to practise. Doctors will be revalidated every five years. These reforms were a long time coming and it is unfortunate that it has taken high profile scandals to provoke them.

At first sight, it appeared that the regulatory system at last recognised that a doctor who qualified over thirty years ago needs to be re-tested to ensure continued competence. Formal periodic reassessment is required for the continued practice of many other professions where incompetence can lead to the death or serious injury of others. Fire-fighters and airline pilots are two examples. Unfortunately, the licence to practise procedure that the GMC had intended to implement fell short of its potential. The fifth Shipman report scathingly attacked the GMC's proposals, arguing that the proposed system of revalidation fell short of proper "summative evaluation of each individual doctor's fitness to practise".[70]

The 2007 White Paper, endorsing most of the recommendations of the CMO, proposed further changes. Revalidation is to have two strands: relicensing and specialist recertification.[71] *Relicensing* is to encompass both summative and form-ative components, thereby requiring doctors to prove their continued compe-tence relative to the GMC's general standards. *Specialist recertification*, which will only apply to doctors on the specialist or general practice registers, will require doctors to demonstrate their continued competence relative to the standards of their medical speciality. Since the GMC cannot feasibly directly supervise, inspect, and evaluate the work of 150,000 doctors, relicensing will be conducted through local systems of clinical governance.[72] It is too early to judge how successful this new system will be.

2.3.1.4 The fitness to practise procedures

Doctors who are seriously incompetent or who abuse their position can endanger the health or life of their patients and the reputation of the medical profession as a whole. Consider the male GP locum who used his position to

---

[69] Medical Act 1983 ss.29A–29J. See further *http://www.gmc-uk.org*.
[70] Shipman Inquiry 2004, para.26.205.
[71] See HM Government 2007, ch. 2 and DH 2008c.
[72] See DH 2008c, esp. para.4.3.

carry out unnecessary intimate examinations of women.[73] When acting as a locum in Nottingham, he carried out an unnecessary breast examination on a patient complaining of *earache* and even attempted to give her an unnecessary internal examination. Later, as a locum in Manchester, he touched the breast of another patient who had no medical need for a breast examination. To make matters worse he sent Christmas cards to the home addresses of both women as subsequent disciplinary procedures were in motion against him, knowing that they would be witnesses at the hearing. Not surprisingly this doctor was struck off as a result of those disciplinary procedures.[74] Such behaviour is clearly an abuse of the position of power and intimacy entrusted to a doctor. Fortunately, it is extremely unusual.

Misconduct is only one of the problems that the professional disciplinary procedures are designed to address. New procedures were introduced at the beginning of November 2004.[75] Under these procedures, the Investigation Committee will investigate allegations that a doctor's "fitness to practise" is impaired (s.35C). The grounds for such a finding of impairment will be examined below, only one of which is misconduct (s.35C(2)). Any complaints that would not, if proven, call into question a doctor's fitness to practise will be referred directly to local procedures for consideration.[76] If the Committee considers there to be substance in an allegation, the issue can be referred to a Fitness to Practise Panel (s.35C(4)).[77] Where the Committee considers referral to be inappropriate, it may give a warning to the doctor regarding his future conduct or performance (s.35C(6)). Also, the matter can be referred to the Interim Orders Panel,[78] which has the power to suspend or place conditions on a doctor's registration pending a full investigation. This is a wide range of powers for an investigative panel. These reforms ironed out some of the problems presented by the old system. The GMC (including its licensing authority) can now act on its own initiative and refer a doctor to the Investigative Committee, rather than having to wait for a complaint (s.35CC(3)).[79] Further, the new revalidation procedure is likely to mean a substantial increase in the Investigative Committee's workload as a result of increased referrals (s.29C)

A Fitness to Practise Panel has much greater powers to address matters of discipline and performance than the Investigative Committee. In addition to being able to issue a warning (s35D(3)), a panel finding that a doctor's fitness to practise is impaired can erase the doctor's name from the register (except where a doctor is unfit to practise due to ill health), suspend him for up to 12 months, or make his registration conditional on compliance with conditions laid down by the panel for up to three years (s.35D(5)). Both suspension and erasure are harsh sanctions removing the livelihood of the doctor for their

---

[73] See BMA 2004, 56.
[74] See also the similar case of *Council for the Regulation of Health Care Professionals v GMC & Basiouny* [2005] EWHC 68.
[75] Medical Act 1983 (Amendment) Order 2002/3135, Sch.2.
[76] See GMC 2005.
[77] The "Adjudicator", once the Health and Social Care Act 2008 comes into force.
[78] The "Adjudicator", once the Health and Social Care Act 2008 comes into force.
[79] This was a flaw in the previous system: see *Krippendorf v GMC* [2001] Lloyd's Rep. Med. 9.

duration. I say "for their duration" because even erasure is not necessarily permanent. After five years, an erased doctor can apply to have his name restored, though he will need to satisfy a Fitness to Practise panel that he is fit to practise (s.41). Erasure carries negative connotations that are thought to be inappropriate in a health case; other responses are sufficient to protect the public. In an extreme case of ill health, after two years a panel can suspend a doctor indefinitely (s.35D(6))—though he can apply to have the suspension lifted every two years thereafter (s.35D(7)).

An appeal against a decision of the Fitness to Practise Panel (excluding decisions on warnings) is available to the High Court (s.40).[80] Previously appeals were directed to the Privy Council. There is some debate in the case law as to the role of the High Court in appeal hearings under this provision. The Court of Appeal in *Meadow v GMC* expressed the view that the court would not interfere unless the decision or sanction was "wrong".[81] It went further by declaring that the court must bear in mind the fact that decision-making tribunal has specialist expertise (deserving respect), has had the benefit of hearing and seeing the witnesses, and has performed a role akin to that of a jury with regard to questions of the facts and over-all value judgments.[82] Without referring to that judgment, the Court of Appeal in *Raschid v GMC* apparently took a more interventionist line by declaring that

> the High Court will correct material errors of fact and of course of law and it will exercise a judgment, though distinctly and firmly a secondary judgment, as to the application of the principles to the facts of the case.[83]

While the lower courts have recognised a difference in emphasis, hitherto it has been held to be irrelevant to the facts before them.[84]

The substantive test for determining whether a doctor's fitness to practise is impaired has also changed. There is now a single all-embracing concept of "impaired fitness to practise" by reason of misconduct, deficient professional performance, a conviction, adverse physical or mental health, or a determination of another regulatory body (s.35C(2) and 35D(1)). This replaces the old grounds of "serious professional misconduct",[85] "conviction", "seriously deficient performance"[86] and "serious impairment of fitness to practise by reason of a physical or mental condition". Notice the dropping of the phrase "serious professional" before misconduct, and "seriously" before "deficient" performance. These changes should make it easier for a relevant committee to

---

[80] In Scotland appeals are to the Court of Session and in Northern Ireland appeals are to the High Court of Justice in Northern Ireland: s.40(4).

[81] [2006] EWCA Civ 1390, paras 119 and 125 (Auld L.J.).

[82] [2006] EWCA Civ 1390, para.197.

[83] *Raschid v GMC* [2007] EWCA Civ 46, para.20 (Laws L.J.).

[84] *Cohen v GMC* [2008] EWHC 581, paras 19–26; *Rumbold v GMC* [2007] EWHC 2569, paras 17–30; and *Lamming v GMC* [2008] EWHC 266, para.20.

[85] "Serious professional misconduct" was not restricted to dishonesty or moral turpitude, it encompassed all conduct falling short of the standards expected from the profession that were serious in nature or degree: *Doughty v General Dental Council* [1988] A.C. 164.

[86] The leading case on which is *Krippendorf v GMC* [2001] Lloyd's Rep. Med. 9. See Grubb 2001a.

find a doctor unfit to practise.[87] In the fifth Shipman report, however, Dame Janet Smith argued that the new all-embracing test was "not easy to define" as "it means different things in different circumstances, it is almost without meaning".[88] She further suggested that the five categories are not exhaustive.[89] Her concern was that an allegation of an isolated or nearly isolated incidence of serious negligence could fall through the net. She therefore recommended that s.35C of the Medical Act be amended to add a further route to a finding of impaired fitness to practise, i.e. "deficient clinical practice".[90] This recommendation, which was not taken up by the Health and Social Care Act 2008, is arguably unnecessary in the light of recent court decisions. In *R. (Calhaem) v GMC*, for example, Jackson J. upheld a fitness to practice panel's finding of impairment through misconduct where the doctor has made a series of serious mistakes during a single episode of treatment.[91] His Lordship ruled that the authorities supported the view that "a single negligent act or omission, *if particularly grave*, could be characterised as 'misconduct' " and if "very serious indeed" could even constitute "deficient professional performance".[92]

Another reform addresses the *standard of proof* for disputed facts before a fitness to practice panel. (The burden of proof remains on the GMC.) Historically, as a matter of custom and practice, the standard of proof was the *criminal standard*. That is to say that a disciplinary panel would require disputed facts to be proven "beyond any reasonable doubt" (sometimes expressed as "satisfied so as to be sure") or they would find in favour of the doctor. Yet, except where the conduct is tantamount to a crime (where art.6 of the Convention probably requires the criminal standard or equivalent), the courts had indicated that the criminal standard is unnecessary.[93] Following much discussion, the more flexible *civil standard* was adopted at the end of May 2008.[94] The civil standard generally requires the facts to be judged as "more likely than not" (known as the "balance of probabilities"). It can, however, take account of circumstances and the gravity of individual cases, so as to require a greater degree of probability for more serious matters. Indeed, in matters of sufficient gravity, the sliding civil standard is virtually indistinguishable from the criminal standard.[95]

---

[87] The GMC has provided guidance on good medical practice declaring that "serious or persistent failure to follow this guidance will put your registration at risk" (GMC 2006a, 5).
[88] Shipman Inquiry 2004, para.25.46.
[89] See Shipman Inquiry 2004, paras 25.70–25.71.
[90] Shipman Inquiry 2004, para.27.212.
[91] [2007] EWHC 2606.
[92] [2007] EWHC 2606, para.39 (my emphasis).
[93] *McAllister v GMC* [1993] A.C. 388, 339 and *Sadler v GMC* [2003] UKPC 59, paras 73–74.
[94] The GMC (Fitness to Practise) (Amendment in Relation to Standard of Proof) Rules Order of Council 2008/1256 and Health and Social Care Act 2008 s.112 (which inserts s.60A, Health Act 1999). Discussion leading up to this reform can be found in GMC 2001b, para.51; Shipman Inquiry 2004, para. 27.256; HM Government 2007, ch. 4; and GMC 2007.
[95] See *B v Chief Constable of Avon and Somerset Constabulary* [2001] 1 W.L.R. 340, 354; *R (McCann and Others) v Crown Court at Manchester* [2002] UKHL 39, para.37; *Campbell v Hamlet* [2005] UKPC 19, para.25; and *R. (Doshi) v Southend-on-Sea PCT* [2007] EWHC 1361.

These reforms should lead to an increase in the number of doctors found to be unfit to practise. Doctors who would previously have been found guilty of "serious professional misconduct" by the GMC's "Professional Conduct Committee" will still be found guilty of "misconduct" by a "Fitness to Practise Panel" or the panel set up by the OHPA.[96] Many more, who would have previously got off scot-free, should now be warned or otherwise sanctioned. Interestingly, the BMA has objected to the reforms announced in the 2007 *White Paper* and included in the Health and Social Care Act 2008.[97] The BMA opines that these moves—removing the professional-domination of the GMC, lowering the standard of proof in disciplinary cases, passing the GMC's adjudicatory function to the OHPA, and creating responsible officers—threaten the profession's confidence in its regulation. Where one stands on this will inevitably turn on whether one prioritises the public's or the profession's confidence in the regulation of the medical profession.

2.3.2 Patient complaint procedures

Of the 380 million treatments provided on the NHS each year, around 100,000 give rise to a formal complaint.[98] The system dealing with those complaints has received a great deal of attention in recent years—so much so that those who have complained before will often have little better understanding of the process than complaint first-timers. Major reforms to the NHS complaints system effected in 1996 have been followed by reforms in 2003, 2006, and, yet again, in 2009. The Government's hope and belief is that the new system will be clearer and better structured; yet quicker and more responsive.[99]

It is too early to tell how much closer the new procedure will bring us towards a truly effective complaints process: one able to prevent the escalation of genuine concerns, remedy genuine grievances, while neutralising the grumpy gripes of petulant patients. It promises to be a simpler process for patients to understand and less drawn out for both patients and health professionals.[100] This should help to stem escalation and reduce the harm caused to hard-working health professionals by spurious complaints. It will operate alongside the reforms introduced by the NHS Redress Act 2006, so as to combine investigation, explanation, and compensation for claims below £20,000. This promises to provide remedies for genuine grievances while

---

[96] Doctors found guilty of serious professional misconduct by the Professional Conduct Committee include the two cardiac surgeons whose conduct led to the Bristol Inquiry and the doctor who, as Chief Executive of that NHS Trust, had failed to take action when concerns had been raised about the adequacy of the cardiac surgery: *Roylance v GMC* [2000] 1 A.C. 311. Sexual relations with patients were likely to result in such a finding: see e.g. *Wentzel v GMC* [2004] EWHC 381.

[97] See BMA 2007b.

[98] See Healthcare Commission 2007, 4. There are no official collated statistics on the number of complaints received by the independent sector.

[99] See DH 2007a.

[100] See the comments of the Health Service Ombudsman 2008, 7.

avoiding many of the flaws and hurdles of clinical negligence litigation. The assistance of the NHS Redress Act towards delivery on this promise will be examined in the next chapter (3.6.4). Our concern here is with the complaints procedure itself.

Not all patient concerns will lead to a formal complaint. Every Trust has a Patient Advice and Liaison Service (PALS) to listen to patients' concerns and offer information, advice, and support. This service seeks to deal with problems before a formal complaint is made and, where possible, nip them in the bud before they escalate. Where escalation to a formal complaint is necessitated, the PALS acts as a gateway to the Independent Complaints Advocacy Services (ICAS), which seek to assist patients with the complaints systems. Launched in 2003, ICAS supported some 10,422 complaints in its first year alone.[101] While this is actually only around 10% of complaints, this seems to have overburdened ICAS. Their report provides some insight into what patients are complaining about: the top three complaints are about clinical treatment, the attitude of staff, and communication with patients.

2.3.2.1 Overview: A history of change

The formal NHS complaints system was established in 1966, but that system was partial and fragmented. Following the recommendations of a special review committee,[102] the Government responded with a new three-stage procedure. This procedure was to apply throughout the NHS:

(1) local resolution;

(2) independent review; and

(3) review by the NHS Ombudsman (formally known as the Health Service Commissioner).

Despite these reforms the complaints systems continued to attract criticism.[103] The second stage was widely perceived to lack the independence required to ensure patient confidence and compliance with art.6 of the Convention. The problem was that the Convenor, who was to conduct the review with an independent lay person, was usually a non-executive director of the NHS body complained about.

The Government's response was to empower the Secretary of State to make provision for further reform. This was enabled by s.113 of the Health and Social Care (Community Health and Standards) Act 2003. Soon after the NHS (Complaints) Regulations 2004/1768 (*hereafter the 2004 Regulations*) were issued. The 2004 Regulations left the local resolution stage broadly unchanged, except for some consolidation and rationalisation of the statutory requirements, and entrusted a reformed independent review stage to the Healthcare

---

[101] See ICAS 2004, 4.
[102] See the Wilson Report (DH 1994a) and the Government's Response (DH 1995b).
[103] See Longley 1997, Wright 2004, and DH 2001a, paras 3.11–3.13, 2001c, 2001d, and 2003a.

Commission. Further reform was compelled by criticisms in the reports of a number of major inquiries, most notably the fifth report of the Shipman Inquiry.[104]

The next year saw the implementation of the NHS (Complaints) Amendment Regulations 2006/2084 (*hereafter the 2006 Regulations*).[105] These interim reforms made provision for increased coordination between the NHS and social care complaints systems, and adjusted the time limit for NHS bodies to respond to complaints to allow more thorough investigation of complex complaints. As I write, the NHS complains procedures is in the process of being replaced by a procedure that applies to both health and social care. A new regulator, the Care Quality Commission, replaced the Healthcare Commission at the beginning of April 2009 (see 2.2.3, above). The Care Quality Commission is to have no role in investigating individual complaints. Instead, the regulator will focus on the standard of complaints handling and the implementation of learning from complaints by those tasked with responsibility for local resolution. This new two-stage procedure will place much greater responsibility on NHS organisations to resolve complaints locally.

2.3.2.2 Details of the procedure

All NHS bodies (Strategic Health Authorities, NHS Trusts, Foundation Trusts, and PCTs) and primary care practitioners (GPs, dentists, opticians, and pharmacists) must have procedures for local resolution of complaints. At the time of writing, the Health and Social Care Act 2008 has yet to be implemented. Since the 2009 reforms are likely to re-enact some aspects of the 2004/2006 Regulations, it is worthy briefly outlining their key features.

The ground rules for the pre-2009 system were laid down by the 2004 and 2006 Regulations. Since the latter simply amended the former, all references will be to the 2004 Regulations as amended. These Regulations also applied to private hospitals providing care to NHS patients (reg.3(4)), but not to primary care practitioners.[106]

The 2004 Regulations required NHS bodies to have a person dedicated to hearing complaints: a complaints manager (reg.5). Complaints could be about any matter reasonably connected with healthcare provision within the remit of the NHS body (reg.6). Regulation 7 provided for a number of exclusions. One of these required the complaints procedure to cease if the complainant states in writing that he intends to take legal proceedings (reg.7(h)).[107] This was to discourage patient litigation, despite the fact that the complaints system could not award compensation. Another ensured that the complaints procedure did not operate where disciplinary proceedings were proposed or taking place

---

[104] See Shipman Inquiry 2004, esp. chs 7 and 27.
[105] See also the relevant Department of Health guidance: DH 2006c.
[106] To which other regulations applied. See e.g. NHS (General Medical Services Contracts) Regulations 2004/291.
[107] Before 2004 the procedure stopped if the claimant explicitly indicated an intention to take legal proceedings: see NHSE 1996, para.4.38.

against the subject of the complaint (reg.7(i)). The purpose of this exclusion was to reduce the likelihood that clinicians will take an overly defensible attitude towards the complaints procedure, but defensible attitudes were widely regarded as continuing.

Time played a key role under the Regulations (as it had under the 1996 system). Complaints were ordinarily required to be lodged within six months of the incident or the complainant becoming aware of the incident (reg.10). Complaints managers did, however, have the discretion to extend this time limit where the complainant was thought to have had good reason to delay and it was still possible to investigate the matter. The complaints manager's refusal to extend the time limit was itself potentially the subject of a complaint. Time limits applied to both sides. The complaints manager must acknowledge the complaint in writing within two working days (reg.11(1)). Under the 2004 Regulations, a written response was required to be sent to the complainant within 20 working days or as soon as reasonably practicable thereafter, but that was changed to 25 days by the 2006 Regulations (reg.13(3), as amended).

Until 2009, complainants who were not satisfied with local resolution were able to refer their case to the Healthcare Commission (reg.14). It had wide powers to deal with complaints, including the power to investigate further or refer the complaint to an independent regulatory body (such as the GMC) or the Ombudsman (reg.16(2)). It did not, however, have the power to award compensation.

As previously stated, the new procedure will remove the second stage altogether. The first stage, local resolution, will become more structured. In line with the recommendations of the fifth report of the Shipman Inquiry, complainants will be able to choose whether to complain to the provider (such as her GP) *or* directly to the commissioning body (usually the PCT).[108] The aim being to balance patients' fears that complaining will undermine their relationship with their healthcare provider with the need to ensure that the problem is dealt with efficiently.

There is no doubt that local resolution was in need of reform. The Healthcare Commission had reported that up to one third of received requests for independent review had been inappropriate as local resolution had not been completed.[109] What such statistics also reveal, however, is that there is significant patient demand for independent review. Indeed, it was expected that the Healthcare Commission would deal with around 3,000 cases a year, but it received nearly 7,000 requests to review complaints within the first ten months of taking over responsibility for second stage complaints.[110] In 2006–2007, the Healthcare Commission received 7,500 requests for independent review.[111] The Healthcare Commission also reported that around a quarter of complaints fell outside of its jurisdiction and these were "typically cases where the complaint had not yet been made to the trust".[112] Thus, if the abolition of the Healthcare

---

[108] See Shipman Inquiry 2004 and DH 2007a, paras 5.24–5.25.
[109] See Healthcare Commission 2007, 8 (33%) and Healthcare Commission 2008, 2 (26%).
[110] See National Audit Office 2005, 47.
[111] See Healthcare Commission 2008, 2.
[112] See Healthcare Commission 2008, 6.

Commission's investigatory role is not to result in the Ombudsman being overwhelmed, patients must be prepared to consider PCTs as sufficiently independent of the GPs and NHS Trusts whose services they have commissioned. In 2006–2007, the Ombudsman's workload was around a seventh of that of the Healthcare Commission.[113] She expects this to increase, but does not expect to take on the same number of complaints for investigation as the Healthcare Commission has done.[114] Demand for review by the Ombudsman will clearly be a key test of the success of the new beefed up local resolution procedure.

2.3.2.3 The Ombudsman

The Health Service Commissioners Act 1993 establishes the NHS Ombudsman for England and the NHS Ombudsman for Wales (s.1).[115] In practice, these posts are held by one person who is also the Parliamentary Ombudsman (officially the Parliamentary Commissioner for Administration). The current holder of these positions is Ann Abraham. She and her staff act independently of both the NHS and the Government and operate with a jurisdiction encompassing both administrative and clinical complaints within the NHS. On the face of it, this appears to be a very wide jurisdiction, but there are a number of notable limitations.[116]

First, a time limit of one year is imposed on her jurisdiction (s.9(4)).[117] Although the Ombudsman can hear a complaint after this period if she "considers it reasonable to do so", complaints made after a year are rarely investigated. The justification for this time limit lies with the evidential difficulties created by the passing of a long period of time and the need to protect professionals "from being in permanent jeopardy".[118] This justification mirrors that for the imposition of limitation periods in civil litigation, which raises questions as to why the period should differ from the three years placed on personal injury litigation.[119]

Second, the Ombudsman's jurisdiction is restricted to complaints that a patient has sustained "injustice or hardship", as a result of a "failure in a service" provided by a health service body or "maladministration" by a health service body (s.3(1)). Where the complaint concerns a matter of clinical judgment, the injustice or hardship need not be the result of maladministration (s.3(7)). The Ombudsman has indicated that her view on whether the exercise of clinical judgment satisfies the statutory test is essentially a question of whether or not the clinician has behaved "reasonably" or fallen below a "reasonable standard". Thus, the High Court has held, the Ombudsman misdirects herself if she does

[113] *http://www.ombudsman.org.uk/improving_services/annual_reports/ar07/fig_5.html.*
[114] See Health Service Ombudsman 2008, 7.
[115] This provision also established an ombudsman for the Scottish NHS. References to this 1993 Act below are to it as amended by the Health Service Commissioners (Amendment) Acts 1996 and 2000.
[116] See Harpwood 1996.
[117] This runs from the date on which the person aggrieved first had notice of the matters alleged in the complaint
[118] William Reid, a previous Ombudsman, quoted in Harpwood 1996, 221.
[119] See the Limitation Act 1980 s.11 (as amended). See further Harpwood 1996, 221–222.

not actually apply what is, in effect, the standard of care required by the law of negligence (i.e. the *Bolam* test).[120]

Third, the Ombudsman can only investigate where the complainant has exhausted the NHS processes, unless it is not reasonable to expect the complainant to invoke or exhaust these procedures (s.4(5)). Since these processes are meant to be separate from disciplinary processes, she has no jurisdiction over the conduct of disciplinary procedures (s.7).

Fourth, the Ombudsman cannot investigate where the complainant might have a remedy in the courts unless she is satisfied that it is not reasonable to expect the complainant to resort to that remedy (s.4(1)). Although many cases before the Ombudsman would not give rise to a legal action or are not worth suing on, this is one of the most significant limitations on the Ombudsman's jurisdiction. Litigation is often a lottery, legal aid is heavily limited, and many potential litigants cannot afford to bring an action in the courts, though the NHS Redress Act 2006 should address many of the problems for those with claims amounting to less than £20,000 (see Ch.3). In practice, the Ombudsman reinforces this limitation on the overlap with the courts by requiring patients to agree not to sue before investigating conduct that could give rise to a possible claim in negligence. The Ombudsman cannot, however, prevent a patient from initiating litigation, even if such an assurance has been given. Harpwood argues that this limitation seeks to prevent "fishing expeditions" at public expense, as "it would be unfair if the Commissioner proceeded with an investigation and upheld a complaint, only to open the way to litigation by having produced all the relevant evidence and made a recommendation in favour of the complainant".[121] With respect, I cannot agree. As we shall see in the next chapter, potential litigants with claims falling outside of the NHS Redress scheme face considerable burdens, so why should a patient unsatisfied by the complaints procedure be denied the benefit of the evidence produced by that procedure? As Harpwood recognises, the courts have far greater compensatory powers and can award compensation for pain and suffering, psychological injury, bereavement, and so on, whereas the Ombudsman can, at most, recommend an ex gratia payment of the patient's out-of-pocket expenses (under s.11(4)). Further consideration should be given to extending the Ombudsman's compensatory powers and extending her jurisdiction.

Despite these and other limitations, the Ombudsman's powers can be legitimately described as extensive. She has the power to demand the production of documents and records, and compel staff to testify (ss.11(3) and 13). These powers are equivalent to those of the High Court! After completing the investigation the Ombudsman will send a report to the complainant, the relevant NHS body, any person against whom a complaint was made, and the Health Secretary (s.14(1)). She may recommend a remedy, such as an apology or an ex gratia payment of the patient's out-of-pocket expenses. The Ombudsman's report has absolute privilege for the purposes of the law of defamation (s.14(5)). On paper there appears to be huge gap in the Ombudsman's powers, because

---

[120] R. *(Atwood) v Health Service Commissioner* [2008] EWHC 2315, esp. paras 26–35.
[121] Harpwood 1996, 223.

if she finds a complaint justified she cannot require the relevant health service body to do anything. But this misses the teeth of the powerful indirect enforcement mechanism that she has at her disposal in the power to lay a special report before both Houses of Parliament (s.14(3)). Fear of the adverse publicity that this can generate provides a considerable incentive for health services bodies to act on the Ombudsman's report.

2.4 Access to healthcare and resource allocation

The NHS's ability to supply healthcare services has been significantly outpaced by demand since it was first set up in 1948 by the National Health Service Act 1946. Unfortunately, this problem has grown as the average age of the population has increased and patients have come to expect and demand access to new, increasingly expensive treatment. Ironically, the NHS is itself partly responsible for these increased pressures. Over the last six decades the NHS has had a significant impact on average life expectancy, the development of healthcare knowledge and services, and the development of patient expectations. The "paradox of healthcare" is that improvements in healthcare lead to greater patient demands.[122]

No government can afford to resource healthcare services to the extent needed to treat all those who might benefit. Albert Weale has argued that the basic principle of the NHS—to provide comprehensive, high quality medical care to all citizens on the basis of medical need without financial barriers to access—threatens to become an "inconsistent triad".[123] Any two can co-exist but not all three simultaneously:

> Perhaps we can have only a comprehensive service of high quality, but not one available to all. Or a comprehensive service freely available to all, but not of high quality. Or a high quality service freely available to all, but not comprehensive. Each of these three possibilities defines a characteristic position in the modern debate about healthcare costs and organisation.[124]

In the modern NHS it is simply unavoidable that funding factors will sometimes play a role in the decision not to provide a service. The reality of the NHS is that healthcare is rationed by *restrictive access* (e.g. it is difficult to obtain access to cosmetic surgery, some forms of infertility treatment, and sterilisation reversal on the NHS) or by *dilution in quality* (e.g. delays, waiting lists, and understaffing).[125] Need this be so? While some argue that all medical needs can be affordably met if all unnecessary care was eliminated and available resources were diverted

---

[122] See Campbell et al. 2001, 251–252.
[123] See Weale 1998. These goals can be found in the patient guide to the NHS: DH 2001b, 2.
[124] Weale 1998.
[125] Further examples of rationing within the NHS can be found in Witting 2001, 444–450.

from other areas,[126] most opponents of rationing simply hold that rationing can be significantly reduced. According to Light, those who argue that rationing is inevitable in the healthcare system as a whole assume, without empirical evidence, that "health needs are bottomless".[127] He argues that experience in countries such as Germany and the Netherlands shows that well funded, efficient healthcare does not result in infinite demands on the health system. This leads him to conclude that rationing is avoidable and can be minimised by eliminating waste, such as "overtesting, inappropriate prescribing, the organisation of follow up for new outpatients, and the provision of care by doctors that can be done by nurses".[128] While efficiency gains might well be possible, around 70 per cent of the NHS's budget is spent on wages, and efficiency gains here will require redundancies, wage reductions, longer working hours, more effective working practices, or some combination of these.[129] Moreover, it is only possible to meet *all* medical needs if those needs are themselves limited, either by restrictive definition or restrictive assertion by patients.[130] Despite Light's assertions to the contrary, Germany and the Netherlands do not provide *unrationed* medical care that is comprehensive, high quality, and freely available to all on the basis of medical need alone.[131] Similarly, a study has estimated that providing all potentially beneficial healthcare to every French citizen would cost five and a half times the gross national product,[132] yet France topped the World Health Organization's last ranking of national health systems.[133] Reform of the NHS might reduce rationing or hide it more effectively, but it will not remove it.[134]

There are a number of grounds on which challenges to the allocation and funding decisions of healthcare bodies can reach the courts. A patient denied access to treatment might be able to bring an action for

(a) judicial review;

(b) negligence;

(c) breach of statutory duty;

(d) breach of a Convention right under the Human Rights Act 1998; or

---

[126] Relman argues that efficiency gains in the US would create "a realistic hope for an affordable system that will guarantee access to an acceptable standard of care for all Americans, without resort to rationing of any kind" (1990a, 1810). See also Relman 1990b. Cf. Callahan 1990 and Hall 1994.

[127] Light 1997, 113.

[128] Light 1997, 113.

[129] Statistic from Geldman 2002. Light wants greater controls over what he called "parasitic forms of privatisation" (1997, 115). The NHS Plan proposes breaking down boundaries between the professions to avoid wastage (see DH 2000b, 27).

[130] Light recognises that "To minimise the danger of provider induced demand, it is vital that agreement be met and criteria set for the levels of need to be attended" (1997, 112).

[131] Light claims that these countries have "an adequately funded free health services with no waiting lists" (1997, 113), but one has only to look at the Dutch who travel to other countries to avoid waiting lists in the Netherlands (see e.g. *Müller Fauré, van Riet* (C-385/99) [2003] E.C.R. I-4509, discussed below).

[132] See Lamm 1992, 1513.

[133] See WHO 2000.

[134] This has been explicitly recognised by both the Court of Appeal (*R. (Watts) v Bedford PCT* [2004] EWCA Civ 166, para.7) and the ECJ ((C-372/04) [2006] Q.B. 667, para.20).

(e) where the costs of alternative treatment in another EU country are refused, an action under the free movement provisions.

As we shall see, the courts are understandably reluctant to interfere with the political hot potato of resource allocation. The first four possibilities are explored in the following section (2.4.1), whereas the possibilities presented by EU law are addressed later in 2.5.

From an ethical point of view, given the necessity of resource allocation, these decisions must be made on defensible ethical criteria by appropriate persons or bodies. The principal competing criteria for ethical decision-making are explored in 2.4.2.

2.4.1 Challenging rationing decisions in the courts

As we shall see, patients have a difficult time challenging decisions to withhold treatment in the courts. While judicial action is by no means universally hopeless, patients cannot be said to have an *enforceable* right to general healthcare.

2.4.1.1 Judicial review

The traditional grounds for judicial review are relatively limited: the claimant must establish some illegality, irrationality, or procedural impropriety on the part of the public body in question.[135] In the early cases, these weapons have proved to be of little use to a patient denied treatment as the courts were very reluctant to interfere with resource allocation practices. One of many possible examples is the decision in *R. v Central Birmingham HA Ex p. Walker*.[136] In this case, a heart operation on a premature baby had been postponed on a number of occasions due to a shortage of nurses. The mother's application for judicial review was refused. Sir John Donaldson M.R. declared that decisions on the allocation of resources were not for the court to make and the court

> could only intervene where it was satisfied that there was a prima facie case, not only of failing to allocate resources in the way in which others would think that resources should be allocated, but of a failure to allocate resources to an extent which was *Wednesbury* unreasonable … Even then, of course, the court has to exercise a judicial discretion. It has to take account of all the circumstances of the particular case with which it is concerned.[137]

Less than two months later, the Court of Appeal refused to quash another decision of the same Health Authority.[138] The Health Authority's concession that this other child required an urgent operation was not enough for the court

---

[135] *Council of Civil Service Unions v Minister for the Civil Service* [1985] A.C. 374 at 410 (Lord Diplock).
[136] (1987) 3 B.M.L.R. 32.
[137] (1987) 3 B.M.L.R. 32 at 35.
[138] *R. v Central Birmingham HA Ex p. Collier* (1987) (Lexis)

to distinguish *Walker*. However, this later case is difficult to reconcile with later cases, such as *Ex p. A, D & G*.[139]

Ex p. A, D & G is a notable example of a successful case. In this case the Health Authority had refused to fund the referral of three applications to the country's only specialist clinic offering gender reassignment surgery. The Authority regarded such surgery as a low priority, on a par with tattoo removal, face lifts, and hair transplants, and had adopted a policy of not funding such treatment in the absence of "overriding clinical need" or other exceptional circumstances. The Court of Appeal held that the Authority, by adopting what in practice was a blanket exclusionary policy, had fettered its discretion and acted "irrationally". The court indicated that it would have accepted the Authority's policy if it had *genuinely* acknowledged that transsexuality is an illness and made provision for *genuine* consideration of individual cases. This reasoning does not furnish patients with any substantive rights to priority in the allocation of resources. Its focus is primarily procedural, requiring little more than the provision of genuinely personalised reasons for not funding treatment. Furnished with such reasons, the best course of action for patients is probably political, rather than judicial.

Successful judicial review actions are undoubtedly on the increase with the courts now requiring a clear decision-making process utilising explicit individualised reasoning.[140] Another worthy of note is *R. (Rogers) v Swindon PCT*.[141] The Court of Appeal held that the Swindon PCT's policy for the funding of the (then) unlicensed drug Herceptin was irrational. The use of the drug for early stage breast cancer was not licensed (though it was licensed for some forms of late-stage breast cancer), nor was it approved by NICE. Swindon PCT had a policy of not funding such off-licence use of the drug, but would consider whether an individual patient presented exceptional circumstances sufficient to justify treatment. Applying this policy, Ann Marie Rogers was denied treatment for her early breast cancer. In reaching the decision that her case was not exceptional, the PCT declared that the cost of the treatment (about £26,000) was not relevant to its decision. In so doing, the Court of Appeal held, there was no rational basis on which to refuse to treat Mrs Rogers. A rational policy, the Court held, would be one that

> had involved a balance of financial considerations against a general policy not to fund off-licence drugs not approved by NICE and the healthcare needs of the particular patient in an exceptional case.[142]

---

[139] *R. v North West Lancashire HA Ex p. A, D & G* [2000] 1 W.L.R. 977. Newdick (2004, 44) has expressed the view that "*Ex p. Collier* should now be regarded as wrongly decided for failing to assess the reasons for the decision to refuse treatment".

[140] e.g. *R. v North Derbyshire HA Ex p. Fisher* [1997] 8 Med. L.R. 327 (where the HA was held to have ignored a Department of Health circular and acted unlawfully by operating a blanket policy against funding the provision of an expensive new drug to patients with multiple sclerosis) and *R. v North and East Devon HA Ex p. Coughlan* [2001] Q.B. 213 (where the HA sought to renege on a promise to provide a "home for life" for the applications, which the Court of Appeal held to give rise to a "legitimate expectation"). Cf. the decision in *R. (Pfizer) v Secretary of State for Health* [2002] EWCA Civ 1566, discussed in Syrett 2004.

[141] [2006] EWCA Civ 392.

[142] [2006] EWCA Civ 392, para.73.

Thus, the policy would have been lawful if it had turned on financial consider-ations, combined with consideration of the patient's clinical need and indi-vidual circumstances.[143] Any approach that fails to fully articulate and apply criteria for exceptionality that take account of such factors—such as one that treats exceptionality as a concept that cannot belong to a group of patients[144]—will be unlawful.

Even where the ligation is itself unsuccessful, the adverse publicity gener-ated by the case will sometimes make a positive contribution to the patient's case. A father who challenged a health authority's decision not to fund experi-mental leukaemia treatment for his daughter lost in court, but an anonymous benefactor subsequently came forward to pay for her treatment.[145] Similarly, a woman who challenged a health authority's decision not to fund her infertility treatment on the grounds of her age lost in court, but later gave birth to a baby boy after successful treatment paid for by an anonymous benefactor.[146] There have been other incidents where the NHS has agreed to fund expensive treatment following *threatened* legal action and the adverse publicity thereby generated. Before the case against the Swindon PCT (considered above) was heard, for example, adverse publicity seems to have been a factor behind Somerset Coast PCT reversing its decision not to fund the treatment of a patient's early stage breast cancer with Herceptin.[147]

2.4.1.2 Negligence and breach of statutory duty

In theory, patients will have actions against funding bodies if they can show that they have breached either a common law or a statutory duty. The former involves relying on the general tort principles imposing liability for negligence (see Ch.3). A patient faced with the non-provision of a service as a result of resource allocation will usually find it difficult to establish that he is owed a duty of care, but once a duty of care has been established the courts will not usually allow a general lack of resources to operate as a defence for a failure to reach the relevant standard of care.[148] Breach of statutory duty requires the claimant to establish damage caused by the failure to perform a statutory duty that exists for the benefit of a limited class of the public and that Parliament intended those individuals to have a private right of action for breach of that duty.[149]

The success of an action for breach of statutory duty will turn on the proper interpretation of the statute in question. At first sight, two particular statutes appear to be promising sources of statutory duties to provide particular

---

[143] For discussion see Newdick 2007.
[144] See e.g. *R. (Ross) v West Sussex PCT* [2008] EWHC 2252.
[145] *R. v Cambridge HA Ex p. B* [1995] 2 All E.R. 129, examined in 1.4. The patient, Jaymee Bowen, died 14 months after the hearing: see Harm 1999, 1259.
[146] *R. v Sheffield HA Ex p. Seale* (1994) 25 B.M.L.R. 1. On the benefactor, see Cooper 1996.
[147] See BBC 2005f.
[148] *Wilsher v Essex AHA* [1987] Q.B. 730 and *Bull v Devon AHA* [1993] 4 Med. L.R. 117, esp. 141 (Mustill L.J.). See also Ch.3 (3.4.2), Harpwood 2001, 58–60, and Witting 2001.
[149] *X v Bedfordshire CC* [1995] 2 A.C. 633.

treatment and capable of giving rise to a private law cause of action. *First*, as we saw earlier, s.1 of the NHS Act 2006 imposes a duty on the Health Secretary to promote "a comprehensive health service". Section 3 further requires the Secretary to meet, to such extent as he thinks necessary, "all reasonable require-ments" including hospital accommodation and other medical services. *Second*, s.117(2) of the Mental Health Act 1983 imposes a duty on PCTs and health authorities to provide "after-care services" for those covered by the Act until such a person "is no longer in need of such services". Neither Act expressly provides for a private law remedy for breach of these duties.

It is now apparent that an action for breach of the statutory duties under the NHS Act 2006 (which were previously imposed by the 1977 Act) is unlikely to succeed. In *Ex p. Hincks*,[150] the applicant sought to challenge the failure to provide additional orthopaedic services at a hospital on the grounds of cost. Wien J. held that the Secretary of State was granted the discretion to provide services "to such extent as he considers" necessary and so no breach would be established unless no reasonable minister could have acted in that way and, even then, the Act did not give rise to a private law action for damages. The Court of Appeal upheld the decision on its facts without commenting on whether breach of this duty could give rise to a private law remedy. Subsequently, in *Re HIV Haemophiliac Litigation*, the Court of Appeal rejected such a claim on the case before it and expressed considerable doubt that the Act could be construed as imposing a statutory duty enforceable by an individual in a private law action for damages.[151]

Despite its more specific wording it has also proven difficult to establish a private law action for breach of statutory duty under s.117 of the Mental Health Act. In *R. (K) v Camden and Islington HA* the Court of Appeal held that this section did not establish an absolute obligation on health authorities (and by implication PCTs), rather it allowed for some discretion so that such bodies can take account of their budgetary demands.[152] This should be read with the earlier decision of *Clunis v Camden and Islington HA*,[153] where the Court of Appeal held (as a second reason for its decision) that s.117 was not intended to create a private law cause of action.

Consequently, patients have limited prospects of successful claims for breach of statutory duty under either the NHS Act or the Mental Health Act. It remains possible, however, that an exceptional case could give rise to liability.

2.4.1.3 The Human Rights Act 1998

The HRA 1998 introduced a further weapon into a patient's armoury. In contrast to certain other international instruments,[154] the Convention does not

---

[150] *R. v Secretary of State for Social Services Ex p. Hincks.* High Court: (1979) (Lexis); Court of Appeal: (1980) (Lexis).
[151] [1996] P.I.Q.R. P220, 237 (Ralph Gibson L.J.), and 248 (Bingham L.J.).
[152] [2001] EWCA Civ 240. See, in particular, para.29 (Lord Phillips M.R.).
[153] [1998] Q.B. 978, esp. 991.
[154] e.g. the Universal Declaration of Human Rights 1948 (art.25) and the European Social Charter 1961, as revised in 1996 (arts 11 and 13).

directly proclaim a right to health. Yet, at least three articles appear relevant to disgruntled patients denied treatment: art.2 (the right to life), art.3 (prohibition of inhuman and degrading treatment), and art.8 (the right to respect for private and family life).[155] As we shall see, there are situations where these Convention rights might be invoked by patients, but these rights do not grant a means of challenging the vast majority of resource allocation decisions. It should be borne in mind that s.2 of the HRA 1998 requires the domestic courts, when interpreting the Convention rights, to take into account the Strasbourg jurisprudence.

Article 2 has been held by the Strasbourg court to impose an obligation on the State to take positive steps to protect life,[156] but it is unclear to what extent, if any, these positive steps include healthcare. In *Scialacqua v Italy*[157] the European Commission rejected the applicant's claim that art.2 required the Italian public health service to refund the cost of (allegedly life-saving) herbal medicines, because they were not on the list of officially recognised medicines. Interestingly, the Commission did not dismiss out of hand the applicant's attempt to rely on art.2 when challenging the refusal of the health service to cover the costs of treatment obtained in another country.

Reliance on art.8 looks problematic in the light of Auld L.J.'s obiter statement that "Art 8 imposes no positive obligations to provide treatment" in the *Ex p. A, D and G* case examined above.[158] Other decisions have made it clear that where art.8(1) is invoked, resources are an important factor to be considered in the balancing exercise under 8(2).[159] The Strasbourg jurisprudence does, however, offer some hope to patients denied treatment on resource grounds. It has, for example, been held that an undue delay in providing treatment that has a serious impact on a patient's health could raise an issue under art.8.[160] Article 8(1) has been held to be breached by unduly burdensome requirements imposed on a patient wishing to claim the costs of gender reassignment surgery from a state insurance system.[161] In *Sentges v The Netherlands*,[162] in the course of dismissing as inadmissible the claim of a Dutch patient who wished to recover the costs of an expensive robotic arm against the Dutch health authorities, the Court reiterated that art.8 can, in exceptional cases, impose positive obligations on the State in the area of healthcare. However,

> It is incumbent on the individual concerned to demonstrate the existence of a special link between the situation complained of and the particular needs of his or her private life.

---

[155] Note also that art.14 also prohibits discrimination with regard to the enjoyment of these rights.
[156] *Osman v UK* (2000) 29 E.H.R.R. 245.
[157] (1998) 26 E.H.R.R. CD 164.
[158] See also *R. (Watts) v Bedford PCT* [2003] EWHC 2228 (counsel did not even argue the HRA on appeal: [2004] EWCA Civ 166).
[159] See e.g. *R. (F) v Oxfordshire Mental Healthcare NHS* [2001] EWHC Admin 535, para. 79, and *R. (Haggerty) v St Helens Council* [2003] EWHC 803, para.60.
[160] *Passannante v Italy* (1998) 26 E.H.R.R. C.D. 153.
[161] *van Kück v Germany* (2003) 37 E.H.R.R. 973.
[162] No.27677/02, 8 July 2003.

Also, States have a large "margin of appreciation" and

> this margin of appreciation is even wider when, as in the present case, the issues involve an assessment of the priorities in the context of the allocation of limited State resources.

It is clear that a patient denied treatment will have a difficult time establishing a violation of art.8. The door has been left slightly ajar for future exceptional cases, but it could not be said to be truly open.

Can art.3 provide any assistance to patients denied treatment? In the *Ex p. A, D & G* case, the Court of Appeal held that this provision was not designed to cover circumstances where NHS bodies were allocating finite funds between competing demands. The European Court of Human Rights has, however, used art.3 to prevent the deportation of persons with AIDS to a country without provision for treatment.[163] It is, therefore, conceivable that denial of treatment could, in an exceptional case, constitute a violation of art.3.[164] In practice, it is likely that such cases would be dealt with under art.8.

2.4.2 Ethical rationing strategies

Where a patient might benefit from a particular treatment the decision not to provide it is not a purely clinical decision. It is only purely clinical if the doctor genuinely believes, on medical criteria alone, that the proposed treatment is likely to be ineffective or do more harm than good. To deny treatment for any other reason is to ration. The decision not to fund the treatment might not have been the doctor's, but withholding treatment in such circumstances is rationing even if it takes place under the guise of clinical judgment. We have seen that rationing is to some degree inevitable. This raises questions about what (procedural *and* substantive) criteria should be used. In particular: should rationing decisions be open and explicit, who should make them, and how should they be made?

The procedural question of who should make rationing decisions is more complex than it appears. Two candidates are the *public* and *doctors*. NHS reforms are increasing the contribution of public participation and doctors cannot escape rationing decisions because, in a context of limited resources, every decision to treat a patient takes resources that could be used for others. Yet the *population as a whole* does not have sufficient time or expertise to weigh all the relevant variables and make all the decisions. Selective public involvement raises the question of who should be selected to participate. The views of

---

[163] *D v UK* (1997) 24 E.H.R.R. 423.
[164] See e.g. *Tanko v Finland* No. 23634/94, 19 May 1994, where the European Commission indicated that "lack of proper care in a case where someone is suffering from a serious illness could in certain circumstances amount to treatment contrary to Article 3". See also *Hurtado v Switzerland* No.17549/90, 28 January 1994 and *Keenan v UK* (2001) 33 E.H.R.R. 913.

individuals are likely to depend on factors such as whether they see themselves principally as patients or taxpayers. There is a tension between accurately representing public opinion and ensuring minority views are adequately considered. *Doctors and other healthcare professions* have medical expertise but they have no special ethical expertise. They have no special status as ethical decision makers, despite their special knowledge of the data on which these ethical decisions are to be based. As Harris points out, the opinion of mine engineers might be an important part of the data upon which to base a decision as to whether or not to attempt a rescue of trapped miners, but that does not make the decision an engineering decision.[165] Decisions on allocating scarce resources are not purely medical. (While on this point, neither is the advice on the cost-effectiveness of specific drugs and treatment given by the National Institute for Health and Clinical Excellence (NICE).) Yet, the majority of decisions actually taken by doctors are ethical, they are about "what ought to be done, in the light of certain values".[166] Leaving rationing and other morally-loaded decisions largely in the hands of doctors encourages the view that medical ethics is something for doctors alone.

The substantive question is arguably even more difficult. Access to medical care can be rationed using innumerable criteria. These include need, the ability to pay, societal contribution, individual age, cost of treatment, and the patient's responsibility for illness. The weight attached to these (and other) criteria will depend on what is considered to be the purpose of healthcare. Maximising welfare (as required by many versions of utilitarianism) will often produce very different outcomes to protecting hierarchical, non-aggregate interests (as required by rights and duty-based theories). Many initially plausible criteria merely gloss over the underlying difficulties. To allocate according to need, for example, raises questions as to what should count as a need, how an individual's needs are to be ranked, and how one individual's needs are to be weighed against those of others. Such questions are not evaded by simply prefacing the word "need" with the word "clinical",[167] as where resources are limited it will remain necessary to be able to rank and weigh clinical needs. Similarly, allocating according to the responsibility of individuals for their own ill-health raises questions as to how responsibility is to be determined and weighed, taking account of varying levels of prior pressures and the varying degrees of privacy invasion required to investigate individual life-style choices.[168] Once again we will find almost as many divisions between theorists

---

[165] See Harris 1985, 56.
[166] Kennedy 1981, 83. See further Kennedy 1981, ch.4, and Kennedy 1988, ch.2.
[167] Cf. the guidance of the Senate of Surgery of Great Britain and Ireland 1997, 26.
[168] The impact of these variables leads Harris (1995a) to reject allocating according to individual responsibility for one's own adverse health. The GMC guidance tells doctors: "You must not refuse or delay treatment because you believe that patients' actions have contributed to their condition" (GMC 2006b, para.7). NICE also declares it should not take into account whether a condition was "self-induced", unless "the behaviour is likely to continue and can make a treatment less clinically effective or cost effective" (see NICE 2008, para.6.6).

within a moral group as between the moral groups.[169] To avoid undue repetition I propose to focus on three criteria: ability to pay, age, and the Quality Adjusted Life-Year.

2.4.2.1 Ability to pay

Ability to pay will have particular appeal to those who deny that the state has positive duties to provide healthcare. Robert Nozick, for example, famously argued that taxation was a prima facie wrong and akin to forced labour where used in violation of the negative rights of individuals to spend their own justly acquired resources as they wish.[170] Although recognising that the freedom of individuals within complex societies requires the protection of a "minimal state", Nozick considers that "any state more extensive violates people's rights".[171] Nozick would not be willing to extend his vision of a justified "night-watchman state" to encompass anything like the modern NHS.[172] Most bioethicists support a much more interventionist role for the state and few moral positions are compatible with a totally free market in healthcare provision. It has been pointed out that a totally free market would severely disadvantage those who are already disadvantaged, because it would fail "to allow for the vulnerability and disadvantage created by the illness itself".[173] The ill and disabled are not well placed to earn the cost of their treatment, especially if their working life has and will continue to be marred by chronic illness or disability.

At first sight, the NHS appears to represent the very antithesis of allocating according to ability to pay, because it is committed to the principle that treatment should be available according to need, rather than ability to pay. However, in practice, some types of treatment are extremely difficult to get under the NHS. Examples include sterilisation reversal, infertility treatment, and cosmetic procedures such as hair transplants, face lifts, and tattoo removals. For those who have the ability to pay, access to such procedures is more readily available in the private sector.

Rationing by ability to pay should not be taken out of context. Just about all publicly funded services are rationed (by access or dilution), so that those able to pay can gain access to services not available at all or at equivalent quality in the public sector. Those who can pay can gain access to private schools, private security firms, and high-paid lawyers, just as easily as they can gain access to private healthcare. The question is to what extent the needs and demands of

---

[169] On the general problem created by scenarios affecting different numbers of people, see Thomson 1985.

[170] See e.g. Nozick 1974, 169: "Taxation of earnings is on a par with forced labor".

[171] Nozick 1974, 149.

[172] See Nozick 1974, 234–235. When responding to another theorist, Nozick rejects the idea that society should make provision for the medical care of its members. He argues that the "claim that society (that is, each of us acting together in some organized fashion) should make provision for the important needs of all it members . . . ignores the question of where the things or actions to be allocated and distributed come from".

[173] Campbell et al. 2001, 253.

patients should be subject to the ability to pay, and this depends on the extent of the positive duties on individuals and the State.

2.4.2.2 Age

Age is a controversial criterion for healthcare rationing. Despite appearances to the contrary, the major groups of moral theories do not automatically commit adherents to a particular view on the relevance of age. It might, for example, appear that rights-based theories are likely to reject reliance on age as a rights-violating "ageist" prejudice and utilitarians are likely to see directing treatment to the young as a way of maximising utility, but theorists from both camps can be found on both sides of the debate on the permissibility of using age as a selection criterion.

Norman Daniels, who seeks to apply a rights-based theory based on the theory of John Rawls (examined in Ch.17), argues in favour of using age in rationing decisions.[174] Daniels argues that age as a criterion of allocation differs from criteria such as sex or race, because everyone gets old. An institutional practice prioritising the young will, when viewed over our lifespan, treat everyone equally and benefit everyone. He postulates an individual who does not know his future healthcare needs, wealth or family situation, but knows that he has a fixed (and just) allocation of lifetime healthcare. He argues that such an individual would maximise the chances of reasonable longevity by reserving life-extending technologies for his younger years. Daniels applies this "Prudential Lifespan Account" of justice to resource allocation at a societal level and argues that it commits us to prioritising the young over the old when allocating the resources necessary for life-extending treatment.

John Harris argues, from an implicitly utilitarian position (examined in Ch.17), that age should be given only limited relevance when making hard choices over which patients to treat.[175] Harris asserts that in hard cases we can face a tension between the anti-ageist principle (emphasising that the value of life does not depend on age) and the fair innings principle (emphasising that an older person has had the benefit of a life that a young person has not). According to Harris,

> If we remember . . . that it will remain wrong to end the life of someone who wants to live or to fail to save them, and that the fair innings argument will only operate as a principle of selection where we are forced to choose between lives, then something workable might well be salvaged.[176]

He holds that his mid-way position will only operate at the extremes and in those "hopefully rare cases" where we have no choice but to choose between candidates who differ only in that one has had a fair innings (according to the views of reasonable people) and then we "we should choose to give as many

---

[174] See Daniels 1988, esp. ch.3. There are other supporters of using age, see e.g. Shaw 1994.
[175] See Harris 1985, ch.5.
[176] Harris 1985, 93.

people as possible the chance of a fair innings".[177] Thus, Harris does not see age as a general criterion for rationing healthcare resources. Nor will any moral theory rejecting the relevance of age to one's moral status or the weighing of one's moral interests. Indeed, some theories reject the fair innings approach altogether as morally irrelevant (see Ch.17 (17.3.2)). Some feminists have also rejected reliance on age on the basis that such a criterion would disproportionately affect women. Bell has noted there are more elderly women than men, and they tend to make a heavier demand on healthcare resources.[178]

2.4.2.3 Quality Adjusted Life-Years (QALYs)

In recent years, attempts to find an objective framework for determining treatment priorities have led to the development of a calculation based on "quality adjusted life-years" (QALYs). This calculation seeks to rank treatments according to the cost of providing a treatment relative to the number of years of life expectancy gained by such treatment, where life years are discounted according to ill-health, disability, and other factors affecting quality of life. This process involves a calculation wherein an additional year of healthy life expectancy counts as one, an additional year of less than healthy life expectancy counts as less than one, and death counts as zero. The idea is that priority should be given to those treatment services with the lowest cost-per-QALY (i.e. cost per additional year of quality adjusted life expectancy).

To apply the QALY calculation we need to assess both the quality of life (represented by a number between zero and one) and the life expectancy of the patient. The patient's quality of life must then be multiplied by the patient's life expectancy. The QALY score will be the difference between the product of this calculation before and after treatment. Imagine, for example, that a patient has a quality of life score of 0.5 and a live expectancy of 18 years, and that the treatment is expect to improve the patient's quality of life by 0.25 and life expectancy by two years. The QALY score of providing this treatment to this patient will be 6 ($0.75 \times 20 - 0.5 \times 18$). If the cost of the treatment is £6,000, the cost per QALY will be £1,000.

The idea is that the cost per QALY can be used to compare either alternative treatments for this patient or treatments for other patients. Consider, for example, an alternative treatment for the above patient, which for a cost of only £900 would improve her quality of life by the same amount but would not improve her life expectancy. In this case the cost per QALY would be only £200 ($900 / (0.75 \times 18 - 0.5 \times 18)$). Thus, the alternative treatment would be more cost effective. Imagine instead that the £900 for providing this treatment could be used to provide another patient with 9 QALYs. In that case, the cost per QALY would be only £100.

The QALY calculus is the preferred measure of NICE.[179] NICE says that it would be unlikely to reject a medicine with a ratio of £5,000–£15,000 per QALY

---

[177] Harris 1985, 102. See also Harris 1985, 93–94 and 101–102.
[178] See Bell 1992.
[179] See House of Commons Health Committee 2008, paras 97–102.

on cost grounds alone, whereas it would need special reasons for accepting medicines with costs of over £25,000–£35,000 per QALY.[180]

The QALY calculation can be criticised on a number of grounds. It requires medical prognoses to be treated as certain and a value to be attributed to a patient's quality of life.[181] What is more, using QALYs to prioritise the allocation of scarce medical resources in a population requires a distinctly utilitarian maximisation of health gains. This is only consistent with utilitarianism and compromise positions tending towards utilitarian-type reasoning and, even then, it is not consistent with all forms of utilitarianism. Many moral theories would have difficulty prioritising anti-smoking leaflets over kidney dialysis or hip replacement operations, even though this would provide many more QALYs per pound.[182] Saving life is usually given priority over enhancing life, irrespective of the relative QALY values.

Harris has argued that QALY calculations are weighted against the elderly and the permanently disabled due to the effects of their condition on their quality of life and remaining life years.[183] What is more, to use QALY calculations will put those unlucky enough to face a poor quality of life and life expectancy in "double jeopardy" in that these same disadvantages will be used to give them less priority in the resource competition. For Harris, a person's preference for continued existence should be treated as equal to that of anyone else.[184] In opposition, Peter Singer et al. present an example in which treating a victim of a serious car accident will produce more QALYs than treating a victim of a less serious accident for the same cost.[185] Their point is that QALY calculations measure the relative *change* in a person's health brought about by medical intervention. While they accept that there will sometimes be some kind of double jeopardy, they argue that when hard choices are required by scarce resources it is not unfair to give lower priority to those with incurable conditions negatively affecting their quality of life. In essence, this argument reduces to a conflict over the underlying moral assumptions being made.

2.4.2.4 Other issues

The determination of when rationing is required is morally loaded. The rationing of any resource or service is only morally defensible when there are more important and competing claims on limited funding. Where the same funds could provide life-saving cancer treatment or a culturally-important art gallery, cancer treatment is only justifiably rationed if the art gallery takes moral priority.

---

[180] See Rawlins and Culyer 2004, 225. See also the explanation of its decision-making framework in House of Commons Health Committee 2008, para.101.

[181] Singer et al. 1995 suggest that patients can make their own assessment of their quality of life by asking them what "period of life in the given health condition they would be prepared to trade for one year of normal health" (ibid., 144). For example, if the patient would give up 2 years of bedridden life for 1 year of normal health, the discount for being bedridden would then be 0.5.

[182] See Harris 1987, 123.

[183] See Harris 1995b, esp. 153. See also Harris 1987.

[184] See Harris 1995b, 151.

[185] See Singer et al. 1995, 145.

The allocation of healthcare resources is, therefore, merely a sub-instance of the problem of allocating societal resources. It is a sub-problem of the wider distributive justice debate. Once we get beyond the general rejection of criteria such as race, sex, or political views, we find that there are deep divisions over what justice requires. While it is tempting to offer my views on justifiable allocation criteria, this is not the place. The place for this is after arguing for the ethical premises on which to base such a view in Ch.17. Any complex moral theory will produce some situations in which a principled allocation is impossible to calculate with certainty. This might well require random allocation or, in some situations, even the non-availability of particular treatments or services.[186]

2.5 Patient consumerism, tourism, and mobility

The NHS has seen a growth in patient choice as part of a growing climate of general consumer empowerment. Reforms of professional regulation, patient complaints procedure reforms, the Patients Charter,[187] the NHS Plan,[188] the NHS Constitution,[189] and the removal of barriers to obtaining treatment elsewhere in the EU have, at least on their face, moved healthcare services towards a more consumer-driven, patient-centred orientation.

Within the NHS, patients now have the power to choose the provider of their primary care,[190] facilitated by the creation of league tables of clinical performance and relaxation of the GMC's rules prohibiting advertising by medical practitioners.[191] And the evidence suggests that patients are increasingly become cognisant of these moves. Recent reports of the National Patient Choice Survey reveal that nearly half (47%) of patients recalled being offered a choice of hospital for their first outpatient appointment and that three-quarters of patients choosing a hospital took account of cleanliness and low infection rates.[192] The NHS Constitution, introduced at the end of January 2009 with the intention of "setting our existing legal rights and pledges for the first time in one place", will surely increase patient reliance upon their consumer-type rights.[193]

Affluent patients can also vote with their feet by seeking access to private treatment (whether within or outside the UK). Patient tourism can have a

---

[186] See e.g. Ch.17 (17.3.2.3), and Beyleveld and Pattinson 2004a.
[187] DH 1995a.
[188] DH 2000b.
[189] See DH 2009a and 2009b.
[190] s.28F (doctor) and 28G (dentist), NHS Act 1977 (as amended), and NHS (Choice of Medical Practitioner) Regulations 1998/668. These rights are subject to the consent of the healthcare professional concerned and, in the case of medical practitioners, limits on the total number of patients accepted.
[191] The GMC's actions were provoked by a reference to the Monopolies and Mergers Commission. Doctors are still subject to constraint on what they may say in advertisements: GMC 2006a, paras 60–62.
[192] See DH 2008e.
[193] DH 2009b, 2. See also the NHS Constitution itself: DH 2009a.

serious impact on the NHS both *directly* (where patients seek reimbursement from the NHS) and *indirectly* (where the NHS picks up where alternative providers leave off). There are many examples of this indirect impact on the NHS. Private infertility services have increased pressure on NHS maternity provision, patients paying for treatment abroad often return to the NHS if complications arise, and, if something goes drastically wrong, few private hospitals have intensive care facilities. It is, however, the direct costs to the NHS that are attracting the most attention. The most notable developments are in European law, as interpreted by recent rulings of the European Court of Justice (hereafter the ECJ). It is towards these developments that we will now turn.

2.5.1 ECJ jurisprudence on claiming the costs of treatment abroad

European law offers two legal paths for those who wish to obtain medical treatment in another Member State: the EC Treaty Provisions on the free movement of services and art.22 of Regulation 1408/71. These two sets of complementary provisions require some explanation.

Article 49[194] of the EC Treaty prohibits restrictions on the free movement of services. Services are defined in art.50[195] as those normally provided for remuneration, including the activities of the professions. In addition to these provisions, a patient can sometimes rely on the EC Treaty provisions on the free movement of goods (arts 30 and 36).

Article 22 of Regulation 1408/71 (as amended) specifically addresses cross-border medical care. Article 22(1) provides that if the conditions in the national legislation for entitlement to relevant social benefits are satisfied, any insured citizen is entitled to such benefits in another Member State *if* the condition requires immediate attention *or* there has been prior authorisation. Article 22(2) provides that prior authorisation must be granted *if* the treatment is among the benefits provided for by legislation of the Member State in which the patient resides *and* the treatment cannot be given within the time normally necessary for obtaining the treatment in that country, taking into account the patient's current state of health and the probable course of the disease.

While at first sight it might appear that art.22 of this Regulation presents the greatest support for patients wishing to travel abroad for treatment, it is drafted in quite restrictive language. In contrast, the apparently vague Treaty provisions have provided fruitful ground for judicial policy making. As noted by the Court of Appeal, the ECJ has "put in place on the foundation of art.49 a substantial edifice not immediately apparent from its literal terms".[196] As we shall see, the ECJ has used the free movement of goods and services provisions

[194] Formerly art.57. The provisions of the EC Treaty were renumbered by the Treaty of Amsterdam.
[195] Formerly art.60.
[196] *R. (Watts) v Bedford PCT* [2004] EWCA Civ 166, para.31.

to fashion relatively extensive support for patient mobility, while recognising that uncontrolled patient and provider freedom has the potential to destroy public medical provision.

The first of cases on the free movement provisions held that the refusal by the Luxembourg social insurance system to reimburse the costs of treatment abroad were contrary to those provisions and not objectively justified.[197] Thus, one claimant (Mr Decker) was able to recover the costs of purchasing spectacles from Belgium and another (Mr Kohll) was able to recover the cost of her daughter's dental treatment in Germany.

Soon after, in *Geraets-Smits, Peerbooms*, the ECJ was asked to consider whether two Dutch patients could reclaim the costs of their hospital treatment abroad.[198] In contrast to the Luxembourg system, the Dutch health insurance system entitles insured persons to free medical treatment, not reimbursement of the costs of medical treatment. Treatment abroad will be paid for by this scheme only if the insured person has applied for prior approval (which is subject to two conditions). The ECJ ruled that restrictions on the freedom to provide services were only allowed if objectively justified in the "general interest". Following *Kohll*, aims of a purely economic nature could not justify a barrier to the freedom of services, but sufficient justification could be provided by

(1) the risk of seriously undermining the financial balance of the social security system;[199]

(2) the maintenance of a balanced medical and hospital service open to all in the interests of public health, insofar as this contributes to a high level of health protection;[200] and

(3) the maintenance of treatment capacity or medical competence essential for the public health, and even the survival of the population.[201]

The conditions for prior approval of treatment abroad imposed by Dutch law were that (a) the treatment be judged normal by medical professional opinion and (b) the same or equally effective treatment be unavailable in the Netherlands without "undue delay". The Dutch insurance system argued that these conditions were justified in the general interest, and sought to rely on the first of these to refuse reimbursing the cost of treating Mrs Geraets-Smits' Parkinson's disease in Germany and Mr Peerbooms' neurological problems in Austria. The ECJ ruled that although the Dutch legislation was contrary to free movement, both of the grounds in the Dutch legislation for refusing authorisation were justifiable in the general interest, provided that the first condition

---

[197] *Decker v Caisse de Maladie des Employés Privés* (C-120/95) [1998] E.C.R. I-1831 (free movement of goods); and *Kohll v Union des Caisses de Maladie* (C-158/96) [1998] E.C.R. I-1931 (free movement of services).
[198] (C-157/99) [2001] E.C.R. I-5473.
[199] See *Kohll*, 41, and *Geraets-Smits*, 72.
[200] See *Kohll*, 50, and *Geraets-Smits*, 73.
[201] See *Kohll*, 51, and *Geraets-Smits*, 51.

was interpreted to refer to what is sufficiently tried and tested by international medical science.

Geraets-Smits left many questions unanswered, particularly on the meaning of "undue delay" and the extent to which this ruling might enable patients to travel abroad to avoid waiting lists. This arose for consideration in the *Müller-Fauré, van Riet* case.[202] Ms Müller-Fauré had been refused reimbursement for dental treatment received in Germany. Ms van Riet had been refused reimbursement for an arthroscopy and other treatment received in Belgium. Ms van Riet's case is the most interesting because she had travelled abroad primarily to avoid the six-month waiting time in the Netherlands. The Dutch health insurer accepted that both refusals were infringements on free movement but argued that they were justified on the basis of the general interest. They argued that Mrs van Riet's delay was not "undue" because it was no more than was normal in the Netherlands.

This case has extra significance for our purposes because the UK made many forceful interventions, drawing the court's attention to the special characteristics of the NHS. They argued that the NHS, as a special non-profit making body, did not provide services "for remuneration" as required by art.50 for the application of art.49 on the free movement of services. It was also argued that to allow patients to opt out of NHS arrangements at its expense would "have damaging consequences for its management and financial viability".[203] Insofar as the ECJ addressed and rejected these arguments for the uniqueness of the NHS, the UK could be thought to have shot itself in the foot by making the decision directly relevant to the NHS.[204]

The ECJ's ruling revolves around the distinction between hospital and non-hospital treatment. The ECJ accepted that restrictions on free movement of services could be objectively justified in the case of *hospital* treatment.[205] The need for planned and stable medical care provision could justify restricting free movement and requiring prior authorisation. Any such system of prior authorisation must, however, be based on objective, non-discriminatory criteria that are known in advance and a procedural system that is accessible, capable of giving objective decisions within a reasonable time, and judicially challengeable. Any restriction on the provision of treatment abroad to situations where it is not available domestically without undue delay must take account of the circumstances of each specific case, including the patient's medical condition and medical history. Normal waiting times should not be conclusive.[206] In contrast, the ECJ ruled against restrictions on *non-hospital* treatment provided abroad.[207] The court thought that restrictions were not necessary for the planning and stability of the healthcare system. Also, it did not think that removing the requirement of prior authorisation would cause large numbers to

[202] (C-385/99) [2003] E.C.R. I-4509.
[203] [2003] E.C.R. I-4509, para.58.
[204] See [2003] E.C.R. I-4509, para.103 and Davies 2004, 98.
[205] [2003] E.C.R. I-4509, paras 76–81.
[206] [2003] E.C.R. I-4509, paras 89–92.
[207] [2003] E.C.R. I-4509, para.93–95.

travel abroad for treatment because of linguistic barriers, geographic distance, and the costs of travelling abroad.[208] It was also apparent that the fact that just about all secondary and specialist care is provided in hospitals in the UK does not imply that it will be classified as hospital treatment for Treaty-compliance purposes.[209]

The ECJ's interpretation of arts 49 and 50 appears to raise questions about the validity, or at least utility, of art.22 of Regulation 1408/71. In response to another application in *Inizan*,[210] the ECJ ruled that art.22 of the Regulation was compatible with arts 49 and 50 of the Treaty. The court went on to rule that the condition as to delay under art.22(2) of the Regulation (see above) is, in effect, the same as the court has applied under art.49 of the Treaty. Thus, prior authorisation can only be refused under art.22 of the Regulation where the same or equally effective treatment can be provided without undue delay, taking account of the patient's specific medical condition and history.[211] This is, to say the least, a bold move. The vagueness of the Treaty provisions over those of the Regulation has been used to fashion greater patient mobility rights, which have then been used to re-interpret art.22 of the Regulation.

2.5.2 The Watts case

The *Watts* case was the first in which the free movement provisions had to be applied to an NHS patient.[212] Mrs Watts, a woman in her seventies, sought reimbursement of the cost of a hip replacement operation carried out abroad to avoid the waiting period in the UK. She had initially applied for prior authorisation to have the operation in France under Regulation 1408/71 (using an E112 form), but the PCT refused and reduced her waiting time to three to four months. She went ahead with the operation in France anyway because of her constant pain.

At first instance, Munby J. held that the free movement provisions did apply to the NHS.[213] Further, "undue delay" was not to be determined solely by reference to NHS waiting lists. According to his Lordship, while a wait of one year for Mrs Watt would have been undue, her wait following the PCTs re-classification of her condition was not undue.[214] Both Mrs Watts and the Health Minister appealed.

The Court of Appeal expressed considerable concern that the combined effect of the ECJ's decisions was, contrary to its declared intent, "to dictate an increase in what may be an already strained national health service budget; or

---

[208] [2003] E.C.R. I-4509, para.95.
[209] Note the ECJ's approach to the treatment provided for Mrs Riet ([2003] E.C.R. I-4509, para.93).
[210] (C-56/01) [2003] E.C.R. I-12403.
[211] [2003] E.C.R. I-12403, paras 44–46.
[212] *R. (Watts) v Bedford PCT* [2004] EWCA Civ 166.
[213] [2003] EWHC 2228.
[214] [2003] EWHC 2228, paras 173–174.

to force the postponement of more urgent treatment needed by others".[215] Consequently, the Court asked for preliminary rulings from the ECJ on no fewer than eight questions.[216] The final of which poignantly asked whether the NHS was obliged to pay for the patient's treatment in another Member State when it is not so obliged to pay for that treatment to be carried out privately in the UK.

The ECJ ruled that reliance on a proposed waiting time would only be acceptable where it did not exceed the period indicated by "an objective medical assessment to the clinical needs of the person concerned in the light of all the factors characterising his medical condition".[217] Thus, the NHS cannot use its waiting times to define "undue delay". Further, a system of prior authorisation of treatment abroad was compatible with the free movement provisions where it is based on "objective, non-discriminatory criteria which are known in advance".[218] The NHS regulations, however, were held not to set out such criteria and therefore made it difficult to bring a legal challenge to a refusal of prior authorisation.[219] Thus, as McHale points out, the judgment requires the NHS to establish a prior authorisation system for hospital treatment abroad that (a) is non-discriminatory, easily accessible, impartial, and efficient; (b) capable of being challenged by judicial review; (c) produces clear reasoned explanations; and (d) provides a mechanism for the reimbursement of costs.[220] It is fortunate for NHS finances that the free movement provisions do not oblige the NHS to pay for private treatment in the UK (the answer to the Court of Appeal's question, above, is undoubtedly "yes"). NHS finances are also benefited by the reality that that other EU jurisdictions are not as geographically accessible from the UK as they are from continental countries and that many patients will not have the resources to pay for treatment before seeking reimbursement from the NHS. Nonetheless, such patient consumerism has the potential to significantly reshape the NHS.

2.6 Conclusion

This chapter has focused on present regulatory attempts to balance the needs, powers, and rights of doctors, patients, and the general public. The patient, through increased consumer-like powers, is no longer required to be a purely passive recipient of NHS services. The growing private sector can only increase this consumer-driven ethos, as the whole rationale of private healthcare is ineluctably tied to consumer demand. This chapter's focus on the NHS is no accident. While private doctors are still regulated by the GMC, the vast

---

[215] [2004] EWCA Civ 166, para.110.
[216] See [2004] EWCA Civ 166, para.112.
[217] (C-372/04) [2006] Q.B. 667, para.79.
[218] (C-372/04) [2006] Q.B. 667, para.116.
[219] (C-372/04) [2006] Q.B. 667, para.118.
[220] See McHale 2007, 105.

majority of the law covered in this chapter (from the NHS complaints procedure to judicial review actions) does not apply to the private patient. The private sector is *comparatively* lightly regulated. If current trends continue, the private sector is likely to play an increasing part in healthcare provision (treating both private and NHS patients). Increased impact, however, brings pressures for increased regulation. To what extent regulatory oversight of the private sector will increase is unclear, but increase it will.

The suggestion that there is a growing consumer-orientation within healthcare provision needs to be kept in perspective. Unfortunately, consumer-like powers and mechanisms do not benefit all patients equally. Some patients are culturally uncomfortable with questioning the doctor, challenging medical opinion, or seeking alternative treatment. A middle-class patient in a large city is likely to be more comfortable articulating and exercising the wish to, say, change family doctor than a working-class patient from a small village. Financial limitations can also prevent patients exercising some options, particularly the option of seeking private treatment. Seeking reimbursement for treatment obtained outside the UK is, for example, only feasible if one is able to obtain the means of paying for the treatment in the first place. Further, government rhetoric emphasising the patient-driven nature of NHS reforms should not mask the economic motivation often underlying such reforms.

This chapter has focused on the issues facing the UK and the NHS. The *global inequality* of resources, especially economic resources, is such that the preoccupations of this country are not those of most developing countries. A major pressuring facing poorer countries is that of *practitioner tourism*, whereby their medical practitioners (and other health professionals) are attracted abroad by financial opportunities available in richer countries. In response to this, there is currently a ban on NHS recruitment from poorer countries, but its success is open to question.[221]

It should also be noted that the content of this chapter is particularly prone to rapid development. Readers should be alert to the possibility that the position on some of the issues covered will have changed since this chapter was written.

2.7 Further reading

Professional regulation and context

Quick, Oliver (2006) "Outing Medical Errors: Questions of Trust and Responsibility." 14(1) *Medical Law Review* 22–43.

Rationing and challenging rationing decisions

King, Jeff A. (2007) "The Justifiability of Resource Allocation." 70(2) *Modern Law Review* 197–224.

Newdick, Christopher (2005) *Who Should We Treat? Rights, Rationing and Resources in the NHS.* (2nd ed.) (Oxford: Oxford University Press).

---

[221] See Hinsliff 2004.

Syrett, Keith (2004) "Impotence or Importance? Judicial Review in an Era of Explicit NHS Rationing." 67(2) *Modern Law Review* 289–304.

Witting, Christian (2001) "National Health Service Rationing: Implications for the Standard of Care in Negligence." 21(3) *Oxford Journal of Legal Studies* 443–471.

Rights under EU Law

Hervey, Tamara K. and McHale Jean V. (2004) *Health Law and the European Union*. (Cambridge: Cambridge University Press).

Chapter 3

CLINICAL NEGLIGENCE

3.1 Introduction

In the time before anaesthetic, a good surgeon was a quick surgeon and Robert Liston was a great surgeon. He was reputed to be the fastest in the business, being able to amputate a limb in less than $2^1/2$ minutes. Towards the end of his career he was the first in Europe to perform a major operation with ether anaesthesia. Unfortunately his mistakes were as startling as his successes. Three of these mistakes are particularly striking.[1] On one occasion he poured scorn on a house surgeon's claim that a pulsatile tumour on a boy's neck was an aneurysm of an artery, insisting that it had to be an abscess because an aneurysm could not occur in one so young. He took out his surgeon's knife and lanced it. Out leapt the arterial blood and the patient died soon afterwards. On another occasion, while rapidly amputating a leg, he accidentally removed the patient's testicles. On a third occasion, while removing another patient's leg, he accidentally slashed through the observing surgeon's coattails and took off his assistant's fingers. The observing surgeon died of shock (falsely believing that he had lost his manhood), and both the assistant and patient later died of gangrene. Everyone makes mistakes but Liston's had particularly serious consequences.

Liston's escapades serve as a reminder that in medical practice the price of error can be very high. Even in a contemporary setting, a momentary error by an overworked doctor on a busy ward can cost the life or health of a patient. More than a million patients a year are victims of mistakes in NHS hospitals.[2] Some of these mistakes will be recognised by the law as amounting to clinical negligence.

3.1.1 Overview of clinical negligence actions

Clinical negligence law is largely the application of the *tort of negligence* to a clinical setting. A person claiming clinical negligence has to satisfy the general conditions for establishing liability in the tort of negligence:

(a) that the defendant owed him a duty of care,

(b) that there has been a breach of that duty (i.e. negligence), and

(c) that the harm of which the victim complains was caused by that breach of duty, and that harm was not too remote.[3]

Each component of the tort is examined in this chapter: duty of care (3.2), breach of duty (3.3), and factual causation and remoteness (3.4). Claims can also fail if the defendant makes out a defence. Defences will not be explored in this chapter.[4]

In addition to a remedy in the tort of negligence, which will be available to NHS patients able to satisfy the above conditions, private patients will sometimes be able to sue for breach of contract. Private patients enter into a

---

[1] See Gordon 1983, 13–15, and Magee 1999.
[2] See National Audit Office 2005, 1. For the year 2004–2005, there were 974,000 reported adverse incidents and near misses, and many more are thought to have been unreported.
[3] *Burton v Islington HA* [1993] Q.B. 204 at 224 (Dillon L.J.).
[4] For defences, readers should consult a general tort textbook. See e.g. Deakin, Johnston, and Markesinis 2008, ch.24.

contractual relationship by paying for the service (directly or by insurance), whereas the relationship between an NHS doctor and patient is based upon a statutory obligation rather than a contract.[5] Thus, in contrast to an NHS patient, a private patient can sue in either contract or negligence. In practice it rarely matters which. While a private health provider could, in theory, promise to reach a higher standard of care than that imposed in tort, the courts have been very reluctant to accept that private health providers have made such promises. In a case where a couple claimed that their private doctor had guaranteed the success of a vasectomy operation, Nourse L.J. emphatically declared that "a doctor cannot be objectively regarded as guaranteeing the success of any operation or treatment unless he says as much in clear and unequivocal terms".[6] In medical law, the customer is not always right.

Where the health professional's actions have been grossly negligent, there might also be criminal liability. We will consider this possibility below (3.7). Criminal liability for clinical negligence is unusual. Civil liability is far more common. Civil liability for clinical negligence is more about compensating victims than punishing culpable doctors or nurses. That is not to suggest that the present system entirely separates compensation and blame—it does not. But, as we shall see, the law is prepared to regard as negligent an inevitable error caused by the tiredness or inexperience. Injured patients do not, however, have it all their own way. It can be very difficult to establish negligence where there is a clash of medical opinion. Judicial deference to the medical profession is a ghost whose chains continue to shackle the development of medical law, though these shackles are being loosened. Just as limiting are the practicalities of establishing a link between negligent conduct and a patient's injury. Many clinical negligence claims continue to fail on causation. When combined with a litigation process that is often slow, inequitable, and expensive, clinical negligence actions are far from ideal. In response, the NHS Redress Act 2006 sets up a framework for a new redress system for claims worth less than £20,000. As we shall see (3.6.4ff), this system addresses some, but by no means all, of the flaws of civil litigation.

The application of the tort of negligence to questions of liability arising from the provision of information and liability arising from incidents before birth is addressed elsewhere (Chs 4 and 9, respectively). Here, before examining the details of clinical negligence law and the weaknesses of the litigation process, we need to address defendants within the NHS.

3.1.2 Who to sue

Not every careless act, even if grossly careless, will give rise to a civil action in negligence. The person sued must have negligently caused harm and owe the claimant a duty of care (*primary liability*). Alternatively or additionally, the person

---

[5] See *Reynolds v Health First Medical Group* [2000] Lloyd's Rep. Med. 240, applying *Pfizer Corporation v Ministry of Health* [1965] A.C. 512.

[6] *Thake v Maurice* [1986] Q.B. 644 at 688. Neill L.J. was of the same view (685), whereas Kerr L.J. dissented on this point.

sued must employ someone who has caused harm in the course of that employment and owes the claimant a duty of care (*vicarious liability*). This means that where an NHS patient can establish a case against an individual working within the NHS, that patient can sue that individual directly or, as is more usual, sue the NHS body for which that individual works.[7] In any event, the employing NHS body will pay the damages. The NHS Indemnity Scheme ensures that NHS bodies[8] accept full financial liability for the negligence of their staff.[9] A lawyer will therefore usually advise against suing individuals working for NHS bodies directly. Suing individuals personally, or even naming them in a claim against an NHS body, might encourage or increase defensive action by individuals who perceive their professional reputations to be on the line.[10] General practitioners (GPs) are different. Like family dentists, pharmacists, and optometrists, GPs are not directly employed by NHS bodies and are therefore not covered by the NHS Indemnity Scheme. Instead, the financial costs of liability for the negligence of family doctors will be met by the medical defence organisations, principally the Medical Defence Union and the Medical Protection Society.

A patient (or a relative) wishing to bring a legal action will face a number of practical issues. These will be discussed below (3.5) after we have examined the substantive law of clinical negligence.

3.2 Duty of care

Establishing a duty of care is straightforward for patients who have suffered personal injury at the hands of their doctor or hospital. In the words of the Chief Medical Office, "In practice, within the NHS, the existence of a duty of care is seldom challenged".[11] A duty of care is owed by family doctors to the patients on their lists and by hospitals and their staff to those admitted for treatment. Complications arise where the harm suffered is purely psychological or financial, or where the individual in question is not a patient. The law does not impose a blanket duty of care.

In those instances where the existence or scope of a duty of care is unclear, guidance is provided by the House of Lords in *Caparo Industries v Dickman*.[12] This case held that development of a duty of care must proceed incrementally, on a case-by-case basis, by analogy with previously decided cases. A duty of care would then arise when there was (a) *foreseeability* of damage, (b) sufficient *proximity* between the parties, and (c) it was *just and reasonable* to impose a duty

---

[7] There is dicta suggesting that an NHS body (such an NHS Trust) is liable for the negligence of the medical professionals employed by it whether or not those professionals are its employees: *Cassidy v Ministry of Health* [1951] 2 K.B. 343 at 262 (per Denning L.J.). See below. See also the in-depth discussion of who to sue in Lewis 2006, ch.21.

[8] PCTs, Strategic Health Authorities, Special Health Authorities, NHS Trusts, and NHS Foundation Trusts.

[9] See DH 1996a and the guidance in DH 1996b.

[10] See Brazier and Cave 2007, 188.

[11] CMO 2003, 51.

[12] [1990] 2 A.C. 605.

of care.[13] This is not a straightforward three-limbed test. These three intertwined limbs contain vague labels. Its application is entangled with policy questions over whether the imposition of liability is supported by considerations beyond the interests of the litigants.[14] The courts have apparently abandoned any attempt to understand duty of care (let alone negligence as a whole) as a unified system of coherent principle. The result is an anti-academic, pragmatic approach in which we can only be certain that there is a duty of care when the courts have held this to be so (for an alternative approach, see 3.8.2.)

3.2.1 Duty to assist

English law does not impose a general duty to assist or rescue a person in need. Usually the relationship between two strangers will not be considered sufficiently *proximate* or it will not be considered *just and reasonable* to impose liability. No such problem occurs if the potential rescuer has in some sense assumed responsibility for the person in need.[15] It follows that any health professional taking responsibility for treating a patient will thereby owe that patient a duty of care.[16] An NHS body (such as the NHS Trust running a hospital) might also be taken to have assumed such a responsibility.

In *Barnett v Chelsea and Kensington Hospital*, three night watchmen presented themselves to a casualty department complaining of vomiting after drinking tea.[17] The nurse on duty followed the instructions of a doctor, given over the telephone, and sent them home to bed with instructions to see their GP in the morning. Later that night one of the watchmen died from arsenic poisoning. Nield J. was in "no doubt" that the nurse and the doctor owed a duty of care to the deceased and that there was a duty of care "imposed upon the hospital" to the deceased.[18] It seems to follow that an NHS hospital running an open casualty department will be deemed to undertake a duty to treat or at least assess those who present themselves for emergency treatment. No such undertaking will be imposed if the casualty department has closed its doors and has put up a notice declaring that no patients can be received.[19] By implication, no duty of care will be imposed on NHS hospitals adopting the widespread practice of displaying a notice declaring that they do not accept accident and emergency patients.

More recently, in *Kent v Griffith*, the Court of Appeal held that by accepting an emergency call the Ambulance Service will usually undertake to provide

---

[13] This test applies to all negligence claims (but is more easily satisfied by some types of damage): *Marc Rich v Bishop* [1996] A.C. 211.

[14] See e.g. *Hill v Chief Constable of West Yorkshire* [1989] A.C. 53, esp. 63 (emphasising the impact on society as a whole) and *Islington LBC v UCL Hospital NHS Trust* [2005] EWCA Civ 596, esp. 49 (on the policy-based nature of the *Caparo* test).

[15] See e.g. *Barrett v Ministry of Defence* [1995] 3 All E.R. 87.

[16] For an early expression of this view, see Lord Hewart C.J. in the criminal case of *R. v Bateman* [1925] All E.R. Rep. 45.

[17] [1969] 1 Q.B. 428.

[18] [1969] 1 Q.B. 428 at 436.

[19] [1969] 1 Q.B. 428 at 435.

assistance to a person in need within a reasonable time.[20] In this case the Ambulance Service received a call from a doctor requesting an ambulance to take the victim of an asthma attack to hospital immediately. Despite two further telephone calls, the ambulance took 40 minutes to arrive from a base that was no more than a 20-minute drive away. No explanation was offered for the delay. In fact, a member of the ambulance crew was found to have falsified a record to show an earlier arrival! The Court of Appeal found that a duty of care was owed (and on the facts that the duty had been breached). Once a call has been accepted the Ambulance Service is dealing with a named individual who will usually abandon any attempt to find alternative means of transport to the hospital. This was thought sufficient to reject the defendant's submission that the requirement of *proximity* was not met.[21] This decision could have wider implications. Primary Care Trusts (PCTs) might be judged to assume responsibility for named individual patients who rely on them to make arrangements for urgent life-saving treatment within a reasonable time.[22] Note, however, that Lord Woolf M.R., giving the Court of Appeal's judgment, declared that it was significant that "there is no question of an ambulance not being available or of a conflict in priorities" and that the decisions on the allocation of resources were "not suited for resolution by the courts".[23] This suggests that a future court will look favourably on an Ambulance Service able to back up a plea of resource limitations. Courts do not wish to directly interfere with political decisions on resource allocation and funding priorities. Though, since every successful compensation claim against an NHS body or employee takes valuable resources that could be used to save the lives of patients, the courts cannot avoid indirectly influencing such decision-making.

As a rule, an undertaking to assist does not arise simply because there is a doctor present. A doctor who witnesses a road accident or hears a call for a "doctor in the house" at the theatre is not usually under a legal duty to attend.[24] Indeed, if assistance is provided, the doctor could be liable for administering negligent treatment.[25] There is an exception for GPs in the location of their practice, who can be required to provide treatment.[26] It is plausible that the absence of a common law duty might be subject to challenge under the Human Rights Act (HRA) 1998, as art.2 of the European Convention on Human Rights (hereafter the Convention) imposes positive duties on the State to protect life.[27] In any event, professional

---

[20] [2001] Q.B. 36.

[21] Distinguishing *Capital and Counties v Hampshire* CC [1997] Q.B. 1004 (fire service), *Alexandrou v Oxford* [1993] 4 All E.R. 328 (police), and *OLL v Secretary of State for Transport* [1997] 3 All E.R. 897 (coastguards).

[22] See Brazier and Beswick 2006.

[23] [2001] Q.B. 36 at 53.

[24] See *Capital and Counties v Hampshire* CC [1997] Q.B. 1004 at 1035 (Stuart-Smith L.J.), and *Re F* [1990] 2 A.C. 1 at 77–78 (Lord Goff) respectively.

[25] Since such treatment provided by a hospital doctor will fall outside the remit of the NHS Indemnity Scheme, hospital doctors would be well advised to become or remain members of a medical defence organisation. If a doctor does intervene the victim would surely become his patient and he would have to act as a reasonably competent doctor. However, Stuart-Smith L.J. has stated obiter that a doctor would only have to reach the lower standard of simply not making matters worse: *Capital and Counties v Hampshire* CC [1997] Q.B. 1035 at 1035.

[26] NHS (General Medical Services Contracts) Regulations 2004/291, reg.15(6)

[27] *Osman v UK* (1998) 29 E.H.R.R.149.

consequences may follow where a doctor fails to offer assistance, because GMC guidance tells doctors that: "In an emergency, wherever it arises, you must offer assistance, taking account of your own safety, your competence, and the availability of other options for care".[28] Similarly, Nursing and Midwifery Council guidance provides that "In an emergency, in or outside the work setting, [nurses] have a professional duty to provide care".[29]

The ethical issues raised by a failure to assist a person in need are, in the absence of any form of prior commitment, coterminous with the limits of *positive duties*. Positive duties are recognised by most major moral theories (see 1.3.2ff). Utilitarians recognise that a failure to act can produce negative consequences for utility, most duty-based theories impose duties of beneficence, most rights-based theories recognise positive rights,[30] and a willingness to assist those in need is surely a virtue recognised by most virtue theories. Such obligations are not specific to health professionals. Medically trained persons are especially equipped to help those in need of immediate medical care, just as lifeguards are especially equipped to help those who are drowning, but many rescues can be undertaken just as effectively by anyone present. Anyone will, for example, suffice to shout a warning to a pedestrian who is ignorantly strolling into the path of an oncoming vehicle or to call the emergency services if the pedestrian fails to hear that warning in time. The moral obligation to assist in such circumstances will not be absolute (e.g. many moral positions hold that positive duties do not require the assister to give up anything of comparable moral significance).[31] Nonetheless, positive moral obligations fit uneasily with the absence of a legal duty.[32] Most moral theories will question the moral basis of the law calling for a prior undertaking before requiring some action from a hospital doctor who knowingly walks past a man having a heart attack. No such prior undertaking is required under French law. Fortunately, the willingness of the courts to find implied "undertakings"[33] and the existence of appropriate professional guidance have rendered this limitation more apparent than real.

3.2.2 The primary duty of care of healthcare providers

We have seen that patients are owed a duty of care by health professionals and providers who undertake to treat them. This means that NHS bodies can be

---

[28] GMC 2006a, para.11.

[29] NMC 2002, para.8.5.

[30] One notable exception is the rights-based theory of Nozick (1974).

[31] See e.g. Harris 1985, 57 (implicitly utilitarian position), Singer 1993, 229–232 (utilitarian position), and Gewirth 1978, 217–220 (rights-based position). The moral limitations on the duty to assist will differ from theory to theory, but see Pattinson 2009 for a discussion of generally accepted background conditions for the existence of prima facie positive obligations.

[32] See e.g. *Stovin v Wise* [1996] A.C. 923 at 931. For an argument that it is now time for the law to go beyond this point, see Williams 2001.

[33] There are, of course, limits on the ability of the courts to find implied undertakings. A doctor providing contraceptive advice does not, e.g., assume responsibility for the future sexual partners of his patient: *Goodwill v BPAS* [1996] P.I.Q.R. P197.

vicariously liable for the negligence of their employees and *primary* liable for their own negligence. A healthcare provider owes a primary duty to provide competent staff and proper facilities.[34] In *Bull v Devon AHA*, for example, the Court of Appeal held a Health Authority liable for the damage caused by a substantial delay before the arrival of specialist assistance in the delivery of Mrs Bull's son.[35] This delay was attributed to the system for summoning assistance, which involved staff travelling between two maternity sites situated a mile apart. Slade L.J. thought that it was "indisputable" that the health authority owed a duty of care directly to the patient.[36]

For a time it looked like there might be a second way in which NHS bodies could be primarily liable: a *non-delegable duty* to ensure that reasonable care is taken in the provision of medical care to patients.[37] If such a duty were to exist, then NHS bodies could be liable for the negligent care provided by private companies with whom they sub-contract even if they are not negligent in the selection of such companies. In *M v Calderdale HA*, Judge Garner held that a Health Authority had such a non-delegable duty and was thereby responsible for the negligent performance of an abortion that it had arranged to be carried out at a private hospital.[38] If this approach had been affirmed by a higher court, PCTs might have become frequent defendants in clinical negligence actions.[39] Judge Garner was extending the law in a way that was later said not to represent the current state of the law by the Court of Appeal in *A (A Child) v Ministry of Defence*.[40] This case held that the Ministry of Defence did not owe a non-delegable duty to ensure that a patient receives careful treatment. It now seems unlikely that an NHS body will be held to have such a non-delegable duty.[41]

3.2.3 Psychiatric injury

Many victims of *purely* psychological harm have greater difficulty than victims of physical harm when it comes to establishing sufficient *proximity* and that it is *just and reasonable* for a duty of care to exist.[42] Special rules apply in this area. The law divides such persons into "primary" and "secondary" victims. This categorisation is a mixed question of fact and law, and the boundaries are not yet settled.[43] In general terms, *primary victims* are those who are in some sense directly involved as participants in the traumatic event. This encompasses (1) those

---

[34] In addition to the case below see *Wilsher v Essex AHA* [1987] Q.B. 730 and *Robertson v Nottingham HA* [1997] 8 Med. L.R. 1.

[35] [1993] 4 Med. L.R. 117.

[36] [1993] 4 Med. L.R. 117 at 126.

[37] Based on the obiter dicta of Denning L.J. in *Cassidy v Ministry of Health* [1951] 2 K.B. 343, 359–360, and *Roe v Ministry of Health* [1954] 2 Q.B. 66 at 82.

[38] [1998] Lloyd's Rep. Med. 157.

[39] See Brazier and Beswick 2006, 188.

[40] [2004] EWCA Civ 641, esp. para. 52.

[41] Though, this point is not finally settled: see [2004] EWCA Civ 641, para.55.

[42] Psychological harm consequent upon physical injury, as in *Donoghue v Stevenson* [1932] AC 562, will not pose additional difficulties.

[43] See *Cullin v London Fire* [1999] P.I.Q.R. P314 and *W v Essex CC* [2001] 2 A.C. 592, 601, respectively.

within the range of foreseeable physical injury,[44] (2) those with a contractual claim for work-related stress as identifiable individual employees suffering from foreseeable psychiatric harm,[45] and, arguably, (3) those who are negligently made to feel responsible for harm inflicted on another.[46] All other victims of psychiatric harm are *secondary victims*. Paradigmatically, someone who suffers psychiatric harm after hearing news about a traumatic event is a secondary victim. Thus, a patient who suffers psychological harm as a result of his doctor's negligence towards him will be a primary victim, whereas a patient's relative who witnesses his negligent medical treatment will usually be a secondary victim.

Only those, primary and secondary victims, who suffer from a recognised psychiatric illness are owed a duty of care. Grief or distress will not be enough unless experienced to such an abnormal degree as to give rise to a psychological condition ("pathological grief disorder").[47] This prevents the relatives of most victims of clinical negligence having a claim in their own right.

Primary victims of a recognised psychiatric illness are owed a duty of care *if* psychiatric *or* physical harm was reasonably foreseeable.[48] Secondary victims need to satisfy additional criteria of foreseeability and proximity concretised in the leading case of *Alcock v Chief Constable of South Yorkshire Police*.[49] They need to show that the claimant

(a) experienced a single shocking event that would have caused psychiatric injury to a person of reasonable fortitude;

(b) had sufficiently close ties of love and affection to the primary victim (which is presumed if they are married or if the victim is the parent/child of the other);

(c) was present at the traumatic event or its immediate aftermath; and

(d) directly perceived the traumatic event or its immediate aftermath by their own unaided senses.

---

[44] *White v Chief Constable of South Yorkshire Police* [1999] 2 A.C. 455.

[45] *Sutherland v Hatton* [2002] EWCA Civ 76 (a conjoined appeal, an appeal from one of which was later heard by the House of Lords on the issue of whether the duty had been breached on the facts: *Barber v Somerset CC* [2004] UKHL 13). See also *Hartman v South Essex Mental Health* [2005] EWCA Civ 6.

[46] *Dooley v Cammell* [1951] 1 Lloyd's Rep 271, *W v Essex CC* [2001] 2 A.C. 592, esp. 601, and *Salter v UB Frozen and Chilled Foods* 2003 S.L.T. 1011 (Scottish case).

[47] *Vernon v Bosley* [1997] P.I.Q.R. P255 and *North Glamorgan NHS Trust v Walters* [2002] EWCA Civ 1792.

[48] *Page v Smith* [1996] A.C. 155, *White v Chief Constable of South Yorkshire Police* [1999] 2 A.C. 455, and *Donachie v Chief Constable of the Greater Manchester Police* [2004] EWCA Civ 405.
    In *Group B v MRC* [2000] Lloyd's Rep Med 161 the claimants, who had been given human growth hormone that was later discovered to be a potential cause of Creutzfeldt-Jakob Disease (CJD), were allowed to claim for psychiatric illness resulting from worry that they would get CJD in the future. Morland J. ruled that they had to prove that psychiatric injury was reasonably foreseeable (which he held they had done because the relationship between the parties was "akin to that of doctor and patient"). If this case was correctly decided, then either not all primary victims are covered by the ruling in *Page v Smith* or not all secondary victims need to satisfy the *Alcock* requirements (discussed below). The judge seemed to prefer the latter approach, as he likened the claimants to primary victims whilst considering that "they should not be treated as primary victims".

[49] [1992] 1 A.C. 310, building on *McLoughlin v O'Brian* [1983] 1 A.C. 410.

It is not difficult to envisage circumstances where these requirements can operate harshly, particularly where the claimant is classified as a secondary victim. They are intended to keep the liability of defendants within responsible bounds, but smack of arbitrariness.[50] There is, however, some flexibility in the application of these requirements.[51] To take just one example, while a prolonged period attending intensive care and gradually realising that clinical negligence could have caused the victim's injuries will not constitute a single shocking event,[52] it is not necessary to show that the traumatic event was confined to a short moment in time. In *North Glamorgan NHS Trust v Walters* a mother successfully recovered from a pathological grief reaction suffered after waking from anaesthetic when her newborn baby was having a fit and, 36 hours later, having her baby die in her arms after its life-support treatment was withdrawn.[53] The 36-hour period was regarded as a seamless, drawn-out experience.[54] Most of those who suffer from psychiatric injury following the negligent treatment of a close relative will fall on the wrong side of this line. This case could, though, be taken to represent a movement towards a more pro-claimant approach.[55]

This apparent arbitrariness of the law in this is the result of explicit reliance on policy, stemmed from the belief that the duty of care requirement does not reflect any general overarching principle. This belief has been challenged by a number of modern commentators (see 3.8.2).

3.2.4 Other grey areas

We have briefly explored two areas where the courts have displayed reluctance to recognise a general duty of care: the failure to act in the absence of a prior relationship or some other form of undertaking, and purely psychiatric injury. There are many others. In some cases, policy can operate as an explicit barrier to the existence of a duty of care.[56] It can also be difficult to establish a duty of care where the claimant was not a patient of the doctor, as the doctor's duty is usually to his patient alone.[57]

---

[50] See Law Commission 1998.
[51] See *W v Essex CC* [2001] 2 A.C. 592, esp. 601. In *Alcock*, Lords Keith, Ackner, and Oliver suggested that, in extreme circumstances, a bystander without ties of love and affection to the victim might have a claim, but see *McFarlane v Wilkinson* [1997] 2 Lloyd's Rep 259.
[52] *Sion v Hampstead HA* [1994] 5 Med. L.R. 170.
[53] [2002] EWCA Civ 1792.
[54] [2002] EWCA Civ 1792, para.34.
[55] A radically pro-claimant approach to what may constitute a single shocking event was taken towards the husband and son's psychological injury claims in *Froggatt v Chesterfield and North Derbyshire Royal Hospital NHS Trust* [2002] All E.R. (D) 218.
[56] See e.g. *McKay v Essex AHA* [1982] Q.B. 1166 (wrongful life claim), as discussed in Ch.9 (9.4.1).
[57] See e.g. *Powell v Boldaz* (1997) 39 B.M.L.R. 35 (no duty to inform those outside the doctor-patient relationship when something has gone wrong) and *Palmer v Tees HA* [2000] P.I.Q.R. P1 (insufficient proximity on the facts to establish that the HA owed a duty of care to the victim of the psychiatric patient). Difficulties are also created when a doctor negligently examines a patient for the benefit of another, such as an employer: see Harpwood 2001, 18–21, and Brazier and Cave 2007, 159.

The current House of Lords has been proactive in redrawing the boundaries of liability through manipulation of the duty of care requirement.[58] This proactiveness is perhaps influenced by the European Court of Human Rights' decision in *Osman v UK*.[59] In *Osman*, the European Court (mis)interpreted the denial of a duty of care as a restriction on the art.6 right to have determinations of one's civil rights and obligations made by an independent and impartial tribunal. Although the European Court has since backtracked,[60] the duty of care mechanism can no longer be regarded as the conveyor of blanket protection from liability.

3.3 Breach of duty

Not every medical mishap or mistake will result in a finding of negligence. If a case makes it to trial the patient will have to prove that the defendant (or the health professional for whom the defendant is responsible) failed to meet the standard of a reasonably competent professional with the relevant skills. A doctor must reach the standard of a reasonably competent doctor, a nurse the standard of a reasonably competent nurse, and so forth. Even if the professional reaches this standard on average or just about always, he will still be liable on those occasions when his performance does not reach it.[61]

In theory, the standard of care is a question of law and its application to the evidence a question of fact. The two merge when the standard of care is mapped against the facts of specific cases. In practice medical evidence is relevant to both, at least insofar as the courts determine what is required of medical professionals by reference to what is accepted within the profession. The relevance and weight to be attributed to medical views is but one of the many questions surrounding breach. Others include the extent to which breach should be attached to culpability and claimants should be aided by evidential inferences.

Breach of duty tends to focus on the actions of individuals. This is unfortunate. Individuals are likely to take a finding of negligence as a professional sleight and modern medical care is often provided by a team. It should not be forgotten that a finding of negligence indicates no more than that for one isolated instant the conduct in question was such as to give a patient a claim for compensation.[62]

Before examining the case law, we should take a look at s.1 of the Compensation Act 2006. This states:

> A court considering a claim in negligence or breach of statutory duty may, in determining whether the defendant should have taken particular steps to meet a stan-

---

[58] See e.g. *Hall v Simons* [2002] 1 A.C. 615 and *W v Essex CC* [2001] 2 A.C. 592.
[59] (2000) 29 E.H.R.R. 245.
[60] *Z v UK* (2002) 34 E.H.R.R. 97, esp. 100–101.
[61] *Wilsher v Essex AHA* [1987] Q.B. 730 at 747 (Mustill L.J.).
[62] See Brazier 2003, 169.

dard of care (whether by taking precautions against a risk or otherwise), have regard to whether a requirement to take those steps might—

(a) prevent a desirable activity from being undertaken at all, to a particular extent or in a particular way, or
(b) discourage persons from undertaking functions in connection with a desirable activity.

Paragraph 17 of the Explanatory Notes indicates that this provision is meant to "reflect the existing law and approach of the courts". It is not meant to change the law. It was enacted to reassure those who were avoiding desirable activities out of undue fear of liability. The Lord Chancellor suggested that the fear of liability for injury had led to local authorities not opening public spaces and schools not organising class trips.[63] Thus, it is difficult to dissent from Brazier and Cave's view that the provision is unlikely to have any effect on clinical negligence.[64] The present standard of care is far from a standard of strict liability (see 3.3.1) and thereby does take account of the desirability of health professionals being able to exercise their own rights.

3.3.1 The standard of care

In what is probably the most quoted direction ever given to a jury, McNair J. stated that,

> A doctor is not guilty of negligence if he has acted in accordance with a practice accepted as proper by a responsible body of medical men skilled in that particular art.[65]

McNair J. went on to comment on situations where there is a difference in medical opinion,

> Putting it the other way round, a doctor is not negligent, if he is acting in accordance with such a practice, merely because there is a body of opinion that takes a contrary view.[66]

This direction has become known as the *Bolam test* and has been adopted by the House of Lords as the standard of care for treatment, diagnosis, and disclosure of information.[67] It applies to any profession or calling that requires special skill, knowledge, or experience.[68] In fact the Bolam test has taken on a life of its

---

[63] See BBC 2005g.
[64] Brazier and Cave 2007, 160.
[65] *Bolam v Friern Hospital Management Committee* [1957] 2 All E.R. 118 at 122.
[66] [1957] 2 All E.R. 118 at 122.
[67] *Whitehouse v Jordan* [1981] 1 All E.R. 267 (treatment), *Maynard v West Midlands RH* [1985] 1 All E.R. 635 (diagnosis), and *Sidaway v Bethlem Royal Hospital* [1985] A.C. 871 (disclosure of information). Discussion of disclosure is left to the next chapter.
[68] *Gold v Haringey HA* [1988] Q.B. 481 at 489 (Lloyd L.J.).

own and has played a key role in medical law outside negligence. It has, for example, been used by the House of Lords in cases on the sterilisation of incapacitated adults and the withdrawal of food and water from persons in a persistent (permanent) vegetative state.[69]

It is apparent that McNair J. intended the standard of care to be normative: a doctor is negligent if he departs from practices that *ought* to be accepted by the profession. This interpretation is suggested by McNair J.'s use of the word "responsible" before "body of medical men" and bolstered by his use of the prefix "reasonable" elsewhere in his judgment. Yet, if emphasis is placed on other phrases, it is possible to read a descriptive standard of care into his direction, whereby actual professional practices determine what is negligent.[70] In most cases this distinction is more apparent than real. Compliance with practices accepted by the profession will usually ensure compliance with a normative standard of what a professional ought to do if he is to act reasonably competently. Some standard practices might not, however be defensible from an objective point of view. A professional standard might be a product of custom and practice, rather than considered opinion. Outside the medical context, consider the facts of *Wong v Johnson*.[71] In this case, it was the customary conveyancing practice of Hong Kong solicitors, when completing a contract for the sale of land, for the purchaser's solicitor to forward the purchase price to the vendor's solicitor in exchange for an undertaking that the documents of title would be duly executed. Objectively this widely accepted practice runs a very high risk that the vendor will take the money and run, with foreseeably devastating consequences for the client of the purchasing solicitor. Not surprisingly the Privy Council held the defendant solicitor to be negligent when this happened.

While the normative reading of *Bolam* dominated, there was a body of dicta attaching the standard of care more firmly to what is accepted by the profession. When giving the judgment of the House of Lords in *Maynard v West Midlands RHA*, Lord Scarman declared:

> a judge's preference; for one *body of distinguished professional opinion* to another also professionally distinguished is not sufficient to establish negligence in a practitioner whose actions have received the seal of approval of those whose opinions, truthfully expressed, honestly held, were not preferred. . . . For in the realm of diagnosis and treatment negligence is not established by preferring one re*spectable body of professional opinion* to another. Failure to exercise the ordinary skill of a doctor (in the appropriate speciality, if he be a specialist) is necessary.[72]

Here Lord Scarman appears to equate a "reasonable" or "responsible" body of medical opinion with a "distinguished" or "respectable" body of medical opinion. Received opinion seems to be automatically elevated to reasonable opinion. In the later case of *Sidaway v Bethlem Royal Hospital*, Lord Scarman summarised the *Bolam* test by saying that "the standard of care is a matter of

---

[69] *Re F* [1990] 2 A.C. 1 at 73 (sterilisation) and *Airedale NHS Trust v Bland* [1993] A.C. 789 (PVS).
[70] This was highlighted at the time by Montrose (1958).
[71] [1984] A.C. 296.
[72] [1985] 1 All E.R. 635 at 639 (my emphasis).

medical judgment".[73] The descriptive reading of *Bolam* is exceedingly deferential and, in effect, lets the medical profession set its own standard of care without external oversight. This reading has been bolstered by rulings that the relevant body of opinion can be small. In one case the Court of Appeal held that it was not negligent to perform a spinal operation that only 11 spinal surgeons (out of well over 1,000) considered safe.[74]

The decision of the House of Lords in *Bolitho v City and Hackney HA* makes it clear that the normative reading is the correct one.[75] In this case, the standard of care had to be considered to address the defendant's assertion that Patrick Bolitho would have died even if she had attended to him promptly, because she would not have performed the only intervention that was likely to have saved his life. She argued that the risks of intubation would have prevented her from using this invasive procedure to clear the obstruction of his bronchial air passages. An expert for the defendant indicated that he would not have intubated in these circumstances, though five experts for the claimant thought that the two-year-old should have been intubated. Giving the judgment of the House of Lords, Lord Browne-Wilkinson stated,

> In the vast majority of cases the fact that distinguished experts in the field are of a particular opinion will demonstrate the reasonableness of that opinion. . . . But if, *in a rare case*, it can be demonstrated that the professional opinion is *not capable of withstanding logical analysis*, the judge is entitled to hold that the body of opinion is not reasonable or responsible.[76]

His Lordship had earlier noted that requiring the exponents of the body of opinion relied on to demonstrate a logical basis meant that the judge needs to weigh the risks against the benefits:

> the judge before accepting a body of opinion as being responsible, reasonable or respectable, will need to be satisfied that, in forming their views, the experts have directed their minds to the question of *comparative risks and benefits* and have reached a *defensible conclusion* on the matter.[77]

I have added emphasis to the two quotes above. Combined they show that while the standard required of a medic is not left solely in the hands of the medical profession and requires a considered weighing of risks and benefits, it will remain rare for a body of medical opinion to be dismissed as negligent. Demonstrating the likely rarity of a finding that a body of opinion does not withstand "logical" analysis, his Lordship went on to find in the defendant's favour on the facts before the court.

Setting and applying the standard of care does pose difficulties for the court. On the one hand, matters of technical medical knowledge and judgment fall

---

[73] [1985] A.C. 871 at 881.
[74] *De Freitas v O'Brien* [1995] P.I.Q.R. P281. For obvious reasons it is doubtful that one person can constitute a "body" of opinion, see *Walsh v Gwynedd HA* [1998] C.L.Y. 3977.
[75] [1998] A.C. 232.
[76] [1998] A.C. 232 at 243 (my emphasis).
[77] [1998] A.C. 232 at 242 (my emphasis).

within the expertise of the medical profession, not the judiciary. This is partic-ularly so where there is a conflict of expert opinion on the relative risks and benefits of particular procedures and approaches. On the other hand, few medical decisions are purely matters of medical expertise. Weighing the risks and benefits is value-laden and medical expertise does not entail ethical expertise or legitimacy. Thus, at the very least, some judicial oversight is required to ensure that doctors do not abuse their position, whether by intent, inadvertence, or indolence.

Is the illogicality test invoked by Lord Browne-Wilkinson the best way to balance these difficulties? Many commentators have noted that a defendant's conduct can be unreasonable even if it is logical.[78] It is, however, arguable that the emphasis placed on weighing risks and benefits indicates that he used the phrase "logical analysis" to mean something beyond the avoidance of contra-diction and other logical errors. Only time will tell to what extent "reasonable" will be used to ensure the objective defensibility of a body of opinion. As one of Chairman Mao's Prime Ministers is reputed to have said when asked his opinion of the French revolution: "It is too early to tell". Interpreting the case law presents three difficulties. *First*, analysis of decided cases does not reveal how many cases have been settled out of court because of fears that the health professional's actions were not objectively defensible despite the support of other experts. The NHS Litigation Authority (see 3.5.3) has an incentive to keep cases that could result in the development of the law out of court and NHS bodies will want to limit opportunities for adverse publicity. *Second*, many of the cases clearly rejecting expert opinion (but by no means all)[79] were concerned with the disclosure of information, which Lord Browne-Wilkinson expressly excluded from consideration in *Bolitho*.[80] *Third*, medical opinion can also be rejected on grounds other than its failure to stand up to logical analysis as a body of opinion on proper practice. It is not always clear whether medical opinion is being rejected because the trial judge does not accept that view of the facts in issue or does not accept that it represents a body of opinion on proper practice. *Bolam/Bolitho* is strictly not relevant to determinations of fact concerning what happened or whether a view is held by others.[81] In *Reynolds v North Tyneside HA*, for example, Gross J. was prepared to hold that any body of opinion supporting the defendant's conduct would not be defensible, but was not satisfied that any such a body of opinion existed.[82]

Academic views on the true impact of *Bolitho* vary.[83] The then Lord Chief Justice argued, extra-judicially, that it presents a move away from excessive deference to the medical profession.[84] *Bolitho* does not, of course, remove all

---

[78] See e.g. Teff 1998, 481 and Jones 1999a, 238–239.

[79] See e.g. *Clarke v Adams* (1950) 94 Sol Jo 599 (where the standard warning given by radiologists before giving the treatment in question was held to be negligent).

[80] *Bolitho v City and Hackney HA* [1998] A.C. 232 at 243. See the discussion in Ch.4 (4.4.2.1).

[81] See *Marriott v West Midlands RHA* [1999] Lloyd's Rep. Med. 23 and *Penney v East Kent HA* [2000] Lloyd's Rep. Med. 41. These cases are discussed in Harpwood (2001, 51–53).

[82] (2002) Lloyd's Rep. Med. 459, para.47.

[83] Cf. Grubb 1998a, 380 ("Eureka! The courts have got it at last") with Keown 1998, 250 ("*Bolitho* is a step in the right direction, but the road is long").

[84] See Woolf 2001.

deference to the profession; some judgments are properly left to doctors. Expert opinion is not to be rejected without due consideration of potential counter responses. In *Burke v A*, the Court of Appeal ordered a retrial as the judge had been too quick to reject the doctor's diagnostic approach.[85] It had the support of medical experts for both parties. The judge should therefore have given the expert witnesses the opportunity to explain and justify their practice before ruling that the doctor had been negligent for failing to ask the patient's mother specific questions.

3.3.2 Application of the standard of care

Bolam tells us that the standard of care is that of a person competent in the speciality in question.[86] A GP must exercise the skill of a reasonably competent GP[87] and a specialist must exercise the skill of a reasonably competent specialist.[88] The choice of the appropriate group of specialists is usually straightforward, though it is unavoidably value laden. Consider the cases of *Shakoor v Situ* and *Knight v Home Office*.[89] In *Shakoor*, a patient died of acute liver failure after suffering an unusual reaction to a herbal remedy prescribed by a practitioner of traditional Chinese herbal medicine. The court held that the appropriate standard was that of a reasonably competent practitioner of alternative medicine, not a reasonably competent practitioner of either orthodox medicine or Chinese herbal medicine. The judge considered the alternative standards of care to be inappropriately too high or low. Similarly, in *Knight* the court thought it appropriate to hold a prison hospital to the standard of a prison hospital rather than the higher standard of a psychiatric hospital outside prison. It is clear that Pill J. was influenced by the fact "that resources available for the public service are limited and [the view] that the allocation of resources [is] a matter for Parliament".[90] *Knight* does not, however, apply to all medical services given in prison[91] and needs to be narrowly interpreted in the light of the HRA 1998.[92]

---

[85] [2006] EWCA Civ 24.

[86] *Maynard v West Midlands RH* [1985] 1 All E.R. 635 at 638 (Lord Scarman), and *Sidaway v Bethlem Royal Hospital* [1985] A.C. 871 at 897 (Lord Bridge).

[87] See e.g. *Chin Keow v Government of Malaysia* [1967] 1 W.L.R. 813 (GP fell below the standard of a reasonably competent GP by failing to inquiry about the possibility of an allergy before injecting penicillin).

[88] See e.g. *Ashcroft v Mersey Regional Health Authority* [1983] 2 All E.R. 245 (where the defendant surgeon fell below the standard of a reasonably competent ear surgeon).

[89] [2000] 4 All E.R. 181 and [1990] 3 All E.R. 237, respectively.

[90] [1990] 3 All E.R. 237. It is well established that the failure to reach the relevant standard of care cannot be justified by a general lack of resources: *Wilsher v Essex AHA* [1987] Q.B. 730 and *Bull v Devon AHA* [1993] 4 Med. L.R. 117. See also Harpwood 2001, 58–60 and Montgomery 2002, 180–182.

[91] A pregnant woman in prison is entitled to the same standard of obstetric medical care as a woman at liberty: *Brooks v Home Office* [1999] 2 F.L.R. 33.

[92] *Keenan v UK* (2001) 33 E.H.R.R. 913.

The duty imposed by the common law is to act as is reasonable *in all the circumstances*. It follows that the application of the standard of care is largely a question of fact and the decided cases illustrate relevant factual parameters, rather than operate as strict authorities. What is appropriate in, for example, an emergency might not be appropriate generally,[93] though those who are trained to deal with emergencies will be held to the standard of someone with such expertise.[94]

What is appropriate will depend on the facts. Those facts are to be assessed in the light of the knowledge available at the time of the incident rather than the time of trial. In *Roe v Minister of Health*, the patient had been paralysed because the anaesthetic given during his operation had been contaminated by seepage through invisible cracks in the glass.[95] The Court of Appeal held that there was no negligence. The risk was known at the time of the trial but had not been known when the accident occurred in 1947. In the words of Denning L.J.: "We must not look at the 1947 accident with 1954 spectacles".[96] Further, professionals are not expected to know *everything* that was known at the relevant time. One article published in the *Lancet* six months before the operation in question was not, for example, sufficient to render an anaesthetist negligent in *Crawford v Charing Cross Hospital*.[97]

3.3.2.1 Inexperience

Just as a learner driver cannot plead inexperience,[98] medical students and newly qualified doctors are not excused by their inexperience.[99] In *Wilsher v Essex AHA*, a junior and inexperienced doctor inserted a catheter into a vein rather than an artery and then asked a senior registrar to check its position.[100] The registrar failed to spot the error and the baby was subsequently discovered to be blind, possibly as a result of the excess oxygen. The majority of the Court of Appeal (the point was not considered in the House of Lords) held that the same standard of care needs to be shown by both inexperienced doctors and their more experienced colleagues. Mustill L.J. added that the standard of care should take account of the "post" of the doctor but not his "rank" or "status", so a member of a specialist unit (whether a house officer or a registrar) would be expected to reach the standard of a professional in that unit.[101] An inexperienced doctor can sometimes discharge his duty by asking a more experienced colleague for advice. In this way the junior doctor in *Wilsher* was held to have passed responsibility on to the registrar.

---

93 *Wilsher v Essex AHA* [1987] Q.B. 730 at 749 (Mustill L.J.). See also *Watt v Hertfordshire CC* [1954] 2 All E.R. 368.

94 See *Cattley v St John's Ambulance Brigade* (1998) (Lexis).

95 [1954] 2 Q.B. 66.

96 [1954] 2 Q.B. 66 at 84. See also *Abouzaid v Mothercare* (2000) (Westlaw).

97 (1953) *The Times*, December 8, CA.

98 *Nettleship v Weston* [1971] 2 Q.B. 691.

99 In addition to the case considered below, see *Jones v Manchester* [1952] 2 Q.B. 852, esp. 871.

100 [1987] Q.B. 730, CA.

101 [1987] Q.B. 730 at 751. Glidewell L.J. did not comment on this and Browne-Wilkinson V.-C. dissented, holding that the standard was that of a doctor with the same qualifications and experience.

The determination of the standard of care owed by the inexperienced raises a tension between the compensation needs of patients and the need to find wrongdoing on the part of the health professionals in question. On the one hand, patients can legitimately expect to be treated competently and compensated if unavoidably injured, but will not usually know the level of experience of those who treat them. On the other hand, health professionals learn on the job and will inevitably make mistakes that could be avoided if they had the experience to know when and how to act or ask for advice. The position adopted by the Court of Appeal in *Wilsher* favours the compensation needs of patients (though it is defensible from the perspective of corrective justice: see 3.8.2).

3.3.2.2 Departure from guidance

As we saw in Ch.2, the NHS has procedures for issuing and monitoring the implementation of national standards. The National Institute for Health and Clinical Excellence (NICE), for example, is specifically tasked with responsibility for issuing guidance on best practice. In addition, guidance is frequently issued by the professional bodies, such as the Royal Colleges, the British Medical Association, and the General Medical Council.[102] While such guidance lacks the direct legal force often mistakenly attributed to it by health professionals, it can have indirect legal force via the law of negligence. Such guidance can be important for the application of the standard of care, because it represents evidence of what is considered to constitute proper practice.[103] The courts have sometimes explicitly endorsed professional guidance. In *Airedale NHS Trust v Bland*, for example, Lord Goff expressed the view that the BMA's guidance on the issue before the court represented a responsible body of opinion.[104] In another case, a nurse was found to be negligent for failing to follow the procedure operated at her health centre, which required that a patient complaining of a lump in her breast be referred to a doctor.[105] However, *Bolitho* makes it clear that any course of action must be logical and defensible. In appropriate circumstances it could be logically indefensible to blindly follow guidance, just as it could be to depart from guidance without good reason.

3.3.2.3 Proving breach

The burden of proving negligence rests with the claimant. The claimant needs to prove on the balance of probabilities the defendant (or a person for whom the defendant is vicariously liable) fell below the standard of a reasonably competent person exercising those professional skills. It is not difficult to see how this could operate harshly against patients. In theory at least, a patient facing an unexpected outcome following treatment is not well placed to determine whether his doctor, nurse, surgeon, or anaesthetist has been negligent.

---

[102] See, in particular, GMC 2006a.
[103] See Teff 2000.
[104] [1993] A.C. 789 at 871.
[105] *Sutton v PSFPP* (1981) (Lexis transcript). See also *Clark v MacLennan* [1983] 1 All E.R. 416.

The patient is likely to lack medical expertise and might even have been unconscious at the relevant time. In some (exceptional) cases, the courts have aided the patient by applying the maxim *res ipsa loquitur* ("the thing speaks for itself"). This has been applied in cases where the medical outcome is so obviously suggestive of negligence that its mere occurrence is sufficient to make it more likely than not that there was negligence. Where, for example, a patient has surgery to treat two stiff fingers and ends up with four stiff fingers,[106] or where a patient dies when a swab is left in his body for three months after an abdominal operation.[107] In these cases the outcome speaks of negligence and the Court of Appeal applied this maxim accordingly.

A patient who cannot show what actually happened can rely on this maxim where he can show that the defendant was in control (primarily or vicariously) of the circumstances preceding the injury and that an injury of this type would not occur in the ordinary course of events.[108] At one time it was hotly debated whether the effect of this maxim is to reverse the burden of proof, but the balance of opinion is that it does no more than establish a prima facie inference of negligence.[109] Hobhouse L.J. suggested that it would help if the Latin tag were dropped and replaced by the phrase "a prima facie case".[110] Understood in this way the maxim is of little use to most claimants. In practice, the courts are reluctant to allow claimants to establish a prima facie case of negligence early on in the proceedings where the facts are disputed. Where the court is willing to draw such an inference, the defendant will still be able to rebut it by showing that there is a plausible explanation of how the outcome might have occurred without negligence on his part.

A detailed analysis of the current ambit of this maxim can be found in *Ratcliffe v Plymouth and Torbay HA*.[111] In this case, counsel for the injured patient based much of their appeal on the trial judge's failure to support their use of the maxim. The Court of Appeal supported the trial judge, displaying a desire to minimise use of the maxim. The court made it clear that the maxim, with or without the Latin tag, can only be used in exceptional, straightforward cases. Should this be so? In the modern litigation context does the historical rationale for the maxim have less potency? Claimants who make it to trial will have had the benefit of medical evidence and will have obtained disclosure of relevant materials from the defendant. Nonetheless, limiting use of this maxim makes it difficult for claimants to establish negligence in a medical case. The compensatory needs of patients lose out here to the fault-based nature of the claim (as they should if the function of the tort system is to achieve corrective justice: below).

---

[106] *Cassidy v Ministry of Health* [1951] 2 K.B. 343.

[107] *Mahon v Osborne* [1939] 2 K.B. 14.

[108] See e.g. *Scott v London & St Katherine Docks* (1865) 3 H. & C. 596 at 601 and *Fryer v Pearson* [2000] (Westlaw).

[109] There are suggestions that the maxim reverses the burden of proof in some older cases, such as *Mahon v Osborne* [1939] 2 K.B. 14. This has been rejected in more recent cases, such as *Ratcliffe v Plymouth & Torbay HA* [1998] P.I.Q.R. P170 at 186 (Hobhouse L.J.) and 178 (Brooke L.J., selectively citing earlier judgments).

[110] [1998] P.I.Q.R. P170 at 189. See also May L.J. in *Fryer v Pearson* [2000] (Westlaw), at para.18.

[111] [1998] P.I.Q.R. P170.

3.4 Causation and remoteness

To succeed in a clinical negligence action the claimant must prove, on the balance of probabilities, that the damage was caused by the health professional's negligence. This is often the most difficult part of a negligence claim.

In some cases the evidence will simply go against the claimant. Where, for example, non-negligent treatment would have made no difference because the background factors were independently sufficient to cause the outcome. In the case of *Barnett*, which we looked at earlier, the night watchmen would have died of arsenic poisoning even if the doctor had properly assessed and treated him.[112] Similarly, in *Robinson v Post Office*, the Court of Appeal held that even if the doctor had taken the precaution of administering a test dose of the anti-tetanus serum, it was unlikely that the patient's allergy would have been revealed in time, so the doctor would have administered the injection anyway.[113] In such cases the claimant is unable to satisfy the "but for" test, i.e. is unable to show on the balance of probabilities that "but for" the negligent conduct the injury would not have occurred.

In other cases, the evidence is inconclusive. Patients are usually suffering from some pre-existing illness or have been exposed to other risk factors and it can be very difficult to prove that a patient's injury was caused by negligence rather than the pre-existing illness or risk factors. We have already briefly looked at *Wilsher v Essex AHA* in which a premature baby had been negligently administered excess oxygen. The baby developed *retrolental fibroplasias*, which led to total blindness in one eye and seriously damaged the vision in the other. The problem was that negligence was only one of five possible causes, and the trial judge had, in effect, required the defendants to show that their negligent conduct had not caused the injury. The House of Lords held that the onus of proving causation rested with the claimant, who had to show that the negligence had caused, or at least materially contributed to, the injury.[114] Thus, a retrial was ordered in which the claimant would have to show that the negligent conduct had actually made a *material contribution* to his injury.

3.4.1 Materially increasing the risk of harm

The *Wilsher* approach fits uneasily with the earlier decision of the House of Lords in *McGhee v NCB*,[115] which has recently been reinterpreted and applied in

---

[112] [1969] 1 Q.B. 428. See also *Kay v Ayrshire & Arran Health Board* [1987] 2 All E.R. 417, where over prescribing penicillin to a child was found to be incapable of causing the meningitis that deprived the child of his hearing.

[113] [1974] 1 W.L.R. 1176.

[114] [1988] A.C. 1074. The material contribution test was developed in *Bonnington Castings v Wardlaw* [1956] A.C. 613.

[115] [1972] 3 All E.R. 1008.

Fairchild v Glenhaven.[116] In *McGhee*, the claimant had suffered dermatitis *as a result* of exposure to brick dust, but he could not show that the material brick dust was that to which he was not negligently exposed or that to which he was negligently exposed (by the failure to provide after-work washing facilities). The House of Lords allowed the claim to succeed, apparently on the basis that the claimant had shown that the negligent conduct had "materially increased the risk" of harm. In *Wilsher*, the House of Lords refused to overrule *McGhee*. Instead it was explained away as a case in which there was sufficient evidence to make the necessary inference of a causal link between fault and damage. Lord Bridge said that the Law Lords in *McGhee* had simply taken "a robust and pragmatic approach to the undisputed primary facts".[117] This explanation was rejected in *Fairchild*.[118] In this case, the claimants suffered from mesothelioma, after being negligently exposed to asbestos in the course of successive jobs. Each claimant could prove, on the balance of probabilities, that his mesothelioma was caused by negligent exposure in the course of his employment, but could not show which defendant employer had actually caused his condition. The House of Lords held all the defendant employers liable, as each had materially increased the risk of harm to their employees.[119] Policy considerations were, in effect, used to escape the harshness of the strict rules of causation.

What effect does *Fairchild* have on *Wilsher*? Apparently very little. Lord Hoffman distinguished *Wilsher* from *McGhee* and *Fairchild* on policy grounds relating to the distinction in context between general employers and the NHS:

> the political and economic arguments involved in the massive increase in the liability of the National Health Service which would have been a consequence of the broad rule favoured by the Court of Appeal in Wilsher's case are far more complicated than the reasons given by Lord Wilberforce [in *McGhee*] for imposing liability upon an employer who has failed to take simple precautions.[120]

When, then, will the material increase in risk test apply? Is it restricted to fact situations that are substantially the same as those of *McGhee* and *Fairchild*? On this their Lordships offered slightly differing approaches to the conditions necessary to invoke the more relaxed causation test. Lord Bingham stated the conditions so precisely (six in total) that they would only apply to the particular factual situation in hand.[121] Lord Hoffman laid down five conditions, which limit the principle to circumstances where the duty is intended to protect employees against being unnecessarily exposed to a particular disease or substance, where the risk was proportionate to the exposure.[122] Lord Hutton

---

[116] [2002] UKHL 22.
[117] [1988] A.C. 1074 at 1090.
[118] [2002] UKHL 22.
[119] *Barker v Corus UK* [2006] UKHL 20 later held that where more than defendant was in breach of duty, each was to be liable only to their relative degree of contribution to the risk. Thus, the damages paid by each defendant would be proportionate to the claimant's asbestos exposure resulting from that defendant's negligence. The effect of this on mesothelioma claims was removed by s.3 of the Compensation Act 2006.
[120] [2002] UKHL 22, para.69.
[121] [2002] UKHL 22, paras 2 and 34.
[122] [2002] UKHL 22, paras 61, 67, and 73.

explicitly confined his decision to the facts of *Fairchild*.[123] Lord Nicholls also carefully avoided a generalised principle.[124] Only Lord Rodger was prepared to lay down more general conditions.[125] While there are situations where the *McGhee* approach will probably apply,[126] it is difficult to envisage clinical negligence scenarios where the courts will take such a claimant-friendly approach. As Lord Hoffman made clear, the courts are heavily influenced by the financial constraints faced by the NHS. Here, the compensation needs of patients lose out to the financial needs of the NHS and the law abandons any claim to having a coherent principled rationale.

3.4.2 Loss of a chance

As we have seen, *Wilsher* remains good law. The all or nothing balance of probabilities test remains the general rule. If the claimant establishes that on the balance of probabilities the negligent conduct caused or materially contributed to the injury, he gets full compensation. The *Fairchild* exception aside, if the claimant establishes a probability of less than 51 per cent, he gets nothing. Further scope for making exceptions to the balance of probabilities test arose for consideration on the facts of *Hotson v East Berkshire HA*.[127] In this case a boy had injured his hip when he fell out of a tree when swinging on a rope. The hospital negligently failed to diagnose the fracture for five days and the hip joint was irreparably damaged by the loss of blood supply to its cartilage. The trial judge found that at the time of the misdiagnosis there was a 25 per cent chance that enough of the blood vessels remained intact to save the joint. He went on to hold that the boy's permanent disability was *partially* caused by the negligent failure to diagnose and treat his injury promptly, and awarded him 25 per cent of the full damages. The House of Lords rejected this reasoning and held that the claimant had not established that, on the balance of probabilities, the defendant had caused or materially contributed to the injury. There was a 75 per cent chance that the injury had already occurred by the time the claimant got to the hospital.

In the case of *Gregg v Scott* the courts returned to the issue of loss of a chance in a personal injury claim.[128] In this case, the negligent misdiagnosis of the claimant's tumour caused a nine-month delay in the start of treatment. The trial judge held that this delay had reduced the claimant's chance of a cure (defined as survival for more than 10 years) from 42 per cent to 25 per cent. The trial judge and majority of the Court of Appeal considered *Hotson* to have prevented

---

[123] [2002] UKHL 22, para.118.
[124] [2002] UKHL 22, para.43.
[125] [2002] UKHL 22, para.170.
[126] Consider the factual situations of *Cook v Lewis* [1951] S.C.R. 830 (a Canadian case) and *Fitzgerald v Lane* [1987] Q.B. 781. Lord Rodger was inclined to the view that *Fitzgerald* was correctly decided (para.170) and Lord Nicholls approved the decision in *Cook* (see paras 39–40).
[127] [1987] A.C. 750.
[128] [2005] UKHL 2.

the claimant recovering for the loss of the (roughly 20 per cent) chance of a cure. The majority of the Law Lords were not prepared to make an exception to the balance of probabilities test. Lords Nicholls and Hope dissented.

Lord Nicholls would have distinguished the *Hotson-type* case (where the claimant could not establish on the balance of probabilities that he had not already suffered the harm prior to the negligent diagnosis/treatment) from the *Gregg-type* case (where the claimant could establish that he had not, at the time of the alleged negligence, already suffered the harm for which he is claiming, but could not establish on the balance of probabilities that non-negligent treatment would have prevented the harm).[129] His Lordship was concerned that any other ruling would render the doctor's duty hollow where the chance that non-negligent diagnosis and treatment would have made a difference was less than 51 per cent.[130]

The majority were simply not prepared to depart from conventional causation principles. Lord Hoffmann was concerned that any method of keeping liability for loss of a chance within reasonable bounds would be "artificial" and "lacking in principle".[131] Lord Phillips thought that allowing a claim on the facts before him would undermine the coherence of our common law.[132] Baroness Hale was particularly concerned that allowing the appeal would mean that there would be liability in almost every case.[133] Significantly, Lord Phillips was not prepared to rule out the possibility that a loss of a chance case could succeed on different facts, where "medical treatment has resulted in an adverse outcome and negligence has increased the chance of that outcome".[134] (Gregg was still alive over eight years after the misdiagnosis and his argument that he had been negligently deprived of the chance of surviving for more than 10 years was weakening with time.) Nonetheless, no such reservation is evident in the judgments of Lord Hoffmann or Baroness Hale. The net effect of the decisions seems to be the reaffirmation of the standard causation rules, on which *Fairchild* must continue to be read as a narrow exception. The position of Lord Phillips does, however, leave some room for argument in future cases.[135] Whether this is merely illusionary has yet to be seen.

3.4.3 Legal causation and remoteness

Additional complexity is raised by legal causation and remoteness. As we shall see, the case law displays a difficult combination of legal principle and policy.

---

[129] [2005] UKHL 2, paras 34–41.
[130] [2005] UKHL 2, esp. para.43.
[131] [2005] UKHL 2, paras 86–88.
[132] [2005] UKHL 2, para.72.
[133] [2005] UKHL 2, para.215.
[134] [2005] UKHL 2, para.190.
[135] However, see Foster 2005, 249, who argues that other more subtle arguments will now have to be presented.

It is, therefore, fortunate that such matters are rarely in dispute in clinical negligence actions.

Where there is more than one independently sufficient cause of harm to the claimant, the court has the task of determining whether the defendant's breach of duty is to be treated as *the legal cause* of damage. Even where it is clear that the negligence conduct did play a necessary role in the occurrence of the claimant's harm, the court still has to attribute legal responsibility for that harm to the defendant. The harm suffered by the claimant must be within the foreseeable area of risk created by the negligent conduct. Where another's conduct intervenes between the negligent conduct and the harm, the court could hold that the intervening act breaks the chain of causation and thereby constitutes a *novus actus interveniens*. Where there is something very unusual about the harm sustained in the circumstances, the court could hold that it is "too remote" from the negligent conduct.

Legal causation and remoteness are mechanisms for attributing legal responsibility. The rules governing independently sufficient causes are relatively settled and turn on whether they are both tortious.[136] At first sight, the rules governing *novus actus* and remoteness also appear to be straightforward. A subsequent intervention will not break the chain of causation if it is "reasonable" and "foreseeable",[137] and unusual harm will not be too remote if the "type of harm sustained" was "reasonably foreseeable".[138] However, both the legal tests and their application are value-laden and the judicial outcome is not always predictable. Much of the case law in this area appeals to value judgments about the *fair* extent of the defendant's legal responsibility for the harm,[139] on which judges can disagree.[140] Fortunately, as stated earlier, legal causation and remoteness are rarely in dispute in clinical negligence cases. Only rarely, for example, will a patient's conduct be so unreasonable that the courts will be willing to hold that it breaks the chain of causation. While the refusal to terminate a pregnancy following a negligently conducted sterilisation operation will not constitute a *novus actus*,[141] the decision to have sexual intercourse in the knowledge that the sterilisation operation has failed could.[142] Here we find that the law usually favours patients.

---

[136] If both events are tortious, responsibility is borne by the defendant who is liable for the first tort: *Baker v Willoughby* [1970] A.C. 467. If the subsequent event is *non-tortious*, it relieves the defendant of responsibility as soon as it occurs: *Jobling v Associated Dairies* [1982] A.C. 794.

[137] See e.g. *Knightley v Johns* [1982] 1 W.L.R. 349 (the court asked whether the intervention was a "natural and probably consequence of the defendant's negligence" and "reasonable foreseeable") and *McKew v Holland* [1969] 3 All E.R. 1621 (the court asked whether the intervening action of the defendant was reasonable).

[138] *The Wagon Mound (No.1)* [1961] A.C. 388.

[139] See *Roe v Minister of Health* [1954] 2 Q.B. 66 at 85 (Denning L.J.).

[140] See e.g. the different variations in framing the question as to what must have been reasonably foreseeable in the remoteness cases. In particular, compare *Hughes v Lord Advocate* [1963] A.C. 837 with *Doughty v Turner* [1964] 1 Q.B. 518, and *Bradford v Robinson* [1967] 1 All E.R. 267 with *Tremain v Pike* [1969] 1 W.L.R. 1556.

[141] *Emeh v Kensington and Chelsea AHA* [1985] Q.B. 1012.

[142] *Sabri-Tabrizi v Lothian Health Board* (1998) S.L.T. 607 (Scottish case).

3.5 Further procedural issues

Those wishing to bring an action for clinical negligence face a number of practical hurdles. These include the need to bring the claim relatively promptly (3.5.1) and have or acquire the means to fund it (3.5.2). The NHS, in turn, has set itself up to respond to and defend against these claims (3.5.3). Both parties must deal with the civil justice process; a process that is still reverberating from the impact of significant reform a decade again (3.5.4).

3.5.1 The limitation period

A legal action does not remain an open possibility indefinitely. If the action is not started within the *limitation period*, the claimant loses the right to sue.[143] There are good reasons for placing limits on tardiness. For a start, keeping the prospect of litigation for past acts perpetually alive could impose significant burdens upon potential defendants, at least some of whom will not actually have committed a tort. The passing of time can also hinder fact-finding as memories fades and personnel change. On the other hand, there can be good reasons for not suing immediately, such as where the person was unaware of the injury until much later, which support flexibility over blanket rules.

Under the Limitation Act 1980 claimants usually have six years to bring a tortious action (s.2), which reduces to three years in the case of death or personal injury claims (s.11). In the case of personal injury the three years runs from the date on which the cause of action accrues *or* the date of the claimant's knowledge, whichever is later (s.11(4)).[144] If the claimant dies without initiating an action within the three-year limitation period, that period is extended by a further three years either from the death or from the date of knowledge of the personal representative (s.11(4)–(6)).

The courts have the discretion under s.33 to extend liability in personal injury actions falling within s.11. Such actions must be for "negligence, nuisance or breach of duty of care" (s.11(1)) and, in *Stubbings v Webb*, the House of Lords ruled that this excluded intentional trespass to the person.[145] This meant that actions for assault or battery were subject to the six-year limitation period under s.2, which was not extendable. Just over 15 years later, in *A v Hoare*, the House of Lords overturned this ruling.[146] It held that personal injury actions for intentional trespass to the person did fall within s.11(1) and there is therefore judicial discretion to extend the limitation period when it appears equitable to do so.

---

[143] See further James 1998.
[144] The date of knowledge is defined in s.14. On the meaning of which see *A v Hoare* [2008] UKHL 6.
[145] [1993] A.C. 498.
[146] [2008] UKHL 6.

3.5.2 Funding a negligence claim

Litigation can be very expensive. Patients without a proverbial silver spoon or large earnings will therefore struggle to bring a negligence claim, unless they had the foresight to take out appropriate insurance, are sufficiently impecunious to obtain legal aid, or are able to take advantage of a conditional fee agreement.[147] The legal aid scheme is run by the Legal Services Commission under the Access to Justice Act 1999. Conditional fee agreements were set up, in July 2003, under s.58 of the Courts and Legal Services Act 1990.

In 2003, a consultation document issued by Chief Medical Officer noted that nearly 90 per cent of clinical negligence cases received the support of a *legal aid* contribution.[148] This is despite many potential litigants being unable to obtain legal aid because availability is assessed (rationed) by a combination of financial eligibility criteria and the predicted prospects of success relative to the costs of litigation. Less than half the adult population can satisfy the financial eligibility criteria. Children, in contrast, usually have much less difficulty because parental income is not taken into account.[149] In future, the Legal Services Commission will probably expect potential litigants of low value hospital claims to have properly utilised the NHS redress scheme (3.6.4) before legal aid will be forthcoming.

The Government has been seeking to reduce reliance on legal aid and push litigants towards *conditional fee agreements*. These, sometimes called "no win no fee" agreements, allow solicitors to provide legal services without charging a fee unless and until the claim succeeds, at which point they are permitted to charge an increased fee.[150] Conditional fees are not to be confused with US-style *contingency fees*, which would allow the lawyer to claim a percentage of the final award. Both types of fee arrangement have one thing in common: they provide a significant financial incentive for lawyers to get a settlement in their client's favour.[151] Further, they are not well suited for complex and unpredictable claims, which clinical negligence claims can be.[152] In practice, the claimant must have a sufficiently strong case for a solicitor to take the risk and needs to be able to afford the cost of insurance to cover the defendant's costs in the event of losing.

3.5.3 The defence of clinical negligence claims

There are also practical issues affecting the defendants of clinical negligence actions. Negligence claims against GPs are handled by the medical defence organisations. However, the majority of claims are brought against secondary care providers and the bodies responsible for managing health services, principally

---

[147] More a more detailed discussion of funding issues than is presented here, see Lewis 2006, ch.3.
[148] See CMO 2003, 67.
[149] Access to Justice Act 1999 s.7.
[150] That increased fee cannot exceed 25% of the damages recovered: see Lewis 2006, 46.
[151] See Lewis 2006, 32.
[152] See Lewis 2006, 32–33.

NHS Trusts, NHS Foundation Trusts, and Primary Care Trusts (PCTs). These bodies are discouraged from taking out commercial insurance to cover their clinical negligence litigation costs. Instead they are encouraged to pool their resources by joining the Clinical Negligence Scheme for Trusts (CNST).[153] Currently all NHS Trusts, Foundation Trusts and PCTs in England belong to this scheme. It requires the adoption of *risk management measures* on the pain of higher contribution fees.[154] (In this vein, it is also worth nothing that the *National Patient Safety Agency* exists to develop a culture of reporting and investigation of errors and potential errors, and to disseminate the lessons learned.)[155]

Both the CNST and the Existing Liabilities Scheme (which covers litigation claims from before the CNST was set up) are administered by a Special Health Authority known as the NHS Litigation Authority.[156] The impact of the Litigation Authority should not be underestimated. It now manages all clinical negligence litigation within the NHS, offers advice to the Department of Health on litigation, and seeks to ensure that claims that could impact on the NHS as a whole are not settled locally. It deals with thousands of clinical negligence cases a year. The Chief Medical Officer, at least, considers the Litigation Authority to have dramatically improved the efficiency of claims handling.[157] Practitioners are less enthusiastic.[158]

3.5.4 The civil justice system after the Woolf reforms

The civil litigation process was radically reformed following the final report of a review committee chaired by Lord Woolf.[159] These reforms were intended to be long-term solutions to two of the principal problems of the litigation system: expense and delay. They sought to encourage alternative dispute resolution (mediation), early settlement, and the use of a single expert for both parties. They sought to introduce faster and more cost effective procedures for small claims, facilitate judicial case management, and reduce reliance on expensive disclosure. This is not the place for a full exposition of all aspects of civil justice procedure, but it is worth briefly exploring some of the principal features of the post-Woolf procedure.[160]

The principal result of Lord Woolf's recommendations was the introduction a new procedure code for the County Court and High Court known as the *Civil*

---

[153] This scheme applies to claims arising from incidents since April 1995. It was set up by the NHS (Clinical Negligence Scheme) Regulations 1996/251, made under s.21 of the NHS and Community Care Act 1990.
[154] See NHSLA 2003.
[155] See *http://www.npsa.nhs.uk/*.
[156] The Authority was set up under s.21(3) of the NHS and Community Care Act 1990. See DH 2002b.
[157] See CMO 2003, esp. 11–12.
[158] See e.g. Lewis 2006, 17–18.
[159] See Woolf 1996.
[160] The following discussion owns much to Lewis 2006.

Procedure Rules (CPR).[161] These rules recognise, among other things, pre-action protocols (3.5.4.1) and limits on the use of expert witnesses (3.5.4.2). A related reform to private law procedure that will be briefly considered below is the introduction of periodical payments (structured settlements) (3.5.4.3).

3.5.4.1 The pre-action protocol

The Pre-action Protocol for the Resolution of Clinical Disputes was introduced in response to the Woolf report and came into force in April 1999.[162] The latest version was issued in April 2006. It sets out "a code of good practice" in the form of a set of "ground rules" for dealing with disputes that have the potential to lead to litigation (paras 1.6 and 3.1). Its general aim is to maintain and restore the rela-tionship between the parties while resolving any disputes without recourse to litigation (para.2.1). To achieve this, it seeks to encourage openness, timeliness, and awareness of options (para.2.2). In essence, it seeks to engender a "cards on the table" approach to early communication so that cases can be investigated swiftly, records volunteered, and settlements reached without the involvement of the court. It therefore provides for a timed sequence of steps that are to be followed before litigation proceedings are formally launched.

If the dispute leads to proceedings, it will be for the court to decide whether to sanction the parties and their solicitors for non-compliance with the pre-action protocol (para.1.13 and CPR 3.9). The court could, for example, refuse to extend time limits, disallow costs, or (under CPR 3.1(5)) order payment into court.

3.5.4.2 Expert evidence

How does an injured patient prove breach of duty and causation? Expert evidence is a large part of the answer.[163] Unfortunately, experts are expensive and tend to side with those who have instructed them.[164] Part 35 of the CPR seeks to address these concerns. The CPR explicitly declares that the primary duty of the expert is to the court, which overrides any obligation to the instructing client or paymaster (CPR 35.3). Expert evidence is to be restricted to what is reasonably required to resolve the case (CPR 35.1) and the introduction of expert evidence requires the court's permission (CPR 35.4).

The CPR also provide that the court has the power to direct the appointment of a single joint expert (CPR 35.7). Joint reports, by experts whose appointment has been agreed by the parties, saves time and money in straightforward cases and on issues on which professional disagreement is unlikely. In more complicated disputes over liability and causation, separate experts are usually unavoidable.

---

[161] Civil Procedure Rules 1998/3132 (enacted under the Civil Procedure Act 1997).

[162] See *http://www.justice.gov.uk/civil/procrules_fin/pdf/protocols/prot_rcd.pdf* (April 2006 edition) and the discussion in Lewis 2006, 10.

[163] See Lewis 2006, ch.9.

[164] See the comments of Lord Bingham in *Abbey National Mortgages v Key Surveyors Nationwide* [1996] 1 W.L.R. 1534 at 1542 (a professional negligence case, albeit not a clinical negligence case).

We should not forget that, as recent inquiries have highlighted,[165] doctors are often reluctant to publicly criticise each other. Also, a proper understanding of the issues could require investigation of different professional views. In some cases the litigants will need more than one separate expert. In one case, the Court of Appeal acceded to the claimant's wish to have two experts to put the parties on an equal footing in the light of the fact that the defence not only had their own expert but the two consultant defendants would be giving their own view during the hearing.[166]

3.5.4.3 Periodical payments

Until recently, compensation for clinical negligence (and negligence more generally) was paid as a "once and forever" lump sum.[167] This inevitably meant that some successful claimants would be overcompensated (e.g. dying earlier than expected leaving a "windfall" for surviving relatives) or undercompensated (e.g. living longer than expected and requiring expensive nursing care). In response *structured* settlements, now known as *periodical payments*, were introduced as a payment vehicle for higher value settlements. Initially these required the agreement of both parties, but the courts now have the power to impose an order for such payments without consent.[168] The idea is that the part of the lump sum (granted for future losses) is used by the defendant to purchase an annuity to provide payments each year to meet the claimant's future needs. Where the defendant is the NHS, the annual payments under such settlements are drawn from NHS funds.[169] One more point worth mentioning is that Pt 36 of the CPR, which deals with offers to settle, has specific provisions for periodical payments (CPR 36.5).

3.6 Reform and redress

Clinical negligence actions operate in a context of competing demands: those of injured patients, health professions, the health service, and lawyers. While no system can satisfy all these demands to everyone's satisfaction, the current system seems wide off the mark. The current clinical negligence system is inefficient, expensive, and frustrating for patients and health professionals alike (3.6.3). Reforms have to be considered (3.6.2 and 3.6.3). The Government's response has been to engage in what many view as an experiment. The NHS Redress Act 2006 (3.6.4) has evoked both hope and dismay. As I write, it remains difficult to be sure of how this new redress scheme will work.

---

[165] See e.g. Kennedy et al. 2001 and the discussion in Ch.2 (esp. 2.1).
[166] *E S v Chesterfield and North Derbyshire Royal Hospital NHS Trust* [2003] EWCA Civ 1284.
[167] See CMO 2003, paras 64–67.
[168] Damages Act 1996 ss.2–2B (as amended).
[169] See CMO 2003, para.66.

3.6.1 Problems with the ligation system

The costs of the clinical negligence system are enormous. The NHS paid out £423 million to settle clinical negligence claims in 2003–2004 alone,[170] rising to £500 million the following year.[171] While this is slightly less than 1 per cent of the NHS's annual expenditure, it is substantially more than it would have cost to build, run, and staff a new hospital that year.[172] What is more, provisions for outstanding clinical negligence claims were over £2 billion in the same period.[173] It hardly bares thinking about the medical care that such a sum could fund. Perhaps not surprisingly, politicians tend to blame lawyers for sucking money out of the NHS. One Health Secretary famously declared that "the best place for a lawyer is on the operating table".[174] At an average rate of over £300 per hour, clinical negligence claims are potentially very lucrative for lawyers.[175] It is difficult not to see a conflict of interest in the president of the Association of Personal Injury Lawyers' declaration that, "it is important for injured patients to be able to retain their right to litigate if they wish".[176] Practising lawyers cannot, however, be saddled with responsibility for a system that is flawed on so many levels.

The clinical negligence system is uncertain, costly, and an inefficient means of getting compensation to those in need. In England, some 21 per 100,000 tried to make a claim, but only eight per 100,000 succeed.[177] As Michael Jones has memorably pointed out, the last six clinical negligence cases to reach the House of Lords leave the score as Claimants 0, Defendants 6.[178] Since then one case has been won before the House of Lords and another has lost, so the score is now 1–7.[179] Litigation after the event is inevitably piecemeal and erratic. It requires injured parties to recognise a legal claim, have the resources or support required to sue, and have sufficient evidence to link the injury to the legal conditions for liability. Legal actions also create great uncertainty until they are resolved; a patient who alleges clinical negligence might need to convert his accommodation in response to the injury but cannot do so in the knowledge that his costs will be met later. Defendants face the same uncertainties in the litigation lottery but will probably have advantages that the patient does not: deep pockets and litigation experience. This does not, however, enable the NHS to avoid all unmeritorious claims because the costs of fighting claims will sometimes be disproportionate to the costs of settling. Nor does it enable healthcare professions to avoid internalising worry: "It has been estimated that 38% of doctors

---

[170] National Audit Office 2005, 1. This does not include the costs of litigation against GPs, which remain within the remit of the medical protection organisations.

[171] See DH 2006a, 14.

[172] See CMO 2003, 26 and Woolf 2003, 3–4, respectively.

[173] See National Audit Office 2005, 1.

[174] Frank Dobson, quoted in Harpwood 2000, 49.

[175] See CMO 2003, 69. That figure will no doubt have subsequently increased.

[176] Quoted in Dyer 2003.

[177] See CMO 2003, 106.

[178] Jones 1999a, 236.

[179] See *Chester v Afshar* [2004] UKHL 41 (addressed in Ch.4) and *Gregg v Scott* [2005] UKHL 2, respectively.

who are the subject of a clinical negligence claim suffer clinical depression as a result of the process".[180]

The clinical negligence system is meant to provide compensation for injured patients, hold those responsible to account, and create an incentive for careful conduct.[181] Yet the Bristol Inquiry found that the system actually serves as a barrier and disincentive to openness within the NHS and creates a culture of blame and fault. Accountability was found to be "an entirely haphazard process" and the system was found to "fare equally poorly" as a deterrent. Accordingly,

> the culture and the practice of clinical negligence litigation work against the interests of patients' safety. The system is positively counterproductive, in that it provides a clear incentive not to report, or to cover up, an error or incident. And, once covered up, no one can learn from it and the next patient is exposed to the same or a similar risk.[182]

The present system was not the product of any grand design. Clinical negligence law and procedure developed in piecemeal fashion over a considerable period of time. It is apparent that the resulting system would be difficult to justify from any moral theory. A high cost system leaving many dissatisfied is not an obviously effective means of maximising utility, protecting individual rights, enforcing duties, or facilitating the development of virtues.

The problems should not, however, be over exaggerated. Problems have not reached the magnitude of those in the US, nor are they likely to. The estimated cost of medical litigation in the US is estimated to represent 0.2 per cent of the entire Gross Domestic Product, compared with 0.04 per cent in the UK.[183] However, the US has a very different health and legal system: it does not have a national health service, awards are made by juries, contingency fees operate, there is more of a litigation culture, and doctors are paid by the patient (when paying, directly or indirectly, dissatisfied patients are likely to be more eager to litigate).[184]

The risk of *defensive medicine*, said to have manifested in the US, should also be put into perspective. Medicine is said to be practised defensively when patients are *over or under treated* merely to avoid subsequent litigation. Such claims are controversial for two reasons. *First, if* doctors are treating defensively in England and Wales this must be because they have not received sufficient legal education because *Bolam/Bolitho* defer to medical practice. *Second*, evidence of defensible practice is equivocal. The increase in Caesarean sections, for example, is often held out as evidence of defensive practices involving over treatment, but they are also on the increase in countries where litigation is rare[185] and women are increasingly requesting Caesarean sections.[186] Interpretation of the evidence is beset by the difficulty of disentangling the promotion of good

---

[180] CMO 2003, 43.
[181] See Kennedy et al. 2001, 364–366, and CMO 2003, 52.
[182] Kennedy et al. 2001, 366.
[183] See DH 2003a, 11.
[184] See Montgomery 2002, 207–209, and Brazier and Cave 2007, 204–205.
[185] See Montgomery 2002, 209–211.
[186] Usually for quite defensible reasons: see Fisk and Paterson Brown 2004.

practice from negative defensive practices: some practices encouraged by the fear of litigation result in better patient treatment.[187]

Whatever the truth of fears of defensive medicine, the government has acknowledged that there is a perception of a "compensation culture" by enacting the Compensation Act 2006. In addition to stating that the standard of care is not to be set so high as to discourage desirable activities (s.1, discussed above), the Act states that "an apology, an offer of treatment or other redress" does not in itself amount to an admission of negligence (s.2). These provisions appear to have changed little. The courts, for example, had routinely accepted that an apology by itself does not automatically amount to acceptance of blame. More pressing problems with clinical negligence litigation remain.

3.6.2 Types of reforms

There are degrees of tinkering. Reform can be intended to create a permanent solution or can function as a short-term stopgap until the implementation of something more radical. We have already examined the Woolf reforms above (3.5.4). These were intended to make the civil litigation process quicker, cheaper, and fairer. They were intended as a long-term solution to many of the problems inherent in the litigation system. As we have seen, these reforms go well beyond the cosmetic; well beyond replacing "plaintiffs" with "claimants" and limiting the use of Latin. No procedural reforms of this could, even if completely successful, remove the problems stemming from the content of the law and the essentially adversarial nature of litigation.

In 2003, the Chief Medical Officer (CMO) issued a consultation document on clinical negligence claims, entitled *Making Amends*. In addition to the proposal that became the NHS Redress Act 2006, the CMO suggested two changes to the existing system. *First*, the revocation of s.2(4) of the Law Reform (Personal Injuries) Act 1948.[188] This would prevent awards for the costs of future *private* care. It is anomalous that such costs can currently be obtained without the claimant having to undertake to actually use private care.[189] *Second*, the CMO suggested the introduction of statutory provisions to encourage openness in the reporting of adverse events. This was envisaged to include a *duty of candour* requiring health-care professions to inform patients about adverse events or medical errors, an exception from disciplinary action for those reporting these (except where there is a criminal offence or where it would not be safe for the professional to continue to treat patients), and legal privilege for reports and information identifying adverse events except where the information was not recorded in the medical record.[190]

---

[187] Jones (1996, 6–7) goes further and argues that some over-treatment might actually be "positively beneficial" to the patient by discovering unsuspected problems or reassuring the patient.

[188] See CMO 2003, 127.

[189] Brown 2003 objects: "This [reform] raises the spectre that, in future, claimants will be shackled with a care package that will not allow them to be cared for in their own home with appropriate levels of care".

[190] CMO 2003, esp. 18. See also Recommendation 12.

Neither has been taken up. Nor do such reforms address the nature of tort litigation as a costly and an uncertain lottery for claimants. The Bristol Report, whose recommendation led to the CMO's consultation, recommended that consideration be given to alternative systems of compensation.[191] Tort litigation for clinical negligence could be abolished or restricted, and (partially or wholly) replaced by private insurance or some type of state compensation scheme. Some consider the best solution to be a no fault compensation scheme.[192]

3.6.3 No fault compensation schemes

As the label suggests, no fault compensation schemes are intended to remove the need to find someone legally at fault to trigger compensation. Different forms of state compensation schemes have been tried both here (e.g. the criminal injuries compensation scheme and the vaccination damages scheme) and abroad. No fault schemes for medical injury have been introduced in most Nordic countries (Denmark, Finland, Norway, and Sweden), and New Zealand.[193] Sweden provides no fault compensation for avoidable injury caused by treatment or examination and injuries caused by a drug. The New Zealand accident compensation scheme provides for compensation for "personal injury", defined to include "treatment injury", without the need to prove fault.[194] This scheme is administered by the Accident Compensation Corporation (ACC).[195] Unlike the New Zealand system, the Swedish system still allows patients to sue, although few choose to do so.

Experience suggests that state compensation systems provide compensation more efficiently (claimants obtaining a greater percentage of the funding put into the system), quickly, and to a greater number of people. They also tend to reduce the tensions created by the adversarial nature of litigation. Unfortunately, such systems have proven to be more expensive overall and place less emphasis on responsibility and investigation into what went wrong. The CMO thought that a comprehensive no fault scheme would be unaffordable for the NHS,

> Estimates suggest that even with a 25% reduction in the current level of compensation the cost of a true no-fault scheme would vary between £1.6bn per year (if 19% of eligible claimants claimed) to almost £4bn (if 28% of eligible claimants

---

[191] See Kennedy et al. 2001, 367 and recommendation 37.

[192] See e.g. Kennedy et al. 2001, 367; BMA 1987; and Brazier 1993. Cf. the Pearson Report (Person et al. 1978), which rejected a non-fault compensation scheme for medical accidents.

[193] See CMO 2003, ch.6. The American States of Virginia and Florida have introduced a more limited scheme, providing no-fault compensation only for babies with birth-related neurological injuries.

[194] The Injury Prevention, Rehabilitation, and Compensation Act 2001, as amended by the amended by the Injury Prevention, Rehabilitation, and Compensation Amendment Act (No.2) 2005, and the Injury Prevention, Rehabilitation, and Compensation Amendment Act 2008. See, in particular, ss. 26, 32–33.

[195] See *http://www.acc.co.nz*.

claimed). This compares with the £400 million spent on clinical negligence in 2000/01.[196]

New Zealand seems to have had less success than Sweden or Finland, but this might be due to excessive political interference and few seem to want the tort system back.[197] The New Zealand system has now been in operation for 35 years and has recently been significantly reformed. Medical compensation for treatment injury no longer requires negligent medical error, or rare and severe treatment outcomes.

Of course, separating compensation and blame will require the adoption of an alternative system of accountability. Otherwise an aggrieved patient is left without the means of airing grievances and the (limited) deterrence effect of the tort system is removed without an equivalent replacement.[198]

3.6.4 NHS Redress Act 2006

The CMO also proposed a new NHS redress scheme. Special arrangements were proposed for two types of case. *First*, where there were "serious shortcomings in the standards of care", "the harm could have been avoided" and "the adverse outcome was not the result of the natural progression of the illness".[199] This would encompass medical errors or mishaps but not the consequences of the illness or the unavoidable risks of treatment. Damages would be limited to £30,000. *Second*, where a baby suffers brain damage and the birth took place "under NHS care", there is "severe neurological impairment (including cerebral palsy) related to or resulting from the birth", the claim is made within eight years of the birth, and the damage was not the result of "genetic or chromosomal abnormality".[200] Only the first of these proposals has been acted on. With some changes, this has become the NHS Redress Act 2006. The recommendation concerning a no fault redress scheme for severely neurologically impaired babies has, as yet, not been acted upon. This is, perhaps, surprising for a Government apparently obsessed with cost cutting. Clinical negligence damages tend to be the highest in these cases—the costs of taking care of such child for the rest of their lives can be huge. Maybe the Government simply wishes to finalise the details of one radical move in the area before moving on to the next.

3.6.4.1 The Act's structure

The NHS Redress Act 2006 enables the establishment of a redress scheme that will operate *without the need to go to court* (s.1). The scheme is to provide for investigation when things go wrong and, where appropriate, remedial treatment and

---

[196] CMO 2003, 112.
[197] See Merry and McCall Smith 2001, 223–229.
[198] See Brazier 1993, 63.
[199] CMO 2003, 120.
[200] CMO 2003, 120–121.

care, explanations and apologies, and financial compensation (s.3(2)). The aim is to create a cost effective and speedy alternative to litigation for low value claims. The Act itself provides no more than a framework. It establishes the parameters of the cases to which the scheme is to apply and grants powers to the Secretary of State to set out the detailed rules of the scheme in regulations. This approach is meant to provide the Government with the flexibility to adapt the scheme without the need for full Parliamentary discussion.[201] With this in mind it intends to review the scheme three years after implementation.[202] Implementation in England was originally envisaged to be in April 2008,[203] but draft implementing regulations are still not available a year after this date.

The scheme will initially only apply to cases giving rise to *liability in tort* in connection with *hospital care provided by the NHS in England* (s.1(2), (5)). It thereby seeks to supplement the existing tort system rather than replace it. Patients can opt-out before settlement and seek redress in the courts, but those accepting compensation or other settlement under the scheme would waive their right to sue (ss.2(1) and 6(5)). While the scheme only covers NHS-provided care, it does not matter whether the hospital treatment takes place in the UK or abroad (s.1(5)). Primary care services (dental, general practice, and pharmaceutical services) are excluded whether provided by the NHS or not (s.1(6)).

The scheme is not intended to be primarily triggered by applications from injured patients. Providers of NHS hospital services in England—NHS Trusts, NHS Foundation Trusts, and independent providers—will be required to "actively indentify" potentially eligible cases.[204] Further, the Secretary of State has a duty to arrange assistance to individuals seeking redress (s.9). This assistance should include the provision of free independent legal advice in relation to the offer and any settlement agreement (s.8(2)), and may include the provision of jointly instructed medical experts (s.8(1), (4)).[205]

3.6.4.2 Evaluating the Act

The NHS Redress Scheme is to provide low cost, non-litigious redress for low value tort claims. It was originally envisaged to apply to all hospital claims under £30,000, as had been suggested by the CMO. The current plan is for the scheme limit to be £20,000.[206] With this payout cap the financial impact of the scheme is estimated to be anything from a £7m saving to a £48m loss.[207] Over ten years the impact is predicted to range from a £15.4m saving to a £70.5m

---

[201] Under the Act, only regulations establishing a scheme are subject to positive resolution by both Houses of Parliament, other regulations are simply subject to annulment by resolution: ss16(6), (7).

[202] See DH 2005h, para.1.

[203] See DH 2006a, 24. The Welsh Parliament has enacted its own framework legislation: NHS Redress (Wales) Measure 2008.

[204] NHS 2005h, para.49. See also s.12.

[205] Also potentially benefitting to free independent legal advice, see Farrell and Devaney 2007, 635.

[206] See e.g. DH 2005h, para.36.

[207] See DH 2006a, 15.

loss.[208] These figures are proportional to the payout cap, so the higher the cap the greater the potential savings and loses. If the impact proves to be financially beneficial to the NHS, we can expect enthusiastic increases to the payout cap. The Government expects increased costs in the short term: "more patients may receive compensation as scheme members take an active approach to identifying eligible cases and providing redress".[209] Nevertheless, it expects these costs to be offset over time by savings on legal fees. This, it has to be said, will depend on how many new claims are brought into the system and how many accept the settlement offered. In the absence of an appeal mechanism, it is likely that patients convinced that the courts would be more generous than the settlement offered will want to litigate. The complaints procedure (to be set up under the Act) will only be concerned to identify and respond to "maladministration" in the handling and consideration of the complaint (ss.14 and 15).

The biggest concern of critics is that the Government proposes to appoint the NHS Litigation Authority as the scheme authority (under s.11).[210] This would mean that the Litigation Authority would deal directly with claims under the scheme and then would act as the defendant in the litigation of claims outside of the scheme (see 3.5.3). This move will no doubt save the NHS money but perhaps at the expense of public confidence in the impartiality of the system. Another concern, also related to the Government's desire to cut costs, is that the Government proposes to pay fixed fees for medico-legal advice, apparently with little consultation as to whether those who could provide such advice would be willing to do so on this basis.[211]

It also remains unclear how the redress system will fit with the patient's complaints system examined in Ch.2 (2.3.2ff). Both intend to address patient grievances; both will offer explanations and apologies where appropriate. In Ch.2 we saw that complaints system is to become more geared towards local resolution and above we saw that providers of NHS hospital services are to consider potential eligibility for redress in cases before then. If the result is increased local recognition of potential tortious liability and many more complaints leading to compensation, will the Government rapidly utilise the flexibility of the regulation-based system to reduce costs? Maybe we should not be surprised that the Government has taken much longer than anticipated to implement the redress system. The longer it waits, however, the longer patients will miss out on the benefits of this new system, such as remedies beyond compensation.

3.7 Criminal negligence

Early in 2000 two surgeons made a very serious mistake. After looking at an x-ray back to front, a surgeon oversaw a colleague remove a pensioner's healthy

---

[208] See DH 2006, 33.
[209] DH 2005h, para.11.
[210] On the Government's intention see e.g. DH 2005h, para.27. For criticism see e.g. Farrell and Devaney 2007, esp. 643–644.
[211] See Farrell and Devaney 2007, 635–636.

kidney instead of the diseased one that was supposed to be removed. The 70-year-old patient died five weeks later. This proved to be one of those rare cases where negligence leads to criminal prosecution for manslaughter. Although on the increase, criminal prosecution of doctors is rare and few of those who are prosecuted are successfully convicted.[212] These two surgeons, for example, were cleared of manslaughter after a prosecution pathologist told the court that he could not be sure that the pensioner's death had been caused by the mistake.

Should they have been tried at all? The justifiability of criminal liability is tied to its moral objectives and notions of individual culpability. In general terms, duty, rights, and virtue-based theories will focus on *individual* wrong-doing of some type, whereas some forms of communitarianism and utilitarianism will also allow the imposition of criminal liability for the greater good. Utility could plausibly be maximised by criminalising certain conduct (e.g. conduct falling below an objective standard even in the absence of individual culpability) where it will influence the caution exercised by others facing similar circumstances. There are, however, grounds for disagreement between and within the five moral camps outlined in Ch.1.

Killing a patient by negligence will only give rise to criminal liability for manslaughter if that negligence is "extreme" or "gross". This goes far beyond civil negligence. The leading case is the decision of the House of Lords in *R. v Adomako*.[213] Dr Adomako, an anaesthetist, failed to notice that the endotracheal tube delivering oxygen to his patient had become disconnected for over four minutes. The patient suffered a cardiac arrest and subsequently died. One prosecution witness described the standard of care as "abysmal" and the other stated that a competent anaesthetist should have noticed the disconnection within 15 seconds. At trial, the defendant conceded that he had been negligent but denied criminal negligence. His conviction was upheld on appeal.

Lord Mackay held that the determination of whether the doctor's conduct amounted to criminal negligence was a matter for the jury:

> The jury will have to consider whether the extent to which the defendant's conduct departed from the proper standard of care incumbent upon him, involving as it must have done a risk of death to the patient, was such that it should be judged criminal.[214]

He recognised that this involved "an element of circularity": the jury being told, in effect, that it was a crime if they thought it was a crime. Despite this, Lord Mackay (with whom the other judges agreed) refused to elaborate further. He did, however, affirm the two previous decisions[215] and the Court of Appeal's decision in this case.[216]

---

[212] Ferner (2000) found a massive increase in manslaughter charges against doctors in the 1990s compared to earlier decades (17 doctors in the 1990s compared with two in each of the two preceding decades). This rate continues to increase: see Dyer 2002a, Holbrook 2003, and Quick 2006b.

[213] [1995] 1 A.C. 171.

[214] [1995] 1 A.C. 171 at 187.

[215] *R. v Bateman* [1925] All E.R. Rep. 45 and *Andrews v DPP* [1937] A.C. 576.

[216] [1994] Q.B. 302.

The Court of Appeal had heard Dr Adomako's appeal with two others. One of these was the appeal of Prentice and Sullman, who had killed a patient by mistakenly injecting a substance into his spine rather than his arm.[217] Dr Prentice, who administered the injection, had not performed a spinal injection before, and Dr Sullman, who supervised, was unfamiliar with the drug used. They succeeded on appeal because the trial judge had misdirected the jury. If he had not, they might still have been convicted—another doctor has recently been convicted after making a similar mistake.[218]

The Court of Appeal, extrapolating from the case law, gave four examples of situations where criminal negligence could be found.[219] Where a doctor

(a) displays an indifference to an obvious risk of injury to his patient;

(b) displays an awareness of a risk but decides to run it;

(c) attempts to avoid a known risk but does so with such a high degree of negligence as to deserve to be punished;

(d) displays inattention or failure to avert to a serious risk, going beyond mere inadvertence.

Situation (d) could capture Prentice and Sullman, and the surgeons who removed the wrong kidney. Thus, a doctor can be convicted for a gross failure to reach an objective standard. McCall Smith has argued that a doctor should only be prosecuted for criminal negligence if he "deliberately and culpably took a risk with their patients" and those who are "merely incompetent should be dealt with in other ways".[220] There is a great deal of force in the argument that gross incompetence without subjective wrongdoing (situations (c) and (d) above) should be left to professional disciplinary procedures. The escapades of Dr Shipman et al. appear, however, to have made the courts reluctant to revisit the law in this area.

The Court of Appeal has applied *R. v Adomako* in a number of subsequent cases.[221] In the most recent of these, *R. v Misra*, it had been argued that the crime of gross negligence manslaughter was not compliant with the Convention rights laid down in art.6 (the right to a fair trial) and art.7 (the prohibition of criminal conviction in the absence of a pre-existing criminal offence). The Court of Appeal dismissed the appeal, holding that the decision in *Adomako* clearly defined the elements of the offence and left no uncertainty.[222] A doctor, it was said, could be advised that he may be convicted of manslaughter where his treatment exposes his patient to the risk of death, and thereby causes the patient's death, if a jury is satisfied that his treatment was grossly negligent.

---

[217] The other was the appeal of Mr Holloway, an electrician whose wiring of a central heating system had killed a man.

[218] See Holbrook 2003.

[219] [1994] Q.B. 302 at 323.

[220] McCall Smith 1993, 349. See also Mason and Laurie 2006, 344–347.

[221] *R v Becker* (2000) (Westlaw and Lexis), *R. v Mark* [2004] EWCA Crim 2490, and *R. v Misra* [2004] EWCA Crim 2375.

[222] [2004] EWCA Crim 2375, para.64.

3.8 Ethics and other theoretical considerations

It should now be apparent that the tort system faces many ethical and practical tensions. From an ethical point of view, the best compensatory system will be one that best succeeds in asserting and achieving defensible ethical objectives. Many readers will be attracted by the view that the current tort system is not best designed to maximise utility, protect individual moral rights, enforce moral duties, or track virtues. Before examining whether the tort system represents an ethically justifiable compensation system, it is instructive to examine the debate over whether the existing tort system tracks corrective justice alone or also tracks distributive justice.

3.8.1 Corrective and distributive justice

The distinction between corrective and distributive justice was first drawn by Aristotle in Book V of *Nicomachean Ethics*.[223] *Corrective justice* is concerned with "voluntary and involuntary transactions"[224] and with correcting the imbalance caused to the claimant injured by the defendant's wrong. *Distributive justice* is concerned with the just distribution of benefits and burdens among members of society.

Lord Steyn has argued that the tort of negligence tracks both corrective and distributive justice.[225] According to his Lordship,

> While one thinks of an innocent plaintiff and a wrongdoing defendant one instinctively thinks in terms of corrective justice. If one shifts the focus to an enquiry whether the plaintiff should recover from the National Health Service (or ultimately the taxpayer) one's perception of the dictates of fairness may change.[226]

These words relate to *McFarlane*, where the House of Lords held that no duty of care was owed to parents with regard to the costs of rearing an unwanted healthy child born as a result of negligent sterilisation advice (see further 9.5.1). From the perspective of corrective justice, his Lordship opined, the parents' claim "must succeed".[227] Yet, from the perspective of distributive justice "it may become relevant to ask commuters on the Underground" whether the claimant should be able to recover. Asked whether there should be liability he was "firmly of the view that an overwhelming number of ordinary men and women" on the Underground would emphatically say "No". Thus, Lord Steyn holds that:

---

[223] See Aristotle BCE, as translated in Crisp 2000. For a helpful discussion, see Weinrib 2002a.
[224] See Aristotle BCE, 1132a, as translated in Crisp 2000, 87. This translation refers to "rectificatory" justice, which most lawyers would refer to (as I have) as "corrective" justice.
[225] See *McFarlane v Tayside Health Board* [2000] 2 A.C. 59 at 82 and Steyn 2002.
[226] Steyn 2002, 5.
[227] [2000] 2 A.C. 59 at 82.

(a) negligence liability tracks both corrective and distributive justice;

(b) in cases such as *McFarlane*, liability is to be determined by reference to matters of distributive justice; and

(c) matters of distributive justice are to addressed from "the judge's . . . perception of prevailing community standards"[228] (represented by a hypothetical opinion poll in *McFarlane*).

No reason was given for the prioritisation of distributive over corrective justice or for reliance on the judge's intuitions concerning prevailing community standards, beyond the assertion that "judges' sense of the moral answer to a question, or the justice of the case, has been one of the great shaping forces of the common law".[229] Indeed, a strong case can be made for rejecting judicial reliance on distributive justice in tort cases (3.8.2) and his Lordship's criterion for determining matters of distributive justice presupposes adoption of a compromise position (in fact, a form of communitarianism) interpreted by reference to moral intuitionism.

3.8.2 Negligence as a system of corrective justice[230]

The account of the substantive law of clinical negligence adopted in this chapter (3.2–3.4) attempts to mirror the reasoning and practice of the courts. While no explication of the law of negligence can be free of interpretative gloss, this approach accords with what Stephen Smith labels the "descriptive" account.[231] An alternative is the "interpretative" account, which aims

> to enhance understanding of the law by highlighting its significance or meaning . . . [T]his is achieved by explaining why certain features of law are important or unimportant and by identifying connections between those features—in other words, by revealing an *intelligible order* in the law, so far as such order exists.[232]

This approach seeks the most coherent understanding of the decisions, even when this is inconsistent with the reasons individual judges have had for reaching those decisions.[233]

Since the case law on clinical negligence does not represent a seamless web of coherent rules and doctrines, some decisions will need to be reinterpreted or disregarded by those seeking any form of coherence. The prevalent view is that negligence liability cannot be determined solely by reference to the rules and

---

[228] Steyn 2002, 12.
[229] [2000] 2 A.C. 59 at 82.
[230] The following discussion owes much to Beever 2007.
[231] Smith 2004, 4–5. Smith identifies three other approaches to any area of law: historical, prescriptive, and interpretative accounts.
[232] Smith 2004, 5 (original emphasis).
[233] See Beever and Rickett 2005, esp. 327.

doctrines of the law, as policy considerations have an inescapable justificatory role. Liability for negligently inflicted injury must be subject to "control mechanisms" or what is "fair, just and reasonable".[234] Explicit appeal to such policy considerations is endemic (see e.g. the discussion of the *Caparo* test and the nervous shock cases above). Yet, in the absence of any general principle determining what is to count as a legitimate policy, appeals to policy considerations are little more than appeals to individual intuitions.

Justificatory appeals to considerations beyond the existing legal rules and the legal rights of the litigants raise a challenge to democracy and the rule of law. Is it appropriate for private law litigation to be resolved by appeals to the case-by-case application of the judges' sense of prevailing community standards? Does this not raise the spectre of "unelected, unaccountable officials enforcing their personal political preferences on a sometimes unwilling public"?[235] Is there any alternative account of the law of negligence?

Some commentators argue that *corrective justice* is capable of providing an alternative, in the sense of a principled foundation for the law that is consistent with democracy and the rule of law. Beever, for example, argues that the law of negligence is properly understood as seeking to *correct interpersonal legal wrongs between litigants*, according to which a person wrongs another when that person interferes with that other's rights.[236] He urges us to "rediscover" the principled coherence of the law of negligence as represented by five major cases.[237] From these cases Beever derives a unifying principle: "a defendant is liable to a claimant if and only if the defendant created an unreasonable risk of the actual injury suffered by the claimant".[238] On this account, *breach of duty* is the unreasonable creation of the risk: determined by application of the objective test as one that is fair between the parties. A *duty of care* exists if the claimant is placed at an unreasonable risk: determined by whether it was reasonably foreseeable that the claimant would be injured by the defendant's action. The injury is not *too remote* if the actual injury suffered, and the way it came about, was a reasonably foreseeable consequence of the defendant's breach of duty. The actionable injury itself is determined by the claimant's legal rights.[239]

This approach has significant explanatory force. It grounds the objective standard in corrective justice, as one seeking a fair balance between the parties.[240] Strict liability in this context is rejected as it would protect the claimant at the expense of the defendant and a subjective standard (taking account of the defendant's idiosyncrasies) would protect the defendant at the expense of the claimant. Only where the relationship between the parties is characterised by

---

[234] See the discussion in Beever 2007b.
[235] Beever 2007a, 14.
[236] See Beever 2007a, esp. 45. See also the work of Weinrib (e.g. Weinrib 1983, 38).
[237] *Donoghue v Stevenson* [1932] A.C. 562, *Palsgraf v Long Island Railroad* (1928) 248 N.Y. 339, *Bolton v Stone* 1951] A.C. 850, *The Wagon Mound (No.1)* [1961] A.C. 388, and *The Wagon Mound (No.2)* [1967] 1 A.C. 617.
[238] See Beever 2007a, 512. See also Beever 2007, chs 3 (on breach), 4 (on duty and remoteness), and 5 (on duty).
[239] See e.g. Beever 2007a, esp. 120.
[240] Beever 2007a, 491.

the peculiarities of either party will the standard take account of those peculiarities, such as in the case of doctor and patient, where the doctor must reach the standard of a reasonable doctor.

Yet, this approach requires reinterpretation of many cases whose reasoning (but often not result) is inconsistent with corrective justice, including just about all the duty of care cases decided by the House of Lords in the last two decades.[241] For the nervous shock cases it requires abandonment of the distinction between primary and secondary victims[242] and their reclassification as cases on remoteness rather than duty of care. And, with regard to remoteness, it requires the abandonment of the "egg-shell skull" ("thin skull") rule.[243] Consequently, this approach is contrary to many modern precedents and cannot be straightforwardly applied by the lower courts.

3.8.3 Further ethical considerations

Corrective and distributive justice are both purely formal justificatory structures. They are forms of justice, rather than theories of justice. They require criteria to determine the content of what is to be restored between two individuals (corrective justice) or distributed among society (distributive justice).[244] In the case of distributive justice, those criteria could derive from any of the five moral camps outlined in Ch.1. Corrective justice is more restrictive, as its focus on interpersonal or bipolar equality is incompatible with collective aggregation, such as that required by utility maximisation within act utilitarianism. Indeed, it fits most comfortably with rights-based and duty-based moral theories, in which wrongdoing is understood as infringing the entitlements of individuals. Weinrib notably suggests that the moral theory underpinning negligence law is "an Aristotelian corrective justice structure with a Kantian content".[245]

Even if the existing tort law system is not interpreted as solely concerned with the restoration of equality between two individuals, it is an insufficient means of satisfying the demands of distributive justice. Distributive justice requires a fair distribution of benefits and burdens within society as a whole. The question therefore arises as to whether a no fault scheme or other distributive compensation scheme should be put into place. Such schemes are obviously not concerned with the realisation of corrective justice; they are simply not about restorative redress between a wrongdoer and his victim.

---

[241] Note, in particular, the explicit appeals to distributive justice in *McFarlane v Tayside Health Board* [2000] 2 A.C. 59 at 82–84 (Lord Steyn), and *White v Chief Constable of South Yorkshire Police* [1999] 2 A.C. 455, 504 at 510 (Lord Hoffman).
[242] See Beever 2007a, 405–406.
[243] See Beever 2007a, 31, 162–166.
[244] See Weinrib 1983 and Cane 2001, esp. 407.
[245] See Weinrib 1983, 38.

3.8.3.1 The needs of medical accident victims

A distributive scheme seeking to satisfy the *needs of medical accident victims* would surely have to be a no fault or social insurance scheme, rather than a tortious system.[246] If need *as such* were the only relevant consideration, however, it would be difficult to justify providing compensation at all where those resources could be used to satisfy greater needs. Harris has pointed out that compensation awarded to the victims of medical negligence is obtained from the same limited pot of healthcare resources that provides for publicly-funded medical treatment.[247] He argues that guaranteeing the victims of negligence priority is unjust (from the point of view of distributive justice) where this priority does not take account of individual need and the weight of competing demands on these resources. No fault compensation schemes address the needs of a wider category of medical accident victim than the tort litigation system. They do not restrict compensation to the victims of those medical accidents caused by negligence. Nonetheless, they do not address the needs of all those with medical needs. This raises the question of whether there is an ethical distinction between the victims of a medical blunder and the victims of other accidents or naturally occurring events. The needs of an adult who loses his sight do not depend on whether he was blinded by a naturally occurring condition or a medical blunder. Therefore, operating alone, the rationale of need provision would require a general disability scheme, not a no fault compensation scheme. It is also worth noting that need provision cannot be a distributive rationale at all for those (few) ethical theories that rule out positive duties (which must also challenge the very foundation of the NHS).[248]

3.8.3.2 Deterring medical accidents

It is often suggested that *deterrence*, in the sense of influencing behaviour through the prospect of liability, is a goal of the tort system. A no fault compensation system would surely be less of a deterrent to those responsible for medical errors than negligence liability. Does this mean that the goal of deterrence requires tortious liability? Not quite. We need to distinguish two types of deterrence: weak and strong. *Weak deterrence* applauds deterrence as a consequence of the compensation mechanism, but does not grant it a role in defining the content of the norms of compensation. In other words, deterrence is regarded as a positive side-effect of the system, but not a rationale for it. *Strong deterrence* regards deterrence a role in defining the nature of the wrong, so that the compensatory mechanism can be triggered by norms that are designed to deter a class of persons. In other words, deterrence is regarded as a rationale for the system. It should be clear that only weak deterrence is consistent with corrective justice,[249] so a tortious system built on corrective justice would not support the rationale of strong deterrence.

---

[246] See Weinrib 1983, 47.
[247] See Harris 1997.
[248] See e.g. Nozick 1974.
[249] See Weinrib 2002b.

There are limits to the ability of any compensatory mechanism to deter medical mistakes by encouraging joined-up thinking and the adoption of suitable safety systems. The fear of litigation might deter dangerous cuts in services and encourage risk management practices, but the Kennedy Report found that litigation was often counter-productive in this regard (see 3.6.1). Individuals do not pay damages themselves and the threat and reality of litigation leads to secrecy and cover-ups. Also, the focus of litigation on a particular incident can obscure the broader issues and institutional context, which require consideration if accidents are to be prevented in the future. The incentive currently provided to NHS bodies to prevent medical accidents is the result of the link between the costs of compensating victims (through the tort system) and the ability to control those by effective risk management and safety systems,[250] but that link does not depend on the tort system. In theory, tort-based or state-compensation systems could all operate effectively as part of a system designed to encourage risk reduction within the NHS. The difference is that a no fault or other forms of state compensation system require innovation in the creation of the relevant financial link.

3.8.3.3 Punishing those responsible

At first blush, it would appear that if the compensation system is meant to provide retribution for past wrong doing, then nothing less than a fault-based system would be sufficient. A no fault scheme is clearly not connected to the rationale of punishing wrongdoers. Neither, however, is a tort system based on corrective justice, because the conception of corrective justice examined above does not turn on moral fault in the sense of personal moral responsibility.[251] Indeed, we have seen that liability for clinical negligence cannot be equated with moral culpability. Duty of care, breach of duty, and causation are not established by culpability alone and could be established in the absence of any real culpability. Also, the reality of clinical negligence litigation practice is that individuals rarely defend against or directly pay the financial consequences of litigation. Insofar as punishment of those responsible for medical accidents is our aim, we should look towards criminal, professional, and disciplinary procedures, rather than tort litigation or no fault compensation schemes.

3.9 Conclusion

No compensation system will satisfy everyone; nor can any compensation system be ethically neutral. The moral camps outlined in Ch.1 are, however, too broadly defined to provide much guidance on the ethical objectives of a defensible compensatory system. What can be said is that *if* the current tortious system

---

[250] See 3.5.3, above, on the NHS risk management strategy that operates on the back of the tort system.
[251] See Beever 2008.

is coterminous with corrective justice, it will not be compatible with those moral theories that have purely collective distributive concerns. The current tort system does not satisfactorily maximise utility. Indeed, distributive concerns are generally better addressed by a state compensation scheme than by tortious litigation. Nonetheless, insofar as tort law can be (re)interpreted by reference to the notion of corrective justice, one powerful argument for its replacement with a no fault scheme (the conceptual incoherence created by reliance upon policy considerations) thereby disappears.

Readers will have to keep a close eye on the implementation of the NHS Redress Act 2006. It represents a change to position of patients injured by negligence that is significantly more dramatic than the impact of the Compensation Act 2006 or, arguably, the Woolf reforms. The criticisms directed at the current tort system are, however, far from removed by this Act and it is possible that its implementation could exacerbate some of the difficulties faced by those injured by medical error.

3.10 Further reading

Clinical negligence law and practice
CMO (Chief Medical Officer) (2003) *Making Amends: A consultation paper setting out proposals for reforming the approach to clinical negligence in the NHS.* (London: Department of Health).

Harpwood, Vivienne (2001) *Negligence in Healthcare: Clinical Claims and Risk.* (London: Informa).

Lewis, Charles J. (2006) *Clinical Negligence: A Practical Guide.* (6th ed.) (Haywards Heath: Tottel Publishing).

Criminal Negligence
Quick, Oliver (2006) "Prosecuting 'Gross' Medical Negligence: Manslaughter, Discretion, and the Crown Prosecution Service." 33(3) *Journal of Law and Society* 421–450.

Ethics and other theoretical considerations
Harris, John (1997) "The Injustice of Compensation for Victims of Medical Accidents." 314 *British Medical Journal* 1821–1823.

Weinrib, Ernest J. (1983) "Toward a Moral Theory of Negligence Law." 2(1) *Law and Philosophy* 37–62.

Williams, Kevin (2001) "Medical Samaritans: Is There A Duty To Treat?" 21(3) *Oxford Journal of Legal Studies* 393–413.

Chapter 4

CONSENT I: INFORMATION, VOLUNTARINESS, AND PUBLIC POLICY

4.1 Introduction

Consent is a precondition of autonomous decision-making and a requirement of lawful medical treatment. Anyone who intentionally or recklessly touches another without that person's consent will generally commit both a tort and a crime. Health professionals administering medical treatment to a patient with capacity therefore need to obtain a valid consent. Failing to do so can give rise to an action for battery or negligence[1] and can constitute the crime of assault.[2]

---

[1] That is, for negligent failure to obtain the patient's consent where this leads to actionable harm.

[2] "There are now three types of assault in ascending order of gravity, first common assault, secondly assault which occasions actual bodily harm and thirdly assault which inflicts grievous bodily harm" (per Lord Templeman in *R. v Brown* [1994] 1 A.C. 212 at 230). See s.39 of the Criminal Justice Act 1988, and ss.47 and 20 of the Offences Against the Person Act 1861, respectively.

Criminal prosecution is, however, unusual and private law claims are more often in negligence than battery. Since the consent requirements for battery and criminal assault are largely the same, this chapter will only draw attention to the latter when the situation is otherwise.

For a patient's decision to be truly autonomous, it must be freely made with sufficient information and understanding. For consent to be legally valid it must satisfy three requirements: the patient must give it voluntarily, have the capacity to consent, and understand the nature of the treatment in question. This chapter focuses on information and voluntariness (along with the public policy requirement of the criminal law). The next chapter will address capacity. Before addressing any of this, we need to consider the historical development of the law of consent.

4.2 The development of the law of consent

Many features of the law of consent are tied up with its intimate connection to the tort of trespass to the person. Trespass to the person has medieval origins. It was developed to address fist and sword fights, rather than the problems of modern medical practice.[3] It comprises three distinct torts—assault, battery, and false imprisonment:

> An assault is an act which causes another person to apprehend the infliction of immediate, unlawful, force on his person[,] a battery is the actual infliction of unlawful force on another person . . . [and] false imprisonment . . . is the unlawful imposition of constraint on another's freedom of movement from a particular place.[4]

In medical law, battery is the most important of these torts, though false imprisonment can sometimes play a role in the context of detention of mentally disordered patients. Like all these torts, battery has its origins in the ancient writ of trespass, the features of which still shape the modern law. One feature of the writ of trespass was that it was actionable per se. The claimant did not need to prove damage. The modern tort remains actionable without proof of damage or physical injury (although damage is relevant to the level of compensation that will be awarded). For battery, the actionable harm is the uninvited contact, rather than the consequences of that contact. It follows that a patient may sue where a doctor performs an operation without consent *even if the operation is medically required and improves the patient's health*. Another feature of this ancient writ was that the interference complained of had to have been the *direct* result of the defendant's act.[5] The other side of the coin was that the defendant was

---

[3] See Grubb 2004, 133.
[4] *Collins v Wilcock* [1984] 3 All E.R. 374 at 377–378 (Goff L.J.).
[5] This requirement was interpreted very broadly: see *Scott v Shepherd* (1773) 2 W. Bl 892. If the interference was *indirect*, then the action was different and was known as an action on the case or simply "case".

liable for all the direct consequences of the unlawful contact, no matter how unforeseeable. This explains why damages can be recovered in the modern tort of battery for the unforeseen medical complications of an unlawful procedure, even though damages would not be recoverable in negligence.

Historically, conduct that was neither intentional nor reckless could give rise to an action in trespass.[6] The last century has, however, seen the rise and tremendous growth of a tort specifically addressing careless conduct: the tort of negligence. This has led to judicial statements to the effect that actions for battery should be confined to intentional acts: Lord Denning (with the support of Danckwerts L.J.) took this view in *Letang v Cooper*,[7] as did the Court of Appeal in *Wilson v Pringle*.[8] These statements might be regarded as inconclusive— Lord Denning also decided *Letang* on an alternative ground and *Wilson* was concerned with an intentional act—but, in practice, they have probably settled the issue. An intentional act is required. It is worth pausing to note that the intention relates to the defendant's act, not the harm suffered by the claimant.[9] After all, the defendant need not prove any harm at all (battery is actionable per se).

4.2.1 Hostility

For the touching of another to amount to a battery, it had to be a touching "in anger".[10] According to the Court of Appeal in *Wilson v Pringle*, this requirement still applies, so the "touching must be proved to be hostile touching".[11] The Court of Appeal did not define hostility except to say that it "cannot be equated with ill-will or malevolence" and "must be a question of fact".[12] In *Re F*, Lord Goff rejected the "hostility" requirement as being "difficult to reconcile with the principle that any touching of another's body is, in the absence of lawful excuse, capable of amounting to a battery and trespass".[13] Although one obiter statement cannot overrule the ratio of an earlier Court of Appeal decision, it is submitted that the hostility requirement must be either read as requiring no more than the touching be unlawful[14] or taken as implicitly overruled by their Lordships' subsequent failure to insist on it as a separate requirement, at least in medical cases.[15] *Bartley v Studd* provides some support for the former

---

[6] See *Weaver v Ward* (1617) Hob. 134.

[7] [1965] 1 Q.B. 232.

[8] [1987] Q.B. 237.

[9] *Wilson v Pringle* [1987] Q.B. 237 at 249.

[10] See *Cole v Turner* (1794) 6 Mod. 149 (Holt C.J.).

[11] [1987] Q.B. 237 at 253.

[12] The actions of the policewoman in *Collins v Wilcock* [1984] 3 All E.R. 374 were cited as an example, on the basis that although her actions were intended to do no more than restrain, "she was acting unlawfully and in that way was acting with hostility" ([1987] Q.B. 237 at 253).

[13] *Re F* [1990] 2 A.C. 1 at 73. (This case is also known as *F v West Berkshire HA*.)

[14] See e.g. Lord Jauncey's speech in *R. v Brown* [1994] 1 A.C. 212 at 244.

[15] See e.g. Lord Keith's speech in *Airedale NHS Trust v Bland* [1993] A.C. 789 at 857: "it is unlawful, so as to constitute both a tort and the crime of battery, to administer medical treatment to an adult, who is conscious and of sound mind, without his consent".

approach.[16] In this case, the High Court made a finding of battery against a surgeon who removed a woman's ovaries without her consent during a hysterectomy operation, holding that "hostility" did not require malevolence or ill-will: "It is sufficient that the touching is against the will of the person being touched".[17] In the more recent *Ms B* case, Butler-Sloss P. did not consider it necessary to mention the hostility requirement at all when holding doctors liable for continuing to ventilate against the will of a competent patient.[18] Thus, the hostility requirement, if required at all in medical cases, is satisfied where an adult with capacity is subjected to unauthorised treatment.

4.2.2 Burden of proving consent

One issue that was not explicitly addressed until modern times was whether the absence of consent was a component of the tort or consent was a defence to it. This is relevant to the burden of proof. Does *the claimant* need to establish the absence of consent to establish his claim *or* is it left to *the defendant* to prove consent if he is to rely on it as a defence? Surprisingly, there is only one case explicitly addressing this point: *Freeman v Home Office*.[19] In this case, a prisoner claimed that he had been administered drugs forcibly against his will. McCowan J. accepted the defendant's argument that the tort of battery is "the unconsented to intrusion of another's bodily integrity . . . [and] that the burden of proving absence of consent is on the [claimant]".[20] This has been taken to have settled the question in a way contrary to the position in many other jurisdictions, notably Australia and Canada.[21] This is particularly harsh on claimants who are unlikely to have made contemporaneous notes of the details of their visit to the doctor. *Freeman* is consistent with the historical deference to the medical profession, but was, perhaps, the result of the prisoner's case failing to evoke the sympathy of the court. It is unfortunate that the Court of Appeal chose to uphold McCowan J.'s judgment on appeal without addressing this issue.[22] The dearth of case law on this point is probably explained by the tendency of claimants to plead negligence instead of battery and the eagerness of the courts to support this approach. Also, in practice, once the claimant has presented evidence casting doubt on the presence of consent, it will be treated as if it were a defence.

[16] (1995) 2(8) *Medical Law Monitor* 1.
[17] (1995) 2(8) *Medical Law Monitor* 1, 2.
[18] *Re B* [2002] EWHC 429.
[19] [1984] 1 Q.B. 524.
[20] [1984] 1 Q.B. 524 at 539.
[21] *Department of Health and Community Services v JWB* (1992) 175 C.L.R. 218 at 310–311 and *Sansalone v Wawanesa Mutual Insurance* (2000) 185 D.L.R. (4th) 57, respectively. In the former, McHugh J. rejected the English position as "inconsistent with a person's right of bodily integrity": (1992) 175 C.L.R. 218 at 311.
[22] In the Court of Appeal, Sir John Donaldson simply asserted that "in this context, [consent] deprives the act of its tortious character" ([1984] 1 Q.B. 524 at 557). See Murphy 2007, 238 for support for this position.

A similar issue arises with regard to a *criminal charge* of assault. Where consent could negate the offence (on which see 4.6ff), is the absence of consent constitutive of the definition of the offence or its presence a defence to it? To put it another way, does the prosecution need to prove beyond reasonable doubt that the victim did not consent? In *R. v Brown* their Lordships did not speak with one voice on this matter, but the dominant view seems to have been that, where consent is relevant, it is a defence to be made out by the defendant.[23] In the subsequent case law on reckless transmission of HIV, consent has been treated as a defence.[24]

4.2.3 Declaratory procedure and clinical judgment

One development has radically reshaped the law of consent and its application to medical practice: the extension of the declaratory procedure. This power was first recognised at common law[25] and now s.15 of the Mental Capacity Act 2005 explicitly grants the Court of Protection the power to make declarations on whether a person has capacity and the lawfulness of any action in relation to that person (see further Ch.5). Thus, the courts are able to declare the legal position in advance, rather than wait until the unlawful conduct has taken place. Where there is some doubt as to the legality of an action, health professionals can (and often do) seek a court declaration to protect themselves from subsequent litigation or prosecution. Others may also seek to clarify the legality of proposed treatment.

In contrast to the development of declaratory relief, the courts have been reluctant to allow mandatory injunctions to be granted against doctors. In *Re J*, the Court of Appeal overturned the trial judge's interim injunctive order directing that life-prolonging treatment be provided if the patient was to suffer a life-threatening event.[26] Both Lord Donaldson and Balcombe L.J. declared that in no circumstances would the court order a doctor to treat contrary to his clinical judgment.[27] Leggatt L.J. more cautiously noted that he was not required to rule on all possible factual situations.[28] In any event, by the time that the case got to the Court of Appeal, the consultant in question was prepared to provide life-prolonging treatment. It is not difficult to see how the majority's unqualified blanket assertion could operate in a way that is inconsistent with those

---

[23] *R. v Brown* [1994] 1 A.C. 212. Lord Templeman treated consent as a defence to common assault and battery (234), Lord Jauncey noted that if it had been necessary to decide this issue, he would have held that consent could be a defence (246–247), and Lord Lowry agreed with both. In contrast, Lord Slynn approved Glanville Williams' statement that consent is "inherent in the conception of assault and battery" (279) and Lord Mustill rejected the theory of consent as a defence as "forced" (259).

[24] See *R. v Dica* [2004] EWCA Crim 1103 and *R. v Konzani* [2005] EWCA Crim 706, and the discussion in Weait 2007, ch.5.

[25] *Re F* [1990] 2 A.C. 1. See also the discussion of when to involve the court in Ch.5 (5.4).

[26] *Re J (A Minor)* [1993] Fam. 15.

[27] [1993] Fam. 15 at 26–27 (Lord Donaldson), 29 (Balcombe L.J.).

[28] [1993] Fam. 15 at 30.

moral theories requiring the protection of the sanctity of life or otherwise imposing relevant duties to intervene to treat a patient.

A patient faced with a doctor unwilling to comply with a court declaration might take some comfort from the fact that, in practice, a willing doctor would usually be found.[29] In *R. (Burke) v GMC*, Munby J. noted that that there had been a number of legal developments since *Re J*, including reduced judicial deference to the medical profession and the coming into force of the HRA 1998.[30] Munby J. was considering a challenge to the legality of General Medical Council (GMC) guidance,[31] which the applicant, Mr Burke, read as permitting doctors to withdraw nutrition and hydration from him against his will. The judge was prepared to accept that the court will not grant a mandatory order requiring an individual doctor to treat a patient against his clinical judgment.[32] He opined, however, that a doctor could still be under a legal duty to transfer a patient into the care of another doctor who is willing to provide treatment. Further, in an appropriate case a court could

> grant both declaratory and mandatory relief against a NHS trust or other health authority. Thus the court can by appropriate orders ensure that a patient who ought to be treated is, if need be, transferred to the care of doctors who are willing to do so.[33]

The Court of Appeal later overturned the judge, ruling that his declarations had extended well beyond the law relating to the applicant.[34] Mr Burke was not receiving artificial nutrition and hydration, let alone facing doctors who wished to withdraw it. Munby J.'s declarations on mandatory relief were not specifically mentioned by the Court of Appeal and must now be viewed as obiter. The Court of Appeal did not consider mandatory relief to be relevant with regard to Mr Burke's situation. The court opined that it did not believe that it has ever been open to doubt that the common law (and art.2 of the Convention) imposes a duty on those who care for a capacitated patient to provide artificial nutrition and hydration to him as long it prolongs his life and is in accordance with his expressed wishes.[35] Significantly, the Court of Appeal undermined the authority of Munby J.'s declarations on this point by counselling strongly against selective use of his judgment in future cases.[36] The High Court has subsequently reasserted that a doctor cannot be required to treat contrary to his *bone fide* clinical judgment.[37]

---

[29] As in *Re B* [2002] EWHC 429. See also the guidance MCA Code of Practice guidance on conscientious objections: Department for Constitutional Affairs 2007, paras 9.61–9.63.
[30] [2004] EWHC 1879, para.189.
[31] See GMC 2002a.
[32] [2004] EWHC 1879, para.191.
[33] [2004] EWHC 1879, para.213. See further paras 192–194.
[34] [2005] EWCA 1003.
[35] [2005] EWCA 1003, para.40.
[36] [2005] EWCA 1003, para.24.
[37] *Re Wyatt* [2005] EWHC 2293, para.32.

4.3 Valid consent

We cannot know another's inner thoughts. Yet, consent is an internal state of mind. Consent to what would otherwise be a battery is, in the words of Lord Diplock, "a state of mind personal to the victim of the battery".[38] The best that we can do is act on the observable features of another's thoughts. Consent is a process that might not be complete even where the patient has signed a form, so a completed "consent form" can be no more than evidence of consent.[39] A patient's conduct can, however, lead us to believe that there is consent. The law does not require a written or an explicit verbal agreement. Patients who visit a doctor complaining of something in their eye and put their head back so that the doctor can take a look, need not expressly state that they agree to the doctor placing fingers on either side of their eye. Paradoxically, this means that patients can be taken to have consented even when they do not actually consent. In one American case, an immigrant who had held out her arm to a doctor at a vaccination point on a ship entering the US was taken to have consented to vaccination.[40] Her conduct prevented her suing for trespass.

There are many ways in which a patient's conduct could reasonably be taken to signal consent. These can be quickly summarised here (see further 6.3.1.1). The patient could use explicit words or conduct (*express consent*) or suggestive conduct (*implicit consent*). Consent to an activity could also be reasonably taken to be implied where it is a necessary means of fulfilling a purpose for which express consent has been obtained and the patient is reasonably expected to be aware of this connection (*implied consent*). Not every (express, implicit, or implied) agreement will, however, be recognised as a valid consent in law. Where it is, for example, obtained by coercion or deception, any apparent consent will not amount to real consent. For the consent to be valid, the person giving the consent must

(a) have the capacity to consent;

(b) be acting voluntarily; and

(c) be broadly aware of what he is consenting to (in a treatment context, broadly aware of the "nature and purpose of the treatment").

Where these three requirements—capacity, voluntariness, and information—are present, no action for battery can succeed. Satisfying these three requirements will not, however, protect a doctor who acts contrary to public policy from prosecution for assault occasioning actual or grievous bodily harm (or, for that matter, murder). This is one area where the criminal law diverges from the civil law.

---

[38] *Sidaway v Bethlem Royal Hospital* [1985] A.C. 871 at 894.
[39] *Chatterton v Gerson* [1981] 1 Q.B. 432 at 443.
[40] *O'Brien v Cunard* (1891) 28 N.E. 266.

As stated in the introduction, this chapter will start by examining the information requirement before examining voluntariness and public policy. Capacity is addressed in the next chapter.

4.4 Information

To be a valid consent the patient must have understood what is being agreed to. This raises two related questions: how "informed" does that consent have to be and what legal consequences follow if the physician has been less than candid when disclosing the risks of the procedure? It would be impractical for the law to require a doctor to disclose *all* the known risks of a procedure to all patients. A patient is not usually in a position to understand or absorb all that information, or resolve conflicts in professional opinion. Conversely, a patient who knows nothing about a procedure cannot be said to have consented to it. The law requires something between these two extremes. There are two overlapping causes of action, both of which require the patient to understand something between all possible risks and none of the risks: an action for battery (4.4.1) and an action for negligence (4.4.2). The information requirement for the criminal law of assault is largely the same as that for battery. To put it another way, conduct giving rise to an action for battery will usually also amount to the crime of assault, exceptions will be considered below.

4.4.1 Information and battery

An action in battery has many advantages for claimants. As we have seen, there is no need to prove physical harm or injury (but any harm directly flowing from the uninvited contact will be recoverable), or that, had the patient been adequately informed, he would have rejected the treatment. The information threshold for battery is, however, very low. In *Chatterton v Gerson*,[41] Bristow J. held that to succeed in trespass, the patient had to show that there had been a lack of real consent, but

> once the patient is informed in broad terms of the nature of the procedure which is intended, and gives his consent, that consent is real, and the cause on which to base a claim for failure to go into the risks and implications is negligence, not trespass.[42]

No battery is committed where the patient understands the broad nature of the treatment, even if this understanding derives from sources other than the doctor. In practice, where a patient consents to a medical procedure he will just about always be broadly aware of its "nature". This information threshold

---

[41] [1981] 1 Q.B. 432.
[42] [1981] 1 Q.B. 432 at 443.

effectively means that an action in battery is only available if the doctor treats the patient *against that patient's will*, administers *a different treatment*, or obtains the patient's consent by *fraud*. As an example of where trespass could be pleaded, Bristow J. referred to a case "in the 1940s in the Salford Hundred Court where a boy was admitted to hospital for tonsillectomy and due to administrative error was circumcised instead".[43] Having one's foreskin removed is a very different procedure from having one's tonsils removed! When an administrative error leads a doctor or surgeon to administer the wrong treatment there is simply no defence. Such cases will just about always be settled out of court.

In a case that did make it to court, a dentist was found liable in battery after he conducted large-scale, unnecessary treatment on patients.[44] The dentist was found liable, apparently on the ground that the consent was not real. The claimants would not have consented had they known the true position. The implication of this judgment is that the "nature" of an unnecessary medical procedure is different from that of a necessary medical procedure, or that a fraudulent misrepresentation as to the need for treatment will invalidate an apparent consent.

The effect of a *fraudulent* misrepresentation might be different for the civil and criminal law. There is a plethora of criminal cases holding that apparent consent will be invalid where a person is mislead about the "nature or quality" of what was being done to them or the identity of the accused.[45] However, in *R. v Richardson (Diane)*, the Court of Appeal quashed the conviction of a dentist for criminal assault where she had failed to inform her patients that she had been struck off the dental register.[46] Otton L.J. noted that on this point "the criminal and the civil law do not run along the same track"; the accused's conduct was "reprehensible and may well found the basis of a civil claim for damages".[47] The criminal law is usually more restrictive than the civil law, so civil action for battery could be founded on the facts of subsequent criminal cases where fraud as to the "quality" of the act invalidated the victim's consent. In one such case, a man was convicted of indecent assault having carried out breast examinations in such a way as to mislead the women into believing that he had medical qualifications or training.[48] In another, an embryologist was convicted of assault when he replaced the embryos that were to be implanted into his victims with saline solution.[49] The victims' consents were not real, they were induced by fraud.

[43] [1981] 1 Q.B. 432 at 443.

[44] *Appleton v Garret* [1996] P.I.Q.R. P1.

[45] See e.g. *R v Williams* [1923] 1 K.B. 340, where a choir master was convicted of rape having persuaded a 16-year-old girl to have sex with him under the pretence that it was an operation to help her breathing so that she could produce her voice properly. More recently, see *R. v Dica (Mohammed)* [2004] EWCA Crim 1103, which held that consent to sexual intercourse does not imply consent to the risk of infection from HIV or any other sexually transmitted disease (overruling *Clarence* (1888) 22 Q.B. 23). On consent in relation to HIV transmission, see also *R. v Konzani* [2005] EWCA Crim 706 and Pattinson 2009.

[46] [1999] Q.B. 444.

[47] [1999] Q.B. 444 at 450.

[48] *R. v Tabassum* [2000] 2 Cr. App. R. 328.

[49] See BBC 2002b.

4.4.1.1 *Performing an additional procedure on an unconscious patient*

The scope of a patient's consent is particularly important where, having obtained consent for one procedure, a surgeon discovers the need to carry out another procedure on an unconscious patient. In *Devi v West Midlands RHA* a surgeon who was performing minor gynaecological surgery discovered that his patient's womb had ruptured and decided to perform a sterilisation operation as the abdomen was open and he considered this to be in the interests of the patient.[50] The surgeon was found liable, as the patient had not consented to sterilisation. Although the authority of this case is not beyond question,[51] there have been other similar cases. In *Bartley v Studd*, mentioned earlier (in 4.2.1), a finding of battery was made against a surgeon who removed the ovaries of a woman for what he considered to be justifiable clinical reasons, as although the patient had consented to a hysterectomy she had not consented to the removal of her ovaries.[52] The "nature" of the procedure should not, however, be read too narrowly. In *Davis v Barking*, for example, McCullough J. held that consent to a general anaesthetic was sufficient to cover a local anaesthetic by way of caudal block (i.e. a form of epidural involving the injection of an anaesthetising drug into the lower spine).[53] McCullough J. reasoned that there was a difference between two separate operations, for which specific consents are required whether or not they are performed on two occasions or one, and the details of one procedure, for which one consent will be sufficient. The dividing line between two separate procedures and one multifaceted procedure was said to be "a question of fact and degree".[54] It is evidently one that is difficult to draw other than by analogy with the decided cases.

What if, although the additional procedure clearly falls outside the scope of the unconscious patient's prior consent, it is required to address a life-threatening medical emergency arising during the course of the surgery? In neither *Devi* nor *Bartley* were the doctors' actions immediately necessary to save the women's lives. While there are no English cases on this issue, there are two Canadian cases. The first, *Marshall v Curry*, concerned the removal of a patient's left testicle during the course of a hernia operation.[55] The testicle was diseased and in danger of becoming gangrenous. The court held that the additional procedure was necessary to protect the patient's health and life, and it would have been "unreasonable to postpone the removal to a later date".[56] In the second case, *Murray v McMurchy*, the surgeon performing a Caesarean section sterilised a patient upon discovering that her womb was in such a state as to make any future pregnancy hazardous.[57] The court held the operation to be unnecessary. A similar conclusion could be reached applying the Mental

---

[50] [1980] C.L.Y. 687.
[51] When it reached the Court of Appeal on the assessment of damages, it was indicated that this case should not be treated as authority on the assault point.
[52] (1995) 2(8) *Medical Law Monitor* 1.
[53] *Davis v Barking Havering and Brentwood HA* [1993] 4 Med. L.R. 85.
[54] [1993] 4 Med. L.R. 85 at 90.
[55] [1933] 3 D.L.R. 260.
[56] [1933] 3 D.L.R. 260 at 275–276.
[57] [1949] 2 D.L.R. 442.

Capacity Act 2005 (which will be examined in depth in the next chapter). Section 5 of that Act grants health professionals a general authority to act in the best interests of a patient who (temporarily or permanently) lacks capacity. Under s.4, the determination of the patient's best interests must take account of all relevant circumstances, which will include the patients' past wishes, the length of time it will take for the patient to regain capacity, and the urgency of the situation. Thus, where there is no evidence of the patient's wishes on such an additional procedure and it is immediately necessary to save his life or preserve his long-term health, it can be lawfully performed.

What if the additional unauthorised contact is part of the training of medical students? Is separate consent needed for medical students to perform, say, intimate examinations on unconscious women undergoing gynaecological surgery? Unless the patient is explicitly informed about this practice, she is unlikely to have it in mind when consenting to a procedure. Since it is not for the benefit of that particular patient, it cannot be part of the nature of the procedure or necessary to protect the health or life of that patient. GMC guidance requires doctors to "obtain consent prior to anaesthetisation, usually in writing, for the intimate examination of anaesthetised patients" and a medic supervising students "should ensure that valid consent has been obtained before they carry out any intimate examination under anaesthesia".[58] Unfortunately it appears that this is not always the practice.[59] This issue is not simply a matter of whether the interests of the general patient population (who benefit from the training of future doctors) can outweigh the self-determination interests of a particular patient. Insofar as failure to obtain consent is likely to have a detrimental impact on women's confidence in seeking health advice, even a utilitarian would require the patient's knowledge and consent.[60] For obvious reasons, an even stronger line will be taken by rights-based and feminist moral approaches; the former being autonomy-based and the latter emphasising the interests of the female patient.

4.4.1.2 Questioning the low information threshold

Why is the information threshold for a valid consent for the purposes of the law of trespass so low? As we have seen, an action for battery is only available if the patient lacks information as to the broad nature of the treatment and, so, any complaint relating to the failure to disclose the risks of the treatment must be brought in negligence.[61] According to Bristow J., "it would be very much

---

[58] GMC 2006b, paras 18 and 19, respectively. See also BMA 2004, 48.

[59] See Coldicott et al. 2003, 97, who found that, in their sample, up to a quarter of intimate examinations on anaesthetised or sedated patients appeared to have taken place without adequate consent from patients. For comments on the US practice see McCullough and Surendran 2003.

[60] Cf. Coldicott et al. 2003, 97.

[61] There is ample authority from the Court of Appeal and below on this point (see e.g. Lord Donaldson in *Freeman v Home Office* [1984] Q.B. 524 at 556). When *Sidaway* ([1985] A.C. 871) reached the House of Lords, this point was conceded without argument by counsel for the claimant. This is consistent with the legal position in other jurisdictions, see e.g. *Reibl v Hughes* [1980] 2 S.C.R. 880 at 890–892 (Canada), and *Rogers v Whitaker* (1992) 109 A.L.R. 625 (Australia).

against the interests of justice" to allow a claimant who was broadly aware of the nature of the procedure to plead in trespass.[62] In *Sidaway*, Lord Scarman, following Hirst J. in *Hills v Potter*,[63] declared that "it would be deplorable to base the law in medical cases of this kind on the torts of assault and battery".[64] However, it might be objected that consent in ignorance of the details and implications of a procedure cannot be real consent, and negligence does not protect patients from all uninvited contact (it requires the contact to lead to harm in circumstances where, had adequate information been given, the patient would have at least delayed the treatment). Along these lines Feng has argued that the dividing line between trespass and negligence has been inappropriately drawn and attention should be "focussed on the *degree* of non-disclosure in the medical advice instead of the *type* of medical information that is not communicated".[65]

It should be remembered that trespass has drawbacks as a means of protecting a patient's "right" to information. Two deserve particular mention. *First*, a battery action is stigmatising. A finding that a doctor has "battered" a patient carries emotive connotations.[66] Is a doctor who fails to inform a patient of a risk because of misplaced paternalism no more than a vicious mugger in clinical robes? Battery is, after all, intimately connected with the crime of assault. *Second*, since battery traditionally requires some physical contact,[67] it has hitherto not been applied to drugs or other treatment administered without physical contact, or treatments not even offered to the patient. Should different rules on disclosure apply to drug treatment?

Neither of these drawbacks need be fatal, as the law is not immutable.[68] A further response could be the creation of a *sui generic* action. Brazier has, for example, argued that fiduciary duties could derive from the doctor–patient relationship as in Canada.[69] She suggests that within a reformulated fiduciary relationship "the doctor's duty would be to make available to the patient that information that it seems likely that individual patients would need to make an informed choice on treatment".[70] Insofar as the case law only imposes fiduciary relationships where property interests are at stake, Brazier has argued that the

---

[62] *Chatterton v Gerson* [1981] 1 Q.B. 432 at 443.

[63] [1984] 1 W.L.R. 641.

[64] [1985] A.C. 871 at 883.

[65] Feng 1987, 160.

[66] See Brazier and Cave 2007, 109.

[67] *Collins v Wilcock* [1984] 3 All E.R. 374 at 377. Cf. *Kaye v Robertson* [1991] FSR 62 at 68, where Glidewell L.J. stated that he was prepared "to accept that it may well be the case that if a bright light is deliberately shone into another person's eyes and injures his sight, or damages him in some other way, this may be in law a battery". This obiter statement runs counter to authority by requiring physical harm/damage, yet not requiring physical contact of any type.

Cf. the crime of assault occasioning actual bodily harm for which unlawful physical contact is no longer required: *R. v Ireland; R. v Burstow* [1998] A.C. 147; *R. v Dica (Mohammed)* [2004] EWCA Crim 1103.

[68] Indeed, an additional drawback listed in the last edition of this book (Pattinson 2006, 108) is no longer a concern in the light of the decision of the House of Lords in *A v Hoare* [2008] UKHL 6, overruling *Stubbings v Webb* [1993] A.C. 498.

[69] See Brazier 1987 and 2003, 110, Brazier and Lobjoit 1999, and Brazier and Glover 2000, 379. See also Bartlett 1997.

[70] Brazier 2003, 110.

patient "does entrust his most precious property to the doctor" and asks whether equity is really too rigid to remedy the inflexibility of tort within the common law.[71] This proposal is unlikely to be implemented, as it was dismissed by both the Court of Appeal and the House of Lords in *Sidaway* and there is no political will for legislative intervention. Also, developing the notion of fiduciary duty has not received universal academic support: Kennedy has argued that the fiduciary's obligation to act in the other's best interests might actually encourage doctor paternalism.[72] It is now appropriate to consider the law of negligence.[73]

4.4.2 Information and negligence

What information must a doctor disclose to avoid liability in negligence? In *Bolam*, McNair J. applied the same standard of care to the claimant's claim that the defendants were negligent in failing to warn him of the risks of electro-convulsive therapy as he did to the claim that the defendants were negligent in the administration of this treatment. What became known as the *Bolam* test was applied to both. Nearly 30 years later the House of Lords considered this issue in *Sidaway v Bethlem Royal Hospital*.[74] Mrs Sidaway had been partially paralysed by an operation to remove recurrent pain in her arms and shoulders, which had carried a risk of injury to a nerve root or her spinal cord of between 1 and 2 per cent.[75] She claimed that this risk had not been disclosed to her. Unfortunately, her claim was beset with evidential problems exacerbated by the passing of time: the case came to trial eight years after the operation had taken place, by which time the surgeon had died, and it was not until two years later that the case reached the House of Lords! These evidential difficulties made the case, in Lord Diplock's words, "a naked question of legal principle".[76] All but one of their Lordships applied the *Bolam* test and held that a doctor need only disclose such information as would be disclosed by a reasonable body of medical opinion. Since many neurosurgeons would not have warned Mrs Sidaway about the risk to the spinal cord, she lost.

Although lack of evidence caused Lord Scarman to concur with the majority's dismissal of Mrs Sidaway's appeal, he was not prepared to support the application of the *Bolam* test. Lord Scarman thought that the court should be primarily concerned with the "patient's rights" from which the doctor's duty arises. Since, he reasoned, to ask what that particular patient would consider a significant risk requiring disclosure would be impractical and too subjective, the court should ask what "a reasonably prudent patient" would

---

[71] Brazier 1987, 190–191. On the idea of property in the body, see further Ch.14 (14.4).

[72] See Kennedy 1996, esp. 137–140.

[73] For the approach adopted in New Zealand, which abolished medical negligence actions in 1972, see Manning 2004.

[74] [1985] A.C. 871.

[75] The risk of damage to the spinal cord in isolation from the other risk was less than 1%.

[76] [1985] A.C. 871 at 892.

want disclosed, subject only to "therapeutic privilege" (i.e. the doctor could still rely on a reasonable belief that disclosure of a risk would prove psychologically damaging to a patient: see below).[77] The speeches of the majority displayed subtle differences. Lord Bridge (with whom Lord Keith agreed) and (possibly) Lord Templeman applied *Bolam* with the rider that there might be some risks that no reasonable doctor would fail to disclose, irrespective of normal practice.[78] Lord Diplock applied *Bolam* without such a rider.

4.4.2.1 Developments since Sidaway

Early attempts to restrict *Sidaway* to its facts were quickly quashed by the Court of Appeal.[79] It has received considerable academic criticism for placing a large amount of discretion in the hands of the medical profession. The reasonable doctor test does not protect the self-determination of patients.[80] The doctor's medical training qualifies him to diagnose and carry out medical procedures, but should it qualify him to determine what a patient needs to know? What if there is no common professional view?[81]

The differences between their Lordships' speeches in *Sidaway* proved to be a hostage to fortune. For a time it looked like Lord Diplock's "doctor knows best" approach might take hold.[82] More recently the House of Lords has reconsidered the ambit of the *Bolam* test on which it is based. As discussed in Ch.3 (3.4.1), the House of Lords in *Bolitho v City and Hackney HA* made it clear that the *Bolam* test referred to a *responsible*, rather than a *received* body of opinion.[83] It was not simply a find-any-supportive-expert standard, as medical opinion must have a "logical basis". However, when delivering the only substantial judgment, Lord Browne-Wilkinson stated, in parentheses: "I am not here considering questions of disclosure of risk".[84] It would be unreasonable to interpret Lord Browne-Wilkinson as suggesting that the find-any-supportive-expert standard applies to disclosure of information because he was so emphatic that this was

---

[77] This is broadly consistent with decisions in other common law jurisdictions, such as Australia (*Rogers v Whitaker* [1992] 109 A.L.R. 625), Canada (*Reibl v Hughes* [1980] 2 S.C.R. 880), and some states in the US (*Canterbury v Spence* (1972) 464 F. 2d. 772).

[78] See [1985] A.C. 871 at 900 and 903, respectively. Lord Templeman did not refer explicitly to *Bolam* and appears to be have been less inclined to give *Bolam* a free reign: "the court must decide whether the information afforded to the patient was sufficient to alert the patient to the possibility of serious harm of the kind in fact suffered" (903). The proper interpretation of this judgment is not entirely clear: see Kennedy 1988, 205–209.

[79] See e.g. *Gold v Haringey HA* [1988] Q.B. 481 (*Sidaway* applied to sterilisation for contraceptive purposes, rather than restricted to therapeutic procedures).

[80] There are a number of judicial statements to the effect that "The concept of informed consent forms no part of English law" (per Dunn L.J., *Sidaway* [1984] 1 All E.R. 1018 at 1030). One must be careful with such statements because here "informed consent" is merely used as shorthand for the "prudent patient" test as adopted in other jurisdictions.

[81] See Kennedy 1988, 189. In some instances there is a clear medical view: see e.g. *Gowton v Wolverhampton HA* [1994] 5 Med. L.R. 432 at 433 (failure to warn of the risk of recanalisation following a vasectomy operation).

[82] See the Court of Appeal decisions in *Gold v Haringey HA* [1988] Q.B. 481 and *Blyth v Bloomsbury HA* [1993] 4 Med. L.R. 151.

[83] [1998] A.C. 232.

[84] [1998] A.C. 232 at 243.

a misinterpretation of *Bolam* and there is no suggestion that he thought *Sidaway* ripe for overturning. His Lordship was most probably either indicating that the facts of the case before him did not raise any issue of disclosure of risk or suggesting that the find-any-supportive-expert standard had not taken hold in the disclosure of risk cases.[85] Whatever was meant, *Sidaway* and *Bolitho* have now been combined and reconciled by Lord Woolf in *Pearce v United Bristol Healthcare NHS Trust*.[86] Lord Woolf, in effect, equated Lord Brown-Wilkinson's requirement that the position have a logical basis with the rider that Lord Bridge put on *Bolam* in *Sidaway*.

The facts of *Pearce* are straightforward. Mrs Pearce was overdue by two weeks with what was to be her sixth child. She begged her consultant to induce the birth or give her a Caesarean section. The consultant considered medical intervention to be inappropriate and discussed the risks and disadvantages of induction and Caesarean section. He did not advise her of the increased risk of a stillbirth associated with non-intervention, estimated at 0.1 to 0.2 per cent. Five days later the child was delivered stillborn. Mrs Pearce claimed that the consultant had been negligent in failing to advise her of the increase risk of a stillbirth.

According to Lord Woolf, with whom Roch and Mummery L.JJ. agreed,

> if there is a significant risk which would affect the judgment of a reasonable patient, then in the normal course it is the responsibility of a doctor to inform the patient of that significant risk . . . In the Sidaway case Lord Bridge recognises that position. He refers to a "significant risk" as being a risk of something in the region of 10 per cent.[87]

On the facts, the consultant was not negligent in failing to disclose "that very, very small additional risk", as it was not a "significant risk". Despite the outcome for Mrs Pearce, this judgment is very pro-claimant. This reading of Lord Bridge's rider to the *Bolam* test brings the English legal position very close to Lord Scarman's "prudent patient" test. In the passage quoted above, Lord Woolf explicitly defines a significant risk as one "which would affect the judgment of a reasonable patient". Apparently, a "reasonable doctor" must disclose the information that a "reasonable patient" would want to make an informed decision! Since Lord Bridge dismissed the prudent patient test "as quite impractical in application",[88] Lord Woolf's move is both bold and ingenious.[89] Nonetheless, Lord Woolf's view was endorsed by the House of Lords in *Chester v Afshar*, where Lord Steyn added:

> In modern law medical paternalism no longer rules and a patient has a prima facie right to be informed by a surgeon of a small, but well established, risk of serious injury as a result of surgery.[90]

---

[85] See Brazier and Miola 2000, 108.
[86] [1999] P.I.Q.R. 53.
[87] [1999] P.I.Q.R. 53 at 49.
[88] [1985] A.C. 871 at 899.
[89] Compare Maclean 2004 who dismisses the view that the two tests are being brought together, also expressed by Brazier and Miola 2000, as "seeing the judgment though rose-tinted glasses" (Maclean 2004, 408–409).
[90] [2004] UKHL 41, para.16.

While *Chester* was an appeal on causation (the parties having conceded breach of duty), there is little doubt that the law has now adopted a more patient-orientated standard.[91]

Lord Woolf's judgment still leaves the question as to what is a significant risk. It must be judged by reference to the possible benefits of the procedure and depend on both the severity and likelihood of possible harm. A high likelihood of a minor itch lasting a few minutes on waking from an anaesthetic is not significant, but is a low risk of major irreversible pain? Might it be less significant (in terms of the risk/benefit ratio) if the procedure is aimed at treating a life-threatening condition than if the procedure is aimed a treating a minor ache? We have seen that Lord Woolf cited Lord Bridge who had given as an example the 10 per cent risk of a stroke suffered by the patient in the Canadian case of *Reibl v Hughes*.[92] In *Sidaway*, Lord Bridge did not consider a risk of around 1 per cent per cent of damage to the spinal cord (and a risk of up to 2 per cent risk of damage to either the spinal cord or nerve roots) to be significant and Lord Woolf in *Pearce* did not consider a 0.1–0.2 per cent risk of still-birth to be significant. Lord Bridge's notion of "significant", at least, is far from favourable to claimants. (These percentages should not lead us to forget that medical prognosis and risk calculation is inherently uncertain and lacking medical consensus.)[93]

What if the physician knows that the patient attaches particular importance to something? *Pearce* indicates that this will not render a "very, very small additional risk" significant, but does it add to the significance of the risk? Is, say, a 5 per cent risk of bleeding so as to require a transfusion more significant when the physician knows that the patient is a Jehovah's Witness and would reject a blood transfusion? What if surgery on a patient's sightless right eye carries risk of rendering the patient totally blind when the patient had made it clear that he fears damage to her left eye? This second question arose for consideration by the High Court of Australia in *Rogers v Whitaker*.[94] Applying the prudent patient test, Australia's highest federal court found the surgeon negligent despite the surgeon's actions attracting the support of a body of medical opinion, and the risk in question being only "slightly greater" than 1 in 14,000. Will the reasonable doctor taking account of the reasonable patient come to the same decision as the reasonable patient? Maclean has argued that requiring disclosure of the information that a reasonable patient would want to be disclosed is very different from requiring disclosure of "those risks that the reasonable doctor believes the reasonable patient ought to find significant to a decision".[95] According to Maclean, Lord Woolf adopted the latter test. Whether this distinction has any practical significance is yet to be seen. I doubt it.

---

[91] Meyer 2006 argues that *Chester* is far more noteworthy for defining the scope of the doctor's duty to warn, than has been recognised by commentators. See the discussion of this view in Pattinson 2007, 257–258.

[92] [1980] 2 S.C.R. 880. Mr Reibl also faced the risks of a stroke and of resulting death if he did not have the operation in question.

[93] See Katz 1993, esp. 81–82.

[94] (1992) 109 A.L.R. 625.

[95] Maclean 2004, 204.

Even before *Pearce* there were a few cases—but only a few cases—where the courts had found a doctor negligent for a failure to disclose information where that decision was supported by medical opinion. In one case, a man succeeded in an action because he had not been warned of the risk of impotence inherent in an operation to repair a rectal prolapse, despite expert evidence that a body of surgeons did not warn patients of that risk.[96] Citing Lord Bridge in *Sidaway*, it held that by 1988 the failure to warn the patient of such a risk was "neither reasonable nor responsible".[97] In another, it was held that no responsible body of medical opinion would have supported the defendant's failure to disclose the risks associated with a particular type of brain surgery, rejecting the supporting testimony of one of the defendant's expert witnesses.[98] There were a number of cases holding that it was not defensible to fail to warn a patient that a vasectomy operation can reverse naturally.[99] More recently, it was held that the failure to explain that the patient would be catheterised during penile surgery was "logically indefensible".[100]

A recent case, *Birch v UCL Hospital NHS Foundation Trust*, went further and held that a doctor who had informed the patient of the significant risks of the procedure administered was nonetheless negligent for failing to inform her that an alternative procedure carried fewer or no risks.[101] Cranston J. refused to state, in general terms, when the duty to inform a patient of such comparative risks would arise. On the facts, he held that "no reasonable, prudent medical practitioner" would have failed to disclose the relative risks of the procedures, especially since (unknown to the patient) the less risky option had been specifically recommended for the patient by a senior neurologist.[102]

4.4.2.2 *Patient questions*

What if the patient asks a specific question? *Sidaway* is peppered by strong obiter statements to the effect that if a patient were to ask about the risks of a proposed procedure the physician should, in Lord Bridge's words, "answer both truthfully and as fully as the questioner requires".[103] Subject, perhaps, to therapeutic privilege, *Bolam* was thought to have no application where the patient has asked for the information. Despite this, in *Blyth v Bloomsbury HA* the Court of Appeal concluded that what a claimant should be told in response to "a general enquiry cannot be divorced from the *Bolam* test, any more than when no such enquiry is made" (per Kerr L.J.).[104] More strikingly, Kerr L.J. opined that he was unconvinced "that the *Bolam* test is irrelevant" even if a specific inquiry is made; Neill L.J. thought that the *Bolam* test applied "as a general

[96] *Smith v Tunbridge Wells HA* [1994] 5 Med. L.R. 334.
[97] [1994] 5 Med. L.R. 334 at 339.
[98] *McAllister v Lewisham and North Southwark HA* [1994] 5 Med. L.R. 343.
[99] See *Gowton v Wolverhampton HA* [1994] 5 Med. L.R. 432 at 433 and *Newell v Goldenberg* [1995] 6 Med. L.R. 371.
[100] *E v Castro* [2003] EWHC 2066, para.171.
[101] [2008] EWHC 2237.
[102] [2008] EWHC 2237, para.79.
[103] [1985] A.C. 871 at 898. See also 891 (Lord Diplock) and 902 (Lord Templeman).
[104] [1993] 4 Med. L.R. 151 at 157.

proposition" when a patient asked questions; and Balcombe L.J. agreed with both.[105] Since the trial judge had found that the patient had made only general enquiries, these remarks on the application of the *Bolam* test to a specific enquiry are technically obiter. To confuse matters, in *Pearce* Lord Woolf asserted that counsel for the claimant "correctly submits that it is clear that, if a patient asks a doctor about the risk, then the doctor is required to give an honest answer".[106] This obiter statement is easy to reconcile with their Lordships' speeches in *Sidaway*, but Lord Woolf made no reference to *Blyth*. However, the retreat from *Bolam* indicated by *Pearce* makes it unlikely that the obiter statements in *Blyth* will be followed.

In *Chester v Afshar*, the claimant specifically asked about the risks of the spinal operation in question. The consultant was held to be in breach of duty when he light-heartedly deflected her inquiries with the remark: "Well, I have never crippled anybody yet".[107] This aspect of the case was not even argued in the later appeal (on causation) to the Court of Appeal and House of Lords. Also, the latest GMC guidance states that doctors "must answer patients' questions honestly and, as far as practical answer as fully as they wish".[108] The conclusion that we must reach is that doctors should be advised to fully answer a patient's questions about the risks inherent in a procedure, save, perhaps, in exceptional cases. In the past, it has been objected that disclosing more to an inquisitive patient unfairly advantages the inquisitive over the noninquisitive, and the inquisitive are likely to be the educated, middle class patients.[109] The courts, at least, appear to consider it more culpable to deliberately evade a request for information than to fail to volunteer that information, hence the greater duty to the inquisitive patient.

4.4.2.3 The changing direction of the law

There are other moves in the direction of informing a patient.

First, art.5 of the European Convention on Human Rights and Biomedicine (hereafter the Biomedicine Convention) states that,

> An intervention in the health field may only be carried out after the person concerned has given free and informed consent to it. . . . This person shall beforehand be given appropriate information as to the purpose and nature of the intervention as well as on its consequences and risks.

The Biomedicine Convention has not been signed or ratified by the UK and, even if it had, it would have no direct force in domestic law. It might, however, provide an interpretative reference for the Convention rights given domestic force by the HRA 1998, as suggested by dicta in the jurisprudence of the European Court of

---

[105] [1993] 4 Med. L.R. 151 at 157, 160.

[106] [1999] P.I.Q.R. 53 at 54.

[107] Quoted in the Court of Appeal: [2002] EWCA Civ 724, para.6.

[108] GMC 2008b, para.12.

[109] See Brazier 1987, 188–189 and 1992, 87 (this comment is not repeated in later editions of that book).

Human Rights.[110] It would therefore be difficult for the domestic courts to retreat to a more paternalistic position, at least where the rights in the Convention are involved. The art.8(1) Convention right to "private life" has already been held to protect personal autonomy.[111]

Second, the medical profession itself is moving in the direction of a more patient-centred approach. The current guidance of the General Medical Council for example, states that doctors "must . . . share with patients the information that they want or need in order to make decisions" and they "should not make assumptions about . . . the information a patient might want or need".[112] Since the medical profession's own standards form the starting point for the law, such professional moves towards greater disclosure feed directly into the standard of disclosure required by law. Also, few doctors will knowingly risk a disciplinary hearing in front of the GMC, as discussed in Ch.2 (2.3.1).

Also, the courts appear to be taking a more relaxed attitude to causation in negligence actions for failure to disclose a risk (see below).

4.4.2.4 Causation

Causation is often the claimant's biggest hurdle. To succeed the claimant must establish that the defendant's negligent failure to obtain a valid consent in some sense caused his injury. This requires that the claimant prove that he (or, maybe, a reasonable patient)[113] would not have consented had he not been negligently deprived of information. There are two ways in which the courts have indicated a more pro-claimant approach to causation.

First, the lower courts have displayed a willingness to draw inferences in the claimant's favour. In *McAllister v Lewisham*, for example, the judge found that the patient would not have consented if she had been fully informed, despite her admission that it was "almost impossible" to know what she would have done.[114] This has been bolstered by the Court of Appeal's reluctance to interfere with the findings of fact made by first instance judges.[115]

Second, the House of Lords has recently held that it was not necessary for a claimant to prove that he would never have consented to the operation in the future. In *Chester v Afshar*, the trial judge had accepted that the patient would not have consented to the surgery if she had been told about its risks, but she might still have consented to the surgery at a future date.[116] Since the risk was unavoidable, Miss Chester would have faced the same risk of injury whenever

---

[110] See *Glass v UK* (2004) 39 E.H.R.R. 15, para.58. See the discussion in Ch.1 (1.5).

[111] *Pretty v UK* (2002) 35 E.H.R.R. 1, para.63. See also the judgment of Munby J. in *R. (Burke) v GMC* [2004] EWHC 1879, esp. para.80, which was overruled on other grounds by the Court of Appeal: [2005] EWCA 1003.

[112] GMC 2008, paras 2 and 8.

[113] In *Chester v Afshar* [2002] EWCA Civ 724, paras 16–17, the Court of Appeal was prepared to accept that proof of causation depends on what *a reasonable claimant in the patient's position* would have done.

[114] [1994] 5 Med. L.R. 343.

[115] *O'Keefe v Harvey-Kemble* (1999) 45 B.M.L.R. 74.

[116] [2004] UKHL 41.

she had the operation. This meant that Miss Chester could not succeed on conventional causation principles, which require the negligent conduct to have caused or materially contributed to the injury. The majority simply made an exception to conventional causation principles, the minority were not prepared to do so. Lord Hoffmann, who dissented with Lord Bingham, declared that the failure to warn had simply made no difference. He rejected the claimant's argument because he considered it about as logical as saying that if one discovers that the odds of a number coming up at roulette were only 1 in 37, one's chances might have improved by returning at another time or going to a different casino.[117] The majority held that it was necessary to depart from conventional causation principles to vindicate Miss Chester's right to autonomy.[118] They held that the claimant had a right to be informed and had suffered damage in a context where the surgeon had breached his duty to inform of that very risk. For the majority, it was not decisive that there was no causal connection between the breach of duty and the damage. Lord Hope considered that any other decision "would render the duty useless in the cases where it is needed the most", because it would discriminate against those who honestly admit to the possibility that they would not have declined the operation once and for all.[119]

Chester is a very pro-claimant, patient-centred decision. A doctor who fails to disclose sufficient information thereby triggers potential liability even if that failure does not actually cause the patient any physical harm. All that is required is that the patient is thereby deprived of the opportunity of exercising a choice, which seems to require him to prove only that he would not have consented to the treatment at that time. This proviso is not certain, as a question remains about what a future court will say to a claimant who cannot prove that he would have delayed at all because the risk is one which a reasonable person would have run. Their Lordships did not make it clear whether they wish to limit their reasoning to situations where the claimant is able to show, on the balance of probabilities, that he would have delayed treatment if he had been properly informed. In any event, the decision represents a radical change in the law. It was heavily influenced by a leading Australian case and a great deal of academic commentary.[120] It recognises the difficulty that a patient has proving that he would never have consented to a particular procedure in the future. It explicitly recognises that causation is not morally neutral and moves towards a position tracking maximal patient autonomy (see below). The decision thereby weakens the argument that the law of negligence is incapable of protecting autonomy interests. Of course, *Chester* still requires the claimant to suffer harm, because negligence remains actionable upon proof of damage, rather than actionable per se.

---

[117] [2004] UKHL 41, paras 30–31.
[118] [2004] UKHL 41, *esp.* paras 24 (Lord Steyn), 85–87 (Lord Hope).
[119] [2004] UKHL 41, para.87. See also para.101 (Lord Walker).
[120] In *Chappel v Hart* [1998] H.C.A. 55 the majority of the Australian High Court had reached essentially the same conclusion.

4.4.3 Disclosure from a moral point of view

What level of disclosure should the law require? Should a doctor be judged against the standards of the medical profession (the "professional standard" as personified by the *Bolam* test), a reasonable patient, a particular patient, or against a hybrid standard? As we have seen, the professional standard is the most paternalistic while the particular patient test is the most patient-centred. The reasonable patient test sits somewhere between these two; by focusing on a hypothetical patient, it supports the patient's informational interests only insofar as that patient wishes to know what a typical (or ideal-typical) patient would wish to know. The major moral camps detailed in Ch.1 are too broad to provide much guidance on this. There are as many variants within the major moral camps as between them. The level of disclosure required turns on the moral weight attached to *patient autonomy* (self-determination) and the level of *moral responsibility* for this placed on the shoulders of the doctor (or other health professional).[121] In general, the facilitation of patient autonomy is important to all the major theories of medical ethics, because it is considered to be required or implied by the patient's rights (for rights-based theories), the patient's bests interests (for duty-based theories), the maximisation of preferences or interests (for many utilitarian theories), and human flourishing (for many virtue theories). However, the level of disclosure required is not uniform for all moral theories.

None of the major moral theories will impose an absolute duty on doctors to disclose detailed information. Some theories are reluctant to impose positive duties to assist,[122] which could limit the informational duties of health professionals. It is relevant to all the major moral positions that extensive disclosure requirements can also have negative consequences for healthcare resources (it costs time and money to disclose information)[123] and for patient autonomy (overemphasis on information over communication can actually hinder patient autonomy). It is also impractical for patients to be given a comprehensive education in a clinical context. A non-absolute duty to provide information is, nonetheless, compatible with theories within all the major moral camps. *Rights-based theories* can support a patient's right to information, but will require a patient's rights to be balanced against any competing rights of others. *Utilitarians* will recognise the utility-maximising consequences of full and frank disclosure (such as boosting the doctor–patient relationship and the quality of the healthcare), but will also recognise the potential negative consequences of doctors (and patients) devoting disproportionate attention to tiny risks. *Duty-based theories* impose few if any absolute duties and place less emphasis on autonomy than rights-based theories (because they do not hold that the benefi-

---

[121] For convenience, the addition of "or other health professional" is dropped in the discussion below. The importance of other health professionals is specifically addressed at the end of this section.

[122] See e.g. the rights-based theory of Nozick 1974.

[123] Perhaps, the existence of the NHS goes some way towards explaining why the professional (*Bolam*) standard on disclosure has been more entrenched here than in other countries.

ciary of every duty may waive that duty).[124] For *virtue theories*, there are no absolute duties of conduct, because the focus must be on the virtues exercised by the doctor and patient. The interaction between the carer and the patient is the focus, rather than the patient's rights or the specific information provided.

The most demanding moral theories will require the doctor to seek to maximise the patient's ability to make a decision that is as autonomous as possible in the circumstances.[125] Maximal autonomy requires that a patient be given the maximal opportunity to reach an autonomous decision. Maximal autonomy requires that patients have *access* to all relevant information capable of influencing their choice. This requires a doctor to seek to discover what might influence *that* patient's decision. Accordingly, this would seem to suggest that a doctor should disclose everything that a reasonable patient would regard as material *and* anything that the doctor knows, or ought to know, that the patient actually regards as material or relevant. We have seen that the law does not go quite that far. Yet, ensuring the maximal autonomy of individuals is in fact required by many moral theories. It is, in particular, required by many rights-based and preference-utilitarian theories (though utilitarians are always led by the overall utility balance).[126] It should also be pointed out that in the context of healthcare provision, where the medical profession is dominated by males and women are overrepresented in the patient population, feminists will often seek to maximise patient autonomy. Sheldon and Thomson have noted that "many of the cases dealing with medical practice seem to involve female [claimants] (particular those concerning flawed consent)".[127] This suspicion is supported by perusal of the leading cases on consent, notably *Chatterton*, *Sidaway*, and *Pearce*.

The existing law also provides little redress for "dignitarian" harm. For some theories, being deprived of maximal autonomy is itself a dignitarian harm, as it is capable of preventing the exercise of the patient's rights or values. Yet, the tort of battery has a narrow ambit and the tort of negligence requires patients to suffer from some mental or physical harm. Ch.1 outlined two conceptions of dignity, derived from the work of Beyleveld and Brownsword: "dignity as empowerment" and "dignity as constraint".[128] Moral theories adhering to a conception of "dignity as empowerment" must regard the law is at least prima facie morally deficient, as failing to sufficiently protect human dignity.[129] Those adopting a conception of "dignity as constraint" do not place the same level of value on patient autonomy over other dignitarian issues. For such theories,

---

[124] The emphasis that Kant places on autonomy might lead us to question whether he was really a duty-based theorist at all.

[125] The view of "maximal autonomy" developed above is similar to that developed by Harris 1985, 200, from whose work the label derives.

[126] See e.g. Beyleveld and Brownsword 2001 (a rights-based theory) and Harris 1985 (an implicitly preference utilitarian position supporting maximal autonomy and examined in more detail in Ch.17, 17.2.1). For a discussion of the limitations of autonomy from an act-utilitarian perspective, see Singer 1993, esp. 99–10.

[127] Sheldon and Thomson 1998, 8.

[128] See Ch. 1 (1.4.1) and Beyleveld and Brownsword 2001.

[129] See the analysis in Brownsword 2003a.

protecting a patient's dignity can sometimes require the denial of maximal autonomy.

Two ethical issues deserve particular attention: the notion of therapeutic privilege and the "right" to remain ignorant.

4.4.3.1 Therapeutic privilege

Must a doctor be open and honest with a patient dying of cancer? In *Sidaway*, even Lord Scarman accepted that a doctor might use his discretion not to inform a patient of a risk that will harm the patient.[130] The doctrine of therapeutic privilege grants the medical professional protection that is not available to other professions. No other profession can point to the likelihood that informing a client of a likely risk from the activity on which they seek advice would pose a serious threat of psychological harm by causing worry and anxiety. The courts will not allow a financial advisor to escape liability by pleading that the client would have become ill with anxiety if informed about the risk of bankruptcy from a transaction. Other professionals are not usually in a good position to judge the likely psychological or physical effects of disclosure on a client/customer. Is it morally permissible for doctors to do so?

Therapeutic privilege can be defined widely or narrowly. The wider it is defined, the more paternalism triumphs over patient autonomy. If it is not to reduce to a wholesale "doctors knows best" approach, therapeutic privilege must seek to protect the patient from harm other than that likely to be caused by the patient's decision to refuse the treatment in question. GMC guidance, for example, requires doctors not to withhold information unless it is thought that disclosure would cause the patient "serious harm", defined to exclude the patient becoming upset or deciding to refuse treatment.[131] Even interpreted in this way, therapeutic privilege fits uneasily with the obiter statements in *Sidaway* and *Pearce* suggesting that a doctor must answer the inquisitive patient's questions fully and truthfully—unless (as suggested above) the doctor's duty to disclose when questioned is read as being subject to therapeutic privilege.

Therapeutic privilege is inherently paternalistic. It should be clear that rights-based theories are opposed to the application of the notion of therapeutic privilege to a *competent* patient. Since rights-holders are entitled to waive the benefit of all their rights, once it is established that a patient is acting autonomously, that patient's rights cannot justify the failure to disclose information on the basis of the need to protect him from himself. In contrast, not all duty-based theories, utilitarian, or virtue theories are opposed to this doctrine. Unless autonomy always trumps nonmaleficence, therapeutic privilege will have a role to play even when dealing with a competent patient. The precise role will depend on the particular theory.

Campbell et al. suggest that therapeutic privilege is properly relied on only in those exceptional circumstances where a patient is so fragile that full disclosure

---

[130] It was accepted implicitly by the other Law Lords as part of the *Bolam* test.
[131] See GMC 2008, para.16.

would overwhelm them at that time, such as where a road accident victim in a critical condition asks about family members or where a patient asks about the extent of burns or internal injuries at a critical time.[132] Therapeutic privilege can, however, only be consistent with maximal autonomy where a patient is in good faith deemed incompetent or a good faith attempt is being made to assess a patient's competence. These examples of fragility are consistent with such circumstances, but the point of moral controversy arises once a doctor believes that the patient is competent.

4.4.3.2 The "right" to ignorance

Is a patient entitled to remain ignorant of all the facts and risks of a particular procedure? This question has not been directly addressed by the courts. We have seen that a doctor commits a legal wrong if he intentionally applies a procedure to a competent patient who is ignorant of the basic nature of that procedure. This appears to suggest that a doctor should ensure that the patient understands the nature and purpose of the procedure, irrespective of whether the patient wishes to know this information.[133] However, it is difficult to imagine circumstances where, in practice, there would be legal repercussions for a doctor arising because of a failure to provide information before treating a competent patient who had voluntarily refused that information.

From a moral point of view, it is an interesting question whether a patient can validly make a treatment decision when he has refused even minimal information about the treatment options. Some take the view that the lack of minimal information will render the decision non-autonomous or at least not a valid consent/refusal. Harris has argued that some (minimal) disclosure is required, irrespective of the views of the patient.[134] He offers two arguments for this conclusion. First of all, he argues that a patient who consents to treatment without knowing the basic details of that treatment is not truly consenting, so minimal information may be provided to remedy "the defects . . . of information which militate against the individual's capacity for autonomy".[135] He then argues that health professionals should not have to bear responsibility for "the decisions about the patient's state of health that are properly the patient's own", as this is against the interests of the community as a whole.[136] Harris thereby appears to support the force-feeding of basic information to competent patients even when they have made a decision to refuse that information on the basis that no information that the doctor is likely to give would cause him to change his mind. At first sight, this smacks of paternalism derived from utilitarian premises. However, the infringement of the patient's will supported by Harris is temporary and limited in scope, and is potentially compatible with all the major theories. While rights-based theories allow rights-holders to waive

---

[132] See Campbell et al. 2001, 30.
[133] See further Kennedy and Grubb 2000, 752.
[134] See Harris 1985, 211–213.
[135] Harris 1985, 213.
[136] Harris 1985, 212.

the benefit of *all* their rights, they do not prohibit behaviour or procedures designed to ensure that patients are truly waiving the benefit of their rights or those designed to protect the rights of others. Other moral theories could support further force-feeding of information to unwilling patients on the basis that the patient has a duty to be fully informed, either a duty to himself (a view that is compatible with the duty-based camp) or a duty to the community as a whole (a view compatible with communitarianism and some forms of utilitarianism).

4.4.3.3 Practical considerations

The legal test for disclosure has moral significance only insofar as it protects and represents moral interests. What matters is what patients are actually told and understand in practice. In practice, healthcare professions could be more influenced by professional guidance and the general fear of litigation than the standard of care required in a negligence action. What evidence there is suggests that few disclosure cases are successful and the legal test has little direct impact on medical practice generally.[137] Insofar as the legal test is relevant, the case law has a number of notable limitations. *First*, the case law overwhelmingly focuses on doctors, yet, in practice, treatment is usually provided by a team rather than an individual. Other staff, particularly nursing staff, can be very important for ensuring effective communication with a patient. *Second*, the case law focuses on what the doctor must volunteer, whereas a more patient-centred approach would require the doctor to ask the patient what he wants to know. *Third*, the case law focuses on what a doctor is required to tell the patient, whereas the evidence suggests that verbally informing patients of risks is not, by itself, the most effective way of ensuring that they remember enough details to make a sufficiently informed decision.[138] If the standard of care and other relevant (policy and regulatory) mechanisms are to adequately balance the moral interests of patients and health professionals, they must take account of the practical reality of medical care provision. Part of this reality is recognising that not all patients are comfortable with asking for additional information or questioning the doctor's judgment. Adequate communication of information should minimise future litigation, but this is not its ethical raison d'être.

4.5 Voluntariness

A valid consent must be voluntary. Acquiescence in the face of coercion or undue pressure applied by another is no consent at all. If a patient appears to consent as a result of pressure from another, robbing the patient of any genuine independent

---

[137] See Robertson 1991 (on the limited impact of the Canadian Supreme Court in *Reibl v Hughes*). On the English position see Jones 1999b and Skegg 1999, 146–147.
[138] See Jones 1999b, esp. 126.

choice, it cannot truly be said that the patient consented. To put it another way, the justification for inflicting what would otherwise be a moral wrong cannot be the patient's consent if it is not considered to be the result of independent choice. In practice, it is extremely rare for a patient to be forced to acquiesce to medical treatment by a direct, coercive threat.[139] Pressure from a third party amounting to something less than a direct threat is more likely and, in legal terms, the issue is then whether that pressure amounts to "undue influence".

No one acts in a vacuum and some decision-making contexts are inherently pressured. In *Freeman v Home Office* it was argued that prison was a context in which a patient's decision could not be said to be truly free.[140] Counsel claimed that the prison medical officer's power to influence the prisoner's situation and prospects was such that the prisoner cannot be taken to have given free and voluntary consent "at least . . . in the absence of any written consent form".[141] Unsurprisingly, the Court of Appeal made short shrift of this as a general proposition. They held that whether there was actually undue influence will be a question of fact.[142]

There has been only one case where a court has accepted a claim of undue influence in a medical context. This case was *Re T*, where pressure was put on a weakened patient by a close relative.[143] *T* was a pregnant woman who had been injured in a car accident and refused a blood transfusion after a meeting with her Jehovah's Witness mother, despite having previously told nursing staff that she was not a Jehovah's Witness. After undergoing a Caesarean section the patient became unconscious and in need of a blood transfusion. Her father and boyfriend applied to the court for a declaration that it would be lawful to administer one, despite the patient's prior refusal. The Court of Appeal set aside the pregnant woman's prior refusal on the basis that she had been temporarily incapacitated, not properly informed, *and* her will had been overborne by her mother.

On the latter ground Lord Donaldson stated that,

> The real question in each such case is "Does the patient really mean what he says or is he merely saying it for a quiet life, to satisfy someone else or because the advice and persuasion to which he has been subjected is such that he can no longer think and decide for himself?"[144]

He went on to state that when considering the effects of outside influences, two aspects were of crucial importance: the strength of will of the patient and the relationship of the "persuader" to the patient. Butler-Sloss L.J. noted that "in equity it has long been recognised that an influence may be subtle, insidious, pervasive and where religious beliefs are involved especially powerful".[145]

---

[139] Examples of forced sterilisations in developing countries are cited in Jackson 2001, 46–47.
[140] [1984] Q.B. 524.
[141] [1984] Q.B. 524 at 553.
[142] [1984] Q.B. 524 at 555.
[143] [1993] Fam. 95.
[144] [1993] Fam. 95 at 113.
[145] [1993] Fam. 95 at 120.

Feminists and religious adherents might perceive the Court of Appeal in *Re T* to be a little too eager to find that *T's* decision was induced by undue influence. Nonetheless, *Re T* was an advance for patient autonomy, because it indicates judicial acceptance of the effects of external pressures on a vulnerable patient.

A more recent decision on undue influence is *U v Centre for Reproductive Medicine*.[146] This case was concerned with the altogether different situation in which consent to posthumous storage and use of sperm was withdrawn by a patient when pressured to do so by a medical advisor. After the unexpected death of Mr U, the Centre for Reproductive Medicine sought a declaration that he had validly withdrawn his consent (so as to enable them to destroy his sperm), which was opposed by his wife, who wished to have the opportunity to use this sperm in an attempt to bear a child. The case, therefore, turned on whether Mr U's decision to withdraw his consent had been induced by the undue influence of the clinic's staff.

Mr U had initially consented to the posthumous storage and use of his sperm by signing the relevant form and declaring his intention to his wife. At a subsequent meeting with a nursing sister at the clinic Mr U was asked to alter the form, as the "ethical policy" of the clinic (strongly supported by the nursing sister) was against posthumous treatment. This meeting took place two days before Mrs U was due to receive treatment, some four and a half months after the couple's first consultation at the clinic. At first instance, Butler-Sloss P. accepted that "the pressure [put on Mr U by the nursing sister] must have been considerable"[147] and the Court of Appeal noted that the couple "had already committed themselves, mentally, emotionally, and financially, to the course of treatment" and "were both very vulnerable".[148] Nonetheless, the Court of Appeal upheld Butler-Sloss P.'s decision that Mrs U had not shown that the pressure placed on Mr U amounted to undue influence.

According to Butler-Sloss P., "an able, intelligent, educated man of 47, with a responsible job and in good health" would not be expected to succumb to "considerable" pressure put on him by a medical advisor. This is questionable. A patient with no medical training seeking medical treatment is in an inherently vulnerable position and although the factors cited by the then President of the Family Division suggest an ability to think independently, these attributes are likely to be weakened by the degree of trust typically vested in medical opinion and the emotional vulnerability of most patients. The decision in this case seems wrong on its facts.[149]

The moral issue turns on the value placed on patient autonomy over other interests and values (see further 4.4.2). The current law on undue influence in the context of medical treatment is unlikely to satisfy those theories seeking maximal autonomy. Elsewhere I have argued that the courts could give greater protection to patient autonomy by reversing the burden of proof when

---

[146] [2002] EWCA Civ 565.
[147] [2002] EWHC 36, para.22.
[148] [2002] EWCA Civ 565, para.21.
[149] See Pattinson 2002b, 309–310. Cf. Grubb 2002.

reviewing the pressure put on patients in some medical contexts.[150] Patients are particularly vulnerable to directive advice, i.e. pressure from medical advisors who use their medical expertise to press their own ethical views on the patient. One way in which the courts can recognise the particular vulnerability of patients would be to presume undue influence (thereby placing the evidential burden onto the party denying undue influence) where the patient proves that

(a) the relationship between the parties is one of patient and medical advisor;

(b) the medical advisor has put pressure on the patient to reach a particular decision (i.e. the decision reached); and

(c) the patient needs persuasion for reasons other than an initial failure to understand the full details of relevant medical science.

Criterion (a) defines a relationship where one party, the patient, is particularly vulnerable because it is formed where that party seeks to rely on the expertise of the other at a time of need, uncertainty, and, often, ill health. Criteria (b) and (c) specify circumstances where the patient's decision calls for an explanation, so that it is appropriate for the medical advisor to bear the burden of showing that undue influence has not been applied. To be clear, such a presumption would be no more than a rebuttable evidential inference of undue influence where the three criteria above are satisfied, similar to the rebuttable presumptions operating in transaction- based undue influence cases.[151] On the facts of *U*, since Butler-Sloss had held the "evidence was finely balanced", it is clear that the Centre for Reproductive Medicine would not have been able to rebut an evidential inference of undue influence. On other facts, this might not be the case.[152]

As the law stands at present, it is for the party claiming undue influence to prove the existence of undue pressure overbearing that party's will. What *U* shows is that where the patient is educated, mature, and healthy, it is highly unlikely that the court will find undue influence, even if the medical advisor has used her position to deliberately change the mind of the patient for non-medical reasons. Adherents of moral perspectives supporting maximal patient autonomy must hope that the Court of Appeal's decision is restricted to the context of posthumous consent or overruled by the House of Lords. If it is applied to ethical pressure placed on patients from medical advisors generally, then patient autonomy will be eroded. Reversing the burden of proof could increase the administrative burden on healthcare providers but this must be weighed against the value granted to patient autonomy by the moral theory in question.

---

[150] See Pattinson 2002b, 310–314.
[151] See e.g. *Royal Bank of Scotland v Etridge* [2001] UKHL 44.
[152] See Pattinson 2002b, 312.

4.6 Public policy

Outside the medical context, the case law states that the crime of assault occasioning either grievous or actual bodily harm can still be committed where the victim has consented to the assault.[153] The consent of the "victim" was no defence where a man beat a girl of 17 for sexual gratification,[154] where the defendant had been involved in a fist fight,[155] or where genital mutilation had been part of the defendant's sadomasochistic homosexual activities.[156] In law, a person cannot consent to severe bodily harm without a good reason, because this is regarded as against the public interest. Medical treatment is, however, considered a good reason and within the public interest. This means that what is illegal outside the medical context can be legal within it. The law prohibits using fishhooks on another's genitals for sexual gratification (as in *R. v Brown*), but will allow a surgeon to castrate a patient in transsexual surgery performed to protect the patient's mental health.[157]

Where a patient has consented, "bodily invasions in the course of proper medical treatment stand completely outside the criminal law".[158] This was one point on which their Lordships were not divided in *R. v Brown*.[159] This is not, however, to suggest that the law gives physicians carte blanche. Not every act performed by a medical practitioner is ipso facto "proper medical treatment" and in the public interest.

A surgeon who cuts off a man's fingers to assist his dishonest insurance claim cannot rely on that man's consent as a defence to criminal assault.[160] Similarly, an otherwise valid consent will not protect a doctor who circumcises a female for religious reasons.[161] Nor will it protect a surgeon who removes a vital organ, such as a liver or heart, from a healthy patient solely for the treatment of another. There is no legislation or case law on this last example, but this is the consensus view of commentators. According to Edmund Davis L.J., speaking extra-judicially in 1969, "a man may declare himself ready to die for another, but the surgeon must not take him at his word".[162] In all these circumstances

---

[153] There is some confusion over whether the common law crime of maim is "obsolete", which was the view of Lord Mustill in his dissenting speech in *R. v Brown* [1994] 1 A.C. 212 at 262.

[154] *R. v Donovan* [1934] 2 K.B. 498.

[155] *AG's Reference (No.6 of 1980)* [1981] Q.B. 715.

[156] *R. v Brown* [1994] 1 A.C. 212.

[157] *Corbett v Corbett* [1971] P. 83, esp. 98–99. As the Law Commission has pointed out sexual reassignment surgery "may now be funded by the NHS and, since *Corbett*, the legality of the operation itself has never really been questioned" (1995a, 110, para.8.29)

[158] *Airedale NHS Trust v Bland* [1993] A.C. 789 at 891 (Lord Mustill).

[159] According to Lord Mustill, it was legitimate to perform "surgical treatment . . . in accordance with good medical practice and with the consent of the patient" (258–259). See also 231 (Lord Templeman), 245 (Lord Jauncey), and 276 (Lord Slynn). In *AG's Reference (No.6 of 1980)* [1981] Q.B. 715, Lord Lane C.J. had previously cited "reasonable surgical interference" as an example of an activity that is lawful "in the public interest" (718).

[160] See the US case of *State v Bass* (1961) 255 N.C. 42, S.E.2d 580.

[161] Female Genital Mutilation Act 2003.

[162] Edmund Davis 1969, 634. See also Law Commission 1995a, 111, para.8.31 and Kennedy and Grubb 2000, 1758.

the consent of a patient is thought to offer no defence on the grounds of public policy.

A borderline case is the surgical amputation of a healthy limb to treat "amputee identity disorder", also known as "body integrity identity disorder".[163] A Scottish surgeon is known to have amputated the healthy legs of two men who felt a desperate need to be amputees; one in 1997 and the other in 1999.[164] The hospital subsequently instructed the surgeon to not to carry out further operations of this type. In legal terms, the closest analogy is probably sexual reassignment surgery, which is not considered to be against public policy where it is medically indicated.

4.6.1 Self harm from a moral point of view

Is it appropriate for the law to seek to protect a person from voluntarily harming him or herself? The answer depends on the moral theory appealed to. At the generalised level detailed in Ch.1, drawing out the implications of partic- ular moral positions risks oversimplification. What can be said is that the current legal position is easier to reconcile with duty-based positions (and compromise positions tending towards duty-based positions), than with rights- based, utilitarian, or virtue-based positions. Consider, for example, the response of the major moral camps to a father who wishes to donate both his kidneys to his two sons who are suffering from kidney failure.[165] Rights-based theories, which hold that all moral duties derive from rights (the benefits of which are waivable by the rights-holder), must reject the idea that the rights-holder can have direct duties to him or herself. Protecting the patient's interests/rights cannot justify preventing the patient from freely choosing to endanger his or her own life; any constraints on autonomous action must derive from the rights of others. Therefore, such theories cannot appeal to a father's rights to prevent him from freely choosing to donate his kidneys, but could allow medics who object to participating in the operation to appeal to their own rights. Utilitarians do not prioritise individual autonomy in the same way, but act-utilitarians must weigh the consequences of the father's decision against the consequences of the alternatives for the overall utility balance. Relevant considerations would include the objections of medical staff, and the availability and suitability of dialysis and an alternative source of kidneys. Preference utilitarians, seeking to maximise the satisfaction of choices, will give at least prima facie support to the father's free choice. The father's altruistic motives are likely to predispose a virtue-based theory towards supporting the father's decision. Duty-based theories place less value on patient autonomy than rights-based theories and can appeal to the father's own interests to object to him harming himself. The father's freely chosen decision to donate his kidneys could be rejected as a

---

[163] See the discussion of some of the ethical issues in Bayne and Levy 2005.
[164] Dyer 2000.
[165] This example is not purely hypothetical, see Davies 1998, 389.

violation of his dignity—relying on "dignity as a constraint".[166] The reasoning in *R. v Brown* fits comfortably within the duty-based camp *if* it is read as prohibiting the consensual infliction of serious harm *to protect the interests of the victim who is actually consenting*.[167]

More paternalistic moral theories will, however, go further than the law. As indicated above, risky therapeutic procedures performed in accordance with responsible medical opinion and with the full consent of the patient are lawful. Consider the attempt to separate the conjoined twins Ladan and Laleh. Although this separation took place in another jurisdiction, there is no reason to doubt that their separation would have been lawful here. They were both adult and competent and had an overwhelming desire to be separated, despite their brains being interlinked and being turned down by a German neurosurgeon. The surgery proved to be tragic and they both died. Different views as to the permissibility of their separation are taken by different moral theories. On the one hand, theories requiring maximal patient autonomy will leave the decision to the patients, subject only to such protective mechanisms as are necessary to ensure the voluntariness of their decision. (One practical problem where twins are joined at the head is ensuring that one is not coercing the other.) On the other hand, paternalistic examples of duty-based theories, will point to the high chance of death and appeal to conceptions of "dignity as constraint" against the patients' informed decision.[168]

4.6.2 Public policy and refusing treatment

The law is also prepared to reject the exculpatory sufficiency of a *refusal* on the grounds of public policy. It has been claimed, for example, that the law will not allow a patient to refuse to consent to measures designed to maintain basic hygiene and pain relief, because of the effects of such a refusal on nursing staff attending the patient.[169] For present purposes this issue is merely mooted and the law on contemporaneous refusals is considered in more depth in Ch.15 (15.3.1).

It is also worth briefly mentioning that all the major moral theories could accept some limitations on refusals. Even rights-based theories will not allow patients to refuse interventions that are necessary to protect the more important rights of others. An extreme example would be where overriding a competent patient's refusal of treatment is the only way of preventing the spread of a highly infectious, fatal disease. Nonetheless, we have seen that patient autonomy is important to all the major moral theories and overruling other-

---

[166] See the discussion in Ch.1 (1.4.1).

[167] See, perhaps, [1994] 1 A.C. 212 at 255 (Lord Lowry). As is often the case, the decision reached might be also defended from the perspective of other moral theories. For some forms of utilitarianism, for example, sadism involves the desire to do the very opposite of one's moral duties.

[168] See Hawkes 2003 for the opposed views taken by Professor Harris (taking an autonomy-focused position) and Dr Nicholson (taking a duty-based approach and appealing to the "primary" duty of the doctor to "do no harm").

[169] See Grubb 1993a, 85 and 2004, 141.

wise valid refusals involves serious interference with patient autonomy. Any limits on the ability of competent patients to refuse an intervention must be therefore justified by reference to compelling counter-concerns recognised by the tenets of the moral theory in question. The ethical distinctions that are relevant to the ability to refuse life-sustaining treatment are addressed in detail in Ch.16 (especially 16.2).

4.7 Conclusion

Demands for increased patient participation in treatment decisions reflect the patient consumerism that is affecting medical law as whole. Such demands are made from many ethical perspectives. Nonetheless, there is an underlying ethical tension between theories prioritising maximal patient autonomy and those prioritising other duties and communal values. There is a tension between what Beyleveld and Brownsword present as positions adhering to "dignity as constraint" and positions adhering to "dignity as empowerment", as discussed in Ch.1 (1.4.1).

The next chapter will focus on the issue of competence and the legal position with regard to those who lack the legal capacity to consent to, or refuse, treatment on their own behalf because of incompetence or minority.

4.8 Further reading

Consent and information
Brazier, Margaret and Lobjoit, Mary (1999) "Fiduciary Relationship: An Ethical Approach and a Legal Concept." In Rebecca Bennett and Charles Erin (eds) *HIV and AIDS: Testing, Screening, and Confidentiality.* (Oxford: Oxford University Press), 179–199.
Kennedy, Ian (1996) "The Fiduciary Relationship and its Application to Doctors." In P. Birks (ed.) *Wrongs and Remedies in the Twenty-first Century.* (Oxford: Clarendon Press), 111–140.

Consent and public policy
Bayne, Tim and Levy, Neil (2005) "Amputees By Choice: Body Integrity Identity Disorder and the Ethics of Amputation." 22(1) *Journal of Applied Philosophy* 75–86.

The ethics of consent
Beyleveld, Deryck and Brownsword, Roger (2007) *Consent in the Law.* (London: Hart).
Harris, John (1985) *The Value of Life: An Introduction to Medical Ethics.* (London: Routledge), ch. 10.

Chapter 5

CONSENT II: CAPACITY

5.1 Introduction

Ruth has cerebral palsy and lacks even minimal muscular control.[1] She is quadriplegic. She cannot speak or point. She can move little more than her eyes, ears, and nose, and produce ten distinct sounds with her weak vocal cords. Other than this, her body is functionally useless. She was institutionalised and treated as an "imbecile" for most of her early life. Not recognised as able to make even

---

[1] Ruth Sienkiewicz-Mercer: see Sienkiewicz-Mercer and Kaplan 1989. See also Stefan 1993, 763–765.

the simplest decisions. Yet, after nearly 16 years, when two members of staff were talking and making humorous comments about a colleague they noticed that Ruth laughed. The more assistance she was given, the better she was able to communicate. After some years, the staff began to realise that she could say "yes" by raising her eyes and use various other eye, lip, and facial movements for further words. With practice she could also use her eyes to communicate using "word boards"—laminated pieces of white cardboard on which words, phrases, and numbers are arranged in rows and columns. With the aid of these she was able to co-author her autobiography and claim the thing that she had missed the most: the capacity to make her own decisions.

Ruth's story is about capacity. Before proceeding, we need some definitions.[2] As is often repeated throughout this book, the same label can describe different concepts and different labels can describe the same concept. A patient will be described as *competent* when her cognitive faculties are such that she is able to make a decision with respect to the given situation (and will be described as incompetent where she lacks such cognitive faculties). This is a cognitive-functional definition of competence. An individual possessing legally recognised decision-making authority will be said to have *capacity* (and the converse for incapacity). On these definitions, insofar as the law seeks to grant decision-making authority to those who are competent and deny decision-making authority to those who are incompetent, there is little need to draw a distinction between capacity and competence.[3] Ruth lacked capacity only because she was mistakenly perceived to lack competence. As we shall see, however, capacity does not invariably track competence or perceived competence.

5.1.1 The Mental Capacity Act 2005

The law relating to determinations of capacity and the consequences of lacking capacity has been codified and re-shaped by the Mental Capacity Act 2005.[4] This Act is the product of a long process of preparation and consultation. In 1995, following five years of research and consultation, the Law Commission had made detailed recommendations for the introduction of legislation to govern capacity.[5] The Conservative Government proposed to act on those recommendations but took fright after a negative media campaign in which some newspapers accused the Government of taking a permissive approach towards euthanasia.[6] In 1997, the new Labour Government consulted further[7]

---

[2] The following definitions display the influence of Bielby 2005 and Lötjönen 2003, 357.
[3] Note the distinction between competence and capacity drawn here is the opposite way round to that adopted by some US commentators (see Berg et al. 1996, 347–349).
[4] As elsewhere, this chapter is only concerned with the law of England and Wales. Cf. Adults with Incapacity (Scotland) Act 2000.
[5] See Law Commission 1995b.
[6] See Dyer 2004.
[7] A green paper, entitled *Who Decides?*: see Law Chancellor's Department 1997.

and, two years later, set out its proposals for legal reform in a policy document.[8] After many parliamentary changes the Mental Capacity Act received Royal assent on April 7, 2005. It came fully into force on October 1, 2007 and, from April 2009, will be amended by the Mental Health Act 2007 (on which see 5.5).

The Act has three parts. The *first* part deals with "persons who lack capacity". Since the present concern is with capacity to make treatment decisions, the provisions addressing issues not related to treatment will be ignored. I will therefore refer to "patients" rather than the wider term "persons" used in the Act. Also, it should be noted at the outset that the powers under the Act are only exercisable in relation to "adults", defined as those who are 16 or over (s.2(5)). The *second* part of the Act deals with the roles of the new Court of Protection and the Public Guardian. The *third* part is a collection of miscellaneous provisions, principally defining terms and providing for commencement. There are also nine schedules (including the new Schs A1 and 1A).

Much of the 2005 Act merely codifies the pre-existing common law, so pre-Act case law continues to require careful study. The Act does, however, make a number of significant legal changes, not least of which is the recognition of patient-appointed and court-appointed proxy decision-makers (see 5.2.2.2.). It also provides for a Code of Practice to lay down guidance on its interpretation and application (s.42). The current version was issued in February 2007.[9] Health professionals and proxy decision-makers are among those subject to a legal duty to have regard to the provisions of the code (s.42(4)). Failure to do so will be taken into account in any subsequent legal proceedings (s.42(5)).

5.1.2 The ambit of this chapter

Capacity is relevant to many areas of law that are given only passing consideration in this chapter. End of life decisions and life-shortening medical practices are examined in depth in Chs 15 and 16. Those chapters will provide detailed legal and ethical examination of the validity of contemporaneous and advance refusals of life-sustaining medical treatment. Similarly, issues relating to research on human subjects and organ transplantation form the focus of Chs 11 and 13, respectively. These issues are mentioned in this chapter only insofar as necessary to explicate the law and ethics of treating adults and children considered to lack the ability to make their own treatment decisions.

This chapter will not attempt to a full explication and analysis of *mental health law*. Although mental health law is an integral part of the law governing the treatment and care of those with cognitive difficulties, to examine its full details would have unduly distorted this chapter. Nonetheless, a new section below (5.5) presents an overview of the treatment and detention of mentally ill patients.

---

[8] A white paper, entitled *Making Decisions*: see Law Chancellor's Department 1999.
[9] See Department for Constitutional Affairs 2007.

5.2 Incapacitated adults

Since to treat an adult with capacity against his will is to commit a tort and a crime, such a patient is legally entitled to refuse to consent to medical treatment. The legal right to refuse treatment will apply even if the patient will die as a result.[10] This common law principle was reinforced by the Human Rights Act (HRA) 1998. In *Pretty v UK*, the European Court of Human Rights recognised that the art.8(1) right respect for "private life" includes respect for "personal autonomy".[11] Interference with personal autonomy is therefore only permitted to the extent that it is "in accordance with the law and is necessary in a democratic society" for a purpose recognised by art.8(2). Consistent judicial recognition of the right of a person with capacity to refuse treatment indicates how the English courts currently perform this balancing exercise. Article 8(2) is unlikely to change this position[12] and the Mental Capacity Act 2005 is entirely consistent with this aspect of the common law. The 2005 Act did, however, fill a legal lacuna. The common law did not recognise anyone as having the capacity to make treatment decisions on behalf of an adult who lacks capacity.[13] This meant that the treatment of such patients was only lawful by means of the doctrine of necessity, applied by reference to the patient's "best interests". As we shall see, the best interests test remains at the heart of the law. Determinations of capacity and best interests have been particularly controversial where the issue has been the refusal of treatment in late pregnancy (5.2.3) or non-therapeutic sterilisation (5.2.4).

5.2.1 Determining capacity

Competence was defined at the outset of this chapter as the judgment that a patient has sufficient cognitive faculties to be able to make a decision on a particular issue. Competence is thereby defined functionally, as specific to a particular task or decision.[14] An individual's cognitive abilities might be sufficient to make simple decisions requiring consideration of limited variables (such as choosing between two meal options), but insufficient to make decisions

---

[10] See e.g. *Re T* [1993] Fam. 95, 102; *Re MB* [1997] 2 F.L.R. 426 at 432; and *Re B* [2002] EWHC 429. See the detailed discussion in Ch.15 (15.3.1).

[11] (2002) 35 E.H.R.R. 1, esp. para.63. See also *R. (Burke) v GMC* [2004] EWHC 1879, esp. para.80.

[12] Grubb (2004, 132–133) argues that the courts are likely to hold that the only permissible derogations to art.8(1) in this context are those made by Parliament to protect public health, such as public vaccination programmes and mental health legislation.

[13] *Re F* [1990] 2 A.C. 1.

[14] Elsewhere this concept has been described as "specific task competence" or "task specific competence": see Beyleveld and Pattinson 1998; Pattinson 2002a, esp. 78 and 163; and Bielby 2005, esp. 357–359. Since only agents (those able to act on freely chosen purposes) are able to make decisions (understood as considered choices), only agents can be competent. Yet particular tasks or decisions, due to their complexity, require greater cognitive faculties than are required to be an agent *as such*.

involving consideration of complex variables (such as those required to plan a week's meals). An individual could also be able to make a decision of a particular level of complexity at time X but not at time Y, because individuals can develop or lose, or have fluctuating cognitive faculties.

The definition of competence used in this chapter presupposes the capability for rational thought. If a *decision* is understood as a considered choice, then only those able to reflect upon their desires or preferences with regard to the task at hand can be considered competent. There are many difficulties raised by attempts to determine whether an individual is in fact competent. For a start, since we do not have direct access to the mind of another, any assessment of an individual's cognitive capacities has to be indirect. Assessing competence requires a judgment on the evidence available. It thereby requires a point of reference; a model against which the attributes displayed can be assessed. It is inevitable that there will be *hard cases*, i.e. cases over which experts can reasonably disagree over the cognitive faculties actually possessed by an individual and over whether the faculties thought to be possessed are sufficient for that patient to make a decision. I use the qualifier "reasonably" to distinguish hard cases from those situations where doubt or disagreement about the patient's cognitive abilities stems from ignorance or indolence. Examples include ignoring the empirical evidence or failing to take all practical steps to maximise the patient's ability to make a decision in the circumstances—well illustrated by Ruth's story with which this chapter began.

It should be noted that some form of verbal or non-verbal communication is needed with an individual if we are to take account of his decision(s). Consider the condition known as "locked-in syndrome". Some of those suffering from this terrible condition are rendered mute and physically unresponsive but are thought to retain their cognitive faculties. Most can at least move their eyelids, but the most unfortunate are rendered completely immobile with full consciousness.[15] It is not possible to avoid treating such individuals as if they were incompetent. Thus, while the ability to communicate is not required to be competent, it is essential for *acting* on the belief that an individual is competent. It also follows that a minimum condition for possession of *capacity* (i.e. legal decision-making authority) must be the ability to communicate.

Setting and applying criteria for capacity has evident implications for the individual in question. Capacity concerns the freedom and powers of the subject.[16] Different standards for assessing and determining capacity will affect the identity and proportion of those judged to have capacity.[17] If the threshold criteria (or their application) are set at a low level, then some of those with capacity will in fact lack competence. Consent and refusal thereby become fictional. If the level is set at a high level, then patients who can make their own treatment decisions will be disempowered. Competence-based criteria will seek to grant decision-making authority to those who are cognitively able to make a

---

[15] See Smith and Delargy 2005, 406.
[16] See Stefan 1993.
[17] See Grisso and Appelbaum 1995 and 1998, and Wong et al. 1999.

relevant decision at that time and thereby seek to avoid fiction or deliberate disempowerment. With competence-based criteria, the treatment of hard cases will depend on the evidential presumption used. A presumption of competence will mean that where the patient's autonomy interests conflict with his health interests, his autonomy interests will triumph, and vice versa.[18] Capacity need not, however, be competence-based; it need not turn on cognitive-functional assessment.[19] One alternative is to set the capacity threshold purely by reference to whether the decision is considered reasonable (a "reasonable outcome" test). This would deny capacity to those who adopt an internally coherent belief system that is regarded as unreasonable or immoral, whether or not they are considered to be competent. Another alternative is to require only that the patient express a preference for or against treatment (an "expression of a preference" test). This adopts the lowest possible threshold and will inevitably grant capacity to some patients who cannot make autonomous decisions. A third alternative is to set capacity by reference to a status, such as age or IQ (a "status" test). As we shall see, age has relevance in English law (see 5.3.1).

It is worth pausing to distinguish *first person capacity* (i.e. the legal authority to make decisions for oneself) from *proxy capacity* (i.e. the legal authority to make decisions on behalf of another).[20] This section has been primarily concerned with first person capacity. Indeed, unless otherwise stated or evident, capacity is used as shorthand in this chapter for first person capacity.

5.2.1.1 The capacity test

The test of capacity adopted by the Mental Capacity Act 2005 owes much to the previous common law, which it is therefore helpful to examine. At common law, the leading case was the 1993 first instance decision of *Re C*.[21] Even before *Re C* it had been clear that capacity was meant to track competence and was thereby dependent on the particular decision and the complexity of the task at hand. This can be seen from the case of *In the Estate of Park*.[22] On a day shortly before his death, Mr Park had married and a few hours later executed a new will (marriage revokes a previous will). His wife stood to gain a greater share of his property if Mr Park had died without a valid will. She successfully challenged his capacity to enter into the new will. His family then challenged his capacity to get married only a few hours before he had executed this new will. They failed. According to the Court of Appeal, in both cases the question was whether Mr Park had been capable of understanding the nature of the act or

---

[18] There will only be a conflict between a patient's health and autonomy interests where he seeks to refuse treatment that apparently tracks his health interests or seeks to consent to treatment that is apparently against his health interests.

[19] See the discussion in Gunn 1994.

[20] Proxy consent can be a version of *express consent* (where the patient has expressly consented to the proxy representing his will), or a version of *imputed consent* (where the proxy decision-maker is not represented the patient's actual will but is determining the best interests of the patients). For discussion of express, implicit, implied, and imputed consent, see Chs 4 (4.3) and 6 (6.3.1.1).

[21] *Re C* [1994] 1 All E.R. 819, decided in October 1993.

[22] [1954] P. 112.

transaction. The court was prepared to accept that the nature of that particular will was more complex than the nature of marriage, so that he could have capacity to marry but not the capacity to make that will.[23]

The courts had also given some, albeit limited, guidance on capacity to make a treatment decision. In *Re F*, the Court of Appeal had referred to capacity in terms of the ability to exercise a "right of choice".[24] The House of Lords did not elaborate, though some of the Law Lords indicated that capacity required the ability to communicate.[25] The Court of Appeal added to this in *Re T*—a case examined with regard to undue influence in the previous chapter (4.5).[26] This case concerned an unconscious patient who had previously refused to consent to a blood transfusion without which she would die. The court declared that every adult is presumed to have the capacity to make treatment decisions, but that presumption could be rebutted.[27] It was said that an adult could be deprived of capacity by mental illness or temporary factors such as unconsciousness, the effects of shock, fatigue, pain, or drugs.[28] More serious decisions were said to require more ability than less serious decisions.[29]

Re C concerned a 68-year-old patient who had developed gangrene in his foot. Despite being told that without amputation of his leg below the knee he would have only a 15 per cent chance of survival, he had refused to consent to amputation, saying that he would rather die with two feet than live with one. Less dramatic treatment had successfully averted the immediate threat to his life, but the hospital wanted to keep the option of future amputation open. The patient sought an injunction preventing amputation of his leg without his express consent. In earlier cases (including *Re T*) there had been powerful dicta to the effect that a competent adult was entitled to refuse treatment.[30] The question was therefore whether this patient was competent. He was clearly mentally ill. He had paranoid schizophrenia and suffered delusions, including the delusion that he had had an international career in medicine. Nonetheless, Thorpe J. held that he had capacity to refuse to consent to amputation and granted the injunction. C's mental illness did not deprive him of capacity to make the treatment decision in question.[31]

Thorpe J. accepted the view of an expert witness that there were three stages to the decision-making process: "first, comprehending and retaining treatment information, second, believing it and, third, weighing it in the balance to arrive at choice".[32] This was used as, in effect, a three-stage test for capacity:

---

[23] [1954] P. 112 at 122.

[24] [1990] 2 A.C. 1 at 18 (Lord Donaldson M.R.), 31 (Neill L.J.), and 34 (Butler-Sloss L.J.).

[25] [1990] 2 A.C. 1 at 52 (Lord Bridge) and 75 (Lord Goff).

[26] *Re T* [1993] Fam. 95.

[27] [1993] Fam. 95 at 112.

[28] [1993] Fam. 95 at 113 (Lord Donaldson).

[29] [1993] Fam. 95 at 113. The precise meaning of this paraphrase is examined below.

[30] *Re T* [1993] Fam. 95, esp. 102, and *Airedale NHS Trust v Bland* [1993] A.C. 789, esp. 857.

[31] He did, however, lack capacity to refuse treatment for his mental disorder under s.63 of the Mental Health Act 1983 (on which see *B v Croydon HA* [1995] Fam. 133). For another case where a mentally ill patient was held to have capacity to refuse a specific treatment (dialysis) see *Re JT* [1998] 1 F.L.R. 48.

[32] [1994] 1 All E.R. 819 at 823.

(1) Can the patient *understand and retain* the treatment information?

(2) Can the patient *believe* it?

(3) Can the patient *weigh* it sufficiently to make a choice?

The information that the patient needs to be able to understand was said to concern "the nature, purpose and effects" of the proposed treatment.[33] This three-fold common law test of capacity (hereafter referred to as the *Re C* test) was confirmed by the Court of Appeal in *Re MB*.[34] It was emphasised that a patient will only lack capacity if "some impairment or disturbance of mental functioning renders the person unable to make a decision" and the purpose of the three-stage test was to determine whether there is such an inability.[35] Butler-Sloss L.J., giving the opinion of the Court of Appeal, indicated that the information that the patient must able to understand and retain is that "which is material to the decision, especially as to the likely consequences of having, or not having, the treatment in question".[36] While the *Re C* test does not explicitly refer to the ability to communicate, we have already seen that a patient who cannot communicate in any way must lack capacity to make treatment decisions.[37]

As stated earlier, the *Re C* test underpins the test of capacity within the Mental Capacity Act 2005. Nonetheless, those seeking to apply the law to a set of facts must now apply the provisions of the 2005 Act, rather than the common law. Account also needs to be taken of the guidance in the Code of Practice.[38]

Section 1 lays down a set of principles, three of which concern capacity and its determination. These comprise (a) a presumption of capacity, (b) a requirement that "all practicable steps" must be taken to help a patient reach a decision,[39] and (c) an explicit statement that a patient is not to be treated as lacking capacity to make a decision "merely because he makes an unwise decision" (s.1(2)–(4)). All three principles had been recognised by the common law.

Sections 2 and 3 codify the common law definition of (first person) capacity. Capacity remains tied to competence and is to be assessed by reference to the ability of a patient to make the decision in question at that particular time. It is to be determined by a *two-stage test*.

Stage one imposes a diagnostic requirement: a patient will only lack capacity if he is "unable to make a decision for himself in relation to the matter because of an impairment of, or a disturbance in the functioning of, the mind or brain" (s.2(1)). This is a cognitive-functional test of capacity. It is the competence-based test that was adopted at common law. It explicitly includes temporary states of impairment (s.2(2)). As the Code of Practice points out, the impairment or

---

[33] [1994] 1 All E.R. 819 at 823.
[34] [1997] 2 F.L.R. 426 at 437. Butler-Sloss L.J., when giving the judgment of the Court of Appeal, omitted to refer to the second stage of the *Re C* test, but subsequently made it clear that the Court of Appeal approved the *Re C* test: *Re B* [2002] EWHC 429, para.33.
[35] [1997] 2 F.L.R. 426 at 437.
[36] [1997] 2 F.L.R. 426 at 437.
[37] See also *Re F* [1990] 2 A.C. 1, 63 at 75 and *R. (Burke) v GMC* [2005] EWCA 1003, para.10.
[38] On assessing capacity, see Department for Constitutional Affairs 2007, esp. ch.4.
[39] See Department for Constitutional Affairs 2007, ch.3.

disturbance could be caused by delirium, drug misuse, alcohol, and other such factors, as well as mental illness, dementia, and brain damage.[40] This cognitive disability requirement is therefore less stringent than the "mental disorder" requirement of the Mental Health Act 1983 (on which see 5.5).

Stage two of the capacity test is almost identical to the three-stage *Re C* test. Section 3(1) states that a patient will be considered unable to make a decision if he is unable to:

(a) understand the information relevant to the decision;

(b) retain that information;

(c) use or weigh that information as part of the process of making the decision; or

(d) communicate his decision by any means.

While no mention is made of the ability to believe the information, which formed the second stage of the *Re C* test, this could be viewed as part of understanding.

Fluctuating competence, in the sense of being able to retain the information relevant to a decision for only a short period, does not prevent the patient from having capacity under this test (s.3(3)). The Act requires the *ability* to understand the relevant information, rather than *actual* understanding.[41] This is what would be required by a competence-based test,[42] though the former will often be assessed in practice by reference to the latter. The relevant information is, as in the common law, defined to include information about the foreseeable consequences of deciding one way or another, or failing to make the decision (s.3(4)). Thus, what the patient must be able to understand to have capacity (the consequences of treatment versus non-treatment) is greater than what he must actually understand if the doctor is to avoid committing a trespass (the broad nature and purpose of the treatment). Of course, as long as a patient remains able to satisfy the threshold test of capacity, it will be possible to address any defects in his actual understanding.

The substantive requirements for capacity under the Act are therefore essentially the same as those of the common law. The difference is that these requirements have statutory force and the Act explicitly provides that health professionals are to be judged against a standard of reasonable belief that a patient lacks capacity. More specifically, s.5 provides that the same protection is

---

[40] See Department for Constitutional Affairs 2007, para.4.12.

[41] This was the common law position: see e.g. *R. (Burke) v GMC* 2004] EWHC 1879, para.42. Cf. *Re C* [1994] 1 All E.R. 819 at 823.

[42] Conceptually, competence requires that the patient have the dispositional ability to understand *and* be cognitively able to exercise that ability in the context in question. Since competence is task specific, a patient who has the dispositional abilities to make a decision will lack competence if he cannot exercise those abilities in relation to a specific task or decision. A patient who is completely overcome with emotion every time he thinks about his cancer might, e.g., have the dispositional abilities to make a competent decision but will be incompetent with regard to decisions concerning his cancer treatment.

to be given to those treating or caring for a patient as would have been given by a valid consent, as long as: (i) "reasonable steps" have been taken to establish whether the patient lacks capacity; and (ii) the person whose conduct is in question "reasonably believes" that the patient lacks capacity and he is acting in the patient's best interests. There has been no common law decisions addressing the situation where a doctor acts in the face of refusal as a result of falsely believing that the patient lacks capacity. At common law, such a doctor would commit a battery. It has been suggested that the court would have been likely to fashion a defence of reasonable mistake.[43] The Act provides a legislative answer in s.5, *the general legal authority provision*, which effectively gives effect to a legislative version of the common law doctrine of necessity.

As indicated by the Code of Practice, for most day-to-day actions or decisions, capacity will be assessed by the person caring for the patient at the time that the decision is made.[44] Carers will not usually need to invoke a formal assessment process, unless their assessment is challenged by the patient or family. Health professionals proposing treatment in reliance upon s.5 must formally assess a patient's capacity, in a way appropriate to the circumstances, before they can be said to have a "reasonable belief that the patient lacks capacity. In difficult cases conclusions are to be reached on the balance of probabilities (s.2(4)),[45] taking account of the presumption of capacity (s.1(2)).

5.2.1.2 Unwise decisions and the risk of death or irreversible harm

At common law it was repeatedly stated that it does not matter whether the patient's "reasons for making the choice are rational, irrational, unknown or even non-existent".[46] Under the Act this is expressed by the s.1(4) principle that a patient is not to be treated as lacking capacity "merely because he makes an unwise decision". The law is thus only concerned with the rationality of a patient's decision or its basis when it suggests that the patient is unable to satisfy the two-stage capacity test. Treatment decisions made on the basis of religious or other beliefs that others might consider to be unwise or irrational can be legally valid. A Jehovah's Witness refusing blood products does not thereby demonstrate a cognitive impairment rendering him unable to make a decision. Even extremely bizarre behaviour is not automatically inconsistent with satisfaction of the capacity test. In one pre-Act case a prisoner was declared to have the capacity to refuse treatment for self-injuries caused by cutting open his lower leg, keeping the wound open by forcing faeces and foreign objects into it, and placing two taps in his anus so that they could only be removed with surgical intervention.[47] This behaviour had been part of the

---

[43] See Grubb 2004, 161.
[44] See Department for Constitutional Affairs 2007, esp. paras 4.38–4.45.
[45] See also Department for Constitutional Affairs 2007, para.4.48.
[46] *Re T* [1993] Fam. 95 at 102 (Lord Donaldson, citing Lord Templeman in *Sidaway v Bethlem Royal Hospital* [1985] A.C. 871 at 904–905) and 116 (Butler-Sloss L.J.); and *Re MB* [1997] 2 F.L.R. 426 at 432, 436–437.
[47] *Re W* [2002] EWHC 901.

prisoner's campaign to force the prison authorities to have him treated in a special hospital. In *Re MB* the Court of Appeal was emphatic that a patient did not lack capacity even if the decision was "so outrageous in its defiance of logic, or of accepted moral standards, that no sensible person, who had applied his mind to the question to be decided, could have arrived at it".[48]

A patient is likely, however, to fail to satisfy the capacity test where he makes a decision that is based upon a misperception of reality stemming from a mental disorder. In *Re MB*, Butler-Sloss L.J. cited the belief that the "blood is poisoned because it is red" as an example. In a 2004 case, a patient was held to lack capacity to refuse a blood transfusion (needed because she had self-harmed by cutting herself and bloodletting) on the basis that her references to "her blood being evil" were evidence of a mental disorder rendering her unable to "use and weigh the relevant information".[49] Similarly, in a 2006 case, a woman was held to lack capacity to refuse surgery for an ovarian cyst that appeared to be cancerous when she persisted in the belief that she was married and childless (she was actually divorced with two children) and her stomach swelling was "just food".[50] Sir Mark Potter P. held that her mental condition prevented her from understanding that the surgery would remove her pain and that she had cancer. She was therefore unable to weigh the information. The line between delusions that are sufficient to render a patient unable to satisfy the capacity test and those that are not (such as *C's* delusions of grandeur) is not always easy to draw. As long as the decision reached is based upon a "reasonable belief", this line is to be drawn by those seeking to rely upon the general legal authority or the decision of a proxy (ss.5(b), 11(7)(a) and 20(9)).

As already stated, a patient with capacity is entitled to refuse treatment even where this will result in his death. At common law there was, however, some ambiguity as to the extent to which the stringency of the test for capacity varied with the risk of such consequences. In *Re T*, Lord Donaldson said:

> What matters is that the doctors should consider whether at that time he had a capacity which was commensurate with the gravity of the decision which he purported to make. The more serious the decision, the greater the capacity required.[51]

This was approved by the Court of Appeal in *Re MB*. According to Butler-Sloss L.J.,

> The graver the consequences of the decision, the commensurately greater the level of competence is required to take the decision.[52]

It is difficult to be sure what these statements mean. They raise two questions. *First*, what is meant by seriousness of the decision and the gravity of its

---

[48] *Re MB* [1997] 2 F.L.R. 426 at 437.
[49] *NHS Trust v Ms T* [2004] EWHC 1279, esp. paras 61 and 63.
[50] *Trust A v H (An Adult Patient)* [2006] EWHC 1230.
[51] *Re T* [1993] Fam. 95 at 113.
[52] *Re MB* [1997] 2 F.L.R. 426 at 437.

consequences? *Second*, what is meant by varying levels of capacity/competence being required?

Starting with the second question first, we must be careful with the labels used here. As defined earlier, capacity or competence cannot be possessed to degrees or levels, they are all-or-nothing judgments about a specific individual facing a specific task at a specific time: competent or incompetent, capacitated or incapacitated. Lord Donaldson and Butler-Sloss L.J.'s comments were made in the context of discussions as to when a patient is to be treated as having the legal authority to make his own decisions (i.e. when a patient has first person capacity). Their comments therefore indicate that what the common law considered sufficient for capacity varied according to the seriousness/gravity of the decision. Interpreted in this way, what is said to vary must be the abilities required or the level of scrutiny given to a patient's abilities.

The seriousness of the decision and the gravity of its consequences appear to refer to the risk that the decision reached will have a deleterious effect on the patient's health or even life. This suggests a risk-relative sliding scale of capacity with the threshold criteria being set higher for capacity to refuse life-saving treatment than to refuse, say, the treatment of a broken finger. More would generally be required to refuse treatment than to consent to it. Gunn et al. have suggested that Lord Donaldson was simply referring to the complexity of the decision.[53] The complexity of the decision is relevant to the threshold for capacity, but the words "serious" and "gravity" are not words easy to associate with complexity. Lord Donaldson went on to say that,

> Doctors faced with a refusal of consent have to give very careful and detailed consideration to what was the patient's capacity to decide at the time when the decision was made. It may not be a case of capacity or no capacity. It may be a case of reduced capacity. What matters is whether at that time the patient's capacity was reduced below the level needed in the case of a refusal of that importance, *for refusals can vary in importance. Some may involve a risk to life or of irreparable damage to health*. Others may not.[54]

Here his Lordship links seriousness and importance to the "risk to life or of irreparable damage to health".

The 2005 Act makes no reference to the likelihood of a tragic outcome when assessing a patient's capacity. Indeed, both the Act (s.2(3)(b)) and the Code of Practice emphasises that the person assessing the patient's capacity must not assume a lack of capacity because they have a particular diagnosis or condition.[55] Of course, in practice, a patient's ability to refuse treatment that the doctor considers appropriate is more likely to be questioned than his ability to consent to that treatment.[56] Conversely, there is no point in challenging the patient's capacity where he wants the treatment and no disagreement arises about what is the best treatment option, because the treatment can be lawfully

---

[53] See Gunn et al. 1999, 273.
[54] *Re T* [1993] Fam. 95 at 116 (my emphasis).
[55] See Department for Constitutional Affairs 2007, para.4.48.
[56] See Gunn et al. 1999, 281. This point is well illustrated by *Re B* [2002] EWHC 429.

administered in any event (on the basis of his consent if he has capacity and on the basis of his best interests if he lacks capacity).

5.2.1.3 Types of risk-relativity

Whether the threshold criteria for capacity should attempt to track decisional-complexity alone or explicitly take account of decisional-consequences is controversial. A *risks-relative approach* varies the threshold criteria according to the expected harm/benefit of complying with the patient's apparent decision, and will thereby err towards non-interference where the risks of harm are low and towards interference where the risks of harm are high. We need to distinguish two risk-relative approaches: *strong* vs. *weak* risk-relativity.

The *strong risk relativity* approach holds that the threshold criteria for capacity should vary according to the risk that the patient will *intentionally or unintentionally* cause himself irreversible harm. This is incompatible with the competence-based approach, because it could deny capacity to a patient who is genuinely believed to be competent where his conduct carries a high risk of causing irreversible harm and vice versa. This approach is consistent with those moral theories that permit an autonomous decision to be overridden in the patient's own interests and is therefore consistent with what Beyleveld and Brownsword refer to as the "dignity as constraint" position.[57]

The *weak risk-relativity* approach holds that the threshold criteria for capacity should vary according to the risk that the patient will *unintentionally* cause himself irreversible harm. It seeks to maximise patient autonomy by leaving the decision to the patient where doing so does not unduly risk *unintentional* self-harm. It is consistent with the competence-based approach if it is understood as denying legal decision-making authority to a patient where he is uncontroversially considered to be incompetent *or* where there is genuine doubt among experts as to the patient's cognitive ability to make a considered choice *and* complying with his views carries non-trivial risks of death or irreversible damage to health. According to this approach, first person capacity is still determined by competence-assessment, but the treatment of hard cases, where there is genuine doubt among experts, is risk-relative. A patient whose competence is genuinely not clear might, for example, be granted the legal authority to consent to uncontroversially life-saving treatment but not to a risky experimental treatment, participation in research, or to volunteer as an organ donor. Similarly, such a patient might be granted the capacity to refuse minor treatment but not to refuse life-saving treatment of the same level of complexity. This is consistent with the "dignity as empowerment" camp. To reject all forms of the risks-relative approach to first person capacity *in all circumstances* is to claim that no account should ever be taken of the consequences of being wrong either way. This suggests that cases of genuine doubt as to the patient's competence are to be treated as if no doubt exists and no account is to be taken of the level of harm faced in such circumstances. Those

---

[57] See Beyleveld and Brownsword 2001, discussed in Ch.1 (1.4.1).

in the dignity as empowerment camp must therefore allow reliance on weak risk-relativity. The difficulty, from a practical point of view, is that what is claimed to be competence-based risk-relativity (weak risk-relativity) could easily mask what is in reality a rejection of the competence-based approach (strong risk-relativity). This difficulty is unavoidable if hard cases are to be treated in accordance with the principle of precaution, so as to avoid the most probable risk of harm.[58]

5.2.2 The consequences of incapacity

When an adult patient lacks capacity to consent we need to consider: who is to authorise the proposed treatment and on what basis? The common law answer was that no one could provide proxy consent on behalf of an incapacitated adult, but treatment could be lawfully administered in the patient's best interests by virtue of the doctrine of necessity. The 2005 Act's answer is that treatment can be lawful under the s.5 general legal authority, unless there is a proxy appointed to consent on behalf of the patient or the patient validly refused the treatment when he had capacity. Proxy decision-makers and those relying on the general legal authority are to act in the patient's best interests.

The pre-Act common law position will be outlined first (in 5.2.1), before examining the changes made by the 2005 Act (5.2.2). Finally, this section will analyse the ethical issues raised by the best interest test (5.2.3).

5.2.1.1 The common law

The common law answer was provided by Re F.[59] The patient was a 36-year-old woman, who was said to have the mental age of a small child. Her mother and the staff caring for her at the mental hospital at which she was a voluntary patient were concerned that she had started to have a sexual relationship. A declaration was sought to the effect that it would be lawful to sterilise her, despite her manifest inability to consent to the operation. The House of Lords granted the declaration and explained the law governing the treatment of incapacitated adults.

It was held that the ancient jurisdiction enabling the court to consent on behalf of an incapacitated individual—the *parens patriae* jurisdiction—could no longer be exercised on behalf of any adult.[60] In the absence of anyone capable of consenting on behalf of an incapacitated adult, medical interventions were held to be lawful only insofar as they were justified by the doctrine of necessity. The touchstone of necessity in this context was said to be the patient's "best interests". This meant that it was lawful for doctors to undertake treatment to

---

[58] For further discussion of precautionary reasoning, see Ch.17 (esp. 17.3.2.3).
[59] *Re F* [1990] 2 A.C. 1.
[60] As a result of, inter alia, the Mental Health Act 1959.

"preserve the life, health, or well being" of the patient.[61] As Lord Brandon put it, to be in a patient's best interests the treatment must be designed "to save their lives, or to ensure improvement or prevent deterioration in their physical or mental health".[62] What is more, it was held that the declaratory jurisdiction allowed the court to declare whether a proposed treatment was in the best interests of an incapacitated patient. A declaration was not legally required, but there were circumstances (such as those of the present case) where it would be considered good practice to seek prior judicial approval (see further 5.4). For most treatments, a declaration would be unnecessary and the doctor would, in effect, make the decision.

How were the best interests of the patient to be determined? The House of Lords held that the *Bolam* test was to be applied.[63] This is the standard used to determine whether a doctor has been negligent, examined in the clinical negligence chapter (3.4.1). McNair J. famously directed the jury in *Bolam* to the effect that a doctor should not be considered negligent if he acts in accordance with a responsible body of medical opinion.[64] According to their Lordships, when deciding whether the proposed treatment is in the best interests of an incapacitated adult, the doctor must comply with a responsible body of relevant professional opinion. Indeed, this was viewed as *sufficient* to protect the doctor from liability in trespass.[65]

Reliance on the *Bolam* test provoked objections.[66] It seemed to mean that a patient's "best" interests depended on who happened to treat him and, since *Bolam* is concerned with a reasonable body of medical opinion, it seemed to be solely concerned with a patient's *medical* best interests. The decision in *Re F* was, however, narrowly interpreted by the lower courts. They added interpretative gloss by holding that, *first*, satisfying the *Bolam* test is a necessary but not a sufficient condition of treatment being in a patient's best interests; *second*, the court is the ultimate arbiter of a patient's best interests; and, *third*, a patient's best interests go beyond best medical interests.[67]

This interpretative gloss is discussed in more depth in the first edition of this book.[68] It fits most uneasily with the actual decision in *Re F*. The House of Lords had explicitly rejected the view of the Court of Appeal to the effect that the law required something more stringent than *Bolam*.[69] Nonetheless, led by Butler Sloss (L.J., then P.), the Court of Appeal and the Family Division of the High Court chose to overlook this. The determination of a patient's best interests was only to start with responsible medical opinion and was ultimately a legal

[61] *Re F* [1990] 2 A.C. 1 at 52 (Lord Bridge), 74, 75 (Lord Goff).
[62] [1990] 2 A.C. 1 at 55.
[63] *Re F* [1990] 2 A.C. 1, 54 at 66–68, 69, 78.
[64] *Bolam v Friern Hospital Management Committee* [1957] 2 All E.R. 118 at 122.
[65] [1990] 2 A.C. 1 at 54 (Lord Bridge) and 68 (with whom Lord Jauncey agreed without reservation).
[66] See e.g. Jones 1989.
[67] See *Re MB* [1997] 2 F.L.R. 426 at 439; *Re A* [2000] 1 F.L.R. 549 at 555; *Re S* [2001] Fam. 1, 28 at 29; *R. (N) v M* [2002] EWCA Civ 1789, para.29, *Simms v Simms* [2002] EWHC 2734, para.42; and *A Hospital NHS Trust v S* [2003] EWHC 365, para. 43.
[68] See Pattinson 2006, 142–144.
[69] *Re F* [1990] 2 A.C. 1, 54 at 67–68.

decision to be made, if necessary by a court, taking account of "medical, emotional and all other welfare issues".[70]

Re F held that no one could consent on behalf of an incapacitated adult, but this did not mean that the views of friends, relatives, or the previously capacitated patient were irrelevant considerations. In fact, a refusal of medical treatment made by a capacitated adult in anticipation of becoming incapacitated *(an advance refusal)* was said to have same legal force as a contemporaneous refusal if it was "clearly established and applicable in the circumstances".[71] The views of friends and relatives were not themselves binding, but could serve to draw attention to the incapacitated patient's previous views and values. It was therefore good practice to consult friends and relatives if practical to do so.[72] The patient's best interests were to be the focus of the consultation, not the interests of those consulted. Having said that, the Court of Appeal in *Re A* (a case on sterilisation to which we will return later) explicitly left open the question of whether third party interests should ever be considered with regard to the application of the best interests test.[73]

5.2.2.2 The Mental Capacity Act 2005

The 2005 Act replaces the common law on the treatment of incapacitated adults. The legal lacuna created by the common law's failure to recognise proxy decision-makers for incapacitated adults has been addressed. In addition to *the general legal authority* to act in what one reasonably believes to be in the best interests of an incapacitated patient (s.5), the Act provides for "lasting powers of attorney" (ss.9–14: *LPAs* for short) and "court appointed deputies" (s.16–20: *deputies* for short). All such decision-making powers must be exercised in what is reasonably believed to be the best interests of the patient, which we consider shortly. The general legal authority does not authorise actions that are inconsistent with a decision made by a person appointed under a LPA or a deputy, except in relation to life- and health-sustaining treatment given while awaiting a court decision (s.6(6), (7)).

The general legal authority also does not authorise actions contrary to a valid and applicable *advance refusal* (s.5(4)).[74] The previous common law had also recognised that an advance refusal could have the same legal force as a contemporaneous refusal. This had been stated by the Court of Appeal in *Re T*—the case in which an unconscious woman had previously refused to consent to a blood transfusion—but this aspect of the decision was technically obiter, as the court found that the advance refusal in question had not been valid. While support for this position in a later decision of the House of Lords was also obiter,[75] there have been two first instance decisions where specific advance

---

[70] *Re A* [2000] 1 F.L.R. 549 at 555 (Butler-Sloss P.).
[71] *Re T* [1993] Fam. 95 at 103.
[72] *Re F* [1990] 2 A.C. 1 at 78 (Lord Goff).
[73] *Re A* [2000] 1 F.L.R. 549 at 556, 558.
[74] On advance refusals, see the Code of Practice: Department for Constitutional Affairs 2007, ch.9.
[75] *Airedale NHS Trust v Bland* [1993] A.C. 789, esp. 857 (Lord Keith) and 864 (Lord Goff).

refusals were held to be valid.[76] One of these was the *Re C* decision that gave rise to the common law capacity test. Thus, there was little doubt that at common law an advance refusal would be valid it if it complied with the conditions for a contemporaneous refusal being valid, was intended to apply to the specific treatment/circumstances in question, and had not been effectively revoked. The 2005 Act deals with advance refusals in ss.24 to 26. It gives legal effect to an "advance decision" to refuse treatment made by a person who had reached 18 and had the capacity to make it (s.24(1)). To be effective, the advance refusal must be both "valid" and "applicable" (s.25(1)). Since the most challenging are advance refusals of life-sustaining treatment, detailed consideration of the Act's provisions on advance refusals will be left to Ch.15 (15.3).

The Act's provisions on appointing proxy decision-makers require further attention. The *LPA* enables an individual to choose a proxy to act on his behalf when he loses capacity.[77] This power replaces the previous "enduring power of attorney" under the Enduring Powers of Attorney Act 1985, which was limited to financial and property matters. The Act's formalities on LPAs, as laid down in ss.9–10 and Sch.1, are actually more stringent than those applying to advance refusals. The "donor" (the person appointing the proxy) must be at least 18 and have capacity to execute an LPA (s.9(2)). The "donee" or "attorney" (the appointed proxy) must similarly be over 18. An attorney can be granted capacity to make decisions about the donor's personal welfare, including decisions about the continuation of medical treatment, but express provision is required to extend the authority to decisions on life-sustaining treatment (s.11(7), (8)). If more than one attorney is appointed, the donor can specify whether they are to act jointly or severally (s.10(4)). If he fails to do so for the matter in hand, they will be assumed to be appointed to act jointly, so that they must act together for their decision to have force (s.10(5)).

Unlike advance refusals, LPAs need to be registered in accordance with the provisions in Sch.1 (s.9(2)(b)). They must take the form of a written document and include prescribed information about its nature and effect and a signed statement from the donor indicating that they have understood the document. Registration currently costs £150.[78] It can be done by the donor while he is still capable or by the attorney at any time.[79] The task of maintaining the register of LPAs and supervising donees falls to the new *Office of the Public Guardian* (ss.57–60).

Deputies can be appointed by the *Court of Protection* (ss.16(2) and 45).[80] On matters within its jurisdiction this new court has the same legal powers and authority as the High Court (s.47). Appeals from its decisions are to the Court of Appeal (s.53). It has jurisdiction over the entire Act and will be the final arbiter of capacity matters, which it is to decide on the balance of probabilities (s.2(4)). The power to appoint a deputy is to be exercised where there is no

[76] *Re C* [1994] 1 All E.R. 819 and *Re AK* [2001] 1 F.L.R. 129.
[77] See Department for Constitutional Affairs 2007, ch.7.
[78] See OPG 2007, 6.
[79] See Department for Constitutional Affairs 2007, para.7.14.
[80] See also Department for Constitutional Affairs 2007, ch.8.

validly-appointed donee and the court cannot make a one-off decision to resolve all the issues. Like attorneys, deputies must be over 18 (s.19(1)). The deputy will usually be a family member or someone who knows the patient well, unless the court decides that it is necessary or more appropriate to appoint an independent person.[81] The Act places a number of restrictions on the powers of deputies (s.20). A deputy cannot, for example, go against a decision made by an attorney acting under a valid LPA (s.20(4)) or refuse consent to the carrying out or continuation of life-sustaining treatment (s.20(5)).

Those acting under the general legal authority or making a decision as proxy (attorney or deputy) must act in the incapacitated patient's *best interests* (s.1(5)). The best interests test is addressed in s.4.[82] A patient's best interests must be determined by reference to "all the circumstances", including whether and when the patient is likely to have capacity in the future (s.4(2), (3)). So far as "reasonably practicable" the patient must be permitted and encouraged to participate in the decision as far as he is able (s.4(4)). To assist vulnerable patients in this regard a new Independent Mental Capacity Advocate (IMCA) service has been set up under the Act (ss.35–41).[83] Such an advocate must be instructed and consulted for patients lacking capacity who have no-one else to support them when a patient is proposed for serious medical treatment by an NHS body (s.37).

Consideration must be given, as far as is "reasonably ascertainable", to the

(a) patient's past and present wishes and feelings;

(b) beliefs and values that would be likely to influence his decision if he had capacity; and

(c) other factors that he would be likely to consider if he were able to do so (s.4(6)).

In considering these factors, the 2005 Act requires that views of those who know the patient be sought. So, "if it is practicable and appropriate", the decision-maker must consult

(i)   anyone named by the patient as someone to be consulted;

(ii)   anyone engaged in caring for the patient or interested in his welfare;

(iii) any attorney or deputy on matters outside of their direct authority (s.4(7)).

Any consultation must concern the patient's best interests, rather than the interests of those consulted. This is a line that might not be clear-cut in practice. This is well illustrated by 1996 case of *Re Y*.[84] This concerned the legality of

---

[81] See Department for Constitutional Affairs 2007, para.8.83.
[82] See also Department for Constitutional Affairs 2007, ch.5.
[83] See also Department for Constitutional Affairs 2007, ch.10.
[84] [1997] Fam. 110.

performing a blood test and removing bone marrow from an incapacitated adult for the treatment of her sick sister. Connell J. declared that performing these procedures would be in the best interests of the incapacitated donor, Y. The judge took the view that if Y's sister was to die this would have an adverse effect on their mother, potentially depriving Y of her mother's visits. Donating was also considered likely to improve Y's relationship with her sister. This link to the patient's interests in this case was indirect and a cynic might be tempted by the view *Re Y* did not strictly adhere to the patient's best interests at all, especially since she did not appreciate that the lady who visited her was her mother.

5.2.2.3 The ethics of relying on the "best interests" test

Different moral theories will take account of different variables and weigh them differently. Varying levels of weight could be placed on the decisions, views, values, and interests of the patient, friends and loved ones, health professionals, or society in general. The views of the patient when previously competent could be treated as decisive and directive, influential, or irrelevant. Where there are no relevant views from a previous period of competence or they are not treated as decisive, treatment decisions could track the *interests of the patient alone* or *the interests of third parties*.

Applying the patient's prior decision requires there to have actually been an *advance decision* (often called an advance directive), i.e. a prior decision that was made when that patient was competent and was intended to apply once he had lost competence. In the absence of an advance decision, the most autonomy-based approach is to apply the values that the patient had when previously competent. This is what the *substituted judgement approach* requires. It requires a proxy decision-maker to attempt to reach the decision that the patient would have made in the circumstances had he been competent. The view of the patient is, in effect, second-guessed. Some US States take this approach.[85] We have seen that it is not adopted by the 2005 Act. At common law, it had been rejected by the House of Lords in *Bland*.[86] Lord Goff relied on *Re F* without recognising that the test could not have applied in that case because the patient had never been competent and Lord Mustill dismissed the test as "simply a fiction" because he treated it as a mechanism for obtaining the patient's consent. To be clear, the substituted judgment approach presupposes previous competence and, properly understood, it does not seek to obtain the patient's consent but to promote his autonomy interests. It prioritises the patient's prior autonomy interests over his contemporaneous welfare interests. It is, however, subject to many of the ethical objections that are made against the implementation of advance decisions (such as the personal identity objection), which are addressed in Ch.16 (16.3.1). In addition, any attempt to adopt this approach must take a view on the required level of evidence as to what the incapacitated

---

[85] See the historical explanation and use of the doctrine in Harmon 1990. By way of example see *Strunk v Strunk* (1969) 445 S.W.2d 145.

[86] *Airedale NHS Trust v Bland* [1993] A.C. 789 at 871–871 (Lord Goff), 895 (Lord Mustill).

patient's views and values were when he was competent.[87] In the absence of evidence making it at least more likely than not that the individual would have made a particular decision, the substituted judgment test collapses into the *best interests* approach with which it is often contrasted.

The *best interests approach* asks whether the proposed course of action is the best one for the patient all things considered. The relationship between best interests and substituted judgment is not necessarily one of alternative. If the substituted judgment approach is applied, then it could be supplemented by the best interest approach where there are no relevant or applicable views from a previous period of competence. This is not the approach of English law. English law takes the best interests approach as the *primary criterion* for treating an incapacitated adult, rather than as a *secondary or supplementary criterion*. While the patient's views when previously competent are relevant considerations, they are not determinate (s.4(6)). A weaker approach to best interests would be to allow interventions on an incapacitated patient if they are merely compatible with the patient's interests. Treatment can be regarded as not against the interests of the patient without being regarded as in the best interests of the patient. The weaker approach has been explicitly applied in this country to the paternity testing of children.[88]

If the application of the best interests test does not operate according to explicit criteria specifying what are relevant "goods" or "interests" (or at least how they are to be determined) and specifying the approach that is to be taken to weighing those goods where they point in different directions, the best interests test will operate as little more than a cloak for the application of the decision-maker's contingent values. In short, there is an unavoidable element of ethical evaluation inherent in the attempt to determine what is "best" for the patient under the guise of the best interests test.

In theory at least, the substituted judgment and best interests tests could be rejected in favour of a wider test of *overall interests*. This would require *all* competing interests to be balanced. This, uniquely, gives direct consideration to the interests and views of individuals other than the patient. It could require the treatment of an incapacitated patient in a way that could not be considered to be in that patient's interests. English law has not yet been prepared to overtly adopt this approach, although at common law the courts had not authoritatively ruled out the option of taking account of third party interests under the guise of the best interests test.[89] Communitarians and utilitarians could require a patient's welfare or autonomy interests to be balanced against societal interests. Even rights-based theorists could adopt an approach that is not restricted to the patient's interests where the rights of others potentially outweigh those of the incapacitated patient. Virtue ethicists will simply seek to foster and facilitate virtuous conduct (including the virtue of charity). This approach again requires criteria as to what interests are to count and how they are to be weighted.

---

[87] See Lewis 1999, 585–586.
[88] *S v S* [1972] A.C. 24. Discussed below.
[89] Explicitly left open as a possibility in *Re A* [2000] 1 F.L.R. 549 at 556, 558.

Few moral theories would advocate the application of the overall interests approach to the medical treatment of incapacitated patients in general. Even utility-maximising utilitarians would have to take account of the disutility of allowing incapacitated patients to be used for the purposes of others or of directly following the preferences of family members. If the preferences of loved ones were to be taken into account directly, John Harris has noted that those with many loved ones who want them to live would thereby be treated as having more valuable lives than those with few or no loved ones. This has led him to declare that "It seems safer in such cases to stick to the Benthamite maxim that everyone is to count for one and none for more than one".[90] In effect, Harris relies on a form of rule utilitarianism to answer the counter-intuitive consequences of act utilitarianism.

5.2.3 Refusal of treatment in late pregnancy

5.2.3.1 The law

Lord Donaldson in *Re T* added a caveat to the "absolute right" of an adult who satisfied the general capacity test to refuse medical treatment: "The only possible qualification is a case in which the choice may lead to the death of a viable foetus".[91] Within three months, the High Court in *Re S* had to consider whether a Caesarean section could lawfully be performed against the will of a 30-year-old woman.[92] She was refusing to consent on religious grounds. After a hearing lasting less than 20 minutes, Sir Stephen Brown granted a declaration that the intervention would be lawful. The brief judgment relied on the surgeon's evidence that the operation was needed to save the life of the woman and the fetus. There was no real legal analysis and no attempt to assess the woman's competence.

The refusals of other women in late pregnancy were overruled in a string of subsequent first instance decisions.[93] All were urgent hearings requiring instant decisions because the life of the woman or her fetus was considered to be at risk. In these cases, unlike *Re S*, the woman was first declared to lack capacity under the (then applicable) common law capacity test. Johnson J. heard two of these cases in a single day. In the first he held the woman to lack capacity "because she was incapable of weighing up the considerations that were involved".[94] The patient had a history of mental illness and, despite obvious indications to the contrary, denied that she was pregnant. Johnson J. seemed to put great weight on the debilitating effects of the "acute emotional stress and

---

[90] Harris 1985, 105.
[91] *Re T* [1993] Fam. 95 at 102.
[92] *Re S* [1993] Fam. 123.
[93] *Tameside and Glossop Acute Services Trust v CH.* [1996] 1 F.L.R. 762, *Norfolk and Norwich Healthcare Trust v W* [1997] 1 F.C.R. 269, *Rochdale NHS Trust v C* [1997] 1 F.C.R. 274, and *Re L* (December 5, 1996, unreported).
[94] *Norfolk and Norwich Healthcare Trust v W* [1997] 1 F.C.R. 269 at 272.

physical pain [that arises] in the ordinary course of labour".[95] In the second, more controversial decision, he held the woman to be "unable to make any valid decision, about anything of even the most trivial kind" because of the pain and emotional stress of labour.[96] The obstetrician treating the woman considered her to be competent.

In *Re MB*, the Court of Appeal heard an appeal at 11pm from a decision to grant a declaration allowing a Caesarean section made only an hour earlier.[97] The court upheld the declaration, later giving a reserved judgment to support its decision. While the patient ultimately lost—and in fact consented after being told the outcome of the hearing—the court rejected Lord Donaldson's caveat and the approach in *Re S*. The Court of Appeal reiterated the general legal principles of *Re T* and *Re C* and held that they applied with equal force to women in late pregnancy. The fetus' interests could not be relied on to force a Caesarean or other invasive treatment on a woman with capacity under the *Re C* test. Even the court has no "jurisdiction to declare that such medical intervention is lawful to protect the interests of the unborn child even at the point of birth".[98] Doubting Johnson J.'s controversial decision discussed in the last paragraph, the Court of Appeal emphasised that labour *as such* was not to be treated as rendering a woman unable to make a decision:

> The "temporary factors" mentioned by Lord Donaldson MR in *Re T* (confusion, shock, fatigue, pain or drugs) may completely erode capacity but those concerned must be satisfied that such factors are operating to such a degree that the ability to decide is absent.[99]

However, on the facts, MB was not considered to be competent to refuse a Caesarean. She had consented to the Caesarean but then, because of her fear of needles, refused to allow blood samples to be taken or anaesthetic to be administered by injection. She then agreed to anaesthesia by mask but later withdrew her consent to that. An expert witness described her "needle phobia" as such that "at the moment of panic ... her fear dominated all".[100] The Court of Appeal declared MB's acute needle phobia to have deprived her of capacity and the administration of the anaesthetic to be in her best interests.

The determination of MB's best interests was helped by the fact that the patient wanted her child to be born alive and was willing to consent to the most invasive aspect of the treatment (the Caesarean section). Her needle phobia had not prevented MB from competently making that decision. This meant that the court simply had to consider whether the less intrusive procedure of anaesthesia was in her best interests. Unfortunately, the Court of Appeal chose not to provide guidance on determining the best interests of a patient who was (incompetently) refusing a Caesarean.[101] There is evidence that 9 to 15 per cent

---

[95] [1997] 1 F.C.R. 269 at 272.
[96] *Rochdale NHS Trust v C* [1997] 1 F.C.R. 274 at 275.
[97] *Re MB* [1997] 2 F.L.R. 426.
[98] [1997] 2 F.L.R. 426 at 444.
[99] [1997] 2 F.L.R. 426 at 437.
[100] [1997] 2 F.L.R. 426 at 438.
[101] See Michalowski 1999, 122–123.

of Caesareans lead to serious side effects and the risk of maternal mortality is thought to be between two and 11 times higher than for vaginal delivery.[102] In addition, Caesareans vastly increase the likelihood that future pregnancies will have to be delivered in the same way, can hinder maternal-fetal bonding, and leave a scar.[103] The psychological consequences of forced Caesareans (particularly where a patient's phobia has been overridden) can also be serious. Such invasive treatment might not be required to protect the woman's physical health. In *Re MB*, for example, a breech birth (where the feet or bottom will emerge first) posed little physical danger to the woman, as opposed to the fetus.[104] An expert had, however, predicted long-term psychological damage if the operation was not performed and the baby was born disabled or died. If non-intervention is unlikely to have lasting psychological effects, it is difficult to see how a Caesarean could be viewed as in a woman's best interests. The court in *Re MB* rejected reliance on the fetus' interests *even where the woman lacks capacity*:

> The foetus up to the moment of birth does not have any separate interests capable of being taken into account when a court has to consider an application for a declaration in respect of a caesarian section operation.[105]

A later decision of the Court of Appeal, considered in the next paragraph, did recognise that the fetus had legally relevant interests, but supported its early view that the fetus' "need for medical assistance does not prevail over [the woman's] rights".[106]

In *St George's Healthcare NHS Trust v S*, a woman refused to consent to an induced delivery despite being told that without it her life and that of her unborn child would be in danger. Those treating her accepted that she understood the risks and still wanted a natural delivery.[107] She was sectioned for assessment under the Mental Health Act 1983. When she continued to refuse to consent, the hospital authorities applied *ex parte* for a declaration that the treatment could be administered against her will. The baby was delivered by Caesarean and the patient was allowed to discharge herself having received no specific treatment for any mental illness or disorder. She then appealed to the Court of Appeal. Judge L.J., giving the opinion of the court, declared that "while pregnancy increases the personal responsibilities of a woman it does not

---

[102] Figures and studies cited in Michalowski 1999, 122. Donohoe 1996, 200–202 cites similar statistics.
[103] See Robertson 1983, 154.
[104] Butler-Sloss L.J. said: "The risk to the unborn child was assessed as 50%, although there was little physical danger to the mother": [1997] 2 F.L.R. 426 at 429.
[105] [1997] 2 F.L.R. 426 at 444.
[106] *St George's Healthcare NHS Trust v S* [1999] Fam. 26 at 50. *St George's* could be considered as slightly revising the view that the fetus has *no* legally relevant interests, which is suggested by some statements in *Re MB*. Nonetheless, it was part of the ratio of *Re MB* that the fetus' interests are not relevant to determining whether a Caesarean could be lawfully performed on *a woman who lacks capacity*. What was said in *Re MB* was only technically obiter for a woman with capacity.
[107] While she wanted to give birth in a barn in Wales, she clearly satisfied the *Re C* test. For readers who doubt this, consider the extracts from the letter that she wrote at the request of the senior registrar: [1999] Fam. 26 at 39.

diminish her entitlement to decide whether or not to undergo medical treat-ment".[108] A woman's right to reject medical treatment was said to exist even "if her own life or that of her unborn child depends on it" and even if her decision is considered to be "morally repugnant".[109] The Court of Appeal allowed her appeal, holding that she had capacity and the Mental Health Act had been inappropriately used. The declaration given after an *ex parte* hearing could not protect the hospital from liability in trespass. The actions of the hospital were heavily criticised. A court hearing had been arranged without the knowledge of the patient or the solicitor she was consulting and the judge had been falsely led to believe that this was an emergency in which the patient was actually in labour. To avoid such circumstances occurring in the future, the Court of Appeal laid down some general guidelines.[110] They largely affirm the guidance given in *Re MB*, provide for the involvement of the Official Solicitor where the patient is unable to instruct solicitors and require that any judicial hearing should be *inter parties* and involve the production of all accurate and relevant information. They also explicitly declare that it is pointless seeking a declara-tion where there is no doubt as to the patient's capacity.[111]

In *Bolton Hospitals NHS Trust v O*, the Court of Appeal's guidance had been complied with.[112] The woman did not want a lawyer, because she actually agreed with the hospital's application. She was suffering from post-traumatic stress disorder following four previous Caesareans, causing her to withdraw her consent just before the operation was to take place. Butler-Sloss P. held that a patient was temporarily incapacitated where she is unable to "see though the consequences of the act" because of panic.[113] As in *Re MB*, panic deprived this woman of her capacity.

The reasoning in *Re MB, St George's Healthcare NHS Trust*, and *Bolton* is not altered by the implementation of the 2005 Act. There will, however, remain room for some cynicism about whether the courts are truly acting according to their declared principles until a case occurs when the courts actually let a woman and her unborn child die as a result of refusing medical treatment. A cynic might also wonder whether MB's phobia would have been so decisive had she been refusing to consent to surgery to remove a cancerous lump from her breast.

5.2.3.2 Ethical issues

In some cases where Caesareans have been performed on unwilling women, those women have later come to be pleased that their decision was overridden and a healthy child was born as a result. The Court of Appeal in *Re MB* chose to ignore predictions of a future change of mind, because "the alternative

---

108 [1999] Fam. 26 at 50.
109 [1999] Fam. 26.
110 [1999] Fam. 26 at 63–65.
111 [1999] Fam. 26 at 63.
112 [2002] EWHC 2871.
113 [2002] EWHC 287, para.15.

would be an unwarranted invasion of the right of the woman to make the decision".[114] Reliance on future wishes to override present wishes is to allow paternalism to triumph in the false cloak of autonomy. As Harris has put the point, though not addressing forced Caesareans,

> Autonomy is the running of one's own life according to one's own lights. The fact that these lights change colour and intensity over time is no evidence at all that the later lights are either better or more "one's own" than the earlier ones. They're just different. To be autonomous, self-determined, just is to be able to do as one wishes—not to be able to do as one will wish at some future time.[115]

A woman's future autonomy interests cannot be taken to override her present autonomous wishes without the reliance on autonomy becoming fictitious.

Allowing a woman to refuse interventions designed to protect or further *the interests of the fetus* raises questions about the moral relevance of those interests. Ch.1 outlined three basic views on the moral status of the fetus: full, no, or limited status.[116] The *no status* position holds that the fetus has no relevant interests that could come into conflict with those of the pregnant woman. In contrast, the *full status* position will hold that the fetus has the same status as the woman. The fetus is viewed almost as if it were the woman's temporarily conjoined twin. The *limited status* position adopts an approach between these two views holding that the fetus' (fixed or gradualist) moral status is less than the woman's but more than her hair or nails. For all these positions, where the fetus will (or is intended to) develop into a child in the future, the future child/adult could also have relevant interests. In addition, other affected persons (such as the fetus' father) could have moral interests. Whether the interests of the fetus, future child, father, or other affected individuals could ever be sufficient to override the woman's autonomy and bodily integrity interests depends on the specific moral theory being applied. A duty-based position that grants full status to the fetus could, for example, hold that the woman's autonomy and integrity interests cannot override our duties to protect the fetus' life, at least where the consequent invasion of her bodily integrity does not unduly risk the woman's life. In contrast, an autonomy-based position holding that the fetus has little or no status (including many utilitarian and rights-based theories) would be at least prima facie opposed to enforcing risky medical interventions on a woman. Some would even distinguish moral duties that are sufficient to justify their enforcement and moral duties that are insufficient to justify their enforcement: "Finding that there are moral duties to avoid harmful prenatal conduct does not mean that those duties should always have legal standing".[117] A virtue ethicist might, for example, conclude that it would be virtuous for the woman to consent to treatment designed to help the fetus but she has no obligation to consent and, therefore, the law ought not to impose

---

[114] [1997] 2 F.L.R. 426 at 438.
[115] Harris 1985, 199.
[116] The connection between these views and the five major positions on determining moral permissibility is examined in Ch.7 (7.2.1.2).
[117] Robertson 1994, 177. See also Morris and Nott 1995, 60.

a legal obligation to do so. The morally good is thereby distinguished from the morally required.

For those moral theories recognising competing interests that are at least potentially able to override a competent woman's refusal, it will often matter *why* the woman is refusing treatment and *how* invasive the proposed treatment is. A woman refusing to take an antibiotic injection *solely* because the infection is of no risk to her could be viewed very differently from a woman refusing a Caesarean section because she does not want to risk the physical complications of the operation.[118] Many of the arguments are also relevant to the question of whether the mother should have a tortious duty to her unborn child, as addressed in Ch.9 (esp. 9.3.2).

5.2.4 Sterilisation

Like any other medical procedure, the sterilisation of an incapacitated woman can be lawfully performed if it is in her best interests under the 2005 Act. It will be in the woman's best interests if it is performed for unequivocally therapeutic reasons, where alternative treatments have been exhausted or are not available. Performing a hysterectomy to remove a malignant tumour will therefore pose few problems. At the other extreme, it will not be in a patient's best interests to be sterilised for "eugenic" or population control reasons.[119] The judiciary is now wary of the eugenic policies of the early twentieth century and judges are now unlikely to echo the sentiments of Justice Holmes in the US Supreme Court case of *Buck v Bell* to the effect that "three generations of imbeciles are enough".[120] More difficult are those cases between the extremes of pressing therapeutic need and "eugenic" control, where sterilisation is proposed for reasons of contraception or to remedy menstrual inconvenience.

In *Re F*, their Lordships advised that judicial sanction should be sought in such cases.[121] The distinction sometimes drawn between "therapeutic" and "non-therapeutic" sterilisation had been dismissed by the House of Lords in an earlier case involving the sterilisation of a mentally disabled minor for contraceptive purposes as "totally meaningless", "semantic", and "entirely immaterial".[122] Nonetheless, this distinction continues to be drawn by the lower courts. In *Re GF*, for example, Sir Stephen Brown P. ruled that there was no need for a declaration where

> two medical practitioners are satisfied that the operation is: (1) necessary *for therapeutic purposes*, (2) in the best interests of the patient, and (3) that there is no practicable, less intrusive means of treating the condition.[123]

---

[118] Those risks could be very high where the woman is particularly obese. See e.g. Robertson 1983, n.165.

[119] *Re B* [1988] A.C. 199.

[120] *Buck v Bell* (1927) 274 U.S. 200 at 207.

[121] [1990] 2 A.C. 1.

[122] *Re B* [1988] A.C. 199 at 204, 205, 211.

[123] *Re GF* [1992] 1 F.L.R. 293 at 294 (my emphasis).

He had reached a similar conclusion with regard to a mentally disabled minor only a few months before.[124] More recently, but still before the implementation of the 2005 Act, the Court of Appeal has confirmed this guidance.[125]

The two leading cases on determining whether sterilisation is in the best interests of an incapacitated patient are now *Re S* and *Re A*, both decided on common law principles.[126] *Re S* concerned a female patient and *Re A* concerned a male patient.

In *Re A*, the elderly mother of a 28-year-old male with Down's syndrome sought a declaration that a vasectomy operation was in his best interests. The patient had no understanding of the link between sexual intercourse and pregnancy and was incapable of being responsible for a child. His mother disapproved of a man walking away from responsibility. The Court of Appeal, predictably, ruled that the sterilisation of a man was not equivalent to the sterilisation of a woman. A man does not have to go through pregnancy and childbirth. On the evidence, *A* had little to gain from the operation. Thorpe L.J. emphasised that a future application could be made "on fresh evidence".[127]

In *Re S*, the mother of a 28-year-old woman with severe learning difficulties sought to have her sterilised. Her mother was finding it increasingly difficult to look after her and was worried that she might become pregnant. The mentally disabled woman was unable to understand or properly cope with her periods, and would similarly be unable to cope with pregnancy. There was, however, a division of opinion on whether she should have a hysterectomy as a first option (the mother's view) or whether the coil should be tried first (the medical experts' view). At first instance, Wall J. held that both were compatible with the *Bolam* test and therefore both were in the patient's best interests. The Court of Appeal rejected this approach. In the words of Butler-Sloss L.J.: "the best interests test ought, logically to give only one answer". On the facts, they held that it was in the patient's best interests to try the less intrusive method first.

Commentators, feminist commentators in particular, have expressed concern over the willingness of the judiciary to sanction invasive sterilisation procedures that deprive incapacitated women of the opportunity to participate in the reproductive enterprise. In an article published in 1995, Keywood cited a number of problems with the case law on the sterilisation of mentally disabled women, including:

(1) the sterilisation of an incapacitated woman to protect her from the effects of pregnancy does not protect her from the effects of sexual abuse or sexual disease, and could actually increase the risk of sexual abuse;[128]

(2) the sexual needs of incapacitated women are often underplayed or ignored (especially by references to "mental age" suggesting that

---

[124] *Re E* [1991] 2 F.L.R. 585.
[125] *Re S* [2001] Fam. 15.
[126] *Re S* [2001] Fam. 15 and *Re A* [2000] 1 F.L.R. 549.
[127] [2000] 1 F.L.R. 549 at 561.
[128] See Keywood 1995, 135.

incapacitated women are child-like and thereby lack sexual desires and life experience);[129]

(3) the best interests test provides "little or no guidance to carers and healthcare workers contemplating sterilisation for their female charges and leaves the adjudication of sterilisation cases to the unfettered discretion of the judiciary";[130]

(4) judges are too ready to rubber-stamp the doctor's decision;[131] and

(5) little or no consideration is given to alternatives to sterilisation.[132]

Many of these criticisms now have to be re-considered in the light of *Re A* and *Re S*. The Courts of Appeal addressed these concerns, at least to some degree.

With regard to (1), in *Re A* it was explicitly recognised that sterilisation cannot remove the risk of sexually transmitted diseases.[133] *Re A* was concerned with a male patient, but it is evident that the courts are fully cognisant of the fact that sterilisation only prevents pregnancy.

With regard to (2), the sexual needs of the patients are being increasingly recognised. In *Re A*, for example, both Butler-Sloss and Thorpe L.JJ. recognised that the patient masturbated.[134] Thorpe L.J. declared that any "opportunities of replacing with reality the fantasies that stimulate A's isolated masturbatory sexual activity . . . should be grasped".[135]

With regard to (3), the Court of Appeal sought to indicate that best interests went beyond medical interests and this is explicitly the case under s.4 of the 2005 Act. The specific application of the best interests test to the facts of both *Re S* and *Re A* indicates that sterilisation should now be considered an option of last resort. It is, for example, apparent that contraceptive sterilisation will not be in the best interests of a patient who is likely to gain the capacity to make the decision for herself in the future (a relevant factor under s.4(3) of the 2005 Act).[136]

With regard to (4), the Court of Appeal's decisions make it quite clear that the courts will no longer merely rubber stamp the views of doctors, which would, in any event, now be against the tenor of the 2005 Act. Indeed, in both *Re S* and *Re A* the Court of Appeal refused to sanction sterilisation, albeit while leaving it open as a future possibility.

With regard to (5), the Court of Appeal rejected sterilisation in both cases largely on the basis that alternative methods of addressing the relevant concerns should be tried or adopted.

In sum, the law has now stepped towards a far more patient-centred approach to sterilisation. A cynic might note that there are no cases questioning

---

[129] See Keywood 1995, 132–133.
[130] Keywood 1995, 127.
[131] See Keywood 1995, 128–129.
[132] See Keywood 1995, 129.
[133] [2000] 1 F.L.R. 549 at 552.
[134] [2000] 1 F.L.R. 549 at 550, 559.
[135] [2000] 1 F.L.R. 549 at 559.
[136] See also *Re D* [1976] Fam. 185 at 196 (a case concerning a child).

the capacity of a mentally impaired patient who is consenting to sterilisation. Such a cynic might also fear that the small number of sterilisation cases reaching the court might hide a much larger number of sterilisations on mentally impaired patients taking place without judicial sanction. Moral views on the appropriate stringency of restrictions are not unanimous. One American theorist has, for example, argued that seriously mentally disabled individuals who are incapable of fulfilling the responsibilities of parenthood do not have a protectable interest in procreation.[137] Others argue that sterilisation other than where it is necessary to protect the physical health of the patient is always immoral.[138]

5.3 Children

5.3.1 First person and proxy consent

In law, for most purposes a child is someone below the age of 18.[139] Children are sometimes referred to as "minors", reflecting the fact that they have yet to attain the age of majority. Consent for the treatment of a child can be given by

(a) a child who is 16–17;[140]

(b) a child under 16 who has "sufficient understanding and intelligence";[141] or

(c) a proxy (anyone with "parental responsibility" or the court).

Notice that in addition to the capacity of some children to consent, the law provides for proxy (parental and court) consent on behalf of a child (i.e. proxy capacity). The legal lacuna that existed with regard to incapacitated adults, did not exist with regard to children. The role of the doctrine of necessity was therefore restricted to emergency treatment. Where treatment was needed to avert an *immediate and irreversible* threat to the patient's life or health, the doctrine of necessity could be invoked to render lawful treatment without consent.[142]

Readers will remember that the Mental Capacity Act 2005 now applies to anyone who is at least 16 and fails to satisfy the Act's two-stage capacity test. This means that a health professional dealing with a incapacitated patient of 16 or 17 can rely on the s.5 general legal authority *whether or not it is an emergency or they have parental consent*.[143] They must, of course, follow the Act's principles

---

[137] See Scott 1986, esp.832–833.
[138] See the discussion of the position of the Catholic Church in Mason and Laurie 2006, 130.
[139] See e.g. Children Act 1989 s.105(1).
[140] Family Law Reform Act 1969 s.8(1).
[141] *Gillick v West Norfolk and Wisbech AHA* [1986] A.C. 112.
[142] [1986] A.C. 112 at 138, 181–182, 189, 200, 204.
[143] See Department for Constitutional Affairs 2007, ch.12 (esp. paras 12.16–12.22).

and act in the patient's best interest. Since the decision-maker must, where practical and appropriate, consult anyone engaged in caring for the patient or interested in his welfare (s.4(7)), they should usually consult anyone with parental responsibility for the child.

Children with capacity to validly consent (to whom the 2005 Act does not apply) do not automatically have the capacity to validly refuse treatment. The court or anyone with parental responsibility can consent even in the face of a refusal from a competent child.[144] Lord Donaldson once suggested a "keyholder" analogy, whereby there are two "consent keys", one held by the parents and the other by the child, both of which are capable of unlocking the door to treatment.[145] In a later case, however, he rejected this analogy because a key can also lock the door.[146] He thus suggested a "flak jacket" analogy whereby the consent of either the parent or the child will act as a flak jacket protecting the medical profession from liability. On this approach, consent is no longer viewed purely in terms of protecting the child's autonomy or ability to exercise his rights, but as protecting the doctor from a charge of assault or a claim in trespass. The child's welfare (beneficence) is thereby considered to outweigh the child's decision-making freedom (autonomy).

5.3.1.1 Parental consent and parental responsibility

Parental responsibility is defined by s.3(1) of the Children Act 1989 to mean "all the rights, duties, powers, responsibilities and authority which by law a parent has in relation to the child and his property". This includes the capacity to consent to medical treatment on behalf of a child.[147] Under s.2(5), more than one person can have personal responsibility. The child's *mother* will automatically gain parental responsibility at birth (s.2). The child's *father* will have parental responsibility if he is married to the mother at the time of the birth (s.2(1)). Alternatively, the father can gain parental responsibility if he jointly registers the child's birth, makes a "parental responsibility agreement" with the mother, or is granted it by a court order (s.4(1)). Parental responsibility can also be obtained by a person appointed as the child's guardian (s.5(6)), a person who obtains a residence order (s.12(2)), a local authority receiving a care order (s.33(3)(b)), and by a local authority that has obtained an emergency protection order (s.44(4)(c)).

Where more than one person has parental responsibility for a child, the consent of one will usually be sufficient (s.2(7)). There are, however, a small number of important decisions that should not be carried out where those with parental responsibility disagree unless specific approval has been given by the courts, such as sterilisation, change of surname, male circumcision, and immunisation.[148]

---

[144] *Re R* [1991] 4 All E.R. 177 and *Re W* [1993] Fam. 64.
[145] *Re R* [1991] 4 All E.R. 177 at 183.
[146] *Re W* [1993] Fam. 64 at 78.
[147] See e.g. *Re Z* [1997] Fam. 1 at 26.
[148] See e.g. *Re C* [2003] EWCA Civ 1148, paras 15–17.

There is no case law addressing the situation in which the person with parental responsibility would lack capacity to consent to the treatment in question being administered to themselves on the basis of age or mental impairment, i.e. situations where the parent lacks first person capacity. Imagine that, as a result of an accident, a mother and her child both require the same (non-emergency) treatment, but the mother lacks capacity to consent to her own treatment. In my view, she would not be able to consent on behalf of her child. In other words, absence of first person capacity prevents the parent exercising proxy capacity. Any other approach (such as one extending the "flak jacket" analogy) would make a mockery of the need to obtain consent for the treatment of a child. The only sensible exception would be where the reason why the mother lacks first person capacity does not apply when she is making a proxy decision, such as where her clouded judgment prevents her understanding her own diagnosis/prognosis but not that of her child.

5.3.1.2 Judicial consent

The court can make proxy decisions under its inherent (*parens patriae*) jurisdiction, wardship, or s.8 of the Children Act 1989. These powers are very similar. The Crown's *parens patriae* jurisdiction to protect and make decisions on behalf of children is exercised by the High Court as part of its inherent jurisdiction and can be exercised by means of wardship. The only difference between wardship and the exercise of the inherent jurisdiction without invoking wardship is that the court continues to control the care of a ward of court.[149] The court's consent must be obtained before any "important" or "major" step is taken in the life of a ward.[150]

Section 8 of the Children Act 1989 grants the court the power to make a "prohibited steps order" or a "specific issue order". A prohibited steps order will prevent a specific treatment or step taking place, whereas a specific issue order will determine the legality of a specific treatment or issue. Under s.1(1), the court must always take the child's welfare as its paramount consideration. When considering a s.8 order, the court must have regard to the s.1(3) checklist. In particular, the court must take account of the wishes and feelings of the child (considered in the light of his age and understanding), his physical and emotional needs, and any harm which he has suffered or is at risk of suffering.

5.3.2 The competent child

5.3.2.1 The law

Section 8(1) of the Family Law Reform Act 1969 states that the consent of a 16 or 17-year- to "any surgical, medical or dental treatment" is as effective as that of an adult. The adult capacity test is laid down by the Mental Capacity Act

---

[149] See Munby 2004, 227–228.
[150] See e.g. *Re J* [1991] Fam. 33 at 49, and *Re W* [1993] Fam. 64 at 73.

2005. Section 2(3) of the 2005 Act explicitly states that a lack of capacity cannot be established merely by reference to a person's age or appearance. (This provision was included to address concerns about discrimination against the elderly and people with disabilities, but has evident relevance for children.) In sum, the consent of a child of 16 or 17 who satisfies the 2005 Act's two-stage capacity test will be as valid as that of someone over 18.

Both the Family Law Reform Act and silent on the capacity of children below the age of 16. This was addressed in the famous *Gillick* case.[151] The *Gillick* case was a judicial review action brought by the mother of five daughters aged under 16. Mrs Gillick challenged a Department of Health circular that stated that a doctor could prescribe contraceptives to a girl under 16 without the consent or knowledge of her parents. The majority of the House of Lords held that the circular was lawful. A child under 16 could have the capacity to consent if, in the words of Lord Scarman, the child has "sufficient understanding and intelligence to enable him or her to understand fully what is proposed".[152] Lords Scarman, Fraser, and Bridge were prepared to accept that a mature child under 16 could consent to contraception; Lords Templeman and Brandon were not. In the words of Lord Templeman, "there are many things which a girl under 16 needs to practise but sex is not one of them".[153] One way of reading is to take the view that, from the start, there was a debate about whether the *Gillick* test was to be a test of competence or capacity detachable from competence.

The "*Gillick* test" (or "Gillick competence" test) turns on the child's understanding and intelligence.[154] It follows that a mature adolescent could have the capacity to consent to some treatments but not others. Lord Fraser suggested that a child would usually be able to consent to the medical examination of a trivial injury or the setting of a broken arm.[155] Lord Templeman was prepared to accept that an intelligent 15-year-old could consent to a tonsillectomy or even an appendectomy.[156] Their Lordships did not, however, entirely agree on what exactly the child must be able to understand. Lord Scarman expressed the view that the child must fully understand what is proposed including "moral and family questions" and their emotional implications, whereas Lord Fraser only required the child to understand the doctor's advice.[157] The adult test of capacity, as considered above, requires the patient to be able to understand the proposed treatment, non-treatment, and the likely consequences of both (s.3(4), 2005 Act). Lord Scarman's view therefore requires much more of a child than would be required of an adult.

Does *Gillick* imply that a mature adolescent can validly refuse treatment in the face of parental consent? Lord Scarman had expressed the view that "the

---

[151] *Gillick v West Norfolk and Wisbech AHA* [1986] A.C. 112.
[152] [1986] A.C. 112, 189. See also [1986] A.C. 112 at 169, 187, 195, and 201.
[153] [1986] A.C. 112 at 201.
[154] There is a myth that Mrs Gillick has objected to the association of her name with this test: see Wheeler 2006.
[155] [1986] A.C. 112 at 169.
[156] [1986] A.C. 112 at 201.
[157] [1986] A.C. 112 at 189 and 174; respectively.

parental right to determine whether or not their . . . child below the age of 16 will have medical treatment *terminates* if and when the child" satisfied the *Gillick* test.[158] This suggests that when he later said that parental rights "do not wholly disappear until the age of majority", he was referring to parental rights with regard to children who do not satisfy the *Gillick* test.[159] None of their Lordships expressly addressed the capacity to refuse, but it was natural to assume that there was symmetry between the capacity to consent and refuse. To respect only one decision-making outcome would make respect for autonomy contingent and artificial. It would prioritise the child's welfare over the child's autonomy. Yet, this was the view taken in two subsequent cases.

In the first, *Re R*, the 15-year-old girl had a fluctuating mental state.[160] When lucid, she refused the anti-psychotic drugs that were considered necessary to prevent her returning to a psychotic state. The local authority commenced wardship proceedings to obtain authorisation to administer anti-psychotic drugs against her will. The Court of Appeal ruled that R lacked capacity, because she did not satisfy the *Gillick* test and, obiter, the court could consent on behalf of a "*Gillick* competent" child in the exercise of its wardship jurisdiction. Some commentators have suggested that R would also have failed the adult capacity test,[161] others have expressed doubt.[162] Was R able to understand, retain, and weigh the information during her periods of lucidity? The consultant child psychiatrist involved in her care said of her, during one of those periods: "She is of sufficient maturity and understanding to comprehend the treatment being recommended and is currently rational".[163] Whether or not R was actually competent, the *Gillick* test was set at a higher level than the adult capacity test.[164] It was said that a child of fluctuating competence could not be considered to satisfy the *Gillick* test.[165] The Court of Appeal went on to hold that the court's wardship powers can be used to override a "*Gillick* competent" child's consent or refusal. Lord Donaldson went further and declared that parental consent could also override the refusal of a child who satisfied the *Gillick* test. His view was not that much more caution is required for a child when determining competence than with an adult (which could be compatible with weak-risk relativity), but that the refusal of a *competent* child is not determinate (which presupposes strong risk-relativity).[166]

In *Re W*, a local authority caring for a 16-year-old girl with anorexia nervosa sought court authorisation to override her refusal of consent to transfer her to a specialist unit for treatment. Despite considering W to be competent, Thorpe J. provided the authorisation under the court's inherent jurisdiction. His decision was upheld on appeal. The Court of Appeal considered s.8 of the Family Law Reform Act 1969 to allow doctors to rely on the consent of competent children

---

[158] [1986] A.C. 112 at 189–190 (my emphasis).
[159] [1986] A.C. 112 at 184–185.
[160] [1991] 4 All ER 177.
[161] See Brazier and Bridge 1996, 95; Brazier and Cave 2007, 405; and Hagger 2003, 29.
[162] See Grubb 1993, 56–59, Bainham 1992, 200, and Morris 1999, 254.
[163] [1991] 4 All ER 177 at 181.
[164] See Bainham 1992, 200 and Morris 1999, 255.
[165] [1991] 4 All E.R. 177 at 186.
[166] See the discussion of strong v weak risk-relativity above (5.2.1.3).

aged 16 or 17, but not to grant such children the capacity to refuse. Not only was the court considered to have the power to override the refusal of any child, but those with parental responsibility were also considered to have such decision-making authority. A refusal would still be a "very important consideration" and its importance was considered to increase with the child's age and maturity.[167] Some muddying of the waters is, however, created by the fact that Lord Donaldson doubted, obiter, whether W was competent. Both Lord Donaldson and Balcombe L.J. noted that "it is a feature of anorexia nervosa that it is capable of destroying the ability to make an informed choice".[168] If the court had genuine doubts about W's competence, it could be considered to have missed the opportunity to rely on weak rather than strong risk-relativity and hold that a competent refusal would be valid but we should be particularly cautious when determining whether a child is competent.

Re W has been subject to extensive criticism.[169] Their Lordships referred to the possibility that doctors could rely on parental consent to impose an abortion despite the refusal of a child. Lord Donaldson conceded that that was "possible as a matter of law" but thought that "medical ethics" (and here meant professional ethics) rendered this unlikely, Balcombe L.J. simply rejected this as "highly unlikely" to occur in practice, and Nolan L.J. expressed the view that the court should always be involved in such cases.[170] It is a startling possibility when one considers that the 17-year-old girl could be married but still lack the legal authority to refuse such treatment. In practice, the only direct case law on the performance of an abortion on a child was a case where the court held a 15-year-old schoolgirl to have the capacity to consent to an abortion against the wishes of her mother.[171] Also, the language used by Balcombe L.J. and Nolan L.J. suggests that the power to override a competent child's refusal is limited to situations where the treatment is necessary to prevent death or serious, irreversible harm.[172]

On many occasions the courts have overridden the views of teenagers attempting to refuse life-sustaining treatment, often against a background of fervent religious belief. Three cases are especially worthy of note.[173] In Re E, a devout Jehovah's Witness who was just under 16 was considered to have insufficient understanding of the implications of refusing a blood transfusion. He had consented to an alternative form of treatment (said to have a 40 to 50 per cent chance of success) but had refused treatment involving a blood transfusion on the basis that this was incompatible with his religious beliefs (said to have an 80 to 90 per cent chance of success). Ward J. overruled the boy's refusal on the basis that he did not fully understanding the implications of that refusal. He

---

[167] [1993] Fam. 64 at 84.
[168] [1993] Fam. 64 at 81, 84. In a number of subsequent cases, anorexics to whom the Mental Health Act 1983 has been held to apply have be said (obiter) to lack capacity under the Re C test: South West Hertfordshire HA v B [1994] 2 F.C.R. 1051, Re KB (1994) 19 B.M.L.R. 144. See further Lewis 1999.
[169] See e.g. Kennedy 1993.
[170] [1993] Fam. 64 at 79, 90, 94.
[171] Re P [1986] 1 F.L.R. 272.
[172] [1993] Fam. 64 at 88, 94.
[173] Re E [1993] 1 F.L.R. 386, Re L [1998] 2 F.L.R. 810, and Re M [1999] 2 F.L.R. 1097.

died after validly refusing blood transfusions when he reached the age of 18, though it is difficult to believe that any dramatic non-legal change took place on his 18th birthday. In *Re L*, a 14-year-old Jehovah's Witness who had been severely scalded after falling into a hot bath during an epileptic attack had refused to consent to life-sustaining blood transfusions. Sir Stephen Brown authorised the transfusions, holding that L was "certainly not '*Gillick* competent' in the context of all the necessary details which it would be appropriate for her to be able to form a view about".[174] The judge asked whether the patient *actually* understood (rather than was capable of understanding) the consequences of her refusal, which gave her an impossible threshold to reach as she had not actually been told what would happen if she wasn't treated.[175] Despite considering L to be "for her age mature", the judge relied on her "sheltered life" and "limited experience of life", which appear to be ways of depriving her of capacity because of her age.[176] In *Re M*, Johnson J. overrode a 15-year-old's refusal of consent to a heart transplant, without considering it necessary to determine whether or not the girl satisfied the *Gillick* criteria. There is some suggestion that he did in fact consider her able to satisfy the *Gillick* test, because he stated that M could have potentially given a valid *consent*.[177] It is likely, however, that had he expressly addressed the matter, the judge would have decided that she lacked this ability. The judge had noted that the girl had "not been able to come to terms with her situation" and was insisting that she did not want to die.[178]

5.3.2.2 Legal evolution and ethical views

The existing common law view on the capacity of mature children to refuse treatment could, in an appropriate case, be subject to two types of legal challenge. *First*, while the undermining of *Gillick* by the Court of Appeal in *Re W* now binds any court below the House of Lords, it is still open for challenge in the House of Lords itself. *Second*, the existing common law could not stand if it were shown to be incompatible with the Convention rights as given effect by the HRA 1998. It has been argued that the denial of capacity to a *competent* adolescent or even a failure to properly assess or take account of competence could violate the child's Convention rights.[179] Potentially relevant Convention rights include the right not be subject to inhuman and degrading treatment (art.3), not to be deprived of liberty and security of person (art.5), to private and family life (art.8), to have freedom of religion (art.9) and the right not be discriminated against in the enjoyment of any other Convention right (art.14). While not all the Strasbourg jurisprudence is encouraging,[180] it is well-established that the

---

[174] [1998] 2 F.L.R. 810 at 813.
[175] See Grubb 1999, 59–60.
[176] [1998] 2 F.L.R. 810 at 812, 813.
[177] [1999] 2 F.L.R. 1097 at 1097. See the discussion of this point in Morris 1999, 259.
[178] [1999] 2 F.L.R. 1097 at 1100.
[179] See Garwood-Gowers 2001 and Hagger 2003.
[180] See e.g. *Keenan v UK* (2001) 33 E.H.R.R. 38 (on art.3) and *Nielsen v Denmark* (1989) 11 E.H.R.R. 175 (on art.5).

Convention is a "living instrument" that is to be interpreted in the light of evolving social standards. Article 14 could bolster the impact of arts 3, 5, 8, and 9, insofar as the current law discriminates between competent patients on the basis of their age.

The current common law approach to capacity with regard to children is not simply *competence*-based. It takes account of the child's age and the decision reached, and could therefore also be described as *status*-based and *outcome*-based. Before 16 a patient is presumed to lack capacity, whereas after 16 a patient is presumed to possess capacity (to consent, if not to refuse). Before 18 a competent patient cannot validly refuse treatment to which a proxy has consented, whereas after 18 even the court will not overrule a competent patient's refusal.

Rights-based views will be antagonistic to this approach. The practical difficulties presented by an individualised approach to capacity could lead rights-based theories to accept an age-based blanket approach with regard to decisions that affect the rights of others (such as voting), but not with regard to decisions that do not so affect the rights of others (such as consent and refusal of treatment).[181] Properly applied weak risk-relativity can deal with genuine hard cases without completely undermining the protection of adolescent autonomy. Preference utilitarians would also be prima facie antagonistic to denying legal authority to the treatment preferences of competent children,[182] but could allow such restriction if it could be said to maximise utility. One key disutility of generally overriding the refusals of competent adults, the likelihood that this would discourage competent adults from seeking medical treatment in the first place, has less force in the case of a competent child in parental care. The practical difficulties of individualising capacity and assessing the competence of every patient are the same whether the patient is an adult or a child. Overriding the views of some competent children is consistent with those duty-based approaches that prioritise duties of beneficence over duties to protect autonomy and those virtue-ethics approaches that emphasise the caring motives of those seeking to protect competent children from their own decisions. Compromise positions span the range here. Communitarians will uphold the values of the community and will typically attach great importance to the family and parental decision-making. In the end, it all boils down to how much weight is given to a child's autonomy, the hallmark of which has been said to be "the right to be wrong".[183]

5.3.3 The incompetent child

While an incompetent child cannot make a legally valid treatment decision, those with parental responsibility can consent on their behalf. A child over 16 who fails to satisfy the two-stage capacity test in the Mental Capacity Act 2005

---

[181] See Beyleveld and Brownsword 2001, 132–134.
[182] See e.g. Harris 2003b.
[183] Brazier and Bridge 1996, 88.

can also be treated under the general legal authority provision. This means that some disputes concerning the treatment of a young patient can be heard by either a court dealing with family proceedings (the Family Division of the High Court) or the Court of Protection.[184]

All types of decision-making power must be exercised in the child's interests. With regard to parental proxy capacity, Lord Scarman in *Gillick* declared that the "parental right must be exercised in accordance with the welfare principle and can be challenged, even overridden, if it be not".[185] It follows that a court ruling should be sought where there is disagreement over a child's best interests. Such disagreement could be between the parents and the doctors treating their child, or between the parents. Before examining these situations, some general comments should be made about the limits of parental decision-making authority.

5.3.3.1 The limits of parental capacity

Any procedure performed to address a pressing therapeutic need will be readily within parental proxy decision-making authority or, in an emergency, within the remit of the doctrine of necessity. So-called therapeutic sterilisation of a child would, for example, fall within the category.[186] Even apparently "cosmetic" procedures appear to fall within parental capacity as long as they can properly be considered to be in the child's interests. Ear pinning (designed to address "sticky out" ears) and limb-lengthening procedures (designed to increase the patient's height) are, for example, widely considered to be lawful if performed with parental consent as means of preventing deterioration in a child's mental health. There is controversy over those procedures that are performed without any medical indication and, a fortiori, over those procedures that could be considered to be against the medical interests of the child. Consider, for example, ritual male circumcision (addressed below: 5.3.3.3), organ and tissue transplantation (addressed in Chs 13 and13), non-therapeutic research (addressed in Ch.11), and cosmetic facial surgery for those with Down's syndrome.[187]

As a general rule, parental authority is constrained by the child's best interests. There is, however, some authority to suggest that it could sometimes be lawful to rely on a less stringent test, requiring only that the procedure not be against the interests of the child. This test stems from a case that is now over three decades old: *S v S*.[188] This case was a conjoined appeal concerning the refusal of two mothers to allow their ex-husbands to paternity test their children during divorce proceedings. The House of Lords declared that the blood tests were lawful if they were not "against the interests" of the child because of the public interest in justice being done and the minimal harm to the child.

---

[184] See Department for Constitutional Affairs 2007, para.8.6.
[185] [1986] A.C. 112 at 184.
[186] *Re E* [1991] 2 F.L.R. 585.
[187] See Jones 2000.
[188] [1972] A.C. 24.

According to Lord Reid, "a reasonable parent would have some regard to the general public interest and would not refuse a blood *test unless he thought that would clearly be against the interests of the child*".[189] Lord MacDermott, expressing himself in similar terms, said that unless it "would prejudicially affect the health of the infant" the blood test could lawfully be performed, as there is no need to show "that the outcome thereof will be for the benefit of the infant".[190] Paternity tests are now covered by legislation.[191] There are two plausible views on the ambit of the general principle relied on in this case: (a) it only applies to paternity testing and other interventions designed to ensure a fair hearing before a court; or (b) it is capable of applying to other non-therapeutic interventions (such as male circumcision or medical research). The first view is much easier to reconcile with the case law addressing procedures performed on children. Applying a test less stringent than the child's best interests would mean that children would be granted less protection than incapacitated adults under the Mental Capacity Act. In any event, it is clear that if an application is made to the court it will overrule any parental decision that is not considered to be in the child's *best interests*.[192]

5.3.3.2 *Disagreement between the parents and the medical profession*

Parents and doctors can disagree over a child's best interests in two situations: (1) where the parents wish treatment to be administered against the doctors' view of the child's best interests and (2) where the parents refuse to consent to treatment against the doctors' view of the child's best interests. As explained in the last chapter, in situation (1) the courts will not require an individual doctor to administer treatment against his clinical judgment.[193] In both situations, any court asked for a ruling will seek to give effect to the best interests of the child. This section will examine three illustrative cases. Others will be considered in the chapters on end of life decisions.[194]

In *Ex p. Glass*, the relatives of a severely disabled 12-year-old boy, David, wished him to receive whatever treatment was necessary to prolong his life following a respiratory tract infection.[195] The doctors apparently decided that this was not in his best interests. They administered diamorphine (which depresses respiratory function) against his mother's wishes. Without consulting his mother, they also amended David's medical notes to indicate that he was not to be resuscitated in the event of further problems—what is now known as a DNAR (Do Not Attempt Resuscitation) order was put on David's notes. The family forcibly intervened to resuscitate David, took him

---

[189] [1972] A.C. 24 at 44 (my emphasis). Lord Guest agreed entirely with Lord Reid.
[190] [1972] A.C. 24 at 48 and 51.
[191] Family Law Reform Act 1969 s.21 (as amended by the Mental Capacity Act 2005).
[192] See e.g. *Re B* [1990] 3 All E.R. 927, *Re T* [1997] 1 All ER 906, and *Wyatt v Portsmouth Hospital NHS* [2005] EWCA Civ 1181.
[193] See Ch.4 (4.2). They will also be reluctant to challenge resource allocation decisions, see Ch.2 (2.4.1.1).
[194] See, in particular, Ch.15 on the selective treatment of infants (15.5.2.1) and the separation of conjoined twins against the wishes of the patents (15.5.3).
[195] *R v Portsmouth Hospitals NHS Trust Ex p. Glass* [1999] 2 F.L.R. 905.

home, and he was successfully treated by the family doctor. The Trust then wrote to the family to notify them that they could no longer offer life-prolonging treatment to David and explained that any future care should occur at another hospital that was located nearby. The mother applied for judicial review of the Trust's decisions relating to David's care, but the Court of Appeal refused to rule in advance on David's future treatment. It was, however, emphasised that any future disagreement should be brought to court. The case was then brought before the European Court of Human Rights.[196] The European Court of Human Rights held that the administration of diamorphine against the wishes of David's mother, who was his legal proxy, had breached David's art.8 right to respect for his private life, specifically his right to physical integrity.[197] Further, the Court considered that no satisfactory explanation had been given to explain why the Trust had not sought a declaration from the High Court and ruled that the onus had been on the Trust to defuse the situation.[198] Thus, a failure to respect parental views on the best interests of the child can breach art.8 and hospitals should bring disputes with parents before the court.

In cases that have been brought to court, the courts have shown considerable reluctance to reject medical opinion, even where the contested treatment is necessary to prolong the child's life.[199] Yet, the doctors do not always get it right. In *Glass*, one of the judges in the European Court noted that David was still alive six years after the incident, so in that case at least "maternal instinct has had more weight than medical opinion".[200] In 2004, he celebrated his 18th birthday.[201]

The opposite situation, where the doctors wish to administer life-saving treatment against the wishes of the parents, occurred in *Re B* and *Re T*.[202] *Re B* concerned an infant with Down's syndrome complicated by an intestinal obstruction that was likely to be fatal if left untreated. The parents refused to consent to the surgery as they took the view that it would be kinder to let the child die. The High Court refused to authorise the procedure against the wishes of the parents. Later that day, the Court of Appeal reversed the judge's decision, holding that the surgery was in the child's best interests. *Re T* concerned an infant with a life-threatening liver defect. He had previously endured an unsuccessful operation and the unanimous medical opinion was that he should be given a liver transplant. His mother refused to consent to the operation, emphasising the pain and suffering that he had endured following the last operation. An opportunity for a transplant was lost after they moved out of the jurisdiction to join the child's father who worked abroad. The local authority applied to the court for permission to carry out the operation and for the child to be

---

[196] *Glass v UK* [2004] 1 F.L.R. 1019.

[197] [2004] 1 F.L.R. 1019, para.70.

[198] [2004] 1 F.L.R. 1019, para.79.

[199] Recently, see *Re L* [2004] EWHC 2713 (mechanical ventilation) and *Wyatt v Portsmouth NHS Trust* [2005] EWCA Civ 1181 (aggressive treatment).

[200] (2004) 39 E.H.R.R. 15 at 364 (Separate Opinion of Judge Casadevall).

[201] See Dyer 2004c.

[202] *Re B* [1990] 3 All E.R. 927 and *Re T* [1997] 1 All ER 906.

returned to the jurisdiction. The Court of Appeal held that it was not in the best interests of the child for the operation to take place against the wishes of the mother. (The mother is believed to have reconsidered her decision and consented to the liver transplant.)[203]

Re T represents a rare example of the court apparently rejecting medical opinion. Even here, however, the court placed great reliance on the evidence of one of the treating physicians to the effect that the total commitment of the caring parent was crucial to the success of the treatment.[204] There were also a number of unusual factors. *First,* the parents were health professionals.[205] *Second,* the child had already undergone an unsuccessful operation, which had caused him considerable pain and distress.[206] *Third,* they were living abroad (in a "distant Commonwealth country") and would have to have brought their child back to the UK for the transplant.[207]

Emphasising the clinical significance of the mother's objections, Butler-Sloss L.J. went so far as to declare that the mother and child were one for the purpose of this case.[208] This conflation of the interests of the mother and child comes dangerously close to taking direct account of the mother's interests (as an *overall interests approach* would do) while claiming to focus entirely on the patient's interests (as the *best interests approach* should do). Butler-Sloss L.J. sought to distinguish this case from *Re B* on the grounds that,

> Unlike the intestinal obstruction of the Down's syndrome baby which could be cured by a single operation, T's problems require complicated surgery and many years of special care from the mother.[209]

Many commentators remain unconvinced.[210] Long-term special care was required for both children and in both cases the operation was necessary to save the child's life. In any event, the application of the best interests test is factually specific and *Re T* is clearly factually unique.

In every other case the courts have overridden parental refusals where the child's life or health will be put at risk if the proposed treatment is not administered. In *Re C*, for example, a mother's refusal to allow her child to be tested for HIV was overridden, despite her genuine belief that conventional views on the causes and treatment of HIV were wrong and against her child's best interests.[211] Similarly in *A NHS Trust v A*, Holman J. rejected the parent's refusal to allow a bone transplant on the basis that the child had suffered enough, the proposed treatment offered only a 50 per cent chance of a lasting cure, and they had (religious) faith that God would cure the child.[212] The medical opinion was

---

[203] See Dyer 2004d.
[204] [1997] 1 All ER 906 at 914–915, 917, 919.
[205] [1997] 1 All ER 906 at 908, 918.
[206] [1997] 1 All ER 906 at 908.
[207] [1997] 1 All ER 906 at 908, 915, 919.
[208] [1997] 1 All ER 906 at 914.
[209] [1997] 1 All ER 906 at 915.
[210] See Michalowski 1997, 183–184 and Fox and McHale, 703–704.
[211] *Re C (HIV Test)* [1999] 2 F.L.R. 1004.
[212] [2007] EWHC 1696.

firmly in support of the treatment on the basis that without the treatment it was "medically certain" that she would die within a year at most and the chance that the treatment itself would directly kill her was only around 10 per cent. These are mere examples, other are examined in Ch.15. In law, not only are parental wishes not decisive, the courts tend to support medical opinion over parental wishes.

5.3.3.3 Disagreement between the parents

Those with parental responsibility do not always agree on whether a proposed procedure is in the best interests of a child. Two high-profile disputes have concerned immunisation and male circumcision.[213] In *Re C*, the Court of Appeal supported the immunisation of two children at the request of their fathers in the face of objection from their mothers. In *Re J*, the Court of Appeal supported the mother's objection to the circumcision of a child against the religious-based views of his father. Both cases turn on their facts. Non-medical factors potentially play a much larger role with regard to circumcision than with regard to immunisation. The complexities of parental disagreement are well illustrated by this practice and its controversy is such that it is particularly worthy of further discussion.

Ritual circumcision is usually irreversible and involves the deliberate modification or excision of the genitalia for reasons other than therapeutic need. Where the patient is female, this is viewed as contrary to public policy and prohibited by legislation.[214] Ritual male circumcision (which is just about always a less invasive procedure) is not so prohibited and is routinely performed where both parents consent and a willing medical practitioner can be found.[215]

Re J was decided on a relatively straightforward application of the best interests test following the father's application for a specific issue order under s.8 of the Children Act. The child's mother was a non-practising Christian who was unwilling to support the wishes of the child's non-practising Muslim father. The outcome was not surprising given that the child was likely to have an essentially secular upbringing, circumcision is an irreversible procedure carrying risks, there was no medical indication for circumcision, and the mother was the primary carer. Under the HRA 1998, the potential engagement of the art.9(1) right to freedom of religion is now directly relevant, at least where a child is actively being brought up in a religion for which circumcision is usual or required. This right is, however, subject to limitation in art.9(2) where prescribed by law and necessary in a democratic society to protect health.

---

[213] *Re C* [2003] EWCA Civ 1148 and *Re J* [1999] 2 F.L.R. 678.

[214] It is a criminal offence to modify the genitalia of a female where this is not necessary for her physical or mental health or connected with her giving birth to a child: Female Genital Mutilation Act 2003 s.1. Such activities can also have professional disciplinary consequences: see Dyer 2001.

[215] See the guidance of the GMC (2008a, paras 12–16) and the BMA (2003 and 2006). For discussion of the controversy of the practice cf. Hinchley 2007 and Patrick 2007.

While there is evidence that circumcision has protective effects against certain infections and diseases, these could be replicable by less invasive measures.[216] In rare instances, circumcision has been reported to lead to fatal and near fatal complications, and sexual dysfunction in later life.[217] Ritual male circumcision is irreversible, or almost irreversible, and in this respect differs only in degree from ear piercing, tattooing, liposuction, indoctrination of children with belief systems, or female circumcision.[218] It could be performed in later life when the subject is able to consent and able to benefit from any positive effects of circumcision. On the other hand, it is an intimate and valued part of some religious and cultural traditions, its performance in later life will require surgery under general anaesthetic, and interference with parental values can be socially divisive. Consequently, there is a range of moral views on this issue. Different theories will attach different weight to the dangers of driving the practice underground, reinforcing the practice, alienating religious and cultural traditions, allowing avoidable complications, and removing future options from the subject. Feinberg has, for example, argued for a "right to an open future" that could be considered relevant here.[219] The problem with the best interest test is that it cloaks these underlying theoretical tensions in vague language and, indeed, its application to ritual circumcision has been inconsistent with its application to other medically unnecessary irreversible procedures.

In a more recent case, *Re S*, the performance of ritual circumcision on a child was once again held not to be in the best interests of that child.[220] The parents were divided. The eight-year-old boy had been brought up according to the tenets of the father's Jain faith. Upon separation of the parents, the mother applied to have him circumcised and (along with his sister) converted to her Muslim faith. This was opposed by the child's father. Baron J., in a judgment that was upheld on appeal, ruled that:

> Circumcision once done cannot be undone. It may have an effect on K if he wishes to practice Jainism when he grows up. He has been ambivalent about his religion and is not old enough to decide or understand the long-term implications. It is not in his best interests to be circumcised at present. The Muslim religion, whilst favouring circumcision at 10 years and below, does permit of an upper age limit of puberty or later on conversion. By the date of puberty K would be *Gillick* competent and so he could make an informed decision.[221]

This conclusion will be supported by all those opposed to the imposition of irreversible and medically unnecessary surgery on incompetent minors.[222]

---

[216] See Hutson 2003, WHO 2007, and Kalichman et al. 2007.

[217] See Hutson 2003.

[218] One form of female circumcision could be considered comparable to male circumcision: Bibbings 1995, 151.

[219] Feinberg 1980.

[220] *Re S (Children)* [2004] EWHC 1282, upheld by the Court of Appeal: [2004] EWCA Civ 1257.

[221] [2004] EWHC 1282, para.83(k).

[222] See further the discussion in Fox and Thomas 2009.

5.4 When to involve the court

At varying points in this chapter references have been made to the possibility of obtaining a court ruling or declaration. Court involvement is pointless and unnecessary in the vast majority of clinical circumstances. There is, for example, no point in involving the courts where treatment is refused by an adult patient who clearly has capacity.[223] The courts have, however, recognised that some medical procedures, or conflicting views, should be brought before a court. In virtually all cases this was viewed "as a matter of good practice", rather than as a legal requirement.

We have seen that, since *Re F*, the declaratory procedure has been important in the development of the law on the treatment of incapacitated adults.[224] A declaration merely "declares" what the legal position is, it does not change it, so what is declared legal by a declaration would have been legal without it. This was the conclusion of the House of Lords in *Re F*[225] and in the later *Bland* case.[226] In *Re F*, the majority of their Lordships ruled that the sterilisation of an incapacitated woman did not strictly require the involvement of the court, but it was "nevertheless highly desirable as a matter of good practice".[227] (Lord Griffith dissented, holding that court approval should be required as a matter of law.)[228] In *Bland*, their Lordships held that, until a body of experience and practice built up, an application should be made to the High Court before nutrition and hydration is withdrawn from a patient in a permanent vegetative state (PVS).[229] While not all their Lordships were explicit on this, use of the declaratory procedure was viewed as highly advisable, not as a legal requirement. The justification for judicial involvement, offered by Sir Thomas Bingham in the Court of Appeal and approved by the Law Lords, was "the protection of patients, the protection of doctors, the reassurance of patients' families and the reassurance of the public".[230] The Official Solicitor has formally recognised the need for judicial sanction in such circumstances.[231] A similar approach has been adopted with regard to children.[232] Where, however, a child is already a ward of court, judicial sanction is a legal requirement, because the court's consent must be obtained before any "important" or "major" step in the life of a ward of court.[233]

---

[223] *Re JT* [1998] 1 F.L.R. 48 at 51–52, and *St George's Healthcare NHS Trust v S* [1999] Fam. 26 at 63.
[224] [1990] 2 A.C. 1.
[225] [1990] 2 A.C. 1, esp. 63–64 (Lord Brandon).
[226] [1993] A.C. 789, esp. 876 (Lord Lowry) and 889–890 (Lord Mustill).
[227] [1990] 2 A.C. 1 at 57 (Lord Brandon).
[228] [1990] 2 A.C. 1 at 70.
[229] See further Ch.15 (15.5.1).
[230] [1990] 2 A.C. 1 at 815 (Sir Thomas Bingham). In the House of Lords see 859 (Lord Keith) and 874 (Lord Goff).
[231] *Practice Note (Official Solicitor: Declaratory Proceedings: Medical and Welfare Decisions for Adults who Lack Capacity)* [2006] 2 F.L.R. 373. See also the practice note issued by the President of the Family Division with the approval of the Lord Chief Justice and the Lord Chancellor: *Practice Note (Incapacitated Adults: Declaratory Proceedings)* [2002] 1 All E.R. 794.
[232] See Munby 2004, 243–244.
[233] See e.g. *Re J* [1991] Fam. 33 at 49 and *Re W* [1993] Fam. 64 at 73.

There are other circumstances, in addition to withdrawing nutrition and hydration from a patient in PVS, that fall within what has been described as a "special category" of cases where obtaining judicial sanction should be obtained.[234] In such cases, an application for authorisation (in the case of a child) or a declaration (in the case of an adult) should be made even if all the parties are "united in their support of what [is] being proposed".[235] This special category covers controversial proposed interventions that cannot be viewed as necessary or emergency treatment for that patient, such as the donation of bone marrow[236] (and by implication solid organ donation).[237] It also covers situations such as those where there is a question about the capacity of a pregnant woman to refuse a Caesarean section.[238]

The courts have indicated that a prior judicial ruling should also be sought where there is disagreement between those involved. With regard to children, the court should be involved in at least those situations where there is disagreement between those with parental responsibility over whether a child should be circumcised or immunised.[239] The case of *D v An NHS Trust* considered when prior judicial sanction should be obtained for the performance of an abortion on an incapacitated adult[240]—an issue that had previously been held not to fall within the "special category" of cases where prior judicial sanction should be obtained as a matter of good practice.[241] Coleridge J. laid down guidance, which he indicated had the support of the President of the Family Division.[242] He declared that an application should be made where there is "any doubt as to either capacity or best interests", in particular, in those situations "where there is a lack of unanimity amongst the medical professionals as to the best interests of the patient" and "where the patient, members of her immediate family or the foetus' father have opposed, or expressed views inconsistent with, a termination of the pregnancy". Munby J. in *R. (Burke) v GMC* sought to modify this guidance and apply it to withholding or withdrawing artificial nutrition and hydration.[243] He considered cases where there is disagreement among those involved in the light of the decision in *Glass v UK*.[244] In that case, the Strasbourg court had held that art.8 (the right to private and family life) was violated by the failure of the hospital to seek a court ruling where the family had passionately disagreed with treatment decisions made with regard to a disabled child. Munby J. held that the effect of *Glass* was that an *obligation* arises under art.8 to refer such cases to the court,

---

[234] For use of this label, see e.g. *R. (Burke) v GMC* [2004] EWHC 1879, para.195 (Munby J.).
[235] [2004] EWHC 1879.
[236] *Re Y* [1997] Fam. 110 at 117.
[237] A view supported with regard to incapacitated adults by *Re F* [1990] 2 A.C. 1 at 52 (Lord Bridge); and with regard to children by *Re W* [1993] Fam. 64 at 79 (Lord Donaldson) and 94 (Balcombe L.J.).
[238] *Re MB* [1997] 2 F.L.R. 426.
[239] See *Re J* [1999] 2 F.C.R. 345 and *Re C* [2003] EWCA Civ 1148, respectively.
[240] [2003] EWHC 2793.
[241] *Re SG (Adult Mental Patient: Abortion)* [1991] F.L.R. 329.
[242] [2003] EWHC 2793, paras 34 and 37.
[243] [2004] EWHC 1879, paras 200–202.
[244] *Glass v UK* [2004] 1 F.L.R. 1019.

The primary significance of there being the obligation under Article 8 identified in Glass ... is that what was previously only a matter of good practice is now, by reason of the Human Rights Act 1998, a matter of legal requirement. That, it seems to me, is a significant and potentially very important change.[245]

When overturning Munby J.'s judgment, the Court of Appeal took the view that he had misinterpreted the effect of *D* and *Glass*.[246] The Court of Appeal noted that Munby J.'s declaration had "caused considerable concern" and it had been predicted that it would require approximately ten applications to the courts a day.[247] According to the Court of Appeal, the European Court of Human Rights in *Glass* had done no more than consider the implications of the doctor's conduct in the light of what it understood to be English law.[248] Accordingly, since the true effect of a declaration is merely to declare the law and not to authorise what would otherwise be unlawful, a declaration was not required as a matter of law. This was accepted by the European Court of Human Rights, when the case came before it:

> Any more stringent legal duty would be prescriptively burdensome—doctors, and emergency ward staff in particular, would be constantly in court—and would not necessarily entail any greater protection.[249]

The Court of Appeal has, in another case, given guidance on the principles and procedures applying to applications to the court when there is doubt as to a patient's capacity or best interests.[250] Section 15 of the Mental Capacity Act 2005 explicitly grants the Court of Protection the power to make declarations as to when a person has capacity and the lawfulness of any action in relation to that person. Further, the *Code of Practice* advises that serious healthcare and treatment decisions should continue to go to court in accordance with the pre-Act case law.[251]

5.5 Detaining and treating the mentally ill

As stated in the introduction, this chapter will not attempt a detailed analysis of mental health law. This section seeks to provide only a brief overview of the application of the Mental Health Act 1983, as amended by the Mental Health Act 2007. Readers with a deeper interest in that topic should therefore consult specialist works.[252]

Most of those who receive treatment for mental illness do so as out-patients.[253] Of those who receive in-patient treatment in hospital, the vast majority are

---

[245] [2004] EWHC 1879, para.210.
[246] [2005] EWCA 1003, paras 72–80.
[247] [2005] EWCA 1003, para.69.
[248] [2005] EWCA 1003, para.80.
[249] *Burke v UK* (No.19807/06, July 7, 2006).
[250] *St George's Healthcare NHS Trust v S* [1999] Fam. 26.
[251] See Department for Constitutional Affairs 2007, paras 8.18–8.24.
[252] See e.g. Bartlett and Sandland 2007, esp. ch.7.
[253] See Jackson 2006, 394.

admitted informally under s.131 of the 1983 Act. The rest are compulsorily detained or "sectioned" under ss.1–5. What is striking about the latter is that they are potentially subject to compulsory treatment under s.63, which provides an exception to the principle that a capacitated adult can refuse any treatment for any or no reason. Brief further consideration will now be given to compulsory treatment (5.5.1), compulsory detention (5.5.2), and informal admission (5.5.3).

5.5.1 Compulsory treatment

Part IV of the Act permits the compulsory treatment of those detained under its provisions. In particular, s.63 provides that a patient's consent is not required for medical treatment given for a mental disorder from which he is suffering. This only applies to "detained" patients (5.5.2) and to treatment of a "mental disorder". Significantly, it permits treatment to be administered in the face of a refusal by a patient who has capacity under the Mental Capacity Act 2005. There is no need to rely on these compulsory treatment powers where the patient has capacity under the 2005 Act and is consenting (where the normal principles of medical law apply).

Mental disorder is defined as "any disorder or disability of the mind" (s.1(2)). Neither learning disability nor alcohol/drug dependence *as such* are to be treated as mental disorders (s.1(2A)–(4)).[254] The compulsory treatment powers do not apply to treatment for physical conditions unrelated to that disorder. What amounts to treatment for mental disorder has, however, been interpreted widely to include the forced feeding of anorexic patients[255] and even (more controversially) non-consensual Caesarean surgery.[256] *Exceptions and additional safeguards* apply to some of the most controversial treatments (ss.57–58A). Section 57 lays down additional safeguards for surgical treatments that destroy brain tissue or interfere with the functioning of the brain, and hormone implants designed to reduce the male sex drive.[257] This provision stands out as applying to both detained and informal patients (s.56(1)), presumably because of the extremely invasive nature of these procedures. It restricts such procedures to situations where the patient consents and a supportive second opinion has been obtained from a panel appointed by the Care Quality Commission (s.57(2)).[258] Section 58A lays down additional requirements for electro-convulsive therapy. This requires the patient's consent or, if the patient lacks capacity, the treatment to be certified as appropriate and not conflict with a valid and

---

[254] See further the Mental Health Act Code of Practice: DH 2008a, ch.3.

[255] *Re KB (Adult) (Mental Patient: Medical Treatment)* (1994) 19 B.M.L.R. 144 and *B v Croydon Health Authority* [1995] Fam. 133.

[256] *Tameside and Glossop Acute Services Trust v CH* [1996] 1 F.L.R. 762. Note also the Act's definition of "medical treatment" in s.145(1), (4).

[257] The last procedure is specified by secondary legislation issued under s.57(1)(b): Mental Health (Hospital, Guardianship and Treatment) (England) Regulations 2008/1184, reg.27.

[258] The role of the Care Quality Commission was previously performed by the Mental Health Act Commission.

applicable advance refusal or a decision of a donee or deputy (s.58(3)–(5)). Thus, these sections prevent psychosurgery and ECT being imposed against the will of a patient with capacity. An exception is, however, made to the application of ss.57–58A for specified situations of emergency situations, such as where the treatment is immediately necessary to save the patient's life (s.62).

Compulsory treatment need not violate the patient's Convention rights. Even if prima facie degrading, it will not amount to violation of the art.3 prohibition on inhuman and degrading treatment where it is "convincingly shown" to be a "therapeutic necessity".[259] The same justification will also prevent violation of the art.8 right to private life. Despite some judicial reservations about imposing treatment on a competent patient,[260] there are cases where the English courts have ruled that the drug treatments could be imposed on a competent patient without breaching art.3 or 8.[261] Indeed, in one recent case the Court of Appeal reached the conclusion that competence is "not the critical factor in determining whether treatment can be administered without consent" and "when considering the severity of treatment the fact that it is imposed by compulsion is more significant".[262]

The most ethically controversial aspect of mental health law is undoubtedly this power to impose compulsory treatment on competent patients. The upshot is that the law allows a capacitated adult to refuse medical treatment for any or no reason at all *except* where the patient is detained and that treatment is for mental disorder. The mentally ill are thereby treated differently from others *who have the same cognitive-functional ability to make a particular decision*. The justification for this cannot rest on a paternalistic duty to protect patients from themselves (contrary to the tenets of rights-based and other moral theories rejecting the idea of duties-to-oneself), as such a rationale would apply irrespective of whether the patient is physically or mentally ill. Such a distinction, if it can be coherently defended, must therefore track the duty to protect others from harm. But is the non-consensual detention and treatment of a competent patient a justifiable means of protecting others from harm? Here we must be careful to avoid the simplistic assumption that only utilitarian or utilitarian-type reasoning could be compatible with non-consensual interventions designed to protect others. Rights-based and duty-based theories holding that individuals have rights or entitlements that cannot be overridden by the collective welfare, still accept that individual rights can be overridden by the hierarchically more important rights of others. The remaining difficulties (questions as to which rights are engaged and which win out when unavoidable conflict arises) cannot be addressed at the general level of these moral camps as outlined in Ch.1. The most that can be said is that the rights potentially infringed by the non-consensual treatment of a competent adult could only

---

[259] *Herczegfalvy v Austria* (No.10533/83) (1993) 15 E.H.R.R. 437 at 484; *R. (Wilkinson) v Broadmoor Special Hospital Authority* [2001] EWCA Civ 1545, paras 30, 77–79; and *R. (N) v M* [2002] EWCA Civ 1789, esp. para.19 (setting out a check list of seven factors to take into account).

[260] See e.g. *R. (Wilkinson) v Broadmoor Special Hospital Authority* [2001] EWCA Civ 1545, para.30 (Simon Brown L.J.). Cf. *ibid.*, para.80 (Hale L.J.).

[261] See e.g. *R (PS) v Responsible Medical Officer* [2003] EWHC 2335.

[262] *R. (B) v S* [2006] EWCA Civ 28, paras 42 and 50, respectively.

plausibly be overridden by an otherwise unpreventable, significant threat to the most important rights of others (such as the right to life).

5.5.2 Compulsory detention

A mental ill patient can be involuntarily admitted to hospital under s.2 (admission for assessment) or s.3 (admission for treatment) of the 1983 Act. Additionally, there are a number of short-term detention provisions, under which a patient can be detained for no longer than 72 hours. These *include* emergency admission (s.4) and the detention of those initially admitted to hospital informally (s.5).

The powers of compulsory treatment, examined above, apply to patients "liable to be detained" *except* those detained under the short-term detentions provisions (s.56). Thus, these powers can be applied to patients detained under ss.2 and 3, but not those detained under ss.4 and 5. These powers also apply to patients on leave of absence from hospital (under s.17) and those recalled to hospital (under s.17E) having been released under a community treatment order (s.17A).

Admission for assessment under s.2 requires the written recommendation of two medical practitioners to the effect that the patient (a) is suffering from a "mental disorder" that warrants detention in hospital, for at least a limited period and (b) ought to be so detained in the interests of his own health and safety or to protect others (s.2(2), (3)). A patient can be detained for no longer than 28 days under this provision (s.2(4)). A longer period of detention requires reliance on s.3.

Admission for treatment under s.3 requires the two written recommendations to certify that (a) the patient is suffering from a "mental disorder" that makes hospital treatment appropriate, (b) it is necessary for his health and safety or to protect others that he should receive such treatment and it cannot be provided unless he is detained under this section, and (c) appropriate medical treatment is available for him (ss.3(2), (3)). A patient can be detained under this section for up to six months at first (s.20). Upon expiry, this period can be extended for a further six months and thereafter extended for a year at a time. Thus, where the Act's conditions are satisfied, a patient could potentially be detained under s.3 for the rest of his life.

Emergency admission under s.4 requires *one* medical practitioner to confirm that (a) it is of "urgent necessity" for the patient to be admitted and detained, and (b) waiting for another medical practitioner to satisfy the requirements for admission under s.2 would cause "undesirable delay" (s.4(2), (3)). A patient can be detailed for no longer than 72 hours under this provision, after which the patient must be released unless detained under s.2 or 3 (s.4(4).

Detention of patients admitted informally under s.5 requires the medical practitioners in charge of the patient to report to hospital managers that an application for compulsory admission "ought to be made". Some nurses can also detain an informal patient under this section, but only for up to six hours or until the arrival of a medical practitioner with the power to detain the patient (s.5(4)).

5.5.3 Informal admission and the Bournewood gap

A patient who "requires treatment for mental disorder" may be admitted informally under s.131 of the 1983 Act. Notice that s.131 explicitly refers to "*treatment* for mental disorder", which has been taken to mean that it only covers admission for treatment rather than for assessment.[263] This provision applies straightforwardly where the patient has capacity and consents to admission and treatment. In fact, since s.131 does not require the informal patient's consent, it also applies to patients who lack capacity and whose acquiescence means that they do not require formal detention.

Many provisions of the 1983 Act only apply to compulsorily detained patients. What does this mean for informally admitted patients who lack capacity? The common law response was to invoke the principle of necessity, so that patients lacking capacity could be *treated and detained* in their best interests, as long as no force was required. This was the result of *R. v Bournewood Community and Mental Health NHS Trust Ex p. L.*[264]

L was 48 years old, autistic and profoundly mentally disabled. He was unable to speak and had very limited understanding. For nearly 30 years he had lived in a mental hospital but for subsequent three years had lived with paid carers. On a visit to a day centre he became extremely agitated and was informally admitted to hospital. His carers wished him to return home but were refused access to him. They brought an action in L's name for false imprisonment. A majority of their Lordships held that L had not been imprisoned in the hospital. Had he attempted to leave steps would have been taken to detain him, but he had been kept in an unlocked ward and had not attempted to leave. Lord Steyn, in dissent, dismissed the view that L was free as "a fairy tale". Nonetheless, all their Lordships ruled that any detention that had taken place had not been unlawful, as it had been necessary in the patient's bests interests. The upshot was that L was, in effect compulsorily detained without the protection of the safeguards in the 1983 Act.

Before the European Court of Human Rights it was claimed that L's art.5 right to liberty have been violated by his detention.[265] Article 5(1) does permit the detention of "persons of unsound mind", but art.5(4) requires that anyone deprived of his liberty by detention must be able to take proceedings by which the lawfulness of his detention can decided speedily by a court. The Court ruled in favour of L. L had been deprived of his liberty solely on the basis of clinical assessments and the lawfulness of his detention had not been amenable to rapid judicial review. Thus, there was a gap in the UK's mental health law.

The so-called "Bournewood gap" has now been addressed by the amendment of the Mental Capacity Act 2005. It is the 2005 Act (rather than the common law doctrine of necessity) that now governs the lawfulness of acts in connection with the care or treatment of incapacitated adults not covered by

---

[263] *R. v Kirklees MBC Ex p. C* [1993] 2 F.L.R. 187.
[264] [1999] 1 A.C. 458.
[265] *HL v UK* (45508/99) (2005) 40 E.H.R.R. 32. See also *Storck v Germany* (61603/00) (2006) 43 E.H.R.R. 6.

Pt IV of the 1983 Act.[266] The Mental Health Act 2007 inserts new sections (ss.4A, 4B, and 16A) and a new Schedule (Sch.A1) into the 2005 Act. From April 2009, the 2005 Act will only authorise a patient to be lawfully deprived of his liberty in a *hospital or care home* if there is a *standard or urgent authorisation* under Sch.A1 or if it is the result of giving effect to an order of the Court of Protection under the Act (s.4A). There is also provision for emergency deprivation of liberty while a decision is sought from the Court of Protection (s.4B).

Part 4 of Sch.A1 sets out the requirements and procedure for *standard authorisations* of deprivation of liberty in hospitals or care homes. There are six qualifying requirements. The patient must: *first*, be aged 18 or over (the age requirement); *second*, be suffering from a "mental disorder" as defined by the 1983 Act (the mental health requirement); and *third*, lack capacity to decide whether to be a resident in the hospital or care home (the mental capacity requirement). *Fourth*, the deprivation of liberty must be in the patient's best interests, necessary to prevent harm to the patient, and a proportionate response to the likelihood of suffering harm and the seriousness of that harm (the best interests requirement). *Fifth*, the patient must not be excluded from eligibility by, for example, having been detained or treated under the protections of the 1983 Act (the eligibility requirement). *Sixth*, the deprivation must not conflict with a valid and applicable advance refusal or a decision of an attorney or deputy (the no refusals requirement). The authorisation itself must be requested by the "managing authority" of a hospital or care home from the "supervisory body" (which, in the case of hospitals, will usually be the relevant Primary Care Trust).[267]

Part 5 of Sch.A1 addresses *urgent authorisations*. These may be given, while a standard authorisation is being obtained, by the "managing authority" (e.g. the relevant NHS Trust) where the qualifying requirements listed in Part 3 appear to have been met.

This summary is merely the tip of the iceberg of this set of long and complex provisions. The effect of these "deprivation of liberty safeguards" is to create a formal procedure for informally admitting incapacitated patients into hospital. At the time of writing, this procedure is in the process of being implemented.

5.6 Conclusion

There is a general trend in medical law away from paternalistic and status-based thinking towards competence-based thinking tracking patient autonomy. In the last chapter we saw the movement towards patient-centred disclosure and in this chapter we have seen the adoption of competence-based criteria for adult capacity and the movement towards prioritising the autonomy of pregnant women. Yet, the wind is not blowing entirely in one direction. For the time being, the law continues to apply a status-based approach to some matters of adolescent

---

[266] The 2005 Act does not apply where Pt IV of the 1983 Act applies (s.28 of the 2005 Act).
[267] See paras 176, 177, and 179 on the "managing authority" and paras 128, 180, and 182 on the "supervisory authority".

autonomy and competence still cannot be equated with capacity when it comes to the treatment of mental illness under the mental health legislation.

Consent as a notion has importance well beyond its roles as a justification for administering treatment. It is frequently invoked as "justificatory currency"[268] with regard to many of the topics covered in this book. It is, for example, invoked with regard to assisted reproduction, organ transplantation, end of life decisions, and research on human subjects. Consent in the context of medical treatment is generally considered to be undervalued, with most commentators arguing for greater reliance on consent. There is a parallel danger of overvaluing consent.[269] Consent can be "presumed" or "implied" so as to render it entirely fictional and consent can be required or relied on in contexts where it is simply inappropriate. In the context of administering medical treatment, the major moral division is between the "dignity as empowerment" and "dignity as constraint" camps. In other contexts, the divisions between utilitarians, rights-based theories, duty-based theories, virtue-theories, and compromise positions will be more apparent. The relevance and currency of consent will depend on the ethical filter applied, whether that filter derives from utility, rights, duty, virtue, or a combination of these. Consent is not a free-standing moral value, where effective it involves the waiving of an otherwise binding duty, and so its import is theory dependent.

5.7 Further reading

The capacity test

Gunn, Michael (1994) "The Meaning of Incapacity." 2(1) *Medical Law Review* 8–29.

Stefan, Susan (1993) "Silencing the Different Voice: Competency Feminist Theory and Law." 47 *University of Miami Law Review* 736–815.

Mental health law

Bartlett, Peter and Sandland, Ralph (2007) *Mental Health Law: Policy and Practice.* (3rd edition) (Oxford: Oxford University Press), esp. ch.7.

Ritual circumcision

Fox, Marie and Thomson, Michael (2009) "Older Minors and Circumcision: Questioning the Limits of Religious Actions." 9(4) *Medical Law International* 283–310.

Hinchley, Geoff (2007) "Is Infant Male Circumcision An Abuse Of The Rights Of The Child? Yes." 335 *British Medical Journal* 1180–1181.

Patrick, Kirsten (2007) "Is Infant Male Circumcision An Abuse Of The Rights Of The Child? No." 335 *British Medical Journal* 1181.

---

[268] See Brownsword 2004b.
[269] See Brownsword 2004b.

Chapter 6

....

MEDICAL CONFIDENTIALITY AND DATA PROTECTION

6.1 Introduction

Trust is difficult to gain and easy to lose. Medical treatment depends on trust. Patients and potential patients need to believe that those to whom they go to for medical advice, diagnosis, and treatment are competent and discreet. Just as few would go to those they believe to be incompetent, few would go to those who were unable or unwilling to keep a patient's intimate details to them-selves. Readily releasing patient details to the rest of the world without the patient's consent would be likely to embarrass, offend, stigmatise, and, ulti-mately, deter people from seeking medical advice and treatment.[1] It could threaten the greater good, individuals' rights and interests, and a number of virtues. As a result, just about all moral theories will recognise the existence of a duty of confidentiality. Such a duty will not be absolute. The failure to release information about a patient's physical or mental health can itself threaten the greater good, individuals' rights and interests, and many virtues. A blanket and absolute duty of confidence would prevent a doctor from disclosing informa-tion that is necessary for other health professionals to treat the patient effec-tively. Exceptions to the general duty of confidentiality must go beyond patient consent if disclosure is to be permitted to protect others from a patient who, say, intends to murder or carries a highly infectious disease.

The view that protecting patient confidentiality has moral value but not absolute moral value has been widely accepted since at least the time of the Ancient Greeks. The existence of the duty is part of the Hippocratic Oath:

> Whatever, in connection with my professional practice, or not in connection with it, I see or hear in the life of men, which ought not to be spoken of abroad, I will not divulge, as reckoning that all such should be kept secret.

That duty is reiterated in the Declaration of Geneva, which requires doctors to "respect the secrets which are confided ... even after the patient has died".[2] Neither of these instruments is understood as imposing an absolute duty. Similarly, a strict but non-absolute duty is recognised by the guidance of the professional bodies and the NHS.[3] The need for a balance between protecting the secrecy of information and permitting disclosure is explicitly recognised by the common law of confidentiality and the Data Protection Act 1998. It is also recognised by the art.8 right to "private and family life" of the European Convention on Human Rights (hereafter the Convention), as given domestic effect by the Human Rights Act (HRA) 1998.[4] This chapter will address confidentiality, privacy, and data protection as its affects medical practice. Its principal focus will, however, be medical confidentiality.

6.2 The general duty to protect medical information

We have already seen that all the major moral theories will insist that the confi-dentiality of information disclosed to a doctor or other health professional should generally be observed. There is, nonetheless, a divergence of views on

---

[1] See e.g. R. (Axon) v Secretary of State for Health [2006] EWHC 37, para.68.
[2] The Declaration of Geneva was first adopted by the World Medical Association in 1948. It was last amended by the General Assembly in 2006.
[3] See GMC 2004; NMC 2002, para.5; GDC 1997, para. 3.5; and DH 2003d.
[4] See also art.10 of the European Convention on Human Rights and Biomedicine.

the precise ethical justification and function of the obligation of confidence.[5] Different moral theories will focus on different goals and benefits protected by restraining the disclosure of information divulged by a patient. Utilitarians will focus on the likely benefit to the overall utility balance. Respecting confidentiality will generally maximise utility, because it is likely to encourage patients to be open with their doctor and to seek medical assistance in the first place. Duty-based and rights-based theories will focus on individual rights and interests, such as those related to privacy and autonomy. Virtue theories will focus on the virtues, such as trustworthiness and confidentiality. Many of these ethical considerations are broader than confidentiality *as such*. Protecting autonomy interests in the shaping of one's life choices, for example, requires more than the ability to control who knows what about one's personal affairs. Some of these ethical considerations are justifications for maintaining confidentiality and others are justifications for protecting medical information from further dissemination or misuse.

Different moral positions will have different implications for what should count as protected information and when the moral need to protect confidential information should be overridden in favour of other moral interests and considerations. Act-utilitarian reasoning will, for example, favour breaching confidentiality whenever this will maximise utility, whereas a duty or rights-based approach to confidentiality will favour stronger protection of confidentiality. The law reflects these ethical tensions. We shall see that the law adopts a compromise position that simultaneously appeals to the greater good (e.g. the notion of the public interest), individual rights and interests (e.g. the right to privacy), and virtues (e.g. the notion of unconscionability defined by reference to the conscience of the person confided in). The net effect is a strong *presumption* in favour of confidentiality with exceptions that involve a utilitarian-type balancing exercise.

This section will focus primarily on the general duty to protect medical information, leaving detailed examination of the exceptions to this general duty to the next section. We shall begin by looking at the common law duty of confidentiality (6.2.1), before examining the impact of the HRA 1998 and professional guidance (6.2.2), the complexities raised by children and incapacitated adults (6.2.3), and the impact of the Data Protection Act 1998 (6.2.4).

6.2.1 The common law duty of confidentiality

A breach of confidence can sometimes found an action in *contract* or the tort of *negligence*. To found an action in *contract*, the obligation of confidence would need to form an express or implied contractual term. An employee, for example, has a contractual duty of confidence when dealing with the sensitive business information of his employer. Only private patients, however, enter

---

[5] See Montgomery 2002, 253–254.

into a contract with their doctor.[6] To found an action in *negligence*, the obligation of confidence would need to be part of the duty of care, which must have been breached and thereby caused actionable damage. However, the release of patient information, contrary to the behaviour of a reasonable doctor, will not usually cause damage to the patient that is generally actionable damage in negligence. Most patients will suffer embarrassment or a feeling of being violated. An action for breach of confidence can also be brought without the need to satisfy the strict requirements of contract or negligence.[7] Such an action is best characterised as *sui generis*, deriving from the law of *equity*.

The traditional formulation for the action for breach of confidence was laid down by Megarry J. in *Coco v Clark*:

> First, the information itself . . . must have the necessary quality of confidence about it. Secondly, that information must have been imparted in circumstances importing an obligation of confidence. Thirdly, there must be an unauthorised use of that information to the detriment of the party communicating it.[8]

In the first breach of confidence case to reach the House of Lords, often referred to as the *Spycatcher* case, Lord Goff stated that,

> a duty of confidence arises when confidential information comes to the knowledge of a person (the confidant) in circumstances where he has notice, or is held to have agreed, that the information is confidential, with the effect that it would be just in all the circumstances that he should be precluded from disclosing the information to others.[9]

According to this approach, a duty of confidence arises whenever the person receiving information knows, or ought to know, that it is confidential. Stated in the abstract, this is both vague and circular. It does, however, indicate that what matters is the *nature of the information* and *the circumstances of its acquisition*. Lord Goff went on to say that to be confidential, the information must not be in the "public domain" and must not be "useless" or "trivia".[10] Other cases indicate that personal and intimate information will qualify as confidential information.[11] With regard to the circumstances of acquisition, Lord Keith cited the doctor–patient relationship as a well-established example of a relationship that will give rise to an obligation of confidence[12] and other cases have held that this also applies to other health professionals.[13] Thus, the protection of medical

---

[6] See *Reynolds v Health First Medical Group* [2000] Lloyd's Rep. Med. 240, applying *Pfizer Corporation v Ministry of Health* [1965] A.C. 512.

[7] See e.g. *Saltman Engineering v Campbell Engineering* [1963] 3 All E.R. 413, *AG v Guardian Newspapers (No.2)* [1990] 1 A.C. 109, and *Ashworth Hospital Authority v MGN* [2002] UKHL 29.

[8] *Coco v Clark* [1968] F.S.R. 415 at 419. These criteria reflected earlier cases such as *Prince Albert v Strange* [1849] 41 E.R. 1171.

[9] *AG v Guardian Newspapers (No.2)* [1990] 1 A.C. 109 at 281.

[10] [1990] 1 A.C. 109 at 282.

[11] See e.g. *Stephens v Avery* [1988] Ch. 449 (where information relating to sexual conduct of a lesbian nature was held to be confidential information).

[12] [1990] 1 A.C. 109 at 255. This had been established in earlier cases: see e.g. *Hunter v Mann* [1974] Q.B. 767, esp. 772.

[13] *Ashworth Hospital Authority v MGN* [2002] UKHL 29.

information is generally. This remains the case with the recent expansion of the action for breach of confidence to give effect to the art.8 Convention right to "private and family life" (see 6.2.2.1, below).

Whether it is necessary for the claimant to suffer a detriment from the disclosure of his confidential information was moot for some time. Detriment was the third of Megarry J.'s three requirements, but this issue was left open by the House of Lords in the *Spycatcher* case.[14] Subsequent cases demonstrate that it is not usually difficult for the courts to find a detriment.[15] In *Re C*, for example, the Court of Appeal accepted that the infant in question would always remain ignorant of her condition but declared that disclosure of her identity was likely to adversely affect the ability of her carers to care for her.[16] In relation to medical information, it is now generally accepted that the mere fact of disclosure will suffice.[17]

It is often said that the principal justification for respecting patient confidentiality is the public interest. As Lord Goff put it in the *Spycatcher* case, "there is such a public interest in the maintenance of confidences, that the law will provide remedies for their protection".[18] His Lordship reiterated this later in his judgment and noted that the public interest also provided the principal legal justification for disclosing confidential information: "that public interest may be outweighed by some other countervailing public interest which favours disclosure".[19] The law now recognises that confidentiality also protects private interests.

6.2.2 The impact of legislation and professional guidance

The common law duty of confidentiality must be understood in the light of relevant legislation and professional guidance.

6.2.2.1 The impact of the Human Rights Act 1998

In *Campbell v MGN*, the House of Lords interpreted the common law duty of confidentiality in the light of the Convention, as given effect by the HRA 1998.[20]

---

[14] [1990] 1 A.C. 109 at 255–256 (Lord Keith suggested that detriment might not be required), 281–282 (Lord Goff left the at issue open), and 270 (Lord Griffiths considered detriment to be required).

[15] See e.g. *X v Y* [1988] 2 All E.R. 648 at 657–658 (Rose J. considered detriment to be unnecessary but found it anyway) and *Campbell v GMC* [2002] EWHC 499, para.40 (Morland J. easily found a detriment and this issue was not even addressed on appeal).

[16] *Re C (A Minor) (Wardship: Medical Treatment) (No.2)* [1990] Fam. 39 at 47–48 (Lord Donaldson), 51 (Balcombe L.J.), and 54–55 (Nicholls L.J.).

[17] *Cornelius v De Taranto* [2001] E.M.L.R. 12, para.72 (confirmed without addressing this point by the Court of Appeal: [2001] EWCA Civ 1511)), *R v Department of Health Ex p. Source Informatics* [1999] 4 All E.R. 185 (overturned, but the Court of Appeal sidestepped this point: [2001] Q.B. 424, para.35); and *Bluck v The Information Commissioner* (2007) 98 B.M.L.R. 1, paras 14–15 (holding that detriment was not a necessary ingredient in relation to the disclosure of medical information).

[18] *AG v Guardian* [1990] 1 A.C. 109 at 281.

[19] [1990] 1 A.C. 109 at 281, 282.

[20] [2004] UKHL 22.

Although their Lordships were divided over the application of the law to the facts of the case itself, they all agreed that the action for breach of confidence had developed to take account of the art.8 right to privacy. According to Lord Nicholls, "the time has come to recognise that the values enshrined in Arts 8 and 10 are now part of the cause of action for breach of confidence".[21] Breach of confidence was said to address the "misuse of private information".[22] It followed, according to their Lordships, that a person can commit an actionable wrong by unjustifiably disclosing information about one person to another when he knows or ought to know that that information is private. The principal touchstone adopted by the House of Lords (and subsequently applied by the courts below) is to ask whether the facts give rise to "a reasonable expectation of privacy".[23]

Campbell has radically reshaped the action for breach of confidence. Information that, in law, should be recognised as "private" is now protected by this action without the need to establish a confidential relationship. Indeed, in the subsequent case of *Douglas v Hello*, Lord Nicholls went so far as to declare that "developed breach of confidence, or misuse of confidential information, now covers two distinct causes of action, protecting two different interests: privacy, and secret ('confidential') information".[24] His Lordship went on to declare that these two should be kept distinct and information could qualify for protection on grounds of privacy, confidentiality, or both. The relationship between privacy and confidentiality was not, however, examined by the other members of the House of Lords in *Douglas*, because the case itself was concerned with the protection of commercially confidential information for which no claim to privacy under art.8 arose. As suggested earlier, medical information will almost invariably qualify for protection on grounds of both privacy and confidentiality. Indeed, the Court of Appeal in *McKennitt v Ash* declared that information about a person's health was clearly private and "doubly private" when it is imparted in the context of a relationship of confidence.[25] In such cases, the courts will now directly apply the framework of the Convention rights when determining whether disclosure is permissible.

The jurisprudence of the European Court of Human Rights has interpreted respect for "private life" under art.8(1) broadly, so that it extends far beyond information directly relating to one's identity and encompasses wider considerations of dignity and autonomy.[26] In *Pretty v UK*, for example, "private life" was equated with "the ability to conduct one's life in a manner of one's own choosing".[27] Under art.8(2), it is permissible to interfere with this right

---

[21] [2004] UKHL 22, para.17.
[22] [2004] UKHL 22, para.14.
[23] [2004] UKHL 22, paras 21 (Lord Nicholls), 96 (Lord Hope), and 134 (Baroness Hale); *McKennitt v Ash* [2006] EWCA 1714, [2008] Q.B. 73, esp. para.23; and *Murray v Express Newspapers* [2008] EWCA Civ 446, esp. paras 24–30.
[24] *Douglas v Hello (No.3)* [2007] UKHL 21, para.255.
[25] [2006] EWCA 1714, para.23.
[26] See e.g. *X and Y v The Netherlands* (1986) 8 E.H.R.R. 235, para.22, and *Pretty v UK* (2002) 35 E.H.R.R. 1, paras 61–62. See also *R (Burke) v GMC* [2004] EWHC 1879, para.62.
[27] (2002) 35 E.H.R.R. 1, para.62.

provided that the interference is "in accordance with the law and is necessary in a democratic society" for one of a limited number of specified purposes. These purposes are concerned with the protection of "national security, public safety or the economic well-being of the country, for the prevention of disorder or crime, for the protection of health or morals, or for the protection of the rights and freedoms of others". Thus, disclosing private information without consent will violate Art.8, unless privacy is infringed only to the extent required to protect one or more of the specified interests. In other words, only proportional infringement to protect an overriding interest is permitted.

There are currently few cases on the application of art.8 to medical information. In *Z v Finland*, the European Court of Human Rights held the disclosure of a woman's medical records (revealing her HIV status) during the trial of her husband for the rape of other women to be a breach of her rights under art.8.[28] The Court considered the confidentiality of health records to be crucial for a patient's privacy and to preserve confidence in the medical profession and the health service.[29] Accordingly, only "an overriding requirement in the public interest" could justify breaching medical confidentiality.[30] In the circumstances, the disclosure of her records could be justified under art.8(2), because of the importance of pursuing criminal proceedings against her husband. Nonetheless, there had been a breach of art.8 because it had not been necessary for the court to publicly disclose her identity and medical condition in its judgment. Later in the same year, in *MS v Sweden*, the European Court of Human Rights rejected another woman's claim that her art.8 right to privacy had been unjustifiably violated by the release of her medical records to the Swedish Social Insurance office so that they could check the validity of her claim that she had suffered a back injury at work.[31] She was upset because her medical records also recorded the details of an abortion that she had had *as a result of her back problem*. In both cases, the Court held that the disclosure of medical data without consent was a prima facie breach of the right to privacy, but could be justified if the method of disclosure was a proportionate means of addressing a more important interest. The impact of this balancing exercise on the common law of confidence will be examined below.

6.2.2.2 The impact of other legislation

Additional obligations relating to confidentiality are imposed by specific statutes. The Data Protection Act 1998 is the most important and will be addressed both in outline in the next section (6.2.3) and throughout this chapter. Others include the Human Fertilisation and Embryology Act 1990 (s.33A of which imposes non-disclosure obligations upon those who hold information that is on the HFEA's register) and the Abortion Regulations 1991/499 (reg.5 of which imposes restrictions on the disclosure of abortion

---

[28] (1998) 25 E.H.R.R. 371.
[29] (1998) 25 E.H.R.R. 371 at 405.
[30] (1998) 25 E.H.R.R. 371 at 406.
[31] *MS v Sweden* (1999) 28 E.H.R.R. 313.

information, which operates alongside the obligation, under reg.4, to report abortions to the Chief Medical Officer).

6.2.2.3 The impact of professional guidance

Most victims of a breach of confidence do not seek to involve the courts. Litigation is notoriously expensive and is unlikely to provide the remedy sought by a victim of a breach of medical confidentiality. A potentially more attractive option is for the patient to make a complaint to a body such as the General Medical Council (GMC). The NHS and all the professional bodies have guidance reinforcing the duty of confidence,[32] and a breach of that guidance is potentially a disciplinary matter. Consider, for example, the doctor and the dentist who discussed a mutual patient during a round of golf. The doctor casually mentioned that the patient had had an abortion and the dentist repeated this to his wife, who told a friend, who in turn informed the patient. Both were suspended from their professional registers for six months.[33] The courts cannot grant any remedy of such severity for a breach of confidence. Before the breach has occurred a court could grant an injunction, but post-breach the court is restricted to issuing a declaration that a breach has occurred or awarding damages.[34]

A breach of professional guidance is also likely to influence the courts if a civil action is brought. Not only have the courts tended to take account of the GMC's guidance when deciding medical confidentiality cases,[35] but a breach of the guidance will constitute prima facie negligence under the *Bolam* test.[36] The impact of professional guidance is not limited to judicial and disciplinary use. Many health professionals will rely on professional guidance for assistance before they act and, in practice, they are far more likely to read the guidance than the case law. This is significant because, as we shall see, on some issues professional guidance on best practice goes beyond the requirements of the law.

6.2.3 Children, incapacitated adults, and the dead

Three categories of patient raise additional issues when it comes to establishing the existence and ambit of a duty of confidentiality: children, incapacitated adults, and dead patients.

---

[32] See GMC 2004; NMC 2002, para.5; GDC 1997, para.3.5; and DH 2003d.

[33] See BMA 2004, 167. The disciplinary functions of the professional bodies, particularly the General Medical Council (GMC), are examined in Ch.2 (2.3.1).

[34] It was for sometime unclear whether damages for injured feelings were available where the claim is brought in equity. However, modest damages for mental distress are now sometimes awarded. See, e.g., *Archer v Williams* [2003] EWHC 1670 (contractual claim for breach of confidence) and *Cornelius v De Taranto* [2001] E.M.L.R. 12, para.66 (the HRA 1998 has been interpreted to require damages to be available for a breach of art.8.

[35] See e.g. *W v Egdell* [1990] Ch. 359 at 412, 420 and *Lewis v Secretary of State for Health* [2008] EWHC 2196, para.19.

[36] See the discussion in Ch.3 (3.4).

6.2.3.1 Children and incapacitated adults

The obligation of confidence in relation to children and incapacitated adults is a little more complex than for capacitated adults. *First*, if a duty of confidence is to be owed to *all* children and incapacitated adults, then it needs to be founded on the nature of the information alone. Some children and incapacitated adults will simply not be able to form a *relationship* of confidentiality or operate with an *expectation* that information will be kept secret. *Second*, any duty of confidence will need to take account of the role of the patient's primary carer.

In the *Gillick* case, addressed in Ch.5 (5.3.1), the House of Lords recognised that a doctor could in certain circumstances follow a child's wishes to keep information about her medical treatment from her parents.[37] Lord Fraser had opined that the doctor would be "justified in proceeding without the parents' consent *or even knowledge*", provided that the doctor was satisfied on five matters, including the child being able to understand the advice.[38] However, their Lordships were primarily concerned with whether a so-called "Gillick-competent" child could consent to contraceptive treatment in the absence of parental knowledge or consent. It was possible to read their Lordships as linking the duty of confidentiality to the capacity to consent to treatment.[39] Building on this approach, Kennedy and Grubb have argued that it is "analytically preferable" to found the duty of confidentiality on the child's ability to form a confidential relationship or an expectation that the information will be kept secret.[40] They argue that this approach, which would deny a duty of confidence to children who are unable to understand what secrecy entails, fits better with the approach taken to capacity to consent to treatment. Both capacity to consent and capacity to request confidentiality would turn on the child's ability to understand what is entailed by the activity in question.

The idea that the existence of a duty of confidence is determined by the patient's capacity is, however, difficult to reconcile with the case law even before *Campbell v MGN*.[41] There had been a string of cases where injunctions were granted against the publication of the identities of children in which there is powerful dicta to the effect that a duty of confidence is owed to an incompetent child. In *Re C*, the Court of Appeal unanimously declared that a duty of confidentiality was owed to a baby by all those caring for her.[42] In another case, Dame Elizabeth Butler Sloss made it clear that she had no reservations about the existence of a general duty of confidence owed to all children:

> Children, like adults, are entitled to confidentiality in respect of certain areas of information. Medical records are the obvious example.[43]

---

[37] *Gillick v West Norfolk and Wisbech AHA* [1986] A.C. 112.
[38] My emphasis. The so-called Fraser guidelines listed five matters to be considered: [1986] A.C. 112 at 174.
[39] See Loughrey 2003, 511–512.
[40] See Kennedy and Grubb 2000, 1077–1078.
[41] [2004] UKHL 22.
[42] [1990] Fam. 39 at 48 (Lord Donaldson), 52 (Balcombe L.J.), and 54 (Nicholls L.J.).
[43] *Venables v NGN* [2001] Fam. 430 at 469.

In *Re Z*, the Court of Appeal even suggested that in certain circumstances, a parent could be bound by a duty of confidence to their child.[44] None of these cases explained precisely why a duty of confidence is owed to an incompetent child.[45] Since the duty protects all patients, any disclosure needs to be justified in the public interest. Of course, an important variable in the application of the public interest justification would have to be the child's capacity. There is surely a compelling public interest justification for disclosing information to the child's parents where the child lacks capacity,[46] as parental consent would usually be needed before the treatment could be administered lawfully. Where a child can lawfully consent to treatment (i.e. is *Gillick* competent), the public interest in disclosing information to his parents is less compelling.

The approach of the House of Lords in the *Campbell* case was, as already stated, to link the art.8 right to privacy with the action for breach of confidence. It is well established in Convention jurisprudence that children have a right to privacy under art.8(1),[47] so any disclosure of the child's medical information will need to be justified as necessary for the proportionate pursuit of a legitimate aim recognised by art.8(2).

The most controversial situations are those where a child with capacity to consent to treatment insists that the details of her medical consultation on contraception or abortion are kept from her parents. This was the very issue to arise for consideration in *R. (Axon) v Secretary of State for Health*.[48] Over 20 years after *Gillick*, Mrs Axon sought to challenge Department of Health guidance.[49] Mrs Axon argued that the Department of Health guidance had misrepresented the law as stated in *Gillick*. The duty of confidence owed to a child was, she argued, subject to the parent's responsibility for the welfare of their child. Accordingly, health professionals were only under an obligation to maintain the confidence of a child under 16 who sought advice or treatment on sexual matters (contraception, sexually transmitted infections, and abortion) where parental knowledge "would or might prejudice a child's physical or mental health so that it is in the child's bests interests" to maintain the confidence.[50] Further, the parent's right to respect for their privacy and family life under art.8 of the Convention required that they be notified of such matters. Silber J. rejected these claims. The first was held to have been *impliedly* rejected by *Gillick* and inconsistent with the nature of the duty owed to a *Gillick* competent child (which was "a high one" that could only be overridden by "a very powerful reason" beyond "family factors").[51] The parent's art.8(1) right to private and family life was held not to entitle them to be notified of any advice given to their child by a health professional once the child is *Gillick* competent and any such right would, in any event, be limited by the protection of health

---

[44] See e.g. *Re Z* [1997] Fam. 1, 25 (Ward L.J. with whom the other judges agreed).
[45] See Loughrey 2003.
[46] Save in extreme circumstances, such as suspected child abuse.
[47] See e.g. *Gaskin v United Kingdom* (1990) 12 E.H.R.R. 36 and *Glass v UK* [2004] 1 F.L.R. 1019.
[48] [2006] EWHC 372.
[49] See DH 2004b.
[50] [2006] EWHC 372, para.29.
[51] [2006] EWHC 372, para.64.

and the rights of others under art.8(2). Thus, although young persons should be encouraged to inform their parents, if they understand all aspects of the advice they are entitled to have their confidence protected.[52] As Loughrey has pointed out, questions remain about extent of duties owed to children *against their parents* when they are not *Gillick*-competent.[53]

The position of incapacitated adults is similar to that of children. In *R. (S) v Plymouth City Council*, the Court of Appeal recognised that incapacitated adults were owed a duty of confidence and had a right to privacy under art.8.[54] The applicant, S, was the mother of an incapacitated adult and wished to see the medical records of her child. According to Hale L.J.,

> both at common law and under the Human Rights Act, a balance must be struck between the public and private interests in maintaining the confidentiality of this information and the public and private interests in permitting, indeed requiring, its disclosure for certain purposes.[55]

The Court of Appeal agreed on these principles but was divided over the application of this balancing exercise to the facts. The majority ruled that the balance favoured disclosure.

Guidance from the General Medical Council (GMC) and the British Medical Association (BMA) recognise that doctors owe a duty of confidence to children and incapacitated adults.[56] In contrast, the Department of Health guidance links the duty of confidentiality to the capacity to consent. According to the guidance,

> Young people aged 16 or 17 are presumed to be competent for the purposes of consent to treatment and *are therefore entitled* to the same duty of confidentiality as adults. Children under the age of 16 who have the capacity and understanding to take decisions about their own treatment are also entitled to make decisions about the use and disclosure of information they have provided in confidence (e.g. they may be receiving treatment or counselling about which they do not want their parents to know).[57]

Read literally, this approach is narrower than that adopted by the case law. As we have seen, the case law suggests that *all* children (and all incapacitated adults) are owed a duty of confidentiality, so that their capacity is only relevant with regard to the question of whether a breach of confidentiality is permissible.

6.2.3.2 Dead patients

Imagine a woman from a devout Catholic family who wishes to have an abortion. She is anxious that her family never finds out, even after she dies. Imagine another patient who is currently being treated for cancer and who also fears that he might have contracted HIV. He is anxious that no one ever finds out that

---

[52] See further the guidance (based on Lord Fraser's guidance) in [2006] EWHC 372, para.154.
[53] See Loughrey 2008.
[54] [2002] EWCA Civ 388, esp. paras 49 and 50 (Hale L.J.).
[55] [2002] EWCA Civ 388, para.32.
[56] See GMC 2004, para.28 and BMA 2004, 177.
[57] DH 2003d, 30 (my emphasis). See also DH 2003d 40.

he had contracted HIV, if he has, because he fears that it will cause the small community from which he comes to stigmatise his whole family. In both scenarios the patients do not readily draw a distinction between disclosure of their medical information now or after their death. Fear of future disclosure could lead them to avoid complete openness with their doctor. In the HIV scenario, the patient might even avoid seeking further treatment for his cancer if he thought that his doctor would disclose information relating to his HIV status. A significant likelihood of posthumous disclosure could thereby lead these patients to suffer considerable distress and could undermine their confidence in the healthcare system. It is not difficult to see why the major moral theories should be concerned about maintaining the secrecy of patient information even after the patient's death. Even if the dead themselves are not considered to have any interests—which is an issue on which different views are taken—posthumous confidentiality can protect important moral interests.

If further scenarios are needed to demonstrate the potential of posthumous disclosure to infringe patient's rights or expectations, produce significant disutility, or compromise important virtues, readers should consider the scenarios used in the discussion of anonymisation below (under the sub-heading "Teaching, research, and audit": 6.3.3). A Catholic woman who is anxious that her gynaecological information is not used for research into chemical contraceptives is unlikely to consider it relevant whether the research takes place before or after her death.[58] The point is that many of the ethical concerns that give rise to the ethical obligation to protect patient confidentiality continue to have force once the patient has died. It might be easier to justify posthumous disclosure than to justify disclosure during the patient's life time (because a living individual can be harmed directly), but it does not follow that posthumous disclosure is unproblematic.

Until recently, there was no case law addressing the question of whether a duty of confidence can be owed to, or in respect of, a patient who is now dead. Kennedy and Grubb had argued by analogy with the law of defamation (a dead person cannot sue for defamation)[59] that the common law of confidentiality does not apply to disclosures after a patient's death.[60] This analogy has a certain force: if posthumous defamatory statements do not give rise to a cause of action, why should posthumous statements of true medical facts? However, maintaining confidentiality arguably protects wider and more important interests than preventing defamatory statements. Medical confidentiality is intimately connected with maintaining confidence in the medical profession and healthcare system. Perhaps for this reason, the professional guidance of the GMC, BMA, and the Department of Health declare that the obligation of confidence continues after death.[61] As stated earlier, breaching those guidelines could give rise to disciplinary action. The guidance of the GMC and BMA only

---

[58] This hypothetical scenario derives from Beyleveld and Histed 1999, 73–74, who use it in the context of anonymisation.

[59] Law Reform (Miscellaneous Provisions) Act 1934 (as amended) s.1(1).

[60] Kennedy and Grubb 2000, 1082. See also Law Commission 1981, para.4.107 and DH 2003d, 29. Cf. Toulson and Phipps 1996, para.13.17.

[61] See GMC 2004, para.30, BMA 1999, BMA 2004, 179, and DH 2003d, 29.

apply to doctors and the Department of Health guidance only applies to those who work within the NHS or under contract with NHS bodies. Nonetheless, other professional bodies are unlikely to view releasing information about dead patients in a positive light and private employers will also be owed a duty of confidence by their employees.[62] The threat of such disciplinary action might not, however, concern a health professional who is about to retire.

In *Lewis v Secretary of State for Health*, the High Court was asked to consider the disclosure of the medical records of certain deceased patients to an inquiry into human tissue analysis in UK nuclear facilities.[63] Both parties invited the High Court to authorise the relevant disclosure, but differed as to the source of the authority for doing so (i.e. whether the disclosure had been authorised under s.251 of the National Health Service Act 2006 and the relevant regulations, or required another legal justification). Since the parties accepted that the duty of confidentiality of a doctor towards a patient continues after the patient's death, Foskett J. did not find it necessary to reach anything more than a prima facie conclusion, namely, that "it is *arguable* that the duty of confidentiality does survive the death of the patient".[64] This conclusion was reached taking into account the position adopted by the relevant professional guidance, the general expectations of patients, and the likely consequences of holding otherwise.[65] This decision is of particular importance given that the Data Protection Act 1998 does not apply once the patient has died (see below).

6.2.4 The Data Protection Act 1998

The Data Protection Act 1998 implements Directive 95/46/EC. The purpose of this Directive is to protect the free flow of personal data between Member States and the fundamental rights and freedoms of individuals, in particular, their right to privacy.[66] Unfortunately, the implementing Act lacks the brevity of the Directive.[67] The result is a complex statutory scheme regulating the "processing" of "personal data" belonging to "data subjects" by "data controllers" (s.1(1)). The Act introduces eight Data Protection Principles that set standards for information handling (Sch. 1). These principles are backed up by criminal sanctions (e.g. s.21) and a number of personal remedies for data subjects (see below). The scheme has its own enforcement officer, known as the Information Commissioner, or the Commissioner for short.[68] It is often said that the devil is in the detail—and the

---

[62] Releasing patient information supplied by other hospital staff can breach the duty of confidence owed to the hospital: *Ashworth Hospital Authority v MGN* [2002] UKHL 29.

[63] [2008] EWHC 2196.

[64] [2008] EWHC 2196, para.18.

[65] [2008] EWHC 2196, paras 19–31. Foskett J. also cited a decision of the Tribunals Service Information Tribunal that had reached the same conclusion: *Bluck v The Information Commissioner* (2007) 98 B.M.L.R. 1.

[66] Article 1 of the Directive. See Beyleveld 2004a, 5–6 on the proper interpretation of this provision.

[67] The Act has also been subject to minor amendments by the Freedom and Information Act 2000.

[68] Part V of the 1998 Act. Before the enactment of the Freedom and Information Act 2000, the Commissioner was referred to as the "Data Protection Commissioner".

Act contains a lot of detail. This brief overview will start by defining the key terms in the following order: "personal data", "data subjects", "data controllers", and "processing".

6.2.4.1 The key terms

The term "personal data" is defined widely. For present purposes it is sufficient to note that it includes a patient's health record, whether that record is on computer or in manual form (ss.1(1) and 68). Health records are defined in s.68(2), as any record consisting of "information relating to the physical or mental health or condition of an individual" that "has been made by or on behalf of a health professional in connection with the care of that individual". Health professional is defined widely in s.69(1) and includes doctors, dentists, nurses, and the like.

"Data subjects" are those individuals who are the subjects of the personal data. Since s.1(1) requires the data to relate to "living individuals", the Act's requirements do not apply to the posthumous processing of patient data.[69] (The restriction of protection to living individuals raises the same issues that are considered in relation to the law of confidentiality above, 6.2.3.) It follows that all registered patients who are alive will be data subjects.

"Data controllers" are defined in s.1(1) to encompass those who determine the purposes and the manner that personal data is processed. Data controllers can thereby be individuals or collectives. NHS bodies (such as NHS Trusts, Primary Care Trusts, and GP practices) and private healthcare providers (such as private hospitals and clinics) are clearly data controllers.

"Processing" is defined very broadly in s.1(1). It is defined to encompass "*any* operation or set of operations on the information or data*", including any alteration, retrieval, use, disclosure, or erasure. Thus, *any* activity in relation to a patient's health record will constitute processing for the purposes of the Act.[70]

6.2.4.2 The First Data Protection Principle

In essence, the data controller has a legal obligation to ensure that the Act's stringent requirements are complied with when patient health information is stored, used, or disclosed. These requirements turn on *eight* Data Protection Principles. The First Data Protection Principle states that all personal data must be processed "fairly and lawfully". The term "lawfully" imports all other legal requirements into the Act, *including the common law of confidentiality and the provisions of the HRA 1998.* In addition, the processing of any "personal data" must comply with at least one of the conditions of Sch.2 and the processing of "sensitive personal data" must further comply with at least one condition of

---

[69] Unless, of course, the data also relates to another living individual.
[70] See also Information Commissioner 1998, para.2.3. Under s.1(2), unless the context requires otherwise, "using" or "disclosing" in relation to personal data also applies to the "information contained in the data". See also s.55.

Sch.3 (Sch.1 para.1). Health records contain both personal data and sensitive personal data.[71]

Six conditions are given in Sch.2.[72] These conditions, in broad terms, include (i) processing with the data subject's consent, (ii) processing that is necessary to protect the data subject's vital interests, (iii) processing that is necessary in the administration of justice or the exercise of other functions of a public nature exercised in the public interest, and (iv) processing that is necessary for the purposes of the legitimate interests of the data controller.[73] In the view of the Information Commissioner, health sector data controllers will not usually find it difficult to satisfy at least one of these conditions.[74] The ease of satisfying these conditions will turn on how widely they are interpreted. Schedule 2 (unlike Sch.3) does not require the data subject's consent to be explicit, but the lack of definitional detail still leaves some ambiguity as to when consent can (as a matter of law) be taken to have been given in the absence of explicit words of acceptance or equivalent conduct. Some commentators have suggested that consent could be taken as having been given where a patient has not "opted out" after being exposed to prominent notices in hospitals or GP surgeries indicating possible uses of his medical information.[75] The Directive refers to "any freely given specific and informed *indication* of [the patient's] wishes" (art.2(h)). Is the failure to opt out a sufficient indication, taking into account the vulnerable and distracted position of many of those in hospitals or GP surgeries awaiting medical assistance? Over eagerness to infer or impute consent will render the patient's consent no more than a legal fiction (see further 6.3.1). In any event, there are five other conditions that could be used to justify processing under Sch.2 where the patient has not given a specific indication of agreement. Protecting the patient's vital interests should enable additional medically-indicated disclosures to be undertaken. For example, a patient's GP might wish to inform a casualty doctor about any relevant medication that the patient is on.[76] Also, use of patient information might sometimes be necessary for the legitimate purposes of an NHS body, potentially including audit and research.

Further conditions are given in Sch.3 for sensitive personal data.[77] Sensitive personal data is defined in s.2(e) to include information about a person's physical or mental health or condition. These conditions thereby apply to information about a patient's broken arm just as much as information about his HIV status or mental health.

In addition to processing with the data subject's *explicit* consent, processing of such information can also take place in a number of other specified

---

[71] Sensitive personal data includes personal data relating to an individual's "physical or mental health or condition" (s.2(e)).
[72] Art.7 is the equivalent provision in the Directive.
[73] The other two conditions are processing that is necessary for the performance of a contract to which the data subject is or will be a party and processing that is necessary to comply with a non-contractual legal obligation.
[74] See Information Commissioner 2002, 3.
[75] See Laing and Grubb 2004, 614–615, and Brazier 2003, 76.
[76] See Laing and Grubb 2004, 615.
[77] Art.8 is the equivalent provision in the Directive.

circumstances. In particular, information relating to a patient's health can be used where *necessary*

(a) to protect the *vital interests* of a data subject who cannot consent, or where the data controller cannot reasonably be expected to obtain consent, or to protect the vital interests of another person where the data subject has unreasonably withheld consent (para.3);

(b) in connection with legal proceedings or legal rights (para.6), or the administration of justice (para.7); and

(c) for *medical purposes* and undertaken by a health professional or person with an equivalent duty of confidentiality (para.8).

Notice that these exceptions to the duty of non-disclosure are limited by the requirement that the processing be "necessary" for the relevant purpose. The "medical purposes" condition, exemption (c) above, is particularly significant. The Act does not restrict "medical purposes" to medical treatment, but includes "preventative medicine, medical diagnosis, medical research, the provision of care and treatment, and the management of healthcare services" (para.8(2)). Notice that one of these purposes is "medical research" to which we will return below. This was not in the equivalent provision of the Directive (art.8(3)).

The Secretary of State may add further purposes for which sensitive personal data can be lawfully processed and has done so.[78]

Part II of Sch.1 lays down the requirements for data to be processed "fairly" in paras 2 and 3. Where data are obtained from the data subject, specific information must be provided *so far as is practicable*. Where data are *not* obtained from the data subject, specific information must be provided so far as practicable, *unless* doing so would involve disproportionate effort.[79] The specific information that data subjects must be given in these circumstances must include the uses to which the data will be put, the identity of the data controller, the identity of any person to whom the data will be disclosed, and any further information that is necessary to enable the processing to be fair. These provisions are key, because the data subject can only fully exercise the other rights granted to him by the Act if he is provided with the information prescribed by these provisions.[80]

6.2.4.3 The other Data Protection Principles and the Act's remedies

Data Protection Principles two to six seek to ensure that personal data is obtained and used only so far as is required to perform the specified lawful

---

[78] Data Protection (Processing of Sensitive Personal Data) Order 2000/417.

[79] Also, specific information need not be given to the data subject if the data controller is under a non-contractual legal obligation to record the information contained in the data or disclose the data, *or* the Secretary of State has so prescribed by order.

[80] See Beyleveld 2004b. The discrepancies between the Act and the equivalent provisions in the Directive, arts 10 and 11, lead Beyleveld to argue that the UK's implementation is inadequate: see Beyleveld 2004b, esp. 80–83. See also Beyleveld et al. 2004, 419.

purposes (Sch.1 Pt I). The Second Data Protection Principle restricts the obtaining and use of the data to the lawful purposes specified in the registration with the Commissioner or the notice given to the data subject.[81] The Third Principle requires that personal data should be relevant and not excessive in relation to the purposes for which it is processed. The Fourth Principle requires that it be accurate and up-to-date and the Fifth Principle requires that it be kept for no longer than is necessary for those purposes.

The Sixth Data Protection Principle requires that personal data be processed in accordance with the rights of the data subject under the Act. These rights include personal remedies that are far more extensive than those provided by the common law of confidentiality. Under s.10, a data subject is entitled to prevent the processing of data that is likely to cause substantial and unwarranted damage or distress by writing to the data controller. An individual who suffers damage or distress as a result of a violation of the Act's requirements has a right to compensation under s.13. The right to compensation is, however, subject to the defence that the data controller has taken all reasonable care to comply with the Act's requirements. Most significantly, s.14 allows the data subject to apply to the court to correct any inaccurate information held about him. This right is supplemented by rights of access to health records, addressed in 6.4. It is significant that none of these rights are restricted to adults, so any child with legal capacity should be entitled to exercise any of the rights granted by the Act.

6.2.5 The Data Protection Act and the law of confidentiality

The law of confidentiality continues to operate alongside the 1998 Act and, as we have seen, its requirements are imported into the Act as a condition for the lawful processing of data under the First Data Protection Principle. The rest of this chapter will explicate the common law of confidentiality before briefly comparing its requirements to those of the 1998 Act. It should be apparent that the data protection legislation is not coterminous with the common law of confidentiality. The common law will sometimes apply where the 1998 Act does not apply, because not all misuse of confidential/private information will fall within the Act. Conversely, the Act will sometimes apply where the common law does not, because not all processing of personal data will constitute relevant misuse of confidential information.

The 1998 Act only applies to the processing of personal data. The gist of s.1(1) is that information only counts as relevant data if it is held electronically, manually as part of a "relevant filing system", or manually in an "accessible record" (which includes a "health record"). It follows that the Act does not apply to confidential information that has not been recorded in any way. Patients often divulge information about their personal lives to health professionals and much of it will not be recorded in their medical notes. A patient might, for

[81] Sch.1 Pt II para.5.

example, tell his doctor that he has been unfaithful to his partner or that he has suspicions that his partner is being unfaithful. The protection of such information falls to the common law duty of confidence. Some recorded medical information might also fall outside of the 1998 Act. Remember that a health record is defined as a record that "has been made by or on behalf of a health professional in connection with the care of that individual" (s.68(2)). It seems to follow that medical information that is not held in connection with the care of an individual is not a health record. Thus, a medical report prepared by a health professional who is not treating the patient could fall outside of the Act if it is handwritten and not stored in a relevant filing system.

The HRA 1998 could bring the law of confidentiality and the data protection legislation closer together. We have already seen that the common law of confidentiality has been extended by reference to art.8 of the Convention. The Convention rights also affect the way that the 1998 Act must be interpreted. Article 1 of the Directive on which the Act is based states that the Directive seeks to protect the fundamental rights and freedoms of individuals, in particular, their right to privacy. More directly, s.3 of the HRA requires *all* legislation to be interpreted, insofar as possible, so as to give effect the Convention rights (including art.8).

6.3 Permitted disclosure

The duty of confidence is not all-encompassing and is subject to well established exceptions. Even where the existence of a duty of confidence is beyond doubt, doctors and other health professionals are sometimes permitted, and sometimes even required, to disclose patient information.[82] As previously, the material below will initially focus on the common law of confidentiality, before briefly contrasting the common law position with that under the Data Protection Act 1998. The following subsections will examine consent and the patient's interests (6.3.1), the public interest (6.3.2), and teaching, research, and audit (6.3.3).

6.3.1 Consent and the patient's interests

Perhaps the most straightforward instance of permitted disclosure of patient information is where the patient unequivocally consents to the disclosure. Disclosure within parameters of a valid consent will not breach the legal duty of confidence, because the patient's consent operates as a waiver of the duty. This is evident from an early case in which a husband and wife had, in the course of divorce proceedings, written to their doctor to request that he disclose

---

[82] This chapter does not address the absence of medical privilege in criminal proceedings. On a doctor's lack of a legal right to refuse to give testimony, see Michalowski 2003, esp. ch.6.

information related to her venereal disease.[83] Disclosure in the circumstances was held not to amount to a breach of confidence. Similarly, no breach of art.8 occurs if the patient has consented to the disclosure of his private information.[84] The five major moral positions outlined in Ch.1 will support this conclusion. Consent to the disclosure of one's medical information does not usually raise the spectre of autonomous self-harm and therefore tends not to evoke the division over whether there are direct duties to oneself.[85] Information is simply not confidential or private where the subject of that information does not regard it as such. The subject's consent permits disclosure within the parameters of that consent in both law and moral theory.[86]

The courts have not specifically addressed the requirements for a valid consent for the disclosure of what is otherwise confidential information. These requirements are, however, surely the same as those for a valid consent to treatment: a valid consent is one given by an individual who has the capacity to consent, is acting voluntarily, and is broadly aware of what he is consenting to (see Ch.4 (4.3)). The courts have also given very little consideration to the issue of when a patient will be taken to have consented to disclosure.[87] No case has yet turned on this issue. Once again the law on consent to treatment should provide guidance. There is no reason to doubt that, as with consent to treatment, a patient will be taken to be consenting in many circumstances when he has not expressly said that he consents. Where, for example, a patient seeks medical treatment from a doctor other than his own GP, he is surely to be taken to be consenting to that doctor having access to his health record, unless he indicates otherwise. Disclosure to other health professionals for the purpose of treating the patient is generally considered lawful on these grounds. The GMC guidance takes this view, but advises doctors to "make sure that patients are aware that personal information about them will be shared within the healthcare team".[88] Similarly, the Department of Health Code of Practice states that explicit consent is not usually required for disclosure to other members of the team treating the patient, as long as the patient is informed of this and the choices that they have to limit the information that may be shared.[89]

6.3.1.1 Unpacking consent

Addressing consent as a justification for disclosure requires some unpacking of the types of situations where, conceptually, consent could be reasonably taken to have been given.[90] Consent is, in essence, a state of mind that is potentially

---

[83] *C v C* [1946] 1 All E.R. 562.
[84] The art.8(1) right to respect for private life is engaged by the *non-consensual* use of private information, see e.g. *Z v Finland* (1998) 25 E.H.R.R. 371, para.112, *MS v Sweden* (1999) 28 E.H.R.R. 313, paras 34–35, and *Peck v UK* (2003) 36 E.H.R.R. 719, esp. para.81.
[85] See e.g. Chs 1 (1.3.2 and 1.4.1), and 4 (4.6).
[86] French law takes a different approach: see Michalowski 2003, ch. 4, esp. 87.
[87] But see *R. v Department of Health Ex p. Source Informatics* [1999] 4 All E.R. 185 at 192 (first instance), [2001] Q.B. 424 at 443–444 (Court of Appeal), and *Kapadia v Lambeth* [2000] I.R.L.R. 699 at 703 (Pill L.J.).
[88] See GMC 2004, para.10.
[89] See DH 2003d, para.15. See also BMA 2004, 177 and 180.
[90] See Beyleveld and Histed 1999, 75 for distinctions between "implicit", "implied", "presumed", and "imputed" consent.

signalled in many different ways. Consent might even be taken to have been signalled when the patient is not in fact consenting, because the signalling individual has deliberately or inadvertently mislead or the individual interpreting the signals has deliberately or inadvertently misread them.

When may a doctor reasonably take the patient to be consenting so as to rely on that consent as a justification for disclosing information? The most straightforward situation is where the patient appears to expressly signal consent by (written or spoken) words of agreement or by conduct equivalent to words of agreement (such as the nodding of the head). In such situations the doctor could be said to be relying on the patient's *express consent*. A slight variation is conduct that appears to signal consent in the particular context in question but would not in other contexts. A patient could reasonably be taken as signalling consent to an injection by holding out his arm in response to the doctor's recommendation of a tetanus injection, even though holding out his arm would not indicate consent to an injection in many other contexts. Similarly, a patient could reasonably be taken to be signalling consent to the disclosure of her test results in front of her partner if she asks for them while sat next to her partner in a doctor's surgery. In such situations the doctor could be said to be relying on the patient's *implicit consent*.

Where a patient consents to one activity, consent for another could be said to be *implied* where that other is a necessary means of fulfilling the purpose for which express consent has be obtained *and* the patient is reasonably expected to be aware of this connection. Where a patient agrees to have an X-ray at his doctor's suggestion, for example, consent to disclosure of any relevant medical information to the radiologist could reasonably be implied. (A patient who seeks hospital treatment will usually be treated by a team and could similarly be reasonably taken to have impliedly consented to disclosure to all members of that team for the purposes of treating him.) If it is likely that the patient is not aware of the need for the additional activity/disclosure, then the justification for performing it cannot be the patient's consent. If the law were to treat this as an instance of consent, this would have to be on the basis of a legal fiction. A legal fiction would also have to be relied on in most circumstances where the patient has given no signal at all.

To *impute* consent in the absence of any reason for thinking that the patient has actually consented is to rely on a justification other than consent cloaked in the language of consent. In the absence of case law directly on point, it is difficult to be sure when the law will allow reliance on fictional consent as if it were real consent. There is, however, some discussion on this in the leading case on anonymisation addressed below (in 6.3.3).

6.3.1.2 The Data Protection Act 1998

The 1998 Act rejects reliance on fictional consent for the purpose of justifying the disclosure (or other processing) of a patient's health information. As we saw in 6.2.4, if consent is relied on as a justification for disclosure under Sch.3, it needs to be *explicit*. Thus, even if the common law of confidentiality will take a patient to be consenting to disclosure in the absence of explicit consent, the 1998 Act will not.

6.3.2 Public interest

The common law recognises that the disclosure of confidential information can sometimes protect interests that outweigh those protected by maintaining confidentiality. As Lord Goff recognised in the *Spycatcher* case, the public interest in maintaining confidence can sometimes be outweighed by the public interest in disclosure.[91] Since the public interest can potentially pull in both directions, the public interest in disclosure clearly needs to be considerable before non-consensual disclosure will be legally justified. Unfortunately, what little case law there is leaves the ambit of the public interest justification open to some debate. This means that, in practice, health professionals must look to the guidance of the professional bodies and the Department of Health. The GMC, in particular, plays a key role in enforcing the duty of confidentiality.

The non-absolute nature of the duty of confidence is, for the reasons explained earlier, consistent with all the major moral theories. Differences between moral theories appear when determining the relative value given to different competing interests and the method for weighing those interests. The law, as usual, adopts language that seeks to cloak these differences. While the language of the "public interest" smacks of utilitarian reasoning, the language of rights has become increasingly prevalent since the implementation of the HRA 1998. In any event, a public interest enquiry could, in principle, track rights and virtues just as easily as collective utility.[92] I suggest that the law, however, is best interpreted as a compromise position, which grants greater presumptive protection to confidential information than is strictly required by act-utilitarianism but tends to weigh competing factors as if it were seeking to maximise utility rather than balance rights.

The leading case on disclosure in the public interest is *W v Egdell*.[93] The patient was detained in a secure hospital following his conviction for manslaughter after shooting dead five people and seriously injuring two others. To support his application for release to the mental health tribunal, the patient's solicitors sought an independent psychiatric report from Dr Egdell. This report expressed the view that the patient was highly dangerous and had a long standing interest in homemade bombs. Not surprisingly, the patient's solicitors withdrew the application for his release. Dr Egdell took steps to ensure that his report was made available to the medical director of the patient's hospital and the Home Secretary. The patient brought an action for breach of confidence. The Court of Appeal unanimously ruled that the public interest supported release of the report to the medical director and the Home Secretary. The Court was also not prepared to grant an injunction to prevent its further release to the mental health tribunal.

---

[91] *AG v Guardian* [1990] 1 A.C. 109 at 281.
[92] See Townend (2004, esp. 100–101) for an example of a rights-based interpretation of the public interest.
[93] [1990] Ch. 359.

The Court of Appeal considered the issue in *Egdell* to be one of two competing public interests: the public interest in maintaining confidentiality and the public interest in allowing restricted disclosure on the facts.[94] The weighing of these two interests was said to require careful balancing. On the facts, the disclosure was to prevent "a real risk of consequent danger to the public"[95] and had been to a restricted class of those with a legitimate interest in the information.[96] Bingham L.J. stated, obiter as this was prior to the HRA 1998, that he considered this decision to be consistent with art.8 of the Convention.[97] Article 8, contrary to the position adopted by the Court of Appeal in *Egdell*, requires any identifiable individual's *private interests* (particularly, the right to private life) to be weighed in the balance. The effect of this is simply that, in any particular factual situation, the balancing exercise must be between the *public and private interests* in maintaining confidentiality and the *public and private interests* in disclosure.[98] The bringing together of the law of confidentiality and the art.8 right to privacy[99] would not, however, have made any difference on the facts of *Egdell* itself. Article 8(2) accepts lawful and proportionate interference with the right to privacy to protect, among other interests, the rights and freedoms of others and to prevent disorder or crime. Dr Egdell's actions were a proportionate means of protecting legitimate interests.

The balancing exercise required by the public interest justification (and art.8(2)) was relatively straightforward on the facts of *Egdell*. Deriving generally applicable principles is somewhat difficult. Kennedy and Grubb have argued that the Court of Appeal's decision suggests a number of factors that determine the limits of the public interest defence: the disclosure should only be to those whom it is necessary to tell to protect the public, the risk of harm must be "real" rather than fanciful, and the risk must be one of "physical harm".[100] Brazier has argued that if a doctor reasonably foresees that non-disclosure poses a real risk of physical harm to another, the "courts should not be over-zealous in proving him wrong".[101] The adoption of a *reasonable belief* test would cut a mid-way position between requiring objective proof that a risk exists before any action is taken and the blanket deferral to the doctor's opinion. The courts have indicated that, unless it is not practicable or desirable to do so, the confidant should inform the confider that he intends to disclose.[102] The confider should, therefore, usually have an opportunity to seek assistance from the courts before the breach of confidence occurs, enabling the court to judge whether disclosure would be justified.

---

[94] [1990] Ch. 359 at 416 (Stephen Brown P.) and 419 (Bingham L.J.). May J. agreed with both.
[95] [1990] Ch. 359 at 424.
[96] [1990] Ch. 359 at 424. 419. As Bingham L.J. indicates, disclosure to the press, in memoirs, or to a friend would have been treated differently.
[97] [1990] Ch. 359 at 425.
[98] See e.g. *R. (S) v Plymouth City Council* [2002] EWCA Civ 388, para.32 (Hale L.J.).
[99] *Campbell v MGN* [2004] UKHL 22.
[100] Kennedy and Grubb 2000, 1100–1101. See also Brazier 2003, 68, Montgomery 2002, 268, Michalowski 2003, 190–191.
[101] Brazier 2003, 68.
[102] *Woolgar v Chief Constable of the Sussex Police* [1999] 3 All E.R. 604 and *Maddock v Devon County Council* [2003] EWHC 3494.

The professional bodies have provided their own guidance on when disclosure will be justified in the public interest. The Department of Health Code of Practice advises NHS staff that disclosure is permitted, on a case-by-case basis, to prevent abuse or serious harm to others or in relation to detection, investigation, or punishment of serious crime.[103] The risk of a traffic accident or the spread of a serious disease are given as examples of serious harm or abuse that can justify disclosure of information. Murder, manslaughter, rape, treason, kidnapping, and child abuse are given as examples of sufficiently serious crimes. The Code emphasises that "whenever possible" the disclosure should be discussed with the patient beforehand. The GMC and the BMA have provided detailed guidance along the same lines.[104] Sometimes it is not possible to discuss the matter with the patient beforehand, such as where the patient has died. In *Lewis v Secretary of State for Health*, discussed above, Foskett J. authorised the disclosure of confidential information related to deceased patients to an inquiry on the basis that the public interest in protecting that information was outweighed by the public interest in determining what had happened and why in the situation in question.[105]

6.3.2.1 Communicable diseases

Balancing the risk of physical harm to others against the risk of harm caused by breach of confidence poses some particularly interesting questions where the patient has a communicable disease. We are concerned with the common law public interest justification here, but it is worth pointing out two pieces of related legislation. Under s.11(1) of the Public Health (Control of Disease) Act 1984, a doctor is required to notify the relevant official if he becomes aware of, or suspects, that a patient is suffering from a notifiable disease.[106] Under the NHS (Venereal Diseases) Regulations 1974/29, information about sexually transmitted diseases can only be communicated for the purposes of treatment and prevention.[107]

It is possible to envisage many circumstances where a doctor's decision to release confidential patient information about a communicable disease will be justified in the public interest. Perhaps the most frequently discussed communicable disease is HIV/AIDS. HIV/AIDS is not a notifiable disease under the 1984 Act and it is unclear whether HIV/AID transmitted by means other than sexual intercourse would count as a sexually transmitted disease for the purposes of the 1974 Regulations.[108] A patient with HIV could pose a serious risk to the physical health of others if he participates in infection-transferring

---

[103] See DH 2003d, 34–35.
[104] See GMC 2004, paras 22–30 and BMA 2004, 189–194.
[105] [2008] EWHC 2196, esp. paras 58–60.
[106] See also Public Health (Infectious Diseases) Regulations 1988/1546.
[107] As amended and supplemented by the Health and Social Care (Community Health and Standards) Act 2003 (Supplementary and Consequential Provision) (NHS Foundation Trusts) Order 2003/696 and the NHS Trusts and Primary Care Trusts (Sexually Transmitted Diseases) Directions 2000.
[108] On the latter, compare Kennedy and Grubb 2000, 1127 with Laing and Grubb 2004, 594.

activities with uninfected individuals. The patient could have a sexual partner who is unaware of his condition or could be a surgeon who performs risky operations. These risks should not be overestimated. Not all sexual practices carry the same risk and there have only been two reported incidents of HIV transmission from infected healthcare workers to patients.[109] Moreover, many patients will modify their behaviour if properly informed of the risks. Applying the principles of *Egdell* and art.8, a doctor would appear to be permitted to warn those put at risk of HIV-infection by the behaviour of a patient who adamantly refuses to take precautions or inform them himself. GMC guidance is consistent with this position.[110] Doctors should not, however, rely on the public interest justification in all but the most extreme cases, because the public interest in maintaining confidentiality is particularly powerful where the consequence of breaching confidentiality could be to discourage others in a similar position from seeking medical advice or treatment in the first place.

There is professional guidance specifically addressing HIV,[111] but little case law. What little case law there is has been concerned with newspapers wanting to publish details about HIV positive health professionals. In the first, *X v Y*, the judge balanced the public interest in maintaining confidence with the public interest in the freedom of the press to publish the information before ruling in favour of the doctors who wanted to prevent the publication of their details.[112] In the second, *H v Associated Newspapers and N*, the Court of Appeal balanced the healthcare worker's interest in ensuring that no information be published that would lead to his identification with the newspaper's art.10 right to freedom of expression under the HRA 1998.[113] The newspaper had heard about the case when the claimant sought to prevent the Health Authority contacting his patients in a "lookback" exercise. Their Lordships were prepared to prevent publication of the identities of the claimant and the Health Authority, but were not prepared to order that the speciality be kept secret. He was a dentist. The Department has subsequently issued strict guidance on when to contact patients where a healthcare worker is found to be HIV positive. These guidance state that it is not necessary to contact patients *unless* it is possible that the patient has been exposed to the healthcare worker's blood in circumstances that this could have gone unnoticed (such as during the performance of a Caesarean section) or there are "other relevant considerations" (such as evidence of actual exposure or evidence of poor clinical practice).[114]

6.3.2.2 Genetic information

Genetic information is the subject of Ch.12, but it is worth briefly pausing here to note some of the confidentiality issues raised by genetic testing. Diagnosis of a genetic disease, or a genetic predisposition for a disease, will often reveal

---

[109] See DH 2002c, para.2.2. The two were a French orthopaedic surgeon and a Florida dentist.
[110] See GMC 2004, paras 24 and 27.
[111] See e.g. DH 2002c, paras 10.1–10.5.
[112] [1988] 2 All E.R. 648.
[113] [2002] EWCA Civ 195.
[114] See DH 2005c, para.8.13, read in the light of paras 8.4 and 8.13.

information that is relevant to other family members. Unlike psychotic patients and those infected with HIV, however, the risk posed to other family members will not stem from the patient's conduct. Moreover, genetic information is not always useful or desired. The vast majority of those who discover that they are at risk of having inherited Huntington's disease, for example, choose not to have a genetic test for the condition because it is fatal, incurable, and does not usually manifest until middle age or beyond. Nonetheless, where a patient's genetic information reveals that a relative is at a high risk of suffering *serious and preventable physical harm* as a result of a genetic condition that he could be unaware of, in principle, the *Egdell* principles should permit disclosure under the public interest justification.

The British Medical Association (BMA) has made it clear that it does not take the view that where genetic information is involved the real patient is the family.[115] (Some communitarian positions might well adopt such a view.) Instead the BMA emphasises the importance of maintaining patient confidentiality in the absence of a legal obligation or overriding public interest in disclosure.[116] This body has suggested a number of factors that doctors should take into account when deciding whether to disclose genetic information in breach of confidence, including the severity of the disorder, the level of predictability of the information provided by the testing, the actions that informed relatives could take to protect themselves from the risk, the consequences of withholding the information, the reasons given for refusing to share the information, and whether it is possible to identify relatives without the patient's assistance.[117] This guidance has no direct legal force but it is very likely to inform any future judicial consideration of this issue.

6.3.2.3 Could there be a duty to disclose under the law of negligence?

Up until now we have been concerned with when a doctor will be legally permitted to disclose confidential information. Non-disclosure in a situation in which the law would consider disclosure to be in the public interest cannot, for obvious reasons, found an action for breach of confidence. Could non-disclosure amounting to a failure to warn a third party who is subsequently injured by the patient found an action in *negligence*? Consider, for example, a doctor who fails to warn a patient's partner that his patient has HIV or a psychiatrist who fails to warn a patient's girlfriend that his patient has threatened to kill her.[118] For a negligence action to succeed, the claimant must be owed a duty of care by the defendant, the defendant's breach of duty must have caused the damage, and the defendant must have no applicable defence (see Ch.3).

There is no English case law on the failure to warn an identifiable victim of the risk posed by a patient. There is, however, some case law addressing the liability

---

[115] See BMA 2004, 315–317.
[116] See also HGC 2002, 10.
[117] See BMA 2004, 316.
[118] See *Pittman Estate v Bain* (1994) 112 D.L.R. (4th) 257 (Canadian case), and *Tarasoff v Regents of the University of California* (1976) 131 Cal. Rptr. 14 (US case), respectively.

of a doctor to a third party. In *Palmer v Tees HA*, a young girl was abducted, sexually assaulted, and murdered by a mental patient who had previously told those caring for him at a mental hospital that he had sexual feelings towards children and that a child would be murdered after his discharge.[119] The Court of Appeal held that no duty of care was owed, on the facts, to either the murdered child or her mother (who claimed for her own psychological injury). The Court considered there to be no "proximity" between the defendant and the claimant, largely because the claimant had not been identified or identifiable as the victim before her abduction.[120] Without deciding the issue, their Lordships indicated that they might have come to a different conclusion had the patient identified his victim beforehand.[121] This is precisely what happened in a California case, given as an example earlier, where a patient confided to his psychotherapist that he had an overwhelming desire to kill his girlfriend.[122] The psychotherapist informed the police but did not tell the patient's girlfriend, whom the patient later murdered. The California Supreme Court found the defendant liable for failing to breach the patient's confidence and warn his victim. The English courts are extremely reluctant to impose liability for the actions of third parties and, if they were to impose a duty to protect a third party from a patient's conduct, would be unlikely to require that the potential victim be warned as a necessary condition of discharging that duty.[123] While the Californian court was statutorily prevented from imposing liability on the psychotherapist for failing to take all reasonable steps to bring about the patient's confinement, the English courts would not be.

On the facts of the California case, had the psychotherapist chosen to warn the patient's girlfriend and been sued by the patient for breaching confidence, English law would clearly have allowed him to rely on the public interest defence. The public interest defence would, arguably, also have justified disclosure to the girlfriend. Nonetheless, given the law's reluctance to impose liability for the acts of a third party there is a big difference between saying that disclosure is legally permitted and saying that it is legally required. Moreover, the fine balancing required before disclosure is legally permitted surely suggests that doctors will not be required by the law of negligence to disclose confidential patient information in the form of a warning in the HIV or genetic examples given earlier. Whether this is ethically defensible is another matter. A duty to breach confidence so as to warn a third party of a risk would only be consistent with those moral theories recognising extensive (positive) duties to provide assistance capable of requiring infringement of the (negative) duty against breaching confidentiality.

---

[119] [2000] P.I.Q.R. P1.

[120] [2000] P.I.Q.R. P1, esp. P11–12. The Court of Appeal relied on earlier decisions of the House of Lords in *Home Office v Dorset Yacht* [1970] A.C. 1004 and *Hill v Chief Constable of West Yorkshire* [1989] A.C. 53.

[121] [2000] P.I.Q.R. P1, esp. P11–12 and P19 (Pill L.J.).

[122] *Tarasoff v Regents of the University of California* (1976) 131 Cal. Rptr. 14.

[123] In addition to the *Palmer* case, note the decisions in *Home Office v Dorset Yacht* [1970] A.C. 1004 and *Hill v Chief Constable of West Yorkshire* [1989] A.C. 53. There are often other ways of protecting a potential victim, see the Australian case of *PD v Harvey* [2003] NSWSC 487.

6.3.2.4 The public interest and the Data Protection Act 1998

The processing (including disclosure) of data concerning a patient's health is only permitted by the 1998 Act where there has been compliance with the Data Protection Principles (see 6.2.4). The first of these principles requires satisfaction of at least one condition from Sch.2 and one condition from Sch.3. These conditions were discussed in 6.2.4, above. Most are, in effect, specific public interest justifications for processing data.[124] A doctor's disclosure of information relating to a patient's communicable disease, or disclosure of genetic information revealing potential risks faced by the patient's relatives, would need to be justified by reference to the Sch.2 and 3 conditions. The Schedule 3 conditions are more stringent than those in Sch.2. A number of the Sch.3 conditions could potentially be relied on in the communicable disease or genetic information scenarios mentioned earlier. Disclosure might fall within the condition allowing processing that is *necessary* for *medical* purposes, as these are defined to include the purposes of preventative medicine, medical diagnosis, and the provision of care and treatment. In an extreme case, it might even be justified under the condition allowing processing that is *necessary* to protect another's *vital interests* (Sch.3 para.3). What will be sufficient to satisfy the Sch.3 conditions will arguably also be sufficient to render disclosure in the public interest for the purposes of the law of confidentiality. There is no case law on this point, but this surely follows if it is accepted that the Schedule conditions are intended to track public interest considerations.

6.3.3 Teaching, research, and audit

All health professionals need to be trained if they are to become competent, medical research is important for the improvement and development of medical treatments, and audits are important for the effective and competent running of the health service. Yet, access to patient information is often essential for these purposes. Usually the patient's consent is easy to obtain. Where it is not obtained or sought, there is a potential conflict between the interests protected by allowing patients to control the use of their medical information and the interests protected by limiting that control. That balance can be difficult from both a legal and a moral point of view. Not all teaching, research, or audit-related activities are equally important or defensible, but some will be of considerable importance. Medical research is examined in more depth in Ch.11. For present purposes, it should be noted that obtaining consent poses particular difficulties for some research projects. Obtaining consent could be impracticable or impossible where the research needs to involve a huge number of past patients (e.g. historical studies into the relationship between a particular

---

[124] The additional Sch.3 conditions laid down by the Data Protection (Processing of Sensitive Personal Data) Order 2000/417 explicitly require there to be a substantial public interest before the processing takes place.

drug and subsequent cancer) and could be scientifically undesirable where the self-selection of the research subjects is likely to distort the results (the so-called "consent bias").

This section will start with the law of confidentiality, before examining the impact of professional guidance and the Data Protection Act 1998. We have already seen that the use of patient information for *any* purpose within the ambit of the patient's consent will not amount to a breach of the patient's confidence. Some judicial dicta suggests that a patient might sometimes be taken to have given "implied consent" to the use of their medical data for "research, medical advancement or the proper administration" of the NHS.[125] However, reliance on any form of consent is a problematic rationale where the patient is not aware that such disclosures will take place and the disclosures in question are not necessary for the treatment purposes for which the patient has consented.[126] If the patient's consent were to be *imputed* as a matter of law, then the real basis for lawfulness of the disclosure would not truly be consent.

We have already seen that non-consensual disclosures can be lawful if they are in the public interest. Many teaching, research, and audit purposes will undoubtedly be in the public interest. However the case law on the public interest defence has been concerned with relatively specific issues. As one commentator has put it, the "authorities on the public interest defence deal with specific, identifiable and immediate risks to the public rather than potential or generalised risks, such as those posed by not pursuing potential medical advances by research"[127] and, one could add, those posed by not pursuing particular teaching practices or audits. The competing private and public interests against non-consensual disclosure can be considerable, especially where the medical information directly identifies individual patients. The Health Service Commissioner (popularly known as the Ombudsman and discussed in 2.3.3) upheld one complaint from a patient who discovered that a full-face frontal photograph of his naked body had been published in a medical textbook without his knowledge or permission.[128] The GMC guidance states that express consent is usually required where identifying information is to be used "for purposes such as research, epidemiology, financial audit or administration".[129] The BMA seems to distinguish internal "clinical audit", which is concerned with the quality of patient care, from "research, teaching, or financial audit".[130] In the former case, the BMA considers it acceptable to rely on implied consent, whereas in the latter cases "competent patients must be asked to give their express consent".[131]

The courts have yet to consider the use of identifiable information, except by way of an obiter statement in *Ex p. Source Informatics*, which was a case

---

[125] *R. v Department of Health Ex p. Source Informatics* [2001] Q.B. 424, per Letham J., who was addressing the use of anonymised data. Obiter in the Court of Appeal leaned against reliance on implied consent: [2001] Q.B. 424 at 444–445.
[126] See further Beyleveld and Histed 1999, 75–76.
[127] Case 2003, 219.
[128] See Brazier 2003, 418.
[129] GMC 2004, para.16.
[130] See BMA 2004.
[131] BMA 2004, 180 and 177, respectively.

concerned with the use of non-identifying (i.e. anonymised) data.[132] Simon Brown L.J., with whom the other judges agreed, expressed the view that the use of identifiable information for such purposes without consent is "very strictly controlled" and was acceptable "because it falls within the public interest or as is perhaps the preferable view, because the scope of the duty of confidentiality is circumscribed to accommodate it".[133] We will consider this latter approach, which is undoubtedly the most controversial, below.

6.3.3.1 Anonymisation: breach of confidentiality

Imagine a devout Catholic woman who, as a matter of religious conviction, is opposed to the use of chemical contraceptive methods.[134] Suppose further that she goes to see her doctor because she is concerned about her irregular menstrual cycles. If the doctor were to ask her to participate in research on chemical contraceptives, she would refuse. Would it be sufficient for the doctor to anonymise her data before it is used in such research? This will be referred to as the *Catholic woman scenario*.

Imagine another woman who actively campaigns against a company that aggressively markets baby milk in developing countries. She believes that women in developing countries should not be encouraged to rely on artificial baby milk because of the shortage of sterilised water and has helped to organise a consumer boycott of the company.[135] Imagine further that she visits her doctor with lactation problems. She would refuse, if asked, to participate in a research trial run by the company against which she is campaigning. She would, however, be happy for her medical data to be used by publicly-funded enterprises, or even other private enterprises, for this purpose. Would it be sufficient for the doctor to anonymise her data before it is used in such research? This will be referred to as the *baby milk scenario*.

Both of these scenarios are also relevant to the earlier section on the use of medical information derived from patients who are now dead (6.2.3). In that context the question to ask is: would it be sufficient for the doctor to wait until she dies before using her information for such research? Many of the same issues are raised here. If a culture of research using anonymised patient data (or data from dead patients) develops, it is only a matter of time before the data of those with firmly held views is used in contravention of those views. The individual from whom the information is derived might be opposed to the type of research (as in the Catholic woman scenario), the past or present behaviour of those conducting the research (as in the baby milk scenario), or the type of body conducting the research (imagine if in our baby milk scenario the woman was not prepared to allow her data to be used by *any* commercial entity). A blanket overriding of such views, without even giving patients the opportunity to object

---

[132] *R. v Department of Health Ex p. Source Informatics* [2001] Q.B. 424 at 444–445.
[133] [2001] Q.B. 424 at 444.
[134] This hypothetical scenario derives from Beyleveld and Histed 1999, 73–74.
[135] This scenario is hypothetical, despite some similarity to the consumer campaign once organised against a certain manufacturer of baby milk.

to the use of their data for non-essential purposes, could lead to sections of society losing confidence in the healthcare system. This is a form of feared end point argument, capable of being expressed using the metaphor of the slippery slope, as discussed in Ch.1 (1.4.2). The plausibility of the empirical prediction is bolstered by reactions to scandals that have led to public inquiries (such as those concerning Bristol Royal Infirmary and Alder Hey Hospital in Liverpool).[136] All empirical slippery slope arguments require the risk of the endpoint occurring to be assessed by reference to the benefits of running that risk and the cost of alternative mechanisms for preventing that risk manifesting. With regard to the argument in question here, this ethical evaluation must take account of any rights or interests in informational autonomy and privacy possessed by the patient. The argument in play here should lead us to question the acceptability of a blanket approach to the use of anonymised data.

The leading authority on the law in this area is the *Ex p. Source Informatics* case mentioned earlier.[137] Source Informatics, a database company, operated a scheme whereby information was obtained on GPs' prescribing habits from patient's prescriptions. Source Informatics intended to sell this information to pharmaceutical companies for marketing purposes. The scheme was, however, compromised by a Department of Health policy document that warned GPs and pharmacists that participation in such schemes put them at risk of breaching patient confidentiality, even though only anonymised data would be disclosed. Source Informatics sought judicial review of this policy document. The Department of Health argued that it was a breach of confidence to disclose patient information, even if anonymised, as it had been disclosed in confidence for the patient's "care and treatment and wider NHS purposes".[138]

At first instance, Latham J. ruled for the Department of Health, holding that the disclosure of data (irrespective of whether it is anonymised or not) without consent for *any* purpose other than that for which the data was provided was a prima facie breach of confidence.[139] The judge did not consider disclosure to Source Informatics to be justified in the public interest and refused to decide when disclosure for wider NHS purposes was justified. The Court of Appeal unanimously overruled this decision. Simon Brown L.J., with whom the other judges agreed, ruled that the scope of the duty of confidence, where equity provides the basis of the duty, turns on whether the use of the information is fair and the use of patient information by Source Informatics would not be unfair. The touchstone of fairness was said to be *the conscience of the confidant*,

> no more and no less. One asks, therefore, on the facts of the case: would a reasonable pharmacist's conscience be troubled by the proposed use to be made of patient's prescriptions?[140]

[136] See the Bristol Report (Kennedy et al. 2001) and the Alder Hey Report (Redfern et al. 2001).
[137] [2001] Q.B. 424.
[138] [2001] Q.B. 424 at 431.
[139] [1999] 4 All E.R. 185.
[140] [2001] Q.B. 424 at 439.

This was to be answered by reference to the interests at stake and on these facts the law's *only* concern was said to be the protection of the confider's privacy.[141] What is more, privacy was to be interpreted narrowly and was held to be adequately protected by the concealment of their identities by appropriate anonymisation.

The Court of Appeal emphasised that it was not ruling that confidential information loses all protection as soon as it is anonymised, citing with approval a first instance decision where the party proposing to anonymise and disclose the information had obtained it in flagrant breach of confidence.[142] The ratio of the Court of Appeal's decision must, however, be that patient information is no longer subject to a duty of confidentiality once it has been fully and effectively anonymised *by a party who has lawfully obtained it*. (A subsequent case shows that the sufficiency of anonymisation is to be determined in the light of all the evidence.)[143]

As stated earlier, the Court also stated obiter that anonymisation was not always required for use within the NHS for research and management purposes.[144] Many such uses of patient information were said to be potentially justifiable in the public interest or because the scope of the duty of confidentiality does not extend to them. This latter approach would, presumably, involve relying on the conscience test, whereby one asks whether the conscience of a reasonable person *in the position of the confider* would be troubled by the use of identifying data for the purpose in question. The conscience test, by modifying the scope of the duty of confidence, appears to make disclosure easier to justify than it would be under the public interest test, which operates only where a duty of confidence exists. The upshot is that the conscience test is more likely to lead to patient's interests being overridden.

Almost every premise in this reasoning is subject to challenge.[145] In any event, now that the House of Lords in *Campbell* has ruled that the action for breach of confidence should be interpreted in the light of art.8(1),[146] there is surely no room for a narrow interpretation of privacy that is incompatible with the well established approach to that article. As stated earlier, the right to respect for private life protected by art.8(1) is concerned with personal autonomy, not just the concealment of one's identity.[147] While it will be possible to bring some use of anonymised data within art.8(2), the use of the patient's data without their consent must be shown to be *necessary* and *proportionate* for one of the stated interests. This balancing exercise will surely be heavily weighted in the patient's favour where the patient has a conscientious objection to the use of their data for the relevant purpose (as in the Catholic woman and baby milk scenarios).[148] Such patients might also be able to rely on the art.9

---

[141] [2001] Q.B. 424 at 440.
[142] [2001] Q.B. 424 at 435–436, citing *X v Y* [1988] 2 All E.R. 648.
[143] See *H v Associated Newspapers and N* [2002] EWCA Civ 195.
[144] [2001] Q.B. 424 at 444.
[145] See Beyleveld and Histed 2000. Cf. Grubb 2000a, 117–118.
[146] [2004] UKHL 22. See 6.2.2, above.
[147] *Pretty v UK* (2002) 35 E.H.R.R. 1, para.62, and *R. (Burke) v GMC* [2004] EWHC 1879, para.62.
[148] See further Beyleveld and Townend 2004, 79–80.

right to freedom of thought, conscience, and religion.[149] The ratio in *Source Informatics* needs to be narrowly reinterpreted in the light of subsequent developments. It is legally suspect as it stands. The conscience test emphasises the confidant's interests over the rights of the confidant and a blanket exclusion of anonymised data from protection would allow the use of patient data for a contentious purpose even in the face of the express wishes of the patient.

6.3.3.2 Anonymisation: data protection

The provisions of the Data Protection Act were outlined above (6.2.3). It should also be mentioned that s.33 provides that the Second Data Protection Principle (which requires that personal data only be used for the purposes for which it was obtained) is not breached where the processing is for "research purposes", *provided that* (a) no measure or decision relating to a particular individual is based on it and (b) that its use is unlikely to cause substantial damage or substantial distress to any data subject (s.33(1), (2)).[150] The Catholic woman and baby milk scenarios are examples of situations where use of patient data for research purposes could lead to substantial distress, unless the phrase is to be given an artificially narrow interpretation.

At first sight, the application of the Act to the facts of *Source Informatics* appears to be straightforward. Given the Act's broad definition of "processing", the process of anonymisation will involve the processing of sensitive personal data. The First Data Protection Principle requires that any processing of patient health data be "necessary" for a condition under Sch.2 and a condition under Sch.3. In *Source Informatics*, the patients had not provided consent. It is difficult to see how anonymisation for the purpose of selling information to Source Informatics was "necessary" for the legitimate interests of doctors/pharmacists or the exercise of public functions in the public interest under Sch.2.[151] It is also difficult to see how such an activity could be "necessary" for "medical purposes" under Sch.3. "Medical research" is stated to be a "medical purpose" under Sch.3, but not in the equivalent provision of the Directive (i.e. art. 8(3)). "Medical research" therefore needs to be interpreted narrowly if the Act is to be compatible with the Directive. The application of s.33 also turns on what is meant by "research purposes", defined there to include statistical purposes. However, to interpret research purposes as capturing activities solely concerned with marketing by a third party commercial organisation would significantly enfeeble the Second Data Protection Principle and thereby render it inapplicable to the vast majority of data processing. In my view, s.33 cannot be relied on in these circumstances and the Second Principle therefore applies. Moreover, it is hard to see how the Second Principle is satisfied because the data was obtained

---

[149] See Beyleveld and Histed 1999, 74.

[150] Cf. art.6(1)(b) of the Directive.

[151] As Grubb points out (2004a, 119), processing for the data controller's legitimate purposes is also subject to a proviso: "except where the processing is unwarranted in any particular case by reason of prejudice to the rights and freedoms or legitimate interests of the data subject".

for treatment purposes and the data subjects had not been informed that it would also be sold to a commercial organisation. Thus, at first sight, the scheme operated by Source Informatics appears to be inconsistent with the Act.

However, the Court of Appeal in *Source Informatics* considered the scheme not to breach the Directive and, by implication, not to breach the subsequently enacted Data Protection Act. The reasoning of the Court of Appeal is, to say the least, difficult to defend.[152] The Court of Appeal took the view that properly anonymised data falls outside of the scope of the Directive![153] While it might do *after* it has been anonymised, the party anonymising the data must surely satisfy the requirements of the Directive/Act. The Court of Appeal seems to have been unduly distracted by a question that was not in issue on the facts, namely, whether Source Informatics' actions breached the Directive. It is also worth bearing in mind that the First Principle additionally requires that where data are obtained from the data subject, as in the *Source Informatics* scenario, specific information must be provided, so far as is practicable. Patients picking up prescriptions could easily be told that their data is to be anonymised and sold.

6.3.3.3 Statutory exception to the duty of confidentiality

The Department of Health withdrew its petition to appeal *Source Informatics* to the House of Lords.[154] The reason for this was that the Government intended to enact legislation that would enable the Secretary of State to (a) prohibit the processing of patient information for commercial and direct marketing purposes and (b) allow the use of patient information for wider NHS purposes. Political opposition led to the dropping of (a) and this might lead some to rely on the Court of Appeal's dubious views on the application of the Data Protection Directive/Act. The legislative response was s.60 of the Health and Social Care Act 2001, now re-enacted as s.251 of the National Health Service Act 2006. This provision allows the Secretary of State to issue regulations permitting the use of confidential patient information without consent for wider NHS purposes. It can only be relied on where the information will be used for "medical purposes" in the interests of improving patient care or in the public interest (s.251(1)), and where it is not "reasonably practicable" to achieve that purpose by other means (s.251(4)). Such regulations must be laid before Parliament. Before this, the Secretary of State must seek the views of the National Informational Governance Board for Health and Social Care (NIGB) (s.252).[155]

Section 251 empowers the Secretary of State to pass regulations to allow the use of confidential patient information without consent, *despite any obligation of confidence* (s.251(2)(c)). Section 251(7) states that regulations passed under s.251(1)

---

[152] See Beyleveld and Histed 2000, 292–293 and Grubb 2004a, 118–120.
[153] The Court relied on a perverse reading of Recital 26. See further Beyleveld and Townend 2004.
[154] See Beyleveld and Histed 2000, 310 (n.91).
[155] Until the end of 2008, this role was performed by the Patient Information Advisory Group.

may not make provision for the processing of prescribed patient information in a matter inconsistent with the provisions of the Data Protection Act 1998. But s.251(8) goes on to state that s.251(7) "does not affect the operation" of regulations made under s.251(2)(c)). This suggests that the Secretary of State is empowered to act inconsistently with the Data Protection Act by issuing a regulation. Contravention of the Data Protection Act will, however, usually also contravene the Directive and any regulations passed under s.251 will have to be interpreted (as far as possible) consistently with that Directive.[156] One requirement of the Directive (which forms First Principle of the Data Protection Act) is that, where data are obtained from the data subject, the data subject must be provided with information, *so far as is practicable*, on (inter alia) the uses to which the data will be put and the identity of any person to whom the data will be disclosed.

The Health Service (Control of Patient Information) Regulations 2002/1438 were passed under s.60 of the Health and Social Care Act and these remain in force following the replacement of that provision by s.251 of the NHS Act 2006.

Regulation 2 of these regulations provides for the creation of databases for medical purposes related *to* the diagnosis and treatment of neoplasia, i.e. tumours. The intention was to allow cancer patients' information to be entered on to Cancer Registries without consent or anonymisation. Significantly, these regulations do not distinguish between patient information relating to neoplasia and patient information relating to patients with/referred for neoplasia. Read literally this would appear to allow any research without consent using the medical information of patients who happen to have neoplasia. While the regulations explicitly disapply the common law obligation of confidentiality, they do not explicitly mention the Data Protection Act. The provisions of the Data Protection Act still apply.

Regulation 5 grants the Secretary of State the power to authorise the processing of "confidential patient information" for "medical purposes" in circumstances set out in the Schedule of the Regulations. The ambit of this power was examined in *Lewis v Secretary of State for Health*—the case considered above in which High Court was asked to consider the disclosure of the medical records of deceased patients to an inquiry.[157] In this case, it was argued that the relevant disclosure had been authorised by the Secretary of State under the powers granted to him by reg.5 on the basis that the purpose of the disclosure fell within para.5 of the Schedule, namely, "The audit, monitoring and analysing of the provision made by the health service for patient care and treatment". Foskett J. rejected this claim. In the process of reaching this conclusion, he offered the view that the Regulations are restricted to "patient information *generated within the NHS*".[158] In any event, on the facts, the Regulations were held not to apply on the basis that the taking of tissues after death did not amount to

---

[156] Note that national courts are required to interpret domestic law so that it achieves the objectives of Directives *if it is possible to do so: Marleasing SA v La Comercial Internacional de Alimentacion SA* [1990] E.C.R. I-4135, para.8, and *Miret v Fondo de Guarantia Salaria* [1993] E.C.R. I-6911, para.20.

[157] [2008] EWHC 2196.

[158] [2008] EWHC 2196, para.46 (original emphasis). See also paras 48–49.

"care and treatment", as required by the Regulations.[159] Foskett J, nonetheless, authorised the disclosure on other grounds; holding, on general confidentiality principles, that disclosure was justified in the public interest.

6.4 Access to records

6.4.1 The Data Protection Act 1998

Patients not only want to prevent the disclosure of their medical information, they sometimes want to gain access to their medical records. The principal legal route by which a patient can gain access to his medical records is s.7 of the Data Protection Act 1998, which grants data subjects a right to certain information from the data controller. The Act does not say that data subjects must be adults, so it appears that any competent patient can rely on this provision when seeking to gain access to their health records. Those with parental responsibility for a child can arguably also rely on s.7 to gain access to their child's records.[160] For the s.7 rights to be triggered, the data controller must have received a written request, a fee not exceeding the prescribed maximum (under secondary legislation this will usually be £10),[161] and any further information that he requests in order to satisfy himself as to the applicant's identity and to locate the information sought (s.7(2), (3)). Once triggered, the data protection controller must supply the information "promptly" and in any event within 40 days (s.7(8), (10)). If the data controller improperly refuses access, the person making the request may apply to the court (s.7(9)). In addition, such a failure could lead to enforcement or penal sanctions from the Information Commissioner (Pt V).

Access is subject to many exceptions and limitations. Information held for research, historical, or statistical purposes is exempt, unless it is used to support decisions with respect to particular individuals or processing will (or is likely to) cause substantial damage or substantial distress to any data subject (s.33(1), (4)). This exemption should not apply to the Catholic woman and baby milk scenarios that were outlined earlier as processing in those scenarios is

---

[159] [2008] EWHC 2196, paras 45–54.

[160] This is implied by Data Protection (Subject Access Modification) (Health) Order 2000/413, art.5(3). Nonetheless, Laing and Grubb (2004, 635–638) argue that the precise wording of s.7 presents interpretative difficulties for parents or relatives seeking to rely on this provision. Any interpretative difficulties should, however, be read in the light of the purposive approach to interpretation that the appeals courts tend to adopt (see e.g. See *R. (Bruno Quintavalle) v Secretary of State for Health* [2003] UKHL 13 and *R. (Josephine Quintavalle) v HFEA* [2005] UKHL 28). Also, where the child's Convention rights are invoked those rights will be exercisable by the parent as legal proxy (see *Glass v UK* (2004) 39 E.H.R.R. 15), and the Data Protection Act must be interpreted, so far as possible, to ensure compliance with those rights (s.3, HRA 1998).

[161] Data Protection (Subject Access) (Fees and Miscellaneous Provisions) Regulations 2000/191, reg.3.

likely to cause substantial distress. It will, however, cover data held for many research or audit purposes. There are other exemptions. For example, any information that relates to a third party is exempt, unless that person has consented to its release or it is reasonable to release it without consent (s.7(4)). The most significant exemption is undoubtedly the harm exemption laid down by secondary legislation passed under the Act.[162] This allows a health professional to withhold a patient's records where it would be likely to cause serious harm to the physical or mental health of the data subject or any other person.[163]

6.4.2 Other legal routes

To avoid the potential gap created by the fact that the 1998 Act only applies to living patients, some parts of an Act that was otherwise repealed by the 1998 Act remain in force. Section 3(1)(f) of the Access to Health Records Act 1990 continues to grant a prima facie right of access to health records to the executors of the deceased patient's estate or a family member with a potential legal claim arising from the patient's death. The scope and limitations to these rights are similar to those apply to the s.7 right. The 1998 Act is also supplemented by the Access to Medical Reports Act 1988 and the common law. The rights granted by these are limited and, in the case of the common law, far from settled.

The 1988 Act grants a right of access to *medical reports* prepared by the patient's doctor for employment or insurance purposes (s.1 read in the light of s.2(1)). Under s.5, the patient is granted the right to withhold consent to the release of such a report and to request the amendment of anything that he considers to be incorrect or misleading (and, if the doctor refuses to amend the report, the patient may attach an explanatory statement). These rights are limited and subject to a number of exceptions. They are *limited* because they only apply to certain types of reports (i.e. those prepared for employment or insurance purposes) made by doctors responsible for the care of the patient (which a doctor employed by the patient's employer or insurer for the sole purpose of making the report will not be). Also, the only remedy provided is the right to make an application to the court to obtain an order requiring compliance (s.8). The *exceptions* deny the patient a right to gain access where *the doctor* considers that it would be likely to cause serious harm to the patient's or another's mental or physical health, or would reveal the doctor's treatment intentions for the patient (s.7(1)), or where the information in the report also concerns another person who has not consented (s.7(2)). The wording of these exemptions is very similar to the equivalent exemptions applying to s.7 of the Data Protection Act 1998. The only

---

[162] Data Protection (Subject Access Modification) (Health) Order 2000/413, passed under s.30 of the 1998 Act.

[163] Order 2000/413, arts 3(1) and 5. If the data controller is not a health professional, he can only withhold information under this provision if an "appropriate health professional" considers the harm exemption to be satisfied: arts 5(2), 6, and 7.

real difference is that the harm exemption here explicitly turns on a subjective test, i.e. whether "in the opinion of the practitioner" the disclosure would be likely to cause serious harm to health.

Those hoping to supplement the provisions of the 1988 and 1998 Acts by relying on the common law are likely to be disappointed. The leading case on disclosure at common law is somewhat equivocal about whether the patient actually has any rights of access at common law. In *Ex P. Martin*, the patient sought access to records that fell outside of the access rights granted by the legislation then in force.[164] What he really wanted to find out was why a social worker with whom he had fallen in love with had been taken off his case in 1966. The Court of Appeal held that the health authority and the doctor, as the owner of a patient's medical records, could lawfully deny the patient access to them if it is in the patient's best interests to do so, such as where disclosure would be detrimental to the patient's health. On the facts, the health authority had offered to release the information to the patient's doctor to judge whether disclosure would be detrimental to his health. Their Lordships considered that offer to be a complete answer to any claim that the patient might have.[165] This case is distinctly unsatisfactory as a precedent.[166] It remains uncertain whether the common law will ever be any use to patients seeking to gain access to their medical records.

6.5 Conclusion

There are many areas where the impact of the law of confidentiality is still relatively uncertain. The scarcity of case law is likely to remain because litigation is usually far less attractive to patients than complaining to the GMC (or equivalent professional bodies for health professionals other than doctors), the Ombudsman, or the Information Commissioner (under the Data Protection Act). Despite high-profile scandals that have been followed by inquiries (notably those concerning Bristol Royal Infirmary and Alder Hey Hospital in Liverpool),[167] the public as a whole still appear to trust the medical professional to protect the confidentiality of their medical data. One has to wonder, however, whether a scandal along the lines of the Catholic woman or baby milk scenarios might one day alter that. Research publications can make a professional career (see further Ch.11) and the increasing infiltration of financial forces into medical care can only increase the pressure for data to be sold for profit. Dangers, nonetheless, usually lurk around more than one corner and none of the major moral theories places unconditional value on confidentiality and privacy.

---

[164] *R. v Mid-Glamorgan Family Health Services Authority Ex P. Martin* [1995] P.I.Q.R. P103.
[165] [1995] P.I.Q.R. P103 at P108, P110.
[166] See Laing and Grubb 2004, 635–638.
[167] See the Bristol Report (Kennedy et al. 2001) and the Alder Hey Report (Redfern et al. 2001).

6.6 Further reading

Beyleveld, Deryck and Histed, Elise (2000) "Betrayal of Confidence in the Court of Appeal." 4 *Medical Law International* 277–311.

Beyleveld, Deryck (2004) "The Duty to Provide Information to the Data Subject: Articles 10 and 11 of Directive 95/46/EC." In Deryck Beyleveld, David Townend, Ségoléne Rouillé-Mirza, and Jessica Wright (eds) *The Data Protection Directive and Medical Research Across Europe.* (Aldershot: Ashgate), 69–87.

Loughrey, Joan (2008) "Can You Keep A Secret? Children, Human Rights, and the Law of Medical Confidentiality." 20(3) *Child and Family Law Quarterly* 312–334.

Chapter 7

ABORTION

7.1 Introduction

In December 1994, an extreme anti-abortionist opened fire on two neighbouring abortion clinics in Boston, killing two people and injuring at least five others. He then headed 600 miles south and was arrested as he fired shots into another clinic. He later committed suicide in prison. In the same year, another anti-abortionist was convicted of shooting and killing an obstetrician and his driver outside a clinic in Florida. He was executed in 2003.[1] Fortunately such extremism on the abortion issue has not (yet) been seen in Britain. Abortion is a source of considerable controversy but lacks the nasty bite of the crusading killer. Abortion is, after all, really about the value that should be attached to human life. It is about

---

[1] These two incidents are reported on *http://www.news.bbc.co.uk*. See undated article entitled "1994: Gunman kills two women at abortion clinic" and BBC 2003d, respectively.

whether it is permissible to kill a fetus, and whether and when the medical profession should act to free a pregnant woman from an unwanted pregnancy.

The abortion debate is seeped in ethical controversy and the moral position adopted makes a huge difference. The existence of different views and regulatory approaches raises practical issues beyond extremism. Britain's relatively permissive regulatory approach to abortion encourages *medical tourism*, as women (particularly Irish women) travel to this country for treatment not available in their home country. Despite this tourism, the Irish only narrowly rejected the adoption of an even stricter abortion law in a 2002 constitutional referendum.[2] Unlike Ireland, where abortion is permitted only to save the life of the pregnant woman,[3] the legality of abortion on more general grounds has been clear in Britain for nearly four decades. Before examining the detail of the abortion legislation, however, this chapter will seek to map the moral debate.

For convenience, in this chapter I will refer to a human being from conception until birth as a *fetus*. Scientists tend to restrict use of the term "fetus" to eight weeks gestation and beyond. In other chapters, where the focus is only the very early stage of development, I will use the term embryo. Here, however, using the term fetus seems stylistically preferable to constantly saying "embryo and/or fetus" or using the composite "embryo-fetus".

7.2 The ethics of abortion

Abortion is sometimes presented as involving a conflict between the moral interests of the unborn child and those of the pregnant woman. While such an approach is rejected by some virtue and compromise positions, it is unavoidable if one adopts a duty-based, rights-based, or utilitarian position granting direct moral protection to both the fetus and the pregnant women. For there to be a conflict at all a fetus must have *moral value or status*, in the sense of being granted duties of protection. This issue—the moral status of the unborn child—is one of the most hotly debated issues within bioethics.

Conceptually, moral duties towards a being can be imposed in two ways. The first way is for that being to be owed duties *directly*, solely on the basis of its characteristics. The second way is for the being to attract protection *indirectly*, as a means of protecting those (others) who possess moral status. This is often forgotten. We do not need to have duties directly *to* a fetus for us to have duties *in relation to* a fetus. Even if the fetus had no more moral status than a sausage or tomato, it would not follow that anything and everything could permissibility be done to a fetus. In some circumstances deliberately damaging a fetus might harm those to whom we have direct duties. It might, for example, endanger the pregnant woman, violate the property rights of its parents, or demonstrate harmful tendencies likely to lead to the violation of duties to those

---

[2] See Cowan 2002.
[3] The Eighth amendment to the Irish constitution (art.40.3.3), as interpreted by the Supreme Court in *Attorney General v X* [1992] 1 I.R. 1.

who do matter.[4] This whole area is beset with terminological difficulties.[5] What is clear is that the most controversial issue is whether the early human is owed direct duties. If the fetus is owed direct duties, it can be said to have *moral status*. This issue will be addressed, before considering the major arguments over abortion within medical ethics.

7.2.1 The moral status of the fetus

7.2.1.1 Grounds for moral status

Possession of moral status can be grounded on possession of a number of characteristics or properties. There are many possible criteria. Some wish to grant moral status to those who are

(a) living creatures;

(b) sentient, i.e. capable of experiencing pleasure or pain;

(c) biologically human;

(d) agents, i.e. able to act for purposes constituting their reasons for action;

(e) partial agents, i.e. non-agents who possess some of the characteristics of agents; *or*

(f) potential agents, i.e. non-agents who have the potential to become agents.

These are just examples. Each criterion has its supporters and critics. For example, some duty-based positions wish to ground possession of moral status on membership of the species *Homo sapiens*;[6] yet others denounce this criterion as a morally repugnant prejudice comparable to racism and sexism.[7] All attempts to distinguish those possessing moral status from those not possessing moral status will inevitably be considered morally arbitrary by those who take a different view of where this distinction is to be drawn.

The criterion of moral status in play will determine the extent to which our moral obligations to the unborn child's interests can come into conflict with our moral obligations to the pregnant woman. As stated in Ch.1 (1.4.3.1), the value of the fetus is easy to map according to whether and to what extent it is thought to possess moral status. At one extreme are moral positions holding that the fetus deserves the same level of protection as an adult human being. According to what may be called the *full status* position, full moral status is to be granted to the fetus from the moment of its creation. At the other extreme is what may be called the *no status* position, which holds that the fetus itself has no intrinsic value or

---

[4] For a detailed explanation of such arguments for indirect duties, see Pattinson 2002a, 28–33.
[5] What I called *moral status* can be referred to as intrinsic or direct moral status, standing, or value, or even dignity (so that possessing dignity means being the object of direct duties).
[6] See e.g. Noonan 1970 and Finnis 2001.
[7] See e.g. Singer 1995.

status, until at least birth. According to this position, a fetus is no more than a collection of cells whose intrinsic features grant it no special protection. Between these two extremes are *limited status* positions, which hold that the fetus has a status resting somewhere between full and none. The most popular limited position is the *proportional status* position, which holds that the moral status of the fetus increases with gestational development until it obtains full moral status at birth or beyond. Thus, the fetus can be recognised as having moral status to the same degree as the pregnant woman (full status), to a degree less than the pregnant woman (limited status, or where that status increases with gestational development, proportional status), or to no degree at all (no status).

The moral status of the fetus is a key factor in determining the permissibility of abortion. Those adopting the full status position must consider abortion to be morally equivalent to murder. To deliberately induce the termination of a pregnancy is equivalent to poisoning or stabbing an innocent adult. At the other extreme, the no status position must hold that abortion involves no intrinsic wrong. If we ignore its (indirect) effects on others, killing a fetus is no more problematic than cutting one's toenails. Between these two extremes the unborn child cannot be treated as if it has the same status as the pregnant woman or as if it were a mere collection of cells. It follows that, from the limited status position, abortion cannot be left as a free-for-all or prohibited in all circumstances. The proportional status position is more specific. The closer to birth, the greater weight must attach to the fetus and the greater the justificatory burden placed on those who wish to abort.

Some prefer the labels of "pro-choice" and "pro-life" (or "liberal" and "conservative"). These positions reduce to what I have called the no and full status positions, respectively. The "pro-choice" position implies that the fetus has no status, because otherwise abortion cannot always and automatically be solely a matter of choice for the pregnant woman. As Peter Singer has put it, "To present the issue of abortion as a question of individual choice (like sexual behaviour between consenting adults) is already to presuppose that the fetus does not really count".[8] In contrast, the "pro-life" position implies that the fetus has full status. Singer argues that the pro-life label is also misleading because it is human life that advocates tend to value, and then not all human life is valued equally because advocates tend to support killing in war or capital punishment, and focus more on abortion than on saving the lives of existing humans dying from starvation or preventable disease.[9] Although labels are no more than tools for communication, the no, full, and limited status labels should be less misleading.

7.2.1.2 The major moral positions

The major moral camps outlined in Ch.1 do not map straightforwardly on to the no, full, and limited status framework. It cannot be emphasised too strongly that utilitarianism, rights-based, duty-based, virtue ethics, and compromise positions are all collections of moral theories. To locate one's position within

[8] Singer 1994, 85.
[9] Singer 1994, 86.

one of these camps does not automatically commit one to a particular view on the moral status of the fetus. It does, however, commit one to a view on how the interests of the fetus (if it has moral status) are to be weighed against those of the pregnant woman.

Utilitarianism comes in many flavours and is compatible with a number of criteria of moral status. For a utilitarian granting moral status to those capable of *sentience*, the permissibility of abortion depends on the distress inflicted by abortion on the fetus (which usually means the earlier the better) and the distress of the mother if she has to carry the fetus to term. If one assumes that the early fetus is not capable of consciousness and experiencing pain, the fetus has moral status only when this threshold is crossed. For a utilitarian granting moral status only to those capable of *exercising preferences* (understood as choices, not mere interests or pro-attitudes), moral status is grounded in agency. If one assumes that a fetus is not an agent, then the *no status* position follows automatically from this version of utilitarianism.

Peter Singer adopts a version of preference utilitarianism holding that moral status depends on having preferences, understood as interests. According to Singer, to have any moral status at all one must be sentient (which requires consciousness and self-awareness), and those with greater capacity for suffering have greater moral status. Only when the fetus becomes capable of feeling pain—which Singer judges to be at around 18 weeks—does it have any moral interests.[10] According to Singer, it follows that,

> At least when carried out before 18 weeks, abortion is in itself morally neutral. Even later abortions, when some pain may be involved, could be justified if the outcome were to prevent much greater suffering [to any being capable of suffering] . . .[11]

The moral status of a fetus is thus limited. Singer holds that it does not gain full status until well after birth when it becomes a "person". A person is understood as a rational being with a conception of self in the present and future—what I have called an agent.[12] The implications of applying a utilitarian calculus go far beyond abortion. As Singer willingly concedes, it follows that the killing of an early infant can also be permissible, at least when the parents-to-be do not want a child,[13] and more so when the infant is disabled.[14] Singer is not the only utilitarian theorist to rest full status on agency.[15]

---

[10] See Singer 1993, 163–169. See also Singer 1994, esp. 208–210.

[11] Singer 1993, 166. See also Singer 1993, 151.

[12] See Singer 1993, 87. Singer presents a number of reasons why killing a "person" is more serious then killing a merely conscious being (see Singer 1993, ch. 4 and 194). These include the greater disutility generated by killing a being capable of fearing its own death and the disutility of thwarting a desire to go on living.

[13] See Singer 1993, esp. 171–174.

[14] See Singer 1993, esp. 191.

[15] John Harris holds that full status is possessed by "persons", understood as those capable of valuing their own existence (see Harris 1985, ch.1). (He suggests, but does not expressly state, that those who appear to be non-persons have no moral status.) According to Harris, "The capacity to value existence in this sense is a fairly low-level capacity; it does not require rationality in any very sophisticated sense of that term, merely the ability to want to experience the future, or to want not to experience it and the awareness of those wants" (Harris 1985, 18). This suggests that Harris wishes to rely on partial agency.

Rights-based theories—where rights are understood as justifiable moral claims imposing correlative duties, the benefits of which are waivable by the rights-holder—are committed to grounding moral status on agency. Only agents are capable of exercising rights in the sense of waiving the benefit of those rights.[16] As already stated, if one assumes that the fetus is not an agent, the *no status* position automatically follows. This is, for example, the position of Mary Anne Warren, who appears to use the word "person" to refer to what I have called an agent.[17]

The duty-based camp is compatible with any criterion of moral status. Although membership of *Homo sapiens* is of key importance to all Judaeo-Christian religions, not all adopt the full status position of the Catholic Church. The present day official Roman Catholic position noticeably rests possession of moral status on being human, so that all biological humans from conception are regarded as possessing the same level of moral status as you or I.[18] (This position holds that it is always wrong to *intentionally* kill an innocent human—the sanctity of life position—and a human is defined to exist from conception. It follows that bringing about fetal death is only permitted if it is not intentional.)[19] In contrast, Orthodox Judaism does not grant moral status to the early fetus. It is often forgotten that Immanuel Kant's duty-based theory granted moral status only to agents.[20]

Many theorists have argued that resting moral status on *agency* (irrespective of whether one is a utilitarian, duty-based, or rights-theorist) not only denies the fetus moral status, but also denies moral status to infants and mentally disabled adults.[21] Positions holding abortion to be permissible on such a ground thus become positions supporting infanticide and the killing of mentally disabled adults. However, this makes assumptions about the attributes of fetuses, infants, and mentally disabled adults that are not morally neutral. I will argue in Ch.17 that *categorical* moral theories granting moral status only to (actual and prospective) agents cannot treat fetuses, infants, or the mentally disabled as non-agents, even though they do not display the attributes of full agency. It needs to be borne in mind that all moral theories require *both* a criterion of moral status *and* a theory of what beings in the empirical world satisfy the relevant criterion. Applying a criterion of moral status to fetuses can, depending on the moral theory in play, require counter-intuitive moral assumptions about the attributes

[16] Nozick, when presenting his rights-based theory, suggests that moral status requires rationality, free will, moral agency, and "the ability to regulate and guide its life in accordance with some overall conception it chooses to accept": Nozick 1974, 48–51. (He sums these attributes up in terms of the ability "to have or strive for meaningful life".)

[17] See Warren 1973.

[18] See Pope John Paul II 1993. See also Finnis 1973. Until 1869, the Catholic Church regarded quickening (the point at which the movement of the fetus can be felt) as the point when the fetus attains moral status. Some Catholics continue to reject the full status position: see Farley 2001.

[19] Sanctity of life supporters also appeal to the principle of double effect, which distinguishes between intentional conduct and the foreseen consequences of that conduct. See further Ch.16 (16.2.1).

[20] See Kant 1948. Kant's theory is discussed in Ch.17.

[21] See e.g. Abbott 1978, who argues that this is an implication of the concept of a "person" adopted by Tooley 1972 and Warren 1973.

of the being that you are actually dealing with. This complicates the application of many moral theories (see 17.3).

There are also many theories that appeal to *potentiality*. Some uses of potentiality are invalid. It does not follow from the fact that an actual x (agent, human, or whatever) has moral status that a potential x has moral status. Potential qualification is not the same thing as actual qualification.[22] To use the words of John Harris, "We are all potentially dead, but no one supposes that this fact constitutes a reason for treating us as if we were already dead".[23] This logical point does not, however, show that potentiality must be irrelevant to the possession of moral status. Harris raises a further objection:

> if the potentiality argument suggests that we have to regard as morally significant anything which has the potential to become a fully fledged human being, and hence have some moral duty to protect and actualize all human potential, then we are in for a very exhausting time of it indeed.[24]

There are two possible responses to this. *First*, a proponent of potentiality could simply bite the bullet and accept that we are obliged to protect and actualise such potential *insofar as we can*. *Second*, a proponent can take advantage of the "if" and develop a potentiality argument that does not impose a duty to protect and actualise all potential. Potentiality does not have to be used to ground full moral status; it can also be used to ground a fixed level of limited status or status that is proportionate to the degree of potentiality possessed. If potentiality gives rise to less than full moral status, then (depending on the underlying moral theory) protecting the greater needs of those with greater moral status could be a more important moral objective. Also, potentiality itself might only be viewed as morally relevant when it achieves a particular threshold.

It is hardly worth mentioning that the compromise position is compatible with any view of the status of the fetus. Predictably, many of those in the compromise camp are attracted to the limited status position as some form of mid-way between the no and full status positions.[25] In practice, just about all legal systems can only be consistently viewed as adopting compromise positions. (Ireland is an exception.) As will become apparent, the particular compromise position adopted in Britain is best viewed as adopting a *proportional status* position. The legal constraints on what may be done to a fetus increase with gestational development. Before implantation the fetus can be lawfully destroyed without relying upon any of the grounds in the abortion legislation (and, if created outside the body, it must be destroyed unless both gamete donors consent to its storage or use: see Ch.10). The legal grounds for abortion are more restrictive after 24 weeks and *legal* personality is only obtained at birth. Thus, it can be said that fetal development can be divided into three legally relevant stages: preimplantation, implantation to 24 weeks, post-24 weeks to birth.

---

[22] Feinberg and Levenbrook (1993, 206) refer to this as the "logical point about potentiality".
[23] Harris 1998, 50.
[24] Harris 1998, 50.
[25] See e.g. Dworkin 1993.

7.2.2 Other issues raised by abortion

In one of the most famous and influential articles ever written on abortion, Judith Jarvis Thomson tried to avoid the need to settle the question of whether and to what extent the fetus has moral status.[26] She asks you to imagine that you wake up one morning and find yourself in a hospital bed connected to an unconscious man. The man is a world-famous violinist with a kidney disease. He will only survive if he is plugged into someone of the same blood type for nine months, and you are the only person with the suitable blood type. You are in this position because you were kidnapped by the Society of Music Lovers. Do you have to give up your liberty in this way for nine months to save the life of this violinist? Thomson argues that *even if a fetus has moral status equivalent to a normal adult*, a woman has no duty to carry a fetus if she has no duty to remain connected to the violinist in this situation. Further, she holds that you would be under no moral obligation to allow the violinist to use your kidneys for nine months. There appear to be only three lines of response: one can accept that there is a duty in both cases (i.e. it is impermissible to disconnect the violinist or abort the fetus); accept that there is no duty in either case; or identify a morally relevant disanalogy between the two cases.[27]

The third option has attracted the most support. Some commentators wish to rely on a notion of fault, pointing out that, except in the case of rape, a pregnant woman has voluntarily run the risk of pregnancy by having sexual intercourse.[28] However, the woman's "responsibility" can vary in degree. Pregnancy can be the result of a deliberate choice, but it can also be the product of carelessness (e.g. failure to use contraception) or mere unluckiness (e.g. contraceptive failure). To hold the woman morally responsible for the pregnancy, and thus the occurrence of the dilemma, requires a moral judgment that she is morally required to bear the costs of pregnancy avoidance. If contraception is used and fails, is the woman morally responsible on the basis that she failed to take more dramatic steps (sterilisation or abstinence from sex)?[29] The answer unavoidably depends on the underlying moral position adhered to. The freedom to release oneself from physical invasion and one's prior responsibility for the invasion are far from morally neutral.

Thomson's analogy raises more questions than it answers. A proper moral response requires an underlying moral position. As Hare points out,

> If philosophers are going to apply ethical theory successfully to practical issues, they must first have a theory ... [Yet Thomson] simply parades the examples before us and asks what we would say about them. But how do we know whether

---

[26] See Thomson 1971.

[27] Boonin-Vain 1997, suggests a fourth—rejecting the authority of such arguments from analogy. However, insofar as arguments from analogy are merely substitutive instances of the logical principle of universalisability, this is not a defensible option.

[28] See e.g. Warren 1973, 49.

[29] The official position of the Catholic Church regards both abortion and contraception (other than abstinence) as immoral!

what we feel inclined to say has any secure ground? May we not feel inclined to say it just because of the way we were brought up to think?[30]

Some moral positions will reject Thomson's intuition that there can never be a moral obligation to remain attached to the violinist. Peter Singer argues,

> The utilitarian would hold that, however outraged I may be at having been kidnapped, if the consequences of disconnecting myself from the violinist are, on balance, and taking into account the interests of everyone affected, worse than the consequences of remaining connected, I ought to remain connected.[31]

It is open to utilitarianism (and other moral positions holding that the fetus does not have full moral status) to hold that abortion is less problematic than disconnecting the violinist. While Thomson's analogy can lead supporters of the full status position to consider the implications of their position for other situations, it cannot enable us to adjudicate between different implications. A utilitarian will apply a utility calculus, whereas a virtue theorist will analyse the relevant virtues (for if a fetus matters morally, a virtue theorist might reject abortion performed in the absence of a "virtuous" reason).[32] Ethical implications are theory dependent.

Thomson's analogy highlights the complexity of the abortion issue. Abortion is only simply a matter of a pregnant woman choosing to escape bodily invasion if the fetus has no status, otherwise it is complicated by the moral interests of the fetus and the involvement of others (health professionals) in the deliberate killing of the fetus. Feminist theorists point out that the abortion issue impacts more directly on women than it could ever impact on men. Some theories will also point to the consequences of not permitting abortion, which include illegal (and potentially dangerous) backstreet abortions[33] and medical tourism to less restrictive jurisdictions. The likely effects of abortion law even lead some to adopt or argue for laws that do not track their view on the moral status of the fetus, fearing that a restrictive/permissive law could do more harm than good. Here we must operate caution when converting moral principles into legal principles, even in a book like this, which analyses law as an exercise in applied moral reasoning. Outside the abortion context, one commentator has noted,

> For one thing, there are enforcement costs once we convert moral principle into legal prohibition as well as significant inroads into individual choice and freedom; and, although for practical purposes both law and morality demand some degree

[30] Hare 1975, 201.
[31] Singer 1993, 148.
[32] See Hursthouse 1991. Hursthouse claims that "the status of the fetus . . . is, according to virtue theory, simply not relevant to the rightness or wrongness of abortion" (1991, 236) but nonetheless holds that "anyone who genuinely believes that an abortion is comparable to a haircut or an appendectomy is mistaken" (237) because "the cutting off of a human life is always a matter of some seriousness" (238).
[33] When discussing the pressures leading to the enactment of the Abortion Act 1967, Sheldon notes that, "Official estimates showed that 35–40 women died each year as a result of botched abortions, but unofficial sources guessed at a far higher figure" (Sheldon 1997, 20).

of closure and settlement, the integrity of morality is not threatened by ongoing debate, review, and adjustment of position.[34]

With this note of caution, the abortion debate leads us ineluctably towards deeper moral theory, which is the topic of the final chapter. Enough has been said to show the ethical controversy evoked by the legal position outlined below.

7.3 Grounds for legal abortion

The law on abortion is governed by statute. Unfortunately it is not governed by just one statute. The starting point is the Offences Against the Person Act 1861. Section 58 of this Act makes it a criminal offence, punishable by up to life imprisonment, to unlawfully and intentionally attempt to procure a miscarriage. The woman only commits this offence if she is in fact pregnant, whereas anyone else commits an offence whether or not the woman was in fact pregnant. A woman who mistakenly believes that she is pregnant and attempts to procure a miscarriage with another could, nonetheless, be guilty of conspiring to commit this offence.[35] Also, s.59 makes it an offence to supply drugs or other instruments for use in procuring a miscarriage.

There were doubts about whether the 1861 Act covered a fetus during child-birth,[36] so the offence of "child destruction" was created by the Infant Life (Preservation) Act 1929. Section 1(1) provides that any person who intends to destroy the life of a child "capable of being born alive" commits an offence, unless the act was done "in good faith for the purpose only of preserving the life of the mother". Section 1(2) creates an evidential presumption that a 28-week fetus is capable of being born alive. Before 28 weeks the prosecution could still prove that the fetus was capable of being born alive, without the assistance of an evidential presumption. In *C v S*, the Court of Appeal held that an 18–21 week fetus in question would not have been capable of breathing either naturally or artificially, and so was not "capable of being born alive" under the 1929 Act.[37] In *Rance v Mid-Downs HA*, Brooke J. held that a child was capable of been born alive within the meaning of this Act when it possessed the attributes need to breathe "through its own lungs alone, without deriving any of its living or power of living by or through any connection with its mother".[38]

The Abortion Act 1967, as amended in 1990, now provides that no offence is committed under the 1861 or 1929 Acts when a pregnancy is terminated in accordance with its provisions. Thus, the 1929 Act is now of little relevance. It will only apply to late abortions not falling within statutory defences created by the Act 1967 and to situations where an attack on the pregnant woman intentionally kills the viable child that she is carrying.

---

[34] Brownsword 2003a, 418–419.
[35] *R v Whitchurch* [1890] L.R. 24 Q.B.D. 420.
[36] Killing a fetus during childbirth does not appear to involve procuring a miscarriage.
[37] [1988] Q.B. 135.
[38] [1991] 1 Q.B. 587 at 621.

The enactment of the Abortion Act 1967 was driven by concerns about the high mortality rates of illegal abortions[39] and to remove the remaining legal uncertainties. The Act provides that abortion is not unlawful if certain conditions are satisfied. It must be performed by a registered doctor in circumstances where two doctors are of the opinion, formed in good faith, that grounds specified in the Act are met (s.1(1)). Also, the abortion must take place in an approved place (s.1(3)) and Chief Medical Officer must be notified within the time, and in the form, prescribed by regulations (s.2).

What the Act does not do is provide pregnant women with a legally enforceable *right* to abortion. Nor does it require that the statutory grounds be proven to be objectively satisfied. Instead it provides that abortion can lawfully be provided where two doctors are of the good faith opinion that the statutory grounds are satisfied. This means that it is just about impossible to obtain a conviction against a doctor who performs an abortion, unless it can be proven that he failed to fulfil the Act's procedural requirements or did not act in good faith.

There has been only one successful prosecution against a doctor performing an abortion in *bad faith*. In *R. v Smith*, the evidence was that the doctor had made no internal examination, asked no questions about the woman's medical history, and had incompletely performed the abortion.[40] The Court of Appeal refused to overturn his conviction, holding that "The question of good faith is essentially one for the jury to determine on the totality of the evidence".[41] In view of the rarity of past prosecutions and, as we shall see, the ease with which a doctor can plausibly claim that the grounds for abortion are satisfied, prosecution is highly unlikely. Mason and Laurie go so far as to declare that "possibly the only way in which a termination can be carried out in *bad* faith is when it is done without the woman's consent".[42] Prosecutors and juries could adopt such a narrow view of bad faith,[43] but they are not required to do so.

The Abortion Act clearly places considerable power in the hands of doctors. Unfortunately, we shall see that the grounds under which abortion is legal are not purely medical. Doctors are making decisions (indeed are required to make decisions) that are not strictly within their competence. The law has, in essence, medicalised abortion.[44] Abortion is principally seen as a matter for the medical professional.

There are a number of grounds under which abortion is lawful under the Abortion Act as amended. Abortion is permitted *until the 24th week* on therapeutic and social grounds, i.e. where the continuance of the pregnancy involves risk of physical or mental injury to the pregnant woman or any existing children of her family (s.1(1)(a)). Abortion is also permitted *up to birth* to save the life of the woman, to prevent "grave permanent injury" to the physical or

---

[39] In the words of the Lord Chief Justice in *R. v Scrimaglia* (1971) 55 Cr. App. R. 280 at 282, "one of the objects, as everyone knows, of the new Act was to try to get rid of the back-street insanitary operations".

[40] [1974] 1 All E.R. 376.

[41] [1974] 1 All E.R. 376 at 381.

[42] Mason and Laurie 2006, 146.

[43] See Stauch et al. (2006, 435) for a discussion of the unreported case of *R. v Dixon (Reginald)* (1995).

[44] See Sheldon 1995 and 1997.

mental health of the pregnant woman, or on grounds of fetal abnormality (s.1(1)(b)–(d)).

Before examining these grounds in turn, it is instructive to note the official statistics on lawful abortions taking place in England and Wales that are collected under the notification procedure.[45] These statistics highlight a number of practical issues. *First*, in 2007 some 7,100 (principally from Ireland and Northern Ireland) travelled here to have abortions. This is a significant number of women travelling to Britain to escape their home country's restrictive abortion laws, but it is lower than it has been in any year since 1969. From 1995 to 2003, the figure was between 9,000 and 10,000 a year. *Second*, while the majority of abortions for women resident in England and Wales were funded by the NHS (some 89 per cent), just over half of these actually took place in the private sector under NHS contract. *Third*, this figure for abortions funded by the NHS belies notable regional variation. In 2007, the NHS funded 97 per cent of abortions performed in Blackpool and Doncaster compared to only 64 per cent of those performed in Newham. While some suggest that such variations provide sufficient evidence of the inconsistent application of the abortion legislation by doctors in different parts of the country,[46] they might also be accounted for (at least in part) by variations in the ability and willingness of residents in different parts of the country to seek (faster and more convenient) private treatment. Nonetheless, given the vagueness of the grounds for lawful abortion it is to be expected that there will be significant variation in the way that different doctors interpret and apply the legislation, and there is other evidence to support the realisation of this expectation in practice.[47] *Fourth*, since the enactment of the 1967 Act, abortions in England and Wales have increased from 24,000 in 1968 to 205,598 in 2007.[48] Only some of this increase can be explained by the decline in illegal abortions. The total number of abortions is still seeing yearly rises and the 2007 figure shows a 2.5 per cent rise compared to 2006. This suggests that there is an increasing willingness to see abortion as a form of post-conception contraception.

7.3.1 The "social" ground

The vast majority of abortions are performed under s.1(1)(a)—99 per cent of those performed in England and Wales in 2007. This section requires that the continuance of the pregnancy involve risk, greater than if the pregnancy were terminated, of physical or mental injury to the pregnant woman or any existing children of her family. Only 1 per cent of the abortions performed on this ground are undertaken because of the risk to existing children. The other 98 per cent

---

[45] All abortion statistics given in this chapter derive from DH 2008b, unless otherwise stated.

[46] Stauch (2001, 263) cites regional variation to support the claim that "there is ample evidence that doctors apply the Abortion Act divergently in different parts of the country".

[47] See Sheldon 1997, ch.4.

[48] The figure for 1968 is cited in Osborne 2003. The 2007 figure includes the 7,100 abortions performed on women who were not residents in England and Wales.

were performed on the basis of the risk to the pregnant woman, overwhelmingly the risk was reported to be to the woman's mental health.

Section 1(2) states that in determining the risk of injury to the health of the woman or her existing children, "account may be taken of the pregnant woman's actual or reasonably foreseeable environment". This imports the effects of "social" considerations, such as inconvenience and social pressure, which is one reason why this provision is often referred to as the "social" ground.

7.3.1.1 The time limit

This ground for legal termination is the only one with an attendant time limit. This provision requires that "the pregnancy has not exceeded its twenty-fourth week", thereby allowing abortion up to just before the 25th week. After this time, the doctors must rely on one of the three other grounds. When calculating when the pregnancy actually began, the convention is to treat the first day of the woman's last period as the start date, which errs on the side of caution, as the pregnancy will usually have started two weeks later. Scientific precision is currently impossible because not all women are fertile at the same time in the menstrual cycle and hours or days can elapse after sex before the sperm fertilises the egg and the egg then implants. In practice, however, if a criminal case were ever brought to court, the courts would be likely to interpret this provision in the defendant's favour.[49]

The time period chosen was thought to represent the period after which the fetus was viable. Viability had, after all, been important to the application of the Infant Life (Preservation) Act 1929.[50] Fortunately, Parliament avoided directly relying on viability, in contrast to the US Supreme Court decision of *Roe v Wade*.[51] In *Roe*, the court held that a woman's constitutional right to privacy encompassed her right to decide whether or not to have an abortion, and only after viability could the State's interest in protecting fetal life override that right. Viability has been a controversial feature of US abortion law since—though the Supreme Court has modified *Roe* considerably.[52] Viability depends on the changing state of technology and the pregnant woman's access to medical facilities. A fetus that would not have been viable in 1967 might be viable if delivered in the modern maternity hospital of a major British city. Indeed, around 20 to 30 per cent of babies born at 24 weeks now survive.[53] In the last edition, I expressed the view that when Parliament considers the abortion legislation in the future it is inevitable that anti-abortionists will latch on to viability, and its implicit recognition in the 1967 Act, as a way mounting pressure to reduce

---

[49] See further Grubb 1991, 665–666 and Montgomery 2002, 386.
[50] The Act's offence of child destruction required that a fetus be "capable of being born alive", which at least overlaps with viability.
[51] (1973) 410 U.S. 113.
[52] *Webster v Reproductive Health Services* (1989) 492 U.S. 490 and *Planned Parenthood v Casey* (1992) 120 L. ed. 2nd 674
[53] See Arden L.J. in *Evans v Amicus Healthcare* [2004] EWCA Civ 727, para.106.

the relevant time period to take account of technological developments. This happened during the Parliamentary debate on what was to become the Human Fertilisation and Embryology Act 2008 in which MPs rejected a series of private member amendments seeking to reduce the abortion time limit.[54] The closest vote, which attempted to bring the limit down to 22 weeks, was rejected by 304 to 233 votes. The Act eventually passed does not make any changes to the abortion law, but the Government is apparently considering the possibility of allowing time for parliamentary debate on abortion in 2010.

Most other countries have adopted an earlier time limit for their most permissive abortion provisions, but these provisions tend to place less emphasis on medical opinion and more on the rights or desires of the pregnant woman.[55] The least restrictive provisions in the relevant abortion legislation apply to up to 18 weeks in Sweden, 16 weeks in Finland, and up to 12 weeks in Austria, Belgium, Denmark, France, Germany, Greece, Luxembourg, and Portugal. An exception is the Netherlands where abortion is permitted up to fetal viability (in practice 24 weeks), if the woman is in a state of distress and has a genuine desire to terminate. Even in England and Wales, in practice, the majority of abortions (90 per cent) take place before 13 weeks gestation.

7.3.1.2 Establishing social and therapeutic grounds

The actual ground for abortion under this provision is not nearly as stringent as it first appears. Many commentators consider pregnancy and childbirth to carry inherent risk, so that they are just about always more risky than termination. According to Mason and Laurie,

> It is arguable that the risks of an abortion to the health of a woman are always less than those of a full-term pregnancy—particularly if the termination is carried out in the first trimester. Equally, it is obvious that the mental health of a woman who is carrying an unwanted pregnancy must suffer more damage if she is forced to carry her fetus than it would [if] she were relieved of her burden. It can also be argued that simple economics dictate that a *risk* to the well-being of any existing members of the family is occasioned by the advent of another mouth to feed.[56]

While this provision does require a balancing exercise—the termination must carry lower risk when all likely consequences are considered—a doctor can easily provide defensible grounds for certifying that he believes in good faith that this ground is satisfied. It has been argued that the wider effects of the pregnancy on the woman's mental and physical health could provide a basis for abortion on sex selection grounds where the woman faces pressure to have a child of a particular sex.[57]

---

[54] See BBC 2008a, 2008b, and 2008c.
[55] See Pattinson 2002a, Appendix 1.
[56] Mason and Laurie 2006, 145 (original emphasis). See also Grubb 1991, 661 and Dickens 2004a, 1034 (n.49).
[57] See Morgan 1988, 357–358, and Mason and Laurie 2006, 147.

7.3.2 Risk to life and health

Abortion is also lawful to prevent "grave permanent injury" to the physical or mental health of the pregnant women (s.1(1)(b)), or where the continuance of the pregnancy would involve risk to the life of the pregnant woman, greater than if it were terminated (s.1(1)(c)). Together these two grounds accounted for less than 1 per cent of abortions in England and Wales in 2007.

Section 1(1)(b) requires that the abortion be "necessary" to "prevent grave permanent injury". These are two stringent requirements. Abortion is not strictly "necessary" where there are other means of avoiding the injury and not all predicted mental or physical damage to health will be grave *and* permanent.

Section 1(1)(c), like s.1(1)(a), requires a comparison between the risks of continuing pregnancy against the risks of termination (albeit risks to life rather than health). We have seen that continuing pregnancy is inherently risky. Nonetheless, interpreting this provision too generously would effectively remove the need for s.1(1)(a). Something more than the general risk must be required. The existence of this provision is no surprise. Such grounds for abortion exist even in the most restrictive countries. Indeed, this forms the only ground for abortion in Ireland, where abortion is prohibited unless "there is a real and substantial threat to the life, as distinct from the health, of the mother".[58]

Where the termination is "immediately necessary" on the grounds set down by these two sections, the abortion need not be performed by two practitioners in an approved place (s.1(4)). In such an emergency, fulfilling these formal requirements would risk the safety of the pregnant woman. Fortunately, abortions are rarely performed in such circumstances. No precise figure is given for 2007; a single case was reported to have occurred in 2002.[59]

7.3.3 Fetal abnormality

Finally, abortion can be lawful on the grounds of fetal abnormality, i.e. where there is a "substantial risk" that the child would be born "seriously handicapped" (s.1(1)(d)). Only about 1 per cent of the total abortions performed in England and Wales in 2007 were performed under this section. Similar provisions exist in the abortion legislation of most other countries, though many of these are subject to a time limit.[60] Abortion on the grounds of fetal abnormality is, for example, lawful up to 24 weeks in Greece, the Netherlands, and Portugal; up to 20 weeks in Finland, and up to 22 weeks in Spain and Sweden.[61] Many impose additional conditions, such as counselling or the approval of a special

---

[58] See *Attorney General v X* [1992] 1 I.R. 1 at 53–54 (Finlay C.J.) interpreting the Eighth amendment to the constitution (art.40.3.3).
[59] See DH 2003b, para.4.2.2.
[60] See Pattinson 2002a, Appendix 1.
[61] See Pattinson 2002a, Appendix 1.

board. A notable exception is Ireland, where fetal abnormality does not provide a ground for lawful abortion.

Many genetic diagnosis and screening tests for fetal abnormalities carry a small additional risk of spontaneous miscarriage. For amniocentesis, which accounts for 90 per cent of prenatal diagnosis performed in the UK, this additional risk is 0.5–1 per cent and for chorionic villus sampling (CVS) and fetal blood sampling it is 1–3 per cent.[62] In contrast, prenatal ultrasound is not thought to carry risks for the mother or fetus, though it can still be used to detect over 280 congenital malformations, generally at 18–20 weeks gestation.[63]

7.3.3.1 Interpreting the fetal abnormality provision

The Act does not define "seriously handicapped" (or for that matter "substantial risk"). However, in its guidance to practitioners, the Royal College of Obstetricians and Gynaecologists (RCOG) states that consideration ought to be given to the following factors "not all of which will be relevant in every case":

(a) the probability of effective treatment, either *in utero* or after birth;

(b) the probable degree of self-awareness and of ability to communicate with others;

(c) the suffering that would be experienced; and

(d) the extent to which actions essential for health that normal individuals perform unaided would have to be provided by others.[64]

The RCOG go on to declare that "it is not possible to give an authoritative view of the meaning of "seriously handicapped" as this has not been interpreted by the courts".[65] Without such an authoritative interpretation a number of possibilities remain. Morgan, for example, draws an analogy with the fatal non-treatment of severely handicapped neonates, which the law requires to be in their best interests.[66] This analogy requires the justification for decisions in both instances to rest with the interests of the child itself (whether born or unborn)— which is highly questionable.[67] In any event, there is arguably a disanalogy here as the law clearly treats fetuses differently from neonates: only a neonate can have legal rights or standing and a neonate cannot be actively killed.[68]

In 2003, when reading the abortion statistics for 2001, a Church of England curate discovered that a fetus had been aborted under s.1(1)(d) because it had a cleft lip and palate. The curate in question is opposed to abortion, has been

---

[62] See ACGT 2000, 11.

[63] See Connor and Ferguson-Smith 1997, 202, and ACGT 2000, 12.

[64] See RCOG 1996, para.3.3.3. The BMA has laid down a list of similar factors: see BMA 2004, 254.

[65] RCOG 1996, para.3.3.3.

[66] Morgan 1990, 689–691. Morgan is commenting on s.1(1)(b) of the Abortion Act 1967, which became s.1(a)(d) when that Act was amended in 1990.

[67] Compare Morgan 1990, 692–693 with Stauch et al. 2006, 422.

[68] See below and Ch.16, respectively.

successfully treated for a significant facial impairment, and has a brother with Down's syndrome. When the police refused to investigate, she sought judicial review of that decision. Following permission to proceed to a full hearing being granted by the High Court,[69] the police launched an inquiry into the case. In March 2005, the Crown Prosecution Service (CPS) decided not to prosecute on the grounds that they were satisfied that the doctors involved had acted in good faith.[70] Those pushing for the active enforcement of a narrow interpretation of s.1(1)(d) are likely to remain dissatisfied. In this particular case, the degree of disability of the child in question was not made public. A cleft palate can prevent normal feeding and require years of corrective surgery. In a serious case, the skull might not have fused properly, which can impair brain function.[71] Alternatively, it might describe a relatively minor and purely cosmetic abnormality.

At present it is unclear whether the risk of a late onset disorder (revealed by prenatal diagnosis) could fall within the fetal abnormality provision. Huntington's disease is a good example. This disorder usually manifests between the ages of 40 and 50, causing progressive neurodegeneration leading to involuntary movements, loss of motor control, and dementia, with death occurring 10 to 20 years later.[72] It has no cure, the only treatment being symptom relief and support.[73] A fetus with the relevant gene will later die from this, unless something else kills it first. Is such a fetus at "substantial risk" of being born "seriously handicapped"?[74] Even if two doctors are unwilling to certify that it is, they might well be willing to certify satisfaction of the social ground.

7.3.3.2 Ethical issues

What is striking about the fetal abnormality provision is that it grants far less protection to a "seriously handicapped" unborn child than a non-handicapped unborn child. For those theories granting full or limited moral status to the fetus this is problematic for two reasons.

First, so little protection is granted to a fetus judged to be at risk of being born seriously handicapped that neither the pregnant woman nor her family need to be at risk from harm as a result of the birth of such a child. This is only compatible with the fetus having moral status if that moral status is always insufficient to protect it against the mother's desires *or* the abnormality is such that it is in the fetus' interests to die. This latter approach raises the question of whether it can ever be in the moral interests of the fetus to die. This ethical question is raised more directly in the "wrongful life" debate and is explored in some depth in Ch.9 (9.4.2). For present purposes, however, it should be noted that

---

[69] *Jepson v Chief Constable of West Mercia* [2003] EWHC 3318.
[70] See BBC 2005d.
[71] See Hewson 2003 and Furedi 2003.
[72] See e.g. Sermon et al. 1998.
[73] See Braude et al. 1998, 1422.
[74] Morgan (1990, 689) argues that such a wide interpretation requires more specific wording.

even if it was accepted that a particular fetus' quality of life would be so low that it would be better off dead, the fetal abnormality provision is not currently restricted to conditions that could plausibly result in a negative quality of life.[75]

Second, "seriously handicapped" can to be determined by factors that many theories will consider irrelevant to the possession of moral status. Some abnormalities captured by the RCOG guidelines are irrelevant to the humanity, viability, future mental attributes, or the future suffering of a fetus. A viable Down's syndrome fetus, for example, could become a happy child whose mental attributes are compatible with agency, yet in 2007 Down's syndrome accounted for 23 per cent of all abortions under this ground. The law itself has some difficulty with Down's syndrome, because it appears to regard this condition as a reason for killing a fetus, but it does not regard it as a reason for allowing a neonate to die.[76]

The distinction drawn between seriously handicapped and non-handicapped fetuses can also be questioned for other reasons (which are also compatible with the fetus having no moral status). It could be argued, for example, that the destruction of handicapped fetuses is likely to facilitate or encourage discrimination against adults and children with that handicap—though this would require empirical evidence. In general, theories granting no (or very little) moral status to the fetus would not distinguish between an abnormal and a normal fetus—all fetuses could be justifiably aborted. Utilitarians might, however, point to the negative utility of having a disabled child. According to Glover, in some circumstances, "If aborting the abnormal foetus can be followed by having another, normal one, it will be wrong not to do this".[77]

7.4 Affected persons

The pregnant woman and her fetus are clearly those most directly affected by abortion, but they are not the only ones affected. In addition to exploring the legal claims and rights of the fetus (7.4.1) and the pregnant woman (7.4.2), this section will examine those of the father (7.4.3) and the conscientious objector (7.4.4).

7.4.1 The fetus

The fetus lacks the legal status of its mother. There is no crime of feticide. Only when it is born alive does it have the full protection of the civil and criminal law.

---

[75] A similar view is expressed by Sheldon and Wilkinson 2001a, 90 and 93.

[76] See *Re B* [1990] 3 All E.R. 927. This analogy is suggested by Morgan 1990, and Sheldon and Wilkinson 2001a, 91–92.

[77] Glover 1977, 146. See also Savulescu 2001.

In *Paton v BPAS*, when asked to rule on an application to prevent an abortion taking place, Sir George Baker declared that the fetus did not have "a right of its own at least until it is born and has a separate existence from its mother".[78] In the later case of *Re F (in utero)*, the Court of Appeal refused to make a fetus a ward of court to protect it from its mentally disturbed, nomadic mother.[79] The fetus was said to lack the legal personality necessary to make it a ward of court and there was "inherent incompatibility between any projected exercise of wardship jurisdiction and the rights and welfare of the mother".[80] Only upon birth would its status as a legal person with legal rights crystallise.[81] England is not alone in adopting this approach.[82]

While the fetus is not treated as having *full status*, neither is it treated as having *no status*. Abortion is not simply a matter of the woman's consent, nor can the abortion legislation be explained away as protecting the moral interests of others. The view that the fetus has *limited status* has received judicial support in a number of cases that had nothing to do with abortion. In *AG's Reference (No.3 of 1994)*, the House of Lords was asked to rule on whether the requirements for manslaughter could be made out when a severely premature infant's death could be shown to have been caused by injuries inflicted *in utero*.[83] Lord Mustill (with whom their Lordships agreed) was of the view that the fetus was not to be regarded as simply part of its mother. Instead, the fetus was

> an organism *sui generis* lacking at this stage the entire range of characteristics both of the mother to which it is physically linked and of the complete human being which it will later become.[84]

In *St George's Healthcare v S*, when considering whether a pregnant woman could refuse treatment needed to save her fetus, Judge L.J. declared that "Whatever else it may be a 36-week foetus is not nothing: if viable it is not lifeless and it is certainly human".[85] He went on, however, to hold that a competent women had an absolute right to refuse treatment for herself or her fetus, because "Of themselves the perceived needs of the foetus did not provide the necessary justification" for restricting the pregnant woman's autonomy.[86]

Is the fetus' position bolstered by the enactment of the Human Rights Act (HRA) 1998? After all, art.2 of the Convention provides that "everyone" has a

---

[78] [1979] Q.B. 276 at 279.

[79] [1988] Fam. 122.

[80] 135–136 (May L.J.).

[81] 137 (May L.J.). The House of Lords in *Re D (A Minor)* 1987] A.C. 317, had previously decided that the conditions before birth could be taken into account when assessing the likely future of an infant in wardship proceedings. See Ch.9 on negligence actions brought in the name of a child injured before birth.

[82] A more or less identical approach to this issue has been adopted in Canada (*Medhurst v Medhurst* (1984) 9 D.L.R. (4th) 252 and *Tremblay v Daigle* (1989) 59 D.L.R. (4th) 609) and Scotland (*Kelly v Kelly* (1997) S.L.T. 896).

[83] [1998] A.C. 245.

[84] [1998] A.C. 245 at 255–256 (Lord Mustill).

[85] [1999] Fam. 26 at 45.

[86] [1999] Fam. 26 at 50. For further discussion of this issue see Ch.5 (5.2.3.1).

right to life. Section 2 of the HRA requires the courts to take account of the Strasbourg jurisprudence.

When the *Paton* case was brought to the European Commission of Human Rights, the Commission pointed out that the Convention did not define "everyone" or "life".[87] Since the issue before the court involved a woman who was only 10 weeks pregnant, the Commission felt that it was unnecessary to decide whether the fetus was not covered at all or has a "right to life" with implied limitations. Any interests that such an early fetus might have were held to be overridden by the pregnant woman's right to life and health, as to hold otherwise would give the life of the fetus higher value than that of the woman.[88]

The Commission returned to this issue in *H v Norway*, where a man sought to challenge his former partner's decision to abort their unborn child at 14 weeks on social grounds.[89] The Commission noted that national courts have reached different decisions on whether art.2 (or equivalent domestic provision) encompasses the fetus: the Austrian Constitutional Court has held that it does not, whereas the German Federal Constitutional Court has held that it does.[90] Here the Commission simply held that Norway had not gone beyond the wide discretion granted on this issue.[91] Other cases have adopted the same approach, affirming a wide "margin of appreciation" and holding that art.2 has not been violated on the facts.[92]

Fears that art.2 will be used to undermine the abortion legislation, expressed by some MPs during the Parliamentary debate preceding the enactment of the HRA, are undoubtedly misguided.[93] As long as the Strasbourg court continues to allow a wide margin of appreciation, English judges are likely to follow the historical approach of domestic law. The HRA itself retains the force of incompatible primary legislation, subject only to the s.3 duty to interpret legislation "in a way which is compatible with the Convention rights".[94] The English courts are traditionally non-interventionist in this area and will be bolstered in this position by the legislative background on abortion. Thus, in my view, the domestic courts are likely to uphold the existing legal position and hold that the fetus has no legally recognised right to life until birth. Indeed, the Court of Appeal refused to countenance the idea that art.2 offered protection to a stored fetus of less than 14 days old, the Court of Appeal noted "In our domestic law it has been repeatedly held that a foetus prior to the moment of birth does not have independent rights or interests".[95]

---

[87] *Paton v UK* (1981) 3 E.H.R.R. 408.
[88] (1981) 3 E.H.R.R. 408 at 415–416.
[89] (1992) 73 D.R. 155.
[90] (1992) 73 D.R. 155 at 167.
[91] (1992) 73 D.R. 155 at 169.
[92] See e.g. *Open Door Counselling and Dublin Well Woman v Ireland* (1993) 15 E.H.R.R. 244, *Boso v Italy* (no.50490/99), and, most recently, *Vo v France* (no.53924/00).
[93] See e.g. 306 *Hansard (House of Commons)* 828, February 16, 1998 (Mr David Ruffley MP).
[94] See ss.3(2)(b) and 4(6).
[95] *Evans v Amicus Healthcare* [2004] EWCA Civ 727, para.19 (per Thorpe and Sedley L.JJ.).

7.4.2 The pregnant woman

7.4.2.1 Human rights

We have seen that the abortion legislation confers no rights on the pregnant woman. Is this compatible with the HRA 1998? Can a pregnant woman claim that abortion falls within her art.8 right to respect for her private and family life? Whether art.8 poses any real challenge to the 1967 Act turns on two things: the interpretation of "private life" adopted and the protection granted to the fetus under art.2 (because art.8(2) permits interference with this right in "accordance with the law" where it is "necessary in a democratic society" to protect "the rights and freedoms of others"). While Strasbourg has consistently declared that "private life" covers a person's "physical and moral integrity",[96] the Commission has held that abortion cannot be "solely a matter of the private life of the mother".[97] So, it appears that art.8 does encompass abortion but its ambit is subject to a large "margin of appreciation" and the, as yet inconclusive, effects of art.2.

Stauch has argued that the art.8 right could be used to challenge two procedurally restrictive features of the 1967 Act: the lack of any right to abortion conferred on the pregnant woman and the vagueness of the grounds under which abortion is lawful.[98] In practice, it will probably take a clear case to get this issue before a court.

7.4.2.2 Incapacitated women and children

In 2007, 20,289 abortions were performed on girls under 18 in England and Wales, of which 1,171 were performed on girls under 15. The abortion legislation is, however, silent on girls under the age of 18. The general law on consent to medical treatment, discussed in Ch.5 (5.3), therefore applies in addition to the provisions of the abortion legislation. This means that a doctor can perform an abortion on a minor if she has capacity and consents, or if a person with parental responsibility consents. Like any other treatment, an abortion can never be lawfully performed against the will of a competent adult. A competent minor does not, however, have an absolute right to refuse treatment. In the leading case of *Re W*, Lord Donaldson went so far as to declare obiter that it "may be possible as a matter of law" for an abortion to be carried out with the consent of parents in the face of refusal by a 16 or 17-year-old![99] (Though if a mature minor wishes to have an abortion, it appears that doctors are under no obligation to inform her parents.)[100]

If the pregnant girl or woman lacks capacity, any treatment must be in her best interests. In *Re SG* Sir Stephen Brown P. ruled that a declaration is not

---

[96] See e.g. *Costello-Roberts v UK* (1995) 19 E.H.R.R. 112, para.34.
[97] *Brüggemann v Germany* (1981) 3 E.H.R.R. 244, para.61.
[98] See Stauch 2001, 262–264.
[99] *Re W (A Minor)* [1993] Fam. 64 at 79, though he added "I do not see any likelihood [of this] taking account of medical ethics, unless the abortion was truly in the best interests of the child".
[100] See the discussion in Ch.6 (6.2.3).

usually necessary because the 1967 Act already specifies when an abortion will be lawful.[101] This guidance was reconsidered by Coleridge J. in *D v An NHS Trust*.[102] He declared that an application should be made where there is "any doubt as to either capacity or best interests", in particular, in those situations "where there is a lack of unanimity amongst the medical professionals as to the best interests of the patient" and "where the patient, members of her immediate family or the foetus' father have opposed, or expressed views inconsistent with, a termination of the pregnancy".[103]

The few cases that have come before the Court where there has been some disagreement about whether the abortion was in the interests of the incompetent patient, indicate that the wishes of the incompetent patient will be persuasive but not decisive. In *Re P*, a 15-year-old mother who did not want another child became pregnant while in local authority care.[104] Despite her parent's objection, Butler-Sloss J. authorised an abortion as being in her best interests. An abortion was also authorised in *Re B* on behalf of a 12-year-old girl.[105] In that case, the girl's desire for an abortion was supported by her grandparents (with whom she lived), her father, and the local authority. Only her mother, who did not believe in abortion, objected. The later case of *Re SS* is different in a number of respects.[106] In this case the judge ruled that an abortion of a 24-week-old fetus was not in the best interests of the 34-year-old schizophrenic woman, despite her having expressed a (fluctuating) wish to undergo a termination. The judge was heavily influenced by the fact that the expert witnesses thought that a late termination would be just as stressful for her as a normal birth followed by adoption. Disturbingly, the judge indicated that he might have reached the opposite decision had the case been brought to him when the woman first expressed a desire for an abortion. This might appear to present an incentive to those opposed to the termination to delay an application to the court, but the judge did chastise the applicants for taking so long to bring the case to the court and Coleridge J. in *D* was at pains to reiterate "the importance of making necessary applications in good time".[107]

7.4.3 Fathers and other interested parties

The abortion legislation does not grant any legal rights. We have seen that it does not grant pregnant women a right to have an abortion nor does it grant any rights to the fetus. It also grants no rights to the father, not even a right to be informed that an abortion has taken place. In *Paton v BPAP* Sir George Baker

---

[101] [1991] 2 F.L.R. 329.
[102] [2003] EWHC 2793.
[103] [2003] EWHC 2793, paras 34 and 37. Coleridge J. indicated that his guidance had the support of the President of the Family Division.
[104] *Re P* [1986] 1 F.L.R. 272.
[105] [1991] 2 F.L.R. 426,
[106] [2002] 1 F.L.R. 445.
[107] [2003] EWHC 2793, para.36.

rejected the father's application, made both in his own name as the husband of the pregnant woman and on behalf of the fetus, for an injunction to prevent the abortion.[108] The judge declared that the husband "has no legal right enforceable in law or in equity to stop his wife having this abortion or to stop the doctors from carrying out the abortion".[109] On his application to Strasbourg, the Commission held that any rights that the father had under art.8(1) to his private and family life were outweighed by the rights of the mother under art.8(2).[110]

In *Paton* the father had conceded that the abortion was otherwise lawful and had not sought to argue that the doctors had acted in bad faith. What would happen if a father does make such a claim? Even if he lacks rights of his own, can he act as a protector of the public interest? The judge expressed the view, without deciding the point, that the courts would very reluctantly intervene unless there was "clear bad faith" and, even then, prosecution is probably best left to the Director of Public Prosecutions. In *C v S*, the Court of Appeal did not feel the need to address this issue (having held that the abortion in question would not be unlawful) but held that if it had to consider the father's position it would have given "very considerable thought to the words of Sir George Baker".[111]

Fathers have also been unsuccessful in obtaining injunctions (or equivalent) in other jurisdictions, including Scotland and Canada.[112] Other interested parties cannot possibly have any legal rights themselves, but could they have standing to challenge an allegedly unlawful abortion? Any court considering this point will have to consider Sir George Baker's dicta. The situation for fathers and other third parties might, however, be different after the abortion has taken place.[113] Mason and Laurie have argued that the father morally ought to have the right to a hearing before any abortion takes place.[114] Supporters of the full status position who will wish to go further and grant extensive powers to protect the fetus.

7.4.4 Conscientious objectors

The abortion legislation unequivocally recognises the interests of third parties in one, limited way. The conscientious objector is excused from participating in an abortion, unless treatment is "necessary" to save the life of the woman or to prevent grave permanent injury to her health (s.4). While this provision does not say that the treatment must be "immediately" necessary, this seems to be its

---

[108] [1979] Q.B. 276.

[109] [1979] Q.B. 276 at 281.

[110] *Paton v UK* (1981) 3 E.H.R.R. 408.

[111] [1988] Q.B. 135 at 153.

[112] See *Kelly v Kelly* (1997) S.L.T. 896 (Scotland) and Canada (*Medhurst v Medhurst* (1984) 9 D.L.R. (4th) 252 and *Tremblay v Daigle* (1989) 59 D.L.R. (4th) 609).

[113] See *Jepson v Chief Constable of West Mercia* [2003] EWHC 3318, though this is only a decision to allow an action for judicial review to be heard.

[114] See Mason and Laurie 2006, 165.

import. The provision does clearly state that it is for the objector to prove that he has an objection of conscience.

The conscience provision was considered by the House of Lords in *Janaway v Salford AHA*.[115] Mrs Janaway was a devout Roman Catholic who had been dismissed from her employment as a secretary at a health centre for refusing to type abortion referral letters. She challenged her dismissal, relying on the conscientious objector provision. Her action failed. Lord Keith (with whom their Lordships agreed) held that the word "participate" in s.4 meant "actually taking part in treatment administered . . . for the purpose of terminating a pregnancy".[116]

To what extent does the conscience provision protect a doctor who, like Mrs Janaway, views abortion as murder and providing even indirect assistance as assisting murder? In *Janaway*, Lord Keith expressly refused to express a view on whether a doctor could rely on this provision to refuse to certify that a woman satisfied the statutory grounds for abortion.[117] It is less likely that a doctor could refuse to refer a woman. In *Barr v Matthews*, Alliott J. expressed the view that "once a termination of pregnancy is recognised as an option, the doctor invoking the conscientious objection clause should refer the patient to a colleague at once".[118] Kennedy and Grubb have gone further and expressed the view that GPs are actually contractually required to arrange abortion services for their patients, as part of their duties to refer patients for NHS services.[119]

What is clear is that a woman would not be able get a court order requiring her doctor to refer her or to certify that she satisfies the statutory grounds for abortion.[120] In practice, her only legal recourse would be to sue the doctor for negligence *if* she can show that her doctor was in breach of duty and that the breach of duty was the cause of harm (see Chs 3 and 9). In *Barr*, the woman's negligence claim against the doctor failed on the grounds of causation: the doctor had not prevented her from obtaining an abortion. In the earlier case of *Saxby v Morgan*, it was claimed that the doctor had told his patient that her pregnancy had "too far gone" for an abortion, despite her 18–19-week pregnancy clearly falling within the time limit of the 1967 Act.[121] Her claim failed on procedural grounds (being out of time). Claimants are likely to be more successful if a doctor's objections to abortion cause him not to advise her on prenatal screening or abortion in circumstances where the child is at risk of an abnormality and is then born.[122]

The conscience provision was not modified when the abortion legislation was amended in 1990.[123] Thus, we must wait for further judicial clarification of the remaining uncertainties.

---

[115] [1989] A.C. 537.
[116] [1989] A.C. 537 at 570.
[117] [1989] A.C. 537 at 572.
[118] (2000) 52 B.M.L.R. 217.
[119] Kennedy and Grubb 2000, 1446–1447.
[120] *Re J (A Minor)* [1993] Fam. 15. This point is discussed in Ch.4 (4.2).
[121] [1997] P.I.Q.R. P531.
[122] See e.g. *Enright v Kwun* [2003] EWHC 1000 (doctor's Catholicism may have influenced his failure to advise a woman on screening and a possible termination). On wrongful birth actions generally, see Ch.9.
[123] Parliament rejected a proposed amendment that would have required doctors who are conscientious objectors to register on a publicly available list: see Sheldon 1995, 112.

The ethical issues raised by the conscience provision are not coterminous with those raised by the debate on the morality of abortion. A supporter of the full status position is not ethically required to refuse to refer a pregnant woman to a pro-abortion colleague, nor is a supporter of the no status position ethically required to ignore the conscience provision. The fact that Parliament, in the exercise of its powers as a democratically elected body, has chosen to legalise abortion with a provision for conscientious objectors will have procedural ethical force for all moral theories supporting democratic decision-making. Nonetheless, not everyone accepts that Parliament was right to accept the conscience provision. Ian Kennedy has argued that the conscience clause allows a doctor to "legislate morality to others":

> To the doctor who complains that he wants to practise medicine without abortions, the answer must be that he can choose to engage in private practice, and thereby arrange his affairs by agreement with his patients. If he joins the NHS, he should remember the last word of the three, "service", and serve.[124]

7.5 Other issues

Medical technology and understanding have changed more rapidly than the abortion legislation. When the 1967 Act was enacted, abortion required the surgical removal of a fetus by a doctor, now early abortions can be induced by drugs alone. This raises a number of issues, addressed in 7.5.1, with regard to the involvement of health professionals other than doctors, the premises required for an abortion, and the connection between abortifacients and contraception. Additional issues are also raised by advances in ultrasound technology, which have made it possible to selectively terminate a fetus while leaving the woman pregnant with another fetus (7.5.2). Technology might one day make it possible to expel an early fetus from the womb for gestation in an artificial womb. Occasionally health professionals already have to deal with late fetuses that unintentionally survive an abortion operation (7.5.3).

7.5.1 Drug-induced abortion and contraception

In medical law the courts have shown great willingness to read legislation purposively to encompass conduct unanticipated at the time of its passing.[125] The arrival of drugs capable of preventing implantation or development post-implantation has brought a number of issues before the courts.

---

[124] Kennedy 1988, 29.
[125] See e.g. *R (Bruno Quintavalle) v Secretary of State for Health* [2003] UKHL 13 and *R. (Josephine Quintavalle) v HFEA* [2005] UKHL 28.

7.5.1.1 *The involvement of persons other than doctors*

Section 1 of the 1967 Act only offers immunity from the offences under the 1861 Act "when a pregnancy is terminated by a registered medical practitioner". To what extent does this prevent a nurse, or the pregnant woman herself, taking active steps to terminate the pregnancy? This question is particularly important now that early pregnancies can be aborted without any surgical intervention. The now standard procedure for early-term abortion involves the woman taking the oral drug mifepristone (sometimes called RU486 or the "abortion pill"), followed by a vaginal pessary a couple of days later.[126] The courts have not considered whether the woman who takes this mifepristone herself could be guilty of a criminal offence (or whether a woman taking the pill at home would contravene the requirement that the termination of a pregnancy take place in an NHS hospital or in a place approved by the Secretary of State).[127] The House of Lords has, however, ruled that nurses can actively participate in the termination of a pregnancy provided that a doctor makes the decision to terminate, prescribes the treatment, and remains in charge throughout the treatment.[128] Thus, nurses can lawfully administer drugs such as mifepristone and it is probably the case that self-administration by the pregnant woman would also be lawful where a doctor takes full responsibility for all stages of the treatment in this way. Challenging such a view, Kennedy and Grubb point out that doctors exercise a different type of responsibility over a pregnant woman, i.e. not one of control.[129] In both cases, however, a doctor prescribing treatment under instruction is exercising his key responsibility in certifying that, in his view, the legislative grounds for abortion legislation are satisfied. The Department of Health is in fact considering a scheme whereby pregnant women would self-administer at home.[130]

7.5.1.2 *Post-coital contraception*

Post-coital contraceptive drugs (such as the so-called "morning-after" pill) or an intra-uterine device (IUD) fitted after intercourse, can prevent a fertilised egg implanting into the womb. Do these measures procure a "miscarriage" within the meaning of the 1861 Act? If they do, the provisions of the 1967 Act would need to be complied with before they could be administered.

In 1983 the Attorney-General, in response to a Parliamentary question, expressed the view that the word "miscarriage" did not describe the failure to implant.[131] This issue has now been considered by the courts twice. In *R. v Dhingra*, Wright J. agreed with this view and dismissed a charge against a doctor

---

[126] See Osborne 2003.
[127] Section 1(3) Abortion Act 1967. Section 1(3A) could be used by the Secretary of State to authorise the abortion pill being administered at GPs' surgeries.
[128] *Royal College of Nursing v DHSS* [1981] A.C. 800.
[129] Kennedy and Grubb 2000, 1479.
[130] See Osborne 2003.
[131] 42 Parl Deb HC, Written Answers, May 10, 1983, Col 237 (Sir Michael Havers Q.C.).

under s.18 of the 1861 Act for inserting an IUD.[132] More recently, in *R. (Smeaton) v Secretary of State for Health*, Munby J. rejected the Society for the Protection of Unborn Children's (SPUC) claim that allowing the sale of a morning-after pill without prescription contravened the 1861 Act.[133] He held that the term "miscarriage" was to be read as an ordinary English word in the light of current scientific and medical knowledge. Hence it refers to the termination of a pregnancy after implantation.[134] The judge noted that SPUC's arguments would apply to all forms of contraception preventing the implantation of a fertilised egg, which could mean that "some 34% of all women between the ages of 16–49 in Great Britain ... would potentially become guilty of criminal offences".[135] (Though there would be some difficulty proving that the woman was actually pregnant.) Despite being only a first instance decision, this case now appears to have settled the position in English law.

7.5.2 Selective reduction

In 1996, Mandy Allwood hit the headlines when she became pregnant with no fewer than eight foetuses, having ignored advice to avoid sex while having hormone injections and taking fertility drugs.[136] Her situation fuelled the media's interest—she was claiming benefits and in an unstable relationship, and she took the step of hiring a PR consultant and selling her story to the *News of the World*. She was advised to selectively reduce her pregnancies, as multiple pregnancies carry a greatly increased risk of complications for both the pregnant woman and the fetuses. She refused to follow this advice and all eight fetuses eventually died.

The selective termination of one or more fetuses has been technically possible for at least two decades. The procedure remains rare. In 2007, there were only 47 cases of selective reduction and 68 per cent of those terminations were performed under the fetal abnormality provision (s.1(1)(d)). It tends to be performed not only in situations like Mandy Allwood's where multiple pregnancies pose risks to the woman and her other fetuses, but also where one twin is seriously handicapped. To limit the need for selective termination following multiple pregnancies, the body governing IVF restrictively limits the number of embryos that may be transferred to the womb in one treatment cycle.[137]

Until its amendment in 1990 it was unclear whether the abortion legislation covered selective termination where the woman continues to be pregnant.[138]

---

[132] (1991), unreported. This case is quoted extensively in *R. (Smeaton) v Secretary of State for Health* [2002] EWHC 610.
[133] [2002] EWHC 610. Sale without prescription to women aged 16 or over had been authorised by Prescription Only Medicines (Human Use) Amendment (No.3) Order 2000/3231.
[134] [2002] EWHC 610, paras 350–352. For criticism of Munby J.'s reasoning, see Keown 2005.
[135] [2002] EWHC 610, paras 223–234.
[136] There were many newspaper articles published on Mandy in 1996, for a recent summary see Adams 2002.
[137] See the discussion in Ch.8 (8.3.3.3).
[138] See Keown 1987 and Price 1988.

Section 5(2) of the Abortion Act, as inserted by s.37(5) Human Fertilisation and Embryology Act 1990, now makes selective reduction lawful if it complies with grounds for lawful abortion. The application of these grounds presents no issues of particular legal difficulty, except where the reason for selectively terminating a non-handicapped fetus is to improve the remaining fetuses' chances of survival. Here it would be necessary to rely on s.1(1)(a) and, even then, this provision would have to be interpreted rather broadly. The focus of that provision is on the risk to the health of the mother or any existing child, not the fetuses. Whether it would be permissible to choose the fetuses non-randomly, on say their sex, is more controversial.[139] As with the application of the so-called "social" ground generally, it could be argued that sex selection (even selective sex reduction) could sometimes protect the mother from the damaging effects of social and cultural pressures on her health.

7.5.3 The living abortus

In 1988, a 21-week-old fetal girl was reported to have survived an abortion procedure. According to a report in *The Times*, "It lay in a kidney dish for nearly three hours, allegedly gasping for breath and with a heartbeat of 80 beats a minute, and was then wrapped in a plastic bag and incinerated".[140] The coroner's application to the Home Office for authority to hold an inquest was refused.[141] Some years earlier, a gynaecologist was prosecuted for allegedly leaving a 23-week-old fetus to die following an abortion. The magistrates dismissed the prosecution for lack of evidence.[142] Official figures report that in 2005 66 fetuses were born alive following legal termination of pregnancy (predominately on grounds of congenital anomalies), only to die during the neonatal period.[143]

The conflict over the status of the fetus unavoidably dominates the ethical debate over what it is permissible to do with a living abortus, i.e. a fetus that has been aborted but nonetheless survives. Insofar as there is a right or power to have an abortion does this permit the killing of a living abortus or it is no more than a right or power to expel the fetus from the womb? To what extent does one's position on abortion logically commit one to infanticide?

The abortion legislation is silent on what can be done with a living abortus. A doctor performing an abortion cannot be guilty of child destruction under the 1929 Act, but the law regards any fetus born alive as a full legal person. In theory, killing a living abortus, or failing to prevent its death in the absence of

---

[139] The BMA considers abortion on the grounds of sex to be unethical, except for severe sex linked disorders: see BMA 2004, 248. For a discussion of the ethics of sex selection, see the section on sex selecting using preimplantation diagnosis in Ch.8 (8.5.1.2).

[140] Fletcher 1988.

[141] See Mason and Laurie 2006, 160.

[142] See Brazier 2003, 330, and Mason and Laurie 2006, 160.

[143] See CEMACH 2007, 28.

a legally recognised justification, could be manslaughter or even murder. In practice, there have been no successful prosecutions for the death of a living abortus that could have been saved, despite stories such as those above. RCOG guidance recommends that in all termination of pregnancies of gestational age of more than 21 weeks and six days "the method chosen should ensure that the fetus is born dead".[144] Thus, late term fetuses are to have potassium chloride injected into their hearts while they are still in the womb to ensure that they are not born alive following the abortion procedure.

From an ethical point of view, while the protection granted to a fetus might depend on its location, its moral status does not. Any protection granted to a fetus will restrict the pregnant woman's physical liberty in a way that protecting a living abortus will not. It follows that a pregnant woman cannot rely on her moral interest in physical freedom to demand the destruction of a living abortus. A living abortus is quite simply an *unwanted premature child*. Any moral status that it has can only be overridden by more compelling moral considerations. This also has implications for the abortion debate, because even if the fetus does not have sufficient moral status to render attempts to expel it from the womb immoral, it might have sufficient moral status to require that efforts be made to expel it unharmed where possible. In the future it might even be technically possible to gestate a currently unviable fetus in an artificial womb. Such a development will bring the tension between the right to expel and the right to kill to the forefront of the debate. The key issue remains the moral status of the fetus *and* the weight of any conflicting moral considerations.

7.6 Conclusion

Britain has not gone the way of the US, where extremists, such as those mentioned at the outset, have murdered doctors and a candidate's views on abortion can be crucial to electoral success or appointment to the Supreme Court. Faced with the US example our judges are unlikely to allow the Human Rights Act 1998 to be used as a conduit for greater judicial intervention. The Strasbourg jurisprudence also reflects such concern. Abortion presents a real test of judicial deference to the democratic process and, indeed, it presents a real test for that process itself. The democratic process is the only thing that can possibly keep a balance between the non-belligerent at the extremes of the abortion debate—those, at one extreme, holding that abortion is murder and, at the other, holding that restricting abortion is to unjustifiably constrain a woman's basic liberty. The law's medicalisation of abortion has serious attenuated the political controversy of abortion, although treating abortion as an essentially medical matter sits uneasily with the majority of pro- and anti-abortionists. Many pro-abortionists lament the control granted to the medical profession (as opposed to the pregnant woman),[145] and many anti-abortionists lament the ease with which

---

[144] RCOG 2001.
[145] Notably Sheldon 1995.

doctors can legally conduct abortions. The controversy is unlikely to wane. The choice of moral theory is key and we will return to that issue in the final chapter.

7.7 Further reading

Finnis, John (1973) "The Rights and Wrongs of Abortion: A Reply to Judith Thomson." 2(2) *Philosophy and Public Affairs* 117–145.

Sheldon, Sally and Wilkinson, Stephen (2001) "Termination of Pregnancy for Reason of Foetal Disability: Are There Grounds for a Special Exception in Law?" 9(2) *Medical Law Review* 85–109.

Singer, Peter (1993) *Practical Ethics*. (Cambridge: Cambridge University Press), ch. 6; or Singer, Peter (1994) *Rethinking Life and Death: The Collapse of Our Traditional Ethics*. (Oxford: Oxford University Press), ch. 5.

Thomson, Judith Jarvis (1971) "A Defence of Abortion." 1 *Philosophy and Public Affairs* 47–66.

Chapter 8

REPRODUCTIVE TECHNOLOGIES

8.1 Introduction

Louise Brown, the first IVF baby, was born in July 1978. Since then over a million children have been born following IVF worldwide and over 68,000 of these have, like Louise, been born in the UK.[1] IVF, or to give it its full name *in vitro* fertilisation, involves the creation of an embryo outside of the body. It is just one of many ways in which the medical profession can assist a person to become a parent. The development of reproductive technologies has revolutionised the lives of many and redrawn the boundaries of reproduction. To some reproductive medicine simply treats involuntarily childlessness, to others it threatens the essence of the family and society. It is now much easier for the roles of genetic parents, social parents, and the gestational mother to be separated. Medicine is now involved more fully in reproduction through a range of (medically) assisted reproductive techniques. Reproduction is becoming increasingly medicalised.

This chapter seeks to explore the legal and ethical complexities of assisted reproduction (including surrogacy) and its regulation. The law in this area operates under many pressures. One of these is medical tourism, as both patient and research-led *reproductive tourism* are becoming commonplace. In fact, assisted reproduction brings all the major themes of this book together. It is a topic affected by market forces and patient consumerism, the politicisation of medical law, the changing nature of medicine and technology, the Human Rights Act (HRA) 1998, and resource limitations. Since this is a huge topic some aspects are addressed in other chapters. The regulation of embryo and stem cell research, and cloning are, for example, addressed in Ch.10.

8.1.1 The 1990 and 2008 Acts

The Human Fertilisation and Embryology Act 1990 (hereafter *the 1990 Act*) established a detailed regulatory scheme addressing IVF and related assisted reproductive technologies. In particular, it set up the Human Fertilisation and Embryology Authority (hereafter *the HFEA*). As I write this, the 1990 Act is about to be significantly amended by the Human Fertilisation and Embryology Act 2008 (hereafter *the 2008 Act*). The 2008 Act received Royal Assent on November 13, 2008. The plan is for its implementation to be divided into three stages.[2] Stage one will give effect to the revised definitions of parenthood from Pt 2 of the 2008 Act and is planned for April 2009. Stage two will see the other amendments to the 1990 Act take effect and is planned for October 2009. Stage three will give effect to parent orders and is planned for 2010. To avoid this book becoming out-of-date shortly after publication, this chapter has been written as if the principal provisions of the 2008 Act are in force.

---

[1] See HFEA 2004b. IVF and donor insemination now accounts for 1.7% of all babies born in the UK: see HFEA 2008a, 5.

[2] See the HFEA's website (*http://www.hfea.gov.uk/en/1735.html*) (visited in January 2009).

Amending, rather than repealing and replacing, the 1990 Act in this way has the advantage of legal continuity. Unmodified provisions require no additional interpretation and judicial decisions on these remain applicable. The principal disadvantage is that understanding the law requires account to be taken of yet another piece of legislation. The 1990 Act had already been significantly modified, not least by the Human Fertilisation and Embryology (Quality and Safety) Regulations 2007/1522.[3] The 1990 Act must, thus, be read side-by-side with multiple pieces of amending legislation. Readers are therefore advised to read the illustrative amended Act prepared by the Department of Health.[4]

8.2 The ethics of assisted reproduction

The introduction of chloroform in the nineteenth century brought passionate protests.[5] Many considered it "unnatural" or even a satanic intervention, removing the pain inflicted by God to punish us for our sins. Similar concerns were raised following the creation of Louise Brown in 1978. Even six years later, the special committee chaired by Mary Warnock—popularly known as the Warnock Committee—issued a report in which it was thought necessary to address similar arguments. The Warnock Report addresses claims that such techniques are unnatural, an interference with God's will, and, where donated gametes are used, comparable to adultery.[6] Such claims have notorious problems. Medicine exists to defeat the effects of nature (pain, distress, illness, and death), there are difficulties determining what God's will is,[7] and the use of donated gametes lacks most of the features of adultery (it does not involve deceiving a partner for the purpose of sexual gratification).

While many ethical arguments continue to be made against particular technologies or particular uses of the technology, few now reject assisted reproduction *as such*. IVF and assisted reproduction are now generally accepted as means of addressing involuntary childlessness. *Involuntary childlessness* is the physical inability to fulfil the desire to have a biologically-related child. That physical inability can be caused by one's own reproductive dysfunction (e.g. low sperm count or blocked fallopian tubes), the reproductive dysfunction of one's partner, or the absence of a partner of the opposite sex. Infertility and sterility are merely examples of the physical inability to reproduce. The desire to have a biologically related child itself might be the product of, or at least influenced by, social norms. It has been argued that this desire is a social product, and infertility is the medicalisation of these factors and, as such, a medical construct.[8] However, as one commentator put it,

---

[3] These gave domestic effect to the Tissues and Cells Directive (Directive 2004/23/EC).
[4] See DH 2007b.
[5] See Sokol 2004.
[6] See Warnock et al. 1984, paras 2.3, 4.10, 5.6, and 8.10.
[7] See further Ch.17 (17.2).
[8] See Klein (1989, 246) who doubts the validity of women's consent to IVF and the discussion of those radical feminists who hold that involuntarily childless woman are acting out of "mindless socialization" in Jackson 2001, 179–181.

The view that medical infertility is a medical construct and the desire to have a biologically related child a social product does not deny the consequences of such definitions.[9]

Whatever the origins of this desire, it does not follow that its subjects are thereby deprived of the capacity for choice. The empirical evidence suggests that involuntary childlessness can be as distressing as grief, emotionally crippling its victims with feelings of inadequacy, loss, anger, and confusion.[10] It does not suggest that involuntary childlessness is a compulsive or psychotic disorder removing freewill and the capacity for decision-making.

Assisted reproduction can be used to overcome a physical inability, but it rarely permanently removes that inability. Even when successful, assisted reproduction usually only sidesteps that inability in one particular instance. Many are not even this lucky, as success rates remain low. The live birth rate for IVF patients of all ages is still only 23.1 per cent.[11] There is, however, evidence that even where IVF is unsuccessful, it can reduce the suffering of the involuntarily childless by leading to acceptance of the condition.[12]

Assisted reproduction techniques are not restricted to use by those suffering from a physical inability to have a biologically-related child. They can be used for reasons of convenience or to achieve goals that are not connected to any infertility. Assisted reproduction, therefore, raises questions far beyond the interests of potential parents to found a family; it raises questions about the weight of the desire to create *a particular type of family in a particular way*.

8.2.1 The moral status of the *in vitro* embryo

The moral status of the embryo is evidently relevant for abortion and research on *in vitro* embryos (i.e. embryos created outside the body). These issues are addressed in Chs 7 (esp. 7.2.1) and 10 (10.3.1). Less obviously, the moral duties that we owe directly to early human life also have an impact on the moral permissibility of IVF and related forms of assisted reproduction.

If an embryo is owed duties because of what it is, then it has moral status or standing. As explained in Ch.1 (1.4.3.1), the value of the embryo is easy to map according to whether and to what extent it is thought to possess moral status. At one extreme, are moral positions holding that the embryo deserves the same level of protection as an adult human being. According to what may be called the *full status* position, full moral status is to be granted to the embryo from the moment of its creation. At the other extreme, is what may be called the *no status* position, which holds that the embryo itself has no intrinsic value or status.

---

[9] Anleu quoted in Morgan 2001, 72.
[10] See e.g. Menning 1977 and 1980; Hull 1992, 2; and Warnock 1984, para.2.2.
[11] See HFEA 2008a, 4.
[12] See Boivin et al. 1995, 805; Menning 1977 and 1980; Koropatnick et al. 1993, esp. 169; and Lalos et al. 1985.

According to this position, an embryo is no more than a bunch of cells whose intrinsic features grant it no special protection. Between these two extremes are *limited status* positions, which hold that the embryo has a status resting somewhere between full and none. The most popular limited position is the *proportional status* position, which holds that the moral status of the embryo increases with gestational development (as it is implanted and develops) until it obtains full moral status at birth or beyond. Thus, the embryo can be recognised as having moral status to the same degree as you or I (full status), to a degree less than you or I (limited status, or where that status increases with gestational, proportional status), or to no degree at all (no status).

IVF practices pose considerable difficulties for adherents of the full status position. *First*, the present and future development of IVF and related techniques is intimately connected with what is considered to be morally impermissible destructive embryo experimentation. In this sense, these techniques rely on and encourage conduct that a holder of the full status position must regard as equivalent to murder. Destructive embryo research continues and has resulted in both vast improvements to the success of standard IVF and the development of new techniques over the last couple of decades. Some years ago, for example, experimentation led to the development of a technique to help men whose sperm have not developed fully or who lack sufficient sperm to conceive by other means. This technique, known as intra-cytoplasmic sperm injection (ICSI), involves injecting immature sperm directly into an egg outside the body.[13] Even a practitioner of IVF who eschews embryo research will find it practically impossible to avoid utilising the products of continuing embryo research and thereby indirectly encouraging future embryo research. *Second*, IVF can create embryos that are not implanted into the woman receiving treatment. The production of so-called "surplus" embryos is commonplace in countries where the number of embryos produced is not limited to the number that can be implanted in a single treatment cycle. Even in countries where the number created is so limited, surplus embryos are created in practice. Surplus embryos will be created unless women undergoing treatment are *required* to allow *all* these embryos to be implanted (into their body or that of another woman). This would require even potentially abnormal embryos to be properly implanted. *In contrast*, no status positions need not be so troubled by the effects of IVF *on* existing or future embryos, because they hold that the embryo matters no more than the hair on your head or the nails on your fingers. The limited status position is more variable. There are many variants of this position united only by the view that embryos count for something more than nothing but do not have the same value as the child and adult that they could become.

Any moral status that an embryo has will be supplemented by the morally significant consequences of our actions on those (others) who have moral status. Even the no status position does not imply that embryos can be destroyed for fun—the couple who produced the gametes could, for example, have morally relevant interests. Also, if one's intention is to allow an embryo to

---

[13] See Palmero et al. 1992.

develop into a future child, then one's actions towards that embryo must take account of the moral interests that it will have as a child-in-the-future.[14]

The major moral camps outlined in Ch.1 do not map straightforwardly on to the no, full, and limited status framework.[15] Nonetheless, there are clear trends and sometimes even correlations. Compromise positions are, by definition, capable of adopting any view on the moral status of the embryo, but often tend towards limited status. The 1990 Act (before and after amendment) is most coherently explained as depending on the limited status position—more precisely, proportional or gradualist versions of the limited status position (see further Ch.10 (10.3.2.2)). Neither utilitarian nor rights-based positions are compatible with the full status position. For utilitarians, to have moral status a being must be capable of experiencing pain or even capable of making choices (depending on the type of utilitarianism in play). For rights-based theories, only those who can waive the benefit of rights can have rights and, therefore, moral status. (For the complex reasons examined in the final chapter, it does not automatically follow that such theories are committed to the no status position.) In contrast, the duty-based camp is compatible with the full status position. Catholicism, the major full status position, is a duty-based position.[16]

8.2.2 Reproductive tourism

Globalised trade, travel, and communication are now part of the context of our lives. With globalisation comes reproductive tourism, as individuals are free to travel abroad for treatment not offered, or perhaps not even legal, in the their country of origin. There have been a number of high profile cases of reproductive tourism involving patients travelling from this to other countries for treatment. In one case, a woman was able to export sperm for treatment in Belgium, despite not being able to lawfully use it here (it was to be used posthumously without the written consent required by the 1990 Act).[17] In another, a couple went to the US after the HFEA refused to allow them to use diagnostic technology to ensure that their next child would be a suitable donor of cord blood for their sick child (see 8.5.2, below). Reproductive tourism operating the other way, with prospective parents travelling to the UK, is also said to occur.[18]

For some moral theories, particularly those of a utilitarian ilk, it might be better to allow access to a particular technology or freedom here (where some regulatory control can be maintained) than to encourage travel to less regulated jurisdictions. Utilitarians, at least those of the act variety, cannot ignore any disutility generated by patients being attracted by less tightly controlled services available elsewhere. In contrast, rights and duty-based positions could

[14] See Pattinson 2002a, 2.6.
[15] Greater elaboration of the following points can be found in Chs 7 (7.2.1) and 10 (10.3.1).
[16] This is the official position of the Roman Catholic Church: see Pope John Paul II 1993. Some Catholics reject the full status position in favour of a limited status position: see Farley 2001.
[17] See the discussion of *R. v HFEA Ex p. Blood* [1999] Fam. 151, below.
[18] e.g. in relation to surrogacy: see Brazier et al. 1998, para.3.43, and Jackson 2001, 282–283.

consistently maintain a position against allowing a particular reproductive technique or a particular application of that technique, irrespective of such consequences. Some rights-based theories grant persons extensive reproductive rights.[19] From this view, reproductive tourism can be seen as little more than a reflection of a State's unwillingness or inability to recognise those rights.

In practice, reproductive tourism is only an option for those able to obtain the necessary resources. Even when undertaken in this country, assisted reproduction is prohibitively expensive. In the UK, 80 per cent of IVF treatment is private[20] and the cost ranges from £2,000–£4,000 per cycle with the drugs costing up to £1,000 more.[21] This raises a question that has divided many moral positions: the extent of positive duties to assist those in need. Even theories that accept extensive positive duties will not necessarily grant high priority to assisted reproduction, because any public money spent on assisted reproduction could be needed to treat other medical conditions thought to be more urgent or more serious.[22]

8.2.3 Dignitarian concerns

Many of the ethical issues raised by assisted reproduction invite competing dignitarian concerns. Ch.1 distinguished two conceptions of dignity, deriving from the work of Beyleveld and Brownsword: "dignity as empowerment" and "dignity as constraint".[23]

The "dignity as constraint" position resonates throughout the assisted reproduction debate. This position captures the paternalistic concerns of certain duty-based and compromise positions such as those of Kant, Catholics, and communitarians. It rejects certain practices as contrary to human dignity, *irrespective of their consequences or consensual nature*.[24] Where underpinned by Catholicism and some variants of communitarianism, it adheres to the full status position. It generally seeks to maintain the traditional family unit and is thereby opposed to opening up access to assisted reproduction beyond heterosexual couples (sometimes even married heterosexual couples) and is antagonistic to the use of donor gametes or surrogacy. This position also raises dignitarian objections to the use of genetic and selective technology to influence the traits of a future child.

In contrast, the "dignity as empowerment" position captures the autonomy-focused approach of rights-based theories, demanding that one's capacity for free and informed choice be recognised and that one's particular choices be respected. While utilitarians generally reject the species-specific label of "human" dignity,

---

[19] See e.g. Robertson 1994.
[20] HFEA website (*http://www.hfea.gov.uk/en/1681.html*) (viewed January 2009).
[21] See HFEA 2004b.
[22] See further McMillan 2003. For an early objection to the provision of public funding for IVF see Kass 1979, 56–57.
[23] See Ch.1 (1.4.1) and Beyleveld and Brownsword 2001.
[24] See e.g. Anderson who holds that "both pregnancy [surrogacy] contracts and slave contracts wrongly treat someone's inalienable rights as if they were freely alienable" (2004, 23).

many utilitarian concerns can be consistent with the demands of the empowerment camp. With regard to assisted reproduction, the empowerment camp places the onus on those who wish to curtail reproductive freedoms and choices.[25] The traditional family unit is not held to be intrinsically valuable and genetic and selective technologies could have morally permitted (or even required) uses.

This tension is evident in the debate on assisted reproduction. Positions seeking to limit or remove the use of reproduction technologies are constantly in conflict with positions favouring reproductive autonomy.

8.3 The statutory scheme

Before the Human Fertilisation and Embryology Authority (the HFEA) was set up as a statutory licensing body by s.5 of the 1990 Act, the profession had regulated itself using a non-statutory body. The Voluntary Licensing Authority had been jointly set up in 1985 by the Royal College of Obstetricians and Gynaecologists (RCOG) and the Medical Research Council. In 1989, as an indication of the desire that a statutory framework be put in place, this body renamed itself the Interim Voluntary Licensing Authority. When the Warnock Committee reported in 1984, it declared that a statutory authority was necessary as, "None of our . . . recommendations can have any practical impact until such body is set up".[26] The 1990 Act was enacted in (slow) response to that recommendation.

The existing statutory scheme has a number of attributes. The HFEA serves as licensor, regulator, and advisor. A key aspect of its regulatory functions is the issuing of a *Code of Practice* (required by s.25). A new edition is published every few years and the HFEA issues regular updates to the Code. At the time of writing, the seventh edition of the Code, which came into force in July 2007, is in its fourth revision.[27] The eight edition was issued in draft for consultation in November 2008 and deals with the law as it will be after implementation of the 2008 Act.[28]

The Code of Practice specifies what the HFEA considers to be proper conduct in relation to licensed activities. It is not directly binding, but disregard of its provisions would count against a licensed clinic in any civil or criminal proceedings *and* could lead the HFEA to vary, revoke, or refuse to renew a clinic's licence (s.25(6) of the 1990 Act). Another key regulatory device is the power to issue mandatory directions (ss.23–24).[29] Directions can be given for a large number of regulatory purposes. In practice, many of those issued have dealt with payment for gametes and embryos. Failure to comply with a direction empowers the HFEA to revoke a licence (s.18(2)(c)) and, in some cases, it can constitute a criminal offence (s.41(2)(d)).

---

[25] See e.g. Pattinson 2002a; Robertson 1994; Jackson 2001, ch. 5; and Harris 1998.
[26] Warnock et al. 1984, para.13.14.
[27] See HFEA 2007b and HFEA website.
[28] See HFEA 2008b.
[29] See further Freeman 2004, 666–668.

Like the abortion legislation, the 1990 Act also allows conscientious objection. Under s.38, no one will be forced to participate in any activity regulated by the 1990 Act (such as IVF or embryo research) where they have a conscientious objection to those activities.[30]

8.3.1 The HFEA and its licensing remit

In 2001, two leading commentators declared it to be "surprising that the work of the HFEA has drawn so little serious or sustained comment".[31] This is no longer the case. There have now been many legal challenges to the HFEA's regulatory jurisdiction, challenging the Authority's view on the activities requiring a licence and its view on the activities for which it has granted or denied permission.[32] Moreover, there have been a number of controversies over the activities of licensed clinics.[33] Many of these cases have received considerable, serious, and sustained comment.[34] Further, the process leading up to the enactment of the 2008 Act saw many official reports and academic comment, in addition to extensive Parliamentary debate.[35]

8.3.1.1 Membership

The HFEA currently has 22 members. Since late 2005, appointments have been made by the NHS Appointments Committees.[36] The 1990 Act imposes a number of requirements (Sch.1 para.4). It prohibits the Chair, Deputy Chair, and more than half of the other members from having backgrounds as doctors or as persons professionally involved in assisted reproduction or related research. Nonetheless, at least a third must have such backgrounds. This attempts to strike a balance between independence and expertise. Also, when making appointments the Health Minister must have regard to the desirability of ensuring that the proceedings and functions of the HFEA are informed by the views of both men and women. Notably, despite operating in such an ethically controversial area, there is no requirement that any members have ethical expertise. There is also no requirement that its members have legal expertise. In practice, some of its members do and the HFEA has adopted a system of retaining a panel of solicitors whose members are able to sit on Licensing Committees.[37]

---

[30] See further Freeman 2004, 685–687.

[31] Lee and Morgan 2001, 8.

[32] See e.g. *R. v HFEA Ex p. Blood* [1999] Fam. 151, *R. (Bruno Quintavalle) v Secretary of State for Health* [2003] UKHL 13, *R. (Josephine Quintavalle) v HFEA* [2005] UKHL 28, *Rose v Secretary of State for Health and HFEA* [2002] EWHC 1593, and BBC 2008d.

[33] e.g. *Leeds Teaching Hospitals NHS Trust v A* [2003] EWHC 259.

[34] See e.g. the discussion of *R. (Bruno Quintavalle) v Secretary of State for Health* [2003] UKHL 13 in Ch.10 (10.4.2.1) and the footnote reference to the views of other commentators.

[35] See e.g. the official reports and responses issued in 2005 alone: Science and Technology Committee 2005a, 2005b, and 2005c, HM Government 2005 and DH 2005d.

[36] 436 *Hansard (House of Commons)* 2702W, 12 September 2005 (Caroline Flint MP).

[37] In response to the Toft Report: see Toft 2004 and HFEA 2004g, 1.

The appointed nature of the body has opened it up to the criticism that it is undemocratic. In 2002, a House of Commons Select Committee (after considering a particularly controversial decision made by the HFEA) went so far as to declare that "democracy is not served by unelected quangos taking decisions on behalf of Parliament".[38] The undemocratic nature of HFEA can, however, only be taken so far. Its existence, function, and constitution are specified by an Act of Parliament. Parliament has thereby used its own democratic mandate to empower and legitimate the role and function of the HFEA, *as long as it stays within the provisions and principles of the 1990 Act*.[39] There is also specific provision for Parliamentary overview: s.7 of the 1990 Act requires the HFEA to submit an annual report, detailing its past and projected activities. This report is to be laid before Parliament by the Minister. Further, the actions of the HFEA have now received detailed and lengthy consideration by Parliament in the lead up to the enactment of the 2008 Act. Parliament has provided further legislative clarification of the regulatory body's policy-making role. The amended s.8 of the 1990 Act now requires the HFEA to "maintain a statement of general principles" on the carrying-out of activities governed by the Act and in the carrying-out of its functions in relation to these activities. In addition, the HFEA is now required to "carry out its functions effectively, efficiently and economically" and, where relevant, have regard to the "principles of best regulatory practice (including the principles under which regulatory activities should be transparent, accountable, proportionate, consistent and targeted only at cases in which action is needed)" (s.8ZA). As we shall see, some issues that were previously dealt with purely by the HFEA in its guidance and Code of Practice (such as sex selection for social reasons) have now been dealt with directly by legislation. Interestingly, this legislative guidance largely follows the HFEA's past practice.

8.3.1.2 Funding

The Department of Health has set a target for the HFEA to raise 70 per cent of its annual income from licence fees. It exceeded that target a number of years ago.[40] This weakens the independence of the HFEA. It means that the HFEA is required to regulate and maybe even revoke the licenses of the clinics that pay for it to be run. What is more, the increasing number of cases in which the HFEA has to be represented (as a party or an intervener) significantly cut into its limited budget. It has even been suggested that the reason that the HFEA did not appeal one of the key cases brought against it was largely financial.[41]

---

[38] See Science and Technology Committee 2002, para.19.
[39] See further Pattinson 2005.
[40] See HFEA 2004a.
[41] The previous chair of the HFEA has said that "*Had money and pressures been more relaxed*, the HFEA would have been able to establish that there was a public interest to be protected in the Blood case [(1999) Fam. 151] which justified an infringement of the European right of provision of services. . . ." (Deech 2002, 586, my emphasis).

8.3.1.3 *Licensing remit*

The 1990 Act has three regulatory responses to the activities falling within its ambit: (1) outright prohibition, (2) prohibition subject to an authorising licence issued by the HFEA, and (3) prohibition subject to authorisation by either a licence or a third party agreement with a licence-holder. These prohibitions are backed by criminal sanctions.

The HFEA has the power to issue licences for treatment, the provision of non-medical fertility services, the storage of gametes and embryos, and embryo research (s.11). It also has related powers to vary, suspend, or revoke such licences (ss.18, 18A and 19C). Not every form of assisted reproduction, however, requires a licence or even a third party agreement. The Act only regulates activities involving or related to the involvement of embryos, gametes, and cells used to create embryos.

A licence alone may authorise:

(a) the creation of an embryo outside of the body (ss.3(1)(a) and 1(2));

(b) the storage or use of embryos (s.3(1)(b))

(c) storage of gametes (s.4(1)(a));

(d) the use of gametes in the course of providing treatment services for any woman, *except* where it is partner-donated sperm that has been neither processed nor stored (s.4(1)(b).

A licence or third party agreement (i.e. between a licence holder and another) may authorise:

(i) the keeping or processing (without storage) of an embryo intended for human application (s.3(1A)(b));

(ii) the procurement or distribution of an embryo intended for human application (s.3(1B));

(iii) the procurement, testing, processing, or distribution of gametes intended for human application (s.4(1A)).

These lists require some explanation. What it means is that a licence is required for the creation, freezing, or use of *in vitro* embryos; the freezing of gametes; and the use of donated gametes in the course of treatment. A third party agreement will suffice for gamete preparation processes for use in fertility treatment and services providing introductions to sperm donors (referred to by the 1990 Act as "non-medical fertility services").[42] Nonetheless, some medical responses to infertility do not fall within the regulatory framework created by the 1990 Act.

---

[42] "Non-medical fertility services" are defined, in s.2(1), to mean "any services that are provided, in the course of a business, for the purpose of assisting women to carry children, but are not medical, surgical or obstetric services".

Imagine a couple, Janet and John, who have tried for a number of years to have a child. Their family doctor can provide advice or even fertility drugs without falling within the HFEA's licensing remit. This is despite the fact that superovulatory drugs can pose serious risks to a woman's health and can result in multiple pregnancies, sometimes in circumstances where the woman will need to consider selective termination to ensure the survival of at least one fetus.[43] The doctor treating Janet and John could also refer the couple for surgery (e.g. surgical repair of damaged fallopian tubes) without either the referring doctor or the surgeon performing any activity requiring a licence or a third party agreement. Prior to 2007, the doctor could even provide so-called "basic partner treatment services" without a licence. That is to say that no licence was required (and third party agreements did not then exist) to treat a man and woman together with their unstored sperm and eggs. That meant that the doctor could, for example, have mixed the couple's gametes in Janet's fallopian tubes to encourage conception (a technique known as gamete intra-fallopian treatment or GIFT) without a licence. This is no longer the case due to amending secondary legislation, enacted in 2007 to give effect to the EU Tissues and Cells Directive 2004/23/EC.[44] A licence or third party agreement is now required for activities such as the "processing" of gametes. "Processing" is defined in s.2(1) to mean "in relation to gametes or embryos intended for human application . . . any operation involved in their preparation, manipulation or packaging, and related terms are to be interpreted accordingly". This would even seem to capture the doctor artificially inseminating Janet with John's sperm—intrauterine insemination (IUI), intracervical insemination (ICI), and related techniques.

8.3.2 Access to assisted reproduction

There are currently 115 centres licensed to carry out licensed treatment.[45] Many are private. As stated above, only about 20 per cent of IVF treatment is funded by the NHS and cycles cost up to £4,000 plus the cost of the drugs. In February 2004, in an attempt to address the "postcode lottery" whereby NHS-funding varied by region,[46] the National Institute for Health and Clinical Excellence (NICE) issued guidelines designed to effect a common policy in the UK.[47] Under these guidelines, couples with an identifiable cause of infertility or an unexplained cause of infertility of at least three years in which the woman is aged 23–39, should be offered three cycles of IVF.[48] Such guidelines are not binding on Primary Care Trusts (PCTs), the local bodies responsible for securing and planning NHS provision. Despite endorsement of NICE's guidance by Health Secretaries,[49] funding

[43] See further Ch.7 (7.5.2).
[44] The Human Fertilisation and Embryology (Quality and Safety) Regulations 2007/1522.
[45] HFEA website (February 2009).
[46] See e.g. Plomer et al. 1999.
[47] See NICE 2004. See Ch.2 (2.2.2) for an explanation of the role and function of the NICE.
[48] NICE 2004, 5.
[49] See e.g. HFEA 2004b.

still varies from region to region in accordance with different PCT's funding policies. In late 2008, the Interim Report of the Expert Group on Commissioning NHS Infertility Provision reported that 95 per cent of PCTs still do not offer the three cycles recommended by NICE.[50]

8.3.2.1 The welfare of the child requirement

During the parliamentary debate leading up to the passing of the 1990 Act, the House of Lords introduced a proposed amendment that would have restricted the provision of IVF and related services to married couples. That proposal was defeated by a single vote. Instead, 1990 Act s.13(5) declared:

> A woman shall not be provided with treatment services unless account has been taken of the welfare of any child who may be born as a result of the treatment (including the need of that child for a father), and of any other child who may be affected by the birth.

The 2008 Act substituted the words "including the need of that child for *supportive parenting*" for "including the need of that child for *a father*".[51] The previous wording prioritised the traditional family unit of a man and a woman in a stable, or even marital, relationship. It reflected the Warnock Committee's view that "as a general rule it is better for children to be born into a two-parent family, with both father and mother".[52] It nudged fertility doctors towards a particular view of parenthood and family. Some commentators, and the 2005 report of the House of Commons Science and Technology Committee, argued that it constituted unjustified discrimination against the involuntary childless.[53] In any event, the HFEA had, in practice, marginalised the requirement by giving it only passing attention in its Code of Practice.

The 2008 Act removed additional words inserted by the Quality and Safety Regulations 2007/1522 that disapplied the welfare of the child requirement to "basic partner treatment services". The provision now applies, as it did before, to all "treatment services", defined in s.2(1) to mean "medical, surgical or obstetric services provided to the public or a section of the public for the purpose of assisting women to carry children". The HFEA quite properly considers licensed clinics bound by this requirement even when providing unlicensed treatment services.[54]

Section 13(5), even as amended, places considerable power in the hands of doctors. As Kennedy and Grubb pointed out some years ago, the discretion granted to doctors "departs from what would be the normal understanding of a doctor's duty to his patient".[55] What is more, the factors to be taken into account are not purely medical. Doctors are expected to make decisions that are not

---

[50] See Expert Group on Commissioning NHS Infertility Provision 2008.
[51] My emphasis.
[52] Warnock et al. 1984, para.2.11. Cf. Golombok 1998.
[53] See Jackson 2001, esp. 195 and the Science and Technology Committee 2005a, 44–51.
[54] See HFEA 2007b, G.3.2.1 and 2008b, para.8.1.
[55] Kennedy and Grubb 2000, 1272.

strictly within their competence. The law has medicalised access to assisted reproduction. Social judgments about the suitability of the involuntarily childless to be parents are not simply encouraged, doctors are required to make them.[56] The key term, "welfare", is not defined in the Act. Notice also that the provision requires account to be taken of "any other child who may be affected by the birth".

The "welfare of the child" requirement raises conceptual difficulties insofar as it is concerned with the welfare of the child that will be born. Assisted reproduction is usually the only plausible way in which *a particular* child could be brought into existence. Section 13(5) therefore requires the determination of whether to allow access to assisted reproduction to turn on the assessment of the welfare of a future child whose very existence depends on allowing access. Can bringing a child into existence be a wrong to the child brought into existence?[57] Here, I suggest, moral theories could differ. Utilitarians could argue that bringing a child into existence is a wrong to that child, *if* that existence would overall be a burden rather than a benefit.[58] For many utilitarians, it can be wrong to a child to bring that child into a state of disutility, *even if that child could not have existed in any other state.*[59] In contrast, a rights-based theorist would have to hold that even a terrible existence does not violate the child's rights. For a child's rights to have been violated that child would have to have been deprived of an alternative existence in which his rights were fulfilled.[60] A parallel argument can be made for duty-based theories, which only differ from rights-based theories in that they reject the idea that the benefit of any duty is necessarily waivable by the beneficiary. This is an implication of moral theories that define wrongs as distributive and individual-affecting, as considered in more depth in Ch.9 (9.4.2). Virtue theorists would not focus on whether a duty owed to the child has been violated, but on the character and motive of the prospective parent and assisting clinician vis-à-vis the relevant virtues.

According to Freeman, s.13(5) is "incoherent", because,

> It asks us to compare the utilities of not being born to a single mother; surely a nonsense since existence will nearly always (perhaps always) be preferable to non-existence.[61]

Trying to conceptualise the wrong in a different way (so that existence is not been compared to non-existence) runs into other problems. One could, for example, characterise the wrong as having the intention to harm the welfare of the future child, *after it comes into existence.* This approach does not depend on a wrong being inflicted on the child by its existence. Unfortunately, it is very difficult to impute an intention to commit a future wrong in any but the most extreme circumstances.

---

[56] See e.g. Harris 1985, ch.7 and 1998, esp. 92–98.
[57] Parfit called this the "non-identity problem": Parfit 1984, ch.16. This question is also raised by wrongful life actions (Ch.9, 9.4.2) and cloning (Ch.10, 10.4.1).
[58] See e.g. Harris 1998 and 2000.
[59] It could, however, be questioned whether this wrong is correctly characterised as a wrong *to the child*. For utilitarians, wrongs do not need to affect a specific individual.
[60] See Pattinson 2002c.
[61] Freeman 2004, 677. See also Harris 2000, 33; Jackson 2001, 192; and Jackson 2002, 196–199.

Alternatively, some moral theories could characterise the wrong as a wrong not to the future child but to community values (communitarianism), the overall welfare balance (utilitarianism), or other relevant persons. Reconciling s.13(5) with an interpretation that makes philosophical sense is no easy task.

The HFEA significantly revised its guidance on the welfare of the child in November 2005[62] and has modified it on a number of subsequent occasions.[63] The 2005 revision saw the adoption of a presumption in favour of treatment, unless there is evidence that any child born, or any existing child of the family, will face a serious risk of physical, psychological, or medical harm. The draft eighth edition of the Code of Practice states that "the centre should consider factors that are likely to cause a risk of significant harm or neglect, either to the child to be born or to any existing child of the family".[64] The presumption in favour of treatment has become a presumption that all prospective parents will be supportive parents "in the absence of any reasonable cause for concern that either the child to be born, or any other child, may be at risk of significant harm or neglect".[65] As before, the HFEA lists a number of factors that centres are to take into account but retains clinical discretion on the weighting to be given to these factors. The result is that individual clinicians remain free to adopt inconsistent philosophical approaches to the welfare of the child within the broad parameters laid down by the HFEA.

8.3.2.2 Legally challenging the exercise of discretion

Neither the 1990 Act nor the Code of Practice exclude any category of person from access to assisted reproduction. As already indicated, the upshot of the welfare of the child requirement is that clinicians have a great deal of discretion to decide whom to treat. A disgruntled patient could challenge a clinic's decision by judicial review. The few reported cases do not, however, present much hope that a patient will obtain judicial assistance. Back in 1987, Mrs Harriott sought to challenge her removal from a clinic's IVF waiting list.[66] The clinic had removed her after becoming aware that she had been turned down for both adoption and fostering because of her criminal record (for offences relating to prostitution and the running of a brothel) and her allegedly poor understanding of the role of a foster-parent. Only after the ethical advisory committee had offered support for the consultant's decision was Mrs Harriott told the real reason for the decision. Until that time she had been told that she was being removed because of her husband's semen infection, then because of her liver abnormality. Despite this deceit, which the judge charitably put down to the consultant's sense of delicacy, Mrs Harriott failed in her judicial review action against the ethics committee and the consultant. It was held to be both reasonable and lawful for the consultant to apply the adoption criteria and the ethics

---

[62] See HFEA 2005b.
[63] See e.g. HFEA 2007b, G.3 and HFEA 2008b, paras 8.1–8.19.
[64] See HFEA 2008b, para.8.8.
[65] See HFEA 2008b, para.8.9.
[66] *R v Ethical Committee of St. Mary's Hospital Ex p. Harriott* [1988] 1 F.L.R. 512.

committee would not be compelled to give advice or embark on a particular investigation. The decision was not one that "no reasonable consultant could have come to", unlike, the judge suggested, the refusal of treatment on the grounds of religion or ethnic origin.[67]

The only other reported case was one brought by Mrs Seale after being refused NHS-funded treatment because of her age.[68] She was 37 and the defendant health authority only funded treatment for those under 35. This policy had been adopted to ration treatment. The judge refused to quash the decision on any of the standard grounds for judicial review: illegality, irrationality, or procedural impropriety. According to the court, the Health Authority had the discretion to refuse treatment: refusing treatment to those to whom it was "generally less effective" was not *Wednesbury* unreasonable[69] and there was no "procedural hook" on which Mrs Seale could rest her case. The procedural hook surely rested with the claim that the Health Authority had fettered its discretion by failing to consider Mrs Seale's case as an exceptional one falling outside of its policy.[70] Kennedy and Grubb, rightly in my view, state that this was the "best argument for the applicant".[71] Despite the judge's refusal to grant Mrs Seale's application for leave, the Health Authority appeared to have adopted a blanket policy against funding women over 35.

Although Mrs Seale lost in court, she later gave birth to a baby boy after successful treatment paid for by an anonymous benefactor. In 2001, a 56-year-old woman became the mother of twins after being assisted to reproduce by, what is thought to be, the only clinic in this country willing to treat woman over 51.[72] Older women have subsequently been assisted to reproduce.[73] The different treatment polices of IVF clinics are undoubtedly the result of the flexibility inherent in the welfare of the child provision.

8.3.2.3 Human rights issues

To what extent is the HRA 1998 relevant to a refusal of access to assisted reproduction? The Convention recognises the right to respect for private and family life (art.8) and the right to marry and found a family (art.12), both of which are subject to a prohibition of discrimination with regard to their enjoyment (art.14). The ambit of these rights in the context of assisted reproduction is not yet settled, but both rights could potentially be engaged by the denial of access of assisted reproduction. In the *Evans* case, considered below, the Court of Appeal (and later the Grand Chamber of the European Court of Human Rights) accepted that the refusal of assisted reproduction engaged the art.8(1) right to

---

[67] The judge actually used the phrase "a Jew or Coloured".
[68] *R. v Sheffield Health Authority Ex p. Seale* (1994) 25 B.M.L.R. 1.
[69] *Associated Provincial Picture Houses v Wednesbury Corporation* [1948] 1 K.B. 223.
[70] *British Oxygen v Ministry of Technology* [1971] A.C. 610 and *R. v North West Lancashire Ex p. A, D & G* [2000] 1 W.L.R. 977.
[71] Kennedy and Grubb 2000, 1277. Similarly, Freeman finds the judge's conclusion on this point to be "dubious" (2004, 682).
[72] See Branigan 2001.
[73] See e.g. HFEA 2003c (58-year-old woman).

respect for private life.[74] However, the positive aspect of these rights is more restrictive than the negative aspect of this right, which affects the potential of arts 8 and 12 to provide grounds for successful challenge of a refusal under s.13(5) of the 1990 Act.[75] Article 8(2) explicitly restricts the ambit of the (negative and positive) right laid down by art.8(1)[76] and the European Court has held that,

> In determining whether or not a positive obligation exists, regard must be had to the fair balance that has to be struck between the general interest of the community and the interests of the individual, the search for which balance is inherent in the whole of the Convention.[77]

The courts will surely view s.13(5) as providing such a balance. Indeed, in the *Evans* case, the Grand Chamber declared that individual States had a wide margin of appreciation in the interpretation of the positive right to private life, because there was no European consensus on the regulation of IVF and IVF treatment gives rise to "sensitive moral and ethical issues against a background of fast-moving medical and scientific developments".[78]

With regard to art.12, the *Mellor* case decided it does not entitle a married couple to access to artificial insemination falling outside the 1990 Act where the husband is serving a prison sentence.[79] Significantly for our purposes, the Court of Appeal specified a number of factors that could legitimately be used to limit the scope of art.12, including the exceptions listed in art.8(2) and the welfare of the future child.[80] Section 13(5) therefore appears to be compatible with the jurisprudence on the relevant provisions of the HRA 1998. It is, nonetheless, possible to envisage circumstances where these provisions could bolster any challenge to an individual clinic's policy or the application of that policy in a specific case. The adoption of a blanket policy against permitting access to lesbian couples could, for example, invoke both art.8 and 14, and thereby bolster a challenge to the claim that the clinic has fettered its discretion.

8.3.3 Other issues concerning treatment

Access is only one issue relevant to treatment. This section will consider the requirement that patients be given the opportunity to receive counselling and

---

[74] *Evans v Amicus Healthcare* [2004] EWCA Civ 727, paras 60 and 108; and *Evans v UK* (No.6339/05, April 10, 2007) (2008) 46 E.H.R.R. 34. Ms Evans had already been given some treatment, but the approach taken to private life did not turn on that point. In contrast the right to be a legal parent of a child to which one is not biologically related does not appear to invoke art.8(1): *Re R* [2005] UKHL 33, para.44.
[75] See Jackson 2002, 199–201.
[76] Allowing such interference with the art.8(1) right,
> as is in accordance with the law and is necessary in a democratic society in the interests of national security, public safety or the economic well-being of the country, for the prevention of disorder or crime, *for the protection of health or morals, or for the protection of the rights and freedoms of others.* (My emphasis)
[77] *Sheffield and Horsham v UK* (1999) 27 E.H.R.R. 163 at 191.
[78] (2008) 46 E.H.R.R. 34, para.59.
[79] *R. (Mellor) v Secretary of State for the Home Department* [2002] Q.B. 13.
[80] [2002] Q.B. 13 at 25 and 33–34.

provide appropriate consent. In addition, it will examine the issue of the number of embryos that can be implanted.

8.3.3.1 Counselling

Section 13(6) of the 1990 Act states that specified treatment services must not be provided unless the woman and the person treated together with her have been given "a suitable opportunity to receive proper counselling about the implications of her being provided with treatment services of that kind, and have been provided with such relevant information as is proper".[81] The relevant treatment services are defined in Pt 1 of the new Sch.3ZA as those that involve the use of donated gametes or embryos, or the use of an embryo that has been created *in vitro*. A suitable offer of counselling must also be given where two people consent to the parenthood of a child that could be born as a result of the treatment (s.13(6A), (6B) and Sch.3ZA Pt 2) and where an individual or couple seeks to store their gametes or embryos (Sch.3 para.3).

The Code of Practice adds significantly to the Act's requirements.[82] In particular, it requires that any counselling provided comply with current professional guidance on good practice and be undertaken by qualified counsellors. In practice, the take up of counselling is thought to be low. Since patients are usually paying customers, it has been argued that clinics could be viewed as having an incentive not to promote counselling in case it deters them from proceeding.[83] The extent of the incentive effect should not, however, be overstated, because clinics have no shortage of potential customers and many of the involuntarily childless have a desperate desire for a child that is not easily assuaged.

8.3.3.2 Consent

The principle of consent is central to the 1990 Act. Licences granted must comply with the consent provisions in Sch.3, the only exception being for basic partner treatment services (s.12(c)). Paragraph one specifies that any consent given must be in writing and signed by the person giving it.[84] That consent must specify the maximum period for which the gametes or embryos are to be stored, the purposes for which they are to be used, and what is to be done if the person giving the consent dies, subject to the limits laid down by the Act (Sch.3 para.2(2)).

Consent that has not been withdrawn is referred to as "effective consent" (Sch.3 para.1(3)). It can be withdrawn or varied "by notice" given by that person (Sch.3 para.4(1)), which must also be in writing and signed (para.1(2)).[85]

---

[81] See also s.13A(3) and Sch.3 para.3.
[82] As is now required by s.25(2A). See HFEA 2007b, esp. G.1.4 and S.7.6.3; and 2008b, esp. paras 2.13 and 3.1–3.12.
[83] See Lee and Morgan 2001, 188, and Freeman 2004, 694.
[84] The consent giver can direct another to sign on their behalf in their presence and the present of at least one witness if they are physically unable to sign (Sch.3 para.1(2)).
[85] Cf. the previous position: see Pattinson 2006, 255.

That notice may be served by being delivered to the person, left at his proper address, or posted to that address (s.46(2)).

Consent cannot be varied or withdrawn once the gamete, human cell, or embryo has been "used" for treatment services, specified training purposes, or for the purposes of research (Sch.3 para.4(2)). The meaning of the word "used" here was considered by the Court of Appeal in the *Evans* case.[86] Natalie Evans wished to have an embryo implanted that had been created from her eggs and the sperm of the man from whom she had subsequently separated. Since these embryos had been created just before an operation to remove her ovaries, they represented her only chance to have a genetically-related child. The man in question had, however, written to the clinic to notify it of the separation and require the embryos to be destroyed. The Court of Appeal held that the embryos would only be used once they were implanted. In the words of Arden L.J., "*In the context of the withdrawal of consent* (Sch.3 para.4), . . . 'use' refers to the final stage".[87] These words make it clear that *Evans* is perfectly consistent with the case law indicating that removing a single cell from an embryo constitutes the "use" of an embryo for the purposes of s.3(1A).[88] The meaning of "use" in the 1990 Act is clearly context specific. In the context of the *Evans* case, the embryos had not been used before they had been implanted, therefore enabling the man who had provided sperm to withdraw his consent to the storage and use of the embryo.

Natalie Evans subsequently lost her application to the European Court of Human Rights and, ultimately, the Grand Chamber of the European Court of Human Rights.[89] The 2008 Act did make one key modification to the law on withdrawal of consent, but it was not one that would have given Natalie Evans what she wanted. The new para.4A of Sch.3 introduced into the 1990 Act provides for a year-long "cooling off period" when one gamete provider withdraws consent to the storage of an embryo that has been created for use in fertility treatment. This provision allows the embryos to be lawfully stored in case the party withdrawing consent changes his or her mind. If not, after expiry of the one year period, the embryos must be allowed to perish.

In theory, at least, no consent or withdrawal of consent will be valid if induced by undue influence. In *U v Centre for Reproductive Medicine*, the Court of Appeal accepted that if Mr U's decision to withdraw his consent had been induced by undue influence, his consent to posthumous use would still stand.[90] The clinic had put "considerable" pressure on the couple who "had already committed themselves, mentally, emotionally, and financially, to the course of treatment" and "were both very vulnerable".[91] Despite this, the Court of

---

[86] [2004] EWCA Civ 727, para.103.

[87] [2004] EWCA Civ 727, para.103 (my emphasis). See also para.33 (Thorpe and Sedley L.JJ.).

[88] *R. (Josephine Quintavalle) v HFEA* [2003] EWCA Civ 667, implicit in the ruling on appeal [2005] UKHL 28. That relevant part of what is now s.3(1A) was then s.3(1)(b).

[89] *Evans v UK* (No.6339/05) (2008) 46 E.H.R.R. 34 (April 10, 2007, Grand Chamber); affirming: (2006) 43 E.H.R.R. 21 (March 7, 2006).

[90] [2002] EWCA Civ 565.

[91] [2002] EWCA Civ 565, para.21.

Appeal upheld the President of the Family Division's finding that no undue influence had occurred. According to Butler-Sloss P., "an able, intelligent, educated man of 47, with a responsible job and in good health" would not be expected to succumb to what she herself described as "considerable" pressure put on him by the medical advisor.[92] Moral positions of a "dignity as empowerment" persuasion (such as rights-based theories) will surely question this decision.[93] Not only does it seem wrong on its facts, but ethical pressure put on a patient by a medical advisor can seriously undermine a patient's autonomy and goes beyond the medical remit of the advisor. This issue is discussed further in Ch.5 (5.5).

The *U* case was set against the backdrop of posthumous use of sperm, which was also the context of an earlier decision on the Act's consent provisions.[94] In the *Blood* case, Mrs Blood wished to use sperm extracted from her (then unconscious) husband by electro-ejaculation just before he died.[95] The Act requires written consent from the sperm provider for the storage and posthumous use of his sperm (Sch.3 paras 2(2)(b) and 8(1)). This had not been obtained from Mr Blood. The Court of Appeal was therefore forced to rule that the sperm was being stored unlawfully and could not lawfully be used (in this country).[96] Following this decision, Sheila McLean was commissioned by the Government to review the consent provisions in the 1990 Act.[97] The McLean Report concluded that the written requirement should remain. A limited exception was recommended for those situations where a patient was incapacitated but likely to (re)gain capacity after becoming infertile, such as where a child undergoes chemotherapy that is likely to result in infertility.[98] Under para.9 of Sch.3 (introduced by 2008 the Act), gametes from a patient under 18 who lacks capacity can be stored without effective consent, provided: (a) they were lawfully removed and (b) a medical practitioner certifies that the patient's fertility is likely to be significantly impaired by medical treatment and storage of the gametes is in the patient's best interests. Paragraph 10 allows storage of the gametes of an incapacitated adult on the same conditions provided that the medical practitioner also certifies that the patient is likely to have capacity in the future.

Only a month before the enactment of the 2008 Act, the High Court ruled in a case where sperm had been retrieved (with the support of a court declaration) from a deceased person and, like in the *Blood* case, stored without the effective consent required by the Act.[99] The wife of the deceased argued that the need for effective consent to storage or use in the UK was incompatible with her

---

[92] [2002] EWHC 36, para.28.
[93] See Pattinson 2002b. Cf. Grubb 2002a.
[94] For a discussion of the ethics of post-mortem sperm retrieval, see Strong et al. 2000.
[95] *R. v HFEA Ex p. Blood* [1999] Fam. 151.
[96] The Court of Appeal did, however, quash the HFEA's refusal to allow Mrs Blood to export the sperm for treatment abroad, see below.
[97] See the McLean Report: McLean 1998.
[98] See McLean 1998, para.2.6.
[99] *L v HFEA* [2008] EWHC 2149. Charles J. raised serious doubts about the lawfulness of the removal of gametes from a deceased person and therefore the earlier decision of Macur J. declaring that it was lawful in this case, see esp. para.161.

Convention rights. Noting the *Evans* case on the need to balance the Convention rights under art.8 and the wide margin of appreciation granted to States, Charles J. ruled that the legislative bright line was not incompatible with the claimant's right to private and family life.

8.3.3.3 Number of embryos to be implanted

To maximise the number of healthy embryos available for implantation it is normal practice to fertilise more eggs than will be implanted. To maximise the chance of a successful pregnancy many clinicians and patients will want to have more than one implanted; but not many more because a multiple pregnancy will itself reduce the likelihood of a successful live birth. This issue has reached the courts on two occasions. In one case, a woman gave birth to triplets after being mistakenly implanted with three embryos during the course of IVF, rather than the two that had been agreed. She successfully sued in contract.[100] In the other, a woman sought to challenge the HFEA's refusal to authorise the implantation into her of no more than three embryos.[101] The Court of Appeal refused to quash the HFEA's decision to limit the number implanted in this way.

The Code of Practice now states that, where the couple's own eggs or embryos are used no more than two should be transferred to women under 40 and no more than three to women over 40.[102] If donated eggs or embryos are being used, then no more than two are to be transferred at one time, regardless of the woman's age.[103] HFEA Directions (which came into force on January 1, 2009) further require centres to have a documented strategy to minimise multiple births and this must set out the circumstances in which the centre would consider it suitable practice to recommend Single Embryo Transfer (SET) to a patient.[104]

8.4 Donation, storage, and import/export of gametes and embryos

Gametes and embryos can be used for purposes other than the immediate treatment of the providers. The 1990 Act also provides for their storage, donation, import/export, and use in research. Embryo research will be examined in Ch.10.

---

[100] *Thompson v Sheffield Fertility Clinic* [2001] (Westlaw). Damages were settled out of court, no doubt significantly reduced by the limitations put on tortious claims for the birth of a healthy baby in *McFarlane v Tayside Health Board* [2000] 2 A.C. 59: see Ch.9. In a later case Lord Scott expressed the obiter view that "[t]he same result [as *McFarlane*] must be reached whether the claimant was a private patient or an NHS patient": *Rees v Darlington Memorial Hospital NHS Trust* [2003] UKHL 52 at 133.

[101] *R. (Assisted Reproduction and Gynaecology Centre, H) v HFEA* [2002] EWCA Civ 20.

[102] See HFEA 2007b, G.8.5.1 and 2008b, paras 7.3–7.4.

[103] See HFEA 2007b, G.8.5.2 and 2008b, para.7.5.

[104] D.2008/5 Multiple Births Minimisation Strategy.

8.4.1 Donation

Over 25,000 children have been born from donated gametes or embryos since the HFEA register was set up in 1991 and it is estimated that around 12,000 such children were born before that date.[105] Donors must provide effective consent and be given an opportunity for counselling. In practice, the chief concern of prospective users of donated gametes or embryos is likely to be the low success rate. There is, for example, a 89.2 per cent chance that donor insemination will fail.[106] In ethical terms, some of the most pressing questions are about whether donors should be paid, prospective parents should be able to select a donor with desired traits, aborted fetuses should be utilised as donor sources, and whether donors should be able to remain anonymous when the subsequent child desires to discover his genetic origins. Parentage of a child produced using donor gametes will be addressed separately below (in 8.7).

8.4.1.1 Selecting a donor

Stories abound about US gamete banks offering the sperm of Nobel Prize winners and the eggs of models. This is highly controversial. The Warnock Committee thought that only limited information should be revealed to prospective parents, such as the donor's ethnic group and genetic health.[107] The HFEA's Code of Practice goes much further than this. It states that,

> The centre should encourage prospective donors to provide as much other non-identifying biographical information as possible, so that it may be available to prospective parents and resulting children.[108]

The inevitable result is that some donors will be more popular with prospective parents than others. The Code of Practice does limit the number of families that can use the donor's gametes or embryos to have a child to ten, and the donor can specify a lower limit.[109] However, unless the donor has specified a relevant limit, successful patients are allowed to have subsequent children by the same donor. This means that it is possible for significantly more than ten children to be produced from one donor. On this basis, popular sperm donors could father more than twenty children. In large cities the chances of unintentional incest by the donor's offspring should still be relatively remote.

The ethical issues raised by donor selection centre on the acceptability of prospective parents seeking to influence the traits of their future children. Donor selection potentially enables prospective parents to select on the basis

---

[105] See HFEA 2004h.
[106] See HFEA 2008a, 4.
[107] See Warnock et al. 1984, para.4.21.
[108] HFEA 2007b, G.4.7.1 and HFEA 2008b, para.11.15. See also HFEA 2007b, G.5.4.1 and HFEA 2008b, 20(5).
[109] See HFEA 2007b, G.5.11.1(f) and S.7.8.12(c), and HFEA 2008b, paras 11.7(f) and 17.13(b).

of traits far beyond the absence of genetic conditions, such as colour or racial characteristics. Indeed, previous editions of the Code of Practice stated that

> treatment centres are *expected* to strive as far as possible to match the physical characteristics and ethnic background of the donor to those of the infertile partner.[110]

Harris argued that,

> It is difficult not to view this desire, and attempts to implement it, as a form of "ethnic cleansing", it smacks very much of the pressure that so many societies and cultures have put upon their members not to "marry out" or, to put it more bluntly, not to mate with somebody of another tribe or race.[111]

While often not considered in this light, many of the ethical objections raised to seeking to influence particular traits by preimplantation genetic diagnosis (considered below), will also apply to attempts to achieve the same aim by donor selection. As Harris indicates, donor selection can be used to influence the possession or absence of traits that will be irrelevant to the resulting child's moral status. Fortunately, the HFEA's guidance on "matching physical characteristics and ethnic background" no longer appears in the Code of Practice.[112]

8.4.1.2 Paying donors

The payment of gamete donors is, like the payment of surrogates and organ donors, controversial. The HFEA does, however, have some discretion under s.12(1)(e), which grants the Authority the power to issue directions authorising such payments. This provision states that "no money or other benefit" may be given or received for the supply of gametes or embryos, except in accordance with directions. After declaring that it was, in principle, opposed to payments being made to gamete donors, the HFEA launched a consultation in 1998.[113] Following this the HFEA accepted the practical need for payment, albeit limiting payment to a maximum of £15 plus reasonable expenses.[114] Article 12 of the Tissues and Cells Directive (2004/23/EC), however, now requires Member States to "endeavour to ensure voluntary and unpaid donations of tissues and cells". Thus, Directions issued by the HFEA in 2006 no longer allow the payment of a flat-rate to donors. Donors may be reimbursed only for reasonable out-of-pocket expenses, including loss of earnings up to a specified amount.[115] In any event, the practical need for payment is surely reduced by the removal of donor anonymity (examined below), as it is likely that those potential donors who were influenced by the availability of payment will now be put off by the removal of anonymity.

---

[110] See HFEA 2003a, para.3.18 (my emphasis). See also para.3.19.
[111] Harris 2003a, 206.
[112] Also, the 1990 Act now prohibits attempts to select donors in an attempt to ensure that a child will have a particular abnormality: s.13(9).
[113] See HFEA 1998.
[114] See HFEA 2003a, para.4.26 and 2004c.
[115] Directions D.2006/1, Giving and receiving money or other benefits in respect of any supply of gametes or embryos. See also HFEA 2007b, G.4.11.1–G.4.11.3 and HFEA 2008b, paras 13.1–13.7

The HFEA currently permits clinics to offer women who cannot afford to pay for IVF the option of cheaper treatment if they give up some of their eggs (known as "egg sharing").[116]

8.4.1.3 Donor anonymity

Since 1991 the HFEA has kept a record of all donors, licensed treatments and children born as a result of donated sperm, eggs or embryos.[117] Access to that information is limited. One exception is that donor-conceived persons above 16 years old are entitled to find out whether they are related to a person they intend to marry, enter a civil partnership or physical relationship with, or with whom they are having an intimate relationship (s.31ZB). The specified person (i.e. the actual or prospective partner) must provide written consent and both the applicant and the specified person must be given a suitable opportunity to receive counselling. Before the amendment of the 1990 Act, the equivalent provision only applied where the applicant intended marriage, despite marriage not being a prerequisite for sexual intercourse and unwitting incest.

The 1990 Act originally also did not grant donor-conceived persons any entitlement to information about the donor. Donors were entitled to remain anonymous. The issue of donor anonymity evokes pressures pulling in both directions.[118] On the one hand, anonymity appears to encourage donation and those who have already donated were promised anonymity. On the other hand, many children have a (sometimes overwhelming) desire to know their genetic origins. The law has now changed.

In *Rose v Secretary Of State for Health*, a challenge to donor anonymity was brought by a 29-year-old woman and the parents of a six-year-old girl.[119] They argued that a person born as a result of artificial insemination using donor sperm was entitled to know details of their origin, as a result of art.8 of the Convention (the right to private and family life), as given effect by the HRA 1998. The judge, in a ruling on a preliminary issue, held that art.8 was engaged. He emphasised, however, that "the fact that art.8 is engaged is far from saying that there is a breach of it".[120] Article 8(1) grants only a limited right, it is limited by art.8(2), which requires consideration of (among other considerations) the rights and freedoms of others. On the facts, the claimants were not seeking identifying information, realising that it was unlikely that the court would force the disclosure of the identity of an anonymous donor.[121] According to the judge,

---

[116] See Directions D.2006/1, para.5, HFEA 2007b, G.15 and HFEA 2008b, paras 12.1–12.30.
[117] As required by s.31(1).
[118] See Pennings 1997 (who argues for a "double track" policy whereby the participants choose between an anonymity and non-anonymity).
[119] [2002] EWHC 1593.
[120] [2002] EWHC 1593, para.46.
[121] [2002] EWHC 1593, paras 36 and 40. See more recently *Odievre v France* (2004) 38 E.H.R.R. 43 (where it was held that the French legislation permitting anonymous births did not breach art.8, because the French legislature had not overstepped its margin of appreciation in relation to the mother's rights under art.8(2)).

The distinction between identifying and non-identifying information is not relevant at the engagement stage of Article 8, but it is likely to become very relevant when one comes to the important balancing exercise of the other considerations in Article 8(2).[122]

Unfortunately, the records of the 29-year-old woman had been destroyed. When the six-year-old girl comes of age, she could now obtain non-identifying information under the 1990 Act as now amended.

Under s.31ZA donor-conceived persons who are at least 16 years old are entitled to obtain information about their donor. If the applicant is still under 18, that information must be non-identifying (s.31ZA(4)). The specific information falling within the categories of identifying and non-identifying information is specified in secondary legislation: at the time of writing, the HFEA (Disclosure of Donor Information) Regulations 2004/1511. Relevant non-identifying information includes the donor's physical description, year and country of birth, ethnic group, marital status, and details of any screening tests and medical history. Relevant identifying information includes the name, date of birth, appearance, and last known address of the donor. This means that those who donate gametes face the prospect of a child contacting them 18 years later, irrespective of their views on the matter. It is worth noting, however, that those who donated before April 1, 2005 are entitled to remain anonymous, as these Regulations were not retrospective.

Sperm donation did, predictably, seriously decrease with the removal of donor anonymity. By way of context, in Sweden where anonymity for sperm donors was removed many years ago, the result was a change in the number, age, and background of those who donated. It is likely that prospective parents who wish to avoid their child discovering the identity of the gamete donor will travel abroad (as many Swedish couples now do)[123] or keep the fact of donor insemination secret from their child. Studies have shown great reluctance to inform children of the use of donor gametes.[124] One study found that 89 per cent of Swedish parents who had used donor gametes had not told their children of that fact.[125] Secrecy is, however, notably significantly less pronounced where the parents are single women or lesbian couples, presumably because they need to explain the absence of a father to their child and have no need to protect a father from the stigma of infertility.[126] Although it is apparently easy to make a moral case for openness (as opposed to secrecy and deception by omission), moral principle does not always straightforwardly link to regulatory policy. Regulatory mechanisms carry enforcement costs extending far beyond the monetary. Whether parental secrecy can be challenged by a morally acceptable mechanism has been questioned.[127] The 2008 Act does not, as was mooted

---

[122] [2002] EWHC 1593, para.47.

[123] There are reports that fertility treatment services are likely to be set up on ships flying under the flags of countries with laws that protect donor anonymity: see BBC 2005e.

[124] A good summary can be found in Golombok 2004, 286–287.

[125] See Gottlieb et al. 2000.

[126] See Golombok 2004, 286.

[127] See e.g. Patrizio et al. 2001 (who reject mandatory disclosure).

before its enactment, add the words "by donation" to the birth register and birth certificate. Instead it is left to the Code of Practice, which simply emphasises the importance of parents of a donor-conceived child telling that child about its origins early in its childhood on the basis that the evidence indicates "that finding out suddenly, later in life, about donor origins can be emotionally damaging to children and to family relations".[128]

8.4.1.4 Aborted fetuses

The idea of using aborted fetuses as sources of (immature) eggs predictably provokes deep divisions. In addition to divisions over the morality of using the products of abortion (reflecting differing views on the moral status of the embryo), there are divisions over the extent to which the psychological welfare of the future child requires the prohibition of this activity. In any event, s.3A of the 1990 Act prohibits the use of female germ cells derived from an embryo or fetus for the provision of treatment services for any woman.

8.4.2 Storage

There are many situations where patients might wish to freeze their gametes or embryos. Where, for example, that patient is likely to be rendered infertile by medical treatment (such as chemotherapy or surgical removal of malignant reproductive organs) or surplus embryos are created in the course of IVF treatment. The 1990 Act expressly allows the freezing of gametes and embryos under licence (ss.2(2) and 14(1)). While it has been technically possible to freeze sperm since 1949 and embryos since 1983, egg freezing is far more recent and the availability of this service is still much more limited.[129]

The 1990 Act requires gametes or embryos to have been obtained by a licensed person and used thereafter only by licensed persons (ss.3(1A) and 4(1)). It imposes a number of other requirements, particularly with regard to consent. Any consent to storage given under the Act must, for example, state what is to be done with the gametes or embryo if the person who gave the consent dies or is unable because of incapacity to vary the terms of the consent or to revoke it (Sch.3 para.2(2)(b)). They can only be kept frozen for the statutory storage period (s.14(1)(c)). The Act states that the maximum storage period shall be 10 years for gametes and embryos (s.14(3)/(4)), subject to modification by regulation (s.14(5)). Such regulations have been passed extending the storage period where specified conditions are satisfied.[130]

---

[128] See HFEA 2007b, G.5.4.6 and 2008b, para.20.10.
[129] See Jackson 2001, 163–164.
[130] Regulations 1991/1540 and 1996/375.

8.4.3 Import and export

Under s.24(4), the HFEA has the power to issue directions allowing the import or export of gametes or embryos, subject to the provisions of the 1990 Act. A challenge to the HFEA's decision to refuse permission for the export of sperm for treatment services in Belgium was the basis of the notorious *Blood* case, mentioned earlier.[131] The HFEA's decision to refuse export permission to Mrs Blood was consistent with its previous directions[132] and the authority indicated that it considered the removal, storage, and use of the sperm to be unlawful. Mr Blood had not provided his written consent for the storage or use of his sperm posthumously and the Court of Appeal conceded that this meant that "technically" an offence had been committed under the Act.[133] Nonetheless, the Court of Appeal required the HFEA to reconsider its decision on the basis that it had failed to take account of arts 49 and 50[134] of the EC Treaty, and the fact that this would be a one-off case now that the storage of the sperm had been unequivocally declared to be unlawful. These provisions of the EC Treaty, concerning free movement of services, undoubtedly granted Mrs Blood the right to receive medical treatment in another member state, *unless* interference with that right is justified on grounds of public policy.[135] However, there is a powerful argument that the UK Parliament has taken a public policy position on the posthumous use of sperm in the absence of consent. Surely public policy prevents the export of gametes that have been obtained and stored in contravention of domestic law. According to Morgan and Lee,

> in treating rights to access services as though they are unrestricted, pretending that it raises no issues of morality of public policy, the Court effectively constructs a European bypass round the route which the Member State has signposted as carrying its fundamental ethical judgments; the vehicle which transports its national determination of the public policy issues is blocked.[136]

One suspects that the court's decision might have been different had public opinion been the other way. Delaney and Doyle ask us to consider the uproar that would greet a husband who wishes to extract an egg from his unconscious wife and have it mixed with sperm and re-implanted, albeit it in another European country.[137] Mrs Blood did, however, benefit from the Court of

---

[131] *R. v HFEA Ex p. Blood* [1999] Fam. 151.
[132] General Direction 1991/8 Export of Gametes.
[133] Lord Woolf went on to say that there was "no question of any prosecution being brought in the circumstances of this case": [1999] Fam. 151 at 178.
[134] Then Articles 59 and 60, as the provisions of the EC Treaty were renumbered by the Treaty of Amsterdam.
[135] art.46(1), applied to art.49 by art.55, states that,
    The provisions of this Chapter . . . shall not prejudice the applicability of provisions laid down by law . . . providing for special treatment for foreign nationals on grounds of public policy, public security or public health.
[136] Morgan and Lee 1997, 848.
[137] See Delaney and Doyle 1997, 264.

Appeal's decision and has now given birth to her second child from the sperm subsequently exported to Belgium.

The Government subsequently commissioned Sheila McLean to consider the implications of the *Blood* decision and her report was critical of the Court of Appeal's decision.[138] The 2008 Act amendments did not change either the need for effective consent to storage and use in the UK or the provisions concerning the HFEA's powers in relation to the import and export of gametes and embryos. Also, in October 2008 the High Court (in a case considered in 8.3.3.2, above) rejected a claim that the HFEA's policy of requiring effective consent to storage before permitting export of gametes contravened her Convention rights.[139]

8.5 Preimplantation genetic diagnosis and tissue typing

Preimplantation genetic diagnosis (*PGD for short*) involves genetically testing a cell or two after removal from an early embryo. This technique was first successfully used in 1989.[140] As originally enacted, the 1990 Act explicitly allowed a research licence to be granted for the purpose of developing methods of PGD, but was silent on whether a treatment licence could authorise PGD.[141] In practice, the HFEA granted such licences and, in 2005, the House of Lords ruled that a purposive interpretation of the Act supported the conclusion that PGD did fall within the HFEA's licensing jurisdiction.[142] In 2007, the Quality and Safety Regulations 2007/1522 inserted a provision into the 1990 Act stating that a licence could authorise "procuring, keeping, testing, processing or distributing embryos" (Sch.2 para.1(1)(b)). The 2008 Act added a number of further provisions on embryo testing to the 1990 Act.

Embryo testing for treatment purposes is only permitted by the 1990 Act:

(a) to establish if an embryo has an abnormality that might affect its capacity to result in a live birth;

(b) to avoid a serious medical condition;

(c) to avoid a sex-related serious medical condition;

(d) for histocompatibility (tissue typing); or

(e) to establish the identity of gamete providers (Sch.2 para.1ZA).

There are many potential uses of PGD and further guidance on the application of the Act to these can be found in the Code of Practice.[143] The 2008 Act's

---

[138] See the McLean Report: McLean 1997, esp. para.7.4.
[139] *L v HFEA* [2008] EWHC 2149.
[140] See Handyside et al. 1989.
[141] See the first edition of this book: Pattinson 2006, 262–263 and 267–268.
[142] *R. (Josephine Quintavalle) v HFEA* [2005] UKHL 28. The first instance decision in that case had raised doubts about this.
[143] See HFEA 2008b, paras 10.1–10.9.

amendments do not in any way undermine the HFEA's existing practices. This chapter will focus on the use of PGD to select an embryo of a particular sex and to select an embryo that is likely to be a suitable donor.

8.5.1 Sex selection

8.5.1.1 The regulatory position

Alan and Louise Masterton were delighted with the little girl they had tried for 15 years to conceive. At the age of only three, she was tragically killed in a bonfire accident. Since they already had four sons, they sought medical help to ensure that their next child would be a girl. The HFEA refused to allow PGD to be used for this purpose. Selecting the sex of an embryo for social reasons was then prohibited by the Code of Practice.[144] As a result of the 2008 Act, it is now also prohibited by the 1990 Act itself (Sch.2 para.1ZB).

The 1990 Act does not allow prospective parents to use "any practice designed to secure that any resulting child will be one sex rather than the other" (para.1ZB(1)). This is clearly wide enough to prohibit selecting embryos of a particular sex and selecting sperm samples for the purpose of sex selection. There is one key exception. The Act does allow sex selection to avoid severe genetic conditions that are linked to a particular sex, so-called X-linked conditions (Sch.2 paras 1ZA(1)(c) and 1ZB(2),(3)). A brutal example is Lesch-Nyhan syndrome.[145] Boys with this genetic condition are often mentally disabled and suffer extreme pain similar to that associated with gout. What is more disturbing is that its victims compulsively self-mutilate—often chewing off their lips, biting off their finger tips, or gouging out their eyes. They usually die in their teens. Not all X-linked conditions are this extreme. The severity of X-linked conditions varies from colour blindness to more severe conditions, such as haemophilia and Duchenne's muscular dystrophy.

Many other countries adopt a similar distinction between sex selection for social reasons and sex selection to avoid X-linked conditions.[146] The Code of Practice goes further and states that:

> Due to concerns about the reliability of the technique, sperm that has been sorted for sex selection using gradient methods should not be used for medical reasons.[147]

This technique is based on the fact that the sex of an embryo is determined by the sperm (the egg always carrying an X chromosome and the sperm containing either an X or a Y chromosome). Unfortunately it has a misdiagnosis rate of up to 10 per cent.[148]

---

[144] See HFEA 2001, para.9.9. See now HFEA 2007b, G.8.7.2 and 2008b, esp. paras 10.11–12.
[145] See Lesch and Nyhan 1964 and the discussion in Kitcher 1996, esp. 82 and Holm 1998, 184.
[146] See Pattinson 2002a, 4.4.1 and App.2.
[147] See HFEA 2007b, G.8.7.2 and 2008b, para.10.12.
[148] See HFEA 2003b, para.124.

8.5.1.2 The ethics of sex selection

Sex selection can prevent severe harm and distress for some couples facing a significant risk of having a child with a serious X-linked condition. Such predictable harm to prospective parents is not limited to fears of serious X-linked conditions. In some circumstances having a child of one particular sex might cause the parents to be stigmatised or ostracised by their community. Other prospective parents, like the Mastertons, suffer from the effects of an overwhelming desire to have a sex-balanced family. Those moral theories permitting sex selection, holding that it is within the reproductive freedom of prospective parents or an acceptable means of avoiding harm to prospective parents, will challenge the drawing of a sharp line between social and non-social reasons. The negative consequences of having a child of a particular sex are not coterminous with the question of whether that child is at risk from an X-linked condition. If the effects to prospective parents are relevant to the utilitarian calculus or their rights in one case, surely they are relevant in the other.

Some of the most powerful arguments against sex selection for social reasons have been presented using the metaphor of the slippery slope.[149] Sex selection for social reasons will, so the argument goes, gradually lead us to a situation that is morally objectionable. That undesired outcome could be the treatment of an undesired sex as if it were a harmful trait, the re-enforcement of unacceptable gender-role expectations, or an imbalance in the sex ratio to the detriment of society. These claims depend on empirical premises, albeit very plausible empirical premises. Gradually increasing social pressure is a realistic consequence of widespread selection against *any* trait. There is, for example, evidence that routine prenatal diagnosis for thalassaemia in Sardinia has led to women who fail to abort a fetus diagnosed as having the condition being stigmatised by the local community.[150] The argument that selecting sex is likely to display and encourage gender-role expectations is underpinned by the plausible claim that those who desire a child of a particular sex for reasons other than the avoidance of an X-linked condition must have expectations about how such a child will be different from a child of the opposite sex. Those expectations are very likely to include sexual stereotypes and lead to gender expectations being placed (or even forced) on children. The claim that sex selection could alter society's sex ratio is borne out by evidence from countries such as China and India showing a declining proportion of females to males.[151] (However, this data is not transferable to the UK as a whole. In the long-term, any such imbalance between the sexes is likely to be self-rectifying, as social pressures are likely to create a demand for the minority sex.)

More than empirical evidence is required for these arguments to carry moral weight. As argued in Ch.1, for any feared endpoint argument to work, the relevant endpoint must be morally unacceptable and the risk of its occurrence must outweigh the benefits of allowing the starting point. Here the moral theory in

---

[149] See e.g. Pattinson 2002a, 6.2 and HFEA 2002b.
[150] See Black 1998, 45.
[151] See Mudur 1999, Plafker 2002, and Watts 2004.

play will make a difference. The likelihood of reinforced and increased gender-role expectations is, for example, likely to be a far more powerful issue for feminist theories[152] than for theories that value the traditional family structure with its gender-related roles. The HFEA, in its report on sex selection, relied on hypothetical risks to the welfare of a sex-selected child and its family, for which it offered no empirical evidence, beyond simply noting fears expressed in the consultation.[153] More than speculation is required if one starts from a moral presumption in favour of allowing and facilitating individuals' reproductive choices (as will utilitarians and rights-based theorists).[154]

8.5.2 Donor selection (saviour siblings)

Zain Hashmi was born with beta thalassaemia, a serious and potentially fatal blood disorder. His only hope of a cure was a stem cell transplant from someone with matching tissue. In the absence of a suitable donor, his mother attempted to conceive a child for the purpose. The intention was to take stem cells from the blood in the sibling's umbilical cord. Unfortunately, the child Mrs Hashmi conceived was aborted when it became apparent that it also had this hereditary condition and her next child was not a tissue match. One possibility remained. An embryo conceived by IVF could be subjected to PGD to ensure that it was free of this genetic defect and then tissue typed for tissue-compatibility with Zain.[155] A six-year-old American girl, Molly Nash, had already benefited from receiving stems cells from the umbilical cord blood of a specially created donor sibling.[156] After some deliberation, the HFEA granted permission to the Hashmis.

Josephine Quintavalle subsequently brought an action on behalf of a prolife group arguing that the HFEA could not license the tissue-typing of embryos under the 1990 Act. While this succeeded at first instance, it failed before the Court of Appeal and House of Lords.[157] As it had done in the earlier case bought by Bruno Quintavalle on behalf of another prolife group challenging the HFEA's ability to regulate cloning (see further 10.4.2.1),[158] the House of Lords adopted a wide, purposive interpretation of the 1990 Act.

Soon after its decision in the Hashmi case, the HFEA was faced with another request. This it turned down. The HFEA established criteria for such cases: the condition should be severe or life threatening, the embryo conceived should be

---

[152] See e.g. Danis 1995.

[153] See HFEA 2003b, para.139.

[154] Examples of theories starting from strong presumptions in favour of reproductive liberty include Harris 2003d and McCarthy 2001.

[155] Tissue-typing is as a form of PGD, but less confusion is likely to be caused if PGD is defined narrowly for present purposes.

[156] See Orr 2000 and Ledward 2000.

[157] *R. (Josephine Quintavalle) v HFEA* [2002] EWHC 2785, [2003] EWCA Civ 667 and [2005] UKHL 28. This case was examined in more depth in the first edition of this book: see Pattinson 2006, 267–268.

[158] *R. (Bruno Quintavalle) v Secretary of State for Health* [2003] UKHL 13.

at risk from inheriting the condition, all other possibilities should have been explored, the intended recipient should not be a parent, the intention should be to take only cord blood, the couples should have received implications counselling, follow-up studies should be encouraged, and no genetic modification should take place.[159] The Whitakers satisfied all but one of these criteria—Charlie Whitaker's condition was not hereditary. Unlike the Hashmis, it was extremely unlikely that the next child that the Whitakers conceived would suffer from the sick child's disorder. The ethical relevance of the distinction drawn by the HFEA will be examined below (8.5.2.2). In any event, the HFEA subsequently changed its policy and removed the need for the selected embryo to be at risk of the relevant condition.[160] The 2004 guidance also changed two other conditions: it removed the requirement that the intention be to take only cord blood and instead of all other treatment options having to be explored, tissue typing was to be viewed as a "last resort".

The 1990 Act now expressly permits embryo testing for the purpose of tissue typing. Paragraph 1ZA(d) of Sch.3 states that the testing of an embryo for treatment may be permitted where:

> a person ("the sibling") who is the child of the persons whose gametes are used to bring about the creation of the embryo (or of either of those persons) suffers from a serious medical condition which could be treated by umbilical cord blood stem cells, bone marrow or other tissue of any resulting child, establishing whether the tissue of any resulting child would be compatible with that of the sibling.

Paragraph 1ZA(1)(d) provides that the reference to "other tissue" of the resulting child does not include a whole organ. Thus, tissue typing can only be licensed if the intended recipient and the prospective donor are siblings, and the intended recipient suffers from a medical condition that could be treated by umbilical cord blood stem cells, bone marrow or other tissue (excluding whole organs) from a donor sibling. Notice that this position differs slightly from that under the previous HFEA guidance. Unlike the HFEA's 2002 guidance, there is no requirement that the condition be hereditary. Unlike either HFEA's 2002 or 2004 guidance, there is no mention of other treatment options being exhausted or even explored. The legislation, however, only lays down the framework, leaving the details of licences within those parameters to the HFEA. The guidance in the HFEA's Code of Practice makes it clear that tissue typing should not be undertaken lightly.[161] Thus, the 2008 Act's amendments largely concretise existing regulatory practice, though this does mean that the HFEA no longer has the breadth of regulatory discretion that it had before.

8.5.2.1 The ethics of donor selection

Some moral positions will object to the very idea of using tissue-typing to select a suitable donor. Some duty-based positions in the "dignity as constraint" camp

---

[159] See HFEA 2002a.
[160] See HFEA 2004e.
[161] See HFEA 2008b, paras 10.13–10.20.

will be concerned about instrumentalising or harming the embryo and any future child for the benefit of others.[162] Other moral theories will see nothing wrong with at least some instances of donor selection. Utilitarians, for example, will see the potential to maximise utility by saving the life of a sick child (at least if the donor child will be loved and the donation is as non-invasive as cord blood). The parents' loving motives are likely to influence virtue theorists. For rights-based theorists, it is all a matter of whether anyone's rights are violated by donor selection,[163] and the weight of those rights (including any positive rights of the sick sibling).

Was there a morally relevant distinction between the Hashmis and Whitakers? When the HFEA drew such a distinction it argued that the biopsy was a prima facie wrong outweighed by a countervailing consideration in the Hashmi case that did not apply in the Whitaker case. Suzi Leather, then Chair of the HFEA, said that performing a biopsy on an embryo that is to be implanted is a prima facie wrong because "we don't know what the long-term consequences of that will be for the child being created".[164] The difference between the cases was the "benefit" that the Hashmis' embryo was to gain:

> We have to look at the benefit for the embryo, not just the sibling ... HFEA policy states that women are allowed to have treatment only for the benefit of the embryo.[165]

Is this reasoning defensible?

If the biopsy is likely to damage the embryo, it could be regarded as a prima facie moral wrong to the embryo *or* the child later born damaged as a result of the biopsy.[166] Is there a benefit in the Hashmi scenario that does not apply in the Whitaker scenario? In both cases, successful tissue typing followed by implantation and the birth of a suitable donor will benefit the parents and the sick sibling. This is, of course, the purpose of the enterprise. The benefit to the parents and sick siblings is identical in both cases. With regard to the embryos, does the Hashmi embryo gain an additional benefit by being selected for the absence of a serious life-threatening genetic disorder? The difficulty is that PGD is not being used to change the disorder status of an embryo, but to select embryos without Zain's disorder. The rejected embryo could have gained whatever (if any) benefit is given by continued existence.[167] The idea of benefit

---

[162] Sheldon and Wilkinson 2004 summarise and reject three arguments reflecting concerns about "(a) the commodification of babies; (b) a move down a slippery slope towards 'designer babies'; and (c) adversely affecting the welfare of the child created".

[163] There is a powerful argument that any rights possessed by the embryo, or the future child that it will become, are not violated. See below.

[164] Quoted in the *Guardian* 2003.

[165] HFEA spokesperson, quoted in Wright 2003.

[166] Selection by a damaging procedure should not necessarily be viewed as a benefit to the selected embryo. Imagine an evil scientist who decides, on a mere whim, to implant whichever embryos survive being subjected to a small amount of acid. Any surviving embryo would have been damaged by this unnecessary selection process. While it *might* be possible to argue that it is better off relative to the non-selected embryos, it is not better off relative to other possible scenarios leading to its implantation.

[167] Zain's condition, beta thalassaemia, is serious and life-threatening but it does not produce suffering of such magnitude that it could plausibly be argued that it negates the possibility of a worthwhile existence.

to the embryo surely points against the use of biopsy procedures for both the Hashmis and Whitakers. The Hashmi embryos do not benefit any more than the Whitaker embryos.[168]

Depending on the moral theory in play, many reasons could be offered for allowing the Hashmis to conduct PGD.[169] Examples include the parents' moral rights or interests in avoiding having another sick child and, for utilitarians, the disutility of bringing avoidable suffering into the world.[170] It is, however, difficult to see how any of these reasons could turn on the benefit of PGD to the embryos. The distinction originally drawn by the HFEA between the Hashmis and Whitakers was arguably morally irrelevant.

It is worth noting that the Whitakers successfully obtained treatment in the US and Mrs Whitaker subsequently gave birth to a baby that is tissue-compatible with her sick child.[171] Examples of such reproductive tourism from the UK are actually relatively infrequent because of the generally permissive regulatory regime here. What it shows, however, is that any attempt to adopt more restrictive policies will simply divide the rich, who have the resources to jurisdiction shop, from the not so rich.

8.5.3 Selecting for other traits

In the future, PGD might become a precursor to preimplantation gene therapy (see Ch.12). At present, it is used as a way of selecting for implantation or discarding. PGD is therefore rejected in all circumstances by some dignitarian approaches[172] and accepted in some or all circumstances by other moral positions. PGD becomes more controversial when it is used to select against traits other than severe and debilitating genetic disorders. Consider, for example, the possible future ability to select embryos on the basis of eye colour or, though this is unlikely, a predisposition towards sporting prowess.

It is reported that some couples who themselves suffer from a particular disability wish to select embryos who will also have that disability. Examples are couples who wish to have a deaf child (perhaps, to render it more amenable to the deaf culture of its deaf parents),[173] or an achondroplasic child (perhaps, to enable it to fit into the spatially restricted living conditions of parents with such congenitally restricted growth). When selecting embryos for implantation, the 1990 Act now expressly prohibits preference being given to an embryo that is known to have a gene, chromosome or mitochondrial abnormality involving

---

[168] See Pattinson 2003b. A similar argument is made by Sheldon and Wilkinson 2004.

[169] A full status position will, of course, reject PGD: see e.g. Watt 2004.

[170] Some theories might even impose a moral duty to conduct PGD. One utilitarian theorist has argued that, in the abortion context, there could be a moral duty to abort an abnormal fetus if it "can be followed by having another, normal one" (Glover 1977, 146).

[171] See BBC 2003c.

[172] See e.g. the full status position in Watt 2004.

[173] On "Deafness" as a culture, see Ivers 1995 and Davis 1997, 567–575. A deaf lesbian couple have deliberately used a sperm donor with congenital deafness to enable them to have a deaf child: see Spriggs 2002.

a significant risk that the person with the abnormality will develop a serious medical condition (s.13(9)). In moral terms, it is a matter of weighing the relevant duties, rights, or utilities, or assessing the underlying motives and characters.[174] Savulescu has argued, from an implicitly utilitarian position, for what he has called Procreative Beneficence, according to which

> couples (or single reproducers) should select the child, of the possible children they could have, who is expected to have the best life, or at least as good a life as the others, based on the relevant, available information.[175]

According to this principle, couples are *morally required* (but should not be coerced) to maximise the well-being of the children that they have. Thus, all things being equal, Savulescu would support attempts to use PGD to select for sporting prowess or the absence of disease, but would reject attempts to select for deafness or achondroplasia.

8.6 Surrogacy

Not all women are able to carry their own genetic offspring. A woman might be unable to ovulate or carry a pregnancy—perhaps having lost her womb and ovaries to cancer or having never been born with them in the first place. A woman might be able to ovulate but unable to carry a pregnancy—perhaps because of dangerously high blood pressure or kidney disease. By using a surrogate, such women could still raise a child that is their partners' biological child.

Surrogacy, as defined by the Warnock Committee, is the "practice whereby one woman carries a child for another with the intention that the child should be handed over after birth".[176] Defined in this way, surrogacy need not be limited to situations where a woman has been involuntarily robbed of the opportunity to carry her own child. Those using a surrogate might be gay couples, single men, or even women who are able to carry a child but choose surrogacy for convenience.

8.6.1 Ethical issues

Surrogacy evokes ethical division over whether the surrogate is merely lending her womb (full surrogacy) or also provides the egg (partial surrogacy). Ethical division is amplified by the reality that few surrogates act for purely altruistic reasons—surrogacy is not necessarily the personification of virtue ethics. The promise of some form of payment often lurks in the shadows. Supporters of

---

[174] Compare e.g. Freeman 2004, 714, Holm 1998; King 1999; and Pattinson 2002a, 88–90.
[175] Savulescu 2001, 415.
[176] Warnock 1984, para.8.1. See also the Surrogacy Arrangements Act 1985 s.1.

moral positions of a "dignity as constraint" ilk are likely to be uncomfortable with surrogacy's potential to build inroads into the traditional family structure and to commodify children, irrespective of whether the relationship is fully consensual. This approach was adopted by the majority of the Warnock Committee, who condemned surrogacy as presenting an unacceptable danger of exploitation "in almost every case" and went on to declare commercial surrogacy to be "positively exploitative".[177] The Committee noted that some opposition to surrogacy was based on the view that "it is inconsistent with human dignity that a woman should use her uterus for financial profit and treat it as an incubator for someone else's child".[178] In contrast, supporters of moral positions of the "dignity as empowerment" camp are likely to be attracted by the potential to increase reproductive choices and regard commercial surrogacy as just another form of risky, paid labour (perhaps similar to being a boxer, fire-fighter, soldier, or racing driver). The existence of payment, even if one's range of options for alternative forms of payment is limited, is not inconsistent with a free choice considered to be entitled to prima facie respect by rights-based and many utilitarian theories.[179] Feminists are, as is often the case, divided. They are divided by "the conflict between the potential of surrogacy to enhance female reproductive freedom, and its potential to allow exploitation and control by others of women's bodies".[180]

Surrogacy raises many challenges for the law. Who is to be regarded as the mother: the commissioning woman, the woman gestating and giving birth, or the woman who provided the egg? Who is to be regarded as the father: the commissioning man, the surrogate's partner, or the provider of the sperm? What happens if any party reneges on their promises? If, for example, the surrogate changes her mind after giving birth (estimated to occur in only 4–5 per cent of surrogacy arrangements)[181] or the commissioning couple change their mind after discovering that the child is disabled (I know of no such case to have occurred). How should the law deal with different types of payment? Should surrogacy as such be allowed? This section will deal with all but the first two questions—parentage is dealt with in 8.7.

8.6.2 The law

It is thought that at least one baby a week is born to a surrogate mother in the UK.[182] Nonetheless, surrogacy remains controversial and it wasn't until 1996 that the BMA officially recognised surrogacy as an "acceptable option of last resort".[183] Not all forms of surrogacy are regulated. It is perfectly legal to

[177] Warnock 1984, para.8.17.
[178] Warnock 1984, para.8.10.
[179] See e.g. Arneson 1992.
[180] Douglas 1991, 141. Compare, e.g., Arneson 1992 and Satz 1992 who take different views on whether commercial surrogacy reinforces gender inequalities.
[181] See Brazier et al. 1998, para.3.38.
[182] See BBC 1998.
[183] BMA 1996, 59. See also Brazier et al. 1998, para.8.9.

participate in a surrogacy arrangement and, as long as no payment is received, to arrange a surrogacy agreement for others. The involvement of the law is limited to the ambit of the 1990 and 2008 Acts and activities connected with commercial surrogacy agencies.

We have already examined the 1990 Act's ambit. A licence or third party agreement will be required if any regulated activity is undertaken and, then, the s.13(5) welfare of the child requirement will apply. As stated by the Code of Practice, the clinic should assess both the commissioning persons and the surrogate (and her partner, if she has one).[184] This assessment must involve consideration of the possibility of a breakdown in the surrogacy arrangement and its likely consequences.[185] The seventh edition of the Code of Practice goes further, stating that assisted conception techniques should only be used "to produce a surrogate pregnancy where no person commissioning the surrogacy arrangement is able to carry a child" or where doing so could seriously impair her health.[186] No such provision appears in the draft eighth edition of the Code.

There is also an earlier Act, the Surrogacy Arrangements Act 1985. This Act was rushed through Parliament following the adverse media attention given to a British woman (Kim Cotton) who had acted as a paid surrogate for an American couple.[187] It has been amended by the 1990 and 2008 Acts. The Act neither prohibits nor facilitates surrogacy, and, as a result of s.1(2), it does not apply to any arrangement made after the woman has become pregnant. Section 2 makes it a criminal offence for anyone to participate in the setting up of a *commercial* surrogacy arrangement. As a result of amendments made by the 2008 Act, non-profit-making organisations can now recoup their costs by charging for limited purposes, such as establishing and keeping lists of people willing to be a surrogate mother or intended parents. Section 3 makes it a criminal offence to *advertise* about surrogacy, where the advert indicates that someone is entering into (or might be willing to enter into) a surrogacy arrangement or negotiate such an arrangement, or that someone is seeking a surrogate mother. This section does prevent non-profit-making organisations from advertising activities that do not convene s.2 (s.3(1A)). There have been no reported prosecutions.

No criminal offence is imposed under s.2 on the surrogate or the commissioning couple (s.2(2)). This reflects the Warnock Committee's view that it was better for the child if the "the taint of criminality" was avoided.[188] A criminal offence could, however, be committed under s.95 of the Adoption and Children Act 2002 if payments are made *with regard to adoption*.[189]

The Surrogacy Arrangements Act, as amended, provides that surrogacy arrangements are legally unenforceable (s.1A). The consequence is that no one

---

[184] See HFEA 2007b, G.3.2.3 and 2008b, para.8.4.
[185] See HFEA 1997b, G.3.3.4 and 2008b, para.8.10.
[186] HFEA 2007b, S.7.6.9.
[187] *Re C* [1985] F.L.R. 846 (Latey J. granted the commissioning couple custody and permission to take the baby to live with them in America).
[188] See Warnock et al. 1984, para.8.19. See also Brazier et al. 1998, para.4.38.
[189] This provision replaced s.57 of the Adoption Act 1976 on 30 December 2005. Note *Re Adoption Application (Payment for Adoption)* [1987] Fam. 81.

is granted any legal rights by the surrogacy arrangement. The commissioning couple cannot sue for damages or performance, and the surrogate cannot sue for payment. This legal vulnerability is intended to discourage surrogacy arrangements. Whether this is an acceptable goal or an appropriate way of achieving that goal is morally controversial. Sultz has argued, from a feminist perspective, that not only should surrogacy arrangements be legally enforceable, but specific performance might sometimes be an appropriate remedy.[190]

The lack of legal enforceability of a surrogacy arrangement is *irrelevant* to who gets to raise the child if there is a dispute. Here, the welfare of the child will be paramount under s.1(1) of the Children Act 1989. In practice, the child's welfare will just about always require the child to stay with a surrogate who has changed her mind.[191] The recent case of *Re N (Child)* is an exception.[192] The High Court (the judgment of which was upheld by the Court of Appeal 15 days later) held that an 18-month-old boy was to be removed from the care of the gestation mother and placed in the care of his biological father and wife (who had commissioned the surrogacy). Relying on expert evidence, Coleridge J. considered the existing family to be "dysfunctional".[193] He placed particular emphasis on the "culture of deceit/falsehood in their household": the commissioning mother had previously laid false claim to an abandoned child and, on the facts before the High Court, had offered herself as a surrogate with the intention of bearing and raising further children, falsely told the commissioning couple that this child had miscarried, and misled the court on various matters.

The decided cases all involved partial surrogacy (where the commissioning man had provided the sperm), but it should make no difference if the commissioning woman is the genetic mother (as in full surrogacy).[194] The child's welfare will also usually dictate that the child stay with the commissioning parents where the surrogate does not want the child.[195] What if the surrogate changes her mind *after* giving up her child? This was the situation faced by the Supreme Court of New Jersey in the *Baby M* case.[196] The child had been living with the commissioning couple for a year-and-a-half and they sought to enforce the surrogacy arrangement. The court was unwilling to enforce the arrangement, but did grant custody to the commissioning couple and visitation rights to the mother. The closest English case is *Re MW*, where an adoption order was granted to a commissioning couple who had cared for the child for two and a half years.[197] However, by the time that the commissioning couple's application for adoption was made, the surrogate had abandoned her application to bring up the child herself and only sought contact. The adoption order

---

[190] See Sultz 1990, esp. 364–369.
[191] See *A v C* [1985] F.L.R. 445 and *Re P* [1987] 2 F.L.R. 421.
[192] [2008] 1 F.L.R. 198, HC and [2007] EWCA Civ 1053, CA.
[193] [2008] 1 F.L.R. 198, para.50.
[194] In any event, the surrogate will be the child's legal mother: s.27(1), 1990 Act. See the next section.
[195] *Re C* [1985] F.L.R. 846.
[196] In the Matter of *Baby M* (1988) 537 A. 2d. 1277.
[197] *Re MW* [1995] 2 F.L.R. 759.

was granted and the surrogate was denied contact. As this case demonstrates, where the surrogate changes her mind after giving up the child the court will have regard to the length of time that has passed and consider what the circumstances say about the parties' fitness to raise the child.[198]

While many issues concerning *legal parenthood* and *parental responsibility* will be left to the next section, some points are best made here. The surrogate will automatically be the child's legal mother (s.33, 2008 Act). In some circumstances, the man providing the sperm will be the legal father (see 8.7.2, below); but it is possible for neither member of the commissioning couple to be a legal parent. To become legal parents they must then either adopt or apply for a Parental Order under s.54 of the 2008 Act (previously s.30 of the 1990 Act). A Parental Order will result in the re-registration of the child's birth and can thereby make the commissioning couple the child's *legal parents* with *parental responsibility* (i.e. the legal rights and responsibilities that by law a parent has over a child).[199] A number of stringent conditions must be satisfied for s.54 to be invoked. In particular:

(1) the child must be created by a variant of IVF, GIFT, or by artificial insemination, using the gametes of at least one of the commissioning couple (s.54(1));

(2) the commissioning couple must be married, civil partners, or living as partners in an enduring family relationship and not within prohibited degrees of relationship to each other (s.54(2));

(3) the child must already be living with the commissioning couple (s.54(4));

(4) the surrogate and any other person who is a parent of the child (if not a member of the commissioning couple) must consent (s.54(6)); and

(5) the court must be satisfied that no prohibited payment (which excludes reasonable expenses) has been made, unless authorised by the court (s.54(8)).

Clearly, Parental Orders are not to be given away lightly. This provision (unlike adoption) cannot be used against surrogate mothers against their will and a single person cannot apply for a Parental Order. Under the previous provision (s.30 of the 1990 Act), the commissioning couple had to be married and the change in this regard reflects the law's increasing acceptance of same sex couples and other non-traditional family units.

Judicial interpretation of s.30 of the 1990 Act had relaxed its requirements in one crucial way; the courts had held that where payment has been made, the court can authorise that payment retrospectively.[200] In *Re C*, for example,

---

[198] See the unusual approach taken in the Australian case of *Re Evelyn* (1998) Fam. LR 53.
[199] On parental responsibility, see s.3(1) of Children Act 1989 and the discussion in Ch.5 (5.3.1.1).
[200] See *Re Q* [1996] 1 F.L.R. 369 and *Re C* [2002] EWHC 157.

Wall L.J. authorised the payment of expenses for loss of earnings to a surrogate who had suffered no loss of earnings as she was on income support. His Lordship considered that a failure to grant the Parental Order would not be in the child's best interests. If the couple had not been able to obtain a Parental Order, then the only way in which the social mother could have obtained parental responsibility would have been to adopt. The adoption process is difficult and time-consuming. Perhaps not surprisingly, it is thought that "a substantial proportion of commissioning couples are failing to apply to the courts to become the legal parents of the child".[201]

A Government appointed committee, chaired by Margaret Brazier and reporting in 1998, had recommended that the Surrogacy Arrangements Act be repealed and replaced, and that much tighter controls be placed on surrogacy.[202] One of these recommendations was that the s.30 Parental Order process (as it was then) would be tightened, so that payments could not be authorised retrospectively. This has not happened. Nor has the Government implemented recommendations, such as that non-profit-making agencies be required to be registered and comply with a statutory Code of Practice. It has to be said, however, that at the time the Brazier Committee's recommendations did not receive universal support. Freeman, for example, argued that the recommendations pointed to a bleak future for surrogacy.[203]

8.7 Parentage

Assisted reproduction can create difficulties where a person other than the gamete provider wishes to be the legal parent. Historically biology ruled. If the partner of a woman who had given birth to a child produced by *donor* insemination tried to register himself as the father knowing that he was not the biological father, he would have committed perjury.[204] At common law, the legal father of a child born by sperm donation was the biological father even if the woman's husband had fully consented.[205] The 1990 Act solved many problems, but raised some of its own. Whether a person other than the woman's husband was to be the legal father turned on whether the man was receiving "treatment together" with the woman, a phrase that is not as easy to apply as it appears, given that the man in question would not be providing the sperm. Also, the 1990 Act failed to address the possibility that the partner of the woman giving birth to the child could be another woman. The 2008 Act has addressed these issues and the new parentage provisions came into effect on April 6, 2009. These provisions define the legal mother and, where there is one, the other legal parent.

---

[201] Brazier et al. 1998, para.5.7.
[202] See Brazier et al. 1998.
[203] See Freeman 1999.
[204] See Brazier 2003, 284–285 and Freeman 2004, 715.
[205] *Re M* [1997] 2 F.L.R. 90.

8.7.1 The mother

Section 33(1) of the 2008 Act re-enacts the content of s.27(1) of the 1990 Act. This provides that where an embryo or sperm and eggs are placed in a woman who is in the UK at the time, she, and no other woman, will be the child's mother. Thus, the gestational woman is the mother and, to use a phrase from the *Highlander* films, there can be only one. The gestation mother will cease to be the legal mother where the child is subsequently adopted (s.33(2), 2008 Act) or parenthood is transferred through a Parental Order (s.54, 2008 Act).

Freeman (commenting on the identically worded previous provision) suggests that there could also be another situation where the legal mother is not the gestational mother.[206] He notes that the phrase "sperm *and* eggs" could be read as meaning that the provision does not apply where only an egg is placed in a woman and is fertilised by sexual intercourse. At common law, the mother of a donated egg is not conclusively settled. However, the appeal courts have adopted wide, purposive interpretations to avoid gaps being created by narrow, literal readings of legislative provisions of this type.[207] Further, Parliament, when enacting the 1990 Act and later the 2008 Act, surely did not intend a child's parentage to depend on whether a donated egg was implanted on its own or with sperm.

The restriction of legal maternity to one woman by the previous provision has been criticised by Wallbank, who objects to the application of what she terms the "either/or approach" in surrogacy cases.[208] She argues that prioritising the welfare of the child "is not inimical to child sharing" and does not have to privilege the traditional two-parent view of the family.[209] The 2008 Act still restricts the term mother to one parent and, as we shall see, still adopts a two-parent family model.

8.7.2 The other legal parent

The 1990 Act recognised only one other type of parent beyond the legal mother: the legal father. A child either had a legal father or was legally fatherless and thereby had only one legal parent. The 2008 Act now recognises the possibility that the other parent could be a woman. There can still, however, only be two parents: the legal mother and the other legal parent. The rebuttable presumption is that the husband or civil partner is the other parent, though another can become the other parent if a number of conditions are satisfied.

---

[206] See the discussion in Freeman 2004, 716.
[207] See *R. (Bruno Quintavalle) v Secretary of State for Health* [2003] UKHL 13 and *R. (Josephine Quintavalle) v HFEA* [2005] UKHL 28.
[208] See Wallbank 2002.
[209] Wallbank 2002, 293.

8.7.2.1 The father: married mother

The 2008 Act re-enacts the substance of s.28(1) of the 1990 Act. Under what is now s.35 of the 2008 Act, if the gestational mother is *married* and the pregnancy is the result of the placing in her of an embryo, donor sperm and eggs, or donor sperm, her husband will be the child's legal father. There is a significant exception: the husband is not the father where "it is shown that he did not consent" to the treatment. The common law presumption of paternity in the case of marriage is retained by s.38(2), but that is a rebuttable presumption. What this means is that the husband can escape legal fatherhood by showing that he did not consent *and* is not the biological father (using DNA evidence).

Legal fatherhood and parental responsibility are *not* the same thing. Legal fatherhood is about being recognised in law as the father, whereas parental responsibility is about having legal rights over the child. The Code of Practice requires treatment centres to explain this to couples undergoing treatment.[210] The Code of Practice also states that the clinic take all practical steps to ascertain whether the husband consents and obtain his written consent or written evidence that he does not consent.[211]

The husband does not consent where another man's sperm is *mistakenly* used in the provision of treatment services. This was decided by the Court of Appeal in the *Leeds* case, where mixed-race twins were born to a white couple as a result of the wrong sperm being used during IVF.[212] The husband was nonetheless granted parental responsibility and the children will be brought up by this couple.

8.7.2.2 The father: unmarried mothers and married mothers whose husbands do not consent

Under the previous provision, s.28(3) of the 1990 Act, if no man was the father by virtue of being a consenting husband, then any man "treated together" with the woman was the legal father. This concept of receiving treatment services together, which continues to be used by other provisions,[213] was not as straightforward as it appears. Consider the following situation. A woman and her boyfriend seek access to IVF using donated sperm. He consents, acknowledging that he would be the legal father, but the treatment fails and they split up. She then presents herself for a second attempt with her new partner, without drawing her change of partner to the clinic's attention. This second attempt using donor sperm produces a baby girl. Was the ex-boyfriend still receiving treatment together with the woman and thereby the legal father? This situation actually occurred and went all the way to the House of Lords.[214] In

---

[210] See HFEA 2007b, G.6.9.1 and 2008b, para.6.2.
[211] See HFEA 2007b, G.6.9.3 and 2008b, para.6.3.
[212] *Leeds Teaching Hospitals NHS Trust v A* [2003] EWHC 259. This led to the Toft Report (see Toft 2004 and HFEA 2004g).
[213] E.g. s.2(1), 13(6), and Sch.3 para.5(3) (see *Evans v Amicus Healthcare* [2004] EWCA Civ 727, esp. para.29).
[214] *Re R* [2005] UKHL 33.

Re R, it was accepted that "treatment together" did not require that the man also be receiving medical treatment. Instead, it was a test having a "mental element", concerned with whether the couple were engaged in a "joint enterprise", and was to be determined at the time when the embryo was placed in the mother.[215] On the facts, they were no longer receiving treatment together when the embryo was placed in the woman, so her ex-boyfriend was not the legal father. Lord Walker expressed the view that if an unmarried man is to become the legal father of a child of which he is not the biological father, this should be "brought home to the prospective father as clearly as possible".[216] This is precisely what the new provision does and it no longer turns on the notion of treatment together.[217]

Section 36 of the 2008 Act applies where no man is the father by virtue of s.35 (i.e. there is no consenting husband) and no woman is the other parent by virtue of s.42 (i.e. there is no consenting civil partner). This allows another man to be the father of a child created from donor sperm where the implantation takes place in the UK and the "agreed fatherhood conditions" in s.37 are satisifed. The agreed fatherhood conditions are, and here I paraphrase:

(a) licensed treatment was provided to a woman;

(b) a man consents to being treated as the father;

(b) the woman also consents to this;

(c) neither has subsequently withdrawn that consent;

(d) the woman has not subsequently consented to another person being the other parent; and

(e) the man and woman are not within prohibited degrees of relationship to each other (as defined in s.58(2));

(f) these consents (or withdrawals) are in writing and signed by the people giving them.

This provision does not grant paternity to the boyfriend of a woman who conceives as a result of unlicensed "DIY" insemination or sexual intercourse. In such cases, paternity will be determined by the common law rules, which grant paternity to the genetic father. Nor does it grant paternity to boyfriends who travel abroad to support their partner's treatment using donor sperm outside the UK.[218] Moreover, this provision cannot be invoked by a woman's husband, who must rely on s.35.[219]

---

[215] [2005] UKHL 33, para.43.

[216] *Re R* [2005] UKHL 33, para.35.

[217] *Cf* HFEA 2008b, 60, where the draft Code of Practice mistakenly states that the s.37 requires that the woman "be treated together with a male partner".

[218] See also *U v W* [1998] Fam. 29.

[219] This was the position under the 1990 Act's provisions and there has been no change to the relevant wording: *Leeds Teaching Hospitals NHS Trust v A* [2003] EWHC 259.

Applying the agreed fatherhood conditions to the facts of *Re R* would have produced a different result. The man in question had consented to being treated as the father and although his ex-partner had presented herself to the clinic with a new man, she had neither withdrawn her consent nor consented to her new boyfriend being the legal father.

8.7.2.3 A woman as the other legal parent

The 2008 Act treats the mother's female partner in the same way that it would her male partner. Section 42 applies to woman in a civil partnership the same conditions that s.35 applies to husbands. Where the mother is in a civil partnership and the pregnancy is the result of the placing in her of an embryo, donor sperm and eggs, or donor sperm, her civil partner will be the child's other legal parent, unless she did not consent. Section 43 enables another woman to be the other legal parent where neither s.35 nor s.42 apply and the "agreed female parenthood conditions" apply. These conditions are identical, *mutatis mutandis*, to those applying to the situation where the other prospective legal parent is a man. Thus, the mother's female partner can become the other legal parent provided the mother does not have a consenting husband or civil partner, and the relevant written and signed consents have been obtained and remain in force.

8.7.3 Children without another parent

A child can only have one legal mother and one other legal parent (ss.33(1), 38(1) and 45(1)). The Act also creates the possibility of a child with only one legal parent in at least two situations.

First, if a sperm donor gives his effective consent under the 1990 Act, he will not be the legal father (s.41(1), 2008 Act). Freeman asks us to consider a situation where sperm is donated for research purposes but accidentally used for infertility treatment.[220] It is difficult to see how his consent would still be valid, which would make him the child's father if no other person is the legal parent, even if he was passionately against donating for treatment (perhaps, because of the recent removal of donor anonymity). Given Parliament's intentions, the courts would most probably seek to interpret the Act to best avoid this consequence on the facts before them.

Second, where the implantation takes place after the death of the man providing the sperm or, where donor sperm is used and the other prospective parent has died before the implantation takes place, a child will have only one legal parent. The 2008 Act disapplies this restriction where a number of conditions are satisfied.[221] The deceased man providing the sperm can be the legal

---

[220] See Freeman 2004, 720.
[221] It thereby replaces the provisions of the Human Fertilisation and Embryology (Deceased Fathers) Act 2003.

father, *for the purposes of birth registration only*, if he consented (in writing) to the use of the sperm or embryo after his death, to being the child's father, and the mother elects for him to be so treated within 42 days of the child's birth (s.39). Where donor sperm is used, the mother may elect for another person to be treated as the other legal parent where that person was her husband or civil partner and consented in writing (ss.40(1) and 46(1)). If the other person was not the mother's husband or civil partner, the agreed fatherhood or conditions must also be met immediately before that person's death and the embryo must have been created in the course of licensed treatment services (ss.40(2) and 46(2)).

8.8 Conclusion

Reproductive technologies unavoidably evoke moral divisions over issues as fundamental as the value to be attached to early human life. Some issues have been left for later chapters. The pressures faced by the 1990 Act are powerfully shown by the development of cloning and stem cell technology, which will be examined in Ch.10. There are questions about whether the control granted to the providers of gametes and embryos, particularly by the consent requirements, implies an underlying notion of property. Property in the body will be briefly examined in Ch.14 (14.4). There are also questions about the possibility of a prenatal negligence claim if something goes wrong. Prenatal negligence is the subject of the next chapter.

8.9 Further reading

Freeman, Michael D. (1999) "Does Surrogacy Have a Future After Brazier?" 7(1) *Medical Law Review* 1–20.

Holm, Søren (1998) "Ethical Issues in Pre-Implantation Diagnosis." In Harris, John, and Holm, Søren (eds.) *The Future of Human Reproduction: Choice and Regulation*. (Oxford: Clarendon Press, 1998), 176–190.

Jackson, Emily (2002) "Conception and the Irrelevance of the Welfare Principle." 65(2) *Modern Law Review* 176–203.

Chapter 9

PRENATAL NEGLIGENCE

9.1 Introduction

A poorly performed sterilisation, vasectomy, or abortion could result in the birth of an unwanted child. Bungled preimplantation or prenatal diagnosis could lead to the selection of an embryo or fetus that is born with undesired traits or in an undesired condition. So could a failure to properly immunise or advise a woman about the risks of an activity or infection to her future child. Future developments, such as cloning and germ-line gene therapy, both of which are currently illegal (see Chs 10 and 12), can only increase the ways in which unsound advice, diagnosis, and treatment can produce an undesired outcome. There are, thus, many types of prenatal negligence that can lead to the birth of children who would not otherwise have been born or would not have been born with particular traits or prospects.

In many ways the law on prenatal negligence is merely the application of the rules of clinical negligence to conduct relating to the conception or birth of a child. It follows that a claimant needs to establish a duty of care, breach of that duty, and damage caused by that breach of duty (see Ch.3). Establishing a duty of care is, however, fraught with difficulties and specific rules. Prenatal negligence simply raises policy and ethical issues that are not apparent in other clinical negligence cases.

9.2 Types of action

Before starting to explore these issues and the law that has developed around them, we need some terminology. This is another area where it is common for the same label to be used to describe different concepts and different labels to be used to describe the same concept. What one person calls "wrongful birth" might be what another calls "wrongful conception", and what one person calls "wrongful conception" might be called "failed sterilisation" by someone else.

The child and its parents are most likely to want to sue for prenatal negligence. For convenience, it is useful to distinguish the actions capable of being brought in the child's name from those capable of being brought in the parents' name. To be clear, the following definitions are offered for clarity of expression and do not necessarily correlate to usage elsewhere.

9.2.1 Actions by or on behalf of the child

Actions brought by (or on behalf of) the child are relatively straightforward to categorise according to the consequence of the purportedly negligent conduct. I will use the labels "prenatal injury" and "wrongful life" to distinguish two types of outcome.

Prenatal injury actions involve claims brought on behalf of a child born in a damaged condition where the child alleges that he was injured by the negligence of another before his birth. The negligent act or omission might have occurred before conception (e.g. negligent failure to offer the mother preconception immunisation against rubella), before implantation (e.g. negligent *in vitro* fertilisation (IVF) treatment), during gestation (e.g. negligent prescription of drugs to a pregnant woman, or the pregnant woman's negligent use of drugs), or during birth (e.g. negligent delivery). Essentially, it involves a claim for the losses associated with being born injured where the injury is the result of someone's negligent conduct. If the loss is characterised as loss resulting from a failure to abort after the occurrence of the defect, it is a different type of action—it is an action for "wrongful life".

Wrongful life actions involve a child claiming a financial award for its birth with allegedly unsatisfactory traits or prospects, in circumstances where if the alleged negligence had not occurred it would not have been conceived or born at all. The defendant is alleged to have negligently failed to prevent, or negligently facilitated, the child's conception or birth in circumstances leading to its birth with unsatisfactory traits or prospects. This alleged negligent act or omission might occur prior to conception (e.g. failure to advise the parents of the risk of their future child inheriting a genetic defect or the negligent use of a cloning technique to create a child); before implantation (e.g. negligent selection of a less than optimal embryo for implantation); or during gestation (e.g. negligent failure to advise the mother on the likely condition of her child). This action involves a claim, by the resultant child, for the losses consequent on being conceived or born with allegedly unsatisfactory traits or prospects. The twist is that in the absence of the claimed negligence, the claimant would not have existed.

These labels distinguish a child's claim for damages arising from a preventable injury (prenatal injury) from a claim arising from conduct that was a necessary condition for *that* child's existence (wrongful life). Both actions would be brought after birth, if the allegedly negligent conduct causes the child to die before birth, then the action would be one for *wrongful death*. Wrongful death actions, so defined, are not available in this country and will not be addressed in this chapter. (Nor will this chapter address such actions brought by parents.)[1]

9.2.2 Actions by or on behalf of the parents

Classifying the possible claims capable of being brought by aggrieved parents is more complex. A distinction can be drawn between "wrongful conception" and "wrongful birth" on the basis of whether the prenatal negligence occurred before conception or birth.

Wrongful conception actions refer to those situations where the parents were deprived of the opportunity to avoid the conception or pregnancy in the first place. The paradigmatic cases are where there has been a negligently performed sterilisation or vasectomy. It is also possible to envisage cases where the parents wanted a conception but not *that* conception (where e.g. diseased gametes were negligently used for IVF). The claimed loss is the cost of the unwanted pregnancy and its consequences.

Wrongful birth actions refer to those situations where the parents were deprived of an opportunity to avoid continuing with an existing pregnancy. Examples include the negligent failure to perform a scan/diagnosis that would have lead to an abortion, or the negligent performance of an abortion. The claimed loss is the cost of an unwanted birth and its consequences.

A further distinction can be drawn based on the parental wishes frustrated by the prenatal negligence.[2] Wrongful conception and wrongful birth actions

---

[1] If a negligently caused still-birth causes the mother physical injury or causes psychological injury to either parent, the relevant parent might have a claim under ordinary negligence principles for their own injury: see Ch.3.

[2] I previously made this same distinction but used the labels of wrongful conception/pregnancy and wrongful birth (see Pattinson 1999). I now consider that the use of these labels for this purpose is unnecessarily confusing.

can frustrate the parents' wish not to have any children or frustrate the parents' wish not to have a child with those traits.

Prenatal negligence will be said to have caused an *undesired child* when the parents had not wanted any more children. They might later come to want and love the child that is born, but at the time that the prenatal negligence occurred they had decided against having more children or at least had taken measures to prevent it. This captures all unwanted pregnancies (e.g. a negligently performed sterilisation, vasectomy, or abortion; negligent contraceptive advice or device; and negligent fertility diagnosis). Parents are claiming the costs of a negligently produced undesired child; the cost of an unwanted pregnancy. They are claiming damages for the harm caused by the post-negligence pregnancy, childbirth, and the costs of rearing the child.

Prenatal negligence will be said to have caused an *undesired trait* where there has been the negligent failure to prevent the conception/birth of a child with a particular trait (e.g. a congenital defect) or to ensure the birth of a child with a particular trait. When, for example, there is a negligent failure to advise the parents of the risk of having a child with a congenital abnormality, a negligent failure to carry out a prenatal diagnostic technique (at all or with due care) that would have resulted in non-selection or destruction, or, in the future, negligent attempts at conducting germ-line gene therapy or cloning. Parents are claiming for the loss of an opportunity to have a particular child or to avoid that child (paradigmatically, the loss of opportunity to terminate a "defective" fetus), and thus the emotional and financial costs of bringing up the resultant child. Since, *ex hypothesi*, the parents intended to have a child, they have not been forced to pick up the costs of raising a child *as such*.

It is possible for a set of circumstances to give rise to a combination of these actions and frustrated desires. Imagine a woman who does not want any more children but is also against abortion except where it is performed on the grounds of fetal abnormality or to save the pregnant woman's life. If this woman is very unlucky she could become pregnant because of a negligent sterilisation operation and then be deprived of the opportunity to discover that the fetus is abnormal because of negligently performed prenatal diagnosis. The claim stemming from the negligent sterilisation would be one for wrongful conception leading to an undesired child. The claim stemming from the negligent diagnosis would be one for wrongful birth leading to an undesired trait. I use these labels not to draw legally relevant distinctions but to facilitate the ethical discussion. As we shall see, the law does not distinguish between causing an unwanted child and causing an unwanted trait. Instead the law focuses on whether the child is born healthy or unhealthy.

Two leading academic commentators, Kennedy and Grubb, offer different definitions and distinctions. They define "wrongful conception" actions as parental claims for "negligence which has led to the birth of a *healthy child*",[3]

---

[3] Kennedy and Grubb 2000, 1553 (original emphasis).

and "wrongful birth" actions as claims "brought by the parents of a child *born disabled* as a consequence of negligence before its birth".[4] They are not alone in this.[5] I do not use this terminology as it conflates the distinctions made by the terminology in use here. Consider the case of *Emeh v Kensington and Chelsea and Westminster AHA*.[6] This was a case where a failed sterilisation operation resulted in the birth of a girl with congenital disabilities. In my terminology, this action is for wrongful conception producing an undesired child. Applying the terminology of Kennedy and Grubb, since the child was born disabled, this is a wrongful birth action.[7]

It is also worth noting that, at least in the past, the label "wrongful birth" has sometimes been used to encompass what I have called "wrongful conception" actions.[8] Usage is now changing.[9]

9.3 Action brought by the child: Prenatal injury

In the early 1960s hundreds of children were born with serious deformities after their mothers had taken the drug thalidomide during pregnancy. Thalidomide had been thought to be safe. It was not. Many cases were settled out-of-court and the courts never declared that a sufficient causal link had been established, nor was it clear at the time that it was possible to sue for injuries suffered before birth. It is now clear that a child injured in the womb does have a cause of action. As we shall see, a child born after July 22, 1976 is granted a cause of action by the Congenital Disabilities (Civil Liability) Act 1976 and a child born before that date is owed a common law duty of care. This does not, however, mean that a child would have no difficulty establishing liability if a similar tragedy were to occur today. The law does not impose strict liability and, like clinical negligence and product liability claims generally, causation can be a major stumbling block. What is more, the 1976 Act is peppered with hurdles and limitations that make establishing liability more than a little difficult.

---

[4] Kennedy and Grubb 2000, 1586 (original emphasis).
[5] Jackson (1996, 346) declares that the American courts use the "helpful distinction . . . between claims for wrongful pregnancy (where the child is born healthy) and those for wrongful birth (where the child is born with disabilities)".
[6] [1985] Q.B. 1012.
[7] Though somewhat confusingly these respected authors use this case to illustrate the difficulties in establishing causation in wrongful conception cases: Kennedy and Grubb 2000, 1580–1582. This suggests that their assertion that a wrongful conception case is brought on behalf of a healthy child could be an overgeneralisation, rather than a definitional requirement.
[8] See e.g. Fortin 1987, 306, Jackson 1996, 349, and Harris 1998, 100.
[9] For explicit use of wrongful conception and birth as defined here see Lord Clyde in *McFarlane v Tayside Health* [2000] 2 A.C. 59 at 99, and Whitfield 2004, 825. In *Rees v Darlington Memorial Hospital NHS Trust* [2003] UKHL 52, Lord Hope uses the label wrongful or uncovenanted pregnancy (para.56) and Lord Millet "wrongful pregnancy" (para.100) to describe what I have called wrongful conception.

9.3.1 Legal issues

9.3.1.1 The 1976 Act

The Congenital Disabilities (Civil Liability) Act 1976 (*hereafter the 1976 Act*) enables a child to sue for damages in respect of injuries inflicted before birth.[10] It does this by providing a cause of action to a child "born disabled" as a result of another's negligence (s.1(1)). "Born" means "born alive"—there can be no action for wrongful death (s.4(2)(a)). "Disabled" is defined widely to encompass any personal injury: "any deformity, disease or abnormality, including predisposition (whether or not susceptible of immediate prognosis) to physical or mental defect in the future" (s.4(1)).

The Act requires the child claimant to jump a number of hurdles. *First*, the child needs to establish that his disabilities were caused by an "occurrence" that affected (a) either parent's ability to have a normal healthy child, (b) his mother during her pregnancy, or (c) his mother or himself in the course of his birth (s.1(1) and (2)). *Second*, the child needs to establish that the person responsible for this occurrence (the defendant) was liable to the affected parent (s.1(3)). In other words, the child only has a cause of action if a duty owed to one of its parents has been breached. This means that a child damaged in the womb by drugs prescribed to his mother can only sue the doctor if the doctor has thereby acted negligently towards his mother. While the child does not need to establish that his mother has suffered any tangible injury,[11] this can be a significant hurdle for the child to jump. The derivative nature of the claim means that any defects that infect the mother's claim will also apply to the child's claim, and it prevents the child from suing for careless conduct that could only have adversely affected the fetus. A child could not, for example, sue where he was born disabled following his mother's refusal of a Caesarean section, as the doctor will not have breached his duty to the mother as long as she had capacity (on the doctor's duties to the mother here, see Ch.5 (5.2.3.1)). The derivative nature of the child's claim does, however, have a number of advantages. From the claimant's perspective, it is not necessary to prove that the defendant knew, or ought to have known, that his mother was pregnant.[12] From the defendant's perspective, there is no danger that multiple levels of duty will be imposed for the same act (one to the mother and another to the child).

The position of a defendant doctor is aided by s.1(5), which outlines the standard of care imposed by the Act. This section states that a professional treating or advising the parent will not be liable to the child

---

[10] The 1976 Act extends to Northern Ireland but not to Scotland: s.6(2).

[11] Section 1(3) goes on to state: "it is no answer that there could not have been such liability because the parent suffered no actionable injury, if there was a breach of legal duty which, accompanied by injury, would have given rise to the liability".

[12] Also, as Whitfield (2004, 809) notes, giving the child a derivative right allows the child to sue for negligent advice given to the mother.

if he took reasonable care having due regard to then received professional opinion applicable to the particular class of case; but this does not mean that he is answerable only because he departed from received opinion.

This enshrines the standards of the day, along the lines of the common law rule in *Roe v Minister of Health* (in which Denning L.J. famously opined that "We must not look at the 1947 accident with 1954 spectacles").[13] It also enshrines the principle that departure from standard practice is not necessarily negligent, which is part of the common law rule in *Bolam*.[14] It is, however, possible to read the words "received professional opinion" as suggesting that the post-*Bolitho* common law proviso that the position must be logically defensible does not apply.[15] This interpretation is unlikely to be adopted by the courts, as *Bolitho* represents only a minimal level of judicial scrutiny.

With one exception, the Act does not allow a child to sue his mother (s.1(1)). The exception concerns injuries sustained as a result of her negligently driving a motor vehicle (s.2).[16] This is a point of ethical controversy to which we will return shortly. There might be grounds for legal challenge. It has been argued that the maternal immunity could be open to challenge under art.6 (the right to a fair trial for determinations of one's civil rights and obligations) of the Convention as given effect by the Human Rights Act (HRA) 1998.[17] In the face of primary legislation, however, the most that a successful claimant could hope to obtain would be a declaration of incompatibility under s.4(2) of the HRA. The Government could then amend the relevant legislation to remove this incompatibility by making a "remedial order" under s.10. In practice, any declaration of incompatibility would put considerable pressure on the Government to act, though it would not be under a legal duty to do so.

In addition to the limitations implied by the derivative nature of the child's claim (addressed above), the 1976 Act explicitly provides for a number of defences. These include parental knowledge of the risks, exclusion and limitation of liability, and contributory negligence.

Section 1(4) covers circumstances where the parents knew of the risks. More precisely, this section states that,

> In the case of an occurrence preceding the time of conception, the defendant is not answerable to the child if at that time either or both of the parents knew the risk of their child being born disabled (that is to say, the particular risk created by the occurrence); but should it be the child's father who is the defendant, this subsection does not apply if he knew of the risk and the mother did not.

This means that the defendant has a defence if (with regard to a preconception occurrence) the affected parent knows of the risk that the child will be born

---

[13] [1954] 2 Q.B. 66 at 84.
[14] *Bolam v Friern Hospital Management Committee* [1957] 2 All E.R. 118. See the discussion in Ch.3, esp. 3.4.1.
[15] *Bolitho v City and Hackney HA* [1998] A.C. 232.
[16] "Motor vehicle" is defined in s.4(2)(b) to mean "a mechanically propelled vehicle intended or adapted for use on roads". Thus, it includes cars and motorcycles, but not bicycles or horses.
[17] See Stauch 2001, 265–268.

disabled. An exception is made where the child sues his father, as the father can still be liable if he is aware of this risk as long as the mother was not so aware.

Section 1(6) allows the defence of exclusion or limitation of liability, but this is subject to any protection applying to the parents' claim. Thus, a claimant can take advantage of s.2(1) of the Unfair Contract Terms Act 1977, which prevents the exclusion or limitation of liability in respect of personal injury and death.

Section 1(7) allows the defence of contributory negligence by the parents. This section states that if

> the parent affected shared the responsibility for the child being born disabled, the damages are to be reduced to such extent as the court thinks just and equitable having regard to the extent of the parent's responsibility.

This is a partial defence,[18] because, technically, there can be no defence of 100 per cent contributory negligence.[19] (In any event, the child would have no claim if the parent is wholly to blame, because the child's claim is derivative and any parental claim in such circumstances would fail on causation alone.) This provision would apply if the pregnant woman exacerbates her child's injury or disability by, say, ignoring medical advice.

9.3.1.2 At common law

The 1976 Act replaces the common law for any child born after 22 July 1976 (s.4(5)). The common law is not, however, thereby irrelevant. A potential claim brought on behalf of a mentally disabled child born before this date might never become statute-barred. Time does not start to run under the Limitation Act 1980 while the potential claimant is "under a disability" (s.28(1)), which is defined to include infants and those "of unsound mind" (s.38(2)).

The courts did not confirm the existence of a common law duty of care owed to an unborn child until well after the 1976 Act came into force. This was first directly considered in a consolidated appeal brought on behalf of disabled children whose injuries predated the enactment of the 1976 Act: *Burton v Islington HA* and *De Martell v Merton and Sutton HA*.[20] Both cases involved allegations of negligence by health professionals. In *Burton*, it was alleged that a gynaecological operation had been negligently performed on the pregnant mother. In *De Martell*, the claim was of negligent care at the delivery and birth of the claimant. The Court of Appeal held that a duty of care existed, thereby rejecting the objection that at the time of the alleged negligence the claimant was not a legal person.[21] The majority followed a decision of the Supreme Court of Australia in

---

[18] Cf. Whitfield 2004, 813.
[19] *Anderson v Newham College* [2002] EWCA Civ 505 (Court of Appeal decision on s.1(1) of the Law Reform (Contributory Negligence) Act 1945, which has similar wording).
[20] [1993] Q.B. 204. Similar decisions have been reached by Australian, Canadian, Irish, US, and Scottish courts: see Whitfield 2004, 796.
[21] It is well established that birth marks the arrival of legal personality: see Ch.7 (7.4.1).

Watt v Rama.[22] The court was not, however, particularly concerned with the details of the analytic path by which this conclusion can be supported.[23]

Could the common law, in contrast to the 1976 Act, allow a child to sue its mother for prenatal injury? This point has not arisen for consideration by the English courts and may never do so. In *Burton*, Dillon L.J. noted that counsel had pointed

> to the dangers of conflict between the mother and her child, with the child suing for damages for injuries allegedly caused by the negligence of the mother before the child's birth. If the floodgates prove to be open too wide no doubt Parliament can intervene.[24]

This last sentence is ambiguous but suggests that the common law does not grant the maternal immunity of the 1976 Act. There is, however, a more recent decision of the Supreme Court of Canada that is directly on point. In *Dobson v Dobson*, a claim was brought in the name of a child who had been seriously injured in the womb following his mother's allegedly negligent driving.[25] By a bare majority the court supported the maternal immunity on the facts. This decision could influence the English courts.

9.3.1.3 Future reforms

In 2003, in a consultation document entitled *Making Amends*, the Chief Medical Officer (CMO) expressed concern about one type of clinical negligence claim covered by the 1976 Act: birth-related brain damage.[26] These claims account for 5 per cent of all clinical negligence compensation claims and 60 per cent of the clinical negligence budget.[27] In response, the CMO proposed an *NHS Redress Scheme for Severely Neurologically Impaired Babies*, whereby a compensation package would be provided according to the severity of the impairment.[28] As envisaged, the scheme would provide a managed care package for the child, a monthly payment for the costs of care up to £100,000 a year, one-off lump sums for home adaptations and equipment of up to £50,000, and compensation for pain and suffering capped at £50,000. To be eligible, the child would have to suffer brain damage amounting to "severe neurological impairment" as a result of its birth under NHS care. This scheme would not cover damage caused by "genetic or chromosomal abnormality".

---

[22] [1972] V.R. 353 (Winneke C.J., Pape J. and Gillard J.). Potts J. in *Burton* ([1991] 1 Q.B. 638) had preferred the approach of the majority (Winneke C.J. and Pape J.), whereas Phillips J. in *de Martell* ([1993] Q.B. 204) had preferred the approach of Gillard J. For a discussion of the underlying difference, see Kennedy and Grubb 2000, 1503–1505, and Whitfield 2004, 797–799.

[23] According to Dillon L.J., "both [the approach of the majority and that of Gillard J. in *Watt v Rama*] lead to the same conclusion and the differences between them are not . . . significant in the context of the present appeal" ([1993] Q.B. 204 at 230).

[24] [1993] Q.B. 204 at 232.

[25] [1999] 2 S.C.R. 753.

[26] See CMO 2003.

[27] See CMO 2003, 9.

[28] See CMO 2003, 16 and 120–121.

The CMO's proposals were designed to remove the litigation lottery from one type of prenatal negligence claim and, in the process, reduce the costs of such claims to the NHS. This recommendation was not, however, adopted by the NHS Redress Act 2006, which is discussed in Ch.3 (3.6.4). In fact, since the scheme to be set up under that Act will only concerns claims worth less than £20,000, the vast majority of birth-related injuries will fall outside of that scheme.

9.3.2 Ethical issues

If one accepts the ethical defensibility of negligence actions generally, prenatal injury actions seem to raise few complications. The English legal position does, however, provoke a number of questions. The most obvious question is whether the child should be able to sue its mother and whether the maternal immunity unfairly discriminates against fathers. Additionally, there are questions as to the nature of prenatal "injuries" that should be recognised. The 1976 Act's definition of disability is very narrow and does not capture many traits that a child might regard as disabilities. The importance of this question will come to the forefront if prenatal gene therapy becomes a reality (see further Ch.12).

9.3.2.1 Maternal immunity from suit

As stated above, under the 1976 Act prenatal injury actions are not available against the claimant's mother with the limited exception of road traffic accidents. The 1976 Act is largely based on the recommendations of the English Law Commission. In its working paper, the Law Commission's provisional view had been that a child who "suffers antenatal injury caused by his mother's negligence . . . should be entitled to recover damages from her".[29] This view was reversed in the final report, the Law Commission declaring that it had

> under-estimated the number of different ways in which it might be alleged that a mother's negligence caused her child's disability and the extent to which actions or threats of actions might be used in matrimonial disputes.[30]

In contrast, the existence of compulsory insurance with regard to claims arising as a result of the mother's negligent driving was thought to be sufficient to prevent undue "bitterness", or the action "becoming a weapon in matrimonial conflict".[31]

There are three arguments for denying the child a cause of action for prenatal injury in play here. The *first* is the argument that there are too many ways in which a mother can negligently cause her child's disability before its birth. The *second* is that to allow a claim against the mother will cause bitterness,

---

[29] Law Commission 1973, para.34.
[30] Law Commission 1974, para.58.
[31] Law Commission 1974, para.60.

compromising the mother–child relationship. The *third* is that such an action will be used illegitimately by husbands in matrimonial disputes. These were not thought sufficient to prevent a child claiming against its parents for negligently inflicted post-natal injury or claiming against its father for prenatal injury.[32] Yet, the second and third arguments appear to apply to these situations as well. Are these arguments sufficient to justify blanket immunity from suit? In many cases, of course, the mother will simply not have the funds to satisfy any successful damages claim against her or will be the person who would receive any damages given to support her child, but this will not always be so.

The first argument is not so much that a mother has too many opportunities to commit a wrong to the child, but that liability would unduly constrain the mother's conduct. According to Jackson,

> While the fetus is inside the woman's body, protecting it from harm caused by the pregnant woman would be possible only if the woman's freedom to make decisions about her body were suspended for the duration of her pregnancy. In addition, because almost everything the pregnant woman chooses to do or not do might have an impact upon her fetus, in order to minimise fetal harm pregnant women would have to be under almost continual surveillance.[33]

Similarly, McLean has argued that to impose retrospective liability on women for negligent behaviour during pregnancy could effectively require that "all fertile, sexually active women of childbearing age should act at all times as if they were pregnant".[34] Here there is some ethical controversy over whether this concern is best addressed by blanket immunity from suit (irrespective of the circumstances or level of negligence) or by low standard of care (there is no reason why the standard has to be set so high that the mother is effectively confined to the house). Setting the standard of care is itself value-laden,[35] but there are activities (such as performing multiple bungee-jumps while pregnant) that can be avoided at little cost to the pregnant woman. This presents a clear tension between the claims and needs of the pregnant woman and those of her unborn child. Blanket immunity from suit is, in effect, only supported by views holding that either (a) a woman's liberty should *always* take priority over the interests of her fetus and the future child that she intends it to become, or (b) allowing *any* liability would, in practice, result in unjustifiable priority being given to the fetus.[36]

The second argument focuses on the effects on the mother–child relationship of a tortious action, rather than the initial wrong that that is designed to address. Does this concern also apply where the mother–child relationship has already broken down? Consider, for example, the situation where a rich biological mother has given her child up for adoption after recklessly (or even deliberately) inflicting a serious injury on the child as it developed in the womb.

---

[32] Since the child's claim is derivative, for the father to be liable to the child he would have to commit a tort on the mother, by (e.g.) battering her while pregnant.

[33] Jackson 2001, 143.

[34] McLean 1999, 66. See Brazier 1999 for further arguments along these lines.

[35] In *Dobson v Dobson* [1999] 2 S.C.R. 753, para.52 Cory J. opined that setting an appropriate standard of care was "difficult" and "perhaps impossible".

[36] Brazier 1999 presents an argument effectively supporting (b).

The third argument could be answered by simply excluding the use of such an action in or following matrimonial disputes. Prohibiting the action altogether, irrespective of the circumstances, goes much further than the argument. In fact, all three arguments appear to justify a step less than blanket immunity from suit.

Some commentators have noted the potential of liability to deter avoidable injuries to the fetus (and subsequent child) and the need to address blatant wrongs. According to Dickens,

> Requiring mothers to take reasonable care to prevent avoidable injury to their chil-
> dren, such as by not consuming inappropriate amounts of alcohol, caffeine, tobacco
> or known toxic or teratogenic substances, may seem a tolerable limitation upon
> freedom.[37]

The underlying ethical controversy is manifest. In addition to arguments over the appropriateness of tort actions generally (as opposed to state-compensation schemes), there are arguments here over the moral claims of the fetus and future child compared to those of the pregnant woman. It has been pointed out, by feminist theorists in particular, that similar constraints are not put on men, "even though their behaviour before and during pregnancy could prove equally damaging to a foetus".[38]

It should be apparent that ethical controversies underlying a child's claim for prenatal injury do not easily map onto the five major ethical positions. This topic causes as many divisions within such positions as between them.

9.4 Action brought by the child: Wrongful life

Wrongful life actions are the most controversial of the prenatal negligence actions addressed in this chapter. They are actions brought in the name of a child, born with allegedly unsatisfactory traits or prospects, in circumstances where if the alleged negligence had not occurred that child would not have been conceived or born at all. As we shall see, the courts have hitherto set themselves against recognising such actions.

9.4.1 Legal issues

9.4.1.1 At common law

McKay v Essex AHA is the only English case on the feasibility of a wrongful life action.[39] Mrs McKay had contracted rubella in the early months of her pregnancy, causing the claimant to be born deaf and partially blind. It was argued

---

[37] Dickens 1986, 266.
[38] Morris and Nott 1995, 54.
[39] [1982] 1 Q.B. 1166.

that Mrs McKay would not have continued with the pregnancy had she been properly informed that she had contracted rubella, and advised of the risks to her child and of the possibility of a lawful abortion. The child's claim was for wrongful life—the claimant would not have been born but for the negligence of the doctor or the laboratory conducting the tests. The court was, in essence, asked to hold that the doctor was in breach of a duty *to the child* to give its mother an opportunity to terminate its life. The Court of Appeal gave two main reasons for striking out this claim. *First*, to impose such a duty would be contrary to public policy because it would violate the sanctity of human life and devalue the life of a handicapped child.[40] *Second*, there was no proper measure of damages representing the difference between the child's disabled existence and non-existence.[41] The first reason is far from persuasive because the court expressed no difficulty with Mrs McKay's additional action for wrongful birth and the Abortion Act 1967 arguably provides legislative support for the view that abortion on the grounds of fetal handicap is consistent with public policy.[42] The second reason has force only if one tries to define the injury as existence and apply the usual principle that tortious damages should seek to put the claimant in the position that he would have been in but for the negligent act or omission. To avoid this difficulty Mason and Laurie have argued that the compensation given to the child should "look not at a comparison, whether it be between the neonate's current existence and non-existence or with normality, but, rather at the actual suffering that has been caused".[43] Whether this is a "solution" depends on how one defines the harm in question, which will be addressed below. In any event, the courts frequently allow monetary awards for negligently inflicted non-monetary losses. Monetary awards are, for example, routinely awarded where another's negligence has left the claimant deaf or permanently unconscious.[44]

Their Lordships gave other reasons for their decision.[45] Stephenson L.J. opined that neither the doctor nor the mother were under a legal obligation to the fetus to terminate its life.[46] Ackner L.J. thought that neither should be under such a legal obligation.[47] With respect, the doctor had not failed to abort, he had failed to inform the mother of the possibility of her aborting. It surely follows that the legal duty would be a duty to inform the mother, not a duty to abort.[48] Stephenson L.J. also feared that allowing the wrongful life claim would open up "the courts to claims by children born handicapped against their mothers for not having an abortion".[49] However, the imposition of a duty on the doctor

---

[40] [1982] 1 Q.B. 1166 at 1180 (Stephenson L.J.) and 1189 (Ackner L.J.).

[41] [1982] 1 Q.B. 1166 at 1181–1182 (Stephenson L.J.), 1189 (Ackner L.J.), and 1192 (Griffith L.J.).

[42] More so now, because since *McKay* was decided the Abortion Act 1967 has been extended to allow abortion for fetal abnormality up to birth: see Ch.7 (7.3.3).

[43] Mason and Laurie 2006, 196.

[44] See e.g. *Lim Poh Choo v Camden and Islington AHA* [1980] A.C. 174.

[45] Other commentators have declared that there were three, rather than merely two, main reasons given for the decision. Those commentators go on to offer different versions of that additional reason: cf. Whitfield 2004, 815; Brazier 2004, 379; and Kennedy and Grubb 2000, 1537.

[46] [1982] 1 Q.B. 1166 at 1180.

[47] [1982] 1 Q.B. 1166 at 1188.

[48] See Fortin 1987, 307–308. See also Jackson 1996, 352–354.

[49] [1982] 1 Q.B. 1166 at 1181.

(to inform the mother) does not require or imply the imposition of a duty on the mother (to even consider abortion, let alone a duty to actually abort). Even if allowing the claim to succeed opened up this possibility for future courts to consider, we have seen that s.1(1) of the 1976 Act grants the mother immunity from such actions.

Whatever one thinks of the decision, if Mrs McKay's daughter could not sue for being born physically disabled, then a child certainly could not sue for being born illegitimate or being born to a mentally disabled mother.[50] Support is offered for the decision in *McKay* by Lord Steyn (obiter) in a subsequent wrongful conception case[51] and by the finding of the European Commission of Human Rights that the refusal of a claim for wrongful life fell within the State's margin of appreciation.[52]

9.4.1.2 The 1976 Act

The Court of Appeal in *McKay* also expressed the obiter view that if the facts of the case had occurred after the 1976 Act came into force, the child's action under that Act would also have failed. The Law Commission, on whose report the 1976 Act is based, had decided against allowing wrongful life actions[53] and the Court of Appeal thought that the 1976 Act had successfully achieved this objective. This was considered to be the effect of s.1(2)(b), which requires that the relevant "occurrence" be one that affected the mother during her pregnancy "so that the child is born with disabilities which would not otherwise have been present".[54] Their Lordships opined that the occurrence is envisaged by this provision as having led to the child's disabilities, not its existence. This reasoning has been criticised, particularly the reliance on the Law Commission's views over those expressed in Parliament preceding the Act.[55]

Kennedy and Grubb have also pointed out that the 1976 Act still leaves two other possible wrongful life actions.[56] *First*, s.1(2)(a) states that the 1976 Act covers the birth of a disabled child by an occurrence that "affected either parent of the child in his or her ability to have a normal, healthy child". This would appear to allow a child to claim for a pre-conception event that was a necessary condition of its existence (such as the negligent genetic counselling of the parents leading to the conception of a disabled child), subject to the standard defences and limitations imposed on the 1976 Act. *Second*, s.1A allows a disabled child to sue for negligence in the course of infertility treatment. More

---

[50] Such claims have also been rejected in the States: *Williams v State of New York* (1966) 223 N.E. 2d 343 (claim resulting from the rape of a mentally disabled woman rejected by the New York Court of Appeal) and *Stills v Gratton* (1976) 127 Cal. Rptr. 652 (claim resulting from birth out of wedlock rejected by the California Court of Appeal).
[51] *McFarlane v Tayside Health Board* [2000] 2 A.C. 59 at 83.
[52] *Reeve v UK* (1994) 24844/94.
[53] See Law Commission 1974, para.89. Section 2(1)(b) of the 1976 Act is identical to clause 2(1)(b) of the draft bill.
[54] See [1982] 1 Q.B. 1166 at 1187 (Ackner L.J.). See also 1178 (Stephenson L.J.) and 1191 (Griffiths L.J.).
[55] See Jackson 1996, 366–368.
[56] See Kennedy and Grubb 2000, 1551–1552. On the second, see also Jackson 1996, 369–370.

specifically, s.1A(1)(b) covers a disability resulting from an act or omission in the course of the "selection" or "the keeping and use outside the body" of gametes or an embryo. While this will encompass prenatal injury actions (e.g. damage caused by cryopreservation), it also appears to create a cause of action where the negligent use of gametes or embryos was a necessary condition for the claimant's existence.[57] It will be interesting to see whether the judicial objections to wrongful life actions expressed in *McKay* will influence their interpretation of these provisions of the 1976 Act.

As an aside, it should be noted that s.6(3) of the Consumer Protection Act 1987 extends the 1976 Act so that it is possible to sue persons who are liable under the 1987 Act for a defective product that caused ante-natal injury.

9.4.2 Ethical issues

Wrongful life actions have also caused difficulties elsewhere. In France, the supreme civil court (the *Cour de cassation*) has held that wrongful life actions are available on a number of occasions.[58] The court's most recent decision, on facts that were very similar to those of *McKay*, resulted in industrial action by the medical profession and legislation being passed to change the law![59] In the US, wrongful life actions have divided the State courts with many rejecting such actions.[60] Many other jurisdictions have, like our own, rejected the possibility of wrongful life actions.[61] The Dutch Supreme Court has, however, recently allowed a wrongful life claim in what was regarded as an exceptional case.[62] Such actions are manifestly controversial.

The aim of a wrongful life action is to obtain money or other remedy for a child (born with unsatisfactory traits or prospects) who would not have been born had the defendant acted differently. Like any private law action, to be ethically justifiable the claimant must be entitled to the remedy, the action must be an appropriate means of obtaining it, and the defendant must have an obligation to provide it. Let us assume that negligence actions are, all things considered, an appropriate means of obtaining a monetary award for claimants generally.[63] Making this assumption, there are two strategies for arguing that wrongful life actions satisfy the conditions of an ethically justified action. *Strategy one* involves demonstrating that the defendant has inflicted a wrong on

---

[57] Cf. Whitfield 2004, 823–824.

[58] See Morris and Saintier 2003.

[59] The *Perruche* decision (Cass Ass Plén, 17.11.00, J.C.P. G. 2000, II-10438, 2309) is discussed in Morris and Saintier 2003.

[60] The exception is the decision of the Supreme Court of California: *Turpin v Sortini* (1982) 643 P. 2d 954 (which accepted special damages for extraordinary expenses necessary to treat the hereditary ailment in wrongful life cases). While this has been followed by two other States (*Harbeson v Parke-Davis* (1983) 656 P. 2d 483 and *Procanik v Cillo* (1984) 478 A. 2d 755, it has been rejected in many more by judicial decision and even legislation (see e.g. Dickens 1989, 91).

[61] e.g. Germany (see Priaulx 2002, 339).

[62] See Sheldon 2005.

[63] This issue is discussed in Ch.3 (3.6ff).

the claimant and that this wrong entitles the claimant to compensation from the defendant, appropriately obtained by a wrongful life action. *Strategy two* involves demonstrating that a wrongful life action is a defensible means of obtaining a monetary award to which the claimant is entitled for reasons other than being the victim of a wrong inflicted by the defendant. These two justificatory strategies have very different structures: the first adopts the language and structure of corrective justice, whereas the second strategy is one of distributive justice (see further Ch.3, esp. 3.8.1 and 3.8.2).

9.4.2.1 Strategy one

The first justificatory strategy for wrongful life actions fits more comfortably with judicial approaches to negligence actions generally. Negligence actions are commonly understood in terms of corrective justice, i.e. as addressing wrongs done by the defendant to the claimant. Unfortunately, it is very difficult to determine whether a wrong has been done to the claimant in a wrongful life action. The problem is that the claimant would not exist had the allegedly wrongful act not occurred. This raises the complex question of whether an individual can be wronged by conduct that causes his initial existence or even his continued existence to the present time. Can bringing a child into existence be a wrong to the child brought into existence?[64]

The claimant has certainly suffered a wrong if he has been harmed. Philosophers have, however, offered different definitions of harm.[65] Feinberg asks us to consider a couple who conceive a child knowing there is a risk that it will have a genetic deformity. He argues that this couple have not harmed their child, because

> to be harmed is to be put in a worse condition than one would otherwise be in (to be made "worse off"), but if the negligent act had not occurred [the child] would not have existed at all.[66]

In other words, Feinberg claims that to be harmed is to be made "worse off" relative to one's alternatives. According to this definition of harm, a child's conception cannot harm it unless *that specific child* could have been in an alternative less or non-harmed state. This is contested by Harris, who prefers to define harm as putting an individual into a position "in which that individual is disabled or suffering in some way or in which his interests or rights are frustrated".[67] For Harris, to be harmed is to be put in "a disabling or hurtful condition, even though that condition is only marginally disabling and *even though it is not possible for that particular individual to avoid the condition in question*".[68] Thus,

---

[64] Parfit called this the "non-identity problem": Parfit 1984, ch.16. This question is also raised by s.13(5) of the Human Fertilisation and Embryology Act 1990 (Ch.9) and by cloning (Ch.10).
[65] Derek Parfit initially provoked this particular discussion by presenting what he called the "non-identity problem": see Parfit 1984, ch.16, and Pattinson 2002c.
[66] Feinberg 1984, 102.
[67] Harris 1998, 109.
[68] Harris 1998 (my emphasis).

for Harris being made "worse off" relative to one's alternatives is a sufficient but not a necessary condition for being harmed.

What we make of this philosophical discussion will depend on the moral position from which we approach it.[69] Given the definition of a wrongful life action, the simple fact of the matter is that the child would not exist had the alleged negligence not occurred. Rights-based theories, at least, must hold that to be wronged (impermissibly harmed) requires one to have been made worse off relative to one's alternatives.[70] This is simply because to have one's rights violated presupposes that one's rights could have been fulfilled. To be deprived of a right is to be put in a situation that is different from the situation that one would have been in had one's right been recognised. It follows that (from a rights-based perspective) no wrong could be done *to a child* by merely allowing *that child* to be brought into existence, *no matter how bad that existence*. A parallel argument can be made for duty-based theories, which only differ from rights-based theories in that they reject the idea that the benefit of any duty is necessarily waivable by the beneficiary. In my view, this is an implication of moral theories that define wrongs as distributive and individual-affecting.[71] Not all moral theories will, however, define wrongs or harms in this way. Utilitarians could argue that bringing a child into existence is a wrong, if that existence would overall be a burden rather than a benefit. For some utilitarians, it can be wrong to bring a child into a state of disutility, even if that child could not have existed in any other state.[72] (Arguably, whether or not the wrong is truly to the child is not important to moral theories that are aggregative, rather than distributive.)

The approach of virtue-theories also stands out, because for these theories it makes no sense to define harm and wrong in an action-based way. The focus of such theories will be on the motives and behaviour of the parties, relative to the virtues. Yet, there is no reason why such theories could not hold that to be wronged could be defined as being the subject of unvirtuous conduct. Similarly, there is no reason why compromise positions have to be incompatible with the idea of being harmed or wronged where one has not been deprived of any alternative existence. It has, for example, been argued that the law on abortion for fetal handicap and on the withdrawal of treatment of disabled neonates implies that some lives are "not worth preserving".[73] If these laws are properly understood as protecting the child's interests,

---

[69] To make matters more complicated, Feinberg holds that a child could still have been *wronged* without being *harmed*. According to Feinberg, a child that has not been made worse off cannot have been harmed, but that child would still have been wronged where its condition is "so severe as to render his life not worth living" (1984, 102). He also argues that where a child has not been harmed or wronged, the mother's act can still be wrong where it involves "wantonly introducing a certain evil into the world" (Feinberg 1984, 103). Cf. Harris 1998, ch.4.

[70] I have presented the following argument elsewhere: see Pattinson 2002b.

[71] The response of many theorists to the non-identity problem has been to reject this conception of a wrong (see e.g. Brock 1995).

[72] See e.g. Harris 1998 and 2000.

[73] Morris and Saintier 2003, 177. See also Priaulx 2002, 341.

rather than the interests of other affected persons, this implies that the law rejects a distributive, individual-affecting view of what constitutes a wrong to an individual.

9.4.2.2 Strategy two

The second justificatory strategy for wrongful life actions requires a wrong to have been done, but that wrong need not be to the child claimant, as long as it is sufficient to justify holding the defendant liable to pay damages directed towards the claimant's needs. This strategy is controversial. Those theories holding that all wrongs stem from duties owed to individuals (rights-based and duty-based theories) might well consider that it is more appropriate for the action to be brought by, or in the name of, that individual. Theories recognising victimless wrongs will have no such difficulties. Nonetheless, whether wrongful life actions are needed to perform this function (of distributive justice) depends on the existing mechanisms for providing for the child's needs and the suitability of alternative mechanisms. It has been argued that,

> In the UK, . . . there may be somewhat reduced need for the wrongful life action to be available to reinforce principles of social justice. If standards of public provision of health services fall, however, the action may be necessary for maintenance of individual welfare.[74]

The existence of the NHS addresses most medical needs, whether the child's other care-based needs are adequately addressed has been questioned.[75] According to Morris and Saintier,

> it is generally acknowledged that current social welfare support for those who are disabled and those who care for them is inadequate and that there is little sign of political will to meet in full the needs of these children.[76]

Those relying on this strategy could allow damages to track the child's needs and the defendant's wrong, but the purpose of such damages would not be to put the child in the position that he would have been in had the defendant's wrong not occurred. This would make the compensatory rationale different from that of tort actions generally. In *McKay*, their Lordships expressed concerns about the absence of principle by which damages can be granted. This strategy provides a principle, albeit one that sits uncomfortably with existing common law principles. This strategy would probably require the common law to operate on the basis of a legal fiction, i.e. an assumption invoked as a matter of procedure that could well be false. Lee has, for example, argued that,

---

[74] Dickens 1989, 95.

[75] Note, however, the recently implemented Children Act 2004.

[76] Morris and Saintier 2003, 170. For what is arguably further reliance on this second strategy, see Morris and Saintier 2003, 191 and 193.

In order to satisfy the demands of the legal concepts of damage and causation, the plaintiff finds it necessary to assert the preferability of non-existence over life. This is a legal fiction which conceals a far more basic assertion—that handicapped children need financial support.[77]

9.4.2.3 Other comments

Many commentators have rejected the approach of *McKay*. Strategy one is popular, with a number of theorists arguing that the doctor has a duty to the claimant.[78] Some commentators have, however, argued against allowing wrongful life claims. Harris has argued that such actions ought to be rejected in just about all cases.[79] He argues that a child who has a life that is "worth living" has made a net benefit, whereas a child whose life truly is not "worth living" should be compensated as of right and not have to rely on a negligence action. In effect, he is arguing that both strategy one (relying on the wrongs done to the child) and strategy two (relying on the child's needs in the absence of a wrong to the child) point against allowing wrongful life actions. He makes this clear when he concludes that if a disabled child should be compensated, then, "Their need should be the trigger for the compensation, not the claim that their need results from wrongdoing".[80] Harris does, however, favour state compensation schemes over negligence actions generally.[81]

In situations where the child's claim would be for wrongful life, the mother will often have a claim for wrongful conception or wrongful birth. The availability of wrongful life actions would, however, have practical significance where the child cannot gain from any damages awarded to the mother (e.g. where the mother has no claim or has given the child up for adoption).

9.5 Actions brought by the parent: Legal issues

Wrongful conception and birth actions arise where the parents sue in circumstances that would be characterised as wrongful life or prenatal injury actions if the child were the claimant. They also arise where prenatal negligence results in the birth of a healthy child who would not fall within the remit of wrongful life or prenatal injury because the complaint is entirely that of the parents.

The history of wrongful conception and birth actions is chequered. One continuous theme is that the courts have been concerned with whether the prenatal negligence resulted in a child that is healthy or disabled, rather than

---

[77] Lee 1989, 189.
[78] See e.g. Jackson 1996, and Mason and Laurie 2006, 196 (who argue that a handicapped fetus could be understood as having an interest in not being born in a disadvantaged condition). Strategy two also has supporters, e.g. Morris and Saintier 2003 (esp. 170, 191, and 193) invoke arguments that fit most comfortably with strategy two.
[79] See Harris 1998, 117–119.
[80] Harris 1998, 119.
[81] See Harris 1997, discussed in Ch.3.

with whether it is an action for wrongful conception or birth, or has resulted in an undesired child or undesired traits.

9.5.1 Prenatal negligence leading to the birth of a healthy child

Where prenatal negligence results in the birth of a healthy but undesired child, the courts could adopt a number of approaches: granting full compensation, limited compensation (e.g. compensation for the pain, discomfort and inconvenience of the pregnancy and childbirth, but not the cost of rearing the child), reduced compensation (e.g. reduced by a sum representing the benefits of having a child), or no compensation. Different judges have been variously attracted by all these options.

In *Udale v Bloomsbury AHA*, the costs of bringing up a healthy child resulting from a negligently performed sterilisation operation were held to be irrecoverable.[82] Jupp J. rejected recovery of these cost on the grounds of public policy, declaring that the birth of a child "is a blessing and an occasion for rejoicing".[83] The notion of a "blessing" in play here differed from that of the parents, as (like most wrongful conception cases) this was a case of an undesired child. In *Emeh v Kensington and Chelsea and Westminster AHA*, the Court of Appeal then overruled *Udale*, holding the costs of bringing up a child were recoverable.[84] In one of the cases following *Emeh* damages were even allowed in respect of the costs of the future private education of a healthy child.[85] Then, some fifteen years later, the House of Lords overruled *Emeh* in *McFarlane v Tayside Health Board*.[86]

The claimants, Mr and Mrs McFarlane, had followed negligent advice to the effect that Mr McFarlane was no longer fertile following his vasectomy operation. The result was Catherine, their fifth child. A majority of their Lordships allowed Mrs McFarlane to recover for the pain and inconvenience of the pregnancy and birth, along with those financial losses that were directly attributable to the pregnancy and birth.[87] Their Lordships unanimously rejected the couple's larger claim for the costs of rearing Catherine, as constituting purely economic loss. They gave differing reasons.

Lord Steyn directly appealed to considerations of justice and morality, relying on the principle of distributive justice.[88] He accepted that "corrective justice"

---

[82] [1983] 2 All E.R. 522. Damages for the pain and inconvenience of the pregnancy and childbirth were allowed.

[83] [1983] 2 All E.R. 522 at 531.

[84] [1985] Q.B. 1012.

[85] *Benarr v Kettering HA* (1988) 138 N.L.J. Rep. 179. See also *Allen v Bloomsbury HA* [1993] 1 All E.R. 651, 662. However, these cases did not award full compensation, as the Court of Appeal in *Thake v Maurice* [1986] Q.B. 644 had held that the costs to the mother in rearing a healthy child generally were to be off set by the benefits derived from bringing a child to maturity.

[86] [2000] 2 A.C. 59. This was a Scottish case, but it was conceded that the law of England and Wales was the same on this issue. See also the later case of *Greenfield v Flather* [2001] EWCA Civ 113.

[87] Lord Millet dissented on both points, whereas Lord Clyde dissenting only on recovery of the directly attributable financial costs.

[88] [2000] 2 A.C. 59 at 82.

would look solely at the harm that the defendants had inflicted on the claimants without justification and allow recovery of the costs of rearing Catherine. However, his Lordship reasoned that the alternative view of distributive justice,

> requires a focus on the just distribution of burdens and losses among members of a society. If the matter is approached in this way, it may become relevant to ask commuters on the Underground the following question: "Should the parents of an unwanted but healthy child be able to sue the doctor or hospital for compensation equivalent to the cost of bringing up the child for the years of his or her minority, i.e. until about 18 years?" My Lords, I am firmly of the view that an overwhelming number of ordinary men and women would answer the question with an emphatic "No".[89]

Unfortunately, Lord Steyn provides no reason for prioritising corrective over distributive justice (see further Ch.3, 3.81). Further, his reliance on the judge's intuitions on prevailing community standards requires justification. As presented, it smacks of being a compromise position underpinned by moral intuitionism. His Lordships' invocation of a hypothetical opinion poll shows that he sees his underlying moral intuitions on this topic as reflecting communal values.[90] Thus, Lord Steyn appears to presuppose a form of communitarianism.

Lord Millet held that the law regarded the birth of a healthy, normal baby as a blessing and not as a detriment.[91] Making clear that this was just as much a moral as a legal conclusion, his Lordship declared that treating the birth of a healthy baby as a matter for compensation was "morally offensive".[92] On this point, Lord Steyn had also expressed the view that the traveller on the Underground would regard the birth of a healthy child "as a valuable and good thing".[93] Drawing on an example given by Waller L.J. in a later case, it has to be asked where the benefit would be for a poor single mother with four children who will suffer from a mental breakdown upon the birth of her fifth unwanted child.[94] As Waller L.J. points out, under *McFarlane* she won't be able to recover the costs of caring for the child even if this would alleviate the crisis—the birth of an additional healthy child is conclusively regarded as a benefit.

The other Law Lords cloaked their moral judgments. Lord Slynn sought to express himself in purely legal language, but there is an unavoidable moral element to denying that a duty of care exists on the basis that it was not fair, just or reasonable to impose on the doctor for the costs of bringing up a child.[95] Lord Clyde (and less directly Lord Hope) opined that to relieve the parents of the financial obligations of caring for their child went beyond reasonable restitution for the wrong done.[96]

---

[89] [2000] 2 A.C. 59 at 82.
[90] Note the critical comments of Hale L.J. in *Parkinson v St James and Seacroft University Hospital NHS Trust* [2001] EWCA Civ 530, para.82.
[91] [2000] 2 A.C. 59 at 111–114, esp. 114.
[92] [2000] 2 A.C. 59 at 111 and 114.
[93] [2000] 2 A.C. 59 at 82.
[94] *Rees v Darlington Memorial Hospital NHS Trust* [2002] EWCA Civ 88, para. 53.
[95] [2000] 2 A.C. 59 at 76.
[96] [2000] 2 A.C. 59 at 105–106 (Lord Clyde) and 97 (Lord Hope). Cf. Lord Millet, 109.

McFarlane has been subject to powerful criticism. The decision blocks recovery for damages that would be recoverable under ordinary negligence principles, largely for reasons of legal policy.[97] Australia's highest federal court (the High Court) has refused to follow the decision.[98] One commentator went so far as to declare: "I can think of few decisions that are—to their very core— as odious, unsound, and unsafe as this one".[99] Nonetheless, the House of Lords has since refused to reconsider *McFarlane*.[100] Also, the Court of Appeal has rejected attempts to distinguish the case by claiming the lost future earnings (resulting from giving up a job to look after an unplanned child), rather than the costs of rearing the child.[101] Claimants have, however, been more successful where the child has been born disabled.

9.5.2 Prenatal negligence leading to the birth of a disabled child

The House of Lords in *McFarlane* restricted their decision to prenatal negligence claims for the birth of healthy children. In *Parkinson v St James and Seacroft University Hospital NHS Trust*, the Court of Appeal held that the *extra expenses* associated with bringing up a child with a "significant disability" could be claimed.[102] This case concerned a claim for the negligent performance of a sterilisation operation on Mrs Parkinson, who was then living with her husband and her four existing children in a cramped two-bedroomed house.[103] The result was the birth of Scott, who had significant disabilities. How significant these were was to be decided at trial. Their Lordships did comment on what would constitute a "significant disability". Brooke L.J. said that this would have to be decided on a case-by-case basis. He opined that it would cover both mental and physical disabilities, but not "minor defects or inconveniences".[104] His Lordship also agreed with Hale L.J., who indicated that the degree of disability was to be determined by reference to the statutory definitions in the Children Act 1989 and the legislation used since the establishment of the welfare state to identify those whose special needs require special services.[105] Sir Martin Nourse agreed with both.

Section 17(11) of the Children Act 1989 reads,

---

[97] See Pedain 2004, 19. Cf. Beever (2007a, 386–404) who comes to a slightly different view on the application of ordinarily negligence principles (understood in terms of corrective justice).

[98] *Cattanach v Mechior* [2003] H.C.A. 38. See also the critical appraisal of the decision and its effects given by Hale L.J. in *Parkinson v St James and Seacroft University Hospital NHS Trust* [2001] EWCA Civ 530.

[99] Cameron-Perry 1999, 1888.

[100] *Rees v Darlington Memorial Hospital NHS Trust* [2003] UKHL 52.

[101] *Greenfield v Flather* [2001] EWCA Civ 113.

[102] [2001] EWCA Civ 530.

[103] By the time of Scott's birth the pressure of an additional child had apparently led to Mr Parkinson leaving the family home.

[104] [2001] EWCA Civ 530, para.52.

[105] [2001] EWCA Civ 530, para.91.

> a child is disabled if he is blind, deaf or dumb or suffers from a mental disorder of any kind or is substantially and permanently handicapped by illness, injury or congenital deformity or such other disability as may be prescribed.

This, given by Hale L.J. as a definition of "significant disability", is a lot narrower than the definition of "disabled" employed in regard to a child's prenatal injury claim under the 1976 Act (see 9.3.1 above). Moreover, Hale L.J. firmly rejected any implication that a disabled child has any less dignity or status, rather awarding damages for the birth of a disabled child "simply acknowledges that he costs more".[106]

Dicta in *Parkinson* suggested that wrongful conception cases such as this might be different from wrongful birth cases.[107] However, in *Groom v Selby*, the Court of Appeal held that the costs of the disability could be claimed when a negligent failure to detect that the woman was pregnant had deprived her of the opportunity to abort a fetus that was found to be suffering from meningitis shortly after birth.[108] The Court of Appeal (including Brooke L.J. and Hale L.J.) held that wrongful birth cases were to be treated in the same way as failed sterilisation (wrongful conception) cases.

There are clearly many scenarios in which prenatal negligence can lead to the birth of a disabled child. *Parkinson* was a case in which the prenatal negligence had caused an *undesired child*. Claims where prenatal negligence has caused an *undesired trait* are even stronger, because the disability will be the very thing that the claimant was trying to avoid. Consider, for example, the negligent use of preimplantation genetic diagnosis leading to the birth of a child with the very disability that the parents were seeking to avoid.

The status of *Parkinson* was considered (obiter) by the House of Lords in *Rees v Darlington Memorial Hospital NHS Trust*.[109]

9.5.3 Rees v Darlington

In *Rees*, the baby was born healthy, but the claimant herself was disabled. Mrs Rees was virtually blind and had sought sterilisation because she feared that she would be unable to properly care for a child. Unfortunately the operation was negligently performed, resulting in the birth of a healthy boy. A seven-member panel of the House of Lords refused to overrule *McFarlane*, but only a bare majority of four of their Lordships rejected her claim for the extra costs of child care occasioned by her disability. Instead, the majority allowed Ms Rees a conventional award of £15,000 to recognise the harm that she had suffered. This was additional to the damages granted in respect of the pregnancy and the birth.

---

[106] [2001] EWCA Civ 530, para.90.
[107] [2001] EWCA Civ 530 para.46 (Brooke L.J.).
[108] [2001] EWCA Civ 1522. There was also a string of post-*McFarlane* first instance decisions on this issue.
[109] [2003] UKHL 52.

Lord Bingham proposed the conventional sum of £15,000 to "afford some measure of recognition of the wrong done".[110] This attracted the support of Lords Nicholls, Millett, and Scott.[111] Of the dissenting judges, Lords Steyn and Hope emphatically rejected the conventional sum, whereas Lord Hutton was silent on the matter. Lord Steyn declared that there was no precedent to support the imposition of conventional sums, it was "contrary to principle", and Lord Bingham's suggestion (not taken up by the majority) that it should also apply to cases where the child was disabled would overrule *Parkinson* without appeal.[112] He thought that such an approach was more appropriate for Parliament and then "it would be a hugely controversial legislative measure". Lord Hope supported this reasoning and expressed concern about the lack of a non-arbitrary method of setting the amount of the conventional sum.[113] Indeed, it has been pointed out that the choice of £15,000 is £5,000 more than what you get under the Fatal Accidents Act 1976 for losing a child through another's negligence.[114]

What implications does this decision have for *Parkinson*? While not deciding this issue, all their Lordships expressed an obiter view on *Parkinson*. The three dissenting judges expressed support for the decision,[115] whereas Lords Bingham, Nicholls, and Scott expressed disapproval.[116] Lord Millet expressed muted support for *Parkinson*, declaring that he did not find drawing a distinction between a healthy and disabled child to be "morally offensive" but wished "to keep the point open".[117] Thus, a bare majority considered *Parkinson* to be good law. It is hard to avoid the conclusion that the way that a future House of Lords will jump will largely depend on its constitution. A five panel decision could swing either way.

Lord Scott offered an interesting take on the issue. He rejected the distinction between healthy and disabled children and, instead, distinguished prenatal negligence leading to an undesired trait from that leading to an undesired child:

> In my opinion, . . . a distinction may need to be drawn between a case where the avoidance of the birth of a child with a disability is the very reason why the parent or parents sought the medical treatment or services to avoid conception that, in the event, were negligently provided and a case where the medical treatment or services were sought simply to avoid conception. *Parkinson* was a case in the latter category.[118]

Thus, Lord Scott holds that only a parent facing an undesired trait should be able to claim for the extra cost of the disability, and not a parent facing an undesired

---

[110] [2003] UKHL 52, para.8. Lord Bingham was building on a suggestion by Lord Millett in *McFarlane*.

[111] [2003] UKHL 52, paras 17, 19; 125; and 148; respectively.

[112] [2003] UKHL 52, paras 40–47.

[113] [2003] UKHL 52, paras 70–77.

[114] See Pedain 2004, 21.

[115] See paras 35 (Lord Steyn), 57 (Lord Hope), and 91–93 (Lord Hutton).

[116] See paras 9, 18, and 145/147, respectively.

[117] [2003] UKHL 52, para.112.

[118] [2003] UKHL 52, para.147.

child. This seems odd because it is arguable that parents faced with an undesired child have lost even more than those faced with an undesired trait, because in the former case they did not even accept the cost of raising a child *as such*, let alone the cost of a disabled child.

9.5.4 Other legal issues

The law as it currently stands on parental claims for prenatal negligence is thus:

    (a) the mother can recover damages for the pain and distress of pregnancy and childbirth, as well as any directly attributable financial losses;

    (b) a couple cannot claim for the costs of bringing up a healthy child, but they can claim for the additional costs of rearing a disabled child; and

    (c) a disabled mother is entitled to an additional "conventional" award of £15,000.

There are a number of legal issues not yet considered in this chapter.[119] One of which is whether the failure to abort or have the child adopted could break the chain of causation. In *Emeh*, at first instance Park J. had accepted that the Mrs Emeh's failure to have an abortion constituted a *novus actus*, breaking the chain of causation between the defendant's negligence and her loss. This was reversed on appeal.[120] This case did not concern a mother who knows that the child would be born disabled. On this point, it is interesting to note that Slade L.J. added the proviso "save in the most exceptional circumstances" and Purchas L.J. suggested that he might have reached a different decision had "the sole motivation" of the claimant been to advance a legal claim.[121] This point was not argued in *McFarlane*, but their Lordships nonetheless rejected the idea that the failure to have an abortion could break the chain of causation.[122]

Causation does, however, reveal a key difference between a wrongful conception and a wrongful birth claim. In a wrongful birth claim, the claimant has to prove that, if the prenatal negligence had not occurred, she would have terminated the pregnancy.[123] In contrast, in a wrongful conception action the

---

[119] In particularly, the classification of damage (as personal injury or purely economic loss) for the purposes of the Limitation Act 1980, which imposes a 3-year limitation period on personal injury cases and a 6-year period on any other type of negligence case. See further Whitfield 2004, 826–828, 833–834.

[120] [1985] Q.B. 1012.

[121] [1985] Q.B. 1012 at 1024 and 1027, respectively.

[122] See [2003] UKHL 52 at 74 (Lord Slynn), 81 (Lord Steyn), 97 (Lord Hope), 104/105 (Lord Clyde), and 113 (Lord Millet).

[123] See *Deriche v Ealing Hospital NHS Trust* [2003] EWHC 3104, where the claim was dismissed because the claimant did not establish that she would have terminated her pregnancy had she been properly advised on the risk of serious damage to her child arising from the chicken pox she had contracted during pregnancy.

claimant only has to prove that measures would have been taken to prevent the conception or the conception would not have occurred.

9.6 Actions brought by the parent: Ethical issues

In this area of law, judges have been unusually candid about their reliance on moral principles. As a result, many of the opposing ethical arguments are well represented in the case law.

9.6.1 Autonomy and human dignity

The major ethical tension is over the value to be attached to the autonomous decision of those deprived of the opportunity to avoid having a child or a child with particular traits. As Lord Millett noted in *Rees*, in a wrongful conception case, "The pregnancy and birth of a child are the very things which the defendants are employed to prevent".[124] In any prenatal negligence case (whether for wrongful conception or birth) leading to an undesired child, the birth of a child is the very thing that the claimant(s) sought to avoid. Similarly, in any prenatal negligence case leading to undesired traits, the birth of a child with or without the relevant traits is the very thing that the claimant(s) sought. To deny full compensation is to deny full legal protection to the autonomy interests of reluctant parents.

Chapter 1 (1.4.1) invoked the work of Beyleveld and Brownsword to distinguish two conceptions of dignity: "dignity as empowerment" and "dignity as constraint".[125] Dignity as empowerment captures the autonomy-focused approach of rights-based theories, demanding that one's capacity for free and informed choice be recognised and that one's particular choices be respected. Dignity as constraint captures the more paternalistic concerns of duty-based and compromise positions such as those of Kant, Catholics, and communitarians. Dignity as constraint adheres to values such as the sanctity of life, irrespective of the background autonomous choices made. Utilitarians, while rejecting the "human dignity" label, have concerns that are more consistent with the empowerment camp.

In *McFarlane*, it is clear that their Lordships relied on values consistent with dignity as constraint (as evidenced by the emphasis put on the value of human life) to rule out full compensation.[126] As quoted above, Lords Steyn and Millett both made it clear that they regarded the birth of a normal baby as a good, irrespective of the autonomous decision of the reluctant parents. Lord Clyde also recognised that "the 'sanctity of human life' can be put forward as a ground for

---

[124] [2003] EWHC 3104, para.108.
[125] See Beyleveld and Brownsword 2001.
[126] See Brownsword 2003a, 429–430.

justifying the law's refusal of a remedy for a wrongful conception".[127] Reliance was also placed on the value of human life by their Lordships in *Rees*.[128] In supporting the majority decision to award the conventional sum, Lord Millett explicitly recognised the competing conception of human dignity,

> I still regard the proper outcome in all these cases is to award the parents a modest conventional sum by way of general damages, not for the birth of the child, but for the denial of an important aspect of their personal autonomy, viz. the right to limit the size of their family. *This is an important aspect of human dignity*, which is increasingly being regarded as an important human right which should be protected by law.[129]

It is this conception of dignity that dominates Hale L.J.'s judgment in *Parkinson*[130] and the counterargument to the decision in *McFarlane*.

9.6.2 Other ethical arguments

A plethora of ethical arguments have been presented in the context of parental claims for prenatal negligence. The claim that the parents should have aborted or adopted is particularly controversial. According to one commentator,

> In situations in which parents are pleased to keep their children, it is suggested that it is straining the concept of an "injury" to state that one has been suffered by them. It appears contradictory to state that on the one hand that a child is so unwanted that damages should be available for its very existence and upbringing, while on the other confirming that it is so wanted by these parents that they have chosen to keep the child.[131]

With respect, there is no contradiction between the claim that a child was unwanted and the failure to abort or adopt. A failure to have a child aborted or adopted demonstrates only that one considers these options to be worse than keeping that child, it does not demonstrate that one's free choice has been respected. Here supporters of the two conceptions of dignity outlined above are likely to want to reject this argument for different reasons. Supporters of the empowerment conception would emphasise that autonomous choices should be supported in favour of both decisions against having more children and decisions in favour of keeping any that are conceived. Supporters of the constraint conception, at least insofar as they also hold that the embryo or fetus has full moral status, would reject the idea that the parents in any sense ought to have aborted or adopted.

---

[127] [2000] 2 A.C. 59 at 100. Though, he went on to hold that is to be set against the public policy in favour of calculable family planning.
[128] [2003] UKHL 52, paras 16 (Lord Bingham), 68 (Lord Hope), and 134/135 (Lord Scott).
[129] [2003] UKHL 52, para.123 (my emphasis).
[130] [2001] EWCA Civ 530, esp. paras 56, 66–71.
[131] Jackson 1996, 377.

The debate over whether allowing the birth of a disabled child should be recognised as a legal injury is just as divisive. According to Jackson,

> the law should not declare that the birth of a disabled child is an injury to others (in wrongful birth claims, to the child's parents). Society should focus upon ensuring that those with disabilities are treated as equals, not that their very existence constitutes an injury to other members of society.[132]

With respect, a distinction could be drawn between claiming that the existence of the child constitutes a wrong and that depriving the parents of the opportunity to avoid that existence constitutes a wrong. There are, however, a number of ethical arguments that could be in play here. Those theories holding that a disabled fetus has moral status could consistently hold that the failure to offer the parents the opportunity to abort a disabled fetus is not a wrong (because abortion in such circumstances would be wrong).[133] It could also be claimed that treating the birth of a disabled child as an injury is likely to encourage or facilitate increased prejudice against those members of society with those disabilities. This claim would require empirical support.[134]

The debate over whether allowing prenatal negligence actions could lead to psychological costs to the child also requires empirical support. It is equally probable that the subject of a successful award will be grateful for the greater freedom that an award of damages gave to his family. In *Thake v Maurice*, Peter Pain J. expressed the view that the child in question was unlikely to feel rejection following an award of damages: "by the time she comes to consider this judgment (if she ever does) she will, I think, welcome it as a means of having made life somewhat easier for her family."[135] Logically, not wanting another child or a child with that disability does not imply that the parents do not now love the existing child. In the case of a disabled child, the parents might actually have the undesired traits themselves.

9.7 Conclusion

We have seen how prenatal negligence actions can provide a mechanism by which redress can be obtained for certain types of grievance. Novel factual situations could lead to further developments in this area, especially with regard to negligent (non-)use of advances in genetic medicine. Negligent future applications of technologies such as preimplantation genetic diagnosis (Ch.8), cloning (Ch.10), and gene therapy (Ch.12) are likely to encourage incremental extension of the existing boundaries of liability.[136] The actions examined in this chapter

---

[132] Jackson 1996, 379.
[133] See Chs 1 (1.4.3) and 7 (7.2).
[134] See e.g. Pattinson 2002a, ch.6, 6.3.
[135] [1986] Q.B. 644 at 667.
[136] See e.g. the situations explored in Brownsword 2003a.

could therefore become key "genomic torts", by which I mean torts addressing grievances arising from the (non)use of genetic information and technologies.

Even in their current form prenatal negligence actions raise more issues than is at first apparent. This chapter has argued that moral theory can illuminate many of these issues. While the five major groups of moral theories presented in Ch.1 do not always have clear implications, they do rule out certain approaches to at least wrongful life and parental actions for prenatal negligence. Much is still left to the choice of a particular theory within these camps, which is the focus of the final chapter.

9.8 Further reading

Brazier, Margaret (1999) "Liberty Responsibility and Maternity." 52 *Current Legal Problems* 359–391.

Brownsword, Roger (2003) "An Interest in Human Dignity as the Basis for Genomic Torts." 42 *Washburn Law Journal* 413–487.

   (Pages 413–430 are relevant to prenatal negligence actions.)

Whitfield, Adrian (2004) "Actions Arising from Birth." In Andrew Grubb (ed.) *Principles of Medical Law*. (Oxford: Oxford University Press, 2004), 789–851.

Chapter 10

....

EMBRYO RESEARCH, EMBRYONIC STEM CELLS, AND CLONING

10.1 Introduction

Few developments are truly revolutionary. Few are truly dramatic. Few overthrow established beliefs or systems. The birth of what was to become the most famous sheep in history is probably an exception. That sheep, Dolly, was the product of asexual reproduction.[1] As the world's media unhesitatingly announced, she was a clone. She was produced by a technique that only 13 years before had been dismissed as "biologically impossible" by two well respected developmental biologists.[2] Dolly opened up the possibility of cloning existing

---

[1] See Wilmut et al. 1997.
[2] McGrath and Solter 1984. For a wider discussion of the history of cloning, see Kolata 1998.

human beings. Only a year later other possibilities were brought a step closer when it was announced that embryonic stem cells had been successfully extracted from non-cloned human embryos.[3] Dolly has now been dead for years,[4] but many of the legal and ethical issues she evoked are still alive.

The issues raised by human cloning, embryonic stem cell research, and embryo experimentation form the subject matter of this chapter. The regulation of these technologies has a global context. Any regulatory attempts will be affected by patient, researcher, and investor tourism, and by developments elsewhere. These technologies also have a medical context; they enable and bring us closer to new medical practices.

This chapter will not examine the general regulation of the creation of embryos outside the body, for which see Ch.8. Nor will this chapter examine the regulation of research on human beings who have already been born, for which see Ch.11. Only passing attention will be given to stem cell research on cells derived from sources other than embryos and research on fetuses developing in the womb. We will begin with a brief overview of the underlying science.

For convenience, in this chapter I do not distinguish between an embryo and a fetus. Unless otherwise apparent I use the term embryo to include the fetus, i.e. the developing human from eight weeks gestation until birth.

10.1.1 The 1990 and 2008 Acts

Research on embryos, including the derivation of embryonic stem cells and the creation of cloned embryos, is governed by the Human Fertilisation and Embryology Act 1990 (*hereafter the 1990 Act*). This Act prohibits some activities and for others requires a licence from the Human Fertilisation and Embryology Authority (*the HFEA*). Over the last decade the HFEA's jurisdiction has faced sustained attack from groups opposed to the destruction of embryos. Legal challenge has, in particular, been made to the HFEA's licensing jurisdiction with regard to the creation and use of cloned and hybrid embryos.[5] Ultimately these challenges have failed as the courts have (in my view quite properly) given a wide, purposive interpretation to the Act's provisions. The rapidity of social and scientific developments did, nonetheless, put some strain on the Act, leading to the enactment of the Human Fertilisation and Embryology Act 2008 (*the 2008 Act*). This amends, rather than replaces, the 1990 Act. At the time of writing it is yet to come into force, though the key provisions are intended to come into force in October 2009. This chapter has therefore been written as if the 2008 Act is already in force. Any other approach would have either made this chapter disproportionately large or rendered it out of date soon after publication.

---

[3] See Thomson et al. 1998.
[4] Having been put to sleep: see Vogel 2003.
[5] See *R. (Bruno Quintavalle) v Secretary of State for Health* [2003] UKHL 13 and BBC 2008d, respectively. See also *R. (Josephine Quintavalle) v HFEA* [2005] UKHL 28.

10.2 The science

Biological science is advancing rapidly and much of it is not easy for the layperson to understand. Fortunately you don't have to swallow the bottle to get at the liquid inside. Only a basic understanding of modern biological and reproductive science is needed to appreciate the legal and ethical issues raised by its application to humans. Some understanding is, however, essential. We cannot understand the regulation of embryo research unless we understand that embryos can be created outside the body. It has been possible to fertilise a human egg outside the body (known as *in vitro* fertilisation or IVF) for over 30 years. The development of IVF as a method of human reproduction required considerable research using gametes (sperm and eggs) and embryos. Publicity surrounding the creation of Dolly, announced in February 1997, drew the public's attention to the possibility of a human clone. Just as many were beginning to understand what cloning actually is, it started to be linked to a type of cell that few non-scientists realised existed: the stem cell. For reasons that will be outlined shortly, attention initially focused on embryonic stem cells, though other types of stem cell are now receiving increased attention. This section will briefly explain the science behind embryo research, cloning, and stem cells.

10.2.1 Embryo research

Embryos can be used for research purposes that are *therapeutic*, in the sense of intended to benefit the embryo itself, or *non-therapeutic*, in the sense of not intended to benefit the embryo. For convenience, throughout this chapter the term "embryo research" is used to refer to non-therapeutic experimentation on embryos, and the term "experimental treatment" is used to refer to innovative procedures carried out on an embryo that are intended to benefit that embryo. This is an important distinction, because those opposed to the harm or destructive use of embryos are not required to oppose experimental treatment.

Embryo research has had a dramatic impact on the development and use of assisted reproduction techniques and continues to have great scientific potential. In particular, research involving the creation and/or use of embryos outside of the body (*in vitro* embryos) has the potential to

(a) improve basic scientific knowledge;

(b) improve the selection of suitable gametes or embryos for assisted reproduction purposes;

(c) increase the possibilities for creating functional *in vitro* embryos and the understanding of those possibilities (e.g. research into new fertilisation and cloning techniques);

(d) improve the development of *in vitro* embryos (e.g. research directed towards improving the quality of the culture media);

(e) improve the quality of *in vitro* embryos (by, e.g., genetic manipulation techniques); and

(f) lead to the therapeutic use of embryonic cells, particularly embryonic stem cells.

Some of these aims are more ethically controversial than others. In practice, an individual research project might have multiple aims and scientific research often produces unexpected results, which means that research initially performed with one set of aims might actually achieve or facilitate the achievement of other aims.

Some research can only be performed if embryos are created specifically for the purpose of research. According to Gunning,

> Research involving the creation of human embryos is needed particularly in the development of techniques involving gamete manipulation, such as intra-cytoplasmic sperm injection (ICSI) with immature sperm, in order to determine that normal fertilization and embryonic development is likely to result. Allowing research on spare embryos, which have been created for treatment purposes, is not appropriate for this type of research, which nevertheless underpins the safety of assisted conception techniques.[6]

Nonetheless, as will become apparent, specifically creating embryos for research purposes is even more controversial than research on existing embryos.

10.2.2 Cloning

You are the product of fertilisation. Your parent's gametes joined together and developed into an embryo. Occasionally embryos split into two, producing identical (monozygotic) twins. Identical twins are *genetically* identical;[7] they are naturally occurring clones. Embryos created outside the body could be artificially divided in this way to deliberately create human clones, which is known as embryo splitting. Dolly opened up another possibility. Dolly was the product of joining an egg with a body (somatic) cell, rather than with sperm. That somatic cell was taken from the mammary gland of a sheep—Dolly was named after Dolly Parton. The nucleus was removed from an egg and replaced with the nucleus taken from the mammary cell. (If you want a visual image, imagine the cells as chicken eggs. Pictured in this way, the Dolly technique involves replacing the yoke of one egg with the yoke of a different type of egg.)[8]

---

[6] Gunning 2001, 427–428. See also House of Lords Select Committee 2002, para.4.28.
[7] Except for spontaneous genetic mutations.
[8] A human egg carries only half of the genes required to develop, so the chicken egg from which the yoke is removed should be pictured as starting with only half a yoke.

The product was then encouraged to develop by an electric shock, resulting in a cloned sheep.

Dolly was not quite genetically identical to the sheep from which the mammary cell was taken. DNA, which forms the genetic material of most organisms, is carried in the cell nucleus *and* also inside sack-like bodies (called mitochondria) within the cells.[9] (Imagine the mitochondria as little sacks floating in the egg white.) The Dolly technique replaces the egg's nuclear DNA but leaves the mitochondrial DNA.[10] In humans the mitochondria carry 37 of our estimated 25,000 genes.[11] These 37 genes are crucial. More than 50 inherited metabolic diseases are thought to be caused by mitochondrial DNA.[12] Since your mitochondria always come from your mother, you will share your mitochondrial DNA with all those to whom you are biologically related through the maternal line.[13] It follows that unless the provider of the somatic cell is from the same maternal line as the provider of the egg, a child produced by the Dolly technique would not quite be genetically identical to the person cloned.

In theory, a clone could be produced from any living somatic cell in your body. Your clone would not, of course, be an exactly replica of you. Even if you were genetically identical to your clone (like identical twins), you would not be the same person as your clone. We are more than our genes. Our appearance is also shaped by environmental influences (e.g. nutrients in the womb) and our character is also shaped by our upbringing, experiences, and ideas.

Human cloning technology has greater potential than the creation of cloned children. A distinction is often drawn between reproductive and non-reproductive cloning. This is a distinction tracking the aim or result. Both reproductive and non-reproductive cloning involve the use of cloning technology to create a functional embryo. The difference is whether the aim or result is the creation of a child from that cloned embryo. *Reproductive cloning* involves the use of cloning technology as a presently untested and uncertain reproductive technique. In contrast, *non-reproductive cloning* does not involve the implantation or gestation of the cloned embryo, but its destructive use. Since non-reproductive cloning is primarily envisaged as a means of developing therapeutic products, it is sometimes called *therapeutic cloning*. While many objections have been made to this terminology, they all reduce to fears that unjustified implications will be drawn from these labels. Opponents of embryo research, for example, fear that the term "non-reproductive" will lead some to believe that the research subject (the cloned embryo) could not have been used for reproductive purposes.[14] Once warned against drawing such illegitimate inferences, I can see no further objection to drawing a distinction

---

[9] DNA is the acronym of deoxyribonucleic acid. DNA molecules consist of two sugar-phosphate backbones that wind round each other to form a double helix, from which bases jut inwards like the steps of a ladder (see Watson and Crick 1953).

[10] See Evans et al. 1999.

[11] See the Hopkins Tanne 1999, 593 and Watson 2003, 201, respectively.

[12] See DH 2000c, para.22.

[13] E.g. your siblings, your maternal grandmother, your maternal aunty (and her children), and your maternal uncle.

[14] The President's Council on Bioethics (2002, ch.1) has summarised many of these objections. In response, it adopted the labels cloning-to-produce-children (in place of reproductive cloning) and cloning-for-biomedical research (to replace non-reproductive cloning).

between the creation and use of cloned embryos for reproduction (reproductive cloning) and for other purposes (non-reproductive cloning). The fact that some moral theories do not place *moral* weight on this distinction does not remove the distinction itself.

Reproductive cloning is undoubtedly more controversial than non-reproductive cloning. In scientific terms, virtually all new reproductive techniques create risks and uncertainties. A few decades ago many were predicting terrible consequences for IVF babies. James Watson, who discovered the structure of DNA with Francis Crick, warned of another "Thalidomide" tragedy.[15] Watson was referring to a catastrophe of the early 1960s when hundreds of children were born with serious deformities after their mothers had taken the sedative thalidomide during pregnancy, which had wrongly been thought to have been safe. The fear that IVF would be similarly catastrophic proved to be unfounded.[16] We cannot, however, tell whether reproductive cloning will ever be as successful as IVF.[17] The results of experiments on animals are neither conclusive nor encouraging. Dolly was the only successful birth from 277 attempts to transfer a nucleus into an egg.[18] Success rates have been improved in subsequent animal experiments, but the Dolly technique remains very inefficient.[19] Many (animal) clones are lost before implantation or birth. Few survive to term. Some of those born alive die prematurely or are euthanised to prevent suffering. The creation of cloned human embryos has proven to be more difficult than cloned animal embryos.[20] Cloned mice, goats, cows, rabbits, pigs, and horses have now been born. Significantly, many of those that survive to term succumb to a variety of abnormalities. Some of these abnormalities have been found in several species (such as cardiovascular and placental defects), whereas others appear to be species-specific (such as obesity in mice). If these consequences can be understood and prevented, then reproductive cloning could become a more reliable means of avoiding genetic disorders than existing means of assisted reproduction. Successful cloning could replicate genomes that we know to be free of serious genetic disorders. We are, however, nowhere near to that stage and undesired effects might even be an unavoidable consequence of the Dolly technique.

10.2.3 Stem cells

Some see non-reproductive cloning as a potential source of stem cells. Stem cells could be derived from many other sources. These are very special cells

---

[15] See Jackson 2001, 167.

[16] Over a million IVF children have now been born (see HFEA 2004b). One study has, however, concluded that the incidence of a human overgrowth syndrome (Beckwith–Wiedemann syndrome) is increased in children that are produced by IVF (see DeBaun 2003).

[17] The live birth rate for IVF patients is still only 23.1% (see HFEA 2008a).

[18] See Wilmut et al. 1997.

[19] The information presented below is largely derived from Rhind et al. 2003 and Rideout et al. 2001.

[20] The first confirmed report of cloned human embryos only developed to the 6-cell stage (see Cibelli et al. 2001).

with two important biological properties. *First*, they are capable of *self-renewal*. That is to say that they have the capacity to divide to produce more of themselves. *Second*, they can *differentiate* into more specialised cells. All other cell types cannot change their function; they are irreversibly differentiated.[21] A muscle cell cannot become a kidney cell and a kidney cell cannot become a muscle cell. In contrast, stem cells can undergo differentiation into one or more specialised types of cells, so that some stem cells can become muscle or kidney cells.

Stem cells give rise to a number of therapeutic hopes for the future. It is hoped that stem cells could one day be used to treat a wide range of diseases for which there is currently no cure, such as diabetes, Parkinson's disease, and certain types of heart disease. The most widely used stem cell-based therapy is currently bone marrow transplant for leukaemia. It is hoped that future regenerative therapies will enable any diseased or damaged tissue to be repaired. As well as providing tissue for transplantation, it is hoped that some types of stem cells could be used in gene therapy.

Cloned embryos are being considered as a potential source of embryonic stem cells because they are genetically identical to the person from whom the somatic cell was derived. A cloned embryo produced from one of your somatic cells would be genetically identical to you. If transplanted into your body it would not provoke any negative immune response. Your body would not treat it as an invading foreign cell. This is the reason why some consider non-reproductive cloning to have great potential.

There are two types of stem cells: embryonic and adult. Despite their name, *adult stem cells* do not have to come from adults. They are found in many parts of the human body, including bone marrow. *Embryonic stem cells* (*hereafter ES cells*) are more aptly named, as they can only be derived from embryos. These are more flexible than unmodified adult stem cells, as they have the potential to develop into a wide range of tissue types. The degree of flexibility depends on the age of the embryo from which it is derived. The cells in a very early human embryo are "totipotent", i.e. they have the potential to develop into any type of cell or a child.[22] Between 5 and 14 days some of the embryo's cells still have the capacity to develop into other types of cell. These cells are "pluripotent"—they have the potential to develop into any one of 200 or so human cell types. In contrast, adult stem cells are at best "multipotent". They are already differentiated but can give rise to a limited number of other cells or tissue types. Bone marrow stem cells, for example, can regenerate blood cells but are not thought to have the capacity to regenerate skin, brain, or other types of cells. Adult stem cells can also be derived from fetal tissue and umbilical cord blood.[23]

Pluripotent ES cells were first derived from human embryos by an American group headed by James Thomson over a decade ago.[24] Follow up research by a

---

[21] Unless they are subject to the Dolly technique. That technique showed that it was possible to artificially change a differentiated cell.

[22] See IBAC 2001.

[23] For one use for stem cells derived from cord blood see Ch.8 (8.5.2).

[24] See Thomson et al. 1998.

group of Korean scientists publishing in 2004 declared that ES cells had been successfully extracted from cloned human embryos, but those particular results were later shown to have been faked.[25] The scientific prestige that awaits pioneers in this ethically divisive area apparently proved to be too much of a temptation.

The process of removing ES cells from a living embryo involves its destruction. It is worth noting, however, that research published in 2006 reported success in the creation of ES cell lines from "arrested" embryos.[26] Arrested embryos are those that no longer grow but still contain revivable cells. In other words, some of their cells are alive but these embryos cannot develop further and are therefore generally referred to as "dead embryos".

In 2007 an important scientific development was announced by two groups of researchers. James Thomson's group along with a group in Japan headed by Shinya Yamanaka reported that they had successfully reprogrammed adult human cells so that they became pluripotent.[27] These new cells are known as *induced pluripotent stem (iPS) cells*. Clinical applications are still a very long way off, but the hope is that it will be possible to simply take a cell from the patient's body and reprogramme it to perform the necessary function. Further basic research is much needed on both ES and iPS cells. It is not yet entirely clear whether iPS cells really do have the same developmental potential as ES cells and, even if they do, they are currently beset by problems of their own (particularly concerning the viruses used to create them). If these problems can be addressed, iPS cells could remove the need for non-reproductive cloning altogether.[28]

10.2.4 Chimeras and hybrids

There is a shortage of human eggs available for research.[29] The biggest obstacle is a shortage of donors, primarily because egg donation is a physically demanding process. Yet, donated eggs are desperately sought not only by researchers but also by those in need of donor eggs for IVF treatment. Where the eggs are specifically donated for research some will be unsuitable for the creation of stable cell lines, particularly where they were donated for research in the first place because they have failed to properly fertilise. These difficulties have led some scientists to seek to use animal eggs. Embryos created by a cloning technique using animal eggs and human gametes or cells are commonly referred to as *cytoplasmic hybrids*. Such embryos will have purely human nuclear DNA. There are other potential combinations of animal–human source material. Embryos could be created using a combination of human and

---

[25] See Hwang et al. 2004.
[26] See Zhang et al. 2006.
[27] See Takahashi et al. 2007 and Yu et al. 2007.
[28] See Cibelli 2007.
[29] See HFEA 2007a, paras 2.6–2.7.

animal gametes (e.g. an animal egg with a human sperm) or pronuclei,[30] creating *human–animal hybrids*. Embryos could also be created by the introduction of animal DNA into one or more cells of the embryo, resulting in *human transgenic embryos*.

10.3 Research on embryos

We have seen that research on embryos and embryo products has the potential to advance biological understanding, increase knowledge that could assist the involuntarily childless, and assist the development of cures for many otherwise devastating diseases. Why, then, is such research controversial? For some the objections are little more than automatic "yuk" responses, similar to the cries of disgust prolific in the early days of blood transfusion, organ transplantation and *in vitro* fertilisation. Some have much more profound ethical objections to the intentional destruction of early human embryos. Opponents multiply where the research involves the creation and use of a cloned embryo or, even more controversially, a human–animal embryo. The first part of this section (10.3.1) will examine the major ethical issues raised by embryo research and the destructive use of embryos, starting with the issue of the embryo's moral status. The second part (10.3.2) will examine the legal response to these issues under the 1990 Act, as amended.

10.3.1 Ethical issues

10.3.1.1 The moral status of the human embryo

Central to moral divisions over embryo research is the value given to the *human embryo*. We owe moral duties to an embryo in two ways. We could owe duties *directly* to the embryo on the basis of the characteristics possessed by the embryo, or the embryo could attract moral protection *indirectly*, as a means of protecting those (others) who possess moral status. This is often forgotten. We do not need to have duties directly *to* an embryo for us to have duties *in relation to* an embryo. If, for example, a moral theory were to grant you property rights in an embryo, then my harming your embryo without your consent could violate my duties to you. The most difficult issue, however, is determining whether we owe direct duties to an embryo. If we owe direct duties to embryos, they will be said to have *moral status*. Here it is necessary to repeat some of the analysis of Chs 7 (on abortion) and 8 (on assisted reproduction). Some readers can therefore skip the next four paragraphs.

Different moral theories ground possession of moral status on possession of a number of characteristics or properties. Some wish to grant moral status to

---

[30] A pronucleus is the nucleus of a sperm or an egg cell during the process of fertilisation, before they fuse.

those who are alive; sentient (capable of experiencing pleasure or pain); biologically human; agents (capable of reflective purposive action); partial agents (possessing only some of the characteristics of agents); *or* potential agents. These are just examples. Each criterion has its supporters and critics. For example, some theological positions wish to ground possession of moral status on membership of the human species;[31] yet others denounce this criterion as a morally repugnant prejudice ("speciesism") comparable to racism and sexism.[32] The relevance of the developmental *potential* of healthy embryos is also hotly debated and is discussed in Ch.7 (7.2.1.2).

The ground for possession of moral status has implications for the early human being. The different possibilities for the embryo are easy to map (as in Ch.1).[33] At one extreme are moral positions holding that the embryo deserves the same level of protection as an adult human being. According to what may be called the *full status* position, full moral status is to be granted to the embryo from the moment of its creation. At the other extreme is what may be called the *no status* position, which holds that the embryo itself has no intrinsic value or status, until at least birth. According to this position, an embryo is no more than a bunch of cells without any special status. Between these two extremes are *limited status* positions, which hold that the embryo has a status resting somewhere between full and none. The most popular limited position is the *proportional status* position, which holds that the moral status of the embryo increases with development until it obtains full moral status at birth or beyond. Thus, the embryo can be recognised as having moral status to the same degree as you or I (full status), to a degree less than you or I (limited status, or where that status increases with gestational, proportional status), or to no degree at all (no status).

The moral status of the embryo is a key factor in determining the permissibility of embryo research and other destructive uses of embryos. Those adopting the full status position must consider the deliberate destruction of an embryo as equivalent to murder. Embryo research is equivalent to conducting non-consensual, invasive experimentation on an adult. At the other extreme, the no status position must hold that embryo destruction involves no intrinsic wrong. If we ignore its (indirect) effects on others, killing an embryo is no more problematic than cutting one's toenails. Between these two extremes the embryo cannot be treated as if it has the same status as you or I, or as if it were a mere collection of cells. It follows that, from the limited status position, embryo research cannot be left as a free-for-all or prohibited in all circumstances. The proportional status position is more specific. The closer to birth, the greater protection granted to the embryo and the greater the justificatory burden placed on those who wish to destroy embryos. Destructive use of embryos, even if granted little moral status, differs from abortion in that the woman's interest in escaping bodily invasion cannot be used to trump the

---

[31] See e.g. Noonan 1970 and Finnis 2001.
[32] See e.g. Singer 1995.
[33] Some prefer the labels pro-choice (or liberal) vs pro-life (or conservative) to describe what I characterise as no status vs full status.

embryo's status. We need to appeal to other considerations if the embryo's status is to be trumped by the moral interests of those with greater moral status.

The major moral camps outlined in Ch.1 do not map straightforwardly on to the no, full, and limited status framework. Nonetheless, there are clear trends and, sometimes, even correlations.[34] Compromise positions are, by definition, capable of adopting any view on the moral status of the embryo, but often tend towards limited status. Neither utilitarian nor rights-based positions are compatible with the full status position. For utilitarians, to have moral status a being must be capable of experiencing pain or even capable of making choices (depending on the type of utilitarianism in play).[35] For rights-based theories, only those who can waive the benefit of rights (agents) can have rights and, therefore, moral status.[36] (For the complex reasons examined in the final chapter, it does not automatically follow that such theories are committed to the no status position). In contrast, the duty-based camp is compatible with full status position. The official stance of the Roman Catholic Church, the best known full status position, is a duty-based position.[37] Not all duty-based theories, however, adopt the full status position. Orthodox Judaism does not grant moral status to the early embryo (but adopts a limited status position).[38] Immanuel Kant, who is often interpreted as a duty-based theorist, granted moral status only to agents.[39]

10.3.1.2 Specific types of embryo research

Some distinguish between research on human embryos left over from IVF (so-called "surplus" or "spare" embryos) and research on human embryos specifically created for research.[40] This cannot be a distinction between different types of moral status. The initial reason for an embryo's creation says nothing about the embryo's intrinsic features. Surplus embryos are physically identical to embryos intentionally created for research. Any moral distinction drawn must, therefore, rest on something other than the different moral status of these embryos. A common argument relies on the risks to the woman's health created by the removal of eggs, holding that those risks are not justifiably run where the purpose is solely to create an embryo for research purposes.[41] Not all moral theories could support the view that *the moral interests of the woman* could justifiably prevent her from voluntarily choosing (in full knowledge of the risks) to donate her eggs purely for research purposes. Such an approach is, for example, unlikely to maximise utility and is inconsistent with the waivability

---

[34] The points in this paragraph are examined in more depth in the chapter on abortion: Ch.7 (7.2.1.2).

[35] Singer (1993) is an example of the former and Hare (1981) is an example of the latter.

[36] See e.g. Pattinson 2002a, and Beyleveld and Brownsword 2001.

[37] See e.g. House of Lords Select Committee 2002, para.4.18.

[38] See e.g. House of Lords Select Committee 2002, para.4.19.

[39] See Kant 1948 (discussed in Ch.17).

[40] For an early view that it is "especially difficult to justify *creating it* [i.e. an embryo] *solely* for the purpose of experimentation", see Kass 1979, 58 (original emphasis).

[41] See e.g. Discussion Group on Embryo Research 1995, 6.

of all duties recognised by rights-based theories. Another argument is presented by Anleu, who suggests that the restriction of research to spare embryos is a pragmatic mechanism to discourage scientists from using large numbers of embryos purely to maximise their own interests.[42] Even if this mechanism is empirically likely to achieve this aim, not all moral theories will support it. The moral benefits of research on specially created embryos might be thought to outweigh this risk, especially if embryos are considered to have little or no moral status.

Since the derivation of embryonic stem (ES) cells from a living human embryo involves the destruction of that embryo, adherents of the full status position will see such research as equivalent to non-consensual destructive research on you or me. For a (consistent) full status theorist it is morally impermissible to intentionally sacrifice the life of an embryo even if one's purpose is to save the life of an adult. Adherents of the no status position cannot support a principled objection to ES cell research *as such*. Limited status supporters will take a mid-position. The moral status of an embryo is lower than that of the adult whose life could be saved but carte blanche cannot be given to embryo researchers. If the destructive use of embryos is to be permitted at all—and most limited status positions will support at least some embryo research—the creation of therapies to help those suffering serious debilitating and life-threatening diseases is surely among the most important purposes for which it should be permitted. Moreover, to take a stance against all destructive use of embryos, no matter how beneficial the purpose, is difficult to reconcile with acceptance of other activities that unavoidably involve embryo destruction, such as abortion, post-coital contraception, and IVF. Harris points out that anyone who intends to conceive a child by sexual intercourse, or decides to have unprotected sexual heterosexual intercourse, runs the risk of embryo destruction, because even successful pregnancies are usually preceded by many spontaneous miscarriages (most of which will be undetected).[43] He goes on to argue that no one who engages in such activities can consistently object to the principle of embryo research or the use of embryonic stem cells for research or therapy. A full status supporter who is aware that unprotected heterosexual intercourse is likely to result in embryo destruction might appeal to the controversial "principle of double effect", and thereby seek to distinguish the intention behind such actions (having a child) from the unintended but foreseen consequences (embryo destruction).[44] The debate over the moral legitimacy of the principle of double effect is discussed in Ch.15 (15.2.1).

The creation of embryos from a combination of animal and human material raises further complications (see 10.2.4, above). There are two major ethical issues here: the act of creation itself and the status of the resulting entity. These issues are interlinked because the creation of such embryos will be for destructive research purposes. Whatever criterion for possession of moral status is

---

[42] See Anleu 2001, 427.
[43] See Harris 2003c, esp. 362–363.
[44] Harris dismisses this response (2003c, 362) and has presented arguments against the principle of double effect elsewhere (see e.g. Harris 1985, 43–45).

appealed to by supporters of the full or limited status position with regard to the human embryo will surely be displayed by at least some of these embryos. Indeed, if it is likely that the resultant embryo could develop and be born and be visually indistinguishable from other humans, it is difficult to conceive of any major moral position requiring such a child to be treated as having less worth. In addition there are also the moral interests of the animals used as sources of material to consider. Such animals will need to be reared and kept in very particular conditions, as discussed in more depth in relation to using animals as sources of organs in Ch.14 (14.3.2.1).

10.3.2 Legal issues

10.3.2.1 Research on human embryos

The use of *in vitro* embryos for research and other purposes is governed by the 1990 Act, as amended by the 2008 Act. This requires a licence to be obtained from the HFEA for the creation and use of *in vitro* embryos (ss.3(1) and 1(2)). Stringent conditions are imposed on the availability of licences for those practices that are not prohibited outright. Where those conditions are met the HFEA can grant licences for up to three years for individual research projects (Sch.2 para.3(8)). The HFEA Research Licence Committee evaluates applications, renewals, and progress reports and currently aims to process 90 per cent of research licence applications within three months of receipt.[45]

The decision to allow embryo research was the result of a free vote in Parliament leading up to the enactment of the 1990 Act. The Government had offered two mutually exclusive draft clauses: one permitting research under licence and the other prohibiting embryo research. Parliament chose the former.[46] Under the 1990 Act, research is not restricted to embryos left over from IVF (so-called "surplus embryos"), as the creation of embryos specifically for research is explicitly permitted (Sch.2 para.3(1)). A number of conditions are imposed on licensable research on human embryos.

First, embryo research is only permitted up to 14 days after fertilisation or the appearance of the primitive streak, whichever is earlier (ss.3(3)(a) and 3(4)). The 14 days period is to begin with the day on which the process of creating the embryo began.

Second, embryos that have been the subject of research cannot be implanted into the womb (s.15(4)).

Third, the donors whose material produced the embryo must have consented after being provided with "such relevant information as is proper" (Sch.3 para.3(1)(b)) and they may specify conditions on the use of their embryos (para.2(1)). As is the case with all consents required by the Act, the consent must now be in writing and signed by the person giving the consent (or by a person on their behalf in their presence if they are physically incapable of

---

[45] See HFEA website (*http://www.hfea.gov.uk*), last visited in February 2009.
[46] See Brazier 1990a, 127.

signing) (Sch.3 para.1). Before the embryo has been used, any consent given for research can be varied or withdrawn by written notice (Sch.3, paras 1 and 4).

Fourth, the HFEA requires all research proposals to have been approved by a properly constituted ethics committee before an application is made.[47]

Fifth, any research must be "necessary or desirable" for one of the purposes listed by the Act, for providing knowledge capable of being applied for one of those purposes, or for such other purposes as specified in regulations (Sch.2 para.3A). The 1990 Act initially specified five research purposes that were expanded by Regulations in 2001.[48] The 2008 Act brings together the purposes originally listed in the 1990 Act and the 2001 Regulations (which it revoked), while making a number of changes. There are eight research purposes specified by the replacement provision (Sch.2 para.3A(2)):

(a) increasing knowledge about serious disease or other serious medical conditions,

(b) developing treatments for serious disease or other serious medical conditions,

(c) increasing knowledge about the causes of any congenital disease or congenital medical condition that does not fall within paragraph (a),

(d) promoting advances in the treatment of infertility,

(e) increasing knowledge about the causes of miscarriage,

(f) developing more effective techniques of contraception,

(g) developing methods for detecting the presence of gene, chromosome or mitochondrian abnormalities in embryos before implantation, or

(h) increasing knowledge about the development of embryos.

The changes introduced by the 2008 Act have expanded the areas of explicitly permitted research. It is now clearer that the legislation authorises (i) basic research and (ii) research into serious injuries not amounting to a disease, such as spinal cord injuries. Basic research is addressed by the provision permitting research that is necessary or desirable for "providing knowledge" capable of being applied to the specified research purposes (Sch.2 para.3A(1)(b)). Conditions not amounting to disease are captured by the reference to "other serious medical conditions" (in Sch.2 para.3A(2)(a)–(b)), though the HFEA is left to interpret the ambit of this phrase without further legislative guidance.

10.3.2.2 The 1990 Act's position on the moral status of the human embryo

The 1990 Act takes a particular view of the status of the embryo. That view is most coherently explained as a *limited status position*. The Warnock Report, which

---

[47] Further guidance is provided on the HFEA website (*http://www.hfea.gov.uk*).
[48] HFE (Research Purposes) Regulations 2001/188.

formed the basis of the 1990 Act, makes it clear that the underlying view is that "the embryo of the human species ought to have a special status" albeit less than that of a living child or adult.[49] The long title of the 1990 Act states that its purpose is to "make provision in connection with human embryos and any subsequent development of such embryos". What is more, the Act (which also amended the Abortion Act 1967) implicitly grants the embryo *proportional* moral status. Increased protection is given to the embryo according to three legally relevant stages of development: preimplantation, implantation to 24 weeks, and post-24 weeks. We have seen that the Act only permits research on the preimplantation embryo up to 14 days or the development of the primitive streak, whichever is earlier. An *in vitro* embryo cannot be implanted, used for research, or even stored unless both parents consent. In the absence of such consent it must be destroyed (subject to a cooling-off period). In contrast, as explained in Ch.7, after implantation an embryo can only be intentionally destroyed if two medical practitioners certify compliance with one of four legally recognised grounds for abortion, the most permissive of which only applies before 24 weeks gestation. The Act is, therefore, best understood as being underpinned by the view that we owe moral duties to an embryo that increase with its gestational development. This has been explicitly accepted by the 2005 report of the House of Commons' Science and Technology Select Committee and by the Government in its Response.[50] The philosophical basis on which the embryo is granted this (proportional) status is not clear. It is most plausibly interpreted as a compromise position, but the ground for possession of moral status remains obscure. Not all compromise positions are coherent and the absence of clear philosophical foundations leaves questions about the coherence of the position adopted by the 1990 Act unanswered.

Embryo research was an issue that had divided the special committee on whose report the 1990 Act was based. The majority of the committee, chaired by Mary Warnock and popularly known as the Warnock Committee, wished to permit embryo research, subject to the 14-day limit that was later adopted by Parliament. In their view, the formation of the primitive streak about 15 days after fertilisation is a significant marker point, because it marks "the development of the human individual".[51] The 14-day dividing line has the advantage of being clear and measurable, but being essentially stipulative it has been attacked by theorists for being set too early, too late, or as an all or nothing cut off point. This debate is closely connected to the underlying view on the moral status of the embryo and the ground for possession of that status. Public debate over the period for which embryo research is permitted will no doubt return to the foreground when it becomes possible to sustain developing embryos for longer than 14 days outside of the body. The potential to survive will be a key political hook for this debate to surface. Indeed, much of the controversy over what was to become the 2008 Act focused on technological developments that had improved the survival rate for fetuses approaching the 24-week stage that is so crucial to the legal position on abortion.

---

[49] Warnock et al. 1984, para.11.7.
[50] See Science and Technology Committee 2005a, 15–17 and HM Government 2005, paras 1–2.
[51] Warnock et al. 1984, para.11.22.

10.3.2.23 Embryonic stem cells

The 2008 Act's amendments make the HFEA's regulatory discretion with regard to embryonic stem cell research explicit. Even as amended, however, the 1990 Act does not cover non-embryonic stem cell research or the application of cell-based therapies derived from ES cells. Some of those who wish to interpret the 1990 Act narrowly will be attracted by the view that the HFEA's powers concern embryos, rather than embryo products such as ES cell lines. In practice, however, before the HFEA will grant a research licence it requires the applicant to agree to place a sample of all derived cell lines in the UK Stem Cell Bank.[52] It also requires applicants to agree not to conduct secondary research projects on ES cells or transfer ES cells to third parties without the approval of the UK Stem Cell Bank's Steering Committee.[53]

The UK Stem Cell Bank is independent of the HFEA. It is a non-legislative body that seeks to facilitate the sharing of quality controlled stem cell lines by the clinical and research communities.[54] While the Stem Cell Bank's policies are voluntary and therefore do not bind stem cell researchers, the effect of the HFEA's approach is that they do bind ES cell researchers. Is this practice of the HFEA analogous to using the power to regulate the rearing and use of dairy cows to regulate the storage and use of milk? In my view, it is not: the HFEA has not overstepped its jurisdiction. The HFEA should be viewed as empowered to impose any restrictions that are reasonably connected with its roles under the Act as long as those restrictions are consistent with the Act's other provisions. The rationale of protecting embryos surely empowers the HFEA to take steps to minimise the destructive use of embryos and the number of embryos created for research. And the HFEA's other roles under the Act, which include protecting the interests of gamete providers and public confidence in embryo research, arguably permit it to impose these other conditions. In any event, the 2008 Act was enacted following a lengthy consideration of the HFEA's practices, so such a restriction to its jurisdiction must be taken to have been rejected by Parliament.

At the time of writing the UK Stem Cell Bank, which was launched in September 2002, has 14 ES cell lines available. These are all research grade lines. Clinical grade lines (i.e. those capable of being raw materials in the production of clinical products) are likely to be available in the near future. The existence of such cell lines has particular importance in the light of the Act's requirement that no licence for embryo research can be granted unless "any proposed use of embryos . . . is necessary for the purposes of the research" (Sch.2 para.3(5)). The further destructive use of embryos will not be necessary where an existing ES cell line can be used instead or another suitable alternative exists. If iPS cells manifest their full potential, they may also come to represent a suitable alternative to the use of embryos for at least some stem cell research.

---

[52] See HFEA 2007b, Appendix A (d)(viii) and 2008b, 183 respectively. See *http://www.ukstemcell-bank.org.uk.*

[53] See UK Stem Bank 2006, para.3.2.

[54] *http://www.ukstemcellbank.org.uk.*

10.3.2.4 Cloned, hybrid, and chimera embryos

One of the reasons for amending the research provisions of the 1990 Act was to put it beyond doubt that research on cloned embryos fell within its provisions. Doubts about whether the 1990 Act regulated the creation of cloned embryos had been rejected by the House of Lords in 2002 (in a decision that will be examined in 10.4.2.1 below).[55] Some commentators, however, raised questions about whether the purposes for which embryo research was permitted were wide enough to encompass basic research into, say, the development of better techniques for extracting ES cells from cloned embryos.[56] The purposive approach taken by the appeal courts to the interpretation of the 1990 Act was likely to prevent gaps arising from narrow, literal readings of the relevant provisions, but the HFEA's jurisdiction was regularly being challenged in the courts by groups supporting the full status position.[57] It has to be said, however, that such challenges were almost routinely unsuccessful and the HFEA granted many research licenses under the unamended Act. The HFEA granted its first licence for research on cloned embryos in 2004 and a second in 2005.[58]

The 2008 Act amendments also sought to deal with chimera and hybrid embryos. At the end of 2006, the HFEA had received licence applications from two different research teams wanting to derive stem cells from *cytoplasmic hybrids*, i.e. embryos created by putting human genetic material into enucleated animal eggs. The HFEA's response was to launch a consultation.[59] It subsequently granted the research licences to the two teams in January 2008 and granted a further licence to another team in June 2008.[60] Under the unamended legislation the HFEA only had jurisdictional competence with regard to research on live *human* embryos. Some took the view that the animal cytoplasm and mitochondrial DNA in cytoplasmic hybrids meant that they were not strictly human embryos. The purposive approach taken by the appeal courts to the Act's provisions mentioned above rendered it unlikely that such a view would gain judicial approval. Indeed, a legal challenge to the jurisdictional competence of the HFEA with regard to cytoplasmic hybrids was rejected by the High Court at the end of 2008 as "totally without merit".[61]

The 2008 Act amendments explicitly regulate the creation, storage, and use of embryos created by combining animal and human genetic material. The Act adopts the term "human admixed embryo". The provision defining this term, s.4A(6), has five subsections (a) to (e).

Cytoplasmic hybrid embryos are captured by s.4A(6)(a), which states that a "human admixed embryo" includes:

---

[55] See *R. (Bruno Quintavalle) v Secretary of State for Health* [2003] UKHL 13.
[56] See e.g. Brownsword 2002, 579–582.
[57] See e.g. *R. (Bruno Quintavalle) v Secretary of State for Health* [2003] UKHL 13 and *R. (Josephine Quintavalle) v HFEA* [2005] UKHL 28.
[58] See HFEA 2004f and 2005a.
[59] See HFEA 2007a.
[60] See HFEA website (*http://www.hfea.gov.uk*).
[61] See BBC 2008d.

an embryo created by replacing the nucleus of an animal egg or of an animal cell, or two animal pronuclei, with

(i) two human pronuclei,
(ii) one nucleus of a human gamete or of any other human cell, or
(iii) one human gamete or other human cell.

Human–animal hybrid embryos are captured by s.4A(6)(b), which encompasses: "any other embryo created by using (i) human gametes and animal gametes, or (ii) one human pronucleus and one animal pronucleus".

Human transgenic embryos are captured by s.4A(6)(c), which includes in the relevant definition "a human embryo that has been altered by the introduction of any sequence of nuclear or mitochondrial DNA of an animal into one or more cells of the embryo".

Human transgenic embryos fall within s.4A(6)(d), which addresses "a human embryo that has been altered by the introduction of one or more animal cells".

The final subsection, s.4A(6)(e), is a miscellaneous clause covering any other type of embryo that contains both human and animal DNA "in which the animal DNA is not predominant". The word "predominant" has been left undefined and its interpretation will therefore fall to the HFEA and, if challenged, the courts. Since the Secretary of State has the power to amend (but not repeal) all five subsections if it appears "necessary or desirable to do so in the light of developments in science or medicine", any practical problems arising by the use of this word could be addressed relatively quickly without the need for primary legislation.

Research on human admixed embryos is subject to many restrictions. Some of these merely mirror those applying to research on ordinary human embryos. A human admixed embryo can, for example, only be kept until the appearance of the primitive streak or for a period of 14 days, whichever is the earliest (s.4A(3)), and a licence is required to create, use, or store a human admixed embryo (s.4A(2) and Sch.2 para.3(3)). No embryo that has been the subject of research can be implanted and it should therefore be no surprise that the Act makes it an offence to place in a woman a human admixed embryo, any other embryo that is not human, and any gametes other than human gametes (s.4A(1)). It is also an offence to implant a human admixed embryo into an animal (s.4A(4)).

10.4 Reproductive cloning

To some, reproductive cloning raises no more issues than were raised in the early days of IVF. Others consider cloning to be much worse. As we shall see, the ethical debate displays a division between those who argue that reproductive cloning is, or could become, a legitimate exercise of one's reproductive autonomy and those who argue that it violates, or threatens to violate, important human values. An outline of this debate will be presented below before the current legal position is examined. The law undoubtedly favours those who take a restrictive view, but whether it will do so if the technology becomes more reliable is less certain.

10.4.1 Ethical issues

The controversial nature of cloning is obvious. Finding arguments against reproductive cloning has proven to be more difficult than the level of support for its banning would suggest. Here, as is often the case, moral theorists are divided.

10.4.1.1 Arguments against reproductive cloning

The arrival of Dolly provoked a fusillade of arguments against human reproductive cloning. Many of these display fundamental misunderstandings of the technology and its implications or are open to obvious counter responses. The feminist argument that cloning places greater reproductive control in the hands of men,[62] is open to the response that the Dolly technique could enable a child to be born without the involvement or contribution of a man.[63] The argument that cloning violates the clone's right to be the product of two biological parents,[64] invites the response that a clone would be the product of at least two different sources of genetic material: the genetic parents of the DNA donor.[65] The argument that cloning will undermine genetic diversity[66] is open to the response that human clones are highly unlikely to become statistically significant enough to affect human genetic diversity as a whole and humans already share over 99.9 per cent of their genes.[67] The argument that clones have a "right" to a unique identity[68] evokes the response that there is more to identity than genetics and naturally-occurring identical twins are genetically identical (more so than Dolly clones with different mitochondrial DNA).

Adherents of the full status position will inevitably oppose reproductive cloning. In practice, attempts to create cloned children will be preceded by destructive research on cloned embryos. Some potential cloning techniques (such as replacing the nucleus of an embryo) will themselves involve the destruction of embryos. For some, *all* human cloning simply violates human dignity. The "dignity as constraint" position (which is not restricted to

---

[62] According to Andrea Dworkin (1998, 76): "Cloning is the absolute power over reproduction that men have wanted and have destroyed generations upon generations of women to approximate".

[63] Aside, of course, from the man who was originally the genetic father of the cloned person.

[64] According to McLean (1998, 26): "An artificially cloned human being would have been denied the right to be the product of a genetic blueprint having two different sources".

[65] A clone's nuclear and mitochondrial DNA are also likely to be from different sources.

[66] According to Tracy (1998, 192–193), "Human cloning certainly sounds like the ultimate contribution to an undesirable monoculture".

[67] The statistic is from Watson 2003, 259.

[68] According to Callahan (1997), cloning a human being "would be a profound threat to what might be called the right to our own identity."

adherents of the full status position) takes cloning as a paradigmatic violation of dignity.[69] These objections are not answered by the presence of informed consent or any (future) developments rendering the risks identical to long established forms of reproduction.

10.4.1.2 Our duties to the clone

The most popular arguments against cloning claim that it constitutes a wrong to the resultant clone. Many point to the current inefficiency and unpredictability of cloning experiments on animals and fear disastrous results for the health of a human clone.[70] Others predict psychological harm to the clone.[71] Duties to future clones are thought by some to rule out cloning for the time being and, by others, to rule out cloning forever.

Cloning is the only plausible way for particular individuals to be brought into existence at all. Can bringing someone into existence be a wrong to the individual brought into existence?[72] This question was also raised in the chapters on assisted reproduction (Ch.8) and prenatal negligence (Ch.9). As I suggested there, moral theories could offer different answers to this question.[73] Utilitarians could hold that bringing someone into existence is a wrong to that individual where that existence would overall be a burden rather than a benefit.[74] For many utilitarians, it can be wrong to an individual to bring him into a state of disutility, *even if that individual could not have existed in any other state*. In contrast, a rights-based theorist would have to hold that even a terrible existence does not violate that individual's rights. For an individual's rights to have been violated he would have to have been deprived of an alternative existence in which his rights were fulfilled.[75] A parallel argument can be made for duty-based theories, which only differ from rights-based theories in that they reject the idea that the benefit of any duty is necessarily waivable by the beneficiary. (Nonetheless, the idea that cloning wrongs the clone is commonplace in the rights- and duty-based literature.)[76] Virtue theorists would not focus on whether a duty owed to the clone has been violated, but on the character and motive of those bringing about the clone's existence vis-à-vis the relevant virtues.

The conceptual difficulties raised by the notion of a duty not to bring an individual into existence, owed to that individual, can be evaded by re-characterising the relevant duty. Two examples should suffice. No such conceptual difficulty is raised by the idea of duties not to harm the clone *after it comes into existence*, by (for example) forcing the clone to live as if it were someone else (the cloned person). Cloning with the intention of harming the clone-in-the-future could

---

[69] See further Brownsword 2005, where supporters of the dignity as constraint position are referred to as the dignitarian alliance.

[70] See e.g. HFEA and HGAC 1998b, para.4.4; Health Canada 2001, 5; President's Council on Bioethics 2002, 89–94; Jackson 2001, 251; and HM Government 2005, para.18.

[71] See e.g. Deech 1999, 100. Such arguments are addressed in Burley and Harris 1999, 108.

[72] This raises what Parfit called the "non-identity problem": Parfit 1987, ch.16.

[73] See, in particular, 9.4.2, where the arguments below are given greater consideration.

[74] See e.g. Harris 1998 and 2000.

[75] See Pattinson 2002c.

[76] In this context, see Brock's rejection of the non-identity problem: Brock 1995 and 1998, 157.

coherently be dismissed as immoral. Similarly, no conceptual difficulty is created by the idea that there could be duties to others not to bring about the creation of a clone; say, a duty to individuals not to clone them without their consent or (for a communitarian) a duty to society not to infringe communal values.[77]

10.4.1.3 Arguments in favour of reproductive cloning

Given the widespread public antipathy to reproductive cloning it might be surprising to discover that there is an increasing weight of theoretical support for permitting the technique. To argue for cloning is not, of course, necessarily to suggest that it is the preferred option.[78] The vast majority of arguments in favour of reproductive cloning, but by no means all, anticipate and require the health risks to the clone to be reduced to a level equivalent to existing forms of assisted reproduction. Reproductive liberty is the major argument in play here. If presented as no more than an instance of general freedom, then it merely places the burden on the shoulders of those who argue that cloning is wrong. Some, however, wish to take it further and argue that reproductive autonomy is more important than liberty *as such*. This idea has particular appeal for rights-based theories and utilitarians. John Robertson, for example, has argued that once cloning technology has been shown to be "sufficiently safe and effective" it will legitimately be the subject of an individual's right to "procreative liberty", derived from a couple's legitimate "interest in having biologically and genetically related offspring to rear".[79] John Harris has similarly argued for reproductive liberty from an implicitly utilitarian perspective.[80]

The reproductive-autonomy argument is not, however, without dissenters. In the lead up to what was to become the 2008 Act the Government declared that it could see no circumstances in which reproductive cloning could be justified or allowed because there is no "obvious potential benefit to humanity that would be uniquely delivered by human reproductive cloning".[81] Since it is possible to imagine some reproductive goals that would be uniquely deliverable by cloning, this amounts to the claim that this would be no benefit to humanity. The measure of moral benefit is the very issue in question and it is one on which different moral theories will inevitably take different positions.

10.4.2 Legal issues

10.4.2.1 The Pro-Life Alliance case

The creation of Dolly resulted in worldwide fears that this new cloning technology would be applied to human beings. The HFEA was quick to declare

---

[77] The President's Council on Bioethics (2002, 90–91) has drawn attention to the possible risks to the woman who carries a cloned embryo to term.
[78] See Freeman 2003, 620.
[79] See Robertson 2000–2001, 43.
[80] See e.g. Harris 1998 and 2002a, 211.
[81] HM Government 2005, para.19.

that, depending on the method used, cloning was either prohibited or subject to a licensing requirement under the 1990 Act.[82] However, this was only incontestable with regard to the creation of a clone by two methods. *First*, replacing the nucleus of an embryo was directly prohibited by s.3(3)(a)—a provision that was removed by the 2008 Act. *Second*, embryo splitting required (and still requires) a licence because it involves the creation and use of an *in vitro* embryo (ss.3(1) and 1(2)). The creation of a clone using the Dolly technique was not so clearly covered. At the time, the 1990 Act defined "embryo" in s.1(1) to mean "a live human embryo where fertilisation is complete", including "an egg in the process of fertilisation", and many scientists take the view that the Dolly technique does not involve an act of fertilisation.[83]

This issue was brought before the courts by a judicial review action brought by Bruno Quintavalle on behalf of the Pro-Life Alliance.[84] The Pro-Life Alliance wished to get the courts to declare that the Dolly technique did not fall within the 1990 Act. While this might seem a little odd given the pressure group's rejection of cloning and adherence to the full status position, the Pro-Life Alliance was simply trying to force the issue back to Parliament in the hope that Parliament would grant the embryo greater protection and adopt a prohibitive approach. At first instance, Crane J. held that the Dolly technique did not involve the creation of an embryo, because it did not involve an act of fertilisation. The appeal courts were prepared to accept that the Dolly technique did not involve an act of fertilisation, but they were not prepared to hold that it thereby fell outside of the 1990 Act. The House of Lords held that the 1990 Act was to be interpreted purposively in the light of subsequent developments. This purpose was, their Lordships held, to provide for the regulation of live human embryos created outside the body, rather than to regulate only those embryos created by fertilisation. According to Lord Bingham (with whom Lords Hoffman and Scott agreed) the words referring to fertilisation "were not intended to form an integral part of the definition of embryo".[85] In other words, their Lordships ruled that s.1(1)(a) was to be read as specifying no more than when a fertilised egg was to be regarded as an embryo. Interpreted in this way, the 1990 Act applied to any entity that is *functionally* a human embryo in the sense of being theoretically capable of implantation and development in the womb.

Contrary to many commentators, my view is that the House of Lords was correct to hold that the Dolly technique was captured by the 1990 Act.[86] As

---

[82] See HFEA and HGAC 1998a, para.2, and 1998b, para.3.4.

[83] As Dr Wilmut and Professor Bulfield put it, "The oocyte is an egg but it has not been fertilised and it never is fertilised because the nucleus is transferred to it" (quoted in Science and Technology Committee 1997, xii).

[84] *R. (Bruno Quintavalle) v Secretary of State for Health* [2001] EWHC 918, [2002] EWCA Civ 29, and [2003] UKHL 13. See also the earlier academic discussion in Brazier 1999, 189; Beyleveld and Pattinson 2000b, 233; and Lee and Morgan 2001, 93–96.

[85] [2003] UKHL 13, para.14. Cf. the speeches of Lord Steyn (esp. para.26) and Lord Millet (esp. para.45).

[86] See Beyleveld and Pattinson 2004b, 197–201. Cf. Grubb 2002b and Plomer 2002 (commenting on the decision of the Court of Appeal) and Grubb 2003b, Brownsword 2004a, and Morgan and Ford 2004 (commenting on the decision of the House of Lords).

argued above, the 1990 Act is underpinned by the view that we owe moral duties to an embryo that increase with its gestation development. It follows that the Act must be interpreted in the light of this view of the status of the embryo, insofar as it is possible to do so without rendering the Act incoherent on other grounds. Yet, as the appeal courts recognised, if cloned embryos had fallen outside the 1990 Act, then the creation of *functional* embryos would not be regulated at all. This is inconsistent with the moral status of the embryo implied by the Act. Further, even though the 1990 Act did prohibit the replacement of the nucleus of an embryo (by s.3(3)(d)), it could not be taken to be opposed to cloning *as such* because the Act did not prohibit embryo splitting. Indeed, this particular prohibition could itself be explained as protecting embryos, because creating embryos by transplanting the nucleus of an embryo (unlike creating embryos using the Dolly technique) involves the destructive use of embryos.[87]

While I support the appeal courts' attempt to interpret the 1990 Act as encompassing the Dolly technique, the specific interpretative strategy adopted by the House of Lords created regulatory gaps.[88] Written consent was required from the gamete provider, but not from the provider of the somatic cell from which a nucleus is obtained (under Sch.3 para.6, as then worded). Further, the 14-day time limit for which embryos can be kept or used started from the mixing of gametes (under s.3(4), as then worded). While the HFEA could easily cover any such gaps by attaching conditions to licences, they could have been avoided altogether had the courts applied the purposive approach to the terms "fertilisation" and "gamete".[89] Under this approach, fertilisation would be interpreted as the creation of a functional embryo by the joining of genetic material and a gamete would be defined accordingly. This is approach would also have headed off difficulties created if functional gametes are created from stem cells (so-called "artificial gametes"). It was not the approach taken by the 2008 Act, though we shall see that these gaps have now been closed.

10.4.2.2 The 1990 Act as amended

Between the decision of Crane J. and that of the Court of Appeal in the *Pro-Life Alliance* case, Parliament passed the Human Reproductive Cloning Act 2001. This made it a criminal offence to place "in a woman a human embryo which has been created otherwise than by fertilisation" (s.1(1)). It is repealed by the 2008 Act. The 2008 Act amendments redefine the meaning of "embryo" and "gamete" and, under the new s.3(2), only allow the placing in a woman of "permitted" embryos and "permitted gametes".

As amended s.1(1) defines an embryo as "a live human embryo", not including a human admixed embryo. Embryo includes "an egg that is in the process of

---

[87] See also the comments made by Lord Bingham at para.18. This argument is not refuted by the fact that the Act allows destructive use of embryos elsewhere. There is no inconsistency in allowing some destructive use of embryos but not others, at least where the permitted destructive use is held to track the more important moral interests of beings with higher moral status.
[88] See Grubb 2002b, 362–364 and 2003b, 138; and Plomer 2002, 157.
[89] See Beyleveld and Pattinson 2004b, 199–201.

fertilisation or is undergoing any other process capable of resulting in an embryo" (s.1(1)(b)). Gametes (except in s.4A, which concerns non-human gametes) are defined as "live human eggs" (including cells of the female germ line at any stage of maturity) and "live human sperm" (including cells of the male germ line at any stage of maturity" (s.1(4)). Thus, as before, the Dolly technique is not regarded as a process of fertilisation and enucleated eggs and somatic nuclei are not regarded as gametes. This means, alas, that the definitions continue to be circular (embryos are embryos and gametes are gametes). Fortunately, the Act does take the precaution of granting the Secretary of State the power to extend, by regulations, the definitions of "embryo", "eggs", "sperm", or "gametes" in the light of developments in science of medicine (s.1(6)).

A "permitted embryo", which may be placed in a woman, is defined as one that has been created by the fertilisation of a permitted egg by a permitted sperm, whose nuclear or mitochondrial DNA has not been altered and which has not had cells added (s.3Z(4)). "Permitted eggs" are those produced by or extracted from the ovaries of a woman and "permitted sperm" are sperm produced by or extracted from the testes of a man (s.3ZA(2)–(3)). In both cases there must have been no alterations to the gamete's DNA. The upshot is that an embryo created by the Dolly technique could not be lawfully implanted in a woman.[90] Nor could genetically modified embryos or embryos created by artificial gametes. Reproductive cloning (except by embryo splitting) is therefore illegal.

The gaps left following the *Pro-Life Alliance* case have been closed. The consent of the donor of gametes or "human cells" used to create an embryo is now explicitly required (Sch.3 para.6(1)) and the 14-day period now starts from "the day on which the process of creating the embryo began" (s.3(4)).[91]

10.5 The international dimension

The ethical controversy generated by cloning and embryo research and use, predictably divides the international community. Various international instruments will be examined before briefly perusing the domestic regulatory position adopted in other countries.

10.5.1 International instruments

A number of international instruments make prohibitive pronouncements about reproductive cloning,[92] but are less inclined to directly mention embryo

---

[90] A qualification can be made to this: s.3ZA(5) allows regulations the definitions of permitted embryos and permitted gametes to be amended to allow "a prescribed process designed to prevent the transmission of serious mitochondrial disease".

[91] For human admixed embryos the relevant provision is s.4A(3)(b).

[92] e.g. art.11 of the Universal Declaration on the Human Genome and Human Rights states that "Practices which are contrary to human dignity, such as reproductive cloning of human beings shall not be permitted".

research. The European Convention on Human Rights and Biomedicine is an exception. Article 18(1) vaguely requires States permitting embryo research to "ensure adequate protection of the embryo". Article 18(2) is more specific and prohibits the "creation of human embryos for research purposes". The Convention does not define the phrase "human embryos" and a subsequent working party on the protection of the human embryo and fetus has failed to produce an agreed definition. If this provision were interpreted to capture the creation of all *functional* human embryos for research, then it would prohibit non-reproductive cloning. However, such an interpretation is difficult to support because the Convention arguably leaves such decisions to the discretion of individual States.[93] In any event, before signing or ratifying the Convention, any State could make a reservation to this provision under art.36 insofar as it is inconsistent with their pre-existing law. The UK will surely make such a reservation if it eventually signs the Convention. As I have implied, the UK is not one of the 34 States that have so far signed the Convention.[94]

The Convention does not address reproductive cloning. Those who hold that cloning violates human dignity will no doubt point to art.1, which requires parties to the Convention to "protect the dignity and identity of all human beings". This seems tenuous. There is, however, an Additional Protocol on the Prohibition of Cloning Human Beings. Article 1 of the Additional Protocol declares that,

> Any intervention seeking to create a human being genetically identical to another human being, whether living or dead, is prohibited.

Since "genetically identical" is defined, under art.1(2), as "sharing with another the same nuclear gene set", use of the Dolly technique on humans is included within this prohibition. This provision clearly prohibits reproductive cloning, but could it also cover non-reproductive cloning? To foreclose this possibility, when the Dutch government signed the Protocol it added an interpretative statement declaring that it "interprets the term "human beings" as referring exclusively to a human individual, i.e. a human being who has been born".[95] This interpretative statement is arguably unnecessary, because, in the absence of a definition of human being in the Convention itself, States are free to interpret this provision in accordance with their own national policy. Once again, this issue is not directly relevant to the UK. It is, however, important for those countries that have ratified both the Convention and its Additional Protocol, particularly those who lack existing legislation.[96]

The European Union, which has no direct competence in this area,[97] has also expressed reservations about cloning. The Directive on the Legal Protection of

---

[93] Which I would expect to be the outcome in the highly unlikely event that a member state refers this matter to the European Court of Human Rights for interpretation under art.29.

[94] Twenty-two of these have also ratified the Convention: see *http://conventions.coe.int* (status as of 14.2.09).

[95] See *http://www.conventions.coe.int*.

[96] e.g. Portugal (which had no pre-existing legislation), Greece (whose legislation only explicitly prohibits reproductive cloning), and Spain (which has comprehensive legislation in this area).

[97] It does, however, have competence to regulate the common internal and market (arts 94 and 95) and to protect public health (art.152).

Biotechnological Inventions, for example, states that "processes for cloning human beings" are unpatentable.[98] More directly, the European Parliament has passed numerous resolutions in support of a prohibition on the cloning of human beings, such as the Resolution on Human Cloning of September 7, 2000.[99] Similarly, the European Commission has declared that it opposes cloning and will not subsidise experiments. Cloning is also mentioned in some non-legal texts, such as the Charter of Fundamental Rights of the European Union, art.3(2) of which presents "the prohibition of the reproductive cloning of human beings" as something that "must be respected".

10.5.2 Reproductive tourism and regulatory approaches elsewhere

There are no reported incidents of scientists travelling out of the UK to take advantage of more permissible regulation in other jurisdictions. This is probably because of the permissive nature of the UK regulatory position. As we have seen, the vast majority of research activities are regulated, rather than prohibited in the UK. Even before the enactment of the 1990 Act, the UK had established itself as a facilitative environment for research into reproductive technologies. IVF and preimplantation genetic diagnosis (PGD) were, for example, both pioneered in the UK before the enactment of facilitative legislation.

The 1990 Act's position on embryo research stands out in the international community. The UK stands out for allowing the creation of embryos for research. Some countries, notably Austria, Germany, and Ireland have prohibited embryo research, while allowing IVF and other related forms of assisted reproduction.[100] Many other countries have, by various means, permitted embryo research, but prohibit the creation of embryos for research.[101] Permitting the creation of embryos for research, as the UK has done, remains an unpopular legislative move, though this is also the position under the Belgium and Swedish legislation.[102]

Ireland has adopted what appears to be the *full status* position (on the moral status of the embryo), as art.40.3.3 of the Irish Constitution states that,

> The State acknowledges the right to life of the unborn and, with due regard to the equal right to life of the mother, guarantees in its laws to respect, and, as far as practicable, by its laws to defend and vindicate that right.[103]

---

[98] Article 6(2)(a), Directive 98/44/EC.

[99] The European Parliament did, however, reject a resolution against all forms of human cloning in November 2001 (see *http://www.news.bbc.co.uk/1/hi/sci/tech/1682591.stm*).

[100] Law No.275 of July 1, 1992, s.2 (Austria), the Embryo Protection Law 1990, ss.1(1), 1(2), and 2 (Germany), and Art. 40.3 of the Irish Constitution (Ireland).

[101] See Pattinson 2002a, 4.5.2 and App.3.

[102] Law of 11th May 2003, art.4 (Belgium). The Swedish legislation was passed early in 2005.

[103] This provision only adopts the full status position if the "unborn" includes the unimplanted embryo. The Supreme Court has yet to rule on this.

Like the UK, the vast majority of countries are easier to characterise as adopting the *limited status position*.[104] Few, if any, are easy to explain in terms of the *no status* position. Whatever the underlying moral position, the existence of such divergence is problematic for those countries seeking to prohibit or heavily restrict embryo research. The economic and prestige advantage generated by embryo research inevitably places considerable pressure on countries to weaken unfavourably restrictive regulatory stances.[105] This pressure could, however, be removed if IPS cells are found to have the same potential as ES cells. It is to be expected that researchers will prefer permissive regulation, though a clearly regulated system is likely to be preferable to the uncertainty of non-regulation even if it means that some regulatory limits apply. It is certainly noticeable than one of the first moves of the new US President, Barack Obama, was to reverse the restrictions that his predecessor had placed on federal funding for ES cell research.

The regulation of cloning is also the source of much dispute. While the vast majority of the world's legislatures and policy-makers have adopted prohibitive approaches to reproductive cloning, non-reproductive cloning is the source of much regulatory variation. In one study of 30 countries, conducted in 2004, it was found that a narrow majority prohibited non-reproductive cloning and a large minority of countries have yet to enact national legislation addressing cloning at all.[106]

10.6 Conclusion

Both cloning and stem cell technology offer great potential. Reproductive cloning could create an additional means for the involuntarily childless to have a child that is biologically connected to themselves or for those at risk of a genetic (including mitochondrial) disorder to have a healthy child. Stem cells and non-reproductive cloning could offer new cures for diseases that are currently incurable. Neither technology is, however, without ethical complexity. What is a powerful benefit to one moral theory is outweighed by other considerations or not even considered to be a morally relevant factor by other moral theories. Reproductive cloning is likely to remain extremely controversial unless and until it is shown to be no more risky than standard IVF and, even then, theories within the dignity as constraint camp are likely to remain opposed.

10.7 Further reading

Brownsword, Roger (2005) "Stem Cells and Cloning: Where the Regulatory Consensus Fails." 39 *New England Law Review* 535–571.

---

[104] See Beyleveld and Pattinson 2004b for an argument that the prohibitive approaches adopted by Austria and German are difficult to reconcile with a consistent full status position.
[105] See Beyleveld and Pattinson 2001.
[106] See Pattinson and Caulfield 2004.

Morgan, Ryan (2007) "Embryonic Stem Cells and Consent: Incoherence and Inconsistency in the UK Regulatory Model." 15(3) *Medical Law Review* 279–319.

Pattinson, Shaun D. and Caulfield, Timothy (2004) "Variations and Voids: The Regulation of Human Cloning Around the World." 5 *BMC Medical Ethics* 9. (*http://www.biomedcentral.com/1472-6939/5/9*)

Chapter 11

MEDICAL RESEARCH

11.1 Introduction

Just over six decades ago in Nuremberg, 23 German doctors and scientists were prosecuted for what they had done in the name of medicine and medic research.[1] Many were accused of inflicting a range of brutal and lethal pr' dures on the inmates of concentration camps between 1933 and 1945. F'

[1] See Annas and Grodin 1992 and Shuster 1997.

were found guilty and seven (including Hitler's personal physician) were sentenced to death. Ten principles, now known as the Nuremberg Code, were laid down to guide future medical research. While these principles are still relevant today, the international debate has moved on. There is now a plethora of international guidelines and instruments specifically concerned with less extreme forms of medical experimentation. The most famous international ethical guideline is probably the World Medical Association's Helsinki Declaration.[2]

Two European Directives—the Clinical Trials Directive and the Good Clinical Practice (GCP) Directive[3]—have significantly altered the law in this area. The Clinical Trials Directive was implemented by the Clinical Trials Regulations,[4] which were subsequently amended to give effect to the GCP Directive.[5] These Regulations apply only to clinical trials of medicinal products, principally trials of new pharmaceutical products. Other types of medical research—and trials within the Regulations account for only 15 per cent of research applications received by NHS Research Ethics Committees[6]—have no such legal instrument. The result is a regulatory position that is a complex combination of legislation, common law principles, clinical governance, and professional guidance. Before it is explored, the next section (11.2) will examine the nature and practice of medical research and the following section (11.3) will then examine the ethical issues underlying medical research.

This chapter will only address *medical research performed on human beings who have already been born*. Research on embryos was the subject of the last chapter (Ch.10). This chapter will not address confidentiality and data protection (addressed in Ch.6). Nor will this chapter address research involving retained human material, whether from living or deceased persons (which is mentioned in passing in Chs 12 and 13). Readers will benefit from having read the two chapters on consent to medical treatment (Chs 5 and 6). Where necessary, some parts of those chapters will be briefly restated.

11.2 Research and its context

Abusive practices conducted in the name of medical research did not start or end in Nazi Germany. In the infamous Tuskegee study, beginning in the 1930s, over 600 men signed up for a study for which they were given free meals, medical care, and funerals.[7] This was a study of untreated syphilis, but the participants who had syphilis were simply told that they had "bad blood" and would be treated. They were, in fact, given placebos (inactive substances) or

---

[2] See the discussion in 11.4.1, below.
[3] Directives 2001/20/EC and 2005/28/EC, respectively.
[4] The Medicines for Human Use (Clinical Trials Regulations) 2004/1031.
[5] The Medicines for Human Use (Clinical Trials) Amendment Regulations 2006/1928.
[6] See DH 2005b, para.3.2.
[7] See *http://www.tuskegee.edu/global/Story.asp?s=1209870* and Pence 1995.

subjected to purely diagnostic procedures. This continued even after penicillin came into use as a treatment for syphilis in the 1940s. During the course of the study, over 28 died of syphilis, 100 died of related complications, at least 40 wives were infected, and 19 children were infected at birth. All the participants were black. This occurred in the US over a period of 40 years, only ending in the 1970s.

The medical profession, like any other profession, has its fair share of rogues. The trust and confidence typically vested in the medical profession is such that the involvement of any doctors in abusive practices is particularly disconcerting. In 1988, a New Zealand public inquiry examined a senior gynaecologist's study that had been designed to challenge the orthodox view that a positive smear test result was an early warning of cervical cancer.[8] His decision not to treat some of these women until the onset of manifest malignancy caused at least 27 to die prematurely and many others to endure avoidable invasive surgery. Many of his patients were not aware that they were participating in a study. As such extreme cases demonstrate, all patients are potentially vulnerable to abuse in the hands of those responsible for their medical care. Those health professionals who are researchers will often be at the forefront of their speciality, but they could also have considerable self-interest in conducting and publishing research. The New Zealand gynaecologist made a career out of publishing the results of his cervical cancer study. Insofar as career progression and prestige track research publications, researchers have an incentive to produce the research results necessary for those publications.

There can also be considerable financial interests at stake for both researchers (sometimes called investigators) and commercial companies. A successful drug trial can sometimes make or break a pharmaceutical company. A great deal of medical research is now commercial. In fact, the pharmaceutical industry conducts 65 per cent of the UK's health-related research and development, investing some £3.3 billion a year.[9] This has a number of consequences. One consequence is that research money is largely directed at developing lucrative treatments, so that 90 per cent of medical research spending is directed at diseases that cause only 10 per cent of the global disease burden.[10] Another is that private companies increasingly consider it to be in their interests to offer health professionals financial inducements for assistance in the recruitment of research participants. The potential for conflicts of interest is evident.[11] Moreover, financial opportunities linked to research projects provide an incentive for companies and individual researchers to jurisdiction shop. The result can be a form of medical tourism—research tourism. Research tourism out of a jurisdiction is likely to be encouraged by overly stringent regulatory responses, with the consequent loss of research funds, opportunities, and talent.

Medical research is capable of producing immense benefits to the lives and health of those who are ill or potentially ill. It is the linchpin of medical

---

[8] See Cartwright 1988, discussed in BMA 2004.
[9] See House of Commons Select Committee on Health 2005, paras 21–22.
[10] See Kong 2004, 167.
[11] See Shimm and Spece 1991.

progress. Medical research on human subjects is often the only way of satisfactorily establishing that many treatments are safe and effective. Doctors can report the results of their treatment practices on particular patients (in so-called "case notes"), but, in the absence of a well-designed study, those results can lack predictive value. Animal studies can take us so far, but biological differences can hinder their extrapolative relevance. Medical research on human subjects is therefore crucial to the protection of patient lives and health, and thereby required to protect (positive) rights and duties, to maximise utility, and to prevent interference with rights and virtues. We will return to ethical discussion later (11.3), but we first need to consider what medical research actually involves.

11.2.1 What is medical research?

It is important to remember that the same label can be used to describe different concepts and different labels are used to describe the same concept, as discussed in Ch.1 (1.3.2.2). In this chapter, *"medical research"* will be defined broadly as any type of study or experiment performed for the purpose of producing generalisable knowledge related to human health or medical treatment. Medical research performed on human beings could involve observation or some form of intervention (whether physical, chemical, or psychological).[12] Medical research performed on *patients* will be described as *"clinical research"*. Not all medical research is clinical research, so defined. In fact, new pharmaceutical drugs are usually first tested on animals and healthy human volunteers, before they are tested on patient volunteers (see below). Not all clinical research requires direct contact with the patient. Epidemiological research, involving the study of health-related conditions in populations, rarely requires direct contact. Consider, for example, research into the connection between smoking and lung cancer undertaken by reviewing patient health records.

This chapter adopts the modern practice of referring to those who are researched upon as *"participants"*. Many regulatory instruments use the term "subject" instead of "participant". Many commentators prefer "participant", as a less passive term, to emphasise the need to ensure that person's consent or, if the person lacks capacity, at least acquiescence. Both terms have the potential for creating misunderstanding: "participant" might be mistakenly considered to refer to the researcher and "subject" might be mistakenly considered to refer to the thing (such as a new therapy or drug) being tested. Terminological consistency is the best way of avoiding such misunderstandings. The use of "participant" in this chapter should not be taken to imply acceptance or rejection of particular views on the practices of medical researchers. Some feminists have suggested, for example, that, in practice, research *object* is a more accurate description.[13]

---

[12] See CIOMS 2002 (preamble).
[13] See Fox 1998, 122.

11.2.2 Innovative treatment and research

Innovative treatment is a feature of medical care, as doctors at times modify their medical practices in the light of what they learn from patients' experiences and this will sometimes lead to experimentation with a new, untested therapy.[14] This is just one reason why it is not always easy to distinguish treatment and research. The distinction is usually expressed in terms of the healthcare professional's primary aim or intention. The primary aim of medical research is to produce new knowledge for the benefit of future patients. The primary aim of medical treatment is to benefit the immediate patient. Activities can, however, have multiple aims and it is possible to mislead and be misled. A doctor who uses an unproven therapy could intend to benefit future patients as a primary or secondary aim.

Patients are vulnerable to misunderstanding the difference between research and treatment. A research project could be confused with innovative treatment. Even if the participants do not make this mistake, they could hold unrealistic hopes of being cured by their participation. Both are potential dangers of a mind-set known as the *"therapeutic misconception"*, whereby the participant mistakenly assumes that decisions about their participation are made solely with their benefit in mind (see 11.3.1.1, below).[15] Not all hope of a benefit need be based on a mistaken mindset. Some research might directly benefit the participant and is therefore sometimes referred to as *therapeutic research*. In contrast, the participant is not expected to directly benefit from so-called *non-therapeutic research*. All research will, by definition, involve activities or procedures that are non-therapeutic and will involve uncertainty as to the outcome. While not all research-orientated procedures are risky or invasive, some will be. Observational procedures are very different from surgical procedures. Therapeutic research could describe procedures that are identical to those used in innovative treatment or even procedures that are highly unlikely to benefit the participant.

A research project could also potentially benefit one group of research participants but not another. In a *randomised controlled trial* (RCT), which will be examined in depth shortly, one group of participants will receive a different treatment or procedure to the other(s). Groups are allocated at random and participants will not know to which group they have been allocated. If one group receives a new therapy and the other receives a placebo (an inactive substance), then the project is potentially therapeutic for the first group but not for the second group. It is potentially misleading to describe such a project *as a whole* as either therapeutic or non-therapeutic.

In the light of these realities, the World Medical Association's Helsinki Declaration was redrafted to remove references in "therapeutic research". Instead, Part C of the current version of the Declaration refers to "research combined with medicinal care". The conceptual distinction between research from which the

---

[14] See BMA 2004, 491.
[15] Seminally, see Appelbaum et al. 1982, esp. 321.

participant is predicted to gain a medical benefit and research from which the participant is not expected to gain a medical benefit remains. The ethical and regulatory question is whether and when anything should turn on it, particularly taking account of the potential for the therapeutic misconception to operate.

11.2.3 Controlled trials

Many scientific and medical advances were the result of a fortunate accident or innovative treatment, rather than a carefully designed research project. Penicillin is an oft-cited example of serendipity and many modern day surgical techniques were developed as innovative treatments. Whatever the origin and apparent success of a new therapy, evidence of its efficacy is proportionate to evidence that other factors have not contributed to the positive treatment outcome. Controlled trials are designed for the purpose of discriminating between those patient-outcomes caused by the therapy and those caused by other factors, such as the natural progression of the disease and patient expectations.[16]

Controlled trials compare the effects of the therapy on one group (the *test group*) with the effects of alternative approaches on another group (the *control group*).[17] The control group could be a *historical control*, such as where the course of the health condition is uniform in a particular population or otherwise predictable from past experience. Usually, however, a *concurrent control* is needed because the outcome cannot be predicted with sufficient accuracy. The control group should be chosen to eliminate other factors, which will generally require its members to be chosen from the same population as the test group. Bias in the selection of the groups is usually avoided by a random method of allocation. Thus, many studies are randomised controlled trials (*RCTs*). RCTs have been widely considered to represent the "gold standard" for the testing of new therapies since the 1940s.[18]

The treatment given to a control group could be (a) a placebo, (b) no treatment, (c) a slight variation of what is given to the test group, or (d) a different active treatment.[19] A control group given no treatment might still receive palliative care (i.e. care addressing pain and discomfort but lacking curative effect). Typically the control group will receive either a placebo or the standard therapy ((a) or (d)).[20] A control group given a placebo might also receive treatment, such as where both the test group and the control group are given the standard treatment in addition to the new treatment or a placebo. The purpose of the placebo

---

[16] See ICH 2000, 2.
[17] See ICH 2000.
[18] See Miller and Brody 2002, 3.
[19] See ICH 2000, 3.
[20] See Ferguson 2003, 48.

is to eliminate the "placebo effect", whereby the patient's belief that something beneficial is being received leads to some improvement in the symptoms. The placebo effect is well reported to occur in studies of pain interventions and studies where the primary outcome measure is a varying, subjective measure.[21] If the test group does better (in a statistically relevant sense) than a control group given, say, a sugar pill, then this provides evidence that the new therapy is actually effective. Unfortunately, a placebo control cannot counteract all psychological effects, because a modest benefit from the test therapy might increase any psychological effects. In other words, the factors that lead to the placebo effect could be magnified where the patient actually experiences some benefit. Sometimes more than one control group will need to be used if the effects of as many factors as possible are to be counter-balanced.

Whether an individual research participant is in the test or control group could, for many types of research, be kept secret from the participant to limit the effects of bias and expectations. Such trials are said to be *blind*. Blinding is, for obvious reasons, required in all placebo-controlled trials. To limit the effects of researcher bias and expectations, it is sometimes feasible for the researcher to also be kept ignorant of which group a particular participant is in. Such trials are said to be *double blind*. Clearly, blind and double blind trials are only compatible with some types of research. Blind trials are only possible where the research project can be set up in such a way that the participant cannot work out the allocated group from the procedures administered and similarly for double blind trials with regard to the researchers. In drug trials, this could be simply a matter of ensuring that the only difference between the test and control groups is the content of the tablet given to the participants.

In sum, research projects could be therapeutic, controlled (e.g. placebo-controlled), randomised, blinded, or a combination of these things. The vast majority of clinical trials are controlled, randomised, and blinded and it is this form of RCT that is considered to represent the scientific "gold standard".

11.2.4 Phases of research on medicinal products

Pharmaceutical research on humans is often described in terms of four phases (Phase I–IV).[22] Phase I trials usually have non-therapeutic objectives and are conducted to test the toxicity or dose of new drugs. Such trials are usually conducted on a small number of healthy volunteers. Phase II trials are designed to explore the short-term toxicity and therapeutic efficacy of a product on a small group of patients (generally 40 or 50)[23] suffering from the condition in question. Phase III trials are designed to confirm any therapeutic benefit

---

[21] See Albin 2005, 149.
[22] See ICH 1997, 5–8.
[23] See Ferguson 2002, 130.

suggested by a Phase II trial. These usually involve monitoring the effects of supervised use of the product in patients over a long period of time and are usually RCTs. A successful Phase III study is intended to provide support for obtaining authorisation to market the product. Placebo-controlled randomised trials tend to be used for Phase II and III clinical trials.

After the drug is authorised for use, further studies could be conducted, which are referred to as Phase IV trials. Such post-marketing monitoring studies are, in theory, about optimising the use of the product. In practice, manufacturers often see such studies as a form of post-marketing advertising.

11.3 The ethics of medical research

In addition to issues of privacy and confidentiality, addressed in Ch.6, medical research on humans raises many ethical questions on which different views exist. Those theories focusing on the greater good of society (such as utilitarianism and communitarianism) might be expected to take a generally more permissive approach towards medical research than those focusing on the rights and interests of individuals (such as rights-based and duty-based theories). This will sometimes be the case, but such a generalisation must be treated with care. Medical research can track rights, interests, and virtues that are important to all the major moral theories and safeguards are required to maximise utility and protect communal values just as much as they are to protect rights and ensure compliance with duties. Not all activities capable of being described as medical research are equally important or defensible.

Producing the most scientifically valuable results is potentially incompatible with protecting all morally relevant interests. All moral theories will take a view on how to balance the need for evidence-based medicine with the need to protect research participants from avoidable harm. The balance will, in part, depend on the role and validity of the participant's consent (11.3.1) and the approach taken towards the so-called principle of equipoise (11.3.2).

A note of caution should be raised before we discuss the points of divergence among different moral theories. The transition between moral principle and public policy is not always straightforward. In another context, one commentator has noted:

> For one thing, there are enforcement costs once we convert moral principle into legal prohibition as well as significant inroads into individual choice and freedom; and, although for practical purposes both law and morality demand some degree of closure and settlement, the integrity of morality is not threatened by ongoing debate, review, and adjustment of position.[24]

In other words, practical contingencies can affect the application of abstract moral principles.

---

[24] Brownsword 2003a, 418–419.

11.3.1 The role and validity of consent

Consent, understood as valid agreement to the activity in question, poses a number of difficulties. There can be difficulty determining when an individual is actually consenting, because signals can be misinterpreted (see Ch.6 (6.3.1)). There can be difficulty determining whether the individual in question has the competence, voluntariness, or information required for any apparent agreement to be treated as a valid consent (see Chs 4 and 5). These difficulties are underpinned by normative questions stemming from law and moral theory. These include questions about what ought to be taken as sufficient evidence of consent and when ostensible consent ought to be treated as valid. In addition, there are normative questions about the justificatory force of a valid consent.

Where effective, consent removes the burden of an otherwise binding duty. The extent to which consent can be effective as a waiver of the benefit of a duty is theory dependent, because some moral theories allow individuals to waive the benefit of duties that other theories do not. There is a tension between theories placing significant limits on the power of competent individuals to release others from the burden of duties that they owe to them and those theories imposing no such limits. Beyleveld and Brownsword have argued that different views on the role of consent give rise to two opposed conceptions of human dignity: "dignity as constraint" and "dignity as empowerment".[25]

The *dignity as constraint* position holds that human dignity sets non-waivable limits on conduct in a civilised society. It is characterised by the idea that some duties protect an individual *irrespective of that individual's will*, on the basis that these duties reflect non-waivable community values (communitarian view) or duties that an individual also owes to himself (the duty-based view). Orthodox Catholicism and the moral theory of Immanuel Kant are examples of duty-based positions of this type. Hellman and Hellman adopt such a position, which leads them to argue that the patient has "rights" (meaning protected interests) that are implicit in a doctor–patient relationship, including:

> The right to be treated as an individual deserving the physician's best judgment and care, rather than to be used as a means to determine the best treatment of others, is inherent in every person. This right, based on the concept of dignity, *cannot be waived*.[26]

Such a view prevents consent being relied on to justify medical research capable of detrimentally affecting the participant's health or life. In contrast, the *dignity as empowerment* view grants a much greater justificatory role to consent. It holds that duties can only be imposed to protect the interests of those individuals who wish their interests to be protected. Rights-based theories fall

---

[25] See Beyleveld and Brownsword 2001, and the discussion in Ch.1 (1.4.1).
[26] Hellman and Hellman 1991, 1587 (my emphasis).

within the dignity as empowerment camp because they hold that rights-holders are permitted to waive the benefit of *all* their rights. Theories of a utilitarian-ilk, while rejecting both dignity-rationales, are much closer to the empowerment than the constraint camp. What matters for preference utilitarians, for example, is maximising preferences, rather than protecting individuals from themselves. Thus, there are different views on the role of consent at the level of principle.[27]

Radically different views at the level of moral principle do not, however, always result in opposed positions at the level of public policy. Practical impediments might, for example, prevent or restrict reliance on consent in contexts where, in principle, consent would be a complete answer to the moral dilemma under consideration.

11.3.1.1 The therapeutic misconception

The danger of the "therapeutic misconception" goes to the heart of reliance on consent in the context of clinical research. The problem is that participants could, *if adequate precautions are not taken*, mistakenly believe that their participation in a research project is designed to address their specific health needs.[28] This is particularly likely to occur when a doctor suggests that a patient should consider enrolling in a trial that is designed to test a new therapy to treat the condition from which the patient is suffering. Patient volunteers could be expected to have difficulty distinguishing the role of the physician-carer from that of the physician-researcher. Any such difficulty will be exacerbated where the patient sees participation in a research project as the best way of obtaining otherwise unavailable treatments—a notable example being patients with HIV/AIDS who hear about a new therapy that is being tested.[29] In contrast, the therapeutic misconception is much less likely to occur where medical research is conducted on healthy volunteers. Healthy volunteers are unlikely to expect that their taking part in a research project will directly benefit their health. This means that some precautions that could be considered necessary to ensure voluntariness in Phase II and III trials (or combined Phase I/II trials)[30] might not be necessary for Phase I trials.

The therapeutic misconception was seminally reported by Appelbaum et al. who noted the power of this mind-set to skew the participant's understanding of the research trial.[31] Examining two trials, the authors noted that the therapeutic misconception led some of those who were not given contrary information to assume that their participation would advance their therapeutic interests and some of those who were given contrary information to hear only

---

[27] See further Beyleveld and Pattinson 2008, for discussion of the twin dangers of research worship and consent worship.

[28] See Appelbaum et al. 1982 and Appelbaum 2002.

[29] See e.g. the discussion of the HIV/AIDS patient advocacy groups in Dresser 2003, esp. 240.

[30] Where the product being tested is highly likely to be toxic, such as a chemotherapy product for cancer treatments, the first human trials will use patients and are therefore best described as combined Phase I/II trials.

[31] See Appelbaum et al. 1982.

those parts that fitted with their preconception that they would benefit.[32] If this is so, then obtaining informed consent for clinical research would seem to require blunt honesty of a type that is likely to discourage participation. If consent is required by moral principle, then a very clear explanation that the trial's design is not coterminous with their therapeutic needs will be required in practice. Not all moral theories will insist on consent as a matter of over-riding principle. If there is a moral duty to participate in any medical research, then obtaining consent for such a project can only be a procedural safeguard rather than a principled requirement.

11.3.1.2 Duties to participate in research

Whether consent is a *necessary* justificatory condition for all types of medical research on *competent* human subjects is hotly debated. For those moral theories imposing extensive positive duties, particularly those of a utilitarian or commu-nitarian persuasion, participation in some types of medical research could be a moral duty. As already suggested, a strong duty to participate in certain types of research project could, in principle at least, remove the need to ensure that the potential participant is fully informed or even consents at all. Utilitarians could appeal directly to the principle of utility, noting the utility-maximising conse-quences of widespread participation in medical research. Duties to participate in research could also be defended by reliance on a social contract-type argument, whereby it is argued that those who benefit from a public health system are, as quid pro quo, required to contribute to its continued effectiveness by partici-pating in medical research.[33] Some theorists are not prepared to accept such arguments. Hans Jonas, for example, holds that "progress is an optional goal" and rejects the social-contract argument on the basis that society has no right to call in a personal debt that is actually owed to past "martyrs".[34] The debate is essentially over the limits of our positive obligations.

John Harris argues for a moral duty to undertake, support, and even partic-ipate in medical research.[35] His conclusion is restricted to medical research that is "well designed" for the purpose of "preventing serious harm or providing significant benefits to humankind".[36] Further, the burden placed on research participants, individuals, or society must be low relative to the moral benefits of conducting the research. Harris relies on two principles to defend this qual-ified conclusion: the obligation to "do no harm" (interpreted as imposing posi-tive duties to take reasonable steps to prevent serious harm to others) and an appeal to "basic fairness" (whereby "free riders", who accept the benefits of medical advances without being willing to contribute, are said be acting incon-sistently with the principle of fairness). Harris rejects opposed principles in international protocols, such as the statement in paragraph five of the 2000 version of the Helsinki Declaration that "the wellbeing of the human subject

---

[32] See Appelbaum et al. 1982, 328.
[33] See Mackillop and Johnston 1986, 178–179.
[34] Jonas 1980, 105–135.
[35] See Harris 2005.
[36] Harris, 2005, 242.

should take precedence over the interests of science and society".[37] He argues that the interests of participants, as merely one group potentially affected by medical research, should not automatically take precedence over the comparable or more important interests of other groups. He is careful to point out that a moral duty to participate in research does not automatically justify forced conscription, as requiring fully informed consent is usually the best way of preventing the abuse of research participants.[38] He does, however, wish to draw an analogy with instances of mandatory contribution to public goods, such as jury service for British citizens.[39] Moreover, Harris restricts his argument for a moral duty to participate to situations where the costs and risks are minimal and explicitly declares that he is not arguing for a duty to enable industry to profit from our moral commitments.[40]

Harris' argument is consistent with many utilitarian positions. Indeed, the underlying moral position displayed in his other work is arguably best interpreted as a form of (rule) preference utilitarianism for the reasons given in Ch.17 (17.2.1). His argument will have little persuasive force for adherents of moral theories rejecting positive duties, such as the negative rights-based theory of Robert Nozick.[41] In contrast, a rights-based theory accepting extensive positive rights could support the conclusion that we have a prima facie duty to support or even participate in some types of research. Such a theory will, of course, reject any suggestion that the rights of any group potentially affected by medical research could be aggregated so as to outweigh the rights of potential research participants. All theories recognising positive duties will recognise limitations on those duties. Many moral positions hold, for example, that positive duties do not require the assister to give up anything of comparable moral significance (i.e. a "reasonable burden" or "comparable cost" condition).[42] Such limitations on the ambit of positive duties will restrict the types of medical research for which there can be a positive duty to participate. In other words, the choice of moral theory also has an impact on the competing interests or rights that a potential participant can legitimately appeal to as a way of overriding any prima facie obligation to participate.

Harris does not wish limit his arguments to one moral position. His arguments are, however, contingent on the acceptance of certain moral premises. His jury analogy, for example, requires acceptance of the current jury service system. Jury service can place considerable burdens on jurors in relation to freedom of speech and movement during a trial. An extreme example of this is shown by the recent fraud trial that collapsed after two years, largely because of jurors' difficulties.[43] Not all moral theories will accept the imposition of the

---

[37] See Harris 2005, 243. This principle was phrased even more forcefully in 1996 version of the Helsinki declaration and is once again more forceful in the 2008 version: see 11.4.1, below.
[38] See Harris 2005, 245.
[39] See Harris 2005, 244–245.
[40] See Harris 2004, 245 and 246.
[41] See Nozick 1974.
[42] See e.g. Harris 1985, 57 (implicitly utilitarian position), Singer 1993, 229–232 (utilitarian position), and Gewirth 1978, 217–220 (rights-based position). All of whom wish to restrict the ambit of positive duties by such a reasonable burden condition.
[43] See Leigh 2005.

sacrifices required by this or similar jury systems. Moreover, there is arguably a disanalogy with *physically invasive* medical research. Better analogies with regard to invasive research are blood donation, vaccination, and military service, but such activities are not currently subject to a participatory duty in English law.

11.3.1.3 Inducements

Do inducements to participate in medical research threaten or negate the voluntariness of the participant's consent? Such claims are usually made with regard to potentially risky activities such as medical research, surrogacy, or organ donation (on the other two examples see Chs 8 and 13, respectively). The argument must be that payment (or other inducements) that persuade people to participate in such activities amount to coercion or undue influence, or will, in practice, lead to coercion or undue influence.

Theorists who reject the claims of those opposed to payment on the grounds of voluntariness typically rely on two analogies.[44] *First*, it is argued that people are frequently induced to engage in many menial or risky jobs by the offer of payment. Examples of paid activities that are widely regarded as legitimate include the work of a professional boxer, fire-fighter, soldier, and racing car driver. This will be called the *risky employment analogy*. *Second*, it is argued that unpaid participation faces many of the same risks to voluntariness, yet few reject unpaid participation in such activities. This will be called the *unpaid analogy*. Both analogies presuppose acceptance of the view that the allegedly analogous activities are acceptable: that other forms of risky employment are morally acceptable and that unpaid participation in medical research (or organ donation or surrogacy) is acceptable. Like all arguments by analogy, they also require the activities in question to be morally equivalent, so that there is no defensible moral principle capable of demonstrating a disanalogy.

McNeill seeks to reject the risky employment analogy on that basis that,

> The risks of being harmed in our work are usually known in advance and can be minimised by adopting safe practices. The situation is not comparable to research. By definition, research, which involves experimentation on human subjects, exposes those human subjects to risks of harm and those risks cannot be known in advance. ... [Also] the analogy with dangerous or risky work does not apply to research because the results of experiments are not necessary to society in the way in which some dangerous work may be.[45]

The argument that the risks of work activities are known in advance faces obvious counter-examples. The risk of asbestosis faced by those working in industries dealing with asbestos was not known until a few decades ago. The argument that measures can be taken to minimise risks is far from compelling, because the effectiveness of such measures will vary (front-line infantry will always face some risk of death) and measures can also be taken to minimise the

---

[44] See e.g. Wilkinson and Moore 1997. Outside the context of medical research, see Pattinson 2003a.
[45] McNeill 1997, 391–392.

risk from medical research (e.g. prior animal experiments and safety protocols). The argument that the results of experiments are "not necessary to society" in the way that dangerous work could be is subject to the unpaid analogy. It also assumes, as McNeill explicitly states, that medical research is a mere luxury, lacking the potential to significantly benefit society. We have seen that a well-designed research trial is the most accurate way of ensuring that the treatments that are used or considered for use in the future are safe and effective, relative to the alternatives. Knowing whether a treatment is likely to be safe and effective is surely a benefit to those who might be given the treatment in the future. Moreover, if, as other theorists have argued, the benefit of some types of medical research is such as to impose a moral duty to participate, then payment cannot be rejected as undermining voluntariness, because it merely provides an incentive to do what one is already morally obliged to do.

The claim that, in practice, payment will lead to coercion or undue influence involves an empirical prediction. It is a feared end point argument of the type addressed in Ch.1 (1.4.2). As such, it requires that the risk of the feared endpoint occurring, taking account of any preventive measures that could be put in place, outweighs the benefits of allowing the activity in question. Paying participants might have many benefits. It has, for example, been suggested that paying patient-participants might actually aid voluntariness by helping to dispel the therapeutic misconception.[46] Evaluating feared end argument arguments is not, however, always straightforward, because what are benefits or disbenefits and how they are to be weighed will vary from theory to theory.

The majority of those who question the voluntariness of paid participation simultaneously appeal to other arguments to bolster their conclusion that payment should be prohibited or heavily restricted. They often appeal to a supportive conception of exploitation or human dignity. A popular claim is that financial inducements (or inducements removing a financial burden) are most likely to influence the impecunious, who are considered to be particularly vulnerable to exploitation.[47] The counter-argument is that, where those offering the inducement are not responsible for the financial need of the potential participant, offering an inducement simply increases the range of options available to him. Prohibiting or limiting payment appears to be a misguided way of addressing the conditions that make a potential participant vulnerable in the first place. Those who appeal to a moral theory in the dignity as constraint camp can reject the sufficiency of consent outright, irrespective of its voluntariness. Accepting payment could be held to violate one's dignity irrespective of whether or not one consents. Similarly, virtue theorists are likely to lament the tension between commercialisation and the virtue of altruism. This tension is not conclusive because financial volunteers could have altruistic motives for seeking payment, such as wanting to donate the money to charity.

Payment for participation in medical research could also be questioned, irrespective of the issue of consent, on the grounds that payment is likely to have negative consequences for the scientific validity of the results. Payment could,

---

[46] See Dickert and Grady 1999.
[47] See e.g. McNeill 1997, 394–396.

for example, encourage potential participants to withhold information to ensure their eligibility for payment or could render the participants unrepresentative of the population as a whole. Reliance on such concerns could, however, a double-edged sword, where payment is the only or most effective way to attract a scientifically adequate sample. Arguments relying on the contingencies of a particular situation call for responses that are directed towards those contingencies, rather than blanket prohibitions. In short, many of the arguments relying on negative consequences of payment are little more than arguments against particular types of research trials or particular types of payment systems, rather than arguments against payment itself.

Many national and international instruments adopt a compromise position and allow expenses or payments that are kept at modest levels. The guidance of the General Medical Council (GMC) states that doctors must

> not offer payments at a level which could induce research participants to take risks that they would otherwise not take, or to volunteer more frequently than is advisable or against their better interests or judgement.[48]

The international ethical guidance of the Council for International Organizations of Medical Sciences (CIOMS) states that any

> payments should not be so large ... or the medical services so extensive as to induce prospective subjects to consent to participate in the research against their better judgement ("undue inducement").[49]

While such statements can be read as questioning the voluntariness of participation where large payments are offered, they are probably more coherently interpreted as compromise positions accepting elements of the dignity of constraint view. The legal import of such instruments will be examined below (in 11.4.1).

11.3.1.4 The vulnerable

All actual and potential participants are potentially vulnerable when it comes to obtaining their valid consent. Some groups are widely considered to be *particularly vulnerable*, because they face an increased likelihood of succumbing to pressure or an increased likelihood of failing to properly understand the nature of that to which they agree or acquiesce. At one extreme are those who are (temporarily or permanently) unable to consent, such as the unconscious, some mentally disabled adults, and young children. The incapacitated are a special category and will be addressed below (in 11.3.3). Here, we are concerned with those who are able to provide a valid consent, but whose voluntariness or understanding is particularly fragile or open to question. Pressures undermining voluntariness present increased dangers where, for example, the prospective participant is in a relationship of dependency, such as

---

[48] GMC 2002b, para.14.
[49] CIOMS 2002, guidelines 7.

students on courses run by the researchers and prisoners whose freedom is controlled by those seeking their consent. In fact, all patients who seek the assistance of a doctor at a time of need and ill-health are dependent on that doctor and therefore potentially vulnerable to suggestion. We have already seen that understanding can also be undermined by the therapeutic misconception, which can be a significant factor for those who are desperate to participate in a research project and see it as a way of obtaining otherwise unavailable treatment for their terminal illness.[50]

Vulnerability calls for protective mechanisms. Exclusion from research trials is an extreme protective measure that can also be the practical effect of other concerns. Members of groups that are likely to have unusual reactions or face increased susceptibility to adverse consequences tend to be underrepresented or excluded because of the difficulty or inconvenience of obtaining valid consent or because moral limits are placed on the sufficiency of any consent by views of a dignity as constraint persuasion. Blanket exclusion of particular groups from participation in research is, however, likely to have a detrimental impact on the quality of the healthcare given to those groups. The population as a whole does not respond uniformly to medical treatment. Feminists have pointed out that the reluctance to test new therapies on pregnant women, or even women of childbearing age, can have the effect of turning what is standard treatment for men into innovative treatment with uncertain risks for women.[51] The reluctance to test new therapies on the elderly has similar implications for the 18 per cent of the population that is over 65, which happens to be a section of the population that consumes 50 per cent of all prescribed drugs.[52] Research into some conditions requires the participation of particular groups. The study of paediatric diseases requires research on children (children are not, biologically speaking, small adults), the study of mental illness requires research on the mentally ill, and the study of age-related conditions requires participants in the relevant age group. Similarly, emergency research (such as resuscitation research on those who have suffered from cardiac arrest or head trauma) will usually require participants who are unconscious or otherwise incapacitated.[53] Blanket exclusion also means that those groups will be prevented from obtaining the benefits of participation. Remember that some research trials do present hope of directly benefiting the participant (so-called therapeutic research) and others offer indirect benefits (such as the sense of satisfaction often generated by contributing to charity or the positive interaction with health professionals and others facilitated by participation). Moreover, as stated above, enrolment in research trials is sometimes the only way to become a potential recipient of otherwise unavailable experimental treatment—one RCT of HIV drugs was rendered ineffective when patients who were desperate to receive treatment pooled the drugs.[54] Exclusion affects the distribution of the benefits as well as the burdens of medical research. It follows

---

[50] See e.g. Dresser 2003, esp. 240.
[51] See e.g. Fox 1998, 123–124 and 126–128.
[52] See Ferguson 2002, 130.
[53] See further Plomer 2001 and Lötjönen 2002.
[54] See McHale 2004b, 872.

that excluding the particularly vulnerable from participating in research trials could, from some moral positions, be challenged as unjust and discriminatory.[55]

As with the issue of payment, many national and international instruments adopt a compromise position. The Helsinki Declaration, for example, does not exclude those who are in a position of dependency from participating in research, but requires consent to be obtained by "an appropriately qualified individual who is completely independent of this relationship".[56]

11.3.2 Equipoise and placebos

Many moral theories are divided over how to determine when and whether the risks faced by prospective research participants are acceptable.

11.3.2.1 Equipoise and uncertainty

There is ethical debate about the extent to which the outcome must be uncertain for it to be ethically permissible to initiate or continue a controlled trial. A balance of uncertainty over the therapeutic merits of a therapy relative to the control is sometimes described as "equipoise". There is dispute over whether equipoise is a necessary condition of a legitimate clinical trial, the extent to which equipoise continues to be relevant throughout the trial, and how equipoise is to be determined.

In his seminal work, the late Benjamin Freedman argued that "clinical" rather than "theoretical" equipoise is a necessary condition for legitimate research.[57] Freedman considered "theoretical equipoise" to exist where the researcher has no treatment preference, i.e. when the researcher considers the arms of the trial to be balanced with regard to the merit of the treatment offered in each. He considered this to be "overwhelmingly fragile" and disturbed by even a slight accretion of evidence between the arms of the trial.[58] Freedman offered clinical equipoise as an alternative, which he said exists where there is genuine uncertainty *in the medical community* about the comparative therapeutic merit of the different treatment approaches. He argued that

> at the start of the trial, there must be a state of clinical equipoise regarding the merits of the regimens to be tested, and the trial must be designed in such a way as to make it reasonable to expect that, if it is successfully concluded, clinical equipoise will be disturbed. In other words, the results of a successful clinical trial should be convincing enough to resolve the dispute among clinicians.[59]

[55] See e.g. Lötjönen 2000, 197–198; Plomer 2001, 334; and Hagger and Woods 2005, esp. 50 and 55. The European Commission has proposed a Regulation that requires and provides incentives for increased research on children: see Lötjönen 2005, n.17.

[56] Principle 26 of the 2008 version. This principle appeared (though worded slightly differently) in previous versions of the Helsinki declaration.

[57] See Freedman 1987.

[58] Freedman 1987, 143.

[59] Freedman 1987, 144.

Freedman left many questions of detail unanswered, such as how the appropriate medical community is to be identified and what percentage of that community must be divided before equipoise can be said to exist.[60] These questions can only be addressed by reference to the ethical rationale of the principle of equipoise. The difficulty is that the general principle could plausibly be interpreted as the application of a number of differing ethical tenets. The principle of equipoise could be interpreted as a substantive or procedural moral requirement. Interpreted as a substantive moral requirement, it holds that participants must not be disadvantaged by participation in a clinical trial, because they cannot permissibly be asked to risk their health or life in the name of science. This view is consistent with the dignity as constraint position. Interpreted as a procedural moral requirement, it could be understood as a practical safeguard designed to reduce opportunities for abuse presented by, for example, the effects of the therapeutic misconception. The interpretation given will influence the stringency of its requirements and the exceptions made to it, if any.

It should not be assumed that all theories will adopt the principle. Requiring clinical equipoise (let alone theoretical equipoise) will inevitably prevent some scientifically valid research taking place. Miller and Brody are among the theorists who seek to reject the principle on the basis that it ignores the ethically relevant distinction between clinical trials and treatment.[61] The objectives of research and treatment certainly differ; the question is whether non-therapeutic, risky procedures can be legitimately conducted by doctors.

11.3.2.2 Placebos (sham treatment)

Few would question the use of a placebo control in a RCT where no standard treatment exists and there is genuine uncertainty within the scientific community about whether the possible therapy being tested has any therapeutic merit. Placebo controls become ethically controversial where the therapeutic needs of participants appear to be better addressed by allocation to the test group or by not entering the research trial at all. This might be because the test group is using a standard or new therapy that is considered to be effective, so that there is neither individual (theoretical) nor collective (clinical) equipoise. It might also be because receiving the control is itself potentially harmful, the most dramatic example of which is the surgical placebo (sham surgery). In such circumstances there could be a tension between the need for scientific rigour and the health interests of research participants.[62] Some have argued that many placebo-controlled trials are morally required to protect patients from unhelpful and dangerous treatment,[63] even where the placebo has to be surgical.[64] Albin has, for example, argued "that use of surgical placebos is

---

[60] See Johnson et al. 1991 and Alderson 1996, 135.
[61] See Miller and Brody 2002.
[62] Compromise positions are popular here: see e.g. Emanuel and Miller 2001.
[63] See e.g. Cohen 2002.
[64] See Albin 2002 and 2005.

necessary for the rigorous experimental designs needed to exclude false positive trial results".[65]

Research into the use of fetal tissue grafting in those with Parkinson's disease has reignited the debate about surgical placebos.[66] While experiments on animals and trials without placebo-controls were encouraging, it was unclear to what extent the improvement in patients was attributable to the placebo-effect. The placebo-effect is problematic for such trials, relying as they do on the patient's self-reporting of the effects of treatment. Researchers therefore proposed to conduct controlled trials using a surgical placebo, whereby those in the control group would have their skulls drilled but would not be given the fetal tissue grafts that were to be given to the test group. Albin reports that such trials have now taken place and have revealed that there is indeed a significant placebo effect, probably aggravated by dopamine release.[67]

The principal justification for sham surgery emphasises the numbers issue: a large number of future patients could be protected by taking controlled risks with a few research participants. Numbers are directly relevant to those utilitarian theories that are prepared to aggregate the interests of a large group to outweigh the interests of a smaller number in the utility balance. Contrary to appearances, numbers can also be relevant to duty and rights-based theories, albeit it indirectly. In some situations, for example, the greater the number put at risk by a particular action or inaction, the more likely that the most important rights or interests of a single person will be violated or frustrated. In the philosophical literature, the intuitive difficulty created by numbers is represented by two thought experiments, the transplant case and the trolley problem.[68] In the transplant case, mentioned in Ch.1 (1.3.2), a surgeon can save five patients by sacrificing a single patient and using that patient's perfectly compatible organs and tissue. In the trolley problem, a runaway railway trolley is heading towards five workmen but can be diverted to a branch line, where it will collide with only one. Many theorists have sought to justify their intuition that a preference for advancing the interests of the five over the single individual is unacceptable in the transplant case, but acceptable (or even morally required) in the runaway trolley problem.[69] Building on this intuition, Albin has tried to draw an analogy between the trolley problem and the surgical placebo problem.[70] Whether or not such an analogy succeeds depends on the criteria of analogy. No such analogy works, for example, if the rationale for distinguishing the transplantation case from the trolley problem is the need to minimise the risk of losing any life. In any event, rights-based theories will consider that, in principle, surgical placebos pose no such tension, because they are permissible as long as the participants have properly consented. The practical difficulty is that the therapeutic misconception is most likely to operate in clinical research of this type. The difficulty justifying surgical placebos for

[65] Albin 2005, 149.
[66] See Albin 2002.
[67] See Albin 2002 and 2005.
[68] See Albin 2005.
[69] See e.g. Thomson 1976 and 1985.
[70] See Albin 2005.

virtue theories is that the virtue of beneficence would appear to require doctors to seek to do what is best for the patient in front of them. Similarly, many duty-based theories hold that physicians have a therapeutic obligation to do what is best for their patients, as reflected by the principle of equipoise.

Controversy over placebos has resulted in a number of changes between the present and previous versions of the Helsinki Declaration. Paragraph 32 of the latest (2008) version states,

> The benefits, risks, burdens and effectiveness of a new method should be tested against those of the best current proven intervention, except in the following circumstances:
>
> - The use of placebo, or no treatment, is acceptable in studies where no current proven intervention exists; or
> - Where for compelling scientific or scientifically sound methodological reasons the use of placebo is necessary to determine the efficacy or safety of an intervention and the patients who receive placebo or no treatment will not be subject to any risk of serious or irreversible harm. Extreme care must be taken to avoid abuse of this option.

This goes further than any previous version of the Declaration. Indeed, the 1996 version did not include any equivalent to the second of these two exceptions and it is that version enshrined in domestic law (see 11.4.1).

11.3.3 Those who lack capacity

Whatever justificatory force vests in a valid consent, it is clearly not possible to rely on the consent of a participant who lacks the ability to consent, whether as a result of mental disability, age, or temporary factors such as shock or unconsciousness. It is, however, sometimes possible to obtain consent in advance from those who have competence/capacity but are likely to lose it before or during the trial. This might, for example, be a possibility for some types of research into Alzheimer's disease, which is a progressive brain disorder that gradually destroys mental function. Even prospective participants who have never been able to consent might be able to display unwillingness to participate. The participant's acquiescence might therefore be obtainable even where actual consent is not.

To say that an individual cannot provide a valid consent could be to say one of two things. In Ch.5, a distinction was drawn between competence and capacity: *competence* was defined as possession of the cognitive faculties required to make a decision with respect to the given situation, whereas *capacity* was defined as possession of the legal authority to make a decision with respect to the given situation. This cognitive-function definition of competence means that an individual could have the competence to consent to participate in some research projects but not to other, more complex, projects. The distinction between competence and capacity is important insofar as the test for capacity does not seek to track competence. It need not. It was, for example, explained in Ch.5 (5.3.1) that age is sometimes treated as a sufficient reason for depriving a mature child of the legal authority required to refuse treatment, even if that child is considered to be competent.

Views on when research should be conducted on those who lack competence are similar to views that can be taken with regard to treatment (discussed in Chs 5 and 15), with one notable difference—participation in research cannot be justified by reference to the individual's health needs alone.

Where the prospective participant was previously competent, the views and values that were held when competent could be regarded as decisive, influential, or irrelevant. There are practical difficulties treating prospective consent as equivalent to contemporaneous consent stemming from its comparative deficiency in terms of context, immediacy, and safeguards. Some theorists go further and argue that individuals can lose their "personal identity", so that an individual who projects autonomous choices into the future can be viewed as imposing those wishes on a different (incompetent) individual.[71] The "personal identity objection" is examined in some depth in Ch.16 (16.3.1). For this objection to have force it must be accepted that the participant does not share his identity with the decision-maker *and* that it is impermissible to impose the decision-maker's views on the participant. From a moral point of view, there must be limits on the extent to which the past, present, and future selves of any given individual can be regarded as distinct. To regard me as a different person to the one who went to sleep last night is to free me from responsibility for the actions of the person who went to sleep. Any theory imposing moral duties must treat past, present, and future selves as sharing some core identity that is not easily lost.[72] This still leaves a great deal of room for different views on the essential features of personal identity (some form of psychological continuity with one's past self being a popular criterion) and on the permissibility of imposing previously held views on a future incompetent individual (which is clearly connected to the level of moral status possessed by the incompetent individual, mentioned below).[73]

If no consent at all has been obtained or prospective consent is discounted, questions arise as to who (if anyone) should be able to authorise the involvement of that individual in medical research, what criteria such decision-makers should apply, and what degree of moral status should be attributed to the participant. All three issues are controversial.

The authorisation of a proxy might be defended as a procedural safeguard but it is not conceptually identical to the participant's consent. To treat a proxy's consent as if it were the participant's might sometimes be a useful legal fiction, but it is nonetheless a fiction—at least where the proxy was not appointed by the participant so that the proxy's decision could legitimately be said to be an expression of the participant's prior will. It is a fiction (and thereby likely to mislead) because the justification of proxy consent cannot rest with the waivability of the benefits of the duties owed to the recipient. Rights-based

[71] See e.g. Buchanan 1988, 280 (who goes on to partially reject this view).
[72] See further the discussion of related issues in Beyleveld and Brownsword 2001, 107.
[73] See e.g. Buchanan 1988 and Dworkin 1986.

theories, for example, allow rights-holders to waive the benefit of their rights, but this does not imply that a proxy can waive the benefit of all the rights of the rights-holder. The choice of proxy itself raises questions, such as questions over the extent to which the views and values previously held by the individual should be taken into account when appointing a proxy (as such reliance is subject to the objections considered above). Proxies can confuse their own interests with those of the individual for whom they are making decisions. Conflicts of interests might be personal (e.g. a loved one enrolling the participant into a trial to get some free time) or professional (e.g. some doctors might unwaveringly support their researching colleagues or at least unduly support those with whom they share an educational and professional background).

With regard to the criteria for use by decision-makers, the most pressing issue is whether participation in medical research should track the *prospective participant's interests alone* or whether it should also track *the interests of others* (such as those with the condition from which the patient is suffering). The nature of research is such that it would be unusual for the participant's contemporaneous health or welfare interests to support participation. The prospective participant's interests could include the values that were held before the loss of competence (subject to the same type of objections that can be made against reliance on previously held views). This gives rise to three approaches competing for consideration: the substituted judgment approach, the best interests approach, and the overall interests approach. These approaches have been presented with regard to treatment elsewhere, especially in Ch.5 (5.2.2).

The *substituted judgement approach* requires a proxy decision-maker to attempt to reach the decision that the prospective participant would have made in the circumstances. This requires the application of previously expressed or displayed *values* and, as such, presupposes prior competence. It follows that the substituted judgment test, so defined, has no relevance where the prospective participant has never been competent to form views or hold values.[74] This approach is to be contrasted with the *best interests approach*, which requires actions to track what is best for the participant *all things considered*. Relevant interests could be purely medical or could encompass the participant's social or emotional interests. The best interest approach can be applied either where the substituted judgment test provides no answers (i.e. as a secondary criterion) or in place of that test (i.e. as a primary criterion). Both the substituted judgment and best interests tests, as defined, focus on the participant's interests alone. Taken as the primary criterion the best interests approach will generally be opposed to invasive medical research, particularly research that is against the medical interests of the participant.[75] Non-invasive research will be less problematic, particularly where the participant obtains an indirect benefit, such as the benefit of increased attention from health professionals.

Both participant interests tests (i.e. the best interests and the substitutive judgment test) can be rejected or supplemented by a wider test of *overall interests*, which directly requires the interests of others to be taken into account. In

---

[74] Cf. *Strunk v Strunk* (1969) 445 S.W.2d 145.
[75] See further 11.4.5, below.

this context, the overall interests approach is not to be equated with a utilitarian approach.[76] There are three ways in which the prospective/actual participant's interests could count for less than those of others:

(a) the interest in question could be worthy of less protection;

(b) the participant could be worthy of less protection; or

(c) the aggregated interests of others could outweigh the interests of the participant.

The first possibility, (a), merely requires a hierarchy of interests and is thereby potentially compatible with all types of moral theory. Rights-based theories can have a hierarchy of rights where they conflict, duty-based theories a hierarchy of duties, virtue-theories a hierarchy of virtues, and ideal utilitarians hold that there are higher and lower types of utility. To give an example from a rights-based perspective: the positive right to life of those who might benefit from cancer research might outweigh a cancer's patient's negative right to privacy with regard to the use of that patient's health records in some types of cancer research.[77]

The second possibility, (b), is concerned with the participant's moral status, i.e. the direct duties owed to the participant because of that individual's properties and characteristics. The question of whether some human beings count for less than others is highly controversial. It is not, however, only utilitarians who hold that some humans count for less than others.[78] Some theorists adopt a variant of Kant's *Formula of the End in Itself* (which requires us to treat others never as simply means to our ends but also as ends in themselves) to reject the use of any human being for the purposes of others. This interpretation of the Categorical Imperative is actually inconsistent with Kant's own work, as his supreme moral principle applied only to those able to reflect on their own chosen purposes (i.e. agents or, in Kant's words, "rational beings with a will"). In other words, Kant did not grant all human beings full moral status by virtue of their humanity.[79] (Also, this formulation of the Categorical Imperative does not prohibit treating relevant others as means, but *merely* as means.)

The third possibility, (c) is distinctly utilitarian and, as such, is rejected by virtue, rights, and duty-based theories. To attempt to aggregate the lesser interests of a large number so as to outweigh a major interest of one individual is to adopt utilitarianism or a utilitarian-type compromise position.

It follows that all the major moral theories are potentially compatible with *some type* of the overall interests test in the context of the participation of incompetent patients in medical research. The variables used in the application of this test will vary from one theory to another, so some versions of the overall

---

[76] Cf. Lewis 2002, esp. 614.

[77] Different rights-based theories will invoke different hierarchies and conflict resolution criteria.

[78] See further Ch.7 (7.2.1) on the moral status of the fetus and Ch.16 (16.4.1) on moral status in the context of end of life decisions.

[79] See further Chs 1 (1.3.2) and 16.

interests test will be much weaker than others. Since practical considerations can also influence the application of moral theories, it is difficult to draw more specific implications from the general moral positions. Before examining the legal response to these issues (in 11.4.5), we must first examine the general regulatory position on medical research on humans.

11.4 The regulatory position

For many years, research on animals and embryos was more comprehensively regulated than research on humans after birth. Research on "protected animals" that might cause the animal "pain, suffering, distress, or lasting harm" requires a licence under the Animals (Scientific Procedures) Act 1986. Research on human embryos requires a licence under the Human Fertilization and Embryology Act 1990 (see Ch.10). It was not until the implementation of the Clinical Trials Regulations, in 2004, that research on humans started to be regulated to anywhere near this level. These regulations do not cover all such research and they operate against a complex backdrop of guidance, law, and regulatory structures.

11.4.1 Guidance

Guidance on good research practices has been issued by a variety of national and international bodies. The first international guidance of importance was the Nuremberg Code.[80] This laid down ten principles for research on humans, starting with the assertion that obtaining the participant's voluntary consent is "absolutely essential". It also required that experiments be designed to yield fruitful results, be based on the results of animal experimentation, avoid unnecessary suffering and injury, and be terminable at the request of the participant. These principles formed the basis of the Declaration of Helsinki, which takes its name from the place where it was first adopted by the World Medical Association in 1964. This declaration has been amended several times, most recently in October 2008.[81] More detailed guidance has been provided by an international conference bringing together the regulatory authorities of Europe, Japan and the US and experts from the pharmaceutical industry: the International Conference on Harmonisation of Technical Requirements for Registration of Pharmaceuticals for Human Use (ICH).[82] Moreover, the Council for International Organisations of Medical Sciences (CIOMS) in collaboration with the World Health Organization (WHO) has offered guidance on the import of these principles for research carried out in developing countries.[83]

---

[80] The Nuremberg Code is extracted in Annas and Grodin 1992, 2.
[81] The current text is available at: *http://www.wma.net/e/policy/b3.htm*.
[82] See the ICH website (*http://www.ich.org*) and ICH 1996.
[83] For the latest version, see CIOMS 2002.

The impact of the Helsinki Declaration (and through it the Nuremberg Code) is evident from even a cursory glance at the ICH guidance on good clinical practice and CIOMS guidance on biomedical research.[84] The latest versions of these international documents share a set of foundational principles—though there are also many differences in the content of these documents.[85] These shared principles include those requiring the research to be:

(a) scientifically valid;[86]

(b) conducted by those who are sufficiently qualified and experienced;[87]

(c) reviewed by an independent ethics committee;[88]

(d) supported by the participant's (voluntary and informed) consent or, if the participant is not capable of giving legally valid consent, the permission of a legally authorised representative;[89]

(e) designed to protect the participant's rights and inform the participant of these rights, including the right to confidentiality and to withdraw from the trial at any time;[90] and

(f) initiated and continued only if the anticipated benefits justify the risks (where those risks have been minimised).[91]

The medical profession has had a major role in the articulation of these principles—the Nuremberg Code was based on three principles suggested by a medical expert at the Nuremberg trial and the World Medical Association is an international organisation representing physicians.[92] The pharmaceutical industry has also played a major role—directly participating in the ICH on which the Clinical Trials Directive is based. That Directive is "industry-led", as its principal purpose is to make conducting profitable clinical trials in Europe attractive to researchers and their sponsors. Some commentators believe that its implementation "has led to a subtle change of emphasis from the protection of research participants to the facilitation of research".[93]

For completeness, it is also worth briefly mentioning the Council of Europe's Convention on Human Rights and Biomedicine (the Biomedicine Convention) and the 2005 Additional Protocol on Biomedical Research. These instruments seek to translate many of the principles enshrined in the above instruments into legal principles. The UK has not, however, signed the Biomedicine Convention. It

---

[84] See ICH 1996 and CIOMS 2002.
[85] On the differences see Gevers 2001.
[86] See Helsinki Declaration, para.12; ICH 1996, para.2.5; and CIOMS 2002, guideline 1.
[87] See Helsinki Declaration, para.16; ICH 1996, para.4.3.1; and CIOMS 2002, guideline 1.
[88] See Helsinki Declaration, para.15; ICH 1996, para.2.6; and CIOMS 2002, guideline 2.
[89] See Helsinki Declaration, paras 21, 24, and 27; ICH 1996, para.4.8; and CIOMS 2002, guidelines 5–6.
[90] See Helsinki Declaration, paras 23–24; ICH 1996, paras 2.11, 4.3.4, 4.8.10; and CIOMS 2002, guideline 5.
[91] See Helsinki Declaration, paras 18 and 20, ICH 1996, para.2.2, and CIOMS 2002, guideline 8.
[92] See Shuster 1997 and WMA website (www.wma.net), respectively.
[93] See Cave and Holm 2002.

could, however, still have an interpretative impact on the Convention on Human Rights and Fundamental Freedoms (the Convention), as given effect by the Human Rights Act (HRA) 1998[94] and perhaps even other domestic legislation.[95]

All the common principles mentioned above have been incorporated into national law and guidance. Indeed, any trial falling within the ambit of the Clinical Trials Regulations must be conducted "in accordance with the ethical principles that have their origin in the [1996 version of the] Declaration of Helsinki" (Sch.1 Pt 2). This gives effect to the preamble of the Clinical Trials Directive. Article 3 of the Good Clinical Practice (GCP) Directive explicitly requires clinical trials to comply with the 1996 version of the Declaration. Notice that these instruments refer to the *1996* version of the Helsinki Declaration, rather than either the *2000* or *2008* versions. This is so even though the Clinical Trials Regulations were implemented in 2004, and the GCP Directive was adopted in 2005 and implemented in 2006. There are a number of key differences between these versions of the Helsinki Declaration. The importance attached to the interests of participants has, for example, changed from one version to another. Compare:

> Concern for the interests of the subject must always prevail over the interests of science and society. (1996 version, para.1.5)

> In medical research on human subjects, considerations related to the well-being of the human subject should take precedence over the interests of science and society. (2000 version, para.5)

> In medical research involving human subjects, the well-being of the individual research subject must take precedence over all other interests. (2008 version, para.6)

On this principle, the 1996 version was notably stronger than the 2000 version ("must always prevail", rather than "should take precedence"). There are other differences. Unlike the 1996 version, the 2000 and 2008 versions do not draw an explicit distinction between therapeutic and non-therapeutic research (see 11.2.2) and there have been changes concerning references to placebos in the Declaration (see 11.3.2.2). Other differences are mentioned below (see 11.4.4.2). It is, therefore, of some importance that it is the 1996 version that is enshrined in the Clinical Trials and GCP Directives.

Guidance on good practice issued by a variety of national bodies also incorporate these core principles of the major international documents. For example, the 1998 guidance of the Medical Research Council (MRC), entitled *Guidelines for Good Clinical Practice in Clinical Trials*,[96] expressly refers to the 1996 version of the Helsinki Declaration and seeks to apply the principles of Good Clinical Practice from the ICH's guidance on good clinical practice.[97] It follows that all MRC-

---

[94] See e.g. *Glass v UK* [2004] 1 F.L.R. 1019, para.58. Interpreting a binding Convention in the light of a non-binding Convention can surely only be acceptable where the relevant provision from the non-binding Convention is uncontroversial and plausibly implicit in the binding provision (see Ch.1 (1.5)).

[95] Section 30 of the Mental Capacity Act is very similar to art.17(2) of the Biomedicine Convention and the explanatory notes indicate that that provision is based on the Convention's provisions.

[96] See MRC 1998.

[97] See MRC 1998, esp. 10.

funded research, whether or not it falls within the remit of the Clinical Trials Regulations, is required to comply with these international documents. The MRC is a major funder of medical research in the UK. It is not the only national body to have produced guidelines tracking the values contained in international guidance. Guidance has also been produced by the Department of Health and the professional bodies such as the General Medical Council (GMC) and the Royal College of Physicians (RCP).[98] Breach of the guidance of the professional bodies responsible for regulating the professional, such as the GMC, could give rise to professional disciplinary proceedings.[99] A doctor has, for example, had his name erased from the medical register for repeatedly forging ethics committee approval for his research projects and many others have been struck of for scientific misconduct.[100]

11.4.2 Clinical trials

The Clinical Trials Regulations regulate trials of medicines on humans. Medicinal products have been directly regulated by legislation for decades. Even thoroughly tested medicinal products can pose uncertain risks and limitations. Drug reaction is the fourth biggest cause of death in the UK.[101] Moreover, most drugs help fewer than half of the patients to whom they are prescribed. The vice-president of a major pharmaceutical company has publicly admitted that more than 90 per cent of drugs "only work in 30 or 50 per cent of patients".[102] In the future drugs might be tailored to our individual genetic differences but pharmacogenetics is still very much in its infancy and this will require a great many clinical trials.[103] The UK body that is responsible for regulating post-research marketing and use of medical products (and medical devices) is also responsible for regulating the use of medicinal products in clinical trials. That body is the Medicines and Healthcare products Regulatory Agency (MHRA). The Regulations make it a criminal offence to start a clinical trial without having first obtained a "clinical trial authorisation" from the MHRA and the approval of a research ethics committee (regs 12 and 49).[104]

Clinical trials are defined in reg.2 as any *interventional* trial on a human participant that is designed with the object of ascertaining the safety or efficacy of *medicinal products*.[105] It does not matter whether or not the trial is commercially funded. Nor does it matter whether or not the trial takes place within the NHS or uses NHS staff or facilities. Examples of research protocols that are

---

[98] See DH 2005a, GMC 2002b, and RCP 2007, respectively.

[99] See Ch.2 (2.3.1) for a discussion of the disciplinary role of the professional bodies.

[100] See Carnall 1996.

[101] See Morgan 2001, 15.

[102] Allen Roses, worldwide vice-president of genetics at GlaxoSmithKline, as quoted in Connor 2003.

[103] A distinction is sometimes drawn between pharmacogenomics and pharmacogenetics, but these two terms are increasingly used interchangeably (see Evans and Relling 1999, 488).

[104] This second requirement is addressed below (in 11.4.3).

[105] Reg.2 goes on to define "investigational medicinal product", "medicinal product", and "non-interventional trial".

covered include the testing of a new pharmaceutical drug (including Phase I studies), the testing of an existing pharmaceutical drug outside of the ambit of its product licence, the testing of a gene therapy procedure (see Ch.12), and the testing of a medical device that is used to deliver a medicinal product. Not all research protocols will, however, involve interventional investigation using medicinal products. The Regulations do not, for example, apply to the investigation of a new surgical technique (such as research on a new form of keyhole surgery), research into a new form of radiotherapy, non-invasive epidemiological research (such as the collection and analysis of statistics on heart disease), non-invasive observational research (such as observational research on sleeping patterns), or to the use of a pharmaceutical drug within the ambit of its product licence (i.e. phase IV trials).

The Regulations require all those involved in clinical trials to comply with the conditions and principles of "good clinical practice" that are specified in Sch.1 (regs 2 and 28–31) The details of which with regard to consent *and* the involvement of those who cannot consent will be detailed below (11.4.4.3 and 11.4.5.3). For present purposes it is sufficient to note that the conditions and principles of good practice include those that are common to the various international codes and guidance. Thus, the Regulations, in effect, give domestic legal force to principles laid down by the 1996 version of the Helsinki Declaration and other such international instruments. The Regulations actually go much further than that and they have teeth. The MHRA has the power to suspend or terminate the trial, generally or at a particular site, where it is no longer satisfied that the original conditions are satisfied or receives information raising doubts about the safety, conduct, or scientific validity of the trial (reg.31). The MHRA can also issue infringement notices, which can include directions as to the measures to be taken by the person on whom the notice is served (reg.48). Both researchers and sponsors have specific duties to report actual and suspected serious adverse events (regs 32–35). These powers and obligations are backed up by criminal sanctions (regs 49–52). There is also a criminal offence covering the provision of false or misleading information about the safety, quality or efficacy of the product or the trial, or about compliance with the principles of good clinical practice in the course of an application for a clinical trial authorisation or ethics committee approval (reg.50). The offences themselves include no mens rea requirement, but provision is made for due diligence defence. Under reg.51, no offence is committed under the Regulations if all reasonable precautions were taken and all due diligence was exercised. Prima facie proof is sufficient to give rise to a presumption that the defence is made out, only rebuttable if the prosecution proves beyond reasonable doubt that it is not.

11.4.3 Research ethics committees

11.4.3.1 Types

Research Ethics Committees (RECs) have existed in the UK for decades. Their function is to review the ethical acceptability of research proposals (known as protocols) and thereby act as an independent safeguard sitting between the researcher and the potential participant. NHS RECs were first set up in 1968.[106] Some exist outside of the NHS, such as those set up by pharmaceutical companies, universities, and private hospitals. Until 2004, all were non-statutory bodies. Those recognised for the purpose of reviewing clinical trials on medicinal products were put on a statutory basis by the Clinical Trials Regulations (reg.6). Others continue to operate both outside and within the NHS. Thus, there are three types of REC:

(a) *recognised RECs*: those permitted to review clinical trials involving medicinal products (virtually all of which can also review all other medical research on humans);[107]

(b) *authorised NHS RECs*: those within the NHS that are permitted to review all medical research on humans *except* such clinical trials; and

(c) *non-NHS RECs.*

There are currently 155 "recognised" and "authorised" NHS RECs in the UK.[108] Any research using NHS patients, staff, or facilities, or otherwise connected to the NHS, must be approved by an NHS REC.[109] NHS RECs can also consider other studies on request.[110] There was no legal requirement to take research outside of the Clinical Trials Regulations before a relevant REC.

All NHS RECs are now part of the National Research Ethics Service (NRES), which itself is a division of the National Patient Agency (NPSA).[111] Regardless of whether they are recognised or authorised, NHS RECs are subject to the *Governance Arrangements for NHS Research Ethics Committees* (GAfREC) and NREC's standard operating procedures (SOP).[112] Significantly, the SOP make it clear that the policy of the Department of Health and NREC is to apply the research ethics review requirements of the Clinical Trials Regulations more generally.[113] Thus, NHS research falling outside of the Clinical Trials Regulations will be governed and assessed by RECs as if it were covered by the Regulations.

The body responsible for establishing, recognising, and monitoring RECs under the Clinical Trials Regulations is the United Kingdom Ethics Committees Authority (UKECA).[114] There are three types of "recognised" RECS: type 1, 2, and 3.[115] *Type 1* committees are those that are recognised to review phase I trials

---

[106] See McHale 2004, 855.

[107] The exception are the non-NHS type 1 committees, which are only recognised to review clinical trials and not other types of research.

[108] NREC website: *http://www.nres.npsa.nhs.uk/aboutus/what-are-recs* (March 2009).

[109] See COREC 2001, para.3.1.

[110] See COREC 2001, para.3.2.

[111] The NRES has also taken over the functions of the former Central Office for Research Ethics Committees (COREC).

[112] See COREC 2001 and NREC 2008, respectively.

[113] See NREC 2008, 9 (para.3).

[114] Set up by reg.5. It comprises the health ministers of England, Scotland, the Welsh national assembly, and the Northern Irish health department.

[115] See NREC 2008, 28.

of medicinal products on healthy volunteers throughout the UK. Type 1 committees include both NHS and non-NHS RECs. *Type 2* committees are those recognised to review clinical trials of investigational medicinal products (other than phase I trials in healthy volunteers) to take place only at sites within an area defined by the geographical remit of their own appointing authority. *Type 3* committees are recognised to review the same clinical trials as type 2 committees taking place at any site within the UK. This categorisation is not mutually exclusive, as committees recognised as type 1 committees can also be recognised as type 2 or 3.

The Clinical Trials Regulations require ethics committees to take into account various matters before approving a clinical trial. These include the design of the trial; the anticipated risks and benefits; the suitability of the protocol, all those involved, and the facilities; the procedure for obtaining informed consent; the rationale for including any persons incapable of giving informed consent; the provision for compensation in the event of injury or death; and the arrangements for recruitment (reg.15(5)). These Regulations also introduce new criminal sanctions. A researcher who fails to obtain REC approval for the conduct of a clinical trial involving medicinal products commits a criminal offence (regs 12 and 49). This threat bolsters the existing non-criminal sanctions, which are particularly important for protocols falling outside of the Regulations. Failure to obtain or comply with the views of an REC could, in appropriate circumstances, result in disciplinary action by the NHS against employees, disciplinary action by the relevant professional body (as failing to obtain the approval of a REC could amount to professional misconduct), and could cause difficulties for researchers seeking to publish research outcomes in the major journals. Moreover, it could make it easier for an injured participant to succeed in a negligence action against a researcher.

For convenience, unless otherwise stated, all references to RECs will refer to those operating within the NHS.

11.4.3.2 Membership of RECs

We have seen that the Regulations apply to recognised committees and GAfREC apply to all RECs. In addition to imposing review criteria and time limits on decision-making, these lay down membership requirements for RECs. Both GAfREC and Sch.2 of the Regulations limit membership to 18[116] (in practice, such committees tend to have between 12 and 18 members).[117] Both require at least a third of the members to be lay members,[118] as distinct from expert members, such as practising health professionals and those involved in clinical research. Both require at least half of the lay members to meet additional criteria.[119] The purpose of these requirements is clearly to reduce the potential

---

[116] See COREC 2001, para.6.1 and Sch.2 para.3.
[117] See DH 2005b, 10.
[118] See COREC 2001, para.6.3, and Sch.2 para.5(a).
[119] Cf. Sch.2 para.3(4) and para.5(b) and COREC 2001, para.6.7. Note that the definitions of lay members differ slightly between GAfREC and the Regulations.

for researcher-bias without depriving the committee of members who are able to understand research proposals. GAfREC states that members should be drawn from both sexes, a wide range of age groups, and from a "sufficiently broad range of experience and expertise".[120] Beyond this, the expertise of REC members is not defined by their role and function. No members are required to have expertise in ethics, moral theory, or law.[121] In practice, this means that lay members could just as easily identify themselves with future patients who might benefit from any research proposal as with prospective research participants.

Not all members need to be present for a REC to have a quorum. Under the Clinical Trials Regulations, a quorum for a full meeting is seven members including the Chair or a vice-chair, one lay and one expert member (Sch.2 para.6(6)). The NRES SOP adopts the same policy for other NHS RECs.[122]

11.4.3.3 RECs and the law

Imagine an REC faced with a research proposal that contravenes a legal requirement. The Data Protection Act 1998, for example, is a rich source of relevant legal requirements (see Ch.6). Can the committee nonetheless accept the proposal on the basis that it considers the proposal to be entirely ethical? What if the REC suspects that the proposal has unlawful elements but is unsure?

GAfREC states:

> RECs should have due regard for the requirement of relevant regulatory agencies and of applicable laws. It is not for the REC to interpret regulations or laws, but they may indicate in their advice to the researcher and those institutions where they believe further consideration needs to be given to such matters.[123]

The *Research Governance Framework* expresses a similar view:

> It is not for research ethics committees or reviewers to give legal advice, nor are they liable for any of their decisions in this respect. It is the researchers and the health or social care organisations who have the responsibility not to break the law. If a research ethics committee suspects that a research proposal might contravene the law, it is expected to advise both the chief investigator and the appropriate authority. Then the chief investigator and the organisation will need to seek legal advice.[124]

The latest version of the SOP states

> When reviewing research involving human tissue, the role of the REC is to give an ethical opinion rather than to apply the law. The REC's opinion should be informed by and take account of legal requirements but is not limited by them. Where

---

[120] See COREC 2001, paras 6.1 and 6.2.
[121] Such persons could be lay members and would usually also satisfy the additional criteria required of half the lay members.
[122] See also NREA 2008, para.2.3.1.
[123] COREC 2001, para.26.
[124] DH 2005a, para.3.12.7.

difficult issues of legal interpretation arise it is not the role of the committee to provide legal advice. RECs may provide researchers with essential information about the legal requirements. However, researchers should seek their own legal advice and/or consult the HTA for advice where appropriate.[125]

Notice that none of these statements explicitly requires or even advises RECs to reject research proposals that involve unlawful activities. GAfREC requires RECs to have regard to the law, but suggests that they should limit themselves to advising the researcher to consider whether to address such matters. The *Research Governance Framework* states that RECs are expected to advise the lead researcher ("chief investigator") and the "appropriate authority". The SOP states that RECs must be informed by and take account of legal requirements, "but is not limited by them" and "it is not the role of the committee to provide legal advice". There is ambiguity in these statements. Are the statements denying the appropriateness of interpreting laws and giving legal advice meant to indicate that RECs should add appropriate provisos to their rulings or are they meant to suggest that RECs should not reject research proposals on purely legal grounds?[126] Are the statements concerning advising on suspected unlawfulness meant to suggest that RECs should leave the legal issues to the researcher? Does the *Research Governance Framework's* reference to "the appropriate authority" expect or even require RECs that suspect unlawfulness to refer the matter to the relevant regulatory authority (such as the Information Commissioner or the Department of Health)?

There are many reasons why RECs should consider conformity to the law to be *a necessary condition for REC approval* and interpret these guidelines accordingly. For a start, many national and international guidelines indicate that the primary responsibility of RECs is to protect the rights and interests of research participants, without any qualification to the effect that this excludes their legal rights.[127] Moreover, RECs are surely public authorities for the purposes of judicial review at common law or challenge under the HRA 1998.[128] Baker et al. have argued that judicial review proceedings are potentially available if an REC approves a protocol that contravenes a clear legal requirement.[129]

Beyleveld argues that it makes no sense for RECs to treat law and ethics as distinct, even if one accepts legal positivism.[130] He argues that any moral theory recognising the procedural legitimacy of democratic governance must also recognise that the positive law of a democratic society has procedural moral authority. Moreover, the moral authority of the positive law will be greater than the moral authority of the pronouncements of RECs. As Beyleveld puts it, RECs "do not have the role or authority of a high priesthood, whose views on ethics would be

---

[125] NRES 2008, para.11.9.

[126] Beyleveld 2002 argues that the Department Health intended the latter.

[127] See e.g. the Helsinki declaration (esp. paras 6 and 9), ICH 1996, para.2.3, and MRC 1996, para.2.3. See also the starting point of COREC 2001, para. 2.6 cited earlier.

[128] On judicial review of the decisions of ethics committees, see *R. v Ethical Committee of St Mary's Hospital Ex p. Harriott* [1988] 1 F.L.R. 512.

[129] See Baker et al. 2005, 281–283.

[130] See Beyleveld 2002 and 2009. On legal positivism see Ch.1 (1.2).

decisive".[131] It follows that RECs are morally obliged to comply with the law and must treat law as a necessary condition of moral acceptability. If this is right, then RECs must view the law as setting down minimum ethical standards. This does not, of course, prevent a REC from laying down additional ethical requirements, but they should not depart from procedurally legitimate law.

The above quoted guidance suggests an obvious counter-response: RECs are not well-designed to *identify or interpret* the law. Presumably, anyone attempting to rely on such a counter-response would have to concede that recognised RECs must at least comply with the Clinical Trials Regulations on which they rely for their authority. In any event, the argument that RECs must view conformity with the law as a necessary condition for approving research proposals does not imply that RECs must themselves be regarded as legal decision-making bodies equivalent to the courts in expertise and authority. RECs are capable of referring legal questions to the appropriate regulatory bodies (such as the Information Commissioner) or the Department of Health. Beyleveld has gone further and argued that if RECs need expertise in law, then this must be provided.[132] Expertise could, for example, be provided by ensuring that an REC has at least one member with adequate legal competence, can quickly refer matters to an existing body, or by ensuring that RECs operate as only one stage of a two-staged process in which the other stage involves a body with legal expertise.

Research participants are not in a strong position to discover when their interests are being infringed, let alone take legal action in response. RECs are well placed to protect participants. Leaving legal review to researchers is open to the objection that they are interested parties and can be expected to use the law defensively rather than to protect research participants. While different theories will take different views on the interests of research participants that deserve protection, they will surely all accept that a judge in his own cause is likely to be a partial judge.

11.4.4 The participant's consent

The general principles that apply to consent to treatment, addressed in Ch.4, also apply to consent to research. Failure to obtain a valid consent from an adult with capacity will render a researcher potentially liable in *battery* and a failure to ensure that the participant has adequate information could render him liable in *negligence* for any injury that the participant suffers. For an apparent consent to be valid it must be given *voluntarily* in the light of *sufficient information* by a person with *capacity*. Unfortunately, from the point of view of explicating the law, there is a dearth of case law in the context of research.

---

[131] Beyleveld 2009, 11. The moral authority of the REC will depend on the manner of its appointment, its membership, and its expertise, and, in practice, appointment procedures are not democratic.

[132] See Beyleveld 2002, 64–68.

11.4.4.1 Voluntariness

The law with regard to voluntariness in participation in medical research might not differ from the law applying to medical treatment. There is, for example, no judicial suggestion that the courts will be any more willing to invoke presumptions of undue influence in the context of research than in the context of treatment.[133] Given the danger of the therapeutic misconception and the relatively powerful position of the physician-researcher, this is unfortunate, at least insofar as there is no duty to participate. The Clinical Trials Regulations add nothing to the common law position, as they say little more on this issue than consent must be given "freely" (Sch.1 Pt 1 para.3).[134] The GMC guidance is more detailed, asserting that doctors must not put pressure on volunteers to participate and must ensure that no real or implied coercion is put on those in a dependent relationship.[135] These requirements go beyond the common law position as it applies to medical treatment, because at common law more than mere pressure is required to establish undue influence, let alone duress.[136] The GMC guidance will, of course, be of significant importance in any disciplinary proceedings brought before the GMC itself.

The law governing disclosure of information to prospective participants is more developed.

11.4.4.2 Disclosure of information

The law governing disclosure in *the context of treatment* is relatively straightforward and is examined in depth in Ch.4 (4.4.). A brief summary might help. There can be no action in battery where the patient consents having been informed in "broad terms" of the nature of the treatment.[137] For an action to succeed in negligence, the patient needs to show that the doctor has fallen below the standard of a *reasonable* doctor and the courts have indicated that such a doctor would disclose any "substantial" or "significant" risk of adverse consequences to the patient.[138] A significant risk is one that "would affect the judgment of a reasonable patient".[139] Even if the legal principles applying to research were identical to these, it is reasonable to assume that the failure to disclose the fact that the procedure is experimental or conducted primarily for research purposes would render the doctor liable in negligence and in battery. Such information is arguably necessary to understand the broad nature of the procedure and would surely be disclosed by a reasonable doctor (taking account of what would affect the

---

[133] See the discussion of voluntariness in the context of treatment in Ch.4 (4.5).
[134] The other aspects of this provision are addressed below.
[135] See GMC 2002b, paras 8 and 21.
[136] See *U v Centre for Reproductive Medicine* [2002] EWCA Civ 565 and the discussion in Ch.4 (4.5).
[137] *Chatterton v Gerson* [1981] 1 Q.B. 432.
[138] *Sidaway v Bethlem Royal Hospital* [1985] A.C. 871 at 898–900 (Lord Bridge with whom Lord Keith agreed), 903 (Lord Templeman), and *Pearce v United Bristol Healthcare NHS Trust* [1999] P.I.Q.R. 53 at 59 (Lord Woolf with whom Roch and Mummery L.JJ. agreed).
[139] *Pearce v United Bristol Healthcare NHS Trust* [1999] P.I.Q.R. 53, P59. E.g. a 10% risk of a stroke: *Sidaway v Bethlem Royal Hospital* [1985] A.C. 871 at 900 (Lord Bridge citing the Canadian case of *Reibl v Hughes* [1980] 2 S.C.R. 880). See also [1985] A.C. 871, 903 (Lord Templeman).

judgment of a reasonable patient/participant). There are powerful reasons to believe that, if the matter were ever to come to court, the courts would actually require full or at least very detailed disclosure. *First*, judicial developments in the treatment context post-*Sidaway* have tended to favour patient's informational interests.[140] *Second*, the principal argument for failing to disclose the risks of treatment—the so-called "therapeutic privilege", which tracks the patient's medical interests—does not apply to research. *Third*, the professional standard adopted by the law of negligence will take account of the guidance offered in national and international documents and the wider regulatory context.

National and international documents tend to favour very detailed disclosure. Consider, for example, the 2008 version of the Helsinki Declaration.[141] Paragraph 35 declares that *innovative treatment* is permissible where proven treatments do not exist or are ineffective, as long as it might be effective and the "*informed* consent" of the patient has been obtained. Paragraph 24 specifies the depth of information that ought to be conveyed. It requires each participant to be "adequately informed of the aims, methods, sources of funding, any possible conflicts of interest, institutional affiliations of the researcher, the anticipated benefits and potential risks of the study and the discomfort it may entail". Moreover, it requires the participant to be informed of the right to abstain and withdraw from participation, and states that written consent is to be preferred and, if written consent cannot be obtained, consent should be "formally documented and witnessed".

Unfortunately, ensuring that participants are *fully informed* does not ensure that they *fully understand* the information that they are given. Recognising this, the GMC's guidance not only requires that participants be given information that "they want or ought to know" but requires it to be "presented in terms and a form that they can understand".[142] The information that doctors are asked to disclose is very detailed.[143] Participants must also be given time to ask questions and reflect on the implications of participation.[144] A reasonable doctor would surely take account of such professional guidance, so the GMC's guidance will feed directly into the common law standard of care in a negligence action. Disgruntled participants might also complain to the GMC for any breach of its guidance. Complaints do not face the difficulties of the litigation process and might therefore present a more convenient grievance mechanism.

11.4.4.3 The Clinical Trials Regulations

Under the Clinical Trials Regulations, failure to offer sufficient information to prospective participants of clinical trials involving medicines can also give rise to

---

[140] See *Pearce v United Bristol Healthcare NHS Trust* [1999] P.I.Q.R. 53, *Chester v Afshar* [2004] UKHL 41, and the discussion in Ch.4 (4.4.2).

[141] See also the Clinical Trials Regulations (discussed below) and the *Research Governance Framework* (which makes it clear that the researchers are responsible for "selecting means of communication to ensure potential participants are fully informed": DH 2005a, para.3.4.2).

[142] GMC 2002b, para.19.

[143] See GMC 2002b, para.20.

[144] See GMC 2002b, paras 20–21.

criminal liability. Part 3 of Sch.1 lays down the conditions and principles of good clinical practice that apply to those who have (or had) the capacity to consent to their own participation in the trial. It is an offence to fail to comply with these when conducting a clinical trial or performing the functions of the sponsor of a clinical trial (subject to the due diligence defence discussed above) (regs 49 and 51). In particular, the participant must have given "informed consent" to taking part in the trial (Sch.1 Pt 3 para.3) and must have been given an interview with a member of the research team and a contact point to obtain further information about the trial (paras 1 and 5). "Informed consent" is defined to mean a decision that is made freely after the participant has been "informed of the nature, significance, implications and risks of the trial" (Sch.1 Pt 1 para.3). That consent has to be evidenced in writing or, if the participant is unable to sign or mark a document, consent must be given orally in the presence of at least one witness and recorded in writing (Sch.1 Pt 1 para.3). There seems little reason to doubt that a researcher or sponsor convicted for failing to comply with these conditions and principles will also be found negligent if sued by the participant.

The "informed consent" requirements laid down by the Clinical Trials Regulations are, however, less demanding than those in the GMC guidance and the 2008 version of the Helsinki Declaration.[145] Paragraph 24 of the Helsinki Declaration 2008, like the 2000 version, states that all prospective participants must be "adequately informed of the aims, methods, sources of funding, any possible conflicts of interest, institutional affiliations of the researcher". The Regulations, like the 1996 version of the Helsinki Declaration, do not require participants to be given this type of information. This is yet another area where the 1996 and later versions of the Helsinki Declaration differ (see 11.4.1, above).

11.4.5   Children and incapacitated adults

The first of the ten principles of the Nuremberg Code asserts: "The voluntary consent of the human subject is absolutely essential".[146] Such a bold statement requires qualification if research is to be undertaken on those who lack the capacity to consent. A number of questions arise. When can a mentally disabled, mentally ill, or unconscious adult patient be entered into a trial? When can a child be entered into a trial? The answers turn on whether or not the Clinical Trials Regulations apply. This section will address: *first*, the common law position with regard to children; *second*, the application of the Mental Capacity Act 2005 to those over 16; and, *third*, the application of the Clinical Trials Regulations to both children and incapacitated adults.

11.4.5.1 Children and the common law

The involvement of children in research that does not amount to a clinical trial on a medicinal product falls to the common law. It is useful to remind ourselves

---

[145] See GMC 2002b, para.20.
[146] The Nuremberg Code is extracted in Annas and Grodin 1992 and Shuster 1997.

of the law as it applies *in the context of treatment* (addressed in Ch.5). Consent to the treatment of a child can be provided by someone with parental responsibility or, if the child is over 16 or *"Gillick* competent", by the child.[147] The courts have the power to overrule the child and its parents, if it is in the best interests of the child to do so.[148]

The courts have yet to address research on a child. Section 8(1) of the Family Law Reform Act 1969 is limited to therapeutic and diagnostic procedures[149] and the capacity to consent to research was not considered in *Gillick*. Whether a researcher can rely on the consent of a suitably mature and intelligent child in the context of medical research is unclear. The Court of Appeal in *Re W* did not read *Gillick* as protecting a child's autonomy interests, but as protecting a doctor from liability when acting to protect the child's health with that child's consent.[150] Lord Donaldson, in obiter dicta, expressed doubt about whether the consent of a child could authorise a serious non-therapeutic procedure that did not benefit that child.[151] More precisely, his Lordship asserted that it was "highly improbable" that a child would be considered sufficiently mature and comprehending (*Gillick* competent) to consent to such a procedure. It is, nonetheless, unlikely that a court would permit a mature, comprehending child to be involved in a research trial against her will.[152] Thus, for the purposes of the common law, it might be safer for doctors to obtain the consent of the child's parents *and* the child (if the child is suitably mature). In some cases, it might even be advisable to seek judicial authorisation.

The guidance of the Royal College of Paediatrics and Child Health takes a less cautious approach to the legal force of the consent of a child with "sufficient understanding and intelligence to understand what is proposed" and asserts that the implication of *Gillick* is that the consent of such a child is sufficient.[153] It is regrettable that the law is more uncertain than this guidance might lead physician-researchers to believe. Doctors relying on this guidance would be well advised to take special caution before reaching the conclusion that a child whose consent they wish to rely on has the requisite maturity and understanding.

There are two cases that might have some analogical value for younger children: *S v S* and *Simms v Simms*.[154]

In *S v S*, the House of Lords considered the refusal of two mothers to allow their ex-husbands to paternity test their children during divorce proceedings.[155] Their Lordships declared that the blood tests were lawful if they were not "against the interests" of the child because of the public interest in justice being

---

[147] See, in particular, the Children Act 1989 (s.3(1)), Family Law Reform Act 1969 (s.8(1)), and *Gillick v West Norfolk and Wisbech AHA* [1986] A.C. 112.
[148] *Re W* [1993] Fam. 64.
[149] *Re W* [1993] Fam. 64 at 78 and 92.
[150] [1993] Fam. 64.
[151] [1993] Fam. 64 at 78.
[152] Even in the context of treatment, the refusal of a child is "very important consideration" and its importance increases with the child's age and maturity: *Re W* [1993] Fam. 64 at 84.
[153] See Royal College of Paediatrics and Child Health 2000, 180.
[154] [1972] A.C. 24. and [2002] EWHC 2734, respectively.
[155] [1972] A.C. 24.

done and the minimal harm to the child.[156] If the principle laid down in this case applies generally to non-therapeutic interventions, then it is clearly of relevance to medical research. This weaker test is not, however, supported by the general approach in the case law on *medical treatment*, where the English courts have reviewed parental decisions by reference to the child's *best interests*.[157] The Royal College guidance, once again, takes a less cautious approach and simply asserts that the principle in *S v S* applies to research on children.[158] Similarly, the MRC's ethics guide on medical research involving children asserts that since "the benefits of research are not predictable, the researcher must be satisfied that the research *is not contrary* to the child participant's interests".[159]

In *Simms v Simms*, the High Court declared that it was lawful to use innovative treatment on an 18- and a 16-year-old suffering from variant Creutzfeldt-Jakob Disease (vCJD).[160] The treatment was to involve an experimental drug that had a long history of use as treatment for conditions such as thrombosis, but other uses were restricted to early experiments performed on rodents. In determining the best interests of these two patients, Butler-Sloss P. noted that there was some possibility of an unquantifiable benefit and no alternative treatment.[161] Butler-Sloss P. also took account of the emotional effect that refusing the declaration would have on the patients' families.[162] While this was not a case on research, it displays a willingness on the part of the courts to apply the best interest test flexibly.

Participating in a research project will not usually be in the *medical* best interests of a patient. It might be where participation is the only way of getting a chance to receive innovative treatment for an otherwise untreatable condition, as long as the incapacitated patient has not been illegitimately deprived of the opportunity to obtain the innovative treatment outside of a research project. Nonetheless, the medical best interests of the patient can, at most, only permit participation in *therapeutic* research. More leeway is provided if the best interests test is interpreted beyond medical interests. It might be remembered that, in *Re Y*, performing a blood test and removing bone marrow from an incapacitated adult was held to be in her best interests on the basis that donating to her sister would have *indirect benefits* to her.[163] Participation might carry many indirect benefits, such as providing the participant with positive distractions in an otherwise uneventful life. Even this more flexible approach to the best interest tests will not take us very far unless it is replaced by a test that is, in reality, an *overall interests* test that goes beyond the interests of the participant (see above, 11.3.3). The guidance of the Royal College of Paediatrics and Child Health

---

[156] See the discussion in Ch.5 (5.3.2.1).
[157] See e.g. *Re B* [1990] 3 All E.R. 927 and *Re T* [1997] 1 All ER 906.
[158] See Royal College of Paediatrics and Child Health 2000, 180.
[159] MRC 2004, para.4.3 (my emphasis).
[160] [2002] EWHC 2734. CJD is explained below (11.5).
[161] [2002] EWHC 2734, para.61.
[162] [2002] EWHC 2734, para.64.
[163] [1997] Fam. 110. The judge took the view that if the death of Y's sister would have an adverse effect on their mother, potentially depriving Y of her mother's visits, and that donating was also likely to improve Y's relationship with her sister.

certainly holds the view that research on children that is of no direct benefit can be both ethical and lawful.[164]

11.4.5.2 The Mental Capacity Act

The Mental Capacity Act 2005 (the 2005 Act) applies to "intrusive research" on those who lack capacity and are 16 or over (s.2(5)). Intrusive research is defined in s.30(2) to mean research of the kind that would be unlawful to carry out on a person who had capacity without his consent. In other words, research that would involve a trespass if not authorised by consent or other lawful justification. The Act does not apply to clinical trials covered by the Clinical Trials Regulations (s.30(3)) or to research on medical data.[165] Research falling within the Act's remit is therefore largely restricted to the investigation of new surgical techniques and procedures that do not involve the use of medicinal products. The Act requires research on those who lack capacity to be part of a protocol approved by an appropriate body (in effect, an REC) and carried out in accordance with specified conditions (s.30(1)).

Section 31 specifies the requirements for approval. The REC must be satisfied that the research relates to the participant's condition and cannot be done as effectively using those who have capacity (s.31(2)–(4)). This section also requires the benefits of the research to justify the risks in one of two ways. The *first* is where the research has the potential to produce a benefit to the participant that outweighs any risk or burden (s.31(5)(a)). Research of this type is sometimes called "therapeutic research". The *second* is where the research is intended to provide knowledge that will benefit those affected by the same or a similar condition, the risks to the participant are "negligible", and the research will not significantly interfere with the participant's freedom or privacy, or be unduly invasive or restrictive (s.31(5)(b)/(6)). This permits "non-therapeutic research" that is considered to carry minimal risks and involve minimal intrusion and interference.

The conditions imposed by the Mental Capacity Act are slightly more permissive than those imposed by the Clinical Trials Regulations with regard to relevant research that may be carried out on incapacitated participants who are 16 or over. As we shall see, the Regulations require the research to be therapeutic or carry no risks (Sch.1 Pt 5 para.9), whereas the Act will permit research that is non-therapeutic as long as the risks, intrusion, and interference are minimal. The conditions imposed by the Mental Capacity Act are therefore similar to those laid down by art.17(2) of the Biomedicine Convention, rather than those laid down by the Clinical Trials Directive/Regulations.[166] It follows that whether or not the research involves a medicinal product (and thereby falls within the Regulations rather than the Act) could be significant for the lawfulness of some types of (non-therapeutic) research on incapacitated adults.

---

[164] See Royal College of Paediatrics and Child Health 2000, esp. 180.

[165] These could be subject to controls under the Data Protection Act 1998 or the Human Tissue Act 2004.

[166] The difference between the Directive and the Convention on this point is addressed in more detail in Plomer 2001 and Lötjönen 2003.

Section 32 addresses proxy consent and participant acquiescence. Carers (who care for the participant in a non-professional, unpaid capacity) or nominated third parties (who must not be connected to the project) must agree that the participant would want to join an approved research project. Under s.33, the participant must be withdrawn from the project if any sign of resistance is displayed or if there is any other indication of an unwillingness to take part (s.33(2), (4)). The assent (acquiescence) of incapacitated participants is therefore essential under the Act. We shall see that the Regulations merely require the researcher to *consider* any *explicit* dissent (Sch.1 Pt 5 para.7). It might be thought this apparent disparity can be partly explained by reference to differences in the consequences of suddenly stopping a trial if assent is withdrawn. Suddenly stopping the administration of some medicinal products might cause harm to the recipient, whereas this is unlikely to be the effect of stopping other research trials. The provision in the Regulations, however, also applies before any medicinal products have been administered and it is important to note that the provision in the Mental Capacity Act does not require the discontinuation of treatment if the researcher has reasonable grounds for believing that discontinuation would pose significant risk to participant's health (s.33(6)).

11.4.5.3 The Clinical Trials Regulations

The Clinical Trials Regulations apply to both adults and children (defined as those under 16: reg.2). Before a child or an incapacitated adult can be entered into a clinical trial, the Regulations require informed consent to be given on that person's behalf by someone not connected with the trial.[167] To be clear, children (irrespective of their competence) do not have capacity to consent under the Regulations. The Regulations provide a hierarchy of persons who should be approached to consent on behalf of children and incapacitated adults.[168] At the top of the hierarchy are those who have a close personal relationship with the participant. In the case of a *child*, this will be someone with parental responsibility.[169] In the case of an *incapacitated adult*, this will be someone who is a close friend or relative and willing to act as a "legal representative". The Regulations also provide for situations where it is not possible to obtain the consent of a parent or personal legal representative, such as emergencies and situations where there is no one with a sufficiently close relationship to the incapacitated adult. To deal with such circumstances, the Regulations provide for a professional legal representative to consent on behalf of the incapacitated person. The participant's doctor can consent if that doctor is not connected with the conduct of the trial. Where the participant's doctor is unable or unwilling to act as the legal representative, the healthcare provider (e.g. the NHS Trust) may nominate someone else not connected to the conduct of the trial.

---

[167] Sch.1 Pt 4 para.4 (child) and Sch.1 Pt 5 para.4 (incapacitated adult).

[168] This hierarchy is implicit in the definition of the major category of proxy (the "legal representative") in Sch.1 Pt 1 para.2 and, in the case of children, the priority given to those with parental responsibility in Sch.1 Pt 4.

[169] The Regulations refer to a child as a "minor".

The protection offered by the legal representative will depend on who that person is and the relative weight that the representative attaches to the research and the participant's interests. Some legal representatives will inevitably be more supportive of research than others. There must be a danger that, where there is a choice of prospective legal representative, researchers will approach the person most likely to consent. The Regulations do, however, specify that the parent or legal representative must seek to act on the basis of the "presumed will" of the incapacitated patient.[170] Unfortunately, that "presumed will" is not defined. It is likely that it is not restricted to the participant's actual or past will, and thereby relies on fictionalised consent. The legal representative's consent cannot, in fact, be based on the participant's will where the participant was never able to display a will or the legal representative has no evidence of the participant's will.

The Regulations require that the consent provider be given all the information that would be given to a potential participant with capacity.[171] In addition, the incapacitated participant must be given information in accordance with his ability to understand it, regarding the trials and its risks and benefits.[172] The provision of this information to the participant does not, however, imply that the participant has the power to assent or dissent in accordance with his understanding. Instead, the Regulations assert that incapacitated participant's "explicit" wish to refuse to participate or withdraw should be "considered" by the researcher.[173] This was contrasted with the more stringent position under the 2005 Act above. The Regulations do, however, adopt a more stringent position with regard to advance refusals: a refusal before the onset of incapacity is determinate and cannot be overruled by the researcher or the legal representative.[174]

The trial itself must be "designed to minimise pain, discomfort, fear and any other foreseeable risk"[175] and must be essential to validate data obtained by other methods.[176] The clinical trial must satisfy other conditions, which differ depending on whether the incapacitated participant is a child or an adult. With regard to *children*, the Regulations provide that the trial must either relate directly to a clinical condition from which the child suffers or only be capable of being carried out on children, and some direct benefit must be obtained by

---

[170] Sch.1 Pt 4 para.13 (child) and Sch.1 Pt 5 para.13 (incapacitated adult) actually state that the informed consent of the incapacitated adult's legal representative "*shall* represent that adult's presumed will". This must be interpreted in the light of the Directive, which uses the word "must" instead of "shall" (art.5(a)).

[171] See Sch.1 Pt 4 (in relation to those under 16) and Sch.1 Pt 5 (in relation to those 16 or over who lack capacity).

[172] Sch.1 Pt 4 para.6 (child) and Sch.1 Pt 5 para.6 (incapacitated adult).

[173] Sch.1 Pt 4 para.7 (child) and Sch.1 Pt 5 para.7 (incapacitated adult).

[174] Sch.1 Pt 1 para.1(5)(b).

[175] Sch.1 Pt 4 para.14 (child) and Sch.1 Pt 5 para.13 (incapacitated adult).

[176] Sch.1 Pt 4 para.11 (child) and Sch.1 Pt 5 para.10 (incapacitated adult). These provisions are identical save one word. With regard to children, the trial must be "necessary" to validate data, whereas in the case of adults it must be "essential". Since these provisions must be read in the light of the Directive—which uses the word "essential" for both: arts 4(e) and 5(e)—no significance should be attached to this minor difference.

the group of participants involved in the trial.[177] With regard to *incapacitated adults*, the Regulations provide that there must be grounds for expecting that the trial will produce a benefit to the participant outweighing the risks or produce no risk at all, and the trial must relate directly to a life-threatening or debilitating clinical condition from which the participant suffers.[178] This is a potentially significant difference. For adults the research must be therapeutic or carry no risks, whereas for children it need only carry a benefit *for the group* of participants as a whole.[179]

11.4.5.4 Research into Emergency Treatment

Cardiac arrest, severe strokes, anaphylactic shock, severe head injuries, and severed arteries can occur suddenly and kill quickly. These are examples of conditions whose potentially lethal consequences can sometimes be avoided by the immediate administration of appropriate treatment. What if there is doubt about the best treatment to administer? What if, for example, it is unclear whether the administration of a specific medicinal product is better than an alternative form of emergency treatment for out-of-hospital cardiac arrest? This was the question addressed by the international TROICA trial and there are many other valuable clinical questions that cannot be properly answered without research into emergency treatment.[180]

For trials of emergency treatment, *prospective consent* is not an option unless the prospective participants' future need for emergency treatment can be anticipated, so that they can be made fully aware of their possible future entry into the trial. The *no research option* will mean relying on historical treatment or best-guess predictions when administering emergency care. *Proxy consent* is only an option where there is sufficient time to inform and request the agreement of the proxy decision-maker. *Deferred consent*, where a participant or proxy is asked to "consent" after entry into the trial, is not truly consent at all, because the emergency intervention will already have taken place. Thus, from the point of view of advancing medical science, the *no consent* option will sometimes be the best option. This option rejects the safeguard of consent, but is perfectly compatible with the existence of other safeguards.

We have seen that the Clinical Trials Regulations require that incapacitated adults and child are not included in clinical trials unless a number of conditions are satisfied. One of those conditions is that prospective participants or their legal representatives have given informed consent (i.e. prospective consent).[181] As a result of amendments to the Clinical Trials Regulations, an exception to these conditions applies where: (i) treatment is required urgently; (ii) the nature of the trial requires urgent action; (iii) it is not reasonably practicable to meet the relevant Sch.1 conditions; and (iv) the procedure adopted has been

---

[177] Sch.1 Pt 4 paras 9 and 10.
[178] Sch.1 Pt 5 paras 9 and 11.
[179] Cf. Hagger and Woods 2005, esp. 51.
[180] See Spöhr et al. 2005. This and other such trials are discussed in Beyleveld and Pattinson 2006.
[181] Sch.1 Pt 4 para.4 (children) and Sch.1 Pt 5 para.5 (incapacitated adults).

approved by an ethics committee (Sch.1 Pt 1 para.1(6)–(7)). Thus, like the Mental Capacity Act (s.32(8)), the Regulations now adopt the no consent option.[182]

I and a co-author have argued elsewhere that the amendment of the Clinical Trials Regulations, so that prior consent is no longer required, is not consistent with a proper interpretation of the Clinical Trials Directive and, in any event, it would have been better to amend the Directive itself.[183] The problem is that the Directive explicitly requires prior consent (arts 4–5) and any attempt to read the Directive down is hindered by the fact that it also explicitly requires the interests of the participants to be given priority over the interests of science and society (art.5(h)).

11.5 Compensation

Creutzfeldt-Jakob Disease (CJD) is a terrible condition that causes progressive mental deterioration similar to that associated with Alzheimer's disease.[184] It is widely known as the human form of "mad cow" disease, has an incubation period of decades, and is invariably fatal. Indeed, patients diagnosed with this disease survive for an average of only four months. One form has been linked to the human growth hormone that was given to around 1,800 children who were treated for short stature over a period of over 25 years as part of a programme started by the Medical Research Council (MRC) and later taken over by the Department of Health.[185] This programme used growth hormone from the pituitary glands of the dead and started as a clinical trial in 1959. It came to an end after the link with CJD was recognised in 1985. The MRC had been slow to pass on earlier warnings from scientists about the possible link. A number of those in this programme died after developing CJD and many more have become ill worrying about the possibility that they will get CJD in the future. Unfortunately, no compensation system had been set up for the victims of what was at least initially a clinical trial. The unlucky victims of this programme therefore had to resort to bringing actions in the law of negligence.[186] The litigation ended some 13 years later with many participants/patients successfully obtaining compensation after proving that they were owed a duty of care that had been breached (the Department of Health and Medical Research Council having conceded that the human growth hormone treatment had caused CJD).[187] Future cases will now be dealt with

---

[182] Regulations 2006/2984 made an exception with regard to incapacitated adults and Regulations 2008/941 have extended this to include children.

[183] See Beyleveld and Pattinson 2006.

[184] The following information on CJD derives from Boggio 2005.

[185] See Mildred 1998, 251–252 and Boggio 2005.

[186] *Newman v MRC* [1996] 7 Med. L. R. 309 and (2000) 54 B.M.L.R. 85, and *Group B v MRC* [2000] Lloyd's Rep Med 161. See also the Practice Direction of the Lord Chief Justice issued on July 30, 1998 (*http://www.hmcourts-service.gov.uk/cms/901.htm*).

[187] See Boggio 2005.

using a tariff system set up to avoid the need for future litigation.[188] It is striking that the victims had to litigate to get compensation. In 1978 the Pearson Commission recommended that a "no fault" compensation scheme be established for those injured during medical research,[189] but this recommendation was never implemented.

Participants in research trials will often find it very difficult to litigate. We have already seen that no action in battery will exist where the participant had consented having been informed in "broad terms" of the nature of the trial[190] and establishing the requirements of negligence (duty, breach, and causation: see Ch.3) can be very difficult. While researchers clearly owe a duty of care to the participants in their care, it will often be difficult to prove that the researcher was in breach of duty (i.e. negligently designed or implemented the research protocol, or negligently failed to divulge adequate information to the participant) and that that breach caused the claimant to suffer from actionable harm.

11.5.1 Liability of RECs and their members

Some academics have considered whether an action might lie against the REC in negligence if it fails to notice that the protocol is defective.[191] To my knowledge no such action has ever been brought in the UK. In the Canadian case of *Weiss v Solomon*, a successful negligence action was brought on behalf of a research participant who died after being injected with a chemical that caused him to have a heart attack.[192] The Supreme Court of Quebec held that the hospital, through its research committee, was negligent because it had failed to ensure that prospective participants were given adequate information about the risks of the procedure. It is difficult to judge how persuasive such a case will be. In a treatment context, the English courts have historically been more reluctant than the Canadian courts to require detailed disclosure from the primary defendant.[193] As mentioned earlier, the English courts have now moved much closer to the Canadian position with regard to disclosure of information by a doctor in a treatment context.[194] Nonetheless, facts of the *Weiss* case are very different from any of the decided English cases.

Establishing that the REC (or its individual members) has fallen below the standard of a reasonable REC (or REC member) will be no easy task.[195]

---

[188] HL Deb vol. 591 col. WA80, July 1, 1998, Baroness Jay (Minister of State, Department of Health).
[189] See Pearson et al. 1978, paras. 1340–1341.
[190] *Chatterton v Gerson* [1981] 1 Q.B. 432.
[191] See Brazier 1990b and Baker et al. 2005, 284–288.
[192] [1989] R.J.Q. 731.
[193] Cf. *Sidaway v Bethlem Royal Hospital* [1985] A.C. 871 with *Reibl v Hughes* [1980] 2 S.C.R. 880.
[194] See *Pearce v United Bristol Healthcare NHS Trust* [1999] P.I.Q.R. 53 and *Chester v Afshar* [2004] UKHL 41.
[195] There could also be evidential difficulties bringing an action against an individual REC member as a result of the collective decision-making process and the secrecy surrounding discussion of protocols: see Baker et al. 2005, 288.

Similarly establishing causation could pose difficulties, because the claimant would need to show that "but for" the committee's (or member's) negligence, the harm would not have occurred.[196] All this is assuming that a duty of care would be held to exist. Brazier considers that there is "little doubt that the ethics committee, and each of its members owe a duty of care to the aggrieved patient or volunteer".[197] In my view, there is a little room for debate here. For a duty of care to be imposed, the harm (to the participant) must be foreseeable, the relationship (between the REC and the participant) must be sufficiently proximate, and it must be fair, just, and reasonable to impose liability.[198] It will be much easier to show that it is reasonably foreseeable that the negligent approval of a defective research protocol could cause injury to the participant, than to satisfy the proximity and just and reasonableness requirements. The courts are reluctant to impose a duty of care on *public authorities* to protect persons from injury at the hands of a *third party*.[199] While the courts have moved away from blanket denials of a duty of care,[200] an assumption of responsibility would be required. On the one hand, it could be argued that such an assumption of responsibility will be found because participants rely on RECs to safeguard their interests and are not well placed to protect themselves.[201] (This is, indeed, a powerful moral argument.) On the other hand, the majority of REC approvals of research protocols are not straightforwardly analogous to those situations where assumptions of responsibility have previously been imposed, as protocols do not usually identify specific individual participants and the participants might not even be aware of the existence of the REC. Consider, for example, *Kent v Griffith*, where the ambulance service was held to owe a duty to provide an ambulance for the claimant within a reasonable time *because* it had accepted a call dealing with a *named individual* and had thereby *discouraged others* from providing alternative means of transport to the hospital.[202] Thus, while there are clearly circumstances where a duty of care will be owed, the courts are unlikely to impose a blanket duty. In an event, we have already seen that proving breach and causation are onerous obstacles to overcome.

The lack of means to satisfy an award of damages should not, however, deter injured participants from suing RECs or their members. If an action were brought against an NHS REC or an individual member, NHS Indemnity would cover NHS staff, medical academic staff, and staff with honorary contracts.[203] GAfREC state that the appointing authority will also take responsibility for the actions of lay members of RECS as long as they do not involve "bad faith, wilful deceit or gross negligence".[204]

---

[196] *Barnett v Chelsea and Kensington Hospital* [1969] 1 Q.B. 428. The exceptions to the "but for" principle, discussed in Ch.3 (3.5), do not appear to apply in such circumstances.

[197] Brazier 1990b, 187.

[198] *Caparo Industries v Dickman* [1990] 2 A.C. 605.

[199] *Hill v Chief Constable of West Yorkshire* [1989] A.C. 53 and *Palmer v Tees HA* [2000] P.I.Q.R. P1. See also Ch.6 (6.3.2.3).

[200] Arguably influenced by *Osman v UK* (2000) 29 E.H.R.R. 245.

[201] Implicit in Brazier 1990b, 187.

[202] *Kent v Griffith* [2001] Q.B. 36 at 43.

[203] See DH 1996a and the guidance in DH 1996b.

[204] See COREC 2001, para.4.14 See also para.5.9.

11.5.2 Obtaining compensation from the researcher/sponsor

Researchers (and their sponsors) are clearly the principal potential defendants. Researchers should make sure that compensation arrangements exist before the trial begins. The Clinical Trials Regulations require provision to be made for insurance or indemnity to cover the liability of the researcher or sponsor and RECs are required to consider the adequacy of the compensation arrangements.[205] GAfREC also requires RECs to consider such issues.[206] In any event, the adverse publicity that would be generated by a failure to offer compensation to those who are injured after volunteering to participate in research trials will usually lead to an ex gratia payment, particularly where commercial entities are involved. Indeed, the Association of the British Pharmaceutical Industry (ABPI) has issued guidance stating that compensation should be paid for any injury attributable to the administration of a medicinal product under trial, irrespective of fault.[207] This scheme only applies to trials of *non-marketed* medicinal products conducted on *patients* where the trial has been initiated or sponsored by the company providing the product.[208] Thus, this non-fault compensation scheme applies to industry-led Phase II and III trials, but not to Phase I and IV trials. Some participants will inevitably fall through the gaps. Such participants will, like the victims of the human growth hormone programme mentioned earlier, have to rely on the uncertainties of the litigation process. It was argued in Ch.3 (3.6) that many of the justifications offered for clinical negligence liability actually provide greater support for a non-fault compensation scheme. The case for no fault compensation for the victims of medical research is arguably stronger as it is bolstered by the moral benefits of encouraging participation in the first place. The case against is largely financial, but there are other questions would also need to be addressed, such as whether such schemes should apply to all types of research and what eligibility conditions should be imposed.[209]

11.6 Conclusion

Scandals in the UK and overseas should not blind us to the need for well-designed and ethically defensible medical research.[210] Medical research is quite simply the most effective way of ensuring the safety and efficacy of most prospective treatment. Research participants are, however, in an inherently vulnerable position. A rogue in clinical robes can easily abuse his position by

---

[205] Sch.1 para.16, and reg.15 (I)–(k).
[206] See COREC 2001, esp. para.10.6.
[207] See ABPI 1991, esp. paras 1.2 and 1.7.
[208] See ABPI 1991, paras 2.1–2.4.
[209] See further Brazier 2003, 412–414.
[210] For recent scandals in the UK, see Kennedy et al. 2001 (the Bristol Report) and Redfern et al. 2001 (Alder Hey Report).

relying on the generally high regard in which the medical profession is held. If participants are to be safeguarded, then we need strong RECs, monitoring systems, and compensation systems. In this regard the current regulatory structure still has a long way to go.

11.7 Further reading

Duties and incentives for participation

Harris, John (2005) "Scientific Research is a Moral Duty." 31 *Journal of Medical Ethics* 242–248.

Shimm, D. S. and Spece, R. G. (1991) "Industry Reimbursement for Entering Patients into Clinical Trials: Legal and Ethical Issues." 115 *Annals of Internal Medicine* 148–151.

Research ethics committees and the law

Beyleveld, Deryck (2009) "Jurisprudential Views of the Relationship Between Law and Ethics." In D. Beyleveld, D. Townend and J. Wright (eds) *Research Ethics Committees, Data Protection and Medical Research in Europe: Key Issues.* (Aldershot: Ashgate) (forthcoming).

Research into emergency treatment

Beyleveld, Deryck and Pattinson, Shaun D. (2006) "Medical Research into Emergency Treatment: Regulatory Tensions in England and Wales." 5 *Web Journal of Current Legal Issues.*

Research on incapacitated adults

Lewis, Penney (2002) "Procedures that are Against the Medical Interests of Incompetent Adults." 22(4) *Oxford Journal of Legal Studies* 575–618.

Chapter 12

MEDICAL GENETICS: TESTING, THERAPY, AND PATENTS

12.1 Introduction

From birth many of us are told that we resemble our biological parents. Some of us are lucky enough to inherit our mother's or father's endearing features, others inherit less beneficial traits. Many generations of the Habsburg dynasty passed down a distinctively long jaw and droopy lower lip, which became known as the "Habsburg lip". Charles II of Spain, the last of the Habsburg monarchs, had a family lip so pronounced that he could not even chew his own food.[1] This genetic trait was, at least, not life-threatening. Huntington's disease is. Those with this condition usually display no symptoms until they reach

---

[1] See Watson 2003, 4, who uses the alternative spelling of the family name, i.e. "Hapsburg".

middle age or beyond. It then causes progressive neurodegeneration, leading to involuntary movements, loss of motor control and dementia, with death occurring 10 to 20 years later.[2] There is currently no cure.

No special tests were needed to diagnose the Habsburg lip. It was evident to any observer from the moment of birth. In contrast, Huntington's disease can remain undiscovered until the onset of symptoms. Both the Habsburg lip and Huntington's disease can run in families. Not all genetic disorders are similarly associated with a family history. Down's syndrome, for example, is usually the result of a spontaneous mutation, so children with the condition are frequently born to those without any family history of it. Genetic tests can now reveal whether you have certain genes, including the gene that causes Huntington's disease or the extra chromosome that causes Down's syndrome. No test can, however, cure a disorder and curing patients at the genetic level (gene therapy) is still very much in its infancy.

This chapter is concerned with the acquisition, use, and commercialisation of *genetic information* as it impacts on diagnosis, treatment, and medical research. In particular, it will examine genetic testing and screening, gene therapy, and the legal protection granted to genetic technological advances in this field by patent law. To avoid overlap with issues covered in Chs 7–10, the focus will be on postnatal (as opposed to prenatal) genetic testing. I refer readers who are interested in privacy and confidentiality issues to Ch.6, those who are interested in preimplantation genetic diagnosis to Ch.8, and those who are interested in cloning and embryonic stem cells to Ch.10.

12.2 Genetic science

Understanding the legal and ethical issues raised by human genetics requires a basic grasp of genetic science.

12.2.1 Genes and chromosomes

Genes are the units of heredity, enabling traits to be passed from parent to child. They are composed of *DNA*[3] and found scattered along tiny structures within the nucleus of each cell.[4] These tiny structures are called *chromosomes*. (If a cell were a chicken egg, the nucleus would be the yolk and the chromosomes would be tiny X-shaped particles floating around in the yolk.) Each of our cells

---

[2] See e.g. Sermon et al. 1998.

[3] DNA is the acronym of deoxyribonucleic acid. DNA molecules consist of two sugar-phosphate backbones that wind round each other to form a double helix, from which bases jut inwards like the steps of a ladder (see Watson and Crick 1953).

[4] Here, I ignore the mitochondrial DNA, which is discussed in Ch.10 (10.2.2).

has the 46 chromosomes that we inherited from our parents; 23 from each.[5] Every cell in our body therefore contains a combination of our parents' genes. The genes themselves are found at distinct locations (called loci) along the chromosomes. At each locus there are a number of different variants that the gene can take.[6]

We evidently do not see the genes of those around us. What we see is the product of the interaction between their genes and many non-genetic factors.[7] Very few physical traits are the product of one gene alone. For those traits that are directly correlated to one gene, it can make a difference whether the gene variants at one particular locus on each of the paired chromosomes are the same. A *dominant* gene variant will be expressed irrespective of whether it is matched on the other chromosome. A *recessive* gene variant will only be expressed if its effects are not counter-balanced by a different gene variant on the other chromosome.

Huntington's disease is an example of a dominant disorder. Inheriting one copy of the defective gene from either of your parents will mean that you will get Huntington's disease (which will later kill you unless something else kills you first). It also follows that, even without a genetic test, we know that the biological child of someone with Huntington's disease has at least a 50 per cent chance of developing the condition himself.[8] In contrast, phenylketonuria (PKU) is a recessive disorder. Only those born with two copies of the relevant gene variant will be unable to produce the enzyme needed to metabolise the protein phenylalanine. Without this enzyme the normal cellular process that converts this protein into another does not occur. Such individuals will, if brought up on a normal diet, accumulate an abnormal imbalance between these two proteins, which can severely disrupt cognitive development and cause retarded growth, epilepsy, and hyperactivity.

Single gene disorders are comparatively rare. Most traits, including most genetic disorders, are associated with many genes. The interaction between genetic and non-genetic factors can be extremely complicated. The reason for this is that genes act indirectly. Genes can either be expressed—by directing the production of a protein (or part of a protein) in a cell—or they can regulate the expression of other genes. Genes cannot perform either function without an appropriate cellular environment, and the consequences of producing a protein will depend on the protein in question, the other proteins in the body, where in the body it is produced, and an individual's external environment.

---

[5] This simplification requires two qualifications. *First*, two types of cell (sperm and eggs) carry only 23 chromosomes, so that when they join together the resulting conceptus has the full complement of chromosomes. *Second*, occasionally abnormalities can cause slight variation in the number of chromosomes. Most chromosomal abnormalities are incompatible with viability. One notable exception is Down's syndrome, which is caused by an extra copy, or extra part, of chromosome 21.

[6] A gene variant is called an allele.

[7] That product is known as the phenotype.

[8] The child of a parent with one copy of the gene variant responsible for the disorder has a 1 in 2 chance of inheriting it, whereas the child of a parent with two copies of the variant will inevitably inherit it.

The contribution of a specific gene is rarely straightforward. Where a particular gene does contribute to the expression of a particular trait, it can act as a *necessary, sufficient*, or *contributing* condition for the expression of that trait. Few genes are *sufficient* conditions for a trait (in the sense that possession of a specific variant of the gene will lead to the expression of the trait in any individual who survives until the time of onset). Similarly, few are *necessary* conditions for a trait (in the sense that only individuals with that gene variant can express that trait). The vast majority of gene variants associated with complex traits are merely *contributing* conditions. That is to say that the variations of a particular gene can contribute to a trait without being either a necessary or sufficient condition for that trait. For example, a mutation in the BRCA1 gene can increase the chances of a woman developing breast cancer but a woman without such a mutation can still develop breast cancer, and possessing such a mutation does not automatically indicate that the woman will develop breast cancer. The BRCA1 mutation is therefore only a potential *contributor* to the development of breast cancer. Its presence merely indicates increased *susceptibility* to breast cancer.

12.2.2 Some complexities: genetic influence on behaviour

Only a few traits have been mapped to specific genes that are identifiable at the molecular level (i.e. as specific sequences of DNA). Most correlations between genes and traits are little more than statistical associations, not all of which reveal a causal connection. A strong association between having Huntington's disease and watching football would, for example, not suggest that watching football causes Huntington's or that Huntington's causes the development of an interest in watching football.

In recent years a number of genetic claims have been made for various behavioural traits. The most controversial have concerned intelligence, homosexuality, and criminality. In many cases, the samples or results have been statistically unpersuasive and there are difficulties with adequately defining such traits so that the results are meaningful.[9]

In 1978, the existence of a peculiar Dutch family came to the attention of a clinical geneticist working in Nijmegen.[10] Eight of the male members of this family displayed similar levels of violence. One had raped his sister and later stabbed a prison guard, another had deliberately run over his boss after being mildly reprimanded for laziness, and two had been convicted of arson. The scientist discovered that the affected males all shared a mutation on the X-chromosome. They all had a mutated, non-functioning copy of the gene coding for a protein regulating levels of neurotransmitters in the brain.[11] Since it was recessive and on the X-chromosome, this trait was largely restricted to

---

[9] See Pattinson 2002a, ch.3.
[10] See Watson 2003, 415–416; Brunner 1993; and Cases et al. 1995.
[11] Known as Monoamine Oxidase A (MAOA).

males. (Women get two copies of the X-chromosome, so that a recessive gene on one can be counter-balanced by the corresponding gene on the other, whereas men only get one copy of that chromosome.) Here we have a genetic mutation associated with aggressive and violent behaviour. It is, however, misleading to present this as a "gene for criminality" or a "crime gene". Crime is more than aggressive behaviour; criminality is the social characterisation of certain conduct and, as such, is socially (rather than biologically) defined. The legality of certain sexual acts, for example, depends on the jurisdiction in which one acts. In the absence of large-scale population studies it is simply not possible to tell whether this particular gene is also associated with non-criminal aggressive behaviour, such as sporting prowess or entrepreneurial success. Also, since crime is only measured indirectly by its detection, any associations between a gene and crime will be associations with detected or self-attributed crime, rather than crime as such. In any event, an association itself is not proof of a causal link, let alone one of any predictive utility. Loose talk of "criminal" or "crime" genes should be avoided because it could encourage legal and medical interventions based on misunderstandings of the underlying science.[12]

12.3 Genetic screening and testing

Many of us have a false view of the genetic variability of our species. You share 99.9 per cent of your genes with any randomly selected human, which is a tiny degree of difference when compared to differences within other species.[13] Fruit flies have ten times more variation and even chimpanzees are about three times as variable.[14] Our comparatively tiny variations can, however, have significant effects on our lives. The genetic disorders mentioned above provide clear examples. Modern methods of genetic analysis enable the testing of individuals for the presence or absence of particular gene variants. At present, though, direct molecular tests are only available for a small number of genetic disorders. In a few cases, genetic tests can enable treatment to be provided. In others, they can enable individuals to plan for a future event or to reassess their reproductive choices. For some individuals, however, the genetic information obtained will be of no use or, as will be illustrated below, could even be harmful.

A general distinction is often drawn between "genetic testing" and "genetic screening".[15] *Genetic testing* is where an individual patient is tested because he is thought to be at an increased risk of possessing a particular chromosomal or gene variant. An individual with a family history of Huntington's could, for example, be tested for the genetic mutation responsible. *Genetic screening* involves the testing of members of particular populations for a genetic disorder or condition without reliance on evidence that the specific individuals tested

[12] See further Nuffield 2002a.
[13] See HGC 2000, 5 and Watson 2003, 259. You share 99.95% of your genes with either of your parents.
[14] See Watson 2003, 259.
[15] See e.g. BMA 1998, 34–35.

face an increased risk. In this country, for example, newborn babies are routinely screened for PKU, using what is known as the Guthrie or heel prick test.[16] This is done because PKU is a severely disabling condition that, if detected early, is treatable by a special diet.

While the Guthrie test will reveal specific genetic information, it looks for certain substances in the blood rather than for the relevant sequence of DNA. As this highlights, there is some difficulty distinguishing "genetic" from "non-genetic" testing or screening. It is possible to discover some aspects of an individual's genetic makeup by, for example, directly testing for the presence of a particular DNA sequence, testing for the presence of a particular gene product, investigating an individual's family history, or by simply observing an individual. There are thus degrees of directness (and accuracy) by which the presence or absence of a particular chromosome or gene variant can be determined. Most screening methods are meant to reveal those at increased risk (to whom a more direct diagnostic technique can then be applied), so they tend to be less direct than testing methods. For present purposes, a procedure will be referred to as "genetic" if it seeks to detect the presence or absence of a particular gene or chromosomal variant, including an indirect test for a gene product that is primarily indicative of a specific gene or chromosomal variant.

The Guthrie test has particular significance in Australia, where the blood samples taken from newborn infants have been stored on so-called "Guthrie cards" since 1960. Other countries have created tissue banks and genetic databases of their own. These projects have been set up in Estonia (the Estonian Genome Project (EGP)), Iceland (deCODE), Quebec (CARTaGENE), Singapore (Singapore Tissue Network), Sweden (UmanGenomics), and in the UK (the UK BioBank).[17] The UK BioBank is designed to produce a mass database of DNA samples and confidential health information from a representative sample of 500,000 volunteers aged 45–69. The intention is to track the volunteers for up to 30 years. Genetic databases are mentioned here in passing and are not examined further in this chapter. Since large population genetic databases typically contain both information and physical biosamples they tend to be fall within the remit of both data and tissue regulation.[18]

12.3.1 Ethical issues

Genetic information evokes an array of ethical issues. This section will focus on some of the more prominent debates concerning presymptomatic testing for

---

[16] See BMA 1998, 114–115, and Connor and Ferguson-Smith 1997, 207.

[17] See *http://www.geenivaramu.ee*, *www.decode.com*, *http://www.cartagene.qc.ca*, *www.stn.org.sg*, *http://www.umangenomics.com*, and *http://www.ukbiobank.ac.uk*.

[18] For an overview of the law applying to biobanks used for medical research, see Kaye and Gibbons 2008. See also Ch.6 (for discussion of data protection and confidentiality law generally), McHale 2004a (for discussion of data issues in relation to biobanks), Ch.14 (14.3.1.2) (for discussed the Human Tissue (Quality and Safety for Human Application) Regulations 2007/1523, which apply to tissue banks providing tissues of human origin for therapeutic purposes).

late onset disorders, the so-called "right not to know", and the societal consequences of genetic information.

12.3.1.1 Presymptomatic testing for late onset disorders

One of the key figures in the development of a genetic test for Huntington's disease, Nancy Wexler, had lost her mother to the condition.[19] This means that Wexler has a 1 in 2 chance of having the genetic mutation herself. In the absence of a cure, she has chosen not to take the test.[20] Choosing to live with uncertainty in such circumstances is common—only 10 to 19 per cent of those at risk choose to be tested.[21] Predictive testing can have psychological benefits (such as the relief brought by a negative result or the comfort of being able to plan one's final years), but it can also bring significantly increased suffering. One international study recorded a notably increased likelihood of a catastrophic psychological event following a positive test result.[22] Even a negative test result was linked to such consequences for some (albeit a small minority) of those tested,[23] perhaps indicating "survivor guilt" similar to that suffered by wartime soldiers who survive when their friends are killed.[24]

There is no single ethical response to predictive genetic testing, due to differing views on issues concerning patient autonomy, clinical autonomy, and resource limitations. A patient's choice with regard to predictive testing and counselling services can conflict with what a clinician considers to be in the patient's best interests or with the just distribution of limited health resources. Generalisations at the level of the five major groups of moral theories are difficult. What should be clear is that not all moral positions allow reliance on a patient's own interests to defeat their autonomous decisions. Paternalism of this type is, for example, difficult to reconcile with rights-based theories (which hold that rights-holders are entitled to waive the benefit of all the duties owed to them) and some forms of preference utilitarianism (which hold that the satisfaction of choices should be maximised). In contrast, some duty-based and virtue theories will not allow autonomy to trump nonmaleficence. The difficulty in applying moral theories to genetic testing is that the issues go far beyond the interests of the patient. For a start, the effects of presymptomatic genetic testing are rarely limited to the proband (i.e. the individual tested). Whether, and in what circumstances, presymptomatic genetic testing should be

[19] Wexler was a key member of the group that mapped the locus for Huntington's disease on chromosome 4 in 1983 (see Gusella et al. 1983) and the group that later identified the gene in 1993 (see Huntington's Disease Collaborative Research Group 1993).
[20] See Watson 2003, ch.11, esp. 338.
[21] See Report of a Working Party of the Clinical Genetics Society 1994, 791 (citing a figure of 10–15%) and Harper et al. 2000, 570 (who cite a figure of about 19% of those who possess a 1 in 2 chance of having the condition).
[22] See Almqvist et al. 1999 who examined the occurrence of suicides, suicide attempts, and psychiatric hospitalisation. One earlier study had found that the risk of suicide for those with Huntington's disease was almost 4 times greater than for the US Caucasian population generally: see Farrer 1986.
[23] See Almqvist et al. 1999, esp. 1300.
[24] See Wexler 1985, 297–298, and Andrews 1991, 38.

allowed will therefore also depend on the weight given to the interests of third parties. There is also some debate about the extent to which a decision to remain ignorant can be truly autonomous, which we must now address.

12.3.1.2 The right not to know

The results of genetic tests can be difficult to keep from family members. Yet genetic tests can reveal genetic information about the proband's family members. Imagine if Nancy Wexler had a child who, when reaching adulthood, wanted to be tested. A positive result would also reveal that Nancy herself has the disorder. This would undermine her decision not to have herself tested. The decision to have a genetic test can therefore severely affect the autonomy of a close relative. For those willing to use the language of rights, there can be a conflict between one individual's right to know and another's right not to know. This conflict is removed altogether if a right to remain in ignorance of one's own genetic makeup is rejected—as it is by some moral theories.

Harris and Keywood have argued that there is no such thing as a right to remain in ignorance if it is understood as an entitlement trumping competing claims.[25] They reject the idea of a prima facie entitlement to be protected from true or honest information about oneself on the basis that it cannot be justified as an attempt to protect autonomy or liberty. They argue that ignorance of information that bears upon one's life choices is "inimical to autonomy", because "where the individual is ignorant of information that bears upon rational life choices she is not in a position to be self-governing".[26] They argue that ignorance of crucial information about one's genetic makeup cannot be justified by the right to liberty (understood as the right to make free, non-autonomous decisions), because liberty cannot trump the competing claims of others to protection from significant harm or protection of their comparably important rights or liberties.[27] Harris and Keywood are not arguing that it is always in a patient's best interests for them to be told distressing information, nor are they arguing that it is always morally right to force information on unwilling patients. They are arguing that a patient's autonomy and liberty interests alone cannot entitle them to remain ignorant of information that is relevant to their future life choices.

Consider Nancy Wexler's decision to remain ignorant of whether she has inherited Huntington's disease from her mother. Is Nancy's decision to remain ignorant of her disease status, however, really incompatible with her own autonomy interests? Her decision to plan her life without this information is voluntary and informed in the sense that she is fully aware of the nature of the information that she is denying herself. Harris and Keywood argue that some apparently autonomous choices are inconsistent with the idea of autonomy.[28] They give selling oneself into slavery as an example. Selling oneself into slavery

---

[25] See Harris and Keywood 2001.

[26] See Harris and Keywood 2001, 421. See Harris and Keywood 2001, 419–421.

[27] See Harris and Keywood 2001, esp. 426–428.

[28] See Harris and Keywood 2001, esp. 420.

is, however, surely a decision of a very different type. The reason that the decision to sell oneself into slavery is inconsistent with the idea of autonomy, even if it is a fully informed decision, is that slavery is incompatible with self-government. A slave's present and future purposes are subject to another's will. Nancy's decision to remain ignorant of her disease status is not incompatible with self-government of her own future in anything like this sense. The decision to remain ignorant of one's disease status does not foreclose the possibility of changing one's mind in the future and does not defer all future decision-making to the will of another.[29]

Harris and Keywood are, however, right to insist that following a decision to remain ignorant can place huge burdens on others. Many examples could be given as to the burden that Nancy's decision will place on others. Her doctor could find it difficult to properly diagnose a future illness if he is deprived of this relevant information and her family might respond inappropriately to her future behaviour on the basis of a mistaken assumption vis-à-vis her disease status. Nancy's choice to remain ignorant of her disease status does not, however, have to rest on her autonomy or liberty interests alone. Overriding Nancy's freely chosen choice might lead her to suffer significant psychological harm. This will be relevant to the application of many moral theories.

12.3.1.3 Confidentiality

Whether or not a patient has a right to remain in ignorance, just about all moral theories will recognise that there are good moral reasons for generally upholding patient confidentiality (see Ch.6). Patient confidentiality can, however, compromise the interests of others where the proband refuses to authorise the release of genetic information to family members. Imagine, for example, that an individual is shown to have the genetic mutation responsible for a nasty, treatable condition, but does not want to inform close relatives who are oblivious to their own risk. This is simply another example of circumstances where the need to protect patient confidentiality can come into conflict with other needs and interests, which is addressed in Ch.6 (esp. 6.3.2.2). Third party interests present less pressing reasons for breaching confidentiality in those situations where the harm of not releasing the information is not as clear. Where, for example, the genetic mutation is only associated with susceptibility to a disease or condition (e.g. the BRCA1 mutation) or is associated with conditions for which there is no treatment or cure. Here, informing a relative that they are at risk deprives that person of the option of remaining ignorant and infringes confidentiality in a situation where the benefits of releasing this information are far from self-evident. When dealing with any conflict of moral interests the choice of moral theory can be key, because different theories have different approaches to determining how relevant interests are to be weighed against other relevant interests.

---

[29] See also Husted 1997 for an argument that there are both "thick" or "thin" conceptions of autonomy that are relevant to the debate on the right not to know.

12.3.1.4 Societal consequences of genetic information

Revealing genetic information can have wider social consequences. Genetic information is at least potentially relevant to persons such as insurers, employers, the criminal justice system, and public health planners.

Private insurance is less of a necessity to those of us who live in the UK than it is in countries without a similar publicly-funded health service. Nevertheless, many wish, or are required, to take out life insurance. Life insurance is, for example, required for some loans and mortgages. Insurers seek to set their premiums according to the level of risk against which they are insuring. From the insurer's point of view, genetic test results could aid risk-projection (as blood pressure readings or family histories have done for many years) and a customer who has genetic test results, if not required to disclose those results, might be able to play the system against them. From the potential customer's point of view, genetic tests could reveal information that they do not want to know and any requirement to obtain or release such information could affect their ability to obtain insurance at an affordable price or at all.

Employers could also benefit from genetic information about potential and actual employees. Genetic information might, for example, reveal those likely to be affected by future illness or disability, or reveal those likely to be adversely or disproportionately affected by certain types of working condition.

The criminal justice system is increasingly using DNA evidence in the solving of crimes. DNA fingerprints can provide critical evidence as to the presence of the accused at the crime scene. Far more controversially, some hope that so-called "crime genes" or "violence genes" could be used to influence decisions as to the appropriate response to criminal behaviour (see 12.2). Loose talk that encourages misunderstanding of the underlying science could therefore have profound effects on social policy.

In all three contexts, genetic information allows distinctions to be drawn between particular individuals and particular groups, and thereby enables (positive and negative) discrimination. Many fear that genetic information will give rise to new or additional opportunities for *unfair* discrimination, specifically unfair *genetic* discrimination. Unless defined very narrowly, genetic discrimination *as such* does not map on to unfair discrimination, because just about every trait or ability has some genetic contribution and not all acts of differential treatment are unethical.[30] Determining what is unethical treatment is largely theory dependent. Most moral positions will not accept differential treatment with regard to (at least some) important needs or opportunities to turn on factually irrelevant considerations. Consider the high-profile discriminatory policy adopted by the US Department of Defense towards those with a particular genetic mutation in the 1970s.[31] It was known that individuals with two copies of a particular genetic mutation faced a significantly increased risk of collapsing at high altitudes (because such individuals had sickle cell

---

[30] See further Taylor 2004.
[31] See Kitcher 1996, 130–132.

disease). No such increased risk was associated with possession of only one copy of that mutation (because the trait was recessive).[32] Yet, the US Department of Defense carried out a policy of excluding individuals with only one copy from entering the Air Force Academy, which was the most direct way to became a commissioned officer in the air force. This policy has been widely condemned as unfairly discriminatory. Since this mutation is largely restricted to native Africans and those of African descent, this appears to be as much an instance of unfair *racial* discrimination as unfair *genetic* discrimination. Discrimination by insurers and employers on the basis of considerations that are factually relevant to their business activities is more controversial. We have seen that genetic information can be economically relevant to the business activities of insurers and employers. The difficulty is that reliance on genetic information can disadvantage individuals and these disadvantages could increase if discrimination on that basis were to be regarded as legitimate in society as a whole. In these circumstances, there is a difficult balance to be made between the respective utilities, rights, or duties. That balance will depend on the specifics of a particular moral theory, rather than the general moral camp in which the theory rests.

12.3.2 The regulatory position

12.3.2.1 Domestic law

The law governing genetic testing and screening is largely the same as that governing any other diagnostic or screening technique. Many of these issues have been covered in other chapters, namely the chapters covering consent (Chs 4, 5, and 11) and confidentiality and privacy (Ch.6).

There is no law directly addressing genetic discrimination. Current anti-discrimination legislation is restricted to sex, race, disability, religion/belief, sexual orientation, and age.[33] The race or sex discrimination legislation will sometimes apply where a person is discriminated against on the grounds of his genetics if the condition in question primarily affects a particular sex (e.g. haemophilia) or a particular racial group (e.g. sickle cell disease). There is some debate about the extent to which the Disability Discrimination Act 1995 could apply to instances of discrimination against those with disabling genetic traits or against those whose genetic test results suggest a high likelihood of a genetic trait occurring.[34] Section 1(1) of the Act defines "disability" as "a physical or mental impairment which has a substantial and long-term adverse effect on . . . ability to carry out normal day-to-day activities". The Act also states that a

---

[32] Confusingly, such individuals are said to have the sickle cell trait.

[33] See, in particular, the Sex Discrimination Act 1975, the Race Relations Act 1975, the Disability Discrimination Act 1995, Employment Equality (Religion or Belief) Regulations 2003/1660, Employment Equality (Sexual Orientation) Regulations 2003/1661, and Employment Equality (Age) Regulations 2006/1031.

[34] See Mason and Laurie 2006, 237–238.

person who has a progressive condition (such as muscular dystrophy) is to be treated as having an impairment that has substantial effect on his ability to carry out normal day-to-day activities before that effect actually becomes substantial (Sch.1 para.8(1)). Both provisions use the word "has" rather "is likely to have" and both provisions require the impairment to have an effect on the ability to carry out day-to-day activities that is or will become substantial. Many genetic traits and predispositions will therefore fall outside of these provisions. A person possessing a gene indicating a propensity for breast cancer does not have a disability under the Act unless and until that breast cancer manifests. Similarly, a person with a single copy of the gene responsible for sickle cell disease does not have a disability under the Act. Article 14 of the European Convention on Human Rights (the Convention), as given domestic effect by the Human Rights Act 1998, is not so narrowly phrased. This provision prohibits discrimination with regard to the exercise of the Convention rights "on any ground". It is plausible to argue that this includes discrimination on genetic grounds,[35] but this can only operate where an individual is able to rely on a particular Convention right.[36]

Responding to the need to keep the wider effects of genetic technological developments under consideration, the Human Genetics Commission (HGC) was set up in December 1999. This is an independent, non-statutory advisory body tasked with responsibility for promoting coordination between bodies with advisory and regulatory functions in human genetics, and monitoring and advising on the provision of genetic services, including testing and screening procedures. It has taken over responsibility from three predecessor bodies: the Human Genetics Advisory Commission (HGAC), the Advisory Committee on Genetic Testing (ACGT), and the Advisory Group on Scientific Advances in Genetics. It works "with the National Screening Committee and conduct an initial analysis of the ethical, social, scientific, economic, and practical considerations of genetic profiling at birth".[37]

The HGC and its predecessors have already considered many of the issues raised in the last section. The defunct ACGT had, for example, issued a report on genetic testing for late onset disorders.[38] This emphasised the need for consent and, in the case of presymptomatic genetic testing of healthy individuals, advised that the patient's consent be obtained in writing. The presymptomatic testing of young children who have not reached competent adolescence was "not recommended".[39] The ACGT's view that great caution should be

---

[35] A claim that is bolstered by art.21 of the EU Charter of Fundamental Rights (which prohibits discrimination on "any ground such as . . . genetic features"), and art.11 of the Convention on Human Rights and Biomedicine (which prohibits discrimination on the grounds of "genetic heritage").

[36] Moreover, this will only be of use where the defendant is a public body, unless the Act has full horizontal effect (see Ch.1 (1.5)) or the courts are willing to interpret an existing cause of action to give effect to the Convention right (as in *Campbell v Mirror Group Newspapers* [2004] UKHL 22).

[37] DH 2003c, para.3.38.

[38] See ACGT 1998.

[39] Prenatal genetic testing for late onset disorders was not advised against, but was only thought appropriate in the context of full genetic counselling (see ACGT 1998, 5). For an ethical discussion of this issue, see Pattinson 2002a, 79–81.

observed in the testing of children with late onset disorders has been explicitly endorsed by the HGC.[40] The HGC has also built on the work of the ACGT with regard to genetic tests supplied direct to the public. In particular, the HGC has recommended that

- there should be stricter controls on direct genetic testing (such as over-the-counter testing kits), but not a statutory ban;

- there should be a well-funded NHS genetics service that can properly manage and allow access to predictive genetic tests;

- most genetic tests that provide predictive health information should not be offered as direct genetic tests; and

- predictive genetic tests that rely on home testing or home sampling should be discouraged.[41]

These recommendations were meant to provide a framework for future regulation of direct genetic tests, balancing the need for access with the perceived dangers of abuse.

With regard to insurance, the HGC recommended an immediate moratorium on the use by insurance companies of the results of genetic tests.[42] Following this advice, the Government and the Association of British Insurers (ABI) agreed a moratorium on the use of predictive genetic test results, which was later extended to November 1, 2011.[43] This voluntary moratorium applies to life insurance policies up to a value of £500,000 and policies for critical illness, long term care, and income protection up to a value of £300,000. Above these limits, tests can be used where they have been approved by the Government's Genetics and Insurance Committee (GAIC). Compliance with the moratorium falls to the ABI and the GAIC. This means that, for the short-term at least, those at risk of Huntington's disease will face no higher premiums if they receive an unfavourable genetic test result. Their premiums will, however, remain higher than for those without a family history of the condition, as family history is not covered by the moratorium. A patient who has a favourable test result may choose to disclose this to negate the need for an additional premium based on his family history.

There is one further regulatory response that is worthy of mention in this context. Section 45 of the Human Tissue Act 2004 creates an *offence of non-consensual analysis of DNA*. More specifically, under s.45(1) it is an offence to have "bodily material" (defined in s.45(5) as any material that has come from a human body and consists of or contains human cells) intending to analyse the DNA in it without "qualifying consent", subject to certain exceptions. Section 45(2) excludes material from the scope of the offence: embryos outside of the body

[40] See HGC 2002, para.4.38.
[41] See HGC 2003.
[42] See HGC 2001.
[43] See DH and BAI 2005. See also ABI 2008.

(which are regulated separately by the Human Fertilisation and Embryology Act 1990: see Ch.8) and existing holdings of material where the identity of the person from whom it came is not known and is not likely to become known. Part 1 of Sch.4 states that "qualifying consent" means the consent of the DNA source and makes provision for the dead, children, and adults who lack capacity. Part 2 of Sch.4 lists the excepted purposes for which the results of the analysis can be used outside of the scope of the offence. These include the medical diagnosis or treatment of the DNA source and criminal justice purposes (Sch.4 Pt 2 para.5). Thus, in general terms, this provision makes it an offence to genetically screen or test without consent unless the purpose is to treat that person.

12.3.2.2 International instruments

The possibility of medical tourism, specifically genetic tourism, renders it necessary for regulation to operate on an international level. Those denied access to genetic tests or information in one country can easily travel to another or, with even greater ease, simply log on to the internet and purchase a mail order test.

The Council of Europe's Convention on Human Rights and Biomedicine (hereafter the Biomedicine Convention) has a number of provisions that are relevant to genetic testing and screening procedures. Some explicitly address genetic information. Article 12 restricts predictive genetic tests to health purposes and linked scientific research, subject to "appropriate genetic counselling". This would exclude most requests by insurers or employers. Article 11 prohibits discrimination on the grounds of "genetic heritage". Some of the general principles are also applicable in this context, such as the prohibition on interventions in the health field without free and informed consent (art.5) and the right not to know information collected about one's health (art.10(2)). While the UK has not yet signed this Convention, some of these principles could inform interpretation of the general human rights convention, as given domestic effect by the Human Rights Act (HRA) 1998. The art.8(1) right to private and family life will, for example, give protection to the right to consent and the right not to know, subject to art.8(2).[44]

UNESCO's Universal Declaration on the Human Genome and Human Rights 1997 and its later International Declaration on Human Genetic Data 2003 have provisions addressing genetic screening and testing. The 1997 Declaration emphasises the importance of informed consent before any research, treatment or diagnosis is performed concerning an individual's genome (art.5(b)), rejects discrimination on the grounds of genetic characteristics, where this is intended to infringe or will have the effect of infringing human rights (art.6), and specifically includes genetic data within medical confidentiality (art.7). The 2003 Declaration repeats these assertions[45] and goes into much more depth. It is, for

---

[44] See *Glass v UK* [2004] 1 F.L.R. 1019, esp. para.58.
[45] See, in particular, arts 7 (non-discrimination and non-stigmatisation), 8 (consent), and 14 (privacy and confidentiality).

example, considered "ethically imperative" that genetic counselling be available when genetic testing that may have significant implications for a person's health is being considered (art.11) and it is asserted that a person's identity should not be reduced to genetic characteristics (art.3). Both Declarations have been adopted by the General Conference of UNESCO, but neither have legal force.

12.4 Gene therapy and human genetic manipulation

Gene therapy involves the use of genes for therapy. More precisely, it involves the genetic modification of human cells directed at treating, preventing, or curing a condition. The phrase "gene therapy" is often used to refer to genetic modifications that are currently largely experimental.[46] The first apparently successful gene therapy trial took place in the United States in 1990 on two young girls with a terrible immune disorder.[47] It was a genetic disorder causing a lack of an enzyme required for effective immune protection. The experiment targeted immune cells in the blood, which were extracted and grown outside of the body and infected with a virus that had been modified so that it would implant a functional copy of the defective gene. The idea was to put the modified cells back into the girls' blood streams, where they were intended to produce the required enzyme. The girls are healthy today. It is not, however, entirely clear what contribution gene therapy made because the regulatory body had insisted that they be treated with the non-gene therapy replacement enzyme (albeit at a lower dose) at the same time as the gene therapy trial.

In 1999, gene therapy trials saw their first death.[48] An 18-year-old volunteer suffered from a mild case of a genetic disorder that is lethal if untreated, but which can be managed by medication and an appropriate diet. The American research team injected a modified virus containing a functional copy of the gene into his liver and, only three days later, he died following infection, blood clots, and liver haemorrhaging. A later inquiry identified 18 specific violations of the research protocol and a failure to properly supervise and monitor the trial.

In 2003, what had appeared to represent the successful treatment of another immune deficiency—by virally modifying bone marrow cells—was setback by news that the first two patients were suffering from a cancer of the bone marrow (leukaemia).[49] This unfortunate outcome was not in any way attributed to inadequate supervisory procedures. The condition in question is commonly known as "bubble baby syndrome" because of the isolation in which affected children (usually boys) have to live to be protected from infection.[50] Here in the UK, doctors have used a similar gene therapy approach on five children and young

---

[46] A good summary of the science can be found in Staff 2001.
[47] See Watson 2003, 367–369. The disorder was Adenosine Deaminase Deficiency.
[48] See Marshall 1999; Watson 2003, 371–372; and Ciment 2000.
[49] See Hacein-Bey-Abina et al. 2003; and Watson 2003, 372–373.
[50] It is an X-linked form of severe combined immune deficiency (X-SCID).

adults with this condition, and, at present, these patients are progressing well, with none showing any signs of leukaemia.[51] Other trials have subsequently used gene therapy to treat additional conditions.[52]

All the trials mentioned so far were instances of "somatic" (or "somatic cell") gene therapy. This involves the modification of somatic (body) cells. This is to be contrasted with "germ-line" gene therapy, which involves the deliberate genetic modification of germ cells (sperm or eggs), their precursors, or the cells of early embryos where the germ-line has yet to be segregated. The difference is that any germ-line effects will be passed on to future generations.[53]

New genes were first successfully introduced into the germ-line of animals over two decades ago. Mice have, for example, been genetically engineered since the mid-1980s.[54] A strain of mice has even been genetically engineered for susceptibility to cancer (the so-called Oncomouse). Even primates have been genetically engineered.[55] Prenatal gene therapy, whether germ-line or not, might be the only way to prevent some genetic disorders, particularly those causing irreversible damage to the fetus before birth. Prenatal gene therapy might also be the only method by which some prospective parents can have a genetically-related child with particular traits or without particular traits.[56]

As should by now be clear, gene therapy is the genetic modification of human cells directed at treating a medical condition. The phrase "gene therapy" is often used to refer to genetic modifications that are not strictly therapeutic, because these procedures are still experimental and thereby more a matter of research than therapy. Some object to the description of germ-line modifications as "gene therapy" on the basis that they are not directed at something that is recognised as a medical condition or apply to entities that are not recognised as individuals.[57] Here, for convenience, the term gene therapy is used throughout.

12.4.1 The regulatory position

It is now approaching two decades since a special committee was set up to consider the ethics of gene therapy. In its 1992 report, the Clothier Committee

---

[51] See GTAC 2003, iii; and 2004a, vii.

[52] See e.g. Morgan et al. 2006 (cancer) and Maguire et al. 2007 (retinal disease).

[53] It is now possible to envisage a situation where a genetically altered somatic cell is subjected to the Dolly cloning technique, thereby producing a child using the nuclear material of a somatic cell, as explained in Ch.10 (10.2.2),. This possibility will be ignored for present purposes.

[54] For an early study, see Palmiter et al. 1982.

[55] See Chan et al. 2001.

[56] The usefulness of merely relying on selection techniques following genetic testing (i.e. preimplantation genetic diagnosis or prenatal diagnosis) is restricted by the traits possessed by the embryo or fetus being selected. Some couples will be unable to conceive a child with or without certain traits. If, for example, one parent has two copies of a dominant trait, all their offspring will have that trait, unless germ-line gene therapy becomes an option.

[57] For arguments that germ-line manipulations do not treat individuals see e.g. Glannon 1998, 195; and Baird 1994, 571. Cf. Pattinson 2002, 130.

took the view that gene therapy should be confined to somatic cells and such proposals should be considered by a regulatory committee.[58] The Gene Therapy Advisory Committee (GTAC) was established shortly afterwards as a ministerial advisory body. The Medicines for Human Use (Clinical Trials) Regulations 2004/1031 recognise GTAC as the national ethics committee for gene therapy (reg.2).[59] Under the Clinical Trials Regulations, obtaining the favourable opinion of GTAC is a legal requirement for conducting a clinical trial on a gene therapy medical product, unless GTAC has transferred consideration of the trial to another research ethics committee (regs 12 and 14(5)). An opinion must be given within 90 days of receiving a valid application by GTAC or the committee to which it has been transferred (reg.15(10)). This power to transfer was introduced in May 2008.[60] Its aim is to free up GTAC to oversee the ethical review of clinical trials involving stem cells and to facilitate the integration of gene therapy into mainstream medical research.[61] GTAC has issued guidance on the types of clinical trial that will be considered for transfer, namely, those where the application is judged to be "low genetic risk".[62]

Gene therapy also falls within the regulatory remit of the Medicines and Healthcare products Regulatory Agency (MHRA). The MHRA was created in 2003 and is the licensing authority for medical products and clinical trials on such products.[63] This body must be satisfied that any medicinal product is of sufficient safety, efficacy, and quality.[64] It must also ensure compliance with the principles of good clinical practice specified in the Clinical Trials Regulations (see Ch.11). Under these Regulations, the MHRA is prohibited from authorising a clinical trial involving products for gene therapy if it would result in modifications to any subject's "germ line genetic identity" (reg.19(3)).

Some forms of gene therapy also fall within the remit of the Human Fertilisation and Embryology Authority (HFEA). The HFEA was set up by the Human Fertilisation and Embryology Act 1990 to regulate and licence specified activities, including the creation, storage, and use of embryos outside of the body (see Ch.8). The provisions potentially relevant to gene therapy are to be amended when the Human Fertilisation and Embryology Act 2008 is fully implemented in October 2009. Until that date the 1990 Act will continue to prohibit the issuing of a treatment licence to authorise "altering the genetic structure of any cell while it forms part of an embryo" (Sch.2 para.1(4)). The issue of a research licence for such a purpose was permitted by the 1990 Act only by regulations (Sch.2 para.3(4)), though no such regulations exist. The 2008 amendment Act will repeal these provisions. Under the replacement provisions, a treatment licence is not permitted to authorise "altering the

---

[58] See DH 1992.

[59] These regulations implement the Clinical Trials Directive (2001/20/EC) and are examined in depth in Ch.11.

[60] The amendment to the Clinical Trials Regulations was effected by the Medicines for Human Use (Clinical Trials) and Blood Safety and Quality (Amendment) Regulations 2008/941.

[61] See GTAC 2008c, 7.

[62] See GTAC 2008a, para.5 and the transfer guidance: GTAC 2008b.

[63] The MHRA was created by the merger of the Medicines Control Agency and the Medical Devices Agency.

[64] Medicines Act 1968 (as amended) s.19. See also Regulations 2004/1031 reg.19.

nuclear or mitochondrial DNA of a cell while it forms part of an embryo" (new Sch.2 para.1(4)). An exception can be made by regulations (passed under the new s.3ZA(5)), but only where the purpose is to enable an egg or embryo to be altered to prevent the transmission of serious mitochondrial disease. The amendment Act removes the prohibition on research involving alteration of the genetic structure of an embryo. The upshot is that the 2008 amendment legislation enables the HFEA to license embryo research involving the genetic modification of embryos and opens up the possibility of a future regulation permitting the specified modification of an embryo intended for implantation. As before, the Act will not cover any genetic modification of a post-implantation human embryo or other aspects of gene therapy.

Many international instruments take a restrictive approach towards germ-line gene therapy.[65] Article 13 of the Biomedicine Convention states that an intervention "seeking to modify the human genome may only be undertaken for preventive, diagnostic or therapeutic purposes and only if its aim is not to introduce any modification in the genome of any descendants". This prohibits the application of germ-line gene therapy. It does not directly prohibit research into germ-line gene therapy, but art.18(2) prohibits the creation of embryos for research. The UK has yet to sign or ratify this Convention. If it wishes to, it will need to make reservation with regard to arts 13 and 18(2), which it can do under art.36 "to the extent that any law then in force in its territory is not in conformity with the provision". In addition, art.24 of the Universal Declaration on the Human Genome and Human Rights cites germ-line interventions as a practice that "could be contrary to human dignity".[66] Of related interest is art.6(2)(b) of the European Directive on the Legal Protection of Biotechnological Inventions (Directive 98/44/EC), which declares that "processes for modifying the germ-line genetic identity of human beings" are unpatentable. This removes much of the incentive behind any commercial involvement in germ-line gene therapy.

In contrast, somatic cell therapy is not prohibited by any international instrument and currently takes place in the UK. GTAC's terms of reference require it to advise on the acceptability of proposals for gene therapy research on human subjects "on ethical grounds, taking account of the scientific merits of the proposals and the potential benefits and risks".[67] Additionally, it is to provide advice on the "use of unlicensed gene therapy" and has issued specific guidance on the use of gene therapy medicinal products on a named patient outside of the context of GTAC approved clinical trials.[68] GTAC continues to follow the principle that germ-line effects must be avoided[69] and has expressed the view that most forms of prenatal gene therapy are "unlikely to be acceptable for the foreseeable future, in view of the safety and ethical difficulties".[70]

---

[65] See also the laws of other countries examined in Pattinson 2002a, 5.8 and App.5.
[66] See also the requirements of art.5(a).
[67] See GTAC 2008, Annex B.
[68] See GTAC 2005.
[69] See GTAC 2008a, para.12.
[70] GTAC 1998, para.27(e).

In short, it is a criminal offence to start or conduct a clinical trial without ethics committee approval (which, in the case of gene therapy, means the approval of the GTAC or a delegated research ethics committee) and authorisation from the MHRA.[71] Non-compliance with such requirements would also make researchers vulnerable in any private law claim brought if something goes wrong and make it extremely difficult for them to publish the results of the research. In addition there is an EU Regulation addressing "advanced therapy medicinal products" (ATMPs), which includes gene therapy products, and is now in force. The MHRA is the Competent Authority for ATMPs. The Regulation applies, in effect, to the *mass production* and *marketing* of gene therapy products. It does not cover products that are produced on a one-off ad hoc basis for the treatment of an individual patient in accordance with a specific medical prescription (Recital 6).[72]

12.4.2 Ethical issues

As the regulatory position indicates, germ-line is far more controversial than somatic cell gene therapy. Somatic gene therapy research is widely considered to be little more than research into a form of innovative treatment. It has had enough success to satisfy many as to its acceptability, at least as a treatment of last resort for patients with severely disabling or life-threatening conditions. Germ-line gene therapy evokes views that are much more negative. Many, but by no means all, objections to germ-line gene therapy simply emphasise current uncertainties and safety issues. Some have argued for germ-line interventions, noting that it is the only possible way of addressing some deleterious genetic traits and, when it becomes predictable, it could remove the need for repeated somatic cell therapy.[73] Germ-line intervention is still, however, more argued against than for. Some arguments seem to be designed solely for the purpose of declaring that germ-line interventions are wrong, such as arguments that this technique violates the integrity of genetic patrimony, the right to inherit an unmodified genetic endowment, or the right not to be intentionally modified.[74]

12.4.2.1 The slippery slope metaphor

The metaphor of sliding down the slippery slope is sometimes relied on by those arguing against allowing gene therapy. As explained in Ch.1, the underlying argumentative strategy is to argue that allowing the activity in question (*A*) will *lead to* an unacceptable endpoint (*B*). The link between the starting and ending point can be logical, empirical, or a combination of the two.

---

[71] Regulations 2004/1031, regs 12 and 40. Penalties are specified in reg.52.

[72] See also the discussion of the Tissue and Cells Directive as the implementing regulations in Ch.14 (14.3.1.2).

[73] See e.g. Zimmerman 1991, 597–598. See also Juengst 1991, 589–590.

[74] See Agius 1989, Juengst 1991, 590, and Mauron and Thévoz 1991, 654–655.

An example of the former is provided by Berger and Gert:

> if we use the procedures to cure sickle cell anemia and other genetic disorders, we will be unable to draw the line against using gene therapy to improve our species. This is an example of what is known as a "slippery slope" argument. The argument involves denying that a non-arbitrary line can be drawn between negative and positive eugenics, and therefore to protect against positive eugenics, we should not even start with negative eugenics.[75]

For this argument to work there must be no morally defensible stopping point between permitting *A* and the occurrence of *B* (which, incidentally, Berger and Gert argue is not the case), and *B* must be morally impermissible. Similarly considerations apply to empirical versions of this argument. According to Gardner,

> It is widely feared that human gene therapy is at the top of a slippery slope, such that therapeutic engineering of human genes will generate technological change of such momentum that it will force the adoption of genetic enhancement.[76]

The key difficulty for those wishing to rely on such arguments is that opponents are unlikely to concede that genetic enhancement (positive eugenics) is immoral. As Harris has pointed out, there is no obvious moral difference between social enhancement and genetic enhancement, and social enhancement by education is routinely accepted and encouraged.[77] Rising to the challenge, Kass has argued that social engineering mechanisms are "feeble and inefficient" when compared to genetic engineering; do not circumvent the human context of speech, meaning, and choice; and "their effects are in general, reversible, or at least subject to attempts at reversal".[78] Also, Kass asserts, traditional influences "pay tribute to the animal who lives by speech and who understands the meanings of actions".[79] However, the effects of some forms of social indoctrination can be just as difficult to reverse and pay just as little tribute to individual choice as the effects of many future germ-line interventions. Compare being genetically engineered to have a certain eye colour with being brought up Amish.[80] The difference between Harris and Kass is perhaps best understood as a based on different moral starting points. Kass relies on an approach in the "dignity as constraint" camp.[81] Harris rejects appeals to dignity as "comprehensively vague",[82] but (using the definitions offered by Beyleveld and Brownsword) Harris' approach is close to the "dignity as empowerment" approach.

---

[75] Berger and Gert 1991, 674.
[76] Gardner 1995, 65.
[77] Harris 1998, 171–174.
[78] Kass 1988, 18.
[79] Kass 1988, 18.
[80] Both are in a sense reversible, because it is possible to leave the Amish community and possible to change one's eye colour (by contact lenses or surgery), but there are notable costs and difficulties involved with such actions.
[81] See further Ch.1 (1.4.1).
[82] Harris 1998, 31.

There is another type of argument that has more widespread appeal. This argument claims that germ-line interventions, even if properly understood and predictable, could facilitate and perpetuate harmful social attitudes towards certain individuals and their families.[83] Harmful social attitudes can be defined relative to any moral theory, i.e. those that violate individual rights, undermine our duties to others, cause disutility, or are non-virtuous. The claim is that allowing germ-line gene therapy to be used for or against particular traits will lead to a morally unacceptable social distinction being drawn (or more readily being drawn) with regard to possession or absence of morally irrelevant traits. Possession of a trait that is irrelevant to one's moral status (i.e. the moral duties that one is owed) is predicted to become a ground for discrimination between individuals who either possess or lack that trait, or have failed to ensure that their children possess or lack that trait. Beyleveld and Brownsword ask us to consider

> the example of the desire for perfectly shaped teeth that has swept the United States, resulting in children whose parents are unable to afford the treatment that can correct "imperfections" that are now perceived of as deformities, suffering deep traumas as a result.[84]

There are also a number of reported instances of genetic stigmatisation. Routine prenatal diagnosis for thalassaemia in Sardinia led to women who fail to abort a fetus diagnosed as having the condition being stigmatised by the local community.[85] In a village in Greece, researchers tested everyone for the sickle cell gene, assuming that carriers would pair with non-carriers to avoid having children with sickle cell disease.[86] Instead carriers were stigmatised and were thereby forced to marry among themselves, increasing incidence of sickle cell disease in the population. The likelihood of social stigmatisation of certain traits following gene therapy is therefore one that has some empirical plausibility. This argument has force if the trait in question is one for which there is no powerful moral argument for modifying in the first place or at least one for which the reason for modifying in the first place would be outweighed by the risk of such social consequences. It is an argument against allowing germ-line interventions for specific types of traits.

12.4.2.2 Other ethical issues

Genetic intervention remains risky, uncertain, and experimental. In the case of germ-line gene therapy, this has led many advisory bodies and theorists to reject the technology, at least for the present.[87] As the technology currently stands, germ-line interventions are not predictable and are likely to create more

---

[83] See e.g. Juengst 1991, 590; Pattinson 2000 and 2002a, 6.2.2; and Beyleveld and Brownsword 2001, 151.
[84] Beyleveld and Brownsword 2001, 151.
[85] See Black 1998, 637.
[86] Moore 2000, 107.
[87] See e.g. the view of the Clothier Committee (DH 1992) and Lappè 1991, 626.

problems than they solve. A related concern is that use of this technique on an apparently deleterious gene could inadvertently remove any positive effects of that gene.[88] The sickle cell gene, which we considered earlier, is usually cited as an example. Two copies of the (recessive) mutation will cause sickle cell disease, whereas a single copy provides a degree of resistance to malaria. However, examples of such apparently deleterious genes with positive effects are extremely rare[89] and the probability that positive effects will be inadvertently removed must be weighed against the negative effects of the gene to be modified and the probability of these being removed. In the sickle cell example, the disease is severely debilitating and life-shortening, whereas the limited genetic resistance to malaria given by a single copy of the mutation can be replicated by vaccination and is only relevant to those facing an environmental risk of getting malaria.[90]

Some ethical objections are less powerful than they first appear. The claim that germ-line gene therapy unavoidably involves non-consenting subjects,[91] for example, is equally true of any medical intervention performed on an incompetent patient. Any force attributed to this claim must therefore rest on additional premises, such as an implicit declaration that the potential benefits of the intervention do not outweigh the risks to the non-consenting subject.

Some ethical objections to gene therapy have a much wider focus than is at first apparent. It is often noted that gene therapy is a preoccupation of the developed world. In global terms, about 90 per cent of medical research spending is directed at diseases that are responsible for only 10 per cent of the total disease burden.[92] Gene therapy research is likely to lead to high-cost treatments and bring relatively small benefits in terms of global mortality and morbidity.[93] Advances in gene therapy could even reinforce and increase the economic and social divide between the developed and developing world. The ethical concerns implicit in these predictions—the failure to maximise utility, the failure to recognise the rights of those with equal or greater needs, etc.—arise from wider inequalities in the global distribution of economic and healthcare resources. It follows that these are not so much objections against gene therapy as they are objections about allowing current levels of global inequity to continue.

12.5 Patents, Genes, and Medicine

In April 2003, it was announced that the final map of the human genome was complete.[94] Nearly three years before, President Bill Clinton and Prime

---

[88] See e.g. Suzuki and Knudtson 1989, 202, and Coghlan 1994, 15.
[89] Another example is two copies of the recessive mutation responsible for cystic fibrosis appear to grant some protection from typhoid fever (see van de Vosse et al. 2005).
[90] See Harris 1998, 199–202 and Pattinson 2002a, 132–133.
[91] See e.g. Juengst 1991, 590 and Moseley 1991, 642.
[92] See Kong 2004, 167.
[93] See Kong 2004, 167.
[94] See BBC 2003b. 99% of gene containing regions had been sequenced. The gaps were considered to be too costly to fill at that time.

Minister Tony Blair had simultaneously announced that the first *rough* map was complete.[95] Fear that the two leaders would seek to weaken patent protection, based on a misunderstanding of their joint statement, led to a dramatic drop in biotech stocks.[96] Patent protection is economically sensitive, particularly for those biotechnology firms for which patents are their only assets of real value. Whatever its historical rationale, the principal justification now given for patent protection is the encouragement of innovation and investment. Ironically, the needs of unrestricted scientific research and innovation also inform many of the criticisms directed at patents on genes and gene fragments (hereafter *gene patents*). This is a debate with a global context, as globalisation "creates incentives to develop uniform policies on issues affecting economic activity"[97] and ensures that many social and regulatory problems transcend national and regional boundaries. It is a debate that goes straight to the heart of actual and potential use of genetic information for medical practice and research.

Patents are economic tools. They grant the patent holder no legal right to use or exploit an invention. A valid patent on a genetically-engineered virus, for example, does not exempt the patent holder from any laws that ban or control the creation, storage, release, or use of that virus. Instead, it grants the holder the legal right to prevent others from making, using, selling or importing that invention. It is not an absolute right nor does it last indefinitely. In essence, a patent grants those who fulfil specified conditions a time-limited (i.e. 20-year) monopoly over whatever commercial exploitation of the patented invention is legally permitted. In theory at least, the patent holder has given something in return for this monopoly—the very act of applying for a patent involves publicly disclosing the nature of the invention. Also, the exclusionary right is potentially subject to compulsory licences (whereby the patent holder is ordered to allow a third party to use a patented product or process) and does not cover all activities that utilise the patented invention.

The next section (12.5.1) will outline the patent system governed by the Patents Act 1977. This will be followed by an examination of some of the main policy and ethical issues raised by gene patents (12.5.2). The issue to which this is directed is the effect that the legal protection of genetic information by patent law has on the ability to conduct medical research and utilise new therapeutic products.

12.5.1 Patent criteria

The Patents Act 1977 sets out the system under which the UK Intellectual Property Office (UKIPO) may grant a patent.[98] Patents are territorial, rather

---

[95] See BBC 2000. The rough draft comprised 97% of the human genetic code, but the majority of this had not been "proof-read".
[96] See Schehr and Fox 2000.
[97] Caulfield and von Tigerstrom 2005, 130.
[98] UKIPO was previously known as the UK Patent Office (UKPO).

than global, rights. All patent systems, however, operate against an international backcloth. The UK is bound by a number of significant international agreements, including the European Patent Convention (EPC) 2000 and the TRIPS Agreement 1995.[99] In addition, the EU has directly intervened by adopting Directive 98/44/EC on the legal protection of biotechnological inventions (*hereafter* the Biotechnology Directive).

The EPC set up a patent-granting authority for Europe: the European Patent Office (EPO). The EPO can issue patents that are effective in the UK and other countries that have ratified the EPC. In this country, the EPC has been implemented by the Patents Act, which is to be read in conformity with it (s.130(7)). The TRIPS agreement does not create another patent granting authority, but focuses on harmonising and promoting strong patent protection in all the 153 member states of the World Trade Organization (WTO).[100] Similarly, the EU does not have the power to issue multi-territorial patents, though there have been moves towards adopting a European Community Patent.

The Patents Act lays down qualificatory criteria for patentability, which are meant to capture those inventions that are worthy of patent protection. There are three *positive criteria*: the invention must

    (a) be *new* (i.e. it must be novel in the sense of not having been previously made available to the public, anywhere in the world);[101]

    (b) involve an *inventive step* (i.e. it must go beyond a step that was obvious to a person skilled in the relevant field);[102] and

    (c) be capable of *industrial application* (i.e. it must be capable of being made or used in some kind of industry).[103]

There are also *negative criteria*: a list of non-patentable items and a morality clause. Items excluded from patentability[104] include mere discoveries and scientific theories;[105] processes for cloning human beings or modifying the germ-line genetic identity of human beings;[106] and methods of treatment by surgery or therapy and methods of diagnosis.[107] The *morality clause* states that a patent shall not be granted "for an invention the commercial exploitation of which would be contrary to public policy or morality".[108]

---

[99] EPC 2000 is the revised version of the EPC 1973, which entered into force on December 13, 2007. TRIPS is short for the Agreement on Trade-Related Aspects of Intellectual Property Rights. Patent law was already regulated internationally by the Paris Convention 1883 and the Patent Cooperation Treaty (PCT) 1970. The PCT Treaty is administered by the World Intellectual Property Organisation (WIPO) and facilitates patent applications in different countries.

[100] See *http://www.wto.org*.

[101] Ss.1(1)(a) and 2.

[102] Ss.1(1)(b) and 3.

[103] Ss.1(1)(c) and 4.

[104] S.1(2), s.4(4), and Sch.A2 para.3.

[105] S.1(2)(a).

[106] Sch.A2 para.3(b)/(c).

[107] S.4A.

[108] S.1(3).

12.5.1.1 Non-patentable items

When presenting his co-discovered theory on the structure of DNA, James Watson was asked by a fellow scientist whether he would patent it.[109] Watson simply shrugged off this suggestion. Watson and Crick's theory was new and went beyond what was then obvious to those possessing knowledge and experience of genetic science. Nonetheless, it is a good example of something that if developed now would not be patentable under the present legislation. In its abstract form it is excluded from patentability as a mere *scientific theory*.[110] While a great deal of effort and ingenuity can go into the development of abstract scientific theories, patent protection is thought to be unnecessary or against the public interest. It is unnecessary in the sense that the development and public dissemination of this and similar abstract theories does not require the incentive of patent protection. It is against the public interest in the sense that patent protection for abstract theories is more likely to slow or hinder scientific progress than encourage its advancement. If the exclusivity granted by the patent system had been applied to Watson and Crick's theory (or the previous work on which it stood), the goal of advancing innovation and development would surely have been undermined.

The Patents Act also excludes *discoveries* from patentability,[111] on the basis that mere discoveries do not represent anything new or innovative. Does this mean that genes, partial gene sequences, stem cell line, and alike are unpatentable? In practice it does not.[112] Like all exclusions from patentability, this provision has been interpreted restrictively. Discoveries *as such* are distinguished from discoveries that solve a technical problem (and thereby display the necessary novelty and inventive step). The EPO guidelines, for example, state that "a gene which is discovered to exist in nature may be patentable if a technical effect is revealed, e.g. its use in making a certain polypeptide or in gene therapy".[113] This narrow distinction is articulated in art.5 of the Biotechnology Directive. Article 5(1) excludes from patentability, "The human body, at the various stages of its formation and development, and the simple discovery of one of its elements, including the sequence or partial sequence of a gene". Whereas, art.5(2) states that patents are available for elements "isolated from the human body or otherwise produced by means of a technical process, including the sequence or partial sequence of a gene, ... even if the structure of that element is identical to that of a natural element". Very similar words were used in the subsequent amendment to the Patents Act.[114] The net result is that a gene patent can be obtained on *an isolated gene* for which there is a *stipulated industrial application* and the *requisite novelty value*. This remains

---

[109] See Watson 2003, 55.
[110] S.1(2)(a). It would also need to go beyond mere abstract theory to be capable of industrial application.
[111] S.1(2)(a). See also art.52(2)(a) EPC.
[112] Stem cell line are discussed further below (12.5.1.2).
[113] EPO 2007, Pt C Ch. IV para.2.3.1.
[114] See Sch.A2 paras (3)(3)(a) and 5, respectively, as introduced by the Patent Regulations 2000/2037. See also rule 23a of the Implementing Regulations of the EPC.

controversial, not least because an isolated gene holds the same information as the natural, non-isolated version. Many have questioned the defensibility of such a technical distinction.[115] Further guidance is provided by the recent decision of *Eli Lilly v Human Genome Sciences*, where the High Court held a gene patent to be invalid for, inter alia, failing to display the required novelty, inventive step, and industrial application.[116] The gene in question had been discovered by computer modelling (i.e. by "bioinformatics" or "computational biology", rather than traditional laboratory techniques) and the patent contained no more than speculation about how this gene sequence might be useful.

Another exclusion from patentability that has particular relevance for medicine is "a *method of treatment* . . . by surgery or therapy, or . . . a *method of diagnosis* practised on the human . . . body".[117] It therefore prevents the patenting of a new procedure for, say, performing heart surgery, administering a drug, or administering gene therapy.[118] This provision is expressed in narrow terms and is interpreted restrictively. EPO Guidelines, for example, declare that the provision only applies to treatment or diagnostic methods carried out in or on the living human body, and so it does not cover those carried out on a dead body or on substances that have been removed and not returned to the same body.[119] Similarly, the courts have read "methods of treatment" narrowly.[120] As a result of this, many medical inventions are not covered by this exclusion, including genetics tests.[121] What is more, the provision goes on to declare that products, such as pharmaceuticals, are not excluded from patentability merely because they are invented for use in a method of medical treatment or diagnosis.[122] Thus, the exclusion does not prevent the patenting of a new drug, instrument, or apparatus for use in treatment or diagnosis. According to one commentator,

> The inclusion of [the earlier version of] this provision is entirely due to the lobbying power of the pharmaceutical industry and its insistence on the need for strong patent protection to maintain the incentive to develop an ever-burgeoning range of drugs. The threat that innovation will dry up if patent protection is not available is a powerful argument which is used across a range of industries that avail themselves of the benefits of the patent system, but nowhere is that threat more effective than in the realm of pharmaceuticals. Although there is precious little empirical evidence that the denial of a patent has a disproportionately negative effect on innovation, the cost is thought to be too great to challenge the fixity of the pharmaceutical sector.[123]

It is difficult to extract a rationale for these exclusions that is consistent with their apparent narrowness. Reliance on the *general public interest* in ensuring the

---

[115] See e.g. Danish Council on Ethics 2004, 97.
[116] [2008] EWHC 1903.
[117] S.4A(1) (my emphasis). See also art.53(c) EPC.
[118] See e.g. *Merck and Co Inc's Patents* [2003] EWHC 5.
[119] See EPO 2007, Pt C, Ch. IV, para.4.8.1.
[120] See e.g. *Du Pont/Appetite Suppressant* [1987] E.P.O.R. 6.
[121] *R. v CYGNUS/Diagnostic Method* [2002] E.P.O.R. 26. See also *R. v Diagnostic Methods* [2004] E.P.O.R. 46.
[122] S.4A(2)–(4).
[123] Laurie 2004, 1082–1084.

wide availability and freedom from commodification of abstract theories, mere discoveries, and advances in treatment and diagnostic methods would seem to call for wider exemptions. The counter argument is two-fold. *First*, patent applicants have been led by current practice to expect the exemptions to be read narrowly and could be said to have reasonably relied on this practice. Expectations can, of course, be changed for the future. *Second*, patents seek not only to encourage innovation but also to encourage public disclosure of inventions and strong patent protection is plausibly considered to be more likely to incentivise such disclosure. The patent system, thus, raises a number of ethical issues to which we will return below (in 12.5.2).

12.5.1.2 The morality clause

Article 53(a) of EPC excludes from patentability "inventions the commercial exploitation of which would be contrary to 'ordre public' or morality". The equivalent provision in the Patents Act (s.1(3)) replaces "ordre public" with "public policy". Both the EPC and the Patents Act go on to declare that an invention is not to be taken to be so contrary merely because it is prohibited by law.[124]

The effect of the morality clause in the EPC was the main point of contention in the *Oncomouse* case, which concerned a patent on a mouse that had been genetically-engineered for cancer research.[125] The EPO (Examining Division) applied a utilitarian approach and ruled that the benefit of cancer research to humanity outweighs the suffering of the animal, especially since the invention could reduce the amount of animal testing needed to achieve this benefit. This morality clause has subsequently been invoked *unsuccessfully* in other opposition actions[126] taken against patents granted by the EPO: the *Plant Genetic Systems* case (which concerned a patent on a genetically modified herbicide-resistant plant), the *Relaxin* Opposition (which concerned a patent on a genetically engineered human protein, H2-relaxin, and the gene fragment encoding for that protein), and the *Leland Stanford* case (which concerned a patent on a genetically modified mouse intended for use in AIDS research).[127] The morality clause was interpreted narrowly in all these cases.[128]

The *Relaxin* case is currently the leading case on the morality clause in relation to patents involving human genetic material. The relaxin protein is produced naturally by pregnant women and helps the pelvic area stretch during pregnancy and childbirth. The opponents argued that the patent, insofar as it covered the gene fragment that encoded for relaxin, was contrary

---

[124] Art.53(a) EPC and s.1(4) Patents Act 1977. See also art.6(1) of the Biotechnology Directive.

[125] *HARVARD/Oncomouse* [1991] E.P.O.R. 525.

[126] Opposition proceedings allow a third party to challenge a patent within 9 months of it being awarded by the EPO: art.99, EPC. The grounds for challenging patents in opposition proceedings are laid down by art.100.

[127] *Plant Genetic Systems/Glutamine Synthetase Inhibitors* [1995] E.P.O.R. 357, *Howard Florey/Relaxin* [1995] E.P.O.R. 541, and *Leland Stanford/Modified Animal* [2002] E.P.O.R. 2.

[128] See e.g. the *Plant Genetic Systems* case [1995] E.P.O.R. 357 at 367: "the exceptions to patentability have been narrowly construed. . . . In the Board's view, this approach applies equally in respect of the provisions of Article 53(a) EPC".

to the morality clause of the EPC. They presented three specific arguments: (1) it is an offence against human dignity to use a pregnant woman for profit; (2) the granting of the patent is tantamount to slavery, because "it involves the dismemberment of women and their piecemeal sale to commercial enterprises throughout the world"; and (3) it is "intrinsically immoral" because the "patenting of human genes means that human life is being patented".[129] The Opposition Division of the EPO conceded that the patenting of a human gene would be "abhorrent to the overwhelming majority of the public" *if these claims were true*, but emphatically denied that they were.[130] It rejected the first argument on the basis that there was nothing immoral in the act of taking tissue, *as long as the subject had consented*, and many life-saving products (such as blood-clotting factors) had been developed in this way. Here the Opposition Division appears to be relying on a different conception of human dignity than the opponents ("dignity as empowerment" rather than "dignity as constraint").[131] The second argument was rejected as displaying a "funda-mental misunderstanding" of patents, which do not confer any rights whatso-ever over any particular human beings or their tissue. The final argument was rejected on the basis that there is more to human beings than their genes and the opponents could not consistently object to the patenting of genes when not objecting to the patenting of other human substances (such as proteins) for medical purposes. Theorists of within the dignity as constraints view might well applaud the opponent's intentions, but it is difficult to avoid the conclu-sion that their objections were clumsily expressed.

It is apparent that patents on isolated human gene sequences are neither immune from challenge under the morality clause nor always excluded by the clause. Instead, gene patents need to be examined on a case-by-case basis.

Article 6(2) of the Biotechnology Directive has supplemented the morality clause with the statement that

> the following, in particular, shall be considered unpatentable:
>
> (a) processes for cloning human beings;
> (b) processes for modifying the germ line genetic identity of human beings;
> (c) uses of human embryos for industrial or commercial purposes;
> (d) processes for modifying the genetic identity of animals which are likely to cause them suffering without any substantial medical benefit to man or animal, and also animals resulting from such processes.

This additional provision forms the substance of Rule 28 of the Implementing Regulations to the EPC, as amended in December 2006. It has also been imple-mented in domestic law by amendment of the Patents Act (without the words "in particular").[132] The exclusion from patentability of "uses of human embryos

---

[129] [1995] E.P.O.R. 541 at 549.

[130] [1995] E.P.O.R. 541 at 550.

[131] See further Beyleveld and Brownsword 2001, ch.8, and Resnik 2001.

[132] Schedule A2 para.3. This paragraph also implements art.4(1) (which excludes animal and plant varieties from patentability) and art.5(2) (which excludes from patentability the human body and the simple discovery of one of its elements).

for industrial or commercial purposes" has raised particular concern. Until recently, the UK Intellectual Property Office (UKIPO) interpreted this provision as preventing the patentability of only some types of human embryonic stem cell lines—those that are *totipotent* (capable of developing into a human child).[133] Interpreting the provision narrowly, the UKIPO considered stem cells lines that are merely pluripotent or multipotent to be patentable.

The UKIPO has issued new guidance following the decision of the Enlarged Board of Appeal of the EPO in the *WARF/Stem cells* case.[134] The Technical Board of Appeal had referred four questions to the Enlarged Board of Appeal, resulting from its consideration of a patent application that had been filed by the Wisconsin Alumni Research Foundation (WARF) in 1995.[135] The patent application included a method by which primate (including human) embryonic stem cells can be cultured without losing their potential to differentiate. The Enlarged Board of Appeal was asked

(1) whether the exclusion from patentability of "uses of human embryos for industrial or commercial purposes" by Rule 28(c) applied to an application filed before the entry into force of that rule and

(2) if so, does it forbid the patenting of claims directed to products (such as human embryonic stem cell cultures) that at the filing date could only be prepared by a method necessarily involving the destruction of the human embryos from which they are derived.

It answered yes to both questions. Rule 28(c) did not change the patentability criteria, it merely detailed the application of the morality clause. Rule 28(c) does prohibit patenting claims directed to products that could only be prepared by a method involving the destruction of human embryos. Further, when assessing whether a claim contravenes this rule, any technical developments that became publicly available only after the filing date cannot be taken into consideration. Thus, the WARF patent application was rejected, as it concerned an invention that at the filing date could only be realised by destroying the embryo used as the starting material.

In the light of the *WARF* case, the UKIPO has slightly revised its position on the patentability of embryonic stem cells lines. Its latest official statement declares that:

> the Office will continue to grant patents for inventions involving such cells provided they satisfy the normal requirements for patentability and provided that, at the filing or priority date, the invention could be obtained by means other than the destruction of human embryos.[136]

---

[133] See UKPO 2007, paras 98–102. The UKIPO (previously UKPO) does not distinguish between embryos produced by fertilisation and embryos produced by a cloning method (UKPO 2007, para.96). See earlier UKPO 2003.

[134] Case G 2/06, decided November 25, 2008.

[135] [2006] E.P.O.R. 31. WARF.

[136] UKIPO 2009.

Thus, at present, human embryonic stem cell lines derived from an existing line, and not directly from an embryo, remain patentable in the UK.

Other questions arise from the morality clause. There is additional controversy over whether the morality clause denies patentability to inventions based on human biological material originally derived from a person who has not provided informed consent. We have seen that the Opposition Division relied on the consent of the tissue source when dismissing the opposition's arguments in the *Relaxin* case. Consent later proved to be a contentious issue during the negotiation of what was to become the Biotechnology Directive. In the end, the issue was relegated to the recitals in the preamble. Recital 26 states:

> Whereas if an invention is based on biological material of human origin or if it uses such material, where a patent application is filed, the person from whose body the material is taken must have had an opportunity of expressing free and informed consent thereto, in accordance with national law.

The UK has not directly implemented any of the Directive's Recitals.[137] Whether or not the domestic courts are required to give effect to Recital 26 is controversial.[138] If it has domestic force, it is at least arguable that it requires informed consent not only to the taking of the tissue but also to the filing of a patent application.[139] The Directive is after all a patent Directive, rather than one governing the removal of tissue.

There is, as yet, no domestic case law directly concerned with patenting and the consent of the tissue source. In a high-profile American case, John Moore brought a claim after discovering that the doctor treating him for spleen cancer had, with some other researchers, developed and patented a cell-line from his cells.[140] Moore had only consented to the removal of his tissue and cells for the purposes of his treatment. The Supreme Court of California rejected Moore's claim to property in his cells, holding (inter alia) that granting property rights to Moore would "hinder research by restricting access to the necessary raw materials".[141] The patent itself was viewed as "factually and legally distinct from the cells taken from Moore's body".[142] Thus, while Moore had no property rights in his tissue, a third party was able to gain intellectual property rights over a cell-line developed from that tissue.[143] (Moore's specific claim succeeded on other grounds and was settled out of court.)

The extent to which the English courts would be influenced by the *Moore* case has yet to be tested. A later case in a different American jurisdiction, *Greenberg v Miami Children's Hospital*, raises additional food for thought.[144] This was a case concerning a patent over the gene mutation responsible for Canavan disease, a

---

[137] See the Patent Regulations 2000/2037.
[138] See Beyleveld 2000 for an argument that the domestic courts are required to give effect to Recital 26.
[139] See Beyleveld and Brownsword 2001, 203. See also the discussion in Laurie 2004, 1089–1090.
[140] *Moore v Regents of the University Of California* (1990) 51 Cal. 3d 120.
[141] 51 Cal. 3d 120 at 144.
[142] 51 Cal. 3d 120 at 141.
[143] The issue of property in one's body and body parts is addressed in Ch.14.4 (14.4).
[144] (2003) 264 F. Supp. 2d 1064.

devastating and currently incurable childhood condition. The parties who had brought the claim had contributed financial resources and tissue samples that were ultimately used to help identify the mutation and develop a genetic test. In a preliminary judgment, a district judge dismissed many of their claims, including the claim for conversion, but was not prepared to dismiss the claim for unjust enrichment. The case was then settled out of court.[145] Future legal developments should be expected in this area and it is by no means clear that the English courts will follow the approach of *Moore* and *Greenberg*. The English courts could not, for example, rely on the developed notion of fiduciary duty invoked by the California court to recognise the justice of Moore's claim, so were these facts to arise here, the property approach might be considered more favourably. See Ch.14 (14.4) for further discussion of property in the body and its parts.

12.5.1.3 The scope of patent protection

The scope of patent protection is often key to its economic utility, because the scope determines the extent of the patent holder's exclusive rights. A broad scope provides greater financial potential for the patent holder.[146] However, broader patent claims are generally more difficult to defend against challenge and are more likely to cause controversy, particularly where the subject matter is a gene or gene fragment. Since a gene patent can only be obtained on an isolated gene, it cannot provide the patent holder with any rights over the genes in your body. Nonetheless, broad gene patents could grant the patent holder significant power to dictate licensing terms (and thereby control who may use the invention, for what price, and for what purposes), and broad gene patents also create a risk of multiple overlapping patents, which can hinder further research.[147]

Perhaps the most controversial gene patents have been Myriad Genetics' patents over the BRCA1 and 2 (breast cancer) mutations. Myriad had managed to obtain comprehensive patents on the BRCA genes in Europe and North America. Since it is not possible to screen for mutations or develop alternative methods of testing for the mutation without having access to the isolated gene, Myriad's patent seemed to give it extensive control. Myriad stirred up controversy when it sought to ensure that only its own genetic tests were used, which would be undertaken at its laboratories in the US. Healthcare providers in Europe and Canada objected. They claimed that the Myriad test was more expensive than other genetic testing processes and would give Myriad control

---

[145] See the Joint Press Release of September 29, 2003 on the Canavan Foundation Website (*http://www.canavanfoundation.org/news/09-03_miami.php*).

[146] The broadest type of patent is a *product patent*, which protects *all* commercial applications of the invention. It is also possible to obtain a *use patent* (which only protects the specific application of the invention) or a *process patent* (which only protects the invented process by which something is produced).

[147] Heller and Eisenberg (1998, esp. 699) argue that the expense of buying multiple licences can hinder further research by leading to the diversion of resources to less expensive projects or less complete research methods.

over all future research by virtue of its exclusive access to all the relevant samples and the information derived from them.[148] Following opposition proceedings before the EPO, Myriad's European patents on BRCA 1 and 2 were invalidated.[149]

If Myriad's patent had been valid, could it have prevented *any* testing for or isolation of BRCA mutations? The exclusionary right granted by a patent is subject to (a) the exemption from infringement granted to non-commercial activities done for experimental purposes;[150] and (b) the patent office's power to grant a compulsory licence in the public interest.[151] Both provisions are interpreted narrowly.[152] In practice, there is considerable antipathy to the use of compulsory licensing.[153] No compulsory licence has been granted under the 1977 Act. The existence of this measure seems to act more as a threat to encourage patent holders to negotiate or work their patents than as a tool for imposing licences on patent holders.

12.5.2 Ethical and policy issues

No system capable of constraining the freedom of individuals in the interests of others can be morally neutral. While patents do not grant a right to exploit, to grant a patent is to recognise private control over whatever commercial exploitation is permitted. The practical effect of a right to exclusivity can be monopolistic market control.[154] It follows that the EPO and the UKIPO's operation of a presumption in favour of granting a patent (which leads to the exemptions to patentability being interpreted narrowly) is not a morally neutral policy. The recognition of any exclusionary control requires ethical justification and due consideration to be given to the appropriate balance of competing ethical interests.

The appropriate balance is theory and context dependent. The patent system is only justified from a *utilitarian* perspective if it maximises utility.[155] Whether the use and availability of patents results in a net increase in technological developments (by encouraging and rewarding innovation and investment) and greater availability of ideas (by publication in patent specifications) is an empirical question. In the short-term, patents actually restrict the availability of the protected technology as they grant time-limited exclusivity to the patent holder. The assumption of the system is that, viewed over a period of time, it results in greater technological progress and idea dissemination than would

---

[148] See Heller and Eisenberg, 1998 and Caulfield and von Tigerstrom 2005, 132.
[149] See EPO 2004.
[150] S.60(5) of the Patents Act 1977.
[151] S.48. Compulsory licences can also be granted to Government Departments (so-called Crown Use): ss.55–58 Patents Act 1977.
[152] On the "experimental use" exemption, see Warren-Jones 2004, 120–121.
[153] See Laurie 2004, 1097.
[154] See Warren-Jones 2004, 102.
[155] As stated in Ch.1, this book focuses on the utility-maximising version of utilitarianism.

otherwise be the case. Indeed, insofar as the disclosure requirement is adequate, the patent system could also be viewed as giving rise to an immediate benefit. These benefits are weakened if the disclosure requirement is not stringent or, in the case of encouraging future developments, if the invention is a research tool. Patent protection (at least where exemptions and compulsory licences are limited) also has less clear overall utility where unfettered access to the invention in question would save many lives.

Duty- and *rights-based* positions can also appeal to the beneficial consequences of increased technological developments and idea dissemination, albeit measuring the predicted benefits in terms of individual rights and interests rather than collective utility. Such positions can directly appeal to the inventor's moral rights to exploit the product of his creativity and investment. Such a right is recognised by art.27(2) of the Universal Declaration of Human Rights 1948: "Everyone has the right to the protection of the moral and material interests resulting from any scientific, literary or artistic production of which he is the author." The patent system must, however, pay sufficient regard to the rights of others and many such theories grant extensive positive rights to life and health that are likely to restrict the operation of the patent system in a health law context.

It is difficult to draw any implications from *virtue-based* theories here, as these theories focus on character and motivation. A virtue theorist could, however, seek to defend systems that encourage and reward innovation and the dissemination of ideas as attempts to track human flourishing.

In sum, while an ethical rationale for patents can be derived from all the major moral positions, its current application to research tools (needed to develop new and improved medicines) and medicinal products is less secure. Applying the five major moral positions to the patent system poses a number of particular difficulties. *First*, what constitutes an appropriate balance between competing ethical interests divides theories within each camp as much as theories between the camps. Consider, for example, the approach of rights-based theories to the granting of time-limited monopolistic control of inventions capable of producing health benefits. A theory granting extensive negative rights to the product of one's labour and denying positive rights to health or anything beyond a minimal "night watchman" state[156] could be expected to support far stronger patent (or patent-like) protection than one recognising extensive positive rights to those in (immediate) need. *Second*, the current patent system is the result of historical, political and economic pressures, rather than a rational attempt to apply a particular moral perspective. *Third*, the mere existence of the current patent system has created expectations, fostered reasonable reliance, and shaped world-wide commercial practices. These factors are morally significant.

12.5.2.1 The morality clause

The morality clause requires at least some part of the moral evaluation inherent in the patent system to be made explicit. This leads to questions about the

---

[156] See e.g. Nozick 1973.

appropriate criterion of moral assessment and the appropriateness of the current system for performing this task.

The first question has divided the courts and commentators. On one level to consider the appropriate criterion for moral assessment is to consider how and whether the choice between different moral theories can be rationally made. This issue is considered in the final chapter. Another level of approach is to ask whether the legal instruments granting authority to the patent examiners imply any particular criterion for moral assessment, despite not explicitly appealing to any particular moral theory. In practice, the courts and patent examiners have adopted a narrow, non-interventionist interpretation of the morality clause. In the *Relaxin* case the Opposition Division of the EPO declared that:

> Only in those very limited cases in which there appears to be an overwhelming consensus that the exploitation or publication of an invention would be immoral may an invention be excluded from patentability under [the morality clause].[157]

Similarly, in the later case of *Leland Stanford*, the Opposition Division declared that the morality clause was meant to focus on "extreme subject-matter (e.g. letter-bombs and anti-personal mines) which would be regarded by the public as so abhorrent that the grant of a patent would be inconceivable".[158] In contrast, Beyleveld and Brownsword have argued that the appropriate yardstick for moral assessment is the more stringent test of "European critical cultural morality", to be interpreted by reference to international human rights instruments such as the Human Rights Convention.[159] They argue that this is a logical implication of signatory states to the EPC having ratified international human rights instruments. Indeed, in a domestic context, the UKIPO as a public body is now required by the HRA 1998 to act compatibly with the Convention. The less stringent approach has, nonetheless, been defended by patent lawyers. Armitage and Davis have, for example, defended the narrow approach by reference to the historical intention of the EPC's drafters and the practical difficulties of requiring patent offices to apply what they consider to be imprecise and variable moral values.[160]

Few are satisfied with the adequacy of the current system for conducting full-scale moral assessments of all patent applications. Some wish to rely on the limitations of the current system and examiners' declared competence to marginalise or narrowly interpret the morality clause.[161] Others wish to rely on the morality clause to challenge the limitations of the current system and examiners.[162] Given the existence of the morality clause in Biotechnology Directive, it is difficult to

---

[157] [1995] E.P.O.R. 541 at 552.

[158] [2002] E.P.O.R 2, para.51.

[159] See Beyleveld and Brownsword 1993, esp. ch.3. They also argue that the phrase "ordre public" in the EPC is not coterminous with "public order" (the phrase in the Patents Act), as the former is meant to refer to the wider structure of social relations governed by the rule of law: Beyleveld and Brownsword 1993, 58–63.

[160] See Armitage and Davis 1994. They go so far as to express doubt as to whether the morality clause should ever have been included in the EPC: see Armitage and Davis 1994, 74–75.

[161] See e.g. Armitage and Davis 1994 and Warren-Jones 2004, 113–114.

[162] See e.g. Beyleveld and Brownsword 1993.

argue that moral issues do not require direct consideration by patent examiners. The extent to which they should be assisted by other procedural mechanisms is more debatable. Article 7 of the Directive provides the European Group on Ethics in Science and New Technologies (EGE) with a mandate for evaluating all ethical aspects of biotechnology, but this body is concerned with general principles, rather than specific patent applications.[163] Norway has required its Patent Office to confer with an ethics committee if there is any doubt about whether an invention is compatible with the morality clause.[164] This committee is to be staffed by persons with competence in philosophy (ethics), medicine, biotechnology, and animal welfare. Norway's response has attracted support elsewhere,[165] but it must not be forgotten that patent examiners are supposed to be competent to apply the (positive and negative) criteria of patentability, which include the morality clause. Setting up a separate committee to deal with moral issues is not obviously preferable to ensuring that the patent examiners themselves have appropriate qualifications and expertise to do the job for which they are appointed. In the short-term, however, it needs to be recognised that the current patent examiners (for whatever reason) were not appointed with appropriate qualifications and expertise to consider issues of moral philosophy. Whether additional expertise is necessary or even desirable is hotly debated.

It also needs to be asked whether the current presumption in favour of granting a patent can be defended over a presumption against patenting or no presumption either way. In practical terms, such a presumption enables a patent office to maximise its revenue and limit its operational costs.[166] In legal terms, none of the relevant legal instruments requires a presumption in favour of patentability and the adoption of this presumption actually restricts the exemptions from patentability imposed by those documents. This presumption has, however, become a rule of practice thereby inducing reasonable reliance by patent applicants. In ethical terms, most major moral theories require a justification for constraining the freedom of others rather than the other way around. While the freedom of others to use a new invention is constrained by a patent on that invention, it must be remembered that the invention might only be in the public domain at that time at all because of the patent system. There are, thus, morally loaded views for and against the current presumption. It might even be possible to argue that the opposite presumption (i.e. one against granting patents) is not entirely against the interests of patent applicants, because insofar as it would make patents harder to challenge after grant, it might actually increase the commercial value of valid patents.

---

[163] See further Danish Council of Ethics 2004, 13.
[164] See Danish Council of Ethics 2004.
[165] See e.g. Danish Council of Ethics 2004, 13.
[166] Both the EPO and the UKIPO are financed by the fees charged for assessing patent applications. A presumption of patentability is likely to reduce the time spent considering each patent and maximise the likelihood of future renewal fees.

Armitage and Davis (1994, esp. 83) argue for the current presumption on the basis that a patent that is refused cannot be revived. However, easy availability of patents also has costs— costs for persons other than the applicant, especially since challenge to a patent can require significant resources.

12.5.2.2 *Reforms to the patent system*

The costs of developing new genetic and medicinal products can be huge. In 2002 Nuffield Council on Bioethics[167] pointed out that, when all development and regulatory costs are taken into account, it costs about £110 million to develop a new medicine.[168] Patents are perceived as encouraging such investment by facilitating financial return for successful outcomes. Their effectiveness in achieving this goal has been questioned, particularly with regard to gene patents.

In 2003 two non-profit organisations, the US Centers for Disease Control and Prevention and the British Columbian Cancer Agency, applied for a patent on the gene thought to cause SARS. They did this not because they wanted to restrict other researchers or to make a profit, but simply to ensure that the gene remained publicly accessible to all researchers. As Gold has explained, simply publishing the information would not prevent others from patenting uses and products that interact with this gene, thus removing them from the public domain.[169] To this consequence of the patent system Gold objects,

> The goal of the patent system is to serve the public good, here by not only encouraging biomedical research but also providing access to the results of that research. Giving exclusive rights to inventors is simply the means through which the system reaches this goal but is not the goal itself.[170]

The Nuffield Council has also criticised the application of the current system to genes and gene fragments, arguing that the law has tended to be too generous in granting gene patents.[171] They also argue that broad protection of genes, and sometimes even the proteins that they produce, has sometimes granted the patent holder rights over not only the invention and its predicted uses, but also over all new uses that are subsequently developed. Other international voices have been added to these concerns.[172] The *Lilly* case, considered in 12.5.1.1, should alleviate some concerns that the patenting criteria will be applied far less stringently to genes. Other reforms have been suggested. The Nuffield Council, for example, has recommended that more emphasis should be given to compulsory licensing and exclusive licensing should be discouraged.[173]

The existence, scope, and strength of patent protection can no longer be examined as if a full range of viable alternatives were available. The scope for unilateral reform of the patent system is heavily constrained by globalisation. The TRIPS agreement, for example, is premised on the assumption that strong patent protection is necessary to promote innovation and economic growth and

---

[167] The Nuffield Council is an independent body jointly funded by the Nuffield Foundation, the Medical Research Council and the Wellcome Trust.
[168] See Nuffield Council on Bioethics 2002b, 14 (n.3).
[169] See Gold 2003, 2002.
[170] Gold 2003, 2002.
[171] See Nuffield Council on Bioethics 2002b, esp. 47.
[172] See e.g. Danish Council on Ethics 2004, esp. 101, and Thomas et al. 2002, 118.
[173] See Nuffield Council on Bioethics 2002b, 71–72. For analysis of this and other possibilities see Andrews 2002 and Warren-Jones 2004, 116–123.

is binding on all WTO member states. Even gradual reform for any single country would risk a global economic backlash and maybe even legal challenge under international instruments such as the TRIPS agreement.[174] Such practical difficulties are not ethically conclusive, but do place the burden of proof on the shoulders of reformers. In any event, expectations and the reliance placed on those expectations do have moral significance, at least until those expectations are changed.

12.6 Conclusion

This chapter has covered many issues raised by the acquisition, use, and potential use of genetic information. It has not, however, covered the breadth of possible private law mechanisms capable of addressing grievances arising from genetic information and technologies. Torts addressing such grievances—which can be conveniently referred to as "genomic torts"—could be developed by incremental extension of the existing case law or by the development of additional torts. The existing case law does provide some developmental potential with regard to the novel situations created by modern genetics. The prenatal negligence actions addressed in Ch.9 are just one example. Some commentators have considered more controversial legal responses. Brownsword has, for example, considered the possibility of a "blockbuster" dignity-based tort.[175] The possibility of the wholesale replacement of private law actions with state compensation schemes was also mooted in Ch.3 with regard to clinical negligence generally. With regard to tortious actions, genetic science does little more than highlight issues already raised by existing regulatory problems. The possibility of a tortious action for breach of the "right not to know" genetic information about oneself is, for example, a matter falling within the ambit of privacy generally. Genetic science has added new variants of possible grievance, but, as in other areas, the appropriate legal response depends on its likely effectiveness at achieving the desired moral end. This is by no means a straightforward matter.

The topics on which this chapter has focused—genetic testing/screening, gene therapy, and gene patenting—all face a context of global pressures. It is a context in which the regulatory concerns of the UK and similarly developed countries will not be those of developing countries. The acquisition and use of genetic information simply has different implications for developed and developing countries. Globalisation cannot be ignored, because it enables genetic tourism and can severely restrict the ability of any one country to unilaterally regulate and reform its existing approach. Underlying the moral debate it has, once again, been possible to discern a division between positions that are largely facilitative and those that are largely restrictive. Beyleveld and

---

[174] See Caulfield and von Tigerstrom 2005, 136. The US could plausibly get away with unilateral action in a way that other, less economically powerful countries could not.
[175] See Brownsword 2003a.

Brownsword helpfully refer to this division as one between "dignity as empowerment" and "dignity as constraint". The choice of regulatory approach is, as usual, a moral choice.

12.7 Further reading

Harris, John and Keywood, Kirsty (2001) "Ignorance, Information and Autonomy." 22(5) *Theoretical Medicine and Bioethics* 415–436.

Laurie, Graeme (2004) "Patenting and the Human Body." In Andrew Grubb (eds), *Principles of Medical Law*. (Oxford: Oxford University Press), 1079–1101.

Nuffield Council on Bioethics (2002a) *Genetics and Human Behaviour* (London: Nuffield Council on Bioethics).

Nuffield Council on Bioethics (2002b) *The Ethics of Patenting DNA: A Discussion Paper*. (London: Nuffield Council on Bioethics).

Chapter 13

TRANSPLANTATION I:
LIVING AND DECEASED DONORS

13.1 Introduction

The scarcity of human organs is causing preventable death and suffering. Every year many are buried or cremated when their organs could save lives. Every year many are prevented from selling or donating their organs. Every year many suffer or die on waiting lists. This invites moral concern but so do the alternatives. Organs cannot be removed from a living body without risky, invasive surgery. The dead body is regarded as sacred by many religions, cultures, and individuals. Buying and selling organs is widely considered to be morally pernicious. Nascent technologies involving artificial organs, tissue-engineering, and animal organs have practical limitations and evoke varying degrees of moral concern or condemnation. It is no exaggeration to say that the regulation and practice of transplantation is an ethical minefield.

The problem of scarcity is very real. In the UK alone, although over 3,200 solid organ transplants now take place each year, around 9,700 remain on the official waiting lists.[1] What is more, waiting lists do not reveal the whole picture, because the chronic shortage of human organs means that some transplant clinicians are extremely selective about which patients they put on the waiting list.[2] In the US, for example, in 2000 there were over 250,000 patients with end-stage renal disease, many of whom would benefit from transplantation, but there are only about 44,000 on the waiting list.[3]

Although the success rate for transplantation operations is improving, the demand for organs and other tissues is increasing. The population is ageing and transplanted materials often do not last the lifespan of the patient. The survival of transplanted material requires powerful immunosuppressant drugs in virtually all recipients, because the recipient's immune system will attack and destroy any graft it views as foreign. The immune system is not the only barrier to graft survival—many tissues deteriorate rapidly outside of a working cardio-respiratory system and therefore need to be prepared for transplantation with haste. The situation is not entirely bleak. The last fifty years have seen significant improvements in immunosuppressant drugs and techniques designed to prevent the deterioration of tissues and organs before and during transplantation. The lifespan of transplanted material has been extended considerably from the early days of transplantation. UK official statistics report that 88 per cent of kidneys from living donors now survive for at least the five years, though the survival rate is slightly lower for kidney transplants from deceased donors.[4] The success rates for other solid organ transplants are not at quite that level. Only 69 per cent of pancreas grafts survive for a year. In fact, only 70 per cent of solid organ transplants last over five years,[5] with a 9–10 year average for kidneys.[6] Alternatives are limited and, in any event, transplantation is often substantially cheaper than long-term treatment alternatives for protracted kidney, heart, or liver failure. Successful kidney transplantation, for example, saves £128,000 compared to dialysis over a nine-year period (the median graft survival time).[7]

This chapter will examine the legal and ethical controversies raised by the regulation of transplantation from *dead donors* (in 13.2) and *living donors* (13.3). The next chapter will address the issues of payment for transplantable human material (14.2), alternatives to human organs (14.3) and the notion of property in our bodies and body parts (14.4). These chapters will devote no more than passing attention to the removal and use of human material for purposes other

---

[1] Figures from UK Transplant 2008, 4, 7 and 9. During 2007–2008, 3,235 solid organ transplants took place (of which 2,381 were from cadavers and 854 were from living donors). At the end of March 2008, 7,655 were on the active waiting list and further 2,092 on the temporarily suspending waiting list.

[2] See Council of Europe 1999, para.1.2 and DH 2000d, para.3.17.

[3] See Lysaght and Mason 2000, 253.

[4] See UK Transplant 2008, 45–48, 54. The 5-year graft survival rate is 83% for deceased heart-beating donation and 76% for deceased non-heartbeating donation.

[5] See Council of Europe 1999. This is consistent with other estimates of 5-year survival rates, which range from 75% (see Grant et al. 2001, 243) to 65% (see Cooper et al. 2002, 133).

[6] Garwood-Gowers and Summan 2001, 13.

[7] See UK Transplant 2005.

than transplantation. The transfer of materials such as embryos, sperm, and eggs for reproductive purposes is addressed in Ch.10 and the use of materials for treatments such as gene therapy is addressed in Ch.12.

13.1.1 The Human Tissue Act 2004

The *Human Tissue Act 2004* obtained Royal Assent on November 15, 2004 and came fully into force in September 2006. The Act applies to England, Wales, and Northern Ireland.[8] It repeals, inter alia, the Human Tissue Act 1961 (which addressed the use of tissue from the deceased) and the Human Organ Transplants Act 1989 (which addressed organ transplantation from living donors). The old legislation was outdated and littered with holes and ambiguities. The dearth of case law meant that the law was unclear on the many issues that were left to the common law. Unfortunately the 2004 Act is no panacea. Its enactment was provoked by a number of scandals, notably the retention of organs and tissue without the knowledge or consent of loved ones at Bristol Royal Infirmary, Alder Hey Children's Hospital, and elsewhere.[9] We shall see that the result is an Act that is easy to criticise.

The 2004 Act is a long and complex piece of legislation. It is peppered with very similar terms that have different definitions, such as "relevant material", "transplantable material", "controlled material", "bodily material", and "excepted material". It has three Parts, seven Schedules, and extends far beyond transplantation. The 2004 Act regulates the removal, storage, and use of human tissue from cadavers and the storage and use of human tissue from the living. In particular, it seeks to make consent a fundamental principle, and establish the Human Tissue Authority (*HTA*), a licensing system, and a number of criminal offences.

The tissue referred to by the majority of the Act's provisions, "relevant material", is defined in s.53 as all material that "consists of or includes human cells" with specified exclusions. Excluded from the definition of relevant material are gametes and embryos, hair and nails from the body of a living person, and human material created outside of the body (such as cell lines) (ss.53(2) and 54(7)). Gametes and embryos created outside of the body are regulated by the soon to be amended Human Fertilisation and Embryology Act 1990 (see Ch.8). Cell lines for therapeutic use have to meet the quality and safety standards imposed by Regulations 2007/1523. These Regulations apply to activities relating to the donation, storage, and use of human tissues and cells intended for transplantation (except where the cells are the patient's own) and are discussed in the next chapter (see 14.3.1.2)). Aside from these Regulations, the storage and use of hair and nails from a living person is largely unregulated.[10]

---

[8] S.59. The s.45 offence of non-consensual analysis of DNA applies throughout the UK.
[9] See the Alder Hey Report (Redfern et al. 2001) and the Isaacs Report (HM Inspector of Anatomy 2003).
[10] Hair root cells will fall within the definition of "bodily material" for the purposes of the s.45 offence of non-consensual analysis of DNA, see Ch.12 (12.3.2.1).

While hair and nails are routinely discarded (at, for example, hairdressers and manicurists), it is difficult to find a rationale for their exclusion from the 2004 Act beyond pragmatic convenience. Some included material is also routinely discarded (such as saliva and urine),[11] the excluded material can be valuable (consider, for example, hair for wig making), and, as Price points out, hair roots contain keratin producing cells.[12]

The role of the HTA is key to the operation of the Act. Its functions include issuing Codes of Practice, licensing a number of activities, and inspecting to ensure compliance with the Act and the licence conditions. Section 28 of the Act states that failure to comply with a Code of Practice (issued under s.26) will not in itself give rise to liability, but will be taken into account by the HTA when performing its inspecting and licensing functions. There are nine such codes:

Code 1: Consent

Code 2: Donation of solid organs for transplantation

Code 3: Post-mortem examination

Code 4: Anatomical examination

Code 5: Disposal of human tissue

Code 6: Donation of bone marrow and peripheral blood stem cells for transplantation

Code 7: Public display

Code 8: Import and export of human bodies, body parts and tissue

Code 9: Research

Codes 1 to 7 were first issued in July 2006. Code 8 was first issued in May 2007. Draft revisions of the first seven codes and the draft first edition of Code 9 were issued for consultation on August 1, 2008. At the time of writing, the first editions are still in force. These codes flesh out the bare bones of the Act. For convenience, *the Codes will hereafter be referred to by their numbers* (Code 1, Code 2, etc.). The draft codes issued for consultation will be referred to as Draft Code followed by the appropriate number (Draft Code 1, Draft Code 2, etc.).

This chapter will not address every aspect of the 2004 Act. The focus here will be on the Act's application to transplantation. Its application to transplantation from cadavers will be addressed in 13.2.3 and its application to transplantation from living donors will be addressed in 13.3.2. The Act goes much further. It notably creates an offence of non-consensual analysis of DNA in s.45, which is addressed in Ch.12 (12.3.2). It also regulates the removal, storage, and use of human material for public display and for health-related purposes other than transplantation.

---

[11] Saliva and urine will usually contain human cells and can therefore be "relevant material".
[12] See Price 2005, 800.

13.2 Transplantation from the dead

The majority of organs for transplantation are removed from those who are legally dead and most of these are currently obtained from those who are "brain dead", or more correctly, "brain-stem dead". Since the brain-stem dead still have beating hearts, dead organ providers are often divided into heart-beating cadavers and non-heartbeating cadavers. Recent years have seen a drop in the number of dead donors, largely due to better medical treatment preventing early deaths and fewer fatal road accidents (primarily because of increased use of seatbelts).[13] This has intensified the need to consider legal changes and the option of alternative systems of acquisition. Increasing the supply of cadaveric material could only be a partial solution for the huge gap between supply and demand, because there is a limit to the number of people who die with tissue or organs suitable for transplantation and there is already a chronic shortage of transplant surgeons.[14]

Transplantation from the dead has been successfully conducted for many decades. Immune rejection by the recipient is now increasingly controlled by drugs, but the chances of graft and patient survival is still closely connected to the tissue-matching of the graft. Such transplantation need not be restricted to vital organs and tissues (such as kidneys, livers, lungs, hearts, and pancreases), as tissue that is not necessary for survival can also be transplanted (such as corneas and hands).

This section has three main sub-sections. First we will consider the definition of death and its impact on transplantation (13.2.1), before examining other ethical issues raised by the acquisition and allocation of cadaveric material for transplantation (13.2.2), and, finally, we will examine the law on transplantation from the dead (13.2.3). The possibility of paid acquisition of cadaveric material will be considered in the next chapter.

13.2.1 Defining death and preparing for cadaveric transplantation

A famous scene in *Monty Python's Flying Circus* has John Cleese complaining to a shopkeeper about the condition of the parrot that he has recently bought. When the shopkeeper suggests that the parrot's stillness is due to it pining for its homeland, Cleese shouts that it is "stone dead . . . definitely deceased . . . bleeding demised . . . ceased to be . . . a stiff".[15] As Singer points out, these terms do not apply to those warm, breathing, pulsating humans in intensive care units who are declared dead, sometimes only moments before their organs are cut out and given to strangers.[16] If death is to act as a gateway for transplantation and

---

[13] See DH 2000d, para. 3.19.

[14] Only about 1% of people who die are potential donors: see DH 2000d, para.3.5. On the shortage of transplant surgeons, see Carvel 2004.

[15] Cited in Singer 1994, 21.

[16] See Singer 1994, ch.2.

other conduct that would otherwise be prohibited, then its determination cannot be morally neutral. Choosing between different criteria of death (e.g. cessation of brain-stem function versus irreversible cardiopulmonary failure) requires a moral judgment.

The issue is that the term "death" is not restricted to the absence of any biological life, but used as shorthand for the legal acceptability of certain conduct. There are many points in the dying or decaying process when a human being could be treated as dead. At one extreme, death as a legal conclusion could "wait until every cell has degenerated to the point where all that is left of us is some kind of smelly porridge".[17] At the other extreme, those who are senile or merely too elderly to look after themselves could be treated as dead—some native American tribes are said to have left such people for dead, even if they did not actually regard them as dead. No major moral theorist has seriously suggested that either extreme be adopted as the legal designation of dead. To treat those who are merely elderly or temporarily unconscious as dead would violate the tenets of all the major theories. To treat only those who have degenerated into a kind of "porridge" (i.e. those who are putrefied) as dead would also have morally significant implications, such as diverting finite healthcare resources, extending the grieving process, undermining the morale of health professionals, and preventing the use of any human organ or tissue for virtually all beneficial purposes from transplantation to teaching and research. There is a range of options resting between such extremes, many of which carry implications for what it is feasible to do with the "dead". Some consequences of a chosen designation of death could change with future technological developments. Harris, for example, asks us to consider the possibility of freezing a body so that it could be brought back to life in a few centuries.[18]

As already indicated, organ transplantation becomes unfeasible well before putrefaction. The re-usable potential of body parts progressively deteriorates during the dying process and some organs are not transplantable unless they are removed from a body with a beating heart.[19] This means that the point chosen for the purposes of lawful organ removal is crucial. Death acts as the gateway for lawful removal of organs that are likely to affect the health or continued life of the provider—the law is understood to prohibit the removal of life-sustaining organs from a living person on the basis that it is contrary to public policy.[20] Death has traditionally been defined in terms of irreversible cardiopulmonary failure. The arrival of artificial means of maintaining a patient's oxygen supply and heartbeat, however, meant that cardiopulmonary function could be replaced mechanically. Consider the extreme case of a guillotine victim, whose body could be resuscitated and organs kept alive, in the biological sense, for a considerable period.[21] In contrast, brain function cannot be replaced by current mechanical devices. The connection between brain function and death is a complex one. With

---

[17] Kennedy 1988, 10.
[18] See Harris 1985, ch.12 (esp. 243–244).
[19] For a discussion of some issues raised by non-beating heat donation, see Papalois et al. 2004.
[20] See the discussion in Ch.4 (4.6) and below (13.3.2.1).
[21] See Brazier and Cave 2007, 440–441.

assistance, a human being can have biological life with a brain so severely damaged that no future interaction with the world is feasible. Damage to the higher-brain (or cortex), brain-stem, or even the whole brain need not be incompatible with continued life signs in a human body. The higher-brain is associated with the capacity for consciousness, whereas the brain-stem controls respiratory function (but not heart function, which is controlled by the heart itself).[22]

Higher-brain function is apparently irreversibly lacking in those whose "vegetative state" has persisted for long enough to be regarded by doctors as permanent—"permanent vegetative state" or *PVS*. Yet, patients in PVS have hearts that continue to beat, they turn, they sleep, they wake, and their brain-stem continues to function.[23] Similarly, higher-brain function is absent in those who are born with the congenital defect *anencephaly*. This condition is almost the infant version of PVS. Its victims lack major portions of the brain but possess at least rudimentary brain-stem function.[24] Some are born alive and can survive for a few days, although they very rarely survive for longer than ten days. Should PVS patients and those born with anencephaly be considered dead or, even if not, suitable providers of organs?[25]

Some patients are reported to have higher-brains that are substantially intact alongside seriously compromised brain-stem functions. The terrible condition known as *"locked-in syndrome"* does not appear to remove the victim's cognitive faculties but renders them mute and physically unresponsive.[26] Its victims are typically able to move only their eyelids, but are sometimes rendered completely immobile with full consciousness. This condition must induce sheer terror in its poor victims. If the prognosis is irreversibility, should such patients be regarded as dead? Contrast such patients with those suffering from irreversible cessation of brain-stem function, the so-called *"brain-stem dead"*. Such patients are considered to have irreversibly lost consciousness and the capacity to breathe unassisted. They have "no discernable central nervous system activity".[27] Even if such patients are ventilated, their hearts will stop beating within a few days or, at most, within a few weeks.[28] Should such patients be treated as dead (or otherwise considered suitable providers of organs)?

There are, thus, a number of possible criteria of death focusing on brain function alone. The main candidates are higher-brain death and brain-stem death. *Higher-brain death* would capture patients diagnosed with PVS, anencephaly, and cessation of brain-stem function. *Brain-stem death* would only capture those diagnosed with cessation of brain-stem function. Notice that any criteria of death that depend on the brain will define death in a way that could not be applied to plants and, in practice, is not applied to animals.[29] The more

---

[22] See Mason and Laurie 2006, 465–466. Note that the brain also comprises the thalamus: "which roughly regulates our animal existence": Mason and Laurie 2006, 466.

[23] See further Ch.14 (14.5.1).

[24] See Dickens 2004b, 1143.

[25] See Hoffenberg 1997, esp. 1321.

[26] See Smith and Delargy 2005, esp. 406 and the discussion in Ch.5 (5.2.1).

[27] Brazier and Cave 2007, 441.

[28] See DH 1998, para.3.4.

[29] See Singer 1994, 21–22.

exclusive the criteria, the fewer organs will be available for possible transplantation *if death continues to act as a gateway for the lawful removal of organs.*

To treat a human being who still shows life signs as dead is to operate a medical and legal *fiction.* It carries soothing rhetorical force and thereby appears to facilitate activities that would invite greater challenge if thought to be conducted on the living. Disconnecting transplantation from death would be more open and honest, but greater honesty might lead to increased public anxiety about the removal of organs from living (albeit seriously impaired and dying) humans. This could lead to public pressures that would reduce the available supply of human organs even further. Thus, designating as dead certain categories of the dying will be viewed by some as a clandestine way of distracting from the reality of the situation and, by others, as a practical way of persuading society to accept what is morally permissible or even required.

The moral inquiry over when it is permissible to remove organs from the dead and dying is multi-variable. A key issue is the relative moral status of the organ provider and the organ recipient. Indeed, this is an important issue when determining the permissibility of removing organs from anyone for the benefit of another. As mentioned in Ch.1 (1.4.3.2), and examined in some detail in Ch.7 (7.2.1), not all moral theories hold that all humans have equal moral status. Embryos, fetuses, and the severely mentally disabled are examples of those who are sometimes granted *no* or *limited* (as opposed to *full*) *moral status*, depending on the position taken with regard to the moral duties that we owe directly to them. Moral theories are divided over the proper criteria for determining moral status and, consequentially, over the moral status properly granted to those who appear to have irreversibly lost the function of their higher-brain or brain-stem. The lower the moral status of the potential organ provider, the easier it is to justify removing their organs for the benefit of a cognitively normal adult human or any other individual considered to possess full moral status. From a moral point of view, the issue is not whether a potential organ provider is dead, but whether there are sufficient moral reasons to permit the removal of his organs.

13.2.1.1 The Law

We have already seen that the law regards death as a significant gateway. There is, nonetheless, no statutory definition of death. Coroners and the courts have been prepared to accept both "cardiopulmonary death" (irreversible failure of heart-beat and respiration) and "brain-stem death" (cessation of brain-stem function) as sufficient criteria of death for legal purposes. Death is not, however, required for the absence of a legal obligation to continue life-saving or life-extending effort (as explained in Ch.15). There are two key cases on the legal definition of death.

In the first, *Re A*, a young child who satisfied the clinical criteria for brain-stem death was declared to be dead "for all legal, as well as medical, purposes".[30] On admission to hospital the 20-month-old child had been found to have no heart-beat and, after the failure of extensive attempts to resuscitate him, had been

---

[30] *Re A* [1992] 3 Med. L.R. 303 at 305.

placed on a ventilator. The first attempt to remove the ventilator led him to make slight gasping noises, but the young boy had no such response the day after. A consultant considered him to satisfy the clinical criteria for brain-stem death, which was confirmed the day after that by another consultant. Both consultants had been careful to exclude other possible explanations for the patient's state, such as extreme hypothermia and drugs. Johnson J. who heard the case while the boy was kept on ventilation and fed intravenously, held that the child had been dead since the first consultant determined that the brain-stem death criteria were satisfied. While this is only a first instance decision, this approach was subsequently confirmed in the *Bland* case.[31] In that case, the House of Lords considered the lawfulness of removing nutrition and hydration from an adult in PVS. Their Lordships considered Anthony Bland to be alive and proceeded on that basis. In the words of Lord Keith,

> In the eyes of the medical world and of the law a person is not clinically dead so long as the brain stem retains its function.[32]

Their Lordships went on to hold that it was, nonetheless, lawful to remove nutrition and hydration from a patient in PVS.[33]

In sum, the current common law position is that a patient who satisfies the clinical criteria for brain-stem death is legally dead, whereas patients who fail to satisfy those criteria are alive, even if their cognitive capacities are so poor that there is no legal obligation to keep them alive. Thus, the legal definition of death accepts the clinical criteria for brain-stem death. For legal purposes, a warm, pink body kept "alive" on a ventilator is dead as long as it lacks an active brain-stem. (This definition of death has not led to breathing bodies being buried or cremated, because, in practice, they will first be disconnected from the ventilator.)

Clinical diagnostic tests for confirming brain-stem death were laid down in the 1976 statement of the Conference of Medical Royal Colleges and in the Code of Practice issued by the Department of Health in 1983 and revised in 1998.[34] An updated revision of this Code of Practice was issued by the Academy of Medical Royal Colleges in October 2008.[35] This defines death in more or less the same terms as the previous code:

> Death entails the irreversible loss of those essential characteristics which are necessary to the existence of a living human person and, thus, the definition of death should be regarded as the irreversible loss of the capacity for consciousness, combined with irreversible loss of the capacity to breathe. . . . The irreversible cessation of brain-stem function whether induced by intra-cranial events or the result of extra-cranial phenomena, such as hypoxia, will produce this clinical state and therefore irreversible cessation of the integrative function of the brain-stem equates with the death of the individual.[36]

---

[31] *Airedale NHS Trust v Bland* [1993] A.C. 789.
[32] [1993] A.C. 789 at 856. See also [1993] A.C. 789 at 863 (Lord Goff) and 878 (Lord Browne-Wilkinson).
[33] See Chs 14 (14.5.1) and 15 (15.4.2).
[34] See Conference of the Medical Royal Colleges 1976, DH 1983, and DH 1998, respectively.
[35] See Academy of Medical Royal Colleges 2008.
[36] Academy of Medical Royal Colleges 2008, 11.

Significantly, the diagnosis of brain-stem death is to be made by at least *two* experienced doctors *who are not members of the transplant team*.[37]

As already stated, there is no statutory definition of death. The Human Tissue Act 2004 does not define death. Instead, the 2004 Act empowers the HTA to issue a Code of Practice laying down a definition of death *for the purposes of the Act* (s.26(2)(d)). This move has clearly been taken to avoid the inflexibility of statutory definitions and to take account of the likelihood that medical science will move on (as it has from the historical focus on heartbeat and breathing). The HTA is at least operating under the authority of legislation passed by Parliament and thereby possesses indirect democratic legitimacy. The HTA has not issued its own Code of Practice on the definition of death, though the HTA was officially consulted before the Academy of Medical Royal Colleges issued the Code of Practice discussed above.

13.2.1.2 Elective ventilation

In 1988 the Royal Devon and Exeter Hospital adopted a protocol designed to identify potential donors from those who were dying from strokes and similar conditions outside of intensive care units (ICUs).[38] With the consent of their relatives, such patients were given "elective ventilation" and transferred to an ICU until the brain-stem death criteria could be satisfied. The purpose was to maximise the likelihood that their organs would be suitable for transplantation. The hospital increased the organs available for transplantation by 50 per cent during the 19 months that the protocol was in operation. This practice no longer occurs in the UK. In October 1994, the Department of Health issued guidelines stating that elective ventilation for transplantation purposes was illegal.[39] This view was reasserted in the Department's Code of Practice of 1998.[40] The issue was not the removal of the organs, which was to take place when the patients were brain-stem dead, but the ventilation, which was to take place when the patients were still legally alive. At common law, the consent of relatives had no legal force and medical procedures could only be conducted on an incapacitated adult if those procedures were in that patient's best interests.[41] The Department of Health and many commentators took the view that non-consensually prolonging the death of a dying patient could not be in that patient's best interests.[42] The British Medical Association (BMA), which initially supported a change to the law to permit elective ventilation, now takes the view that "there are too many ethical and practical difficulties for a change in the law to be recommended at the present time".[43]

The Mental Capacity Act 2005 retains the common law requirement that the ventilation of an incapacitated adult has to be in that patient's best interests (see

---

[37] See Academy of Medical Royal Colleges 2008, 19 (para.6.3).
[38] See Feest 1990. See also Salih 1991.
[39] DH 1994b.
[40] See DH 1998, 2 and 8.
[41] *Re F* [1990] 2 A.C. 1.
[42] See e.g. Mason 1996, esp. 120–121.
[43] BMA 2000, part 2.

Ch.5). The Act differs from the old common law by recognising proxy decision-makers: the patient can appoint an attorney under a lasting power of attorney or, exceptionally, the court can appoint a deputy. The decision-maker (i.e. proxy or, if there is no proxy, the doctor acting under the s.5 general legal authority) has to act in what he reasonably believes to be in the patient's best interests. Even where a relative is not appointed as proxy, the decision-maker must consult such persons when considering the patient's past wishes and feelings, beliefs, and values (s.4(6)). This highlights the possibility that the decision-maker could reasonably believe elective ventilation to be in the patient's best interests where the patient had previously displayed support for the procedure.

Another way of looking at elective ventilation is suggested by the clinicians who developed the Exeter Protocol. They have argued that when the patient is ventilated he is already dead, so that the protocol merely involves ventilating a corpse to enable confirmation of brain-stem death.[44] The diagnosis of brain-stem death must be retrospective, because the brain-stem death criteria seek to establish that the patient's brain-stem has already ceased to function.[45] However, as we saw in *Re A*, the law ties determination of the moment of death to its certification. Moreover, separating the time of death from its certification effectively weakens the definition of death in use. There are other reasons why elective ventilation provokes ethical controversy. *First*, it requires the use of limited and expensive ICUs, which might thereby become unavailable for those who are far more likely to recover. This was recognised by those operating the Exeter protocol, who argued that transplantation is cost-saving, so, "Some of the savings made by an increased rate of transplantation must be diverted to ICU and theatres to support the increased workload of organ retrieval".[46] It could also be argued that elective ventilation might sometimes prevent an ICU bed going unused and, where a conflict arises, priority could be given to the patient most likely to benefit. *Second*, a patient who is electively ventilated could stabilise in a PVS.[47] This, Mason argues, would be a "clinical disaster which, if publicised, could be catastrophically detrimental to the whole transplantation programme".[48] It also bolsters the claim that elective ventilation is not in the best interests of most patients.

13.2.2 Acquisition: ethical issues

The availability and use of cadaveric organs and tissue is inevitably closely connected to the ability and willingness of the deceased (prior to death) or surviving relatives to veto removal. There are many different permutations of regulatory responses to both the deceased's views and the views of loved ones

[44] See the discussion in Price 1997, esp. 171.
[45] See Mason and Laurie 2006, 472.
[46] Feest 1990, 1135.
[47] See Mason 1996, 121.
[48] Mason 1996, 121.

and surviving relatives. The *deceased's views* could be relied on or ignored, the deceased could have been required to express an official view before death or left to decide whether to express a view, and the law might even operate a rebuttable presumption as to what the deceased's views were. Similarly, *the views of surviving relatives* and loved ones can be treated as persuasive, determinate, or irrelevant. To complicate matters further, the law might allow for a different approach to that operated in practice. Many health professionals are reluctant to ignore the wishes of surviving loved ones, irrespective of the strict legal position.

Some distinctions need to be drawn between different types of systems for the acquisition of cadaveric material. It is important to remember that others may use the same label to describe different concepts or different labels to describe the same concept. There are essentially three ideal-typical systems: opt-in, opt-out, and conscription. The possibility of payment for organ donation will be considered separately (in 13.4).

13.2.2.1 Types of regulatory system

An *"opt-in"* system is one permitting tissue and organs to be posthumously removed for transplantation only with appropriate consent. This is sometimes referred to as a "contracting in" system. As usually envisaged, the consent must have been obtained from the deceased prior to his death. For completeness, a distinction could be drawn between a *narrow* opt-in system, under which only the deceased can opt in, and a *wide* opt-in system, under which surviving loved ones can also permit the removal of the deceased's organs and tissues for transplantation. An opt-in system could operate without any obligation to consider whether or not to opt in *or* could impose an obligation to make a formal decision on the issue. For an narrow opt-in system, an obligated choice could be imposed on attainment of a certain age (say, 18) or could be enforced indirectly, by making a donation decision a condition of (say) obtaining a driving licence, registering with a doctor, or buying a house.

An *"opt-out"* system is one permitting tissue and organs to be posthumously removed for transplantation unless an appropriate objection is made. This type of system is sometimes referred to as "contracting out" or, somewhat misleadingly, as "presumed consent". This is not a consent-based system, because consent is fictionalised in the absence of any positive indication that posthumous removal for transplantation has actually been agreed.[49] As discussed in Ch.6 (6.3.1.1), imputed (as opposed to explicit, implicit, or implied) consent is no consent at all. In an opt-out system, as usually envisaged, the refusal must come from the deceased prior to his death. A distinction can be drawn between systems recognising objections only from the deceased prior to his death (*narrow* opt-out systems) and those recognising the objections of surviving loved ones on after his death (*wide* opt-out systems). Opt-out systems can also differ according to the level of formality required for registering or recording

---

[49] See Erin and Harris 1999, 365.

an objection (and thereby opting out) and according to the grounds for a valid objection (e.g. religious conscientious objection only). Most supporters of an opt-out system envisage a narrow opt-out system in which the objection need only be recorded on a formal register without any reason being required. The British Medical Association (BMA) has, however, argued for a wide opt-out system in which even a verbal objection will suffice.[50]

A *"conscription"* system is one where tissue and organs can be removed posthumously for transplantation, irrespective of any consent or refusal. Under such a system, dead bodies and their parts would become treated as public property either indefinitely or for a limited period before what remains is released for burial.

One would expect the available supply of tissue and organs to be inversely proportional to the emphasis placed on obtaining or complying with the wishes of the deceased and surviving loved ones. It is to be expected that a *strictly followed* narrow opt-out system would supply significantly more transplantable material than either an opt-in system or a wide opt-out system. A system of conscription would be expected to maximise the supply of cadaveric material for transplantation. It is, however, difficult to accurately predict the precise impact of legislation recognising any particular type of system before it is implemented. One difficulty with such predictions is that few countries have adopted strict instances of opt-out or conscription systems and every country has its own unique cultural, historical, and economic features. There is evidence that changing from an opt-in system to an opt-out system has increased the number of organs in Spain, Austria, and Belgium, but this was not achieved by the change in legislation alone.[51] After Belgium adopted opt-out legislation, it is reported that the donation rate remained the same in a clinic that retained a practice of opt-in, whereas in another clinic that implemented the new approach, the number of donors rose from 15 to 40 per year over a three-year period.[52] There is also evidence that adopting opt-out legislation, even if consent is required from relatives in practice, does generally increase willingness to consent.[53] It is, however, unlikely that the universal adoption of even a narrow opt-out system that is operated strictly would eliminate organ shortages.[54] No law or policy could change the fact that many deaths fail to leave usable organs and no country with an opt-out system has of yet managed to supply enough organs for all of its citizens with a medically indicated need.

13.2.2.2 Ethical views on the type of system

The moral acceptability of the systems outlined above turns on the moral interests that are recognised and the weight attached to those interests. A system of

---

[50] See BMA 2000, part 2 and 2004, 434.
[51] See Kennedy et al. 1998, 1650–1652 and Organ Donation Taskforce 2008, ch. 11.
[52] See Kennedy et al. 1998, 1651.
[53] See Kennedy et al. 1998, 1651.
[54] See Jefferies 1998, 639 (detailing the position under the strict opt-out system operating in Austria); Cooper et al. 2002, 134; and New et al. 1994.

conscription requires that neither the deceased nor his surviving loved ones have any relevant moral interest in controlling what happens to the tissue and organs in question or that their moral interests are overridden by (positive) duties to assist those in need of such material. An opt-out system requires that the deceased and his surviving loved ones have little moral claim to control what happens to cadaveric material or that any such moral claims are attenuated by positive duties owed to those in need of cadaveric material.

A note of caution should be raised before we discuss the impact of different moral theories. The transition between moral principle and public policy is not always straightforward, because practical contingencies can affect the application of abstract moral principles. There are enforcement costs once moral principle is converted into public policy through legislation and "although for practical purposes both law and morality demand some degree of closure and settlement, the integrity of morality is not threatened by ongoing debate, review, and adjustment of position".[55]

Utilitarians will require the costs (disutility) of the regulatory requirements to be low relative to their benefits (utility).[56] The costs of removing organs or tissue from a cadaver are the infliction of anticipatory worry on prospective providers (which might include worry that their deeply held beliefs will be violated) and the infliction of emotional harm on surviving loved ones. Cadaver provision could benefit the recipient, by saving his life or health, and thereby also benefit those who care for the recipient. Successful transplantation can also produce substantial financial savings over alternative long-term treatment for protracted organ failure (see 13.1, above). This balance is such that utilitarians will be at least prima facie supportive of a duty to donate and use tissues and organs for posthumous transplantation. *Virtue theorists* are likely to view the decision to donate as virtuous, at least where it is underpinned by a virtuous motive. A virtuous person would surely save another's life where it poses little cost to himself. Theories within the *rights-based, duty-based*, and *compromise* camps are more likely to span the full range of views.

Even if the deceased or surviving loved ones are recognised as having moral claims over cadaveric tissue and organs, many moral theorists accept the existence of (non-absolute) positive duties to assist those in need.[57] A popular limitation on positive duties is the "reasonable burden" or "comparable cost" condition, according to which positive duties cannot require the assister to give up anything of comparable moral significance to what is likely to be received by the individual assisted.[58] In this context of cadaver transplantation, this proviso would not usually hinder posthumous removal for transplantation because the assister will (*ex hypothesis*) have no compelling life-extending need

---

[55] Brownsword 2003a, 418–419.

[56] Remember that, unless otherwise specified, references to utilitarianism refer to the utility-maximising version: see Ch.1 (1.3.2.1). The most popular version, preference utilitarianism, requires the maximisation of preference-satisfaction.

[57] See the discussion of property in the next chapter (14.4) and positive duties in Ch.1 (1.3.3).

[58] See e.g. Gewirth 1978, 217–220 (rights-based position), Harris 1985, 57 (implicitly utilitarian position), Singer 1993, 229–232 (utilitarian position), and Pattinson 2009.

for tissues that are necessary to save the life or health of the prospective recipient. It follows that many moral theories will not object to an opt-out system as a matter of principle.

Systems of conscription are clearly more difficult to defend than opt-out systems. Some theorists do, nonetheless, deny that the interests of the deceased (before or after death) or the interests of surviving relatives can ever outweigh the interests of those who require a life-saving transplant. John Harris, for example, rejects the appropriateness of consent as a "gatekeeper" for cadaver donations.[59] As Harris points out, the moral justification for automatic and mandatory availability of donor organs for the purpose of saving another's life is *at least* as compelling as the justification for compulsory jury service or compulsory autopsies.[60] Harris holds this to be the case, even though he accepts the notion of surviving interests (though he does invoke democratic support as a background condition).[61] Others also argue that not only would conscription be a good thing, it is actually immoral to seek consent for the use of cadaver organs in transplantation.[62] Opponents of such a view must deny the claim of the potential recipient or hold that others have a greater claim to the deceased body and its body parts.[63]

13.2.2.3 Duties on doctors: required request

Whatever the strict legal position, it is health professionals who will have to face grieving loved ones. Many health professionals are understandably reluctant to go against the views of grieving loved ones or, if those views are not offered, ask what their views are. Many attribute low procurement rates to the reluctance to enquire as to the wishes of the deceased and their surviving loved ones. One mechanism that is designed to address such reluctance (in a wide opt-in system) is the imposition of a legal duty on health professionals (or at least doctors) to request the permission of relatives. Such a system, often referred to as "required request", is usually presented as a way of limiting the waste of cadaveric material stemming from a failure to ask for permission. "Required request" legislation has been widely implemented in the US.[64] The duty imposed on health professionals in such systems is usually subject to "professional privilege", to avoid the situation whereby a doctor is obliged to ask when he reasonably considers that the mere question will cause psychological harm. If, however, exceptions are made for professional privilege, required request is likely to be little different from a system of permissible request in which request is actively encouraged. As Mason points out,

> while legislation can cover what must be said, it cannot cover *how* it is said. It is well to leave matters in the capable hands of the transplant coordinators.[65]

---

[59] See Harris 1998, 125; 2002b; and 2003e
[60] See Harris 2003e, 131.
[61] His position is, arguably, a version of rule utilitarianism: see Ch.16 (16.2.1) and Harris 2003e, 131.
[62] See Emson 2003.
[63] For an example of the latter approach see Brazier 2002.
[64] See Mason 1996, 119.
[65] Mason 1996, 119 (original emphasis).

Some also question the effectiveness of such a system. According to the King's Fund Report,

> only 6 per cent of relatives in the UK [which does not have a system of required request] are not approached when an otherwise potential donor is on a ventilator, and many of those would probably have communicated their unwillingness to consider donation by other means.[66]

If this is correct, required request is an issue of little practical significance for the UK.

13.2.2.4 Tissue that is not necessary for survival

Until now much of our focus has been on transplantation intended to save and prolong life. Recent years have seen a number of transplants aimed not at saving life but improving its quality. Hand and face transplants are among the most prominent. Many thousands of patients lack limbs or have been left with facial disfigurements as a result of accidents, surgical removal of tumours, infections, or congenital defects.[67] Alternative treatments to transplantation— such as surgically reattaching the original tissues, transferring tissues from other parts of the patient's body, or using prosthetic materials—are not always possible or satisfactory.[68] Successful transplantation could therefore significantly improve the quality of life of some of these patients. A hand transplant could provide an amputee with lost function and a transplanted face could provide a severe burn victim with a more responsive face and new found confidence.

The first human hand transplant took place in Lyon, France in September 1998.[69] It was transplanted from a 41-year-old brain-stem dead patient to a 48-year-old who had lost his right hand and part of his right forearm in an accident involving a circular-saw. By 2006, 24 hand and forearm transplants had taken place.[70]

Face transplants are more complex. Opinions against such transplants were issued by the Royal College of Surgeons of England in 2003 and the French National Consultative Ethics Committee in 2004.[71] In late November 2005, however, a patient in France became the first recipient of a partial face transplant incorporating the nose and lips.[72] Isabel Dinoire had suffered serious face injuries after being savaged by a dog. The transplant was a complete success and, over three years later, the patient remains pleased with the results. This was followed in April 2006 by a partial face transplant in China on a 30-year-old

---

[66] New et al. 1994, 60.
[67] See Clark 2005a, RA2.
[68] See Clark 2005a, RA2.
[69] See Dubernard 1999, 1315.
[70] See RCS 2006, 3.
[71] See RCS 2003, 20 and CCNE 2004, 21.
[72] See Devauchelle et al. 2006 and 2008.

man who had lost the right-side of his face in a bear attack.[73] Other successful operations have now taken place in France (where such a transplant followed the removal of a large facial tumour)[74] and the US (where 80 per cent of the patient's face was replaced).[75] In 2006, the Royal College of Surgeons revised its guidance on face transplantation.[76] It is now only a matter of time before it takes place in the UK.

Despite these successes, face and limb transplants also raise concerns. Whatever reluctance there is to donate life-saving organs, there is likely to be less eagerness to come forward to donate one's face and limbs or those of deceased loved ones. And insofar as the moral claims of the recipient are weaker, the case for systems of opt-out or conscription for such material is more dependent on the deceased and his loved ones having little or no competing claims. Further, and somewhat paradoxically, even a surgically successful transplant could leave the patient worse off. The transplant could be rejected, as immunosuppressant drugs are not always effective. These drugs carry well-reported side-effects that can actually shorten a patient's life, such as increased incidence of infection, diabetes, hypertension, and cancer.[77] Psycho-social effects could follow if the recipient fails to identify with his new limb or face, or others react negatively.[78]

In the first edition of the Working Party Report issued by the Royal College of Surgeons in 2003, the lack of sufficient reliable data to estimate the risks to physical safety of a face transplant was said to mean that "patients will not be able to choose it in an appropriately informed way".[79] Since the risks are uncertain and could be very high,

> obtaining adequate informed consent to incurring these physical risks appears impossible. There seems no way of coherently aggregating these risks for the purposes of informed decision making in such a way that the duty to respect autonomy overrides the duty to protect patients from unacceptable or unknown levels of potential harm.[80]

Why? Why is a patient who makes a decision *with a clear understanding of what is known*, including knowledge that reliable risk estimates are not available, not adequately informed?[81] The rhetorical power of the quoted words is parasitic upon a conceptual conflation, whereby the conditions for a consent being valid (in the sense of being an adequate indication of the consent-giver's will) are confused with the conditions for the justificatory sufficiency of consent. What is really being contested in that quotation is not whether the consent-giver has exer-

[73] See Guo 2008.
[74] See Lantieri et al. 2008.
[75] See BBC 2008e.
[76] See RCS 2006.
[77] See RCS 2006, 11–12.
[78] See RCS 2006, 14–16.
[79] RCS 2003, 19.
[80] RCS 2003, 19.
[81] See further Pattinson 2009.

cised his will, but whether that will is a morally sufficient justification for proceeding. Thus, the report was relying on the view that a patient cannot release the doctor from his duty not to harm him. In the absence of reliable estimates of non-harm, the patient's consent was deprived of its moral authority. The permissibility of self-harm and running risks of self-harm is an issue that divides the major moral theories. Some moral theories allow individuals to release others from duties owed to them that other theories do not (see further below, 13.3.1). *If* the patient's consent lacks conclusive moral authority as to *his* moral interests, transplants that are not aimed at saving the patient's life might be considered to fare badly in a cost-benefit calculation—at least on the science as it was.[82] In contrast, the second edition of the Working Party Report declares that

> there is no a priori reason why prospective patients who have been shown to be sufficiently autonomous cannot be accurately informed about both known and unknown risks of transplantation—assuming the REC [research ethics committee] has agreed the risk benefit ratio to be acceptable.[83]

This is clearly more supportive of face transplantation than the first edition and represents a change of mind on the underlying ethical issues.

13.2.3 Acquisition: legal issues

The use of cadavers as sources of tissue for transplantation is governed by legislation. For over four decades this was the Human Tissue Act 1961. It is now the much longer and more complex Human Tissue Act 2004. Under the previous legislation, human material could be removed at the prior request of the deceased (s.1(1)) *or* without any request where relatives did not object or indicate that they have reason to believe that the deceased objected (s.1(2)). The 1961 Act thereby combined elements of a narrow opt-in and a wide opt-out system. In contrast, the Human Tissue Act 2004 adopts a wide opt-in system under which the deceased's objection prevents others from opting-in on his behalf. In practice, however, the 1961 Act was never applied as strictly as it could have been.[84] Loved ones and family members were consulted even if the donor had made a valid request, largely because many health professionals empathise with the bereaved and fear the negative publicity that ignoring their views could generate. Relatives were therefore granted the *de facto* power to veto the deceased's opt-in. The 2004 Act does not prevent this practice continuing. Codes 1 and 2 advise health professionals to sensitively encourage relatives to accept the deceased's wishes, while making it clear that the relatives do not have the legal right to veto those wishes (Code 1, para.47 and Code 2, para.40). Code 2 goes further and states that there will be cases where

---

[82] See e.g. Dickenson and Widderhoven 2001, Clark 2005a and 2005b, and RCS 2003.
[83] RCS 2006, 35.
[84] See Price 2003, 8–9 and 2005, 813.

"donation is inappropriate and each case should be considered individually". The legally unnecessary authorisation of relatives is, in fact, acquired in many countries, including many of those that have adopted opt-out legislation, such as Belgium, France, and Sweden.[85]

Relatives are more likely to support donation where their loved one has previously consented. If a person's name is on the Organ Donor Register only 10 per cent of families refuse to consent, compared to the general refusal rate of around 40 per cent.[86] Since the overall donation rate remains low (13.2 per million population, compared to 34.4 per million population in Spain),[87] the Government asked the Organ Donation Taskforce to consider the potential impact of changing to an opt-out system. Its report, published in November 2008, recommends against adopting an opt-out system, concluding that such a move "may deliver real benefits but carries a significant risk of making the current situation worse".[88]

Before outlining the details of the 2004 Act's approach to cadaveric transplantation, it is worth pausing to note some of the problems presented by the previous legislation. The 1961 Act was loaded with omissions and ambiguities, which required untested assumptions to be made in practice. Section 1(1) did not mention children, but the Department of Health advised that children would be able to opt-in under that provision if they were of an age that made it reasonable to believe that they understood what donation involves.[89] The Act did not define the "person lawfully in possession of the dead body", who was the person who could authorise the removal of tissue under s.1(1) and 1(2), but it was widely assumed that this would be the relevant hospital administrator if the deceased had died in hospital.[90] Section 1(2) required "such reasonable enquiry as may be practicable" with regard to the objections of the deceased or any surviving relative, but did not define reasonable enquiry or insist that the surviving relative have a close relationship to the deceased. The Department of Health nonetheless advised that it would usually be adequate to discuss the matter with any *one* relative who has been in close contact with the deceased.[91] Most significantly, the Act itself did not provide any criminal penalty or civil remedy for violation of its provisions. The Act appears to have rested on the assumption that the medical profession can be trusted to act in accordance with the rules—an assumption that the recent scandals involving the retention of organs have led many to doubt. In *R v Lennox-Wright*, Judge Lawson controversially relied on the ancient common law crime of disobedience of a statute to convict a man who had removed parts of a dead body without being medically qualified contrary to s.1(4) of the 1961 Act.[92] This case was probably wrongly

[85] See Kurnit 1994, esp. 423, Jefferies 1998, esp. 637–638, and Price 2003, 9.
[86] See Organ Donation Taskforce 2008, para.1.15 and UK Transplant 2008, 5.
[87] See Organ Donation Taskforce 2008, para.11.3.
[88] See Organ Donation Taskforce 2008, para.1.14.
[89] It also advised that parental consent be obtained "as a matter of good practice": see DH 1998, 8.10. See also Kennedy and Grubb 2000, 1834–1845, and Dickens 2004a, 1045.
[90] See DH 1998, para.5.2. See also s.1(7) of the 1961 Act.
[91] See DH 1998, para.8.8.
[92] [1973] Crim. L. R. 529.

decided. The relevance of this ancient crime was all but removed by a later ruling of the Divisional Court[93] and, in the context of the 1961 Act, s.1(8) explicitly states that s.1 does not render unlawful anything that is lawful apart from the Act. The 1961 Act was therefore little more than a statutory code of practice. In an exceptional case, violation of the Act's provisions could have given rise to a claim in negligence for psychiatric injury.[94]

13.2.3.1 Appropriate consent

The 2004 Act requires "appropriate consent" for, inter alia, the removal, retention and use of tissue from cadavers for transplantation (s.1 and Sch.1 Pt 1 para.7). A person commits an offence if he fails to obtain appropriate consent, unless he reasonably believes that he does the activity with consent or it is one for which consent is not required (s.5(1)). The penalty for conviction on indictment can be up to three years imprisonment, a fine, or both (s.5(7)).

"Appropriate consent" is defined in sections two and three by reference to who may give it. The Act remains silent with regard to the amount of information that the consenter must possess and the circumstances in which it would be acceptable to infer or imply consent (save those situations, outside of the context of tissue donation and transplantation, where written consent is required).[95] In the case of a deceased adult, consent can be given or withheld by *the deceased* before he died, *a nominated representative* (if no prior decision), or *a qualifying relative* (if no prior decision or nominated representative) (s.3(6)). In the case of a deceased child,[96] consent can be given or withheld by *the child* before he died, *a parent* (if no prior decision), or *a qualifying relative* (if no prior decision or parent) (s.2(7)). The deceased's decision need not be written but must be "in force immediately before he died" (ss.3(6)(a) and 2(7)(a)). Most decisions to donate are expressed by signing a donor card or registering on the NHS Organ Donor Register. This Register now has more than 15 million signed up, which represents about a quarter of the population.[97] In sum, the Act adopts a *wide opt-in system* under which the wishes of the deceased take precedence. There have already been attempts made to change this to an opt-out system.[98]

Section 4 states that an adult may appoint a nominated representative in writing (if witnessed) or orally (if two witnesses are present). A parent for the purposes of the Act is a person with *parental responsibility*, as discussed in Ch.5 (5.3.1.1).

---

[93] *R. v Horseferry Road Justices Ex p. IBA* [1987] Q.B. 54.
[94] *Re Organ Retention Group Litigation* [2004] EWHC 644 (in which only one of the claims in this group action was successful: para. 110).
[95] Written consent is e.g. required for an activity involving the storage or use of relevant material for the purpose of public display: ss.2(4) and 3(3). For a discussion of express, implicit, or implied consent, see Ch.6 (6.3.1.1).
[96] Defined as someone under 18: s.54(1).
[97] See Organ Donation Taskforce 2008, para.4.4.
[98] A Private Members Bill, known as the Human Tissue Act 2004 (Amendment) Bill, was introduced into the House of Commons in early 2005 in an attempt to change the legislative position from an opt-in system to an opt-out system. This Bill was dropped upon the prorogation of Parliament in April 2005.

Qualifying relationships, ranked in order in s.27(4), are the individual's (a) spouse or partner, (b) parent or child, (c) brother or sister, (d) grandparent or grandchild, (e) niece or nephew, (f) stepfather or stepmother, (g) half-brother or half-sister, and (h) friend of long standing.[99] Some levels of this ranking appear a little odd. Half-siblings, for example, are ranked below nieces and nephews despite the likelihood that half-siblings will have been brought up as siblings.

Where there is more than one person *at the same level of the hierarchy*, the consent of one will be sufficient (s.27(7)). This means that disputes between the deceased's existing partner and estranged spouse, disputes between the deceased's estranged parents, and other such disputes are to be resolved in favour of the person who actually consents. This is very different from the position under s.1(2) the 1961 Act, where (if the deceased did not consent) *any surviving relative* could veto the removal and use of the deceased's tissue. Code 2 advises that "differences of opinion" are to be treated on a case-by-case basis and, where possible, an agreed position should be reached by inclusive discussion (paras 55–57). Further, it states that the Act's ranking provision should not be used to impose one family member's views on the others where the objection is so strongly held that the distress and resentment would outweigh the benefit. Interestingly, the draft revision of Code 2 contains less detail on this issue. It no longer explicitly deals with conflicts with those who are not of equal ranking, beyond the advice (in para.114) that the person giving the consent should discuss the matter with other family members. Where there is a conflict between persons of equal ranking, the draft revision says only that the matter should be discussed sensitively and a clear explanation of the legal position should be provided (Draft Code 2, para.117). The upshot is that the revised Code is less supportive of family members vetoing the consent of those higher up the hierarchy.

The 2004 Act does not insist on the hierarchical ranking where the relevant person cannot or does not want to make a decision. It permits a person's relationship to be ignored where he does not wish, or is unable, to deal with the issue of consent, or if it is not reasonably practicable to communicate with him in the time available (s.27(8)). Also, in contrast to the 1961 Act, it is made clear that reasonable practicability is to be determined by reference to whether it will be possible for "consent in relation to the activity . . . to be acted on".

13.2.3.2 Other provisions

Section 43 clarifies the legal position with regard to the retention and preservation of the bodies of potential donors in the period between death and contacting the deceased's surviving relatives. This section states that it is lawful to take the minimum steps to retain and preserve a dead body for use for transplantation until it is established that the consent for lawful removal of material for transplantation has not been, and will not be, given.

---

[99] See also ss.27(5) and 54(9). The Secretary of State is given the power to amend the stipulated hierarchy by secondary legislation: s.27(9).

13.2.4 Allocation

In addition to difficult questions about the acquisition of cadaveric material, there are questions about the allocation of such material. There could be a close connection between the system for acquisition and the criteria for allocating tissues and organs obtained from cadavers. An opt-in system could, for example, encourage willingness to consent to posthumous transplantation if priority is thereby given to the donor or their loved ones should they ever require a transplant. Some acquisition and allocation systems would be more difficult to coherently link. It would, for example, be difficult to find a morally coherent rationale for linking allocation solely on the basis of ability to pay with a conscription system.

The limited supply of cadaveric material raises distributive issues beyond those created by the limited financial resources of the NHS, considered in Ch.2 (2.4.2). Despite this, the same basic questions arise: should rationing decisions be open and explicit, who should make them, and how should they be made? If public support for the system is to be maintained, allocation decisions need to be open, explicit, and based on defensible criteria. Perhaps the most controversial issue is whether liver transplants should be offered to alcoholics and reformed alcoholics. Should alcoholics and former alcoholics be denied access on the basis that they have contributed to their own condition and even reformed alcoholics face increased risks of a future lapse that could damage the new liver? The UK does not adopt a blanket regulatory policy on this issue. The late George Best famously received a liver transplant despite his well-publicised alcohol problems.[100] Blanket exclusions would be open to challenge under the Human Rights Act (HRA) 1998 as a potential breach of art.2 (the right to life) read in conjunction with art.14 (the right not to be discriminated against in the exercise of one's rights). Blanket exclusions might also be ethically challenged, at least from some moral positions, on the basis that they would disproportionately affect those from particular backgrounds and involve invasive investigation of individuals' life-style choices.

A Special Health Authority, *NHS Blood and Transplant* (NHSBT), exists to ensure that the limited supply of donated organs is properly matched, allocated, and transported. Thus, operational matters relating to transplantation are dealt with by the Organ Donation and Transplantation Directorate of NHSBT, rather than the HTA.[101] This body uses a computer program to identify the best matched patient or, alternatively, the transplant unit to which the organ is to be offered.[102] The precise criteria differ according to the type of organ. For livers, priority is given to those who face an imminent threat to their

---

[100] See BBC 2002a.
[101] NHSBT was formed by the merger of UK Transplant with National Blood Authority in October 2005: National Blood Authority and United Kingdom Transplant (Abolition) Order 2005/2532. The transplantation directorate of NHSBT continued to operate under the title of UK Transplant until 2008.
[102] See *http://www.nhsbt.nhs.uk* and *www.uktransplant.org.uk*.

life, whose life expectancy is measured in terms of days or even hours. If there are no such urgent patients on the waiting list, the liver will be offered to the nearest transplant centre to minimise delay in its implantation. If the organ cannot be used at the local centre, it is offered nationally according to a "points" system. Centres are allocated points for passing on livers and lose them when they accept one from outside of their area. The allocation of kidneys relies on a points system that takes account of tissue type, blood group, and geographical location. Priority is given to children because they do not do well on dialysis and could suffer growth impairment.

13.2.4.1 Allocation and conditional donation

Another divisive issue is whether the donor or his surviving loved ones should be able to influence allocation decisions. In theory, conditions could be placed on a donation in both opt-in and opt-out systems by making an authorisation conditional upon certain conditions or by limiting an objection by reference to certain conditions. The system must then decide whether to comply with the conditions, not use the organ at all because of the conditions, or use the organ irrespective of the conditions.

In July 1998, an unconscious man was admitted to an ICU at the North General Hospital in Sheffield. The deceased had not provided a legally valid prior consent to cadaveric transplantation. His family agreed to organ donation in the event of his death *on the condition* that the organs went to white recipients. His liver was used to save the life of man who would otherwise have died within 24 hours and his kidneys went to the two people at the top of the waiting list under the renal transplant points system.[103] All the recipients were white. The Department of Health set up a panel to investigate the situation. The panel reported that all the organs had gone to those who would have received them had the donation been unconditional. The panel denounced the acceptance of racist offers and condemned *all* conditions attached to donation.[104] It recognised that not only did the 1961 Act not envisage conditional agreement, but it would have been a breach of the Race Relations Act 1976 for the NHS to have complied with racist wishes.[105] On the day that the report was published, the Government accepted the panel's recommendations and similarly condemned acceptance of *any* donation conditions.[106]

In practice, both then and now, the donor's family will be told that the organs have been transplanted, but not given any details about the recipients.[107] This means that organs donated with conditions could, in theory, be used contrary to those conditions without the donor family finding out. This is not the approach adopted and its adoption would require institutionalised deception and look to the outside world as if the conditions were being complied with. It would also

---

103 See DH 2000d, ch.4.
104 See DH 2000d, para.6.9.
105 See DH 2000d, para.5.3.
106 See also DH 2000e.
107 See DH 2000d, para.3.43.

not answer the panel's stated rationale for objecting to conditional donation, namely, that "it offends against the fundamental principle that organs are donated altruistically and should go to patients in the greatest need".[108] Wilkinson has persuasively argued that this rationale does not support a blanket refusal on accepting conditional donation.[109] He argues that conditional donation could be altruistic, by way of example noting that donating to children is no less altruistic than donating to a children's charity.[110] And, he argues, even where attaching a condition to an offer is non-altruistic or otherwise immoral, it does not follow that accepting that offer is wrong. There is no violation of the principle that organs should go to patients in the greatest need if conditional offers are only accepted where the organ will go to the person in greater need.[111] Wilkinson is surely correct in his observation that the panel's view depends on additional, unarticulated, premises. Others have supported policy responses along the lines of the panel's view—at least where the condition is not that the organ be donated to a specified individual.[112]

13.3 Transplantation from the living

We have seen that the discrepancy between supply and demand for human organs leads to death and distress. Transplantation is the only hope for some of those suffering from organ and tissue failure, and is the preferable treatment option for many others. So far we have focused on the use of deceased (or cadaveric) donors, but life-saving organs and tissues can also be obtained from those who are uncontroversially alive. Living providers are routinely used as sources for regenerative tissues such as blood and bone marrow. The first kidney transplants used live donors and the number of live donors is increasing from year-to-year. The latest figures show a 22 per cent increase in the number of living solid organ donors compared to the year before, as opposed to a mere 2 per cent increase in the number of cadaveric donors over the same period.[113] The total number of solid organ transplants from living donors in 2007–2008 remained small (854), compared to transplants from cadavers (2,381). The vast majority of organs transplanted from living donors are kidneys (829), though there were also 24 liver segment transplants and one lung segment transplant. The majority of the donors are women. Several studies have shown that women are more likely to be living kidney donors than men, but are less likely to receive a kidney from a living donor.[114] It is unclear why this gender disparity exists, though a plausible hypothesis is that it is the result of social inequalities between the sexes.

---

[108] See DH 2000d, para.6.1.
[109] See Wilkinson 2003.
[110] See Wilkinson 2003, 163.
[111] See Wilkinson 2003, 163.
[112] See Pennings 2007.
[113] Unless otherwise stated, all figures below derive from UK Transplant 2008, esp. 4, 8, and 11.
[114] See Kimmel and Patel 2003, esp. 63.

Transplantation from the living offers many technical advantages over transplantation from cadavers. Living donors are obviously healthier than dead donors and the timing of a transplant from a living donor can be controlled, thereby allowing the period in which the organ is degenerating outside of a body to become almost negligible. The result is that using organs and tissue from living providers leads to better graft and patient survival rates than those from cadavers. This is so even where the provider is *unrelated* to the recipient, as live unrelated graft and patient survival rates are almost comparable to living *related* transplantations.[115]

Many tissues, organs, and fluids can, with varying degrees of risk for the provider, be removed from the living. The removal of blood is among the least risky. The removal of whole or parts of solid organs poses much greater risk. In addition to the inevitable pain and scarring, having a solid organ removed carries risks of mortality, morbidity, psychological harm, and long-term complications. In terms of mortality the risks are small, but "a small number, particularly those donating partial livers, have died as a consequence".[116] The mortality rate for kidney donation was estimated at about 0.03 per cent by a survey of members of the American Society of Transplant Surgeons in 1992.[117] One study of 871 kidney donors at a US hospital reported no mortalities and relatively few complications—including only two major complications and minor complications in only 8 per cent of donors, resulting in an overall complication rate of 8.2 per cent.[118] Similarly, although no one has yet died from donating a lung lobe in Britain or the US,

> all general anaesthetics and surgery have some risk and removal of a lung lobe for cancer has a mortality rate of about one per cent. If donation of living lung lobes becomes widespread then eventually a donor will die.[119]

Similar risks are reported for living transplants of pancreas segments[120] and small bowel segments.[121]

Unusually for a solid organ, removed liver segments (lobes) will regenerate. Liver donation between adults involves the organ being cut in half, yet the donor's liver will usually have fully regenerated 12 weeks later.[122] A child recipient need only receive a small part of the living adult's liver (a bit of the left lobe), which will take even less time to regenerate. Many fluids and tissues can also be replaced (regenerated) by the body, including blood, bone marrow, skin, and hair.

---

[115] See Sever et al. 2001, 1481, Cecka 1999, and Sesso et al. 1998.
[116] Cooper 2002, 134.
[117] See Najarian 1992, esp. 807.
[118] See Johnson 1997, esp. 1125.
[119] Hodson 2000, 420.
[120] See Margreiter 1991, esp. 105.
[121] See Deltz 1991.
[122] See Meikle 2005.

13.3.1 The ethical issues

Transplantation from living organ providers is an unusual medical procedure as its purpose is to benefit someone other than the immediate subject.[123] The principal moral issue raised by the fact that the provider of the transplantable material is not the intended beneficiary of the procedure is the issue of whether we have *duties to ourselves*. This divides moral theories. Rights-based and other autonomy-prioritising theories reject the idea that a competent individual can commit a wrong to himself. Since the benefits of all one's moral obligations are waivable by the rights-holder, a rights-holder cannot have an unwaivable obligation to himself. Wrongs involve the violation of the rights of others. From such a perspective, fully consensual self-harm cannot be immoral per se. John Harris, who adopts an implicitly preference utilitarian approach, expresses this view:

> Should I be permitted voluntarily to donate a vital organ like the heart? . . . [I]f I know what I am doing then I do not see why I should not give my life to save that of another if that is what I want to do with my life. Non-voluntary or involuntary donation of vital organs is of course murder and is justified only where murder is justified.[124]

In contrast, some forms of virtue theory hold self-harm and the encouragement of self-harm by others to represent a flaw in one's moral character. Elliot points out that unease with self-sacrifice tends to be proportionate to the degree of risk and the severity of the self-harm, which is why heart transplants from living organ providers are a paradigmatic case.[125] He argues that endorsing the self-sacrifice of others for one's own benefit indicates "a failure of courage, a lapse of moral nerve" and we might be "justifiably suspicious of the character of a doctor who had no . . . reservations" about the infliction harm on a person for the sake of another.[126] (Elliot also holds that the introduction of any financial incentive will strengthen virtue-based objections.) Similarly, some duty-based positions imply that individuals owe duties to themselves, so that to provide one's organs for another's benefit is potentially violation of one's duty not to cause harm to oneself. In the language of dignity, the position that Beyleveld and Brownsword refer to as the "dignity as constraint" view holds that giving one's organs to another can involve a violation of one's dignity, understood as setting non-waivable limits on conduct in a civilised society.[127] This position is characterised by the idea that some duties protect an individual *irrespective of his will*, on the basis that these duties reflect non-waivable community values (communitarian view) or duties that an individual also owes to himself (the duty-based view). This conflict between autonomy-focused theories (such as

---

[123] So-called "domino transplants" are in exception (discussed below, 13.3.2.1).
[124] Harris 1998, 137.
[125] See Elliot 1995, esp. 92.
[126] Elliott 1995, 94 and 95, respectively.
[127] See Beyleveld and Brownsword 2001 and the discussion in Ch.1 (1.4.1).

rights-based theories and preference utilitarian) and more paternalistic moral theories (such as some duty-based, virtue-based, and communitarian theories) has significant import for controls over fully *consensual* organ provision. Views within the "dignity as constraint" camp start from the opposite presumption from those within the "dignity as empowerment" camp.

Although all five of the major groups of moral theories are potentially compatible with tissue and organ donation *as such*, those adopting the more paternalistic "dignity as constraint" view do not accept the removal of *life-sustaining* tissue and organs for transplantation into another. Moreover, not all tissue and organ donation will be viewed in the same light as the risks to the source vary according to his physical health and circumstances, the procedure used, and the type of tissue removed. As stated earlier, the removal of blood is less risky than the removal of bone marrow, which is less risky than the removal of a kidney, which is less risky than the removal of a liver lobe or lung lobe. The risks of organ provision can be put into perspective by a simple analogy: the increased risk of death to a healthy 35-year-old from giving up a single kidney is thought to be equivalent to driving sixteen miles a day to and from work.[128] Other issues of controversy are the use of the young or particularly vulnerable as donors and the issue of paying tissue and organ providers. The issue of payment will be addressed in the next chapter (14.2).

13.3.2 The law

Transplantation from living donors is governed by both legislation and the common law. The removal must be lawful at common law and the requirements of ss.1 and 33 of the Human Tissue Act 2004 Act must be satisfied.

Like any other surgery, removing tissue or organs from a living donor will be unlawful and a criminal assault unless the surgeon properly relies on a valid consent or the provisions of the Mental Capacity Act 2005.

Sections 1 and 33 of the 2004 Act impose additional requirements. Section 1 requires "appropriate consent" for the *storage and use* of "relevant material" from living persons for transplantation. Section 33 places restrictions on the *removal or use* of "transplantable material" from living persons for transplantation.

The relationship between the common law and ss.1 and 33 is not self-evident. The issues are examined below in the following order: the lawfulness of removal at common law; s.1 of the 2004 Act; and then s.33 of the 2004 Act.

13.3.2.1 The common law and the lawfulness of removal

The common law applies where the 2004 Act does not. At common law, inflicting serious bodily harm is usually an offence even if the "victim" has consented. An

---

[128] See Hansmann 1989, 72.

exception is made for proper medical treatment on the basis that such conduct is intended to benefit the patient's health and is therefore not regarded as causing bodily harm (see Ch.4 (4.6)). The difficulty for live organ and tissue donations is that the intended health benefits are usually directed at the recipient, rather than the donor. The only exception are so-called "domino transplants", which involve the removal of transplantable organs from a patient as part of that patient's treatment. It is, for example, technically easier to replace the heart and lungs together of cystic fibrosis sufferers who require lung transplants, and so the patient's removed heart could then become available for transplantation. Domino transplants remain rare—there were no domino heart transplants in the last full year for which there are official statistics. Domino transplants aside, donation does not track the medical interests of a living donor. It is, nonetheless, beyond question that living organ and tissue donation are lawful at common law if conducted in accordance with proper medical practice. Live transplantation of tissue and organs that are essential to maintain the life of the donor appears to remain unlawful, as contrary to public policy.

The position with regard to children and incapacitated adults is more complex. It is useful to remind ourselves of the law applying to *the treatment of incapacitated patients*, as explained and examined in Ch.5. Consent for the treatment of a *child* can be given by someone with parental responsibility or, if the child is over 16 or "*Gillick* competent", by the child.[129] The courts have the power to overrule the child and its parents, if it is in the best interests of the child to do so.[130] Incapacitated patients over 16 are covered by the Mental Capacity Act 2005. No intervention will be lawful unless the decision-maker (proxy or, if there is no proxy, the doctor acting under the s.5 general legal authority) reasonably believes it to be in the patient's best interests. The courts have required approval, as a matter of good practice, in only a handful of circumstances. Adults are presumed to have capacity (i.e. the legal authority to consent), but will lack it if they are unable to make a decision due to an impairment in the functioning of their mind or brain that renders them unable to understand, retain, and weigh the relevant information (ss.1–3).

There is little case law on the lawfulness of using children or incapacitated adults as living donors. There is one case involving an incapacitated adult and only obiter statements addressing child donors. The adult case—decided before the passing of the 2005 Act—was *Re Y*.[131] This concerned the legality of performing a blood test and removing *bone marrow* from an incapacitated adult for the treatment of her sick sister. Connell J. declared that performing these procedures would be in the best interests of the incapacitated donor, Y. He took the view that if Y's sister died this would have an adverse effect on their mother, potentially depriving Y of her mother's visits. Donating was also considered likely to improve Y's relationship with her sister. This link to the patient's interests in this case was indirect and a cynic might be tempted by the view that *Re*

---

[129] See, in particular, the Children Act 1989 (s.3(1)), Family Law Reform Act 1969 (s.8(1)), and *Gillick v West Norfolk and Wisbech AHA* [1986] A.C. 112.

[130] *Re W* [1993] Fam. 64.

[131] [1997] Fam. 110.

Y did not strictly adhere to the patient's best interests at all, especially since she did not appreciate that the lady who visited her was her mother. Connell J. made it clear that his decision turned on its facts and should not be considered a precedent for more invasive donations, as he was influenced by the fact that "bone marrow harvested is speedily regenerated and that a healthy individual can donate as much as two pints with no long term consequences at all".[132]

There is some American case law addressing more invasive donations from incapacitated adults. Connell J. in *Re Y* had readily cited the decision of the Court of Appeals of Kentucky in *Strunk v Strunk*.[133] In *Strunk*, the court authorised a kidney transplant from a 27–year-old man with a mental age of six to his 28-year-old brother who was suffering from kidney disease. The psychiatric evidence suggested that his brother's death would have an "extremely traumatic effect" on the mentally incompetent adult as the relationship between the brothers was very close.[134] The court supported the donation after, somewhat confusingly, purporting to apply the "substituted judgment" test to a patient who had never been competent.[135] Although English law is wedded to the "best interests" test, on facts like these a decision-maker could reasonably believe donation to be in the donor's best interests under the Mental Capacity Act 2005.

Article 20 of the European Convention on Human Rights and Biomedicine (the *Biomedicine Convention*) prohibits the donation of non-regenerative organs and tissue from a person who lacks capacity. It permits the donation of regenerative tissue from the incapacitated only where there is compliance with a number of protective conditions that are prescribed by law: no compatible capacitated donor exists, the recipient is a sibling, the donation is potentially life-saving for the recipient, the potential donor does not object, and the authorisation is in writing and approved by a competent body. The situation in *Strunk* could be brought within these protective conditions. The UK has not signed the Biomedicine Convention, but it could still have an interpretative impact on the Convention on Human Rights and Fundamental Freedoms, as given domestic effect by the HRA1998.[136]

As already stated, there is no directly relevant case law addressing the use of children as living donors.[137] Section 8(1) of the Family Law Reform Act 1969 is limited to therapeutic and diagnostic procedures, and therefore does not apply to donation,[138] and the capacity to consent to transplantation was not considered in *Gillick*.[139] Whether a doctor can rely on the consent of a suitably mature and

---

[132] [1997] Fam. 110 at 116.

[133] (1969) 445 S.W.2d 145.

[134] 445 S.W.2d 145 at 146.

[135] See the discussion of the substituted judgment test in Ch.5 (5.2.2.4).

[136] See e.g. *Glass v UK* [2004] 1 F.L.R. 1019, para.58. Interpreting a binding Convention in the light of a non-binding Convention can surely only be acceptable where the relevant provision from the non-binding Convention is uncontroversial and plausibly implicit in the binding provision (see Ch.1 (1.5)).

[137] There is American jurisprudence. See e.g. *Hart v Brown* (1972) 289 A.2d 386 (the parents were able to consent to the donation of a kidney by a child under 8 to his twin brother).

[138] *Re W* [1993] Fam. 64 at 78 and 92.

[139] *Gillick v West Norfolk and Wisbech AHA* [1986] A.C. 112.

intelligent child is unclear. The Court of Appeal in *Re W* considered the legality of using a child as a donor, though what was said was obiter as the case concerned a 16-year-old girl with anorexia nervosa who was refusing to consent to transfer to a specialist treatment unit.[140] The Court of Appeal did not read *Gillick* as protecting a child's autonomy interests, but as protecting a doctor from liability when he acts to protect the child's health with that child's consent. Their Lordships' obiter statements on organ donation are far from clear. Lord Donaldson declared that consent must be obtained from a proxy or a *Gillick* competent child, but it was "highly improbable" that a child would be *Gillick* competent in these circumstances and "inconceivable" that a doctor would proceed without consent from both the parent and the child.[141] Later in his judgment, his Lordship went on to say that the common law right of a *Gillick* competent child to consent to treatment "which again cannot be overridden by those with parental responsibility . . . extends to the donation of blood or organs".[142] A doctor faced with such "guidance" would be well advised to follow their Lordships' advice and make an application to the court![143] It is hardly surprising that "no currently practising British transplant surgeon would accept a live child as an organ donor; only one such instance, involving an identical twin aged 17 years, has arisen in the United Kingdom in the last 20 years".[144]

A mature child is unlikely to automatically lack capacity to donate, otherwise a 17-year-old married woman would be unable to independently consent to donate blood to her own child, even if her child is in desperate need of a blood transfusion! The Department of Health in a consultation report declared that,

> in theory, . . . a child able to give consent to the donation of an organ . . . or regenerative tissue, such as bone marrow, could refuse to do so—and then have the refusal over-ruled by a person with parental responsibility.[145]

Until a case comes before the courts we cannot be sure whether this is right. The specific facts will be immensely important, especially given the likelihood that a child will face considerable emotional pressure to donate to save the life of a sibling.

Whether the parent's consent must be in the best interests of the child, or could merely be not against the interests of the child, is also unclear. In one case, blood testing was allowed for the purposes of paternity testing a child during divorce proceedings on the basis that it was not against the interests of the child.[146] It is unclear whether this decision is restricted to its facts.[147] In any event, where the potential donor and recipient are siblings, the parent will face

---

[140] [1993] Fam. 64.
[141] [1993] Fam. 64 at 78–79.
[142] [1993] Fam. 64 at 83–84.
[143] [1993] Fam. 64 at 79 (Lord Donaldson) and 94 (Nolan L.J.).
[144] Mason and Laurie 2006, 488.
[145] DH 2002d, para.14.28.
[146] *S v S* [1972] A.C. 24.
[147] See further Chs 5 (5.3.2.1) and 11 (11.4.5).

a problematic conflict of interest. While doubt remains about whether a parent can legally consent for one child to act as a donor for another, it is highly unlikely that they could consent for their child to donate to them.

13.3.2.2 Section 1

Section 1 requires "appropriate consent" to be obtained for the *storage or use* of relevant material taken from a *living* person for the purpose of transplantation (s.1(1)(d),(f) and Sch.1). Appropriate consent is again defined by reference to the person who may give it. It can be provided by a *capacitated adult* or *child* on his own behalf (ss.3(2) and 2(2)). In fact, if the potential donor is an adult with capacity, only that person can consent. Code 1 makes it clear that a valid consent requires "a positive act" and must be voluntary, appropriately informed, and given by a person with capacity (paras 17 and 31). Code 1 also indicates that it is "good practice" to obtain written consent to organ donation (paras 93 and 99).

If a child lacks capacity or has capacity but is unwilling to make a decision, then appropriate consent can be obtained from a person with parental responsibility (s.2(3)). (A child being someone under 18: s.54(1).) During the Parliamentary debate and in the Explanatory Notes to the Act, it was indicated that a child's capacity is to be determined by reference to the common law, which was said to be the "*Gillick* test".[148] Code 1 also states that children may provide appropriate consent "if they are competent" and then summarises the *Gillick* test (para.42). This is certainly the relevant test where the child is under 16, but these documents make no mention of the fact that the *Gillick* case was only concerned with the treatment of children under 16[149] and the Mental Capacity Act 2005 applies to those who are 16 and 17.[150] This point should be considered in the light of the view presented in Ch.5 (5.3.2.1) to the effect that the case law suggests that the *Gillick* test is more difficult to satisfy than the Mental Capacity Act's two-stage test.

Code 2 goes on to declare that "if the child is competent, the decision to consent (under the Act) must be the child's", but it is good practice to consult the child's family (para.33). Thus, a capacitated child's decision to store or use his tissue for transplantation is secure from challenge by the child's parents, even though the same child's decision to refuse treatment could be overridden by the child's parents at common law. This position, although odd from the point of view of the child's autonomy interests, is at least understandable from the point of view of the child's health/welfare interests (once the tissue has been removed) its storage and use threatens much less harm to the child.

Section 6 enables the Secretary of State to specify in regulations the circumstances in which there is "deemed to be consent" to the storage and use of the relevant material of an *incapacitated adult*. Regulations 2006/1659 specify a

---

[148] Explanatory Notes to the Human Tissue Act 2004, para.16.
[149] *Gillick v West Norfolk and Wisbech AHA* [1986] A.C. 112.
[150] See s.2(5) of the 2005 Act. Draft Code 1 does refer to the application of the 2005 Act, but the sentence referring to its different definition of an adult is not clearly drafted (para.146).

number of circumstances.[151] The donor is deemed to have consented where the storage and use of the relevant material for the purpose of transplantation is reasonably believed to be in the donor's best interests (reg.3(2)(a)). It was suggested to Parliament, as an example, that it could sometimes be in the best interests of an incapacitated adult for his tissue to be stored and used for transplantation into a close relative.[152] In practice, it will surely be more difficult to demonstrate that its removal for donation is in the best interests of an incapacitated patient, as required by the 2005 Act. Thus, once it is established that the removal for transplantation is lawful at common law and under the 2005 Act, storage and use for that purpose will usually also be lawful under these Regulations. Conceptual clarity would, however, have been aided if the Act had simply said that consent was not required where specified in regulations, rather than fictionalising consent in this way. Such "deemed" consent is in no way connected to the actual will of the incapacitated donor.

13.3.2.3 Section 33

Section 33 of the 2004 Act states that the *removal* or *use* of "transplantable material" from a living person for the purposes of transplantation is illegal *unless* (a) it is permitted by regulations and (b) the HTA is satisfied that the specified conditions are fulfilled. A person committing an offence under s.33 is liable on summary conviction for a term of imprisonment of up to a year, a fine, or both (s.33(6)). No offence is committed where the person reasonably believes that the exception applies (s.33(5)).

The relevant regulations are those referred above: Regulations 2006/1659. Regulation 10 defines transplantable material for the purposes of s.33 as:

(a) an organ, or part of an organ if it is to be used for the same   purpose as the entire organ in the human body,
(b) bone marrow, and
(c) peripheral blood stem cells,

where that material is removed from the body of a living person with the intention that it be transplanted into another person.

This is narrower than the definition of relevant material, which encompassed any material containing or consisting of human cells with exclusions.

"Organ" is defined in reg.2(2) to mean "a differentiated and vital part of the human body, formed by different tissues, that maintains its structure, vascularisation and capacity to develop physiological functions with an important level of autonomy". This definition excludes all the things excluded from the definition of relevant material—embryos, gametes, cell lines, hair, and nails—because these are not vascularised or not formed by different tissues. It also excludes materials such as plasma blood, heart valves removed from a patient receiving a donated heart, and bone removed for bone grafting into another.

---

[151] Human Tissue Act 2004 (Persons who Lack Capacity to Consent and Transplants) Regulations 2006/1659.
[152] See the Explanatory Notes to the Human Tissue Act 2004, para.22.

The Regulations further narrow the definition of an organ by stating that the primary purpose of removal must not be the medical treatment of the person from whose body it was removed (reg.10(2)). This means that domino transplants are not covered by the s.33 offence.

Transplantable materials only encompass bone marrow and peripheral stem cells where the donor is (i) an adult who lacks capacity or (ii) a child who lacks capacity to consent to the removal (reg.10(3)). Thus, when dealing with a capacitated adult or child, transplantable materials encompasses only organs or parts of organs, so removal of bone marrow from such persons does not require the approval of the HTA.

Where the material does fall within the definition of transplantable material a number of conditions and requirements must be met to avoid committing a criminal offence under s.33.

First, a doctor who has clinical responsibility for the donor must have referred the matter to the HTA (Reg.11(2)).

Second, the HTA must be satisfied that no reward has been given in contravention of s.32 (see further 14.2.1) *and* that the removal was consensual or otherwise lawful. The second part effectively incorporates the requirements of the common law and the Mental Capacity Act into the HTA's decision-making process.

Third, the HTA must have given notice of its decision and, where appropriate, have taken account of the report of interviews with the donor, the person consenting (if different from the donor), and the recipient (regs 11(4)–(10)). The interviews are only required where the removal has not been authorised by a court (reg.11(7)). They are to be conducted by HTA-approved independent assessors (see Code 2, paras 84–85). The reports must cover, among other things, the capacity of the person interviewed to understand the procedure (reg.11(9)(c)). Code 2 also emphasises the common law requirement of good practice that a court declaration be sought before removing an organ from an incapacitated adult or a child (para.82). Since a court declaration would dispense with the need for separately conducted interviews for the purposes of the Regulations, perhaps this explains the Code's insistence that the independent assessor's report should show that he is satisfied that the donor understand the nature of the procedure and the risks and has the capacity to consent (Code 2, para.88). In any event, such donations are expected to be "exceedingly rare" (para.82).

The HTA's decision must be made by a panel of at least three HTA members where:

(a) the donor is a child or an adult who lacks capacity and the material is an organ (reg. 12(2),(3)); or

(b) the donor is an adult with capacity and the case involves (i) paired donations, (ii) pooled donations, or (iii) a non-directed altruistic donation (reg.12(4)).

Cases where an adult consents and the donation is directed to a genetically or emotionally-related recipient are to be regarded as more straightforward and can proceed on the basis of the report of an independent assessor.

"Paired donation" relates to the situation where there are two persons in need of an organ both of whom have a willing donor lined up who is not a tissue match with them but is a tissue match with the other person in need. Imagine, for example, that you are in need of a kidney and your partner wants to donate to you but is not a tissue match. Your partner's kidney could be removed and given to a stranger and you would receive the kidney of a donor close to that stranger.

"Pooled donation" relates to the situation where there is a chain of paired donations, whereby each recipient has a willing donor who is not a tissue match to them. The idea is that the organs are all pooled so that everyone in the pool receives an organ and has a willing donor who donates to someone else in the pool.

"Non-directed altruistic donation" relates to the situation where a person offers to donate an organ to a complete stranger wholly altruistically. The recipient is to be identified in accordance with the procedure that allocates organs from deceased donors (Code 2, para.102).

These three kinds of live donations did not take place in the UK prior to the 2004 Act. To limit the potential for abuse and negative psychological consequences, anonymity between donors and recipients is to be maintained (paras 96 and 99). In the case of paired and pooled donations, the transplants are to occur simultaneously within 6 months of approval by the HTA panel (para.96).

13.4 Conclusion

We have seen that the law addressing transplantation has undergone considerable change over the last few years. Nonetheless, the shortage of human organs continues to cause otherwise preventable death and suffering and the next chapter will address two other responses: paying organ providers and alternatives to the use of human organs.

Chapter 14

TRANSPLANTATION II: PAYMENT, ALTERNATIVES, AND PROPERTY

14.1 Introduction

Few responses to organ failure are as emotive as the notion of paying the poor to provide an organ or using an organ from a non-human animal, such as a pig. This chapter will address the law and ethical controversy behind such responses and an issue that lurks, often unexamined, in the background—the question of whether we have ownership in our bodies or its parts.

14.2 Allowing payment and incentives

It is likely that at least some of those who are reluctant to consent to the donation of transplantable material could be persuaded by the offer of an incentive. The issue of incentives for the provision of organs or tissue is extremely controversial, especially where the incentives in question are financial. Incentives could be offered to prospective organ and tissue providers or their relatives to encourage consent to removal. Where the incentive is to be offered to the prospective provider, it could be offered for removal before or after death. As we shall see in 14.2.1, Parliament has sought to criminalise payment for virtually all types of transplantable material obtained from cadavers *and* living persons. We shall see in 14.2.2, however, that this blanket prohibition is easier to defend by reference to some moral theories than others, and some will support a distinction between payment for cadaveric material and the payment of living tissue and organ providers.

14.2.1 The law

Commercial dealings in human organs were previously addressed by s.1 of the Human Organ Transplantation Act 1989. Those provisions were repealed for England, Wales, and Northern Ireland on October 20, 2005 and replaced by the slightly more extensive provisions of the Human Tissue Act 2004. The 1989 Act was passed at the time of a media outcry over kidneys that were apparently bought for around £3,000 from four Turkish men by a Harley Street kidney specialist.[1] This legislative response was not invited by a regulatory vacuum. The General Medical Council (GMC) already had significant powers to discipline doctors who participate in such commercial dealing (see Ch.2). Indeed, the GMC found the doctors involved in the Turkish kidney dealings guilty of professional misconduct and, more recently in 2002, the GMC has struck of another doctor for allegedly trafficking in human organs.[2] British doctors involved in commercial dealings could, therefore, already lose their livelihood at the hands of the GMC. The 1989 Act, however, was not restricted to doctors and enabled those convicted under its provision to be fined or even imprisoned for *up to three months* (s.1(5)).[3] Under s.32(4) of the 2004 Act, a person who buys or sells an organ can now, on conviction on indictment, be imprisoned for up to *three years*, fined, or both. In 2007, a debt-ridden 26-year-old man who tried to sell his kidney on the internet for £24,000 was convicted under the 2004 Act.[4] He avoided jail, receiving a 12-month suspended jail sentence.

Section 32 of the 2004 Act provides for a number of offences. They all concern activities with "controlled material", which is defined as all human material intended to be used for transplantation with stated exceptions (s.32(8)/(9)). It is, for example, prohibited to make or receive payment for the supply of controlled material and to offer, negotiate, or broker any transaction with controlled material (s.32(1)). The prohibitions do not apply to reimbursement for expenses (incurred in connection with transporting, removing, or storing the material) or loss of earnings (incurred by the person supplying the material) (s.32(7)). There are further exceptions. The Act grants the HTA the discretion to

---

[1] See Parry 1990 and Price 2000, 370.
[2] See Parry 1990 and Allison 2002, respectively.
[3] The possibility of imprisonment only applied to summary conviction under s.1(1).
[4] See BBC 2007.

permit a person to trade in human materials (s.32(3)), thereby enabling the HTA to permit the National Blood Service to purchase blood from abroad. It allows licence-holders (such as commercial tissue banks) to receive payment beyond expenses (s.32(6)). The prohibitions do not apply to gametes, embryos, or "material which has become property by reason of the application of human skill" (s.32(9)).[5] Cell lines created outside of the body are also excluded (s.54(7)).

At first sight the prohibition on voluntary organ sales would appear to be a violation of art.8(1) of the Convention (the right to respect for a private and family life). The Convention does, however, permit proportionate interference with this right on a number of grounds. Article 8(2) permits interference with the right to private and family life where it is in accordance with the law and is necessary for, inter alia, the protection of health or morals, or the protection of the rights and freedoms of others. The legislative prohibition of commercial dealings would undoubtedly be legally justifiable on these grounds.

14.2.2 The ethical issues

Many commentators take the view that it is easier to defend the provision of incentives for posthumous removal than for removal from the living. Lysaght and Mason, for example, assert that the argument against sale of organs is "admittedly stronger" when directed at living donors than cadaveric donors.[6] Similarly, Erin and Harris claim that making an argument "for commerce in the context of organs obtained from cadavers is less morally problematic than in the case of the living".[7] This conclusion is common.[8] It is generally influenced by the fact that someone who permits tissue and organs to be removed while he is alive has more to lose than someone who is dead. The lower burdens facing the dead also mean that it is much easier to support a *positive obligation* to donate posthumously than it is to support a positive obligation to donate while still alive. When alive, removal against one's will is likely to violate the "reasonable burden" (comparable cost) condition mentioned in the last chapter (see 13.2.2). If there is a positive moral duty to permit posthumous removal, then the provision of incentives could be seen as encouraging what one is already required to do. There is evidently little or no need to provide an incentive for consent in a conscription or opt-out system.

Those who accept commercial dealings and private property rights over transplantable material (addressed below, 14.4), face further questions about the type of regulatory system that should be put in place. A popular proposal for a regulatory system applying to commercial dealings in *cadaveric* material involves establishing a "futures market" whereby the right to remove such

---

[5] The human skill exception will be addressed below (14.4.2).
[6] Lysaght and Mason 2000, 255.
[7] Erin and Harris 1994, 135.
[8] See also Blumstein 1993, 25–26 and Cohen 1989, 2.

material upon death would be purchased from the person while alive.[9] A system permitting purchase-in-advance is likely to create tensions between the interests of the seller (who will want to gain maximal use from his tissue and organs while he is alive) and purchaser (who will want to obtain reusable tissue and organs after the seller's death). Such tensions could be reduced by providing incentives only after death. Concerns that any market in transplantable material, whether from living or dead providers, would be dominated by the rich and powerful[10] could be addressed by regulating acquisition and allocation. Erin and Harris, for example, suggest the establishment of a "monopsony" (i.e. a single purchaser for the products of several sellers), which would take responsibility for the equitable distribution of purchased tissue and organs and "prevent rich people using their purchasing power to exploit the market at the expense of the poor".[11] Mason and Laurie suggest that Britain could extend the role of the regulatory authority—previously the Unrelated Live Transplant Regulatory Authority (ULTRA), now the HTA—so that it becomes a purchasing and regulatory body ensuring the protection of relevant rights and interests.[12] The type of regulatory system will be at least partly determined by the ethical justification or rationale for allowing commercial dealings in the first place. If the ethical defensibility of commercial dealings requires the participant's consent, then the regulatory system must be designed to ensure (or maximise the likelihood) that the consent is valid.

14.2.2.1 Paying living providers

We have already seen that paying for the removal of transplantable material from living persons is widely considered to be more controversial than paying for cadaveric transplantable material. Many consider allowing individuals to sell their tissue or organs as a way of reducing the discrepancy between supply and demand. In 1999 when a man from Florida auctioned a kidney on eBay, the price got up to $5.7 million before eBay stepped in and cancelled the auction.[13] Many others might be persuaded to sell their tissue or organs for a financial (or perhaps even a non-financial) incentive. We could imagine, for example, that a middle-aged, relatively well-off man who wishes to obtain enough money to retire early might consider selling a kidney or a young person who wants the money for an expensive holiday or to pay off student debts might consider selling some bone marrow. As the conviction of the debt-ridden 26-year-old in 2007 shows, such examples are not unrealistic. Allowing payment could, however, reduce those who are willing to *donate*, i.e. provide tissue or organs without an incentive.[14] We must, nonetheless, be wary of equating a predicted

---

[9] See e.g. Schwindt and Vining 1986 and 1998; Hansmann 1989, esp. 62–63; and Crespi 1994, esp. 28. See also Cohen 1989, who argues for a system in which payment is made to the deceased's estate when the material is removed.

[10] See e.g. Sells 1992, 2198 (who is focuses on the sale of cadaveric material).

[11] Erin and Harris 1994, 141. See also Erin and Harris 2003.

[12] See Mason and Laurie 2006, 491.

[13] See Bradberry 1999.

[14] See Titmuss 1971; Abouna et al. 1991, 167; Broyer 1991, 199; and Hansmann 1989, 67–68.

reduction in donation with a predicted reduction in the long-term supply of *organs* from the living. It should be noted that there are currently very few living organ donors, those who currently donate would not be able to rely on the market to satisfy all demand, and where there are medical reasons for preferring a related donor to a paid organ provider (such as increased compatibility of the organ or decreased likelihood of disease from the organ) these could be divulged to the relatives to encourage them to donate. In fact, any short-term reduction in living providers would most likely be because of reduced emotional and social pressure to donate—which would not be a bad thing.

Like payment for participation in surrogacy and medical research,[15] payment for organ and tissue removal is extremely controversial. The prohibition of commercial dealings with human organs is widespread.[16] Despite this, all five major groups of moral theories are *potentially* compatible with acceptance of a *regulated, voluntary system* of commercial dealings in human tissue and organs. Systems adopting a blanket prohibition of commercial dealings *or* an entirely unregulated market are much more difficult to defend. It is worthwhile considering the implications of the major positions in some depth. It should be clear that the broad nature of the compromise camp renders it potentially compatible with any regulatory outcome.

Utilitarianism is prima facie predisposed towards allowing some types of commercial dealings in human material, because of the high utility of life-saving tissue and organs for the recipient, the cost savings of transplantation over many other treatment alternatives, the generally high utility of facilitating autonomy, and the likelihood that some form of commercial market from live providers will increase supply. Some utilitarians might, however, take a different view because this general position contains differing theories of value and can lead to different assessments of probable outcome.

Since altruistic motives are more virtuous than purely self-interested motives, theories of *virtue ethics* might be thought to be inherently opposed to the commercialism of human materials. According to Pellegrino, for example, the commercialisation of consent to organ donation is to be rejected because altruism "is a fundamental virtue of good societies and good persons".[17] Not all commercial dealings, however, display an absence of altruism (and not all donations display predominantly other-regarding motives). To take a popular example: a father who sells his kidney to obtain the money for his daughter's medical treatment is acting no less altruistically than one who donates his kidney to treat his daughter's kidney failure.[18] The purchaser might also act altruistically, such as where a mother purchases an organ to save her child's life. The focus of virtue ethics on character and motive is such that very few categories of action can be regarded as immoral per se. Commercialisation does not remove a person's ability to act altruistically—a person who donates without payment in a system in which payment is available has taken the opportunity to act even more altruistically than would

---

[15] See Chs 8 and 11, respectively.
[16] See Pattinson 2003a.
[17] Pellegrino 1991, 1305.
[18] See Radcliffe-Richards 1991, 190–191; Bernat 1995, 187; and Radcliffe-Richards et al. 1998, 1951.

otherwise have been possible. Alternatively, an altruistic person acting within such a system could donate any payment to charity or use the money for other altruistic purposes. Moreover, virtue ethicists do not generally reject the existence of commercial transactions for other life-saving or life-providing goods such as food, water, and shelter. If, however, it is the case that altruism begets altruism— so that the existence of a system prohibiting organ providers from selling their tissue and organs itself increases the altruistic tendencies of society or at least the willingness to donate altruistically—a virtue ethicist might be prima facie in favour of prohibiting organ and tissue sales. A virtue ethicist is not, therefore, straightforwardly committed to prohibiting or permitting commercial dealings. Much will depend on the particular criterion of human flourishing in play and the predicted consequences of allowing persons to sell their organs on the ability to flourish.

We saw earlier that *rights-based theories* reject the idea that a rights-holder can owe direct duties to himself (as all moral duties are said to derive from rights, the benefits of which are waivable). It follows that rights-based theories cannot appeal to the tissue provider's interests to justify preventing him from freely choosing to sell his tissue and organs. Thus, where the organ provider is acting *voluntarily*, rights-based theorists are committed to allowing organ dealings, subject only to such regulatory control as is necessary to ensure this voluntariness and to protect the rights of others. In contrast, *duty-based theories* can impose duties on the tissue provider in that individual's interests. Prohibition of commercial dealings is therefore much easier to defend from a duty-based perspective than from a rights-based perspective.[19]

In sum, aside from rights-based theories and utilitarian theories, at this level of abstraction the major moral theories provide little guidance on the permissibility of allowing persons to sell their tissue and organs. To advance further it is necessary to either adopt one specific moral position from one of these general camps and draw out its precise implications, or argue from premises capable of attracting wide support among these camps. Debate about which moral theory to adopt (and disagreement presupposing opposed theories) can only be addressed at the level of moral epistemology (see further Ch.17). Much of the debate on organ dealings has, however, focused on premises that are relevant to just about all of the camps outlined above.

14.2.2.2 *The contemporary debate on paying living providers*

The principal debate is between those who support a *blanket prohibition* on the payment of tissue providers and those who support a *regulated system* in which tissue providers can be paid.

Those who wish to prohibit payment often question the *voluntariness* of the provider's apparent consent. In response, theorists who wish to reject blanket prohibitions on payment typically tend to rely on two analogies.[20] *First*, it is

---

[19] See Cohen 1999 for an example of such a duty-based position.
[20] See e.g. Wilkinson 2000a, Pattinson 2003a, and Pattinson 2008. These analogies are often also invoked in response to the prohibition of payment for participation in medical research or surrogacy.

argued that people are frequently induced to engage in many menial or risky jobs by the offer of payment. Examples of paid activities that are widely regarded as legitimate include the work of a professional boxer, fire-fighter, soldier, racing car driver, and oil rig worker. This will be called the *risky employment analogy*. Second, it is argued that unpaid participation faces many of the same risks to voluntariness and other values, yet few reject unpaid participation in such activities. This will be called the *unpaid analogy*. This analogy has particular bite because the pressures (particularly emotional pressures) on loved ones to donate without payment can be considerable[21] and the risks to the organ provider operated on in the UK would not turn on whether he is paid or not. Both analogies presuppose acceptance of the view that the allegedly analogous activities are acceptable. Like all arguments by analogy, they also require the activities in question to be morally equivalent, so that there is no defensible moral principle capable of demonstrating a disanalogy.

Those who question the potential tissue provider's voluntariness are often concerned that he will be *exploited* or *coerced*, possibly by family members, middlemen, or moneylenders. There are reports that, where organs have been sold by poor persons,

> The sellers' families, having had access to what that money had bought, sought more—and the kidneys of other family members would be put up for sale.[22]

and

> Moneylenders may also be more aggressive in demanding payment from debtors who live in areas where kidneys are sold to pay off debts.[23]

These reports are largely anecdotal and derive from countries characterised by widespread problems of exploitation and human right abuses. The ethical import of these fears is subject to the analogies just mentioned and the feasibility of alternative regulatory responses less extreme than blanket prohibition. Invoking the *unpaid analogy*, it could be argued that an individual whose mother will die without a kidney is just as vulnerable to family pressure to donate as an individual whose family needs money to survive could be subject to family pressure to sell his organs. Invoking the *risky employment analogy*, it could be argued that there are many menial, dangerous, and, indeed, everyday jobs that few would perform without a financial incentive. The point is that the mere existence of a financial incentive to motivate someone to do something that they would not otherwise have done is not itself exploitative or coercive.[24] An irresistibly attractive offer does not amount to coercion unless the circumstances that make the offer irresistible are illegitimately caused or maintained by those who make the offer. In a sense, the risky employment analogy does not go far enough, because it could be argued that treating the possibility of coercion as a

---

[21] See Kallich and Merz 1995, esp. 145–148.
[22] Nisselle 2002, 74.
[23] Goyal et al. 2002, 1590.
[24] Cf. Sells 1992, 2198.

sufficient justification for blanket prohibitions generally would undermine just about all social institutions and practices. Individuals can be bullied into unwelcome marriages and sexual practices, but few would seek to prohibit marriage and all sexual activity. The upshot is that prohibition must be the most defensible way of addressing issues of potential coercion, *all things considered*. In the context of organ dealings relevant considerations include the effectiveness of feasible alternative regulatory responses, the interests of those who voluntarily wish to sell their organs, and the interests of potential recipients.

The issue of feasible alternatives requires consideration of whether a regulated market could be as effective as blanket prohibition at addressing the issues raised by commercial dealings. Many of these concerns arise from experience of current, unregulated practices in developing countries. Practices in developing countries typically indicate that paltry sums are given to organ providers[25] and there are higher rates of complications, graft rejection, and postoperative dissatisfaction compared to the use of living donors in the developed world.[26] It is likely that poor payment is due to weak bargaining positions or the extraction of value by middlemen. And it is likely that the higher complication and graft rejection rates are a consequence of the black market, unsatisfactory operating facilities, inexperienced surgeons, and poor pre- and post-operative procedures (including the lack of proper compatibility checking, basic information, and counselling facilities). These are aspects of wider, systemic problems in developing countries and should not be assumed to apply to every possible form of regulated market capable of being implemented in the developed world.

The interests of potential recipients underpin two reasons that have been given for prohibiting payment. *First*, it is claimed that altruistic donors provide better quality materials. Titmuss, in his study of the commercialisation of *blood* donations, presents evidence that "commercial markets are much more likely to distribute contaminated blood; the risks for the patient of disease and death are substantially greater",[27] because payment encourages sellers to conceal information and attracts "as donors drug addicts, alcoholics, and carriers of hepatitis, malaria and other diseases".[28] Others have challenged these claims.[29] In any event, the ethical import of such concerns depends on the alternatives available to the potential recipient (who could be facing death without a transplant), whether the potential recipient consents (at least for some moral theories), and the possibility of minimising these risks by less extreme means (e.g. excluding certain categories of provider and undertaking extensive assessment of providers and transplantable material). *Second*, we have already noted that some point to the fact that markets in human materials are easily dominated by the rich and powerful. Since this feared abuse is at the level of acquisition and allocation of the available supply of organs, it is best addressed at those levels. A system of

---

[25] See Sever et al. 1994, 351; Goyal et al. 2002, 1591; Kumar 2003; Sever et al. 2001, 1482; and Abouna et al. 1991, 166.

[26] See Kher 2002, 357; Sever et al. 1994; Sever et al. 2001; and Al-Wakeel 2000.

[27] Titmuss 1970, 246.

[28] Titmuss 1970, 76.

[29] See Price 2000, 400.

commercial dealings need not be a free market system and regulation could limit purchasers, prohibit allocation according to the ability to pay, or both.

The approach taken to fears of exploitation and abuse will be guided by the underpinning moral theory. Autonomy-prioritising theories will, for example, start from a presumption in favour of commercial dealings once systems are put in place to ensure voluntariness. Supporters of such positions often point out that the source is the only one in the transplantation process expected to go without payment.[30] Others, from the transplant surgeon to the provider of immunosuppressant drugs, are routinely (handsomely) paid. The law also seems to be more willing to recognise the property rights of those who manipulate and derive products from human tissue, than of the source of that tissue, as explained (see below, 14.4). Moreover, such theorists often point out that to remove the option of selling one's body parts actually reduces the number of options that one has available. Of course, if selling one's tissue and organs is held to be immoral or a violation of one's dignity *irrespective of its consensual nature or utility*, then the possibility of establishing a regulatory system that would allow commercial dealings while protecting voluntariness is somewhat beside the point.

14.3 Alternatives to existing human organs

Transplanation of human tissue and organs is no panacea for the problems created by failing organs and tissues, because it is hindered by a shortage of transplantable material and by the need for powerful drugs in virtually all recipients. Unfortunately, alternatives to the use of human organs are currently unfeasible or inadequate. The most successful have been artificial organs, but this response has so far had only limited success (14.3.1). Growing tissue and organs in laboratories (known as *tissue engineering*: see 14.3.1) and transplanting animal organs into humans (known as *xenotransplantation*: see 14.3.2) are technologies that are still very much in their infancy, carry significant potential risks, and provoke serious ethical controversy.

Alternatives to using existing human organs are largely viewed as future methods of preventing human life being cut short by organ and tissue failure. The development of these alternatives also raises the prospect that they could be used to extend an individual's lifespan indefinitely or at least until the, apparently irreplaceable, human brain dies.[31] If technologies are developed and applied in this way, they are likely to create a substantial disparity between those who have access to such services and those who do not. Cost will surely prevent universal access. Yet, those who have access to these technologies could have an exponentially longer lifespan than all other humans. The choice of criteria for determining access would be of utmost importance for those wishing

---

[30] See e.g. Lysaght and Mason 2000, 254–255; Pattinson 2003a; and Erin and Harris 2003, 137.
[31] Aspects of the following argument were first presented in Beyleveld and Pattinson 2004a.

to live beyond current biological limitations.[32] The result of unrestricted access for some will be a class of super-humans who will be better placed to dominate society than any other group. Given appropriate circumstances, such individuals (and countries, companies, and other groups possessing such individuals) will have incomparable advantages in relation to accumulated wealth and knowledge. Thus, if biotechnology did render all body parts essentially renewable, those able to gain unrestricted access to such technologies would gain a massive competitive advantage over all other humans (unless, of course, lifespan extension did not involve a corresponding extension of mental youth—fears beautifully personified by the Struldbrugs in Jonathan Swift's *Gulliver's Travels*).[33]

The perpetuation and magnification of social divisions by the creation of a new sub-class would be opposed by many moral theories. Utilitarians are generally opposed to outcomes that elevate one group at the expense of a larger, morally equivalent group and such an outcome would also facilitate conduct that violates rights and duties or displays lack of virtue. There are, however, obstacles to a *feared endpoint argument* to the effect that no individual should be permitted to gain access to replacement therapies that render all body parts essentially renewable.[34] The major obstacle stems from the realisation that indefinitely extended life requires indefinite access to replacement therapies, so the feared endpoint could be prevented by means less extreme than blanket prohibition on any access. Whether such regulatory measures would gain universal support is another matter—if the existence of individuals with super longevity did give rise to the competitive advantages suggested above, then societies would have incentives to grant unrestricted access to some individuals. Those opposed to the creation of a new sub-class must therefore hope that replacement therapies never reach the stage whereby all body parts are rendered renewable. Preventing the development of replacement therapies in the first place is not a realistic hope and, in any event, that would be contrary to the tenets of virtually all moral theories imposing positive duties to save lives. Apocalyptic predictions are faced with a more immediate prediction: unless replacement therapies are developed, many will continue to die of organ and tissue failure.

It is evident that replacement technologies have immense potential for those dying from organ and tissue failure in this and similar countries. These technologies are, however, likely to bring relatively few benefits to poorer countries. The development and utilisation of replacement technologies is expensive. Thus, these technologies bring yet another reminder that the *global inequality* of resources, especially economic resources, is such that the preoccupations of this country are not global preoccupations.

---

[32] This is the problem of resource allocation (addressed in Ch. 2 (2.4.2)) where individual lives are at stake.

[33] In Book Three, Gulliver is first filled with envy at the opportunities bestowed by the super longevity of the Struldbrugs, which quickly turns to pity when he discovers that the reality is one of extended old age, rather than extended youth.

[34] The conditions for a valid feared endpoint argument are discussed in Ch. 1 (1.4.2).

14.3.1 Artificial organs and tissue engineering

14.3.1.1 The technology

Artificial organs and medical devices that replace or supplement the functions of failing tissue have been in use for many decades. Such devices include artificial kidneys (used for dialysis), artificial hearts, heart pacemakers, artificial lungs (ventilators), artificial hips and knees, and cochlear implants. Unfortunately, most artificial organs have not reached the stage where they can be anything other than temporary "bridges" or holding devices until human organs become available or the patient recovers. The artificial kidney, for example, decreases in effectiveness over time and often leaves patients with a relatively poor quality of life.[35] Artificial organs are still a long way from replacing organs that perform complex biochemical functions, such as the liver.

Many vest future hope in *tissue engineering*, sometimes referred to as regenerative medicine. Tissue engineering seeks to develop and produce therapeutic products using a combination of viable human cells and a matrix/scaffold or delivery system.[36] These therapeutic products are intended to act as biological substitutes for failing tissue or organs, or repair, maintain, or enhance the functions of tissue or organs.[37] Tissue engineering thereby represents a future treatment option for those for whom transplantation is currently the preferred option.[38] Scientists are, however, still many years away from being able to create fully tissue-engineered blood vessels or heart valves, let alone bioartificial organs.[39] Some process has been made. Bioengineered skin equivalents are already in use for the treatment of damaged skin (such as burns and ulcers) and many other engineered products are at various stages of development.[40]

The major technical issues raised by tissue engineering concern the cell source, construct fabrication, and the integration of the substitute or repair strategy into patients.[41] Possible *sources of cells* include (embryonic or adult) stem cells and differentiated (tissue specific) cells.[42] These could be obtained from the patient, another human source, or from another species.[43] *Construct fabrication* concerns the engineering of a three-dimensional structure (matrix/scaffold) or delivery vehicle. A suitable scaffold will be one that is biogradable and allows cells to be seeded or recruited. The choice of cell and construct is relevant to the *integration of the product or strategy into a living system* and, eventually, patients. Consider the impact that the choice of cells will have on the potential of a future tissue-engineered product. The patient's immune response will be proportional to the closeness of the cells used to his own. Yet, off-the-shelf availability of tissue-engineered products is much easier to bring

[35] See Rettig 1991, esp. 523; and Anderson 1995, 253 (n.20) and 281.
[36] See MHRA website: *http://devices.mhra.gov.uk*.
[37] See Nerem and Ensley 2004, 36 and Griffith and Naughton 2002, esp. 1009.
[38] See Platt 2004.
[39] See Nerem and Ensley 2004, esp. 41.
[40] See Harding et al. 2002, 162, Lysaght and Hazlehurst 2004, esp. 314–315, and Nerem 2003, 7.
[41] See Nerem and Ensley 2004, 36–37, from which the following paragraph draws.
[42] Stem cells are examined in Ch.10 (10.2.3).
[43] Autologous, allogeneic, and xenogeneic cells, respectively.

about if the cells used are derived from a source other than the patient, such as another human or an animal. Therefore, unless it becomes possible to genetically engineer immune acceptability, the choice of cell source will be pulled in one direction by immunological barriers and in the other by the need for future products to be readily available. Moreover, use of embryonic stems cells (which offer the greatest regenerative potential) or animal cells (which pose fewer availability issues) provokes ethical controversy. These issues are considered in Ch.10 and below (14.3.2), respectively.

14.3.1.2 The regulatory position

The Consumer Protection Act 1987 imposes strict liability for defective products and it has been accepted that "product" includes blood.[44] Those damaged by a defective artificial organ or a tissue-engineered product therefore have a potential action under the 1987 Act. What about the regulatory response before any damage occurs? As a result of various European Directives, a European-wide regulatory distinction is drawn between *medicinal products* (generally pharmaceuticals) and *medical devices*. In the UK, the Medicines and Healthcare products Regulatory Agency (MHRA) is responsible for regulating both. The regulatory scheme that applies generally turns on the principal purpose of the product or the means it uses to achieve that purpose.[45] The principal purpose of a medicinal product is usually achieved by pharmacological, immunological, or metabolic means. In contrast, medical devices usually rely on physical means, such as a mechanical action, physical barrier, or one that replaces or supports organs or body functions.

Artificial organs and related devices are regulated under the Medical Devices Regulations.[46] These define a "medical device" as a product that is intended to be used on humans for diagnostic, preventative, investigative, or treatment purposes, where the principal purpose is not achieved by pharmacological, immunological or metabolic means (reg.2(1)).[47] This captures most devices that replace or supplement the functions of failing tissue or organs, including artificial kidneys and joint replacements. Those whole or partial implants that are powered and intended to remain in the body—such as heart pacemakers—are regulated as "active implantable medical devices" (reg.2(1)).[48] Initially the regulatory scheme applying to medical devices did not apply at all to "transplants or tissues or cells of human origin" or products incorporating or derived from such. The Regulations now make an exception for active implantable medical devices, *in vitro* diagnostic medical devices, and accessories to such devices (reg.3(d), as amended). Most tissue-engineered products, however, continue to fall outside of the Medical Device Regulations.

[44] *A v National Blood Authority* [2001] 3 All E.R. 289.
[45] See European Commission 1998, A2 and Longley and Lawford 2001, 105–107.
[46] Medical Devices Regulations 2002/618, as amended by the Medical Devices (Amendment) Regulations 2007/400. These implement: Council Directive 90/385/EEC (the Active Implantable Medical Devices Directive), Council Directive 93/42/EEC (the Medical Devices Directive), and Directive 98/79/EC (the *In Vitro* Diagnostic Medical Devices Directive).
[47] This implements art.1(2)(a) of Directive 93/42/EEC.
[48] This implements art.1(2)(c) of Directive 90/385/EEC.

In November 2007, the EU passed a Regulation recognising "advanced therapy medicinal products" (ATMPs), which includes tissue engineered products. The ATMPs Regulation 1394/2007 seeks to bridge the regulatory gap whereby some therapeutic products are not regulated as either medicinal products or medical devices. It became applicable on December 30, 2008 (art.30). It is therefore now domestic law, as EU Regulations require no implementing legislation. The MHRA is the Competent Authority for ATMPs. A "tissue engineered product" is one that "contains or consists of engineered cells or tissues" and is presented as having properties for treating humans (art.2(1)(b)). The Regulation applies, in effect, to the *mass production* and *marketing* of tissue-engineered products. It does not cover products that are produced on a one-off ad hoc basis for the treatment of an individual patient in accordance with a specific medical prescription (Recital 6). When ATMPs are derived from human cells or tissues, the donation, procurement, and testing of those cells or tissues have to be made in accordance with the Tissue and Cells Directive (art.3).

The Tissue and Cells Directive and its associated Directives were, in part, implemented by the Human Tissue (Quality and Safety for Human Application) Regulations 2007/1523.[49] These fully came into effect on July 5, 2007. Like the Directive, the Regulations require certain quality and safety standards to be met with regard human tissues and cells intended for transplantation. More specifically, the Quality and Safety Regulations require a licence from the HTA for the procurement, testing, processing, storage, and distribution of human tissues and cells intended for transplantation (reg.7). As a result of the way that "cells", "tissues, and "human application" are defined, the Regulations do not apply to reproductive cells, *in vitro* embryos, organs, blood, or the use of the patient's own cells (reg.5(1)). Reproductive cells and embryos are, however, governed by the Human Fertilisation and Embryology Act 1990, as amended (see Ch.8, esp. 8.3.1.3).

The HTA and MHRA have issued a joint policy statement on the relationship between the ATMPs Regulation and the Quality and Safety Regulations.[50] Products classified as medicinal products or ATMPs are to be regulated under the Quality and Safety Regulations only for the donation, procurement, and testing of tissues and cells. The later stages (such as manufacture, storage, and distribution) are to be regulated by the MHRA. Any difficulties over whether a treatment is an ATMP is to be determined by the MHRA working in conjunction with the European Medicines Agency.

14.3.2 Animal organs (xenotransplantation)

Xenotransplantation, the transplantation of animal organs into humans, is far from being a solution for those suffering from organ failure. There have been no long-term survivors of xenografting, though research has shown that an animal

---

[49] See also the Human Fertilisation and Embryology (Quality and Safety) Regulations 2007/1522, which amended the Human Fertilisation and Embryology Act 1990. The Tissues and Cells Directive (2004/23/EC) is to be read with Directives 2006/17/EC and 2006/86/EC, which lay down the technical requirements in relation to its application.
[50] See HTA and MHRA 2008.

organ can survive and function in a human being.[51] In the most successful xenotransplants to date, a man transplanted with a baboon's liver survived for 70 days and a patient transplanted with a chimpanzee's kidneys survived for almost nine months.[52] The most famous attempt involved the transplantation of a baboon's heart into a 12-day-old baby, "Baby Fae", who survived for only 20 days.[53] The major technical obstacle is that the recipient's immune system attacks foreign material and the severity of the immune response is related to the biological distance between the source and the host.[54] In terms of immune response, primate organs are better than organs from other non-human animals, but (partly because of that closeness to us) the use of primates is ethically controversial. Non-human primates also pose practical difficulties: many are endangered or are too small to provide suitably sized organs.[55] Recent research efforts have therefore been directed at using pig organs, which are approximately the right size for adult humans and are readily available. At present this research is restricted to transplanting pig organs into other animals, including non-human primates. To address the immune response, research is being conducted on immunosuppressant drugs and genetically engineering the pig source. Huge technical barriers remain at present.[56]

The focus here is on transplanting animal *organs* into humans, but much of this discussion applies equally to the xenografting of live animal tissues.

14.3.2.1 Ethical issues

A major concern raised by xenotransplantation is that it might cause new infectious agents (such as viruses) to cross the species barrier. It is feared that a virus from an infected animal organ transplanted into an immunosuppressed human could mutate and infect the host. Even harmless animal viruses—such as the porcine endogenous retroviruses (PERVS) that are carried in every pig cell—could mutate into a deadly human virus.[57] Variant Creutzfeldt-Jakob Disease (vCJD), the human form of bovine spongiform encephalitis (BSE) or "mad cow disease", is a vivid example of an animal virus that has crossed the species barrier with deadly consequences.[58] This terrible disease causes progressive mental deterioration similar to that associated with Alzheimer's disease, has an incubation period of decades, and is fatal. While the recipient of the animal organ might be willing to run the risk of contracting a mutated animal virus, on the basis that the organ will save his life, the introduction of such a virus could have a devastating epidemic effect on the population as a whole. The risk of virus transfer can be reduced, but it is unlikely that science will develop to the point where it could be eliminated. Xenotransplantation will therefore require an ethical judgment as to whether the risk that scientists predict is one that it is

---

[51] See Deschamps et al. 2005, esp. 104, and Cooper et al. 2002, esp. 135–136.
[52] See Starzl 1993 and Deschamps et al. 2005, 104, respectively.
[53] See Deschamps et al. 2005, 99 and 104.
[54] See Cartwright 1996, 251.
[55] See Cooper et al. 2002, 136.
[56] See Cooper et al. 2002.
[57] See Cooper et al. 2002, 142–143.
[58] Rabies is a more commonplace example of virus that can infect humans and other animals.

acceptable to run. There are additional ethical difficulties, to which we will return, attached to many methods of tracking or containing this risk.

Another ethical concern focuses on the moral interests of the animals used as sources or hosts of transplanted organs. These animals will be genetically modified, reared in sterile conditions (in isolation from other animals), and killed for human benefit. One response to ethical concerns about the treatment of animals is to draw an analogy with food production. A Working Party of the Nuffield Council on Bioethics concluded that the use of pigs for the supply of organs for xenotransplantation was acceptable, on the basis that:

> It is difficult to see how, in a society in which the breeding of pigs for food and clothing is accepted, their use for life-saving medical procedures such as xenotransplantation could be unacceptable.[59]

The analogy, however, only applies to some animals (we experiment on non-human primates but do not eat them), requires the types of harm involved to be equivalent,[60] and assumes that current food production is ethically acceptable. The moral debate on the latter issue largely stems from different views on the moral status of non-human animals. Some modern theorists argue that animals should be granted a status that is more or less equivalent to humans, notably Peter Singer and Tom Regan. Peter Singer adopts a form of preference utilitarianism, holding that moral status depends on having interests, and attributes possession of such interests to both humans and animals.[61] In contrast, Tom Regan adopts a duty-based position, holding that equal moral status belongs to all those who are "subjects-of-a-life", including all cognitively normal human and non-human mammalian animals over one-year-old.[62] At the other extreme to Singer and Regan are theorists who hold that animals have no moral status and only deserve protection by virtue of their relationship to those who do have moral status. One example is the rights-based theory of Peter Carruthers, according to which moral status belongs only to those who are able to enter into a hypothetical social contract to protect their interests and this ability is said to be lacked by most animals.[63] There are therefore multiple answers to the question of whether, and to what extent, animals matter morally. The relative weight of the moral interests of animals compared to those of humans depends on three variables: (1) the criterion for possession of moral status, (2) the view taken on what beings in the empirical world satisfy the relevant criterion, and (3) the criteria used for weighing conflicting interests. The choice of moral theory is important for all three aspects.[64]

---

[59] Nuffield Council on Bioethics 1996, para.4.42. In contrast, the Report of the Advisory Group on the Ethics of Xenotransplantation considered that "the analogy between eating animals and using them for transplantation is misleading": DH 1997, para.4.10.

[60] Fox and McHale (1998, 49–50) argue that the Report underplays the harm inflicted on animals used for xenotransplantation research. The suffering inflicted on animals by industrial farming, especially for veal and foie gras, make me doubt whether those wishing to draw an analogy with food production need to underplay the harm of xenotransplantation experiments.

[61] See Singer 1995.

[62] See Regan 1988, esp. 77–78 and 243. Regan uses the language of rights, but does not adopt a rights-based theory as defined in this book.

[63] See Carruthers 1992.

[64] On moral status see Ch.7 (7.2.1); on interaction with the empirical world see Chs 7 (7.2.1.2) and 17 (17.3 and 17.3.2.2); and on the criteria for conflicting interests see Chs 1 (1.3.2) and 17 (17.3).

In regulatory terms, the degree of ethical controversy provoked by the use of animals for the purposes of xenotransplantation raises a compelling case for permitting health professionals to *conscientiously object* to participation. An analogy can be drawn with abortion and assisted reproduction where the existing legislation contains conscientious objection clauses.[65] Excusing conscientious objectors poses few difficulties while xenotransplantation remains experimental, but this will change if xenotransplantation becomes a commonplace treatment of last resort for those suffering from organ failure. The abortion legislation does not excuse a conscientious objector from participating in an abortion where it is "necessary" to save the life of the woman or to prevent grave permanent injury to her health.[66] The abortion analogy can therefore only take us so far. The ethical issues raised by a provision for conscientious objection are complex and raise the very issues that make xenotransplantation controversial in the first place. Moreover, any decision made by Parliament, in the exercise of its powers as a democratically elected body, will have procedural ethical force for all moral theories supporting democratic decision-making.

Additional ethical concerns focus on the human recipient of an animal organ. Xenotransplantation is an experimental technology with uncertain risks. If those risks are to be understood and minimised, the human hosts of xenografts will need to be monitored and subject to restrictions. Possibilities include monitoring family members and sexual partners, and making the performance of an autopsy compulsory. If infection were to occur, protecting others might even require the host to be quarantined. Post-transplantation surveillance and restrictions would make xenografting an unusual procedure. On the one hand, insofar as the principal purpose of xenotransplantation would be to benefit the host (who would otherwise be expected to die from organ failure), it could be viewed as a form of experimental treatment. On the other hand, insofar as activities and procedures are imposed for reasons other than the interests of the human host, xenografting to a human could be viewed as medical research. Its classification is not the important issue, except for the regulatory responses that follow. In the UK, participants in medical research are granted far more regulatory protection than patients receiving medical treatment (see Ch.11). Consequently, the classification of xenotransplantation, for legal purposes, could be of key ethical importance. Unlike most other experimental procedures, xenotransplantation carries risks for non-participants from whom individual consent cannot be obtained in practice.

14.3.2.2 The regulatory position

Xenotransplantation requires compliance with the laws regulating the use of animals and those regulating transplantation of animal organs into a human recipient. As indicated by its title, the Human Tissue Act 2004 does not apply to the transplantation of animal organs.

---

[65] See Chs 7 (7.4.4) and 8 (8.3), respectively.
[66] Abortion Act 1967 s.4(2).

The use of animals is regulated by the Animals (Scientific Procedures) Act 1986. This imposes licensing requirements on experimental or scientific procedures applied to "protected animals" that might cause the animal "pain, suffering, distress, or lasting harm" (s.2(1)). Protected animals are defined as "any living vertebrate, other than man" and such others as specified by Regulations (s.1(1), (3)). Xenotransplantation and its concomitant research clearly fall within the ambit of this regulatory framework. An applicant must therefore persuade the licensing committee (acting on behalf of the Secretary of State) that the likely adverse effects on the animal are outweighed by the likely benefits of the research (s.5(4)). This appears to require the application of a utilitarian calculus, but the Act does not actually specify how the relevant variables are to be weighed against each other.

Xenografting to a human has been specifically addressed by reports from the Nuffield Council on Bioethics and the Advisory Group on the Ethics of Xenotransplantation set up by the Department of Health.[67] These Reports reached similar conclusions.[68] Both considered the risk of cross-species virus transfer to be under-researched and thought that xenotransplantation would be acceptable once such safety issues had been addressed. In 1997, in response to these recommendations, the Government established the Xenotransplantation Interim Regulatory Authority (UKXIRA). No xenotransplantation trials took place in the UK during the period that UKXIRA existed and this body continued to classify such procedures as research.[69] It was disbanded on December 12, 2006 and replacement guidance was issued by the Department of Health.[70] This guidance applies to procedures taking place within the NHS, which must have the approval of a research ethics committee.[71] Xenotransplantation is defined widely to cover the transplantation or infusion into a human of live tissues or organs from animals or of human material that has undergone *ex vivo* contact with living non-human animal material.[72] It follows that pig and cow heart valves that are currently implanted into humans do not fall within the guidance because they are treated before implantation so as to kill their cells (though they would fall within the Medical Device Regulations).

Does xenotransplantation fall within the Medicines for Human Use (Clinical Trials) Regulations 2004/1031, as amended? Procedures covered by these Regulations are required to be approved by the MHRA and receive a favourable opinion from a recognised research ethics committee (REC) (reg.12(3)).[73] These Regulations apply to clinical trials of medicinal products (including xenogeneic medicinal products). Special authorisation procedures apply to medicinal products for gene therapy and somatic cell therapy (including "xenogenic cell therapy": reg.19(1)); and medicinal products with "special characteristics" (defined to include products with an "active ingredient" that derives from a

---

[67] See Nuffield Council on Bioethics 1996 and DH 1997.
[68] See the Nuffield Report (Nuffield Council on Bioethics 1996, esp. viii–x), discussed in Cartwright 199, and the Report of the Advisory Group (see DH 1997, esp. x–xxii), discussed in Fox and McHale 1998.
[69] See UKXIRA 1998, paras 2.6 and 5.3, and DH 2006d, 1.
[70] See DH 2006d.
[71] See DH 2006d, para.3.2.
[72] See DH 2006d, 1. This definition derives from Directive 2003/63/E, Pt IV.
[73] The Clinical Trials Regulations are considered in Ch.11 (see 11.4.2 onwards).

biological product of animal origin: reg.20(1)(ii)).[74] Xenotransplantation trials clearly come within the Regulations if they involve the use of a new pharmaceutical product, gene therapy/somatic cell therapy product, or medicinal product with special characteristics.

Elsewhere, I (with others) have questioned whether whole organs transplanted from animals or humans into humans will ordinarily be considered to be medicinal products.[75] The definition of "medicinal products" (in reg.2) refers to art.1 of Directive 2001/83/EC, which uses identical wording to EC Directive 65/65.[76] While a wide definition, it has not been treated as capturing all experimental human-to-human transplantation and doubts have long been expressed about whether it captures xenotransplantation.[77] Xenotransplantation is now explicitly addressed by Directive 2001/83/EC, which amends Directive 2003/63/E. Part IV of Annex I of that Directive applies to "advanced therapy medicinal products", which include "xeno-transplantation medicinal products".[78] The relevant definitions do not, however, appear to treat removed (human or animal) organs, tissues or cells that are not manipulated after removal as medicinal products merely because they are implanted into a human body.[79] Indeed, the European Commission document on clinical trials provides an algorithm, entitled "Is it a Clinical Trial of a Medicinal Product?", in which trials administering only "tissues except a somatic cell therapy medicinal product" are said not to be clinical trials on medicinal products.[80] This is just one of the regulatory gaps into which xenotransplantation trials could now fall.[81]

14.4 Property in human organs and tissue

In the seventeenth century, John Locke declared that "every man has a property in his own person".[82] Yet, the idea that we have a proprietary relationship with our body or parts of our body remains controversial in both ethics (14.4.1) and

---

[74] Additionally, the stringent time limits (usually 60 days) within which REC are generally required to give their opinions do not apply to clinical trial involving a medicinal product for xenogenic cell therapy (reg.15(4)).

[75] See Beyleveld, Finnegan, and Pattinson 2009. For a different view, see Fovargue 2007, 209.

[76] To paraphrase, medicinal products are substances or combinations of substances that either prevent or treat disease in human beings or are administered to human beings with a view to making a medical diagnosis or to restore, correct or modify physiological functions in humans (art.1(1)).

[77] See the discussion in Williamson, Fox, and McLean 2007, esp. 447–448.

[78] This states: "Advanced therapy medicinal products are based on manufacturing processes focussed on various gene transfer produced bio-molecules, and/or biologically advanced therapeutic modified cells as active substances or part of active substances." See also Recital 9 and note that the definition in Annex I, Part IV, para.4 of "xeno-transplantation" is not a definition of "xeno-transplantation medicinal product".

[79] See further Beyleveld, Finnegan, and Pattinson 2009.

[80] See European Commission 2006. This document is referred to by the Department of Health (2006d, 3) guidance and the MHRA website.

[81] See further Williamson, Fox, and McLean 2007.

[82] Locke 1689, section 27.

law (14.4.2).[83] Theorists disagree about what it actually means to have property in or over something and the scarcity of case law leaves the legal position somewhat uncertain.

14.4.1 Conceptions of property

There is no single conception of property. The only thing that seems to be generally agreed is that property is, in some sense, about ownership and control. For an entity to be my property I must stand in a relationship of ownership to it, whereby I have legitimate claims, powers, and interests relating to it, i.e. property rights. Beyond this, property seems to mean different things to different people. Those who try to ground the notion in usage of the word "property" by lawyers tend to treat property as the collection of rights that capitalist legal systems grant to individuals over land and other chattels, such as prima facie rights to use, exclude others from use, and transfer such rights to others.[84] Whether something is property then becomes a question about whether the rights that attach to it are sufficiently like those that attach to paradigmatic instances of property. Unfortunately, this approach becomes circular when the reason for asking whether something is property is to determine whether certain rights attach to it: "property does not exist unless certain rights normally attach to it; but it may not be possible to determine whether those rights are attached to that subject-matter without first determining whether the subject-matter is property"![85] Definitions are not justifications; they are means of formulating normative questions rather than answering them. Whether organs and tissues are property is a matter of controversy precisely because there is profound disagreement about what legitimate claims, powers, and interests individuals have over the organs and tissue that they were born with. Much of this controversy stems from concern that self-ownership of one's body and body parts (tissues and organs) will have implications for whether consent is required for uses of body parts once they have been removed (or whether the source is entitled to compensation), whether body parts can be sold or traded, and whether subsequent possessors of body parts can obtain property rights in them.

As Beyleveld and Brownsword point out, the broader the definition of property used, the easier it will be to justify the claim that something is property.[86] They present a narrow conception of property that they suggest captures the essence of what capitalist societies traditionally view as private property.[87] According to this conception, property grants *"rule preclusionary"* control to individuals, consisting of prima facie rights to use and exclude others from access or use of what one owns, which *preclude* the owner from having to provide a

---

[83] It has even been argued that Locke in the quotation above was not asserting ownership in the physical body: see Dickenson and Widdershoven 2001, 114.
[84] See e.g. the "bundle of rights" conception used by Resnik (2002, 133).
[85] Dworkin and Kennedy 1993, 293.
[86] See Beyleveld and Brownsword 2001, esp. 174.
[87] See Beyleveld and Brownsword 2000, 94–96 and 2001, ch.8.

specific justification for everything he does with what he owns. Once the claim that something is my property is justified (on the basis of the object's importance to my legitimate interests), then, as a rule, it is to be presumed that I can use it and exclude others from using it without needing to provide a specific justification. Thus, ownership (once established) determines where the burden of proof lies when establishing who has legitimate control over an entity. It should be clear that ownership of body parts under the rule-preclusionary conception has implications with regard to the owner's consent and his power to sell or transfer. Rule-preclusionary control implies a presumption requiring the owner's consent for use by others and places the justificatory burden on those who wish to restrict the owner selling or transferring his property.

Rule-preclusionary control actually appears to underlie a number of legal instruments. In Ch.8, for example, we saw that the Human Fertilisation and Embryology Act 1990 requires the consent of the gamete provider(s) for the storage or use of gametes and embryos, so that the withdrawal of consent before use requires that they be allowed to perish.[88] The gamete provider *need not provide any specific justification* for withdrawing his consent and insisting on the destruction of the gametes or embryo produced by them. The 1990 Act thereby grants negative property (rule-preclusionary) rights to gamete providers. Since property under this conception does not imply absolute control over one's property, it is not fatal that gamete providers face restrictions on their freedom to commercially exploit the value of their gametes and embryos.[89] (For the same reason, this conception of property is consistent with the idea that there can be property in land despite the existence of planning laws, tree conservation orders, and formalities for conveyance, and property in guns despite limitations on their sale, purchase, and use.) Thus, the 1990 Act presupposes property in reproductive material. Indeed, in February 2009, the Court of Appeal adopted similar reasoning to this when it held that sperm stored in accordance with the provisions of the 1990 Act could be property for the purposes of the law of tort and bailment.[90]

Beyleveld and Brownsword argue that property (rule-preclusionary) rights in body parts are implied by Art.22 of Biomedicine Convention.[91] This provision holds that,

> When in the course of an intervention any part of a human body is removed, it may be stored and used for a purpose other than that for which it was removed, only if this is done in conformity with appropriate information and consent procedures.

The requirement that specific consent be obtained for use of excised body parts without the source of the body part needing to present a specific justification (based on, say, his religious beliefs or what was agreed before the body was removed) implies rule-preclusionary control. Beyleveld and Brownsword present art.22 as one of three justifications for the claim that we have rule-preclusionary

[88] See Ch.8 (8.3.3.2) and *Evans v Amicus Healthcare* [2004] EWCA Civ 727.
[89] See Ch.8 (8.4.1.2) on the current limitation on payment: £15 plus reasonable expenses.
[90] *Yearworth v North Bristol NHS Trust* [2009] EWCA Civ 37.
[91] See Beyleveld and Brownsword 2000, 89–93 and 2001, 179–181.

rights over body parts.[92] Their second claim is that *if* I am justified in claiming property (rule-preclusionary) rights over anything, then I must have such rights over my living body and its attached body parts. Or, to put the point the other way round, if I cannot claim rule-preclusionary rights over my living body and its parts, then I cannot own anything in this sense. This argument turns on an implicit premise: my living body (including its parts) is the strongest candidate for an entity that is so important to my legitimate interests that I should be given prima facie rights to do what I want with it without a specific justification for my every purpose. Their argument does not, of course, establish that we do have any rule-preclusionary rights at all. To establish this requires a theory-specific argument, which they present as their third argument (premised on the rights-based moral theory of Alan Gewirth).

Other theorists also claim that we have property in body parts. Robert Nozick takes it to be axiomatic that we own what we start with, i.e. we own ourselves in the sense of our natural assets and body parts.[93] According to Nozick, rights to own parts of our bodies are a paradigmatic instance of property and individuals have a right to control their bodies.[94] He takes property rights to be foundational and builds on Locke's theory for the acquisition of further property rights:

> Whoever makes something, having bought or contracted for all other held resources used in the process (transferring some of his holdings for these cooperating factors), is entitled to it.[95]

Nozick's theory has been heavily criticised. The feminist Susan Moller Okin (who also adopts a rights-based position) has objected to the assumption that each person owns himself and argues that the Lockean-Nozickean theory of acquisition implies that a mother owns her children, since she has made them.[96] This, she argues, means that Nozick's theory leaves individuals "in a condition of matriarchy, slavery, and dystopia".[97] Nozick needs to add further qualifications to his theory if he is to avoid that conclusion. Jim Harris has criticised the Lockean-Nozickean theory as based on a "spectacular *non sequitur*":

> From the fact that nobody owns me if I am not a slave, it simply does not follow that I must own myself. Nobody at all owns me, not even me.[98]

Nozick needs to provide a reason why I own myself that does not depend on the very intuitions and assertions that critics wish to question. Indeed, moral

---

[92] See Beyleveld and Brownsword 2001, 179–186.
[93] "Whether or not people's natural assets are arbitrary from a moral point of view they are entitled to them, and to what flows from them": Nozick 1974, 226.
[94] See Nozick 1974, 206 and 273, respectively.
[95] Nozick 1974, 160.
[96] Okin 1989, ch.4. Nozick himself raises this very question, rejects Locke's responses, and suggests (but does not pursue) two possible solutions: see Nozick 1974, 287–289. Okin persuasively argues that the two possible solutions suggested by Nozick are incompatible with this own theory.
[97] Okin 1989, 80.
[98] See Harris 1996, 71. See also Harris 1996, 68–69 and 71–73.

disputes about whether or not we have property at all easily become disputes over the choice of underlying moral theory (on which see Ch.17).

14.4.2 The law

It has long been a maxim of the common law that there is no property in a dead body or its parts. This maxim probably has its origins in Sir Edward Cokes' *Institutes* and the work of other early common law scholars.[99] Early judicial decisions seem to have been misinterpreted or otherwise lack authority—one case held that a dead body could not *own* property, rather than a dead body could not *be* property, and another was not a decision on point, if it was decided at all.[100] There appears to have been no coherent rationale for the no property rule to have developed in the way that it did.[101] Despite its dubious origins, the no property rule was subsequently confirmed by the Court of Appeal in *Dobson v North Tyneside HA* and *R. v Kelly*.[102]

In *Dobson*, the Court of Appeal rejected the claim that the next-of-kin of a deceased man had property rights in his body and tissue following an autopsy. The claim arose because the family wished to use the brain tissue as evidence in litigation. They discovered that, although the brain tissue had been preserved in paraffin for the autopsy, it had not been kept, and so brought an action against the hospital for failing to keep it. The claim failed.

In *Kelly*, the Court of Appeal upheld the defendant's conviction for the theft of body parts from the Royal College of Surgeons. Following *Dobson* and dicta from an old Australian case, the court applied an exception to the no property rule.[103] According to that exception, a corpse (or body part) can be property if it has "acquired different attributes by virtue of the application of skill, such as dissection or preservation techniques, for exhibition or teaching purposes".[104] Under this exception, property rights appear to be acquired by the application of work and skill with an appropriate intention. The intention appears to be key. In *Dobson*, Gibson L.J. opined that the brain had only been preserved in paraffin to comply with the Coroners Rules and the hospital had had no

---

[99] See Matthews 1983, 197–198; Skegg 1992, 311; Grubb 1998b, 307; and Mason and Laurie 2001, 713.

[100] *Williams Hayne's case* (1614) and *Exelby v Handyside* (1749), respectively, as discussed in Matthews 1983, 197–198 and 208–210. The first case where the no property rule was actually used in support of the decision itself is *Williams v Williams* (1882) 20 Ch.D. 659, but see Matthews 1983, 210–212 for doubt about whether it was really part of the ratio.

[101] Skegg (1992, 314) notes that the rule might have developed, or at least become established, because *buried* corpses were often protected by ecclesiastical law. If so, this was not a good reason for denying property to *unburied* corpses. Ecclesiastical law has declined in importance since the seventeenth century and the vast majority of corpses are now cremated. Moreover, a rationale based on the special status of corpses would not make sense as the no property rule deprives corpses and their parts of the protection applying to property (such as the protection of the law of theft).

[102] [1997] 1 W.L.R. 596 and [1999] Q.B. 621, respectively.

[103] *Dobson v North Tyneside HA* [1997] 1 W.L.R. 596 at 601–601 (Gibson L.J.) and *Doodeward v Spence* (1908) 6 C.L.R. 406, respectively.

[104] [1999] Q.B. 621 at 631 (Rose L.J.).

intention of retaining it for any other purpose.[105] The preservation was said not to have been analogous to a stuffing, embalming, or otherwise preserving a specimen for the purpose of teaching or exhibition. In contrast, the body parts in *Kelly* had been preserved as specimens *for the purpose of retaining* for uses relating to teaching and exhibition, and were therefore regarded as property. Interpreted in this way, these cases can be reconciled but many questions were left unanswered.[106]

The "work-skill" principle of property acquisition used in *Dobson* and *Kelly* is similar to that used by Locke and Nozick. According to these approaches, property rights are acquired by the application of work and skill to legitimately acquired resources. There is, however, a significant difference in the context to which the principle is applied. In the case law, the application of work and skill is used as a reason for making an exception to the rule that we have no property in dead bodies or their parts. In contrast, Nozick uses the application of work and skill intention as a reason for *extending* the property rights that we are said to already have in our living bodies.

In *Kelly*, Rose L.J. went on to declare that

> the common law does not stand still. It may be that if, on some future occasion, the question arises, the courts will hold that human body parts are capable of being property for the purposes of section 4 [of the Theft Act 1968], even without the acquisition of different attributes, if they have a use or significance beyond their mere existence. This may be so if, for example, they are intended for use in an organ transplant operation, for the extraction of DNA or, for that matter, as an exhibit in a trial.[107]

In addition to this obiter *dictum*, the *Dobson-Kelly* approach does not deny that there are rights to possess a dead body prior to its burial or cremation.[108] Also, neither case was concerned with *tissues derived from living persons*. On this there are earlier cases in which the Court of Appeal seems to have assumed that urine and blood samples were property capable of being stolen when they had been taken from the lawful possession of the police by the person from whom they came.[109] The point was not argued in either case. In an even earlier case before a magistrates' court, a man who cut a few locks of hair from the back of a girl's head without her consent was convicted of assault *and larceny*.[110] These decisions fit uneasily with *Dobson* and *Kelly*. One approach to these cases would be to consider the issue of property interests over tissue removed from a living person still open, which would simply leaves the issue for future decisions. Another approach, restricting these cases to their facts, would deprive the law of any coherent rationale. A third approach, already suggested, is to interpret

[105] [1997] 1 W.L.R. 596 at 602.
[106] See e.g. Grubb 1998b, 310–312.
[107] [1999] Q.B. 621 at 631.
[108] [1997] 1 W.L.R. 596 at 601, and *Williams v Williams* (1882) 20 Ch.D. 659.
[109] *R. v Welsh* [1974] R.T.R. 478 (concerned a urine sample and the defendant did not appeal the issue of theft) and *R. v Rothery* (1976) 63 Cr. App. R. 231 (concerned a blood sample and the defendant had pleaded guilty to theft and did not appeal that issue).
[110] *R. v Herbert* (1961) JCL 163.

these decisions by reference to whether the source is alive when the tissue (including organs and fluids) is removed. These cases concern tissue removed from living persons, whereas *Dobson* and *Kelly* concerned tissue removed from dead persons. This approach would enable the English courts to take a different approach to the *Moore* case, which will be examined below. A fourth possibility is to interpret these decisions by reference to the common features of the material in question. Hair, blood, and urine are constantly renewed (i.e. they are regenerative), can be removed with minimal harm, and are usually discarded. This approach would enable nail clippings, ear wax, saliva, and sperm to be property even if they have not been the subject of work and skill. It would not recognise property in an excised appendix (usually discarded, but not regenerative) or a liver lobe (regenerative but its removal when not diseased carries significant risks).

In a high-profile American case, John Moore was expressly denied a remedy based in his property rights in his tissues.[111] He had brought a claim on a number of grounds (including conversion) after discovering that the doctor treating him for spleen cancer had, with some other researchers, developed and patented a cell-line from his cells. Moore had only consented to the removal of his tissue and cells for the purposes of his treatment. The Supreme Court of California rejected Moore's claim to property in his cells, holding (inter alia) that granting property rights to Moore would "hinder research by restricting access to the necessary raw materials".[112] Moore was, nonetheless, able to settle his claim out-of-court as the court also ruled that he had a potential action on other grounds, namely, breach of fiduciary duty and lack of informed consent. These alternative grounds are not as well developed in English law, as the English courts have set themselves against recognising the fiduciary character of the doctor–patient relationship *as such* and take the position of a reasonable doctor as the starting point for duties of disclosure in negligence.[113] The extreme nature of the facts and the apparent justice of Moore's claim are such that it is difficult to believe that the English courts would have denied a remedy to Moore.[114] In the absence of binding case law or legislation to the contrary, the conversion-property approach might have fared better before the English courts. Certainly, the fears of one of the judges that recognising and enforcing a property interest in body tissues could lead to the source being able to commercialise his tissues,[115] are answered by the legislative prohibition on commercial dealings considered earlier.

The removal of tissue from a living person without his consent will involve interference with his physical integrity and constitute a battery, but what protectable interests does the source have once it has been removed with his consent? Denying property rights to the source of excised tissue seems to deprive him of grounds for controlling subsequent use. This would mean that the source

---

[111] *Moore v Regents of the University Of California* (1990) 51 Cal. 3d 120. See also *Greenberg v Miami Children's Hospital Research Institute* (2003) 264 F. Supp. 2d 1064, discussed in Ch.12 (12.5.1.2).

[112] 51 Cal. 3d 120, 144 (Panelli J.).

[113] See the discussion of fiduciary duties and the standard of care for disclosure of information in Ch.4 (4.4.1–4.4.2).

[114] See further Dworkin and Kennedy 1993, 311–314.

[115] 51 Cal. 3d 120 at 149 (Arabian J.).

is denied rights over his tissue that others appear to be able to obtain by applying work and skill to it.[116] Imagine if John Moore had been told of the commercial interest in his cells before they were removed and passionately objected to others making a profit from his cells. Without property rights (whether or not recognised by name), his choice is to consent to the removal with the knowledge that commercial exploitation will take place, refuse the removal in the knowledge that he thereby accepts death by terminal cancer, or find another surgeon who will agree not to commercialise his tissue. If the last option is not available, his choice is between death and his values. Recognising the source as having a prima facie right to property would at least enable him to protect his values where the competing interests were not sufficiently compelling. We have already seen that the idea of property rights in tissue derived from a living patient need not be antagonistic to common law principles. The Human Tissue Act 2004 has a number of direct and indirect consequences.

The 2004 Act adopts a rather odd position towards ownership in human tissues. On the one hand, like the Human Fertilisation and Embryology Act 1990, it recognises some form of rule-preclusionary control (through the "appropriate consent" requirement). On the other hand, the Act largely eschews the language of property. The one time that the Act does refer to property in body parts, it offers support for the work-skill exception to the no property rule. As we have seen, the offence relating to commercial dealings in bodily material intended for transplantation, excludes material "which is the *subject of property because of an application of human skill*" (s.32(9)(c), my emphasis). This provision clearly provides statutory support for the claim that human material can be property where human skill has been applied to it (i.e. the *Dobson-Kelly* position). Material that is property *by virtue of the application of human skill* is excluded from the offence relating to commercial dealings. Expressed in this way, the Act need not be taken to prevent human material being property *by virtue* of some other reason; it merely does not exclude human material that is property for other reasons from the prohibition on commercial dealings. The 2004 Act is therefore not inconsistent with the view that the source can have property in the parts or products of his living body. This view, expressed in the first edition of the book, has been objected to by Herring and Chau on the basis that "it is hard to conceive of a reason" why the exception would single out property acquired by the application of skill from property acquired in some other way.[117] I am here, however, discussing property in human material *belonging to the source acquired as a result of ownership of his own body*. The s.32 prohibition could not make an exception for property rights acquired in this way *if* the source is to be prohibited from selling his material for transplantation.

In February 2009, the view that s.32(9)(c) is not inconsistent with property rights being granted by the common law to bodily parts or products on a broader basis than the application of work and skill was accepted by the Court

---

[116] Broussard J., partially dissenting in *Moore*, noted that it was only the patient who was been deprived of ownership interests: 51 Cal. 3d 120 at 153–154.

[117] Herring and Chau 2007, 39.

of Appeal.[118] *Yearworth v North Bristol NHS Trust*, a case that was briefly considered above, concerned the claims of a group of men whose sperm had been destroyed by being negligently allowed to thaw. The Court of Appeal noted that it could treat the storage of sperm as property within the work and skill exception to the no property rule, which would be entirely consistent with the approach in *Kelly*.[119] It chose not to do so. Instead, the Court rested its decision on a broader basis. It ruled that the men had ownership in their sperm, for the purposes of their claims in negligence, on the basis that it had been generated by their bodies alone and the "sole object of the ejaculation of the sperm was that, in certain events, it might later be used for their benefit".[120] Thus, the common law has developed, as anticipated in *Kelly*.

In reference to the above discussion of the *Moore* case, however, it should be noted that the storage and use of tissue for research after it has been obtained from a living patient is directly addressed by the 2004 Act. The Act requires appropriate consent, but an exception is made by s.1(7). This provision, read in conjunction with s.1(9), removes the need for consent for "the storage of relevant material for use for the purpose of research in connection with disorders, or the functioning, of the human body" where the research project has ethical approval and the researcher cannot identify the tissue source. In these circumstances, no consent is required for the use of tissue removed from living patients that is left over from diagnostic or surgical procedures.[121] Indeed, as Price points out, under the Act it is not even necessary for a patient's refusal to be recorded![122] Rule-preclusionary control is therefore not granted against the interests supporting medical research.

14.5 Conclusion

We saw in the last chapter that the shortage of human organs is causing otherwise preventable death and suffering. A number of methods capable of addressing this shortfall have been examined in this chapter. Many of these (such as, in particular, the development and utilisation of replacement technologies) are only feasible solutions for rich countries like the UK. Countries in which large numbers regularly die from poverty and associated conditions (such as starvation and easily preventable disease) have more pressing priorities. India, for example, lacks both a long-term haemodialysis programme and an effective cadaver transplant programme.[123] These inequalities create markets for donor and patient tourism, and facilitate the evasion of domestic regulatory constraints. These considerations are particularly relevant to the

---

[118] *Yearworth v North Bristol NHS Trust* [2009] EWCA Civ 37, para.38.
[119] [2009] EWCA Civ 37, para.45.
[120] [2009] EWCA Civ 37, para.45.
[121] See also Human Tissue Act 2004 (Ethical Approval, Exceptions from Licensing and Supply of Information about Transplants) Regulations 2006/1260 and Draft Code 9, paras 49–54.
[122] See the discussion in Price 2005, 801–804.
[123] See Reddy 1993, 137.

issue of commercial dealings in human tissue and organs. A free market would almost certainly benefit those in rich countries over those in poorer countries from which the sellers of transplantable material would predominantly derive.

14.6 Further reading

Conditional donation

Pennings, Guido (2007) "Directed Organ Donation: Discrimination or Autonomy?" 24(1) *Journal of Applied Philosophy* 41–49.

Wilkinson, T. M. (2003) "What's Not Wrong with Conditional Organ Donation?" 29 *Journal of Medical Ethics* 163–164.

Elective ventilation

Hoffenberg, R., et al. (1997) "Should Organs from Patients in Permanent Vegetative State be Used for Transplantation?" 350 *The Lancet* 1320–1321.

Opt-in v Opt-out

Organ Donation Taskforce (2008) *The Potential Impact of an Opt Out System for Organ Donation in the UK: An Independent Report from the Organ Donation Taskforce.* (London: DH).

Human Tissue Act 2004

Price, David (2005) "The Human Tissue Act 2004." 68(5) *Modern Law Review* 798–821.

Property in the body

Beyleveld, Deryck and Brownsword, Roger (2001) *Human Dignity in Bioethics and Biolaw.* (Oxford: Oxford University Press), Ch.8.

Xenotransplantation

Cartwright, W. (1996) "The Pig, the Transplant Surgeon and the Nuffield Council." 4(3) *Medical Law Review* 250–269.

McLean, Sheila A.M. and Williamson, Laura (2005) *Xenotransplantation: Law and Ethics.* (Aldershot: Ashgate).

Williamson, Laura, Fox, Marie, and McLean, Sheila (2007) "The Regulation of Xenotransplantation in the United Kingdom After UKXIRA: Legal and Ethical Issues." 34(4) *Journal of Law and Society* 441–464.

Chapter 15

END OF LIFE DECISIONS I: THE LAW

15.1 Introduction

Most people die after a long process of dying, usually in a hospital.[1] Where health professions are involved, and they often are, they face difficult decisions about how much effort to put into keeping patients alive and whether to act in ways that are likely to hasten death. The decisions facing medical practice and the law are complicated by many pressures. To mention just a few, pressures are

---

[1] According to Revill 2003, "around 1,500 people a day die in the UK, mostly in hospitals".

created by technological advances that enable the dying process to be significantly prolonged, the (financial and emotional) costs of prolonging life, and by the potentially conflicting views of patients and other affected individuals, such as family members and the healthcare team. End of life decisions can be immensely difficult. Should a patient considered to be irreversibly in a state of waking unconsciousness, a so-called "permanent vegetative state", be tube-fed and hydrated indefinitely, starved and dehydrated to death, or given a lethal injection? Should a patient be deprived of life-ending assistance that is readily available to those living in a nearby country? What role should the law play? These issues are just some of those raised by life-shortening medical practices. Not all are controversial. Few would deny that there was a legal or ethical basis for convicting Dr Harold Shipman of murder and few would expect (let alone require) doctors to prolong all human life at all cost. Beyond this, there is little ethical agreement and the law is riddled with apparent inconsistencies.

This and the next chapter should be read as if they were two parts of the same chapter. The discussion is spread over two chapters simply to break the text into more manageable parts. Separation of the legal discussion (the focus of this chapter) from the ethical discussion (the focus of the next chapter) is artificial. The law is deeply embroiled in ethical controversy that unavoidably seeps into all discussion. Divergent protagonists can barely resist the temptation to read their own values into the law or dismiss particular features of the law as failing to reflect defensible values or social attitudes. The reason for this is that end of life decision-making raises some of the more divisive issues of modern medicine and the law; it raises questions about the value, purpose, and cessation of human life.

To limit the need for repetition, in this chapter it will be assumed that the reader has read Ch.5 on capacity to refuse or consent to treatment. A list of further reading will not be provided until the end of the next chapter.

15.2 Types of end of life decisions

"Euthanasia" is a word with Greek origins. To some it conjures up images of a gentle passing chosen by a person at peace with himself; to others it conjures up Nazi-inspired fear of the brutal slaughter of unwilling innocents. It originally referred to a gentle death and now frequently means different things to different people.[2] End of life discussions are marred by terminological differences whereby the same word means different things to different people. Once again it is important to remember that the same label can be used to describe different concepts and different labels are used to describe the same concept. Yet, a number of distinctions need to be made, whether or not these are defined as instances of euthanasia. To enter the debate we need to ensure that we are not all talking at cross purposes.

---

[2] E.g. compare Keown 1995b, 1 ("Euthanasia—the intentional killing of a patient, *by act or omission*, as part of his or her medical care") with Lord Goff in *Airedale NHS Trust v Bland* [1993] A.C. 789 at 865 ("euthanasia—*actively* causing his death to avoid or to end his suffering", my emphasis).

Let me say at the outset that the focus on doctors in this chapter is not meant to ignore the contribution of other health professionals. In practice, it is often left to nurses and carers to implement end of life treatment regimes and, in most instances, the same law applies to all health professionals. For convenience, when drawing distinctions I will refer only to the doctor and patient.

15.2.1 The doctor's involvement

The doctor's part in the end of life process could involve (1) administering lethal treatment; (2) withholding life-sustaining support; (3) withdrawing life-sustaining support; or (4) assisting the patient to self-administer lethal treatment (i.e. physician-assisted suicide).

This four-fold classification of the doctor's actions cuts across the distinction that is often drawn between "actively" taking steps to end life (such as administering a lethal injection or giving the patient the means of doing so) and "passively" withdrawing or withholding treatment (such as removing or not attaching a patient to a ventilator). Sometimes this distinction is expressed as "killing" and "letting die", or as "active euthanasia" and "passive euthanasia". It is a controversial distinction. Many doubt its ethical significance. Many doubt whether withdrawing life-sustaining support is properly understood as passive, as a mere omission. The four-fold classification offered above seeks to avoid foreclosing these debates by loaded definitions. These are debates to which we will return.

This four-fold classification does rely on the distinction often drawn between the doctor providing assistance with the preparatory steps for ending life (such as giving a patient drugs with which he can commit suicide) and the doctor actually executing the life-ending action himself (such as administering a lethal injection or removing a ventilator). This is a procedural distinction, the drawing of which will facilitate discussion of the ethical and legal debate.

15.2.2 The patient's involvement

Distinctions can also be drawn with regard to the involvement of the patient. There are situations where the patient is apparently competent to consent or refuse and situations where the patient appears to lack such competence. Where steps are taken to end the life of a competent patient these can be taken either with the patient's consent or against the patient's will. This is sometimes expressed as a distinction between *voluntary* and *involuntary* euthanasia.[3] Where the patient appears to lack the competence to participate in an end of life decision, the decision to end a patient's life is often referred to as *non-voluntary* euthanasia. Non-voluntary euthanasia captures those situations where the patient is simply not capable of understanding the choice between life and

---

[3] See e.g. Singer 1993, 176–179.

death. Withdrawing nutrition and hydration from a patient who is unexpectedly in a vegetative state is an instance of non-voluntary euthanasia, so defined. In sum, the patient's end of life decision could be (a) *voluntary* (where a competent patient consents); (b) *involuntary* (where a competent patient does not consent); or (c) *non-voluntary* (where the patient lacks the competence to make an end of life decision).

15.2.3 Intending and foreseeing

Finally, a distinction is sometimes drawn between two states of mind: *intending* death and merely *foreseeing* death without intending it. This can apply to the state of mind of the doctor or the patient when hastening or not slowing the patient's death. The so-called *principle (or doctrine) of double effect* relies on this distinction, as explained in Ch.1 (1.4.3.1). The moral significance of this is controversial and will be examined in the next chapter (16.2.1).

15.3 The law on refusing and requesting life-prolonging treatment

Life-prolonging treatment could be rejected by the patient either for the present time (a contemporaneous refusal) or for a future time when the patient expects to have lost capacity (an advance refusal). Conversely, a patient could make a contemporaneous or advance direction that a particular type of treatment is to be administered. In addition, a patient who expects to lose capacity could seek to appoint a substitute decision-maker (i.e. an appointed proxy) tasked with responsibility for deciding when future treatment should be refused or tasked with responsibility for interpreting the instructions that the patient leaves. This chapter will use "advance decision" to refer to any expression of a patient's will that is intended to apply at a future date when the patient has lost competence or capacity. Unfortunately, it is once again necessary to warn about definitional differences. Others sometimes restrict the label "advance decision" to advance refusals, or advance requests and refusals, and many others prefer to use the terminology of the "advance directive" or the "living will" as a synonym or narrower term. Readers will be glad to learn, that these distinctions should suffice for now.

15.3.1 Contemporaneous refusal

The courts have repeatedly declared that an adult with capacity has the right to refuse medical treatment, *even where this will result in death*.[4] In fact, the failure

---

[4] See e.g. *Re T* [1993] Fam. 95, esp. 102 and *Airedale NHS Trust v Bland* [1993] A.C. 789, esp. 857, 864.

to respect a free and informed refusal given by a patient with capacity will constitute both the tort of trespass and the crime of assault. A patient dying of heart disease is entitled to refuse a heart transplant, even if it represents his only chance of survival. A patient can refuse to continue taking antibiotics to combat a life-threatening infection, no matter how strongly they are recommended by his doctor. The House of Lords in *Bland* confirmed that compliance with a valid refusal of medical treatment is legally required.[5]

It is generally accepted that there are public policy limitations on refusing "basic care", as opposed to "medical treatment". In *Bland*, their Lordships considered the artificial provision of food and water to be part of the patient's "medical treatment and care".[6] Lord Goff expressly declared withdrawing a nasogastric tube (a tube supplying the stomach via the nose) to be analogous to withdrawing a ventilator.[7] In the view of some commentators, had tube feeding been considered "basic care" then it could not lawfully be withheld or withdrawn,[8] perhaps even in the face of an otherwise valid refusal.[9] According to Grubb,

> the common law may justify interventions against a competent patient's wishes in wholly exceptional circumstances on the grounds of public policy. Consequently, a patient could not refuse measures designed to maintain basic hygiene and pain relief. The explanation for this is twofold: the patient may not require his carers, in effect, to abandon him and also the interests of third parties—such as nurses . . .— outweigh his interests in this singular situation.[10]

While there is no clear authority on this point, this view is consistent with the decided cases. The courts have imposed similar public policy limitations on individual autonomy in other contexts.[11] The Law Commission has suggested that the validity of advance refusals (addressed below) be expressly subject to a prohibition on refusing pain relief or "basic care".[12] No such prohibition appeared in the subsequent Mental Capacity Act 2005. The Code of Practice does, however, state that an advance refusal cannot apply to "basic or essential care", such as "warmth, shelter, actions to keep a person clean and the offer of food and water by mouth".[13]

The views expressed in *Bland* with regard to contemporaneous refusals were technically obiter because the case concerned an apparently irreversibly incompetent patient. These principles have, however, been confirmed and applied to competent patients in more recent cases, notably in the *Ms B* case.[14] The rupture of a blood vessel in her neck had left Ms B paralysed from the neck down and

---

[5] [1993] A.C. 789. See e.g. [1993] A.C.789 at 864 (Lord Goff).

[6] e.g. [1993] A.C. 789 at 858 (Lord Keith).

[7] [1993] A.C. 789 at 870.

[8] See e.g. Keown 2002, 219 commenting on the *Bland* case.

[9] See Grubb 1993a, 83 (commenting on *Re T*), and Grubb 2004, 141.

[10] Grubb 2004, 141.

[11] See e.g. *R. v Brown* [1994] 1 A.C. 212.

[12] See Law Commission 1995b.

[13] See Department for Constitutional Affairs 2007, para.9.28.

[14] *Re B* [2002] EWHC 429. See also *Re C* [1994] 1 All E.R. 819 and *St George's Healthcare NHS Trust v S* [1999] Fam. 26.

in need of a ventilator to breathe. While her life expectancy remained normal, there was no real prospect of recovery. The doctors refused to comply with her repeated requests for the ventilator to be removed (later offering only to "wean her off"). Ms B was left with no alternative but to apply for a court declaration. Butler-Sloss P. reiterated the now well-established principle that an adult with capacity is entitled to refuse all life-prolonging medical treatment. Completely satisfied that Ms B had capacity, Butler-Sloss P. declared that continued ventilation was unlawful. Ms B was transferred to another hospital where she died after being removed from the ventilator.

In the circumstances, the ruling of the court was never in doubt. The refusal to remove the ventilator was apparently motivated by the close relationship that the healthcare team had built with Ms B and their unwillingness to cause her death, rather than a considered view of her competence or capacity. This case highlights a number of practical limitations on a patient's ability to exercise her legal right to refuse. Ms B had to go to court and, even then, she was only able to refuse treatment because another clinician could be found who was willing to comply with her request. Despite the *clear* violation of Ms B's legal rights, Butler-Sloss P. opined that the health professionals treating Ms B (against her will for many months) deserved "the highest praise".[15] Ms B was (at her request) awarded only nominal damages.

As we have seen, the law does not distinguish between the voluntary *withholding* of life-sustaining support and the voluntary *withdrawing* of life-sustaining support. The failure to comply with either type of refusal is unlawful. It might be wondered why withholding or removing medical treatment in the knowledge that it will cause the patient's death is not considered murder, after all consent is not a defence to murder. Murder requires death to be caused by an act or by an omission constituting a breach of duty (the *actus reus*), where the intention is to kill or cause serious bodily harm (the *mens rea*). The *Bland* decision held that withholding *and* withdrawing life-sustaining treatment were, from a legal point of view, omissions. It follows that the *actus reus* of murder can only be made out where the doctor is under a legal duty to administer (or continue to administer) life-sustaining treatment. The logical import of the case law is that a valid refusal to consent suspends the doctor's duty to provide that treatment. It is therefore inconceivable that a doctor who complies with a valid refusal could be guilty of murder. The ethical controversy of this will be left until the next chapter.

15.3.2 Advance refusal

The hero of Homer's *Odyssey*, Odysseus or Ulysses as he is sometimes called, gave detailed advance instructions to his sailors.[16] He wanted to hear the Sirens,

---

[15] [2002] EWHC 429, para.97.

[16] See Homer BCE, as translated in Rieu and Rieu 2003, 158 and 161–162, and the discussion in Morgan 2001, ch.12.

whose sweet song was said to lure men to their death. He instructed his men to tie him to the mast of his ship, plug their ears with beeswax, and tighten his bonds if he begged to be set free. They complied with his wishes, binding him more tightly when he commanded them to release him. This is an early example of an advance decision, albeit outside the context of medical treatment. Complying with Odysseus' previously expressed wishes, in the face of his attempt to retract them, saved his life. Advance refusals of life-sustaining medical treatment are more controversial as, by definition, compliance with their terms is expected to lead to the death of the patient. Nonetheless, a valid and applicable advance refusal has the same legal force as a valid contemporaneous refusal—it is legally binding. This powerful principle is, however, attenuated by the ease with which an advance refusal can be rendered legally ineffective.

Few make formal advance decisions. Most of us never even make a will. Without an advance declaration of a patient's wishes, a comatose, unconscious, or otherwise incapacitated patient will simply be treated under the general legal authority in accordance with his best interests (s.5 of the Mental Capacity Act 2005). This was discussed in depth in Ch.5 (5.2.2.2). Even if the patient had taken the trouble to issue an advance decision, at common law it could not confer capacity on a proxy. The 2005 Act alters this. As explained in Ch.5, ss.9–11 enables a capacitated patient to appoint a proxy to make future treatment decisions in his best interests once he loses capacity. For such a "lasting power of attorney" (LPA) to be effective it must comply with a number of formal conditions. Both the donor and attorney must be over 18 (ss.9(2) and 10). The donor must have capacity at the time of making the LPA and the document must be compliant with the conditions in Sch.1 and registered. For present purposes the most significant restriction is that an express provision is required for the attorney's decision-making authority to encompass life-sustaining treatment (ss.11(8)).

There were a few cases addressing *advance refusals* before the implementation of the 2005 Act. The first was *Re T*, which concerned a pregnant woman who had refused a blood transfusion after being admitted to hospital following a car accident.[17] After undergoing a Caesarean section the patient became unconscious and in need of a blood transfusion. Her father and boyfriend applied to the court for a declaration that it would be lawful to administer blood, despite her advance refusal. The Court of Appeal set aside her refusal on a number of grounds and, in the process, laid down some general principles. The court declared that an advance refusal has the same legal force as a contemporaneous refusal if, in the words of Lord Donaldson, it is "clearly established and applicable in the circumstances".[18] Any doubt, the court declared, was to be interpreted by reference to a presumption in favour of life.[19] These principles were later affirmed by the House of Lords in *Bland*.[20]

An advance refusal was declared to be valid in *Re AK*.[21] The 19-year-old patient was gradually deteriorating as a result of motor neurone disease. (This

---

[17] *Re T* [1993] Fam. 95.
[18] [1993] Fam. 95 at 103.
[19] [1993] Fam. 95 at 112.
[20] [1993] A.C. 789, esp. 857 (Lord Keith) and 864 (Lord Goff).
[21] [2001] 1 F.L.R. 129.

is a muscle wasting condition that eventually causes fatal paralysis. Professor Stephen Hawking is a famous victim of this condition.) For some months he had required a ventilator to breathe and at the time of the hearing was only able to communicate by answering "yes" and "no" to questions using the movement of one eyelid. Using eyelid movement he had asked the doctors to remove his ventilator two weeks after he lost the ability to communicate. Hughes J. granted a declaration that this was a valid refusal of treatment. This judge additionally declared that his ruling was fully consistent with the Convention rights that were shortly to be given effect by the HRA 1998. (Subsequent cases have indicated that protecting "personal autonomy" falls within the art.8(1) right to "private life".)[22]

In *HE v Hospital NHS Trust*, it was declared that a blood transfusion could be lawfully administered to an unconscious patient despite a written advance refusal stating that she was a Jehovah's Witness and only a written statement should be taken to indicate a change of mind.[23] Munby J. ruled that a written statement was not required to revoke *any* advance decision,

> A free man can no more sign away his life by executing an irrevocable advance decision refusing life-saving treatment than he can sign away his liberty by subjecting himself to slavery. Any condition in an advance directive purporting to make it irrevocable is contrary to public policy and void.[24]

The judge also ruled that the burden of proof rests on those seeking to establish the existence and continued validity of an advance refusal and any doubt "falls to be resolved in favour of the preservation of life".[25] This particular advance refusal was said to have been revoked by the patient's subsequent actions, in particular, the fact that she had become engaged to marry a Muslim and had agreed to convert to his faith.[26] Statements of irrevocability were thus treated as *legally irrelevant*. Not only was this particular statement of irrevocability not binding, it was not even interpreted as reversing the burden of proof (on the continued validity of the refusal) or neutralising the presumption in favour of life. On common law principles, few advance refusals were sufficiently precise to be legally binding.[27]

The 2005 Act expressly deals with advance refusals in ss.24 to 26. It gives legal effect to an "advance decision" to refuse treatment made by a person of at least 18 who had the capacity when it was made (s.24(1)). In the process it addresses the incentive to ignore an advance refusal created by the possibility that the legal consequences for following an invalid refusal could be worse than for ignoring a valid refusal. In the absence of a valid refusal, the doctor will usually be under a

---

[22] See *Pretty v UK* (2002) 35 E.H.R.R. 1, para.63. See also *R. (Burke) v GMC* [2004] EWHC 1879, esp. para.80.

[23] [2003] EWHC 1017.

[24] [2003] EWHC 1017, para.37.

[25] [2003] EWHC 1017, para.46.

[26] [2003] EWHC 1017, para.47.

[27] Another case where the patient lacked capacity to make the advance refusal was *NHS Trust v Ms T* [2004] EWHC 1279 (patient self-harmed by cutting herself and bloodletting, believing her blood to be evil).

legal duty to administer life saving treatment that he considers to be in the patient's best interests. This means that a doctor acting on an *invalid* refusal potentially satisfies both the *actus reus* and *mens rea* of murder. In contrast, contravening a *valid* refusal will, at most, make the doctor guilty of criminal assault. This disparity potentially weakens the practical effect of advance refusals. The Act's response is to declare that no liability is incurred for the consequences of withholding or withdrawing treatment if, at the time, the health professional *reasonably believes* that an advance refusal exists that is valid and applicable to the treatment (s.26(3)). A doctor who acts on a reasonable belief no longer risks a murder charge. This move alone should make advance refusals more likely to be followed in practice. The common law might well have come to the same conclusion by fashioning a defence of reasonable mistake,[28] but this is largely a matter of speculation. In practice, the English courts have yet to face the situation where an unconscious patient has been resuscitated despite the existence of a valid advance refusal.[29]

An advance refusal, if valid and applicable to the circumstances, has the same force as a contemporaneous refusal (s.26(1)). This does not, in the words of the Code of Practice, require emergency treatment to be delayed to look for an advance refusal "unless there is a clear indication that one exists".[30] This follows from the Act's declaration that it does not stop the provision of life-sustaining treatment, or the doing of anything that is reasonably believed to be necessary to prevent a serious deterioration in the patient's condition, while a court declaration is sought (s.26(5)).

An advance refusal will only be effective if it is *valid* and *applicable*. It can only be *valid* if it has not directly or indirectly withdrawn by the patient. The Act states that it will not be valid if the patient has:

(a) withdrawn it when he has capacity to do so;

(b) subsequently conferred the authority to make the relevant decision on an attorney (under a valid LPA); or

(c) "done anything else clearly inconsistent with the advance decision remaining his fixed decision" (s.25(2)).

The third, withdrawal by inconsistent conduct, requires some consideration. It clearly covers situations such as arose in *Re HE*. In that case, however, Munby J. expressly left open the question of whether an incapacitated patient could withdraw an advance decision when "it appears to conflict with his current (incompetent) wishes and feelings".[31] Two reasons can be offered as to why s.25(2)(c) should be interpreted as requiring that the inconsistent act take place while the patient has capacity. *First*, if the converse were true, then the requirement that the patient have capacity to explicitly withdraw his decision in s.25(2)(a) would be superfluous because any patient who purports to withdraw whether

---

[28] See Grubb 2004, 161.
[29] See further Gavaghan 2000.
[30] See Department for Constitutional Affairs 2007, para.9.56.
[31] [2003] EWHC 1017, para.38.

capacitated or incapacitated would, on that interpretation, fall within s.25(2)(c). *Second*, the Code of Practice supports this interpretation because the example given of the acts of a patient going against an advance refusal remaining his fixed decision are stated to take place "before his lack of capacity".[32] Having said that, the common law presumption in favour of prolonging life is likely to continue to apply—the European Court of Human Rights has expressed the view (in an advance *request* case considered below) that this presumption "accords with the spirit of the Convention".[33] Thus, if an incapacitated patient desires clinically-indicated life-prolonging treatment on which there is an unequivocally applicable advance refusal, the doctor would be best advised to seek a declaration from the Court of Protection.

There is no formal process to follow to *withdraw or alter* an advance refusal and it can be done, in the words of the Act, "at any time when he has capacity to do so" (s.24(3)). The Act expressly states that "[a] "withdrawal (including a partial withdrawal) need not be in writing" (s.24(4)). Thus, *Re HE* would be decided the same way under the Act as it was under the common law.

An advance refusal cannot be *applicable* if the patient still has capacity at the time that it is to be applied (s.25(3)). To be applicable:

(1) it must specify the treatment in question;

(2) it must not refer to any circumstances that are absent; and

(3) there must not be reasonable grounds for believing that the patient did not anticipate the circumstances if they are such as would have affected his decision (s.25(4)).

Requirement (1) can be expressed in "laymen's terms" (s.24(2)). Requirement (2) captures conditional refusals, where the relevant conditions are not present. Requirement (3) prevents reliance on vague refusals that do not properly capture the patient's will. The Code of Practice gives an example of reasonable grounds for believing that the patient did not anticipate the relevant circumstances that arise.[34] The example is of an HIV-positive patient who had made an advance refusal of specific retro-viral treatments to avoid becoming a research "guinea pig", but when it comes to be applied years later there are many new unanticipated treatment options.

Advance refusals of life-sustaining treatment are treated more strictly than other advance refusals. Such a refusal must be in writing, signed, witnessed, and state clearly that it applies even if life is at risk (s.25(5)/(6)). Further, s.62 explicitly states that nothing in the Act is to be taken to affect the law relating to unlawful killing or assisted suicide. Note, however, that the Government expressly refused to prohibit reliance on an advanced refusal of life-sustaining treatment that displays suicidal intentions.[35]

---

[32] See Department for Constitutional Affairs 2007, para.170.
[33] *Burke v UK* (No.19807/06, July 7, 2006).
[34] See Department for Constitutional Affairs 2007, para.9.44.
[35] See House of Commons Debates, 5 April 2005, Cols 1380–1382.

15.3.3 Requesting life-prolonging treatment

Patients sometimes seek not to refuse life-prolonging treatment, but to make a (contemporaneous or advance) demand that it be administered. Earlier chapters have examined the consistent judicial rulings to the effect that the court will not compel a doctor to act against his clinical judgment (see Ch.4 (4.2)) and the manifest judicial reluctance to interfere with decisions about the allocation of scarce medical resources (see Ch.2 (2.4.1)). These limitations aside, the demands or requests of patients still have legal relevance.

This issue came before Munby J. and then the Court of Appeal in *R. (Burke) v GMC.*[36] The applicant, Mr Burke, was a patient with a degenerative brain condition that would eventually remove his ability to swallow and require him to receive nutrition and hydration by tube if he is to survive. He sought to challenge the legality of General Medical Council (GMC) guidance,[37] which he read as permitting doctors to withdraw *artificial nutrition and hydration (ANH)* from him against his will. Munby J., in a judgment 225 paragraphs long, issued many declarations, including declarations that parts of the GMC guidance were unlawful.[38] Patients with capacity were said to have the right to insist on receiving *ordinarily available*[39] life-prolonging treatment, so that Mr Burke was entitled to insist on the provision of ANH for at least those stages of his illness in which he remained aware of his surroundings. The judge also declared that there were a number of situations where it would be unlawful to withdraw ANH from an incapacitated patient without judicial sanction.[40]

The Court of Appeal overturned Munby J.'s declarations, ruling that they had extended well beyond the law relating to the patient.[41] Mr Burke was not faced with doctors who wished to withdraw life-prolonging ANH against his will and, in the view of the court, he had not made an advance decision.[42] The court ruled that Mr Burke should have sought reassurance from the GMC, whose guidance, if interpreted reasonably, was not unlawful. The Court of Appeal opined that the application had served no useful purpose because it had not been open to doubt that the common law (like art.2 of the Convention) imposes a duty on those who care for a capacitated patient to provide ANH to him as long as it prolongs his life and is in accordance with his expressed

---

[36] [2004] EWHC 1879 and [2005] EWCA 1003, respectively.

[37] See GMC 2002a. See the subsequent draft replacement guidance: GMC 2009.

[38] Paras 13, 16, 32, 42, and 81 of GMC 2002a.

[39] As opposed to experimental/untested treatment and treatment where resources were in issue: [2004] EWHC 1879, paras 27 and 28.

[40] [2004] EWHC 1879, para.202.

[41] [2005] EWCA 1003.

[42] [2005] EWCA 1003, para.22. Mr Burke is not likely to lose capacity before the final stage of his life and the Court of Appeal thought that his concerns did not relate to that stage or, if they did, they were premature. With respect, unless the court is of the view that Mr Burke does not understand his prognosis, he ought to be taken to be making an advance refusal and it makes no sense to dismiss his concerns as not representing an advance refusal on the basis that they are "premature".

wishes.[43] Any doctor who brought an end to a patient's life by withdrawing ANH in such circumstances would be guilty of murder.[44]

The Court of Appeal in *Burke* was at pains to prevent the courts being used as sources of general advice, particularly in ethically controversial areas. Steps were taken to limit future judicial involvement to that of adjudicator of last resort. For a start, the previous position on declarations was reinstated: there was no duty to seek a court declaration before treating an incapacitated adult, even if that treatment involves the removal of ANH (see Ch.5 (5.4)). Faced with an invitation to embroil itself in issues of ethical and political controversy, the Court of Appeal retreated back to the status quo. The appeal court therefore counselled strongly against selective use of Munby J.'s declarations in future cases.[45]

The European Court of Human Rights, to which Mr Burke then took his case, was equally unsupportive of his contentions, ruling that his application was "manifestly ill-founded".[46] The Strasbourg court took the view that English law adequately protected his rights under arts 2, 3, 8, and 14. The court considered itself "satisfied that the presumption of domestic law is strongly in favour of prolonging life where possible, which accords with the spirit of the Convention". Further, there was no duty to obtain judicial authorisation for the withdrawal of ANH, as this would be "prescriptively burdensome", and there was no discrimination in the exercise of his Convention rights contrary to art.14, as neither a capacitated nor incapacitated patient "can require that a doctor gives treatment which that doctor considers is not clinically justified".

The common law position on advanced requests was said by the Court of Appeal in *Burke* to be identical to that under the (not then implemented) Mental Capacity Act 2005.[47] This Act regards advance requests as not binding, but an important consideration when assessing what is in the best interests of a patient (s.4(6)(a)).[48] But just how important can the consideration of a patient's previous views really be when whether or not ordinarily available life-prolonging treatment is to be administered is ultimately to rest on clinical judgment? Only Munby J.'s judgment gave any real weight to prospective patient autonomy and that judgment does not represent English law.

15.4 The law on requesting life-shortening treatment and assistance to die

A patient's life could be shortened by the deliberate administration of life-shortening treatment or by the deliberate provision of assistance for a patient to self-

---

[43] [2005] EWCA 1003, paras 39–40.
[44] [2005] EWCA 1003, para.34.
[45] [2005] EWCA 1003, para.24.
[46] *Burke v UK* (No.19807/06, July 7, 2006).
[47] [2005] EWCA 1003, para.5.
[48] See also Department for Constitutional Affairs 2007, esp. paras 5.44–5.45; and GMC 2009, esp. paras 51–52, 90, and 93.

administer lethal treatment. The law on these issues is relatively straightforward. The doctor commits murder if he causes a patient's death by actively intervening with the intention of killing the patient (15.4.1). The doctor commits at least a criminal offence under the Suicide Act 1961 if a patient successfully takes his own life with the doctor's assistance (15.4.2). The ethical acceptability of the legal position, discussed in 15.5, is less straightforward. The underlying ethical issue is this: should a doctor be allowed to administer anything other than *treatment* designed to cure a patient and *palliative care* (i.e. care addressing the patient's pain and discomfort but lacking curative effect)?

15.4.1 Administration of life-shortening treatment

Intentionally taking another person's life is murder. Legally recognised defences and exceptions do not include consent, compassionate motive, or medical training. What is more, murder carries a mandatory life sentence. It is, however, rare for doctors to be charged with murder. It is even rarer for doctors to deliberately shorten patient lives for reasons other than compassion. Dr Shipman aside, the few doctors who have been tried have tended to elicit noticeable public sympathy.

Dr Cox was faced with an elderly patient who repeatedly begged him and others to end her life.[49] Her rheumatoid arthritis was causing her extreme pain against which conventional pain-relief was proving to be ineffective. He administered a lethal dose of potassium chloride, a drug that stops the heart but has no therapeutic or pain-relieving value. Since she was terminally ill and her body had been cremated, it was difficult to prove that the injection had killed her. Dr Cox was therefore charged with *attempted* murder. He was convicted. Since attempted murder carries no mandatory sentence, Dr Cox was given a 12-month suspended prison sentence. The subsequent disciplinary hearing of the GMC was similarly sympathetic, allowing him to continue practising, subject to compulsory attendance on a training course and supervision.[50]

Dr Cox's actions could not be explained away or legally excused, because he had fully chronicled his actions and clearly satisfied the requirements of attempted murder. It might have been a different story if Dr Cox's choice of life-shortening drug had had therapeutic or pain-relieving value. In an earlier case, Dr Adams had administered large doses of heroin and morphine to an elderly patient who was incurably, but not terminally, ill.[51] He had been named as a beneficiary in her will and was charged with murder. In his direction to the jury, Devlin J. stated that a doctor "is entitled to do all that is proper and necessary to relieve pain and suffering, even if the measures he takes may incidentally shorten human life."[52] Dr Adams was acquitted. Devlin J. had invoked the

---

[49] *R. v Cox* (1992) 12 B.M.L.R. 38.
[50] See Biggs 1996, 243.
[51] *R. v Adams* [1957] *Criminal Law Review* 365.
[52] [1957] *Criminal Law Review* 365, 375.

principle (or doctrine) of double effect. According to this principle, discussed in Ch.1 (1.4.3.1) and in depth in the next chapter (16.2.1), the doctor's intention (to relieve pain) is to be distinguished from what he foresees as a consequence of the treatment (the patient's death), so as to absolve him from a charge of murder. This principle was subsequently affirmed by Ognall J. in his direction to the jury in *R. v Cox*, by other similar directions, and by obiter statements in the appeal courts. In *Bland*, for example, Lord Goff re-affirmed

> the established rule that a doctor may, when caring for a patient who is, for example, dying of cancer, lawfully administer painkilling drugs despite the fact that he knows that an incidental effect of that application will be to abbreviate the patient's life.[53]

A subsequent case, brought by Annie Lindsell, was withdrawn after it became clear that the drug that this sufferer of motor neurone disease wanted her doctor to administer was one that would shorten her life only as a side-effect of easing her pain.[54] The judge indicated that he "thoroughly approved and endorsed the discontinuance" of the case.[55]

However, in *R. v Woollin* the House of Lords outlined the requirements of murder in such a way that they fit uneasily with the principle of double effect.[56] Giving the leading judgment, Lord Steyn applied a direction given in an earlier case, which stated that jury members who are satisfied that

> the defendant recognised that death or serious harm would be virtually certain (barring some unforeseen intervention) to result from his voluntary act ... may find it easy to infer that he intended to kill or do serious bodily harm, even though he may not have had any desire to achieve that result.[57]

What effect does *Woollin* have on the principle of double effect? One possibility is that, in law, the principle only applies to proper medical treatment. Another is that juries who consider the defendant to have foreseen death or really serious bodily harm have discretion as to whether to rely on the principle of double effect or infer intention. Yet, another is that the doctrine no longer applies at all. If the principle of double effect no longer applies, then life-shortening palliative care could still be lawful on other grounds, such as the doctrine of necessity. None of these approaches is without difficulty.

The first approach smacks of arbitrariness. If the distinction between intention and foresight is a morally relevant distinction, then it should not matter whether the context is one of medical treatment. If the distinction is not morally relevant, then to rely on it at all is problematic. Proper medical treatment could be held not to constitute the *actus reus* of murder (an *unlawful* act or omission causing death) without invoking the principle of double effect with regard to the *mens rea* of murder.

---

[53] *Airedale NHS Trust v Bland* [1993] A.C. 789 at 867. See also Lord Donaldson in *Re J* [1991] Fam 33, 46.
[54] This application was reported in the media in 1997. See also Keown 2002, 22–24.
[55] Quoted in Keown 2002, 24.
[56] [1999] 1 A.C. 82.
[57] *R. v Woollin* [1999] 1 A.C. 82 at 96, citing Lord Lane in *R. v Nedrick* [1986] 1 W.L.R. 1025 at 1028.

The second approach could be reconciled with *Woollin*. McEwan has argued that,

> Evidence that a defendant foresaw death or really serious bodily harm is evidence from which a jury *may*, not *must*, infer intention. It appears therefore that there is, before the jury, a "get-out" clause whereby they may decide that although a defendant foresaw death as virtually certain, he or she did not intend it.[58]

If the jury can legitimately choose not to infer intention from foresight of virtual certainty, then proper medical treatment is a context in which this is appropriate. This approach, however, means that doctors administering life-shortening palliative care must always operate under the threat of a murder conviction.

The third approach simply knocks the problem of explaining why life-shortening palliative care is not unlawful on to another aspect of the law of murder. In *Re A*, the only judicial decision to address the difficulty of reconciling *Woollin* and the principle of double effect, the problem was simply left open.[59] The majority held that the principle of double effect did not apply on the facts.[60] Faced with determining whether it would be lawful to separate conjoined twins so that one could survive in the knowledge that the separation would accelerate the death of the other, the majority relied on the doctrine of necessity (see 15.5.3). This provides some judicial support for the third approach to *Woollin*.

A more dramatic view is taken by Keown, who has argued that *Woollin* was wrongly decided and "should be overruled as a matter of urgency".[61] According to Keown, *Woollin* grossly represents the state of mind of doctors engaged in proper palliative care (as they do not intend to kill) and unacceptably doubts the lawfulness of proper palliative care.[62] He argues that the possibility that doctors might have the defence of necessity still suggests that the doctors have done something wrong. Keown's view will appeal to those who hold that the principle of double effect is a moral distinction of sufficient weight to determine morally permissible conduct in such circumstances. Other moral positions rejecting the idea that there is an absolute duty not to intentionally kill may consider the administration of life-shortening palliative treatment to be permissible without needing to appeal to the principle of double effect at all. These issues are addressed in the next chapter (16.2.1).

In sum, the lethal administration of treatment that has no palliative effects is illegal. While doctors are apparently legally permitted to prescribe and administer pain relief even if it shortens the life of the patient, the precise legal basis for this remains unclear.

---

[58] McEwan 2001, 257.
[59] *Re A* [2001] Fam. 147 at 198–199 (Ward L.J.).
[60] Cf. Robert Walker L.J. who did think that a distinction between the intention and the foreseeable consequences could be drawn on the facts: [2001] Fam. 147 at 259 (Robert Walker L.J.).
[61] Keown 2002, 29.
[62] See Keown 2002, 28–29.

15.4.2 Physician-assisted suicide (PAS)

15.4.2.1 The Suicide Act 1961

Despite suicide being decriminalised under s.1 of the Suicide Act 1961, assisting another's suicide is a crime. In theory at least, it does not matter whether the person providing assistance is a doctor or acts from sympathy or even love. Under s.2(1) it is an offence to aid, abet, counsel or procure the suicide or attempted suicide of another, punishable by up to 14 years imprisonment. Unlike murder, there is no mandatory sentence. Also, under s.2(4), a person can only be charged with assisted suicide with the consent of the Director of Public Prosecutions (DPP).

It is highly unusual for a crime to be committed by assisting in an activity that is not itself criminal. The continued criminalisation of assisted suicide is ethically controversial (16.3.2). In law, a patient who refuses life-sustaining treatment is not treated as committing suicide, irrespective of whether or not their intention is to end his own life. In *Bland*, for example, Lord Goff emphasised that when a patient is refusing treatment

> there is no question of the patient having committed suicide, nor therefore of the doctor having aided or abetted him in doing so. It is simply that the patient has, as he is entitled to do, declined to consent to treatment which might or would have the effect of prolonging his life, and the doctor has, in accordance with his duty, complied with his patient's wishes.[63]

As we saw earlier, a doctor who complies with a valid refusal of treatment is not viewed as *actively* ending or assisting in the ending of a patient's life and is, in fact, required to comply with a capacitated patient's wishes. In contrast, a doctor who leaves a lethal pill on a quadriplegic patient's tongue for him to choose to spit out or swallow commits a crime. It does not matter that this patient would commit suicide if he could or would refuse life-sustaining treatment if he were receiving any.

Conduct constituting assisted suicide within s.2(1) was examined in *AG v Able*.[64] In this case, the Attorney General applied for a declaration that the requirements of s.2(1) were satisfied by the supply of a booklet detailing ways to commit suicide for the benefit of those who were considering or intending suicide. Woolf J. held that the distribution of the booklet would only be an offence where it was proved that (a) it was intended that it would be used by someone contemplating suicide and the contents of the manual were intended to assist that person, (b) it was distributed in the knowledge that the recipient planned to use it, and (c) the recipient was actually assisted by the publication to take or attempt to take his own life. While only a first instance decision, this severely restricts the application of s.2(1). More direct and personal assistance should continue to give rise to potential prosecution. However, in *R. v Chard*, a

---

[63] *Airedale NHS Trust v Bland* [1993] A.C. 789 at 864. See also *Re T* [1993] Fam. 95 at 117 (Butler Sloss L.J.).
[64] [1984] Q.B. 795.

teenager was acquitted of aiding and abetting the suicide of a terminally ill friend to whom he had given paracetamol tablets, after the judge directed the jury to return a verdict of not guilty on the basis that more was required than providing someone "with an option of taking her own life".[65] Kennedy and Grubb must be right to conclude that, where a doctor is charged with the offence, much will turn on the jury's view of the facts and the judge's directions to the jury.[66]

15.4.2.2 The Pretty Case

Dianne Pretty was dying from motor neurone disease, a debilitating disease that had rendered her unable to commit suicide without assistance. She sought the DPP's assurance that her husband would not be prosecuted for assisting her to commit suicide. This was refused. Mrs Pretty brought a judicial review action claiming that the Act and the DPP's actions were incompatible with her rights under the Convention, as given domestic effect by the HRA 1998. She lost in the Divisional Court, on appeal to the House of Lords, and in the European Court of Human Rights.[67] She died 12 days after losing in the Strasbourg court.

Mrs Pretty had sought to rely on a number of Convention rights. She sought to rely on art.2 (arguing that the right to life included or implied a right to die), art.3 (which prohibits inhuman or degrading treatment), art.8 (the right to respect for private and family life), art.9 (the right to freedom of thought, conscience and religion), and art.14 (which prohibits discrimination with regard to the enjoyment of the Convention rights). The House of Lords dismissed Mrs Pretty's arguments on all of these Articles. Article 2 was said to protect the sanctity of life and thereby prohibit the intentional taking of life, rather than confer any right to be assisted to die. Article 3 was similarly dismissed. Lord Bingham suggested that the positive aspect of art.3 could not go as far as required by Mrs Pretty, Lord Steyn explicitly declared that it was not engaged, and Lord Hope suggested that Mrs Pretty's treatment did not meet the required minimum level of severity.[68] Article 8(1) was held not to be engaged, because it was said to protect the way in which individuals live their lives, rather than the manner in which they wish to die.[69] If it had been engaged, their Lordships declared, the criminalisation of assisted suicide was justifiable under art.8(2), as seeking to protect the rights of vulnerable persons. While Mrs Pretty was arguably not vulnerable, others were. In the words of Lord Bingham,

> It is not hard to imagine that an elderly person, in the absence of any pressure, might opt for a premature end to life if that were available, not from a desire to die or a willingness to stop living, but from a desire to stop being a burden to others.[70]

---

[65] See Gorman 1993.
[66] See Kennedy and Grubb 2000, 1920.
[67] *R. (Pretty) v DPP* [2001] EWHC Admin 788, [2001] UKHL 61, and *Pretty v UK* (2002) 35 E.H.R.R. 1.
[68] [2001] UKHL 61, esp. paras 15, 60, and 91.
[69] [2001] UKHL 61, paras 26, 61–62, and 100.
[70] [2001] UKHL 61, para.29. See also para.62 (Lord Steyn).

Article 9 was similarly dismissed. It followed that Mrs Pretty could not rely on art.14, because she had no Convention right on which to attach her claim for discrimination in the exercise of that right.

The Strasbourg court, unlike the House of Lords, was prepared to accept that art.8(1) was engaged.[71] Like the House of Lords, however, the court went on to hold that the interference in this case could be justified, under art.8(2), as "necessary in a democratic society" to protect the rights of others. The court accepted that

> section 2 of the 1961 Act, was designed to safeguard life by protecting the weak and vulnerable and especially those who are not in a condition to take informed decisions against acts intended to end life or to assist in ending life. Doubtless the condition of terminally ill individuals will vary. But many will be vulnerable and it is the vulnerability of the class which provides the rationale for the law in question.[72]

Mrs Pretty's autonomy interests were to be sacrificed to protect vulnerable persons in society.

While ethical discussion is largely left to the next chapter, a few points are worth making here on the compatibility of the court's reasoning with the major moral theories. A rights-based theorist could accept that Mrs Pretty's right to privacy is overridden by the more powerful rights of others. A utilitarian could accept that the utility balance requires Mrs Pretty's interests to be sacrificed for the greater good. More difficult to reconcile with a rights-based perspective is the court's approach to art.2. Like the House of Lords, the Strasbourg court held that art.2 could not

> without a distortion of language, be interpreted as conferring the diametrically opposite right, namely a right to die; nor can it create a right to self-determination in the sense of conferring on an individual the entitlement to choose death rather than life.[73]

The second clause is actually incompatible with the nature of a right as utilised by rights-based moral theories. If a right is understood as a justifiable claim the benefit of which is waivable by the rights-holder, then it follows that (contrary to the view above) an individual can waive the benefit of his right to life. While a rights-based theory could restrain the exercise of an individual's rights to protect another's more important rights, an individual would have a prima facie entitlement to choose death rather than life. Thus, the details of the Strasbourg court's approach are easier to reconcile with a duty-based, utilitarian, or compromise approach than a rights-based approach.

Both the House of Lords and the European Court of Human Rights were concerned that judicial development was not capable of putting into place the safeguards that could be enacted by Parliament. Dianne Pretty's case would have been stronger on that ground had she been asking for physician assistance. There is, however, also a vociferous debate about whether even Parliament

---

[71] (2002) 35 E.H.R.R. 1 at 37.
[72] (2002) 35 E.H.R.R. 1 at 39.
[73] (2002) 35 E.H.R.R. 1 at 29.

would be able to enact adequate safeguards for PAS. This is a point to which we will return in the next chapter.

In sum, placing a pill on Mrs Pretty's tongue at her request is *legally* distinguishable from turning off Ms B's ventilator at her request. Both lead to death, but the first is legally prohibited (if the pill has no palliative effect) and the second is legally required (as the doctor has a legal obligation to comply with a valid request that treatment be withdrawn). Whether this is a morally defensible distinction is extremely controversial. In practice, discretion at the stages of prosecution and (for non-murder convictions) sentencing is likely to continue to ameliorate the apparent harshness of the law. In early 2005, a lenient one month suspended sentence was imposed on a retired policeman who killed his terminally ill wife in a suicide pact.[74] He had been convicted of manslaughter, rather than murder or any form of assisted suicide, but this once again displays the ability of the current law to sympathise with the defendant's plight.

15.4.3 Death tourism and other jurisdictions

Patient consumerism is an issue that is relevant to many areas of medical law and voluntary end of life decisions are no exception. In 2003, Reginald Crew travelled to Switzerland to take advantage of more permissive laws on physician-assisted suicide (*PAS*).[75] Mr Crew is reported to have ended his life by taking a fatal dose of barbiturates provided by a doctor. So-called "death tourism" has emerged as a new form of patient tourism. What if, as is often the case, the patient cannot travel abroad to commit without assistance? This issue is addressed below (15.4.3.1). More permissive jurisdictions also offer themselves as working models of alternative systems for the regulation of lethal treatment on request (voluntary lethal treatment: *VLT*) and PAS. This section will therefore go on to consider the regulatory positions in some other jurisdictions and the possibility of future reforms in the UK.

15.4.3.1 Assisting another to travel aboard to commit suicide

Anybody who aids another to travel abroad to obtain PAS could commit an offence under s.2 of the Suicide Act. In 2004, the High Court refused to intervene to prevent a woman with a degenerative brain condition travelling to Switzerland for PAS once it had been established that she had capacity.[76] The judge, nonetheless, stated obiter that he considered it "inevitable" that the husband had contravened s.2(1) by "making arrangements and escorting Mrs Z on the flight".[77] On this view, death tourism could be significantly reduced by the application of the existing law to those who are unable to make the

---

[74] See BBC 2005a.
[75] See BBC 2003a.
[76] *Re Z* [2004] EWHC 2817.
[77] [2004] EWHC 2817, para.14.

arrangements and travel unaided. Yet, although *at least* 90 UK citizens have travelled abroad to obtain access to assisted suicide since October 2002, no prosecution has resulted.[78] In any event, the phrase "aids, abets, counsels or procures the suicide of another" does not straightforwardly capture assisting the travel of someone who intends to commit suicide. Remember that in *R. v Chard*, considered above, it was held that it was not sufficient to merely provide someone with the option of taking her own life. When a patient travels abroad to commit suicide, the actual means to commit suicide are not provided by the person accompanying them, but by the foreign doctor. If merely providing assistance to travel with the requisite knowledge will suffice, then the offence would also be committed by a travel agent who is aware of the purpose of the trip!

In *R. (Purdy) v DPP*, the Court of Appeal was asked to consider the DPP's refusal to declare in advance whether a prosecution will occur for assisting another to travel abroad for suicide.[79] Debbie Purdy had been diagnosed with progressive multiple sclerosis in 1995. She lost the ability to walk six years later and is progressively losing physical strength and control. She believes that at some point she will want to travel aboard to commit suicide lawfully in accordance with Swiss law (on which see below). She would like the option of delaying this trip until a future time when she will need the assistance of her husband. Fearing that her husband may be prosecuted, Ms Purdy brought a judicial review action against the DPP for failure to promulgate a specific policy outlining the circumstances in which a prosecution would be brought for assisting suicide. She relied on art.8 of the Convention. The Court of Appeal, like the High Court before it, ruled that it was bound to follow the decision of the House of Lords in *Pretty* to the effect that art.8 was not engaged by the wish to seek assistance to commit suicide. This ruling was held not to be undermined by the decision of the European Court of Human Rights in *Pretty* or by any subsequent decisions of the House of Lords. Further, the Court considered that if it were wrong on the engagement issue, the inference with the Convention right was justifiable under art.8(2). Article 8(2) requires that any infringement must be "in accordance with the law" and, it was held, that the "statute is clear, not vague" and "the absence of a crime-specific policy" relating to the operation and effect of the DPP's discretion under s.2(1) did not contravene the requirements of art.8(2).[80]

The decision of the Court of Appeal differs in two important respects from that of the High Court before it.

First, the High Court ruled that the European Court of Human Rights in the *Pretty* case did not hold that art.8(1) was engaged, on the basis that there were places where the Strasbourg Court had used "somewhat elliptical wording".[81] In reaching this conclusion the High Court dismissed the unequivocal words used by the Strasbourg court under the heading "The Court's Assessment", which declare that "[t]he Court has found above that the applicant's rights

---

[78] *R. (Purdy) v DPP* [2009] EWCA Civ 92, para.19.
[79] [2009] EWCA Civ 92.
[80] [2009] EWCA Civ 92, paras 72 and 79.
[81] [2008] EWHC 2565, para.46. See also paras 36 and 67.

under Article 8 of the Convention were engaged".[82] It is also worth noting that the Strasbourg court itself has not interpreted *Pretty* so narrowly.[83] It is therefore reassuring that the Court of Appeal rejected this interpretation of the Strasbourg judgment.[84]

Second, the High Court failed to recognise that that Lord Brown's reasoning in *R. (Countryside) Alliance v AG* supports the Strasbourg decision in the *Pretty* case in relation to the engagement of art.8.[85] In contrast, the Court of Appeal accepted this, but concluded that, overall, their Lordships in that case were only concerned with the general principle, rather than the narrow effect of the *Pretty* decision.[86] The Court of Appeal further recognised that "it is highly unlikely that the House of Lords will not bow to a decision of Strasbourg on the question of the engagement of Article 8(1) if the matter should fall to be considered by them".[87] Nonetheless, the Court of Appeal held that it was still bound by the decision of the House of Lords because this was not a "very exceptional case" of "extreme character", such as one where the relevant human rights arguments had not been addressed by the House of Lords.[88] Thus, we are in the unsatisfactory position of having a human rights issue on which the Court of Appeal considers itself bound by a decision that it is convinced the House of Lords will set aside at the first opportunity. What does this say about the Court's view of the nature of fundamental human rights?

The High Court and Court of Appeal did agree on general conclusions and both ruled that even if art.8(1) was engaged, the interference complained of was justifiable under art.8(2). It thereby adopted a restrictive reading of the clarity and foreseeability required to be "in accordance with the law". Such a reading is consistent with other domestic decisions. When interpreting the art.7 requirement that there be no punishment without law, for example, the Court of Appeal has ruled that ingredients of the crime of gross negligence manslaughter were consistent with that requirement and involved "no uncertainty" even though what is sufficiently gross is left largely by reference to the discretion of the jury.[89] In *Purdy*, the DPP's Code of Practice stipulates a clear two-stage process to making a decision on whether to prosecute: consideration of the evidence, then consideration of the public interest. It also lists a number of factors to be taken into account when applying considerations of the public interest.

The Court of Appeal also noted the new DPP's ruling in the case of Daniel James.[90] In December 2008, the DPP ruled out prosecuting parents who assisted their son's trip to a Swiss clinic where he was assisted to commit suicide. Despite possessing sufficient evidence to prosecute, the DPP concluded that a prosecution would not be in the public interest. In reaching this conclusion, the DPP argued that the factors in favour of prosecuting (such as the seriousness of an

---

[82] 35 E.H.R.R. 1, para. 87. See [2008] EWHC 2565, paras 40–41.
[83] See e.g. *Burke v UK* (No.19807/06, July 7, 2006).
[84] [2009] EWCA Civ 92, para.49.
[85] *R. (Countryside) Alliance v AG* [2007] UKHL 52, para.141.
[86] [2009] EWCA Civ 92, paras 60–61.
[87] [2009] EWCA Civ 92, para.62.
[88] [2009] EWCA Civ 92, para.53.
[89] *R. v Misra* [2004] EWCA Crim 2375, para.64. See further, the discussion in Ch.3 (3.7).
[90] [2009] EWCA Civ 92, paras 20–24.

offence under s.2(1)) were outweighed by the factors against prosecuting (such as the parents not having influenced their son, who was of a fiercely independent mind, and their actions causing them distress without prospect of personal gain). The Court of Appeal concluded by declaring that this decision provides "ample" guidance to Ms Purdy's legal advisers on the likelihood of her husband being prosecuted,[91] thereby indicating that the relevant factors also apply to her husband. An appeal to the House of Lords is pending.

15.4.3.2 The Netherlands and Belgium

The Netherlands and Belgium are currently the only countries that have legislation explicitly permitting VLT. The Dutch legislation codifies the law as it has evolved in case law and practice over 25 years.[92] It permits both VLT and PAS. The Belgian legislation is more detailed and operates against a background of previous legal uncertainty.[93] While explicitly permitting VLT, the legislation does not apply to assisted suicide. This gap might indicate that PAS was not considered a crime, but is more plausibly explained by the political context within which the legislation was enacted.[94] It has been suggested that "assisted suicide" came to be understood as referring to killing someone at their request without safeguards and by the time that this was addressed, the Government could no longer afford to delay Parliament further.[95]

VLT and PAS have been openly practiced in the Netherlands for nearly three decades. During this time a body of case law has built up supporting this practice, subject to conditions. In 1984, the Dutch Supreme Court overturned the conviction of a doctor, Dr Schoonheim, who had killed an elderly patient at her explicit and repeated request.[96] The lower courts were admonished for failing to consider the defence of "necessity". This decision was later confirmed in a case concerning a psychiatrist, Dr Chabot, who had been convicted for assisting in the suicide of a patient.[97] The patient in question had not been ill but had been suffering from persistent grief at the loss of her two sons in their early twenties. While the Supreme Court affirmed the conviction, on the basis that the doctor had failed to ensure that the patient was examined by a second doctor, it declined to impose any punishment. In 2000, a lower court acquitted a doctor, Dr Sutorius, following his prosecution for assisting in the suicide of an elderly patient who was merely "tired of living".[98] In December 2002, the Dutch Supreme Court took a different approach to this case and held that the law required that the patient's "hopeless" and "unbearable" suffering be the result

---

[91] [2009] EWCA Civ 92, para.98.

[92] An English translation of the *Termination of Life on Request and Assisted Suicide (Review Procedures) Act of 2002* can be found in de Haan 2002.

[93] The *Act Concerning Euthanasia* of 2002 is analysed and compared to the Dutch legislation in Adams and Nys 2003.

[94] See Adams and Nys 2003, 356–357.

[95] See Adams and Nys 2003, 357.

[96] *Alkmaar (Schooheim)*, H.R. 27 November 1984, N.J. 1985, 106. See Keown 1992, Keown 2002, ch. 8, and de Haan 2002, 59, 63.

[97] *Chabot*, H.R. 21 June 1994, N.J. 1994, 656. See Keown 1995a and 2002, 87.

[98] de Haan 2002, 63. See also Keown 2002, 87.

of a medical condition (i.e. a psychiatric or physical illness that is not itself responsible for the wish to die).[99]

The Dutch Parliament enacted new legislation in 2002. This provides a defence to a doctor who administers lethal treatment at a patient's request or assists in his patient's suicide. By enacting the legislation, the Dutch government hopes to increase transparency and the ability to monitor existing practices.[100] Under this legislation, a doctor has to comply with a new reporting procedure and convince a regional review committee that he has satisfied certain requirements of careful practice. In particular, he must satisfy the committee that:

(a) the patient has made a "voluntary and well considered" request;

(b) the patient's suffering was "lasting and unbearable";

(c) he has consulted with another, independent doctor; and

(d) has terminated the patient's life or assisted in his suicide with due medical care.[101]

While the precise interpretation of these criteria is unsettled, the *Chabot* case indicates that the patient need not be terminally ill or physically suffering (i.e. unbearable psychological suffering is sufficient).[102] It should be noted that the new reporting procedure changes existing practice by ensuring that cases are no longer referred to the Public Prosecution Service unless a committee finds that the doctor has not fulfilled the Act's due care criteria.[103] These committees consist of a lawyer, a doctor, and an ethicist.[104]

The Belgian legislation is based on the Dutch position, but differs in a number of key ways.[105] The Belgian legislation does not, for example, apply to PAS and does not specify what offence is committed by a doctor who fails to comply with its requirements.[106] Significantly, it only applies to patients who are 18 or over. In contrast, the Dutch legislation allows a 16 year-old to request lethal treatment or assistance in consultation with his parents, and a child aged 12 to 15 with his parent's consent.[107]

15.4.3.3 Other jurisdictions

In 1995, the Northern Territory of Australia passed legislation effectively decriminalising VLT and PAS, subject to conditions.[108] This legislation came into

---

[99] Adams and Nys 2003, 369.
[100] See de Haan 2002, 61.
[101] S.2(1), as translated in de Haan 2002, 68.
[102] See de Haan 2002, 62–63.
[103] See de Haan 2002, 66.
[104] See de Haan 2002, 62.
[105] See Adams and Nys 2003.
[106] See Adams and Nys 2003, 359.
[107] Art.2, the Termination of Life on Request and Assisted Suicide (Review Procedures) Act of 2002. See also Adams and Nys 2003, 362.
[108] The Rights of the Terminally Ill Act 1995. See Funk 2000.

force in 1996. Only a handful of people were able to lawfully terminate their lives during the period of less than a year that it was in force. It was effectively invalidated by legislation passed in 1997 by the Australian Parliament.[109] In the US, the federal government attempted to similarly undermine the legislation of the State of Oregon, which was passed in 1994 and came into force in 1997.[110] This legislation permits PAS under certain conditions. After attempts to invalidate the Oregon legislation failed,[111] the US Attorney General sought to undermine its operation by using his powers under existing federal legislation. In 2006, the majority of the US Supreme Court ruled that the relevant federal legislation did not allow the Attorney General to prohibit doctors from prescribing controlled substances for use in PAS under the Oregon legislation.[112]

It is also worth briefly mentioning Switzerland, the jurisdiction to which Reg Crew travelled, and to which Debbie Purdy intends to travel, for access to assisted suicide. Switzerland has adopted one of the world's most liberal positions on assisted suicide. Anybody, *not just doctors*, can legally assist another to commit suicide if the act is done for altruistic (non-selfish) reasons.[113] It is only encouraging or assisting suicide for *selfish motives* that is criminalised. The Swiss approach to PAS therefore represents a rare example of a virtue-based position. Despite this, VLT remains illegal, albeit it subject to less severe sanctions than other types of murder.[114]

15.4.3.4 Brief comments and future reforms

The brief overview above presents no more than a flavour of alternative regulatory positions.[115] All adopt (or, in the case of the Northern Territory, did adopt) detailed safeguards seeking to protect the most vulnerable. The Oregon Act, for example, is limited to Oregon residents, requires patients to be diagnosed by two doctors as having a terminal illness, requires a witnessed written request from the patient, and imposes a 15-day waiting period between the request for assistance and the prescription of lethal medication.[116] Whether any existing safeguards are effective, or any safeguards could be effective, is hotly debated.[117] As we shall see in the next chapter, the practices of other jurisdictions are frequently cited by those with opposed views on the decriminalisation of VLT and PAS. What is clear is that each jurisdiction has its own particular historical background. In the Netherlands, for example, it has been said that the deep trust currently enjoyed between doctors and their patients stems back to the Nazi occupation of the Second World War where, "throughout the five-year

---

[109] The Euthanasia Laws Act 1997.
[110] See Funk 2000.
[111] *Vacco v Quill* (1997) 117 S.Ct. 2293.
[112] *Gonzales, Attorney General*, et al. *v Oregon* et al. (2006) 126 S.Ct. 904.
[113] Art.115 of the Swiss penal code. See the discussion in Hurst and Mauron 2003 and Guillod and Schmidt 2005.
[114] See Hurst and Mauron 2003, 272.
[115] See also House of Lords Select Committee 2005e, ch.5.
[116] See Funk 2000, 165–166, 175.
[117] Cf. Funk 2000 with Keown 2002.

occupation, many Dutch physicians refused to provide the Nazis with their patients' names, choosing instead to go to concentration camps".[118]

Experiences abroad have undoubtedly had an impact on the UK debate. In 1993 to 1994 members of the House of Lords Select Committee on Medical Ethics (*hereafter* the Walton Committee) travelled to some of the countries mentioned above, as did members of the more recent House of Lords Select Committee on the Assisted Dying for the Terminally Ill Bill (*hereafter* the Mackay Committee).[119] Although the terms of reference for these committees differed, both addressed the possibility of reforming the legal position to permit voluntary end of life decisions. The Mackay Committee was set up to consider the Assisted Dying for the Terminally Ill Bill introduced into the House of Lords by Lord Joffe in March 2004.[120] This Bill was unable to make progress because of a shortage of Parliamentary time. The 2004 draft sought to permit a capacitated adult who is *suffering unbearably* as a result of a *terminal illness* to request either VLT or PAS.[121] Under this Bill, a doctor could lawfully accede to a request for assistance where a number of procedures have been followed, including an assessment by an attending physician of the patient's condition, capacity, and the extent of his suffering (clause 2). The Bill required the patient to sign a witnessed, written declaration of intent and imposed a 14-day waiting period from the date that the patient first informed the attending physician of his wish for PAS or VLT (clause 4).

The 2004 draft differs from the legislation adopted in other jurisdictions. Its qualifying conditions combine professional assessment with the patient's subjective view. "Unbearable suffering" is defined in clause 1(2) to mean suffering resulting from the patient's terminally illness that *the patient* considers to be unacceptably severe. "Terminal illness" is defined in the same provision to mean an illness that *the consulting physician* considers to be inevitably progressive, irreversible by treatment, and likely to result in the patient's death within a few months at most.

The Mackay Report recommended the redrafting of a number of provisions. In particular, it recommended that consideration be given to:

(a) distinguishing between PAS and VLT to give Parliament the opportunity to address these courses of action separately;

(b) requiring the psychiatric assessment of all those seeking PAS or VLT to confirm that their request is reasoned and voluntary;

(c) replacing "unbearable suffering" with "unrelievable" or "intractable" suffering in any future bill;

---

[118] Bradbury 2003, 223.
[119] See House of Lords Select Committee 1994 and House of Lords Select Committee 2005, respectively. Members of the Mackay Committee visited Oregon, the Netherlands, and Switzerland. For reasons that are made apparent in the text, some refer to the Mackay Report as the Joffe Report.
[120] Lord Joffe had not long before introduced the Patient (Assisted Dying) Bill.
[121] The text of the Bill can be found in House of Lords Select Committee 2005, Appendix 4.

(d) adding a "cooling off" period to requests for VLT; and

(e) changing the conscientious objection clause (clause 7) to remove the obligation placed on a physician with a conscientious objection to refer the patient to another who does not have such an objection.[122]

A revised Bill, seeking to decriminalise PAS but not VLT, was introduced into the House of Lords in November 2005. It was defeated in the House of Lords by 148 to 100 towards the end of 2006.[123]

15.5 The law on non-voluntary end of life decisions

So far we have focused on voluntary end of life decisions made by those who have competence and capacity. As was shown in Ch.5, the law does not always grant capacity to all those who are apparently competent to make voluntary decisions. That chapter indicated that mature adolescents can lack capacity to refuse life-sustaining treatment even if they are competent. Here the concern is patients who appear unable to make voluntary decisions at the relevant time both in law and in practice. This section has three parts. The first, 15.5.1, will address the special case of patients in what has become known as a "permanent vegetative state" (PVS). The second, 15.5.2, will examine other cases in which the law will consider further life-prolonging treatment to be "futile" or, at least, not in the patient's best interests. The third, 15.5.3, will examine the legal issues raised by the recent decision to separate two conjoined twins to maximise the chances that one would survive in the knowledge that this would accelerate the other's death. All these end of life decisions were non-voluntary as the patients lacked the competence/capacity to make a decision themselves and had not previously made a relevant decision.

15.5.1 Permanent vegetative state

In the UK, at any one time there are between 1,000 and 1,500 people diagnosed as being in a "vegetative state" from which they are not expected to recover.[124] They have suffered serious brain damage, which has deprived them of the capacity for consciousness. Such patients are believed to be unable to see, hear, taste, smell, or feel pain. Yet, their hearts continue to beat, their brain-stem continues to function, they turn, they sleep, they wake, and some even appear to smile and frown.[125] This condition is similar to a coma, except that the patient

---

[122] See House of Lords Select Committee 2005, paras 246, 254, 256, 260, and 261. See further House of Lords Select Committee 2005, para.269.
[123] A negative view on the Bill can be found in Keown 2007.
[124] See Jennett 1997, 172–173.
[125] See Jennett 2002.

has a sleep/wake cycle. With adequate care, a patient can remain in a vegetative state for years or even decades.

Patients who had been in such a wakeful state of unconsciousness for a sustained period of time were first described as being in a "persistent vegetative state" over 35 years ago.[126] After a vegetative state has persisted for a certain length of time, modern practice is to describe it as "permanent" to signify a prognosis of irreversibility.[127] In 1994, the Multi-Society Task Force in the US declared that it was reasonable to assume a "permanent vegetative state" (*hereafter PVS*) after one year in traumatic cases and after three months in non-traumatic.[128] The Royal College of Physicians has recommended a longer period of six months for the latter type of case.[129] According to the Royal College of Physicians, the diagnosis of permanent vegetative state "may reasonably be made when a patient has been in a continuing vegetative state following head injury for more than 12 months or following other causes of brain damage for six months".[130] Other than this, the criteria laid down by these bodies are very similar.

Some continue to doubt whether "permanence" can be judged with sufficient certainty. Permanence is a best guess, "a presumption rather than a certainty".[131] There are well documented cases of misdiagnosis of "vegetative states"[132] and even reported incidents of recoveries after a diagnosis of PVS.[133] However, "many patients who regain consciousness after several months remain speechless and tube fed with very limited ability to communicate" and most become no more than "minimally conscious".[134] Even where the evidence of "permanence" is as compelling as possible, the patient remains legally alive. If a passerby stabs a PVS patient in the heart, or simply removes his feeding tube, he is potentially guilty of murder. Health professionals are not, however, obliged to continue treating, feeding, and hydrating PVS patients indefinitely. This was the effect of the leading case of *Bland*.[135]

15.5.1.1 The Bland case

Tony Bland was a victim of the worst sporting disaster in British history. Hundreds were crushed when fans poured into Hillsborough football ground after the start of a match. On that day in Sheffield, April 15, 1989, 95 died and many more were injured. Tony's lungs were crushed and punctured, interrupting the supply of oxygen to his brain. He suffered catastrophic and apparently irreversible damage to the parts of his brain responsible for consciousness. Those parts of his brain, forming the cerebral cortex, were said to have "resolved

---

[126] Jennett and Plum 1972.
[127] *See* e.g. Multi-Society Task Force on PVS 1994a, and Royal College of Physicians Working Group 1996.
[128] See Multi-Society Task Force on PVS 1994a/1994b.
[129] See Royal College of Physicians Working Group 1996.
[130] See Royal College of Physicians Working Group 1996, 119.
[131] Mason and Laurie 2006, 578.
[132] See e.g. Andrews et al. 1996.
[133] See Dyer 1997, Laing 2002 and Jennett 2002.
[134] Jennett 2002. See further Grubb et al. 1998, 176–177.
[135] *Airedale NHS Trust v Bland* [1993] A.C. 789.

into a watery mass".[136] Yet, his brain-stem continued to function, he was able to breathe unaided, and his digestion continued as normal. For over three years he was given food and water through a tube passing from his nose into his stomach and his bladder was emptied by a catheter. If the assistance had continued and his infections treated, Tony might have lived for decades in a PVS. He died much earlier, from dehydration following the removal of the nasogastric tube providing him with food and water. The decision to remove this tube was declared lawful by the House of Lords. The courts below had made the same decision.

The House of Lords was unable to rely on Tony's previously expressed wishes, because at no time had he given any indication of what those wishes were. Instead, their Lordships decided that artificial nutrition and hydration (ANH) were medical treatment that could be withdrawn if their provision was not in Tony's best interests. Despite the differences between their Lordships' speeches, all rejected the Official Solicitor's argument that stopping treatment would constitute murder. The withdrawal of the nasogastric tube was held to be, in law, a mere *omission* to provide *medical treatment*, rather than a commission or the provision of basic care. Their Lordships held that there was no duty to continue tube-feeding. Lord Goff (with whom Lord Keith agreed) declared that the tube-feeding to be "futile because the patient is unconscious and there is no prospect of any improvement in his condition".[137] Lord Browne-Wilkinson considered Tony to derive "no affirmative benefit from the treatment".[138]

Lords Browne-Wilkinson and Lowry opined that not only would withdrawal of treatment be lawful, but it was legally required.[139] Lord Browne-Wilkinson expressed the view that an incapacitated patient can only lawfully be treated in the patient's best interests,[140] so if a responsible doctor no longer believes that treatment is in the patient's best interests, he must withdraw it to avoid committing a battery. Under the 2005 Act, this equation of the patient's best interests with what a responsible doctor could consider them to be is no longer sustainable. The best interests test now requires (as it came to require at common law) consideration be given to "all the circumstances" and not in any way limited to medical concerns (s.4).

The *Bland* decision has been subject to heavy criticism. Supporters of the sanctity of life position have many reservations about the decision. They point out that, since Tony was still a human being and the majority of their Lordships explicitly accepted that the doctor's intention when withdrawing treatment was to kill,[141] the sanctity of human life was thereby violated.[142] Singer commends their Lordships for "discarding the fig leaf that might have hidden the true nature of their decision: that it can be lawful intentionally to bring about the death of an innocent human being".[143] Their Lordships did not, however, discard

---

[136] [1993] A.C. 789 at 856 (Lord Keith).
[137] [1993] A.C. 789 at 869.
[138] [1993] A.C. 789 at 885.
[139] [1993] A.C. 789 at 883 and 876, respectively.
[140] *Re F* [1990] 2 A.C. 1.
[141] [1993] A.C. 789 at 876 (Lord Lowry), 881 (Lord Browne-Wilkinson), and 896 (Lord Mustill).
[142] See e.g. Finnis 1993 and Keown 1997.
[143] Singer 1994, 73.

all fig leaves. They insisted, for example, that they were not asking whether it was in the patient's best interests to die, but whether it was in his best interests that his life should be prolonged in this way.[144] Given their Lordships' concession that the intention was to kill Tony, it is difficult to see this as anything other than an artificial distinction. In the next chapter we will return to the moral significance of the distinction between withholding/withdrawing treatment and administering lethal treatment (16.2.2).

15.5.1.2 Post-Bland cases

In *Bland*, some general safeguards were suggested as a matter of good practice. They advised that before treatment is withdrawn from a patient in PVS a declaration should be sought from the Family Division—a point considered in Ch.5 (5.4). Lord Goff indicated that their Lordships had agreed on four additional safeguards:

> (1) every effort should be made at rehabilitation for at least six months after the injury; (2) the diagnosis of irreversible PVS should not be considered confirmed until at least 12 months after the injury, with the effect that any decision to withhold life-prolonging treatment will be delayed for that period; (3) the diagnosis should be agreed by two other independent doctors; and (4) generally, the wishes of the patient's immediate family will be given great weight.[145]

These safeguards were meant to prevent any slide down the slippery slope, but subsequent cases have weakened or departed from them.

In *Frenchay Healthcare NHS Trust v S*, the patient had been in a vegetative state for two-and-a-half years following a drug overdose.[146] His feeding tube was accidentally dislodged, probably as a result of his own movement. The hospital sought a declaration that it would be lawful not to conduct the operation needed to replace the tube. Both the hearing and the appeal were rushed, depriving the Official Solicitor of the opportunity to confirm the diagnosis with independent doctors (as required by Lord Goff's third safeguard). Indeed, there was doubt about whether the patient was actually in PVS. Some members of the healthcare team believed that he suffered pain and, at times, he appeared to display voluntary behaviour.[147] Despite accepting that the evidence was not "as emphatic and not as unanimous as that in Bland's case", the Court of Appeal granted the declaration.[148] The possibility of reviewing the situation at leisure, after the operation had been performed, was rejected.

There has been further departure from the second safeguard, which required the patient to satisfy the criteria of PVS at least 12 months after the injury. The PVS requirement was weakened in *Re D*, where Sir Stephen Brown P. declared lawful the withdrawal of ANH from a patient who did not satisfy the definition of "permanent" vegetative laid out in the recommendations of the Royal College of

---

[144] e.g. [1993] A.C. 789 at 868 (Lord Goff), 885 (Lord Browne-Wilkinson)
[145] [1993] A.C. 789 at 870–871.
[146] [1994] P.I.Q.R. P118.
[147] [1994] P.I.Q.R. P118 at P124.
[148] [1994] P.I.Q.R. P118 at P125.

Physicians.[149] Despite the unwillingness of an expert to use the term "permanent", the judge was satisfied that there was "no evidence of any meaningful life whatsoever". In a case soon after, Sir Stephen Brown again granted a declaration that life-sustaining treatment should cease even though the patient did not satisfy every aspect of the Royal College of Physicians' guidelines.[150] It is apparent that those cases satisfying the criteria of the Royal College of Physicians are now to be regarded as the easy cases. In *NHS Trust A v H*, the then President of the Family Division granted a declaration supporting the withdrawal of ANH from another patient who had failed to satisfy the criteria of the Royal College guidelines.[151] Butler-Sloss P. preferred the guidance of the International Working Party Report.[152] Similarly, the time aspect of the second safeguard—that diagnosis PVS should not be considered confirmed until *at least 12 months after the injury*—has been relaxed. The patient in *NHS Trust B v H* had only been in a vegetative state for nine months.[153] Butler-Sloss P. was nonetheless prepared to allow withdrawal of treatment in accordance with the Royal College of Physicians guidelines (the patient had suffered brain damaged for reasons other than a head injury). The movement on this safeguard indicates how closely the law is now connected to medical opinion. What counts as PVS and how long the patient needs to be in that condition are seen as purely medical judgments. The court in these cases appears to see its role as simply ensuring that the patient satisfies medical criteria for PVS, which comes close to leaving the parameters of the law to the medical profession itself.

The third safeguard, requiring the diagnosis to be agreed by two other independent doctors, has also been weakened. In *Re G*, Butler-Sloss P. was happy to rely on the evidence of one expert witness.[154]

The fourth safeguard required that "great weight" be given to the wishes of the patient's immediate family. This safeguard must be seen in the light of an early case, also called *Re G*.[155] In that case Sir Stephen Brown declared that the dissenting views of the patient's mother should not operate a veto and granted a declaration supporting the discontinuation of life-sustaining treatment. The 2005 Act does not change this. The decision-maker applying the best interests test under the Act must, so far as practicable and appropriate, consult (among others) those engaged in caring for the patient or interested in his welfare (s.4(7)). But loved ones have no veto.

Before the implementation of the 2005 Act, end of life decisions were becoming medicalised—increased reliance was being placed on medical criteria and medical decision-making—in a similar way to abortion and aspects of assisted reproduction. Increased medicalisation of PVS is virtually inevitable. The 2005 Act in no way reduces a patient's best interests to medical criteria, but

---

[149] [1998] 1 F.L.R. 411. See Royal College of Physicians Working Group 1996.
[150] *Re H (Adult: Incompetent)* [1998] 2 F.L.R. 36.
[151] [2001] 2 F.L.R. 501.
[152] International Working Party 1996.
[153] [2001] Fam. 348. This case was heard with *NHS Trust A v M*.
[154] *Re G* (2002) 65 B.M.L.R. 6.
[155] [1995] 2 F.C.R. 46.

we should not expect the Act to lead courts in a direction divergent to past practice in dealing with PVS patients.

A recent case worthy of note was one in which a declaration on the lawfulness of removing ANH from a woman who had been in PVS for three years was delayed to allow a new drug to be, in effect, trialled. In this case, *NHS Trust v J*, Sir John Potter P. allowed a three-day course of the new drug to be administered on the back of some (largely anecdotal) evidence based on a case where the drug had been given to settle a restless PVS patient and had caused a momentary neurological response.[156] This drug produced no increased responsiveness and simply made her fall asleep (it was, after all, a sleeping pill). The President of the Family division subsequently granted the declaration originally sought by the NHS Trust.

15.5.1.3 The Human Rights Act 1998

The post-implementation impact of the Human Rights Act in PVS cases was first considered by Butler-Sloss P. in two cases heard on the same day: *NHS Trust A v M, NHS Trust B v H*.[157] The then President of the Family Division held that *Bland* is compatible with the relevant articles of the Convention, i.e. art.2 (the right to life), art.3 (the prohibition on torture, and inhuman or degrading treatment), and art.8 (the right to respect for private and family life). The President's analysis of these articles has not gone without challenge.[158] Her interpretation of art.3, in particular, has received considerable criticism. The President gave two reasons for concluding that art.3 was inapplicable to the withdrawal of ANH from a patient in PVS. *First*, the President cited *Herczegfalvy v Austria*, where it was held that "as a general rule, a measure that is a therapeutic necessity cannot be regarded as inhuman or degrading".[159] She opined that the withdrawal of treatment from patients in PVS in accordance with a "responsible body of medical opinion" is "for a benign purpose in accordance with the best interests of the patient".[160] So, in the President's view of the law, the withdrawal of life-sustaining treatment is to be viewed as in the patient's best interests, which in turn is to be equated with a therapeutic necessity. *Second*, the President concluded that art.3 did not apply to patients in PVS, because it "requires the victim to be aware of the inhuman and degrading treatment which he or she is experiencing or at least to be in a state of physical or mental suffering".[161] This second ground was rejected in *R. (Burke) v GMC* by Munby J., who argued that the President has misinterpreted the only authority that she cited in support of this second proposition.[162] To hold otherwise, the judge opined, would mean that "the Convention's emphasis on the protection

---

[156] [2006] EWHC 3152.
[157] [2001] Fam. 348.
[158] See e.g. MacLean 2001 and Grubb 2000b.
[159] (1993) 15 E.H.R.R. 437 at 484.
[160] [2001] Fam. 348 at 363.
[161] [2001] Fam. 348 at 363.
[162] [2004] EWHC 1879, paras 144–151. That authority was *T v UK* (1999) 7 B.H.R.C. 659, which is virtually identical to the linked case of *V v UK* (1999) E.H.R.R. 121.

of the vulnerable may be circumvented".[163] Indeed, to hold otherwise would mean that an intellectually impaired conscious patient who did not appreciate the significance of abusive behaviour could not be subject to "inhuman and degrading treatment" within the meaning of art.3.

In subsequent PVS cases, Dame Elizabeth Butler-Sloss followed her ruling in *NHS Trust A v M* to the effect that *Bland* is unaffected by the HRA.[164] Unless and until a higher court takes a different view, *Bland* remains good law. The European Convention on Human Rights and Biomedicine (the Biomedicine Convention) is unlikely to change this, even if the UK does sign and ratify it or the courts take it into account when interpreting the Convention rights given effect by the HRA 1998. The most pertinent provision of the Biomedicine Convention is art.6(1), which states that "an intervention may only be carried out on a person who does not have the capacity to consent, for his or her direct benefit". Unless the English courts are explicitly directed otherwise by Parliament—and they are not by the 2005 Act—they are likely to continue to hold the view that ANH is of no benefit to a patient in PVS. The 2005 Act does assert that the determination of a patient's best interests with regard to life-sustaining treatment must not be motivated by a desire to bring about his death (s.4(5)). Such treatment is defined as that which "in the view of a person providing health care for the person concerned is necessary to sustain life" (s.4(10)). While it is possible to interpret s.4(5), read in the light of s.4(10), as altering the common law position in situations such as the *Bland* case where there is an intention to cause death, this reading is most probably misguided. As stated in para.31 of the Act's explanatory notes, it is not meant to impose an obligation on doctors "to provide, or to continue to provide, life-sustaining treatment where that treatment is not in the best interests of the person", but meant to ensure that more than lip service is paid to the best interest test.

15.5.1.4 Other jurisdictions

The European Court of Human Rights has traditionally granted a wide "margin of appreciation" in controversial areas.[165] For this reason, the Strasbourg court is unlikely to interpret the Convention as preventing the withdrawal of ANH from patients in PVS. Such withdrawal is widely accepted by many other European legal systems. The national courts have allowed the withdrawal of ANH from patients in PVS in Germany,[166] Ireland,[167] the Netherlands,[168] and Scotland.[169] While there are some countries where the legal

[163] [2004] EWHC 1879, para.145. When Munby J.'s views were considered by the Court of Appeal, the court refused to discuss art.3 and warned against selective use of his judgment: [2005] EWCA 1003, para.24.
[164] *Re G* (2002) 65 B.M.L.R. 6 and *NHS Trust v I* [2003] EWHC 2243.
[165] See e.g. the recent case of *Vo v France* (no.53924/00).
[166] See Grubb et al. 1998, 180, 193.
[167] *In the Matter of a Ward of Court* [1995] 2 I.L.R.M. 401, where the patient was "very nearly" in PVS.
[168] See Grubb et al. 1998, 180.
[169] *Law Hospital NHS Trust v The Lord Advocate* 1996 S.L.T. 848.

position is not entirely clear (such as France and Greece), the removal of treatment from patients in PVS is a widespread practice in Europe.[170]

15.5.2 Futility and other non-voluntary non-treatment

In *Bland* and subsequent cases the courts have taken the view that the provision of continued ANH to a patient in PVS or very near PVS is "futile".[171] This concept of futility conveys a judgment about the worthwhileness of providing or continuing treatment. It is ethically controversial because what is worthwhile can only be assessed relative to its goal. Providing ANH to patients in PVS fulfils the goal of keeping the patient alive and, in this sense at least, is not futile. To regard such treatment as futile, as the law does, is to consider it to be worthless for some further purpose, perhaps enabling the patient to have a life with experiences. In other words, this usage of "futility" implies a quality of life judgment, a judgment about whether it is worthwhile to keep the patient alive.[172]

Surely no one would contest the futility of treatment that is useless or ineffective. However, consider whether it should be permissible to withhold or withdraw life-prolonging treatment that is:

(a) likely to cause the patient significant suffering;

(b) likely to prolong the patient's life for only very brief time;

(c) unlikely to enable the patient to become conscious; or

(d) unlikely to enable the patient to reach a particular threshold of ability/experience over and above consciousness.

We will return to the ethical debate in the next chapter. For present purposes, it is sufficient to note that the courts have allowed life-prolonging treatment to be withheld/withdrawn from at least some patients who are not in a vegetative state. Virtually all of these cases have concerned newborns and infants where the treatment was considered to bestow no medical benefit or be unduly burdensome for the patient.

15.5.2.1 Selective non-treatment of newborns and infants

The first case to address selective non-treatment was *Re B*, a case concerning an infant with Down's syndrome complicated by an intestinal blockage.[173] With surgery she was expected to live for at least 20 years, yet her parents refused to consent. The Court of Appeal overrode the parental refusal, holding that

---

[170] See further Grubb et al. 1998.
[171] See e.g. *Bland* [1993] A.C. 789 at 869 (Lord Goff), and *NHS Trust A v M, NHS Trust B v H* [2001] Fam. 348, esp. 360.
[172] See Keown 1997.
[173] *Re B* [1990] 3 All E.R. 927.

surgery was in the child's best interests. According to Templeman L.J., the test was "whether the life of this child is demonstrably going to be so awful that in effect the child must be condemned to die".[174] Only a few months later, in *R. v Arthur*, a jury found a doctor not guilty of attempted murder after he had ordered "nursing care only" for a Down's syndrome baby whose parents did not want him to survive. The judge instructed the jury that they should "think long and hard before deciding that doctors, of the eminence we have heard . . . have evolved standards which amount to committing crime".[175] The judge made no reference to *Re B* and the two cases appear to be completely irreconcilable. Fortunately, the case law does not stop there. *R. v Arthur* should not be regarded as having much, if any, force as a precedent.

The next case before the Court of Appeal was less controversial because baby C was hopelessly and terminally ill.[176] The Court of Appeal held that it was in her best interests for her suffering to be eased and her life not to be briefly prolonged by medical treatment designed to address future infection or feeding difficulties. What became the leading case came under a year later: *Re J.*[177] Baby J was not dying, but was severely brain damaged, epileptic, blind, deaf, mute, and quadriplegic. He had been ventilated on two previous occasions. The Court of Appeal supported the doctors' view that it would not be in his best interests to administer artificial ventilation again, should he need it in the future. While the application of the best interests test is factually specific and provides little guidance for future cases, the Court of Appeal did make some more general points. Determining what is in the best interests of the child was said to be a balancing exercise, to be looked at from the assumed view point of the patient, and applied with a strong presumption in favour of a course of action that will prolong life.[178] According to Taylor L.J.,

> the correct approach is for the court to judge the quality of life the child would have to endure if given the treatment, and decide whether in all the circumstances such a life would be so afflicted as to be intolerable to that child.[179]

Guidance from the Royal College of Paediatrics and Child Health describes five situations in which doctors might consider withholding/withdrawing treatment from children.[180] In addition to the brain dead child[181] and the child in PVS, these include:

- the "no chance" situation (where "life sustaining treatment simply delays death without significant alleviation of suffering");

- the "no purpose" situation (where the impairment following treatment "will be so great that it is unreasonable to expect them to bear it"); and

---

[174] [1990] 3 All E.R. 927 at 928.
[175] (1981) 12 B.M.L.R. 1 at 22.
[176] *Re C (A Minor)* [1990] Fam. 26.
[177] [1991] Fam. 33.
[178] [1991] Fam. 33 at 46–47 (Lord Donaldson), 55 (Taylor L.J.).
[179] [1991] Fam. 33 at 55.
[180] See Royal College of Paediatrics and Child Health 1997.
[181] On which see *Re A* [1992] 3 Med. L.R. 303 and the discussion in Ch.13 (13.2.1.1).

- the "unbearable" situation" (where the "child and/or family feel that in the face of progressive and irreversible illness further treatment is more than can be borne").[182]

These guidelines have been considered in subsequent judicial decisions. In *Re C*, Stephen Brown P. relied on *Re J* and accepted medical opinion that the 16-month child was in a "no chance" situation. He supported the doctors' view that ventilation should be withdrawn and not reinstated in the event of a further respiratory arrest.[183] *A NHS Trust v D* was a more recent case where the judge accepted that the child fitted the "no chance" situation and ruled that it would be lawful not to resuscitate him in the event of a future cardio-respiratory arrest.[184] Cazalet J. went on to opine that there was no infringement of art.2 (the right to life), because the course of conduct was in the patient's best interests and no infringement of art.3 (the prohibition of inhuman or degrading treatment), because it encompasses the right to die with dignity.[185] The HRA 1998 was not then in force.

In late 2004, the High Court ruled that it was not in 11-month-old Charlotte Wyatt's best interests for her to be artificially ventilated or subjected to similarly aggressive treatment.[186] This was the unanimous view of her doctors, though there was some medical disagreement about whether there was "no chance" or "no purpose" to the treatment. Hedley J. applied the best interest balancing exercise, refusing to rely on the notion of intolerability to supplement or replace the best interests test.[187] He ruled against the little girl's parents. The judge refused to discharge his declarations in two subsequent hearings[188] and the Court of Appeal dismissed the parent's appeal.[189] Wall L.J., giving the judgment of the Court of Appeal, emphasised that *Re J* had decided that the test was the child's best interests, which was to be judged from the assumed point of view of the patient with a strong presumption in favour of life.[190] The Court of Appeal insisted that the majority of their Lordships in *Re B* and *Re J* had not reduced the best interests test to a test of intolerability, as best interests was much wider, though intolerability could sometimes provide a "valuable guide in the search for bests interests in this kind of case".[191] In a later hearing, Hedley J. considered Charlotte's condition for the fourth time and was satisfied that it had changed sufficiently for his previously declarations to be discharged.[192] Hedley J. was asked to consider the case for yet a fifth time only four months later.[193] Charlotte's parents had separated, making it increasingly difficult to obtain joint decisions, and there had been a

---

[182] Royal College of Paediatrics and Child Health 1997, 7.
[183] [1998] 1 F.L.R. 384.
[184] [2000] 2 F.L.R. 677.
[185] On art.3, his Lordship cited *D v UK* (1997) 24 E.H.R.R. 423. See now *NHS Trust A v H* [2001] 2 F.L.R. 501.
[186] *Portsmouth NHS Trust v Wyatt* [2004] EWHC 2247 (October 2004).
[187] [2004] EWHC 2247, esp. paras 25 and 39.
[188] [2005] EWHC 117 (January 2005) and [2005] EWHC 693 (April 2005).
[189] *Wyatt v Portsmouth Hospital NHS* [2005] EWCA Civ 1181 (October 2005).
[190] [2005] EWCA Civ 1181, para.87.
[191] [2005] EWCA Civ 1181, paras 75–76, 87, and 91.
[192] *Re Wyatt* [2005] EWHC 2293 (October 2005).
[193] *Re Wyatt* [2006] EWHC 319 (February 2006).

"very significant deterioration" in her condition. The judge ruled, in accordance with the unanimous medical evidence and against the wishes of Charlotte's mother, that should the need arise it was in the best interests of Charlotte that her doctors should be free to refrain from further intubation and ventilation. It is to be hoped that such protracted litigation can be avoided in future cases.[194]

The law in this area, but not its application to every factual variation, is now well settled. The courts will act as final arbiters and will apply the best interest test to settle any dispute. Medical opinion will evidentially be a key factor in such cases. The courts have not yet deviated from medical opinion as to whether treatment should be withdrawn from a sick child, at least where that opinion has been unanimous.[195] Gradually the situations where selective non-treatment will be considered proper have been extended in line with medical opinion. The Mental Capacity Act 2005 will not have *direct* impact on this line of cases, as it does not apply to those under 16 (s.2(5)). Cross-fertilisation of the law is nonetheless inevitable. At common law the courts treated the best interests test as a single test irrespective of whether it was applied to an adult or a child, so the considerations laid out under the 2005 Act will undoubtedly be applied *indirectly* by the courts to those under 16.

15.5.2.2 Non-voluntary non-treatment of adults

Re R was the first case to address withholding life-prolonging treatment from an incapacitated adult who was not in a vegetative state.[196] *Re R* concerned the validity of a DNR (Do Not Resuscitate) order, which would now be referred to as DNAR (Do Not *Attempt* Resuscitation) orders to indicate that resuscitation is not always successful.[197] The patient was a seriously physically and mentally disabled adult with severe epilepsy and profound learning difficulties. He was probably both blind and deaf. A DNAR order was placed on his medical notes by the consultant responsible for his care in consultation with R's mother. The health authority sought a declaration when this decision was challenged by the day care centre staff. Drawing on *Re J*, Sir Stephen Brown P. ruled that the over-riding principle to be applied when considering whether the treatment was in the patient's best interests is the same for an incapacitated adult as a child. The judge was also influenced by Taylor L.J.'s view that the issue was whether life would be "so afflicted as to be intolerable". A declaration was granted to the effect that not providing antibiotics for any future infection and not under-taking cardiopulmonary resuscitation would be lawful.

Both the GMA and BMA have published guidance on withholding/withdrawing life-prolonging medical treatment.[198] Combining the decision in *Re*

---

[194] There was even another appeal to the Court of Appeal on whether the Legal Services Commission was responsible for all the Trust's costs: *Portsmouth Hospitals NHS Trust v Wyatt (Costs)* [2006] EWCA Civ 529 (May 2006).

[195] The only case where the medical view did not stand was one where the doctors wanted to administer life-prolonging treatment (a liver transplant) against the mother's wishes: *Re T* [1997] 1 All ER 906. See the discussion in Ch.5 (5.3.3.2).

[196] [1996] 2 F.L.R. 99.

[197] See the joint guidance of the BMA Resuscitation Council and the RCN (2001).

[198] See GMC 2002a (for the draft replacement guidance, see GMC 2009) and BMA 2007a.

R with the ruling in *Bland* to the effect that ANH is to be considered medical treatment, the BMA guidance endorses the withholding/withdrawal of tube-delivered food and water from patients suffering from other conditions not amounting to PVS, such as patients who have suffered a serious stroke or have severe dementia.[199] The guidance advises that additional safeguards should be in place before such treatment is withdrawn, but does not advise that such cases should be routinely subject to court review. Keown has suggested that "were a case involving the withdrawal of tube-feeding from a patient with a serious stroke or severe dementia to come before a court, the court would declare the withdrawal lawful if the doctor had complied with the BMA guidance".[200] There are pre-Mental Capacity Act dicta indicating that the courts will permit the withdrawal of tube-feeding in the absence of a valid advance refusal only if the patient's life would, from the patient's point of view, be intolerable.[201] Under the 2005 Act, the best interests test is clearly an objective test in which the patient's past and present desires are relevant but not conclusive (s.4). The Code of Practice states:

> There will be a limited number of cases where treatment is futile, overly burdensome to the patient or where there is no prospect of recovery. In circumstances such as these, it may be that an assessment of best interests leads to the conclusion that it would be in the best interests of the patient to withdraw or withhold life-sustaining treatment, even if this may result in the person's death. The decision-maker must . . . not be motivated by a desire to bring about the person's death for whatever reason, even if this is from a sense of compassion. Healthcare and social care staff should also refer to relevant professional guidance when making decisions regarding life-sustaining treatment.[202]

A doctor seeking to remove ANH from a non-PVS patient would be well advised to seek a court declaration if he has any doubt at all as to the patient's best interests. Remember, however, that the s.5 general legal authority only requires that the doctor have a "reasonably belief" that the proposed response is in the patient's best interests.

15.5.3 The special case of *Re A*

Re A was concerned with the legality of separating a pair of conjoined twins, given the pseudonyms Jodie and Mary.[203] They were joined at the lower abdomen and shared a bladder and had a common aorta. Mary, the weaker of the twins, was being sustained by the common artery, as she had a very impaired heart and brain, and no lung function. Without separation it was predicted that Jodie's heart would fail in the months ahead. Jodie's chances of survival were

---

[199] See BMA 2007a, para.29.4. For criticism, see Keown 2002, ch.10 (commenting on an earlier edition of the BMA guidance: BMA 2001).
[200] See Keown 2002, 251.
[201] *R. (Burke) v GMC* [2004] EWHC 1879, para.213. See also *Re G* (2002) 65 B.M.L.R. 6 and *W Healthcare NHS Trust v H* [2004] EWCA Civ 1324.
[202] See Department for Constitutional Affairs 2007, para.5.31. See also GMC 2009, esp. 90–91.
[203] [2001] Fam. 147.

thought to be significantly lower following an emergency separation (estimated at 40 per cent) than following an elective separation (estimated at 94 per cent), but an elective separation would kill Mary.[204] The parents refused to consent to elective separation, considering such action to contravene the tenets of their Roman Catholic faith. The hospital made an application to the court for a declaration that separation would be lawful. At first instance, Johnson J. declared that separation would be lawful, as it was not in the interests of either child to remain conjoined and the operation would be a legal omission analogous to the withdrawing of ANH. The Court of Appeal granted the declaration for different reasons. While all three judges reasoned differently, they did agree that separation was compatible with proper application of the best interests test and would not amount to the murder of Mary. The separation went ahead. Mary died in the operating theatre. Jodie returned to the Maltese island of Gozo with her parents.

15.5.3.1 Balancing the best interests of the twins

The operation was clearly in the best interests of the stronger twin, Jodie. While the court focused almost exclusively on the medical prognosis of her future quality of life, it is difficult to see how the court could have come to a different conclusion on Jodie's best interests.[205] The judges were divided over whether the operation was in the best interests of Mary. Ward and Brooke L.JJ. held that it was against Mary's interests, emphasising that the operation would greatly accelerate her death.[206] Robert Walker L.J. supported the view of the first instance judge that the operation was actually in her interests. His Lordship opined that he accepted the conclusion

> that to prolong Mary's life for a few months would confer no benefit on her but would be for her disadvantage. If Mary had been born separated from Jodie but with the defective brain and heart and lungs which she has, and if her life were being supported, not by Jodie but by mechanical means, it would be right to withdraw that artificial life support system and allow Mary to die.[207]

Treating the death of Mary following surgical separation from her twin as equivalent to the withdrawal of life-sustaining treatment represents a dramatic extension of the *Bland* approach. It extends the legal concept of an "omission" to the point of virtual meaninglessness. Walker L.J.'s further opinion that the operation was in Mary's best interests, because it would restore her bodily integrity,[208] treats her physical integrity as more important than her life.[209] Ward and Brooke L.JJ., who rejected this approach, had their own justificatory problems. They needed to explain why it is lawful to perform an operation on a child (Mary) against that child's interests. Ward L.J. stated that there was a

---

[204] Unless put on a heart and lung machine. See McEwan 2001 for a criticism of their Lordships unwillingness to consider this point in depth.
[205] See Michalowski 2002, 382.
[206] [2001] Fam. 147 at 190 (Ward L.J.), 218 (Brooke L.J.).
[207] [2001] Fam. 147 at 246.
[208] [2001] Fam. 147, esp. 251.
[209] See Michalowski 2002, 380.

conflict of duty that could only be dealt with by "choosing the lesser of the two evils and so finding the least detrimental alternative".[210] Weighing these interests, he concluded that "the least detrimental choice, balancing the interests of Mary against Jodie and Jodie against Mary, is to permit the operation to be performed.[211] Does this prioritising of the interest of Jodie presuppose that their lives were not truly equal? Their Lordships thought not (see further below).

15.5.3.2 The criminal law

The Court of Appeal's declaration that the operation was lawful implied that the operation would not constitute the crime of murder. Brooke L.J. relied on the defence of necessity. Walker L.J. relied on the principle of double effect and the defence of necessity. Ward L.J. appealed to a form of self-defence, rather than the defence of necessity. The majority view must therefore be that the defence of necessity applied, i.e. the claim that the operation (which would kill Mary) was necessary to save Jodie's life.[212] The defence of necessity had been rejected in a nineteenth-century case where two victims of a shipwreck had killed and eaten the third, a young cabin boy.[213] Bolstered by later dicta of the House of Lords in a case rejecting the defence of duress to a charge of murder,[214] many considered this case to have adopted a blanket rejection of necessity as a defence to murder.[215] Yet, the majority of their Lordships considered themselves free to rely on the defence of necessity on the facts before them. The choice of the cabin boy had been arbitrary and unfair. The victim had been chosen by the defendants rather than by fate or a fair process. In contrast, according to Brooke L.J., "Mary is, sadly, self-designated for a very early death. Nobody can extend her life beyond a very short span."[216] Does treating Mary as "designated to die" because of her limited life span imply that her life is worth less than that of Jodie? According to Harris, if the law consistently takes the view that the life of both twins is truly equal, then both twins could plead necessity "with equal force and plausibility".[217]

Ward L.J. preferred to rely on a form of "quasi-self-defence". His Lordship noted that an innocent aggressor could be lawfully killed in defence of others, giving the example of a six-year-old boy who indiscriminately shoots others in a school playground yet is too young to be held legally responsible for his conduct.[218] Building on this example, Ward L.J. declared that he could "see no difference in essence between that resort to legitimate self-defence and the doctors coming to Jodie's defence and removing the threat of fatal harm to her presented by Mary's draining her lifeblood".[219] However, to rely on

---

[210] [2001] Fam. 147 at 192.
[211] [2001] Fam. 147 at 197.
[212] [2001] Fam. 147 at 239–240 (Brooke L.J.), 255 (Robert Walker L.J.).
[213] *R v Dudley and Stephens* (1884–85) L.R. 14 Q.B.D. 273.
[214] *R v Howe* [1987] A.C. 417 at 439 (Lord Griffin), 453 (Lord Mackay).
[215] See Sheldon and Wilkinson 1997, 169; Michalowski 2002, 387–388; and McEwan 2001, 247.
[216] [2001] Fam. 147 at 239.
[217] Harris 2001b, 227–228. Michalowski (2002, 389) has pointed out that the courts in other cases have asserted that the last few moments of life are not disposable.
[218] [2001] Fam. 147 at 203.
[219] [2001] Fam. 147 at 204.

self-defence (understood widely as the legitimate defence of another) on the facts is surely to presuppose that the value of the twin's lives is not equal. Insofar as separating the twins could be seen as defending Jodie from premature death, leaving them together could be seen as defending Mary from a premature death. As Harris has argued, "self-defence cuts both ways and cannot be used to protect Jodie rather than Mary".[220]

15.5.3.3 Concluding thoughts

Their Lordships described this case as "difficult" and "unique".[221] Perhaps, what was so difficult was constructing an argument for the conclusion that they wanted to reach. The case erodes the bright-line between acts and omissions and many other aspects of the criminal law. Despite their Lordships' attempts to restrict the case to its facts, many of their views are readily applicable to other separation cases and beyond.[222] Given the questions left unanswered in *Re A*, hospitals would be well advised to seek judicial approval before separating other conjoined children, especially where one is likely to die.[223] It is likely that the courts will continue to attach great weight to medical opinion. In *Re A*, not only did the Court of Appeal side with the doctors over the parents, Ward L.J. stated that he would have supported the doctors' decision not to operate.[224] Thus, *Re A* provides yet further support for the view that doctors have greater decision-making power than is apparent if the law is taken at face value.

The moral issues raised by this, on which we have only briefly touched, will be addressed in more detail in the next chapter (16.4.2.2). From a legal point of view, it is problematic that the decision implies that Jodie's life is not equal to Mary's life. Their Lordships explicitly declared that Mary was a legal person (i.e. had full legal status) because she had been born alive.[225] As Brooke L.J. put it, "in the eyes of the law Mary's right to life must be accorded equal status with her sister Jodie's right to life".[226] Thus, insofar as the judgments imply that Mary had less status than Jodie, they are internally incoherent.

---

[220] Harris 2001b, 229.

[221] [2001] Fam. 147, e.g., 155, 198, 205, 206, 245, 255.

[222] McEwan (2001, esp. 248) argues that the decision (in logic, if not in practice) has wider implications for the administration of lethal treatment.

[223] See the discussion of a more recent conjoined twin case in Huxtable 2002.

[224] [2001] Fam. 147 at 173.

[225] Their Lordships cited many cases for the proposition that legal personality exists from the moment of being born alive, including the judgment of Brooke J. in *Rance v Mid-Downs HA* [1991] 1 Q.B. 587 at 621. Brooke J. had ruled that a child is "born alive" for the purposes of s.1 of the Infant Life (Preservation) Act 1929 if he "exists as a live child, that is to say, breathing and living by reason of its breathing through its own lungs alone, without deriving any of its living or power of living by or through any connection with its mother". In *Re A*, their Lordships considered the test to be live existence independent of the mother, rather than breathing independently (which Mary was not capable of).

[226] [2001] Fam. 147 at 214.

15.6 Tensions and contradictions

Very few doctors who facilitate or accelerate a patient's death will find them-selves in prison. In addition to the broad categories of legally permissible end of life responses, there is an evident reluctance to prosecute, convict, or harshly sentence doctors who act out of sympathy for the patient. If euthanasia has not been let in by the front door, the back door is far from locked. The result is a system that balances competing values and interests uneasily. Different moral theories will point to different tensions and contradictions and for at least this reason this chapter needs to be read alongside Ch.16. As stated at the outset, these two chapters should not be seen as two independent chapters, but two parts of the same chapter.

Chapter 16

END OF LIFE DECISIONS II: ETHICAL CONTROVERSY

16.1 Introduction

The last chapter examined the response of English law to the issues raised by end of life decision-making in the context of modern medical practice. These issues are ethically divisive. There is no single utilitarian, rights-based, duty-based, virtue-based, or compromise view on the moral implications of voluntary or non-voluntary end of life decisions. Divergent regulatory positions could potentially be defended within any one of these moral camps. The tenets of these moral camps do, however, attach different weight to different considerations. This tends to result in some convergence of views within particular moral camps, but differences should not be underestimated. End of life decision-making is among the most ethically controversial topics addressed in this book.

It is worth pausing at the outset to mention one ethical view that is well-represented in the ethical literature: the *sanctity of life* view. It was argued in Ch.1 (1.4.3) that this view is incompatible with rights-based, utilitarian, and virtue-based positions. This view holds that it is always wrong to intentionally kill an innocent human being. The sanctity of life view does not impose a moral obligation to preserve life at all costs—it is thereby distinguishable from "vitalism".[1] Nonetheless, the sanctity of life view must be rejected by most of the major moral camps outlined in Ch.1. Rights-based theories must reject this view as they hold that a competent patient can waive the benefit of his right to life. Utilitarian theories track a utility calculus and reject absolute duties prohibiting intentional killing, particularly where the patient has autonomously chosen death over life. Virtue-based theories track character and motive, and so must also reject absolute duties against intentionally killing. It follows that the objections to practices that appeal directly to the sanctity of life view will only be supported by a particular type of moral theory within the duty-based (or compromise) camp. As suggested, the five major moral camps can pull in different moral directions. Treating patient autonomy (i.e. the ability and freedom to make one's own choices) as a major moral requirement is to reject some moral positions just as much as adopting the sanctity of life view.

Voluntary and non-voluntary end of life decisions raise different ethical issues. Both topics, however, raise questions about the moral significance of distinctions between effects and double effects (16.2.1) and between acts and omissions (16.2.2). After examining these distinctions we will address voluntary end of life decisions (16.3): advance refusals (16.3.1) and the arguments concerning the legalisation of voluntary lethal treatment and physician-assisted suicide (16.3.2). Finally, we will examine non-voluntary end of life decisions (16.4).

16.2 Two disputed distinctions

16.2.1 Effects and double effects

The "principle (or doctrine) of double effect" was outlined in Ch.1 (1.4.3) and the last chapter indicated that it has some legal relevance (15.4.1). The principle has its origins in the moral theology of the Roman Catholic Church.[2] It holds that an act that has two predicted consequences, one good and one bad, can be morally permissible where the intention is to achieve the good and the bad is as unchosen as it is unavoidable. It is a distinction between intention and foresight; between a chosen purpose and a foreseen but unchosen side effect. According to Keown, it is best formulated so as to state that it is permissible to

---

[1] See Keown 1997.
[2] See the use of the principle with regard to the permissibility of self-defence in Aquinas c.1265–1274 (II–II, Qu. 64, art.7), as translated in Dermot 1989, 390.

produce a bad consequence only if "the act one is engaged in is not itself bad", "the bad consequence is not a means to the good consequence", "the bad consequence is foreseen but not intended", and there "is a sufficiently serious reason for allowing the bad consequence to occur".[3] It is ethically controversial. Some reject its moral significance. It can be difficult to non-arbitrarily distinguish intended effects from unintended side-effects (double-effects) and it appears to depend on how the action is described.[4] It can also be difficult to determine whether a particular consequence was intended, both from a "first person" perspective (the individual in question might not be sure what he intends and what he does not intend) and from a "third person" perspective (we cannot enter a doctor's mind at the time that he is acting).[5] Others reject these concerns arguing that the distinction is of moral significance, can be drawn without arbitrariness, is apparent from within a first person perspective, and the evidential difficulties from a third person perspective are no more complex than those facing juries every day.[6]

16.2.1.1 The principle of double effect and end of life decisions

The principle of double effect evolved from the sanctity of life tradition and is staunchly defended by supporters of that position. Its reliance on terms like "good" and "bad" mean that it can only be applied by reference to a position defining those terms. Understood by reference to the sanctity of life, the principle of double effect can apply to end of life decisions in two ways. *First*, it is can be applied to a patient's reasons for refusing life-sustaining treatment or otherwise accelerating his death. Refusing treatment with the intention of committing suicide violates the sanctity of life, whereas refusing treatment in the knowledge that death will result, but without the intention to die, does not. *Second*, it can be applied to a doctor's reasons for administering life-shortening treatment or otherwise accelerating the patient's death. Administering life-shortening treatment with the intention of killing the patient is viewed as morally unacceptable, whereas administering life-shortening treatment with the intention of relieving the patient's pain and distress is considered morally permissible.

   Wilkinson has argued that the principle can only apply in the second way if it is actually true that effective pain management at least sometimes requires life-shortening doses.[7] He argues that if life-shortening interventions are never required, a doctor administering life-shortening drugs must intend death or fail to foresee the lethal side-effect. There is, however, a third possibility: the doctor might mistakenly believe that effective pain-management does sometimes require life-shortening doses. In any event, it is currently widely believed that life-shortening doses are sometimes the only effective form of palliative care.

---

[3] Keown 2002, 20. See also the four conditions laid down by Beauchamp and Childress 2001, 129.
[4] See Harris 1985, 46, Beauchamp and Childress 2001, 128–132, and Singer 1993, 209–210.
[5] See Wilkinson 2000b, 301.
[6] See e.g. Finnis 1995a. This last point derives from the Walton Report (see House of Lords Select Committee 1994, para.243).
[7] See Wilkinson 2000b, 301.

Of course, if the palliative care is not in fact life-shortening, then there is no need to rely on the principle of double effect at all.[8]

16.2.1.2 Conceptual distinction and moral significance

There is a *conceptual distinction* between intending and merely foreseeing a virtually certain consequence of one's intended conduct. Harris, who rejects the moral significance of the distinction, accepts that a person can intend to get drunk without intending the hangover that he foresees will be a virtually certain consequence.[9] Finnis, who considers the distinction to hold significant moral weight, provides another example,

> The British climber in the Andes who, some years ago, finally cut the rope on which his friend was dangling, lest he himself be dragged over the precipice, and who later found (to his amazed delight) that the friend he had thought certain to be killed had fallen unscathed into deep snow, had no intent to bring about death or any lesser harm.[10]

Harris rejects its moral significance because he considers us to be morally responsible for all that we knowingly and voluntarily bring about, irrespective of whether we intend to bring about those consequences.[11] I might not have intended my hangover but if I acted voluntarily knowing that that was a virtually certain consequence of my drinking, then I am responsible for it.[12] Finnis refuses to accept this view of moral responsibility. He goes further and argues that the unintended side-effect need not be altogether unwanted, as hangovers are.[13] He declares that a war-time commander who orders the bombing of a factory is not morally responsible for civilian deaths if he does not intend them, even if he welcomes the "bonus" side-effect that killing civilian deaths will weaken enemy morale. According to Finnis, this side-effect is unintended if the war-time commander "has in no way calibrated or adjusted his plans so as to achieve civilian deaths—not even as a secondary objective—and if he stops the bombing as soon as the factory is destroyed".[14] This is an extremely narrow interpretation of intention.

To some extent the debate between Harris and Finnis turns on their underlying moral position. Harris rejects Finnis' duty-based position in favour of one with distinctly utilitarian features. Utilitarians are concerned with outcomes in that all our choices are evaluated in terms of their consequences for the utility balance. To act with virtual certainty that a consequence will follow is to culpably cause that consequence just as much as if bringing about that consequence were that

---

[8] See e.g. Sykes and Thorns 2003 (who cite studies questioning whether the dosages of opioids and sedatives typically used to control the symptoms of patients with advanced, terminal cancer actually shorten the patient's life).

[9] See Harris 1995d, 37.

[10] Finnis 1993, 332.

[11] See e.g. Harris 1995d, 38, and 1985, 43–45.

[12] If Harris was faced with the scenario presented by the climber in the Andes, he would no doubt refer to his discussion of self-defence in response to an innocent threat: see Harris 1985, 66–73.

[13] See Finnis 1995c, 63–64.

[14] Finnis 1995c, 64.

person's sole purpose. At first sight, it might appear that virtue theories could happily embrace the principle of double effect as distinguishing between motives, but the principle does not turn on motive. A man who commits suicide to protect national secrets that he fears he would divulge to an enemy under torture intentionally takes his own life, even though his motive is virtuous.[15] We have already seen that the sanctity of life view that is usually appealed to in conjunction with the principle of double effect is best viewed as a duty-based position and is incompatible with utilitarian, virtue theories, and rights-based theories. It follows that only duty-based and compromise positions can accept the principle as Finnis envisages it to operate. The absolute nature of the sanctity of life view might, in part, explain why its supporters insist on the moral significance of such a narrow conception of intention. This issue, in short, turns on the justification of competing basic moral premises, to which we will return in the final chapter.

16.2.2 Acts and omissions

We have seen that the law draws a distinction between *actively* and *passively* taking a patient's life. Both withholding and withdrawing life-sustaining treatment are, in law, omissions. No legal wrong is committed by an omission unless there is a legal obligation to act, which there will not be where a patient validly refuses treatment or where the treatment is not in the patient's best interests. There are two issues of controversy here. *First*, whether the distinction between an act and omission is morally sufficient to justify the conclusions drawn by the law. *Second*, whether withdrawing (as opposed to withholding) life-sustaining treatment or care is properly characterised as a mere omission. These questions are important to both voluntary and non-voluntary end of life decisions.

Few consider the distinction between killing and letting die to be one of major moral significance. Even outside the medical context philosophers have criticised or sought to narrow the distinction.[16] Rachels, for example, asks the reader to imagine that there is a starving child in the same room and that the reader has a sandwich that he does not need.[17] The force of this analogy rests with the neutralisation of factors typically invoked by those who argue that killing is worse than letting die, such as the cost to the actor and the probability that death will result. Rachels rejects the distinction because he holds that we owe extensive positive duties (i.e. duties to assist), so that letting someone die becomes as morally unacceptable as killing them. Others reject the distinction for other reasons. Harris and Finnis, who agree on little else, agree that the law's reliance on the distinction is morally indefensible. They argue that there is no morally significant distinction between terminating life by deliberate *omission* and terminating life by deliberate *intervention*.[18] Finnis rejects the distinction because he holds that

---

[15] See Gormally 1995, 134.
[16] See e.g. Thomson 1976 and Rachels 1979.
[17] See Rachels 1979, 160.
[18] See Harris 1995d, 36.

intentionally terminating the life of an innocent human is always wrong whether it is done by an act or an omission (i.e. the sanctity of life position). Harris rejects the distinction because he holds that a person is responsible for anything that he voluntarily and knowingly brings about, irrespective of whether he brings it about by an act or an omission. Harris does not, however, hold that deliberately terminating life by act or omission is always wrong. He presents an account of the "value of life" that takes respect for "persons" as fundamental, where persons are defined as those capable of valuing their own existence.[19] By implicitly relying on preference utilitarianism, he moves from the fact that persons value their own existence to the moral principle that it is a prima facie wrong to kill a person against his will. On this account, persons who do not want to live are not wronged by having their wish to die granted *whether it is by act or omission*. Thus, despite adopting radically different moral positions, Finnis and Harris both reject a bright line between terminating life by act and terminating life by omission.

The distinction between killing and letting die evokes controversy because it does not turn on the outcome (a patient can be killed by an act or an omission), the doctor's state of mind (the doctor can intend to kill by act or omission), or the patient's consent (the patient can be killed or left to die without or with his consent). It is therefore difficult to find a convincing reason why this distinction should be drawn *as a matter of ethical principle*. It is, nonetheless, possible to conceive of theories offering such a reason. Perhaps, for example, a theory that rejects all *positive* duties that have not been voluntarily assumed, according to which letting someone die can only be immoral if it involves a failure to comply with voluntarily accepted responsibilities.[20]

By defining permissible omissions widely the law goes further than simply adopting a contested distinction. Both withholding *and withdrawing* medical treatment are considered to be omissions. In *Bland*, their Lordships were at pains to define the removal of tube-feeding and water from Tony Bland as an omission. They considered it to be on a par with withholding treatment in the first place. Lord Browne-Wilkinson went as far as to declare that the tube that was feeding Tony Bland "itself, without the food being supplied through it, does nothing".[21] The difficulty is that where treatment is being administered, the doctors could be described as omitting to continue treatment or as removing treatment. Here the same situation can plausibly be described in the language of omission or commission, but the situation is not simply one of inaction. Switching off a ventilator and removing a feeding tube are acts that the law treats as omissions. They are interventions without which the patient would continue to live and they would be regarded as actions if performed by a passer-by rather than the doctor in charge of the patient's care. In effect, treating the medical withdrawal of life-sustaining support as a legal omission is little more than a "legal fiction" designed for the purpose of holding the line against actively killing a person.

Reliance on this legal fiction leads us to ask why a quick death is unlawful in circumstances where it is lawful to bring about a slow death following

---

[19] See Harris 1985, 1995c, 1995d, and 1995e. See also Ch.17 (17.2.1).
[20] Such a theory is incompatible with (at least) utilitarianism and virtue theory.
[21] *Airedale NHS Trust v Bland* [1993] A.C. 789 at 882.

non-treatment or even dehydration and starvation. Lord Browne-Wilkinson considered it difficult to find a moral answer to this question.[22] Lord Mustill accepted that such distinctions left the law "morally and intellectually misshapen".[23] Few would dissent from this view. Kass and Lund have, nonetheless, sought to defend the legal distinction between lethal treatment and withholding/withdrawing treatment.[24] They point out that discontinued treatment does not always result in death and invoke the principle of double effect: "What is most important morally is that the physician who ceases treatment does not intend the death of the patient, even if death follows as a result of his action or omission".[25] What if the doctor who withdraws life-sustaining treatment does, in fact, intend the patient's death? After admitting that some doctors abuse the principle of double effect they declare that,

> The relation between law and medical ethics is necessarily indirect. The law cannot teach or inculcate the right attitudes and standards that professionals need if they are to preserve the fragile moral integrity on which the proper practice of medicine depends. But the law can support that ethic by enacting and upholding a bright line rule that coincides with the morally necessary prohibition against doctors becoming agents of death.[26]

This suggests that they support the legal distinction as a practical way of implementing a different moral distinction with which it overlaps in application. They support the maintenance of the current legal position as a means of preventing further developments in the direction of legalising physician-assisted suicide (PAS) and voluntary lethal treatment (VLT). Unfortunately, this means that the law will sometimes not coincide with what Kass and Lund consider to be morally defensible. To the extent that Kass and Lund are prepared to accept a compromise whereby intentional killing by omission is legally permitted, they must be rejecting the sanctity of life view, which imposes an *absolute* prohibition on the intentional killing of an innocent human being. Interpreted in this way, Kass and Lund are, in effect, presenting a moral argument for upholding the current legal distinction that accepts that it is an ad hoc device; a legal fiction rather than a principled distinction.

16.3 Voluntary end of life decisions

End of life decisions evoke the loudest calls for increased patient autonomy. Some patients fear that their life will be sustained beyond the point they consider compatible with a meaningful existence and wish to refuse life-sustaining treatment in advance. Others fear that they will die in pain or distress not capable of being addressed by modern palliative care and wish to

---

[22] [1993] A.C. 789 at 885.
[23] [1993] A.C. 789 at 887.
[24] See Kass and Lund 1996.
[25] Kass and Lund 1996, 420.
[26] Kass and Lund 1996, 423.

be killed or assisted to die. Yet others request VLT and PAS simply as means of exercising their autonomous decision that their life is no longer worth living.

16.3.1 Advance refusals

All five of the moral theories outlined in Ch.1 give weight to protecting and encouraging patient autonomy. Expressions of contemporaneous self-determination have moral force, because respecting patients' autonomous choices generally tracks utility, virtues, rights, and duties (see Ch.4 (4.4.3)). For rights-based theories and many utilitarian theories, autonomy represents the expression of one's moral status. Refusals of life-sustaining treatment are more difficult, because the patient's autonomy must be weighed against his and others' interest in the continuance of his life. We have seen, for example, that duty-based positions adhering to the sanctity of life will view refusals motivated by suicidal intent as immoral. (It does not follow that such positions must require doctors to force treatment on unwilling patients.) In contrast, rights-based and utilitarian theories allow individuals to determine their own interests even in the case of a refusal of life-sustaining treatment. (It does not follow that such positions do not allow an individual's interests to be outweighed by the interests of others.)

Advance refusals are more controversial than contemporaneous refusals. Advance refusals could be viewed as expressions of "future-orientated" or "prospective" autonomy.[27] They are made for a future situation when the patient is no longer able to competently make or express a refusal. Advance refusals can also be viewed as reassuring patients that they will not be treated unnecessarily in the future and as reducing the burden on others by relieving them of responsibility for making such decisions.[28] Advance refusals can thus be regarded as persuasive or binding in a similar way to contemporaneous refusals. Prospective refusals, however, lack the context, immediacy, and safeguards of contemporaneous refusals. They rely on hypothetical facts or best-guess predictions[29] and, as Buchanan has argued,

> when the decision to forgo life-sustaining treatment is a remote and abstract possibility it is less likely to elicit the same protective responses that are provoked in family members and health care professionals when they are actually confronted with a human being who they believe can lead a meaningful life but who chooses to die.[30]

Prospective autonomy interests can conflict with contemporaneous welfare interests and, unlike contemporaneous decisions, an incompetent patient can no longer change his mind. Some go further and argue that an individual can lose his "personal identity", so that the individual who projects his autonomous

---

[27] Cantor 1992.
[28] See Docker 1996, 185 and Buchanan 1988, 277–278.
[29] See Cantor 1992, esp. 15.
[30] Buchanan 1988, 279.

choices into the future can be viewed as imposing his wishes on a different (incompetent) individual.[31]

There is no morally neutral position on whether advance refusals should be enforced or even enforceable. There is no reversing a patient's death and, as long as active measures to end life are prohibited, the effects of successfully administrating unwanted life-saving treatment are irreversible. This section will focus on two issues: the personal identity objection, and the conflict between prospective autonomy and contemporaneous welfare.

16.3.1.1 The personal identity objection

The personal identity objection questions the validity of relying on advance decisions as expressions of self-determination. According to this objection, the competent individual who projects his autonomous choices into the future does not share his identity with the incompetent individual to whom the projected choice is meant to apply.[32] The claim is that prospective autonomy interests have no more force than the interests of any other third party. The past self would be imposing his views on a different individual. To be clear, this objection is not restricted to advance refusals. It applies to any form of advance decision and any attempt to take account of the incompetent patient's previous views or values (including the substituted judgment test).

For the personal identity objection to undermine reliance on the views and values expressed by the previously competent patient, it must be accepted that the patient does not share his identity with the decision-maker *and* that it is impermissible to impose the decision-maker's views on the patient. From a moral point of view, there must be limits on the extent to which the past, present, and future selves of any given individual can be regarded as distinct. To regard me as a different person to the one who went to sleep last night is to free me from responsibility for the actions of the person who went to sleep. Any theory imposing moral duties must treat past, present, and future selves as sharing some core identity that is not easily lost.[33] There must be moral limits on what can be legitimately viewed as identity change and moral constraints on the interpretation that can legitimately be placed on the empirical evidence. This still leaves a great deal of room for different views on the essential features of personal identity and on the permissibility of imposing prior views on a future incompetent individual.

Buchanan considers the view that a necessary condition of personal identity is *psychological continuity with one's past self*.[34] (This criterion is, at least, potentially consistent with being the bearer of moral duties and is capable of being lost.) He argues that, on this criterion, an incompetent patient can still have personal identity if the requisite level of psychological continuity is not set too high. On this view, the personal identity objection would not undermine all

---

[31] See Buchanan 1988, 280.
[32] See e.g. Dresser 1986, Buchanan 1988, esp. 280, and Lewis 2002, 581–583.
[33] See further the discussion of related issues in Beyleveld and Brownsword 2001, 107.
[34] See Buchanan 1988, esp. 280.

advance decisions (because not all incompetent patients would have lost their past personal identity). He also argues that the personal identity objection only works if the patient who has lost his past personal identity is still a *person*.[35] He argues that imposing advance decisions on another *person* involves their subjugation (in the same way that slavery would), whereas non-persons can legitimately be subject to the "surviving interests" of the past person they used to be. By way of example, he says that the permanently unconscious and those who suffer from profound, permanent dementia are not persons and so cannot be subject to the personal identity objection. Buchanan's view restricts the force of the personal identity objection to a limited sub-category of incompetent patients (i.e. those who have lost their personal identity but continue to have full moral status as persons). It is not difficult to see how different conclusions follow from different views on personal identity and the criterion of moral status. We will return to the competing criteria for possession of moral status and their implications for end of life treatment alternatives for incompetent patients (see 16.4).

16.3.1.2 The conflict between past autonomy interests and present welfare interests

Even if the personal identity objection is answered or does not apply, there is still an issue about how much weight should be given to the autonomy interests of the previously competent individual as opposed to the welfare interests of the currently incompetent patient. Sometimes these two interests point in the same direction but they can come into conflict. Where, for example, a simple blood transfusion will save the patient and return him to full health but he has made an advance refusal on the basis of his faith as a Jehovah's Witness. We have already seen that some moral theories give little weight to contemporaneous autonomy interests over present welfare, let alone prospective autonomy interests over present welfare. Here, once again, different moral premises lead to different conclusions.

Dworkin asks us to consider Margo.[36] Margo is described in an article in a leading medical journal by a medical student who visited her regularly.[37] When he first began visiting her she was a 45-year-old victim of Alzheimer's disease who lived at home with the help of an attendant. When the medical student arrived he was always greeted warmly, but Margo never used his name. She would often be reading mysteries, but her place in the book seemed to jump randomly from day to day and the student wondered whether reading was always a mystery to her. She also enjoyed attending an art class, but painted much the same picture every day. Despite her apparent problems making new memories and the rapid fading of her old memories, the student considered Margo to be "one of the happiest people I have ever known". Dworkin asks us

---

[35] Person is being used here to refer to those properties necessary to possess full moral status. Moral status is explained in Ch.7 (7.2.1). Buchanan 1988, 284 lists a number of popular criteria for personhood.

[36] See Dworkin 1993, ch.8.

[37] See Firlik 1991.

to suppose that Margo had years ago, when fully competent, directed that if she were to develop Alzheimer's disease "she should not receive treatment for any other serious, life-threatening disease she might contract. Or even that in that event she should be killed as soon and as painlessly as possible".[38] Dworkin argues that we should give effect to her prior wishes, despite the joy that she appears to gain from life as a victim of Alzheimer's disease.

Dworkin considers the values of autonomy, beneficence, and sanctity of life by reference to two kinds of interests that are said to guide our lives.[39] "Experiential interests" are those things that we value because we enjoy experiencing them, such as listening to music. "Critical interests" are the hopes and aims that give value and meaning to our lives beyond experiential preferences, such as close relationships. Dworkin considers our critical interests to take priority over our experiential interests and explain why we care about what will happen to us at the end of our lives. Building on this, he argues for an interpretation of the reasons for valuing autonomy and beneficence that accords priority to Margo's prior views as a competent person. He argues that we should support the "integrity view of autonomy", which enables us to explain why we allow a competent individual to act against his best interests.[40] The integrity view, he argues, requires us to give effect to Margo's "precedent autonomy", reflecting her views on the overall shape of the life that she wanted to live. Margo's "contemporary autonomy" as a demented person is thereby overridden by the "precedent autonomy" of the person that she was before.[41] The upshot, he argues, is that "personal identity does survive even the most serious dementia".[42] With respect, his conception of critical interests presupposes a rejection of the personal identity objection and cannot therefore be a response to it.

Other theorists have also presented arguments emphasising the moral interests of competent individuals to shape their lives according to their own values, even after loss of competence.[43] In opposition, Dresser has rejected the accordance of priority to what Dworkin calls "precedent autonomy" and what Cantor calls "prospective autonomy".[44] She accepts the personal identity objection and, in any case, believes that prospective autonomy interests are overridden by our duties to protect the welfare of incompetent patients and display compassion towards them. Kadish similarly holds that prospective/precedent autonomy lacks the force of contemporary autonomy in a Margo-type scenario and is morally overridden by considerations of human compassion.[45] This debate turns on different views on what are defensible moral premises. It is a debate that can occur within the general moral positions almost as much as between them.

---

[38] Dworkin 1993, 226.
[39] See Dworkin 1993, ch. 7, esp. 201–202.
[40] See also Dworkin 1986.
[41] See, e.g. Dworkin 1986, 11.
[42] Dworkin 1986, 6.
[43] See e.g. Cantor 1992.
[44] See Dresser 1994 and 1995.
[45] See Kadish 1992.

16.3.2 Legalising voluntary lethal treatment and PAS

In the last chapter we saw that there are limits on the voluntary end of life decisions that the law will allow to be lawfully implemented. At the request of a patient, it is lawful to withhold/withdraw life-prolonging treatment or administer palliative treatment that incidentally shortens life, but it is not lawful to administer lethal treatment or assist a patient to self-administer lethal treatment. A patient who happens to be able to commit suicide without assistance, is receiving life-prolonging treatment, or is in need of painkillers that are potentially life-shortening is able to exercise a voluntary decision to die that is legally denied to others. The debates over legalising voluntary lethal treatment (*VLT*) and physician-assisted suicide (*PAS*) are closely connected. It is difficult to see how VLT could be coherently permitted if PAS were not, because PAS is more firmly linked to patient autonomy in the sense that the patient controls the final act. (In Ch.15, however, it was noted that Belgium appears to have adopted the unusual position of permitting VLT but not PAS.) Similarly, permitting PAS will bolster the argument for permitting VLT, because suicide attempts are not always possible or successful. Proponents of legalisation argue that a permissive approach is required by important moral principles or would at least be better than the current position. Opponents argue that legalisation would contravene important moral principles or would be worse than the current position (or would lead to a situation that is much worse). Support for the status quo is largely founded on opposition to legalising PAS and VLT, rather than the view that the current position draws all the right moral distinctions.[46]

16.3.2.1 Arguments advanced by proponents of legalisation

Proponents of the legalisation of PAS and VLT often appeal to *patient autonomy* and argue that legalisation is required to realise maximal patient autonomy.[47] In the last chapter we saw that countries that permit PAS and/or VLT have adopted additional safeguards that go beyond ensuring that the patient's decision is autonomous (see 15.4.3). The Dutch legislation requires the patient to be suffering unbearably and hopelessly and the Oregon legislation requires the patient to be terminally ill. Similarly, the (now rejected) Bill introduced into Parliament by Lord Joffe only permits a doctor to lawfully accede to a request for VLT or PAS if the patient is a capacitated adult who is suffering unbearably as a result of a terminal illness. These additional safeguards require a justification beyond patient autonomy. They must be viewed as either principled safeguards tracking other morally relevant considerations or as politically necessary compromises required to gain sufficient political support for any sort of permissive regulatory regime. Viewed as principled safeguards they could be interpreted as relying on virtues or duties of beneficence that require a

---

[46] See, however, McCall Smith 1999.
[47] See e.g. Harris 1995c and Law 1996, 298–299.

reduction in needless pain and suffering or the provision of psychological reassurance to dying patients.[48]

Many commentators have doubted whether safeguards can sufficiently ensure that a patient's request for assistance to die is autonomous. Patients requesting assistance to die could be suffering from depression and be dependent on health professionals and family members to whom they might feel a burden. According to Wolf,

> Terminal patients are quite unlike independent rights-bearers freely negotiating in business transactions. Instead, they are profoundly dependent, often at the mercy of health professionals for everything from toileting to life-saving care, and may be experiencing too much pain, discomfort, or depression to make independent and truly voluntary decisions.[49]

In the last chapter, we saw that this type of reasoning influenced both the House of Lords and the European Court of Human Rights in the Dianne Pretty case (see 15.4.2.2). The fear was not that Dianne Pretty's decision was not sufficiently autonomous, but that the court had no way of ensuring that the decisions of others would be sufficiently autonomous. Such concerns are, however, equally applicable to refusals of life-sustaining treatment and to requests for life-shortening palliative care. The irony is that more permissive jurisdictions have greater procedural safeguards to ensure that a patient who seeks PAS or VLT is acting autonomously than they do to ensure that a patient who seeks to refuse treatment or request life-shortening palliative care is acting autonomously. Concern for those who are particularly vulnerable does not, without further moral premises, justify the blanket prohibition of PAS or VLT.

16.3.2.2 Arguments advanced by opponents of legalisation

Opponents of the legalisation of PAS and VLT appeal directly to restrictive moral principles (such as the sanctity of life) or to the alleged harmful consequences of legalisation. Those who consider *suicide* to be immoral thereby adopt at least the first approach. It is, of course, possible to favour the prohibition of PAS and VLT without favouring the prohibition of suicide or without even considering suicide to be immoral. One supporter of the sanctity of life position (which considers suicide to be immoral) has argued that those who attempt suicide "need understanding and help rather than condemnation and punishment", but it "remains reasonable to use [the law] against those who would assist or encourage suicide".[50] Criminalising suicide has many undesirable consequences, such as discouraging those who have unsuccessfully attempted suicide from seeking medical assistance and further stigmatising loved ones left behind by successful suicide attempts. Similarly, PAS and VLT could be rejected without holding

---

[48] See Emanuel 1999, 631–635. Emanuel goes on to argue that focusing on VLT and PAS impairs, rather than improves, the care of those reaching the end of lives by diverting resources.

[49] Wolf 1998, 1077–1078.

[50] Keown 2002, 55.

suicide to be immoral at all, because (say) the involvement of the doctor is considered to undermine the doctor–patient relationship.[51]

The dominant approach of opponents of PAS and VLT is to appeal to the allegedly harmful consequences of legalisation.[52] One fear is that of abuse, whereby PAS and VLT will take place without proper informed consent, because patients will be coerced, their mental illness or incompetence will be overlooked, or optimal palliative care will not be offered or available. Other fears are directed at the wider consequences of allowing PAS and VLT, such as the likelihood that psychological distress will be caused to surviving family members or to patients who fear that their doctor will kill them against their will. These empirical claims are frequently made using the metaphor of the slippery slope.[53]

Slippery slope arguments were explained in Ch.1 (1.4.2) as feared end point arguments whereby it is usually argued that allowing an apparently innocuous practice will lead to another unacceptable practice. Put in empirical form, where an appeal is made to the likely negative consequences of allowing a particular practice, such an argument is potentially compatible with all five moral camps. Rights- and duty-based theories will be concerned about a practice that it likely to lead to the violation of individuals' rights or interests. Utilitarians will be concerned if a particular practice will lead to a situation of increased disutility. Virtue-ethicists will be concerned if a practice is likely to undermine or in any way threaten virtuous motives. It follows that if a suitable end point is chosen, one that is widely considered to be unacceptable, such arguments potentially appeal to supporters of theories within any of the five groups of moral positions. For this reason, many opponents of the legalisation of PAS or VLT appeal to end points that attract almost universal commendation, such as the intentional killing of innocent persons against their will.[54] As indicated in Ch.1, however, in addition to empirical evidence and an unacceptable end point, it needs to be shown that the risk of the outcome occurring does not outweigh the moral benefits of taking the first step on to the supposed slippery slope. Also, the risk must not be removable by adequate safeguards.

In the context of end of life decisions, the empirical slippery slope metaphor is sometimes used to convey the argument that allowing PAS or VLT will cause us to slide towards unacceptable practises as respect for life ebbs away. The claim is that allowing these practices will lead to a shift towards increased instances of induced or assisted death in circumstances where appropriate treatment or palliative care exists, where the patient is not terminally ill, where the patient is not ill at all, and, eventually, where the competent patient has not provided any consent at all. Keown is a leading supporter of an empirical slippery slope argument along these lines.[55] He cites statistics from the Netherlands, which show a

---

[51] See Frey 1998, 27.
[52] See Emanuel 1999.
[53] For a list of such claims see House of Lords Select Committee 2005, paras 91–103.
[54] There is no universal agreement on what constitutes an "innocent person". In theory, act-utilitarian theories could allow the murder of an innocent person where it maximised utility.
[55] See Keown 2002. Keown's version of this argument is considered in depth by Smith 2005a, who argues that the current evidence does not support the empirical claims that it relies on.

startlingly high incidence of lethal treatment and PAS without consent.[56] He also takes the view that the safeguards in the Oregon legislation have proven to be inadequate and ineffective.[57] Others offer more sanguine views on experiences elsewhere.[58] In any event, it is not enough to show that abuse occurs in permissive countries. It also needs to be shown that the abuse occurs *because* PAS (or VLT) is permitted. Evidence of an outcome is not evidence of a causal connection—to hold otherwise is to appeal to a logical fallacy.[59] Singer has, for example, argued that

> the Dutch figures cannot possibly show an "increasing practice" of anything, because to show that we would need figures from two or more different years, preferably separated by a substantial gap. No such figures exist.[60]

Many proponents of legalisation argue that abuses occur just as frequent in countries where PAS and VLT are criminal offences. Practices such as withdrawing life-sustaining treatment are also open to abuse and do not currently need to comply with safeguards such as formal reporting mechanisms. Baron cites evidence that suggests that health professionals covertly assist suicide in US States where such practices are illegal "in percentages that rival those in Holland".[61] Surveys in Britain have also revealed a similarly high incidence of patient requests for assistance to die and doctors who have been willing to comply with such requests.[62] Thus, the view that allowing VLT will lead to incremental deterioration in medical practice until we end up with involuntary lethal treatment is hotly contested.

To bolster his claim Keown draws an analogy with the regulation of abortion.[63] A slippery slope argument has been made to the effect that abortion on health grounds should be rejected because permitting it will tend to lead to abortion for social convenience. Keown claims that this prediction has been borne out by experience following the implementation of the Abortion Act 1967: "Even ardent prochoicers would have to concede that, although the Abortion Act 1967 permits abortion for medical but not social reasons, abortion for social reasons has become the norm, or at least commonplace".[64] It is indeed the case that abortion has gained wider social acceptance and is now increasingly available for social reasons. It is more debatable whether this change in

---

[56] See Keown 2002, chs 9–13. See also Fenigsen 2004.
[57] See Keown 2002, ch.15.
[58] See e.g. Brock 2000 (who considers the experience in Oregon to provide reassurance that abuse can be avoided) and Griffiths 1995 (who argues that there is no evidence that abuses are more frequent in the Netherlands than elsewhere, rather the system is simply more transparent).
[59] Sometimes referred to by the Latin phrase *post hoc ergo proctor hoc* (after therefore because of).
[60] Singer 1994, 153.
[61] See Baron 1997, 15 (citing Back et al. 1996 and Asch 1996). See also Brock 2000, 306 and Griffiths 1995.
[62] See e.g. Ward and Tate 1994 (reporting that over three quarters of the doctors surveyed had been asked to take active steps to hasten death, of these 32% had complied with the request). See also House of Lords Select Committee 2005, paras 76–79.
[63] See Keown 2002, 71.
[64] Keown 2002, 71.

attitude was brought about by the 1967 Act, as it could be argued that wider acceptance of abortion for social reasons led to the Act. More significantly, it is controversial whether this end point is impermissible and whether its occurrence outweighs the benefits of permitting abortion for health reasons. As with end of life decisions, there is serious moral debate about what outcomes are truly impermissible relative to the alternatives. Abortion is more fully addressed in Ch.7.

Keown has also argued that VLT should not be allowed, because once VLT is allowed there is a powerful logical argument for allowing non-voluntary lethal treatment (NVLT).[65] He argues that any case for allowing VLT in cases of unbearable suffering is logically a case for lethal treatment without the patient's consent, because any such case must turn on the view that some lives are no longer worth living. In support of this "logical link" Keown notes that many of the leading supporters of VLT also support NVLT in at least some circumstances, including Harris, Singer, Kuhse, and Glover.[66] The existence of theorists who, in appropriate circumstances, support both VLT and NVLT does not, however, do anything to confirm a "logical link". Moreover, the theorists cited by Keown all adopt theories that have distinctly utilitarian features. Unlike the sanctity of life approach adopted by Keown, utilitarianism does not value all human life equally and holds that some lives are not worth living. It is open to theories that reject the sanctity of life approach to reject the absolute impermissibility of NVLT and therefore hold that VLT is not morally impermissible *even if* it logically implies acceptance of NVLT.

The logical link that Keown claims to establish is also subject to challenge. Those accepting VLT are not logically required to accept NVLT if they can show that there is a morally relevant difference. Keown rejects the idea that the patient's autonomous decision can amount to a morally relevant difference because, he argues, advocates of VLT and PAS impose conditions beyond those designed to ensure that the patient's request is autonomous.[67] However, advocates of VLT and PAS need not, *as a matter of principle*, limit VLT and PAS to cases where the patient satisfies conditions such as suffering unbearably or suffering from a terminal illness. Even if they do, Smith has pointed out that the patient's request and the doctor's judgement that the patient is suffering unbearably could consistently *both* be viewed necessary conditions for such practices to be permissible.[68] Moreover, contrary to Keown's view, a doctor providing lethal treatment or assistance on request is not necessarily making the judgment that he considers the patient's life to be of no benefit.[69] Such a doctor need only accept that he is permitted to implement the patient's own decision on the value of that patient's life.

---

[65] See Keown 2002, 76–79.
[66] See Keown 2002, 79. For the views of these theories see Harris 1985, Singer 1994, Kuhse 1987, and Glover 1977.
[67] See Keown 2002, 79.
[68] Smith 2005b, esp. 230.
[69] Cf. Keown 2002, 77.

16.4 Non-voluntary end of life decisions

16.4.1 Criteria and debate

Non-voluntary end of life decisions are at least as divisive as voluntary end of life decisions. Two issues are particularly controversial: the criteria that should be used to determine whether treatment is appropriate and whether all human beings have equal moral value.

Just as a previously competent patient's prior views can be regarded as decisive, influential, or irrelevant, so can a previously competent patient's prior values. Where there are no prior views and values or they are not treated as decisive, a further question arises. This is the question about whether end of life decisions should track the *patient's interests alone* or should also track *the interests of third parties*, such as family members. To track the patient's interests alone is not to ignore the views of family members, but to take them into account only insofar as this is required to uphold the patient's interests. In the absence of prior views, there are three major approaches competing for consideration: the substituted judgment approach, the patient's best interests approach, and the overall interests approach. These approaches were addressed in Ch.5 (5.2.2.4). A summary might help. The *substituted judgement approach* requires a proxy decision-maker to attempt to reach the decision that the patient would have made in the circumstances. This requires the application of the patient's previously expressed or displayed values and, as such, presupposes prior competence. It follows that the substituted judgment test, so defined, has no relevance where the patient has never been competent to form views or hold values.[70] This approach is often contrasted with the *best interests approach*, which requires actions to track what is best for the patient all things considered. This either applies where the substituted judgment test provides no answers (i.e. as a secondary criterion) or in place of that test (i.e. as a primary criterion). Both the substituted judgment and best interests tests, as defined, focus on the patient's interests alone. These can be rejected or supplemented by a wider test of *overall interests*, which directly requires the interests of others to be taken into account.

The choice between the *substituted judgment* and the *best interests approach* as the primary criterion in end of life decision-making rests on the extent to which the former approach is thought to protect prospective autonomy and the extent to which prospective autonomy is valued over the patient's contemporaneous welfare interests. Theories prioritising the patient's contemporaneous welfare interests over his prospective autonomy in cases where the patient had made an advance refusal will similarly favour the best interests approach over the substituted judgment approach. If the patient's prior views are not decisive, the

---

[70] The last chapter examined the case of *Re J* [1991] Fam. 33 (see 15.5.2). In that case, Taylor L.J. said that: "The test must be whether the child in question, if capable of exercising sound judgment, would consider the life tolerable" ([1991] Fam. 33 at 55). This could be read as a misguided attempt to apply the substituted judgment test to a child who had never been competent.

patient's prior values must be even less relevant. In contrast, those theories prioritising prospective autonomy will tend to lean towards the substituted judgment test over the best interests test.

The choice between the patient's interests test and the overall interests test is closely connected to the patient's moral status, i.e. the direct duties owed to the patient because of his properties and characteristics. With regard to end of life decision-making, taking direct account of the interests of affected individuals in addition to the patient will mean that the fate of at least some patients will rest on the value of their life to others. Resource allocation issues aside, few moral theories are prepared to allow the fate of a patient *with full moral status* to rest on the interests of other affected individuals. While communitarians and utilitarians could require a patient's welfare or autonomy interests to be balanced against familial and societal interests, many are not prepared to do this where the patient has full moral status. John Harris has, for example, argued that to do so would mean that those with many loved ones who want them to live would thereby be treated as having more valuable lives than those with few or no loved ones. This has led him to declare that "It seems safer in such cases to stick to the Benthamite maxim that everyone is to count for one and none for more than one".[71] (In effect, Harris relies on a form of rule utilitarianism to answer the counter-intuitive consequences of act utilitarianism.)

If the patient has less than full moral status, then the interests of those with full moral status could potentially outweigh his interest in being kept alive. This is so just as much for rights- and duty-based theories as utilitarian theories. If a patient is considered to have no rights or less powerful rights than you or I, then his moral interests could be outweighed by ours. Not all theories will accept that *all* incompetent humans have the same moral status as all competent humans. Like beginning of life decisions (e.g. those concerning abortion and embryo research), end of life decisions often turn on the moral status of the subject. As explained in Ch.1 (1.4.3.2), "patients" could be granted *full, no,* or *limited* moral status, depending on the position taken with regard to the moral duties that we owe directly to them. For present purposes it will be assumed that competent, cognitively normal adult humans have full moral status—this is certainly the position of all the major moral theorists. Views on embryos, the permanently unconscious, and the like are more variable. Such individuals could be viewed as entitled to the same protection as you or I (the *full status* position), no status (the *no status* position), or a fixed or gradual status between those two extremes (the *limited status* position). To take the no status position is to hold that the patient in question has no interests, so the best interests test can no longer apply[72] and the overall interests test could legitimately be applied. To take the full status approach is to reject the overall interest approach unless one adopts a (utilitarian or compromise) position that allows one person's life to be sacrificed in the interests of others. What are often called deontological moral theories—paradigmatically, rights- and duty-based theories—do not allow the

---

[71] Harris 1985, 105.

[72] This criticism can be levelled at the *Bland* case where the best interests test was applied, despite some of their Lordships considering Tony Bland to have no interests.

lives of those with full moral status to be weighed against the less important interests of others. Adopting the limited status position is compatible with adopting the patient's interests test or the overall interests test, depending on the precise value given to the patient in question.

16.4.2 Applying this ethical framework

Examples should help to put some flesh on these dry theoretical bones. The sanctity of life position, as supported by John Finnis, John Keown, and Luke Gormally, is a duty-based position holding that *all* biologically human beings have full moral status.[73] This position treats the intentional killing of a seriously mentally impaired human (such as a patient in PVS or seriously brain damaged newborn) as murder. From this position, the appropriate test to apply to an incompetent patient is the best interests test, but it could never be in the best interests of a patient to be intentionally killed whether by act or omission. Compare that to the position of John Harris, who adopts an implicitly utilitarian position granting full moral status only to *persons*, defined as those capable of valuing their own existence.[74] For Harris, end of life decisions for non-persons (such as patients in PVS) can legitimately be made according to the overall interests test. An individual not capable of understanding the choice between life and death would be a non-person and a potential subject of a *non-voluntary* end of life decision. The value of a non-person's life is closely connected to its "quality" and some lives will be considered not worth living. Some utilitarians would go further and allow the overall interests test to apply to persons, which would potentially lead to the *involuntary* killing of an innocent, fully competent adult. As already indicated, Harris is unwilling to go this far. Similarly, Singer argues that even a utilitarian should "rule against involuntary euthanasia" on the basis that cases of justifiable involuntary euthanasia are unlikely to ever occur in practice.[75]

Ethical disputes on non-voluntary end of life decisions are multi-variable. Consider the dispute between the "vitalist" and "sanctity of life" positions.[76] Both are duty-based positions granting full moral status to all biological humans. Yet, they are divided over whether life must be preserved at all costs: the "vitalist" position holds that it should, the "sanctity of life" position does not. Thus, these positions will adopt different views on the application of the best interests test to a patient whose life can be prolonged but for only a brief, pain-racked time. What is *futile*, in the sense of not worthwhile, to one theory will not be futile to others. This is one reason why the legal concept of "futility" (examined in the last chapter, 15.5.2) is potentially ethically divisive. The worthwhileness of treatment can only be assessed relative to its ethical goal and what is an acceptable goal is theory dependent. Extremely painful and distressing treatment that prolongs a patient's

---

[73] See e.g. Finnis 1995a, Keown 2002, and Gormally 1995, esp. 114–115.
[74] See Harris 1985, 1995c, 1995d, and 1995e.
[75] See Singer 1993, 201. Singer invokes Hare's distinction between critical and intuitive levels of moral thinking, addressed in the final chapter (17.3).
[76] See further Keown 1997 and the discussion in Ch.1 (1.4.3.1).

life for only a short time could be regarded as worthwhile by a vitalist and futile (as disproportionate) by a sanctity of life supporter.[77] Similarly, a utilitarian assessing the worthwhileness of treating a severely disabled patient could come to a different view to a supporter of the sanctity of life, as a consequence of the utilitarian rejection of the idea that all human patients have lives of equal value.[78]

16.4.3 Patients in PVS and the special case of *Re A*

Bland and *Re A* are two of the most hotly debated decisions in English medical law.[79] Both cases go straight to the heart of disputes on moral status, on whether all human beings are morally equal or some are more equal than others.

16.4.3.1 Patients in PVS

Patients in PVS have a prognosis of irreversible unconsciousness until death. They are not brain-stem dead. They usually require tube-feeding and hydration but do not usually require artificial ventilation. Of the major moral positions, only those duty-based theories resting the possession of moral status on membership of the human species will grant full moral status to patients in PVS. It does not follow that all other theories will permit all life-sustaining care to be withdrawn from all patients in PVS. Given the apparent absence of suffering and the remote possibility that some of these patients could recover, if there were no conflicting moral interests, all theories granting any moral status to patients in PVS would require treatment to continue indefinitely. Conflicting interests will include the interests of other affected persons and could include the prospective autonomy interests of the previously competent patient. In reality, there are always conflicting interests. Continued treatment of PVS patients has significant resource implications in the sense that the cost and equipment could be used to save the lives of patients with much better prognoses. As Morgan has poignantly noted, "there is a sense in which Tony Bland is a hostage to the fortune which the British public health service no longer has".[80] Also, continued treatment can be distressing for relatives and loved ones (many of whom cannot properly grieve until the loved one is dead and buried) and can harm the morale of healthcare workers (who are treating a patient who will most probably never improve or recover consciousness). The best interests test is not directly concerned with the interests of individuals other than the patient. In my view, the test applied by the House of Lords in *Bland* must therefore be considered an impure best interests test verging on an overall interests test. Suggestions to the effect that *Bland* has no interests at all[81]

---

[77] See Keown 2002, ch.4.
[78] Compare Keown 1997, 485–486, with Harris 2001b, 225–226.
[79] *Airedale NHS Trust v Bland* [1993] A.C. 789 and *Re A* [2001] Fam. 147, respectively.
[80] Morgan 2001, 220.
[81] [1993] A.C. 789 at 897 (Lord Mustill).

are only strictly compatible with the no status position (because only a being owed no moral duties of any sort can have no moral interests).

Most grounds capable of supporting the view that it is morally permissible to withdraw life-sustaining treatment from a patient in PVS would equally support the view that it is permissible (or even required) for such patients to be killed quickly by the administration of lethal treatment. The competing interests of those waiting for resources and those suffering distress usually favour the patient's quick death over his slow death by dehydration and starvation.

16.4.3.2 Re A

The case of *Re A*, involving the separation of conjoined twins to save the stronger of the two, was examined in the last chapter (15.5.3).[82] Like all end of life decisions, there are two central ethical issues: what criteria should be applied and who should apply them. The choice of criteria for determining whether conjoined twins should be separated needs to take account of their moral status. If moral status turns on actual and prospective cognitive development, then Mary could be viewed as having less moral status than Jodie.[83] If, however, moral status is considered to be grounded in membership of the human species, then Mary and Jodie have the same moral status. Harris points out that if Jodie and Mary were truly considered to have full moral status then the same conclusion would have to be reached if the twins had been "competent individuals with biographical lives".[84] He therefore imagines a hypothetical case of conjoined twins, Gilbert and George, who are in their twenties and competent, but whose medical condition has deteriorated so that the medical facts mirror those of Jodie and Mary,[85] and argues that deliberately terminating the life of Gilbert to save George "would not be permissible in English law; neither would it be ethical".[86] The view that separation is inconsistent with full status is supported by Watt who argues that the principle of double effect could not justify Mary and Jodie's separation because, although the medics might not have intended Mary's death, they did intend to wrongfully mutilate her.[87]

The relative moral status of twins is not the only morally relevant issue. Positions holding that Mary has less moral status than Jodie still have to consider whether the parents' views have moral relevance. Parental opinion could have moral relevance because of the parents' status as proxy decision-makers or because of their status as individuals directly affected by the decision. Most theorists have focused on the parents' position as proxy decision-makers. Freeman, for example, has argued that "There are more important rights to confer on children than the right to autonomous parents".[88] Harris has argued that *Re A* represents

---

[82] *Re A* [2001] Fam. 147.
[83] See e.g. the rights-based view grounding moral status according to the likelihood that a being is an agent (i.e. is able to act for a voluntarily chosen purpose) in Clucas and O'Donnell 2002.
[84] Harris 2001b.
[85] See Harris 2001b, 224.
[86] Harris 2001b, 235.
[87] See Watt 2001.
[88] Freeman 2001, 279.

"a finely balanced judgment but perhaps because it is, the reason for neglecting the parent's views is absent".[89] Harris could be arguing that the parent's views as proxies should be respected, because the grounds for challenging their decision are so weak. Alternatively or additionally, he could be arguing that the parent's views as directly affected parties should be respected, because (as persons) they have much greater moral status than the children. While Harris does not explicitly say so, his statement that following the parents' views would not have involved the premature death of any *persons*,[90] suggests that he was relying on the parents' moral interests qua affected persons. Whether or not this is correct, this must be a possibility for theories holding that the parents have a much greater moral status than the twins. The distress caused by contravening the parent's firmly held religious convictions appears to have been considerable.

16.5 Conclusion

Technological advances have amplified the need for end of life decision-making. Potentially effective life-sustaining treatment is increasingly available in circumstances where it is unwanted, considered too burdensome, or simply extremely expensive. There is also increased demand for life-shortening treatment and assistance by patients dissatisfied with palliative care or simply wanting to die. The topic of end of life decisions displays many of the book's reoccurring themes. It has its own form of patient tourism, *death tourism*, and has been subject to *medicalisation* in a similar way to the law on abortion and assisted reproduction. Death and dying are increasingly managed by medicine and medicine continues to shape our understanding and expectations. The limits of medicine are, however, very evident. David Glass[91] and the scientist Stephen Hawking (who, when he was 21, was told that he had only two years to live)[92] did not die as was predicted. The patient in *Re C* who believed that he was a world famous surgeon did not get gangrene as predicted.[93] These examples serve as a timely reminder that whatever options medicine puts before us, medicine is not a science of mathematical certainties.

The law on end of life decisions raises many ethical questions. There is an evident judicial coyness with regard to key underlying issues such as the value to be attached to human life and the difficulties presented by the economic cost of life-prolonging care and treatment. Legal usage of the best interests test has allowed such issues to be hidden or addressed only indirectly. The problem is that these issues are profoundly controversial. The next chapter will ask whether there is any way of choosing between the competing ethical views underlying this controversy.

---

[89] Harris 2001b, 236.
[90] See Harris, 2001b, 236.
[91] *R v Portsmouth Hospitals NHS Trust Ex p. Glass* [1999] 2 F.L.R. 905.
[92] See THES 2004.
[93] *Re C* [1994] 1 All E.R. 819.

16.6 Further reading

Present v prospective interests

Buchanan, Allen (1988) "Advance Directives and the Personal Identity Problem." 17(4) *Philosophy and Public Affairs* 277–302.

Dworkin, Ronald (1986) "Autonomy and the Demented Self." 64(2) *Milbank Quarterly* 4–16.

The legalisation of voluntary lethal treatment and physician-assisted suicide

Emanuel, Ezekiel J. (1999) "What is the Great Benefit of Legalizing Euthanasia of Physician-Assisted Suicide?" 109(3) *Ethics* 629–642.

Keown, John (eds) (1995) *Euthanasia Examined: Ethical, Clinical and Legal Perspectives.* (Cambridge: Cambridge University Press).

Smith, Stephen W. (2005) "Evidence for the Practical Slippery Slope in the Debate on Physician-Assisted Suicide and Euthanasia." 13(1) *Medical Law Review* 17–44.

Chapter 17

A MORAL APPROACH TO MEDICAL LAW

17.1 Introduction

If we are to understand an ethical claim we need to understand the perspective from which it is advanced. That is not always easy. Ch.1 detailed the breadth of possible criteria for distinguishing the morally permissible from the morally impermissible and subsequent chapters have gone some way towards explaining the application of some of these positions. Unfortunately, there is a general tendency towards moral imprecision. The bioethical literature often leaves the reader to guess the underlying moral theory in play. Occasionally, bioethicists deliberately choose not to make their underlying position clear to encourage consideration of arguments on their own terms. Labels can be misused and are often "attached to philosophical positions for people to assume that if they reject a particular school of philosophy in general, or adhere to a different philosophical tradition or approach, they can safely ignore or reject arguments from another school of philosophy".[1] Usually, however, where the underlining ethical position

---

[1] Harris 1998, 5–6.

of a writer is unclear, it is as unclear to the writer as the reader. This book has also sought to encourage readers to reflect on their own position. The first step towards moral awareness is to become aware of the inconsistencies and assumptions made in one's pre-reflective moral reasoning.

This book has focused on a number of key categories of moral positions. The tenets of these positions incline or commit supporters to certain conclusions. Rights-based theories, for example, peg all moral duties to moral rights possessed by rights-holders. They are autonomy-based, action-based, and reject duties to oneself. It follows that rights-based theories are supportive of autonomous, informed choices and thereby prima facie supportive of patients being informed to the extent required by maximal autonomy, voluntary lethal treatment/euthanasia, voluntary sales of tissue and organs, and reproductive autonomy. They must reject the idea that a being can be wronged by its mere creation, which is relevant to the debates on wrongful life, assisted reproduction, and reproductive cloning. In contrast, utilitarian theories peg all moral duties to a consequential evaluation of likely outcomes, and plead collective benefits against individual entitlements. For utilitarians, if the general good is best served by doing something then it ought to be done. Utilitarianism is typically supportive of practices designed to direct treatment, research, and resources to those most likely to benefit, so as to maximise utility. We have seen that utilitarianism is prima facie supportive of both abortion and withdrawing treatment from those who are in a permanent vegetative state (PVS).

Is a doctor really given any guidance by being told that a rights-based theorist would do X, a utilitarian Y, or that a virtue ethicist (or, for that matter a principalist or casuist) would take account of X, Y, and Z? If moral theory is to provide any useful guidance it needs to go beyond stamp collecting. The problem is two-fold. *First*, the broad brush implications of the major moral theories are frequently too abstract to be useful in most clinical settings. The moral positions presented in Ch.1 require considerable padding out if they are to be capable of generating guidance. *Second*, as soon as the concrete implications of a particular moral approach are drawn out, we enter the realm of the controversial. The reality of moral pluralism is that adherents of particular moral values and theories will reject the implications of conflicting moral theories.

Is there a way out of this *impasse?* There are many justificatory strategies claiming to provide good reasons for choosing one criterion of moral permissibility over others. Whatever moral position is adopted it should seek to avoid the twin horns of indeterminacy and dogma. Its adequacy will depend on the reasons capable of being offered in favour of it. Any such position should be adopted provisionally, because no justificatory strategy is infallible. Moral reasoning is not about dogma. A good moral argument will lead you to question your pre-reflective views. Unfortunately, "Nothing is so difficult in philosophical writing as to get people to be sympathetic enough to what one is saying to understand what it is".[2] I trust that the reader will now be sympathetic to moral theory. The need for it should now be apparent.

---

[2] Hare 1981, 65.

17.2 Moral objectivism reconsidered

Whatever else morality is about, it is about obligation. It is about doing what is right, what is permissible. It is *prescriptive* or action-guiding. At least, morality is usually defined in this way. What makes something a "moral" matter, in the sense of falling within the field of morality, depends on one's definition of morality. A definition of morality must enable us to distinguish the moral from the non-moral. Many possible definitions are available. Moral requirements are often defined as *other-regarding* or *impartial* in the sense of requiring one to act in the interests of others and treat them as equal to one's own interests. According to some theorists moral requirements are also *categorical*, i.e. they override other demands and are independent of one's desires or inclinations. All definitions are essentially stipulative. We must take care with definitions if we are to understand the claims of any particular theorist (particularly when dealing with virtue ethicists).[3] Stipulating a definition of morality does not, however, tell us how to distinguish the morally permissible from the morally impermissible, nor does it help us to understand why moral requirements are binding on us. Definitions are merely tools for conveying ideas, they are not justificatory mechanisms. A justificatory mechanism is something that provides good reasons for accepting a view. We need to define our starting point if we are to avoid talking at cross purposes and ensure that we are really answering the same question, but definitions are not themselves reasons.

Moral philosophers often ask for good reasons for accepting a particular view. To ask whether good reasons can be given for adopting a particular moral theory could be to ask one of two questions:

(1) can good (non-moral) reasons be offered for adopting the moral point of view; or

(2) can good reasons be offered for accepting one criterion of moral permissibility over others?

Different answers can be given to these two questions. Some hold that one, both, or neither of these questions can be answered in the affirmative. If good reasons can be offered for adopting the moral point of view (as asked by question 1), then we have a justification for accepting that we ought to act or think in a way that falls within the moral field. If good reasons can be offered for accepting one criterion or moral permissibility (as asked by question 2), then we have a justification for accepting a particular view on what it is morally right for us to do or believe. Labels must be used cautiously. If used carefully they can help us to understand the range of possible answers. To question (1), an "amoralist" would answer no and a "strong moral objectivist" would answer yes.[4] To question (2),

---

[3] Since virtue ethics does not treat obligation and action as central, any definition of "ethics" or "morality" used by such theorists is unlikely to include such requirements.

[4] For completeness, a "moral agnostic" would answer neither yes nor no. Also, it should be noted that the more stringent the definition of morality, the more difficult it is to justify a positive answer to question (1).

a "moral objectivist" would answer yes and a "moral relativist" would answer no.[5] Different answers to these two questions distinguish the strong and weak moral objectivist. Only the strong moral objectivist will answer yes to the first question. Both the strong and the weak moral objectivism answer yes to the second question.[6]

This appears to be more complex than it is. The issue is that moral objectivism can mean either the rejection of amoralism and moral relativism (strong moral objectivism) or merely the denial of moral relativism (weak moral objectivism). Let me try to put that in simpler terms. Some claim that morality is objective because those who reject morality can be offered good non-moral reasons for accepting a moral position (strong moral objectivism). Others claim that morality is objective because, if you are prepared to reason morally then good reasons can be offered for accepting one moral position over another (weak moral objectivism).

The difference between strong and weak moral objectivism can be seen in the work of Immanuel Kant. Kant thought that there was a supreme moral principle, the Categorical Imperative. (Kant held this to be a *moral* principle because it is prescriptive, categorical, and other-regarding.) In his book *Groundwork of the Metaphysic of Morals*, he sought to justify that principle in two ways.[7] He did this in three short chapters. In the first two chapters, Kant argued for the Categorical Imperative *from* a moral point of view. He sought to show that anyone who accepted the "common idea" of morality is logically required to accept the Categorical Imperative. In effect, he adopted weak moral objectivism. For reasons that will be examined later, he was not inclined to leave moral reasoning there. In chapter three of the *Groundwork*, Kant attempted something much more radical. He attempted to argue *for* the moral point of view itself. He sought to show that any "rational being with a will", whatever that being's views on morality, is logically required to accept the Categorical Imperative.[8] In effect, he adopted strong moral objectivism.

Kant was writing in the eighteenth century. Most recent philosophers reject the very possibility of defending a strong moral objectivist position. The vast majority of modern bioethicists adhere to some form of weak moral objectivism. They demand rational argument and the justification of moral conclusions, but they believe that rational argument can only go so far. The consensus, insofar as there is any consensus, seems to be that there is no one correct theory but the various theoretical alternatives are to be viewed as "partial contributions to a comprehensive, although necessarily fragmented, moral vision".[9] Another dominant view is that there is a correct moral theory, but it can only be justified to those who already accept morality. The vast majority of such

---

[5] For completeness, the mid-position (neither yes nor no) should be seen as a version of moral relativism.

[6] It is, therefore, possible for a weak moral objectivist to be an amoralist or a moral agnostic.

[7] The "sole aim" of the *Groundwork* was "to seek out and establish *the supreme principle of morality*" (Kant 1785, as translated in Paton 1948, 57 (original emphasis)).

[8] Kant seeks to establish the Categorical Imperative "as a necessary law *for all rational beings*" by showing that it is "connected (entirely *a priori*) with the concept of the will of a rational being as such" (1785, as translated in Paton 1948, 89).

[9] Steinbock et al. 2003, 9.

theorists are utilitarians. Various guises of this position can be seen in the work of Jonathan Glover, R. M. Hare, John Harris, and Peter Singer. In contrast, there are those who reject the very idea of justifying moral beliefs. Communitarians, for example, usually hold that no justification is needed or available beyond acceptance by a particular group or community. I reject these views. Below I will argue that one particular moral theory, that of the late American philosopher Alan Gewirth, offers a *plausible* claim to being *the* correct theory. This is a rights-based theory. What is more, its justification does not depend on prior acceptance of morality or specific moral intuitions. As the reader is no doubt aware, this is a very controversial claim to make.

At this point an explanation as to why this book has not given much attention to theology is probably called for. Ch.1 characterised religious ethics as moral positions typically falling within the duty-based camp, but little attention has been given to religious faith as a source of moral truth. The reader might consider belief in God to provide answers to many of the questions considered in this book. However, Plato showed us long ago why the belief that something is God's will is not sufficient to tell us whether it is morally right.[10] There is a circularity problem in claiming that God's will is good while simultaneously holding that what is good is determined by God's will. Logically, either what is good can be determined independently of God's will or good is no more than God's arbitrary inclinations. To define "good" purely in terms of God's will is to deprive it of prescriptive force. It follows that if we can establish what is morally right, then those who believe that God only wills what is morally right are thereby given a reason to choose between rival interpretations of God's will.[11]

17.2.1 Weak moral objectivism

Most bioethicists are weak moral objectivists using reason within morality rather than for morality. They attempt to provide *moral* reasons for adopting a particular criterion of moral permissibility. According to Jonathan Glover, for example, when asked to defend a moral belief about what ought to be done we might be able to supply a chain of reasoning reducing to moral axioms, but these moral axioms cannot themselves be proven.[12] This position is popular. Earlier chapters have frequently referred to the work of theorists supporting this position. Peter Singer explicitly concedes that he has not, and cannot, show that those who reject utilitarianism from a non-moral point of view can be shown to be in error or irrational.[13] Another theorist whose work we have frequently referred to, John Harris, relies on a form of rational intuitionism by

[10] In the debate between Socrates and Euthyphro: see Plato BCE, 10a, as translated in West and West 1998, 52.
[11] See Harris 2001a, 20. For a much more sophisticated analysis of the implications of accepting a categorical moral principle on belief in God, see Beyleveld and Brownsword 2001, ch.6.
[12] See Glover 1977, 24.
[13] See Singer 1993, esp. ch.12 and 334.

seeking to derive moral conclusions from reflection on moral intuitions. Harris holds that we can rationally test our basic values and the principles derived from those values.[14] These are tested, first, against hypothetical counter-examples (to show that those values hold good "in any imaginable or possible world") and, second, by asking whether those values "taken as a whole are well calculated to make the world a better place".[15]

As Harris would no doubt concede, his methodology is morally loaded. The starting point, pre-reflective moral views, and the premises of the mechanisms by which these are tested, are moral. Moreover, the moral assumptions made by Harris are of a particular sort. In his published works he dresses his essentially utilitarian position in the clothing of a non-utilitarian compromise position. He is wary of labels distracting from his underlying argument. Yet, despite appearing to be drawing out the implications of generally accepted values, the position presented in his work has significant utilitarian tendencies. As defined in Ch.1, utilitarianism seeks to achieve the best balance of good over bad and holds that individuals and their interests can be meaningfully added together and compared. Harris' position has these features. Harris explicitly rejects rights-based theories[16] and allows the aggregation of individuals and their interests:

> Precisely because each individual's life is individually valuable, two lives are more valuable than one. So that in cases where we have to choose between lives where we cannot save all at risk, we should choose to save as many lives as we can.[17]

In *Clones, Genes and Immorality,* he declares support for the principle of equality, i.e. "the principle that people's lives and fundamental interests are of equal importance and that they must in consequence be given equal weight".[18] In *The Value of Life,* he explicitly adopts "the Benthamite maxim that everyone is to count for one and none for more than one".[19] In essence, Harris adopts a form of preference utilitarianism requiring persons to treat the preferences of other persons (particularly their preference for life) as if they were their own when assessing the collective good. It is a negative form of utilitarianism, whereby we have duties to avoid deliberately bringing about avoidable harm or suffering to those capable of valuing their lives and preferences.[20] And, his reliance on general principles suggests that (at least on one level) it is a version of rule-utilitarianism. Unfortunately, Harris fails to explicitly declare his underlying moral theory, and some of its key premises, which makes it more difficult for a reader to check his consistency in applying that theory.[21] There is a further problem. Harris does not provide those readers who do not share his starting

---

[14] See, in particular, Harris 1985 and 2001a.
[15] Harris 1985, 236.
[16] See Harris 1998, 257 (where Harris describes his position as "broadly consequentialist" and states that he does not believe "that rights have any special status"), and Harris 1985, xvi.
[17] Harris 1985, 21. See also Harris 1985, 73.
[18] Harris 1998, 231.
[19] Harris 1985, 105.
[20] See e.g. Harris 1998, 257–258.
[21] See Häyry 2001, ch.5.

intuitions with a reason for accepting them. Instead he draws out the implications of particular intuitions and moral views. I use the work of Harris as no more than an example. By way of contrast, Ronald Dworkin and Robert Nozick are examples of rights-based theorists who famously take their (very different) views on the rights that we possess to be self-evident.[22]

17.2.1.1 Logical analysis of the moral point of view

Even if I accept that I owe moral obligations to others, why must I accept the tenets of any particular moral theory? R. M. Hare, another preference utilitarian within weak moral objectivism, seeks to answer this question. In his book *Moral Thinking*, he does not claim to be able to show that there is a rationally inescapable justification for morality itself. He is not a strong moral objectivist. According to Hare, the best answer to the question why should I accept morality is that morality is required by prudence, i.e. required to maximise one's satisfactions over a lifetime.[23] Hare does, however, claim to be able to derive preference utilitarianism from conceptual analysis of the moral point of view. His method, "rational universal prescriptivism", is to analyse moral oughts, understood as "universalisable", "prescriptive", and "overriding".[24] His claim is that anyone who holds that there are things that we *morally ought* to do is logically committed to preference utilitarianism.[25]

Kant also attempted to derive a particular criterion of moral permissibility from a purely logical analysis of the moral point of view. As mentioned earlier, in the first two chapters of *The Groundwork to the Metaphysic of Morals*, Kant argued that anyone who believes that there are morally binding requirements on action must, logically, consider the criterion of permissible action to be the Categorical Imperative. Here I do not propose to analyse the details of the arguments of Hare or Kant.[26] If their justificatory strategies are to work, the criterion of rationality must not contain hidden premises. The criterion of rationality in play is supposed to be pure logic. Logic is formal, not substantive. The rules of logic[27] do not require us to take account of the interests of others, let alone treat those interests as if they were one's own. The rules of logic are about coherent reasoning, they are not other-regarding or impartial in the sense of requiring us to *value* the interests of others. If logical analysis of the moral point of view is to work, any impartiality or other-regardingness in the conclusion must be

---

[22] See Nozick 1974, ix (this first sentence simply asserts as a starting assumption that "Individuals have rights") and Dworkin 1977, xv.

[23] Hare 1981, ch.10 and 219. This cannot provide an adequate non-moral justification for morality, because Hare defines morality as categorical.

[24] Notice that Hare defines morality as action-guiding and categorical. Indeed, he even goes as far as holding that (at the crucial level) moral requirements are absolute: Hare 1988, 153; 178.

[25] For a collection of comments and Hare's response, see Seanor and Fotion 1988.

[26] For a summary of Kant's argument see Beyleveld and Brownsword 2001, 88–91.

[27] There are a number of principles or laws of logic, sometimes called the rules of thought. These include the principle of identity, the principle of non-contradiction, the principle of implication, and the principle of universalisability (or sufficient reason). These are often misunderstood. The principle of non-contradiction, e.g., states that no statement, about the same set of circumstances, can be simultaneously true and false. It does not hold that every statement is either true or false (this is the controversial principle of the excluded middle).

established or taken as an assumed premise. I point this out because the standard response to both Kant and Hare has been to accuse them of assuming that rationality is impartial rather than agent-relative. According to Gauthier, for example, both Kant and Hare adopt a universalistic (impartial) concept of rationality, holding that whether it is rational to pursue an interest does not depend on whose interest it is.[28] If this is so, then both Kant and Hare fail to do what they claim to: they fail to show that anyone who reasons morally must, logically, accept a particular moral principle.

Peter Singer, in his book *Practical Ethics*, accepts that no one criterion of moral permissibility has been successfully derived purely logically from a bare, purely formal definition of morality.[29] Singer himself offers a less ambitious justification for accepting a particular moral principle that he considers to be "persuasive, although not conclusive".[30] His argument for accepting preference utilitarianism is a version of that offered by Hare. Singer starts by noting that no moral viewpoint is assumed if individuals choose between two courses of action by considering the effect of those actions on their interests, understood broadly as anything that those individuals desire. Singer argues that if an individual thinks *morally* about his own interests, by adopting a universal point of view, that individual cannot give weight to his own interests simply because they are his own.[31] Thus, he argues, any individual reasoning within the universal aspect of ethics must accept that everyone's interests have the same weight as his own. Singer then opines that this requires the individual to "weigh up all these interests and adopt the course of action most likely to maximise the interests of those affected".[32] This, Singer concludes, is sufficient to place "the onus of proof on those who seek to go beyond utilitarianism".[33] He opines he has shown the utilitarian position to be "a minimal one, a first base", so that "[w]e cannot, *if we are to think ethically*, refuse to take this step."[34] Singer's argument moves from maximising one's own interests to maximising the interests of all those affected by assuming a particular conception of impartiality. This conception of impartiality requires me to treat the desires of others as equivalent to my own *and* aggregate those desires as if I were experiencing them. (Since no one experiences the desires of another, I seem to be required to pretend to do something that no one can in fact do, i.e. metaphysically aggregate the desires of different individuals.) Unfortunately, this type of reasoning will only be persuasive to those who are willing to adopt a utilitarian conception of impartiality from the outset.

17.2.1.2 Moral contractarianism

Some theorists within weak moral objectivism have explicitly used criteria of rationality beyond logic alone. Some theorists have attempted to use prudence,

[28] See Gauthier 1986, 6–7. Beyleveld and Brownsword (2001, 90–91) direct a similar criticism at Kant.
[29] See Singer 1993, chs 1 (esp. 12–14) and 12.
[30] Singer 1993, 12.
[31] Singer defines morality as universalisable (see Singer 1993, esp. 317).
[32] Singer 1993, 13.
[33] Singer 1993, 14.
[34] Singer 1993, 14 (my emphasis).

i.e. reasoning from self-interest. Prudence is used in combination with moral assumptions in moral contractarianism. Moral contractarianism seeks to show that an agent reasoning morally and prudentially would agree to certain moral constraints on their conduct. John Rawls' book *A Theory of Justice* can be interpreted as adopting a moral contractarian approach, attempting to justify certain principles of justice by showing that persons reasoning prudentially would agree to them.[35] Rawls famously argued that the key principles of liberal justice could be established by adopting the viewpoint of a utility maximising person in the "original position" behind a "veil of ignorance". The original position is the imaginary position of individuals about to enter society, and the veil of ignorance deprives these individuals of knowledge of the powers, characteristics, and social positions they will occupy.[36] To understand Rawls' argument, imagine the following scenario.[37]

You have just woken up after a long period of sleep. You do not know how long you have been asleep and you can remember nothing about yourself. You cannot even remember your name, let alone your sex, nationality, education, or cultural upbringing. You cannot see or hear, and you cannot move. It appears that you have been asleep for a long time. You cannot tell whether your inability to see, hear and move will wear off with the effects of the long sleep. You hear a voice in your head. It informs you that you are on a long haul space voyage to a planet where you will spend the rest of your life. You are told that the voice comes from a computer, which is communicating with you telepathically. It informs you that there are many others onboard. Like you, they can remember nothing about themselves. The computer tells you that before you can land on your new home planet, you and your fellow passengers must agree on principles of justice under which you will all live. You will only be able to communicate telepathically so that you will know as little about everyone else as they know about you. The computer will answer any question you have about the planet on which you are about to land, including its history, its resources, and its cultures. It will not tell you anything about yourself or your place in society or history. You will not realise this, but the planet is Earth, so the computer will be providing you with information about Earth. What principles of justice would you and your fellow passengers agree to?

Rawls argues that behind such a veil of ignorance, rational self-interested persons would choose liberal principles of justice. According to Rawls you would choose to have all social values—liberty and opportunity, income and wealth, and the bases of self-respect—distributed equally unless an unequal distribution of any or all of these values was to everyone's advantage.[38] If you were to chose an unequal distribution (by, say, accepting slavery) when you find out who you are, you might discover that you are a slave. Despite Rawls'

---

[35] See Rawls 1973. Rawls' focus is justice, not individual morality. It is a work of political theory, rather than moral theory.

[36] Rawls 1973, 136–161.

[37] I have constructed this scenario to mirror most of the conditions of the original position.

[38] See e.g. Rawls 1973, 62. He sets out two specific principles of justice: a principle of liberty (the Principle of Greatest Equal Liberty) and a principle of equality (with two parts: the Difference Principle and the Principle Equality of Opportunity).

denial,[39] this seems to assume that all those in the original position do not favour risk. So, in the spaceship scenario, you will not gamble with your future prospects by betting that you will be a rich and powerful monarch.

Rawls adds another methodological mechanism by requiring that the solutions derived from the contractarian procedure be placed in "reflective equilibrium" with our most firmly held convictions.[40] This requires us to go back and forth between the conditions imposed on those in the original position and one's moral convictions, until the procedure "both expresses reasonable conditions and yields principles which match our considered judgments duly pruned and adjusted".[41] (Rawls does not explicitly consider whether reflective equilibrium could require those behind the veil of ignorance to be risk adverse. If so, he has an answer to the problem of gamblers, namely, reflective equilibrium requires those behind the veil of ignorance to be ignorant of their actual view of risk *and* be risk adverse.)[42]

The result is a version of *moral contractarianism*. The methodology is contractarian because it relies on the hypothetical agreement of prudent persons. It is best understood as *moral* contractarianism because Rawls' use of this methodology is morally loaded. The original position is set up to display the moral requirement of impartiality. Understood in this way, Rawls is a weak moral objectivist. He has not attempted to refute the amoralist by providing reasons for the adopting of the moral point of view, but argues that if you adopt the moral point of view you are committed (by prudence) to certain principles of justice. Even understood on those terms, however, Rawls' methodology is open to substantial criticism. The original position as envisaged by Rawls is weighted heavily towards the principles that he wishes to derive from it and requires us to abstract ourselves from our identity and the world in which we live.

A Theory of Justice has had a profound effect on applied ethics. It is largely responsible for reinvigorating contemporary applied ethics. Ronald Dworkin famously held that the "right to equal concern and respect", which he took to be axiomatic, was consistent with the Rawlsian justificatory strategy.[43] Susan Moller Okin has built a feminist contractarian theory by injecting an explicit gender focus into Rawls' theory.[44] She argues that Rawls fails to address gender injustice by assuming that families are just and by failing to take sufficient account of the (special) perspective of women when constructing the original position. Okin proposes that those in the original position should imagine themselves in the position of others (men and women) in turn and formulate principles for a just division of work and power within the family.

The most influential aspect of *A Theory of Justice* is Rawls' concept of *reflective equilibrium*. This continues to hold great sway in applied ethics, including

---

[39] See Rawls 1973, 172:

> The essential thing is not to allow the principles chosen to depend on special attitudes toward risk. For this reason the veil of ignorance also rules out the knowledge of these inclinations: the parties do not know whether or not they have a characteristic aversion to taking chances.

[40] See Rawls 1973, 48–52.
[41] Rawls 1973, 20.
[42] Rawls appears not to agree with the latter part of this.
[43] See Dworkin 1977, ch.6.
[44] See Okin 1989, esp. ch.5.

medical ethics. The label is not often used, but many theorists attempt to render our moral intuitions coherent so as to achieve some form of reflective equilibrium. Beauchamp and Childress, for example, derive their four principles from "considered judgments in the common morality and medical traditions, both of which form . . . [their] starting point".[45] Considered judgments, traditions, and convictions are, in effect, considered intuitions. Many of the theorists mentioned in this book rely on some form of moral intuitionism but are wary of pre-reflective or unconsidered intuitions. Moral intuitions differ from individual to individual and culture to culture. Consider, for example, intuitions on the permissibility of abortion. Reliance on intuition alone provides no basis for rejecting conflicting intuitions. Yet we have seen that theorists from Rawls to Harris want to reject some intuitions as unconsidered prejudices, encapsulating moral blindness.[46] Even those who accept that intuitionism raises problems are reluctant to dispense with it entirely. According to Mason and Laurie,

> Intuition may have a limited appeal as a basis for moral philosophy but it should not be wholly discounted and this . . . is especially so in the field of healthcare. Intuitions may point in the direction of a value which may not always be articulated formally but which may none the less be very important.[47]

The problem is that even "considered", "rational", or "reflective" intuitions might be no more than internally consistent prejudices. Intuitionism cannot provide a reason for someone who does not share those intuitions to adopt them as criteria of moral permissibility. All forms of moral intuitionism are rendered impotent when faced by conflicting, but equally considered, intuitions. Such limits on reason should not be accepted until the alternatives have been examined.

17.2.2 Strong moral objectivism

Few theorists have attempted to defend strong objectivism by providing reasons for adopting the moral point of view itself. Kant, Gauthier, and Gewirth are rare exceptions.

17.2.2.1 Transcendentalism

At the end of chapter two of his *Groundwork to the Metaphysics of Morals*, Kant declares the need to go beyond weak moral objectivism. His arguments in chapters one and two only work *if* the assumed starting point—the "common idea" of morality—is accepted. This means that morality could be a mere "phantom of the brain".[48] If the Categorical Imperative is to be established as

---

[45] Beauchamp and Childress 2001, 23.
[46] Harris adopts the ethical methodology of reflective equilibrium in all but name: see Harris 2001a, 17.
[47] Mason and Laurie 2006, 10. See also Mason and Laurie 2006, 567.
[48] Kant 1785, as translated in Paton 1948, 106.

the supreme principle of morality, Kant argued, it must be shown to be "a necessary law *for all rational beings*".[49] For this to be the case, "it must already be connected (entirely a priori) with the concept of the will of a rational being as such".[50] That is to say, Kant thought that it must be demonstrated that the Categorical Imperative is connected by reason alone with the concept of the will of a rational being. Such a project is very ambitious. It involves demonstrating that the application of pure logic commits such a being to this particular criterion of moral permissibility. It involves showing that a rational being with a will contradicts itself, by denying that it is such a being, if it denies the Categorical Imperative.[51] It is, predictably, very controversial.[52]

Kant's strong moral objectivism argument is complex and hard to discern. I will not attempt to summarise it in any detail here.[53] The basic argument holds that:

(a) free will and the Categorical Imperative are reciprocal (in the sense of implying each other),

(b) a being with a will denies that it is such a being if it denies that it is free,

therefore,

(c) a rational being with a will in considering itself to be free must also consider itself to be bound by the Categorical Imperative.

This seems to rest on an equivocation with regard to the conception of free will in play.[54]

Few other theorists have attempted to provide rational grounds for strong moral objectivism. There are two notable exceptions: Gewirth and Gauthier. Gewirth utilises a similar methodology (see 17.2.3), whereas Gauthier's methodology is radically different.

17.2.2.2 Non-moral contractarianism

Gauthier, in his book *Morals by Agreement*, attempts to argue using a form of non-moral contractarianism. He seeks to show that the moral point of view must be accepted on prudential grounds, i.e. to maximise one's own self-interest. Like Rawls, Gauthier adopts contractarianism and holds that agents act rationally only

---

[49] Kant 1785, as translated in Paton 1948, 89 (original emphasis).

[50] Kant 1785, as translated in Paton 1948, 89.

[51] See Beyleveld 1999.

[52] Some claim that Kant later changed his mind on the feasibility of such a project in his *Critique of Practical Reason*: see e.g. Paton 1967, 172 and Allison 1990, 2–3. Others claim that Kant consistently maintained the feasibility of the project: see e.g. McCarthy 1982, esp. 170, and Beyleveld 1999, 109. Yet others appear to claim that, contrary to appearances, Kant never attempted such a project.

[53] See Kant 1785, as translated in Paton 1948, esp. 107–109 and 446–448. More detailed summaries of this argument can be round in Beyleveld and Brownsword 2001, 102–103, and Hill and Zweig 2002, 132–136.

[54] See Beyleveld and Brownsword 2001, 102–105. The validity of Kant's derivation of the Categorical Imperative is explored in innumerable works. See e.g. Hill 1985, McCarthy 1985, and Copp 1992.

if they act to maximise their considered preferences.[55] Unlike Rawls, Gauthier seeks to start from morally neutral premises. In his words, he is "committed to showing why an individual, reasoning from non-moral premisses (sic.), would accept the constraints of morality on his choices".[56] He defines morality as action-guiding and impartial (but not categorical).[57]

According to Gauthier, utility maximisers are required to accept moral constraints on their actions if they are to interact with others rationally. If the world was a perfectly competitive market, Gauthier argues, it would be to the greatest advantage of all to allow the unconstrained pursuit of self-interest.[58] Alas, he argues, perfectly competitive markets do not exist. Thus, social inter-action requires us to interact, co-operate, and accept moral constraints on our conduct if we are to maximise our own self-interest. To understand Gauthier's argument, imagine the following scenario.[59]

Imagine that a particular vaccine will protect those who receive it from succumbing to a new virus. The vaccine takes the form of an extremely cheap, easy to obtain, and easy to administer biological substance. The virus is highly contagious and kills many of its victims. It is only spread by contact with those who have contracted it, but there is no way to identify those with the virus until they have died. You face a high chance of coming into contact with infected persons. Unfortunately, the vaccine itself can cause death, albeit the chances of dying from the vaccine are significantly lower than chance of dying if you get the virus. The vaccine will only protect those who receive it for 10 years, after which they will need to be vaccinated again. Clearly, the best possible scenario for you would be if everyone you were to come into contact with had been vaccinated and you had not. But if no one else was vaccinated, your best option would be to be vaccinated every 10 years. A utility maximiser would see that if everyone acts out of their own self-interest, his self-interest would be maximised by everyone agreeing to be vaccinated. That would eliminate the need for future vaccinations.

In this scenario, like the Prisoner's Dilemma and the Arms Race scenarios used by Gauthier, the best result that you can achieve in practice is what is, in theory, the second best result. But that result can only be achieved with mutu-ally agreed principles of constraint. Constrained maximisers will do better than unconstrained maximisers. Of course, constrained maximisers would need to avoid being tricked by free-loaders, i.e. those who seek to benefit from breaking their bargains while others keep theirs. A free-loader might, for example, lie about having been vaccinated so as to gain the benefits of everyone else being vaccinated without the disbenefits of being vaccinated himself.

Gauthier's argument has many details and qualifications.[60] He contrasts a constrained maximiser (i.e. those with the disposition to uphold their agreements when cooperating with other like-minded individuals) with a straightforward

---

[55] See Gauthier 1986, ch.1 and 38.
[56] Gauthier 1986, 5.
[57] See Gauthier 1986, ch.1, esp. 4 and 7.
[58] See Gauthier 1986, 13.
[59] Gauthier uses the Prisoner's Dilemma and the Arms Race. This scenario is my own.
[60] See Gauthier 1986 for a discussion of, in particular, the Principle of Minimax Relative Concession, the Principle of Maximin Relative Benefit, and the Lockean Proviso.

maximiser. His point is not that the constrained maximiser will always do better than a straightforward maximiser in every possible situation. Gauthier's argument is that a constrained maximiser will do better *overall*, because he will have more opportunities to cooperate successfully to his advantage. Thus, Gauthier holds that the free-loader will lose out in the long-run (others will not trust him) and so a disposition to comply with morality is utility maximising.[61] Unfortunately, this assumes that an individual is unable to conceal his bargain-breaking or escape its consequences *and* that he must prefer his long-term interests over his short-term (immediate) interest. As Moore has objected,

> In Gauthier's world, it seems, there are no good poker players; there are no people who find it rational to cultivate their considerable powers of deception rather than simply accept Gauthier's argument that the threat of being recognized will result in fewer opportunities for beneficial cooperation.[62]

A key difference between Kant and Gauthier's justificatory strategies is reflected in their starting points and conclusions. Unlike Kant, Gauthier does not define morality as categorical. His argumentative strategy cannot establish categorical requirements. Non-moral reasons for accepting a *categorical* principle would need the support of a rational necessary justificatory strategy. In this sense at least, Kant's project was more ambitious than attempted by Gauthier.

17.2.3 The strong moral objectivism of Gewirth

Gewirth also attempts to provide a rationally necessary justification for morality. He defines morality as action-guiding, categorical, and other-regarding.[63] Like Kant, Gewirth claims to establish a supreme principle of morality without reliance on any form of moral intuition, consensus, or contingency. He seeks to establish an imperative that is uniformly obligatory for all those capable of understanding its prescriptions.

In *Reason and Morality*, Gewirth argues that the supreme principle of morality is the Principle of Generic Consistency (hereafter the *PGC*).[64] Gewirth's theory draws out the self-reflective implications of being an *agent*, where an agent is a being that has the ability to pursue chosen purposes. For our purposes an agent is indistinguishable from what Kant called a "rational being with a will".[65] Reasoning from the viewpoint of an agent, Gewirth adopts a methodology that has much in common with that used by Kant in the third chapter of the *Groundwork*.[66] Gewirth adopts what he terms the "dialectically necessary

---

[61] See e.g. Gauthier 1986, ch.6, esp. 173, 174–175, and 183. See also Gauthier 1986, 232.
[62] Moore 1994, 216.
[63] See Gewirth 1978, 1.
[64] See Gewirth 1978.
[65] The two conceptions might not be identical, but they have sufficient similarities to be treated as equivalent for our purposes here.
[66] See above, Beyleveld 1999, and Beyleveld and Brownsword 2001.

method". It is "dialectical" because it is conducted in the form of an internal dialogue, beginning with claims that are made within this first-person perspective. It is "necessary" because all the steps of the argument follow logically (hence necessarily) from premises that cannot be coherently rejected within this perspective.

In essence, Gewirth argues from the claim of an agent to be an agent within the first-person perspective of that agent. His argument is best considered in three stages. The *first stage* seeks to establish that an agent must value its having those conditions that are necessary for it to act at all or with general chances of success (i.e. the generic features of agency). The *second stage* seeks to show that this commits the agent to claiming rights to the generic features (i.e. the generic rights). The *third stage* of the argument seeks to establish that an agent must accept that all agents have the generic rights (i.e. Gewirth's supreme principle of morality). Here, I will attempt no more than a skeletal outline of its principal claims and inferences.[67]

In *stage one*, an agent recognises that since it is, by definition, a being that has the capacity to act for freely chosen purposes, it must perceive any purpose that it pursues (or intends to pursue) as "good", in the sense of worth pursuing. Since an agent must proactively value its purpose, it must attach at least instrumental value to anything that is necessary for it to achieve that purpose. Thus, an agent must (if it is to avoid the self-contradiction involved in denying that it is an agent) attach at least instrumental value to those conditions that are necessary for it to act at all or with general chances of success. These conditions for sake of brevity are collectively referred to as the "generic features of agency". So, it is dialectically necessary for an agent to accept that its generic features are good for achieving *whatever* purpose that agent has. It must regard the generic features as categorically instrumentally good.

In *stage two*, an agent recognises that if it is to avoid denying what has just been established, it must claim that it (categorically instrumentally) ought to pursue and defend its possession of the generic features. Since an agent needs to have the generic features in order to pursue and defend its possession of them, an agent must be against interference with its possession of the generic features against its will. For the same reason, an agent must also be in favour of others helping it to secure possession of the generic features, when it wishes to have such help and is unable to secure them without help. Thus, the agent must claim that other agents categorically ought not to interfere with its having the generic features *against its will*, and ought to aid it to secure them when it cannot do so by its own unaided efforts, *if it so wishes*. Re-rephrased in the terminology of a rights-claim, it is dialectically necessary for an agent to claim that it has negative and positive rights to have the generic features. Collectively these rights are referred to as the "generic rights".

---

[67] More detailed summaries and defences are attempted elsewhere: Gewirth 1978 and Beyleveld 1991. This section draws heavily from the more detailed summary that I presented in Pattinson 2002a, ch.1.

Stage three seeks to get from the agent's claim that it has the generic rights to the claim that all agents have the generic rights.[68] To do this Gewirth looks towards the "logical principle of universalisability".[69] This purely logical principle, claims that *if* having Q is a sufficient reason for possession of P, *then* anyone with Q also has a sufficient reason for possession of P. Before this principle can be applied, Gewirth must first establish that an agent must regard the fact that it is an agent as the sufficient reason for its claim that it has the generic rights. He needs to show that the agent's claim that it has the generic rights (established in stage two) entails the claim that it has the generic rights *because* it is an agent. He does this using what he terms the "Argument from the Sufficiency of Agency" (the ASA).[70] Applying the principle of universalisability now, he establishes that "every agent has the generic rights *because* it is an agent". This dialectically necessary claim, when combined with the agent's previous dialectically necessary claim that it has the generic rights, entails the dialectically necessary claim that all agents have the generic rights. Applying the principle of universalisability to this, since an agent denies that it is an agent if it does not accept that all agents have the generic rights, it follows that every agent denies that it is an agent if it does not accept that all agents have the generic rights. Thus, it is dialectically necessary for every agent to accept that all agents have the generic rights. This is the Principle of Generic Consistency—the PGC for short.

This argument is very controversial. Every stage of the argument has been critically probed by some of the world's most respected philosophers. The consensus is that there is a flaw in the argument, although there is no consensus as to where this flaw is.[71] Despite this, as far as I can tell, no one has yet raised a successful objection. Gewirth has addressed many of his critics, and Beyleveld has addressed just about all criticisms made up until 1990.[72] Although objections

---

[68] This step seeks to move from this self-regarding (albeit other-referring) claim to an other-regarding claim.

[69] See Gewirth 1978, 105:

> if some predicate P belongs to some subject S because S has the property Q (where the "because" is that of sufficient reason or condition), then P must also belong to all other subjects $S_1, S_2 \ldots,$ S_n that have Q. If one denies this implication in the case of some subject, such as S_1, that has Q, then one contradicts oneself. For in saying that P belongs to S because S has Q, one is saying that having Q is a sufficient condition of having P; but in denying this in the case of S_1, one is saying that having Q is not a sufficient condition of having P.

> Properly understood, this principle is no more than an explanation of what the word "because" means when it is used to import the concept of sufficient reason.

[70] See Gewirth 1978, 110. All that the ASA does is make explicit what has already been shown to be dialectically necessary. This argument takes the form of a *reductio ad absurdum* in that it seeks to show that by denying the claim that it has the generic rights *because* it is an agent, the agent denies that it has the generic rights. This is because denying that it has the generic rights for the sufficient reason that it is an agent, requires the agent to assert that it has the generic right because it has a property that is not necessarily possessed by all agents. However, this implies that if the agent lacked this property it would not have the generic rights, which contradicts the previously established statement, made on the basis of its claim to be an agent, that it has the generic rights. Thus, it is dialectically necessary for an agent to claim that it has the generic rights because it is an agent.

[71] The argument to the *PGC* does, however, have its supporters: see the list in Pattinson 2002a, 9 (n.12). For collected papers criticising and defending the argument, see Regis 1984 and Boylan 1999.

[72] See Beyleveld 1991.

are still being made, few take account of the responses already made and, in my opinion, all are variations of previously answered criticisms.[73]

Even if the dialectically necessary argument is ultimately unsuccessful, *dialectically contingent arguments* can also be advanced to support the conclusion that the *PGC* is the supreme principle of morality. Such arguments are contingent in the sense that they start from moral premises that can be coherently denied. In other words, the argument to the *PGC* could also be defended within weak moral objectivism. Beyleveld has argued that the *PGC* follows logically from the claim that there are human rights, categorical other-regarding requirements on action, or categorically binding requirements on action.[74] *The argument from rights*[75] points out that to recognise rights to anything requires one to recognise the necessary means of exercising that right, if one is to avoid contradicting oneself. This requires one to grant rights to the generic features of agency as the necessary conditions for exercising any rights irrespective of their specific content. Also, since only agents can meaningfully exercise a right, agents must be the relevant subjects and recipients of these rights. Thus, granting rights requires one to recognise generic rights of agents. If this reasoning is sound, it follows that supporters of rights-based theories are logically required to accept the *PGC* as supreme principle of morality. Similarly, if the corollary arguments from categorical, and categorical other-regarding, requirements on action are sound, then supporters of many of the moral theories considered in this book would be committed to the *PGC* (virtue ethics would be a notable exception).

17.3 Moral application

Whatever criterion of moral permissibility is adopted, it needs to be applied to the real world. In practice, the application of complex action-based moral theories must have a procedural component. People simply do not have time to work out the implications of complex action-based theories for every act that they perform. Thus, unless the moral theory in question has only a few, easy to reconcile moral principles or is virtue-based, its application will require the development of rules-of-thumb, and procedural mechanisms to make decisions and offer practical solutions to the problem of conflicting views.

Even action-based theories, which reject the central tenets of virtue ethics, must require the development of those virtues conducive to automatic and intuitive compliance with that theory's principles.[76] According to Hare, moral thinking has two levels: the intuitive and the critical level.[77] Hare's intuitive level comprises "relatively simple, prima facie, intuitive principles or disposi-

---

[73] See Pattinson 2002a, ch.1, and Beyleveld and Brownsword 2001, ch.4.
[74] See Beyleveld 1996. See also Pattinson 2002a, 11–13 and Beyleveld and Brownsword 2001, 77–82.
[75] Remember that rights were defined in Ch.1 (1.3.2.2) as justifiable claims imposing correlative duties, *the benefits of which are waivable by the rights-holder*.
[76] See e.g. Gewirth 1985 and Pattinson 2002a, 70–71.
[77] See Hare 1981, 39–53. For related arguments on the procedural component of morality, see Beyleveld and Brownsword 1994.

tions", justified at what he calls "the critical level".[78] He argues that the critical level is necessary because the intuitive principles

> are not self-justifying; we can always ask whether the upbringing was the best we could have, or whether the past decisions were the right ones, or, even if so, whether the principles then formed should be applied to a new situation, or, if they cannot all be applied, *which* should be applied. To use intuition itself to answer such questions is a viciously circular procedure; if the dispositions formed by our upbringing are called into question, we cannot appeal to them to settle the question.[79]

Thus, Hare's critical level does not permit appeals to intuition; instead all answers are to be worked out by application of justified principles of morality. Hare is a preference utilitarian. He argues that the intuitive level should comprise rule-utilitarianism, and the critical level should comprise act-utilitarianism. This distinction has been adopted by other utilitarians.[80] The basic idea can and should apply to other complex, action-based theories. Rights-based and duty-based theories can utilise rules-of-thumb comprising simple rights or duties (such as the duty not to lie and the right not to be lied to) at the intuitive level, while holding that these rights or duties can be overridden by more important rights or duties at the critical level.

Going beyond Hare, it should be recognised that the critical level must be understood as having both a substantive and procedural component. In complex societies, attempts to apply complex action-based theories will produce uncertainties and conflicts. Persons and bodies, appointed by mechanisms consistent with the moral theory in question, are required to deal with such situations. Without such procedural mechanisms, complex societies will collapse into ethical chaos. Decision-making methods must, however, be legitimate in the sense of being appointed by ethically defensible procedures and seeking (to the best of their ability) to apply ethically defensible norms.[81] It follows that all complex, action-based theories will require political and legal institutions.[82] If such institutions are to apply the moral theory in question, however, they cannot treat all ethical views as equivalent. Moral constraints on political decision-making making will, of course, depend on the tenets of the underlying moral theory. The moral objectivist project has to live with the reality of ethical pluralism, but does not have to be defined by it.

We have seen great diversity in the tenets of moral theories. None of the theories examined or referred to grant duties directly to every living entity. To put it another way, not every living entity is granted moral status or value. Being alive is not taken to be sufficient for being owed direct duties by any of the

---

[78] Hare 1981, 40.
[79] Hare 1981, 40 (original emphasis).
[80] e.g. Singer 1993, 92–94.
[81] Beyleveld and Brownsword (1994, chs 7–9) argue that applications of the PGC must be made by legitimately appointed persons, conducting a "good faith" attempt to apply the PGC. Gewirth (1978, 319–322) also argues for the "method of consent".
[82] This is not the place to consider whether and to what extent it is permissible for judges to be unelected, unrepresentative, and unanswerable.

theorists examined in the book. Singer, for example, holds that all sentient beings have moral status, whereas Kant holds that only "rational beings with a will" have moral status. Whatever one's criterion of moral status, it does not automatically follow that those beings who appear to lack the relevant property have no moral status and are only owed indirect duties. Those theories that are *categorical*, in the sense of obligatory and overriding, cannot treat empirical evidence as to the properties actually possessed by another being as conclusive. The absence of empirical evidence suggesting that gametes or early embryos can feel pain does not, for example, demonstrate *with certainty* that they cannot feel pain. Pain is partly a mental phenomenon and we do not have access to the minds of other creatures (if, indeed, they have minds). Limits on what we can know for certain are important for categorical theories, because the violation of a categorical moral requirement is (by definition) absolutely impermissible. Thus, a categorical moral theory will require us to treat those who might possibly possess moral status as if they do, unless doing so threatens to violate the tenets of that theory. This reasoning is probably more than a little unclear. It will be developed and explained in relation to a particular categorical theory below (see 17.3.2). For now it is sufficient to note that the implications of some categorical moral theories for abortion and embryo research are not as straight-forward as they first appear.

The next two sections will focus on the application of the specific moral theories whose justificatory strategies have been explored in this chapter.[83]

17.3.1 Applying specific moral theories

All the justificatory strategies considered in this chapter have implications for medical law. Yet, applying moral theories is no easy task. We have seen that the general groups of moral positions do not provide "add water and stir" instant solutions and the application of specific theories can be just as difficult. This section will outline some relevant issues with regard to the application of the moral theories of Kant, Gauthier, Rawls, and Hare. A slightly more detailed examination of the application of the moral theory of Gewirth will be presented below (17.3.2).

17.3.1.1 Kant

Kant has received considerable citation in the bioethical literature, despite his frequent lapses into the dense and impenetrable. Two formulations of his Categorical Imperative have a prominent place in medical ethics. These are the *Formula of the Universal Law* (which requires us to take as guiding principles only those principles that can be willed as universal laws) and the *Formula of the*

---

[83] Some applications of the theories of Peter Singer and John Harris have been explored in earlier chapters. See, e.g., Ch.7 (7.2.1.1) for a discussion of some of Singer and Harris' views on abortion. The points raised in that and other chapters will not be repeated below.

End in Itself (which requires us to treat others never as simply means to our ends but also as ends in themselves). Kant regarded all formulations of the Categorical Imperative as equivalent.

The Formula of the Universal Law requires us to evaluate a proposed action according to whether it can be consistently willed as a universal law. We must ask: can I, as a rational being, consistently will that everyone faced with such a situation should act in this way? In Kant's words, we must "Act only on that maxim through which you can at the same time will that it should become a universal law".[84] This is meant to test the sufficiency of a maxim or guiding principle. It does not allow us to give special treatment to ourselves. It rejects acting on guiding principles that would be, in some sense, contradictory if universalised. Consider, for example, a guiding principle that said: "Where there is a queue, I ought to receive treatment first". This could not be consistently willed as a universal law. Logically, everyone cannot be first, so such a maxim would be both impossible to follow and self-defeating. This type of approach is suggested by Kant's example of a lying promise. He argued that if a maxim permitting a lying promise were a universal law it would undermine the institution of promise-keeping and thereby undermine its goal (obtaining a benefit by making the promise):

> For the universality of a law that every one believing himself to be in need can make any promise he pleases with the intention not to keep it would make promising, and the very purpose of promising, itself impossible, since no one would believe he was being promised anything, but would laugh at utterances of this kind as empty shams.[85]

Unfortunately Kant's reasoning on the application of the Categorical Imperative is not always clear. There are a number of conflicting views on how Kant meant it to be applied and support for all of them can be found in Kant's writings.[86] Kant himself explicitly distinguished two ways in which one's maxims would lead to inconsistency if universalised.[87] Kant's emphasis on a maxim being raised to a universal "law of nature"[88] and some of his examples, has even led some to suggest that Kant thought that a maxim would be contradictory if it were inconsistent with some natural purpose.

One of the examples given by Kant in his *Groundwork* appears to have implications for the permissibility of physician assisted suicide. Kant famously argued that suicide was morally wrong, as it cannot be consistently willed as a

---

[84] Kant 1785, as translated in Paton 1948, 83–84.

[85] Kant 1785, as translated in Paton 1948, 85.

[86] See Korsgaard 1985, esp. 25.

[87] In the *Groundwork*, Kant declares that some maxims "cannot even be conceived as universal laws of nature without contradiction", whereas others "do not find this inner impossibility" but are still contradictory if universalised (Kant 1785, as translated in Paton 1948, 86–87). See O'Neill 1998 for an excellent discussion of the difference between "contradictions in conception" and "contradictions in the will", respectively. In crude summary, "contradictions in conception" involve one simultaneously willing and not willing the same thing, whereas "contradictions in the will" involve attempting to will something that is inconsistent with the means that are necessary for its realisation.

[88] See Kant's Formula of the Law of Nature (Kant 1785, as translated in Paton 1948, 84).

universal law.[89] His reasoning is far from clear. He argued that a suicidal individual must be acting on the principle that it is permissible "to shorten my life if its continuance threatens more evil than it promises pleasure". However, he argues, the function of the desire to avoid evil is "to stimulate the furtherance of life" (by which he seems to mean "to preserve one's life"). Thus, committing suicide cannot be consistently universalised because it requires me to act from self-destruction and self-preservation at the same time. This reasoning is distinctly unsatisfactory. Kant appears to be smuggling his own moral values into the maxims being universalised. Nonetheless, if rational suicide does violate the Categorical Imperative, then it must surely follow that a physician who assists in a patient's suicide also violates Kant's imperative.

17.3.1.2 Gauthier

Gauthier's theory requires rights to property and person as preconditions of a rational bargain,[90] but, since morality is justified as the outcome of a hypothetical contract or bargain, it rejects any moral constraint "outside the context of mutual benefit".[91] It follows that Gauthier's moral theory would have significant implications for the treatment of fetuses, children, and the mentally ill because it does not directly proscribe the coercive treatment of those whose capacities do not make cooperation with them mutually advantageous.[92] If morality is grounded in the notion of mutual benefit, then we are only constrained by the wishes of those from whom we can benefit.

Similarly, this methodology cannot generate positive duties to assist those in need. According to Gauthier,

> the rich man may feast on caviar and champagne, while the poor woman starves at his gate. And she may not even take the crumbs from his table, if that would deprive him of his pleasure in feeding them to the birds.[93]

This appears to support the absence of a general duty to assist in the law of negligence. This focus on individual utility and autonomy does, however, point towards a more permissive approach than the current legal position on physician assisted suicide.

17.3.1.3 Rawls

Rawls claims to have established two principles of justice: a principle of liberty (the Principle of Greatest Equal Liberty) and a principle of equality (with two parts: the Difference Principle and the Principle Equality of Opportunity). Since

---

[89] See Kant 1785, as translated in Paton 1948, 85. For his further thoughts on "murdering oneself" as a violation of one's duties to oneself, see also Kant 1797, as translated in Gregor 1991, 218–219.

[90] See Gauthier 1986, ch.7, esp. 222.

[91] Gauthier 1986, 16.

[92] See Gauthier 1986, 17–18 and 268.

[93] Gauthier 1986, 218.

these principles are derived from a hypothetical agreement made by those in the original position, it might be thought that his principle of equality is necessarily restricted to those able to participate in such an agreement, i.e. agents. Nonetheless, Rawls includes potential agents within the scope of his principle of equality. He argues,

> Since infants and children are thought to have basic rights (normally exercised on their behalf by parents and guardians), this interpretation of the requisite conditions seems necessary to match our considered judgments.[94]

Thus, Rawls unashamedly manipulates the conditions of hypothetical agreement to grant rights to some humans who appear to be non-agents. He does, however, admit that those with irreparable intellectual disabilities "may present a difficulty".[95] This willingness to rely on his intuitions adds another level of uncertainty to the application of his theory.

On physician assisted suicide, it appears that Rawls' principle of liberty favours allowing persons to choose the manner and timing of their death, whereas his principle of equality would protect the weak and vulnerable. It seems to follow that physician assisted suicide must be regulated so as to promote autonomy while protecting the vulnerable. Also, in contrast to Gauthier, Rawls does recognise positive duties to assist those in need.[96]

17.3.1.4 Hare

The application of Hare's preference utilitarianism requires us to imagine ourselves in the position of all those likely to be affected by our actions, as if we experienced their preferences first-hand, so that we can act to maximise preferences. Many critics, raising a standard concern invoked against act-utilitarians, object that this could result in counter-intuitive conclusions. Imagine, for example, that the aggregate preferences in favour of using a certain group of people as involuntary organ and tissue donors outweigh the preferences of this group against their use in this way. Since Hare rejects intuitive judgments at the critical level, it is open to him to reject the concern that some applications of his principle at that level are counter-intuitive. Nonetheless, his preferred response is to argue that such counter-intuitive conclusions, while logically possible, will not arise in practice.[97] This is, to say the least, an optimistic view of human nature and preferences. More everyday issues of medical ethics will arise in a way more readily amenable to the intuitive level of application of his moral theory. Maximising preferences will, for example, require prima facie principles applicable at the intuitive level that are supportive of informed consent and patient's decisions.

---

[94] Rawls 1973, 509.
[95] Rawls 1973, 510.
[96] See Rawls 1973, 114.
[97] See Hare 1981, esp. 134, and Hare 1988, 203 (responding to the Harsanyi 1988).

17.3.2 Applying Gewirth's theory

Kennedy and Grubb argue that human rights provide the "intellectual coherence" of medical law.[98] Morgan is among the theorists who have argued that "Rights are not, and should not be, the only foundation for the practice of modern medicine".[99] If Gewirth is right, rights provide the only intellectually coherent basis for medical law and medical ethics. Gewirth's moral theory is a rights-based moral theory. The argument for the Principle of Generic Consistency (PGC) makes rights foundational.[100]

17.3.2.1 Understanding the generic rights

Gewirth's argument (outlined in 17.2.3) creates a full array of hierarchically ranked rights. All agents have generic rights, i.e. rights to the generic features of action. The generic features can be sub-divided into those capacities necessary to act at all and those necessary to act successfully. Gewirth refers to the capacities necessary to act at all as "basic" capacities. The further capacities necessary for successful action can be divided into the capacities necessary to maintain one's current level of purpose-fulfilment ("nonsubtractive" capacities), and those necessary to increase one's current level of purpose-fulfilment ("additive" capacities). This creates a hierarchy of potential generic harm according to the degree that the relevant generic capacity is needed for purpose-fulfilment. This leads Gewirth to the conclusion that the degree of generic harm or need can be measured by the "criterion of degrees of needfulness for action".[101] Thus, in a situation of conflict, the generic rights are to be ranked hierarchically in descending order: basic, nonsubtractive, then additive generic rights. By way of example, interference with an individual's life (as a basic capacity needed for us to act at all) is worse than depriving an individual of the accurate information needed to act successfully (by, say, breaking promises or lying), which is worse than depriving individuals of the means to obtain the additional skills needed to improve their capacity for successful action.

Also, the duty to aid another agent to secure its generic features is limited by two other provisos.[102] According to the "own unaided effort" proviso, I (any agent) have a duty to aid another agent to secure its generic features only where it is unable to do so by its own unaided effort. According to the "comparable cost" proviso, I only have a duty to aid another agent to secure its generic features when my doing so does not deprive me of the same or more important generic capacities, as measured by the degree of needfulness for action. It follows that a doctor is not morally required to make every passer-by his patient at risk to his own health, life, and safety, but neither is he entitled to walk by all those in need whose plight is desperate when addressing their medical needs would be

---

[98] Kennedy and Grubb 2000, 3. See also Kennedy 1988, esp. vii.
[99] Morgan 2001, 210.
[100] Though, strictly, it is a theory of "agent" rather than "human" rights.
[101] See Gewirth 1996, 45–46. See also Gewirth 1978, esp. 53–58.
[102] See 17.2.3 and Gewirth 1978, 217–230.

no more than an inconvenience. This stands in contrast to the duties recognised by the law of negligence (see Ch.3, 3.3).

Who must I treat as an agent? Agents are beings capable of reflecting on their ability to act for chosen purposes. This captures all those capable of understanding and following moral requirements. The PGC grants such beings full moral status, but what about those beings that do not appear to be agents? Do they lack moral status? Gewirth himself holds that the PGC also grants moral status to various beings that he classifies as non-agents, such as young children, the seriously mentally disabled, and fetuses.[103] He argues that the "Principle of Proportionality"[104] operates to extend the population to which the PGC applies in the abstract to encompass those who have only some of the characteristics necessary for agency—"partial agents". According to Gewirth, partial agents have the generic rights in proportion to their approach to agency. If he is right, this means that the PGC supports the *proportional status* position, with moral status increasing with gestational development (see 7.2). Unfortunately, the Principle of Proportionality cannot operate on the PGC in this way.[105] The generic rights have benefits waivable by the rights-holder and impose correlative duties, but non-agents cannot waive benefits or exercise duties. Also, the principle is a quantitative not qualitative manipulator. On its own it can only be used to manipulate the quantitative variables, it cannot alter the quality of a variable. It cannot be used to derive moral duties for partial agents from the proposition that agents have generic rights. Thus, the PGC, even operating with a quantitative manipulator, cannot grant duties to non-agents. Neither can the PGC grant moral status to potential agents (i.e. non-agents who have the potential to become agents). The argument to the PGC draws out the implications of an agent denying that it is an agent, and an agent cannot deny that it is an agent by refusing to accept that possession of a property *it cannot possibly possess* is sufficient for some moral status.[106]

17.3.2.2 Precautionary reasoning

It does not follow that those who appear to be non-agents have no moral status! The PGC does not allow us to assume that those who appear to lack the capacities of agency are not agents. This point was made earlier.[107] To understand it we need to take a step back. As defined, an agent has a special kind of mental attitude—the ability to reflect on its proactively valued purposes. I (any agent)

---

[103] See Gewirth 1978, 121–124; 140–145.

[104] See further Gewirth 1978, 121. This principle states that,

When some quality Q justifies having certain rights R, and the possession of Q varies in degree in the respect that is relevant to Q's justifying the having of R, the degree to which R is had is proportional to or varies with the degree to which Q is had). . . . Thus, if x units of Q justify that one have x units of R, then y units of Q justify that one have y units of R. (Gewirth 1978, 121).

[105] See Beyleveld and Pattinson 1998 and 2000; and Pattinson 2002a, ch.2. The application of this principle has also been criticised by Hill 1984; and Pluhar 1995, ch.5.

[106] See Beyleveld and Pattinson 2000a, 46–49; and Pattinson 2002a, 21–22.

[107] The argument referred to above and detailed below was first developed and presented at its fullest in Beyleveld and Pattinson 1998. This argument is also used in Beyleveld and Pattinson 2000a; Beyleveld and Brownsword 2001, ch.6; and Pattinson 2002a, ch.2.

have direct access to my mind and cannot even deny my self-reflective existence without thereby demonstrating that very thing. I cannot, however, know that any other being is an agent in this way. I do not have direct access to the mind of another being. The best that I can do is judge another being's characteristics and behaviour against what I would expect of an agent. However, even if that being displays all the characteristics and behaviour expected of an agent (as most adult human beings do), we can only say that it is ostensibly an agent. It remains logically possible that an "ostensible agent" is merely a cleverly programmed automaton without a mind.

There are many contingent responses to the problem of other minds, not least of which is that those presenting this objection must be assuming, for practical purposes, that the person they are interacting with is an agent.[108] The PGC provides a categorical, moral solution to the problem of other minds. If I mistakenly treat a non-agent as an agent, I restrict the exercise of some of my rights. If I mistakenly treat an agent as if it were not an agent, I deny its status as a rights-holder. All things being equal, the consequences of being wrong are much worse if I mistakenly assume that a being is not an agent, than if I mistakenly assume that it is an agent! Since the PGC is categorically binding, it can never be justifiable to run the risk of violating it where this can be avoided. Therefore, I must do whatever I can to avoid denying the agency of others, provided only that the actions taken do not conflict with the hierarchically more important requirements of the PGC.

Ostensible agents can, by definition, be treated as agents possessing the generic rights. I must, therefore, ignore the metaphysical possibility that an ostensible agent is not an agent.[109] Where that other being appears to be only a partial agent, I cannot meaningfully treat it as if it were an agent. I cannot treat gametes, embryos, fetuses and newborn children as if they were agents. They display some related characteristics and behaviour, but the evidence persuasively suggests that they are not agents. The goal-driven behaviour of gametes, embryos, and newborn babies appears to be the product of hardwiring, rather than reflective choice. They do not appear to be able to exercise the generic rights or act in accordance with the generic rights of others. Despite this, I cannot be certain that these are not in fact agents. It remains possible—though admittedly counter-intuitive and not at all likely—that a being who does not display ostensible agency is in fact an agent. A failure to display ostensible agency does not conclusively prove that a being is not an agent. So, if I suppose that it is not an agent and act accordingly, I could thereby be depriving it of the protection required by the PGC. I cannot treat such beings as agents with the generic rights, but I can grant them "duties of protection". That is, therefore, what the PGC requires. Agents are required to assist and refrain from harming those who do not appear to be agents in ways that protect the benefits that they would receive if they had the generic rights and chose to exercise them.

What if we are faced with a conflict between two such beings? Remember that we must treat all possible agents as agents *except* where this threatens to violate

---

[108] See further Beyleveld and Pattinson 2000a, 41–42.
[109] With one proviso, see Pattinson 2002a, 24.

the more important requirements of the PGC. Thus, all things being equal, such conflicts are to be handled by the "criterion of avoidance of more probable harm".[110] I am more likely to violate the PGC by treating a being that is more probably an agent as a non-agent, than by treating a less probable agent as a non-agent. Thus, my duties of protection to those who are more probably agents take precedence over my duties of protection to those who are less probably agents. The only relevant information, however, that I have when dealing with entities in the empirical world is the display of ostensible agency, and characteristics and behaviour similar to those displayed by ostensible agents. It follows that the moral protection granted to those who are apparently only partial agents is proportional to their approach to ostensible agency.

This conclusion is similar to Gewirth's. In its application, the PGC grants *full status* to ostensible agents and *proportional status* to those who approach ostensible agency. Moral status is proportional to the degree of agency-related behaviour and characteristics displayed.[111] It might seem strange to view characteristics and behaviour that are manifestly below what we would expect of an agent in this way. Strange or not, we are morally obliged to treat even the most implausible hypothesis of agency seriously. When faced with a direct conflict between such hypotheses, the least plausible has less force. Less force is not, however, no force. The consequence is a proportional or gradualist view of the value of the embryo, so that its moral status gradually increases during its gestational development.

17.3.2.3 Applying the PGC to medical issues

It should be clear that the principles of application just outlined enable us to say more about substantive issues than reasoning from a general category of rights-based moral theory. To use an issue examined in Ch.2 as an example: when allocating scarce societal resources, including medical resources, some potential criteria are clearly incompatible with the equal generic rights of all. The Quality Adjusted Life Year (QALY) calculation, for example, aims to maximise health gains, rather than protect generic rights. Neither age nor ability to pay are acceptable allocation criteria, because age (when not connected with the likely effectiveness of treatment) is not connected to generic need and financial resources in this society are not distributed solely according to need and merit. Under the PGC, competing (generic) needs and rights are to be ranked according to the criterion of degrees of needfulness for action. It follows that, as a first principle of allocation, priority should be given to those who face an immediate threat to their lives. Since all agents have equal rights, it also follows that some potential advances in biotechnology that cannot be made available to all must be randomly allocated (e.g. by a lottery or queue) or, in some cases, perhaps even given to no one at all.[112] Moreover, for the reasons stated earlier, the application of the PGC requires procedural mechanisms.

---

[110] Beyleveld and Pattinson 2000a, 44. The "criterion of degrees of needfulness of action", above, is an instance of this principle.

[111] See Pattinson 2002a, 26–27, for an explanation of such behaviour and characteristics.

[112] See Beyleveld and Pattinson 2004a.

Drawing out the implications of the PGC for other issues addressed in this book would itself take a work at least as large as this. Elsewhere, I have addressed the implications of the PGC for many of the issues addressed in Chs 7 (on abortion), 8 (on assisted reproduction), and 10 (on embryo research and cloning). In *Influencing Traits Before Birth*, I argued that the proportional status of the early human and the autonomy focus of the PGC point against blanket prohibitions in favour of generally facilitative regulation.[113]

17.4 The future of medical law

Moral theory enables us to review the adequacy of ethical reasoning on its own terms and to question those terms. In practice, the future of positive medical law doctrine is likely to be driven more by social, technological, and political pressures than by abstract moral theories. A good understanding of medical ethics should, however, make us more aware of the difficult task faced by attempts to regulate medical practice against a backdrop of moral pluralism in which many regulatory decisions will have advocates and opponents whose views are (witting or unwittingly) tied to opposed underlying moral positions.[114] Globalisation increasingly enables the realisation of moral pluralism through *medical tourism*, whereby those opposed to domestic regulatory restrictions simply travel across jurisdiction boundaries. In essence, moral pluralism poses an enduring problem for the law. If the law does not embody a partisan moral position, background moral differences will seep in and challenge its coherence; and if the law does adopt a partisan position, there will be problems maintaining respect for the law in the population as a whole. Can the authority of the law be ring-fenced without presupposing some form of legal and ethical objectivism?

We have also seen that there are many bodies whose purpose is to advise the Government, medical professionals, or the general public on the ethical issues raised by medical practice. If ethical consideration is to be adequate, we should encourage the functioning of such bodies. At present, existing bodies overlap but have specific jurisdictional limitations. The professional bodies, such as the GMC, are limited to regulatory and advisory functions related to that particular profession.[115] The Law Commission only reviews specific legal scenarios on an ad hoc basis and, although it consults widely, is a legal reform body. The existing regulatory bodies, some of which have a statutory basis, are limited to particular areas. For example, the HFEA is principally concerned with reproductive medicine and the HGC with genetic issues. There is no general body with all-encompassing ethical jurisdiction for proactive, multi-disciplinary ethical evaluation. The UK has no equivalent to the French National Consultative Ethics Committee (CCNE), the Danish Council of Ethics, or the Health Council of the Netherlands.[116] The Nuffield Council of Bioethics is probably the closest

---

[113] See Pattinson 2002a.
[114] See further Brownsword 2004a.
[115] For a discussion of the limitations of the GMC's ethical role see Miola 2004.
[116] See a point also made by Brazier 2003, ch.20.

that we have to an advisory body with general jurisdiction on the ethics of medical practice. Given the importance of ethical consideration of the topics raised in the book, a case could be made for establishing a body tasked with responsibility for considering medical ethics and removing existing evaluative gaps and the duplication of effort.[117] However, for the time being at least, the Government has rejected the need for such a body.[118]

Could the ethical lacuna be properly filled by clinical ethics committees?[119] Medical expertise is not, after all, ethical expertise. Similarly, when populating such committees it should also be remembered that clerics and other religious advisers are also not necessarily experts in moral theory (which is not to suggest that the role of such persons can be ignored within a pluralistic society). It is often said that we can have too much of a good thing and, if badly constituted, populated, or run, clinical ethics committees can be a bad thing. At their worst, such committees could replace the unrepresentative, unqualified ethical decision-making of one group (the medical profession) with another group (what Siegler and Singer refer to as the "God squad" or "ethics police").[120] An unrepresentative and unqualified body would only add to the existing bureaucratic burden and ethical illegitimacy. Balancing acceptance, representation, independence, and competence is by no means straightforward. This is a problem faced by every political and regulatory mechanism within a modern polity. There are other dangers specific to clinical ethics committees. Some commentators fear that these committees could undermine the decision-making autonomy of clinicians and endanger patient care by allowing clinicians to defer responsibility.[121] While such dangers are real, the alternative is a clinical curtain cloaking ethical decision-making by those whose technical expertise provides neither ethical expertise nor ethical legitimacy. Would educating medics in ethics be better than relying on a properly constituted clinical ethics committee? Here the danger is one of self-serving interpretation and application. Whoever makes the hard decisions that need to be made in medical practice will not have the freedoms of armchair philosophers; time and the ability to hedge are likely to be absent friends. On balance, clinical ethics committees and tailored medical education offer at least the opportunity of greater ethical reflection. Such committees will need to be aware of legal as well as ethical principles, because, in democratic societies, the law carries considerable ethical weight by virtue of its procedural legitimacy.

The creation of new bodies is merely the first step towards ethically defensible regulation and oversight. Ethical analysis is more than procedural. What we need is sustained ethical consideration of medical practice as it develops. The future of medical law lies with those who are prepared to do this. The future of

---

[117] See Brazier (2003, ch. 20) suggests the establishment of a "Commission on Health Care Law and Ethics", but this suggestion is not reiterated in the latest edition of that book (see Brazier and Cave 2007).

[118] See HM Government 2005, para.112.

[119] Clinical ethics committees are relatively new in the UK, though there are now over 85 such committees. The functions and membership of these committees vary. See the UK Clinical Ethics Network website: *http://www.ethics-network.org.uk* and the report of a working party of the Royal College of Physicians (RCP 2005).

[120] Siegler and Singer 1988, 760.

[121] Siegler and Singer 1988, and Siegler 1986.

medical law lies with you. We must not be put off from taking this step and questioning preconceptions. In medicine, the problems are quite literally problems of life and death. Yet, to use the eloquent words of Ian Kennedy, "If you go to Africa thinking that a lion has stripes, you will see striped lions, though you may not see what everyone else would regard as lions."[122] Awareness of the underlying theoretical issues should lead you to give strong moral objectivism serious consideration.

17.5 Further reading

On the justificatory strategies of particular theorists

Gauthier
Gauthier, David (1986) *Morals by Agreement*. (Oxford: Clarendon Press).
Vallentyne, Peter (ed.) (1991) *Contractarianism and Rational Choice*. (Cambridge: Cambridge University Press).

Gewirth
Gewirth, Alan (1978) *Reason and Morality*. (Chicago: University of Chicago Press).
Beyleveld, Deryck (1991) *The Dialectical Necessity of Morality: An Analysis and Defence of Alan Gewirth's Argument to the Principle of Generic Consistency*. (Chicago: Chicago University Press).
Regis, Edward (ed.) (1984) *Gewirth's Ethical Rationalism: Critical Essays with a Reply by Alan Gewirth*. (Chicago: Chicago University Press).

Hare
Hare, R. M. (1981) *Moral Thinking: Its Levels, Method, and Point*. (Oxford: Clarendon Press).
Seanor, Douglas and Fotion, N (eds) (1988) *Hare and Critics: Essay on Moral Thinking*. (Oxford: Clarendon Press).

Kant
Kant, Immanuel (1785) *Groundwork of the Metaphysic of Morals*. Translated by H. J. Paton as *The Moral Law*. (London: Routledge, 1948).

Rawls
Rawls, John (1973) *A Theory of Justice*. (Oxford: Oxford University Press).
Daniels, Norman (ed.) (1975) *Reading Rawls: Critical Studies on Rawls' A Theory of Justice*. (Oxford: Blackwell).

---

[122] Kennedy 1988, 30.

On applied moral theories

Beyleveld, Deryck, and Brownsword, Roger (2001) *Human Dignity in Bioethics and Biolaw*. (Oxford: Oxford University Press).

Brownsword, Roger (2004) "Regulating Human Genetics: Novel Dilemmas for a New Millennium." 12(1) *Medical Law Review* 14–39.

Harris, John (1985) *The Value of Life: An Introduction to Medical Ethics*. (London: Routledge).

Pattinson, Shaun D. (2002) *Influencing Traits Before Birth*. (Aldershot: Ashgate).

Singer, Peter (1993) *Practical Ethics*. (Cambridge: Cambridge University Press).

BIBLIOGRAPHY

Abbott, Philip (1978) "Philosophers and the Abortion Question." 6(3) *Political Theory* 313–335.

ABI (Association of British Insurers) (2008) *Genetic Tests and Insurance: What You Need to Know.* A Guide for Consumers. (London: ABI) (June 2008).

Abouna, G. M., Sabawi, M. M., Kumar, M. S. A., and Samhan, M. (1991) "The Negative Impact of Paid Organ Donation." In W. Land and J. B. Dossetor (eds) *Organ Replacement Therapy: Ethics, Justice, Commerce.* (Berlin: Springer-Verlag), 164–172.

ABPI (Association of the British Pharmaceutical Industry) (1991) *Clinical Trial Compensation Guidelines.* (London: ABPI).

Academy of Medical Royal Colleges (2008) *A Code of Practice for the Diagnosis of Confirmation of Death.* (Academy of Medical Royal Colleges).

ACGT (Advisory Committee on Genetic Testing) (1998) *Report on Late Onset Disorders.* (London: Health Departments of the United Kingdom).

ACGT (Advisory Committee on Genetic Testing) (2000) *Prenatal Genetic Testing: Report for Consultation.* (London: Health Departments of the United Kingdom).

Adams, Maurice and Nys, Herman (2003) "Comparative Reflections on the Belgian Euthanasia Act 2002." 11(3) *Medical Law Review* 353–376.

Adams, Tim (2002) "When the Story's Over." *The Observer*, 27 January.

Agius, Emmanuel (1989) "Germ-line Cells—Our Responsibilities for Future Generations." 203 *Concilium* 105–115.

Al-Wakeel, Jamal, Mitwalli, Ahmed H., Tarif, Nauman, et al. (2000) "Living Unrelated Renal Transplant: Outcome and Issues." 11(4) *Saudi Journal of Kidney Diseases and Transplantation* 553–558.

Albin, R. L. (2002) "Sham Surgery Controls: Intracerebral Grafting of Fetal Tissue for Parkinson's Disease and Proposed Criteria for Use of Sham Surgery Controls." 28 *Journal of Medical Ethics* 322–325.

Albin, R. L. (2005) "Sham Surgery Controls Are Mitigated Trolleys." 31 *Journal of Medical Ethics* 149–152.

Alderson, P. (1996) "Equipoise as a Means of Managing Uncertainty: Personal, Communal and Proxy." 22 *Journal of Medical Ethics* 135–139.

Allison, Henry E. (1990) *Kant's Theory of Freedom.* (Cambridge: Cambridge University Press).

Allison, R. (2002) "Doctor in Organ Sale Scandal Struck Off." *The Guardian*, 31 August.

Almqvist, Elisabeth W., Bloch, Maurice, Brinkman, Ryan, Craufurd, David, and Hayden, Michael R. (1999) "A Worldwide Assessment of the Frequency of Suicide, Suicide Attempts, or Psychiatric Hospitalization after Predictive Testing for Huntington Disease." 64 *American Journal of Human Genetics* 1293–1304.

Andalo, Debbie (2004) "Surgeon Requests Swifter Hearing Over 'Wrong Kidney' Charge." *The Guardian*, 12 January.

Anderson Mark F. (1995) "The Future Of Organ Transplantation: From Where Will New Donors Come, To Whom Will Their Organs Go?" 5 *Health Matrix: The Journal of Law Medicine* 249–310.

Anderson, Elizabeth S. (2004) "Why Commercial Surrogate Motherhood Unethically Commodifies Women and Children: Reply to McLachlan and Swales." 8 *Health Care Analysis* 19–26.

Andrews, Keith, Murphy, Lesley, Munday, Ros, and Littlewood, Clare (1996) "Misdiagnosis of the Vegetative State: Retrospective Study in a Rehabilitation Unit." 313 *British Medical Journal* 13–16.

Andrews, Lori (1991) "Legal Aspects of Genetics Information." 6(4) *Yale Journal of Biology and Medicine* 29–40.

Andrews, Lori (2002) "The Gene Patent Dilemma: Balancing Commercial Incentives with Health Needs." 65 *Houston Journal of Health Law and Policy* 65–106.

Anleu, Roach S. L. (2001) "The Legal Regulation of Medical Science." 23(4) *Law and Policy* 417–440.

Annas, George J. and Grodin, Michael A. (eds) (1992) *The Nazi Doctors and the Nuremberg Code*. (Oxford: Oxford University Press).

Appelbaum, Paul S. (2002) "Clarifying the Ethics of Clinical Research: A Path toward Avoiding the Therapeutic Misconception." 2(2) *American Journal of Bioethics* 22–23.

Appelbaum, Paul S., Roth, Loren H., and Lidz, Charles (1982) "The Therapeutic Misconception: Informed Consent in Psychiatric Research." 5 *International Journal of Law and Psychiatry* 319–329.

Aquinas, St Thomas (c.1265–1274) *Summa Theologiae*. Translated by Timothy Dermot, as *Summa Theologiae: A Concise Translation*. (Texas: Christian Classics, 1989).

Aristotle (BCE) *Nicomachean Ethics*. Translated by Roger Crisp. (Cambridge: Cambridge University Press, 2000).

Armitage, Edward and Davis, Ivor (1994) *Patents and Morality in Perspective*. (London: Common Law Institute of Intellectual Property).

Arneson, Richard J. (1992) "Commodification and Commercial Surrogacy." 21(2) *Philosophy and Public Affairs* 132–164.

Arras, John D. (1991) "Getting Down to Cases: The Revival of Casuistry in Bioethics." 16(1) *Journal of Medicine and Philosophy* 29–51.

Asch, David A. (1996) "The Role of Critical Care Nurses in Euthanasia and Assisted Suicide." 334 *New England Journal of Medicine* 1374–1379.

Back, Anthony L., Wallace, J. I., Starks, H. E., and Pearlman, R. A. (1996) "Physician-Assisted Suicide and Euthanasia in Washington State: Patient Requests and Physician Responses." 275 *Journal of the American Medical Association* 919–925.

Baker, Stephen, Beyleveld, Deryck, Wallace, Susan, and Wright, Jessica (2005) "Research Ethics Committees and the Law in the UK." In D. Beyleveld, D. Townend and J. Wright (eds) *Research Ethics Committees, Data Protection and Medical Research in European Countries*. (Aldershot: Ashgate), 271–289.

Bainham, Andrew (1992) "The Judge and the Competent Minor." 108 *Law Quarterly Review* 194–200.

Baird, Patricia A. (1994) "Altering Human Genes: Social, Ethical, and Legal Implications." 37(4) *Perspectives in Biology and Medicine* 566–575.

Baron, Charles (1997) "Physician Assisted Suicide Should Be Legalized and Regulated." 41 *Boston Bar Journal* 12–29.

Bartlett, Peter (1997) "Doctors as Fiduciaries: Equitable Regulation of the Doctor-Patient Relationship." 5(2) *Medical Law Review* 193–224.

Bartlett, Peter and Sandland, Ralph (2007) *Mental Health Law: Policy and Practice.* (3rd edition) (Oxford: Oxford University Press).

Bayne, Tim and Levy, Neil (2005) "Amputees By Choice: Body Integrity Identity Disorder and the Ethics of Amputation." 22(1) *Journal of Applied Philosophy* 75–86.

BBC (British Broadcasting Corporation) (These documents can be found at *http://news.bbc.co.uk/*).

BBC (1998) "Review Proposes Regulation for Surrogacy." *BBC News*, 16 October.

BBC (2000) "Scientists Crack Human Code." *BBC News*, 26 June.

BBC (2002a) "George Best Out of Intensive Care," *BBC News*, 1 August.

BBC (2002b) "Embryologist Fooled IVF Patients." *BBC News*, 11 December.

BBC (2003a) "Briton's Assisted Suicide Goes Ahead." *BBC News*, 20 January.

BBC (2003b) "Human Genome Finally Complete." *BBC News*, 14 April.

BBC (2003c) " 'Designer Baby' Is Perfect Match." *BBC News*, 21 July.

BBC (2003d) "US Anti-Abortionist Executed." *BBC News*, 4 September.

BBC (2005a) "A Retired Policeman Who Killed his Terminally Ill Wife and then Tried to Kill Himself Has Been Spared Jail." *BBC News*, 14 January.

BBC (2005b) "Frozen Embryo Case goes to Europe." *BBC News*, 14 February.

BBC (2005c) "Tories 'Using Op Case as Stunt'." *BBC News*, 3 March.

BBC (2005d) "No Charges in Late Abortion Case." *BBC News*, 17 March.

BBC (2005e) "Sperm Ships for Fertility Seekers." *BBC News*, 16 September.

BBC (2005f) "Nurse Wins Breast Cancer Drug Row." *BBC News*, 3 October.

BBC (2005g) "Compensation fears 'gripping UK'." *BBC News*, 3 November.

BBC (2007) "Body Parts Sale Man Avoids Jail." *BBC News*, 11 May.

BBC (2008a) "MPs Reject Cut in Abortion Limit." *BBC News*, 21 May.

BBC (2008b) "MPs' Bid to Change Abortion Laws." *BBC News*, 8 July.

BBC (2008c) "MPs Support Embryology Proposals." *BBC News*, 23 October.

BBC (2008d) " 'Hybrid Embryo' Legal Block Lost." *BBC News*, 9 December.

BBC (2008e) "Doctors Explain Face Transplant." *BBC News*, 18 December.

Beauchamp, Tom L. and Childress, James F. (2001) *Principles of Biomedical Ethics.* (5th ed.) (Oxford: Oxford University Press).

Beever, Allan (2007a) *Rediscovering the Law of Negligence.* (Oxford: Hart Publishing).

Beever, Allan (2007b) "Policy in Private Law: An Admission of Failure." *University of Queensland Law Journal* 287–306.

Beever, Allan (2008) "Corrective Justice and Personal Responsibility in Tort Law." 28 *Oxford Journal of Legal Studies* 475–500.

Beever, Allan and Rickett, Charles (2005) "Interpretive Legal Theory and the Academic Lawyer." 68(2) *Modern Law Review* 320–337.

Bell, Nora Kizer (1992) "If Age Becomes a Standard for Rationing Health Care." In Helen Bequaert Holmes, and Laura M. Purdy (ed.) *Feminist Perspectives in Medical Ethics.* (Bloomington: Indiana University Press), 82–90.

Berg, Jessica Wilen, Appelbaum, Paul S., and Grisso, Thomas (1996) "Constructing Competence: Formulating Standards of Legal Competence to Make Medical Decisions." 48(2) *Rutgers Law Review* 345–396.

Berger, Edward M. and Gert, Bernard M. (1991) "Genetic Disorders and the Ethical Status of Germ-line Gene Therapy." 16 *Journal of Medicine and Philosophy* 667–683.

Bernat, Erwin (1995) "Marketing of Human Organs?" 14(3/4) *Medicine and Law* 181–190.

Beyleveld, Deryck (1991) *The Dialectical Necessity of Morality: An Analysis and Defence of Alan Gewirth's Argument to the Principle of Generic Consistency.* (Chicago: Chicago University Press).

Beyleveld, Deryck (1996) "Legal Theory and Dialectically Contingent Justifications for the Principle of Generic Consistency." 9 Ratio *Juris* 15–41.

Beyleveld, Deryck (1997) "The Trouble with Tendential Slippery Slope Arguments." 2 *Biomedical Ethics: Newsletter of the European Network on Biomedical Ethics* 42.

Beyleveld, Deryck (1999) "Gewirth and Kant on Justifying the Supreme Principle of Morality." In Michael Boylan (eds) *Gewirth: Critical Essays on Action, Rationality, and Community.* (New York: Rowman & Littlefield), 97–117.

Beyleveld, Deryck (2000) "Why Recital 26 of the EC Directive on the Legal Protection of Biotechnological Inventions Should Be Implemented in National Law." 1 *Intellectual Property Quarterly* 1–26.

Beyleveld, Deryck (2002) "Law, Ethics and Research Ethics Committees." 21 *Medicine and Law* 57–75.

Beyleveld, Deryck (2004a) "An Overview of Directive 95/46/EC in Relation to Medical Research." In Deryck Beyleveld, David Townend, Ségoléne Rouillé-Mirza, and Jessica Wright (eds) *The Data Protection Directive and Medical Research Across Europe.* (Aldershot: Ashgate), 5–21.

Beyleveld, Deryck (2004b) "The Duty to Provide Information to the Data Subject: Articles 10 and 11 of Directive 95/46/EC." In Deryck Beyleveld, David Townend, Ségoléne Rouillé-Mirza, and Jessica Wright (eds) *The Data Protection Directive and Medical Research Across Europe.* (Aldershot: Ashgate), 69–87.

Beyleveld, Deryck (2009) "Jurisprudential Views of the Relationship Between Law and Ethics." In D. Beyleveld, D. Townend and J. Wright (eds) *Research Ethics Committees, Data Protection and Medical Research in Europe—Key Issues.* (Aldershot: Ashgate) (forthcoming).

Beyleveld, Deryck and Brownsword, Roger (1993) *Mice, Morality, and Patents.* (London: Common Law Institute of Intellectual Property).

Beyleveld, Deryck and Brownsword, Roger (1994) *Law as a Moral Judgement.* (Sheffield: Sheffield Academic Press). (Previously published by Sweet & Maxwell, 1986).

Beyleveld, Deryck and Brownsword, Roger (2000) "My Body, My Body Parts, My Property?" 8(2) *Health Care Analysis* 87–99.

Beyleveld, Deryck and Brownsword, Roger (2001) *Human Dignity in Bioethics and Biolaw.* (Oxford: Oxford University Press).

Beyleveld, Deryck and Brownsword, Roger (2007) *Consent in the Law.* (London: Hart).

Beyleveld, Deryck, Finnegan, Tom, and Pattinson, Shaun D. (2009) "The Regulation of Hybrids and Chimeras in the UK." in Jochen Taupitz and Marion Weschka (eds) *Chimbrids: Chimeras and hybrids in comparative European and international research: scientific, ethical, philosophical and legal aspects.* (Berlin: Springer).

Beyleveld, Deryck, Grubb, Andrew, Townend, David, Morgan, Ryan, and Wright, Jessica (2004) "The UK's Implementation of Directive 95/46/EC." In Deryck Beyleveld, David Townend, Ségoléne Rouillé-Mirza, and Jessica Wright (eds) *The Implementation of the Data Protection Directive in Relation to Medical Research in Europe.* (Aldershot: Ashgate), 403–428.

Beyleveld, Deryck and Histed, Elise (1999) "Case Commentary: Anonymisation is Not Exoneration." 4 *Medical Law International* 69–80.

Beyleveld, Deryck and Histed, Elise (2000) "Betrayal of Confidence in the Court of Appeal." 4 *Medical Law International* 277–311.

Beyleveld, Deryck and Townend, David M. R. (2004) "When is Personal Data Rendered Anonymous? Interpreting Recital 26 of Directive 95/46/EEC." 6(2) *Medical Law International* 73–86.

Beyleveld, Deryck and Pattinson, Shaun D. (1998) "Proportionality under Precaution: Justifying Duties to Apparent Non-Agents." (Unpublished paper available from this author).

Beyleveld, Deryck and Pattinson, Shaun D. (2000a) "Precautionary Reasoning as a Link to Moral Action." In Michael Boylan (ed.) *Medical Ethics.* (Upper Saddle River New Jersey: Prentice-Hall, 2000), 39–53.

Beyleveld, Deryck and Pattinson, Shaun D. (2000b) "Legal Regulation of Assisted Procreation, Genetic Diagnosis, and Gene Therapy." In Hille Haker and Deryck Beyleveld (eds) *The Ethics of Genetics in Human Procreation.* (Aldershot: Ashgate, 2000), 215–276.

Beyleveld, Deryck and Pattinson, Shaun D. (2001) "Embryo Research in the UK: Is Harmonisation in the EU Needed or Possible?" In Minou Bernadette (ed.) *Embryo Experimentation in Europe.* (Bad Neuenahr-Ahrweiler: European Academy), 58–74.

Beyleveld, Deryck and Pattinson, Shaun D. (2002) "Horizontal Applicability and Horizontal Effect." 118 *Law Quarterly Review* 623–646.

Beyleveld, Deryck and Pattinson, Shaun D. (2004a) "Individual Rights, Social Justice, and the Allocation of Advances in Biotechnology." In Michael Boylan (ed.) *Public Health Policy and Ethics.* (The Hague, Kluwer International), 59–72.

Beyleveld, Deryck and Pattinson, Shaun D. (2004b) "Globalisation and Human Dignity: Some Effects and Implications for the Creation and Use of Embryos." In Roger Brownsword (ed.) *Global Governance and the Quest for Justice. Volume IV: Human Rights.* (Oxford: Hart), 185–202.

Beyleveld, Deryck and Pattinson, Shaun D. (2006) "Medical Research into Emergency Treatment: Regulatory Tensions in England and Wales." 5 *Web Journal of Current Legal Issues. (http://webjcli.ncl.ac.uk/2006/issue5/beyleveld5.html).*

Beyleveld, Deryck and Pattinson, Shaun D. (2008) "Moral Interests, Privacy and Medical Research." In Michael Bolan (ed.) *International Public Health Policy and Ethics.* (Springer), 45–57.

Bibbings, Lois S. (1995) "Female Circumcision: Mutilation or Modification?" In Jo Bridgeman and Susan Millns (eds) *Law and Body Politics: Regulating the Female Body.* (Aldershot: Dartmouth), 151–170.

Bielby, Phillip (2005) "The Conflation of Competence and Capacity in English Medical Law: A Philosophical Critique." 8(3) *Medicine, Health Care and Philosophy* 357–369.

Biggs, Hazel (1996) "Decisions and Responsibilities at the End of Life: Euthanasia and Clinically Assisted Death." 2(3) *Medical Law International* 229–245.

Black, Julia (1998) "Regulation as Facilitation: Negotiating the Genetic Revolution." 61(5) *Modern Law Review* 621–660.

Blumstein, James F. (1993) "The Use of Financial Incentives in Medical Care: The Case Of Commerce in Transplantable Organs." *Health Matrix: Journal of Law-Medicine* 1–30.

BMA (British Medical Association) (1987) *No Fault Compensation Working Party*. (London: BMA).

BMA (1996) *The Changing Conceptions of Motherhood: The Practice of Surrogacy in Britain*. (London: BMA).

BMA (1998) *Human Genetics: Choice and Responsibility*. (Oxford: Oxford University Press).

BMA (1999) *Confidentiality and Disclosure of Health Information*. (London: BMA).

BMA (2000) *Organ Donation in the 21st Century: Time for a Consolidated Approach*. (London: BMA).

BMA (2001) *Withholding and Withdrawing Life-prolonging Treatment: Guidance for Decision-Making*. (2nd ed.) (London: BMJ Books).

BMA (2003) *The Law and Ethics of Male Circumcision: Guidance for Doctors*. (London: BMA).

BMA (2004) *Medical Ethics Today: The BMA's Handbook of Ethics and Law*. (2nd ed.) (London: BMJ Books).

BMA (2006) *The Law And Ethics Of Male Circumcision—Guidance For Doctors*. (London: BMA) (June 2006).

BMA (2007a) *Withholding and Withdrawing Life-prolonging Treatment: Guidance for Decision-Making*. (3rd ed.) (London: BMJ Books).

BMA (2007b) *Regulation of the Medical Profession: Health and Social Care Bill*. (22 Nov. 2007). (*http://www.bma.org.uk/ap.nsf/Content/HealthandSocialCareBill*).

BMA Resuscitation Council and the RCN (Royal College of Nursing) (2001) *Decisions Relating to Cardiopulmonary Resuscitation*. (Feb. 2001) (*http://www.resus.org.uk/pages/dnar.htm*).

Boggio, Andrea (2005) "The Compensation of the Victims of the Creutzfeldt-Jacob Disease in the United Kingdom." 7(2) *Medical Law International* 149–167.

Boivin, Jacky, Takefman, Janet E., Tulandi, Togas, and Brender, William (1995) "Reactions to Infertility Based on the Extent of Treatment Failure." 63(4) *Fertility and Sterility* 801–807.

Boonin-Vain, David (1997) "A Defense of 'A Defense of Abortion': On the Responsibility Objection to Thomson's Argument." 107 *Ethics* 286–313.

Boylan, Michael (eds) (1999) *Gewirth: Critical Essays on Action, Rationality, and Community*. (New York: Rowman & Littlefield).

Bradberry, Grace (1999) "Online Bidders' Stake in Kidney." *The Times*, 4 September.

Bradbury, Lisa W. (2003) "Euthanasia in the Netherlands: Recognizing Mature Minors in Euthanasia Legislation." 9(1) *New England Journal of International and Comparative Law* 209–257.

Branigan, Tania (2001) "Doctor Backs Mother-To-Be, 56." *The Guardian*, 23 January.

Braude, Peter R., de Wert, Guido M. W. R., Evers-Kiebooms, Gerry, Pettigrew, Rachel A, and Geraedts, Joep P. M. (1998) "Non-disclosure Preimplantation Genetic Diagnosis for Huntington's Disease: Practical and Ethical Dilemmas." 18 *Prenatal Diagnosis* 1422–1426.

Brazier, Margaret (1987) "Patient Autonomy and Consent to Treatment: The Role of the Law?" 7 *Legal Studies* 169–193.

Brazier, Margaret (1990a) "The Challenge for Parliament: A Critique of the White Paper on Human Fertilisation and Embryology." In Dyson and John Harris (ed.) *Experiments on Embryos.* (London: Routledge), 127–141.

Brazier, Margaret (1990b) "Liability of Ethics Committees." 6 *Professional Negligence* 186–1990.

Brazier, Margaret (1992) *Medicine, Patients and the Law.* (2nd ed.) (London: Penguin).

Brazier, Margaret (1993) "The Case for a No-Fault Compensation Scheme for Medical Accidents." In Sheila McLean (ed.) *Compensation for Damage.* (Aldershot: Dartmouth), 51–74.

Brazier, Margaret (1999) "Liberty Responsibility and Maternity." 52 *Current Legal Problems* 359–391.

Brazier, Margaret (2002) "Retained Organs: Ethics and Humanity." 22(4) *Legal Studies* 550–569.

Brazier, Margaret (2003) *Medicine, Patients and the Law.* (3rd ed.) (London: Penguin).

Brazier, Margaret (2005) "Editorial: Times of Change?" 13(1) *Medical Law Review* 1–16.

Brazier Margaret and Beswick, Joanne (2006) "Who's Caring for Me?" 7(3) *Medical Law International* 183–199.

Brazier, Margaret and Bridge, Caroline (1996) "Coercion or Caring: Analysing Adolescent Autonomy." 16 *Legal Studies* 84–109.

Brazier, Margaret and Cave, Emma (2007) *Medicine, Patients and the Law.* (4th ed.) (London: Penguin Books).

Brazier, Margaret and Glover, Nicola (2000) "Does Medical Law Have a Future?" In David Hayton (eds) *Law's Future.* (Oxford: Hart, 2000), 371–388.

Brazier, Margaret and Lobjoit, Mary (1999) "Fiduciary Relationship: An Ethical Approach and a Legal Concept." In Rebecca Bennett and Charles Erin (eds) *HIV and AIDS: Testing, Screening, and Confidentiality.* (Oxford: Oxford University Press), 179–199.

Brazier, Margaret and Miola, José (2000) "Bye-Bye Bolam: A Medical Litigation Revolution?" 8(1) *Medical Law Review* 85–114.

Brazier, Margaret, Campbell, Alastair, and Golombok, Susan (1998) *Surrogacy: Review for Health Ministers of Current Arrangements for Payments and Regulation* (Cm 4068) (London: HMSO).

Bridgman, Jo (1995) "Declared Innocent?" 3(2) *Medical Law Review* 117–141.

Brock, Dan W. (1995) "The Non-Identity Problem and Genetic Harms—The Case of Wrongful Handicaps." 9 *Bioethics* 269–275.

Brock, Dan W. (1998) "Cloning Human Beings: An Assessment of the Ethical Issues Pro and Con." In Martha C. Nussbaum, and Cass R. Sunstein (eds) *Clones and Clones: Facts and Fantasies About Human Cloning.* (New York and London: W. W. Norton & Company), 141–164.

Brock, Dan W. (2000) "Misconceived Sources of Opposition to Physician-Assisted Suicide." 6 *Psychology, Public Policy, and Law* 305–313.

Brown, Eric (2004) "The New Foundation Trust Regime." 154 *New Law Journal* 930.

Brown, Nick (2003) "Making Adequate Amends?" 153 *New Law Journal* 1095.

Brownsword, Roger (2002) "Stem Cells, Superman, and the Report of the Select Committee" 65(4) *Modern Law Review* 568–587.

Brownsword, Roger (2003a) "An Interest in Human Dignity as the Basis for Genomic Torts." 42 *Washburn Law Journal* 413–487.

Brownsword, Roger (2003b) "Bioethics Today, Bioethics Tomorrow: Stem Cell Research and the 'Dignitarian Alliance'." 17 *Notre Dame Journal of Law, Ethics and Public Policy* 15–51.

Brownsword, Roger (2004a) "Regulating Human Genetics: Novel Dilemmas for a New Millennium." 12(1) *Medical Law Review* 14–39.

Brownsword, Roger (2004b) "The Cult of Consent: Fixation and Fallacy." 15 *Kings College Law Journal* 223–251.

Brownsword, Roger (2005) "Stem Cells and Cloning: Where the Regulatory Consensus Fails." 39 *New England Law Review* 535–571.

Broyer, M. (1991) "Aspects of Living Organ Donation with Emphasis on the Fight Against Commercialism." In W. Land and J. B. Dossetor (eds) *Organ Replacement Therapy: Ethics, Justice, Commerce.* (Berlin: Springer-Verlag), 197–202.

Brunner, H. G., Nelen, M., Breakefield, X. O., Ropers, H. H., and van Oost, B. A. (1993) "Abnormal Behavior Associated with a Point Mutation in the Structural Gene for Monoamine Oxidase A." 262 *Science* 578–580.

Buchanan, Allen (1988) "Advance Directives and the Personal Identity Problem." 17(4) *Philosophy and Public Affairs* 277–302.

Burley, Justine and Harris, John (1999) "Human Cloning and Child Welfare." 25 *Journal of Medical Ethics* 108–113.

Butler, Tom. 2001. "Competency and Risk-relativity." 15(2) *Bioethics* 93–109.

Buxton, Richard (2000) "The Human Rights Act and Private Law." 116 *Law Quarterly Review* 48–56.

Callahan, Daniel (1990) "Rationing Medical Progress: The Way to Affordable Health Care." 322 *New England Journal of Medicine* 1810–1813.

Callahan, Daniel (1997) "A Step Too Far." *New York Times*, 26 February, A23.

Cameron-Perry, J. Ellis (1999) "Return of the Burden of the 'Blessing'." 149 *New Law Journal* 1887–1888.

Campbell, Alastair, Gillett, Grant, and Jones, Gareth (2001) *Medical Ethics.* (3rd ed.) (Oxford: Oxford University Press).

Cane, Peter (2001) "Distributive Justice and Tort Law." 20 *New Zealand Law Review* 401–420.

Cantor, Norman L. (1992) "Prospective Autonomy: On the Limits of Shaping One's Postcompetence Medical Fate." 8 *Journal of Contemporary Health Law and Policy* 13–48.

Carnall, Douglas (1996) "Doctor Struck Off for Scientific Fraud." 312 *British Medical Journal* 400.

Carruthers, Peter (1992) *The Animals Issue: Moral Theory in Practice.* (Cambridge: Cambridge University Press).

Cartwright, Silvia R. (1988) *The Report of the Committee of Inquiry into Allegations Concerning the Treatment of Cervical Cancer at National Women's Hospital and into Other Related Matters.* (Auckland, New Zealand: Government Printing Office).

Cartwright, W. (1996) "The Pig, the Transplant Surgeon and the Nuffield Council." 4(3) *Medical Law Review* 250–269.

Carvel, John (2003) "Patients to Choose their NHS Hospital." *The Guardian*, 17 July, 5.

Carvel, John (2004) "Donated Kidneys Lost for Lack of Surgeons." *The Guardian*, 11 June, 11.

Case, Paula (2003) "Confidence Matters: The Rise and Fall of Informational Autonomy in Medical Law." 11(2) *Medical Law Review* 208–236.

Cases, Olivier, et al. (1995) "Aggressive Behavior and Altered Amounts of Brain Serotonin and Norepinephrine in Mice Lacking MAOA." 268 *Science* 1763–1766.

Caulfield, Tim and von Tigerstrom, B Barbara (2005) "Globalization and Biotechnology Policy: The Challenges Created by Gene Patents and Cloning Technologies." In Belinda Bennett and George F. Tomossy (eds.) *Globalization and Health: Challenges for Health Law and Bioethics*. (Springer: International Library of Ethics, Law and the New Medicine) 129–149.

Cave, E. and Holm, S. (2002) "New Governance Arrangements for Research Ethics Committees: Is Facilitating Research Achieved at the Cost of Participants' Interest." 28 *Journal of Medical Ethics* 318–321.

CCNE (Comité Consultatif National d'Ethique: National Consultative Ethics Committee) English translations of the opinions and reports of the CCNE can be found at *http://www.ccne-ethique.fr*.

CCNE (2004) *Composite Tissue Allotransplantation (CTA) of the Face (Full or Partial Face Transplant)* (No. 82).

Cecka, J. M. (1999) "Results of More Than 1000 Recent Living-Unrelated Donor Transplants in the United States." 31 *Transplantation Proceedings* 234.

CEMACH (Confidential Enquiry into Maternal And Child Health) (2007) *Perinatal Mortality 2005*. (London: CEMACH). (April 2007).

Chan, A. W. S. et al. (2001) "Transgenic Monkeys Produced by Retroviral Gene Transfer into Mature Oocytes; 12 *Science* 309–312.

Cibelli, Jose (2007) "Is Therapeutic Cloning Dead?" 318 *Science* 1879–1880.

Cibelli, Jose B., et al. (2001) "Somatic Cell Nuclear Transfer in Humans: Pronuclear and Early Embryonic Development." 2 *e-biomed: The Journal of Regenerative Medicine* 25–31.

Ciment, James (2000) "Gene Therapy Experiments put on 'Clinical Hold'." 320 *British Medical Journal* 336.

CIOMS (Council for International Organizations of Medical Sciences) (2002) *International Ethical Guidelines for Biomedical Research Involving Human Subjects*. (Geneva: CIMOS).

Clark, Peter A. (2005a) "Face Transplantation: A Medical Perspective." 11(1) *Medical Science Monitor* RA1–6.

Clark, Peter A. (2005b) "Face Transplantation: Part II—An Ethical Perspective." 11(2) *Medical Science Monitor* RA41–47.

Clothier C., MacDonald, C. A., and Shaw, D. A. (1994) *The Allitt Inquiry: Independent Inquiry relating to Deaths and Injuries on the Children's Ward at Grantham and Kesteven General Hospital During the Period February to April 1991*. (London: HMSO).

Clucas, Bev and O'Donnell, Kath (2002) "Conjoined Twins: The Cutting Edge." 5 *Web Journal of Current Legal Issues*. (*http://webjcli.ncl.ac.uk/2002/issue5/clucas5.html*).

CMO (Chief Medical Officer) (2000) *Stem Cell Research: Medical Progress with Responsibility*. (London: Department of Health). (June 2000).

CMO (2003) *Making Amends: A consultation paper setting out proposals for reforming the approach to clinical negligence in the NHS.* (London: Department of Health). (June 2003).

CMO (2006) *Good Doctors, Safer Patients: Proposals to strengthen the system to assure and improve the performance of doctors and to protect the safety of patients.* (London: DH). (July 2006).

Cohen, Cynthia B. (1999) "Selling Bits and Pieces of Humans to Make Babies: The Gift of the Magi Revisited." 24(3) *Journal of Medicine and Philosophy* 288–306.

Cohen, Lloyd R. (1989) "Increasing the Supply of Transplant Organs: The Virtues of a Futures Market." 58 *George Washington Law Review* 1–51.

Cohen, Peter J. (2002) "Failure to Conduct a Placebo-Controlled Trial May be Unethical." 2(2) *American Journal of Bioethics* 24.

Coghlan, A. (1994) "Hidden Costs of a Clean Inheritance." 142 *New Scientist* 14–15.

Coldicott, Yvette, Pope, Catherine, and Roberts, Clive. 2003. "The Ethics of Intimate Examinations—Teaching Tomorrow's Doctors." 326 *British Medical Journal* 97–99.

Conference of the Medical Royal Colleges and their Faculties in the United Kingdom (1976) "Diagnosis of Brain Stem Death." *British Medical Journal* 1187–1188.

Connor, Michael, and Ferguson-Smith, Malcolm (1997) *Medical Genetics.* (5th ed.) (Oxford: Blackwell Science).

Connor, Steve (2003) "Glaxo Chief: Our Drugs Do Not Work on Most Patients." *The Independent*, 8 December, 1.

Cooper, David K. C., Gollackner, Bernd, and Sachs, David H. (2002) "Will the Pig Solve the Transplantation Backlog?" 53 *Annual Review of Medicine* 133–147.

Copp, David (1992) "The 'Possibility' of a Categorical Imperative: Kant's Groundwork, Part III." 6 *Philosophical Perspectives* 261–284.

Cooper, Glenda (1996) "IVF couple 'will fight for others'." *The Independent*, 1 March.

COREC (2001) *Governance Arrangements for NHS Research Ethics Committees.* (London: Department of Health). (August 2001).

Council of Europe (1999) *Meeting the Organ Storage.* (Strasbourg Cedex).

Cowan, Rosie (2002) "Irish Reject Tougher Law on Abortion." *The Guardian*, 8 March, 2.

Crespi, Gregory S. (1994) "Overcoming the Legal Obstacles to the Creation of a Futures Market in Bodily Organs." 55 *Ohio State Law Journal* 1–77.

Crisp, Roger (trans) (2000) Aristotle, *Nicomachean Ethics.* (Cambridge: Cambridge University Press).

Daniels, Norman (ed.) (1975) *Reading Rawls: Critical Studies on Rawls' A Theory of Justice.* (Oxford: Blackwell).

Daniels, Norman (1988) *Am I My Parents' Keeper? An Essay on Justice Between the Young and the Old.* (New York: Oxford University Press).

Danis, Jodi (1995) "Sexism and 'The Superfluous Female': Arguments for Regulating Pre-Implantation Sex Selection." 18 *Harvard Women's Law Journal* 219–264.

Danish Council of Ethics (2004) *Patenting Human Genes and Stem Cells.* (Copenhagen: Danish Council of Ethics).

Davies, Gareth (2004) "Health and Efficiency: Community Law and National Health Systems in the Light of Müller-Fauré." 67(1) *Modern Law Review* 94–107.

Davies, Michael (1998) *Textbook on Medical Law*. (2nd ed.) (London: Blackstone).

Davis, Dena S. (1997) "Genetic Dilemmas and the Child's Right to An Open Future." 28 *Rutgers Law Journal* 549–592.

de Haan, Jurriaan (2002) "The New Dutch Law on Euthanasia." 10(1) *Medical Law Review* 57–75.

DeBaun, M. R., Niemitz, E. L. & Feinberg, A. P. (2003) "Association of *In Vitro* Fertilization with Beckwith–Wiedemann Syndrome and Epigenetic Alterations of LIT1 and H19." 72 *American Journal of Human Genetics* 156–160.

Deakin, Simon, Johnston, Angus, and Markesinis, Basil (2008) *Markesinis and Deakin's Tort Law*. (6th ed.) (Oxford: Oxford University Press).

Deech, Ruth (1999) "Cloning and Public Policy." In Justine Burley (ed.) *The Genetic Revolution and Human Rights: The Oxford Amnesty Lectures 1998*. (Oxford: Oxford University Press), 95–100.

Deech, Ruth (2002) "Losing Control?—Some Cases." In Marie-Thérése Meulders-Klien, Ruth Deech, and Paul Vlaardingerbroek (eds) *Biomedicine, the Family and Human Rights*. (The Hague: Kluwer Law International), 581–598.

Delany, Linda, and Doyle, Kathy (1997) "Fathers—Who Needs Them?—HFEA and Blood." 27 *Family Law* 261–264.

Deltz, E. (1991) "Medical Risk and Benefit in Living Small-Bowel Segment Donors." In W. Land and J. B. Dossetor (eds) *Organ Replacement Therapy: Ethics, Justice, Commerce*. (Berlin: Springer-Verlag), 110–116.

Department for Constitutional Affairs (2007) Mental Capacity Act: Code of Practice. (London: TSO). (Feb. 2007) (*http://www.dca.gov.uk/legal-policy/mental-capacity/mca-cp.pdf*).

Dermot, Timothy (trans) (1989) *Summa Theologiae: A Concise Translation*, by St Thomas Aquinas. (Texas: Christian Classics).

Deschamps, J-Y., Roux, F. A., Saï, P., and Gouin, E. (2005) "History of Xenotransplantation." 12(2) *Xenotransplantation* 91–109.

Devauchelle B., Badet L., Lengele B., et al. (2006) "First human face allograft: early report". 368 *Lancet* 203–209.

Devlin, Patrick (1959) "The Enforcement of Morals." 45 *Proceedings of the British Academy* 129–151.

Devlin, Patrick (1965) *The Enforcement of Morals*. (Oxford: Oxford University Press).

DH (Department of Health) (The majority of these documents can be found at *www.dh.gov.uk*).

DH (1983) *Cadaveric Organs for Transplantation: A Code of Practice including the Diagnosis of Brain Death*. (London: HMSO).

DH (1992) *Report of the Committee on the Ethics of Gene Therapy* (Cm 1788). (London: HMSO).

DH (1994a) *Being Heard: The Report of a Review Committee on NHS Complaints Procedures*. (London: DH).

DH (1994b) *Identification of Potential Donors of Organs for Transplantation*. (HSG(94)41 NHS Executive).

DH (1995a) *The Patient's Charter and You*. (HSG(92)4. (London: DH).

DH (1995b) *Acting on Complaints* (EL(95)37). (London: HMSO).

DH (1996a) *NHS Indemnity: Arrangement for Handling Clinical Negligence Claims Against NHS Staff.* (HSG(96)48).

DH (1996b) *NHS Indemnity: Arrangements for Clinical Negligence Claims in the NHS.* (Oct. 1996).

DH (1997) *Animal Tissue into Humans: A Report by the Advisory Group on the Ethics of Xenotransplantation.* (The Stationery Office: DH).

DH (1998) *A Code of Practice for the Diagnosis of Brain Stem Death, including Guidelines for the Identification and Management of Potential Organ and Tissue Donors.* (London: DH). (March 1998).

DH (2000a) *An Inquiry into Quality and Practice within the National Health Service arising from the Actions of Rodney Ledward.* (London: DH). (June 2000).

DH (2000b) *The NHS Plan.* (Cm 4818–I) (London: HMSO). (July 2000).

DH (2000c) *Stem Cell Research: Medical Progress with Responsibility: A Report from the Chief Medical Officer's Expert Group Reviewing the Potential of Developments in Stem Cell Research and Cell Nuclear Replacement to Benefit Human Health.* (London: HMSO). (June 2000).

DH (2000d) *An Investigation into Conditional Organ Donation: The Report of the Panel.* (London: HMSO). (Feb. 2000).

DH (2000e) Press Release: *Lord Hunt Announces Modernisation of Transplant Services.* (2000/0106).

DH (2001a) *Assuring the Quality of Medical Practice.* (London: DH). (Jan. 2001).

DH (2001b) *Your Guide to the NHS.* (London: DH). (Jan. 2001).

DH (2001c) *NHS Complaints Procedure: National Evaluation.* (London: DH). (March 2001).

DH (2001d) *Reforming the NHS Complaints Procedure: A Listening Document.* (London: DH). (Sept. 2001).

DH (2002a) *Reform of the General Medical Council: Report on the Consultation.* (London: DH). (Sept. 2002).

DH (2002b) *The National Health Service Litigation Authority: Framework Document.* (Dec. 2002).

DH (2002c) *HIV Infected Health Care Workers: A Consultation Paper on Management and Patient Notification.* (London: DH). (July 2002).

DH (2002d) *Human Bodies, Human Choices: The Law on Human Organs and Tissue in England and Wales. A Consultation Report.* (London: DH). (July 2002).

DH (2003a) *NHS Complaints Reform: Making Things Right.* (London: DH).

DH (2003b) *Abortion Statistics, England and Wales: 2002.* (London: DH).

DH (2003c) *Our Inheritance: Our Future: Realising the Potential of Genetics in the NHS.* (London: The Stationary Office). (June 2003).

DH (2003d) *Confidentiality: NHS Code of Practice.* (London: DH). (Nov. 2003).

DH (2004a) *Reconfiguring the DH's Arm's Length Bodies.* (London: DH). (July 2004).

DH (2004b) *Best Practice Guidance For Doctors and Other Health Professionals on the Provision of Advice and Treatment to Young People Under 16 on Contraception, Sexual and Reproductive Health.* (London: DH). (July 2004).

DH (2005a) *Research Governance Framework for Health and Social Care.* (2nd edition) (London: DH). (April 2005).

DH (2005b) *Report of the* Ad Hoc *Advisory Group on the Operation of Research Ethics Committees*. (London: DH). (May 2005).

DH (2005c) *HIV Infected Health Care Workers: Guidance on Management and Patient Notification*. (London: DH). (July 2005).

DH (2005d) *Review of the Human Fertilisation and Embryology Act: A Public Consultation*. (London: DH). (Aug. 2005).

DH (2005h) *NHS Redress: Statement of Policy*. (London: DH). (Nov. 2005).

DH (2006a) *Full Regulatory Impact Assessment*. (London: DH). (March 2006).

DH (2006b) *The Regulation Of The Non-Medical Healthcare Professions*. (London: DH). (July 2006).

DH (2006c) *Supporting Staff, Improving Services—Guidance to support implementation of the: National Health Service (Complaints) Amendment Regulations 2006*. (London: DH). (Aug. 2006).

DH (2006d) *Xenotransplantation Guidance*. (London: DH). (Dec. 2006).

DH (2007a) *Making Experiences Count: The Proposed New Arrangements for Handling Health and Social Care Complaints: Detailed Policy Background*. (London: DH). (June 2007).

DH (2007b) *Human Fertilisation and Embryology Act 1990: An Illustrative Text*. (London: DH). (Nov. 2007).

DH (2008a) *Code of Practice: Mental Health Act 1983*. (London: DH). (May 2008).

DH (2008b) *Abortion Statistics, England and Wales: 2007*. (London: DH). (June 2008).

DH (2008c) *Medical Revalidation—Principles And Next Steps: The Report of the Chief Medical Officer for England's Working Group*. (London: DH). (July 2008).

DH (2008c) *Responsible Officers and their Duties Relating to the Medical Profession*. (London: DH). (July 2008).

DH (2008e) *Report of the National Patient Choice Survey, England: March 2008, and provisional headlines for May 2008*. (London: DH). (Sept. 2008).

DH (2009a) *The NHS Consitution*. (London: DH). (Jan. 2009).

DH (2009b) *The Handbook to the NHS Consitution*. (London: DH). (Jan. 2009).

DH and ABI (Association of British Insurers) (2005) *Concordat and Moratorium on Genetics and Insurance*. (London: DH). (*http://www.dh.gov.uk/assetRoot/04/10/60/50/04106050.pdf*).

Dickens, Bernard M. (1986) "Abortion, Amniocentesis and the Law." 34 *American Journal of Comparative Law* 249–270.

Dickens, Bernard M. (1989) "Wrongful Birth and Life, and Wrongful Death before Birth, and Wrongful Law." In Sheila McLean (eds) *Legal Issues in Human Reproduction*. (Aldershot: Gower), 80–112.

Dickens, Bernard M. (2004a) "Donation and Transplantation of Organs and Tissues." In Andrew Grubb (eds) *Principles of Medical Law*. (Oxford: Oxford University Press), 1025–1077.

Dickens, Bernard M. (2004b) "Death." In Andrew Grubb (eds) *Principles of Medical Law*. (Oxford: Oxford University Press), 1133–1154.

Dickenson, Donna, and Widdershoven, Guy (2001) "Ethical Issues in Limb Transplants." 15(2) *Bioethics* 110–124.

Dickert, Neal and Grady, Christine (1999) "What's the Price of a Research Subject? Approaches to Payment for Research Participation." 341(3) *New England Journal of Medicine* 198–203.

Discussion Group on Embryo Research (1995) *Research on Human Embryos in Canada: Final Report of the Discussion Group on Embryo Research.*

Docker, Chris (1996) "Advance Directives/Living Wills" in Sheila McLean (ed.) *Contemporary Issues in Law, Medicine and Ethics.* (Aldershot: Dartmouth), 179–214.

Donaldson, Liam (2007) "Introduction by the Chief Medical Officer for England" in HM Government, *Trust, Assurance and Safety—The Regulation of Health Professionals in the 21st Century.* CM 7013. (Feb. 2007) (London: The Stationery Office), 13–21.

Donohoe, Margaret M. (1996) "Our Epidemic of Unnecessary Caesarean Sections: The Role of the Law in Creating it, the Role of the law in Stopping It." 11 *Wisconsin Women's Law Journal* 197–241.

Douglas, Gillian (1991) *Law, Fertility and Reproduction.* (London: Sweet and Maxwell).

Dresser, Rebecca (1986) "Life, Death, and Incompetent Patients: Conceptual Infirmities and Hidden Values in the Law." 28(3) *Arizona Law Review* 373–405.

Dresser, Rebecca (1994) "Missing Persons: Legal Perceptions of Incompetent Patients." 46 *Rutgers Law Review* 609–719.

Dresser, Rebecca (1995) "Dworkin on Dementia: Elegant Theory, Questionable Policy." 25(6) *Hastings Center Report* 32–38.

Dresser, Rebecca. (2003) "Patient Advocates in Research: New Possibilities, New Problems." 11 *Washington University Journal of Law and Policy* 237–248.

Dubernard J.M., Lengele B., Morelon E., et al. (2007) "Outcomes 18 months after the first human partial face transplantation." 357 *New England Journal of Medicine* 2451–2460.

Dubernard, J. M., Owen, E., Herzberg, G., et al. (1999) "Human Hand Allograft: Report on First 6 Months." 353 *The Lancet* 1315–1320.

Dworkin, Andrea (1998) "Sasha." In Martha C. Nussbaum, and Cass R. Sunstein (eds) *Clones and Clones: Facts and Fantasies About Human Cloning.* (New York and London: W. W. Norton), 73–77.

Dworkin, Gerald and Kennedy, Ian (1993) "Human Tissue: Rights in the Body and its Parts." 1(3) *Medical Law Review* 291–319.

Dworkin, Ronald (1973) "The Original Position." 40 *University of Chicago Law Review* 500–533.

Dworkin, Ronald (1977) *Taking Rights Seriously.* (London: Gerald Duckworth).

Dworkin, Ronald (1986) "Autonomy and the Demented Self." 64(2) *Milbank Quarterly* 4–16.

Dworkin, Ronald (1993) *Life Dominion: An Argument about Abortion and Euthanasia.* (London: Harper Collins).

Dyer, Clare (1997) "Hillsborough Survivor Emerges from Permanent Vegetative State." 314 *British Medical Journal* 993.

Dyer, Clare (2000) "Surgeon Amputated Healthy Legs." 320 *British Medical Journal* 332.

Dyer, Clare (2002a) "Doctors Face Trial for Manslaughter as Criminal Charges Against Doctors Continue to Rise." 325 *British Medical Journal* 63.

Dyer, Clare (2002b) "Surgeons Cleared of Manslaughter after Removing Wrong Kidney." 325 *British Medical Journal* 9.

Dyer, Clare (2003) "Reform of Compensation for Medical Negligence." *The Guardian*, 1 July, 8.

Dyer, Clare (2004) "Bill Will Set Up Court of Protection for those Lacking Mental Capacity." 484 *British Medical Journal* 328.

Dyer, Clare (2004c) "Parents Who Want to Save Baby Charlotte Fight Doctors Who Say It's Cruel to Let Her Live." *The Guardian*, 1 October, 5.

Dyer, Owen (2001) "GP Stuck Off For Agreeing To Perform Female Circumcision." 322 *British Medical Journal* 9.

Eaton, Lynn (2002) "Politicians Must Stop Exploiting Patients." 325 *British Medical Journal* 6.

Edmund Davis, Lord Justice (1969) "A Legal Look at Transplants." 62 *Proceedings of the Royal Society of Medicine* 633.

Elliott, Carl (1995) "Doing Harm: Living Organ Donors." 21 *Journal of Medical Ethics* 91–96.

Emanuel, Ezekiel J. (1999) "What is the Great Benefit of Legalizing Euthanasia of Physician-Assisted Suicide?" 109(3) *Ethics* 629–642.

Emanuel, Ezekiel J. and Miller, Franklin G. (2001) "The Ethics of Placebo-Controlled Trials—A Middle Ground." 345(12) *New England Journal of Medicine* 915–919.

Emson, H. E. (2003) "It is Immoral to Require Consent for Cadaver Organ Donation." 29(3) *Journal of Medical Ethics* 125–127.

EPO (European Patent Office) (2004) " 'Myriad/Breast Cancer' Patent Revoked After Public Hearing." EPO Press Release, 18th May 2004 (www.european-patent-office.org/news/pressrel/2004_05_18_e.htm).

EPO (2007) *Guidelines for Examination in the European Patent Office*. (Munich: EPO). (Oct. 2007).

Erin, Charles A. and Harris, John (1994) "A Monopsonistic Market: or How to Buy and Sell Human Organs, Tissues and Cells Ethically." In I. Robinson (ed.) *The Social Consequences of Life and Death Under High Technology Medicine*. (Manchester: Manchester University Press), 134–157.

Erin, Charles A. and Harris, John (1999) "Presumed Consent or Contracting Out." 25 *Journal of Medical Ethics* 365–366.

Erin, Charles A. and Harris, John (2003) "An Ethical Market in Human Organs." 29 *Journal of Medical Ethics* 137–138.

Expert Group on Commissioning NHS Infertility Provision (2008) *Interim Report of the Expert Group on Commission NHS Infertility Provision*. (London: Department of Health).

European Commission (1998) *Guidelines Relating to the Demarcation Between Directive 90/385/EEC on Active Implantable Medical Devices Directive 93/42/EEC on Medical Devices and Directive 65/65/EEC Relating to Medicinal Products and Related Directives*. MEDDEV 2.1/3, Rev. 5.1, March 1998. (European Commission).

European Commission (2006) *The Rules Governing Medicinal Products in the European Union. Volume 10. Notice to Applicants: Questions & Answers*. Brussels, F2/BL D (2006) April. Available at: *http://ec.europa.eu/enterprise/pharmaceuticals/pharmacos/docs/doc2006/04_2006/clinical_trial_qa_april_2006.pdf*.

Evans, H. M. (2005) "Should Patients be allowed to Veto their Participation in Clinical Research?" 30 *Journal of Medical Ethics* 198–203.

Evans, Matthew J., et al. (1999) "Mitochondrial DNA Genotypes in Nuclear Transfer-Derived Cloned Sheep." 23(1) *Nature Genetics* 90–93.

Evans, W. E. and Relling, M. V. (1999) "Pharmacogenomics: Translating Functional Genomics into Rational Therapeutics." 286 *Science* 487–491.

Farley, Margaret A. (2001) "Roman Catholic Views on Research Involving Human Embryonic Stem Cells." In Suzanne Holland, Karen Lebacqz, and Laurie Zoloth (eds) *The Human Embryonic Stem Cell Debate*. (Cambridge, Massachusetts and London: MITT Press), 113–118.

Farrell, Anne-Maree and Devaney, Sarah (2007) "Making Amends Or Making Things Worse? Clinical Negligence Reform And Patient Redress In England." 27(4) *Legal Studies* 630–648.

Farrer, Lindsay A. (1986) "Suicide and Attempted Suicide in Huntington Disease: Implications for Preclinical Testing of Persons at Risk." 24 *American Journal of Medical Genetics* 305–311.

Feest T. G., Riad, H. N., Collins, C. H., et al. (1990) "Protocol for Increasing Organ Donation after Cerebrovascular Deaths in a District General Hospital." 335 *Lancet* 1133–1135.

Feinberg, Joel (1980) "The Child's Right to an Open Future." Reprinted in Joel Feinberg, *Freedom and Fulfillment: Philosophical Essays*. (Princeton, New Jersey: Princeton University Press, 1992), 76–97.

Feinberg, Joel (1984) *The Moral Limits of the Criminal Law. Volume 1: Harm to Others*. (Oxford: Oxford University Press).

Feinberg, Joel, and Levenbrook, Baum Barbara (1993) "Abortion." In Tom Regan (eds) *Matters of Life and Death: New Introductory Essays in Moral Philosophy*. (New York: McGraw Hill), 195–234.

Feng, Tan Keng (1987) "Failure of Medical Advice: Trespass or Negligence?" 7 *Legal Studies* 149–168.

Fenigsen, Richard (2004) "Dutch Euthanasia: The new Government Ordered Study." 73 *Issues in Law and Medicine* 73–79.

Ferguson, Pamela R. (2002) "Selecting Participants when Testing New Drugs: the Implications of Age and Gender Discrimination." 70(3) *Medico-Legal Journal* 130–134.

Ferguson, Pamela R. (2003) "Legal and Ethical Aspects of Clinical Trials: the Views of Researchers." 1(1) *Medical Law Review* 48–66.

Ferner, R E (2000) "Medication Errors that have led to Manslaughter Charges." 313 *British Medical Journal* 1212–1216.

Finnis, John (1973) "The Rights and Wrongs of Abortion: A Reply to Judith Thomson." 2(2) *Philosophy and Public Affairs* 117–145.

Finnis, John (1993) "Bland: Crossing the Rubicon?" 109 *Law Quarterly Review* 329–337.

Finnis, John (1995a) "A Philosophical Case Against Euthanasia." In John Keown (ed.) *Euthanasia Examined* (Cambridge: Cambridge University Press), 23–35.

Finnis, John (1995b) "The Fragile Case for Euthanasia: A reply to John Harris." In John Keown (ed.) *Euthanasia Examined* (Cambridge: Cambridge University Press), 46–55.

Finnis, John (1995c) "Misunderstanding the Case Against Euthanasia: Response to Harris's First Reply." In John Keown (ed.) *Euthanasia Examined* (Cambridge: Cambridge University Press), 62–71.

Finnis, John (2001) "Abortion and Cloning: Some New Evasions." *Lifeissues.net*.

Firlik, Andrew D. (1991) "Margo's Logo." 265 *Journal of the American Medical Association* 201.

Fisk, Nicholas and Paterson Brown, Sara (2004) "Caesarean Controversy: 'The safest method of birth is by caesarean': The Doctor's Tale." *The Observer*, 2 May, 18.

Fletcher, Martin (1988) "Inquest on Foetus that 'Fought For Life' Urged." *The Times*, 25 February 1988, 2.

Fortin, Jane E. S (1987) "Is the 'Wrongful Life' Action Really Dead?" *Journal of Social Welfare Law* 306–311.

Foster, Nigel (2005) "Last Chance for Lost Chances." 155 *New Law Journal* 248–249.

Fox, Marie (1998) "Research Bodies: Feminist Perspectives on Clinical Research." In Sally Sheldon and Michael Thomson (eds) *Feminist Perspectives on Health Care Law*. (London: Cavendish), 115–134.

Fox, Marie and McHale, Jean (1997) "In Whose Best Interests?" 60(5) *Modern Law Review* 700–709.

Fox, Marie and McHale, Jean (1998) "Xenotransplantation: The Ethical and Legal Ramifications." 6 *Medical Law Review* 42–61.

Fox, Marie and Thomson, Michael (2009) "Older Minors and Circumcision: Questioning the Limits of Religious Actions." 9(4) *Medical Law International* 283–310.

Fovargue, Sara (2007) " 'Oh Pick Me, Pick Me'—Selecting Participants For Xenotransplant Clinical Trials." 15(2) *Medical Law Review* 176–219.

Freedman, Benjamin (1987) "Equipoise and the Ethics of Clinical Research." 317(3) *New Journal of Medicine* 141–145.

Freeman, Michael D. (1999) "Does Surrogacy Have a Future after Brazier?" 7(1) *Medical Law Review* 1–20.

Freeman, Michael D. (2000) "Can We Leave the Best Interests of Very Sick Children to their Parents?" 3 *Current Legal Issues* 257–268.

Freeman, Michael D. (2001) "Whose Life is it Anyway?" 9(3) *Medical Law Review* 259–280.

Freeman, Michael D. (2003) "A Time to be Born and a Time to Die." 56 *Current Legal Problems* 603–649.

Freeman, Michael D. (2004) "Medical Assisted Reproduction." In Andrew Grubb (ed.) *Principles of Medical Law*. (Oxford: Oxford University Press), 639–738.

Frey, R. G. (1998) "Distinctions in Death." In Gerald Dworkin, R. G. Frey, and Sissela Bok (eds) *Euthanasia and Physician-Assisted Suicide (For and Against)*. (Cambridge: Cambridge UP), 17–42.

Fuller, Lon L. (1978) "The Forms and Limits of Adjudication." 92(2) *Harvard Law Review* 353–409.

Funk, Margaret M. (2000) "A Tale of Two Statutes: Development of Euthanasia Legislation in Australia's Northern Territory and the State of Oregon." 14 *Temple International and Comparative Law Journal* 149–179.

Furedi, Ann (2003) "Trust Doctors on Abortion, Not Lawyers." *The Guardian*, 2 December, 26.

Gandjour, Afschin and Lauterbach, Karl W. (2003) "Utilitarian Theories Reconsidered: Common Misconceptions, More Recent Developments, and Health Policy Implications." 11 (3) *Health Care Analysis* 229–244.

Gardiner, P. (2003) "A Virtue Ethics Approach to Moral Dilemmas in Medicine." 29 *Journal of Medical Ethics* 297–302.

Gardner, William (1995) "Can Human Genetic Enhancement be Prohibited?" 20(1) *Journal of Medicine and Philosophy* 65–84.

Garwood-Gowers, Austen (2001) "Time for Competent Minors to have the Same Right of Self-Determination as Competent Adults with Respect to Medical Intervention?" In Austen Garwood-Gowers, John Tingle, and Tom Lewis (eds) *Healthcare Law: The Impact of the Human Rights Act 1998.* (London: Cavendish), 225–242.

Garwood-Gowers, A. and Summan, S. (2001) "Should Animal-to-Human Organ Transplants be Legal?" 7(8) *Health Care Risk Report* 13–15.

Gauthier, David (1986) *Morals by Agreement.* (Oxford: Clarendon Press).

Gavaghan, Colin. 2000. "Anticipatory Refusals and The Action Of 'Wrongful Living'." 5(1) *Medical Law International* 67–80.

GDC (General Dental Council) (1997) *Maintaining Standards: Guidance to Dentists on Professional and Personal Conduct.*

Geldman, Adam (2002) "Q&A: the NHS Pay Deal—Agenda for Change." *The Guardian http://society.guardian.co.uk/NHSstaff/story/0,7991,844036,00.html.*

Gevers, Sjef (2001) "Medical Research involving Human Subjects: Towards and International Legal Framework?" 8(4) *European Journal of Health Law* 293–298.

Gewirth, Alan (1978) *Reason and Morality.* (Chicago: University of Chicago Press).

Gewirth, Alan (1985) "Rights and Virtues." 33 *Review of Metaphysics* 739–62.

Gewirth, Alan (1996) *The Community of Rights.* (Chicago: Chicago University Press).

Gillon, Raanan (1995) "Defending 'The Four Principles' Approach to Biomedical Ethics." 21 *Journal of Medical Ethics* 323–324.

Glannon, Walter (1998) "Genes, Embryos, and Future People." 12(3) *Bioethics* 187–211.

Glover, Jonathan (1977) *Causing Death and Saving Lives.* (London: Penguin).

GMC (General Medical Council) (These documents can be found at www.gmc-uk.org).

GMC (2001a) *Effective, Inclusive and Accountable: Reform of the GMC's Structure, Constitution and Governance.* (London: GMC).

GMC (2001b) *Acting Fairly to Protect Patients: Reform of the GMC's Fitness to Practise Procedures.* (London: GMC).

GMC (2002a) *Withholding and Withdrawing Life-prolonging Treatments: Good Practice in Decision-making.* (London: GMC). (Aug. 2002).

GMC (2002b) *Research: The Role and Responsibility of Doctors.* (London: GMC).

GMC (2004) *Confidentiality: Protecting and Providing Information.* (London: GMC). (April 2004).

GMC (2005) Press release: *GMC changes complaints handling process.* (17 October 2005).

GMC (2006a) *Good Medical Practice.* (London: GMC). (Nov. 2006).

GMC (2006b) *Maintaining Boundaries.* (London: GMC). (Nov. 2006).

GMC (2006c) *The GMC's Proposals on Healthcare Professional Regulations.* (London: GMC). (Nov. 2006).

GMC (2007) *General Medical Council Consultation.* (London: GMC). (Aug. 2007).

GMC (2008a) *Personal Beliefs and Medical Practice.* (London: GMC). (March 2008).

GMC (2008b) *Consent: Patients and Doctors Making Decisions Together.* (London: GMC). (June 2008).

GMC (2009) *End of Life Treatment and Care: Good Practice in Decision-Making: A Draft for Consultation*. (London: GMC). (March 2009).

Gold, E. Richard (2003) "SARS Genome Patent: Symptom or Disease?" 361 *The Lancet* 2002–2003.

Golombok, Susan (1998) "New Families, Old Values: Considerations Regarding the Welfare of the Child." 13(9) *Human Reproduction* 2342–2347.

Gordon, Richard (1983) *Great Medical Disasters*. (London: Hutchinson).

Gorman, Edward (1993) "Teenager Cleared of Aiding Suicide." *The Times* 23 September.

Gormally, Luke (1995) "Walton, Davies, Boyd and the Legalization of Euthanasia." In John Keown (ed.) *Euthanasia Examined*. (Cambridge: Cambridge University Press), 113–140.

Gottlieb, C., Lalos, O. and Lindblad, F. (2000) "Disclosure of Donor Insemination to the Child: The Impact of Swedish Legislation on Couple's Attitudes." 15 *Human Reproduction* 2052–2056.

Goyal, Madhav, Mehta, Ravindra L., Schneiderman, Lawrence J., and Sehgal, Ashwini R. (2002) "Economic and Health Consequences of Selling a Kidney in India." 288(13) *Journal of the American Medical Association* 1589–1593.

Grant, David, Mendicino, Michael, and Levy, Gary (2001) "Xenotransplantation: Just Around the Corner?" 129(3) *Surgery (Saint Louis)* 243–247.

Gregor, Mary (1991) Translation of *The Metaphysics of Morals*, by Immanuel Kant. (Cambridge: Cambridge University Press).

Griffith, Linda G. and Naughton, Gail (2002) "Tissue Engineering—Current Challenges and Expanding Opportunities." 295 *Science* 1009–1114.

Griffiths, John (1995) "Assisted Suicide in the Netherlands: the Chabot Case." 58 *Modern Law Review* 232–248.

Grisso, Thomas and Appelbaum, Paul S. (1995) "Comparison of Standards for Assessing Patients' Capacities to Make Treatment Decisions." 152 *American Journal of Psychiatry* 1033–1037.

Grisso, Thomas and Appelbaum, Paul S. (1998) *Assessing Competence to Consent to Treatment: A Guide for Physicians and Other Health Professionals* (New York and Oxford: Oxford University Press).

Grubb, Andrew (1991) "The New Law on Abortion: Clarification or Ambiguity." *Criminal Law* 659–670.

Grubb, Andrew (1993a) "Treatment Without Consent: Adult: *Re T. (Adult: Refusal of Treatment)*." 1(1) *Medical Law Review* 84–87.

Grubb, Andrew (1993b) "Treatment Decisions: Keeping it in the Family." In Andrew Grubb (ed.) *Choices and Decisions in Health Care*. (Chichester: John Wiley & Sons).

Grubb, Andrew (1994) "Treatment Without Consent: Adult: *Re C (Refusal of Medical Treatment)*." 2(1) *Medical Law Review* 92–95.

Grubb, Andrew (1998a) "Negligence: Causation and Bolam: *Bolitho v City & Hackney Health Authority*." 6(3) *Medical Law Review* 378–386.

Grubb, Andrew (1998b) " 'I, Me, Mine': Bodies, Parts and Property." 3(4) *Medical Law International* 299–317.

Grubb, Andrew (1999) "Refusal of Treatment (Child): Competence: *Re L (Medical Treatment—Gillick Competence)*." 7(1) *Medical Law Review* 58–61.

Grubb, Andrew (2000a) "Breach of Confidence: Anonymised Information: *R v Department of Health ex parte Source Informatics*." 8(1) *Medical Law Review* 115–120.

Grubb, Andrew (2000b) "Incompetent Patient (Adult): *Bland* and the Human Rights Act 1998: *NHS Trust 'A' and 'M'; NHS Trust 'B' and 'H'.*" 8(3) *Medical Law Review* 342–349.

Grubb, Andrew (2001a) "The General Medical Council and Serious Deficient Conduct: *Krippendorf v General Medical Council.*" 9(1) *Medical Law Review* 63–67.

Grubb, Andrew (2001b) "Euthanasia in England—A Law Lacking Compassion?" 8(2) *European Journal of Health Law* 89–93.

Grubb, Andrew (2002a) "Infertility Treatment: Posthumous Use of Sperm and Withdrawal of Consent: *The Centre for Reproductive Medicine v U.*" 10(2) *Medical Law Review* 204–206.

Grubb, Andrew (2002b) "Regulating Cloned Embryos?" (2002) 118 *Law Quarterly Review* 358–363.

Grubb, Andrew (2003a) "Problems of Medical Law." In Simon Deakin, Angus Johnston, and Basil Markesinis (eds) *Markesinis and Deakin's Tort Law.* (Oxford: Oxford University Press, 2003), 261–327.

Grubb, Andrew (2003b) "Cloning. (Cell Nuclear Replacement): The Scope of the Human Fertilisation and Embryology Act 1990: *R (On the Application of Quintavalle) v Secretary of State for Health.*" 11(1) *Medical Law Review* 135–138.

Grubb, Andrew (2004) "Consent to Treatment: The Competent Patient." In Andrew Grubb (ed.) *Principles of Medical Law.* (Oxford: Oxford University Press), 131–203.

Grubb, Andrew, Walsh, Pat, and Lambe, Neil (1998) "Reporting on the Persistent Vegetative State in Europe." 6(2) *Medical Law Review* 161–219.

GTAC (Gene Therapy Advisory Committee) (2005) *Guidance & Application From for Named Patient Use of Gene Therapy Products.* (1st ed.) (London: GTAC Secretariat). (Oct. 2005).

GTAC (1998) *Report on the Potential Use of Gene Therapy In Utero.* (London: Department of Health).

GTAC (2008a) *Operational Procedures for the Gene Therapy Advisory Committee in its Role as the National Ethics Committee for Gene Therapy Clinical Trials and those with Products Derived from Stem Cell Lines.* (7th ed.) (London: GTAC Secretariat). (May 2008).

GTAC (2008b) *Supplementary Operational Procedures for the Gene Therapy Advisory Committee:: Transfer of applications under the Clinical Trials Amendment Regulations 2008.* (London: GTAC Secretariat). (May 2008).

GTAC (2008c) *Fourteenth Annual Report: Covering the period from January 2007 to December 2007.* (London: Health Departments of the UK). (July 2008).

Guardian (2003) "The Price of Life: Review the Law on Embryo Selection." *The Guardian*, 20 June, 23.

Guillod, Olivier and Schmidt, Aline (2005) "Assisted Suicide under Swiss Law." 12(1) *European Journal of Health Law* 25–38.

Gunn, Michael (1994) "The Meaning of Incapacity." 2(1) *Medical Law Review* 8–29.

Gunn, M. J., Wong, J. G., Clare, I. C. H. and Holland, A. J. (1999) "Decision-Making Capacity." 7(3) *Medical Law Review* 269–306.

Gunning, Jennifer (2001) "Regulating Assisted Reproduction Technologies." 20 *Medicine and Law* 425–433.

Guo, S., Han, Y,. Zhang, X., et al. (2008) "Human Facial Allotransplantation: A 2-year Follow-up Study." 372 *The Lancet* 631–638.

Gusella J.F., et al. (1983) "A Polymorphic DNA Marker Genetically Linked to Huntington's Disease." 306 *Nature* 234–238.

Hacein-Bey-Abina, S., et al. (2003) "LMO2-Associated Clonal T Cell Proliferation in Two Patients after Gene Therapy for SCID-X1." 302 *Science* 415–419.

Hagger, Lynn (2003) "Some Implications of the Human Rights Act 1998 for the Medical Treatment of Children." 6(1) *Medical Law International* 25–51.

Hagger, Lynn, and Woods, Simon. 2005. "Children and Research: A Risk of Double Jeopardy?" 12 *International Journal of Children's Rights* 47–68.

Hall, Mark A. (1994) "Rationing Health Care at the Bedside." 69 *New York University Law Review* 693–780.

Ham, Chris (1999) "Tragic Choices In Health Care: Lessons From The Child B Case." 319 *British Medical Journal* 1258–1261.

Handyside, Alan H. (1998) "Clinical Evaluation of Preimplantation Genetic Diagnosis." 18 *Prenatal Diagnosis* 1345–1348.

Handyside, Alan, et al. (1989) "Biopsy of Human Preimplantation Embryo and Sexing by DNA Amplification." 1 *Lancet* 347–349.

Hansmann, Henry (1989) "The Economics and Ethics of Markets for Human Organs." 14(1) *Journal of Health Politics, Policy and Law* 57–85.

Harding, K. G., Morris, H. L., and Patel, G. K. (2002) "Healing Chronic Wounds." 324 *British Medical Journal* 160–163.

Hare, R. M. (1975) "Abortion and the Golden Rule." 4(3) *Philosophy and Public Affairs* 201–222.

Hare, R. M. (1981) *Moral Thinking: Its Levels, Method, and Point.* (Oxford: Clarendon Press).

Hare, R. M. (1988) "Comments." In Douglas Seanor and N. Fotion (eds) *Hare and Critics: Essay on Moral Thinking.* (Oxford: Clarendon Press), 199–293.

Harmon, Louise (1990) "Falling off the Vine: Legal Fictions and the Doctrine of Substituted Judgment." *Yale Law Journal* 1–70.

Harper, Peter S, et al. (2000) "Ten Years of Presymptomatic Testing for Huntington's Disease: The Experience of the UK Huntington's Disease Prediction Consortium." 37 *Journal of Medical Genetics* 567–571.

Harpwood, Vivienne (1996) "The Health Service Commissioner: An extended role in the new NHS." 3 *European Journal of Health Law* 207–229.

Harpwood, Vivienne (2000) "The Manipulation of Medical Practice." In Michael Freeman, and Andrew Lewis (ed.) *Law and Medicine: Current Law Issues.* (Oxford: Oxford University Press, 2000), 47–66.

Harpwood, Vivienne (2001) *Negligence in Healthcare: Clinical Claims and Risk.* (London: Informa).

Harris, J. W. (1996) "Who Owns My Body?" 16(1) *Oxford Journal of Legal Studies* 55–84.

Harris, John (1975) "The Survival Lottery." 50 *Philosophy* 81–87.

Harris, John (1985) *The Value of Life: An Introduction to Medical Ethics.* (London: Routledge).

Harris, John (1987) "QALYfying the Value of Life." 13(3) *Journal of Medical Ethics* 117–123.

Harris, John (1995a) "Could We Hold People Responsible for their Own Adverse Health?" 12 *Journal of Contemporary Health Law and Policy* 147–153.

Harris, John (1995b) "Double Jeopardy and the Veil of Ignorance—A Reply." 21 *Journal of Medical Ethics* 151–157.

Harris, John (1995c) "Euthanasia and the Value of Life." In John Keown (ed.) *Euthanasia Examined*. (Cambridge: Cambridge University Press), 6–22.

Harris, John (1995d) "The Philosophical Case Against the Philosophical Case Against Euthanasia." In John Keown (ed.) *Euthanasia Examined*. (Cambridge: Cambridge University Press), 36–45.

Harris, John (1995e) "Final Thoughts on Final Acts." In John Keown (ed.) *Euthanasia Examined*. (Cambridge: Cambridge University Press), 56–61.

Harris, John (1997) "The Injustice of Compensation for Victims of Medical Accidents." 314 *British Medical Journal* 1821–1823.

Harris, John (1998) *Clones, Genes, and Immortality: Ethics and the Genetic Revolution.* (Oxford: Oxford University Press).

Harris, John (2000) "The Welfare of the Child." 8 *Health Care Analysis* 27–34.

Harris, John (2001a) "Introduction: The Scope and Importance of Bioethics." In John Harris (ed.) *Bioethics*. (Oxford: Oxford University Press), 1–22.

Harris, John (2001b) "Human Beings, Persons and Conjoined Twins: An Ethical Analysis of the Judgment in *Re A*." 9(3) *Medical Law Review* 221–236.

Harris, John (2002a) "Cloning and Balanced Ethics." 52 *Nijhoff Law Specials* 207–211.

Harris, John (2002b) "Law and Regulation of Retained Organs." 22(4) *Legal Studies* 527–549.

Harris, John (2003a) "Assisted Reproductive Technological Blunders. (ARTBs)." 29 *Journal of Medical Ethics* 205–206.

Harris, John (2003b) "Consent and End of Life Decisions." 29 *Journal of Medical Ethics* 10–15.

Harris, John (2003c) "Stem Cells, Sex, and Procreation." 12 *Cambridge Quarterly of Health Care Ethics* 353–371.

Harris, John (2003d) "Sex Selection and Regulated Hatred." *Journal of Medical Ethics Online* (*http://jme.bmjjournals.com/cgi/data/27/6/DC1/7*).

Harris, John (2003e) "Organ Procurement: Dead Interests, Living Needs." 29(3) *Journal of Medical Ethics* 130–134.

Harris, John (2005) "Scientific Research is a Moral Duty." 31 *Journal of Medical Ethics* 242–248.

Harris, John and Keywood, Kirsty (2001) "Ignorance, Information and Autonomy." 22(5) *Theoretical Medicine and Bioethics* 415–436.

Harsanyi, John C. (1988) "Problems with Act-Utilitarianism and with Malevolent Preferences." In Douglas Seanor and N. Fotion (eds) *Hare and Critics: Essay on Moral Thinking*. (Oxford: Clarendon Press), 89–99.

Hart, H. L. A. (1963) *Law, Liberty and Morality*. (Oxford: Oxford University Press).

Hawkes, Nigel. 2003. "Opinions differ on whether operation should have gone ahead." *The Times*, 9 July, 3.

Häyry, Matti (2001) *Playing Good: Essays on Bioethics*. (Helsinki: Helsinki University Press).

Health Canada (2001) *Proposals for Legislation Governing Assisted Human Reproduction: An Overview*. (Health Canada).

Healthcare Commission (2006) *Investigation into 10 maternal deaths at, or following delivery at, Northwick Park Hospital, North West London Hospitals NHS Trust, between April 2002 and April 2005.* (London: Healthcare Commission). (Aug. 2006).

Healthcare Commission (2007) *Spotlight on Complaints: A report on second-stage complaints about the NHS in England.* (London: Commission for Healthcare Audit and Inspection) (Jan. 2007).

Healthcare Commission (2008) *Spotlight on Complaints: A report on second-stage complaints about the NHS in England.* (London: Commission for Healthcare Audit and Inspection) (April 2008).

Health Service Ombudsman (in England) (2008) *Remedy in the NHS: Summaries of Recent Cases.* (London: Stationery Office). (13 Jun 2008).

Heller, Michael A. and Eisenberg, Rebecca S. (1998) "Can Patents Deter Innovation? The Anticommons in Biomedical Research." 280 *Science* 698–701.

Hellman, Samuel and Hellman Doborah S. (1991) "Of Mice but Not Men. Problems of the Randomized Clinical Trial." 30 *New England Journal of Medicine* 1585–1589.

Herring, Jonathan (2008) *Medical Law and Ethics.* (2nd ed.) (Oxford: Oxford University Press).

Herring, Jonathan, and Chau, P-L (2007) "My Body, Your Body, Our Bodies." 15(1) *Medical Law Review* 34–61.

Hervey, Tamara K. and McHale Jean V. (2004) *Health Law and the European Union.* (Cambridge: Cambridge University Press).

Hewson, Barbara (2003) "Abortion Law in the Doc." 147 *Solicitors Journal* 1408.

HFEA (Human Fertilisation and Embryology Authority) (The majority of these documents can be found at www.hfea.gov.uk/).

HFEA (1998) *Consultation on the Implementation of Withdrawal of Payments to Donors.* (London: HFEA).

HFEA (2001) *Code of Practice.* (5th ed.) (London: HFEA).

HFEA (2002a) "HFEA Confirms that HLA Tissue Typing May Only Take Place When Preimplantation Genetic Diagnosis is Required to Avoid a Serious Genetic Disorder." Press Release, 1 August.

HFEA (2002b) *Sex Selection: Choice and Responsibility in Human Reproduction.* (London: HFEA).

HFEA (2003a) *Code of Practice.* (6th ed.) (London: HFEA).

HFEA (2003b) *Sex Selection: Options for Regulation. A Report on the HFEA's 2002–03 Review on Sex Selection including a Discussion of Legislative and Regulatory Options.* (London: HFEA).

HFEA (2003c) "Following the Announcement that a 58 year old woman had given birth to an IVF baby." Press Release, 3 February.

HFEA (2003d) "HFEA Issues Guidance on Egg Giving." Press Release, 1 December.

HFEA (2004a) *Fact Sheet 2: About the HFEA.* (London: HFEA).

HFEA (2004b) *Fact Sheet 3: About IVF.* (London: HFEA).

HFEA (2004c) "Embryo Splitting and Cloning Statement." Press Release, 15 January.

HFEA (2004d) "HFEA Confirms UK Position on Payment for Egg Donors." Press Release, 25 February.

HFEA (2004e) "HFEA Agrees to Extend Policy on Tissue Typing." Press Release, 21 July.

HFEA (2004f) "HFEA Grants the First Therapeutic Cloning Licence for Research." Press Release, 11 August.

HFEA (2004g) *The HFEA Response to Professor Brian Toft's Report: "Independent Review of the Circumstances Surrounding Four Adverse Events that Occurred in the Reproductive Medicine Units at Leeds Teaching Hospitals NHS Trust, West Yorkshire"*. June 2004.

HFEA (2004h) "HFEA Launches Public Consultation on Donor Assisted Conception." Press Release, 11 November.

HFEA (2005a) "HFEA Grants Embryonic Stem Cell Research Licence to Study Motor Neuron Disease." Press Release, 8 February.

HFEA (2005b) *Tomorrow's Children: Report of the Policy Review of Welfare of the Child Assessments in Licensed Assisted Conception Clinics*. (London: HFEA).

HFEA (2007a) *Hybrids and Chimeras: A Consultation on the Ethical and Social Implications of Creating Human/Animal Embryos in Research*. (London: HFEA). (April 2007).

HFEA (2007b) *Code of Practice*. 7th ed. (London: HFEA). (July 2007).

HFEA (2008a) *Facts and Figures 2006: Fertility Problems and Treatment*. (London: HFEA). (Oct. 2008).

HFEA (2008b) *Code of Practice: 8th edition (Consultation Draft)*. (London: HFEA). (Nov. 2008).

HFEA and ACGT. (Advisory Committee on Genetic Testing) (1999) *Consultation Document on Preimplantation Genetic Diagnosis*. (London: HFEA & ACGT).

HFEA and HGAC (Human Fertilisation and Embryology Authority and Human Genetics Advisory Commission) (1998a) *Cloning Issues in Reproduction, Science and Medicine: A Consultation Document*. (London: HMSO).

HFEA and HGAC (1998b) *Cloning Issues in Reproduction, Science, and Medicine*. (London: HMSO).

HGC (Human Genetics Commission) (2000) *Whose Hands on Your Genes? A Discussion Document on the Storage Protection and Use of Personal Genetic Information*. (London: HGC).

HGC (2001) *The Use of Genetic Information in Insurance: Interim Recommendations of the Human Genetics Commission*. (London: HGC).

HGC (2002) *Inside Information: Balancing Interests in the Use of Personal Genetic Data*. (London: HGC).

HGC (2003) *Genes Direct: Ensuring the Effective Oversight of Genetic Tests Supplied Directly to the Public*. (London: HGC).

Hill, James F. (1984) "Are Marginal Agents 'Our Recipients'?" In Edward Regis (ed.) *Gewirth's Ethical Rationalism: Critical Essays with a Reply by Gewirth*. (Chicago: Chicago University Press), 180–191.

Hill, Thomas E. (1985) "Kant's Argument for the Rationality of Moral Conduct." 66 *Pacific Philosophical Quarterly* 3–23.

Hill, Thomas E. And Zweig, Arnulf (2002) *Kant: Groundwork for the Metaphysics of Morals*. (Oxford: Oxford University Press).

Hinchley, Geoff (2007) "Is Infant Male Circumcision An Abuse Of The Rights Of The Child? Yes." 335 *British Medical Journal* 1180–1181.

Hinsliff, Gaby (2004) "NHS Crackdown on Headhunting African Nurses." *The Observer*, 22 August, 9.

HM Government (2005) *Government Response to the Report from the House of Commons Science and Technology Committee: Human Reproductive Technologies and the Law* (Cm 6641). (London: The Stationary Office).

HM Government (2007) *Trust, Assurance and Safety—The Regulation of Health Professionals in the 21ˢᵗ Century.* CM 7013. (London: The Stationery Office). (Feb. 2007).

HM Inspector of Anatomy (2003) *The Investigation of Events that followed the Death of Cyril Mark Isaacs.* (London: The Stationary Office).

Hodges, Christopher (2004) "The Regulation of Medicinal Products and Medical Devices." In Andrew Grubb (eds) *Principles of Medical Law.* (Oxford: Oxford University Press), 911–984.

Hodgson, John (2001) "The Human Rights Act 1998 and the Common Law, a Health Law Perspective." In Austen Garwood-Gowers, John Tingle, and Tom Lewis (eds) *Healthcare Law: The Impact of the Human Rights Act 1998.* (London: Cavendish, 2001), 13–29.

Hodson, Margaret E. (2000) "Transplantation using Lung Lobes from Living Donors." 26 *Journal of Medical Ethics* 419–421.

Hoffenberg, R., Lock, M., Tilney, N., Casabona, C., Daar, A. S., Guttmann, R. D., Kennedy, I., Nundy, S., Radcliffe-Richards, J., and Sells, R. A. (1997) "Should Organs from Patients in Permanent Vegetative State be Used for Transplantation?" 350 *The Lancet* 1320–1321.

Holbrook, Jon (2003) "The Criminalisation of Fatal Medical Mistakes." 327 *British Medical Journal* 1118–1119.

Holm, Søren (1998) "Ethical Issues in Pre-Implantation Diagnosis." In Harris, John, and Holm, Søren (eds) *The Future of Human Reproduction: Choice and Regulation.* (Oxford: Clarendon Press), 176–190.

Homer (BCE) *The Odyssey.* Translated by E. V. Rieu and D. C. H. Rieu. (London: Penguin Classics, 2003).

Hopkins Tanne, Janice (1999) "Dolly's other DNA Came from Donor Egg." *British* 319 *Medical Journal* 593.

Houses of Commons Heath Committee (2008) *National Institute for Health and Clinical Excellence: First Report of Session 2007–08. Volume I: Report, together with formal minutes. (HC 27-I)* (London: The Stationary Office).

House of Commons Select Committee on Health (1999) *Procedures Related to Adverse Clinical Incidents and Outcomes in Medical Care.* (HC 549–1, Session 1998–1999).

House of Commons Select Committee on Health (2005) *The Influence of the Pharmaceutical Industry: Fourth Report of Session 2004–05. Volume I.* (London: Stationary Office).

House of Lords Select Committee (1994) *Report of the Select Committee on Medical Ethics Volume I—Report (Session 1993–1994).* (London: HMSO).

House of Lords Select Committee (2002) *Report on Stem Cell Research* House of Lords Paper 83(i) (Report). (London: HMSO). (*http://www.parliament.the-stationery-office.co.uk/pa/ld200102/ldselect/ldstem/83/8301.htm*).

House of Lords Select Committee (on the Assisted Dying for the Terminally Ill Bill) (2005) *Assisted Dying for the Terminally Ill Bill [HL]. Volume I: Report.* HL Paper 86–I. (London: The Stationary Office).

Howard-Hassmann, Rhoda E. (1995) *Human Rights and the Search for Community.* (Boulder: Westview Press).

HTA (Human Tissue Authority) and MHRA (Medicines and Healthcare products Regulatory Agency) (2008) *Policy Statement on the Relationship between the Advanced Therapy Medicinal Products (ATMP) Regulation and the Quality and Safety Regulations.* (London: HTA and MHRA). (March 2008).

Hull, Michael (1992) *Infertility Treatment: Needs and Effectiveness. A Report from the University of Bristol Department of Obstetrics and Gynaecology.* (Serond Laboratories).

Hunt, Murray (1998) "The 'Horizontal Effect' of the Human Rights Act." *Public Law* 423–443.

Huntington's Disease Collaborative Research Group (1993) "A Novel Gene Containing a Trinucleotide Repeat that is Unstable and Expanded on Huntington's Disease Chromosomes." 72 *Cell* 971–983.

Hurst, Samia A. and Mauron, Alex (2003) "Assisted Suicide and Euthanasia in Switzerland: Allowing a Role for Non-physicians." 326 *British Medical Journal* 271–273.

Hursthouse, Rosalind (1991) "Virtue Theory and Abortion." 20(3) *Philosophy and Public Affairs* 223–246.

Husted, Jørgen (1997) "Autonomy and A Right Not to Know." In Ruth Chadwick, Mairi Levitt and Darren Shickle (eds) *The Right to Know and the Right Not to Know.* (Aldershot: Avebury), 55–68.

Hutson, J. M. (2003) "Circumcision: A Surgeon's Perspective." 30 *Journal of Medical Ethics* 238–240.

Huxtable, Richard (2002) "Separation of Conjoined Twins: Where Next For English Law." *Criminal Law Review* 459–470.

Hwang, Woo Suk, et al. (2004) "Evidence of a Pluripotent Human Embryonic Stem Cell Line Derived from a Cloned Blastocyst." 303 *Science* 1669–1674.

IBAC (Independent Biotechnology Advisory Council) (2001) *Cloning and Stem Cell Research: Developments in Biotechnology which could lead to new ways of treating some serious diseases but raise ethical issues.* (www.ibac.org.nz).

ICAS (Independent Complaints Advocacy Services) (2004) *The First Year of ICAS: 1 September 2003–31 August 2004.* (London: Department of Health).

ICH (International Conference on Harmonisation of Technical Requirements for Registration of Pharmaceuticals for Human Use). (These documents can be found at www.ich.org).

ICH (1996) *Guideline for Good Clinical Practice.* 10 June 1996.

ICH (1997) *General Considerations for Clinical Trials.* (E8) 17 July 1997.

ICH (2000) *Choice of Control Group and Related Issues in Clinical Trials.* (E10) 20 July 2000.

Information Commissioner (These documents can be found at www.informationcommissioner.gov.uk).

Information Commissioner (1998) *Data Protection Act 1998: Legal Guidance.* Version 1.

Information Commissioner (2002) *Use and Disclosure of Health Data: Guidance on the Application of the Data Protection Act 1998.* (May 2002).

International Working Party (1996) *International Working Party Report on the Vegetative State.* (London: Royal Hospital for Neurodisability).

Ivers, Kathryn (1995) "Towards a Bilingual Education Policy in the Mainstreaming of Deaf Children." 26 *Columbia Human Rights Law Review* 439–482.

Jackson, Anthony (1996) "Wrongful Life and Wrongful Birth." 17 *Journal of Legal Medicine* 349–381.

Jackson, Emily (2001) *Regulating Reproduction: Law, Technology and Autonomy.* (Oxford: Hart).

Jackson, Emily (2002) "Conception and the Irrelevance of the Welfare Principle." 65(2) *Modern Law Review* 176–203.

Jackson, Emily (2006) *Medical Law: Text, Cases, and Materials.* (Oxford: Oxford University Press).

James, Richard (1998) "The Limitation Period in Medical Negligence Claims." 6(1) *Medical Law Review* 62–98.

Jefferies, David E. (1998) "The Body as Commodity: The Use of Markets to Cure the Organ Deficit." 5 *Indiana Journal of Global Legal Studies* 621–658.

Jennett, Bryan (1997) "Letting Vegetative Patients Die." In John Keown (ed.) *Euthanasia Examined: Ethical, Clinical and Legal Perspectives.* (Cambridge: Cambridge UP), 169–188.

Jennett, Bryan (2002) "The Vegetative State." 73 *Journal of Neurology Neurosurgery and Psychiatry* 355–357.

Jennett, Bryan and Plum, Fred (1972) "Persistent Vegetative State after Brain Damage." 1 *Lancet* 734–737.

Johnson, Eric M., Remucal, M. J., Gillingham, K. J., Dahms, R. A., Najarian, J. S., and Matas, A. J. (1997) "Complications and Risks of Living Donor Nephrectomy." 64(8) *Transplantation* 1124–1128.

Johnson, Nicholas, Lilford, Richard J., and Brazier, Wayne (1991) "At What Level of Collective Equipoise Does a Clinical Trial Become Ethical?" 17(1) *Journal of Medical Ethics* 30–34.

Jonas, Hans (1980) *Philosophical Essays: From Current Creed to Technological Man.* (Chicago: University of Chicago Press).

Jones, Michael A. (1989) "Justifying Medical Treatment without Consent." 5 *Professional Negligence* 178–183.

Jones, Michael (1996) *Medical Negligence.* (London: Sweet & Maxwell).

Jones, Michael (1999a) "The Bolam Test and the Responsible Expert." 7(3) *Tort Law Review* 226–250.

Jones, Michael (1999b) "Informed Consent and Other Fairy Stories." 7(2) *Medical Law Review* 103–134.

Jones, R. B. (2000) "Parental Consent to Cosmetic Facial Surgery in Down's Syndrome." 26 *Journal of Medical Ethics* 101–102.

Juengst, Eric T. (1991) "Germ-line Gene Therapy: Back to Basics." 16 *Journal of Medicine and Philosophy* 587–592.

Kadish, Sanford H. (1992) "Letting Patients Die: Legal and Moral Reflections." 80 *California Law Review* 857–888.

Kalichman, Seth C., Eaton, Lisa, and Pinkerton, Steven D. (2007) "Male Circumcision in HIV Prevention." 369 *The Lancet* 1597.

Kallich, Joel D., and Mertz, Jon F. (1995) "The Transplant Imperative: Protecting Living Donors from the Pressure to Donate." 20 *Journal of Corporation Law* 139–154.

Kant, Immanuel (1785) *Groundwork of the Metaphysic of Morals.* Translated by H. J. Paton as *The Moral Law.* (London: Routledge, 1948).

Kant, Immanuel (1797) *The Metaphysics of Morals*. Translated by Mary Gregor. (Cambridge: Cambridge University Press, 1991).

Kass, Leon R. (1979) " 'Making Babies' Revisited." 54 *Public Interest* 32–60.

Kass, Leon R. (1988) *Toward a More Natural Science: Biology and Human Affairs*. (New York: Free Press).

Kass, Leon R. and Lund, Nelson (1996) "Physician-Assisted Suicide, Medical Ethics *Contemporary Health Law and Policy* 69–91.

Kaye, Jane and Gibbons, Susan M. C. (2008) "Mapping the regulatory framework for human genetic databases in England and Wales." 9(2) *Medical Law International* 111–130.

Kennedy, Ian (1981) *The Unmasking of Medicine*. (London: George Allen & Unwin).

Kennedy, Ian (1988) *Treat Me Right: Essays in Medical Law and Ethics*. (Oxford: Clarendon Press).

Kennedy, Ian (1993) "Treatment Without Consent (Anorexia Nervosa): Child: *Re W (A Minor) (Medical Treatment: Court's Jurisdiction)*." 1(1) *Medical Law Review* 87–92.

Kennedy, Ian (1996) "The Fiduciary Relationship and its Application to Doctors." In P. Birks (ed.) *Wrongs and Remedies in the Twenty-first Century*. (Oxford: Clarendon Press), 111–140.

Kennedy, Ian (1997) "Consent: Adult, Refusal of Consent, Capacity: *Re MB (Medical Treatment)*." 5(3) *Medical Law Review* 317–325.

Kennedy, Ian and Grubb, Andrew (2000) *Medical Law*. (3rd ed.) (London: Butterworths).

Kennedy, Ian, Howard, Rebecca, Jarman, Brian, and Maclean, Mavis (2001) *Learning from Bristol: The Report of the Public Inquiry into Children's Heart Surgery at the Bristol Royal Infirmary 1984–1995* (CM 5207). (www.bristol-inquiry.org.uk).

Kennedy, I., Sells, R. A., Daar, A. S., et al. (1998) "The Case for 'Presumed Consent' in Organ Donation." 351 *The Lancet* 1650–1652.

Keown, John (1987) "Selective Reduction of Multiple Pregnancy." 137 *New Law Journal* 1165.

Keown, John (1992) "The Law and Practice of Euthanasia in the Netherlands." 108 *Law Quarterly Review* 51–78.

Keown, John (1995a) "Physician-Assisted Suicide and the Dutch Supreme Court." 111 *Law Quarterly Review* 394–396.

Keown, John (eds) (1995b) *Euthanasia Examined: Ethical, Clinical and Legal Perspectives*. (Cambridge: Cambridge University Press).

Keown, John (1997) "Restoring Moral and Intellectual Shape to the Law after Bland." 113 *Law Quarterly Review* 482–503.

Keown, John (1998) "Reining In the Bolam Test." 57 *Cambridge Law Journal* 248–250.

Keown, John (2002) *Euthanasia, Ethics and Public Policy: An Argument Against Euthanasia*. (Cambridge: Cambridge University Press).

Keown, John (2005) " 'Morning After' Pills, 'Miscarriage' and Muddle." 25(2) *Legal Studies* 296–319.

Keown, John (2007) "Physician-Assisted Suicide: Lord Joffe's Slippery Bill." 15(1) *Medical Law Review* 126–135.

Keown, John and Gormally, Luke (1999) "Human Dignity, Autonomy and Mentally Handicapped Patients: A Critique of Who Decides?" 4 *Web Journal of Current Legal Issues*. (*http://webjcli.ncl.ac.uk*).

Keywood, Kirsty (1995) "Sterilising the Woman with Learning Difficulties—In Her Best Interests?" In Jo Bridgeman and Susan Millns (eds) *Law and Body Politics: Regulating the Female Body*. (Aldershot: Dartmouth), 125–150.

Kher, Vijay (2002) "End-stage Renal Disease in Developing Countries." 62 *Kidney International* 350–362.

Kimmel, Paul L. and Patel, Samir S. (2003) "Psychosocial Issues in Women With Renal Disease." 10(1) *Advances in Renal Replacement Therapy* 61–70.

King, David S. (1999) "Preimplantation Genetic Diagnosis and the 'New' Eugenics." 25(2) *Journal of Medical Ethics* 176–182.

King, Jeff A. (2007) "The Justifiability of Resource Allocation." 70(2) *Modern Law Review* 197–224.

King's Fund (2006) *Local Variations In NHS Spending Priorities*. (London: King's Fund). (Aug. 2006) Online: *http://www.kingsfund.org.uk/publications/briefings/local_variations.html*.

Kirejczyk, M. (1999) "Parliamentary Cultures and Human Embryos: The Dutch and British Debates Compared." 29(6) *Social Studies of Science* 889–912.

Kitcher, Philip (1996) *The Lives to Come: The Genetic Revolution and Human Possibilities*. (London: Penguin Books).

Kittay, Eva Feder (1998) *Love's Labor: Essays on Women, Equality and Dependency*. (London: Routledge).

Klein, Renate (1989) "Resistance: From the Exploitation of Infertility to an Exploration of In-fertility." In Renate D. Klein (ed.) *Infertility: Women Speak Out About Their Experiences of Reproductive Medicine*. (London: Pandora Press), 229–295.

Kolata, Gina (1997) *Clone: The Road to Dolly and the Path Ahead*. (London: Penguin Books).

Kong, Wing May (2004) "The Regulation of Gene Therapy Research in Competent Adult Patients, Today and Tomorrow: Implications of EU Directive 2001/20/EC." 12(2) *Medical Law Review* 164–180.

Koropatnick, Stephanie, Daniluk, Judith, and Pattinson, H. Anthony (1993) "Infertility: a Non-event Transition." 59(1) *Fertility and Sterility* 163–71.

Korsgaard, Christine M. (1985) "Kant's Formula of Universal Law." 66 *Pacific Philosophical Quarterly* 24–47.

Kuhse, Helga (1987) *The Sanctity-of-Life Doctrine in Medicine*. (Oxford: Clarendon Press).

Kumar, Sanjay (2003) "Police Uncover Large Scale Organ Trafficking in Punjab." 326 *British Medical Journal* 180.

Kurnit, Melissa N. (1994) "Organ Donation in the United States: Can We Learn From Successes Abroad?" 17 *Boston College International & Comparative Law Review* 405–452.

Laing, Jacqueline. 2002. " 'Vegetative' State—The Untold Story." 152 *New Law Journal* 1272.

Laing, Judith, and Grubb, Andrew (2004) "Confidentiality and Medical Records." In Andrew Grubb (eds) *Principles of Medical Law*. (Oxford: Oxford University Press), 553–638.

Lalos, A, Lalos O., Jacobson, L., and von Schoultz, B (1985) "Psychological Reactions to the Medical Investigation and Surgical Treatment of Infertility." 20 *Gynecologic and Obstetric Investigation* 209–17.

Lamm, Richard D. (1992) "Rationing of Health Care: Inevitable and Desirable." 140 *University of Pennsylvania Law Review* 1511–1523.

Lappè, Marc (1991) "Ethical Issues in Manipulating the Human Germ Line." 16 *Journal of Medicine and Philosophy* 621–639.

Lantieri, L., Meningaud, J-P., and Grimbert, P et al. (2008) "Repair of the lower and middle parts of the previous termfacenext term by composite tissue allotransplantation in a patient with massive plexiform neurofibroma: a 1-year follow-up study." 372 *Lancet* 639–645.

Laurie, Graeme (2004) "Patenting and the Human Body." In Andrew Grubb (eds) *Principles of Medical Law*. (Oxford: Oxford University Press), 1079–1101.

Law Commission (1973) *Working Paper No.47: Injuries to Unborn Children*. (London: HMSO).

Law Commission (1974) *Report on Injuries to Unborn Children*. Report No. 60. (Cmnd 5709). (London: HMSO).

Law Commission (1981) *Breach of Confidence*. Report No. 110. (London: HMSO).

Law Commission (1995a) *Consent in the Criminal Law: A Consultation Paper*. Consultation Paper No. 139. (London: HMSO).

Law Commission (1995b) *Mental Incapacity*. Report No. 231. (London: HMSO).

Law Commission (1998) *Report on Liability for Psychiatric Illness*, Report No. 249. (London: HMSO).

Law, Sylvia A. (1996) "Physician-Assisted Death: An Essay on Constitutional Rights and Remedies." 55 *Maryland Law Review* 292–342.

Ledward, Sally (2000) " 'Designer Babies' Raise the Spectre of Genetic Manipulation." *The Independent*, 4 October.

Lee, Robert (1989) "To Be or Not to Be: Is that the Question? The Claim of Wrongful Life." In Robert Lee and Derek Morgan (eds) *Birthrights: Law and Ethics at the Beginnings of Life*. (London: Routledge), 172–194.

Lee, Robert G. and Morgan, Derek (2001) *Human Fertilisation & Embryology: Regulating the Reproductive Revolution*. (Oxford: Blackstone).

Leigh, David (2005) Jury Protest Forces Fraud Trial Collapse After 2 Years." *The Guardian*, 23 March.

Lesch, M. and Nyhan, N. L. (1964) "A Familial Disorder of Uric Acid Metabolism of Central Nervous System Function." 36 *American Journal of Medicine* 561–570.

Lewis, Charles J. (2006) *Clinical Negligence: A Practical Guide*. (6th ed.) (Haywards Heath: Tottel Publishing).

Lewis, Penney (1999) "Feeding Anorexic Patients Who Refuse Food." 7(1) *Medical Law Review* 21–34.

Lewis, Penney (2002) "Procedures that are Against the Medical Interests of Incompetent Adults." 22(4) *Oxford Journal of Legal Studies* 575–618.

Light, Donald W. (1997) "The Real Ethics of Rationing." 315 *British Medical Journal* 112–115.

Lind, Craig (2003) "Case Commentary—Re R (Paternity of IVF Baby)—Unmarried Paternity Under The Human Fertilisation And Embryology Act 1990." 15(3) *Child and Family Law Quarterly* 327–340.

Little, George Bradbury (1997) "Comparing German and English Law on Non-Consensual Sterilisation: A Difference in Approach." 5(3) *Medical Law Review* 269–293.

Locke, John (1689) *Two Treatises of Civil Government*. Extracted in Micheal L. Morgan (ed.) *Classics of Moral and Political Theory* (Indianapolis: Hackett Publishing, 1992), 736–817.

Longley, Diane (1997) "Complaints After Wilson; Another Case of too Little too Late?" 5(2) *Medical Law Review* 172–192.

Longley, Diane and Lawford, Pat (2001) "Engineering Human Tissue and Regulation: Confronting Biology and Law to Bridge the Gaps." 5(2) *Medical Law International* 101–115.

Lord Chancellor's Department (1997) *Who Decides? Making Decisions on Behalf of Mentally Incapacitated Adults* (Cm 3803, Dec. 1997).

Lord Chancellor's Department (1999) *Making Decisions: The Government's Proposals for Making Decisions on Behalf of Mentally Incapacitated Adults* (Cm 4465, October 1999).

Lötjönen, Salla (2000) "Medical Research on Children in Europe–For or Against Human Rights?" 11 *Finnish Yearbook of International Law* 163–200. (Printed in 2003).

Lötjönen, Salla (2002) "Medical Research in Clinical Emergency Settings in Europe." 28 *Journal of Medical Ethics* 183–187.

Lötjönen, Salla (2003) "Regulation of Clinical Medical Research on the Decisionally Impaired Adults in Europe." *Oikeustiede—Jurisprudentia* 351–420.

Lötjönen, Salla (2005) "Research on Human Subjects." In J. K. M. Gevers, E. H. Hondius, and J. H. Hubben (eds) *Health Law, Human Rights and the Biomedicine Convention.* (Leiden: Koniniklijke Brill NV), 175–190.

Loughrey, Joan (2003) "Medical Information, Confidentiality and a Child's Right to Privacy." 23(3) *Legal Studies* 510–535.

Loughrey, Joan (2008) "Can You Keep A Secret? Children, Human Rights, and the Law of Medical Confidentiality." 20(3) *Child and Family Law Quarterly* 312–334.

Lyons, David (1965) *The Forms and Limits of Utilitarianism.* (Oxford: Oxford University Press).

Lysaght, Michael J. and Hazlehurst, A. L. (2004) "Tissue Engineering: The End of the Beginning." 10(1/2) *Tissue Engineering* 309–320.

Lysaght, M. J. and Mason, J. (2000) "The Case for Financial Incentives to Encourage Organ Donation." 46(3) *Asaio Journal* 253–256.

McCall Smith, Alexander (1993) "Criminal Negligence and the Incompetent Doctor." 1(3) *Medical Law Review* 336–349.

McCall Smith, R. A. (1999) "Euthanasia: the strengths of the middle ground." 7(2) *Medical Law Review* 194–207.

McCarthy, David (2001) "Why Sex Selection Should be Legal." 27 *Journal of Medical Ethics* 302–307.

McCarthy, Michael H. (1982) "Kant's Rejection of the Argument of Groundwork III." 73 *Kant-Studien* 169–190.

McCarthy, Michael H. (1985) "The Objection of Circularity in Groundwork III." 76 *Kant-Studien* 28–42.

McCullough, Marie and Surendran, Aparana (2003) "Pelvic-exam Debate Starts with Consent." *Philadelphia Inquirer*, 10 March.

McEwan, Jenny (2001) "Murder by Design: The 'Feel-Good Factor' and the Criminal Law." 9(3) *Medical Law Review* 246–258.

McGrath, James and Solter, Davor (1984) "Inability of Mouse Blastomere Nuclei Transferred to Enucleated Zygotes to Support Development In Vitro." 226 *Science* 1317–1319.

McHale, Jean V. (2004a) "Regulating Genetic Databases: Some Legal and Ethical Issues." 12(1) *Medical Law Review* 70–96.

McHale, Jean V. (2004b) "Clinical Research." In Andrew Grubb (eds) *Principles of Medical Law*. (Oxford: Oxford University Press), 853–910.

McHale, Jean V. (2007) "Rights to Medical Treatment in EU Law." 15(1) *Medical Law Review* 99–108.

McHale, Jean and Fox, Marie (2006) *Health Care Law: Text and Materials*. (2nd ed.) (London: Sweet & Maxwell).

Mackillop, W. J. and Johnston, P. A. (1986) "Ethical Problems in Clinical Research: The Need of Empirical Studies of the Clinical Trials Process." 39 *Journal of Chronic Diseases* 177–188.

McLean, Jim (1998) "Human Cloning: A Dangerous Dilemma." 43(3) *Journal of the Law Society of Scotland* 24–26.

Maclean, Alasdair R. (2001) "A Crossing of the Rubicon on the Human Rights Ferry." 64(5) *Modern Law Review* 775–794.

Maclean, Alasdair R. (2004) "The Doctrine of Informed Consent: Does it Exist and Has it Crossed the Atlantic?"24(3) *Legal Studies* 386–413.

McLean, Sheila (1999) *Old Law, New Medicine*. (London: Pandora).

McLean, Shelia A. M. (1998) *Review of the Common Law Provisions Relating to the Removal of Gametes and of the Consent Provisions in the Human Fertilisation and Embryology Act 1990*. (London: Department of Health).

McLean, Sheila A. M. and Williamson, Laura (2005) *Xenotransplantation: Law and Ethics*. (Aldershot: Ashgate).

McMillan, J. R. (2003) "NICE, the Draft Fertility Guideline and Dodging the Big Question." 29 *Journal of Medical Ethics* 313–314.

McNeill, Paul (1997) "Paying People to Participate in Research: Why Not?" 11(7) *Bioethics* 390–396.

Magee, Reginald (1999) "Robert Liston: Surgeon Extraordinary." 69(12) *Australian and New Zealand Journal of Surgery* 878–881.

Maguire, A. M., Simonelli F., Pierce E. A., *et al* (2008). "Safety and Efficacy of Gene Transfer for Leber's Congenital Amaurosis." 358 *New England Journal of Medicine* 2240–2248.

Manning, Joanna (2004) "Informed Consent To Medical Treatment: The Common Law And New Zealand's Code Of Patients' Rights." 12(2) *Medical Law Review* 181–216.

Marchant, Stuart (2004) "Capacity to Legislate." 154 *New Law Journal* 23.

Margreiter, R. (1991) "Medical Risk and Benefit in Living Pancreas Segment Donors." In W. Land and J. B. Dossetor (eds) *Organ Replacement Therapy: Ethics, Justice, Commerce*. (Berlin: Springer-Verlag), 102–105.

Marshall, Eliot (1999) "Gene Therapy Death Prompts Review of Adenovirus Vector." 286 *Science* 2244–2245.

Mason, J. K. (1996) "Contemporary Issues in Organ Transplantation." In Sheila McLean (ed.) *Contemporary Issues in Law, Medicine and Ethics*. (Aldershot: Dartmouth), 117–141.

Mason, J. K. and Laurie, G. T. (2001) "Consent or Property? Dealing with the Body and its Parts in the Shadow of Bristol and Alder Hey." 64(5) *Modern Law Review* 710–729.

Mason, J. K. and Laurie, G. T. (2006) *Mason & McCall Smith's Law and Medical Ethics*. (7th ed.) (Oxford: Oxford University Press).

Matthews, Paul (1983) "Whose Body? People as Property." *Current Legal Problems* 193–239.

Mauron, A. and Thévoz, J-M. (1991) "Germ-line Engineering: A Few European Voices." 16 *Journal of Medicine and Philosophy* 649–666.

Meikle, James (2005) "NHS Prepares for Adult Living Liver Transplants." *The Guardian*, 8 November.

Menning, Barbara Eck (1977) *Infertility: A Guide for the Childless Couple*. (Englewood Cliffs, New Jersey: Prentice Hall).

Menning, Barbara Eck (1980) "The Emotional Needs of Infertile Couples." 34(4) *Fertility and Sterility* 313–319.

Merry, Alan, and McCall Smith, Alexander (2001) *Errors, Medicine and the Law*. (Cambridge: Cambridge University Press).

Meyers, David (2006) "Chester v Afshar: Sayonara, Sub Silentio, Sidaway?" In S.A.M. Mclean (ed) *First Do No Harm*. (Aldershot: Ashgate), 255–271.

Michalowski, Sabine (1997) "Is it in the Best Interests of a Child to Have a Life-Saving Liver Transplantation?—Re T (Wardship: Medical Treatment" 9 *Child and Family Law Quarterly* 179–189.

Michalowski, Sabine (1999) "Court-Authorised Caesarean Sections—The End of a Trend?—*Re MB (An Adult: Medical Treatment)*." 62(1) *Modern Law Review* 115–127.

Michalowski, Sabine (2002) "Sanctity of Life—Are Some Lives More Sacred than Others?" 22(3) *Legal Studies* 377–397.

Michalowski, Sabine (2003) *Medical Confidentiality and Crime*. (Aldershot: Ashgate).

Mildred, Mark (1998) "The Human Growth Hormone (Creutzfeldt Jakob Disease) Litigation." *Journal of Personal Injury Litigation* 251–270.

Miola, José (2004) "Medical Law and Medical Ethics—Complementary or Corrosive?" 6(3) *Medical Law International* 251–274.

Miller, Franklin G. and Brody, Howard (2002) "What Makes Placebo-Controlled Trials Unethical?" 2(2) *American Journal of Bioethics* 3–9.

Montgomery, Jonathan (2002) *Health Care Law*. (2nd ed.) (Oxford: Oxford University Press).

Montrose, L (1958) "Is Negligence an Ethical or a Sociological Concept?" 21 *Modern Law Review* 259–264.

Moore, Adam D. (2000) "Owning Genetic Information and Gene Enhancement Techniques: Why Privacy and Property Rights May Undermine Social Control of the Human Genome." 14(2) *Bioethics* 97–119.

Moore, Margaret (1994) "Gauthier's Contractarian Morality." In David Boucher and Paul Kelly (eds) *The Social Contract from Hobbes to Rawls*. (London and New York: Routledge), 211–225.

Morgan, Derek (1988) "Foetal Sex Identification, Abortion and the Law." 18 *Family Law* 355–359.

Morgan, Derek (1990) "Abortion: The Unexamined Ground." *Criminal Law Review* 687–694.

Morgan, Derek (2001) *Issues in Medical Law and Ethics*. (London: Cavendish).

Morgan, Derek and Ford, Mary (2004) "Cell Phoney: Human Cloning After Quintavalle." 30 *Journal of Medical Ethics* 524–526.

Morgan, Derek and Lee, Robert G. (1997) "In the Name of the Father? Ex parte Blood: Dealing with Novelty and Anomaly." 60(6) *Modern Law Review* 840–856.

Morgan, Jonathan (2004) "Privacy in the House of Lords, Again." 120 *Law Quarterly Review* 563–566.

Morgan, R. A., Dudley M. E., Wunderlich, J.R., et al. (2006) 314 *Science* "Cancer Regression in Patients after Transfer of Genetically Engineered Lymphocytes." 126–129.

Morgan, Ryan (2007) "Embryonic Stem Cells and Consent: Incoherence and Inconsistency in the UK Regulatory Model." 15(3) *Medical Law Review* 279–319.

Morris, Anne E. (1999) "Treating Children Properly: Law, Ethics and Practice." 15(4) *Professional Negligence* 249–266.

Morris, Anne and Nott, Susan (1995) "The Law's Engagement with Pregnancy." In Jo Bridgeman and Susan Millns (eds) *Law and Body Politics: Regulating the Female Body.* (Aldershot: Dartmouth), 53–78.

Morris, Anne and Saintier, Severine (2003) "To Be or Not to Be: Is That The Question? Wrongful Life and Misconceptions." 11(3) *Medical Law Review* 167–193.

Moseley, Ray (1991) "Commentary: Maintaining the Somatic/Germ-Line Distinction: Some Ethical Drawbacks." 16 *Journal of Medicine and Philosophy* 641–647.

MRC (Medical Research Council) (1998) *Guidelines for Good Clinical Practice in Clinical Trials.* (Surrey: Aldridge Print Group).

MRC (Medical Research Council) (2004) *MRC Ethics Guide: Medical Research Involving Children.* (London: MRC).

Mudur, Ganapati (1999) "Indian Medical Authorities Act on Antenatal Sex Selection." 319 *British Medical Journal* 410.

Mullender, Richard (1996) "Judicial Review and the Rule of Law." 112 *Law Quarterly Review* 182–186.

Multi-Society Task Force on PVS (1994a) "Statement on Medical Aspects of the Persistent Vegetative State (First of Two Parts)." 330 *New England Journal of Medicine* 1499–1508.

Multi-Society Task Force on PVS (1994b) "Statement on Medical Aspects of the Persistent Vegetative State (Second of Two Parts)." 330 *New England Journal of Medicine* 1572–1579.

Munby, James (2004) "Consent to Treatment: Children and the Incompetent Patient." In Andrew Grubb (ed.) *Principles of Medical Law.* (Oxford: Oxford University Press), 205–310.

Murphy, John (2007) *Street on Torts.* (12th ed.) (Oxford: Oxford University Press).

Najarian, J. S., Chavers, B. M., McHugh, L. E., and Matas, A. J. (1992) "20 Years or More of Follow-Up of Living Kidney Donors." 340 *The Lancet* 807–810.

National Audit Office (2005) *A Safer Place for Patients: Learning to Improve Patient Safety.* (HC 456 2005–2006) (London: National Audit Office). (Nov 2005).

NRES (National Research Ethics Service) (2008) *Standard Operating Procedures for Research Ethics Committees.* Version 3.5. (London: DH). (May 2008).

Nerem, R. M. (2003) "Tissue Engineering: Confronting the Transplantation Crisis." In Y. Murat Elçin (ed.) *Tissue Engineering, Stem Cells and Gene Therapies (Advances in Experimental Medicine and Biology).* (New York: Kluwer Academic), 1–9.

Nerem, R. M. and Ensley, A. E. (2004) "The Tissue Engineering of Blood Vessels and the Heart." 4 (Suppl. 6) *American Journal of Transplantation* 36–42.

New, B, Solomon, M., Dingwall, R., and McHale J. (1994) *A Question of Give and Take: Improving the Supply of Donor Organs for Transplantation*. (London: King's Fund Institute).

Newdick, Christopher (2004) "The Organisation of Health Care." In Andrew Grubb (ed.) *Principles of Medical Law*. (Oxford: Oxford University Press), 3–82.

Newdick, Christopher (2005) *Who Should We Treat? Rights, Rationing and Resources in the NHS*. (2nd ed.) (Oxford: Oxford University Press).

Newdick, Christopher (2007) "Judicial Review: Low-Priority Treatment and Exceptional Case Review." 15(2) *Medical Law Review* 236–244.

NHSE (National Health Service Executive) (1996) *Complaints: Listening . . . Acting . . . Improving. Guidance on Implementation of the NHS Complaints Procedures*. (London: Department of Health).

NHSLA (NHS Litigation Authority) (2003) *Clinical Negligence Scheme for Trusts: Clinical Risk Management Standards*. (Aug. 2003).

NICE (National Institute for Clinical Excellence) (2004) *Fertility: Assessment and Treatment for People with Fertility Problems*. (London: NICE). (Feb 2004).

NICE (National Institute for Clinical Excellence) (2008) *Social Value Judgments: Principles for the Development of NHS Guidance*. (2nd ed.) (London: NICE). (Aug. 2005).

Nisselle, P. (2002) "Editor's Comments." 3(5) *Medicine Today (New South Wales)* 73–74.

NMC (Nursing and Midwifery Council) (2002) *Code of Professional Conduct 2002*. (London: NMC).

Noonan, John (1970) *The Morality of Abortion: Legal and Historical Perspectives*. (Cambridge, MA: Harvard University Press).

Nozick, Robert (1974) *Anarchy, State and Utopia*. (Oxford: Blackwell).

Nuffield Council on Bioethics (1995) *Human Tissue: Ethical and Legal Issues*. (London: Nuffield Council on Bioethics). (April 2005).

Nuffield Council on Bioethics (1996) *Animal-to-Human Transplants: The Ethics of Xenotransplantation*. (London: Nuffield Council on Bioethics). (March 1996).

Nuffield Council on Bioethics (2002a) *Genetics and Human Behaviour* (London: Nuffield Council on Bioethics). (Oct. 2002).

Nuffield Council on Bioethics (2002b) *The Ethics of Patenting DNA: A Discussion Paper*. (London: Nuffield Council on Bioethics). (July 2002).

Okin, Susan Moller (1989) *Justice, Gender, and the Family*. (New York: Basic Books).

O'Neill, Onora (1998) "Consistency in Action." In James Rachels (eds) *Ethical Theory*. (Oxford: Oxford University Press), 504–529.

OPG (Office of the Public Guardian) (2007) *Office of the Public Guardian and Court of Protection: Fees, Exemptions and Remissions*. (OPG506) (London: OPG). (Oct. 2007).

Organ Donation Taskforce (2008) *The Potential Impact of an Opt Out System for Organ Donation in the UK: An Independent Report from the Organ Donation Taskforce*. (London: DH). (Nov. 2008).

O'Rourke, Mary and Holl-Allen, Jonathan (2004) "Regulating Health Care Professions." In Andrew Grubb (ed.), *Principles of Medical Law*. (Oxford: Oxford University Press), 83–128.

Orr, Deborah (2000) "When a 'Designer Baby' Can Be Right." *The Independent*, 5 October.

Osborne, Susannah (2003) "DIY Abortions at Home 'Should Be Given Trial Run'." *The Daily Telegraph*, 28 July.

Palmero, G., Joris, H., Devroey, P., and van Steirteghem, A. (1992) "Pregnancies After Intracytoplasmic Sperm Injection of Single Spermatozoon into an Oocyte." 340 *The Lancet* 17–18.

Palmiter R. D., et al. (1982) "Dramatic Growth of Mice that Develop from Eggs Microinjected With Metallothionein-Growth Hormone Fusion Genes." 300 *Nature*. 1982 611–615.

Panting, Gerard (2001) "Medical Complaints, Discipline and the Human Rights Act 1998." In Austen Garwood-Gowers, John Tingle, and Tom Lewis (eds) *Healthcare Law: The Impact of the Human Rights Act 1998*. (London: Cavendish), 113–125.

Papalois, Vassilos et al. (2004) "Ethical Issues in Non-heart-beating Donation." 202 *Bulletin of Medical Ethics* 13–20.

Parfit, Derek (1984) *Reason and Persons*. (Oxford: Clarendon Press; repr. corr.1987).

Parry, Gareth (1990) "Struck-off Specialist Defends Kidney Sale." *The Guardian*, 5 April.

Paton, H. J. (1948) Translation of *Groundwork of the Metaphysic of Morals* by Immanuel Kant. (London: Routledge).

——. (1967) *The Categorical Imperative: A Study in Kant's Moral Philosophy*. (New York: Harper and Row).

Patrick, Kirsten (2007) "Is Infant Male Circumcision An Abuse Of The Rights Of The Child? No." 335 *British Medical Journal* 1181.

Patrizio, Pasquale, Mastroianni, Anna C., and Mastroianni, Luigi (2001) "Gamete Donation and Anonymity: Disclosure to Children conceived with Donor Gametes should be Optional." 16(1) *Human Reproduction* 2036–2038.

Pattinson, Shaun D. (1999) "Wrongful Life Actions as a Means of Regulating Use of Genetic and Reproductive Technologies." 7 *Health Law Journal* 19–34.

Pattinson, Shaun D. (2000) "Regulating Germ-Line Gene Therapy to Avoid Sliding Down the Slippery Slope." 4(3&4) *Medical Law International* 213–222.

Pattinson, Shaun D. (2002a) *Influencing Traits Before Birth*. (Aldershot: Ashgate).

Pattinson, Shaun D. (2002b) "Undue Influence in the Context of Medical Treatment." 5(4) *Medical Law International* 305–317.

Pattinson, Shaun D. (2002c) "Reproductive Cloning: Can Cloning Harm the Clone?" 10(3) *Medical Law Review* 295–307.

Pattinson, Shaun D. (2003a) "Paying Living Organ Providers." 3 *Web Journal of Current Legal Issues*. (*http://webjcli.ncl.ac.uk/*).

Pattinson, Shaun D. (2003b) "Designing Donors." In Jennifer Gunning and Søren Holm (eds) *Ethics, Law and Society*. (Aldershot: Ashgate, 2005), 251–256. Originally published in *CCELS (Cardiff Centre for Ethics, Law and Society) Issue of the Month* (July 2003) (*http://www.ccels.cardiff.ac.uk/issue.html*).

Pattinson, Shaun D. (2005) "Some Problems Challenging the UK's Human Fertilisation and Embryology Authority." 24 *Medicine and Law* 391–401.

Pattinson, Shaun D. (2006) *Medical Law and Ethics*. (1st ed.) (London: Sweet & Maxwell).

Pattinson, Shaun D. (2007) "First Do No Harm." 8(3) *Medical Law International* 251–276.

Pattinson, Shaun D. (2008) "Organ Trading, Tourism, and Trafficking within Europe" 27 *Medicine and Law* 191–201.

Pattinson, Shaun D. (2009) "Consent and Informational Responsibility." 35(3) *Journal of Medical Ethics* 176–179.

Pattinson, Shaun D. and Caulfield, Timothy (2004) "Variations and Voids: The Regulation of Human Cloning Around the World." 5 *BMC Medical Ethics* 9. (*http://www.biomedcentral.com/1472-6939/5/9*).

Pearson, Lord, et al. (1978) *The Royal Commission on Civil Liability and Compensation for Personal Injury: Report* (Cmnd 7054-I). (London: HMSO).

Pedain, Antje (2004) "Unconventional Justice in the House of Lords." 63(1) *Cambridge Law Journal* 19–21.

Pellegrino, Edmund D. (1991) "Families' Self-interest and the Cadaver's Organs: What Price Consent?" 265(10) *Journal of the American Medical Association (JAMA)* 1305–1306.

Pence, Gregory E. (1995) "The Tuskegee Study", extract from Gregory E. Pence, *Glass Cases in Medical Ethics* (McGraw-Hill), reprinted in Tom L. Beauchamp and LeRoy Walters (2003) *Contemporary Issues in Bioethics* (sixth edition) Belmont, California: Wadsworth).

Pennings, Guido (1997) "The Double Track Policy for Donor Anonymity." 12 *Human Reproduction* 2839–2844.

Pennings, Guido (2007) "Directed Organ Donation: Discrimination or Autonomy?" 24(1) *Journal of Applied Philosophy* 41–49.

Plafker, Ted (2002) "Sex Selection in China sees 117 Boys Born for Every 100 Girls" 324 *British Medical Journal* 1233.

Plato (BCE) *Euthyphro*. Translated by Thomas G. West and Grace Starry West in *Four Texts on Socrates: Plato & Aristophanes*. (New York: Cornell University Press, 1998).

Platt, Jeffrey L. 2004. "Preface: Future Approaches to Replacement of Organs." 4 (Suppl. 6) *American Journal of Transplantation* 5–6.

Plomer, Aurora (2001) "Protecting the Rights of Human Subjects in Emergency Research." 8(4) *European Journal of Health Law* 333–352.

Plomer, Aurora (2002) "Beyond the HFE Act 1990: The Regulation of Stem Cell Research in the UK." (2002) 10(2) *Medical Law Review* 132–164.

Plomer, Aurora, Smith, Iain, and Martin-Clement, Norma (1999) "Rationing Policies on Access to *In Vitro* Fertilisation in the National Health Service, UK." 7(14) *Reproductive Health Matters* 60–70.

Pluhar, Evelyn B. (1995) *Beyond Prejudice: The Moral Significance of Human and Nonhuman Animals*. (Durham: Duke University Press).

Pope John Paul II (2003) "The Unspeakable Crime of Abortion." In *Evangelium Vitae*, Encyclical Letter, 16 August 2003. Reprinted in Bonnie Steinbock, John Arras, and Alex London (eds) *Ethical Issues in Modern Medicine*. (New York: McGraw-Hill, 2003), 461–463.

President's Council on Bioethics (2002) *Human Cloning and Human Dignity: An Ethical Inquiry*. (Washington DC).

Priaulx, Nicollette M. (2002) "Conceptualising Harm in the Case of the 'Unwanted' Child." 9(4) *European Journal of Health Law* 337–359.

Price, David (1988) "Selective Reduction and Feticide: The Parameters of Abortion." *Criminal Law Review* 199–210.

Price, David (2000) *Legal and Ethical Aspects of Organ Transplantation*. (Cambridge: Cambridge University Press).

Price, David (1997) "Organ Transplant Initiatives: The Twilight Zone." 23 *Journal of Medical Ethics* 170–175.

Price, David (2003) "From Cosmos and Damian to Van Velzen: The Human Tissue Saga Continues." 11(1) *Medical Law Review* 1–47.

Price, David (2005) "The Human Tissue Act 2004." 68(5) *Modern Law Review* 798–821.

Price, David, and Mackay, Ronnie (1991) "The Trade in Human Organs: Part 2." 141 *New Law Journal* 1307–1309.

Quick, Oliver (2006a) "Outing Medical Errors: Questions of Trust and Responsibility." 14(1) *Medical Law Review* 22–43.

Quick, Oliver (2006b) "Prosecuting 'Gross' Medical Negligence: Manslaughter, Discretion, and the Crown Prosecution Service." 33(3) *Journal of Law and Society* 421–450.

Rachels, James (1979) "Killing and Starving to Death" 54 *Philosophy* 159–171.

Radcliffe-Richards, Janet (1991) "From Him that Hath Not." In W. Land and J. B. Dossetor (eds) *Organ Replacement Therapy: Ethics, Justice*, Commerce. (Berlin: Springer-Verlag), 190–196.

Radcliffe-Richards, J, et al. (1998) "The Case For Allowing Kidney Sales." 351 *The Lancet* 1950–1952.

Rawlins, Michael D. and Culyer, Anthony J. (2004) "National Institute for Clinical Excellence and its Value Judgments." 329 *British Medical Journal* 224–227.

Rawls, John (1973) *A Theory of Justice*. (Oxford: Oxford University Press). (First published 1971).

RCOG (Royal College of Obstetricians and Gynaecologists) (1996) *Termination of Pregnancy for Fetal Abnormality in England, Wales and Scotland*. (London: RCOG). (Jan. 2006).

RCOG (2001) *Further Issues Relating to Late Abortion, Fetal Viability and Registration of Births and Deaths*. (London: RCOG). (April 2001).

RCP (Royal College of Physicians) (2005) *Report of a Working Party—Ethics in Practice: Background Recommendations for Enhanced Support*. (June 2005) (London: Royal College of Physicians).

RCP (2007) *Guidelines on the Practice of Ethics Committees in Medical Research With Human Participants*. (4th edition) (London: RCP).

RCS (Royal College of Surgeons) (2003) *Facial Transplantation: Working Party Report*. (1st ed.) (London: Royal College of Surgeons). (Nov. 2003).

RCS (2006) *Facial Transplantation: Working Party Report*. (2nd ed.) (London: Royal College of Surgeons). (Nov. 2006).

Reddy, K. C. (1993) "Should Paid Organ Donation be Banned in India? To Buy or Let Die!" 6(3) *National Medical Journal of India* 137–139.

Redfern, Michael, Keeling, Jean W., and Powell, Elizabeth (2001) *The Royal Liverpool Children's Inquiry Report* (HC 12–11) (www.rlcinquiry.org.uk).

Regan, Tom (1988) *The Case for Animal Rights*. (London: Routledge). (First published in 1984).

Regis, Edward (ed.) (1984) *Gewirth's Ethical Rationalism: Critical Essays with a Reply by Alan Gewirth*. (Chicago: Chicago University Press).

Relman, Arnold S. (1990a) "Is Rationing Inevitable?" 322 *New England Journal of Medicine* 1809–1810.

Relman, Arnold S. (1990b) "The Trouble With Rationing." 323 *New England Journal of Medicine* 911–913.

Renard, Jean-Paul, et al. (1999) "Lymphoid Hypoplasia and Somatic Cloning." 353 *Lancet* 1489–1491.

Report of a Working Party of the Clinical Genetics Society (UK) (1994) "The Genetic Testing of Children." 31 *Journal of Medical Genetics* 785–797.

Resnik, David B. (2001) "DNA Patents and Human Dignity." 29 *Journal of Law, Medicine and Ethics* 152–163.

Resnik, David B. (2002) "The Commercialization of Human Stem Cells: Ethical and Policy Issues." 10 *Health Care Analysis* 127–154.

Rettig, Richard A. (1991) "Artificial Kidneys and Artificial Hearts." 65 *Southern California Law Review* 503–528.

Rhind, Susan M., et al. (2003) "Human Cloning: Can It Be Made Safe?" 4 *Nature* 855–864.

Richardson, Henry S. (2000) "Specifying, Balancing, and Interpreting Bioethical Principles." 25(3) *Journal of Medicine and Philosophy* 285–307.

Rideout, William M., Eggan, Kevin, and Jaenisch, Rudolf (2001) "Nuclear Cloning and Epigenetic Reprogramming of the Genome." 293 *Science* 1093–1098.

Rieu, E. V. and Rieu, D. C. H. (trans) (2003) *The Odyssey* by Homer. (London: Penguin Classics).

Robertson, G. (1991) "Informed Consent Ten Years Later: The Impact of Reibl v Hughes." 70(3) *Canadian Bar Review* 423–447.

Robertson, John A. (1983) "Procreative Liberty and the Control of Conception, Pregnancy and Childbirth." 69 *Virginia Law Review* 405–462.

Robertson, John A. (1990) "Prior Agreements for Disposition of Frozen Embryos." 51 *Ohio State Law Journal* 407–424.

Robertson, John A. (1994) *Children of Choice*. (Princeton University Press).

Robertson, John A. (2000–2001) "Why Human Reproductive Cloning Should Not in All Cases be Prohibited." 4 *NYU Journal of Legislation and Public Policy* 35–43.

Royal College of Paediatrics and Child Health (1997) *Withholding or Withdrawing Life Saving Treatment in Children: A Framework for Practice*. (London: Royal College of Paediatrics and Child Health).

Royal College of Paediatrics and Child Health (2000) "Ethics Advisory Committee Guidelines for the Ethical Conduct of Medical Research involving Children." 82 *Archives of Disease in Childhood* 177–182.

Royal College of Physicians Working Group (1996) "The Permanent Vegetative State." 30(2) *Journal of the Royal College of Physicians London* 119–121.

Salih, M. A., Harvey, I., Frankel, S., Coupe, D. J., Webb, M., and Cripps, H. A. (1991) "Potential Availability of Cadaver Organs for Transplantation." 302 *British Medical Journal* 1053–1055.

Satz, Debra (1992) "Markets in Women's Reproductive Labor." 21(2) *Philosophy and Public Affairs* 107–131.

Savulescu, Julian (2001) "Procreative Beneficence: Why WE Should Select the Best Children." 15 *Bioethics* 413–426.

Schehr, Robert and Fox, Jeff (2000) "Human Genome Bombshell." 18 *Nature Biotechnology* 365.

Schwindt, Richard and Vining, Aidan (1986) "Proposal for a Future Delivery Market for Transplant Organs." 11(3) *Journal of Health Politics, Policy and Law* 483–500.

Schwindt, Richard and Vining, Aidan (1998) "Proposal for a Mutual Insurance Pool for Transplant Organs." 23 *Journal of Health Politics, Policy and Law* 725–739.

Science and Technology Committee (also known as the House of Commons Committee on Science and Technology) (Publications can often be found at: www.parliament.uk/parliamentary_committees/science_and_technology_commit tee.cfm).

Science and Technology Committee (1997) *Fifth Report: The Cloning of Animals from Adult Cells* Session 1996–97; HC 37 3-I. (London: HMSO).

Science and Technology Committee (2002) *Developments in Human Genetics and Embryology: Fourth Report of Session 2001–02.* (HC 791). (London: HMSO).

Science and Technology Committee (2005a) *Human Reproductive Technologies and the Law: Fifth Session 2004–2005. Volume I: Report, together with formal minutes.* (HC 7-I) (London: The Stationary Office).

Science and Technology Committee (2005b) *Human Reproductive Technologies and the Law: Fifth Session 2004–2005. Volume II: Oral and Written Evidence.* (HC 7-II) (London: The Stationary Office).

Science and Technology Committee (2005c) *Inquiry into Human Reproductive Technologies and the Law: Eight Special Report of Session 2004–2005.* (HC 491) (London: The Stationary Office).

Scott, Elizabeth S. (1986) "Sterilization of Mentally Retarded Persons: Reproductive Rights and Family Privacy." *Duke Law Journal* 806–865.

Seanor, Douglas and Fotion, N (eds) (1988) *Hare and Critics: Essay on Moral Thinking.* (Oxford: Clarendon Press).

Sells, R. A. (1992) "The Case Against Buying Organs and a Futures Market in Transplants." 24(5) *Transplantation Proceedings* 2198–2202.

Senate of Surgery of Great Britain and Ireland (1997) *The Surgeon's Duty of Care: Guidance for Surgeons on Legal and Ethical Issues.* (London: Senate of Surgery of Great Britain and Ireland).

Sermon, K., et al. (1998) "Preimplantation Diagnosis for Huntington's Disease (HD): Clinical Application and Analysis of the HD Expansion in Affected Embryos." 18 *Prenatal Diagnosis* 1427–1436.

Sesso, Ricardo, Josephson, Michelle A, Ançāo, Meide S., et al. (1998) "A Retrospective Study of Kidney Transplant Recipients from Living Unrelated Donors." 9(4) *Journal of the American Society of Nephrology* 684–691.

Sever, M. S. Ecder, T. Aydin, A. E., and Türkmen, A. (1994) "Living Unrelated (Paid) Kidney Transplantation in Third-World Countries: High Risk of Complications Besides the Ethical Problem." 9(4) *Nephrology Dialysis Transplantation* 350–354.

Sever, Mehmet #alSükrü, et al. (2001) "Outcome of Living Unrelated (Commercial) Renal Transplantation." 60(4) *Kidney International* 1477–1483.

Shaw, A. B. (1994) "In Defence of Ageism." 20 *Journal of Medical Ethics* 188–191.

Sheldon, Sally (1995) "The Law of Abortion and the Politics of Medicalisation." In Jo Bridgeman and Susan Millns (eds) *Law and Body Politics: Regulating the Female Body.* (Aldershot: Dartmouth), 105–124.

Sheldon, Sally (1997) *Beyond Control.* (London: Pluto).

Sheldon, Sally and Thomson, Michael (1998) "Health Care Law and Feminism: A Developing Relationship." In Sally Sheldon and Michael Thomson (eds) *Feminist Perspectives on Health Care Law.* (London: Cavendish), 1–13.

Sheldon, Sally and Wilkinson, Stephen (1997) "Conjoined Twins: The Legality and Ethics of Sacrifice." 5(1) *Medical Law Review* 149–171.

Sheldon, Sally and Wilkinson, Stephen (2001a) "Termination of Pregnancy for Reason of Foetal Disability: Are There Grounds for a Special Exception in Law?" 9(2) *Medical Law Review* 85–109.

Sheldon, Sally and Wilkinson, Stephen (2001b) " 'On the Sharpest Horns of a Dilemma': *Re A (Conjoined Twins)."* 9(3) *Medical Law Review* 201–207.

Sheldon, Sally and Wilkinson, Stephen (2004) "Hashmi and Whitaker: An Unjustifiable and Misguided Distinction?" 12(2) *Medical Law Review* 137–163.

Sheldon, Tony (2005) "Dutch Supreme Court Backs Damages for Child for Having Been Born." 330 *British Medical Journal* 747.

Shimm, D. S. and Spece, R. G. (1991) "Industry Reimbursement for Entering Patients into Clinical Trials: Legal and Ethical Issues." 115 *Annals of Internal Medicine* 148–151.

Shipman Inquiry (The reports are available online at: *http://www.the-shipman-inquiry.org.uk*).

Shipman Inquiry (2002) *First Report: Death Disguised.* (London: The Stationary Office). (July 2002).

Shipman Inquiry (2004) *Fifth Report: Safeguarding Patients. Lessons from the Past—Proposals for the Future* (Cm 6394). (London: The Stationary Office). (Dec. 2004).

Shultz, Marjorie Maguire (1990) "Reproductive Technology and Intent-Based Parenthood: An Opportunity for Gender Neutrality." *Wisconsin Law Review* 297–398.

Shuster, Evelyne (1997) "Fifty Years Later: The Significance of the Nuremberg Code." 337(20) *New England Journal of Medicine* 1426–1140.

Siegler, Mark (1986) "Ethics Committees: Decisions by Bureaucracy." *Hastings Center Report* (June): 22–24.

Siegler, Mark and Singer, Peter A. (1988) "Clinical Ethics Consultation: Godsend or 'God Squad'?" 85(6) *American Journal of Medicine* 759–760.

Sienkiewicz-Mercer, Ruth and Kaplan, Steven B. (1989) *I Raise My Eyes to Say Yes.* (London: Grafton Books).

Singer, Peter (1993) *Practical Ethics.* (2nd ed.) (Cambridge: Cambridge University Press).

Singer, Peter (1994) *Rethinking Life and Death: The Collapse of Our Traditional Ethics.* (Oxford: Oxford University Press).

Singer, Peter (1995) *Animal Liberation.* (2nd ed.) (London: Pimlico).

Singer, Peter, McKie, John, Kuhse, Helga, and Richardson, Jeff (1995) "Double Jeopardy and the Use of QALYs in Health Care Allocation." 21 *Journal of Medical Ethics* 144–150.

Skegg, P. D. G. (1992) "Medical Uses of Corpses and the 'No Property' Rule." 32(4) *Medicine, Science and the Law* 311–318.

Skegg, P. D. G. (1999) "English Medical Law and 'Informed Consent': An Antipodean Assessment and Alternative." 7(2) *Medical Law Review* 135–165.

Smart, J. J. C. (1973) "An Outline of a System of Utilitarian Ethics." In J.J.C. Smart and Bernard Williams, *Utilitarianism: For and Against*. (Cambridge: Cambridge University Press), 1–74.

Smith, Eimear and Delargy, Mark (2005) "Locked-in Syndrome." 330 *British Medical Journal* 406–409.

Smith, Stephen A. (2004) *Contract Theory*. (Oxford: Oxford University Press).

Smith, Stephen W. (2005a) "Evidence for the Practical Slippery Slope in the Debate on Physician-Assisted Suicide and Euthanasia." 13(1) *Medical Law Review* 17–44.

Smith, Stephen W. (2005b) "Fallacies of the Logical Slippery Slope in the Debate on Physician-Assisted Suicide and Euthanasia." 13(2) *Medical Law Review* 224–243.

Sokol, Daniel K. (2004) "In Medicine, 'Yuk' Is not a Useful Guide." *International Herald Tribute*, 18 May.

Spriggs, M. (2002) "Lesbian Couple Create a Child Who is Deaf Like Them." 28 *Journal of Medical Ethics* 283.

Spöhr, F., Arntz, H. R., Bluhmki, E., et al. (2005) "International Multicentre Trial Protocol to Assess the Efficacy and Safety of Tenecteplase during Cardiopulmonary Resuscitation in Patients with Out-of-Hospital Cardiac Arrest: The Thrombolysis in Cardiac Arrest (TROICA) Study." 35(5) *European Journal of Clinical Investigation* 315–323.

Staff, Anne Catherine (2001) "An Introduction to Gene Therapy and its Potential Prenatal Use." 80(6) *Acta Obstetricia et Gynecologica Scandinavica* 485–491.

Starzl, T.E., et al. (1993) "Baboon-to-Human Liver Transplantation." 341 *The Lancet* 65–71.

Statman, Daniel (1997a) (ed.) *Virtue Ethics*. (Edinburgh: Edinburgh University Press).

Statman, Daniel (1997b) "Introduction to Virtue Ethics." In Daniel Statman (ed.) *Virtue Ethics*. (Edinburgh: Edinburgh University Press), 1–41.

Stauch, Marc (2001) "Pregnancy and the Human Rights Act 1998." In Austen Garwood-Gowers, John Tingle, and Tom Lewis (eds) *Healthcare Law: The Impact of the Human Rights Act 1998*. (London: Cavendish), 259–271.

Stauch, Marc, Wheat, Kay, and Tingle, John (2006) *Text, Cases & Materials on Medical Law*. (London: Routledge-Cavendish).

Stefan, Susan (1993) "Silencing the Different Voice: Competency Feminist Theory and Law." 47 *University of Miami Law Review* 736–815.

Steinbock, Bonnie, Arras, John D., and London, Alex John (2003) "Introduction: Moral Reasoning in the Medical Context." In Bonnie Steinbock, John Arras, and Alex London (eds) *Ethical Issues in Modern Medicine*. (New York: McGraw-Hill, 2003), 1–41.

Stern, Kristina (1994) "Advance Directives." 2(1) *Medical Law Review* 57–76.

Steyn, Johan (Lord) (2002) "Perspectives of Corrective and Distributive Justice in Tort Law." 37 *Irish Jurist* 1–15.

Strong, Carson, Gingrich, Jeffrey R. and Kutteh, William H. (2000) "Ethics of Postmortem Sperm Retrieval: Ethics of Sperm Retrieval After Death or Persistent Vegetative State." 15(4) *Human Reproduction* 739–745.

Suzuki, David and Knudtson, Peter (1989) *Genethics: The Ethics of Engineering Life*. (London: Unwin Hyman).

Sykes Nigel and Thorns Andrew. 2003. "The Use of Opioids and Sedatives at the End of Life." 4(5) *Lancet Oncology* 312–318.

Syrett, Keith (2002) "Nice Work? Rationing, Review and the 'Legitimacy Problem' in the New NHS." 10(1) *Medical Law Review* 1–27.

Syrett, Keith (2003) "Legitimating 'Fourth Hurdle' Pharmaceutical Regulation in Europe: Learning the NICE Way." 9(4) *European Public Law* 509–532.

Syrett, Keith (2004) "Impotence or Importance? Judicial Review in an Era of Explicit NHS Rationing." 67(2) *Modern Law Review* 289–304.

Takahashi, Kazutoshi, Tanabe, Koji, Onhnuki, Mari, et al. (2007) "Induction of Pluripotent Stem Cells from Adult Human Fibroblasts by Defined Factors." 131 *Cell* 861–872.

Taylor, M. J. (2004) "Problems of Practice and Principle if Centring Law Reform on the Concept of Genetic Discrimination." 11(4) *European Journal of Health Law* 365–380.

Teff, Harvey (1998) "The Standard of Care in Medical Negligence—Moving from Bolam?" 18(3) *Oxford Journal of Legal Studies* 473–484.

Teff, Harvey (2000) "Clinical Guidelines, Negligence, and Medical Practice." In Michael Freeman, and Andrew Lewis (eds) *Law and Medicine: Current Law Issues.* (Oxford: Oxford University Press), 67–80.

THES (Times Higher Education Supplement) (2004) "Stephen Hawkings." *Times Higher Education Supplement*, 16 April 2004, 2.

Thomas, Sandy, Hopkins, Michael and Brady, Max (2002) "Shares in the Human Genome—The Future of patenting DNA." (2002) 20 *Nature Biotechnology* 1185–1188.

Thomson, J. A., et al. (1998) "Embryonic Stem Cell Lines Derived from Human Blastocysts." 282 *Science* 1145–1147.

Thomson, Judith Jarvis (1971) "A Defence of Abortion." 1 *Philosophy and Public Affairs* 47–66.

Thomson, Judith Jarvis (1976) "Killing, Letting Die and the Trolley Problem." 59 *Monist* 204–217.

Thomson, Judith Jarvis (1985) "The Trolley Problem." 94 *Yale Law Journal* 1395–1415.

Titmuss, R. M. (1970) *The Gift Relationship: From Human Blood to Social Policy.* (London: George Allen & Unwin).

Toft, Brian (2004) *Independent Review of the Circumstances Surrounding Four Adverse Events that Occurred in the Reproductive Medicine Units at Leeds Teaching Hospitals NHS Trust, West Yorkshire.* (London: Department of Health).

Tooley, Michael (1972) "Abortion and Infanticide." 2 *Philosophy and Public Affairs* 37–65.

Toulson, R. G. and Phipps, C. M. (1996) *Confidentiality.* (London: Sweet & Maxwell).

Townend, David (2004) "Overriding Data Subjects' Rights in the Public Interest." In Deryck Beyleveld, David Townend, Ségoléne Rouillé-Mirza, and Jessica Wright (eds) *The Data Protection Directive and Medical Research Across Europe.* (Aldershot: Ashgate), 89–101.

Tracy, David (1998) "Human Cloning and the Public Realm: A Defense of Intuitions of the Good." In Martha C. Nussbaum, and Cass R. Sunstein (eds) *Clones and Clones: Facts and Fantasies about Human Cloning.* (New York & London: W. W. Norton), 190–203.

ULTRA (Unrelated Live Transplant Regulatory Authority) (2004) *Report 2002–04.* (London: Department of Health).

UK Stem Cell Bank (2006) *Code of Practice for the use of Human Stem Cell Lines. Version 3.* (UK Stem Cell Bank). (Aug. 2006).

UK Transplant (These documents can be found at www.uktransplant.org.uk).

UK Transplant (2004) *More Transplants—New Lives. Transplant Activity in the UK, 2003–2004.* (Bristol: UK Transplant).

UK Transplant (2005) *The Cost-Effectiveness of Transplantation.* (Bristol: UK Transplant).

UK Transplant (2008) *Transplant Activity in the UK: 2007–2008.* (Bristol: UK Transplant). (Aug. 2008).

UKIPO (UK Intellectual Property Office) (2009) *Inventions Involving Human Embryonic Stem Cells.* . (Newport: Intellectual Property Office). (Feb. 2009).

UKPO (UK Patent Office) (2003) *Inventions Involving Human Embryonic Stem Cells.* . (Newport: The Patent Office).

——. (2007) *Examination Guidelines for Patent Applications relating to Biotechnological Inventions in the UK Patent Office.* (Newport: The Patent Office).

UKXIRA (Xenotransplantation Interim Regulatory Authority) (1998) *Guidance on Making Proposals to Conduct Xenotransplantation on Human Subjects.*

Vallentyne, Peter (ed.) (1991) *Contractarianism and Rational Choice.* (Cambridge: Cambridge University Press).

van de Vosse, E., Ali, S., de Visser, A.W., et al. (2005) "Susceptibility to Typhoid Fever is Associated with a Polymorphism in the Cystic Fibrosis Transmembrane Conductance Regulator (CFTR)." 118(1) *Human Genetics* 138–40.

Vogel, Gretchen (2003) "Dolly goes to Greener Pastures." 299 *Science* 1163.

Wade, H. W. R. (2000) "Horizons of Horizontality" 116 *Law Quarterly Review* 217–224.

Wakayama, T. et al. (2001) "Differentiation of Embryonic Stem Cell Lines Generated from Adult Somatic Cells by Nuclear Transfer." 292 *Science* 740–743.

Wallbank, Julie (2002) "Too Many Mothers? Surrogacy, Kinship and the Welfare of the Child." 10(3) *Medical Law Review* 271–294.

Ward, B. J. and Tate, P. A. (1994) "Attitudes Among NHS Doctors to Requests for Euthanasia." 308 *British Medical Journal* 1332–1334.

Warnock, Mary, et al. (1984) *The Report of the Committee of Inquiry into Human Fertilisation and Embryology* (Cmnd 9314). (London: HMSO). Republished as Mary Warnock (1985) *A Question of Life.* (Oxford: Basil Blackwell).

Warren, Mary Anne (1973) "On the Moral and Legal Status of Abortion." 57 *Monist* 43–61.

Warren-Jones, Amanda (2004) "Patenting DNA: A Lot of Controversy Over A Little Intangibility." 12(1) *Medical Law Review* 97–124.

Watson, James (2003) *DNA: The Secret of Life.* (London: Arrow Books).

Watson, James D, and Crick, Francis H. C. (1953) "A Structure for Deoxy-Ribo Nucleic Acid." 171 *Nature* 737–738.

Watt, Helen (2001) "Conjoined Twins: Separation as Mutilation." 9(3) *Medical Law Review* 237–245.

Watt, Helen (2004) "Preimplantation Genetic Diagnosis: Choosing the 'Good Enough' Child." 12(1) *Health Care Analysis* 51–60.

Watts, Jonathan (2004) "China Offers Parents Cash Incentives to Produce More Girls." *The Guardian*, 16 July, 10.

Weale, Albert (1998) "Rationing Health Care." 316 *British Medical Journal* 410.

Weait, Matthew (2007) *Intimacy and Responsibility: The Criminalisation of HIV Transmission*. (London: Routledge-Cavendish).

Weinrib, Ernest J. (1983) "Toward a Moral Theory of Negligence Law." 2(1) *Law and Philosophy* 37–62.

Weinrib, Ernest J. (2002a) "Corrective Justice in a Nutshell." 52(4) *University of Toronto Law Journal* 349–356.

Weinrib, Ernest J. (2002b) "Deterrence and Corrective Justice." 50 *UCLA Law Review* 621–638.

West, Thomas G. and West, Grace Starry (trans) (1998) *Four Texts on Socrates: Plato & Aristophanes*. (New York: Cornell University Press).

Wexler, Nancy S. (1985) "Genetic Jeopardy and the New Clairvoyance." 6 *Progress in Medical Genetics* 277–304.

Wheeler, Robert (2006) "Gillick or Fraser? A Plead for Consistency Over Competence in Children." 332 *British Medical Journal* 807.

Whitfield, Adrian (2004) "Actions Arising from Birth." In Andrew Grubb (ed.) *Principles of Medical Law*. (Oxford: Oxford University Press, 2004), 789–851.

WHO (World Health Organization) (2000) *World Health Report 2000. Health Systems: Improving Performance* (Switzerland: WHO).

WHO and UNAIDS (2007) *New Data on Male Circumcision and HIV Prevention: Policy and Programme Implications*. (Geneva, Switzerland: WHO & UNAIDS). (March 2007) (*http://www.who.int/hiv/mediacentre/MCrecommendations_en.pdf*).

Wilkinson, Martin, and Moore, Andrew (1997) "Inducement in Research." 11(5) *Bioethics* 373–389.

Wilkinson, Stephen (2000a) "Commodification Arguments for the Legal Prohibition of Organ Sale." 8 *Health Care Analysis* 189–201.

Wilkinson, Stephen (2000b) "Palliative Care and the Doctrine of Double Effect." In Donna Dickenson, Malcolm Johnson, Jeanne Samson Katz (eds) *Death, Dying and Bereavement*. (2nd ed.) (London: Sage), 299–302.

Wilkinson, T. M. (2003) "What's Not Wrong with Conditional Organ Donation?" 29 *Journal of Medical Ethics* 163–164.

Williams, Kevin (2001) "Medical Samaritans: Is There A Duty To Treat?" 21(3) *Oxford Journal of Legal Studies* 393–413.

Williamson, Laura, Fox, Marie, and McLean, Sheila (2007) "The Regulation of Xenotransplantation in the United Kingdom After UKXIRA: Legal and Ethical Issues." 34(4) *Journal of Law and Society* 441–464.

Wilmut, I, et al. (1997) "Viable Offspring Derived from Fetal and Adult Mammalian Cells." 385 *Nature* 810–813.

Witting, Christian (2001) "National Health Service Rationing: Implications for the Standard of Care in Negligence." 21(3) *Oxford Journal of Legal Studies* 443–471.

Wolf, Susan M. (1998) "Pragmatism in the Face of Death: The Role of Facts in the Assisted Suicide Debate." 82 *Minnesota Law Review* 1063–1101.

Wong, J. G., Clare, I. C. H., Gunn, M. J., and Holland, A. J. (1999) "Capacity to Make Health Care Decisions: Its Importance in Clinical Practice." 29(2) *Psychological Medicine* 437–446.

Woolf, Lord (1996) *Access to Justice: Final Report to the Lord Chancellor on the Civil Justice System in England and Wales*. (London: HMSO).

Woolf, Lord (2001) "Are the Courts Excessively Deferential to the Medical Profession?" 9(1) *Medical Law Review* 1–16.

Wright, George (2003) "Call for Debate Over 'Designer Baby' Laws." *The Guardian*, 19 June.

Wright, Tim (2004) "A Renovated Complaints Procedure." 154 *New Law Journal* 1372.

Yu, Junying, Vodyanik, Maxim A., Smuga-Otta, Kim, et al. (2007) "Induced Pluripotent Stem Cell Liens Derived from Human Somatic Cells." 318 *Science* 1917–1920.

Zhang, Xin, Stojkovic, Petra, Przyborski, et al. (2006) "Derivation of Human Embryonic Stem Cells from Developing and Arrested Embryos." 24 *Stem Cells* 2669–2676.

Zimmerman, Burke K. (1991) "Human Germ-line Gene Therapy: The Case for its Development and Use." 16 *Journal of Medicine and Philosophy* 593–612.

INDEX

Note that "ff" indicates that the heading number should be taken to include its subheadings, whereas the number alone should be taken to refer only to the text immediately below the cited heading.